The Oxford Handbook of Climate Change and Private Law

The Oxford Handbook of Climate Change and Private Law

Edited by

DOUGLAS A. KYSAR

and

ERNEST LIM

OXFORD
UNIVERSITY PRESS

OXFORD
UNIVERSITY PRESS

Oxford University Press is a department of the University of Oxford.
It furthers the University's objective of excellence in research, scholarship,
and education by publishing worldwide. Oxford is a registered trade mark of
Oxford University Press in the UK and in certain other countries.

Published in the United States of America by Oxford University Press
198 Madison Avenue, New York, NY 10016, United States of America.

Library of Congress Cataloging-in-Publication Data
Names: Kysar, Douglas A. editor | Lim, Ernest, 1977– editor
Title: The oxford handbook of climate change and private law /
Edited by Douglas A. Kysar and Ernest Lim.
Description: 1. | New York : Oxford University Press, 2026. |
Series: Oxford handbooks series | Includes bibliographical references and index.
Identifiers: LCCN 2025048951 (print) | LCCN 2025048952 (ebook) |
ISBN 9780197809167 hardback | ISBN 9780197809174 epub |
ISBN 9780197809181 | ISBN 9780197809198
Subjects: LCSH: Climatic changes—Law and legislation | Environmental law |
Tort liability of corporations | Liability for environmental damages |
Environmental responsibility | Sustainable development—Law and
legislation | Environmental law—Economic aspects
Classification: LCC K955 .O94 2026 (print) | LCC K955 (ebook)
LC record available at https://lccn.loc.gov/2025048951
LC ebook record available at https://lccn.loc.gov/2025048952

DOI: 10.1093/9780197809198.001.0001

Printed by Integrated Books International, United States of America

The manufacturer's authorized representative in the EU for product safety is
Oxford University Press España S.A. of Parque Empresarial San Fernando de Henares,
Avenida de Castilla, 2–28830 Madrid (www.oup.es/en or product.safety@oup.com).
OUP España S.A. also acts as importer into Spain of products made by the manufacturer.

Note to Readers

This publication is designed to provide accurate and authoritative information in regard to the subject matter covered. It is based upon sources believed to be accurate and reliable and is intended to be current as of the time it was written. It is sold with the understanding that the publisher is not engaged in rendering legal, accounting, or other professional services. If legal advice or other expert assistance is required, the services of a competent professional person should be sought. Also, to confirm that the information has not been affected or changed by recent developments, traditional legal research techniques should be used, including checking primary sources where appropriate.

(Based on the Declaration of Principles jointly adopted by a Committee of the American Bar Association and a Committee of Publishers and Associations.)

For Zora and Wells
Douglas A. Kysar

For Mom
Earth-maker, life-giver, and pain-bearer
Ernest Lim

FOREWORD

To a large extent and for a long period the world put the risks associated with climate change to the back of its mind, regarding them essentially as a future threat that would impact on later generations. The Paris Agreement of 2015 and public law measures, such as the UK's Climate Change Act 2008, sought to create a framework for the reduction of carbon emissions, but have not succeeded in reversing the global trend of such emissions.

It is now clear that the risks posed by climate change can no longer be regarded as a problem which only has to be confronted far in the future. They are materialising in the present and are being experienced by all of us with increasing effects. The years 2023 and 2024 were in turn the hottest on record, with 2024 becoming the first year to breach the Paris Agreement's 1.5°C warming threshold. These rising temperatures are driving a cascade of other environmental consequences, including an increase in both the frequency and intensity of extreme weather events. The UK had a severe drought in 2022, which was the joint hottest summer on record, and 2024 brought severe floods and the wettest twelve months in England since 1836. There have been wildfires in Argentina, Australia, Chile, Southern Europe, and the United States, to mention but a few places, many of which have been among the worst ever recorded. Beyond extreme weather, climate change is also causing profound biological and ecological disruption. Shifts in rainfall patterns and rising sea levels are altering ecosystems, with some species facing extinction while others migrate, threatening biodiversity and food supplies. Human health is also affected, as warming expands the range of vector-borne diseases and exacerbates food and water insecurity. These environmental changes are in turn creating widespread physical and economic damage, including the destruction of property, personal injury, and financial losses from business and supply chain disruptions.

The effects of climate change are placing mounting pressures on human societies and their ways of life. This inevitably places pressure in turn on the legal systems which have developed over the *longue durée* to provide practical and conceptual resources to manage the fair distribution of responsibility for coping with losses arising from human interactions, and in particular those arising from unexpected natural disasters, so-called acts of God. The acts of God are impacting the world with increasing frequency and ferocity. The speed of change in the increase of the pressures being experienced has been considerable. The result is that the legal systems and legal concepts which have been developed over time are struggling to adapt to the new environment. The very idea of an act of God has come to be challenged by a sense that it is human agency which is driving the changes; not so much act of God as act of man. But the relevant human agency is very widespread and diffuse in nature, so again the established legal systems and concepts struggle to react to accommodate what is happening within established ideas of legal responsibility.

Techniques for the fair distribution of responsibility, in the sense of distribution of legal rights and legal liabilities, are the essence of private law. Therefore the mounting pressures on societies from climate change are posing challenges—increasingly severe challenges—for private law across the whole field of its operation. This is the context in which the present volume has been produced, to give a comprehensive account written by experts in their fields of how private law is morphing and buckling under the general and increasing pressure of climate change. It need hardly be said that it is most timely. No longer are the risks from climate change something which can be pushed to the background. They are coming to fruition now. Societies need to find ways to live with them. The legal system, and the conceptual regimes it incorporates, need to develop ways to accommodate them and to absorb their impact while trying to maintain their intellectual coherence and sense of shape. The essays in this book provide valuable guidance as to how that might be achieved. The volume's importance as a research handbook for climate change and private law will only grow as the necessity for such work becomes ever more apparent.

Lord Sales
Justice of the Supreme Court
of the United Kingdom

ACKNOWLEDGEMENTS

Speaking with regard to orchestras, the composer Franz Liszt said that "the principal task of a conductor is not to put himself in evidence but to disappear behind his functions as much as possible". We believe the task of editors is comparable and we are mainly content to let the remarkable intellectual contributions made by the authors of this handbook serve as evidence of its worth. We do, however, want to briefly acknowledge and appreciate the many people in addition to the authors who contributed to the success of this project.

Early planning conversations for this handbook included the late Dr. Emily Webster, assistant professor in environmental law in the Department of Land Economy at the University of Cambridge. Dr. Webster's sudden passing was a tragedy to her family and friends, as well as to the entire field of environmental law. We hope that all who encounter this volume will think of the many other sparks and insights she was poised to gift to the world.

Fay Gibbons at Oxford University Press provided invaluable feedback on the initial handbook proposal, as did three anonymous peer reviewers. We are grateful to Fay for believing in this project and for making it better through her every contact throughout its production.

Early versions of this handbook's chapters were workshopped during a conference held at Yale Law School on the 11th and 12th of April, 2025. We are grateful to the co-organisers of that conference: the Yale Law School Center for Private Law, and the Law, Environment, and Animals Program at Yale Law School. We are also indebted to the conference funders: the Oscar M. Ruebhausen Fund at the Yale Law School and the EW Barker Centre for Law & Business at the Faculty of Law, National University of Singapore. The event itself could not have happened without the dedicated and frequently heroic organisational efforts of Kevin Borchert, Laura Capasso, Nick Cifarelli, David Hoover, Jennifer Marshall, Laurie Sellars, Ashley Tucker, and Caroline Zhang. We are grateful to Daina Bray, Malte Deutschmann, Daniel Esty, Eugene Fidell, Joshua Galperin, Jeff Gordon, Viveca Morris, Mark Ortega, Stephanie Safdi, Laurie Sellars, and Garrett West for serving as moderators and commentators alongside the conference authors to ensure the success of the gathering. Additional peer review outside the conference setting was generously provided by Cea Mittler.

Our project editors at OUP, Jordan Burke and Katherine Lowe, and our project manager at NewGen, Suresh Selvamani, all provided admirable stewardship of the handbook throughout the latter and most trying periods of production. In addition, publication of the handbook could not have occurred without the dedicated and inordinately competent assistance of our students. We are especially grateful to Jae D'Alessandro and Param Pandya, who undertook the bulk of the labour with us to ensure that the handbook was complied with all relevant substantive and stylistic guidelines. We are also extremely grateful to Thomas Peterson, Tomás Russo, Victoria Siebor, Amit Singh, and Grant Tucker, who also offered invaluable research assistance.

CONTENTS

Table of Cases xv
Table of International Instruments xxxiii
Editors' Bios li
List of Contributors liii

1. Introduction 1
DOUGLAS A. KYSAR AND ERNEST LIM

PART I Theoretical Approaches to Private Law

2. Law and Economics 17
MICHAEL FAURE

3. Critical and Social Theory 36
K-SUE PARK

4. Relational Justice 49
AVIHAY DORFMAN

PART II Law of Obligations

5. Consumer Climate Contracts 67
ERIC W. ORTS

6. Contract Law 85
IRINA SAKHAROVA

7. Common Law Torts 103
DAVID BULLOCK

8. Causation in Tort 119
MARK A. GEISTFELD AND SANDY STEEL

9. Civil Law Torts 138
ELBERT R. DE JONG

10. Products Liability 156
DOUGLAS A. KYSAR

11. Consumer Protection 173
TIFFANIE CHAN, JULIANA VÉLEZ ECHEVERRI, JOANA SETZER, AND CATHERINE HIGHAM

12. Unjust Enrichment 192
MAYTAL GILBOA, YOTAM KAPLAN, AND ROEE SAREL

13. Fiduciary Law 207
SETH DAVIS AND GREGORY SHAFFER

PART III Property

14. Property Law 229
J. B. RUHL AND JIM ROSSI

15. Cultures of Land Use and Ownership 246
NICOLE GRAHAM

16. Intellectual Property 261
GRAHAM REYNOLDS

17. Trusts 278
CARLA SPIVACK

PART IV Corporate and Commercial Law

18. Corporate Law and Governance 297
ERNEST LIM

19. Climate Disclosure in the Global South 319
MARIA EDUARDA LESSA AND MARIANA PARGENDLER

20. Finance 340
ARJUNA DIBLEY

21. Competition Law 359
JULIAN NOWAG AND THOMAS CHENG

22. Insurance Law 377
FRANZISKA ARNOLD-DWYER

23. Securities Regulation 397
VIRGINIA HARPER HO

24. Bankruptcy Law 416
JOSHUA C. MACEY

25. International Commercial Arbitration 426
YING ZHU

26. Labour Law 442
FRANCES FLANAGAN

27. Maritime Law 459
MARTIN DAVIES

28. Investor–State Disputes 472
KYLA TIENHAARA

29. Corporate Sustainability and the European Union 491
BARBARA POZZO

30. Non-Governmental Organisations and Private Standard Setting 513
CYNTHIA A. WILLIAMS

31. Private Environmental Governance 532
MICHAEL P. VANDENBERGH AND PAUL C. STERN

32. Private International Law 548
EKATERINA ARISTOVA AND UGLJEŠA GRUŠIĆ

PART V Area Perspectives

33. The European Union 571
HARRO VAN ASSELT AND JESSICA CROW

34. The United Kingdom 590
KIM BOUWER

35. The United States 607
JOHN C. DERNBACH

36. India 627
UMAKANTH VAROTTIL

37. Australasia 645
JACQUELINE PEEL

38. East and Southeast Asia 664
JOLENE LIN

39. Africa 680
UZUAZO ETEMIRE

40. China 697
YUE ZHAO AND YI FENG

41. Brazil 716
DANIELLE DE ANDRADE MOREIRA

PART VI Emerging Issues

42. Legal Education 737
CANDIDA LEONE

43. Lawyers and Law Firms 755
CAMILA BUSTOS

44. Artificial Intelligence 774
JAN-ERIK SCHIRMER

45. The Horizontal Effect of Fundamental Rights 791
OLHA O. CHEREDNYCHENKO AND BOUDEWIJN DE BRUIN

46. Indigenous Peoples 808
SAM BOOKMAN

Index 827

TABLE OF CASES

European Union

Court of Justice of the European Union

Albany International (Case C-67/96) EU:C:1999:430 367
Asnef-Equifax, Servicios de InformaciónsobreSolvencia y Crédito SL (Case C-238/05) ECLI:EU:C:2006:734. 374–75
BIDS (Case C-209/07) EU:C:2008:643 366
Budapest Bank Nyrt. and Others (Case C-228/18) EU:C:2020:265. 366–67
Card Bancaire v Commission (Case C-67/13P) EU:C:2014:2204 366–67
Carvalho and Others v Parliament and Council, Case (C-565/19 P) ECLI:EU:C:2021:252. 575
Consten and Grundig v Commission, (Cases 56 and 58–64) ECLI:EU:C:1966:41 372
Deo Antoine Homawoo v GMF Assurances SA (Case C-412/10) ECLI:EU:C:2011:747 561–62
Dole Food and Dole Fresh Fruit Europe v Commission (Case C-286/13P) EU:C:2015:184 366–67
Dumez France SA v Hessische Landesbank (Case C-220/88) ECLI:EU:C:1990:8 559
Generics (UK) Ltd and Others (Case C-307/18) EU:C:2020:52. 366–67
GlaxoSmithKline (Cases C-501/06P, C-513/06P, C-515/06P and C-519/06P) EU: C:2009:610 366
Handelskwekerij G J Bier BV v Mines de potasse d'Alsace SA (Case 21-76) ECLI:EU:C:1976:166. . . . . .558, 559
HSBC v Commission (Case C-883/19P) EU:C:2023:11. 366–67
Lundbeck, P, (Case C-591/16P) EU:C:2021:243 366
Marinari v Lloyds Bank Plc (Case C-364/93) ECLI:EU:C:1995:289 559
MasterCard and Others v Commission (Case C-382/12 P) ECLI:EU:C:2014:2201. 374–75
Owusu v N B Jackson, trading as 'Villa Holidays Bal-Inn Villas' (Case C-281/02) ECLI:EU:C:2005:120 560
Poland v Parliament and Council, (Case C-401/19) CJEU ECLI:EU:C:2022:297 270
Shevill v Presse Alliance SA (Case C-68/93) ECLI:EU:C:1995:61 559
T-Mobile Netherlands and Others (Case C-8/08) EU:C:2009:343. 366–67

European Court of Human Rights

Airey v Ireland, ECHR (1979) Series A, No. 32 798–99
Ashby Donald and others v France, ECHR 36769/08 [5th section], 10 January 2013 270
Dimici v Turkey, No. 70133/16, 5 July 2022 798–99

Duarte Agostinho and Ors v Portugal and others App no 39371/20 (ECtHR, 9 April 2024) 795
Lopez Ostra v Spain App no 16798/90 (ECtHR, 9 December 1994) 794–95
Marckx v Belgium, ECHR (1979) Series A, No. 31 798–99
Neij and Sunde Kolmisoppi v Sweden, App no 4037/12, IHRL 2038 (ECHR 2013), 19 February 2013 270
Pla and Puncernau v Andorra, ECHR (2004) Reports 2004-VIII (2006) 42 EHRR 25 798–99
Tyrer v the United Kingdom App no 5856/72 (ECtHR, 25 April 1978) 793
Verein KlimaSeniorinnen Schweiz and Others v Switzerland, App No. 53600/20, Judgment (Grand Chamber), 9 April 2024 . . . . . 150–51, 585–86, 791, 794–95, 801–2
X and Y v The Netherlands, ECHR (1985) Series A, No. 91 798–99

General Court of the European Union

Carvalho and Others v Parliament and Council, (Case T-330/18) ECLI:EU:T:2019:324 575

International Cases

African Court of Human and Peoples' Rights (AfCHPR)

Kennedy Gihana and others v Republic of Rwanda, App no 017/2015, AfCHPR (28 November 2019) 686–87
Robert John Penessis v United Republic of Tanzania, App no 013/2015, AfCHPR (28 November 2019) 686–87

International Centre for Settlement of Investment Disputes

Azienda ElettricaTicinese v Federal Republic of Germany (ICSID Case. No. ARB/23/47), Claimant's Memorial (26 July 2024) 483, 486
Azienda ElettricaTicinese v Federal Republic of Germany (ICSID Case. No. ARB/23/47), Respondent's Counter-Memorial (26 March 2025) 486–87
Eco Oro Minerals Corp v Republic of Colombia [2021] ICSID Case No. ARB/16/41, Decision on Jurisdiction, Liability and Directions on Quantum 478
Mathias Kruck, Frank Schumm, Joachim Kruck, Jürgen Reiss and others v Kingdom of Spain [2022], ICSID Case No. ARB/15/23, Partial Dissenting Opinion of Zachary Douglas 475
Rockhopper Italia S.p.A., Rockhopper Mediterranean Ltd, and Rockhopper Exploration Plc v Italian Republic, ICSID Case No. ARB/17/14, Final Award (23 August 2022) 475, 480
RWE AG and RWE Eemshaven Holding II BV v Kingdom of the Netherlands (ICSID Case No ARB/21/4) Claimant's Memorial (18 December 2021) 481–82, 486
RWE AG and RWE Eemshaven Holding II BV v Kingdom of the Netherlands (ICSID Case No ARB/21/4) Respondent's Counter-Memorial (5 September 2022) 488

RWE AG and RWE Eemshaven Holding II BV v Kingdom of the Netherlands (ICSID Case No ARB/21/4) Order of the Tribunal Taking Note of the Discontinuance of the Proceeding and Decision on Costs (12 January 2024). 482
Uniper SE, Uniper Benelux Holding BV and Uniper Benelux NV v Kingdom of the Netherlands (ICSID Case No. ARB/21/22), Claimant's Memorial (20 May 2022). 481–82
Westmoreland Coal Company v Government of Canada (ICSID Case No. UNCT/23/2) Award (17 December 2024) 484
Westmoreland Mining Holdings, LLC v Canada (ICSID Case No. UNCT/20/3) Award (31 January 2022) 484
Westmoreland Mining Holdings, LLC v Canada (ICSID Case No. UNCT/20/3) Statement of Defence (26 June 2020) 488

International Court of Justice

Obligations of States in respect of Climate Change, Advisory Opinion, 2025 ICJ Rep No 187 (July 23) 211, 448–49, 683, 685, 690, 793–94

National Cases

Australia

Abrahams v CBA (No 2) NSD864/2021 <https://comcourts.gov.au/file/Federal/P/NSD864/2021/actions> accessed 2 March 2025 651
Abrahams v CBA, Consent Order, 13 April 2023 <https://comcourts.gov.au/file/Federal/P/NSD864/2021/3921677/event/31377494/document/2089025> accessed 2 March 2025 651
AGL Energy Limited v Greenpeace Australia Pacific Limited [2021] FCA 625. 656
Australasian Centre for Corporate Responsibility v Santos Ltd NSD858/2021 656
Australian Competition and Consumer Commission v Volkswagen Aktiengesellschaft [2019] FCA 2166; [2021] FCAFC 49. 654
Australian Securities and Investments Commission v LGSS Pty Ltd (Active Super) [2024] FCA 587. 652–53
Australian Securities and Investments Commission v Mercer Superannuation (Australia) Limited [2024] FCA 850 652–53
Australian Securities and Investments Commission v Vanguard Investments Australia Ltd [2024] FCA 308 652–53
Barrier Branch of the Amalgamated Miners' Association of Broken Hill v The Broken Hill Proprietary Company Limited, The (1909) 3 CAR 1 34. 452–53
Beere v National Australia Bank, NSD715/2024 651–52
Catherine Rossiter v ANZ Group Holdings Limited NSD1315/2023. 651–52
Clancy v Butchers' Shop Employees Union (1904) 1 CLR 181 449
Coldwater First Nation v Canada 2020 FCA 34 823
Ex parte H.V. McKay (1907) 2 CAR 1 452
Gippsland Coastal Board v South Gippsland Shire Council [2008] 1545 (VCAT) . . . 698

Greenpeace Australia Pacific Limited v Woodside Energy Group Ltd NSD1520/2023. 654
Guy Abrahams & Kim Abrahams as trustee for the Guy & Kim Abrahams Family Trust v Commonwealth Bank of Australia (CBA) NSD864/2021 176–77
John Pfeiffer Pty Ltd v Rogerson [2000] HCA 36 564–65
Master Builders' Association (NSW) v Australian Building Construction Employees and Builders Labourers Federation (1974) 23 FLR 356 455
Milirrpum v Nabalco (1971) 17 FLR 141 259
Minister for the Environment v Sharma [2022] FCAFC 35 . . . . . 110–11, 648, 657–58, 660, 661, 663
Pabai v Commonwealth of Australia VID622/2021 (Statement of Claim, 26 October 2021). 658, 814–15
Regie National des Usines Renault SA v Zhang [2002] HCA 10 564–65
Sharma by her litigation representative Sister Marie Brigid Arthur v Minister for Environment [2021] FCA 560 . . . . . 109–11, 648, 657, 658
Uren v Bald Hills Wind Farm Pty Ltd [2022] VSC 145 657
Voth v Manildra Flour Mills Pty Ltd (1990) 171 CLR 538 560
Waratah Coal Pty Ltd v Youth Verdict Ltd & Ors (No 6) [2022] QLC 21 484

Belgium

VZW Klimaatzaak v Kingdom of Belgium 2015/4585/A (17 June 2021) 109–10

Brazil

AMOREMA e AMORETGRAP v Sustainable Carbon and others [2021] ACP 1045416-11.2021.4.01.3900. . . . . 179–80, 182, 183, 185–86, 187–88, 189, 191
CarbonextTecnologiaemSoluçõesAmbientais Ltda. v Amazon Imóveis (Voluntary Carbon Market), 1072768-63.2021.8.26.0100, Decision (1 July 2021) 428–29
Instituto Arayara v Copel, Instituto Água e Terra e outros (UTE Figueira), ACP 5015788-26.2024.4.04.7001/PR, TJDFT 728–29
Instituto Brasileiro de Defesa do Consumidor (IDEC) v Gol LinhasAéreas S/A [2025] Interpelação Judicial 1007633-65.2025.8.26.0100 185
Instituto Brasileiro de Defesa do Consumidor (IDEC) v Localiza Rent A CAR S/ A [2025] 1007605-97.2025.8.26.0100 185
Ministério Público Federal e ANAB v União e outros (Litígioestruturalsobredesa streclimático no RS). 730–31
Ministério Público Federal e INCRA v Joel de Souza (Desmatamento e danoclimático no PAE Antimary) Justiça Federal da 1a Região 7ª Vara Federal Ambiental e Agrária da SJAMP ACP 1022425-07.2021.4.01.3200 729–30

Canada

Attorney-General v Ewen (1895) 3 BCR 468 (BCSC) 108
Club Resorts Ltd v Van Breda 2012 SCC 17 . . . . . 559, 560
Clyde River (Hamlet) v Petroleum Geo-Services Inc. [2017] 1 SCR 1069. 821–22
Cook v Lewis [1951] SCR 830 . . . . . 133, 134

George v Newfoundland and Labrador (2016) 399 DLR (4th) 440 106
Guerin v R [1984] 2 SCR 335 . . . . 809–10, 821–22
Haida Nation v British Columbia [2004] 3 SCR 511 821–22
Mikisew Cree First Nation v Canada [2018] 2 SCR 765 821–22
Pro-Swing Inc v Elta Golf Inc [2006] 2 SCR 612 567
R v Sparrow [1990] 1 SCR 1075 821–22
Snell v Farrell [1990] 2 SCR 311 194–95
Tolofson v Jensen [1994] 3 SCR 1022 564–65
Tsihqot'in Nation v British Columbia [2014] 2 SCR 257 (SCC) 812
Tsleil-Waututh Nation v Canada 2018 FCA 153 822–23
United States of America v Ivey 30 OR (3d) 370, 139 DLR (4th) 570 567
Vancouver Aquarium Marine Science Centre v Charbonneau, 2017 BCCA 395 270

China

Beijing Fengtai District Source Lovers Environmental Research Institute and others v Shenzhen China Optoelectronics (Shenzhen) Co., Ltd. [2019] No. 3509 Yue 03 Min Chu (Shenzhen Intermediate People's Court of Guangdong Province) 711
Deng Peng v Cheng Tianjie [2021] No. 3356 Chuan 0682 Min Chu (Shifang City People's Court of Sichuan Province) 714
Fan Min v Jinke Smart Service Group Co., Ltd. [2022] No. 2470 Chuan 0105 Min chu (Qingyang District People's Court of Chengdu City) 709–10
Fujian Green Home Environmental Friendliness Center v Dingyu Building Materials (Zhangzhou) Co., Ltd. [2021] No. 3933 Min 06 Min Zhong (Zhangzhou Intermediate People's Court of Fujian Province) 710–11
Fujian Green Home Environmental Friendliness Center v Zhao'anHanxin Stone Co., Ltd. [2021] No. 3932 Min 06 Min Zhong (Zhangzhou Intermediate People's Court of Fujian Province) 710–11
Fuzhou Railway Building Co., Ltd. v Fuzhou Federal Commercial Co., Ltd. [2016] No. 7871 Min 0102 Min Chu (Gulou District People's Court of Fuzhou City, Fujian Province) 711–12
Hua Jianwei v Guangdong Zhong'ao Property Management Co., Ltd. [2017] No. 12202 Zhe 0109 Min Chu (Xiaoshan District People's Court of Hangzhou City) 708
Huang Moukai v Xiamen XX Property Management Co., Ltd. [2022] No. 11758 Min 0203 Min Chu (Siming District People's Court of Xiamen City, Fujian Province) 713
Li Ruirui v Tianjin Binhai Real Estate Management Co., Ltd. [2018] No. 3451 Jin 0116 Min Chu (Binhai New Area People's Court of Tianjin Municipality) 714
Ma Hong. Chengdu Zhonghewei Property Group Co., Ltd. [2022] No. 3673 Xin 0109 Min Chu (Midong District People's Court of Urumqi City, Xinjiang Uygur Autonomous Region) 709–10
Qingdao Moore Property Management Co., Ltd. and Qingdao Gome Electrical Appliances Co., Ltd. [2022] No. 1868 Lu 0203 Min Ch (Shibei District People's Court of Qingdao City, Shandong Province) 712

Shang Siming v Luoyang Yingfu Property Management Co., Ltd. [2022] No. 2821 Yu 0303 Min Chu (Xigong District People's Court of Luoyang City, Henan Province) 706–7, 708
Wu Lingjie v Henan Hongjiang Real Estate Development Co., Ltd. [2018] No. 696 Yu 0102 Min Chu (Zhongyuan District People's Court of Zhengzhou City, Henan Province) 714
Xinjiang Xintao Silicon Industry Co., Ltd. v Yang Peng [2022] NO.2201 Xin 2105 Min Chu (Yizhou District People's Court, Hami, Xinjiang Uygur Autonomous Region, China) 704
Yu Tianrong v The Owners Committee of YundingHuating Community [2022] No. 4810 Yue 0783 Min Chu (Kaiping City People's Court of Guangdong Province) 706
Zhangxin v Yifeng [2019] No. 37355 Jing 0102 Min Chu (Xicheng District People's Court of Beijing Municipality) 704
Zhao v SipingFengyi Property Management Co., Ltd.[2023] No. 3588 Ji 0303 Min Chu (Tiedong District People's Court of Siping City, Jilin Province) 708

Colombia

Members of Indigenous community 'Gran Cumbal' v SVP Business SAS, Global Consulting and Assessment Services SA, Deutsche Certification Body SAS, COLCX and the Indigenous authority of 'Gran Cumbal' [2023] 2023000095-00 185
Pirá Paraná Indigenous Council and Association of Indigenous Traditional Authorities of river Pirá Paraná 'ACAIPI' v Ministry of Environment and Sustainable Development and others [2024] T-9.312.858 . . . . 185, 186, 190

France

Notre affaire à tous et autres v TotalEnergies (Complaint, English Version, unofficial translation) 28 January 2020 587–88
Notre affaire à tous et autres v TotalEnergies, n° RG 23/14348, 18 June 2024 . . . . 583, 587–88

Germany

BGH, 27.6.2024–IZR 98/23, ECLI:DE:BGH:2024:270624 UIZR98.23.0 589
BGH, I ZR 98/23 (27 June 2024), ECLI:DE:BGH:2024:270624UIZR98.23.0 581–82
BVerfG, Neubauer v Germany, 1 BvR 2656/18 (24 March 2021) 575
Luciano Lliuya v RWE AG Case number 5 U 15/17 OLG Hamm (Germany) 395
Saúl Luciano Lliuya v RWE AG Case I-5 U 15/17 (Oberlandesgericht Hamm, 28 May 2025) 23–24, 122, 130, 138–40, 147–48, 150, 552, 554, 557, 561–62, 563–64, 568, 587, 589, 698, 731–32

Hong Kong

Fong Chak Kwan v Ascentic Ltd [2022] HKCFA 12 . . . . 559, 560

India

Energy Watchdog v Central Electricity Regulatory Commission 2017 INSC 338 640

Goa Foundation v Union of India (Goa Foundation) (2014) 6 SCC 590 . . . . . 632–33, 635
Goel Ganga Developers India Pvt Ltd v Union of India (Goel Ganga Developers) 2018 INSC 696 . . . . . 633–34, 635
Gujarat Urja Vikas Nigam Limited v Renew Wind Energy (Rajkot) Private Limited 2023 INSC 366 641
Hindustan Zinc Ltd v Rajasthan Electricity Regulatory Commission (2015) 12 SCC 611 640–41
Indian Council for Enviro-Legal Action v Union of India (Indian Council for Enviro-Legal Action) 1996 INSC 237 . . . . . 632, 633
Kaushal Kishor v State of Uttar Pradesh (Kaushal Kishor) 2023 INSC 4 629
Kotah Transport Ltd v Jhalawar Transport Services Ltd, AIR 1960 Raj 224. 564–65
M.C. Mehta v Kamal Nath 1996 INSC 1482 630
M.C. Mehta v Union of India (Oleum Leak Case) 1986 INSC 281. 631–32
Maharashtra State Electricity Distribution Co. Limited v Adani Power Maharashtra Limited 2023 INSC 400 640
Maharashtra State Electricity Distribution Company Limited v Adani Power Maharashtra Limited 2023 SCC OnLine SC 233 591–92
Manoj Mishra v Delhi Developmental Authority 2016 SCC OnLine NGT 114 . . . 633–34
Mayar (HK) Ltd v Owners and Parties, Vessels MV Fortune Ltd AIR [2006] SC 1828 560
M.K. Ranjitsinh v Union of India (M.K. Ranjitsinh 2021) 2021 INSC 257 . . . . . 638, 639
MK Ranjitsinh v Union of India 2024 INSC 280. . . . . . 628, 629, 634–35, 794–95
Municipal Council, Ratlam v Vardhichand 1980 INSC 138 630
National Textile Workers' Union v PR Ramakrishnan 1983 INSC 57 639
Rajkot Municipal Corporation v Manjulben Jayantilal Nakum 1997 INSC 34 635
Rural Litigation and Entitlement Kendra, Dehradun v State of U.P. 1985 INSC 49. . . 629
Sona Devi v Anil Kumar [2011] 3 TAC 552 564–65
Sterlite Industries (India) Ltd v Union of India 2013 INSC 204. 632–33
Sushil Bhatt v Moon Beverages Ltd 2022 SCC OnLine NGT 76 633–34
T.N. GodavarmanThirumulpad v Union of India 2005 INSC 439 632
Tata Consultancy Services Limited v Cyrus Investments Pvt. Ltd.(Tata Consultancy Services Limited) 2021 INSC 217 639
Vellore Citizens Welfare Forum v Union of India (Vellore Citizens Welfare Forum) 1996 INSC 952. 632

Ireland

Friends of the Irish Environment v Government of Ireland [2020] IESC 49. 575

Kenya

Osman & 164 others (Suing on Their Behalf and Behalf of Residents of Merti Sub-County, Chari, and Cherab Wards in Isiolo County) v Northern Rangelands Trust & 8 others (Petition E006 of 2021) [2025] KEELC 99 (KLR) (24 January 2025) 180
Save Lamu and Others v National Environmental Management Authority and Amu Power Co Ltd [2019] KLR (High Court of Kenya) 666–67

Malaysia

American Express Bank Ltd v Mohamed Toufic Al-Ozeir [1995] 1 MLJ 160 (SC).... 560

Mexico

Greenpeace v Energy Regulatory Commission [2023] Amparo No. 239/2023 ... 179–80
Nuestros Derechos al Futuro y Medio Ambiente Sano and CEMDA v Energy Regulatory Commission [2023] Amparo No. 256/2023 179–80

Nepal

Shrestha v Office of the Prime Minister and others (2018) 074-WO-0283 (Supreme Court of Nepal).. 698

Netherlands

Aidstest II HR 12 December 2003, NJ 2004, 117............................... 800–1
Bonser-Lain v Texas Commission on Environmental Quality, 2012 WL 3164561 (Texas District Court August 2, 2012) 283
Fossielvrij v KLM C/13/719848/HA ZA 22-524, 20 March 2024 583
FossielVrij NL and ReclameFossielvrij v Koninklijke Luchtvaart Maatschappij N.V. (KLM), Amsterdam District Court, Case No. C/13/710651/HA ZA 22-836 588
Gerechtshof Den Haag, 12 November 2024, ECLI:NL:GHDHA:2024:2099 ....138, 141, 147, 150, 152–53
Maimonides HR 22 January 1988, NJ 1988, 891 800–1
Mensendieck I HR 31 October 1969, NJ 1970, 57............................. 800–1
Milieudefensie et al. v Royal Dutch Shell plc (2021) District Court of The Hague, Case No C/09/571932/HA ZA 19-379, ECLI:NL:RBDHA:2021:5339, Judgment of 26 May 2021........153, 200–1, 223–24, 551–52, 554, 557, 561–62, 563–64, 568, 575, 583, 584, 586, 587, 589, 590, 596, 598–99, 668–69, 791–92, 796–97, 801
Netherlands v Urgenda Foundation, Case 19/00135, (Supreme Court of the Netherlands), ECLI:NL:HR:2019:2007 (20 December 2019) 223
Royal Dutch Shell Plc v Vereninging Mileudefensie, Case 200.302.332/01, (Hague Court of Appeal), RBDHA, C/09/571932, ECLI:NL:GHDHA:2024:2100 (12 November 2024)............... 22, 27, 109–10, 138–40, 148, 150, 153, 154, 223–24, 552, 584–85, 586, 587, 630–31, 634–35, 660, 697–98
Shell and others v Vereniging Milieudefensie and others [2024] Hague Court of Appeal, 200.302.332/01, ECLI:NL:GHDHA:2024:2099........ 791–92, 801–2, 804
State of the Netherlands v Urgenda Foundation (Supreme Court of the Netherlands, 20 December 2019) ECLI:NL:HR:2019:2007, Case No. 19/00135........... 20–21, 22, 27, 109, 150–51, 152, 200–1, 575, 584, 586, 791, 794–95, 801–2
Urgenda Foundation v Netherlands (District Court of the Hague), Case C/09/456689/HA ZA 13-1396, ECLI:NL:RBDHA:2015:7196 (14 June 2015) 223, 586, 590, 596–97

New Zealand

Attorney-General v Abraham and Williams Ltd [1949] NZLR 461 (CA). 113, 815
Consumer NZ & Ors v Z Energy, [2024] NZHC 2018 . . . . 645, 659
Ellis v R (Continuance) [2022] NZSC 114, [2022] 1 NZLR 239. . . . . 116, 812
Lawyers for Climate Action & Ors v Firstgas, Advertising Standards Complaint Board, Complaint 21/194, Decision 6 July 2021 . . . . 645, 659
Medical Assurance Society New Zealand Ltd v East [2015] NZCA 250 383–84
Michael John Smith v Fonterra Co-Operative Group Limited [2024] NZSC 5. . . . . .590, 591–92, 634–35, 645–46, 658, 659–63
Nireaha Tamaki v Baker (1901) NZPCC 371 116
Proprietors of Wakatū v Attorney-General [2017] NZSC 17, [2017] 1 NZLR 423 809–10
R v Symonds (1847) NZPCC 387. 116
Rea v Wellington City Council [2007] NZRMA 449 (HC) 107
Runanganui o Te Ika Whenua Inc Soc v Attorney-General [1994] 2 NZLR 20 (CA) 116
Smith v Attorney-General [2024] NZCA 692 822–23
Smith v Fonterra [2024] NZSC 7. . . . . 812, 813, 814, 815, 822–23
Smith v Fonterra Co-Operative Group Limited [2021] NZCA 552 (Court of Appeal of New Zealand, 21 October 2021). 660
Smith v Fonterra Co-operative Group Ltd [2020] NZHC 419, [2020] 2 NZLR 394 111
Smith v Fonterra Co-Operative Group Ltd [2021] NZCA 552, [2022] 2 NZLR 284 . . . . 104, 106–7, 108–9, 111–12, 129, 145, 152, 170
Smith v Fonterra Co-Operative Group Ltd [2022] NZSC 35 109–10
Smith v Fonterra Co-Operative Group Ltd [2024] NZSC 5, [2024] 1 NZLR 134. . . . . .112, 113, 116, 117–18
Smith v Fonterra Co-operative Group Ltd, SC 149/2021 [2024] NZSC 5154 145–46
Takamore v Clarke [2012] NZSC 116. 812
Trans-Tasman Resources Ltd v Taranaki-Whanganui Conservation Board [2021] NZSC 127, [2021] 1 NZLR 801 . . . . 116, 812

Nigeria

Centre for Oil Pollution Watch (COPW) v Nigerian National Petroleum Corporation (NNPC) (2019) 15 NWLR 1666 . . . . 688–89, 691, 694–95
Chinda & Ors v Shell Petroleum Development Co. Ltd (1974) 2 RSLR 1 686–87
Gbemre v Shell Petroleum Development Company Nigeria Ltd and Ors Unreported, Suit No: FHC/B/CS/53/05 (14 November 2005). 690–91
Oronto Douglas v Shell Petroleum Development Company Nigeria Limited and Ors Unreported Suit No: FHC/L/CS/573/96 (17 February 1997) 688

Pakistan

D. G. Khan Cement Company v Government of Punjab [2019] C.P.1290-L/2019 (Supreme Court of Pakistan) 698

Philippines

FCF Minerals Corporation v Lunag and Others (896 Phil 806; 119 OG No 36, 6997, 4 September 2023) 665

Singapore

Rappo v Accent Delight International Ltd [2017] 2 SLR 265 560
Rickshaw Investments Ltd v Nicolai Baron von Uexkull [2006] SGCA 39 564–65
Zero Greenwashing Alliance, Case File: S/T/02—Scoot (2023) 674–75
Zero Greenwashing Alliance, Case File: S/T/03—Singapore Airlines (2023) 674–75

South Africa

Earthlife Africa Johannesburg v Minister of Environmental Affairs (65662/16) [2017] ZAGPPHC 58 682
Gonggose v Minister of Agriculture [2018] ZASCA 87 815–16
Maledu v IterelengBakgatla Mineral Resources [2018] ZACC 41 815–16
Philippi Horticultural Area Food & Farming Campaign v MEC for Local Government, Environmental Affairs and Development Planning: Western Cape (16779/17) [2020] ZAWCHC 8 682

South Korea

Constitutional Court of South Korea, Do-Hyun Kim and 18 others v South Korea, judgment of 29 August 2024 671–72

Uganda

Mbabazi v The Attorney General and National Environmental Management Civil Suit No. 283 of 2012 682

United Kingdom

A Local Authority v W [2005] EWHC 1564 (Fam) 803–4
Adams v Cape Industries Plc [1990] 1 Ch 433 (CA) 557, 567
Addis v Gramophone Co Ltd [1909] AC 488 (HL) 92–93
Airbus Industrie GIE v Patel [1999] 1 AC 119 (HL) 567
Anonymous (1535) YB Mich 27 Hen 8, f 27, pl 10 106
Attorney-General v Birmingham (1858) 4 K & J 528, (1858) 70 Eng Rep 220 108
Attorney-General v Leeds Corporation (1870) 5 Ch App 583 108
Bailey v Ministry of Defence [2008] EWCA Civ 883 127
Baker v Willoughby [1970] AC 467 131
Banque Keyser Ullmann SA v Skandia (UK) Insurance Co Ltd [1990] 1 Q.B. 665 . . . 388
Barker v Corus [2006] 2 AC 572 . . . . . . 125, 134
Beauchamp v National Mutual Indemnity Insurance Co [1937] 3 All E.R. 19 382–83
Blair v Deakin (1887) 57 LT 522 (Ch) 108
Bonnington Castings Ltd v Wardlaw [1956] AC 613 (HL); [1956] 1 All ER 615 . . . . 107, 130
Boyd v Ineos Upstream Limited [2019] EWCA Civ 515 110–11
Breyer Group plc and others v Department of Energy and Climate Change [2014] EWHC 2257 (QB) 601–3

Breyer Group plc and others v Department of Energy and Climate Change [2015] EWCA Civ 408 601–3
British South Africa Co v Companhia de Moçambique [1893] AC 602 (HL) 557, 559
Brunei Investment Agency v Fidelis Nominees Ltd [2008] Jersey LR 337 567
BTI 2014 LLC v Sequana SA [2022] UKSC 25 .... 304, 307
Campbell v MGN Newspaper Ltd [2004] UKHL 22 801
Carter v Boehm (1766) 3 Burr. 1905 388
Castellain v Preston (1883) 11 QBD 380 (CA) 386 .... 383–84, 390
Cavendish Square Holding BV v Makdessi, ParkingEye Ltd v Beavis [2015] UKSC 67, [2016] AC 1172 95
Chaplin v Boys [1971] AC 356 (HL) 564–65
ClientEarth v Shell's Board of Directors [2023] EWHC 1137 (Ch); [2023] EWHC 1897 (Ch); [2023] EWHC 2182 (Ch) 225, 297, 300, 598–601, 650, 661
Conservative and Unionist Central Office v Burrell [1982] 1 WLR 522 (CA) 100
Co-operative Insurance Soc Ltd v Argyll Stores (Holdings) Ltd [1998] AC 1 (HL) 93–94
Cowan v Scargill [1985] Ch 270 (Ch) 598–99
Crossley and others v Volkswagen and others [2021] EWHC 3444 603
Crossley and Sons Ltd v Lightowler (1867) LR 2 Ch App 478 108
Delos Shipholding SA v Allianz Global Corporate and Specialty SE [2024] EWHC 719 (Comm) 392
Douglas v Hello! Ltd [2001] QB 967 C.A. 800–1
Drax Power Ltd and Infinis Energy Holdings v HM Treasury and Secretary of State for Climate Change [2016] EWHC 228 602–3
Dunlop v New Garage [1915] AC 79 (HL) 95–96
East Suffolk Rivers Catchment Board v Kent [1941] AC 74 597–98
Fairchild v Glenhaven Funeral Services [2003] 1 AC 32 .... 134, 135
Financial Conduct Authority v Arch Insurance [2021] UKSC 1 126
Foss v Harbottle (1843) 2 Hare 461 (Ch) 600
FS Cairo (Nile Plaza) LLC v Brownlie [2021] UKSC 45 559
Galoo Ltd v Bright Grahame Murray [1994] 1 WLR 1360 (CA) 1370) 92
Gatwick Investment Ltd v Liberty Mutual Insurance Europe SE [2024] EWHC 124 (Comm) 395
Grand View Private Trust Co. v Wong (No 2) [2022] UKPA 47 210
Harper v GN Haden & Sons [1933] Ch 298 (CA) 106–7
Harries v Church Commissioners for England [1992] 1 WLR 1241 (Ch) 605
Hesperides Hotels Ltd v Aegean Turkish Holidays [1979] AC 508 (HL) 557
Hickman v Kent or Romney Marsh Sheep-Breeders' Association [1915] 1 Ch 881 ... 309
HM Treasury and another v Global Feedback Limited and another [2025] EWCA Civ 624 594
Holbeck Hall v Scarborough [2000] 2 ALL ER 705 597–98
Holmes v Poeton Holdings Ltd [2023] EWCA Civ 1377 130
Infinis Energy Holdings Ltd v Her Majesty's Treasury and HM Revenue & Customs [2016] EWCA Civ 1030 602–3

Integrated Container Service v British Traders Insurance Co [1984]
1 Lloyd's Rep. 154 393
Investment Trust Companies (in liquidation) v Revenue and Customs
Commissioners [2017] UKSC 29, [2018] AC 275 195
Jobling v Associated Dairies [1982] AC 794 131
John Edwards and Co v Motor Union Insurance Co Ltd [1922] 2 KB 249 394–95
Johnson v Spiller (1784) 3 Doug 371 103
Kuwait Airways Corp v Kuwait Insurance Co SAK No.1) [1999]
1 Lloyd's Rep. 803 391
Leeds City Council v Barclays Bank [2021] EWHC 363 (Comm) 603
Linelevel Ltd v PowszechnyZakladUbezpieczen SA (the Nore Challenger) [2005]
2 Lloyd's Rep. 534 393
Lingké v Christchurch Corporation [1912] 3 KB 595 (CA) 106–7
Lubbe v Cape Plc [2000] 1 WLR 1545 (HL) 560
Malik v Bank of Credit and Commerce International SA [1998] 1 AC 20 (HL) 93
Marks & Spencer Plc v BNP Paribas Securities Services Trust Co (Jersey) Ltd
[2015] UKSC 72 389
McGaughey v Universities Superannuation Scheme Ltd (CA) [2023]
EWCA Civ 873 .... 598–99, 600
McGaughey v Universities Superannuation Scheme Ltd [2022]
EWHC 565 (Ch) 598, 600
Metall und Rohstoff AG v Donaldson Lufkin & Jenrette Inc [1990]
1 QB 391 (CA) 558
Murungaru v Secretary of State for the Home Department [2008]
EWCA Civ 1015 602
National Oilwell (UK) Ltd v Davy Offshore Ltd [1993] 2 Lloyd's Rep 582 391
Netherlands v Youell [1998] 1 Lloyd's Rep. 236 392
Noble Resources and Unirise Development v George Albert Greenwood
(The Vasso) [1993] 2 Lloyd's Rep. 309 393
Nyang v G4S Care & Justice Services Ltd [2013] EWHC 3946 (QB) 194–95
Pattni v Ali [2006] UKPC 51 567
Phillips v Eyre (1870) LR 6 QB 1 564–65
Photo Production Ltd v Securicor Transport Ltd [1980] AC 827 (HL) 94–95
Quadrant Visual Communications Ltd v Hutchison Telephone (UK) Ltd [1993]
BCLC 442 (CA) 95
R v Brown [2022] EWCA Crim 6 110–11
R v L [2008] EWCA Crim 1970, [2009] 1 All ER 786 100
R v Rimmington [2005] UKHL 63; [2006] 1 AC 459 113
R (Homesun Holdings Ltd) v Secretary of State [2012] EWCA Civ 28 601–2
R (oao Friends of the Earth, ClientEarth and Good Law Project) v Secretary of
State for Energy and Net Zero (Net Zero II) [2024] EWHC 995 (Admin) 595–97
R (oao Friends of the Earth, Kevin Jordan and Douglas Paulley) v the
Secretary of State for Environment, Food and Rural Affairs [2024]
EWHC 2707 (Admin) 597–98

R (on the application of Finch on behalf of the Weald Action Group) v Surrey County Council and others [2024] UKSC 20 595–96
R (on the application of Friends of the Earth Ltd and others) v Secretary of State for the Business, Energy and Industrial Strategy (Net Zero I) [2022] EWHC 1841 (Admin) 595–97
R (on the application of Homesun Holdings) v Secretary of State for Energy and Climate Change [2011] EWHC 3575 (Admin) 601–2
R (on the application of Miller and another) v Secretary of State for Exiting the European Union [2017] UKSC 5 595–96
R (on the application of Sarah Finch on behalf of the Weald Action Group) v Surrey County Council and others [2022] EWCA Civ 187 595–96
Red Sea Insurance Co Ltd v Bouygues SA [1995] 1 AC 190 (PC, appeal from Hong Kong) 564–65
Reynolds and Anderson v Phoenix Insurance Co [1978] 2 Lloyd's Rep. 440 383–84
Roberts v R [2018] EWCA Crim 2739 110–11
Robinson v Harman (1848) 1 Exch 850 (Ex Ct) 855 92–93
Rothwell v Chemical & Insulating Co Ltd; Re Pleural Plaques Litigation [2006] EWCA Civ 27, [2004] 4 All ER 1161 107
Royal Boskalis Westminster NV v Mountain [1997] L.R.L.R. 523 393
Royal Boskalis Westminster NV v Mountain [1999] QB 674 . . . . 391, 393
RTI Ltd v Mur Shipping BV [2024] UKSC 18, [2024] 2 W.L.R. 1350 393
Rylands v Fletcher (1868) LR 3 HL 330 . . . . 116, 631–32
S (Identity: Restrictions on Publication), Re [2004] UKHL 47 803–4
Sarah Butler-Schloss and others v The Charity Commissioner for England and Wales v The Attorney General [2022] EWHC 974 (Ch) 604–5
Sartex Quilts and Textiles Ltd v Endurance Corporate Capital Ltd 2019] EWHC 1103 383–84
Saunders v Vautier [1841] EWHC Ch J82, (1841) 4 Beav 115 (1841) 49 ER 282 . . . . 291, 292
Saxon Woods v Costa [2025] EWCA Civ 708 599
Seele Austria GmbH & Co v Tokio Marine Europe Insurance Ltd [2007] EWHC 1411 391
Sharp Corp Ltd v Viterra BV [2024] UKSC 14 392
Skatteforvaltningen v Solo Capital Partners LLP [2023] UKSC 40 567
Sky UK Ltd v Riverstone Managing Agency Ltd [2024] EWCA Civ 1567 . . . . 379–80, 390–91, 392
Solaria Energy UK Ltd v Department for Business, Energy and Industrial Strategy [2020] EWCA Civ 1625 602–3
Soltau v De Held (1851) Sim (NS) 133 106–7
Star Sea, The [2001] UKHL 1 389
Stonegate Pub Co Ltd v MS Amlin Corporate Member Ltd [2022] EWHC 2548 395
Szalatnay-Stacho v Fink [1947] KB 1 564–65
Tijani v Secretary Southern Nigeria [1921] 2 AC 399 116
Tindall v Chief Constable of Thames Valley Police [2024] UKSC 33 597–98
Veba Oil Supply & Trading GmbH v Petrotrade Inc [2001] EWCA Civ 1832, [2002] 1 All ER 703 107

White & Carter (Councils) Ltd v McGregor [1962] A.C. 413 393
Wildtree Hotels Ltd v Harrow London Bourgh Council [2001] 2 AC 1 (HL) 106–7
Woodyear v Schaefer 57 Md 1 (1881) 108
Woolfall and Rimmer v Moyle [1942] 1 K.B. 66 382–83
Yorkshire Water Services Limited v Sun Alliance London Insurance Plc [1997] C.L.C. 213 391
Yorkshire Water Services Ltd v Sun Alliance and London Insurance Plc [1997] 2 Lloyd's Rep 21 391

United States

ABC Learning Centres Ltd, In re 728 F3d 301, 306 (3rd Cir 2013) 422
Alec L. v Jackson, 863 F. Supp. 2d 11 (D.C. 2012) 282
Alliance to Protect Nantucket Sound v Energy Facilities Siting Board, 932 NE 2d 787 (Mass 2010) 284
Allied Tube v Indian Head, Incorporated 486 US 492 (1988) 369
American Electric Power Co Inc v Connecticut 564 US 410 (2011) 110, 194
Ark Land Co v Harper (W Va 2004) 39–40
Aronow v Minnesota, 2012 WL 4476642 (2012) 284
Asahi Metal Industry Co v Superior Court of California, 480 US 102 (1987) 559
Belmont Association Inc. v Farwig 381 N.C. 306, 873 S.E.2d 486 (N.C. 2022) 238
Berrin v Delta Air Lines Inc 2:23 cv 04150 CD Cal 177, 178
Berrin v Delta Air Lines Inc, slip op, 2024 WL 3304815 (CD Cal, 28 March 2024) 78
Black v Kroger 527 SW2d 794 (Tex App–Houston [1st Dist.] 1975) 57
Board of Trade of City of Chicago v United States 246 US 231, 238 (1918) 361–62
Boomer v Atlantic Cement Co (1970) 257 NE2d 870 39–40
Bremen v Zapata Off-Shore Co., The 407 US 1 (1972) 746, 747
Bristol-Myers Squibb Co v Superior Court of California, 137 S Ct 1773 (2017) 559
Broadcast Music v Columbia Broadcasting System 441 US 1 (1979) 367–68
Brown v Superior Court, 751 P 2d 479 (Cal 1988) 134
Bush v Rust-Oleum Corp, slip op, 2024 WL 422080 (ND Cal, 5 February 2024 78
Butler v Brewer, 2013 WL 1091209 (Ariz App 14 March 2013) 283
California Dental Association v Federal Trade Commission 526 US 766, 781 (1999) 361, 362
Caremark Int'l Inc Derivative Litig, In re 698 A. 2d 959 (Del. Ch. 1996) 221
Caronia v Phillip Morris USA, Inc., 5 N.E.3d 11, 14 (N.Y. 2013) 125
Chamber of Commerce of the US v US Dep't of Labor, 885 F.3d 360 (5th Cir. 2018) 612
Chernaik v Brown, 475 P 3d 68 (OR 2019) 283–84
City & County of Honolulu v Sunoco Case No. 20-cv-00163-DKW-RT (D. Haw. 5 March 2021) 591–92
City & County of Honolulu v Sunoco LP SCAP-22-0000429, 31 October 2023 109
City of Hoboken v Exxon Mobil Corp No 003179-20 (Amended Complaint) (NJ Super Ct Law Div 21 Apr 2023) 169–70, 176
City of New York v BP Plc, 325 F Supp 3d 466 (SDNY 2018) 566

City of New York v Chevron 993 F3d 81 (2d Cir 2019) .170
City of Oakland v BP Plc, 325 F Supp 3d 1017 (ND Cal 2018) 550–51, 555, 566
City of Oakland v BP Plc, 969 F 3d 895 (9th Cir 2020) 566
Claflin v Claflin [1889] 20 NE 454 .291, 292
Commissioners of Pub. Works of City of Charleston v Costco Wholesale Corp No 2:21-CV-42-RMG, 2021 WL 5908758 (DSC 13 Dec 2021) 164–65
Conservation L Found Inc v ExxonMobil Corp No 1:16-cv-11950-MLW (Amended Complaint) (D Mass 20 Oct 2017) 166
Cotnam v Wisdom 104 SW 164 (Ark 1907) .197
Daimler AG v Bauman, 571 US 117 (2014) .557
Dass v Tosco Corp 280 F Appx 571, 571 (9th Cir 2008) .197
Dollar General Corp. v Mississippi Band of Choctaw Indians, 578 US 545 (2016) .815
Dorris v Danone Waters of America, slip op, 2024 WL 4792048 (SDNY, 14 November 2024) 78
Eldred v Ashcroft, 537 US 186 (2003) 190 270
Exxon Mobil Corporation v Arjuna Capital LLC and others (No. 4:24-cv-00069-P) (17 June 2024) 311
Exxon Valdez, In re 1994 W.L. 182856 (D. Alaska); affirmed 104 F.2d 1196 (9th Cir., 1997) .813–14
Fink v Miller (1995) 896 P.2d 649 .241
Fojtik v Charter Med Corp 985 SW2d 625 (Tex Ct App 1999) 57
Ford Motor Co v Montana Eighth Judicial District Court 592 US 351 (2021) .558
Fuel Industry Climate Cases, In re (Sup Ct Cal, 8 October 2024) .550–51, 557, 558
Giglio v Conn Light & Power Co 429 A2d 486, 488 (Conn 1980) .163
Gold & Honey Ltd, In re 410 BR 357 (Bankr EDNY 2009) 422
Goodyear Dunlop Tires Operations SA v Brown, 564 US 915 (2011) .557
Gulf Oil Corp v Gilbert, 330 US 501 (1945) 560
Hall v Du Pont de Nemours & Co 345 F Supp 353 (EDNY 1972) 164–65
Hanson v Denckla, 357 US 235 (1958) .558, 559
Held v State 560 P 3d 1235 (MT 2024) .218–19
Hoover v Colville Confederated Tribes, 3 CTCR 43, 6 CCAR 16 (2002) .819
Hurtado v California 110 US 516, 530 (1884) .103
Illinois Central Railroad v Illinois, 146 US 387 (1892) 282
International Shoe Co v State of Washington, 326 US 210 (1945) .556
J McIntyre Machinery Ltd v Nicastro, 564 US 873 (2011) .559
Jefferson Parish Hospital District No. 2 v Hyde 466 US 2 (1984) 367
Jones v H.F. Ahmanson & Co 460 P.2d 464 (Cal. 1969) .312
Juliana v United States 2015 WL 4747094 (D Or 2015) 211, 282
Juliana v United States, 145 S Ct 1428 (2025) .283
Juliana v United States, 217 F Supp 3d 1224 (D Or 2016) .283
Katko v Briney 183 NW2d 657 (Iowa 1971) 57
Keenan v Russ, No. 2023-3021, Okla. Dist. Ct. (May 7, 2024) .617–18
Kelley v 1250 Oceanside Partners 140 P.3d 985 (Haw. 2006) 282
Kiobel v Royal Dutch Petroleum Co, 569 US 108 (2013) 566

Lawing v Univar USA Inc 415 SC 209 (2015) 164–65
Leichtamer v American Motors Corp 424 NE2d 568, 579 (Ohio 1981) 160
Loper Bright Enterprises v Raimondo, 603 US 369 (2024) 414–15
Lucas v South Carolina Coastal Council 505 US 1003 (1992) 39–40, 229–30
Macquarie Infrastructure Corporation et al v Moab Partners, LP, 144 S Ct 885 (2024) 410–11
Makah Indian Tribe v ExxonMobil Corp., Case No. 2:24-cv-157 (Dist. Ct Wash, 26 March 2025) 813–14
Martin v Lessee of Waddel 41 US 367 (1842) 282
Massachusetts v Exxon Mobil Corp, 462 F Supp 3d 31 (D Mass, 2020) 80
Mayor and City Council of Baltimore v BP PLC Case No: 24-C-18-004219 165–66
McRitchie v Zuckerberg 315 A.3d 518 (Del Ch. 2024) 220, 297–98, 301–4, 309
Methyl Tertiary Butyl Ether (MTBE) Prod Liab Litig, In re 175 F Supp 2d 593, 625 (SDNY 2001) 164–65
Milliken v Meyer, 311 US 457 (1940) 557
Minnesota v American Petroleum Institute 62-CV-20-3837 (Minn Dist Ct 14 Feb 2025) 164
Montana v United States, 450 US 544 (1981) 815
Morrison v National Australia Bank, 561 US 247 (2010) 566
Municipalities of Bayamon v Exxon Mobil Corp, No CV 22-1550 (SCC)(HRV), 2025 WL 600430 (DPR 20 Feb 2025) 161–62, 164–65
Municipalities of Puerto Rico v Exxon Mobil, No. 3:22-cv-01550 (DPR 22 Nov. 2022) 156
National Collegiate Athletic Association v Board of Regents of the University of Oklahoma (NCAA) 468 US 85 (1984) 362, 368, 373–74
National Federation of Independent Business v Department of Labor, 595 US 109 (2022) 414–15
National Society of Professional Engineers v United States 435 US 679 (1978) 362, 368, 373
Native Vill of Kivalina v ExxonMobil Corp 663 F Supp 2d 863 (ND Cal 2009), aff'd, 696 F3d 849 (9th Cir 2012) 110, 170, 810, 813–14
Northern Pacific Railway Co. v United States 356 US 1 (1958) 361
Northwest Wholesale Stationers v Pacific Stationery & Printing Co. 472 US 284 (1985) 367
Ohio v American Express Co. 585 US 529 (2018) 374–75
Palsgraf v Long Island R Co 162 NE 99, 99 (NY 1928) 51
Parsons & Whittemore Overseas Co. v Societe Generale de L'Industrie du Papier (RAKTA), 508 F.2d 969 (2d Cir. 1974) 437
People of the State of California v Southern California Gas Co (Cal Super Ct, 19 October 2023) 80
Piper Aircraft Co v Reyno, 454 US 235 (1981) 560
Ridge Renewables LLC v Hale Cnty. Wind Farm LLC No. A43616-2012 (64th Dist. Ct., Hale County, Tex. 11 May 2023) 234–35
Riggs v Palmer 22 NE 188 (NY 1889) 196

RJR Nabisco v European Community, 579 US ___ (2016) 566
Rozenfeld v Medical Protective Co., 73 F.3d 154 (7th Cir. 1996) 125
Rutherford v Owens-Ill. Inc., 941 P.2d 1203 (Cal. 1997) 127
Schwartz v Accuratus Corp 7 F Supp 3d 490 (ED Pa 2014) 165–66
Sears Hometown and Outlet Stores, Inc. Stockholder Litigation,
In re 2024 WL 262322 (Del. Ch. Jan. 24, 2024) 312
SEC v Jarskey, 608 US (2024)..414–15
Securities Industry and Financial Markets Association v Ashcroft,
745 F.Supp.3d 783 (W.D. Mo. 2024)........................ 612–13, 614, 618–19
Sindell v Abbott Laboratories (1980) 26 Cal 3d 588............................133–34
Slack Techs, LLC v Pirani, 598 US 759 (2023)................................410–11
Sosa v Alvarez-Machain, 542 US 692 (2004) 566
State ex rel Jennings v BP Am Inc 2024 WL 98888 (Del Super Ct 2024)............ 164
State of Vermont v Exxon Mobil Corp (Vermont Super Ct, 2024) 80
Stone v Ritter, 911 A 2d 362 (Del. 2006) 221
Sullivan v Werner Co 306 A3d 846 (Pa 2023) 160
Summers v Tice (1948) 33 Cal 2d 80 .... 133–34, 135–36
Tincher v Omega Flex Inc 104 A3d 328 (Pa 2014) 160
Toft, In re 453 BR 186 (Bankr SDNY 2011) 422
TSC Industry, Inc v Northway, Inc, 426 US 438 (1976).........................611–12
United States v Automobile Manufacturers Association, 307 F. Supp. 617
(C.D. Cal. 1970)... 364
United States v Brown University 5 F.3d 658 (3d Cir 1993) 368
United States v Microsoft Corp 253 F.3d 34 (D.C. Cir. 2001) 361–62, 372–73
United States v Socony-Vacuum Oil Co. 310 US 150 (1940)..................... 367
Unites States v Winans, 198 US 371 (1905) 288
Utah v Micone, 766 F.Supp.3d 669 (N.D. Tex. 2025)...........................612–13
Walden v Fiore, 571 US 277 (2014)...559
Webster v L Romano Eng'g Corp 34 P2d 428 (Wash 1934)...................... 160
West Virginia v EPA, 142 S Ct 2587 (2022) 414–15
Winters v Unites States, 207 US (1954)..................................... 288
Zajac v United Airlines, slip op, 2024 WL 3784535 (D Md, 13 August 2024) 78

TABLE OF INTERNATIONAL INSTRUMENTS

Treaties and Conventions

Agreement on Trade-Related Aspects of Intellectual Property Rights, 15 April 1994, Marrakesh Agreement Establishing the World Trade Organization, 1869 UNTS 299, 33 ILM 1197 (1994) (TRIPS Agreement) 269–70, 275–76, 825
Annex 1C 269
Association of Southeast Asian Nations (ASEAN)-Australia-New Zealand Free Trade Agreement (AANZFTA) 485
Convention on Biodiversity 825
Convention on Jurisdiction and the Recognition and Enforcement of Judgments in Civil and Commercial Matters (signed 30 October 2007, entered into force 1 January 2010) (Lugano Convention) 552–53, 556
Art 2(1) 552–53, 557
Art 60 557
Convention on the Recognition and Enforcement of Foreign Arbitral Awards, 10 June 1958, 21 U.S.T. 2517, 330 U.N.T.S. 3 (New York Convention) 426, 432–34, 435, 437, 441
Art V(1) 432–33
Art V(1)(e) 435
Art V(2) 432–33
Art V(2)(b) 436–37
Convention on the Recognition and Enforcement of Foreign Judgments in Civil or Commercial Matters (signed 2 July 2019, entered into force 1 September 2023 . . . . 549, 567–68
Art 1 567–68
Art 2 567–68
Art 3(1)(b) 567–68
Art 3(2) 567–68
Art 5(1)(a) 567–68
Art 5(1)(d) 567–68
Art 5(1)(i) 567–68
Art 5(1)(j) 558–59
Energy Charter Treaty (ECT) 434, 472–73, 490
European Convention on Human Rights (ECHR) 223, 585–86, 791, 798–99, 800–1
Art2 . . . . . 150–51, 223, 585–86, 697–98, 791–92, 794–95, 801–2
Art 3 795
Art 8 . . . . . 150–51, 223, 585–86, 697–98, 791–92, 794–95, 801–2
First Protocol, Art 1 601–2
International Convention for Prevention of Pollution by Oil, 12 May 1954, 327 UNTS No 4714 (1959) 460
International Convention for the Prevention of Pollution from Ships (MARPOL) 461
Art 1 461
Protocol of 1978 relating to the International Convention

for the prevention of pollution from ships 1973, 17 February 1978, 1340 UNTS No 22484 (1983) (MARPOL 73/78). 461, 462
Art 16(2) 462
Art 16(2)(c) 462
Art 16(2)(d). 462
Art 16(2)(f)(i) 462
Art 16(2)(f)(ii) 462
Art 16(2)(f)(iii). 462
Annexes I–V. 461
Annex VI. 461, 462–64, 465, 466, 467
International Convention for the Safety of Life at Sea, 1 November 1974, 1184 UNTS 18961 (1980) 465
Regulation 3-1 of Pt A-1 of Chapter II-1 465
International Covenant on Civil and Political Rights, 19 December 1966, 999 UNTS 171 . . . . 267, 791
International Covenant on Economic, Social and Cultural Rights, 16 December 1966, 993 UNTS 3. 267
Kyoto Protocol to the United Nations Framework Convention on Climate Change (adopted 11 December 1997, entered into force 16 February 2005) 2303 UNTS 148 . . . . . . 136, 267, 496, 573
Annex B. 573–74
Malé Declaration on the Human Dimension of Global Climate Change (2007). . . 793–94
Montreal Protocol on Substances that Deplete the Ozone Layer (1987) 214
Paris Agreement to the United Nations Framework Convention on Climate Change (adopted 12 December 2015, entered into force 4 November 2016) . . .69–70, 71–72, 84, 173, 201–2, 214, 264, 267, 290, 341, 343, 351, 352, 378, 428, 472–73, 501, 509, 516, 551, 578, 581, 583, 588, 598–99, 604–5, 666–67, 683, 697–98, 765–66, 786–87
Preamble 267–68
Art 2. 69–70
Art 2(1) 378
Art 2(1)(a) .583
Art 2(1)(c) 340–41, 343, 344, 347, 399
Art 3. 69–70
Art4 . . . . 69–70, 343
Art 6. 190
Art 9. 343
Art 9(1) 347
Art 9(3) 343, 347
Art 9(5) 347
Art 13 69–70
Art 14. 69–70
Singapore-Australia Free Trade Agreement 484–85
Treaty on the Functioning of the European Union
Art 3(11). .783
Art 101 . . . . .360–62, 366–67, 371
Art 101(1). 360–62, 367, 370, 371
Art 101(3). 360–62, 371, 375
UN Convention on the Law of the Sea (UNCLOS)
Art 17 466
Art 19(1). 466
Art 21 466
Art 24. 466
Art91(1) 463
Art 218 466
Art 219 466
UNCITRAL Model Law on Cross-Border Insolvency(1997) 422

United Nations Declaration on the Rights of Indigenous Peoples (UNDRIP) 274–75
United Nations Framework Convention on Climate Change, 9 May 1992, 1771 UNTS 107 (entered into force 21 March 1994) 267, 320–21, 342–43, 344, 378, 428, 581, 677, 697–98, 724
Art 4.3 342–43
Art 4.4 342–43
World Intellectual Property Organization, Marrakesh Treaty to Facilitate Access to Published Works for Persons Who Are Blind, Visually Impaired or Otherwise Print Disabled, 27 June 2013, 3162 UNTS (Marrakesh Treaty) 269–70
World Trade Organization, 'Ministerial Declaration of 14 November 2021', WTO Doc WT/MIN(01)/DEC/1, 41 ILM 746 (2002) (Doha Declaration)
s 4 269–70

Arbitration Rules

Hague Rules on Business and Human Rights Arbitration 434
HKIAC Arbitration Rules (2024)
Art 45.1 438
Art 45.2 438
International Chamber of Commerce (ICC) Arbitration Rules (2021) 426, 435, 439
Art 21(1) 435
Art 22(3) 439
Art 25(2) 432
Art 25(3) 432
LCIA Arbitration Rules (2020) 438
Art 20(1) 432
Art21 432
Art 30(1) 438
Art 30(3) 438
PCA Optional Rules for Arbitration of Disputes Relating to the Environment and/or Natural Resources 432, 436, 440–41
Introduction 440–41
Art 6(2) 432
Art 7(2)(b) 432
Art 8(3) 432
Art 23 432
Art27(5) 432
Art 33 436
SCC Arbitration Rules (2023)
Art 3 438
SIAC Arbitration Rules (2025)
Art 59.1 438
UNCITRAL Arbitration Rules 2021 . . . . 426, 435, 436, 439
Art 27(2) 432
Art 29 432
Art 34(5) 439
Art 35(1) 435, 436
UNCITRAL Rules of Transparency in Treaty-Based Investor–State Arbitration 439
United Nations Convention on Transparency in Treaty-Based Investor–State Arbitration (Mauritius Convention) 439
Preamble 439
Art 3 439
Art 4 439
Art 5 439
Art 6 439
Art 7 439

European Union

Charter of Fundamental Rights
Art 16 799–800
Art37 491
Consolidated Version of the Treaty on European Union [2008] OJ C115/13 491
Single European Act [1987] OJ L 169 . . . 491

Treaty establishing the European Economic Community 491, 573
Treaty on European Union (Maastricht Treaty) (signed 7 February 1992, entered into force 1 November 1993) [1992] OJ C191/1 221
Preamble 491
Art 2 . . . . 221, 491
Art 3 491
Art 21 491

Decisions

Decision No 1753/2000/EC of 22 June 2000 establishing a scheme to monitor the average specific emissions of CO2 from new passenger cars [2000] OJ L 202. . . . 497
Decision No 1600/2002/EC of the European Parliament and of the Council of 22 July 2002 laying down the Sixth Community Environment Action Programme: 'Environment 2010: Our future, Our choice' [2022] OJ EC L 242/1 493–94
Recital 6 493–94
Decision No 1386/2013/EU of the European Parliament and of the Council of 20 November 2013 on a General Union Environment Action Programme to 2020 [2013] OJ L 354/171 494
Recital 33 494
Pt 10 494
Pt 17 494
Decision No 2022/591/EU of the European Parliament and of the Council of 6 April 2022 on aGeneral Union Environment Action Programme to 2030 [2022] OJ L 114/22. 494

Directives

Directive 85/611/EEC of 20 December 1985 on the coordination of laws, regulations and administrative provisions relating to undertakings for collective investment in transferable securities [1985] OJ L 375, 3–1 (UCITS) 510–11
Directive 92/75/EEC of 22 September 1992 on the Indication by Labelling and Standard Product Information of the Consumption of Energy and Other Resources by Household Appliances [1992] OJ L297/16
Art 1 573
Directive 2003/51/EC of 18 June 2003 Amending Directives 78/660/EEC, 83/349/EEC, 86/635/EEC and 91/674/EEC on the Annual and Consolidated Accounts of Certain Types of Companies, Banks and Other Financial Institutions and Insurance Undertakings [2003] OJ L178/16 577–78
Directive 2003/87/EC of the European Parliament and of the Council of 13 October 2003 establishing a scheme for GHG emission allowance trading within the Community and amending Council Directive 96/61/EC [2003] OJ L275/32 . . . . .19–20, 140, 496, 563, 571
Directive 2004/35 of 21 April 2004 on Environmental Liability with regard to the Prevention and Remedying of Environmental Damage [2004] OJ EC L 143/56. . . . 495
Recital 13 22
Art4(5) 22

Directive 2005/29/EC of 11 May 2005 concerning unfair business-to-consumer commercial practices in the internal market and amending Council Directive 84/450/EEC, Directives 97/7/EC, 98/27/EC and 2002/65/EC of the European Parliament and of the Council and Regulation (EC) No 2006/2004 of the European Parliament and of the Council (Unfair Commercial Practices Directive)
Art 6(2)(d) . . . 582
Annex I, para 4a . . . 582
Annex I, para 4c . . . 582
Directive 2009/29/EC of 23 April 2009 Amending Directive 2003/87/EC so as to Improve and Extend the Greenhouse Gas Emission Allowance Trading Scheme of the Community [2009] OJ L140/63
Art 10a . . . 574–75
Directive 2009/138/EC of 25 November 2009 on the taking-up and pursuit of the business of Insurance and Reinsurance (Solvency II) (recast) [2009] OJ L 335, 1–155 . . . 510–11
Directive 2011/61/EU of the European Parliament and of the Council of 8 June 2011 on Alternative Investment Fund Managers and amending Directives 2003/41/EC and 2009/65/EC and Regulations (EC) No 1060/2009 and (EU) No 1095/2010 [2011] OJ L 174, 1–73 (AIFMD) . . . 510–11
Directive 2013/34/EU of 26 June 2013 on the annual financial statements, consolidated financial statements and related reports of certain types of undertakings, amending Directive 2006/43/EC of the European Parliament and of the Council and repealing Council Directives 78/660/EEC and 83/349/EEC . . . 507
Art 19a . . . 577–78
Art 29a . . . 577–78
Art 29b . . . 578
Directive 2014/65/EU of 15 May 2014 on markets in financial instruments and amending Directive 2002/92/EC and Directive 2011/61/EU [2014] OJ L 173, 349–496 . . . 510–11
Directive 2014/95/EU of 22 October 2014 amending Directive 2013/34/EU as regards disclosure of non-financial and diversity information by certain large undertakings and groups [2014] OJ L330/1 (NFRD) . . . 336–37, 415, 501, 505–6, 507, 577–78
Recital 6 . . . 506
Recital 9 . . . 506
Art 1(1) . . . 577–78
Art 1(3) . . . 577–78
Directive 2016/97/EU of 20 January 2016 on insurance distribution (recast) [2016] OJ L 26 19–59 (IDD) . . . 510–11
Directive 2021/1269/EU of 21 April 2021 amending Delegated Directive (EU) 2017/593 (MiFID II) as regards the integration of sustainability factors into the product governance obligations . . . 510–11
Directive 2021/1270/EU of 21 April 2021 amending Directive 2010/43/EU as regards the

sustainability risks and sustainability factors to be taken into account for Undertakings for Collective Investment in Transferable Securities (UCITS)....................510–11
Directive 2022/2464/EU of the European Parliament and of the Council of 14 December 2022 amending Regulation (EU) 537/2014, Directive 2004/109/EC, Directive 2006/43/EC, and Directive 2013/34/EU, as regards corporate sustainability reporting [2022] OJ EU L 322/15 (CSRD) 3, 140, 214, 222, 224, 298, 304–6, 324–25, 332, 400–1, 415, 505–6, 507, 578, 579, 586, 589, 625, 784–87, 788–90
Recital 11 506
Recital 60...................... 507
Art 1(4)........................578
Art 1(7)........................578
Art 1(8)........................578
Art 3 784–85
Art 19(2)(a)(iii)................ 787
Art 19a(1).................. 784–85
Directive 2023/959/EU Amending Directive 2003/87/EC Establishing a System for Greenhouse Gas Emission Allowance Trading within the Union and Decision (EU) 2015/1814 Concerning the Establishment and Operation of a Market Stability Reserve for the Union Greenhouse Gas Emission Trading System [2023] OJ L130/134 573
Directive 2023/1791/EU of 13 September 2023 on Energy Efficiency and amending Regulation (EU) 2023/955 (Recast) [2023] OJ L231/1
Art 4(1).....................573–74
Directive 2023/2413/EU of 18 October 2023 amending Directive (EU) 2018/2001, Regulation (EU) 2018/1999 and Directive 98/70/EC as Regards the Promotion of Energy from Renewable Sources, and Repealing Council Directive (EU) 2015/652 [2023] OJ L2023/2413
Art 1(2)(a) 573–74
Directive 2024/825/EU of 28 February 2024 amending Directives 2005/29/EC and 2011/83/EU as Regards Empowering Consumers for the Green Transition through Better Protection against Unfair Practices and through Better Information [2024] OJ L2024/825 (ECGT Directive) 571–72, 582, 588, 589
Recital 12 582
Art 1(2)(b) 582
Annex I, para 2 582
Directive 2024/1760/EU of the European Parliament and of the Council of 13 June 2024 on corporate sustainability due diligence and amending Directive (EU) 2019/1937 and Regulation (EU) 2023/2859 [2024] OJ L 202/1 (CSDDD) ...3, 140, 214, 222, 224, 298, 304–6, 415, 508, 509, 510, 554, 566, 571–72, 580, 581, 586, 588, 589, 625, 786–87, 788
Recital 4...................... 508
Recital 16 508
Recital 38 304
Art 2.................. 508, 786–87
Art 7 508

Art 10 508
Art 11 508
Art 12 509
Art 15 509
Art 16 509
Art 19(2)(b) 581
Art 22 . . . . 151, 222, 509, 588, 786–87
Art 22(1) 581, 786–87
Art 22(3) 786–87
Art 29 . . . . 304, 509, 581
Art 29(1)(a) 509
Art 29(1)(b) 509
Art 29(7) 566
Art 37 509
Annex II, Pt II 581
Proposal for a Directive of the European Parliament and of the Council amending Directives 2006/43/EC, 2013/34/EU, (EU) 2022/2464, and (EU) 2024/1760 as regards certain corporate sustainability reporting and due diligence requirements, COM(2025) 81 final 2025/0045 (COD) 224, 304, 785–86
Proposal for a Directive of the European Parliament and of the Council amending Directives (EU) 2022/2464 and (EU) 2024/1760 as regards the dates from which Member States are to apply certain corporate sustainability reporting and due diligence requirements, COM(2025) 80 final 2025/0044 (COD) 224, 304–5, 336
Proposal for a Directive of the European Parliament and of the Council on Substantiation and Communication of Explicit Environmental Claims (Green Claims Directive) COM(2023) 166 final, 22 March 2023 (Green Claims Directive proposal) 571–72, 582–83, 586, 589
Recital 12 582–83

Regulations

Regulation (EC) 864/2007 of 11 July 2007 on the law applicable to non-contractual obligations (Rome II) OJ L 199 . . . . 565–66, 576–77
Arts 1, 2, 31, 32 561–62
Art 3 562
Art5(1) 562–63
Art 7 . . . . . . 551–53, 558, 559, 561–65, 568
Art 14 . . . . 552, 561–62, 563–64
Art 17 . . . . 561–62, 563, 564, 568
Regulation (EU) 1215/2012 of 12 December 2012 on jurisdiction and the recognition and enforcement of judgments in civil and commercial matters (recast) OJ L 351 (Brussels I bis) 551, 556, 557, 558, 559, 560, 567–68, 576–77
Art 1 567–68
Art 2(a) 567–68
Art4(1) 551, 552–53, 557
Art 7(2) 551, 553, 558, 559, 562
Arts 29–34 560
Art 30 560
Art 45(1)(e) 567–68
Art 45(2) 567–68
Art 45(3) 567–68
Art 63(1) 557
Art 63(2) 557
Regulation (EU) 2015/757 of the European Parliament and of the Council of 29 April 2015 459–60
Regulation (EU) 2016/1011 of 8 June 2016 on indices used

as benchmarks in financial instruments and financial contracts or to measure the performance of investment funds and amending Directives 2008/48/EC and 2014/17/EU and Regulation (EU) No 596/2014 [2014] OJ L 171, 1 510–11
Regulation (EU) 2019/2088 of 27 November 2019 on sustainability-related disclosures in the financial services sector [2019] OJ L 317/1 (SFDR). 214, 347, 386, 408, 504, 505–6, 578–79
Recital 5 505
Recital 10 505
Art 2(17). 505
Art 9(3) 579
Regulation (EU) 2019/2089 of 27 November 2019 amending Regulation (EU) 2016/1011 as Regards EU Climate Transition Benchmarks, EU Paris-Aligned Benchmarks and Sustainability-Related Disclosures for Benchmarks [2019] OJ L317/17 578–79
Regulation (EU) 2020/852 of 18 June 2020, on the establishment of a framework to facilitate sustainable investment and amending Regulation (EU) 2019/2088 (EU Taxonomy Regulation) 503, 578–79
Art 8 579
Regulation (EU) 2020/1818 of 17 July 2020 Supplementing Regulation (EU) 2016/1011 of the European Parliament and of the Council as Regards Minimum Standards for EU Climate Transition Benchmarks and EU Paris-Aligned Benchmarks [2020] OJ L406/17 578–79
Regulation (EU) 2021/1119 of 30 June 2021 establishing the framework for achieving climate neutrality and amending Regulations (EC) No 401/2009 and (EU) 2018/1999 [2021] OJ L 243/1 (European Climate Law) 501, 502, 573–74, 581
Recital 22 501
Art 2 573–74
Art 4(1). 573–74
Art 9 501
Regulation (EU) 2021/1253 of 21 April 2021 amending Delegated Regulation (EU) 2017/565 (MiFID II) as regards the integration of sustainability factors, risks and preferences into certain organisational requirements and operating conditions for investment firms. 510–11
Regulation (EU) 2021/1255 of 21 April 2021 amending Delegated Regulation (EU) No 231/2013 as regards the sustainability risks and sustainability factors to be taken into account by Alternative Investment Fund Managers (AIFM) 510–11
Regulation (EU) 2021/1256 of 21 April 2021 amending Delegated Regulation (EU) 2015/35 (Solvency II) as regards the integration of sustainability risks in the governance of insurance and reinsurance undertakings . . .510–11
Regulation (EU) 2021/1257 of April 2021 amending Delegated Regulations (EU) 2017/2358 and (EU) 2017/2359 (IDD) as regards the integration of sustainability factors, risks and preferences into the product oversight and governance requirements for insurance undertakings and

insurance distributors and into the rules on conduct of business and investment advice for insurance-based investment products. 510–11
Regulation (EU) 2021/2139 of 4 June 2021 supplementing Regulation (EU) 2020/852 of the European Parliament and of the Council by establishing the technical screening criteria for determining the conditions under which an economic activity qualifies as contributing substantially to climate change mitigation or climate change adaptation and for determining whether that economic activity causes no significant harm to any of the other environmental objectives [2021]OJ L 442 . . . . 503, 578–79
Regulation (EU) 2021/2178 of 6 July 2021 supplementing Regulation (EU) 2020/852 of the European Parliament and of the Council by specifying the content and presentation of information to be disclosed by undertakings subject to Articles 19a or 29a of Directive 2013/34/EU concerning environmentally sustainable economic activities, and specifying the methodology to comply with that disclosure obligation [2021] OJ L 443/9 503
Regulation (EU) 2022/1214 of 9 March 2022 amending Delegated Regulation (EU) 2021/2139 as regards economic activities in certain energy sectors and Delegated Regulation (EU) 2021/2178 as regards specific public disclosures for those economic activities, C/2022/631 [2022] OJ L 188/1 . . . . 504, 578–79
Regulation (EU) 2023/956 of the European Parliament and of the Council of 10 May 2023 establishing a carbon border adjustment mechanism, [2023] OJ EU L 130/52 . . . . 140, 571
Regulation (EU) 2023/2485 of 27 June 2023 amending Delegated Regulation (EU) 2021/2139 establishing additional technical screening criteria for determining the conditions under which certain economic activities qualify as contributing substantially to climate change mitigation or climate change adaptation and for determining whether those activities cause no significant harm to any of the other environmental objectives, C/2023/3850 [2023] OJ L 2023/2485. 504
Regulation (EU) 2023/2486 of 27 June 2023 supplementing Regulation (EU) 2020/852 of the European Parliament and of the Council by establishing the technical screening criteria for determining the conditions under which an economic activity qualifies as contributing substantially to the sustainable use and protection of water and marine resources, to the transition to a circular economy, to pollution prevention and control, or to the protection and restoration of biodiversity and ecosystems and for determining whether that economic activity causes no significant harm to any of the other environmental objectives and amending Commission Delegated Regulation (EU) 2021/2178 as regards specific public

disclosures for those economic activities, C/2023/3851 [2023] OJ L 2023/2486 504
Regulation (EU) 2023/2631 of the European Green Bonds and optional disclosures for bonds marketed as environmentally sustainable and for sustainability-linked bonds [2023] OJ L 347, 510–11, 578–79
Art 4 579
Annex I 579
Regulation (EU) 2023/2772 of 31 July 2023 supplementing Directive 2013/34/EU of the European Parliament and of the Council as regards sustainability reporting standards [2023] OJ L2023/2772 (ESRS) 324–25, 506, 787, 789–90
Regulation (EU) 2024/1252 of 11 April 2024 Establishing a Framework for Ensuring a Secure and Sustainable Supply of Critical Raw Materials and Emending Regulations (EU) No 168/2013, (EU) 2018/858, (EU) 2018/1724 and (EU) 2019/1020 [2024] OJ L2024/1252 574–75
Regulation (EU) 2024/1689 of the European Parliament and of the Council of 13 June 2024 laying down harmonised rules on artificial intelligence and amending Regulations (EC) No 300/2008, (EU) No 167/2013, (EU) No 168/2013, (EU) 2018/858, (EU) 2018/1139 and (EU) 2019/2144 and Directives 2014/90/EU, (EU) 2016/797 and (EU) 2020/1828 (EU AI Act)
Art 3(1) 775
Art5 (1)(a) 780–81
Article 53–xx 776
Regulation (EU) 2024/1735 of 13 June 2024 on Establishing a Framework of Measures for Strengthening Europe's Net-Zero Technology Manufacturing Ecosystem and Amending Regulation (EU) 2018/1724 [2024] OJ L2024/1735 574–75
Regulation (EU) 2024/1781 of the European Parliament and of the Council of 13 June 2024 establishing a Framework for the setting of Ecodesign Requirements for Sustainable Products, amending Directive (EU) 2020/1828 and Regulation (EU) 2023/1542 and repealing Directive 2009/125/EC [2024] OJ L 2024/1781 499
Regulation (EU) 2024/3005 of the European Parliament and of the Council of 27 November 2024 on the Transparency and Integrity of Environmental, Social and Governance (ESG) Rating Activities, and Amending Regulations (EU) 2019/2088 and (EU) 2023/2859 [2024]OJ L 2024/2005 409

National Legislation

Australia

Competition and Consumer Act 2010
Pt VII, Div 1, s 90 363
Sch 653–54
Conciliation and Arbitration Act 1904 452
s 2 452
Corporations Act 2001 (Cth) 651, 653–54
s 180(1) 649
s 181(1) 649
s 247A 651
Fair Work Act 455
Federal Court Rules 2011 (Cth)
r 10.42(g) 557

Native Title Act 1993 812
Shipping Registration Act 1981 (Cth)
s 15A 463
s 56(1) 463
s56(2) 463
Superannuation Industry
(Supervision) Act 1993 (Cth) 650
s 52(2)(b) 650
s 52(2)(c) 650
Treasury Laws Amendment
(Financial Market Infrastructure
and Other Measures) Act 2024 346
Uniform Civil Procedure Rules
2005 (NSW)
Sch, r 6(g) 557

Austria

Federal Act against Cartels and
other Restraints of Competition
(Cartel Act 2005—KartG 2005)
s 2(1) 371

Belgium

Civil Code
Art1382 109–10
Art1383 109–10

Brazil

Arbitration Act 2015 (Law 13,129/2015)
Art 1(1) 440
Art 2(3) 440
Civil Code (2002)
Art 393 720
Art 942 719
Code of Civil Procedure
Art 373(1) 722
Constituição Federal [Constitution] 1988
Art 127–xxx 729
Art225 . . . . 290, 716, 717–18
Art 225(3) 719
Art 237 290–91
Decreto 2.652/1998 724
Anexo, Art 1, 3 724
Federal Law No. 9.985/2000 183
National Environmental Policy Act
(Lei 6.938/1981) 719, 724
Art 3, I 724
Art 3, II 724
Art 3, III 724
Art 3, IV 719
Art 14(1) 719
National Policy on Climate
Change (Política Nacional sobre
Mudança do Clima, Lei 12.187/
2009) 724–25
Art 2 724–25
Art 2, II 726
Art 3 724–25

Canada

Quebec Civil Code
Art 3134 557
Art 3148(1) 557
Rules of Civil Procedure (Ontario),
RRO 1990
Reg 194, r 17.02(p) 557
Uniform Court Jurisdiction and
Proceedings Transfer Act 2021
r 3(d); 557

China

Civil Code 698–99
Arts 4–9 699–700
Art 4 699–700
Arts 5–7 700
Art 5 700
Art9 (Green Principle) 697, 698–99, 701, 703–4, 705, 706, 707–12, 713–14, 715
Art 153 . . . . 701, 705
Art153(2) (Public Order
and Good Morals
Principle) 704, 705
Art240 706
Art272 . . . . 706–7, 708–9
Art 322 712
Art 509 . . . . 701, 707–8

Art 558 701
Art 577 707
Contract Law
Art 54 700
Art 97 711–12
Environmental (Ecological) Code ... 702
Property Law
Art 322 711–12

France

CivilCode.......................... 565–66
Art 1832 100
Code de commerce 1807
Art. L225-37.......................... 336–37
Art L225-51-51 782
Art. L225-102-1 336–37
ArtL. 225-102-4.......................... 222, 587–88
Loi no 2001-420 du 15 mai 2001
Art 116 (V).......................... 336–37
Loi no 2010-788 du 12 juillet 2010
Art 225 336–37
Loi no 2015–992 du 17 août 2015 relative à la transition énergétique pour la croissance verte
Art. 173.......................... 336–37
Loi no 2017-399 du 27 mars 2017 relative au devoir de vigilance des sociétés mères et des entreprises donneuses d'ordre, JORF no 0074 du 28 mars 2017 (Duty of Vigilance Act) 222, 225, 508, 553–54, 565–66, 571–72, 580, 587–88
Art 1 .... 222, 580

German

Act against Unfair Commercial Practices 176, 581–82, 588
Act on Corporate Due Diligence Obligations in Supply Chains (Lie ferkettensorgfaltspflichtengesetz) of 16 July 2021 (BGBl. I p 2959) 508
s 2(3).......................... 580
Civil Code (Bürgerliches Gezetsbuch, BGB)
s 90a.......................... 59
s 138(1).......................... 798
s242 798
s 684.......................... 122
s 705.......................... 100
s 812 122
s 823(1).......................... 59
s 1004.......................... 122, 139–40, 552
Climate Protection Act 575
Basic Law (Grundgesetz)...... 797–98
Art 20a.......................... 783
Insurance Contact Law Act (Versicherungsvertragsgesetz)
s 82 392–93
Securities Trading Act 1998 (WpHG)
s 80(2)–(5).......................... 780–81
Supply Chain Due Diligence Act 2021 .... 222, 580
Stock Corporation Act 1965
s 76(3) 782

Hong Kong

Rules and Guidance
AppC1 346
Hong Kong Securities and Futures Ordinance
s 307A(1) 440

India

Code of Civil Procedure, 1908....... 636
Companies Act, 2013 638
s 135.......................... 638
s 166 639
s 166(2).......................... 637, 638, 639
Sch VII.......................... 638
Constitution 628
Art 14 794–95
Art 21 .... 628, 629, 794–95
Art32 .... 631–32, 636–37

Art 142 636–37
Art 226 . . . . 631–32, 636–37
Contract Act, 1872
s 56 640
Environment (Protection) Act, 1986 . . . 638
s 2(a) 638
National Green Tribunal Act, 2010
. . . . 630–31, 633, 643
Preamble 633
s 2(m) 633
s 14 633
s 15(4) 633
s 17(1) 633
s 20 633
Sch II 633
Public Liability Insurance
Act, 1991 630–31
Securities and Exchange Board
of India (Listing Obligations
and Disclosure Requirements)
(Amendment) Regulations, 2015
(22 December 2015) 327–28
Securities and Exchange Board of
India (Listing Obligations and
Disclosure Requirements) (Fifth
Amendment) Regulations, 2019
(26 December 2019) 327–28

Indonesia

Consumer Protection Act No. 8 of 1999
Art 4(3) 674
Art 8 674
Otoritas Jasa Keuangan, OJK
Regulation No. 51/POJK.03/2017
(27 July 2017)
Art 1(13) 335
Art 10(1)-(3) 335
Art 12 335

Ireland

Climate Action and Low Carbon
Development Act 575

Japan

Civil Code
Art 709 668–69
Art 719 668–69

Kazakhstan

Civil Procedure Code
Art 416(1) 557

Kenya

Climate Change Act 2016
s 2 694
s 16 694
s 17(3)–(4) 695
s 23 694–95
s 33 695
Climate Change (Duties and
Incentives) Regulations 2021
(draft) 693–94

Samoa

Constitution
s 111 812

South Korea

Constitution
Art35 791
Framework Act on Carbon
Neutrality and Green Growth for
Coping with the Climate Crisis 671

Mauritius

Climate Change Act 2020
s 25 694–95
s 28 695

Mexico

Code of Civil Procedure for the
Federal District
Art 156(IV) 557

Federal Code of Civil Procedure
Art 24(IV) 557

Netherlands

Civil Code (Dutch Burgerlijk Wetboek, BW) 223
Art3:305a 801
Art 6:162.........139–40, 551, 584, 586, 669, 697–98, 801–2
Art 6:162(2) 223
Coal Ban Act 2019...............481–82

New Zealand

Fair Trade Act
s 9 659
High Court Rules 2016............. 660
r 15.1(1)(a) 660
Resource Management Act 1991 818
Te Urewera Act 2014................821
Te Awa Tupua (Whanganui River Claims Settlement) Act 2017.......821
s 13 819
Tohunga Suppression Act 1907 811

Nigeria

African Charter Act 691
Art 4...................... 690–91
Art 16 690–91
Art 24...................... 690–91
Associated Gas Re-Injection Act
s 3 691
Climate Change Act 2021
s 23 695
s 24(1)–(2) 694
s 24(3)......................... 694
s 32 694
s 34(1)......................... 695
s 34(2)......................... 695
s 35 694
Constitution
s 1(3) 691
s 33 794–95
s 33(1) 690–91
s 34 794–95
s 34(1)..................... 690–91
EIA Decree No. 86 of 1992 688
Laws of the Federation of Nigeria (Cap A9) 690–91
Laws of the Federation of Nigeria, 2004 (Cap A25)..................691
Laws of the Federation of Nigeria, 2004 (Cap 23) 688
Petroleum Industry Act 2021 (PIA) 684–85
s 53(3)..................... 684–85
s 53(5)–(6) 684–85
s 64(a) 684–85

Philippines

Climate Accountability Act (CLIMA).................. 677–78
Indigenous Peoples' Rights Act of 1997...................... 677–78

Singapore

Consumer Protection (Fair Trading) Act 674–75
Reciprocal Enforcement of Foreign Judgments Act (Chapter 265)
s 4(4) 567
Rules of Court 2021
Order 4, Rule 6 675

South Africa

Climate Change Act 2024
s 26 694
s27(1) 694

Switzerland

Cartel Act1995
Art 8..........................363
Civil Code
Pt 5 552–53
Art 28.......................552–53

Code of Obligations
Art 41 552–53
Insurance Contract Act (Versicherungsvertragsgesetz)
Art. 38c I 392–93
Private International Law Act
Art 51 552–53
Art 133 552–53
Art 138 . . . . . 552–53, 564

Uganda

Constitution 2010
Art 237 290–91
National Climate Change Act 2021
s 1 694
s 13(4) 695
s 18(7) 695
s 23 . . . . . 694, 695
s 26 694–95

Ukraine

Law on Private International Law
Art 76(1)(2) 557

United Kingdom

Charter of the Forest 1217 281–82
Civil Jurisdiction and Judgments Act 1982
s 30 557
s 42(4) 557
Civil Procedure Rules
r 6.9(2) 557
PD 6B, para 3.1(1) 557
PD 6B, para 3.1(9)(a) 559
PD 6B, para 3.1(9)(b) 558
PD 19A, para 2 600–1
Climate Change Act 2008 595–96
Companies Act 2006 . . . . . 307–8, 598–99
s 156A(1) 782
s 172 . . . . . 307, 599, 600
s 172(1) 598
s 172(1)(d) 598
s 172(2) 304, 307
s 174 . . . . . 599, 600
s 260(1) 598
s 261(2) 600
s 263(2)(a) 600
s 414CA 386
s 1139(1) 557
Companies Act 2006 (Strategic Report and Directors' Report) Regulations 2013, SI 2013/1970
Pts 7, 15, 20 336–37
Consumer Rights Act 2015
s 62 382–83
Companies (Strategic Report) (Climate-related Financial Disclosure) Regulations 2022 346
Consumer Insurance (Disclosure and Representations) Act 2012
s 2(2) 388
Insurance Act 2015
s 3(1) 388
s 10 382–83
s 11 382–83
s13A 383
s14(3) 388
Law Reform (Contributory Negligence) Act 1945
s 1(1) 392
Magna Carta
Clause 23 281
Clause 33 281
Clause 47 281
Marine Insurance Act 1906
s 17 388
s 67 383–84
s69 383–84
s69(1) 383–84
s 78 391
s 78(1) 391
s 78(4) 391
s79(2) 395
Merchant Shipping (Monitoring, Reporting and Verification of Carbon Dioxide Emissions)

(Amendment) (EU Exit)
Regulations 2018 471
UK Listing Rules
r 6.6.9 386

United States

17 C.F.R.
s 229 612
s 230 401–2
s 232 401–2
s 239 401–2
s 240.14a-8(i)(7) 406–7
s 270 401–2
s 274 401–2
29 C.F.R.
s 2550.404(a) (2022) 612
11 U.S.C
s 101(24) 422
s 1501–xxx 422
s 1506 422
s 1509(b)(2) 422
15 U.S.C
s 780 402
29 U.S.C
ss 1001–1461 612
Alien Tort Statute (ATS) 566
Bankruptcy Abuse Prevention and Consumer Protection Act 2005 . . . 422
Bankruptcy Code
Ch 15 422
Clayton Antitrust Act 1914 442–43
Clean Air Act 39, 110, 495–96
Constitution 281–82
Fifth Amendment 283, 556
Fourteenth Amendment 556
Dodd-Frank Wall Street Reform and Consumer Protection Act, Pub. L. No. 111 - 203,124 Stat. 1376, 1871 (2010) 398–99
§ 929-Z 402
Employee Retirement Income Security Act (ERISA) 219, 611, 612–13
Endangered Species Act 39
Enhancement and Standardization of Climate-Related Disclosures for Investors, 89 Fed Reg 21668 (March 6, 2024) 346
Federal Trade Commission Act . . . 174–75
Inflation Reduction Act (IRA) 537, 574–75
Infrastructure Investment and Jobs Act (IIJA) 537
Investment Company Act
r 35d-1 401–2
National Cooperative Research and Production Act 369
National EnvironmentalPolicy Act 533–34, 537–38
Private Securities Litigation Reform Act of 1995 (PSLRA) 410–11
Sarbanes-Oxley Act of 2002, Pub L 107-204, 116 Stat 745 . . . . . 398–99, 402
s 11 402
s 15 402
s 18 402
s 28 402
Securities Act of 1933 400
Securities Exchange Act of 1934 400
r 10b-5(b) 410–11
r 14a-8(i)(7) 413–14
Sherman Antitrust Act 1890
s 1 . . . . . 361, 375
Standards Development Organization Act 2004 369
Uniform Commercial Code 1989
s 2-718 53–54
Uniform Prudent Investor Act 291
s 5 291

Domestic Statutes / State Law

Ala. Code Ann. (2023)
§ 24-2-802(1) 615–16
§ 24-2-803 614
§ 24-2-805(a) 615, 616
§ 24-2-805(b)(2) 615
§ 24-2-805(e) 616
§ 41-16-160 617
Cal. Consumers Legal Remedies Act . . . 176

Cal. Gov't Code (2015)
§ 7513.75 620–21
§ 7513.75(b)(5) 620–21
§ 7513.75(b)(6) 620–21
§ 7513.75(c) 620–21
§7513.75(d) 620–21
§7513.75(e)(2) 620–21
§ 7513.75(f) 621
Colo. Rev. Stat. (2023)
§ 24-51-220(2)(b) 620
Del. Corporate Law
s 122(18) 311
Del. General Corporation Law (1899)
§ 141(b) 782
Fla. Stat. (2023)
§ 17.57 614
§ 112.662(3) 615, 616
§ 112.662(4) 614, 616
§ 215.4755 615
§ 215.681 618
§ 280.025 618
§ 287.05701 618
§ 1010.04 618
Ga. Code Ann. (2024)
§ 47-20-88(b)(4) 614
Idaho Code (2022)
§ 26-2155 617
§ 67-2345(1) 614
§ 67-2345(3) 615, 616
§ 67-2739 617
Idaho Sess. Laws (2023)
Ch. 129 618
Ill. Comp. Stat. (2019)
Ch. 238, § 20(a) 620
Ch. 238 § 20(b) 620
Ch. 238 § 20(e) 620
Ind. Code (2023)
§ 5-10.2-14-1 to -13 614
§ 5-10.2-14-10 615
§ 5-10.2-14-11 616
Kan. Stat. Ann. (2023)
§ 40-2c01 618
§ 74-4921 616
§ 75-42a01(a)(7)(A) 615
§ 75-42a01(a)(7)(B) 615
§ 75-42a03 615
§ 75-42a03(h) 615–16
Ky. Rev. Stat. Ann. (2023)
§ 21.450(2)(a) 614
§ 21.450(2)(b) 615
§ 21.450(2)(b) 615
§ 21.540(9)(b) 615–16
§ 41.470(3)-(7) 617
§ 41.470(8) 617
§ 41.472(1)(c) (2022) 616–17
§ 41.474(1)-(4) 617
§ 41.474(4) (2022) 616–17
§ 94.030 614
§ 21.450(2)(b) 616
Ky. Rev. Stat. Stat. (2022)
§ 41.472(3) 617
Md. Code Ann. (2022)
§ 21-116.1(a) 620
§ 21-116.1(b)(1) 620
§ 21-116.1(b)(3) 620
§ 21-116.1(d) 620
§ 21-116.1(h) 620
Me. Rev. Stat. (2021)
tit. 5, § 1957 (2024) 620–21
tit. 5, § 1957.1(C) 621
tit. 5, § 1957.2 621
tit. 5, § 1957.3 621
Minn. Stat.
§ 500.30 234–35
Mont. Code(2011)
s 70-17-403 234–35
Mont. Code Ann. (2023)
§ 17-6-232 614
§ 17-6-233 615
§ 17-6-233(1) 616
§ 17-6-233(2) 616
§ 17-6-233(3) 615–16
Mont. Constitution 218–19
Mont. Environmental
Protection Act 218–19
N.C. Gen. Stat. (2023)
§ 143–62.6 (c) 618
§ 147-69.7(5) 614
N.D. Cent. Code (2023)
§ 17-04-03 (2005) 234–35

§ 21-10-08.1 . . . . 614, 615
§ 26.1-04-03(7) 614, 618
§ 54-06-39(2). 615–16
N.H. Rev. Stat. Ann. (2023)
§ 100-A:15, VIII(b) 614
N.J. Industrial Site Recovery Act. 353
Navajo Nation Code Ann.
Tit. I, § 205(D) (2005). 819
Tit. 4 § 901 (2010) 819
Okla. Const.
Art 23, § 12 617–18
Okla. Stat. (2022)
Tit. 74, §§ 12001–12006 616–17
Or. Rev. Stat. (2024)
Ch. 79 620–21
Ch. 79 § 2(1). 620–21
Ch. 79, § 2(2) 621
S.C. Code Ann. (2023)
§ 9-4-1401 614
§ 9-4-1401(2) 615
§ 9-4-1401(2)(C) 614
§ 9-4-1402 614
§ 9-4-1403(a) 615
§ 9-4-1403(b) 615
§ 9-16-10(10) 614, 615
§ 9-16-30(G)(1)-(2) (2024). 615
§ 9-16-50(A)(5) (2024) 614
§ 9-16-320 616
§ 45-1-128 (2024) 618
§ 56-8-114 (2024) 618
S.D. Codified Laws(1996)
§ 43-13-17 234–35
Tex. Gov't Code Ann. (2021)
§ 809.001(1). 616–17
§§ 2276.001–2276.002 616–17
Tex. Ins. Code Ann. (2023)
§ 565.005 618
§ 565.006 618
Utah Code Ann. (2023)
§ 13-63-201(1). 617
§ 49-11-203(1)(q). 614
§ 51-7-14(2)(b). 614
§ 51-7-14(4)(a). 616
W. Va. Code (2023)
§ 12-6-11a(d)(1) 615–16
§ 12-6-11a(5)(2024) 614
§ 12-6-11a(d) 615
§ 12-6-11a(d) 616
W. Va. Code Ann. (2023)
§ 12-6-11a(c)-(e) 615
§ 12-6-11a(f). 616
Wyo. Statutes
§ 34-1-151(e). 234–35

Zambia

Green Economy and Climate Change Act 2024
s 32 694–95
s 44 695
s 46(2)(o) 694

EDITORS' BIOS

Douglas Kysar is Joseph M. Field '55 Professor of Law at Yale Law School and faculty director of the Law, Environment and Animals Program. His teaching and research areas include torts, environmental law, climate change, animal law, products liability, and risk regulation. Kysar was previously on the faculty at Cornell Law School. He received his BA summa cum laude from Indiana University in 1995 and his JD magna cum laude from Harvard Law School in 1998. Following law school, he clerked for the Honorable William G. Young of the United States District Court for the District of Massachusetts.

Ernest Lim is the Chan Sek Keong Professor of Private Law and a vice dean at the Faculty of Law, National University of Singapore. His research expertise in comparative corporate governance and private law addresses critical global challenges: sustainability and artificial intelligence. At its core, his research seeks to reconceptualise the law to advance social and ecological justice. He holds a doctorate from Oxford University and a master's from Harvard Law School. He previously practised law at Davis Polk & Wardwell LLP in New York and Hong Kong.

CONTRIBUTORS

Danielle de Andrade Moreira Associate Professor, Pontifical Catholic University of Rio de Janeiro

Ekaterina Aristova Senior Lecturer in Private Law, University of Surrey; Academic Fellow, The Honourable Society of the Middle Temple

Franziska Arnold-Dwyer Associate Professor, Faculty of Laws, University College London

Sam Bookman Lecturer, Melbourne Law School

Kim Bouwer Associate Professor in Law, Durham University

Boudewijn de Bruin Professor, University of Groningen and the University of Gothenburg

David Bullock Partner, LeeSalmonLong, New Zealand

Camila Bustos Assistant Professor of Law, Elisabeth Haub School of Law, Pace University

Tiffanie Chan Policy Analyst, Grantham Research Institute on Climate Change and the Environment, London School of Economics and Political Science

Thomas Cheng Professor of Law and Associate Dean, Faculty of Law, University of Hong Kong

Olha O. Cherednychenko Professor of European Private Law and Comparative Law, University of Groningen

Jessica Crow Centre Researcher, Cambridge Centre for Environment, Energy, and Natural Resource Governance, University of Cambridge

Martin Davies Niels F. Johnsen Chair of Maritime Law and Director, Tulane Maritime Law Center, Tulane University Law School

Seth Davis Professor of Law, University of California, Berkeley

John C. Dernbach Emeritus Professor of Law, Widener University, Commonwealth Law School

Arjuna Dibley Assistant Professor, Faculty of Law, National University of Singapore

Avihay Dorfman "The Friends of Joe Jamail" Regents Chair in Law, University of Texas at Austin

Uzuazo Etemire Professor of Law and Head of the Department of Jurisprudence and International Law, Faculty of Law, University of Port Harcourt

Michael Faure Professor of Comparative and International Environmental Law, Faculty of Law, Maastricht University; Professor, Erasmus School of Law, Rotterdam; Adjunct Professor, Faculty of Law, Universitas Indonesia

Yi Feng Environmental Researcher, Sichuan University

Frances Flanagan Lecturer, Faculty of Law, University of Technology Sydney

Mark A. Geistfeld Sheila Lubetsky Birnbaum Professor of Civil Litigation, New York University

Maytal Gilboa Associate Professor, Faculty of Law, University of Western Ontario

Nicole Graham Professor of Law, University of Sydney

Uglješa Grušić Professor of Private International Law, Faculty of Laws, University College London

Catherine Higham Senior Policy Fellow, Grantham Research Institute on Climate Change and the Environment, London School of Economics and Political Science

Virginia Harper Ho Professor of Law, School of Law, City University of Hong Kong

Elbert R. de Jong Professor of Private Law and Director of the Utrecht Centre for Accountability and Liability Law, Utrecht University

Yotam Kaplan Frieda & Solomon Rosenzweig Professor of Law, Hebrew University Law School

Douglas A. Kysar Joseph M. Field '55 Professor of Law, Yale University

Candida Leone Associate Professor of Private Law, University of Amsterdam

Maria Eduarda Lessa LL.M. Candidate, Harvard Law School

Ernest Lim Chan Sek Keong Professor of Private Law and Vice Dean, Faculty of Law, National University of Singapore

Jolene Lin Associate Professor and Director of the Asia Pacific Centre for Environmental Law, Faculty of Law, National University of Singapore

Joshua C. Macey Associate Professor of Law, Yale University

Julian Nowag Associate Professor, Faculty of Law, University of Hong Kong, and Faculty of Law, Lund University

Eric W. Orts Guardsmark Professor of Legal Studies and Business Ethics, The Wharton School, University of Pennsylvania

K-Sue Park Professor of Law, University of California, Los Angeles

Mariana Pargendler Beneficial Professor of Law, Harvard University

Jacqueline Peel Redmond Barry Distinguished Professor, Melbourne University

Barbara Pozzo Full Professor of Comparative Law, Faculty of Law, University of Insubria

Graham Reynolds Associate Professor, Peter A. Allard School of Law, University of British Columbia

Jim Rossi Judge D. L. Lansden Chair in Law, Vanderbilt University

J. B. Ruhl David Daniels Allen Distinguished Chair in Law, Vanderbilt University

Irina Sakharova Assistant Professor in Commercial Law, Durham University

Roee Sarel Junior Professor of Private Law and Law and Economics, Institute of Law and Economics, University of Hamburg

Jan-Erik Schirmer Full Professor, Chair of Civil Law, Commercial and Corporate Law, Compliance and Sustainability, European-University Viadrina

Joana Setzer Associate Professorial Research Fellow, Grantham Research Institute on Climate Change and the Environment, London School of Economics and Political Science

Gregory Shaffer Scott K. Ginsburg Professor of International Law, Georgetown University

Carla Spivack David Josiah Brewer Distinguished Professor of Law, Albany Law School

Sandy Steel Professor of Law and Philosophy of Law, Faculty of Law, University of Oxford

Paul C. Stern President, Social and Environmental Research Institute

Kyla Tienhaara Canada Research Chair in Economy and Environment and Associate Professor, School of Environmental Studies and Department of Global Development Studies, Queen's University

Harro van Asselt Hatton Professor of Climate Law, Department of Land Economy, University of Cambridge

Michael P. Vandenbergh David Daniels Allen Distinguished Chair in Law, Vanderbilt University

Umakanth Varottil Professor of Corporate Law, Faculty of Law, National University of Singapore

Juliana Vélez Echeverri Visiting Senior Fellow, Grantham Research Institute on Climate Change and the Environment, London School of Economics and Political Science

Cynthia A. Williams Roscoe C. O'Byrne Chair in Law, Maurer School of Law, Indiana University

Yue Zhao Associate Professor, School of Law, Sichuan University

Ying Zhu Assistant Professor, Faculty of Law, University of Hong Kong

CHAPTER 1

Introduction

DOUGLAS A. KYSAR AND ERNEST LIM

1. Overview

CLIMATE change is a collective action problem of global proportions with vast destabilising, destructive, and even existential consequences at stake. As such, climate change poses an unprecedented challenge to human governance. Ordinarily, scholars understand and address the governance challenges of climate change through public law lenses such as human rights, constitutional, national security, and regulatory law. But climate change also will both impact and be impacted by private law fields such as contract, tort, and property law. *The Oxford Handbook of Climate Change and Private Law* seeks to offer the first ever comprehensive scholarly assessment of the implications of climate change for private law and vice versa.

The handbook brings together a global team of leading experts to examine the interface between private law and climate change, including such issues as how existing private law can respond to the drivers and impacts of climate change, and whether private law itself might be impacted by climate change in addition to being called to address it.

The handbook has six parts:

- Part I, "Theoretical Approaches to Private Law", outlines various schools of private law theory (law and economics, social and critical theories, and relational justice), with particular emphasis on how they might perceive and respond to the challenges and opportunities climate change poses to private law.
- A significant number of subject matter-based chapters that are placed under three major categories (Part II, "Law of Obligations"; Part III, "Property"; and Part IV, "Corporate and Commercial Law"), in which scholars analyse the implications of climate change both in the sense of how existing bodies of private law will bear on climate-related issues and also how climate change may shape those areas of law themselves.
- In Part V, "Area Perspectives", authors analyse variations regarding the intersection of private law and climate change within particular geographical areas (the EU, the US, the UK, China, India, Southeast Asia, Australasia, Brazil, and Africa).
- Part VI, "Emerging Issues", addresses concerns such as the implications of climate change for legal education and private law firms, and the relationship between climate change and matters such as artificial intelligence, the horizontal effect of human rights, and Indigenous private rights.

The authors of these chapters have sought to make original intellectual contributions, rather than just survey or rehash existing scholarship. As such, this handbook serves as a launching pad for scholarly analysis of climate change and private law for years to come.

2. Six Major Themes

Rather than summarising the chapters in a sequential order, a more challenging and rewarding task is to draw out the major themes that have emerged from all the chapters in the handbook. These are:

- The relationship between private law and public law or public considerations
- The relationship between the government or mandatory regulation and private or voluntary action
- Private law as a double-edged sword to promote or undermine climate action
- The role of courts in private law adjudication
- From individualism to interconnectedness
- Endogenous impacts of climate change on private law and society

2.1 Theme 1: The Relationship between Private Law and Public Law or Public Considerations

Traditional pillars of private law—property rights, tort liability, contractual freedom—were conceived in an era when environmental externalities appeared manageable within localised frameworks. Climate change challenges this assumption, creating a temporal and spatial disconnect between private actions and their systemic consequences.

Climate change may require private law to grapple with intergenerational equity, global justice, human rights breaches, and systemic risk—considerations that traditional private law has historically externalised to the public sphere. Thus, a reconceptualisation of how legal systems can coherently address challenges that transcend the organising assumptions of both public and private legal orders is warranted. At the very least, it is no longer tenable to divorce the aims and outcomes of private law from public considerations.

For example, Tiffanie Chan, Juliana Vélez Echeverri, Joana Setzer, and Catherine Higham (Chapter 11, "Consumer Protection") argue that climate-washing litigation challenges the divide between private law and public law as corporate misrepresentation intersects with human rights and climate justice issues. Through an analysis of three key cases in Brazil and Columbia, they argue that litigation targeting climate-washing in carbon markets challenges corporate climate strategies in ways that directly affect land rights, self-determination, and community involvement in environmental governance.

In a similar vein, Graham Reynolds (Chapter 16, "Intellectual Property") argues for a human rights-based approach to the intersection of climate change and intellectual property (IP), one that is based on the human rights principles of substantive equality and non-discrimination, participation and empowerment, accountability and access to justice, transparency, and the rule of law. To him, applying this approach to IP and climate change could create new reform opportunities directly tied to achieving human rights objectives; integrate values into IP systems that differ from traditional IP law principles, and provide greater flexibility for implementing solutions at local, national, or regional levels.

Indeed, a number of chapters implicitly call into question the formalist or non-instrumentalist premise that private law should not be deployed as a tool to achieve substantive social or economic goals. But if private law or private transactions facilitate climate change, which endangers human flourishing, the notion that private law should be primarily or solely concerned with corrective justice such as the vindication of rights and the enforcement of duties between bilaterial parties needs to be reconsidered.

For instance, Douglas A. Kysar (Chapter 10, "Products Liability") suggests that climate change lawsuits challenging greenhouse gas intensive consumer products invite courts to conceive of tort liability as a private law mechanism for achieving systemic, public law aims. With its peculiar focus on "products" rather than "persons" as agents of responsibility, products liability law is a field of private law that encourages inspection beyond the narrow confines of dyadic, interpersonal rights and duties.

The use of private law to achieve substantive public goals is also illustrated by Maytal Gilboa, Yotam Kaplan, and Roee Sarel (Chapter 12, "Unjust Enrichment"). They argue that carbon pools can be treated as atmospheric commons belonging to the public, serving as a shared resource essential to maintaining climate stability, and this can form the basis of an unjust enrichment claim in which the extractors who exploit this common resource for private profit at the public's expense can be sued by private litigants. They argue that the focus on wrongful gains rather than causation of harm is a more effective deterrence tool.

Fiduciary law is another important area of law which has been used to facilitate climate goals. Seth Davis and Gregory Shaffer (Chapter 13, "Fiduciary Law") demonstrate why and how climate activists and scholars have sought to use fiduciary law to advance climate goals in relation to companies, institutional investors, and nation-states. However, using fiduciary law to achieve substantive goals such as climate change mitigation is not without challenges. Some of the problems highlighted by the authors with such use include what they term the "sword-and-shield problem", the "legitimacy trap", and the "interface problem".

In a different context, Ernest Lim (Chapter 18, "Corporate Law and Governance") argues that directors of state-owned enterprises, which are among the worst greenhouse gas emitters in the world, can and should address climate-related risks and other negative externalities, even if it is unconnected to firm-specific shareholders' financial interests. The justification, as he demonstrates, is that because state-owned enterprises are formed to pursue socio-economic goals, in addition to profit-generation, the duties of the three kinds of fiduciaries—the director, the state as the controlling shareholder, and the state as an asset owner or diversified investor—are aligned. Thus, corporate fiduciary law should evolve beyond its narrow focus on directors' obligations to the company for firm-specific shareholders' benefit; it should be reconceptualised to confront climate change and other systemic risks and opportunities, even when doing so does not financially benefit shareholders (at least in the short term).

Climate-related disclosure—often regarded as part of the material risks and opportunities that companies are required to apprise shareholders of as part of their disclosure obligations—is not merely a private tool to protect shareholders' financial interests, but is underpinned by public goals. Maria Eduarda Lessa and Mariana Pargendler (Chapter 19, "Climate Disclosure in the Global South") demonstrate that Global South approaches to climate disclosure have fostered greater stakeholder integration and tied climate change to broader policy and distributional objectives.

Not only are climate disclosure regimes embedded within or connected to public law or public considerations, even supposedly private law type regulations such as the EU Corporate Sustainability Due Diligence Directive and EU Corporate Sustainability Reporting Directive operate within a public law framework, as demonstrated by Harro van Asselt and Jessica Crow (Chapter 33, "The European Union"). This framework is characterised by its market-based approach, heavy reliance on target-setting mechanisms, emphasis on enhancing the EU's global competitiveness, and rising judicial scrutiny of climate policy goals and their implementation at both national and European levels.

The impact of public law on private law claims relating to climate change adjudication is no more evident than in how and to what extent fundamental rights can and should influence private law in climate change cases. That is the question that is being critically analysed by Olha O. Cherednychenko and Boudewijn de Bruin (Chapter 45, "The Horizontal Effect of Fundamental Rights"). They use the concepts of direct and indirect horizontal effect to examine how fundamental rights interact with private law in climate litigation. Their analysis reveals that the horizontal application of fundamental rights creates both obstacles and possibilities for combating climate change.

Serious public concerns raised by private law claims relating to climate change also shed light on the problem of whether matters should be decided in a private forum. For example, Ying Zhu (Chapter 25, "International Commercial Arbitration") examines whether commercial disputes that have significant climate implications can be addressed in private arbitration, or, given their connections to matters of grave public significance, should be exclusively adjudicated in courts.

On a separate but related point, certain private forms of dispute resolution may do more harm than good in addressing climate change. For example, Kyla Tienhaara (Chapter 28, "Investor–State Disputes") demonstrates that investor state dispute settlement—designed to foster a legal environment conducive to private investment—is a major obstacle to climate action to phase out fossil fuels as it allows investors to challenge government climate policies through arbitration, seeking compensation for stranded assets.

If public law or public considerations can or have influenced private law in relation to climate change, the reverse is also true: Private law also influences public law. For example, Umakanth Varottil (Chapter 36, "India") argues that the lines between private and public law are blurred in India because private law principles like tort, corporate, and contract law have been adapted and expanded within public law adjudication related to environmental and climate issues. Specifically, constitutional courts have incorporated private law concepts like the polluter pays principle and absolute liability into public law jurisprudence.

The chapters that have been grouped under the first theme reveal a deeper theoretical challenge: Climate change exposes the inadequacy of treating private and public law as discrete domains. The climate crisis demands legal responses that transcend traditional boundaries, suggesting that future legal frameworks must be conceived more holistically.

2.2 Theme 2: The Relationship between the Government or Mandatory Regulation and Private or Voluntary Action

The relationship between mandatory regulation and voluntary private action in climate governance reveals a complex dialectic that challenges traditional binary thinking about state versus market solutions. Rather than viewing these approaches as competing alternatives, contemporary private law increasingly demonstrates their interdependent and mutually constitutive nature, even if either regulation or private action takes on a more active role.

Michael Faure (Chapter 2, "Law and Economics") analyses the question of which are the optimal combination of legal rules to promote efficient mitigation and adaptation of climate change. On mitigation, he argues that while ex ante regulation by the state is to be preferred, liability rules laid down in private law cases can usefully complement ex ante regulations. On adaptation, he argues that the most effective form of compensation for potential victims of climate change disaster is mandatory first-party insurance supplemented by the government as a reinsurer of last resort.

That both regulation and voluntary action are complementary rather than exclusionary is another theme that emerges from the work by Michael P. Vandenbergh and Paul C. Stern (Chapter 31, "Private Environmental Governance"). They investigate how private environmental governance institutions have emerged at local, regional, and global levels. They demonstrate that these institutions work alongside—not instead of—government to reduce global carbon emissions. The authors examine what drives private climate governance and assess its impacts. In the process, they consider both advantages and drawbacks, identify sources of opposition, analyse spillover effects on public policy, and propose strategies for enhancing effectiveness.

However, for the roles of mandatory regulation or voluntary action to be complementary or reinforcing, it has to be assumed that the government is willing and able to come up with effective regulation to address climate risks. But in light of the hostility that the Trump administration has displayed towards climate action, a greater role needs to be accorded to voluntary action. Hence, Eric W. Orts (Chapter 5, "Consumer Climate Contracts") envisions the important role to be played by engaged and activist consumers, what he calls consumer-citizens (who bear in mind political meaning and social consequences in their consumption decisions), and citizens-consumers (who aim to take political action that help consumers make better decisions).

The significance of voluntary action, albeit in a different form, is subject to critical analysis by Cynthia A. Williams (Chapter 30, "Non-Governmental Organisations and Private Standard-Setting"). She begins by acknowledging the blurry distinctions between mandatory regulation and voluntary actions, followed by a critical analysis of the roles played by private standard setters. She distinguishes (a) market-enhancing standards such as expanded disclosure by the Task Force on Climate-Related Financial Disclosures (now incorporated into the International Sustainability Standards Board) or those developing new markets (such as climate bonds) and (b) market-limiting standards (such as boycotting the financing of coal advocated by the Glasgow Financial Alliance for Net Zero). She argues that the former is likely to be more tenable than the latter.

However, there are drawbacks to voluntary action. One such instance is environmental, social, and governance (ESG)—construed as actions that go beyond compliance with existing law, a voluntary form of action—which has recently attracted intense backlash in the US as a result of anti-ESG laws enacted by more than fifteen states. John C. Dernbach (Chapter 35, "The United States") examines the anti- and pro-ESG laws in the US. He argues that both kinds of legislation are ultimately constrained by fiduciary duties—which are often mandatory—and concludes that these state laws are likely to have limited impact on the overall trajectory of ESG, which is largely driven by private actors.

Understanding private law's climate role requires us to examine how legal institutions can optimise the interaction between public authority and private initiative, recognising that climate governance's legitimacy and effectiveness increasingly depend on this delicate calibration rather than the dominance of either approach alone.

2.3 Theme 3: Private Law as a Double-edged Sword to Promote or Undermine Climate Action

Private law operates as a paradoxical force in climate governance, simultaneously enabling and constraining meaningful climate action through its structures and doctrines. This duality emerges from private law's inherent tension between protecting established rights and facilitating necessary transformation.

A distinctive issue in contract law is whether the voluntary character of contractual obligations could either reduce or worsen the problems that arise when using private law mechanisms to address problems related to climate change. Irina Sakharova (Chapter 6, "Contract Law") examines the potential application of standard contract law remedies to climate-related obligations that parties choose to include in their agreements. She identifies challenges that arise both when applying conventional remedial measures to breaches of these climate commitments and when enforcing specific remedies that contracting parties may have agreed upon for such breaches.

The double-edged sword of private law is also illustrated by Carla Spivack (Chapter 17, "Trusts"). She argues that while the flexible structure of trusts benefits conservation and can drive legal evolution to address climate threats, these same characteristics enable tax avoidance and wealth consolidation. This creates a fundamental tension, as trusts both offer tools for climate response and contribute to the inequality that accelerates climate change and worsens its impacts.

Arjuna Dibley (Chapter 20, "Finance") argues that while climate disclosure laws and climate risk stress tests have produced better and more comparable climate-related information, they have also resulted in transferring, rather than reducing, high carbon assets and climate-related risks to entities outside the climate-information ecosystem. To address the problem of carbon and climate risk transfer, he argues that disclosure laws should be reformed to include carbon risk shifting activities, among other measures.

The double-edged sword of another important area of private law is well illustrated by Ekaterina Aristova and Uglješa Grušić (Chapter 32, "Private International Law"). They argue that because private international law can enable or block access to remedies by determining which courts have jurisdiction and which laws apply, and given that certain courts and legal systems are more open to climate arguments than others, the role of private international law becomes particularly significant.

The Janus-faced effect of private law is evident not only in legal doctrines, but also in the actors who interpret and advise on them such as law firms. Camila Bustos (Chapter 43, "Lawyers and Law Firms") argues that the legal profession plays a crucial role in either perpetuating or transitioning away from carbon-intensive economic models through their selection of clients, the advice they provide, and the professional standards of responsibility lawyers (largely) set for themselves. In light of the climate emergency, Bustos challenges the traditional notion of lawyer neutrality regarding client selection, particularly when representing what she terms "climate wreckers".

For certain areas of private law, the interaction with climate change may give rise less to a double-edged sword and more to a situation that can be seen as both a sword and a shield. Julian Nowag and Thomas Cheng (Chapter 21, "Competition Law") take that view in regard to competition law. They see the field operating as a sword in furtherance of climate-friendly technologies because competition authorities have taken action against cartels for limiting innovation in sustainability features. Simultaneously, they identify competition law as a shield as it increasingly allows cooperation among companies on sustainability matters notwithstanding a surface appearance of anticompetitive behaviour.

On the one hand, climate action may have to operate within frameworks that simultaneously protect property rights, contractual arrangements, and economic structures that underpin carbon-intensive systems. On the other hand, the chapters on this theme suggest how we can tap into private law's transformative potential to overcome its conservative tendencies. This requires systematic attention to three interdependent variables: the doctrinal flexibility of legal instruments, the institutional capacity of legal actors to interpret existing rules in climate-conscious ways, and the alignment of economic incentives with climate objectives. Private law thus functions as a site of ongoing contestation where incremental legal decisions aggregate into either reinforcement of existing carbon dependencies or gradual institutional transformation. The cumulative effect of these day-to-day choices in legal interpretation and application by different actors across subject areas becomes a decisive factor in determining whether private law ultimately advances or obstructs broader climate governance objectives.

2.4 Theme 4: The Role of Courts in Private Law Adjudication

Across diverse legal systems—from the pragmatic tort frameworks of common law jurisdictions to the constitutional principles embedded in civil codes—judges are being asked to translate broad climate imperatives into concrete legal obligations for private actors. This judicial engagement reveals profound tensions between traditional private law concepts and the unprecedented temporal, spatial, and causal complexities of climate harm. As courts navigate these uncharted waters, their decisions illuminate not merely doctrinal evolution but fundamental questions about the separation of powers, the limits of legal reasoning, and the capacity of private law to respond to global challenges that transcend conventional boundaries of causation and remedy.

For example, Mark A. Geistfeld and Sandy Steel (Chapter 8, "Causation in Tort"") demonstrate that causation requirements in tort law pose a problem for climate litigants under most tort causes of action and argue that public nuisance is a better pathway given its collective conception of harm. They draw a distinction between the attenuated-causation problem and the causal-proof problem. The former addresses how individual responsibility is affected when an actor's actions are neither individually necessary nor individually sufficient to produce an outcome, yet some plausible causal connection remains. The latter arises when the claimant's harms likely resulted from background risks, making it impossible to distinguish between the causal effects of those background risks and the risk created by the defendant's conduct.

Through a comparative analysis of Dutch and German courts, E. R. de Jong (Chapter 9, "Civil Law Torts") examines six interrelated "adaptability indicators"—characteristics within a civil law tort system that determine its capacity for judicial development of corporate climate mitigation responsibility through tort law. These include the institutional positioning of civil courts, the pertinent regulatory landscape, substantive liability rules, handling of scientific uncertainty, the influence of EU harmonisation, and the effectiveness of single-actor responsibility.

Kim Bouwer (Chapter 34, "The United Kingdom") argues that under English private law, courts are unlikely to change and adapt doctrines in any significant way in climate change adjudication because of the conservatism of English legal culture. She demonstrates this through an analysis of classic climate litigation cases (such as torts and derivative actions) and regulatory and self-directed cases (such as disputes arising from climate regulations or voluntary climate commitments). Her chapter challenges purely structural explanations for English private law's climate limitations.

However, courts in other parts of the world seem less conservative. For example, Jacqueline Peel (Chapter 37, "Australasia") shows that Australia (and to some extent New Zealand) are "innovative testbeds" for corporate climate litigation, with nearly ninety cases deploying various legal frameworks such as directors' duties, disclosure laws, consumer protection laws, and the duty of care in negligence.

In a similar vein, Jolene Lin (Chapter 38, "East and Southeast Asia") demonstrates that contrary to the widespread assumption that Southeast and East Asia are laggards when it comes to climate litigation, there are several groundbreaking litigation cases that target companies using tort law, constitutional rights, and human rights frameworks to establish corporate duties regarding climate change.

Yue Zhao and Yi Feng (Chapter 40, "China") examine how the "Green Principle" enshrined in China's Civil Code—requiring activities pursued by individuals and entities under civil law to be conducive to conserving resources and protecting the environment—has been applied by Chinese courts in eighty-one climate related cases based on torts, contracts, and property law. The Green Principle reflects an incorporation of public law values into private law, another major theme discussed above. However, they caution against the use of the Green Principle to determine the validity of civil acts for reasons including the hortatory rather than mandatory nature of the principle, and the ensuing legal uncertainty and unpredictability should courts invoke the principle to nullify or prohibit certain acts.

The landscape of climate litigation in private law reveals courts as both constrained actors and creative interpreters, operating within institutional limitations while simultaneously pushing the boundaries of legal imagination. From the Netherlands to Australia, from China's Green Principle to the cautious conservatism of English courts, judicial approaches to climate change reflect deeper cultural and constitutional commitments about the proper role of law in addressing societal transformation. Yet despite this variation, a common thread emerges: Courts are increasingly recognising that climate change poses fundamental challenges to the architecture of private law itself—challenges that cannot be resolved through doctrinal refinement alone but require reimagining the relationship between individual responsibility and collective harm, between present action and future consequence, and between legal systems and planetary boundaries.

2.5 Theme 5: From Individualism to Interconnectedness

The transition from individualism to interconnectedness represents one of the most profound shifts occurring within contemporary private law, driven by the urgent recognition that our legal frameworks must evolve to address the ecological crises of our time.

Avihay Dorfman (Chapter 4, "Relational Justice") examines whether tort law can and should impose duties of care towards living organisms other than humans. He advocates for an affirmative position, arguing that relational justice provides the theoretical framework to extend tort law in this direction while remaining consistent with tort law's foundational principles. Relational justice focuses on determining just terms for interpersonal interactions from the outset, not merely at the remedial stage. Under this framework, private responsibility for non-human life emerges as a natural extension of tort law rather than an aberration. His approach prioritises substantive over formal equality by accounting for the interests and vulnerabilities of all interacting parties.

David Bullock (Chapter 7, "Common Law Torts") takes the view that the narrow, classical liberal tort paradigm—rooted in atomistic individualism and anthropocentric Enlightenment philosophy—appears increasingly inadequate given planetary ecological limits. He argues that Indigenous legal frameworks offer transformative potential through relational worldviews. Tikanga Māori exemplifies this approach, emphasising interconnectedness over individualism, recognising communal victimhood and wrongdoing, and establishing stewardship obligations governing human-environment relations. Tikanga encompasses spiritual and physical dimensions beyond interhuman relationships. New Zealand's judicial recognition of tikanga Māori as integral to common law demonstrates the practical feasibility of incorporating Indigenous principles into established tort frameworks.

In a similar vein, Nicole Graham (Chapter 15, "Cultures of Land Use and Ownership") argues that First Peoples' legal systems fundamentally differ from Anglo-American law by positioning humans as integrated components of their natural environment rather than separate entities. These Indigenous frameworks derive legal principles from specific geographical conditions, emphasising relational obligations over individual property rights. Key features include land-based education where land teaches social relationships, universal stewardship duties, and kinship systems including non-human beings. She contends that more effective climate responses require engaging with First Peoples' legal authorities, whose systems demonstrate proven capacity for sustainable land management within local ecological limits across extended timeframes, offering superior models for addressing environmental challenges.

Together, these chapters illuminate a convergence: the recognition that effective climate responses demand not merely technical legal adjustments, but a fundamental reimagining of the relationships that law both reflects and constructs. Whether through Dorfman's expansion of relational justice to encompass non-human life, Bullock's integration of tikanga Māori principles into common law structures, or Graham's emphasis on land-based stewardship obligations, each approach challenges the artificial boundaries that have long constrained private law's ecological potential. Their work suggests that the path forward lies not in wholesale replacement of existing legal frameworks, but in their careful cultivation towards forms of responsibility that honour both human relationships and the larger web of dependencies within which all legal subjects—human and non-human alike—are embedded. In this light, the evolution from individualism to interconnectedness emerges not as a radical departure from private law's foundations, but as the fulfillment of its deepest aspirations towards justice in an interconnected world.

2.6 Theme 6: Endogenous Impacts of Climate Change on Private Law and Society

Much of the focus of climate law scholarship is on how different areas of law might be utilised to address the sources and impacts of climate change. Given its deep and pervasive effects, climate change will not just be impacted *by* law but will also impact *on* law, including by necessitating shifts and changes in substantive areas of law (including but not limited to property, insurance, products liability, bankruptcy, labour law, and maritime law); in the private law regimes of specific jurisdictions (such as the EU, Brazil, and Africa); in the normative traditions and understandings of specific groups of people (such as Indigenous peoples); in the governance and deployment of critical societal technologies and phenomena (such as artificial intelligence); and, last but not the least, in legal education itself.

J. B. Ruhl and Jim Rossi (Chapter 14, "Property") argue that climate change has undermined a key assumption underlying property law: that is, planetary-scale natural systems like the polar ice caps or the circulation patters of the oceans fluctuate within a consistent range, an assumption the authors refer to as "Earth system stationarity". In light of increasing evidence that humanity has pushed several of these planetary systems towards new equilibrium states, property law needs to be reformed to address mitigation and adaptation against a backdrop of more dramatic and unpredictable change, an assumption of "Earth system of *non*-stationarity". They argue that mitigation policies—covering low-carbon energy, transportation electrification, and carbon capture—raise three property law issues: ownership design, use restrictions, and novel disputes. For adaptation, they argue that property law plays three roles: applying existing doctrines to intensified traditional risks (flooding, wildfires), creating new approaches for overwhelming or novel risks (sea-level rise), and managing private adaptation initiatives responding to public policy. Both mitigation and adaptation require careful integration of property law principles with climate objectives.

While insurance traditionally serves as a private market response to disasters after they occur, Franziska Arnold-Dwyer (Chapter 22, "Insurance") argues that insurance companies could take a more proactive role in preventing losses and building resilience before disasters strike, on the basis of the urgency of climate change and sound business reasoning. She investigates how insurance contract law might enable bottom-up solutions through individual insurance agreements in two key ways: first, by facilitating the exchange of knowledge about risk reduction and disaster preparedness between insurers and policyholders; and second, by enabling insurers to fund loss prevention initiatives.

Joshua C. Macey (Chapter 24, "Bankruptcy Law") analyses the potential complications arising from uncoordinated, piecemeal reorganisation of fossil fuel enterprises amid the energy transition, particularly when nations fail to harmonise their restructuring frameworks for financially distressed multinational energy companies. He demonstrates how fundamental bankruptcy principles—notably the automatic stay provision and absolute priority rule—create a dual dynamic in the context of fossil fuel corporate bankruptcies: They enable past claimants to push for firm reorganisation and continued production in order to maximise their recovery, while sacrificing the interests of future stakeholders who would be better served by systematic dissolution and absolute retirement of fossil fuel assets. He advocates for reforms to transnational insolvency frameworks designed to enable coordinated, orderly dissolution of international fossil fuel corporations facing financial distress during the energy transition.

Frances Flanagan (Chapter 26, "Labour Law") notes that labour law's bilateral contract framework excludes most workers and ignores environmental impacts, creating climate blind spots. She argues that historically, labour law emerged during coal-dependent industrialisation with theoretical justifications favouring fossil fuel industries, giving those workers superior wages and political influence that now enables opposition to climate policies. She contends that this creates a troublesome paradox: While labour law's substantive protections support climate adaptation, its embedded advantages for carbon-intensive sectors simultaneously obstruct decarbonisation, requiring fundamental reconceptualisation of the field rather than marginal reform.

Martin Davies (Chapter 27, "Maritime Law") examines the impact of climate change on maritime-related regulations and enforcement. Three key points emerged from his chapter. Firstly, if US opposition can be overcome, the shipping industry will become uniquely subject to some of the first internationally uniform, legally enforceable regulations for carbon emission reduction aiming for net zero by 2050. Secondly, the regulatory environment is multilayered with enforcement distributed among flag states (often delegating to classification societies) and port states. Finally, the performance-based system relies on market mechanisms, but significant compliance costs will be passed to global consumers, affecting the price of internationally traded goods.

Virginia Harper Ho (Chapter 23, "Securities Regulation") explores how securities regulation increasingly addresses climate change concerns. In her view, while securities law cannot directly compel companies to reduce environmental harm, it can encourage investors and corporations to tackle climate risks through market-based approaches. Her analysis tracks the emergence of required climate disclosures and green finance initiatives, spurred by growing recognition of financial vulnerabilities. However, she notes that despite efforts towards international coordination, different jurisdictions show substantial variation in their climate regulation strategies within securities frameworks, shaped by regulatory capacity and political factors.

In addition to the impacts of climate change on substantive areas of private law, the private law regimes of certain jurisdictions are no doubt impacted by climate change. For example,

Danielle de Andrade Moreira (Chapter 41, "Brazil") argues for a reinterpretation of traditional tort law to tackle the complex nature of climate-environmental damage in Brazil. These legal mechanisms include the adoption of strict liability (eliminating fault requirements), application of the "absolute risk" theory (no traditional defenses allowed), and establishment of the joint and several liability for direct and indirect polluters under the polluter-pays principle. She contends that climate damage is a dimension of environmental damage, requiring full reparation encompassing direct harm to the climate system and indirect impacts.

Uzuazo Etemire (Chapter 39, "Africa") advocates for horizontal climate litigation mechanisms across African jurisdictions, wherein private entities face accountability for climate harm through inter partes proceedings. He contends that conventional governmental regulatory frameworks have proven inadequate, while vertical litigation against state actors, though prevalent, fails to address private sector contributions to carbon-intensive activities. He surveys existing legal doctrines—including tort, environmental, and human rights law—identifying both limitations and emerging opportunities, particularly through evolving human rights jurisprudence and liberalised standing requirements. The chapter evaluates nascent climate-specific legislation's capacity to facilitate horizontal enforcement mechanisms, noting that while certain statutory frameworks provide private enforcement avenues and remedial structures, implementation deficiencies and jurisdictional variations across African legal systems present ongoing challenges.

Barbara Pozzo (Chapter 29, "Corporate Sustainability and the European Union") traces the evolution of European Union environmental and sustainability policy from a traditional "command-and-control" regulatory approach to a comprehensive market-based framework that increasingly relies on private sector engagement and disclosure obligations to achieve environmental objectives. She argues that this evolution represents an "irreversible" transformation in European legal culture, where sustainability principles have become constitutionally embedded and culturally normalised. However, the challenge lies in finding the optimal regulatory balance that achieves environmental objectives without imposing excessive compliance costs that undermine business competitiveness.

Climate change not only affects substantive areas of law or the private law regimes of particular jurisdictions, but it also impacts on certain groups of people or legal systems. For example, Sam Bookman (Chapter 46, "Indigenous Peoples") analyses the complex relationship between Indigenous legal systems, private law doctrines, and climate change jurisprudence. He demonstrates how Indigenous communities face disproportionate climate impacts while simultaneously serving as essential actors in global mitigation efforts through distinct legal frameworks. He explores the challenges inherent in integrating Indigenous private law within colonial legal structures, examining its relevance across climate tort liability, land use regulation for adaptation measures, fiduciary obligations, reparative justice, and traditional ecological knowledge protection. This chapter highlights the strategic legal choices confronting Indigenous peoples as they navigate competing sovereignty claims while pursuing climate justice and self-determination.

Traditional ecological knowledge and artificial intelligence (AI) might seem to be on opposite ends of a spectrum of human enquiry, but both interlace with climate change in complex ways that cannot be ignored. Jan-Erik Schirmer (Chapter 44, "Artificial Intelligence") examines the relationship between corporate climate governance and AI. He argues that while widespread institutional AI adoption—pursued for presumptive operational efficiencies—generates substantial carbon emissions and attendant climate risks, the technology simultaneously offers instrumental value in optimising climate disclosure protocols and environmental risk assessment mechanisms. The chapter advances a framework advocating measured AI deployment that incorporates rigorous risk-benefit analysis, maintaining cognizance of environmental externalities while harnessing technological capabilities for substantive climate governance objectives, consistent with established corporate stewardship principles.

Last but not the least, climate change must impact on legal education. This handbook is written by law professors and academically inclined practitioners who care deeply about the implications of climate change on private law and who understand the importance of deploying and reimagining private law to address the issues arising from climate change. For example, K-Sue Park (Chapter 3, "Critical and Social Theory") undertakes a comprehensive survey of various methodological approaches to legal scholarship that share a common commitment to critically examining foundational tenets and assumptions in a given field, unearthing in the process the field's hidden biases and faulty assumptions, while also shining light on relations of oppression and exclusion that all too often appear normalised or natural through orthodox lenses. Park's survey underscores the centrality of topics such as race, history, and power to any understanding of the private law and its role in causing—and not just failing to prevent—environmental injustice, including the ever-growing injustice of climate change.

Such critical analysis of private law must also be accompanied by a serious evaluation of private law education in law schools, which can either facilitate or undermine climate action. Candida Leone (Chapter 42, "Legal Education") argues that private law education is systematically embedded within a "growth paradigm"—the assumption that continuous economic expansion is both inevitable and desirable. Drawing on the distinction between "weak sustainability" (which assumes natural and manufactured capital are substitutable) and "strong sustainability" (which treats natural capital as non-substitutable), she advocates for making legal education "agnostic with respect to growth". In her view, taking strong sustainability seriously would require fundamentally rethinking how we teach private law such as by moving away from pure wealth maximisation towards recognising non-negotiable ecological constraints. The chapter identifies how legal education shapes growth-dependent professional identities through law firm models, skills training, and career pathways. While acknowledging structural constraints, the author suggests potential interventions.

The chapters under this last theme collectively demonstrate that climate change is not only an external force that private law can be marshalled to address from the outside, but rather a transformative phenomenon that is reshaping the internal logic and fundamental assumptions of private legal systems worldwide. From the erosion of stationarity in property law to the emergence of "failure to adapt" theories in products liability, from the reconceptualisation of insurance as a proactive risk prevention mechanism to the challenging integration of Indigenous legal systems with colonial private law structures, we witness legal orders in transition. Perhaps most significantly, this transformation extends beyond doctrinal evolution to encompass the very foundations of legal education and professional identity, challenging the growth paradigm that has long shaped how we understand the purpose and function of private law and private lawyers themselves.

3. Concluding Thoughts: Moving Forward

Future research must grapple with how to construct truly integrated legal frameworks that narrow the artificial public/private divide, refine the dynamic calibration between state action and private initiative, and systematically harness private law's transformative potential beyond its traditional constraints. It calls for deeper inquiry into the evolving capacity of courts in navigating unprecedented complexities, the practical methods for embedding principles of ecological interconnectedness and relational justice into legal education and professional practice, and the foundational reforms necessary across core private law doctrines—from property and contract to corporate governance and torts—to align with a non-stationary world. The task before us is not merely to adapt existing legal frameworks to accommodate climate realities, but to also envision a new private law that embraces uncertainty, experiments with hybrid forms of responsibility, and remains open to learning from the more-than-human world. Only then can private law effectively address climate change. The stakes could not be higher: The future of private law, and perhaps law itself, depends on our ability to reimagine legal relationships for a planet in transition.

PART I

Theoretical Approaches to Private Law

CHAPTER 2

Law and Economics

MICHAEL FAURE

1. Introduction

CAN private law respond to the drivers and impacts of climate change? And how does climate change affect private law? In this chapter, I will try to examine how law and economics would address those specific questions.

The starting point in the economic analysis is usually that the goal of law in general, and therefore also of private law, is to correct market failures. Climate change undoubtedly creates such a market failure, more particularly a negative externality. In very simple terms the goal of law in general and therefore also of private law is to make sure that that negative externality would be internalised. The starting point for the economic analysis of law is the theorem developed by Ronald Coase, holding that when transaction costs are zero or low, there should not necessarily be an intervention by the law, as the internalisation could also be the result of efficient bargaining between parties.[1] However, climate change is obviously the type of risk where bargaining between potential victims and potential injurers is not feasible, given the high transaction cost setting.

We are therefore in the domain of accidents and economists have more particularly paid attention to the question of which type of instruments can provide incentives to internalise the negative externality created by climate change. The instruments that come to mind are government-initiated instruments such as regulation, but certainly also private law instruments such as torts and insurance. With this, the law and economics literature on instrument choice certainly has a message concerning the optimal rules to mitigate greenhouse gas emissions.

As I will show in Section 2, the law and economics scholarship has advocated that even though private law may not be the primary instrument to control mitigation of greenhouse gas emissions, it can play a very important supplementary role. That role is more particularly to fill gaps where (as a result of effective lobbying by industry) standards for mitigation (for example in an emissions trading scheme, or ETS) have been suboptimal. For that reason, so it will be argued, climate change litigation can certainly be understood from an economic perspective,[2] and, so it will also be argued, how economists would view the "public life of private law"[3] as far as climate change is concerned.

Also, as far as adaptation and loss and damage are concerned—and more particularly compensation of victims of climate change—law and economics literature has addressed the most

[1] Ronald H Coase, 'The Problem of Social Cost' (1960) Journal of Law and Economics 1–44.

[2] Michael Faure and Marjan Peeters, *Liability and Climate Change: Oxford Research Encyclopedia of Climate Science* (OUP 2019).

[3] Doug Kysar, 'The Public Life of Private Law: Tort Law as a Risk Regulation Mechanism' (2018) 9 European Journal of Risk Regulation 48–65.

efficient (and effective) instruments to provide compensation for harms related to climate change (more particularly "natural" disasters such as heavy rain, hurricanes, or flooding).[4]

The type of adaptation that economists have addressed focuses especially on compensation for harm arising from climate change, which is often caused by disasters such as flooding. The traditional (economic) reaction has been that this constitutes primarily a distributional issue and that compensation is therefore worthwhile only if it can create incentives for prevention. However, economists increasingly argue that certainly when climate change creates catastrophic losses, there may be reasons to consider structural ex ante solutions.[5] The reason is that climate change is a so-called systemic risk which can (for example with large-scale flooding) lead to a total disruption of particular societies and of the financial system. Therefore, from an economic perspective also, the question of whether effective compensation for this type of climate change related harm can be provided is justified.

Again, the choice of optimal instruments has been extensively discussed in the law and economics literature. Economists have advocated particular changes to the private law system in order to allow for better adaptation. For this particular domain, the question therefore arises of which legal rules are optimal to provide incentives towards efficient mitigation and adaptation. At the same time, not surprisingly, economists will also ask the question of how these goals can be achieved at the lowest (administrative) cost possible. These issues will be addressed in Section 3. Section 4 concludes the chapter.

2. Mitigation of Climate Change Emissions: Liability Versus Regulation

2.1 Preference for Regulation

At first sight, it might seem odd to use liability rules as an instrument to achieve a reduction of greenhouse gas emissions. The classic law and economics paper addressing when to use liability rules and when to rely on regulation instead is obviously the paper by Steven Shavell in which he presents criteria for regulation.[6] Shavell first points to the importance of information: Regulation requires information from administrative agencies; the application of liability rules requires information from either the judge (under a negligence rule) or the injurer (under a strict liability rule). As far as the problem of climate change is concerned, it can easily be argued that the regulator and administrative agencies can be expected to have better information than either the parties or the courts to set efficient standards for greenhouse gas mitigation. A second criterion relates to the insolvency risk: If the potential damage is so high that it will exceed the wealth of an individual injurer, liability rules may not provide optimal incentives. If an injurer is not exposed to the threat of a liability suit, a problem of under-deterrence will arise.[7] Safety regulation can overcome this problem of under-deterrence caused by insolvency by setting standards ex ante and using non-monetary sanctions as an enforcement

[4] Michael Faure, 'Financial Compensation for Victims of Catastrophes: A Law and Economics Perspective' (2007) 29(3) Law & Policy 339–67.

[5] Reimund Schwarze and Gerhard Wagner, 'In the Aftermath of Dresden. New Directions in German Flood Insurance' (2004) 29(2) Geneva Papers on Risk and Insurance 154–68.

[6] Steven Shavell, 'Liability for Harm versus Regulation of Safety' (1984) Journal of Legal Studies 357–74.

[7] Steven Shavell, 'The Judgment Proof Problem' (1986) 6 International Review of Law and Economics 43–58.

mechanism.[8] The damage related to climate change can obviously be substantially higher than the individual wealth of an emitter; as a result, the insolvency risk is real.

The third criterion is whether there is a sufficient threat from a lawsuit. Latency (a long-time lapse between an emission and the damage), as well as causation problems, could endanger the applicability of liability rules to provide incentives for greenhouse gas mitigation. Because climate change will lead to worldwide damage of many different kinds, it may be impossible to have ex ante foresight of the potential ex post liability. Causation problems in climate change[9] may therefore reduce the possibility to apply liability rules. In addition, the private enforcement of liability rules can also be presumed to be relatively weak. As the damage resulting from climate change is widespread over the entire society, the individual incentives for victims to bring a lawsuit may be limited. For all of those reasons, Shavell's criteria indicate a strong preference for emission regulation as the primary instrument to control the emission of greenhouse gases. Emission regulation should obviously not necessarily take the form of traditional command and control regulation, but can also, as has often been proposed (and introduced) for reducing greenhouse gas emissions, be based on market-based instruments like taxes or an ETS.[10] But market-based instruments also require a regulatory framework (and enforcement)[11] and are therefore regulation in the sense of Shavell's criteria.

2.2 The Private Interest (Public Choice) Perspective

Even though there are strong arguments to give priority to government intervention (regulation, including market-based instruments) to reduce greenhouse gas emissions and not to rely primarily on tort liability, there are many reasons why regulation may not be perfect either. One important reason is provided by an alternative school of thought, public choice, that has powerfully shown that (environmental) regulation is not always made in the public interest, but often merely to serve private interests, more particularly special interests representing industry. Special interest groups will seek regulation that confers particular advantages to them. Mancur Olson indicates that especially when the information costs for the public at large are high and the transaction costs for the group to get organised are relatively low, rent-seeking by interest groups may be successful.[12] Those conditions are often fulfilled in the case of environmental regulation. Environmental regulation, including regulation of greenhouse gas emissions, is often highly technical; as a result, it is often very difficult, if not impossible, for the public at large to discover that rent-seeking has been going on. In this respect, it is especially important that in the case of climate change, some of the harm may affect future generations. They are not represented in the regulatory process, as a result of which there is a great likelihood that their interests will not be sufficiently taken into account when setting standards for greenhouse gas reduction.

The influence of lobbying can clearly be discovered at various places in climate law. One important aspect obviously relates to instrument choice: Economists have, as mentioned in the introduction, since the seminal work of Pigou, advocated carbon taxes as the optimal

[8] Steven Shavell, 'Criminal Law and the Optimal Use of Non-monetary Sanctions as a Deterrent' (1985) 85 Columbia Law Review 1232–62.

[9] See Mark Geitsfeld and Sandy Steel, Chapter 8 of this handbook.

[10] See in this respect the contributions in Jody Freeman and Charles D Kohlstad (eds), *Moving to Markets in Environmental Regulation: Lessons from 20 Years of Experience* (OUP 2007).

[11] Michael Faure and Roy Partain, *Environmental Law and Economics: Theory and Practice* (CUP 2019) 120–21.

[12] Mancur Olson, *The Logic of Collective Action* (Harvard University Press 1971).

instrument to internalise externalities in general[13] and for reducing greenhouse gas emissions in particular.[14] That advice has, however, to a large extent been neglected, as industry often prefers command-and-control regulation, since that allows for the creation of barriers to market entry via grandfathering.[15] Also, when the European ETS was introduced in the EU,[16] initially a large part of the allowances were awarded to existing industry via grandfathering. This, combined with an overallocation to national industries via national allocation plans led (in the initial phase) to a large overallocation of emission rights.[17] As a result of private interest, one can therefore hold that even though there are strong (public interest) arguments in favour of ex ante government regulation, there is a danger that the regulation is not always set at the optimal level, due to the influence of private interest and other reasons.

2.3 Complementary Role of Liability Rules

There are also indeed other reasons that justify a complementary role for liability rules for ex ante regulation. One reason is that ex ante government regulation is often static and not sufficiently dynamic. As a result of changing scientific insights (which is obviously the case with respect to optimal techniques to reduce greenhouse gas emissions), the optimal standard may change compared to what has been laid down in regulation. Scientific insights, for example on the effects of emissions and the optimal care levels to reduce emissions, may quickly develop as a result of which the regulatory standard could be outdated. The effectiveness of regulation can also be flawed as regulation is strongly dependent upon enforcement, which is never optimal. In other words, even though there may be a priority for greenhouse gas emission control via ex ante regulation (given the assumption of better information with regulatory authorities), regulation has particular inherent flaws as well. The major advantage of enforcing emission reductions via the court is that courts are less subject to the influence of lobby groups and may adapt optimal care levels in a more dynamic manner than regulatory authorities. From all of those perspectives, it can certainly be understood that when plaintiffs in a collective action lawsuit are of the opinion that (for a variety of reasons) the standard laid down in regulation to reduce greenhouse gas emissions is not optimal, liability rules could play an important role as a complement to greenhouse gas regulation.[18]

Climate change litigation could, from that perspective, be the result of a trade-off: Public authorities may have better information but incur a higher risk of lobbying by special interests; the judiciary may have less information but a better likelihood of making a decision in the public interest. It is precisely because of this trade-off that it is not surprising that NGOs (such as in the case of *Urgenda v Netherlands*[19]) have investigated the possibilities of using liability

[13] Arthur C Pigou, *A Study in Public Finance* (MacMillan 1951).

[14] Reuven S Avi-Yonah and David Uhlmann, 'Combatting Global Climate Change: Why a Carbon Tax is a Better Response to Global Warming than Cap and Trade' (2009) 28 Stanford Environmental Law Journal 3.

[15] See James Buchanan and Gordon Tullock, 'Polluters' Profits and Political Response: Direct Controls versus Taxes' (1975) 65 American Economic Review 139–47.

[16] Council Directive 2003/87 of 25 October 2003 establishing a scheme for greenhouse gas emission allowance trading within the Community and amending Council Directive 69/61/EC 2002 OJ L 275.

[17] Edwin Woerdman, Stefano Clo, and Alessandra Arcuri, 'European Emissions Trading and the Polluter-Pays-Principle: Assessing Grandfathering and Over-allocation' in Michael Faure and Marjan Peeters (eds), *Climate Change and European Emissions Trading: Lessons for Theory and Practice* (Edward Elgar Publishing 2008) 128–50.

[18] See Faure and Peeters.

[19] ECLI:NL:HR:2019:2007 (Supreme Court, 20 December 2019), English translation in (2020) 59 ILM 811.

rules to reach a further abatement of greenhouse gas emissions. This does not yet indicate that it is a desirable development; it merely shows that law and economics can explain why plaintiffs seek to use the supplementary role of tort law to force either governments or companies to take more ambitious actions to reduce greenhouse gas emissions via tort law.

This is also in line with the analysis of legal literature concerning climate change litigation where it is held:

> The advantage of liability law, as compared to these regulatory instruments, is based on its ability to establish a fine-tuned incentive structure for potential damaging parties because, in principle, parties are only burdened with the damages they have actually caused. The risk of market distortion by way of over- or under-deterrence is therefore lower compared to regulatory instruments.[20]

2.4 Choosing the Smart Instrument Mix

The mere fact that courts intervene in the case of a regulatory failure with respect to the setting of optimal standards for greenhouse gas emissions is, within the optimal mix of policy instruments, not that surprising. According to Shavell's criteria, regulators should have primary responsibility for standard-setting and decision-making. However, when regulators cannot establish standards at optimal care levels—due to information gaps or effective lobbying by interest groups—judicial intervention in this supplementary role becomes predictable. As some would argue, this is not "activism", but an application of applicable (Dutch) tort law and human rights.[21]

Moreover, the intervention of the judiciary in cases of regulatory failure could even be considered as an example of a smart mix of the various instruments available to curb greenhouse gas emissions.[22] It does, however, raise the question of how courts obtain information on optimal standards and how, in other words, climate change can enter the courtroom. This is an important issue, but the intervention of the judge in environmental policy in cases where standardisation via regulation fails is certainly not limited to the case of greenhouse gas emissions. An interesting case in point is the example of India. Given the large failure of environmental standard setting (and especially enforcement) by administrative agencies in India, the judiciary (and more particularly the Supreme Court of India) stepped in to effectively make environmental policy, in many cases most of which were initiated by M. C. Mehta. Again, this environmental policymaking via the judiciary could certainly be considered "second best" (given the regulator's primary role), but empirical evidence showed that some of the decisions (for example ordering the transformation of the entire bus fleet in Delhi from diesel to LNG) were effective in that they led to an improved air quality. Also in those cases, the question arose of how the judiciary could obtain adequate information on optimal standards. The Supreme Court of India solved it by asking not only experts from the administrative agencies,

[20] Monika Hinteregger, 'Civil Liability and the Challenges of Climate Change: A Functional Analysis' (2017) 2 Journal of European Tort Law 238–60.

[21] Jaap Spier, 'Injunctive Relief: Opportunities and Challenges: Thoughts about a Potentially Promising Legal Vehicle to Stem the Tide' in Jaap Spier and Ulrich Magnus (eds), *Climate Change Remedies, Injunctive Relief and Criminal Law Responses* (Eleven 2014) 1–120.

[22] See further on this concept of smart mixes, Judith van Erp and others (eds), *Smart Mixes for Transboundary Environmental Harm* (CUP 2019), following the seminal work of Gunningham and Grabosky on smart regulation (Neil Gunningham and Peter Grabosky, *Smart Regulation. Designing Environmental Policy* (Clarendon Press 1998)).

among others, but also from consultancy firms, and incorporated their insights into the judicial decision-making.[23]

In the two landmark Dutch climate change cases (*Urgenda* and *Shell*[24]), the judges relied heavily on reports from the Intergovernmental Panel on Climate Change and other authoritative scientific bodies to support their decision-making. Obviously, this may imply a shift of decision-making powers with respect to climate change from the regulator to scientists.[25] Moreover, especially in *Urgenda*, the Supreme Court gave detailed attention to the question of whether the judge would take a political decision by ordering the state to reduce greenhouse gas emissions. As the court did not order in which manner (through which specific measures) the state would have to reach the required emissions reduction level, the court held that their decision was in conformity with the separation of powers principle as it still respected the discretionary power of the democratically elected legislator to choose the way in which the necessary emission reductions could be achieved. This use of liability law by the judiciary is qualified (and praised) by some as an example of judicial risk regulation.[26] This concept refers to the fact that tort law is no longer only used as an instrument to achieve victim compensation in individual cases, but also as a tool to regulate important risks with which modern society is confronted, such as climate change, among other things.

2.5 Increasing the Effectiveness of Private Law

If someone had posited thirty years ago that liability rules and private enforcement could be used in climate change litigation, many would have argued that this is impossible, as it is typically an example of widespread damage where no individual victim had a sufficient interest to file a lawsuit. Moreover, causation issues might probably also have prevented a climate change claim. It is in that respect perhaps not surprising that in the EU Environmental Liability Directive, pollution of a widespread, diffuse character is explicitly excluded.[27]

Yet, over the past thirty years in many jurisdictions, changes have taken place facilitating private enforcement and paving the road for climate change litigation. Many of those changes can be considered as improvements from an economic perspective and facilitate the supplementary role of private enforcement in the instrument mix.

[23] Michael Faure and A V Raja, 'Effectiveness of Environmental Public Interest Litigation in India: Determining the Key Variables' (2010) XXI(2) Fordham Environmental Law Review 239–94.

[24] With respect to *Shell*, see in particular the decision in first instance of the District Court of the Hague of 26 May 2021 obliging Shell to reduce its emissions by 45% compared to 2019 by 2030. In a decision of 12 November 2024, the Court of Appeal of the Hague reversed that decision and denied the injunctive relief requested by the NGO plaintiff, Milieudefensie. *Shell plc v Milieudefensie* et al ECLI:NL:GHDHA:2024:2100 (Court of Appeal, The Hague, 12 November 2024).

[25] See Marjan Peeters, 'Climate Science in the Courts' in V Abazi, J Adriaensen, and Th Christiansen (eds), *The Contestation of Expertise in the European Union, European Administrative Governance* (Palgrave Macmillan 2021) 145–72; Edwin H P Brans, *Klimaataansprakelijkheid, negatieve emissies en herstel van biodiversiteit*, Inaugural Lecture University of Utrecht, 23 March 2022 (Boom Juridische uitgevers 2022) 10–12.

[26] Elbert R de Jong and others, 'Judge-made Risk Regulation and Tort Law: An Introduction' (2018) 9(1) European Journal of Risk Regulation 6–13.

[27] See Recital 13 preceding the EU Environmental Liability Directive 2004/35 of 21 April 2004, OJ L143. It is argued that in those cases 'it is impossible to link the negative environmental effects with acts or failure to act of certain individual actors'. Therefore, Article 4(5) provides that the Directive shall only apply 'where it is possible to establish a causal link between the damage and the activities of individual operators'.

Take for example the problem of the widespread nature of climate change-related damage. It is a typical example of what economists would call a collective action problem, leading to a lack of incentives for individual victims to bring a liability suit. This phenomenon has been referred to as rational apathy by Schafer:[28] When the damage is dispersed over a large number of individuals, social costs can be huge, but the individual harm suffered by every individual may be relatively small. No single individual would therefore have sufficient incentives to bring a lawsuit because of the risk of free-riding by others. As a result, individuals remain "rationally disinterested" and the model of individual lawsuits fails. The fact that especially in environmental cases the damage is often widespread implies that each individual victim may lack the motivation to take on the expense of litigation. This is an important argument in favour of allowing a lower threshold of standing in case of environmental harm and to grant standing to environmental NGOs.[29] The fact that many jurisdictions now allow standing by NGOs or (different forms of) collective or representative actions has also facilitated private enforcement in cases of a widespread nature of the damage, such as climate change.[30]

The same is true for the problem of causal uncertainty. Several decades ago, the plaintiff would have to prove that it is "more likely than not" that its harm was caused by the defendant's wrongful action. It often led to the application of a so-called threshold liability rule; that is, there would have to be a greater than 50% chance that a particular activity caused the harm of the plaintiff.[31] Economists (again like Shavell) criticised this threshold liability rule as it could lead either to under-deterrence (if the probability of causation was systematically below 50%) or over-deterrence (in the case where the probability of causation would just pass the 50% threshold). They therefore advocated a proportionate liability rule, implying that the defendant would only be held liable to the extent that their behaviour contributed to the damage.[32] That proportionate liability rule is now accepted in many more jurisdictions and can for example be found in the Principles of European Tort Law.[33] It was a principle directly applied by Mr Saul Lliuya, who in 2015 filed a lawsuit against the large energy producer RWE to pay for the protective structure for his house at the foot of the Andes. He claimed to be in danger of damage from a glacial flood, which would be the result of global warming to which

[28] Hans-Bernd Schafer, 'The Bundling of Similar Interests on Litigation. The Incentives for Class Actions and Legal Actions Taken by Associations' (2000) 9 European Journal of Law and Economics 183.

[29] Michael Faure, Manuela Mühl, and Niels Philipsen, 'Incentives, Costs and Benefits: A Law and Economics Analysis' in Michael Faure and Niels Philipsen (eds), *Access to Justice in Environmental Matters: A Socio-Economic Analysis* (Eleven International Publishing 2014) 23–74; Faure and Raja 239–94.

[30] Jonathan W Kuyper, Björn-Ola Linnér, and Heike Schroeder, 'Non-state Actors in Hybrid Global Climate Governance: Justice, Legitimacy, and Effectiveness in a Post-Paris Era' (2018) 9 WIREs Climate Change e497, 9–10 <https://wires.onlinelibrary.wiley.com/doi/full/10.1002/wcc.497> accessed 8 July 2025.

[31] Douglas A Kysar, 'What Climate Change Can Do About Tort Law' (2011) 41 Environmental Law 1, 3031.

[32] Steven Shavell, 'Uncertainty over Causation and the Determination of Civil Liability' (1985) Journal of Law and Economics 587–609.

[33] See Art. 3:103(1) of the Principles of European Tort Law, which reads: 'In case of multiple activities, where each of them alone would have been sufficient to cause the damage, but it remains uncertain which one in fact caused it, each activity is regarded as a cause to the extent corresponding to the likelihood that it may have caused the victim's damage' (European Group on Tort Law, Principles of European Tort Law: Text and Commentary, Vienna, Springer, 2005, 47). See further Michael Faure, 'Attribution of Liability: An Economic Analysis of Various Cases' (2016) 91(2) Chicago-Kent Law Review 60–635.

RWE had contributed through its greenhouse gas emissions.[34] In December 2016, the claim was denied by the District Court of Essen, which held that the chain of causality was too diffuse and too complex. The plaintiff had claimed approximately €70.000 which would be 0.47% of the costs (the estimated contribution of RWE to climate change).[35] But the plaintiff was more successful before the Court of Appeals of Hamm, which held that liability cannot be ruled out just because a large number of polluters contributed to global warming. The court requested an on-site hearing of the evidence in Peru, which was apparently delayed as a result of the pandemic.[36] One can notice that the plaintiff directly uses a proportional liability rule as a basis for its claim which would have been impossible under the old threshold liability regime.

Those are both examples where developments in environmental liability litigation (and also in climate change litigation) have affected private law rules, and, as they increase the effectiveness of private enforcement, in an economically desirable direction.

3. Adaptation and Loss and Damage

As outlined in the introduction, economists have paid attention to the optimal instruments to compensate for climate change-related harm, often caused by disasters, such as hurricanes and flooding. It was already mentioned in the introduction that for economists the crucial issue is that an ex post compensation mechanism should also provide incentives for ex ante prevention.

At the same time, the question also arises of which instruments can provide the best guarantee of effective compensation (and thus adaptation) in the case of a climate change-related disaster.

I will review four different mechanisms[37] (liability rules, ex post government compensation, first party insurance, and government intervention as last resort) on the basis of three criteria: First, I will review whether the particular instrument is able to provide compensation; then I address the effect of the instrument on prevention; and finally, I specifically ask the question of the extent to which it is suited for climate change-related damage. Given the scope of this chapter, this overview obviously follows the economic approach and literature to those compensation mechanisms.

3.1 Liability Rules

- What is the instrument?

A liability rule is, in very simple terms, a private law mechanism according to which a tortfeasor (injurer) has to pay compensation for the losses suffered by the victim. This liability in

[34] For a detailed analysis, see Gerhard Wagner, *Klimahaftung vor Gericht. Eine Fallstudie* (C. H. Beck 2020), 17–22.

[35] Hinteregger (n 20) 244.

[36] Ümit Yoker, 'The Climate Gets the Benefit of the Doubt' (*Horizons*, 3 March 2022), <https://www.horizons-mag.ch/2022/03/03/the-climate-gets-the-benefit-of-the-doubt/> accessed 1 July 2025; Wagner (n 31) 21–22. In a decision of 28 May 2025, the court decided that major greenhouse gas emitters can be held liable for climate change related harms. However, the claim of Mr Lliuya was rejected because of a lack of evidence of imminent danger to his property. *Saúl Luciano Lliuya v RWE AG* Case I-5 U 15/17 (Oberlandesgericht Hamm, 28 May 2025).

[37] In fact, there is a fifth one (a government financed compensation fund), which I, for reasons of space, will not discuss further (as it is also very much comparable to charity by government). I discuss the difference between a fund solution and ad hoc compensation in Michael Faure, 'Financial Compensation for Victims of Catastrophes: A Law and Economics Perspective' (2007) 29(3) Law & Policy 353–54.

tort can be either fault/negligence-based (requiring the victim to show that the tortfeasor violated a due care standard) or strict liability (in which case the victim only needs to prove that the injurer's behaviour caused the victim's losses).

- Compensation

With respect to compensation, the picture is rather confused. Generally, the tort system is considered highly selective. Meta studies providing an overview of how many victims get actual compensation via the tort system indicate that it is a highly selective system and it is shown that less than 10% of injured people would take action, and even less (2%) would file a lawsuit.[38] For those victims who do file a lawsuit, it is not certain they will succeed in court as there may be high thresholds for obtaining compensation. However, for those who eventually succeed, the tort system provides generous compensation, that is, the goal of the tort system is to put the victim, in principle, back in the same situation as if the tort had not occurred. This means that a successful claimant can, in principle, not only claim income losses, but also compensation for all costs, both pecuniary and non-pecuniary, in principle without financial limits. Some therefore qualify the tort system as a lottery[39] (as only a few victims may effectively be compensated under the tort system), but at the same time it is a luxury system as well. Those who symbolically hit the jackpot get the "luxury" of full compensation.

As far as a specific focus on disasters is concerned, only under a strict liability regime will the injurer be forced to provide compensation to the victim. Under negligence, the tortfeasor will have incentives to follow the efficient care level required by the legal system. As a result, the tortfeasor would not be held liable and the victim would not be compensated. Moreover, even if there were a strict liability rule, an insolvency problem could arise, also referred to as the "judgment proof problem". This would therefore require the introduction of mandatory financial guarantees such as compulsory liability insurance.[40] Without such a financial security, there is always the danger that the magnitude of the damage caused as a result of the (climate change) disaster would outweigh the assets of the individual tortfeasor.

There is, however, a more serious problem concerning the ability to use liability rules to compensate for damage caused by a climate change disaster. The problem is that natural disasters are often deemed "acts of God". As a result, no liable tortfeasor can be found, for example, in the case of damage caused by sea-level rise, flooding, or hailstorms. The only possibility to apply tort law in the case of natural disasters is to argue that public authorities were at fault, such as by failing to prevent the disaster or not taking adequate measures to mitigate the damage. It could, for example, be argued that public authorities failed to give adequate warnings of, say, a flood, or failed to take sufficient preventive measures. The only liability questions that therefore arise after natural catastrophes are often linked to the liability of public authorities. This was, for example, largely the case after Hurricane Katrina.[41] However, legislators

[38] See for an overview of these empirical studies, Ben van Velthoven, 'Empirics of Tort' in Michael Faure (ed), *Tort Law and Economics* (Edward Elgar Publishing 2009) 463–65.

[39] Some victims may receive (generous) compensation via the tort mechanism if they are successful, whereas others may receive no compensation whatsoever (Michael Faure, 'Towards Effective Compensation for Victims of Natural Catastrophes in Developing Countries' in Michael Faure and Andri Wibisana (eds), *Regulating Disasters, Climate Change and Environmental Harm. Lessons from the Indonesian Experience* (Edward Elgar Publishing 2013), 252).

[40] Shavell, 'The Judgment Proof Problem' 43–58.

[41] See Vicki Bier, 'Hurricane Katrina as a Bureaucratic Nightmare' in Ronald J Daniels, Donald G Kettl, and Howard Kunreuther (eds), *On Risk and Disasters: Lessons from Hurricane Katrina* (University of Pennsylvania Press 2006) 243–54; J Walters and Donald Kettl, 'The Katrina Breakdown' in Daniels et al 255–61.

have often reacted by creating (partial) immunities for public authorities in order to limit the scope of liability, or a high threshold is imposed for such liability to be accepted (for example requiring the proof of gross negligence). In the literature it has been argued that there may be good reasons to limit the scope of liability of public authorities, as they are considered multi-task agents who have to weigh different externalities. As a result, they need a wide margin of discretion, as too extensive liability might lead to so-called chilling effects.[42] In summary, liability rules may only work in legal systems that widely accept governmental liability, but even then, the road for victims to receive compensation via tort law may be a complicated one. Therefore, liability rules are certainly not the ideal mechanism to provide compensation for most victims of climate change disasters.

- Effect on prevention

As far as prevention is concerned, the question arises as to whether liability rules would provide incentives for all stakeholders that could either have prevented the risk of natural hazards occurring or could have mitigated the damage after the disaster occurred. An advantage of liability rules is that in principle they have a deterrent effect, thus providing incentives for prevention to the potential injurer exposed to liability. In the case of climate change, the question obviously arises as to who the injurer is. Seeking compensation from greenhouse gas emitters would, given attribution and causation issues, not be an easy route to go. To the extent that public authorities could have prevented the climate change disaster from occurring, it could be argued that an exposure to liability could provide them with incentives for prevention. However, it is questionable whether the liability mechanism is efficient in providing incentives for prevention to public authorities.

Public authorities are not utility maximising individuals and may be exposed to different incentives; thus, there are doubts about the effectiveness of deterrence in this particular context.[43] To the extent that victims should also be given incentives to mitigate losses, this could be achieved via a comparative negligence defence. As a result, the claim of the victim would be reduced proportionally, based on the extent to which the victim failed to take optimal preventive measures where this would have been possible. However, for the reasons mentioned above, it is doubtful that liability rules will have this preventive effect. More particularly, given the high barriers in the tort system, only a few victims may effectively bring a claim, as a result of which tortfeasors (presumably only public authorities) would not be seriously deterred by a liability suit.

- Fit for climate change damage?

From the previous paragraphs, it follows that victims of climate change disasters may face impressive hurdles if they want to use liability rules to obtain compensation. Given these high thresholds and the fact that only public authorities can be addressed as defendants in the case of a climate change disaster, liability rules do not have the possibility of providing substantial compensation for a large amount of victims in a structural manner.

[42] See Gerrit De Geest, 'Who Should Be Immune from Tort Liability?' (2012) 41(2) Journal of Legal Studies 291–319; Jef De Mot and Michael Faure, 'Discretion and the Economics of Defensive Behaviour by Public Bodies' (2016) 23(4) Maastricht Journal of European and Comparative Law 595–610.

[43] Hans-Bernd Schäfer, 'Can Member State Liability for the Infringement of European Law Deter National Legislators' in Thomas Eger and Hans-Bernd Schäfer (eds), *Research Handbook on the Economics of European Union Law* (Edward Elgar Publishing 2012) 82–94.

As indicated in Section 2, there is a possibility to use liability rules in addition to regulation. However, most of the (increasingly successful) climate change claims against either governments (as in the *Urgenda* case) or operators (as in the case of *Milieudefensie v Shell*) were aimed at obtaining mitigation—in other words a reduction of CO_2 emissions, not compensation. It is also held that climate change liability should not aim at seeking compensation, as this may lead to insurmountable causation problems.[44]

Climate change litigation is still rather exceptional and entails the problem that liability rules will only lead to ad hoc recovery (if successful) for particular victims who are successful in the "tort law lottery". It would, however, not provide a structural solution that can provide recovery for most victims of climate change disasters.

3.2 Ex Post Governmental Compensation

- What is the instrument?

Ex post government compensation is compensation that is paid from the public budget by the government. Note that this is about ex post recovery, not about immediate relief at the moment of the disaster. This type of ex post compensation can take different forms, but the essence is that it is ad hoc and ex post. Ad hoc refers to the fact that the government decides on the basis of the nature and the scope of the disaster whether it will provide compensation and what particular type of compensation will be provided.[45] In other words, this ex post government compensation does not give a right to compensation to victims. The payment is from the public budget (and therefore from taxpayers) and the decision is made ex post. This implies that only after the disaster occurred will the government decide if, and how much, compensation will be provided to victims.

- Compensation

At first glance, this type of intervention looks attractive as it can provide ex post compensation for victims who need, for example to finance the rebuilding of their houses after flooding has occurred. However, also from the victim's perspective this ex post compensation is in fact not ideal. The first (major) problem is that the choice of whether to provide this compensation ex post or not, is basically a political one. As mentioned earlier, when the scope of the disaster is large and there is substantial media coverage, there will be strong (political) pressure to provide compensation for victims ex post.[46] However, there is no ex ante structural regime that would give victims a right to compensation in case a disaster might happen. In other words, if the disaster is considered sufficiently large and gets a lot of media coverage, there may be political pressure for ex post compensation, but if that is not the case, the government may simply decide not to provide this compensation at all. Victims are, in other words, left in uncertainty. As some victims of disasters may receive compensation and others not, this may also be problematic from the perspective of the equality principle. Moreover, even in cases where

[44] See Michael Faure and Marjan Peeters, 'Concluding Remarks' in Michael Faure and Marjan Peeters (eds), *Climate Change Liability* (Edward Elgar Publishing 2011) 255–74.

[45] In some cases the ex post government compensation is not ad hoc, but takes place structurally via a compensation fund. This is not discussed separately as many of the objections against ex post government compensation will also arise in the case of a government funded compensation fund.

[46] Giuseppe Dari-Mattiacci and Michael Faure, 'The Economics of Disaster Relief' (2015) 37(3) Law & Policy 183.

the government decides to provide ex post compensation, it is not certain how much will be paid. Usually, a symbolic lump sum *ex gratia* payment is provided, but there is no guarantee of full compensation. Again, the amounts paid for one disaster may be different than that for another.[47]

- Effect on prevention

There are several problems with this type of ex post government intervention. The first problem is that when there is an expectation that the government will compensate ex post, no incentives are provided for potential victims to take effective preventive measures. Of course it depends on the nature of the disaster—whether it is realistic for victims to take preventive measures. Large structural measures, for example, to protect a country against the risk of flooding, will primarily be a government task. However, there are certainly measures which individual potential victims can take. Those are not so much focused on the prevention of the likelihood of a disaster but rather aim to mitigate the losses. In the case of flooding, damage could be prevented such as by not building in flood-prone areas, or by not installing the most valuable objects in the cellar or on the ground floor. The problem is that charity by the government can reduce or even eliminate those incentives for prevention. This is referred to in the literature as the Samaritan's dilemma: The government grants ex post compensation even if this is likely to have negative ex ante effects on incentives.[48] This problem is also referred to as the "charity hazard".[49] It is for this reason that Epstein qualified ex post compensation as "catastrophic responses to catastrophic risks".[50]

The second problem is that if victims count on government compensation, they may no longer have an incentive to purchase insurance and instead simply free-ride on the state.[51] In the words of Gollier: "Solidarity kills market insurance".[52] This is not only a theoretical issue. Empirical studies confirm that the availability of ex post compensation does have a significant negative impact on the willingness, for example, of farmers, to purchase crop insurance.[53] An empirical study comparing compensation for damage caused by flooding in Austria, Switzerland, and the German state of Bavaria came to the same conclusion.[54]

[47] See for examples of different ex post payments made by the (Dutch) government for (technological) disasters, Ton Hartlief and Michael Faure, 'Vergoeding van schade bij rampen in België en Nederland' (2015) 3/4 Tijdschrift voor Privaatrecht 1014–18.

[48] S Coate, 'Altruism, the Samaritan's Dilemma, and the Government Transfer Policy' (1995) 85 American Economic Review 46–57.

[49] Paul Raschky and Hannelore Weck-Hannemann, 'Charity Hazard—Real Hazards to Natural Disaster Insurance' (2007) 7 Environmental Hazard 321–29.

[50] Richard A Epstein, 'Catastrophic Responses to Catastrophic Risks' (1996) 12 Journal of Risk and Uncertainty 287–308; and see Louis Kaplow, 'Incentives and Government Relief for Risk' (1991) 4(2) Journal of Risk and Uncertainty 167–75.

[51] See Saul Levmore and Kyle D Logue, 'Insuring against Terrorism—and Crime' (2003) 102 Michigan Law Review 268–327.

[52] Christian Gollier, 'Some Aspects of the Economics of Catastrophe Risk Insurance' in *Catastrophic Risks and Insurance* (OECD Publishing 2005) 13–30.

[53] Marcel APM. van Asseldonk, Miranda PM Meuwissen, and Ruud BM Huirne, 'Belief in Disaster Relief and the Demand for a Public–Private Insurance Program' (2002) 24(1) Review of Agricultural Economics 196–207.

[54] Paul Raschky, Reimund Schwarze, Manijeh Schwindt, and Hannelore Weck-Hannemann, *Alternative Financing and Insurance Solutions for Natural Hazards: A Comparison of Different Risk Transfer Systems in Three Countries—Germany, Austria and Switzerland—Affected by the August 2005 Floods* (AlpS GmbH, Centre for Natural Hazard and Risk Management 2009).

A third problem with ex post government compensation is simply distribution. The effect of using taxpayers' money to bail out victims of disasters ex post may be that those victims (who for example purchased houses at lower prices in flood-prone areas) de facto free-ride on the general taxpayers who finance the ex post compensation. It could even be argued that they are compensated twice: Once ex ante when they purchased their house in a flood-prone area (the lower housing price reflecting the flooding risk), and a second time when taxpayers' money is used for compensation.

- Fit for climate change damage?

For all the reasons mentioned above, ex post government compensation is not a suitable mechanism to provide compensation. From the victim's perspective, the problem is that the ad hoc nature of the charity by the government creates inequality. If a disaster receives less attention in the media, and thus becomes politically less sensitive, there is a danger that government compensation could be absent. Moreover, from a societal perspective this type of ex post compensation is dramatic, as it was shown to provide negative incentives for prevention. Vulnerable uninsured victims may require more ex post compensation, which in turn makes the disaster more salient and politicians more eager to stage a rescue. This negative spiral results in a less-safe environment and higher death tolls.[55] However, even though ex post compensation is considered problematic, it is still very likely that politicians will keep providing it. The reason, as indicated by Depoorter, is that the political rewards for ex post compensation may be very strong, as a result of which there may be an oversupply of ex post compensation, notwithstanding the devastating effects on prevention.[56]

3.3 First Party Insurance for Natural Disasters

- What is the instrument?

First-party insurance is insurance that is taken out by the person who suffers the loss, that is, the victim. This is distinguished from third-party insurance where a person takes out insurance to cover the risk that he or she would have to pay to a third party. A typical example of third-party insurance is liability insurance. Specifically, because, as has been explained above, liability will in principle not be an instrument of major importance for compensating the damage caused by climate change disasters, the focus here is on the role of first-party disaster insurance. This is a model where the insured, in principle, demands coverage according to his or her own particular needs and preferences.[57]

- Compensation

The major advantage of a first-party disaster insurance model is that it can provide both certainty of compensation and an adequate amount of compensation. In the case of insurance, potential victims are no longer dependent (as with ad hoc ex post compensation) on the political will of the government. The conditions under which the insurance company has to

55 See Justin Pidot, 'Deconstructing Disaster' (2013) 2 Bringham Young University Law Review 213–57.

56 Ben Depoorter, 'Horizontal Political Externalities: The Supply and Demand of Disaster Management' (2006) 56 Duke Law Journal 101–25.

57 First-party insurance has especially been advocated as a tool to deal with disasters. See Howard Kunreuther, 'The Case for Comprehensive Disaster Insurance' (1968) 11(1) Journal of Law and Economics 133–63; George Priest, 'The Government, the Market and the Problem of Catastrophic Loss' (1996) 12 Journal of Risk and Uncertainty 219–37.

intervene are laid down in the insurance policy. There is, in other words, a contractual obligation of the insurer to compensate the victim once the conditions in the policy materialise (such as a flooding with particular characteristics). Moreover, in contrast to government provided compensation (where the compensation is often limited to capped lump sum amounts), in the case of insurance, the insurance company, in principle, pays the amount agreed upon in the policy. This can, depending upon the formulation of the policy conditions (and obviously upon the corresponding premium), amount to full compensation. From the victim's perspective, insurance therefore provides both certainty and adequacy of compensation for climate change disasters.

- Effect on prevention

A major advantage of insurance is that the insurer will have to control the moral hazard risk.[58] This means that the insurer will apply risk differentiation based on the particular risk. For the area of (climate change) disasters, this could, among other things, imply that the insurer would charge a higher premium for risky activities (such as building a house on a flood plain), or reward the good risks (such as those who construct their dwellings using materials that are less vulnerable to disasters). Through the charging of risk-dependent premiums, insurance would have the effect of contributing to the prevention of the risk.[59]

- Fit for climate change damage?

Notwithstanding the theoretical advantages of first-party insurance, there are also problems, both on the supply and the demand side. As far as the demand side is concerned, it is striking that in jurisdictions where disaster insurance is widely available, there is only a limited number of potential victims that demand this type of insurance. For example, after the "Jahrhundert flood" of the Elbe in Germany,[60] as well as after the Katrina disaster in the US,[61] it appeared that only a limited number of victims had adequate insurance coverage.

There are several explanations for the problem of under-insurance. First, individuals apparently have difficulties in assessing risks which have a very low probability (such as natural disasters) in a correct manner. As the probability of occurrence is very low, individuals wrongly assume that this implies that the risk is in fact zero.[62] Second, individuals apparently consider insurance as a type of investment. The problem with disaster insurance is that the insured will be confronted with a certain loss on a yearly basis (this being the payment of the premium), whereas there is only a small expectation that a return on this investment will follow.[63] Third, the literature points to the fact that potential victims count on ex post government compensation, which reduces the incentives to take insurance cover.[64] Here one recognises again the problem of the *charity hazard* discussed earlier.

[58] Steven Shavell, 'On Moral Hazard and Insurance' (1979) Quarterly Journal of Economics 541–62.

[59] George Priest, 'The Government, the Market and the Problem of Catastrophic Loss' (1996) 12 Journal of Risk and Uncertainty 219–37. See also Franziska Arnold-Dwyer, Chapter 22 of this handbook.

[60] Alfred Endres, Cornelia Ohl, and Bianca Rundshagen, 'Land unter! Ein institutionsökonomischer Zwischenruf' (2003) 29(3) List-Forum für Wirtschafts- und Finanzpolitik 284–94.

[61] See the different contributions in Daniels et al.

[62] Howard Kunreuther, 'Mitigating Disaster Losses through Insurance' (1996) 12 Journal of Risk and Uncertainty 175.

[63] See further, Paul Slovic and others, 'Preference for Insuring against Probably Small Losses: Insurance Implications' (1977) 44(2) Journal of Risk and Insurance 237–58.

[64] See on that, for example, Scott E Harrington, 'Rethinking Disaster Policy' (2000) 23(1) Regulation 40–46.

There are also problems on the supply side. Insurers complain that the occurrence of disasters is hard to predict. Disasters can also suffer from an adverse selection problem, that is, disaster cover would only be attractive for high-risk individuals (for example those living in a flood-prone area). As a result, insurers could be stuck with only the bad risks, which is typically the anti-selection problem that could lead to uninsurability.[65]

Moreover, disasters can have a systemic character, implying that they are not limited to one incident, but that in case of a disaster, a large number of losses can accumulate for the insurer. The compensation which the insurer needs to pay in case of a loss should, in principle, be provided by the collection of all the premiums paid by the insured. However, in the case of a disaster, the total amount of premiums could simply be too low to cover the totality of the damage caused by a climate change disaster. Reinsurance can partially deal with this problem, but also has its limitations.[66]

The literature has, however, also developed solutions for these problems. As far as the problems on the demand side are concerned, already in 1968, Kunreuther pleaded in favour of a comprehensive system of disaster insurance. More particularly, he supported a mandatory add-on for disaster cover in addition to voluntarily concluded insurance.[67] The advantage of this model would be that when disaster cover is combined with insurance against more usual risks (for example a fire in a house), there would also be a greater willingness on the part of the insured to accept this type of cover.[68]

As far as the limited supply of disaster cover is concerned, it has been suggested that the government should intervene in a different way in the compensation of (climate change) disasters. This implies that the government would no longer provide ex post ad hoc compensation (leading to the charity hazard), but would rather act as a reinsurer of last resort. This is the last model to be discussed in the next section.

In sum, first-party disaster insurance can be an adequate instrument to compensate damage suffered as a result of climate change disasters. However, it is important that the government facilitates this insurance by: (1) creating a mandatory comprehensive cover for disasters (to deal with demand-side problems), and (2) to intervene as reinsurer of last resort (to deal with supply-side problems).

3.4 Government Intervention as Reinsurer of Last Resort

- What is the instrument?

Under this approach, the State assumes at least part of the risk of losses resulting from catastrophes. Some refer to this role of the government as a "private and public insurance response",[69] whereas others refer to it as "public–private partnerships" consisting of various layers to provide insurance against natural disasters.[70] In practice, there are many different mechanisms

[65] George Priest, 'The Current Insurance Crisis and Modern Tort Law' (1987) Yale Law Journal 1521–90.

[66] See further on these problems with the supply of disaster insurance, Michael Faure and Veronique Bruggeman, 'Catastrophic Risk and First-party Insurance' (2008) 15 Connecticut Insurance Law Journal 1–52.

[67] Kunreuther 133–63.

[68] See further on this issue, Slovic et al 60–61 and 70–71.

[69] Levmore and Logue (n 51) 278.

[70] Howard Kunreuther and Mark Pauly, 'Rules Rather than Discretion: Lessons from Hurricane Katrina' (2006) 33(1) Journal of Risk and Uncertainty 112–13.

in which the government could play this particular role.[71] The core, however, is that the State (in one form or another) supports the failure of traditional insurance markets, given their inability to supply full coverage in case of disasters of a large scale.[72]

- Compensation

When the government plays a role as reinsurer of last resort, it does not directly provide the compensation to the victims. That will usually be done by the primary insurer. However, this role of the government is of crucial importance for the simple reason that it can increase the capacity to provide compensation and, in that sense, it plays a crucial role in guaranteeing that compensation can also be provided for larger losses, that is, in the case of climate change disasters.

One advantage of government intervention is that the government has the capacity to diversify the risks across the entire population and to spread past losses to future generations. The government can thereby create a form of cross-time diversification which the private market could not achieve.[73] Another advantage of government intervention is that to some extent, the occurrence of the disaster may be in the government's control. After all, the government can take measures (such as building levees and dykes) aiming at the prevention or mitigation of losses.[74]

- Effect on prevention

There are different ways in which this role of the government can be viewed. Some economists are very critical of this type of government intervention, based on the fear that the government would, acting as reinsurer, charge a lower price than the market price.[75] They argue that the lower-price signal would lead to market distortion. They would therefore even be in favour of ad hoc solutions where compensation is provided to accident victims on an ex post basis, thus avoiding victims being aware that the government will guarantee compensation. The criticism is in fact not directed towards the intervention of the government as such, but it is based on the assumption that the government will not charge premiums that reflect market prices. A similar criticism is shared by Levmore and Logue, who argue that such a regime (the government acting as reinsurer of last resort) may lead to substantial subsidies from the government.[76] They are sceptical of these types of government interventions in the market and argue that without government intervention "the market would probably have been able to provide the necessary coverage".[77]

[71] Veronique Bruggeman, Michael Faure, and Tobias Heldt, 'Insurance against Catastrophe: Government Stimulation of Insurance Markets for Catastrophic Events' (2012) XXIII(1) Duke Environmental Law & Policy Forum 185–241.

[72] Veronique Bruggeman, Michael Faure and Karine Fiore, 'The Government as Reinsurer of Catastrophic Risks?' (2010) 35 Geneva Papers on Risk and Insurance Theory 369–90.

[73] Howard Kunreuther and Erwann Michel-Kerjan, 'Challenges for Terrorism Risk Insurance in the United States' (2004) 18 Journal of Economic Perspectives 210.

[74] Howard Kunreuther and Erwann Michel-Kerjan, 'Insurability of (Mega-)Terrorism Risk: Challenges and Perspectives' in *Terrorism Risk Insurance in OECD Countries* (OECD Publishing 2005) 107–48.

[75] Anne Gron and Alan O Sykes, 'A Role for Government?' (2002) 25(4) Regulation 44–51; Anne Gron and Alan O Sykes, 'Terrorism and Insurance Markets: A Role for the Government as Insurer?' (2003) 36 Indiana Law Review 447–63.

[76] Levmore and Logue (n 51) 304.

[77] ibid 311.

These arguments against government intervention are mainly based on the assumption that the government will not charge a competitive premium for its reinsurance. That would amount to a subsidy for catastrophe insurance. It is also based on the argument that without governmental support the insurance coverage would have been provided by the market anyway. However, the reality in the case of natural disasters is that without government intervention the capacity of insurance and reinsurance markets is de facto limited. This means that if a disaster of a magnitude larger than the available insurance cover were to occur, the government might have to intervene anyway, with ad hoc ex post compensation. This has, as noted earlier, the major disadvantage of diluting incentives for prevention.

The major advantage of the government acting as reinsurer of last resort therefore is that ex post compensation through the public purse (with negative incentive effects) can be avoided. When the government acts as reinsurer of last resort, at least those exposed to risk can still be charged an actuarially fair premium. At the same time, potential victims are made aware of their exposure to the disaster risk. It is for this reason that others argue that the government's role in assisting the supply side of insurance precisely allows for avoiding the inefficiencies and inequities associated with government provided compensation.[78]

- Fit for climate change damage?

Given the fact that climate change damage is often of a catastrophic nature, it is very likely that it will be of a magnitude largely exceeding the possibilities of the insurance and reinsurance market. The fact that the government would in that case play a role as reinsurer (de facto adding a third layer in addition to compensation provided by the insurer and reinsurer) could have the advantage that the total amount of compensation would be larger and that the beneficial incentive effect of insurance on prevention would still be safeguarded. In that sense, this type of government intervention should be welcomed, as it is to be preferred to ad hoc ex post compensation. However, it is important to structure this type of government intervention in such a way that the positive incentive effects can indeed be safeguarded.[79] For this type of government intervention to be efficient, the following conditions would have to be met:

It should be clear that there is an absence of market solutions, in other words: There is no cover available beyond the capacity provided on the insurance and reinsurance market;

the government should charge risk-based premiums for its intervention, thus avoiding a situation where the government-provided reinsurance would amount to a subsidy;[80]

the reinsurance by the government should also be organised in such a way that market solutions are stimulated, for example by charging a high premium for its reinsurance, thus stimulating the development of market solutions;

insurers should obviously be left free to choose state reinsurance; and

the government's intervention as reinsurer of last resort should, in principle, also have a temporary character (that is, there should be so-called sunset provisions), again in order to provide incentives for the market to develop its own solutions.

[78] This is especially argued by Kunreuther and Pauly 113.

[79] Bruggeman et al 377–79.

[80] Levmore and Logue (n 51) 304.

3.5 Assessing the instruments

Looking once more at the four instruments discussed, more particularly from the perspective of their ability to provide adequate and certain compensation on the one hand and incentives for prevention on the other, the following can be concluded as far as their ability to provide compensation for climate change damage is concerned:

> Liability rules are not an ideal instrument for providing compensation for climate change disasters. They can provide high compensation if all the conditions for liability are met, but the liability system seems more like a lottery and may therefore not provide certain compensation for victims. In the case of natural disasters it is, moreover, only public authorities that usually could be targeted as a defendant, which means that a high threshold for liability often applies.
>
> Ex post government compensation is not attractive from two perspectives: First, it cannot provide certainty of compensation for victims (as it may depend upon a political decision to compensate or not) and, second, often no full compensation, but a limited lump sum amount is provided. Moreover, this type of ex post compensation has negative effects on incentives for prevention or mitigation of losses.
>
> The best instrument to provide certain and adequate compensation for potential victims of climate change disasters is first-party insurance. This also has positive effects on the incentives for prevention. Given the low demand, this type of insurance requires government intervention in order to make comprehensive insurance mandatory, and it may also require government intervention to deal with supply side shortages.

For this reason, the government can support the mandatory first-party insurance system by intervening as reinsurer of last resort. In that way, compensation can also be guaranteed for larger losses (like in the case of disasters). Provided that the government charges a (risk-based) premium for its intervention (rather than providing a subsidy), government intervention as reinsurer of last resort could be a smart public–private (government and insurers) partnership that provides adequate and certain compensation on the one hand and incentives for prevention on the other.

4. Conclusion

This chapter used the economic approach to law to examine two aspects of the relationship between climate change and private law. They relate both to mitigation and adaptation, with implications as well for climate change loss and damage. As far as mitigation is concerned, it was argued that the primary instrument to control the mitigation of greenhouse gas emissions may be regulation (either command and control or market-based). However, public choice literature has indicated that there may be a variety of reasons why standard-setting through regulation may be suboptimal. For that reason, liability rules are often called upon in those cases where (in economic terms) optimal care levels would be higher than the care levels required via regulation. In that sense, climate change litigation, whereby liability rules are used to step in where regulation may fail, is understandable. Moreover, it was equally indicated that in many legal systems changes have taken place to facilitate liability suits; this applies also when damage is widespread and of a diffuse character. The increasing introduction of proportional liability rules (to deal with causal uncertainty), as well as the increasing acceptance of standing for NGOs and collective action are developments in private law that make sense from an economic perspective.

Also, as far as adaptation is concerned, economics has interesting messages for the role of private law instruments, and in this particular case, insurance. Economists argue that the ex post compensation mechanism (as a structural preparation and adaptation to climate change) should also provide incentives for prevention and more particularly for mitigation of losses. That can hardly be realised via government provided compensation. In this respect, the private law instrument of insurance has several advantages. As insurers control the moral hazard risk, they apply principles of risk differentiation, thus providing incentives for prevention and mitigation of losses. However, insurance for climate change induced disasters may not emerge spontaneously given problems on the demand as well as on the supply side. For that reason, this chapter advocated, in line with the literature, an intervention in private law, more particularly to mandatorily provide cover for natural catastrophes in addition to voluntarily concluded insurance policies (like a housing or fire insurance). And in order to deal with the supply side problems, the government could act as reinsurer of last resort. That has the major advantage that the negative incentive effects (inherent in government providing direct compensation) can be avoided and that private law solutions (more particularly insurance) can be promoted. In that way, a structural solution could be provided to the systemic risk resulting from climate change disasters.

CHAPTER 3

Critical and Social Theory

K-SUE PARK

1. Introduction

WHAT do we mean by critical and social theory? It is difficult to avoid overgeneralising when attempting to describe a methodological approach. Many points of disagreement will inevitably arise among the community of people who associate themselves with it. Contestation is likely less in fields that are well-established and dominated by a strong orthodoxy, whereas the risk is higher in newer fields that are inherently interdisciplinary and in the process of rapid development. "Critical theory" and "social theory", as used to describe legal scholarship today, are strong examples of the latter.

For this reason, and because these terms have recently been the subject of much opinion and debate, it is worth beginning this chapter by giving some attention to how we understand them. It is unclear what criteria—whether lineage, self-identification, or something else—should determine the membership of those groups, and who should make this judgment. One way of giving them some precision, for example, would be to associate them with scholars who explicitly engage the work of European philosophers to whom they were originally attached (as "critical theory" has to members of the Frankfurt School, and "social theory" has to thinkers such as Comte, Marx, Weber, Durkheim, and Bourdieu).[1] Another is to attribute them to scholars who use them to describe their own work. After all, scholars do identify as part of groups that have taken up the term "critical" and added various qualifiers related to social categories: for example, critical legal studies, critical race studies, critical disability studies, and so on. Some, though by no means all, of these scholars engage the work of the European thinkers referred to above. Finally, and at the same time, it is common to hear the terms used broadly, to group together scholars who may neither draw from nor identify with these scholarly traditions or groups, but who simply focus on topics such as race, gender, sexuality, and disability (among others); the history and legacies of colonisation and enslavement; and the economic systems that encompass capitalism. This wide-ranging attribution unfortunately aligns with, though it should be distinguished from, the ongoing political reaction to such scholarship that mobilises the terms to point to it and create the spectre of a threat.[2]

[1] For examples of scholarly attempts to trace the lineage of these terms see Douglas Kellner, 'Critical Theory', <https://pages.gseis.ucla.edu/faculty/kellner/essays/criticaltheory.pdf> accessed 13 June 2025; and Johan Heilbron, 'The Emergence of Social Theory' in Peter Kivisto (ed), *The Cambridge Handbook of Social Theory* (CUP 2020).

[2] These various uses of the terms suggest that they come as close to functioning as Rorschach blots for the academic community and public as methodological nomenclature can. Their capacity to serve as interpretive screens is facilitated by the fact that their constituting words provide almost no specific content. 'Critical', which derives from the Greek *Kritikos*, meaning 'able to discern', is, in its most obviously relevant meaning here, defined as nothing more than careful judgment or judicious evaluation. Meanwhile, 'social', in its most basic sense, refers merely to the study of human society and

For the purposes of this chapter, I am interested in what possible productive rationale there might be behind the broad use of these terms to group together a range of scholarship which is highly eclectic in fact—not only in terms of topic but methods of investigation, use of materials, research questions, and scholarly aims. Perhaps it is possible to find a connection between contemporary scholars, and between them and lineages with which they may not even be familiar, in meta-characteristics of the work related to their function in academic discourse. We might consider the following propositions, generalisations though they may be: Scholars identified with critical theory, social theory, and its variants have been willing to question even the foundational premises of the fields to which they contribute. Consequently, the work has placed the very notion of orthodoxy into question and challenged established scholarship's claims to objectivity. Further, by offering alternatives to prevailing narratives, they have often challenged the idea of a single truth. Often, in the service of these projects, these scholars have analysed how power works in society to shape knowledge, social relations, and institutional practice, which has also entailed attending to the material relations between those with power and those without it.

The several areas of inquiry that now fall under the terms "critical" and "social theory", then, may present perspectives and subjects that were underexplored or altogether neglected within fields. By showing where the negative space lies within fields, or what was long left out, these several subjects reveal substantive fault lines within disciplines themselves—the patterns and perspectives that have organised prevailing ways of doing things.[3] The specific content of those interventions, of course, must depend on the ways that fields have developed in the past. The relatively recent establishment of departments and programmes to foster the study of race, ethnicity, gender, sexuality, and disability, and their historical contexts of colonisation and enslavement, however, provides a clue: These are topics to which many disciplines—including the study of capitalism, literature, history, politics, and other fields across the humanities and social sciences—were long closed to exploring, such that the emergence of these new areas of study has in many ways reshaped their fields. These particular transformations, albeit on a slower timeline, have also reached the study of law. To the extent that the pursuit of these long unacknowledged lines of inquiry has destabilised previously clear parameters of fields, it was perhaps inevitable that the work would be viewed by some as disruptive and generate concerted attacks. It may even be that the boundaries of critical and social theory are determined by the *effect* that work has on a field and how it contributes to its orthodoxy or its evolution, rather than its self-avowed goals.

organisation, a broad category to which law clearly pertains; Johan Heilbron notes that shortly after a French encyclopaedia in 1765 described 'social' as a 'word newly introduced into language', Mirabeau called it 'dangerous' 'because of the multiplicity of "vague ideas it has allowed to emerge" '; Heilbron (n 1) 2. Under these definitions, all legal scholarship ought to constitute a variant of critical and social theory.

[3] This phenomenon of distinction invokes another resonance of 'critical', which after all comes from *krinein*, meaning 'to separate' or 'to sieve'. The process of revealing what has been omitted or suppressed often also leads to the charge of being divisive and threatening to the status quo. In both longstanding divisions maintained through existing arrangements *and* new projects of distinguishing between versions of the truth, this process of separation reveals vectors of power. Communities of scholarship reflect and justify similar patterns of social power beyond academia, so such work arises not only as a challenge to tradition within those fields, but as a challenge to power itself. This phenomenon helps to account for the reactionary interest in these terms and their conversion into political lightning rods, rather than neutral or even accurate descriptors of work. See, e.g., Chris Kahn, 'Many Americans Embrace Falsehoods about Critical Race Theory' *Reuters* (New York, 15 July 2021) <https://www.reuters.com/world/us/many-americans-embrace-falsehoods-about-critical-race-theory-2021-07-15/> accessed 25 March 2025.

In the next sections, I focus on the examples of private law and critical and social theory that I know best: property law and race and law, in the context of the US. Although this choice reflects the limitations of my own expertise, I make it with the hope that the dynamics of epistemic and institutional development and dominance I describe will resonate with the observations of scholars working in other areas of private law and critical and social theory around the globe and invite dialogue with them.

2. Exploring the Intersection Between Private Law, the Environment, and Race

The need for a volume such as this one on climate change and private law comes precisely out of the potential that lies in yet little explored cross-sections of fields. Those areas that are ripe for scholarly attention themselves often arise from the way that conventions of scholarly emphasis and path-dependence in fields have created entrenched habits of omission. For example, the field of environmental law, the primary field that takes up the question of climate change, has long been considered a public law field, dominated by the study of federal and state agencies and treaties, statutes, and regulations concerning air quality, water quality, waste management, chemical safety, and endangered species protection. This focus, of course, has made a great deal of sense, and stems from the well-known history of the passage of major environmental legislation and creation of the Environmental Protection Agency in the 1960s and 1970s.[4] One consequence of this focus is the idea that the field has mid-twentieth-century origins and is relatively new. The work of environmental historians, however, has examined a range of other laws that have permitted, regulated, and otherwise shaped the degree, geography, and nature of significant environmental harms. Those accounts suggest that we might view the legal system that impacts and addresses environmental harm and health as a much older topic for study, and one that includes additional varieties of law, including many kinds of private law.[5] In other words, we might consider a different framework for the field. And a big-picture reassessment of a field and attention to long-neglected areas—in this case, the role of private law in driving, addressing, or making it more difficult to address climate change—creates the potential, in turn, for new ideas and approaches to problems, and indeed to shift the direction of scholarship and practice.

The critical and social theory fields discussed above developed in a similar vein. To take the example of race and law, this topic also has been considered a new area of study in part because the civil rights movement, like the environmental justice movement, seemed to bring these topics into law—into major federal law, anyway. These legal developments newly legitimised these topics of study in law schools, and the creation, in the 1990s, of a field like critical race studies. As with the environment and law, this bedrock impetus likely had, as a consequence, the fact that the lion's share of scholarship on race and law for several decades focused on public law topics, namely, civil rights legislation, Supreme Court cases, and questions of Constitutional law stemming from the civil rights movement and its aftermath.[6] With some

[4] Joshua Galperin and Douglas Kysar, 'Uncommon Law: Judging in the Anthropocene' in Jolene Lin and Douglas Kysar (eds), *Climate Change Litigation in the Asia Pacific* (CUP 2020) 15–16.

[5] See, e.g., William Cronon, *Changes in the Land: Indians, Colonists, and the Ecology of New England* (Hill and Wang 1983); William Cronon, *Nature's Metropolis: Chicago and the Great West* (W. W. Norton 1991).

[6] For example, see the great majority of the contents of the foundational volume: Kimberlé W Crenshaw, Neil Gotanda, Gary Peller, and Kendall Thomas (eds), *Critical Race Theory: The Key Writings That Formed the Movement* (The New Press 1995).

notable exceptions, such as Adrienne Davis's work on estates and Patricia Williams's writing on contracts, the field, as it was forming, did not often take up questions of private law.[7] As with the case of environmental law, however, the contemporaneous work of historians and legal historians on race (primarily, but not exclusively of slavery, Reconstruction, and Jim Crow[8]) at the same time described a wide range of private laws that played major roles in constructing the relationship between law and race.[9] Though it seems evident in hindsight that private law should be considered central to the study of race and law, however, such a categorical rethinking of the field did not occur for decades.

I note these parallel tendencies between environmental law and race and law, particularly as they have informed the choices made for classroom curricula, in order to foreground the questions of disciplinary siloing and develop a more holistic view of our disciplines. The kind of path dependence I am describing also impacts the relationship *between* disciplines, as students readily note, but professors do not always know how to address. Specifically with respect to the relationship between environmental law and race law, it is the particularities of how they emerged in the academy that likely have made it harder to see what each of these subjects has to do with the other. Although Black, Indigenous, and immigrant communities have played catalytic roles in the environmental justice movement for decades,[10] it is not immediately clear how to connect standard curricula topics—to show what the Clean Air Act or the Endangered Species Act have to do with race or gender, for example, let alone civil rights law topics like public accommodations or fair housing. Bridge-building is underway, but individual professors must still make choices to depart from standard curricula or choose a critical variation to show the deep intersection between these topics. The irony, then, is that the term "critical" comes to cover attempts to remediate the shortcomings of earlier norms, in a designation that preserves accounts as standard-bearers even when they have been shown to be limited in many ways.

The reinforcement of disciplinary silos occurs throughout a greater system. For example, traditional approaches of private law subjects have bolstered the tendency to marginalise consideration of private law in the environmental law and race and law fields through their treatment, or lack thereof, of race *and* the environment. Neither race nor environmental issues are uniformly considered essential topics of private law.[11] While other parts of this handbook will better treat the nexus of the environment and private law subjects, here I can offer some general observations from a comprehensive study of property law casebooks over time about the extent to which the subjects of environment and race appear. Some texts include cases involving hazardous pollution, but none treat climate change or environmental protection as a

[7] In 1999, Adrienne Davis argued that private law might play at least as significant a role as public law in the construction, recognition, and reinforcement of racial and sexual relationships. Adrienne D Davis, 'The Private Law of Race and Sex: An Antebellum Perspective' (1999) Stanford Law Review 221; see also Patricia Williams, *The Alchemy of Race and Rights* (Harvard University Press 1991).

[8] There are notable exceptions, e.g., Robert Williams Jr., *The American Indian in Western Legal Thought: The Discourses of Conquest* (OUP 1990).

[9] For accounts of how private law operated in colonisation and slavery, see, e.g., Yasuhide Kawashima, *Puritan Justice and the Indian White Man's Law in Massachusetts, 1630–1763* (Wesleyan University Press 1986); A Leon Higginbotham Jr., *In the Matter of Color: Race & the American Legal Process: The Colonial Period* (OUP 1978); Thomas D Morris, *Southern Slavery and the Law, 1619–1860* (University of North Carolina Press 1996); Eric Foner, *Reconstruction: America's Unfinished Revolution, 1863–1877* (Harper & Row 1988).

[10] See K-Sue Park, 'This Land Is Not Our Land' (2020) 87 University of Chicago Law Review 1977, 2019–23 (and associated footnotes).

[11] With the exception, perhaps, of toxic torts in tort law.

key substantive topic for property law.[12] In my examination of their treatment of race, I found that during the first decades of modern legal education, casebooks uniformly acknowledged that colonisation and enslavement were central to the formation of American property law, though without analysing their ideological dependence on racial hierarchy. However, casebook authors just as uniformly began to omit this information beginning in the 1940s, and this erasure of the specific history of property in America made race the marginal, inconsistent, and optional topic in property law courses that it remains today.[13]

Recently, there has been a fluorescence of work on race and private law to similarly highlight, fill in, and in some cases diagnose the gaps left by these disparate paths of field development. Some of it has attempted to map the space of the gaps, while others have concentrated on field-specific topics. In 2020, Justin Simard published an article that showed how virtually every aspect of commercial law, including civil procedure, statutory interpretation, torts, contracts, and property, has dealt with the question of property in enslaved persons, and therefore has been shaped by the history of slavery and race.[14] The new scholarship that has appeared across this range of subjects is too voluminous to list comprehensively, but includes a number of remarkable contributions in contract law and corporate law in particular.[15] In 2024, as a result of the efforts of several scholars, the Association of American Law Schools established a section for the study of race and private law.

The nexus of climate change and private law, like that between private law and race, is similarly ripe for expansion and in the process of growth. In considering what a critical or social theory approach can contribute to this growth, it is important to recognise where the fields themselves are already growing and what questions from their margins the centre might

[12] There are cases heavily implicating environmental issues that are present in every property law casebook, such as *Boomer v Atlantic Cement Co* and *Lucas v South Carolina Coastal Council*, concerning the nuisance created by a cement factory and a state law prohibiting development on a receding coastline, respectively, as well as others that appear in many, such as *Ark Land Co v Harper*, concerning the question of partition in kind or by sale of a property co-owned by a large family and a coal mining company. See *Boomer v Atlantic Cement Co* (1970) 257 NE2d 870; *Lucas v South Carolina Coastal Council* (1992) 505 US 1003; *Ark Land Co v Harper* (W Va 2004). However, across the property casebooks offered on the market today there is typically no discussion of the implications of the property issue for the environment, let alone climate policy.

[13] K-Sue Park, 'The History Wars and Property Law: Conquest and Slavery as Foundational to the Field' (2022) 131 Yale Law Journal 1062, 1071–88 (and associated footnotes).

[14] Justin Simard, 'Citing Slavery' (2020) 72 Stanford Law Review 79. In this vein, Carliss Chatman also recently published an article on teaching slavery and commercial law. Carliss N Chatman, 'Teaching Slavery in Commercial Law' (2023) 28 Michigan Journal of Race and Law 1 (observing that many business and commercial law professors do not teach slavery, despite the foundational role of slavery in developing those fields).

[15] From the last five years, for example, see field-reorienting works on contract by Dylan Penningroth, Brittany Farr, and Erik Encarnacion, among others. See Dylan C Penningroth, 'Race in Contract Law' (2022) 170 University of Pennsylvania Law Review 1199 (revealing the hidden role of race in the development of contract law as a field); Brittany Farr, 'Breach by Violence: The Forgotten History of Sharecropper Litigation in the Post-Slavery South' (2022) 69 UCLA Law Review 674 (highlighting the historically significant role of racial violence in contract formation and breach); Erik Encarnacion, 'Section 1981 as Contract Law' (2025) 111 Virginia Law Review 1605 (arguing that the Civil Rights Act of 1866, prohibiting racial discrimination in virtually all aspects of contract law, should be studied and taught as a major law governing contract). For contributions to corporate law, see, e.g., Gina-Gail S Fletcher and H Timothy Lovelace Jr., 'Corporate Racial Responsibility' (2023) 124 Columbia Law Review 361; Atinuke Adediran, 'Racial Targets' (2024) 118 Northwestern University Law Review 1455; Martin Sybblis, 'Corporate Law as Decolonization' (2024) 71 UCLA Law Review 798.

fruitfully take up. A significant portion of the work feeding the current examination of private law and race is by, or builds upon, the work and cues of legal historians; it less purports to discover new data than to highlight and reframe information that has long been available, or hidden in plain sight, and show it to be salient, even central to the prominent questions of a field. As the next section discusses, this insight may be useful for exploring the nexus of climate change and private law as well. The perspectives of groups that have not previously been centred in the literature—our working hypothesis of what constitutes critical or social theory in this chapter—introduce different sets of background presumptions. These unfamiliar points of departure both highlight how much the assumptions of private law fields permeate current approaches to climate change and reveal other ways of approaching the issue—other priorities, goals, and possibilities.

3. Property Law as an Obstacle to Addressing Climate Change

Taking into account a wide range of perspectives, especially long marginalised perspectives, has the benefit of raising some of the most central and urgent questions about climate change for governments at every level. Climate change, as it is so often said, affects everyone, wreaking devastation across and within borders, but not equally. In addition to seeking to understand the ways that private law can help to address the issue of climate change, as so many pieces in this handbook explore, this section discusses a complementary point that these perspectives repeatedly reveal: that private law, and more specifically, property law, have been major factors contributing to this unevenness, and often constitute obstacles to addressing climate change. The point is not new, by any means. For a well-established example, as several scholars have observed, the history of US property law and real estate has created inequities that continue to dictate what communities are more likely to be placed in harm's way, including harm from climate change. This distribution also determines, as an initial matter, which communities are more equipped with the resources to face and recover from climate disaster. Further, the logic and institutions of property law, as a major part of the entrenched private legal infrastructure that organises resources in our society, impinge massively on the choices made now and in the future. It both independently affects peoples' ability to navigate the upheavals wrought by climate change and deeply informs the legal systems designed for social provision and disaster response.

The special role that property law must play as we evaluate possibilities for responding to climate change is also an observation that multiple scholars are making in current conversations. Jill Fraley, for example, has argued that property law presents "the single largest limitation on our ability to respond effectively to the climate change crisis", largely because of the way it prevents governments from controlling land use for collective benefit. For Fraley, this obstacle stems from the "extraordinary power and significance" of property law in American law and individual property ownership in American culture, as well as from actual doctrines that constrain the government, such as regulatory takings.[16] Mark Nevitt also writes critically about the chilling effect of regulatory takings on ambitious government action on behalf of the collective, and despairs of the individuated approach of disaster compensation and relief

[16] Jill M Fraley, 'Climate Change, Sustainability, and the Failure of Modern Property Theory' (2020) 104 Marquette Law Review 93.

as a response to climate change, describing instances where people have filed insurance claims to rebuild their homes which have flooded many dozens of times over.[17] Their joint warning about the difficulty of collective, systemic action due to existing property interests and entrenched practices that protect them is a crucial starting point for understanding the nexus between private law and climate change.

In seeking, then, to appreciate the ramifications of this initial observation, it is equally crucial to learn from the experiences of communities that have been most severely affected. There are two immediately obvious reasons why. From the front line, their experiences provide us with the most information about how our current legal system is not working to respond to climate change, and therefore, how to think about these systems as we anticipate building upon and adapting them for the future. Further, they relay their experiences from community perspectives that frequently do not share mainstream assumptions of US private law and property law, but that do represent the views and priorities of many communities around the globe. The distance between the needs and values of communities and the priorities of the private property system places in serious doubt whether the status quo has the capacity to meet the needs of a diverse collective in the face of new challenges, or to avoid extending and exacerbating the harms of the past. If it cannot do either, its shortcomings highlight the specific values and needs that it is unequipped to address, which could serve as guiding priorities for imagining a different system, with different capacities and goals concerning what to accommodate and protect.

The continuity between the historical development of property law and the way property logic informs the failure of current disaster responses is not at all lost on scholars who work with marginalised communities or those communities themselves. For example, private property issues dominated in the challenges that arose for several communities facing rising sea levels, including the Isle de Jean Charles Choctaw Nation of Louisiana, communities on the western coast of Alaska, and communities in floodplains, such as in Kinston, North Carolina; consequently, a collective of scholars working in collaboration with these communities, including Alessandra Jerolleman, Elizabeth Marino, and Nathan Jessee, entitled the volume of their findings *People or Property*.[18] This useful book, like many other studies, explores challenges and possibilities in processes of relocation and resettlement, or migration as a strategy of adaptation to climate change; but somewhat uniquely, it is rooted in the worldviews and goals of those communities, as well as observations about their on-the-ground experiences of rising sea levels, disasters, and relocation processes.[19] It is likely that in other contexts, such as wealthy communities where affected persons might largely share and embrace the individuation and monetary calculations that supersede other values in the US private property system, the theme of property critiques might not have risen into such strong relief. However, against the background perspectives of these communities, the assumptions about property goals in current relocation processes emerge lucidly, along with their limited capacity to achieve the outcomes desired by affected communities.

The example of the Jean Charles Choctaw Nation is particularly instructive for understanding how the property logics that permeate climate adaptation programmes can undermine Tribal sovereignty, as well as preservation of a community more broadly. Tribal leaders, as Jerolleman, Marino, and Jessee relate, began planning resettlement in 2002, when their

17 Mark Nevitt, 'Destroy, Rebuild, Repeat: How to Break the Climate Disaster Cycle' (2025) 78 Vanderbilt Law Review 493.

18 Alessandra Jerolleman, Elizabeth Marino, and Nathan Jessee, *People or Property: Legal Contradictions, Climate Resettlement, and the View from the Shifting Ground* (Palgrave Macmillan 2023).

19 ibid.

traditional homelands were excluded from the US Army Corps of Engineers' planned regional hurricane protection.[20] By then, the Tribe already had extensive historical experience with land loss, displacement, and increasing flooding on the Isle de Jean Charles, which particularly affected the two-lane road on which residents depended to access the island. The situation worsened after FEMA refused to fund "enhancements" to protect the road, and many Tribal members and leaders left the island because of flooding of their homes and roads.[21] The Tribe's plans for resettlement focused on cultural survival—a process that they viewed as continuing from the Tribe's multigenerational experience of community fragmentation—and prioritised reunifying kinship-linked Tribal community members and rebuilding collective modes of land and resource stewardship as well as other aspects of traditional communal life in the new location. This plan would have gone some way towards repairing the harms of the past, in addition to securing a more stable future for the group. In 2014, the state decided to support the Tribal leaders' efforts to seek federal funding. In 2016, the Department of Housing and Urban Development, through the National Disaster Resilience Competition, awarded the state $48.3 million for the Tribal leaders' proposal.[22]

However, the framework that state officials then imposed upon resettlement surprised Tribal leaders, frustrating the goals and vision that they had carefully articulated and built over several years. The state's administration of the grant created multiple options for individual households, depending on whether or not they lived on the island at the time of the grant allocation or had left after 2012, as well as on their fiscal resources. The only option available to those who had left prior to 2012 was to receive an empty lot in the new location, but only for former island residents who could demonstrate they had the financial capacity to build a new house on the lot themselves. Low-income former island residents were thereby barred from moving near their friends and family. Others were deterred from moving by the requirement that those who resettled had to give up other properties (though the state abandoned an initial attempt to force island residents to entirely give up their island property, it imposed many restrictions on their ability to maintain and preserve their island property).[23] The state's individuating approach to relocation frustrated Tribal leaders' carefully considered plan for bringing together families that had already been displaced by floods and families still on the island, despite its having invoked these very values through their joint proposal to win the award.

On the one hand, this set of decisions failed to recognise and respect the Tribe as a sovereign collective entity and Tribal leaders' authority to make decisions on behalf of that collective. On the other hand, it failed to recognise value in community cohesion and kinship in several ways. Namely, it created artificial divisions between people who remained on the island past a certain date, long after the challenges of staying there had begun; it unnecessarily discouraged people from rejoining their community in the new location by forcing them to choose between this community and their existing property interests; and it made no provision for low-income members of the community "who could have benefited most from the resilience plans Tribal leaders had envisioned" (a value based on a wealth-hierarchy that permeates US law, but which is not shared by the Tribe).[24] Finally, after dividing and deterring Tribal members from relocating in this way, it allowed for public auctioning of properties unclaimed by Tribal members and public use of common areas, so that the new settlement would become a

20 Jerolleman et al (n 17) 91.
21 ibid 46.
22 ibid 92.
23 ibid 46.
24 ibid.

new suburb where a mixed community had equivalent use rights within the area, rather than community property for the Tribe.[25] By privileging individual ownership and property holdings and management over the opportunity to foster kinship ties, community cohesion, and cultural survival, Jerolleman, Marino, and Jessee observe a pattern in which government agencies "foreground and work to diminish risks to *property*, instead of risks to *people*".[26]

This example raises important questions about what it could mean to implement "community-led resettlement", and further and more specifically, *Tribal* community-led resettlement. After all, in order to receive federal recognition as a Tribe at all, among other things, a Tribe must show that it "comprises a distinct community and demonstrates that it existed as a community from 1900 until the present"; and in meetings with officials from Louisiana's Office of Community Development (OCD), Tribal members emphasised their own understanding of the contours of their community, the social networks between on- and off-island Tribal members, and the importance of Tribal leadership. One of their partners from the Lowlander Center, a local non-profit, insisted that the concept be drawn from the proposal itself: "We must agree that the community is the entire Tribe, and not just those who remain on the Island."[27] These arguments did not deter OCD officials from pursuing a different plan, which entailed individual households negotiating with a subcontracted market analysis team that never met with the Tribe nor took its particular needs into account. Rather, this team made recommendations for land use schemes based on calculations of the "highest and best use" of the site; and the lead state resilience administrator working on the resettlement compared the project to "founding any new town over the course of Western history . . . it's all wrapped around the idea of, how do we generate revenue?"[28] In accordance with this notion, throughout the process, the administrator repeatedly made the statement that "at its core, the resettlement is essentially a very complicated real estate transaction".[29]

For the state and the organisations with which it contracted to carry out the plan, this observation undoubtedly felt like a necessary—perhaps the only conceivable—starting point. Yet the value of community that cannot be monetised—the history and kinship that people share with one another, and the ways they sustain one another through cooperative networks, collective support, and material aid—will not find translation through real estate transactions and the logic of private property in the United States. Rather, the principles inherent in those tools have expressed themselves through histories of colonial extraction, racially restrictive covenants, redlining, racially motivated fraud, repeated rounds of gentrification, and many more forms of dispossession and displacement, and while some of the most obvious problems of the system have been abolished, it has never been reformed to substantially transform the patterns of its effects. Communities that have nevertheless managed to sustain themselves in place over time continue to be challenged by such transactions and logics and even destroyed by them. If the state and these professional organisations cannot conceptualise an approach to climate change without these tools, they fail to cognize the needs and historical position of the communities they purport to try to help. Given that it is in large part the long, consistent history of US real estate and property that shapes the new threats to these communities emerging with the advent of climate change, it is very clear to the communities themselves that this "help" purports to bring a "cure" in the form of the same poison that produced the need for that "help".

[25] ibid 46–48.
[26] ibid 10.
[27] ibid 98–99.
[28] ibid 46.
[29] ibid 45.

To take another example from the same volume to illustrate this point, many communities of colour in the southern United States, like the neighbourhood of Lincoln City in Kinston, North Carolina, were originally built outside of official city limits in floodplains, where non-whites could obtain land during the era of Jim Crow. Those areas now appear to planners scanning the landscape for risk as "neighborhoods that should not have been there in the first place".[30] Despite the rationality of this view of history, this framing glosses over the multigenerational experience of a Black community in which people "loved each other . . . fed each other, clothed each other, and . . . took care of each other's children".[31] This neighbourhood was mourned, upon its demolition, by the people whose parents and grandparents grew up there, and shared the sense that "a piece of important black identity and history, a community identity" had been eradicated.[32] The same property logic that forced this neighbourhood to this undesirable place also made it a target for buyouts and erasure. It also made the people who had nevertheless persisted candidates for displacement and diminished opportunity, yet again. Homes in such places are at greater risk than others' homes in an age of more frequent storms and floods; they are more damaged due to floods and assessed at a lower value than homes at higher elevations. This damage also makes homeowners less likely to be able to comply with elevation requirements, leaving them with fewer options.[33] In general, the poor and communities of colour "may be more likely targeted by local jurisdictions for buyouts";[34] and due to the lower value of their homes, if residents relocate through a buyout programme, they may not be able to purchase a home, or a home of comparable value in a less hazardous area nearby, in proximity to one another.[35]

It must be said that the logics that Jerolleman, Marino, and Jessee describe are not substantially different from observations made decades ago by scholars and advocates from the environmental justice movement. In their 2001 book on environmental racism and the rise of the environmental justice movement, for example, Sheila Foster and Luke Cole pointed out how correlating patterns of race and toxic exposure stemmed from racist histories of segregation, the linkage—created by the real estate market and industry—between non-white presence and low property values, the relegation of people of colour to undesirable areas, and zoning and other choices to site industry in neighbourhoods of colour (or what Yale Rabin has called "expulsive zoning").[36] In other words, Foster and Cole, too, noted the primacy of the property system and real estate logic in the determination of communities' exposure to environmental risk. Not only was risk more likely to be foisted on communities of colour and the poor, but as they observed, in a housing market characterised by scarcity and unaffordability, risk is a hazard of low opportunity; people of colour and poor people also "move to areas that surround waste facilities because those neighbourhoods offered the cheapest available housing".[37]

The dynamics that Cole and Foster described persist. Further, the circumstances that Jerolleman, Marino, and Jessee describe reveal a new system of adaptation to climate change

[30] ibid 75.
[31] ibid 74.
[32] ibid 85–85.
[33] ibid 76–66.
[34] ibid 152.
[35] ibid 76.
[36] Sheila Cole and Luke Foster, *From the Ground Up: Environmental Racism and the Rise of the Environmental Justice Movement* (New York University Press 2001) 68–73 (citing Yale Rabin, 'Expulsive Zoning: The Inequitable Legacy of Euclid' in Charles M Haar and Jerold S Kayden (eds), *Zoning and the American Dream* (Routledge 1990).
[37] ibid 60–61.

that layers more property logics over the long-standing, entrenched, and unequal private property system, which amplifies its effects in cases where communities are facing or will imminently face acute, life-endangering crises. In recognition of this continuity, Jerolleman, Marino, and Jessee recognise "path dependencies that coalesce around property rights, property ownership, and individual property holders in relocation scenarios and find that prevailing paths extend some of the worst injustices expressed throughout U.S. history".[38] Further, they wryly observe that people experiencing repetitive flooding and harm across the United States today face "multiple overlapping risk-producers: climate, weather, wind, rain, racism, redlining, colonialism, and theft".[39] In the bigger picture, scholars find, the wealth in home ownership that people have accrued also determines whether they get to stay in their homes: "[M]edian home value correlates positively with shoreline armouring and negatively with the occurrence of buyouts"; and, as a consequence of which communities own higher value homes, it is also the case that "the percent[age] of the population that identifies as people of colour correlates positively with buyouts and negatively with shoreline armoring". Elevation grants, too, are more likely to go to wealthy and/or mostly white communities, affecting not only who can stay and who must leave their homes and face community fragmentation, but also who will benefit from reduced insurance costs and the equity from increased property values.[40]

The stories from Isle de Jean Charles, coastal Alaska, and Kinston that Jerolleman, Marino, and Jessee share give meaning to the stakes, complexity, and the potential of the basic observation that private property and property law pose obstacles to collective action on climate change. Preexisting systems pose obstacles to such obstacles through their tenacity, and new systems replicate and extend the roadblocks that already litter the field. Repeatedly, we see that state actors find opportunities to serve certain communities and maximise their gains from real estate transactions in resettlement programmes, while disregarding affected communities' needs. Since the Jean Charles Choctaw resettlement funding allocation, the state has moved to protect and enhance the Island Road whose deterioration occasioned the resettlement plan—not to preserve Tribal members' ability to remain on the island but to build up the island for recreational hunting and fishing.[41] Alaska has protected homes and businesses on its coasts with sea well revetments and other infrastructure projects, but not the subsistence equipment, land, and seascapes critical to Alaska Native ways of life; "[t]hese prioritizations", Jerolleman, Marino, and Jessee write, "create the ecological and sociopolitical conditions which lead to relocation". Similarly, they note, Louisiana state "continue to issue land use permits for industrial actors and for the engineering of mega-projects along a sinking coastline, while the inland migration and largely uncompensated abandonment of traditional lands by Indigenous, Black, and other marginalised communities is treated as a foregone conclusion".[42]

When Nevitt and Fraley make the diagnosis of conflict between property values and collective action, for example, they focus on the capacities of government, or the limits placed on government action by property laws—an important issue in thinking about the mechanics

[38] Jerolleman et al (n 17) 8.

[39] ibid 11.

[40] ibid 153 (citing A R Siders and J M Keenan, 'Variables Shaping Coastal Adaptation Decisions to Armor, Nourish, and Retreat in North Carolina' (2020) 183 Ocean and Coastal Management 105023; Thomas Frank, 'How FEMA Helps White and Rich Americans Escape Floods' *Politico* (Wilson, 27 May 2022) <https://www.politico.com/news/2022/05/27/unfair-fema-climate-program-floods-00032080> accessed 12 June 2025).

[41] ibid 56.

[42] ibid 27.

of any future change, to be sure. In their account, Jerolleman, Marino, and Jessee show us the complex property interests driving both private and public action, or what states choose to do when they do have the power to act. It is not encouraging. Further, by highlighting the interests at stake for affected communities, these authors also show the range of private interests that threaten those communities. After all, private property owners who are highly invested in the status quo will aim to hold on to their holdings or pursue developing them at all costs (a phenomenon, it is worth remembering, that is neither natural nor inevitable, but whose history entails centuries of choices to invest in individuals in this system and their private holdings to begin with). These interests can defeat public interests in multiple ways. For example, as Nevitt describes, $2.2 million of taxpayer money can go towards rebuilding the same property forty-four times, as was done with one house in the Outer Banks, North Carolina. To this story suggesting one person's engrossment of an outsized proportion of public funds, Jerolleman, Marino, and Jessee add a bigger picture of public policy that rewards those with the money to turn high-risk land into more money-making real estate, while it pushes those without such resources from their long-time homes. They tell the story of an elder in Louisiana whose home flooded multiple times as she faced rising insurance rates and overwhelming damage. Under these pressures, she sold her land, which was mostly undeveloped, to the highest bidder—who then built a bigger house and subdivided the remaining property for more development.[43]

Scholars and journalists who track these stories observe that people often hold deep attachment to their homes, which may or may not have been in their families for generations, and do not wish to take governmental aid to leave. Nor do they relish the options that an increasingly unaffordable housing market presents elsewhere.[44] They hold these values and priorities whether they are rich or poor, regardless of their families' histories on the land, or how they came to their present circumstances. As scholars have pointed out before, there are values that cannot be captured by conversions into economic transactions.[45] Holding to the default baseline assumption that people's fates can be determined by the dollar amounts that they possess, have access to, or that their properties are worth, wilfully ignores the warnings delivered many times over from scholars and communities themselves, over years during which their urgency has only multiplied and spread.

4. Conclusion

This chapter described the various ways that property law and its logic inform current responses to climate change as revealed by the experiences of marginalised communities facing climate-induced dislocation. It further raised the question of whether the value of learning from these experiences is one that can be relegated to a critical or social theory perspective

43 ibid 31–32.

44 For another example, see an account from North Carolina following Hurricane Helene in 2024. Zack Coleman, 'Why North Carolinians Probably Won't Take the Federal Buyouts After Hurricane Helene' *Politico* (16 October 2024) <https://www.politico.com/news/2024/10/16/north-carolina-helene-federal-money-00183503> accessed 12 June 2025.

45 See the foregoing discussion in this section as well as Lisa Heinzerling's recent piece on the *LPE Blog* and her more extended treatment of this issue in her indispensable book with Frank Ackerman. Lisa Heinzerling, 'Climate Change, Racial Justice, and Cost-Benefit Analysis' *LPE Blog* (28 September 2021) <https://lpeproject.org/blog/climate-change-racial-justice-and-cost-benefit-analysis/> accessed 12 June 2025; Frank Ackerman and Lisa Heinzerling, *Priceless: On Knowing the Price of Everything and the Value of Nothing* (2004).

deemed to be marginal to more traditional or mainstream approaches,[46] and suggested that if it is, that designation may be one more way of minimising perspectives that have long been marginal or suppressed, in the interests of preserving various aspects of the status quo—distributions of power and resources and epistemic dominance, among others. In their volume, Jerolleman, Marino, and Jessee observe that property-oriented plans fail to "foreground the legitimate, empowered, claims of entitlement to land, culture, continuity, and risk protection that we find most prevalent in conversations on the ground and within communities facing repetitive flooding".[47] They raise questions that go to the heart of the discussion of the present handbook—whether US legal tools have the capacity to protect the interests of these communities, and if they do, how. Can the community of scholars and practitioners sincerely invested in meeting the challenge of climate change afford to ignore the warnings posed by scholars of environmental racism long ago—that the way risk and opportunities to maintain one's home, community, and material stability in the face of climate disaster is heavily determined by the extensive history of inequity in property law and the creation of the real estate system? On top of these background conditions, they must contend with the many ways that the systems currently in place to respond to climate disaster operate according to property logics and distribute and deny resources in ways that extend and exacerbate rather than mitigate or avoid those historical patterns.

The history of the dispossessed and displaced—so continuous with the history of the communities facing imminent dispossession and displacement again as a result of climate change—shows that what Nevitt and Fraley describe as paralysis may rather be the result of another set of motivations.[48] The failure of collective action is rooted in the difficult and unprecedented nature of contemplating action on behalf of the collective—the *entire* collective, not simply propertied people driven by property interests. In this respect, the nature of the problem presented by private law and climate change does not differ greatly from the difficulty our legal system has perennially had in attempting to solve other collective action problems concerning the basic safety and well-being of the populace, for example, housing or healthcare. In one sense, the consistency of outcomes in the history of this struggle is extremely disheartening. But in another, the same history is replete with rich ideas for alternative arrangements, programmes, and systems. At the least, this long history forces us to recognise, as a starting point, that a system already exists. That system is comprised of property law and property-driven public programmes, and it serves enough of a class to hold the effects of climate change emergencies more or less at bay for that group of people. As in the past, the power of that system is in the gains that it offers to those who are able to use it, at the direct expense of those who are not, and any attempt to answer or redress its harms must contend with those incentives above all.

46 See, for example, work that treats Tribal governmental experience with conservation for what it is: additional, relevant, often overlooked, and potentially helpful data on the problem at hand. Sarah Krakoff and Ezra Rosser (eds), *Tribes, Land and the Environment* (Routledge 2012); Alejandro Camacho, Elizabeth Kronk Warner, Jason McLachlan, and Nathan Kroeze, 'Adapting Conservation Governance Under Climate Change: Lessons from Indian Country' (2024) 110 Virginia Law Review 1549.

47 ibid 6.

48 Fraley's account focuses on the power of property *theory* to make two intriguing claims: first, that 'Environmental law is effectively impossible in a system where the theory of property espouses a model of near complete control by private landowners'; and second, that property law is 'the foundational limit of environmental law'. Fraley (n 15) 95. This chapter contemplates these propositions given the power of property law over the material world. It joins the scholars from whose work it draws in suggesting that the sheer extent of land comprised by private property and the resources governed by property law poses an obstacle to environmental and climate law and policy as well.

CHAPTER 4

Relational Justice

AVIHAY DORFMAN

1. Introduction

It is well-established that law constantly adapts to changing circumstances and evolving convictions. On many occasions, the fitting response introduces only marginal adjustments to the existing framework. At other times, however, the necessary response is more transformative. The looming danger of global warming and, in particular, the significant role humans have played in causing it, may prompt such a transformative response. One aspect of this response concerns the possibility and desirability of extending *tort law*—the law governing the involuntary duties of individuals to respect the rights of others—to protect non-human animals and plants.[1] Simply put, can and should tort law require individuals to take some measure of care and respect for some or all living organisms?

The ambition of this chapter is to explore the case for an affirmative answer to both questions. I argue that relational justice offers the potential to point tort law in the right direction and, further, that this direction represents an extension of, rather than a break from, tort law's substantive and institutional foundations. Accordingly, the idea of private responsibility for the life and well-being of non-human animals and plants should be best viewed not as an exception to, but rather as a consequence of, subjecting tort law to the demands of relational justice, particularly to relational justice's commitment to substantive equality.[2]

More concretely, there are two basic hurdles—substantive and institutional—that might lead one to believe that tort law has, and should have, nothing to say about our terms of interactions with non-human animals and plants. First, substantively, can tort duties be owed to non-human animals and plants? The underlying difficulty here is that tort duties reflect, as they should, a conception of relating as equals. Can such a conception support duties of care and respect for non-human animals and plants? I answer in the affirmative, drawing on the important connection between a certain conception of transactional equality among persons—that is, a substantive conception of relational equality—and fairness towards other living organisms.

The second, institutional hurdle concerns the impossibility, in the case of non-human animals and plants, of occupying the plaintiff position. In particular, can there be tort duties to entities that lack the threshold agency to pursue claims against those who harm them? I defend the view that standing, power, or even the very right to pursue wrongdoers in a court does not

[1] Another subset, discussed in Hanoch Dagan and Avihay Dorfman, 'Public Nuisance for Private Persons' (2024) 74 University of Toronto Law Journal 198, concerns involuntary duties in connection with other people's rights to use and enjoy public spaces.

[2] Relational justice stands on two, self-standing commitments: Substantive equality and self-determination. In these pages, I focus on the implications of substantive equality for the question of extending tort law to protect non-human living organisms.

occupy tort law's moral centre. In this case, lacking the requisite capacity is beside the point of tort law.

Asking whether tort law can and should incorporate certain involuntary duties towards non-human living organisms presupposes a certain understanding of the place of tort law within the larger social universe. According to this view, tort law is not merely a legal reflection of the sum of all existing political and social forces that lead to the creation of a specific tort duty. Instead, tort law is primarily a realm of normative ideas and commitments that guide those who create and apply the law. Therefore, the key question is which ideas and commitments—compelling on their own, yet compatible with and integral to tort law—can rise to the challenge. I argue that relational justice offers the normative framework whose basic ideas and commitments meet this requirement. I claim that relational justice is not only suitable but necessary *if* considered alongside its two main alternatives: corrective justice and civil recourse.

One last methodological clarification will be apt. The legal institution known as tort law consists of many different ideas and doctrinal rules, managed by various institutional and private actors. Although these elements evolve in response to changing circumstances and revised convictions, some are rightly considered foundational. Remove them, and tort law becomes an entirely different enterprise. Of course, it is quite complicated to identify which elements are truly foundational.[3] For instance, New Zealand's tort reform and US workers' compensation schemes are often presented as leading examples of doing away with tort law,[4] though this characterisation is likely misleading and (in my view) ultimately false.[5] For the purpose of the current argument, I focus on identifying two elements that many leading tort theories explicitly or implicitly deem foundational. My ambition is to explain why duties to protect non-human animals and plants are not antithetical to tort law but rather expand its normative enterprise.

The argument proceeds in the following stages. Section 2 sets the stage by introducing two significant hurdles—the irrelevance of equality and the lack of standing—that challenge the idea that the legal imposition of private responsibility for the life and well-being of non-human animals and plants represents an extension of tort law in response to changed circumstances and revised convictions. Sections 3 and 4 argue that relational justice possesses the normative resources necessary to overcome these hurdles. Section 3 argues that tort duties to non-human animals and plants represent the extension of tort law from the principle of relational justice to relational fairness, whereas Section 4 argues that except for categories of cases unrelated to non-human animals and plants, victims' standing to pursue wrongdoers is of instrumental value only. In doing so, I argue that some other familiar normative theories of tort law lack the resources to achieve the same outcome. Thus, relational justice emerges as a necessary framework when considered alongside these alternatives. Finally, Section 5 clarifies the nature of the

[3] See Sandy Steel, 'On the Moral Necessity of Tort Law: The Fairness Argument' (2021) 41 Oxford Journal of Legal Studies 192. Steel focuses on victims' rights of action (which he calls 'Tort Plus'), whereas I shall focus mainly on primary or substantive rights and duties (which he calls 'Tort Minus').

[4] See Ernest J Weinrib, *Reciprocal Freedom: Private Law and Public Right* (OUP 2022) 110–11; Alan Brudner with Jennifer M Nadler, *The Unity of the Common Law* (2nd edn, OUP 2013) 315; John C P Goldberg and Benjamin C Zipursky, *Torts* (OUP 2010) 267, 394–95. See also John Fabian Witt, *The Accidental Republic* (Harvard University Press 2004) 202, 206. A leading study advocating doing away with tort law (particularly, tort actions for personal injuries) is Stephen D Sugarman, 'Doing Away with Tort Law' (1985) 73 California Law Review 555.

[5] Avihay Dorfman, 'Relational Justice and Torts' in Hanoch Dagan and Benjamin Zipursky (eds), *Research Handbook on Private Law Theory* (Edward Elgar Publishing 2020) 321, 326–28.

connection between our private responsibility for non-human animals and plants and the humanistic sentiments underlying relational justice.

2. Two Challenges: Equality and Standing

2.1 Tort Duties and Equality

Tort law consists of a variety of discrete torts. While the types of injuries they recognise and the standards of proper conduct they establish partially overlap, each of these torts articulates its own theory of mistreatment. That said, the primary duties underlying these torts take a similar form. In particular, they impose an obligation on individuals to moderate their conduct to avoid injuring others. In a liberal legal order where all people's lives are equally important, primary tort duties reflect a commitment to one or another conception of equality.[6] Thus, risk-creators are not permitted to prioritise their interests over those of the individuals they expose to risk because, and insofar as, tort law requires us to relate to one another as equals.[7] For this reason, tort duties call for moderation without subjugation, meaning that risk creators are not required to shun all risky activities when discharging these duties. Put abstractly, such duties construct egalitarian terms of interaction.

To take an example from the tort of negligence, a risk-creator fulfils the primary duty by giving "impartial consideration to the harm likely to be done to the interests of the other as compared to the advantages likely to accrue to [that actor's] own interests".[8] To be sure, impartiality can invite a number of interpretations, depending on the substantive account of tort duties, their correlative rights, and equality. This is true not only for relational and corrective justice accounts of tort law but also for accounts that make no explicit reference to justice, impartiality, and, ultimately, equality. For instance, the economic analysis of tort law identifies primary tort duties with a mechanism for the optimal allocation of scarce resources in society. At the same time, however, it presupposes a conception of equality. Requiring the risk-creator to sacrifice their resources, including time and energy, whenever it maximises society's total resources is a form of equal treatment, as it insists that no one's resources count for more or less than anyone else's.

The intimate connection between tort duties and equality in a liberal legal order manifests itself in various doctrinal rules.[9] It also aligns with the reduction of non-human animals and plants to mere things for the purpose of imposing tort duties and liabilities. Ordinarily, people do not owe tort duties—say, against committing trespass, conversion, and so on—to the things themselves, but rather to the owners of those things. Similarly, non-human animals and plants do not directly attract tort duties; instead, duty-bearers may have to moderate their conduct but only because the animals or plants are the property of the person to whom the tort duty is owed.

Against this backdrop, the challenging question is whether tort duties can be owed to non-human animals and plants without violating tort law's longstanding commitment to equality.

[6] Avihay Dorfman, *Conflict between Equals: Tort Law beyond Wrong, Harm, and Cost* (OUP 2026) ch 14.

[7] ibid.

[8] Restatement (Second) of Torts 1965, s 283 cmt e.

[9] For instance, the celebrated observation (made originally by Pollock) that 'proof of negligence in the air . . . will not do' implies that the impermissibility of conduct must not be assessed independently of its adverse implications for our fellow creatures and, more specifically, those people whose existence within the zone of danger can be foreseeable. See *Palsgraf v Long Island R Co* 162 NE 99, 99 (NY 1928).

Note that this is not a question about the possibility or desirability of legal duties to non-human animals and plants in general. Rather, it is a question of internal normativity: Do these duties reflect tort law's core morality? If so, imposing them would represent a warranted addition to what tort law in a liberal society is already about.

2.2 The Standing to Pursue One's Wrongdoer

The second challenge to the tortification of personal responsibility towards non-human animals and plants concerns the basic right of tort victims to sue their wrongdoers. The problem is that non-human animals and plants cannot hold such a right as they lack the requisite agency to become right-*holders*. One might protest that there is nothing particularly special about this problem. After all, infants and individuals with certain cognitive disabilities (to give two familiar examples) may also lack the necessary agency. Hence, standing to sue is a well-known issue that has, more or less, satisfying solutions. This is largely true in the case of human beings; for example, infants will one day possess the requisite agency to become plaintiffs.

That said, the challenge at issue is entirely different for two reinforcing reasons: Non-human living organisms are permanently and categorically without agency, and leading tort theorists consider such agency essential to the idea and appeal of tort law. Some of the most influential rights-based approaches in the field identify tort law with the victim's right of action. As a result, removing this right amounts to nothing less than eliminating tort law. Notice that this is not a definitional claim. Rather, it reflects a normative conviction about what lies at the *moral* centre of tort law, namely, the tort victim in their capacity as a plaintiff.

In these approaches, being empowered to pursue one's wrongdoer is central to why a legal order that fails to place the victim at the heart of the process of vindicating primary rights is considered "deficient".[10] Civil recourse theorists even suggest that this deficiency undermines the victim's basic freedom, stating "[a] free person—the opposite of a slave—is . . . one who is not left powerless to respond to violations of rights granted to her by law".[11] For their part, corrective justice theorists (of the Toronto School) develop a different theory of why tort law matters, but they go in a somewhat similar direction, namely, that the right to enforce substantive rights in the law of torts belong to the victim, and the victim alone. On this theory, independence and formal equality are the exclusive normative foundations of tort law. Thus, because inflicting an injury on the person or property of the victim involves either using or damaging their means, the victim's right to sue the wrongdoer is akin to a property entitlement to what this victim already possesses.[12] What is valuable in possessing such a right to sue is not merely the prospects of repair. After all, there are other ways to bring about the desired repair (on which more, see text accompanying note 44). Rather, it is the entitlement to decide whether or not to pursue the wrongdoer that gives effect to the victim's status as an independent and formally equal person. It is the right to sue itself, rather than merely the manner in which it is employed or the ensuing consequences (such as repair), that matters.

The challenge is straightforward, then. Non-human animals and plants can be victims of wrongs, but they cannot assume the role of plaintiffs, properly conceived. While they can hold both substantive rights and rights of repair, they necessarily lack the right of action as they do not have the requisite agency to obtain satisfaction, as civil recourse theory suggests, or to

[10] John C P Goldberg and Benjamin C Zipursky, *Recognizing Wrongs* (Harvard University Press 2020) 112.

[11] ibid 129–30.

[12] Arthur Ripstein, *Private Wrongs* (Harvard University Press 2016) 43–51.

rectify the wrong, as corrective justice theory suggests. It turns out, therefore, that the inclusion of non-human animals and plants in the tort system seems doomed from the outset. Or so civil recourse and corrective justice theorists may argue.

3. From Substantive Equality to Fairness

An analytically possible though normatively questionable way out is to generalise the liberal ideal of human equality to encompass the equal status of all living organisms.[13] On this approach, imposing tort duties towards non-human animals and plants is perfectly compatible with tort law's underlying commitment to equality simply because the egalitarian category consists of all living organisms, human or otherwise. Appeal to equality, however, might threaten to unsettle the reflective equilibrium between the equality theory of torts and our moral intuitions about equality.[14] Part of the concern is that the category of non-human living organisms includes many animals and plants that may not warrant the same level of consideration as human or other non-human organisms.

Can a better strategy be found? The challenge is to identify a normative principle that maintains the *right* distance from the liberal commitment to equality. On the one hand, it must not ascribe an all-encompassing scope to the principle of equality. On the other hand, it must maintain a strong connection to equality and, more specifically, to tort law's underlying commitment to equality.

I argue that an appeal to fairness could meet this challenge. On this view, fairness is compatible with treating others as equals but it does *not* require doing so. For example, we can ask a friend to play fair in a pick-up basketball game or to treat another with fairness, but doing so does not make essential reference to equal treatment or treating someone as an equal. Hence, fairness and equality can be distinct. That said, the two can be strongly connected in the following way: Equality is a species of the genus fairness, meaning that the former is a special case of the broader commitment to the latter.

The reason I argue that the two *can* be related is that much turns on what we mean by equality in the torts context. As I will show, the corrective justice conception of tort law's equality does not fit the bill. This is because its basic normative element is sui generis, making it incompatible with being viewed as a special case of fairness. By contrast, the relational justice conception of tort law's equality makes an appealing case for linking equality, the species, with fairness, its genus. I begin by briefly explaining what fairness is and then explore the possible connection between this principle and equality in tort law.

3.1 Fairness

I explore the concept of fairness as a *standard* for evaluating decisions, events, or states of affairs. As a standard, fairness is widely employed in both informal, everyday practices and institutional settings, including the law. For instance, a child who cannot get on a swing at the playground because another child refuses to let go might say "that's not fair". Similarly,

[13] The case for equal moral considerability among sentient animals is famously made in Peter Singer, 'All Animals are Equal' in Peter Singer (ed), *Applied Ethics* (OUP 1986) 215, 225; Peter Singer, *Animal Liberation* (Harper Collins 1975). For a nuanced discussion of equality in the context of animal rights, as opposed to all living organisms, see Christine M Korsgaard, *Fellow Creatures: Our Obligations to Other Animals* (OUP 2018) 64–66.

[14] See further Jeff McMahan, *The Ethics of Killing: Problems at the Margins of Life* (OUP 2002) 197. cf John Rawls, *A Theory of Justice* (Harvard University Press 1971) 505, 512.

students often complain that an exam was unfair because it was "unbelievably hard". In contract remedies law, courts use ex post fairness review to determine whether a liquidated damages clause imposes a de facto penalty on the breaching party.[15] They do so by considering the contracted sum in relation to the actual loss suffered by the aggrieved party. Lastly, in some jurisdictions, including Delaware, courts apply an "entire fairness review" to assess transactions that may appear structurally suspicious, such as when a controlling shareholder buys out minority shareholders without their consent. In these cases, both the process and the price of the transaction are subject to court scrutiny.[16]

What, then, does fairness consist of? A holistic account of fairness should be able to render intelligible our pre-theoretical understanding of this standard in both informal and institutional contexts.[17] On this account, fairness is a standard used to assess whether a decision, event, or state of affairs strikes the right balance between competing considerations. Thus, the child who bullies other swing-users inflates the importance of his desire to use it while downplaying the interests of these others. The overdemanding teacher fails to render the exam commensurate with the knowledge and abilities of her students. In the case of liquidated damages, courts are reluctant to treat remedies as penalties because breaching a contract does not amount to committing a tortious wrong. Finally, the "entire fairness" standard addresses concerns about subordinating the interests of minority shareholders and the corporation to the financial interests of the controlling shareholder. Notice that this characterisation of fairness is purely formal in the sense that it does *not* specify what the relevant considerations are or how to determine the proper balance between them. Rather, it focuses on the structure of the fairness standard by identifying the relationship of appropriateness between outcomes (such as decisions impacting the interests of the decisions' addressees) and the considerations they reflect.[18]

At first glance, a moral standard of equality might seem like a special case of the standard of fairness.[19] Both fairness and equality concern a class of pertinent considerations and how they affect decisions, events, and states of affairs. However, equality takes into account certain considerations (such as the respective interests and conditions of the parties involved), to the exclusion of others. Further, equality introduces its own specific version of fairness when the decisions, events, or states of affairs at its centre are based on human relationships. Thus, an extremely difficult exam might count as unfair but it does not necessarily imply inequality (as the teacher-pupil relationship is hierarchical by design). So, too, facing a broken swing might be viewed as unfair, but judging this situation does not implicate human relationships and, in particular, egalitarian relations.

This view of equality as a special case of fairness might support the view that tort duties to non-human animals and plants represent a warranted expansion of tort duties' commitment to

[15] See U.C.C. 1989, s 2-718; Restatement (Second) of Contracts 1981, s 356.

[16] See, e.g., Morgan White-Smith, 'Revisiting Revlon: Should Judicial Scrutiny of Mergers Depend on the Method of Payment?' (2022) 79 University of Chicago Law Review 1177, 1181–82.

[17] The concept of fairness has been widely discussed in philosophy, legal theory, and elsewhere. John Rawls's theory of justice as fairness is perhaps the most celebrated contribution. Rawls focuses on the principle of fairness as the ground for imposing obligations on individuals to support just institutions and practices. My discussion of fairness as a standard, rather than as a grounding principle, does not turn on the Rawlsian principle of fairness. See Rawls (n 14) 111–14, 342–50.

[18] Compare with the human-centred account of fairness defended in John Broome, 'Fairness' (1990–91) 91 Proceedings of the Aristotelian Society 87, 95.

[19] Some thinkers tend to believe that equality and fairness are 'part and parcel of a single concern'. Larry Temkin, 'Equality as Comparative Fairness' (2017) 34 Journal of Applied Philosophy 43, 45. My brief exposition of fairness does not share this assumption, however.

equality. However, I argue that for this inference to hold, the conception of equality underlying tort duties must, first, reject corrective justice's influential account of equality and, second, embrace instead that of relational justice. It turns out that not all conceptions of equality are special instantiations of fairness.

3.2 Corrective Justice and the Formal Conception of Equality

The prevailing theoretical orthodoxy holds that tort law's moral responsibility to achieve justice can be either corrective or distributive.[20] Some advocate for the former, others for the latter, and even those who critique the either/or picture of tort law's justice argue for a combination of both.[21] A key aspect of the corrective/distributive division of justice is equality. Corrective justice is said to manifest a principle of transactional equality which is most accurately described as formal equality: the idea that the terms of interactions fixed by tort law treat the parties as equals, irrespective of differentiating factors such as powers, vulnerabilities, needs, and virtues.[22] Weinrib, for example, suggests that "we cannot understand the normative character of corrective justice until we elucidate the normative significance of its equality".[23] His analysis indicates that equality "consists in abstracting from the parties' particularities".[24] In this view, to say that parties subject to tort law are formally equal is to suppose that all that matters, for the sake of doing corrective justice, is conceiving of them as constituting no more, and no less, than a generic *capacity for choice.*

There are several difficulties with this conception of tort law equality. Some are conceptual: The distinction between corrective and distributive justice is not a dichotomy, nor can it exhaust the logical space of alternative, non-formal conceptions of transactional equality.[25] Others are normative: The formal conception of tort law equality fails to provide a compelling articulation of what relating as equals in a liberal society requires.[26] Finally, the corrective justice conception also fails on doctrinal grounds: Contemporary tort law contradicts the formal conception of transactional equality. It regularly draws on considerations that align with a competing understanding of what it means for parties in a tort interaction to relate as equals—hence, rather than overlooking these factors, tort law frequently determines rights, duties, and liabilities based, in part and within limits, on the particularities or personal characteristics of the parties.[27]

[20] Corrective justice consists of different approaches and variations. The focus of the discussion going forward is the Toronto School of corrective justice, for it has developed the most comprehensive and sophisticated theory of transactional equality in the law of torts.

[21] See John Gardner, *Torts and Other Wrongs* (OUP 2019) ch 3; Hanoch Sheinman, 'Tort Law and Distributive Justice' in John Oberdiek (ed), *Philosophical Foundations of the Law of Torts* (OUP 2014) 354.

[22] Ernest J Weinrib, *The Idea of Private Law* (Harvard University Press 1995) 77–83; Arthur Ripstein, 'Civil Recourse and Separation of Wrongs and Remedies' (2011) 39 Florida State University Law Review 163, 181.

[23] ibid 77.

[24] ibid 81.

[25] Avihay Dorfman, 'Private Law Exceptionalism? Part II: The Basic Difficulty with the Argument from Formal Equality' (2018) 31 Canadian Journal of Law & Jurisprudence 5.

[26] ibid. See also Dorfman, *Conflict between Equals* (n 6); Hanoch Dagan and Avihay Dorfman, *Relational Justice: A Theory of Private Law* (OUP 2024). The normative difficulties with formal equality go beyond tort law, to be sure. See Karl Marx, 'Critique of the Gotha Program' in L H Simon (ed), *Karl Marx: Selected Writings* (1994) 320–21.

[27] Dorfman, *Conflict between Equals* (n 6).

Most importantly for present purposes, however, the corrective justice conception is sui generis—it is, at its core, human-centric. Therefore, it cannot represent a special case of fairness. If tort duties reflect this conception of equality, then extending tort duties to non-human animals and plants would necessarily represent a substantive departure from tort law's moral centre.

To unpack these claims, recall that the conception of equality at issue singles out the capacity for choice (or purposiveness) as the basic moral criterion for determining what relating as equals requires. This means that choices, as opposed to the very capacity for making them, do not count; nor do interests, needs, vulnerabilities, and other features that define who we are or implicate our condition in the world. The immediate problem here is that non-human animals and plants do not, at least not universally or typically, possess a capacity for choice or anything approximating it. For this reason, embracing the corrective justice conception of equality as the foundation for tort duties makes tort duties to non-humans and plants impossible. Notice that the conclusion is not that such duties should not exist at all. Rather, it is that they have nothing to do with the legal institution we recognise as tort law. Tort law, on this view, has no normative space for living organisms other than human beings as holders or beneficiaries of duties.

3.3 Relational Justice and the Substantive Conception of Equality

Unlike the corrective justice conception, relational justice offers a promising connection between its conception of equality in tort law and the principle of fairness mentioned above. However, before explaining this claim, it will be apt to outline the main themes of relational justice as a theory of private law.

Relational justice articulates the normative foundations of private law in a liberal legal order. Private law, in turn, governs daily interactions between private persons in a variety of settings where people encounter one another—on the road, in the neighbourhood, at the workplace, in the market, and more. It does the "governing" by constructing the terms of these interactions, such as by fixing and imposing duties of care. Relational justice addresses the question of which terms of interpersonal interactions are just—not only at the remedial stage but also, and more importantly, at the get-go stage. This means private law has a *constructive* role. There are two key elements in how relational justice approaches private law terms of interactions.

The first element concerns the relational form of these terms. Relational justice assesses their justness by focusing on whether the participants relate to one another as free and equal persons. In doing so, relational justice treats the terms of interpersonal interactions as a source of concern and value *in themselves*, rather than as a means or a stepping stone towards maximising overall social welfare or reducing distributive injustice in society. The second element is substantive as it explores what it means for the interacting parties to relate as free and equal persons. Within the relational justice framework, private law terms of interaction should abide by the fundamental liberal principle of reciprocal respect for self-determination and substantive equality. This means, among other things, that relational justice is not content with formal equality but seeks at establishing substantive equality by taking the interests and vulnerabilities of the interacting parties into account, rather than ignoring them.

Whereas corrective justice's conception of equality begins and ends with human beings, as just explained, relational justice starts with human beings—rooted in the humanistic tradition of liberalism—but it can, and should, extend its normative reach beyond tort law's current focus on humans. Key to this expansion is the possibility of viewing equality as a special case of fairness.

The substantive equality underlying relational justice does not presuppose people's capacity for choice (in the context of nonvoluntary interactions). Instead, it singles out both the interests they have and the conditions they face as the key metrics for determining the egalitarian terms of interaction between risk-creators and risk-recipients.[28] Interests refer to people's bodily integrity and well-being (among other things) whereas conditions refer to circumstances that adversely affect a person's ability to deliberate, choose, or act (including refraining from acting). Dearth of information and its resulting epistemic a-symmetry, inadequate experience, insufficient physical, mental, or cognitive abilities, and imminently dangerous situations are paradigm cases of conditions that can hinder the ability to relate as substantive equals. More generally, the moral aim of substantive equality in relational justice is to assess the justice or injustice of terms of interaction based on the relative importance of interests and conditions. Unlike the formal conception of equality, egalitarian terms of tort law interactions must account for both interest and condition differentials.[29]

Thus, to illustrate, parties in an interaction governed by tort law cannot relate as equals if the terms of their interaction fail to account for the difference between one party's life and limb and the other party's interest in fungible property.[30] Nor can they relate as equals if one party is adversely affected by a condition (such as disability or power asymmetry) to which they are subject.[31] Rather than setting aside interest and condition differentials, as the formal conception of equality does, the relational justice conception of transaction equality gives rise to rights, duties, liabilities, and remedies that take such differences into account, at least in some measure.[32]

Notice that the interests and conditions at issue are those of human beings. That said, they are not uniquely tied to human beings. Interests such as bodily integrity are morally good because their object—human life—is valuable, meaning that people are "self-originating sources of valid claims".[33] Non-human animals and plants can also possess value. They can be instrumentally valuable and, *arguably*, they can have non-instrumental value, quite apart from their contribution to humanity, the ecosystem, and more.[34] Based on this presupposition, an injured animal (or a sick plant) is something to be lamented even if it does not adversely affect the environment or the humans benefitting from it.

This is not to say that the freestanding value of living organisms makes them equally valuable to human beings. Living organisms can be sources of valid claims, but these claims need not be on par with those originating from human beings. Shifting from equality to fairness reflects precisely this distinction. That said, possessing *some* freestanding value justifies caring for these living organisms, and failing to do so raises legitimate concern. Hence, talk of the interests of non-human animals and plants is neither artificial nor incoherent. Instead, it reflects the recognition of these entities as (arguably) valuable.

Now consider "condition", which is the other metric of the substantive conception of tort law equality. It, too, can extend its normative implications beyond circumstances that adversely affect human beings. The extension mirrors the shift from human interests to interests

[28] For a detailed discussion, see Dorfman, *Conflict between Equals* (n 6).

[29] ibid.

[30] A straightforward illustration concerns the limited scope of the defense of an unoccupied farmhouse. See, e.g., *Katko v Briney* 183 NW2d 657, 657–58 (Iowa 1971).

[31] Consider, for example, the implication of inexperience and power imbalance on determining liability for false imprisonment by comparing *Black v Kroger* 527 SW2d 794 (Tex App–Houston [1st Dist.] 1975) with *Fojtik v Charter Med Corp* 985 SW2d 625, 630 (Tex Ct App 1999).

[32] Dorfman, *Conflict between Equals* (n 6).

[33] John Rawls, 'Justice as Fairness: Political not Metaphysical' (1985) 14 Philosophy & Public Affairs 223, 242.

[34] cf Martha C Nussbaum, *Justice for Animals: Our Collective Responsibility* (Simon & Schuster 2023).

of non-human living organisms. Just as non-human animals and plants are presumed to possess value, facing certain adverse conditions can undermine their existence and well-being as well. Accordingly, the concept of condition influences how we should relate not only to humans but also to other living organisms. Once again, the normative materials that shape the substantive conception of relational justice can extend from the ideal of human equality to illuminate how tort law should govern our interactions with non-human animals and plants. The task is guided by the principle of fairness.

Thus, the underlying commitment to equality in tort duties could be modified by appealing to the more abstract ideal of equality, namely, fairness. When tort duties cannot, and should not, take the form of relating as equals, they can, nonetheless, construct *fair* terms of interaction between a person and a non-human animal or plant. For these terms to count as fair, they should incorporate, and appropriately weigh, the interests and conditions of both the human duty-holder and the non-human duty-beneficiary, ensuring they conform to the demands of fairness. Shifting from relational justice to relational fairness, then, requires the development of a *fairness calculus* to articulate the content of the tort duties we owe to non-human living organisms.[35]

Although the goal of this chapter is to explore the possibility of tort duties to non-human animals and plants, it will be appropriate to identify, rather than pursue, what might follow if, as I argue, such duties are normatively consistent with, perhaps even warranted by, tort law's core commitment to equality. Thus, the next step is to consider how these duties could be determined. At this stage, the task of determination faces (at least) two questions. One is institutional, concerning whose responsibility it is to call these duties into law. The other is substantive, addressing what fairness requires and, in particular, what fairness-based tort duties entail. I take each in turn.

Casting tort duties to non-humans animals and plants into law depends on a prior question: Does it matter whether courts assume this responsibility, or should it fall to the legislature or another public body, such as an administrative agency? The conventional wisdom typically takes an instrumental approach. According to this view, the choice between these (and other) lawmaking institutions need not affect the substance of the duties we owe to non-human animals and plants. The most important question, in this perspective, is institutional competency—expertise, tradition, motivation, and other factors that determine which institution is best suited for the task.

As I argue elsewhere, by contrast, the choice of institution might matter in a non-instrumental sense.[36] This is because a lawmaking institution affects the normative status of the enacted duty. To see this, consider the difference between a legislature- and a judge-made duty against deliberately injuring a harmless animal. Although the duties can be semantically identical, they are qualitatively different. In particular, they carry different values. A statutory duty reflects what the majority of people currently demand, prefer, or judge to be just. Its normative status makes an essential reference to its acceptability by the people. In contrast, a judge-made duty is binding independently of our choices. Its normative status is (ideally) based on justice and—in the case of non-human animals and plants—fairness, rather than on what is deemed to be fair by our contemporary, contingent will.

[35] I defend substantive equality's egalitarian calculus in Dorfman, *Conflict between Equals* (n 6).

[36] Avihay Dorfman and Alon Harel, Constitutionalism and Majoritarianism Reconciled (unpublished manuscript); Avihay Dorfman and Alon Harel, *Reclaiming the Public* (CUP 2024) ch 3; Avihay Dorfman and Along Harel, 'The Necessity of Institutional Pluralism' (2023) 43 Oxford Journal of Legal Studies 753.

Thus, it is one thing to benefit from being owed a duty that reflects the actual choice of the people; quite another to benefit from a similarly worded duty that arises from fairness and is independent of any actual choice (other than the choice to recognise that a duty is obligatory, and that its obligatory nature does not stem from such choice). To be sure, I do not argue that legislatures are not committed to fairness or that their enactments only coincidentally meet the demands of fairness. Rather, the argument is that their resort to fairness is necessarily mediated by majoritarian will.

The distinction between statutory and judge-made tort duties is particularly consequential in the context of the fair treatment of non-human animals and plants. Benefiting from a statutory duty is doubly deficient. Not only are non-human animals and plants necessarily voiceless, but a statutory duty also reflects the voice of the majority, rather than what people should be duty-bound to respect in any case. Hence, a judge-made tort duty is normatively superior to a similar duty enacted by the legislature.[37] This does not mean that the legislature would have no role in systematising and refining tort duties to non-human animals and plants. Rather, it means that the legal *source* of the duty is the court.

Now, consider the substantive side of determining what fairness requires, specifically what fairness-based tort duties entail. Tort law can follow the example set by existing, human-centred tort duties. For instance, the current tort of harmful battery[38] could have a parallel tort for intentionally harming non-human animals and plants. Alternatively, tort law could adopt the civil law tradition of articulating general involuntary obligations. Unlike the common law's bottom-up, incremental creation of discrete torts, this tradition imposes general duties of care and concern. For instance, the current general tort duty in German tort law prohibits intentionally, negligently, or unlawfully injuring the "life, limb, health, freedom, property or some other right of another person".[39] A parallel tort duty towards non-human animals and plants could then follow a similar structure, though its content might differ substantially, particularly regarding the standards of wrongful behaviour and the rights requiring protection (for example, eliminating the appeal to property rights and revising what it means to have a right to freedom).[40] In practice, the general tort duty is subject to further refinement and contextualisation in light of real-life questions and changing circumstances. I will leave the comparison between the common law and the civil law methods of determining tort duties to non-human animals and plants for another occasion.

4. Rights of Action Put in the Right Context

Can there be tort duties to entities who lack the agency to pursue claims as plaintiffs against those who harm them? More generally, can tort law survive the disappearance of the victim's role as a holder of a right of action? I defend the view that standing, power, or even the right to pursue wrongdoers in court is not at the moral centre of tort law. In this view, lacking the requisite agency is beside tort law's point.

37 There is (at least) one downside, though—strictly speaking, the legislature can abolish common law rights and duties.

38 Battery is de facto, if not de jure, divided into harmful and offensive battery. Extending the former to other living organisms poses less intricate questions than in the case of the latter.

39 See German Civil Code (aka BGB), s 823(1).

40 Interestingly, the German Code notes that 'Animals are not things'. At the same time, however, it is said that 'The provisions that apply to things are to be applied accordingly to animals, unless otherwise provided'. ibid s 90a.

To set the scene, it is useful to situate my argument within the broader analytical framework of rights in the law of torts. In particular, it is helpful to distinguish between three types of rights.[41] There is the primary or substantive right, such as a right to bodily integrity, property, reputation, privacy, and so on. Then there is the secondary right, often referred to as right of repair. This right entitles holders of primary rights one or another form of remediation—such as redress or rectification—following the violation of their primary rights. Finally, there is the tertiary right, the right to seek an appropriate remediation. Rights of action are the most familiar instantiation of tertiary rights—to wit, they provide the legal mechanism by which victims of wrongs can pursue those who violated their primary rights.

Against this backdrop, I reject the essentialist view of the centrality of tort victims' rights of action. With some exceptions that do not obtain in the case of non-human animals and plants, rights of actions are only *instrumentally* valuable. To see this, consider the importance of the following question: Need we worry, or might we even wish, that this right be replaced with a better mechanism for redress? My answer is that save for two categories of cases I outline below, we should not worry and, depending on the alternative available, we might even welcome such a change.[42]

Let us begin with the two categories of cases in which victims' rights of action are non-instrumentally valuable. The first category picks out deliberate wrongdoing. It features an additional or parasitic dimension of wrongfulness triggered by the wrongdoer's illicit behaviour. For instance, someone who deliberately attacks an innocent victim is not only causing harm to the person of the victim but also intends, in the sense of *means*, this much. Unlike the case of inadvertently causing serious bodily harm, the deliberate wrongdoer also executes a plan to inflict harm. This planned action constitutes a second, parasitic wrong to the victim's *autonomy*. More specifically, by deliberately striking another person, the injurer wrongs the victim by undermining her autonomous being.

Notice that the setback to the victim is substantive, not superficial. It does not merely threaten to thwart this or that plan of the victim (such as crossing the street safely) but rather seeks to deny the victim the very status of an autonomous agent, one who is entitled to decide whether and what plans to make in the first place. Moreover, the setback to the victim's autonomous being also has an irreducibly relational dimension. This is because autonomy is not only a relationship between a person and their choices (or actions), but also a relationship between that person and others. Specifically, the significance of autonomy is partly defined by an interpersonal element—autonomy requires that *others* treat us in a certain way, namely, as self-determining agents who are entitled to write their own life stories. Deliberately striking an innocent person brings out the relational dimension of autonomy as it reflects the active rejection on the part of one person—the injurer—of the very idea that another person—the victim—is an autonomous being.

Against this backdrop, having the tertiary right to sue the deliberate wrongdoer, quite apart from the secondary right to material redress, might matter to the victim. This is because while material redress could be a fitting response to the physical injury the victim suffers, it does not fully address the setback to their autonomy. Simply put, redress without a right of action may leave the relational aspect of the victim's autonomy setback intact.[43]

[41] See John Gardner, *From Personal Life to Private Law* (OUP 2018) 213–14.

[42] The following discussion draws on Hanoch Dagan, Avihay Dorfman, and Issi Rosen-Zvi, 'It's (Not All) Personal: Civil Litigation and the Values of Rights of Action' 75 American University Law Review (forthcoming 2026) <https://papers.ssrn.com/sol3/papers.cfm?abstract_id=5045336> accessed 14 June 2025.

[43] The reason why awarding punitive damages may not be sufficient is that it does not require the injurer to treat and, so, to recognise the victim as an agent. Instead, the injurer is duty-bound to treat

A right of action, then, constructs terms of interaction under which victims are entitled to *reassert their autonomy* vis-à-vis their injurers. Thus, the right is not only a means to achieve material redress but is also valuable in itself, quite apart from whether it is the most effective legal mechanism to secure adequate material redress.

The second category of cases that calls for personal rights of action involves the impairment of a special relationship of a certain character. This category has a distinctive property: The wrongdoer not only harms the person or property of the victim but also disrupts the relationally equal terms of an ongoing interaction between them (say, a landlord/tenant or workplace relationship). This setback reflects the additional, parasitical wrong that constitutes what I call relational wrongdoing.

A secondary right to redress falls short of repairing the impaired relationship between the parties. While material redress may increase the likelihood of better enforcement of egalitarian terms of interaction in the future, it cannot set right the already damaged relationship. It leaves intact the victim's past subjection to inegalitarian terms of interaction.

To properly address her relational predicament, the victim should be able to *reassert her equal standing*, that is, her entitlement to have been treated as an equal by her injurer. Treating her as an equal means that the injurer should have exercised the quality and quantity of care considering the victim's vulnerability to being harmed. As with reasserting agency in relation to a deliberate wrongdoer, reasserting her equal standing begins with granting the victim the right to decide whether to sue the injurer. It further means that if she chooses to do so, the victim should have the right to confront her injurer under terms that reflect their equal standing. Suing, therefore, enables the victim not only to enforce her secondary right to repair but also to reassert her *equal standing* with respect to the defendant, with whom she stands in this special relationship.

The preceding discussion of deliberate and relational wrongdoings suggests that rights of action are *sometimes* non-instrumentally valuable, in which case fully and satisfactorily executed secondary rights of repair fall short of vindicating primary rights. The qualified language—sometimes, as opposed to "always" or even "typically"—is doubly important. First, contrary to influential rights-based accounts of tort law, such as civil recourse and the Toronto School of corrective justice, victims' rights of action do not capture the moral centre of tort law. To render more vividly this point, compare a case of a manufacturer of a defective product accidentally causing property damage to the product's user with a case of deliberate sexual harassment (which can easily amount to deliberate and/or relational wrongdoing). Is the right to seek material redress in a product liability case and the right to pursue a perpetrator in a sexual harassment case different applications of the same moral commitment? I think not as only in the latter case can the victim right of action matter in a *non*-instrumental way. By implication, rights of action in respect to many paradigmatic torts, including negligence, products liability, and nuisance, are merely means to secure the vindication or enforcement of victims' primary and secondary rights.

Second, and more importantly for the present purpose, the qualified case for victims' right of action has *no* bearing on the case for tort duties towards non-human animals and plants. Recall that the non-instrumental value of rights of action is grounded in the value of reasserting one's autonomy and equal standing in response to suffering deliberate and relational wrongdoings, respectively. As argued before, the case for tort duties towards non-human

the victim as a patient in the form of a payee who is entitled to receiving the injurer's money. Thus, the deliberate disregard of the victim's autonomy remains a going concern for the terms of interaction between the two even as the victim receives a hefty award of punitive damages.

animals and plants does not depend on extending the argument from either (human) autonomy or equality (or both) to non-human animals and plants. These duties need not make essential reference to (human) autonomy and equality. Therefore, the non-instrumental value of rights of action does not apply to victims in the category of non-human animals and plants.

By implication, the rights of action of these victims are, at best, of instrumental value only. They reflect one mechanism, among others, for enforcing or vindicating what really matters, namely, the primary rights of non-human animals and plants. To be sure, reducing the value of tort-law rights of action to an instrument in the service of primary and secondary rights does not imply that the choice between different enforcement (or vindication) mechanisms is straightforward or technical. Tort law and civil procedure law have introduced some such mechanisms—attorneys general in the case of public nuisance and class action and other forms of representative litigation in the case of civil procedure.[44] Other mechanisms can certainly suggest themselves, including in particular in response to the challenge of vindicating the primary rights of non-human animals and plants.[45] The important point to make at this stage, however, is that victims' rights of action do not stand in the way of imposing tort duties to protect non-human animals and plants.

5. Conclusion

Relational justice is a normative theory of private law within a liberal legal order. It places liberalism's commitment to self-determination and substantive equality at the moral centre of private law. As I have argued above, tort duties towards non-human animals and plants are not inconsistent with this commitment. In fact, they can present a welcome expansion of current tort duties in response to our convictions about both the value and urgency of holding private persons accountable for the life and well-being of our fellow living organisms.

The case for tort duties towards non-human animals and plants emphasises the important normative relationship between substantive equality and fairness. As I have argued, liberal-egalitarian duties create the opening for fairness-based duties. This relationship is a microcosm of a more fundamental question concerning humanism and, in particular, its relationship with the natural world.[46]

To begin with, relational justice, as a liberal theory of private law, is closely tied to the humanistic tradition. The question, then, is whether humanism is compatible with recognising non-human animals and plants as worthy of freestanding moral and legal consideration. This is not a descriptive or historical question, as different interpretations of humanism may either support or oppose viewing (some or all) non-human animals and plants as sources of concern and value in themselves. Instead, the question is normative—it asks whether the doctrine of humanism should extend its moral commitments beyond human beings to include other living organisms.

On this normative front, the basic challenge is to adjudicate between two approaches to humanism's place in moral space. According to one approach, humanism is a doctrine of exclusivity, that is, only human beings have intrinsic value and nothing else has value unless it is valuable *for* humans.[47] If humanism's appeal lies in this approach, then relational justice

[44] See Dagan and Dorfman (n 1) 217–19; Dagan, Dorfman, and Rosen-Zvi (n 42).

[45] cf Pablo Magaña, 'The Political Representation of Nonhuman Animals' (2022) 48 Social Theory & Practice 665.

[46] The following discussion emphasises one aspect of humanism—vis-à-vis the natural world—and sets to one side another, historically prominent aspect, which contrasts humanism with theism.

[47] See, e.g., Ted Benton, 'Humanism = Speciesism? Marx on Humans and Animals' (1988) 50 Radical Philosophy 4, 7.

cannot support the extension of tort duties to protect non-human animals and plants. That said, it is difficult to see what could substantiate this version of humanism's normativity, which can be characterised as anthropocentric in the pejorative sense.

The other approach, by contrast, substitutes exclusivity with distinctiveness. Humanism, in this view, does not entail species-centred arrogance towards other living organisms. Instead, it emphasises the distinctive values underlying human existence and the distinctive concerns that arise in connection with *human* relations (consisting of both human cooperation and human conflict). Accordingly, relational justice determines terms of tort law interactions for substantively free and equal persons. In doing so, its humanist aspirations leave ample normative space for considerations of relational fairness to determine what we owe to non-human animals and plants within the law of torts. Relational justice and relational fairness, therefore, do not represent a contrast, let alone a dichotomy; rather, the latter domain of relational duties supplements the former, bringing our private responsibility closer to the demands of right reason.

PART II

Law of Obligations

CHAPTER 5

Consumer Climate Contracts

ERIC W. ORTS

Consumers of the world, unite![1]

1. Introduction

ENVIRONMENTAL contracts exist in different forms and at different levels of law and society.[2] At the most abstract level, social contracts envision or imagine, often in the style of thought experiments, how governments and laws emerge through the exercise of rational will formation.[3] For Thomas Hobbes, no democratic volitional element is needed: The order provided by any government, including an absolutist monarchy or dictatorship, is better than the chaos of a "state of nature".[4] John Locke and Jean-Jacques Rousseau, among others, believed that respecting human rights and some representation of citizens in government are needed too.[5] Governments that overstep the boundaries of legitimacy by trampling on foundational rights or imposing laws without adequate popular representation justified rebellion or even revolution. The influence of Locke, Rousseau, and other philosophers of the Enlightenment paved the way for modern democratic republics, which began to appear in Europe and North America in the late eighteenth century.[6] Absolute monarchies were overthrown. New democratic forms

[1] cf Matthew Hilton, *Prosperity for All: Consumer Activism in an Era of Globalization* (Cornell University Press 2009) ch 4.

[2] Geoffrey C Hazard Jr and Eric W Orts, 'Environmental Contracts in the United States' in Eric W Orts and Kurt Deketelaere (eds), *Environmental Contracts: Comparative Approaches to Regulatory Innovation in the United States and Europe* (Kluwer Law International 2001); Eric W Orts, 'Climate Contracts' (2011) 29 Virginia Environmental Law Journal 197.

[3] I do not hold that social contract theories provide a complete philosophical foundation for morality and ethics. The 'triple theory' proposed by Derek Parfit is helpful along these lines. Parfit argues that social contract theories are consistent with deontological and consequentialist approaches. Derek Parfit, *On What Matters* (OUP 2011) vol 1, 411–19; vol 2, 244–59. From different philosophical perspectives, many readers may agree with Parfit's conclusion about the climate challenge: 'What now matters most is that we rich people give up some of our luxuries, ceasing to overheat the Earth's atmosphere, and taking care of this planet in other ways, so that it continues to support intelligent life.' Parfit, 419.

[4] Thomas Hobbes, *Leviathan* (first published 1651; Edwin Curley 1994).

[5] John Locke, *The Second Treatise of Government* (1690; Hackett Publishing reprint 1980); Jean-Jacques Rousseau, *On the Social Contract* (1762; Judith R Masters tr, St. Martin's Press 1978).

[6] For an account of the international impact of the American Revolution, see Jonathan Israel, *The Expanding Blaze: How the American Revolution Ignited the World, 1775–1848* (Princeton University Press 2017).

of government were established based on an ideal of popular consent.[7] Organised collectives of "the people" in nation-states declared they would rule themselves through law and constitutional government.[8]

Individuals under these new democratic governments were conceived as citizens rather than subjects, with expanding civic rights of participation to vote, run for office, and serve on juries or in government administration.[9] The American, English, and French Revolutions put various versions of democratic theories of a general social contract into practice.[10] The rise of a global political economy based on the authority and power of the rising democratic nation-states, which enabled and supported an expansion of business enterprises and economic markets, formed the framework of the post–World War II international legal order.[11] In this world order, more and more people began to live as individual citizens, as well as individual consumers, with legally enforceable rights and duties. It is possible that the world is at the cusp of devolving into one of "competitive authoritarianism" rather than an expanding global legal network led by democratic governments.[12] It is also still possible to avoid the fate of this "very dark place".[13]

In political theory and philosophy, conceptions of social contracts continue to be influential, especially in the reworking of basic principles by John Rawls and his imaginative "veil of ignorance" and "original position" thought exercises.[14] Similar reasoning has expanded to include the dependence of the human species on our natural environment in Michel Serres's ideal of a "natural contract"[15] and to encompass moral duties to what Christine Korsgaard calls our "fellow creatures" as well as ourselves.[16]

[7] There is a vast literature on political theories of consent. For a defense of consent as a basic democratic principle, see Ilya Somin, 'Revitalizing Consent' (2000) 23 Harvard Journal of Law and Public Policy 753.

[8] See Rogers M Smith, *Political Peoplehood: The Roles of Values, Interests, and Identities* (University of Chicago Press 2015). Relapses into autocracy and barbarism are of course still possible; see R G Collingwood, *The New Leviathan or Man, Society, Civilization and Barbarism* (1942; OUP reprint 1992).

[9] These political rights were of course originally restricted to property-owning self-designated 'white' men in European-based societies. The history of the world since the founding of these modern democratic nation-states can be told in part as a story of ever-expanding recognition of rights to include all people. For suggestions that the origin of a broadening of rights even to all adult white males followed an earlier assertion of rights of women, see Sophia Rosenfeld, *The Age of Choice: A History of Freedom in Modern Life* (Princeton University Press 2025); Wendy Steiner, *The Beauty of Choice: On Women, Art, and Freedom* (Yale University Press 2024).

[10] The Russian Revolution and its influence in sparking revolution in China and elsewhere had a different dynamic, though one reading of the communist and socialist theories that inspired these transformations emphasises the interests of individuals who are oppressed or alienated by extant political and economic systems. The main hitch in these ideologies has been that the 'dictatorship of the proletariat' imagined to be temporary turned out to have a permanence and a ferocity that were quite a bit greater than original theorists such as Karl Marx foresaw.

[11] See Tony Judt, *Postwar: A History of Europe Since 1945* (William Heinemann 2005). On the primacy of the political state with respect to business forms including corporations, see Taisu Zhang and John D Morley, 'The Modern State and the Rise of the Business Corporation' (2023) 132 Yale Law Journal 1970.

[12] Steven Levitsky and Lucan A Way, 'The Path to American Authoritarianism: What Comes After Democratic Breakdown' (*Foreign Affairs*, March/April 2025) 36–51.

[13] Hal Brands, 'The Renegade Order: How Trump Wields American Power' (*Foreign Affairs*, March/April 2025) 22–35.

[14] John Rawls, *A Theory of Justice* (rev edn, Harvard University Press 1999) ch 3; cf T M Scanlon, *What We Owe to Each Other* (Harvard University Press 1998).

[15] Michel Serres, *The Natural Contract* (Elizabeth MacArthur and William Paulson tr, University of Michigan Press 1995).

[16] Christine Korsgaard, *Fellow Creatures: Our Obligations to Other Animals* (OUP 2018).

Without pausing to defend one or more of these philosophical approaches, I extend the general idea of social and natural contracts into thinking about how the law operates at various levels of society. Consider "climate contracts" as an organising conception or metaphor.[17] If one overlays concern about the climate crisis onto a global legal map, there is an understandable tendency to assume that the scale of the problem requires a similarly comprehensive solution. This view has been particularly attractive to some economists who have argued that "putting a price on carbon" at the global level is the best or even the only effective approach to adopt.[18] Even if a comprehensive "price on carbon" would theoretically provide a first-best efficient economic solution to the climate crisis, it has proven politically impractical.[19] Other solutions need to be considered, including those that are less top-down (as in imposing carbon taxes from above) and more bottom-up (such as individuals organising to pursue climate-friendly lifestyles and exerting pressure on institutions and organisations to change). Note that top-down and bottom-up solutions are not mutually exclusive: They can be used together—and, given the scale and urgency of the climate emergency, they should.

2. Challenges to Public Climate Law and the Need for Private Law Alternatives

Even as the human global economy roars towards overwhelming the physical limits of our atmosphere, and even as the powers of our scientific knowledge now predict with near certainty the horrendous consequences of this trajectory, the software of our global governance system cannot be easily reprogrammed to stop the damage. Today, we have a system of nation-states loosely organised into an international legal and economic order. International public law may assist in addressing the climate crisis, but it is much too weak alone solve it.[20]

The Paris Agreement adopted in 2015 by 196 nation-states nevertheless represents a positive development at the international level.[21] Unlike previous international efforts, the Paris Agreement respects the fact that nation-states continue to hold the greatest power to move the needle towards climate solutions through legal reform, while recognising the anarchical nature of the global political order.[22] The key innovation is an intermediate approach which is both

[17] Orts, 'Climate Contracts' (n 2).

[18] See, e.g., Noah Kaufman, Michael Obeiter, and Eleanor Krause, *Putting a Price on Carbon: Reducing Emissions* (World Resources Institute 2016); Jeff Todd, 'The Economic Rhetoric of Carbon Pricing' (2025) 90 Brooklyn Law Review 421.

[19] A primary reason for failure is that most attempts to impose carbon taxes have been regressive, triggering popular outrage; see Simon Copland, 'Anti-Politics and Global Climate Inaction: The Case of the Australian Carbon Tax' (2019) 46 Critical Sociology 623; Daniel Driscoll, 'Populism and Carbon Tax Justice: The Yellow Vest Movement in France' (2023) 70 Social Problems 143.

[20] Weaknesses of comprehensive international public law solutions include: (1) too many people and too many countries; (2) economic competition among nation-states; (3) moral conflicts about the fairness and justice of who should bear the burdens of climate solutions; (4) a mismatch between short-term time horizons of individuals and long-term climate consequences; (5) inadequate institutional infrastructure for monitoring and enforcement; and (6) significant regulatory and economic 'leakage' among nation-states. Orts, 'Climate Contracts' (n 2) 207–14.

[21] Paris Agreement of 12 December 2015 to the UN Framework Convention on Climate Change, entered into force 4 November 2016.

[22] See Eric W Orts, 'The Paris Agreement Delivers a Champagne Moment' (*Regulatory Review*, 22 December 2015) <https://www.theregreview.org/2015/12/22/orts-the-paris-agreement-delivers-a-champagne-moment/> accessed 11 May 2025. On the anarchical nature of the global order, see Hedley Bull, *The Anarchical Society: A Study of Order in World Politics* (4th edn, Palgrave Macmillan 2012).

top-down and bottom-up. The Paris Agreement requires contracting nation-states to submit "nationally determined contribution" reports on climate action plans and their progress.[23] An "enhanced transparency framework" aims to assure the reliability of the national reports. This framework generates a "global stocktake" every five years to measure and assess progress towards global climate goals.[24] With respect to mitigation, the Paris Agreement sets targets to limit the average global temperature increase to "well below 2.0°C above pre-industrial levels" by 2030—and to use best efforts to limit this increase to 1.5°C.[25] Because greenhouse gas emissions would have had to peak by 2025 in order to hit the 1.5° target, and because emissions are instead continuing to increase, we have most likely already missed this interim goal.[26]

The return to power of President Donald Trump and his decision again to withdraw the US from the Paris Agreement is huge blow to climate progress. Nonparticipation by the US will likely cut greenhouse gas reductions accomplished under the Paris Agreement by more than one third.[27] Trump rejects the findings of climate science and calls the entire climate problem a "hoax".[28] This is foolhardy. The consequences of inaction, if not reversed, will almost certainly lead by the end of the century to the deaths of tens of millions of people from heatwaves, storms, flooding, droughts, and other disasters.[29] No US President since the nation's founding on Enlightenment-based principles has ever so thoroughly, ignorantly, and obstinately rejected scientific findings. One can only conclude that Trump and those backing him exemplify the saying of Upton Sinclair (slightly paraphrased): It is difficult to get someone to understand something when their salary—or their business model or political campaign—depends on their not understanding it.[30]

Indeed, to explain the re-election of Donald Trump one need only follow the fossil-fuel money. There are of course other explanations too, including the rise of white Christian nationalism and the fact that many everyday working Americans felt abandoned by Democrats as well as Republicans, but fossil-fuel interests played an outsized role. The industry contributed around US$445 million to Trump and other Republican candidates in the 2024 federal election.[31] This support corresponded to Trump's pitch to fossil-fuel executives to give him

[23] Paris Agreement (n 21) arts 3, 4.

[24] ibid arts 13, 14.

[25] ibid art 2.

[26] Paris Agreement (n 21); Emanuele Bevacqua, Carl-Friedrich Schleussner, and Jakob Zscheischler, 'A Year Above 1.5°C Signals That Earth Is Most Probably Within the 20-Year Period That Will Reach the Paris Agreement Limit' (2025) 15 Nature Climate Change 262; Mark Poynting, Erwan Rivault, and Becky Dale, '2024 First Year to Pass 1.5C Global Warming Limit' (*BBC News*, 9 January 2025) <https://www.bbc.com/news/articles/cd7575x8yq50> accessed 11 May 2025.

[27] Mario Larch and Joschka Wanner, 'The Consequences of Non-Participation in the Paris Agreement' (2024) 163 European Economic Review 104699.

[28] Mark Joyella, 'On Fox, Donald Trump Calls Climate Change a "Hoax": "In the 1920s They Were Talking About Global Freezing"' (*Forbes*, 21 March 2022) <https://www.forbes.com/sites/markjoyella/2022/03/21/on-fox-donald-trump-calls-climate-change-a-hoax-in-the-1920s-they-were-talking-about-global-freezing/> accessed 11 May 2025.

[29] Jorge Gastelumendi, 'The US Retreat on Climate Comes with Steep Costs for the Economy and the American People' (*New Atlanticist*, 21 January 2025) <https://www.atlanticcouncil.org/blogs/new-atlanticist/americans-will-pay-the-price-for-trumps-withdrawal-from-the-paris-agreement/> accessed 11 May 2025.

[30] Upton Sinclair, *I, Candidate for Governor: And How I Got Licked* (first published 1934, University of California Press 1994).

[31] Dharna Noor, 'Big Oil Spent $445m in Last Election Cycle to Influence Trump and Congress, Report Says' (*The Guardian*, 23 January 2025) <https://www.theguardian.com/us-news/2025/jan/23/big-oil-445m-trump-congress> accessed 11 May 2025.

large donations in return for regulatory rollbacks.[32] Other energy-intensive industries contributed heavily too, including those making big bets on generative artificial intelligence and cryptocurrency, both of which are huge energy hogs.[33]

Trump's campaigns in both 2016 and 2024 were also supported by Russia, a leading petrostate with long-standing connections to Trump.[34] Russia faces an existential economic risk when oil and gas are phased out in a global energy transition. Other petrostates such as China also stand to gain from a breakdown of the postwar liberal international order, so they ally with Russia and other illiberal regimes which will not rock the boat on fossil fuels.[35] Trump's global tariffs make sense when considered as part of a larger strategy to break the postwar legal order which has, sadly and ironically, been previously led by the US.[36]

In addition, the oil and gas industry in the US has a large interest in opposing the pro-climate policies promoted and adopted by Democrats, including President Barack Obama's leadership in the adoption of the Paris Agreement and President Joe Biden's passage of a large energy transition law.[37] Trump has made a priority for his administration to reverse all of Biden's regulatory accomplishments on climate policy.[38] The re-election of Trump and a

32 Ben Lefebvre, 'Trump Pressed Oil Executives to Give $1 Billion for His Campaign, People in Industry Say' (*Politico*, 9 May 2024) <https://www.politico.com/news/2024/05/09/trump-asks-oil-executives-campaign-finance-00157131> accessed 11 May 2025.

33 Raphael Hernandes, Lauren Aratani, and Will Craft, 'Revealed: The Tech Bosses Who Poured $394.1m into US Election—and How They Compared to Elon Musk' (*The Guardian*, 7 December 2024) <https://www.theguardian.com/us-news/2024/dec/07/campaign-spending-crypto-tech-influence> accessed 11 May 2025. Elon Musk contributed an unprecedented amount totaling more than a quarter of a billion dollars to the Trump and related Republican campaigns in 2024. He also purchased Twitter for US$44 billion, renamed it X, and politically weaponised it; see Kate Conger and Lauren Hirsch, 'Elon Musk Completes $44 Billion Deal to Own Twitter' (*New York Times*, 27 October 2022), <https://www.nytimes.com/2022/10/27/technology/elon-musk-twitter-deal-complete.html> accessed 11 May 2025.

34 American Constitution Society, 'Key Findings of the Mueller Report' <https://www.acslaw.org/projects/the-presidential-investigation-education-project/other-resources/key-findings-of-the-mueller-report/> accessed 11 May 2025; Huo Jingnan, 'Foreign Influence Efforts Reached a Fever Pitch During the 2024 Elections' (*NPR*, 12 November 2024) <https://www.npr.org/2024/11/09/nx-s1-5181965/2024-election-foreign-influence-russia-china-iran> accessed 11 May 2025. On Trump's Russian connections, see Larry Diamond, 'The Manchurian President' (*Substack*, 28 February 2025) <https://substack.com/inbox/post/158090379> accessed 11 May 2025.

35 China seems to be playing a double game. Recognising that it will suffer severe climate consequences, China is investing heavily in renewable energy, and at the same time it has become the leading source of greenhouse gas emissions in part through the continued building of new coal plants. See Ernest Lim, Chapter 18 of this handbook.

36 See Daisuke Wakabayashi and River Akira Davis, 'A Stunned World Reckons with Economic Fallout from Trump's Tariffs' (*New York Times*, 3 April 2025) <https://www.nytimes.com/2025/04/03/business/trump-tariffs-global-reaction.html> accessed 11 May 2025; Rachel Abrams, 'The Trump Tariffs Poised to Remake Global Trade' (*New York Times*, 3 April 2025) <https://www.nytimes.com/2025/04/03/podcasts/the-daily/trump-tariffs-global-trade.html> accessed 11 May 2025; William Kristol, 'It All Falls Apart' (*The Bulwark*, 4 April 2025) <https://www.thebulwark.com/p/lamps-going-out-around-us-trump-markets-nato-american-decline> accessed 11 May 2025.

37 Adam Vaughan, 'Obama's Clean Power Plan Hailed as US's Strongest Ever Climate Action' (*Our World*, 5 August 2015) <https://ourworld.unu.edu/en/obamas-clean-power-plan-hailed-as-uss-strongest-ever-climate-action> accessed 11 May 2025; Jim Tankersley, 'Biden's Climate Law is Reshaping Private Investment in the United States' (*New York Times*, 13 September 2023) <https://www.nytimes.com/2023/09/13/us/politics/biden-climate-law-investment.html> accessed 11 May 2025.

38 David Gelles and Maxine Joselow, '"Full on Fight Club": How Trump Is Crushing US Climate Policy' (*New York Times*, 2 March 2025) <https://www.nytimes.com/2025/03/02/climate/trump-us-climate-policy-changes.html> accessed 11 May 2025.

pro-Trump Republican Congress will therefore reverse progress made on climate policy in the US and inhibit climate progress internationally.

Given this bleak situation with respect to the rollback of public law solutions in the US and the abdication of US global climate leadership, combined with the continuing intrinsic weakness of public international law, the moment is ripe to revisit other alternatives along the spectrum of available climate contracts.[39] Progress remains possible in other countries, as well as at regional, state, and local levels in the US.[40] Private business firms may continue with pro-climate policies, though many in the US and elsewhere may downplay their efforts to avoid scrutiny and retribution from the anti-climate Trump.[41] It is likely that the political pendulum in the US and elsewhere will swing back towards pro-climate policies as more deadly heatwaves, monster storms, fierce wildfires, and epic floods bring increasingly bad news.[42] Yet a darker global political outcome is also possible. The postwar liberal order based on a framework of international law could break down, and we could enter into an illiberal authoritarian world of "climate leviathans".[43] In such a new Dark Age, competing authoritarian states would go to war over increasingly scarce energy, water, and food—with no global governance by which scientifically informed responses could be deployed effectively to stave off a climate apocalypse. The greenhouse emissions and physical destructiveness of the wars themselves would only accelerate the onset of a climate dystopia.[44]

3. Consumer Climate Contracts

Against this troubling background, one can look for solutions in some first principles about how the global legal order is constructed and how people can act to choose a more positive climate future. Individuals can act as citizens, at least in nation-states that continue to have

[39] Orts, 'Climate Contracts' (n 2).

[40] ibid 221–25; cf Heather K Gerken, 'Federalism as the New Nationalism: An Overview' (2014) 123 Yale Law Journal 1626.

[41] Orts, 'Climate Contracts' (n 2) 229–31. It would be helpful along these lines to revise corporate fiduciary duties to allow and perhaps mandate consideration of climate issues by business firms and institutional investors; see Eric W Orts, 'Is There Really a Fiduciary Duty to Destroy the Climate?' (*CLS Blue Sky Blog*, 17 March 2025) <https://clsbluesky.law.columbia.edu/2025/03/17/is-there-really-a-fiduciary-duty-to-destroy-the-climate/> accessed 11 May 2025. See also Seth Davis and Gregory Shaffer, Chapter 13 of this handbook.

[42] See Alec Tyson, Cary Funk, and Brian Kennedy, 'What the Data Says About Americans' Views of Climate Change' (*Pew Research Center*, 9 August 2023) <https://www.pewresearch.org/short-reads/2023/08/09/what-the-data-says-about-americans-views-of-climate-change/> accessed 11 May 2025; Sarah Wray, 'Climate Concerns Persist in 2025 But Faith in Government Action Wanes' (*Global Government Forum*, 1 August 2025) <https://www.globalgovernmentforum.com/climate-concerns-persist-in-2025-but-faith-in-government-action-wanes/> accessed 11 May 2025.

[43] See Geoff Mann and Joel Wainwright, *Climate Leviathan: A Political Theory of Our Planetary Future* (Verso 2018); cf Robert D Kaplan, *Waste Land: A World in Permanent Crisis* (Random House 2025); Richard Seymour, *Disaster Nationalism: The Downfall of Liberal Civilization* (Verso 2024).

[44] For fictional accounts of climate dystopias, see, e.g., Paolo Bacigalupi, *The Windup Girl* (Night Shade Books 2009); Omar El Akkad, *American War: A Novel* (Vintage 2021); Tochi Onyebuchi, *War Girls* (Razorbill 2019); Edward L Rubin, *The Heatstroke Line: A Cli-Fi Novel* (Sunbury Press 2015). For a classic vision, see Octavia E Butler, *The Parable of the Sower* (Four Walls Eight Windows 1993); *The Parable of the Talents* (Seven Stories Press 1998). For a hopeful version for the future that imagines solving the climate emissions problem by 2050, see Kim Stanley Robinson, *The Ministry for the Future* (Orbit 2020). For a darker but still optimistic view focusing on the power of youth movements, see Allegra Hyde, *Eleutheria* (Vintage 2022).

democratic institutions of political decision-making. Here, I focus instead on how individuals act as consumers and how they might cooperate to move towards more positive climate futures.[45]

The role of individual consumers merges into the role of citizens—so it makes sense to speak instead of *consumer-citizens* or *citizen-consumers*, and I will return to this distinction in a moment.[46] Suffice it to say now that individuals have the capacity to act in at least two important roles with respect to the climate: as citizens in political decision-making (such as in voting, joining campaigns, volunteering, and interacting with their elected representatives) and as consumers in the everyday practice of making purchases in markets and otherwise interacting with producer firms. Collaborative action by individuals can also cross the production-consumer divide through cooperative methods of collective organisation.

Considering the private economy in general terms, an initial observation is that markets are in principle and practice divided into sellers and buyers, supply and demand, producers and consumers. At the same time, governments play major economic roles as both sellers/producers (such as state-owned energy companies) and buyers/consumers (such as military contracts for fighter jets or aircraft carriers). The same goes for nonprofit organisations. Colleges and universities, for example, both supply services for a fee (tuition) and purchase goods, services, and information to support their teaching and research. To keep things tractable for analytical purposes, though, consider first only sellers and buyers acting in private producer-consumer markets.

In private markets, sellers are usually denominated as *firms* in economic and legal theory, and they can range from one-person sole proprietorships to massive multinational corporations with many subsidiaries.[47] In this sense firms are *producers*. Individuals who purchase their goods, services, or information are *consumers*.[48]

A complication is that business firms act as consumers too when they purchase from suppliers as part of their production process. In this connection, firms can also embrace a role of becoming climate-friendly consumers, and a leading example has been Walmart and its supply chain contracts requiring sustainability criteria as conditions of doing business.[49] Here, I focus instead on individual consumers, that is, all of us who constitute the general category

[45] This treatment expands on climate contracts at the level of everyday consumer transactions; see Orts, 'Climate Contracts' (n 2) 231–33.

[46] cf Douglas A Kysar, 'Preferences for Processes: The Process/Product Distinction and the Regulation of Consumer Choice' (2004) 118 Harvard Law Review 525.

[47] See Eric W Orts, *Business Persons: A Legal Theory of the Firm* (rev paperback edn, OUP 2015) ch 5.

[48] This distinction can also be understood in terms of 'production metamarkets' and 'consumption markets'; ibid 175–78; see also Adolf Berle, Introduction, in Adolf A Berle and Gardiner C Means, *The Modern Corporation and Private Property* (first published 1932, revised edn, Harcourt, Brace & World 1968) xxiii ('My thesis is that "property"is now divided into two categories: (1) consumption property on the one hand; and (2) productive property on the other—property devoted to production, manufacture, service or commerce, and designed to offer, for a price, goods or services to the public from which a holder expects to derive a return').

[49] See Michael P Vandenbergh and Patricia A Moore, 'Environmental Governance by Contract: The Growing Role of Supply Chain Contracting' (2022) 12 Michigan Journal of Environmental and Administrative Law 1; Michael P Vandenbergh, 'The New Wal-Mart Effect: The Role of Private Contracting in Global Governance' (2007) 54 UCLA Law Review 913. It is also possible that Walmart's sustainable supply chain practices are intended to distract from allegations of retrograde employment practices.

of "mass consumers" and play both consuming and producing roles in the complex, differentiated division of labour of our contemporary global civilisation.[50]

Some contemporary economists are unfortunately prone to oversimplify our world and reduce it to a sea of individuals who follow their own utility maximising preferences regardless of the role they play as producers or consumers. With respect to the climate, this perspective runs into trouble because "the economy" is conceived as a giant human system that runs autonomously according to the laws of supply and demand. The greenhouse gas emissions that cause atmospheric disruptions are seen as negative "externalities" to the economic system. The most effective and efficient solution from this economic perspective is to "internalise" the costs of this climate externality into the operating system of the economy. The problem of course is that this is much more easily said than done. "Putting a price on carbon" in this fashion requires a central (even imperial) policymaker to somehow stand outside of the economic system from which to assess and impose the correct "prices".[51] In other words, this economic perspective assumes a position of "regulating from nowhere".[52] The economic approach of methodological individualism runs aground on the complexity of the real-world institutions that organise economic and political relationships. Also, to characterise climate damage as an externality gives primacy to the self-operating internalities of the economic system. Flipping this metaphor makes the point more salient. We should arguably consider preserving the habitability of our planet as a primary and overriding concern, and if the global economic system poses a serious threat to the global climate that supports habitability, then it is the economic system that is posing an external problem. In other words, the economy is the externality that is causing severe disturbance to the more important and indeed essential physical self-regulating global ecosystem.

Returning to institutional reality, we can further divide *producers* into categories of owners and employees. In sociological, legal, and economic terms, owners and employees work together in formally organised agency relationships known as firms.[53] In other words, business firms (including state-owned companies) combine both capital and labour. One way to conceive of environmental problems, including the climate challenge, is to focus on the behaviour of producing firms. Traditional methods of so-called command-and-control such as the setting of pollution limits (either performance-based or technology-forcing) typically target the producers of the pollution, namely, business firms. Market-based regulatory approaches also

[50] On the history of mass consumption, see Lizabeth Cohen, *A Consumers' Republic: The Politics of Mass Consumption in Postwar America* (Knopf 2003). The distinction between consumers and producers can break down when ostensible 'consumers' contribute to the 'production' of what they consume. Social media applications, for example, blur this boundary to the extent that the labour of those interacting with various websites as 'consumers' translates into the 'production' of the website processes (i.e., when the website's firm captures the value of its consumer-produced information). A hybrid category of 'prosumption' can supplement, though not replace, the primary distinction between consumption and production; cf George Ritzer, 'Prosumer Capitalism' (2015) 56 Sociological Quarterly 413; cf Yochai Benkler, 'Coase's Penguin, or, Linux and the Nature of the Firm' (2002) 112 Yale Law Journal 369.

[51] For a critical perspective discussing how 'putting a price on carbon' is sometimes used in an unhelpful manner, see David Driesen, 'Putting a Price on Carbon: The Metaphor' (2014) 44 Environmental Law 695.

[52] Douglas A Kysar, *Regulating from Nowhere: Environmental Law and the Search for Objectivity* (Yale University Press 2010); cf Bruno Latour, *After Lockdown: A Metamorphosis* (Julie Rose tr, Polity 2021) ch 7.

[53] See Orts, *Business Persons* (n 47) ch 2.

usually focus on producers, such as in tradeable permit schemes designed to reduce acid rain or to reduce greenhouse gas emissions in particular economic sectors.[54]

Another regulatory approach focuses on the *individual consumers* who may want to include the climate-related qualities of a product or a service as a motivating factor in their decisions, in addition to factors such as price, quality, or fashion. A government may entirely preempt consumers from making any such decision or choice, such as by simply banning them from buying specific products (such as those that contain ozone-depleting chemicals),[55] or by encouraging or "nudging" behaviour by putting a tax or charge on products or services deemed harmful (the preferred method of economists).[56] In the climate context, for example, there is a good case for banning thermal coal energy.[57] Another example of a "green nudge" is to make solar energy a default option in a consumer's energy choice of a public utility.[58] Providing consumers with more and better climate-related information about products can empower them with greater capacity and choice in their decision-making and exercise of "consumers' sovereignty".[59] Although the "climate footprint" idea originated in a corporate campaign to shift feelings of responsibility to consumers rather than the producers of fossil fuels, reliable climate information of this kind can still serve a positive role.[60] This general legal approach goes by the name of "informational regulation".[61] Energy efficiency labels for cars or appliances, for example, may provide consumers with both economic and environmental information. The European Union is moving forward with directives requiring information to consumers relevant to the energy transition away from fossil fuels.[62] These directives will likely have a "Brussels effect" on all firms selling into the European market.[63] Informational

[54] For an overview of different regulatory approaches, see Sarah E Light and Eric W Orts, 'Parallels in Public and Private Environmental Governance' (2015) 5 Michigan Journal of Environmental and Administrative Law 1.

[55] See Frederike Albrecht and Charles F Parker, 'Healing the Ozone Layer: The Montreal Protocol and the Lessons and Limits of a Global Governance Success Story' in Mallory E Compton and Paul T Hart (eds), *Great Policy Successes: Or, A Tale About Why It's Amazing That Governments Get So Little Credit for Their Many Everyday and Extraordinary Achievements as Told by Sympathetic Observers Who Seek to Create Space for a Less Relentlessly Negative View of Our Pivotal Public Institutions* (OUP 2019).

[56] Cass R Sunstein and Richard H Thaler, *Nudge: The Final Edition* (Penguin Books 2021).

[57] Daria Shapovalova, 'Ban on Coal: Rationale and Legality for Restrictions on Coal Production, Sale, and Use' (2024) <http://dx.doi.org/10.2139/ssrn.5084001> accessed 11 May 2025.

[58] Rory Van Loo, 'The Public Stakes of Consumer Law: The Environment, the Economy, Health, Disinformation, and Beyond' (2023) 107 Minnesota Law Review 2039, 2054–55.

[59] W H Hutt, 'The Concept of Consumers' Sovereignty' (1940) 50 Economic Journal 66.

[60] On the corporate jujitsu, see Auden Schendler, *Terrible Beauty: Reckoning with Climate Complicity and Rediscovering our Soul* (Harvard Business Review Press 2025) 7.

[61] Paul R Kleindorfer and Eric W Orts, 'Informational Regulation of Environmental Risks' (1998) 18 Risk Analysis 155; Katherine Renshaw, 'Sounding Alarms: Does Informational Regulation Help or Hinder Environmentalism?' (2006) 14 NYU Environmental Law Journal 654; but cf Omri Ben-Shahar and Carl E Schneider, *More Than You Wanted to Know: The Failure of Mandated Disclosure* (Princeton University Press 2014); Katrina Fischer Kuh, 'Informational Regulation, the Environment, and the Public' (2022) 105 Marquette Law Review 603.

[62] See European Commission, 'New EU Rules to Empower Consumers for the Green Transition Enter into Force' (27 March 2024) <https://energy.ec.europa.eu/news/new-eu-rules-empower-consumers-green-transition-enter-force-2024-03-27_en> accessed 11 May 2025; European Parliament, Legislative Train Schedule, 'Empowering Consumers for the Green Transition' <https://www.europarl.europa.eu/legislative-train/theme-a-european-green-deal/file-consumers-in-the-green-transition> accessed 11 May 2025.

[63] cf Anu Bradford, *The Brussels Effect: How the European Union Rules the World* (OUP 2020).

regulation can also fight greenwashing by penalising firms who lie to or otherwise mislead consumers about the climate or other environmental benefits of their products or services.[64]

At the same time, informational regulation relies on the good faith of government. The Trump administration, for example, has forfeited any good faith in this context by rolling back climate-related informational regulation. In fact, it opposes *any* climate-related regulation, preferring to pretend there is no problem.[65] Also, different consumers have different political and personal priorities. Some may hold pro-climate values and perhaps be willing to pay a "green premium" for climate-friendly products, while others may not and prefer only to pay the lowest economic cost.[66]

Because of the ineffectiveness and often the absence of any reliable government-vetted informational regulation, consumers are left with good reason to doubt any pro-climate claims made by producing firms or governments. This raises questions about how pro-climate consumers might be able to cooperate, in the absence of recourse to government regulation, to advance their interests. As a substitute for unreliable government informational regulation or business firms' representations about the climate qualities of their products and services, which in the absence of reliable policing can easily fall into the category of greenwashing, consumers could cooperate among themselves to create and disseminate reliable, scientifically verified information.

Rather than consider the question of the role of consumers qua consumers, it is better in the climate context to conceive of consumers as involved at the same time in the role of citizens. Even if consumers act with no thought of the political or moral implications of their purchasing behaviour, their purchases nevertheless carry implicit political consequences. Acting as a passive, unthinking consumer or paying spectator cedes a significant amount of authority and power to business producers. Apathetic consumers simply reinforce the status quo. In addition, mass consumers of this kind put themselves in a vulnerable position—or are conditioned to be in a vulnerable position. Thoughtless and uninformed consumers leave themselves open to psychological manipulation or outright fraud.[67]

The recognition of the power of relatively concentrated producers, especially in large firms, compared with relatively dispersed individual consumers reveals that consumers are inevitably making choices that are consciously or unconsciously "political". When consumers make choices that do not take account of politics at all, they adopt an attitude that has been described as "reconcilement".[68]

[64] William S Laufer, 'Social Accountability and Corporate Greenwashing' (2003) 43 Journal of Business Ethics 253; Amanda Shanor and Sarah E Light, 'Greenwashing and the First Amendment' (2022) 122 Columbia Law Review 2033. See also Tiffanie Chan et al, Chapter 11 of this handbook.

[65] The Trump administration is scrubbing government websites of information related to 'climate'. Kiley Price, 'As Trump Administration Purges Climate Data and Web Pages, Research Groups Scramble to Save Information' (*Inside Climate News*, 4 February 2025) <https://insideclimatenews.org/news/04022025/todays-climate-trump-climate-data-purge-archive/> accessed 11 May 2025. No rational explanation for these actions has been provided. In the background lie raw economic self-interests and perhaps unspoken religious justifications or quasi-religious radical market-anarchy social theories.

[66] cf James Q Whitman, 'Consumerism Versus Producerism: A Study in Comparative Law' (2007) 117 Yale Law Journal 340, 347.

[67] This problem and many examples of it has kindled many consumer movements. Cohen, *A Consumers' Republic* (n 50); Hilton, *Prosperity for All* (n 1).

[68] Bernd Schmitt, J Joško Brakus, and Alessandro Biraglia, 'Consumption Ideology' (2022) 49 Journal of Consumer Research 74, 83, and fig 1.

Some individuals instead consume products or services addictively or otherwise harmfully to themselves or others. This attitude has been described as one of "alienation".[69] Unfortunately, there is significant evidence emerging that current consumption patterns on social media—and driven by social media—result in psychologically negative effects, including increased incidence of depression and even suicide among young adults.[70] More active and reflective attitudes towards consumption may lead to healthier psychological grounding for many people who are otherwise in the thrall of clever or addictive marketing practices.

From the point of view of the climate problem (and in favour of positive, conscious living in the world), more active consumer orientations are recommended: "engagement" and "activism".[71] A more robust politically oriented conception of the role of consumers would consider engaged or activist consumers to be either consumer-citizens or citizen-consumers. The difference between the two lies in the primary direction of a particular action, while being conscious of how one's individual behaviour may influence the wider world, even if only in a small way.

4. Consumers as Citizens, and Citizens as Consumers

A consumer-citizen makes a consumption decision, such as buying a sweater, but with some conscious thought about the political meaning and social consequences of the action. For example, the consumer might buy a sweater from Patagonia based on a perception of the company's reputation as an ethical sustainable company—or might reconsider the need to buy a sweater at all.[72] A consumer who simply buys a fast-fashion sweater following a purely aesthetic recommendation on TikTok, however, would not act as a consumer-citizen, caring only about self-interest and personal taste or even whim. This kind of consumer is either reconciled to the status quo or alienated from it. Note that algorithms such as those on TikTok and other social media, and the rise of social media "influencers" to provoke or encourage consumption, raise other questions about layers of potential manipulation and responsibility in contemporary consumer markets.[73]

Empirical surveys suggest that consumers in the US and elsewhere at least sometimes make decisions with climate and other environmental issues in mind. According to one study, 31% of consumers rewarded a company for a perceived positive climate reputation, and 21% punished companies with a perceived negative record.[74] The general point is that if there are in

[69] ibid.

[70] Rory Van Loo, 'Consumer Agents' (2025) 103 Washington University Law Review 705, 707–08.

[71] Schmitt, Brakus, and Alessandro, 'Consumption Ideology' (n 68) 83 and fig 1. In these terms, 'activism' is the stronger orientation with respect to climate issues in most circumstances.

[72] See Patagonia, 'Don't Buy This Jacket, Black Friday and the New York Times' (25 November 2011, updated 2022) <https://www.patagonia.com/stories/dont-buy-this-jacket-black-friday-and-the-new-york-times/story-18615.html> accessed 11 May 2025.

[73] Schmitt, Brakus, and Biraglia, 'Consumption Ideology' (n 68) 86–87 (discussing TikTok). For one philosophical approach, see Sophie Gibert, 'The Wrong of Wrongful Manipulation' (2023) 51 Philosophy & Public Affairs 333.

[74] Connie Roser-Renouf, Edward Maibach, and Anthony Leiserowitz, 'Consumer Activism on Global Warming' (*Yale Program on Climate Change Communication*, 2016) <https://climatecommunication.yale.edu/publications/consumer-activism-global-warming/> accessed 11 May 2025; Connie Roser-Renouf and others, 'The Consumer as Climate Activist' (2016) 10 International Journal of Communication 4759. Surveys of consumers, however, should be qualified by recognising that there is often a large difference between what people say and what they do.

fact a number of consumer-citizens who take the climate seriously in purchasing decisions, then they can collectively, if there are enough of them spending enough money, significantly affect the demand side of the producer-consumer equation. Consumer-facing producer firms would then have strong economic incentives to adopt pro-climate policies in their governance and their production and distribution methods to appeal to or retain climate-oriented consumer-citizens.

In a mass consumption society, the main hurdle for climate consumer-citizens is the collective action problem.[75] Individual consumers can follow a particular climate-friendly trend, such as traditional methods of brand identification (e.g., Patagonia), making a specific pro-climate purchasing decision (such as buying an electric car), or joining a pro-climate related boycott (such as Tesla when the wealthy owner flips politically to oppose climate laws). To make these trends stick, though, consumer organisation and coordination are needed. Otherwise, individuals following momentary and fleeting trends may feel good—what some theorists call "warm glow altruism"—but their collective actions will not have measurable large-scale, long-term effects.[76]

There is some evidence that this kind of climate consumer-citizen coordination is occurring or beginning to occur. *Consumer Reports*, for example, publishes a Guide to Sustainable Living which at least implicitly includes environmental sustainability considerations as a factor in providing independent ratings and labels for some consumer products.[77] *Consumer Reports* does not appear, however, to take an activist or even a strongly engaged approach on climate issues. A tension between a reconciling approach and an activist or engaged approach appears in the historical origins of Consumer Reports as an organisation.[78] In this historical context, Ralph Nader is the epitome of a leader taking an activist consumer approach, exemplifying another consumer-based strategy: private litigation.[79] Examples of consumer-focused climate litigation include cases brought (with mixed success so far) against airlines for false or deceptive claims about carbon offsets or carbon neutrality goals[80] and cases against companies for broad "Earth friendly" or similar environmentally related product claims.[81]

Other examples of organisations that provide independent information include LeafScore and Sustainability Tracker. LeafScore rates consumer products along environmental criteria, though the focus appears to be mainly product safety and health risks rather than climate.[82]

[75] Mancur Olson, *The Logic of Collective Action* (Harvard University Press 1971); see also Angela Kalhoff, *Climate Justice and Collective Action* (CUP 2021).

[76] See James Andreoni, 'Impure Altruism and Donations to Public Goods: A Theory of Warm-Glow Giving' (1990) 100 Economic Journal 464; Felix Oberholzer-Gee, 'Your Contribution Counts! An Empirical Analysis of the Decision to Support Solar Energy' in Orts and Deketelaere (eds), *Environmental Contracts* (n 2) ch 18; Patrick Hartmann and others, 'Warm Glow vs. Altruistic Values: How Important Is Intrinsic Emotional Reward in Proenvironmental Behavior?' (2017) 52 Journal of Environmental Psychology 43.

[77] Consumer Reports, 'Guide to Sustainable Living: Eco-Friendly Products and Simple Solutions for a Green Home' (updated 20 March 2025) <https://www.consumerreports.org/guide-to-sustainable-living-a9484645439/> accessed 11 May 2025.

[78] Hilton, *Prosperity for All* (n 1) ch 1.

[79] ibid chs 1, 6. Other examples of successful consumer activism have focused on labour standards and civil rights; see Kysar, 'Preferences for Processes' (n 46) 584–87.

[80] *Berrin v Delta Air Lines Inc*, slip op, 2024 WL 3304815 (CD Cal, 28 March 2024); *Zajac v United Airlines*, slip op, 2024 WL 3784535 (D Md, 13 August 2024).

[81] *Bush v Rust-Oleum Corp*, slip op, 2024 WL 422080 (ND Cal, 5 February 2024); but see *Dorris v Danone Waters of America*, slip op, 2024 WL 4792048 (SDNY, 14 November 2024).

[82] LeafScore, 'About LeafScore' <https://www.leafscore.com/> accessed 11 May 2025.

Sustainability Tracker also provides assessments and information about various brands, products, and services.[83] What seems still lacking is a coordinated, reliable consumer organisation focused on the climate dimension of consuming different products and services, which may, again, often mean *not* buying anything. One possibility is whether some major nonprofit environmental organisation such as Greenpeace or the Sierra Club, or a consortium of them, might provide this kind of climate consumer coordination.[84]

With respect to the role of the citizen-consumer, the direction of primary influence travels in the other direction. As a citizen who is also often a consumer, a citizen-consumer seeks to act politically in a manner that will enable improved consumer decision-making. For example, a citizen-consumer may wish to lobby for laws—or vote for candidates who support laws—to make environmental information more reliable.[85] Many consumers do not trust environmental or sustainability claims made by companies and for good reason: Greenwashing is rampant.[86] A citizen-consumer would not likely vote for anti-climate candidates such as Donald Trump, but there are many reasons that voters choose candidates.[87] In addition, citizen-consumers may want administrative agencies such as the Environmental Protection Agency and the Federal Trade Commission to rigorously police false or misleading advertising claims and marketing statements made by companies.[88] Another potential reform would permit bringing private lawsuits by citizen-consumers for "environmental fraud".[89]

Even in these examples, however, there is a sense in which consumers and citizens are acting at arm's length with respect to both the governments and economic producers. An individual consumer or citizen acting alone faces a huge collective action challenge. How can climate consumers organise to get more clout?

[83] Sustainability Tracker <https://www.sustainabilitytracker.com/> accessed 11 May 2025.

[84] In this sense, legacy environmental organisation could build on previous campaigns that have focused on 'selling' the view that certain parts of the natural environment, such as national parks, should not be sold or commodified; see Joseph Sax, *Mountains Without Handrails: Reflections on the National Parks* (University of Michigan Press 1980).

[85] For an example of an organisation that vets political candidates in US elections, see Give Green, <https://www.givegreen.com/> accessed 11 May 2025.

[86] Nancy Furlow, 'Greenwashing in the New Millennium' (2010) 10 Journal of Applied Business and Economics 22; Maneola Costa Policarpo and others, 'Social Cynicism, Greenwashing, and Trust in Green Clothing Brands' (2023) 47 International Journal of Consumer Studies 1950.

[87] Note that there is evidence that younger Trump voters believe that climate is an important issue for politicians to take seriously. Amelia Thomson-Deveaux, 'Trump Won More Young Voters, But Many Don't Agree with Him on Issues: AP VoteCast' (*Associated Press*, 15 November 2024) <https://apnews.com/article/trump-climate-change-immigration-tariffs-young-voters-e4bd29e491d42fd989c32be8eeb2a2cb> accessed 11 May 2025.

[88] On informational regulation of environmental marketing, see Wynn Heh, 'Who Certifies the Certifiers?' (2015) 16 Vermont Journal of Environmental Law 688; Ciara Peacock, 'Misleading Markets: Consumer Protection in the Age of Climate Washing' (2023) 126 West Virginia Law Review 367; Robin M Rotman, Chloe J Gossett, and Hope D Goldman, 'Greenwashing No More: The Case for Stronger Regulation of Environmental Marketing' (2020) 72 Administrative Law Review 417. For the most part, at least in the United States, this kind of regulation in the climate context does not appear to have been very effective. See Luca Enriques, Alessandro Romano, and Andrew F Tuch, 'Green Gatekeepers' (2024) 109 Minnesota Law Review 609.

[89] Eric W Orts, 'Conclusion: The Moral Responsibility of Firms: Past, Present, and Future' in Eric W Orts and N Craig Smith (eds), *The Moral Responsibility of Firms* (OUP 2017) 206–09; cf Patrick Reilly, 'False Claims, Real Climate Harm: How Whistleblowers Can Fight Fraud in the Renewable-Energy, REC, and Carbon-Offset Markets' (2023) 35 Georgetown Environmental Law Review 541.

5. Empowering Pro-Climate Consumers

So far, I have discussed the following three possibilities for climate consumer collective action.

1. *Consumer-produced climate information.* In response to government failure to do so, consumers may self-organise to create and disseminate reliable climate information about products and services, keeping in mind that often the best climate decision is not to buy. Key to preserving reliability is scientific verifiability and avoiding conflicts of interest. Again, nonprofit environmental organisations might expand to provide this kind of consumer-oriented climate information.[90] Internet technologies should reduce the costs of dissemination of this kind of climate consumer information, though the difficulty of sifting out false or misleading information promoted by others will remain.
2. *Consumer lawsuits.* Consumers can organise through bringing lawsuits, privately and sometimes by class actions, or through public representatives such as state attorneys general.[91] Direct consumer lawsuits have been mentioned above. Cases brought by state attorneys general may also be brought on behalf of consumers for misleading climate claims.[92]
3. *Procurement policies.* Governments and other nonprofit organisations can affect pro-climate market demand because they are large consumers of products and services. In this role of procurement, governments can encourage and even mandate climate-friendly purchasing standards.[93] In the US for example, the federal government has at least in the past played a very large climate-friendly procurement role.[94] Although a second Trump administration will likely put a brake on this development at the federal level, state governments and municipalities—as well as business firms—may continue to use their procurement decisions, such as for renewable energy, to incentivise pro-climate markets. Pennsylvania, for example, requires that "green options" must be considered in procurement decisions to "encourage[] the production and sale of affordable,

[90] Nonprofit environmental organisations could also themselves be assessed on this score, that is, who provides the best climate information about companies and their products and services?

[91] See Lisa Benjamin and Alexandra Guillot, *Global Perspectives on Corporate Climate Legal Tactics: United States of America National Report* (British Institute of International and Comparative Law, February 2024) <https://www.biicl.org/documents/12175_global_perspectives_on_corporate_climate_legal_tactics_-_usa_national_report_v1.pdf> accessed 11 May 2025; see also Van Loo, 'The Public Stakes of Consumer Law' (n 58).

[92] See *Massachusetts v Exxon Mobil Corp*, 462 F Supp 3d 31 (D Mass, 2020); *People of the State of California v Southern California Gas Co* (Cal Super Ct, 19 October 2023); *State of Vermont v Exxon Mobil Corp* (Vermont Super Ct, 2024).

[93] See Sarah E Light and Eric W Orts, 'Public and Private Procurement in Environmental Governance' in Michael Faure (ed), *Elgar Encyclopedia of Environmental Law, Volume VIII: Instruments for Environmental Policy* (Edward Elgar Publishing 2020) 2022–32; Light and Orts, 'Parallels in Public and Private Environmental Governance' (n 54) 13 tbl 1, 46–50.

[94] For a compilation of federal procurement criteria for sustainable purchasing that was at least not yet taken down from the web as of this writing, see US General Services Administration, *General Procurement Compilation* <https://www.gsa.gov/governmentwide-initiatives/federal-highperformance-buildings/resource-library/sustainable-acquisition/green-procurement-compilation> accessed 11 May 2025.

environmentally-friendly and health conscious products".[95] Other states have followed suit in adopting pro-sustainability procurement policies.[96]

4. *Consumer climate cooperatives.* A fourth possibility is to revitalise consumer cooperatives to focus on the climate problem.

6. Climate Cooperatives

Cooperatives have a long history,[97] and the time is perhaps ripe to consider this form of organisation as a possible climate solution given that the United Nations has named 2025 the Year of Cooperatives, following up on a similar designation in 2012.[98]

Cooperatives come in a wide variety of forms organised for different purposes, and they straddle the producer-consumer divide. Some cooperatives are *producer cooperatives*, that is, essentially a kind of firm. They are "cooperative" in terms of their internal organisation, usually including employees as equity owners with rights of not only a share of profits of the enterprise but also a share of control through democratic decision processes. The International Cooperative Alliance claims that there are three million cooperatives worldwide providing for as much as 10% of total global employment.[99] These are largely producer cooperatives such as those organised in rural agricultural settings. A typical example might be a farming cooperative: owned and governed by a small local group of farmers who sell their produce in the market and then share profits and losses. There are also industrial-scale producer cooperatives, but they are not widespread.[100]

Consumer cooperatives are organised primarily on the other side of the producer-consumer divide. Take the consumption of food, for example. Consumer cooperatives organise purchasers of food to economise on costs and to increase leverage on price, such as having the power to make wholesale purchases and then split savings with "members" rather than paying a private intermediary, such as a for-profit grocery store, retail prices.[101] Housing can also be

[95] Commonwealth of Pennsylvania, *Green Procurement* <https://www.pa.gov/agencies/dgs/programs-and-services/materials-and-services-procurement/green-procurement.html> accessed 11 May 2025.

[96] National Association of State Procurement Officials, *Sustainable Purchasing* <https://www.naspo.org/research-and-innovation/sustainable-purchasing/by-state/> accessed 11 May 2025.

[97] For a source providing wide geographical scope, see Mary Hilson, Silke Neunsinger, and Greg Patmore (eds), *A Global History of Consumer Co-operation since 1850: Movements and Businesses* (Brill 2017). See also Jonathan Michie, Joseph E Blasi, and Carlo Borzaga (eds), *The Oxford Handbook of Mutual, Cooperative, and Co-Owned Business* (OUP 2017).

[98] United Nations, *Year of Cooperatives* <https://2025.coop/> accessed 11 May 2025; United Nations, *International Year of Cooperatives 2012* <https://social.un.org/coopsyear/> accessed 18 July 2025.

[99] International Cooperative Alliance, 'Facts and Figures' <https://ica.coop/en/cooperatives/facts-and-figures> accessed 11 May 2025.

[100] Producer cooperatives often face difficulty in terms of competition in various producer and consumer markets due to various challenges in terms of economies of scale and scope, as well as the economic efficiency of internal organisation. For a standard account of the economic difficulties faced by many producer cooperatives, see Henry Hansmann, *The Ownership of Enterprise* (Harvard University Press 2000). See also Henry Hansmann, 'When Does Worker Ownership Work? ESOPS, Law Firms, Codetermination, and Economic Democracy' (1990) 99 Yale Law Journal 1749. An interesting exception appears in the city-sized industrial cooperatives of Mondragón. See Xabier Barandiaran and Javier Lezaun, 'The Mondragón Experience' in Michie, Blasi, and Borzaga, *The Oxford Handbook of Mutual, Cooperative, and Co-Owned Business* (n 97) 279–94.

[101] There is a consumer cooperative in my neighborhood of West Philadelphia organised along these lines. See West Philadelphia Mariposa Food Co-op <https://mariposa.coop/> accessed 11 May 2025.

organised in a cooperative. Oberlin College, for example, has long offered a student housing option of "co-ops" rather than cafeteria-style dining halls. In an Oberlin co-op, students join as members who live together (usually in a large house) and cook their own food together. They act cooperatively as an economic household. The Oberlin Student Cooperative Association provides an organising centre for the household co-ops and acts as a consumer cooperative by the joint sourcing of food and beverages from outside providers.[102]

Consumer cooperatives provide another pathway by which individual consumers could organise their purchasing power in a pro-climate direction. They could, for example, purchase only products and services that are certified in some way as "climate friendly". They could also participate in boycotts of companies or products that are in some sense anti-climate. The spontaneous mass boycott of Tesla and the protests organised against the company's dealerships as an expression of disapproval and opposition to the alliance of its principal owner Elon Musk with the anti-climate Trump provides one example that could be generalised and made more powerful through cooperative organisation.[103] One might imagine large organised boycotts not only of Tesla but other firms that support Trump and his administration's anti-climate policies, such as Amazon, Google, and Facebook, the CEOs of which stood shoulder-to-shoulder with Trump at his inauguration.[104]

Cooperatives can also provide an example of a form of organisation that combines elements of both production and consumption. Some scholars call this "prosumption", an awkward term.[105] Better might be *hybrid producer-consumer cooperatives* or simply *hybrid cooperatives*.[106] Large cooperative grocery stores provide one example. A cooperative grocery store can act as a consumer in the sense that it makes contracts for supplies of food and beverage products from producer firms. At the same time, it adopts an internal organisation as a producer of the retail service of sharing and distributing groceries to its members and in retail sales to the public.

Local renewable energy cooperatives could provide another climate solution that could be scalable in terms of replication and connections to the larger electric energy grid. For example, a local cooperative could organise solar power generation and collection, and then both share

[102] Oberlin Student Cooperative Association <https://www.oberlin.edu/housing/options/osca> accessed 11 May 2025.

[103] Bernard Condon, 'Tesla Sales Tumble 13% as Musk Backlash, Competition and Aging Lineup Turn Off Buyers' (*Associated Press*, 2 April 2025) <https://apnews.com/article/tesla-deliveries-trump-musk-protests-boycott-67da667cd1267789fecf68376f2b5d14> accessed 17 June 2025.

[104] Ali Swenson, 'Trump, a Populist President, Is Flanked by Tech Billionaires at His Inauguration' (*Associated Press*, 20 January 2025) <https://apnews.com/article/trump-inauguration-tech-billionaires-zuckerberg-musk-wealth-0896bfc3f50d941d62cebc3074267ecd> accessed 11 May 2025.

[105] See Ritzer (n 50). For the origin or at least an early use of the term 'prosumption', see Alvin Toffler, *The Third Wave* (Bantam Books 1980).

[106] Loren Rodgers, 'Hybrid Cooperatives Challenges and Advantages' *National Center for Employee Ownership* (30 January 2008) <https://www.smu.ca/webfiles/HybridCooperatives.pdf> accessed 11 May 2025. Another term used is 'multi-stakeholder cooperatives'; ibid; see also Margaret Lund and Sonja Novkovic, 'Multi-Stakeholder Cooperatives' in Mathew Elliot and Michael Bolds (eds), *Handbook of Research on Cooperatives and Mutuals* (Edward Elgar Publishing 2023) 531–48; USDN, *Sustainable Consumption Toolkit, Multi-Stakeholder Cooperatives* <https://sustainableconsumption.usdn.org/initiatives-list/multi-stakeholder-cooperatives> accessed 11 May 2025. For reasons analogous to why the term 'stakeholders' is problematic in theories of business ethics, this term is too vague and imprecise to be useful. For critical assessment in business ethics, see Eric W Orts and Alan Strudler, 'The Ethical and Environmental Limits of Stakeholder Theory' (2002) 12 Business Ethics Quarterly 215; Eric W Orts and Alan Strudler, 'Putting a Stake in Stakeholder Theory' (2009) 88 Journal of Business Ethics 605.

this power acting as a consumer cooperative with its members and then sell any excess power to either other nonmember households in the community or back into the larger grid.[107] In Germany, energy cooperatives have been advanced through legislation.[108]

In the climate context, then, one can imagine cooperative coordination of various kinds. Climate cooperatives can produce reliable climate-related information to inform purchasing decisions. They can promote education about climate science and the connection between the global climate and everyday consumer choices. They can bring consumer-based lawsuits. They can organise consumer boycotts. And they can act politically in terms of favouring pro-climate candidates and pro-climate legislation. Climate cooperatives of different kinds could then help to provide the organisation needed to force government and business to take the climate emergency seriously.[109]

Wendell Berry observes that "[t]he global economy institutionalizes a global ignorance, in which producers and consumers cannot know or care about one another, and in which the histories of all products will be lost".[110] Reviving cooperative methods of organisation may help to reverse this loss of knowledge with greater awareness about everyday choices in markets.

7. Conclusion

Humanity needs to work all available levers in its toolbox to confront the run-away climate crisis.[111] So far, the emergency brake has been elusive. The problem is not primarily technical or scientific: Humanity has the means to address and solve the climate problem.[112] The problem is mainly political, economic, and legal.

[107] See Seikatsu Club Consumers' Co-operative Union, *A Guide to the Seikatsu Club Group* (2024) <https://seikatsuclub.coop/excludes/rengou/img/about/coop/group2024e.pdf> accessed 11 May 2025. See also Rafael Leal-Arcas and Antonio Morelli, 'The Resilience of the Paris Agreement: Negotiating and Implementing the Climate Regime' (2018) 31 Georgetown Environmental Law Review 1, 30, 60.

[108] See Markus Hanisch, 'Co-operatives and the Transformation of the German Energy Sector' in Michie, Blasi, and Borzaga, *The Oxford Handbook of Mutual, Cooperative, and Co-Owned Business* (n 97) 321–34; Nils Hellmuth and Eva-Maria Jakobs, 'Energy Cooperatives as Energy Transition Actors' (2023) 94 Human Factors in Software and Systems Engineering 166.

[109] Cooperatives are more popular in some countries rather than others. One variable might lie in whether and how cooperative methods of organisation are encouraged or provided for legally. See European Community of Consumer Cooperatives, 'Climate Change and Consumer Co-operatives: Taking the Challenge Forward' (2012); International Cooperative Alliance, *Blue Skies Above: An Anthology of Consumer Co-operatives in Protecting Environment* (1997); Carolin Schröder and Heike Walk, 'Co-operatives and Climate Protection: Housing Co-operatives in Germany' in Anthony Webster, Linda Shaw, and Rachael Vorberg-Rugh (eds), *Mainstreaming Co-operation: An Alternative for the Twenty-First Century?* (Manchester University Press 2016) 201–20); Sustainability Solutions Group, *A Co-operative Solution to Climate Change* (2014) <https://www.ssg.coop/wp-content/uploads/2015/03/141205_Co-ops-and-climate-change_v4.pdf > accessed 11 May 2025. The origins of modern cooperatives seem to have their deepest roots in Germany and in the United Kingdom. See Mary Hilson, Silke Neunsinger, and Greg Patmore (eds), *A Global History of Consumer Co-operation since 1850: Movements and Businesses* (Brill 2017).

[110] Wendell Berry, 'The Whole Horse' in Norman Wirzba (ed), *The Art of the Common-Place: The Agrarian Essays of Wendell Berry* (Counterpoint 2002) 236, 244, quoted in Kysar, 'Preferences for Processes' (n 46) 536.

[111] See Wake Smith, *Pandora's Toolbox: The Hopes and Hazards of Climate Intervention* (CUP 2022).

[112] ibid; Mark Z Jacobson, *No Miracles Needed: How Today's Technology Can Save Our Climate and Clean Our Air* (CUP 2023); Michael Lenox and Rebecca Duff, *The Decarbonization Imperative: Transforming the Global Economy by 2050* (Stanford University Press 2021).

Although the Paris Agreement represents an improvement at the global level, recent events among nation-states—including so-called great powers that are also petrostates such as the US, Russia, and China—show a radical backsliding into economic competition and boosting of the fossil-fuel industry that will, if unchecked, throw the Earth far above the 2.0°C limit above which catastrophic consequences are almost certain to occur for humanity and Earth's biodiversity. Our civilisation with an out-of-control, fossil-fueled economic system is verging on the suicidal.

Here, I have sketched out one response at the opposite end of the climate contracts spectrum from international legal regulation. Individual people in their everyday lives make daily decisions that impact the climate in their patterns and practices of consumption. It is naïve to think that any individual climate-friendly action makes a big difference if it is not collectively organised in some fashion to have a larger impact. But collective action problems can be overcome. At least in democratic nation-states, individuals can get involved in politics and promote pro-climate candidates and issues: They can vote the climate. Even in less democratic countries, citizens as consumers can get involved. There is a great deal of opacity and intentional ignorance in the business processes of production of goods and services related to the use of greenhouse gases and other attributes important to climate damage.[113] However, these informational hurdles can be cleared, as examples of climate-focused cooperatives and nonprofit organisations demonstrate. As individuals, we can act as both pro-climate consumer-citizens and citizen-consumers in our everyday lives and activities.

There are good reasons to doubt whether humanity can avoid entering a Dark Age of climate apocalypse and civilisational decline.[114] However, there remains constructive hope that we can still act soon enough as citizens and consumers to avoid the worst climate outcomes and preserve a temperate home planet for our collective future.[115]

[113] cf Kysar, 'Preferences for Processes' (n 46).

[114] See Dale Jamieson, *Reason in a Dark Time: Why the Struggle Against Climate Change Failed—and What It Means for Our Future* (OUP 2014).

[115] cf Loren Goldman, *The Principle of Political Hope: Progress, Action, and Democracy in Modern Thought* (OUP 2022).

CHAPTER 6

Contract Law

IRINA SAKHAROVA

1. Introduction

WHILE climate change has traditionally been seen as a "public law problem",[1] there has also been a growing body of literature exploring both how climate change could affect private law and how private law could be deployed to help tackle challenges posed by climate change. Both questions—which entail an examination of existing private law doctrines, as well as pondering their actual and potential evolution[2]—have been approached from a general private law perspective and from the perspective of specific branches of private law, most notably, tort law. Such studies have explored both the potential and limitations of private law as a tool to address issues related to climate change.[3] Contract law, which could be said, at least in some sense, to be "most private" within private law, is said to have at least initially been overlooked[4] but has increasingly been coming into focus, in particular, in relation to some types of contract.[5]

As with private law more generally, similar questions arise in relation to contract law. First, there is a question about the extent to which contract law, as well as the practice of contracting, has been or may be affected by climate change. A prominent example is the concept of foreseeability, which transcends private law[6] and which is particularly relevant in contract law in the context of frustration and force majeure clauses, both of which have been examined by

[1] 'Not surprisingly', as some have emphasised: See Jim Rossi and J B Ruhl, 'Adapting Private Law for Climate Change Adaptation' (2023) 76(3) Vanderbilt Law Review 827, 830.

[2] Climate change has been conceptualised as 'legally disruptive in that it requires lawyers and legal scholars to reconcile the legal issues raised by climate change with existing legal orders'. Elizabeth Fisher, Eloise Scotford, and Emily Barritt, 'The Legally Disruptive Nature of Climate Change' (2017) 80 Modern Law Review 173, 173.

[3] See, e.g., Douglas A Kysar, 'The Public Life of Private Law: Tort Law as a Risk Regulation Mechanism' (2018) 9(1) European Journal of Risk Regulation 48; Douglas A Kysar, 'What Climate Change Can Do About Tort Law' (2011) 41(1) Environmental Law 1.

[4] See, e.g., Kateřina Peterková Mitkidis, 'Using Private Contracts for Climate Change Mitigation' (2014) 2(1) Groningen Journal of International Law 54, 67–69; Pia Rebelo, *Green Shipping Contracts: A Contract Governance Approach to Achieving Decarbonisation in the Shipping Sector* (Hart 2024), 19–24.

[5] Most notably, supply chain contracts, which are not a specific focus of this chapter, have been examined from various perspectives. For a private law analysis, see, e.g., Kateřina Peterková Mitkidis, 'Sustainability Clauses in International Supply Chain Contracts: Regulation, Enforceability and Effects of Ethical Requirements' (2014) 1 Nordic Journal of Commercial Law 1.

[6] See Rossi and Ruhl (n 1) 828 (observing that '[t]he principle of foreseeability—central to numerous doctrines . . . across tort, property, and contract law—is likely to face some of the strongest pushback as we confront climate adaptation' and proposing the "foreseeability of nonstationarity" principle while evaluating "what that might mean for some core private law doctrines" '). See also ibid 863–71, 879–90.

scholars.[7] Secondly, there is a question about the extent to which contract law could be deployed to respond to challenges posed by climate change. As with other branches of private law, addressing this question entails examining how suitable contract law is for dealing with issues arising in the context of climate change and, relatedly, whether, and if so how, contract law rules could and should change and develop. However, one difference between contract law and the rest of the law of obligations is that contract law, first and foremost, provides a legal framework for *voluntarily* undertaking obligations. In doing so, contract law both facilitates the undertaking of obligations (including by default rules) and sets limits on which and how *enforceable* obligations can be undertaken (including through mandatory rules). An interesting question, which is unique to contract law, is therefore whether the voluntary nature of contractual obligations might alleviate or indeed exacerbate some of the difficulties associated with a private law response to challenges posed by climate change.

It can be, and has been, asked: "Why do governments not simply oblige companies to include sustainability clauses in all their business contracts?"[8] Radical as it may sound, mandatory rules, which have traditionally been kept to a minimum in contract law, have been taking up more and more space, governing terms of even such paradigmatic contracts as contracts for sale, even between business parties, but also, and more extensively, consumer contracts, or (moving even further from what has typically been seen as the core of contract law) employment contracts. Such rules are often designed to protect parties with a weaker bargaining position, but certain types of contract can also be affected by mandatory rules applicable to activities mediated by such contracts (such as construction contracts), and indeed more and more environmental law rules have become relevant to the practice of contracting.[9] Questions that might arise about introducing in contract law any mandatory rules related to climate change are, in many ways, like questions that have been debated about other mandatory rules in contract law, as well as in private law more generally. At a more practical level, there is a question of such rules' positive or negative effect on the practice of contracting, including on incentives or disincentives to enter into specific types of contract or contracts with specific parties. At a more theoretical level, there is the perennial debate about the divide between private law and public law,[10] including a question of the extent to which the proliferation of mandatory rules is inimical to the very nature of private law. Regardless of the answers, this

[7] See, e.g., Myanna Dellinger, 'An "Act of God"? Rethinking Contractual Impracticability in An Era of Anthropogenic Climate Change' (2016) 67 Hastings Law Journal 1551; Jocelyn L Knoll and Shannon L Bjorklund, 'Force Majeure and Climate Change: What is the New Normal?' (2014) 8(1) American College of Construction Lawyers Journal 29; Jessica R Murfree and Anita M Moorman, 'An Examination and Analysis of Division I Football Game Contracts: Legal Implications of Game Cancellations due to Hurricanes' (2021) 31 Journal of Legal Aspects of Sport 123; Geoffrey F Palachuk, 'The New Decade of Construction Contracts: Technological and Climate Considerations for Owners, Designers, and Builders' (2020) 11(1) Seattle Journal of Technology, Environmental & Innovation Law 171.

[8] Mitkidis, 'Sustainability Clauses' (n 5) 5. Sustainability clauses are typically understood as covering 'a broad range of clauses that implement minimum social and/or environmental standards' (Rebelo (n 4) 21). It has also been emphasised that sustainability clauses 'cover social and environmental issues which are not directly connected to the subject matter of the specific contract'. See Mitkidis, 'Sustainability Clauses' (n 5) 5. Reducing emissions in the production process would be one example, while avoiding child labour would be another.

[9] For an example of how mandatory rules related to climate change can affect freedom of contract, see Gonzalo Vial Fourcade, 'The Relevance of Climate Change to Contract Law' (2023) 16(1) Mexican Law Review 3, 20.

[10] For a critical discussion of such a divide, see, e.g., Thomas W Merrill, 'Private and Public Law' in Andrew S Gold and others (eds), *The Oxford Handbook of the New Private Law* (OUP 2020) 575.

question comes into sharp focus in contract law precisely because of the voluntariness that has traditionally been seen as the hallmark of the practice of contracting.

More interestingly, it can be asked if the practice of contracting itself might offer a tool to address issues related to climate change regardless of any relevant mandatory rules in contract law. After all, it seems that contracting parties always can, if they choose, voluntarily undertake climate obligations, such as commitments related to reducing emissions. In this respect, voluntariness associated with the practice of contracting can be seen both as a curse and as a blessing. On the one hand, contracting parties can, but in the absence of any relevant mandatory rules do not have to, choose to undertake climate obligations (and even if contracting parties do, they then can, but do not have to, enforce such obligations if they are not complied with voluntarily), suggesting that as a tool to address issues related to climate change such climate obligations are in contracting parties' complete discretion. On the other hand, if contracting parties do choose to undertake climate obligations, they can commit to more than might otherwise be required by any relevant mandatory rules (and there is, at the very least, always somebody, that is, one party, with the power to enforce the other party's climate obligations if they are not complied with voluntarily), suggesting that if opted for, such climate obligations might have advantages as a tool to address issues related to climate change.

All this naturally raises questions about contracting parties' (legal and non-legal) incentives to voluntarily undertake climate obligations and, relatedly, about a legal framework that would be conducive, or at the very least would not be hostile, to undertaking and upholding contractual climate commitments. While there could be different reasons why parties might choose, and have chosen, to include climate commitments in their contracts, as far as upholding such commitments is concerned, it appears that more reliance might so far have been placed on ways of encouraging compliance which are predominantly outside of contract law. As far as contract law itself is concerned, there has been scepticism about enforceability of climate obligations that parties stipulate in their contracts.[11] One question is, of course, how effective non-enforceable climate commitments can be. Another question is what any potential issues with enforceability of climate commitments tell us about the contractual nature of climate obligations, as well as about the nature of contractual obligations.

This chapter explores whether and how the general contract law remedial regime[12] might be applied to climate obligations that parties can voluntarily undertake, and have undertaken, in their contracts, focusing on commitments related to reducing emissions and highlighting difficulties[13] with resorting to traditional contract law remedies in the case of a breach of such obligations or with upholding agreed remedies that parties might stipulate in their contract for a breach of such obligations (Section 2). In the process of this exploration, the chapter demonstrates that the difficulties associated with contractual enforceability of voluntary climate obligations are linked to the specificity of such obligations, which typically do not conform to the orthodox model of contracting that the general contract law remedial regime prioritises. However, far from concluding that voluntary climate obligations could never be enforceable

11 See, e.g., Mitkidis, 'Contracts for Climate Change Mitigation' (n 4) 74. For a more detailed analysis, see Mitkidis, 'Sustainability Clauses' (n 5) 12–23.

12 Doctrinal observations in the chapter are mostly made with English law in mind, even though they could, in many instances, be generalised and applied to contracting practices governed by other (common law) systems.

13 'Daunting challenges', as has been put more strongly in a broader context. See Fabrizio Cafaggi, 'Transnational Private Regulation of Environmental Sustainability through Commercial Contracts. Reassessing Contractual Governance in Global Supply Chains' (2024) 20(1) European Review of Contract Law 25, 60.

in contract law by definitional fiat, the chapter suggests a different lens to examine the nature of climate commitments to show that they are yet another, but also in some ways unique, challenge to what can be regarded as the paradigmatic understanding of contracting (Section 3). Not only does appreciating the contractual nature of climate commitments, as well as the often-overlooked diversity of existing models of contracting, invite revisiting the question of contract paradigms,[14] but it also informs a more practical question of enforceability of contractual climate clauses.

2. Climate Clauses and Contractual Enforceability

As mentioned in Section 1, contract law has been increasingly coming into focus as a potential source of a private law response to climate change, but asking why it is said to have initially been overlooked is important for the discussion in this chapter. While one could think about different reasons, and some have been suggested in the literature,[15] two interconnected points are worth highlighting here: one relates to the nature of (commercial) contracts, and another to central features of (general) contract law. These reasons are also a source of continuing scepticism about enforceability of contractual climate clauses.

As far as (commercial) contracts are concerned, they have been described as an unusual place to accommodate climate commitments. For example, with respect to supply chain contracts, it has been observed that such "contracts were traditionally drafted with the sole purpose to regulate behaviour regarding the exchange of goods and money between two parties",[16] while "provisions whose aim is to protect third parties' interests rather than economic interests of the contracting parties . . . do not directly relate to the subject matter of a contract".[17] Similarly, with respect to maritime contracts, it has been observed that they are "notoriously traditional and are not ordinarily used to achieve non-commercial objectives".[18] Such observations can certainly be generalised and applied to other (commercial) contracts, which have traditionally been seen as arm's-length exchanges between self-interested parties with antagonistic (profit-driven) interests. As far as *voluntary* climate obligations are concerned, it might not be immediately clear why parties to (commercial) contracts so understood would *choose* to include such obligations in their contract unless they must do so to comply with whatever mandatory rules that might be applicable to their contract, and assuming the parties "will always opt to contract out of default rules that will increase their costs".[19]

An intuitive reason why contracting parties would choose to include climate clauses in their contract is that they might simply be committed to addressing climate change. Suggesting such a reason would perhaps challenge, at least to some extent, the assumption that (commercial) contracts are (profit-enhancing) exchanges between self-interested parties, even though it might also be observed that acting on the commitment to contributing to climate change mitigation does not necessarily have to be seen as inconsistent with the aim of enhancing profit.

[14] See Irina Sakharova, 'The Power to Contract and the Quid Pro Quo "Straitjacket": (Re) Conceptualising Obligation' (on file with the author).

[15] For further discussion, see, e.g., Mitkidis, 'Contracts for Climate Change Mitigation' (n 4) 67–69; Rebelo (n 4) 19–24.

[16] Mitkidis, 'Contracts for Climate Change Mitigation' (n 4) 67.

[17] ibid.

[18] Rebelo (n 4) 2.

[19] ibid (reference omitted).

However, putting this intuitive reason to one side and focusing on the proverbial self-interest, two types of reason might be highlighted: one could be said to relate to external pressure, and the other to internal motivation. From the external perspective, contracting parties might choose to include climate clauses in their contracts to respond to what might be described as the pressure to adopt sustainable approaches to commerce and business. Such pressure might be felt from various actors, such as industrial associations, investors, consumers, or NGOs and can translate "into various types of private regulation, such as transnational public–private initiatives, industrial and corporate codes of conduct, or reporting, monitoring and auditing schemes".[20] From the internal perspective, contracting parties might choose to include climate clauses in their contracts to ensure securing the benefit (or profit) that they expect to receive from their contract or, as the case might be, avoiding detriment (or loss). Focusing on ensuring profits or avoiding financial losses related to a specific contract, one example might be the buyer's interest in ensuring the anticipated profit from reselling the supplied product with a specific carbon footprint label that a product would bear given the way it would be manufactured by the supplier.[21] Focusing on ensuring non-financial benefits or avoiding non-financial detriments, an obvious example would be contracting parties' reputational interests.

There is, of course, no opposition or strict division between financial benefits and detriments, on the one hand, and non-financial benefits and detriments, on the other hand, which an example of damaged reputation leading to lost profits demonstrates most clearly, even though the focus on reputational interests might often mean looking beyond benefits and detriments related to a specific contract. Moreover, there is also no opposition or strict division between what has been identified as external pressure and internal motivation: By not responding to external pressure, especially materialised in some types of "private regulation" mentioned above, contracting parties "run reputational damage risks that can lead to public shaming in the media, drop in demand for their products, outflow of financing from environmentally responsible investors and losing competitive advantage against their peers".[22] Acknowledging such a connection would also often mean looking beyond benefits and detriments related to a specific contract and considering broader commercial and business interests of contracting parties. If contracting parties are corporations, including climate clauses in contracts might be part of corporate governance and, in particular, of corporate social responsibility commitments, which can also be motivated by complex reasons related to multifaceted corporate interests.

Whatever reasons contracting parties might have for choosing to include climate clauses in their contracts, as a matter of fact, contracting parties do include such clauses in their contracts. It has to be admitted that it might be difficult to ascertain the extent to which climate clauses are used in practice,[23] not least because of confidentiality associated with contracting, which might indeed be protected by non-disclosure obligations.[24] Anyone who is not privy to any given contract, including a researcher, might have to rely on template clauses made publicly

20 Mitkidis, 'Contracts for Climate Change Mitigation' (n 4) 55.

21 ibid 68.

22 ibid 55.

23 See Michael P Vandenbergh, 'Private Environmental Governance' (2013) 91(1) Cornell Law Review 129, 159.

24 Mitkidis, 'Contracts for Climate Change Mitigation' (n 4) 68 (listing confidentiality associated with contracting as a reason why contracts have been overlooked as a potential source of responding to climate change).

available by companies or public associations.[25] Still, there is evidence that climate clauses are being used in practice.[26] In the UK context, it has recently been observed that "[b]ased on currently discernible trends in UK legal practice and markets, . . . climate change drafting for contracts will likely become increasingly necessary and predominant in the legal sector".[27] An impressive project that might be seen both as a response to the demand for climate clauses and as a potential source of facilitating their broader use is the rapidly developing Chancery Lane Project, which currently offers more that 170 template clauses, mainly designed with the jurisdiction of England and Wales in mind, but also including clauses designed to be used in other common law jurisdictions (the US, New Zealand, Australia, and Ireland) and in civil law jurisdictions (Germany, Italy, and Japan). The Project demonstrates how climate clauses can be and have been used in a number of sectors and maintains a database of diverse case studies providing evidence of climate clause implementation by various organisations.[28]

All this paints a rather optimistic picture, but at this point it might be worth revisiting the question of why contract law might have been initially overlooked as a potential source of a private law response to climate change. Apart from reasons related to the nature of (commercial) contracts, considered above, contract law itself might also be thought to be, and has been described in the literature as, not particularly friendly to climate clauses. The two sets of reasons are, of course, not unrelated: If contract law, and its remedial regime, has been designed to facilitate arm's-length exchanges between self-interested parties with antagonistic (profit-driven) interests and enforce obligations pertaining to such exchanges, it might indeed be "largely inept"[29] at enforcing climate clauses, which can also be said about sustainability clauses more generally; such clauses might not naturally fit into such exchanges' established architecture. It has been said about English contract law, in particular, that it "struggles with environmental or sustainability provisions because it was designed to pursue an entirely different set of priorities".[30] Overall, there is scepticism about the enforceability of climate clauses, which are regarded as not legally enforceable in most cases.[31]

Poor prospects of sustainability clauses' enforceability suggest that while contracting parties might, and do indeed, choose to include climate clauses in their contracts, the effectiveness of

[25] Rebelo (n 4) 20–21.

[26] See, e.g., Michael P Vandenburgh and Patricia A Moore, 'Environmental Governance by Contract: The Growing Role of Supply Chain Contracting' (2022) 12(1) Michigan Journal of Environmental and Administrative Law 1.

[27] Thomas L Muinzer, 'A Survey of Climate Change Law in the United Kingdom' (2024) 14 Climate Law 233, 259.

[28] *The Chancery Lane Project* <https://chancerylaneproject.org> accessed 15 March 2025. See also Jenifer Ramos, 'Shifting the Mindset of Commercial Lawyers to Rewire Contracts, to Mitigate Climate Change More Effectively in Practice: The Chancery Lane Project' (2021) 23(1) Environmental Law Review 3; Jenni Ramos and The Chancery Lane Project, 'The Role of Contracts to Address Environmental Impacts in Supply Chains' in Susan A Maslow and David V Snyder (eds), *Contracts for Responsible and Sustainable Supply Chains: Model Contract Clauses, Legal Analysis, and Practical Perspectives* (ABA Publishing 2023) 183.

[29] Rebelo (n 4) 21.

[30] ibid. See also Vibe Ulfbeck and Ole Hansen, 'Sustainability Clauses in an Unsustainable Contract Law?' (2022) 6 CEPRI Studies on Private Governance <https://jura.ku.dk/privategovernance/english/research/working-paper-series/> accessed 15 March 2025 (arguing that 'today's contract law is less well equipped to deal with contracts pursuing sustainability goals, since it was not designed to work in this context').

[31] See Mitkidis, 'Contracts for Climate Change Mitigation' (n 4) 74. For a more detailed analysis, see Mitkidis, 'Sustainability Clauses' (n 5) 12–23.

such clauses might be questioned. At this point, however, it might be asked whether in focusing on *enforceability*, in particular in the context of climate clauses' *effectiveness*, we are not missing the woods for the trees. After all, there are reasons to believe that climate clauses might be effective even if they are not legally enforceable.[32] With respect to such clauses, reliance might be placed on voluntary compliance and non-legal incentives to comply, consistent with how private governance is usually understood.[33]

Nonetheless, two questions could be posed. First, *contract* governance is thought of as capable of overcoming deficiencies normally associated with other forms of private governance (related to private governance's legitimacy, effectiveness, and monitoring and enforcement),[34] not least because of the fact that *contractual* obligations arise from the contract to which its parties agree and could potentially be *enforced* by the parties. However, if climate clauses are not legally enforceable in most cases, is contract governance not falling short of fully overcoming deficiencies normally associated with other forms of private governance? Perhaps contract governance would still have some advantages,[35] but their strength might be questioned. Secondly, and more importantly, even if non-enforceable climate clause can still be effective, is it not somewhat odd that such clauses are regarded as not legally enforceable in most cases, assuming they are not illegal or contrary to public policy? After all, is it not the case that on the (oft-criticised) traditional view, "[c]ontract law should do no more than facilitate what is the will of the parties?"[36] What are, more precisely, potential issues with climate clauses' enforceability?

Sustainability provisions, and in particular climate provisions, can vary significantly both in the way they may be incorporated into contracts and in their content. Depending on the method of incorporation, it might be easier or more difficult to establish that sustainability provisions constitute terms of a given contract. However, even if sustainability provisions are (properly) incorporated into a contract, such terms would still need to be interpreted, and what kind of obligation they stipulate might influence their enforceability.[37] On the one hand, the variety of the content of climate clauses might make any discussion of climate clauses' enforceability too abstract and general. On the other hand, a typical feature of climate clauses, as has already been emphasised, is that they tend to stipulate obligations that are not (directly) related to the main subject-matter of the contract. A focus on this typical feature might help make the discussion of climate clauses' enforceability more concrete and specific. To contextualise the discussion even further, this section uses the example of one such climate clause,

[32] See Mitkidis, 'Sustainability Clauses' (n 5) 24.

[33] See generally Vandenbergh (n 23). cf Rossi and Ruhl (n 1) 874 (distinguishing 'between "private governance"—voluntary, noncollective solutions among stakeholders—and "private law"—which relies on judicial enforcement to effectuate a collective response through the common law').

[34] See Mitkidis, 'Contracts for Climate Change Mitigation' (n 4) 61–64, 75.

[35] For a discussion, see Mitkidis, 'Sustainability Clauses' (n 5) 24–29 (discussing, in particular, 'hardening of soft law effects'). Among other things, the author identifies 'legalisation' of social corporate responsibility as a major contribution of contract law and emphasises, rather intriguingly, that 'legalisation' 'does not necessarily mean that contractual form transforms legally unenforceable soft requirements into legally enforceable hard ones, but rather transforms soft regulation into less soft'. ibid 24. See also Mitkidis, 'Contracts for Climate Change Mitigation' (n 4) 72–75.

[36] Ulfbeck and Hansen (n 30).

[37] See Mitkidis, 'Sustainability Clauses' (n 5) 15 (observing that '[t]he content of [sustainability contractual clauses] varies greatly in relation to the topic and protected interests as well as the style, length and specificity of language, and hence may influence their enforceability').

David's Clause,[38] from the Chancery Lane Project's toolkit (although not purporting to limit the discussion of climate clauses' enforceability to this clause only).

2.1 Judicial Remedies

Section 1 of David's Clause is designed to stipulate contracting parties' climate obligations, which for the purpose of the discussion in this chapter can be summarised as follows: (1) to set a public net-zero target and interim greenhouse gas reduction targets within a certain period of entering into the contract; (2) to develop and implement a net-zero transition plan within a certain period of entering into the contract; (3) to measure and report annually and publicly on the parties' carbon footprint and progress towards their net-zero target; and (4) to provide an environmental and sustainability training programme on a regular basis (at least annually) for employees, personnel and contractors during their usual working hours.[39]

If some climate obligations, such as those stipulated in Section 1 of David's Clause, are breached, what would a remedial response be, and are there any issues with enforceability that might be envisaged from the doctrinal perspective? It might be thought that a potential *contractual* claim would, at least prima facie, not be vulnerable to some of the difficulties identified in the literature with respect to other potential (private law) claims in the context of climate change, such as (most importantly) tort law claims. The reason is broadly related to individuation of duties. Contractual duties, as well as the correlative contractual rights, are specified at contract formation, and are in fact created by entering into a specific contract. This amounts to *undertaking* the duties, leaving little doubt about the identity of both the duty-bearer and the right-holder, and suggesting reasonable clarity as to who could potentially be the (appropriate) claimant and the (appropriate) defendant.

As far as contract damages are concerned, causation is also not regarded as a major topic in contract law. Although the claimant must show, in order to recover more than nominal damages, that the loss was caused by the breach of contract, "[t]he courts have avoided laying down any formal tests for causation: they have relied on common sense to guide decisions as to whether a breach of contract is a sufficiently substantial cause of the claimant's loss".[40] Yet, even though *contractual* duties are specified at contract formation (and correlate with contractual rights), and causation might be less of an obstacle to a possible contractual claim in the context of climate change (compared to possible tort claims), establishing the *loss* (caused by the breach of contract) is necessary for making a claim for more than nominal damages. This latter requirement might present a challenge from the perspective of the general contract law remedial regime.

Staying on the subject of damages, which are the *primary* remedy for breach of contract in English law, "[t]he rule of the common law is, that where a party sustains a loss by reason of a breach of contract, he is, so far as money can do it, to be placed in the same situation with respect to damages, as if the contract had been performed".[41] This statement encapsulates what is

[38] 'David's Clause: SME's Net Zero Objectives' (*The Chancery Lane Project*, 7 March 2023) <https://chancerylaneproject.org/clauses/smes-net-zero-objectives/> accessed 15 March 2025.

[39] ibid (for Section 1 in full).

[40] HG Beale (ed), *Chitty on Contracts* (35th edn, Sweet and Maxwell 2023) para 30-075 (quoted with approval in *Galoo Ltd v Bright Grahame Murray* [1994] 1 WLR 1360 (CA) 1370). It is remoteness that 'tends to be the prominent issue in cases of liability for damage in the law of contract'. *Chitty on Contracts* (n 40) para 30-075. On causation in torts, see Mark Geitsfeld and Sandy Steel, Chapter 8 of this handbook.

[41] *Robinson v Harman* (1848) 1 Exch 850 (Ex Ct) 855 (Parke B).

known as the *expectation* measure of damages. Contract damages are *forward-looking* and are assessed with reference to a hypothetical (future) position in which the contract is performed. This could potentially (although not always actually) translate into a more generous monetary award (compared to tort law damages), but contract damages are normally still compensatory: They are meant to *compensate* the claimant for the *loss* caused by the breach of contract; moreover, punitive damages are not available in contract law.[42]

Taking a notional look at climate clauses, and in particular considering the climate obligations stipulated in Section 1 of David's Clause, it is not immediately clear what loss the *other* contracting party might suffer in the case of one party's breach (for example, if one party is not providing an environmental and sustainability training programme for employees, personnel, and contractors). Depending on the nature of the contract in which a climate clause is included, a breach of a climate obligation by one party could potentially cause the other party's pecuniary or non-pecuniary losses. As already mentioned,[43] an example of pecuniary loss might be a loss of profit on reselling the supplied product that would not bear a specific carbon footprint label because the supplier failed to comply in manufacturing the product with climate obligations stipulated in the supply contract.[44] However, the price or marketability of a product will not always be affected[45] because of the supplier's breach of a climate obligation and the example itself is, of course, limited to a specific type of contract.[46] One example of non-pecuniary loss is a loss of reputation by reason of the breach of climate obligations. However, as a matter of English law, although the claimant might sometimes be able to recover damages for *financial* loss caused by the loss of reputation by reason of the breach of contract[47] (even though it might not be easy to prove such a loss), damages for the loss of reputation per se cannot be recovered in a contractual claim.[48] If, however, the innocent party does not suffer any loss in the case of the other party's breach of climate obligations, which might be the case more often than not,[49] damages would only be nominal.

Any potential availability of specific performance, which is an equitable, and not common law, remedy in English contract law, is not clear. As a *secondary* remedy, it will not be ordered if damages (or the award of an agreed sum) are an adequate remedy, and even if the main bar to specific performance (the adequacy of damages) is overcome, there are multiple other bars, of which "constant supervision" might be worth mentioning.[50] It is similarly not particularly clear whether injunctions, another equitable remedy, might be readily available for the breach of climate obligations. To the extent that climate obligations are positive (rather than negative) undertakings, which climate obligations stipulated in Section 1 of David Clause are, mandatory (rather than prohibitory) injunctions would come to mind, but mandatory injunctions, as a remedy to restore the situation which would have prevailed had the defendant not breached

42 *Addis v Gramophone Co Ltd* [1909] AC 488 (HL).

43 See text accompanying (n 21).

44 See Mitkidis, 'Contracts for Climate Change Mitigation' (n 4) 68.

45 If they are affected, the relevant loss might, of course, still be remote.

46 Special remedies that might be available for a breach of a specific type of contract, such as sale of goods, which might be particularly important in the context of supply chain contracts, are not discussed in this chapter.

47 *Malik v Bank of Credit and Commerce International SA* [1998] 1 AC 20 (HL).

48 *Addis* (n 42).

49 Cf Cafaggi (n 13) 65 (observing that '[c]ompensation is not often used as a contractual remedy since the party who is seeking the remedy is not the victim in case of environmental harm').

50 *Co-operative Insurance Soc Ltd v Argyll Stores (Holdings) Ltd* [1998] AC 1 (HL).

the contract, are "not as readily granted as prohibitory injunctions",[51] as "courts are reluctant to compel *positive* action by mandatory injunctions".[52]

It might be that resorting to the remedy of termination, which is a *self-help* remedy in English contract law, could be more promising, but this remedy would not always be available to the claimant.[53] Moreover, it might also not always be desirable by the claimant in the case of a breach of climate obligations.[54] However, as far as *judicial* remedies for breach of contract are concerned, it appears that they might not be a straightforward avenue for one party to pursue in the case of the other party's breach of climate obligations.[55] A general observation, which could be made about potential issues with applying judicial remedies in the case of a breach of climate obligations and which will be explored in more detail below, is that the *other* party might not necessarily be the only or even the main *beneficiary* of such obligations.[56]

However, yet another distinctive feature of contract law is that not only can persons *create* contractual obligations, but they can also stipulate in their contract the consequences of the breach of such obligations, resorting in particular to various *agreed remedies*, such as, most importantly, agreed damages. Could "agreed remedies" be a solution to potential problems with applying the general contract law remedial regime to climate obligations?

2.2 Agreed Remedies

David's Clause is particularly interesting to discuss because in addition to stipulating contracting parties' climate obligations, it is also designed to stipulate the consequences of the breach of these obligations. Section 2 of David's Clause, entitled "Breach of climate obligations", provides that if either party breaches any of the climate obligations, it shall (1) inform the other party, within a certain period of the breach, of the breaching party's plans to remedy the breach, (2) remedy the breach within a certain period of the breach, and (3) if the breaching party fails to remedy the breach within a certain period of the breach, pay to a climate charity nominated by the other party a specified sum of money for each day (or other period) that the breach continues (up to a specified maximum).[57]

It might seem that agreed remedies could be seen as a possible solution to potential problems with applying the general contract law remedial regime to climate obligations. Indeed, some reasons for stipulating agreed remedies, and in particular agreed damages, in contracts include: certainty (meaning that parties know where they stand), avoiding the costs of resolving disputes through the courts, avoiding under-compensation by the courts, ensuring adequate compensation of the parties, and deterring breach or ensuring performance. However,

[51] Jack Beatson, Andrew Burrows, and John Cartwright, *Anson's Law of Contract* (31st ed, OUP 2020) 588.

[52] Mindy-Chen Wishart, *Contract Law* (7th ed, OUP 2022) 597 (emphasis in original).

[53] For a critical discussion, see Neil Andrews, 'Breach of Contract: A Plea for Clarity and Discipline' (2018) 134 Law Quarterly Review 117, 125–36.

[54] For a discussion of the remedy of termination in the context of international contracts for sale, see Mitkidis, 'Sustainability Clauses' (n 5) 20–22.

[55] cf Mitkidis, 'Sustainability Clauses' (n 5) 23 (observing that 'awarding damages for breaches of [sustainability contractual clauses] under international contract law . . . is not feasible' and that 'specific performance actually cannot be used in relation to [such clauses]').

[56] A discussion of the possibility of, and difficulties with, any enforcement by third party beneficiaries, which would also require revisiting the question of individuation of duties discussed above, is beyond the scope of this chapter.

[57] See David's Clause (n 38) (for Section 2 in full).

agreed remedies, including agreed damages, are not always enforceable. Moreover, as far as enforceability is concerned, one difference between *primary* (or *substantive*) obligations and *secondary* (or *remedial*) obligations[58] stipulated in contracts is that the latter have historically attracted more judicial control than the former.

It is not entirely clear how an obligation to inform the other party of the breaching party's plans to remedy the breach (1) is supposed to be enforced. Perhaps it is not meant to be enforced but rather is included in response to what has been identified as a general problem of discoverability of breaches of climate obligations,[59] or indeed sustainability obligations more generally. For example, subject to obvious caveats, it would normally be reasonably clear to the buyer whether the supplier has performed its obligation to deliver the goods; it might, however, not be immediately apparent to the buyer whether the supplier complied in manufacturing the goods with climate obligations stipulated in the supply contract.[60]

It might be queried how the obligation to remedy the breach (2) could be understood. If the parties are agreeing to specific performance, the enforceability of such a remedial obligation is questionable: Given that specific performance is a discretionary remedy, agreeing to it in the contract is regarded as tantamount to ousting the jurisdiction of the court to determine whether this remedy is appropriate at the time it is claimed.[61] However, perhaps the (main) effect of the obligation to remedy the breach is to give the breaching party a reasonable opportunity to remedy the breach before the subsequent payment obligation is triggered.[62]

The obligation to pay to a climate charity nominated by the other party a specified sum of money for a certain period that the breach continues (3) is the most interesting. One question that might be asked is whether this obligation, as specifying a particular sum of money payable on breach, could be unenforceable as a *penalty*. Applying the traditional test set out by Lord Dunedin in the House of Lords decision in *Dunlop v New Garage*,[63] a specified sum of money payable to a climate charity would hardly amount to a genuine pre-estimate of loss that is likely to be caused by the breach of climate obligations stipulated in Section 1 of David's Clause. However, the obligation to pay a specified sum of money to a climate charity could also be potentially unenforceable as a penalty if what the breaching party is supposed to pay is *not proportionate* to a *legitimate interest* that the innocent party has in the performance of the obligation, applying the test as widened in the UK Supreme Court decision in *Cavendish Square Holding BV v Makdessi, ParkingEye Ltd v Beavis*.[64]

Understanding which considerations might be relevant to establishing the innocent party's legitimate interest would be of particular significance. It is worth noting that in *Makdessi*,[65] the Lords gave much more prominence to Lord Atkinson's speech than to Lord Dunedin's

[58] As articulated in *Photo Production Ltd v Securicor Transport Ltd* [1980] AC 827 (HL) 846–51 (Lord Diplock).

[59] See Mitkidis, 'Sustainability Clauses' (n 5) 20.

[60] cf ibid (observing that 'we cannot see from the goods' appearance that children were used to produce it'). It has, however, also been observed in the context of supply chains that the use of new digital technologies is increasingly helping to 'directly or indirectly source information about compliance'. Cafaggi (n 13).

[61] *Quadrant Visual Communications Ltd v Hutchison Telephone (UK) Ltd* [1993] BCLC 442 (CA).

[62] This would also be consistent with the idea that '[r]emedies [for breaching environmental obligations] are generally articulated in an escalating form', with 'corrective remedies' coming first. See Cafaggi (n 13) 64.

[63] [1915] AC 79 (HL) 85–90.

[64] [2015] UKSC 67, [2016] AC 1172.

[65] ibid.

speech in *Dunlop*,[66] precisely because of the attention that Lord Atkinson had given to broader considerations in determining the nature and the extent of the party's interest in the performance of the relevant obligation. It could be discussed whether an appeal to broader considerations[67] might be pivotal in approaching enforceability of the obligation to pay a specified sum of money to a climate charity.[68] This is, of course, assuming that the penalty rule would be engaged in the first place, that is, assuming that the obligation in question is *remedial* (or *secondary*). In fact, even though such a sum of money is supposed to be payable *on breach*, it might be tempting to try to conceptualise the obligation to pay the money to a climate charity as, in some sense, being closer to a *conditional primary* obligation, and there could indeed be a discussion about whether some way of redrafting Section 2 of David's clause might help solidify such conceptualisation, potentially preventing the penalty rule from being engaged. Relatedly, it should be borne in mind that this obligation is atypical in not stipulating that such a sum of money is payable, by the breaching party, *to* the innocent party.[69]

A general observation that could be made about the obligations stipulated in Section 2 of David's Clause is that they do not naturally fit into the traditional catalogue of agreed remedies, which mirrors the difficulties with applying the general remedial regime to substantive climate obligations outlined above. The obligations stipulated in Section 2 of David's Clause, especially relating to paying a specified sum of money to a climate charity, could hardly be said to be stipulated with the view of putting the *other* party into the position they would have been in had the contract been performed, *in particular*, by compensating the *other* party's loss. This is, of course, not surprising, as each party's substantive obligations stipulated in Section 1 of David's Clause, as has already been emphasised, might not necessarily be stipulated with a view to conferring a benefit only or even mainly on the *other* party, which might also be the source of difficulties with applying the general remedial regime to such obligations.

The next section will focus on the idea that difficulties with contractual enforceability of voluntary climate obligations are linked to the specificity of such obligations, which do not tend to follow the model of contracting that the general contract law remedial regime prioritises. The next section will adopt a different lens to examine the nature of climate commitments to show that they present yet another, but also in some ways unique, challenge to what can be regarded as the paradigmatic understanding of contracting. This analysis suggests that appreciating both the contractual nature of climate commitments and the often-overlooked diversity of existing models of contracting invites us to revisit the question of contract paradigms, while informing the practical question of enforceability.

[66] *Dunlop* (n 63) 90–97.

[67] For a discussion, see Solène Rowan, 'The "Legitimate Interest in Performance" in the Law on Penalties' (2019) 87(1) Cambridge Law Journal 148, 164–74.

[68] For questioning whether broader considerations, such as public interest, should be 'allowed to trump the outcome that would be reached if balancing the interests of the contracting parties alone', see Andrew Summers, 'Unresolved Issues in the Law on Penalty' [2017] Lloyd's Maritime and Commercial Law Quarterly 95, 113 (while concluding that '[f]or better or worse, it seems that judges must now be prepared to engage (for the first time) directly with public interest arguments in applying the penalties rule'). ibid (footnote omitted)).

[69] A question that can be asked is whether the breaching party's obligation to pay a specified sum of money to a climate charity nominated by the innocent party can be enforced by such a charity; the question is particularly interesting if the charity is seen as a beneficiary of a remedial, and not substantive, obligation. As already indicated, considering the third-party beneficiaries' perspective is beyond the scope of this chapter.

3. Climate Commitments and Contract Paradigms

In the context of discussing whether "climate change ill fits the existing tort paradigm",[70] it has been eloquently observed:

> Implicit conceptual dichotomies often lurk beneath the surface of tort doctrine: physical is contrasted with emotional, individual with communal, manmade with natural, immediate with distant, present with future, and so on. One side of these pairings is privileged over another, often on the theory that tort cannot provide redress for all wrongs and thus must establish some system of triage. Surfacing tort law's deep structures and subjecting them to critique has been a major and fruitful focus of feminist tort scholarship for some time now. Intriguingly, climate change litigation may aid this cause by making more visible tort law's disfavored interests. Certain forms of injury that have been rationalized away as incidental or marginal may come to appear more significant when presented in this dramatic new light.[71]

Conceptual dichotomies, as well as favouring some interests over others, are, of course, not unique to tort law. As explained in the previous section, one reason for scepticism about contract law as a potential source of a private law response to climate change has been related to understanding contracts as arm's-length exchanges between self-interested parties with antagonistic (profit-driven) interests: Climate commitments might be thought to be a poor fit for contracts so understood.

Even if it is accepted that this understanding of contracts does not illuminate relations that may obtain in some types of contract (such as consumer contracts or employment contracts, which have indeed received special legal treatment), this understanding can still be said to be reflected in many central doctrines of general contract law. Such reflection constitutes a related reason for scepticism about contract law as a potential source of a private law response to climate change: Contract law might be thought to be ill-equipped to provide a legal framework for undertaking climate commitments. Understanding contracts as arm's-length exchanges between self-interested parties with antagonistic (profit-driven) interests has also been central to contract theory, where such understanding has also not been unchallenged, and a prominent challenge comes from the relational theory of contract,[72] which, among other things, emphasises that a focus on antagonism obscures cooperation, which is important in contracting, or that a focus on self-interest obscures each party's recognition of the other party's interests, which is no less important. In contrasting discrete with "relational" contracts, one-off with long-term contracts, or simple with complex contracts, the relational theory of contract can be understood as diverting attention away from the contract paradigm and drawing attention to underappreciated aspects of contractual relations.

Referring to the relational theory of contract has also been prominent in analyses of climate obligations stipulated in contracts,[73] which is not surprising considering the complex

[70] Douglas A Kysar, 'What Climate Change Can Do About Tort Law' (2012) 42(8) Environmental Law Reporter 10739, 10740.

[71] ibid 10743.

[72] See, e.g., Ian MacNeil, *The Relational Theory of Contract: Selected Works of Ian MacNeil* (David Campbell ed, Sweet & Maxwel 2001). For a recent relational account of contracting, see David Campbell, *Contractual Relations: A Contribution to the Critique of the Classical Law of Contract* (OUP 2022).

[73] See, e.g. Mitkidis, 'Contracts for Climate Change Mitigation' (n 4) 73; Mitkidis, 'Sustainability Clauses' (n 5) 6; Rebelo (n 4) 29.

structure of contracts that may include climate commitments and a likely long-term and co-operative character of contractual relations to which such contracts would give rise. However, important as it is, this perspective might not necessarily be a powerful enough lens through which the nature of climate commitments might be brought to light, especially with a view to understanding the potential for their contractual enforceability. As a side note, it appears that a focus on a relational approach in existing analyses of climate obligations stipulated in contracts tends to point to ways of encouraging compliance with such obligations which are predominantly outside of contract law.[74]

More importantly, as has been poignantly observed, "the contract containing sustainability clauses brings in yet a new element of a corrosion of the classical paradigm".[75] Even if a relational perspective is acknowledged, the interests climate obligations serve may still differ from those served by the contractual obligations that have predominantly been the focus of relational contract theory's criticism. In this respect, it has been emphasised that sustainability clauses are meant to "protect societal interests in their own right"—"interests that are external to the parties"—rather than merely "to integrate social considerations into the contract for the protection of the parties to the contract (as in consumer and labour law)".[76] Even more interestingly, however, undertaking climate commitments, as has already been emphasised in the previous section, does not have to be seen as inconsistent with pursuing self-interest and might in fact be motivated by contracting parties' financial and non-financial interests.[77] Nor is a relational outlook on contracting itself inconsistent with seeing contracting parties as pursuing self-interest, in doing which a party might *have to* cooperate and to recognise the other party's self-interest to make the exchange possible.[78]

This section suggests a different lens to examine the nature of climate commitments and explore the *internal* resources of contract law that might be resorted to in order to approach such commitments' enforceability. A typical feature of climate clauses, as has repeatedly been emphasised, is that they tend to stipulate obligations that are not (directly) related to the main subject-matter of the contract in which such clauses are included, which feature has been acknowledged in the literature.[79] Adopting, as this chapter does, a more "technical" approach to examining what this feature means for understanding the nature of climate commitments

[74] See Mitkidis, 'Sustainability Clauses' (n 5) 20–22 (distinguishing remedies and 'relational enforcement tools' and emphasising that 'enforcement is not always of a formal legal character' but 'the effectiveness of the relational tools is grounded in the threat of formal legal sanctions'). See also Cristina Poncibò, 'The Contractualisation of Environmental Sustainability' (2016) 12(4) European Review of Contract Law 335, 350 (observing in the context of pursuing sustainable development goals that on the 'cooperative ethics' approach to assessing contractual obligations, which is central to the relational theory of contract, 'resorting to the formal law of remedies upon breach misses the mark').

[75] See Ulfbeck and Hansen (n 30).

[76] ibid.

[77] It is worth noting that while it has been emphasised that sustainability clauses in contracts 'protect rather general public interests than private interests of the contractual parties' (Mitkidis, 'Sustainability Clauses' (n 5) 6) or 'societal interests that are external to the parties' (Ulfbeck and Hansen (n 30)), it has also been acknowledged that such 'interests are to some extent "internalised" when incorporated into the contract if the pursuance of the goals are a true objective of the contract' (ibid). This has also been referred to as the *contractualisation* of 'economic, social and environmental values': 'the parties define their own interests' by agreeing to contractual obligations reflecting such values (Poncibò (n 74) 344).

[78] For a discussion, see David Campbell, 'Adam Smith and the Social Foundation of Agreement: *Walford v Miles* as a Relational Contract' (2017) 21(3) The Edinburgh Law Review 376.

[79] See Mitkidis, 'Sustainability Clauses' (n 5) 5; Mitkidis, 'Contracts for Climate Change Mitigation' (n 4) 67. See also Li-Wen Lin, 'Legal Transplants through Private Contracting: Codes of Vendor Conduct in Global Supply Chains as an Example' (2009) 57(3) American Journal of Comparative Law 711, 717.

entails putting under scrutiny what could be more accurately described as the contract paradigm—the quid pro quo (QPQ) model of contracting, which contract law and contract theory could be said to have been prioritising. On the one hand, the QPQ model of contracting, as understood in this chapter, is not inconsistent with a relational approach to contracting. On the other hand, the QPQ model of contracting does not exhaust all models of contracting that *are* recognised, but underappreciated, in contract law and contract theory. Placing contracts containing climate commitments on the map of *existing* models of contracting might provide a better framework for understanding the nature of such commitments and for exploring the *internal* resources of contract law to try to approach such commitments' enforceability.

Traditional exchanges, such as contracts for sale and for services, represent typical examples of QPQ contracts, which expression is used in the chapter to refer to a particular way in which the parties' contractual rights and duties, as well as their interests in contracting, may be connected. Each party's duty *correlates* with the other party's right, such as A's duty to pay for the goods correlates with B's right that A pay, and B's duty to deliver the goods correlates with A's right that B deliver. Each party's interest in contracting is seen as the interest in the other party's performance of its duty—the interest in the *counterperformance*. It is to realise this interest that each party is thought to assume and perform its own duty, to "pay for" (the right to) the other party's performance or "promise", as it is often said.[80] It can be said that a party's interest in contracting is linked to obtaining the other party's performance and is embodied in the right that the other party perform.

Contracting parties' interests can also be said, at least in some sense, to be "antagonistic", even though not necessarily in the sense that is often supposed. Contracting parties' interests are not infrequently portrayed as antagonistic in the sense of being "hostile", and a challenge to this outlook comes, once again, from the relational theory of contract, which draws attention to cooperative patterns of contracting, as different from contracting at arm's length. However, in a QPQ contract, the parties' interests may or may not be, in the circumstances, antagonistic in the sense of being "hostile", while being "antagonistic" in the sense of being *opposite* or rather *oppositely directed*: for example, A is interested in getting the goods and is prepared to part with a particular amount of money, while B is interested in getting this amount of money and is prepared to part with these goods. A and B might still "have to" cooperate and recognise each other's opposite (but not necessarily "hostile") interest if they are to fulfil their expectations for the sale. The QPQ contract is the paradigmatic, but by no means the only, model of contracting.

Another model of contracting underlies *joint project* contracts, which expression is used here to signal a different interrelation between, on the one hand, the contracting parties' rights and duties, and, on the other hand, between their interests in contracting. One example is the contract underlying an unincorporated association,[81] in which the parties are pooling resources for a common purpose. In contrast to QPQ contracts, the whole concept of *counter*performance is simply not applicable to joint project contracts. Each party's interest in contracting cannot be directly linked to receiving the *other* party's performance and cannot be said to be embodied in each party's right that the *other* party perform. Far from being *oppositely directed*, the parties' *shared* interest in contracting is *directed at one and the same common purpose*. This interest is embodied in the parties' rights, but these rights are not rights to some

[80] See, e.g., Jennifer Nadler, 'Freedom from Things: A Defense of the Disjunctive Obligation in Contract Law' (2021) 27 Legal Theory 177, 187.

[81] For a recent critical analysis, see Alec J Morris, 'Unincorporated Associations and the Property Problem: The 'Contract-Holding' Theory as the Ace of Clubs?' (2023) 87(1) Conveyancer and Property Lawyer 9.

other party's (counter)performance. They are rights to all the "fruits" of all parties' performances; they are not *opposite*, rather they *mirror* each other.

This is not to say, of course, that each party is not interested in each of the other parties performance of their individual duties. The idea is rather that their performance is not to be understood to be beneficial to the parties taken one by one but in terms of the *collective* benefit the performance of the individual duties secures. Parties to a joint project contract might be compared, at least in some sense, to players on a team where, although each relies on the others playing their parts, the intended result (winning the game) does not accrue to each player individually, but to them all as a group—the team wins, not the players individually.

In modern civil law systems, the joint project model of contracting underlies the contract of "society" or partnership (e.g., *der Gesellschaftsvertrag*[82] in German law or *la société*[83] in French law), in which the model of the Roman contract of *societas* survived with certain modifications,[84] and which bear some similarity to contracts underlying unincorporated associations and partnerships in common law. Regardless of which jurisdiction or which legal system is in question, the joint project model can conveniently serve a variety of arrangements. In relation to unincorporated associations, it has been observed that "[t]here are probably almost as many different types of unincorporated association as there are forms of human activity".[85]

Joint project contracts have been on the periphery of contract theory, if they are ever seriously analysed at all. They are also typically not considered in doctrinal discussions of contracts and sometimes need to be explicitly mentioned as representing exceptions to general rules (such as in relation to the offer-and-acceptance analysis of contract formation).[86] Yet, as much as QPQ contracts, such as contracts for sale and for services, joint project contracts create *mutually obliging*,[87] and not unilaterally obliging, relations;[88] they *have* traditionally been conceptualised as *contracts*, even though they could not be more different from the QPQ paradigm.

Still, while QPQ contracts and joint project contracts represent very different models of contracting, this might be a misleading dichotomy. QPQ contracts are far less homogeneous than it might seem at first sight. There are various relations that take the QPQ model of contracting and yet are "poor" candidates to exemplify the QPQ paradigm. In particular, there are contracts in which the parties' rights and duties *do* correlate, and the parties' interests in

[82] See BGB §705.

[83] See Article 1832 of the Code civil.

[84] For discussion of the Roman contract of *societas*, see, e.g., David Daube, 'Societas as Consensual Contract' (1938) 6 Cambridge Law Journal 381; Reinhard Zimmermann, *The Law of Obligations: Roman Foundations of the Civilian Tradition* (Clarendon Press 1996) 451–66.

[85] *R v L* [2008] EWCA Crim 1970, [2009] 1 All ER 786, 790 (Hughes LJ).

[86] For references and discussion, see Irina Sakharova, 'The Power to Contract and the Offer-and-Acceptance Analysis of Contract Formation' (2024) 37 Canadian Journal of Law and Jurisprudence 261, 273–76.

[87] As Barry Nicholas emphasises when discussing the Roman law contract of *societas*, such contract was, like sale and hire, 'perfectly bilateral': 'Each party must make some contribution, either of capital, skill, or labour. Otherwise the transaction will be one not of partnership but of gift.' Barry Nicholas, *An Introduction to Roman Law* (Clarendon Press 1976) 186. In English law, mutuality of the parties' undertakings (duties and obligations) is emphasised in a well-known definition of unincorporated associations given by Lawton LJ in *Conservative and Unionist Central Office v Burrell* [1982] 1 WLR 522 (CA) 525.

[88] For terminological explanations, see Irina Sakharova, 'The Bilaterality of Contract' in Mindy Chen-Wishart and Prince Saprai (eds), *Research Handbook on the Philosophy of Contract Law* (Edward Elgar Publishing 2025) 178.

contracting *are* linked to receiving the counterperformance. Still, such interests are not *limited* to receiving the counterperformance. For example, in a contract to restore a sculpture between A (the owner) and B (the restorer), A is deemed to perform in order to have the sculpture restored, and B is deemed to perform in order to get paid. In this sense, at least, A's and B's interests can be said to be *opposite* or *oppositely directed*. At the same time, A's and B's interests *in contracting* may concur, at least to some extent, if B is also interested in the *project* of restoring the sculpture *in its own right*; as far as getting the sculpture restored is concerned, A and B have a *common* purpose in contracting that gives one and the same direction to *some* of their interests, they have a joint project at a higher, and perhaps, more abstract level.

In QPQ contracts, it must be acknowledged, not all interests that are unlinked to counterperformance would be legally significant, but some undoubtedly are. Further, some contracts taking the QPQ model and yet hardly exemplifying the QPQ paradigm—such as employment contracts—have, of course, received special treatment, including a special remedial regime, which is, among other things, designed to respond to interests that might generally be seen as less significant in the QPQ paradigm. It goes without saying that the remedial regime applicable to some joint project contracts, such as contracts underlying unincorporated associations, is also special in relation to the general contract law remedial regime, which could be said to have been prioritising the orthodox QPQ model of contracting. Importantly, however, joint project contracts, as well as contracts that take the QPQ model but hardly exemplify the QPQ paradigm, are *still* seen as legally enforceable.[89]

Climate commitments incorporated into (commercial) contracts are a very interesting case from this perspective. While a contract in which such commitments are included may take the QPQ model (e.g., a contract for sale or for services) as far as many or even most obligations stipulated by such a contract are concerned, climate obligations (e.g., directed at reducing emissions[90]) undertaken by the parties to such a contract might, and often would, take the joint project model.[91] That is, the parties *mutually* undertake such obligations not *in order to* secure counterperformance. Rather, with respect to such obligations, the parties pursue a *common purpose*, meaning that the obligations themselves are not *oppositely directed*, but have *one and the same direction* (i.e., the parties' duties are not *different*, but are the *same*, as required by the joint project model of contracting).[92]

In such contracts with climate commitments, the two models of contracting coexist in the sense that different obligations stipulated in the contact take different models. Not only does this make such contracts different from both joint project contracts and QPQ contracts, but it

[89] For a more extensive discussion of models of contracting in a different context, see Sakharova, 'The Power to Contract and the Quid Pro Quo "Straitjacket"' (n 14).

[90] See David's Clause (n 38).

[91] It must be reiterated that climate clauses vary, and it can also be observed that the *same* climate obligations are not always supposed to be undertaken by *both* parties to a contract containing such obligations. In such cases, the contracting model that these obligations follow might require further analysis. For a study drawing attention to issues associated with imposition of sustainability obligations on the supplier in supply chain contracts and the need to protect the supplier as the weaker party, see Ulfbeck and Hansen (n 30).

[92] It might be worth emphasising that if the focus is on some recognised *examples* (or types) of contracts that take the joint project model, such as the contract underlying an unincorporated association in common law or the contract of 'society' or partnership in civil law, contractual climate obligations might appear a bit different, but if the focus is on the joint project *model* of contracting, and, in particular, on the distinctive interrelation between the contracting parties' rights and duties, on the one hand, and between their interests in contracting, on the other, it is clear that climate obligations such as stipulated in David's Clause do take this model.

also makes them different from contracts taking the QPQ model and yet hardly exemplifying the QPQ paradigm, as discussed earlier in this section. Interestingly, even though some of the latter contracts have attracted a special (remedial) regime, judicial decisions about disputes over such contracts have been feeding into the general contract law regime. A relevant example is employment cases in which claimants were able to recover damages for financial loss caused by the loss of reputation by reason of a breach of contract. It might be that appreciating the *model* of contracting that climate commitments may take, as well as the often-overlooked diversity of *existing* models of contracting, might be a good starting point in thinking about a suitable remedial regime for climate commitments.

4. Conclusion

This chapter has suggested the lens of models of contracting to examine the nature of climate obligations that parties may voluntarily undertake in their contracts, illuminating the contractual nature of climate commitments, which might otherwise be obscured if the main emphasis is only on how "alien" such commitments are to the type of contract in which they may be included. While this might only be a first step in addressing, and certainly not a ready recipe for resolving, difficulties associated with contractual enforceability of voluntary climate obligations, this step is also one towards revisiting the question of contract paradigms.

CHAPTER 7

Common Law Torts

DAVID BULLOCK

1. Introduction

THE goal of this chapter is twofold: to examine both what common law tort doctrine means for climate action, but also what climate change will mean for the development of tort law.[1] To answer these questions it is instructive to look to the past, the present, and the future. It is easy to become lost in the expanse of climate change. One can forget that while climate change is a collective action problem of unprecedented scale and complexity, the legal challenges it poses are not wholly new. The common law of torts grappled with complex collective action problems for centuries. Looking at how the courts used tort—in particular, the tort of public nuisance—to respond to these types of problems can, and should, provide a groundwork for tort law's future in a changing world.

Equally, it would be naïve to disregard the exceptionality created by the "super wicked" features of climate change,[2] and to ignore its enormity. A great asset of the common law is its flexibility and its ability to change with the world.[3] The doctrine used by the Victorian courts to tackle the pathologies of the Industrial Revolution was not found writ upon stone tablets; rather, doctrine was developed as the courts performed their constitutional role of deciding the disputes being presented to them. Those disputes reflected changes in technology, society, and the economy. In the same way, climate change will necessarily drive developments in the common law of torts. It will also drive changes in the way we think about tort law.

I advance three propositions designed to test the sceptic's view of the role of the common law of torts in responding to climate change. First, tort law has never been limited to some narrow, binary world in which "A harms B". In fact, the common law courts long ago developed tort doctrine, through the tort of public nuisance, to address the reality that private wrongs are not always so neatly framed or so tightly packaged. Second, to allow the common law to develop, we should not be afraid to let judges judge. Litigation is rarely the optimal solution to any problem involving significant externalities or complexities. But the job of judges is not to solve social problems; it is to decide the cases that come before them according to law. Judges deal with many disputes that touch on wider social issues, and that social overlay does not stop them from determining the dispute between the parties before them. It is by doing so

[1] Those questions being inexorably linked, see Douglas A Kysar, 'What Climate Change Can Do About Tort Law' (2011) 41(1) Environmental Law 1, 4, 71.

[2] Richard J Lazarus, 'Super Wicked Problems and Climate Change: Restraining the Present to Liberate the Future' (2009) 94 Cornell Law Review 1153, 1160.

[3] This is not some new idea. As Lord Mansfield remarked of the common law in *Johnson v Spiller* (1784) 3 Doug 371, 373 'as the usages of society alter, the law must adapt itself to the various situations of mankind'. See also *Hurtado v California* 110 US 516, 530 (1884): 'This flexibility and capacity for growth and adaption is the peculiar boast and excellence of the common law'.

that the common law develops. Third, to the extent there might seem to be a disconnect between the prevailing dominant theories of tort law and the features of a problem like climate change, then we should think critically about how our understandings of tort law derive from our worldviews. Have we missed a trick? If tort law is to stay relevant—if it is not to be confined to being the law-of-small-wrongs—then we should be open to the possibility that our view of tort law has been unduly constrained by how we see the world.

2. Lessons from the Past

Douglas Kysar's description of climate change as the "paradigmatic anti-tort" resounds whenever one embarks upon an examination of how tort law can engage upon the harms occasioned by the release of greenhouse gases into the atmosphere.[4] On one view, climate change is a global collective action problem of such scale, complexity, and polycentricity that it is inapt for a common law response through the law of torts; instead, it is only capable of being addressed by comprehensive and collaborative policymaking in domestic legislatures and through international treaties.[5] On this view, as the New Zealand Court of Appeal in *Smith v Fonterra Co-Operative Group Ltd* put it, "climate change simply cannot be appropriately or adequately addressed by common law tort claims pursued through the courts. It is quintessentially a matter that calls for a sophisticated regulatory response at a national level supported by international co-ordination".[6]

On another view, climate change caused by emissions of greenhouse gases gives rise to *wrongs* connected to interferences with *rights*.[7] Such matters are the traditional—albeit non-exclusive—province of tort law and the common law courts.[8] While climate change presents a problem of unique scale and complexity, the common law has a long history of using tort to determine disputes arising out of collective action problems and it has developed a set of doctrinal tools developed to that end in the form of the tort of public nuisance.[9]

[4] Kysar, 'What Climate Change Can Do About Tort Law' 4.

[5] See, for example, James E Krier, 'Marketable Pollution Allowances' (1994) 25(2) University Toledo Law Review 449, 451 (explaining that legislative regulation of pollution was necessitated as 'pollution spread beyond the common law's grasp'); Thomas W Merrill, 'Global Warming as a Public Nuisance' (2005) 30(2) Columbia Journal of Environmental Law 293; David A Dana, 'The Mismatch Between Public Nuisance Law and Global Warming' (2010) 18 Supreme Court Economic Review 9; David T Buente Jr, Quin M Sorenson, and Clayton G Northouse, 'A Response to What Climate Change Can Do About Tort Law' (2012) 42 Environmental Law Report News & Analysis 10,749, 10,751; Laura Burgers, 'Should Judges Make Climate Change Law' (2020) 9:1 Transnational Environmental Law 55, 57–58.

[6] [2021] NZCA 552, [2022] 2 NZLR 284 [16] (*Smith (CA)*).

[7] See, for example, Jonathan H Adler, 'Taking Property Rights Seriously: The Case of Climate Change' (2009) 26(2) Social Philosophy and Policy 296; Jonathan Zasloff, 'The Judicial Carbon Tax: Reconstructing Public Nuisance and Climate Change' (2008) 55 UCLA Law Review 1827 at 1882 (observing 'It thus seems somewhat unrealistic to criticize the nuisance system on the grounds that it is unwieldly, imperfect, and continually contentious. Yes, it is, and so is everything else. Litigation very often fails, and so does legislation'); Robert F Blomquist, 'Comparative Climate Change Torts' (2012) 46:4 Valparaiso University Law Rev 1053.

[8] As Galperin and Kysar have argued, a climate case brought under a tort framework does not require the courts to 'fundamentally alter the normative underpinnings of the framework'. This can give tort law an advantage over environmental statutes, which have substantive environmental foundations that may become obsolete or unworkable as the environment, or science, changes. Joshua Galperin and Douglas A Kysar, 'Uncommon Law Judging in the Anthropocene', in Jolene Lin and Douglas Kysar (eds), *Climate Change Litigation in the Asia Pacific* (CUP, 2020) 35.

[9] David Bullock, 'Public Nuisance and Climate Change: The Common Law's Solutions to the Plaintiff, Defendant and Causation Problems' (2022) 85(5) Modern Law Review 1136.

The sceptic's view of tort law and climate change wrongly paints tort as the law-of-small-wrongs. History paints a different picture. For centuries, the common law courts deployed tort law as a response to harms caused by significant social perils, notwithstanding the scale and structural complexity of those problems.[10] The modern tort of negligence was born not from snails in bottles, but from the increased frequency of accidents caused by new and dangerous working conditions associated with an increasingly industrialised society.[11]

Beyond accidents, tort law was instrumental in addressing harms associated with other problems arising from the Industrial Revolution: the pollution of the natural environment. Some of the most socially significant problems of industrialisation were the pollution of water and the air, and these serve as useful analogues for the challenge presented by climate change. When viewed in its time, the calamitous nature of earlier industrial pollution should not be underestimated. The Industrial Revolution that took place in England in the late eighteenth century brought with it massive social upheaval. Urban centres grew rapidly, and technological developments saw resources being utilised in new and inconsistent ways. A largely agricultural society was transformed into one where factories were situated near homes and farms, making use of the air as a ready resource into which smoke and toxic gases could be disposed. Acid rain and acrid chemical exhausts left the landscape around industrial cities like St Helens appearing to be "the landscape of Hell . . . foreshadowed".[12]

In England's industrial heartland, water was central to both the operation of new industrial processes—including manufacturing processes like dye works, and to make steam to generate energy—and also as a means of disposing the wastes and by-products of such processes and the cities providing their workforces. The resources that were available for these purposes were in many instances viewed as having limitless or almost limitless abundance and carrying capacity.[13] Because the waste disposed into common resources often shifted the problem onto others, or no one in particular, there was little reason for polluters to do anything different.[14]

The pollution of waterways was also a consequence of efforts to avoid other social ills—especially health issues that plagued England's industrial cities—and a desire to further the economic and political power of Britain and its empire. The scale of England's sanitation problem was immense. For factory workers living in England's new industrial towns, life was miserable. In these towns, "the lack of sanitation and any provision for the disposal of sewage and rubbish meant that ill health was endemic" and "the death rate in the industrial cities [in the 1840s] was staggering" with "the particular misery of the workers [being] matched by the more general and pervasive environmental abuse caused by the factories".[15]

As waterborne illness ravaged England's rapidly growing industrial cities, Parliament began to impose requirements on city authorities to develop reticulated sewer systems to replace

[10] See, for example, Ben Pontin, *Nuisance Law and Environmental Protection: A study of nuisance injunctions in practice* (Lawtext Publishing, 2013); Kate Markey, 'Air Pollution as Public Nuisance: Comparing Modern-Day Greenhouse Gas Abatement with Nineteenth-Century Smoke Abatement' (2022) 120(1) Michigan Law Review 1535.

[11] Ken Oliphant, 'Tort Law, Risk, and Technological Innovation in England' (2014) 59 McGill Law Journal 820; Donald G Gifford, 'Technological Triggers to Tort Revolution: Steam Locomotives, Autonomous Vehicles, and Accident Compensation' (2018) 11 Journal of Tort Law 71; Guido Calabresi, *The Costs of Accidents* (Yale University Press, 1970).

[12] W G Hoskins, *The Making of the English Landscape* (first published 1954, Penguin Books, 1970) 222.

[13] William R Catton Jr, 'Understanding Humanity's Damaged Future' (2009) 79:4 Sociological Inquiry 509, 519–20.

[14] John P S McLaren, 'Nuisance Law and the Industrial Revolution: Some Lessons from Social History' (1983) 3:2 Oxford Journal of Legal Studies 155, 163.

[15] ibid 164.

traditional privies. The goal was improved sanitation and public health, and ultimately, sustained economic growth. Of course, the sewage had to go somewhere, and the obvious solution—indeed, a solution sometimes mandated by legislation—was for cities to drain their sewers into the nearest river. This did succeed in improving urban sanitation, but the communities living downstream from those cities saw their once clean rivers transform into open sewers. Battle lines were drawn across a rural and urban divide, with a strong case made by the cities that this was a necessary evil: Industrialisation required urbanisation, urbanisation required sanitation, and sewers had to be drained because the alternatives, including purification, came with prohibitive expense.

Tort law—in the form of the tort of public nuisance—and thus the courts, were at the forefront of this battle. Interferences with common resources—especially rivers, fisheries, and the air—became increasingly frequent through the eighteenth, nineteenth, and early twentieth centuries, and were often the subject of actions in public nuisance.[16] Between the 1850s and the 1890s nearly every major urban centre in England had faced actual or threatened actions in public nuisance connected to sewage pollution.[17]

Like some other torts, public nuisance developed as a crime.[18] It regulated activities that interfered with "public rights", being rights held in common by members of the public.[19] Public rights included specific recognised rights, like the right to pass and repass on the highway or over navigable waters, and were extended to a wider range of activities that endangered public health or public safety. As the courts developed public nuisance, a private action was recognised for those who had been particularly injured by such a nuisance,[20] following the general trend of the common law allowing actions on the case where a wrong caused damage.[21]

The Anglo-American cases on pollution of water and air during the Industrial Revolution provide a doctrinal blueprint for solving what I have called the "plaintiff problem", the "defendant problem", and the "causation problem" of climate change, at least in the context of a public nuisance action seeking to enjoin a polluting activity.[22] The plaintiff problem concerns the fact that everyone is injured by the emission of greenhouse gases. This is solved by the standing rule in public nuisance, which requires a claim to either be brought in the name of the attorney general or to be brought by a plaintiff who can show particular injury, meaning some tangible physical injury—and not merely some theoretical injury—from the nuisance.[23] There might be very many people in this class, but it is a determinate class nonetheless.

The defendant problem concerns the fact that there is ubiquity in contributions to climate change. Every person on Earth contributes in some way to climate change by creating some amount of greenhouse gas emissions. One Justice of the Supreme Court of New Zealand posed this problem rhetorically during oral argument in *Smith v Fonterra*: "Well, I've got a Land Rover. Sue me! Why don't you sue me?"[24] The answer to this problem arises from the fact that

[16] See, for example, McLaren (n 14). In the United States, see Markey (n 10).

[17] Pontin (n 10) 53.

[18] For an extended discussion of the history and classification of the tort, see David Bullock 'Public Nuisance is a Tort' (2022) 15(2) Journal of Tort Law 137.

[19] J R Spencer, 'Public Nuisance—A Critical Examination' (1989) 48 Cambridge Law Journal 55 at 80.

[20] *Anonymous* (1535) YB Mich 27 Hen 8, f 27, pl 10.

[21] AK Kiralfy, *The Action on the Case* (Sweet & Maxwell Ltd, 1951) at 69.

[22] Bullock, 'Public Nuisance and Climate Change' (n 9).

[23] *George v Newfoundland and Labrador* (2016) 399 DLR (4th) 440 at [115], citing with approval Allan M Linden and Bruce P Feldthusen, *Canadian Tort Law* (9th edn, LexisNexis Canada, 2011) at 575–76.

[24] Douglas A Kysar, 'The Duty of Climate Care' (2024) 73(2) DePaul Law Review 487, 511 (quoting reporting of a question posed from the bench by Kós J).

not all emissions are created equal. The law of nuisance has long recognised that people can interfere with the rights of others in a way that is not legally wrong or even legally relevant. A reasonable exercise of a public right will not be a wrong merely because it adversely affects the ability of someone else to do the same. The paradigm example of a public right is the right to pass and repass on a public highway;[25] yet those caught in a traffic jam do not commit a public nuisance despite impeding the passage of others: "There would be none on the highways if every obstruction of the highway constituted a legal obstruction".[26] This means that there is an inherent element of "give and take" in the exercise of public rights and that users of resources governed by public rights "must expect to be obstructed occasionally. It is the price users pay for the privilege of obstructing others".[27] By contrast, uses of a road which are more than temporary or that are unusual, "what may be termed excessive user . . . if he uses his rights in a manner incompatible with the fair exercise of their rights by the rest of the public", would be a public nuisance.[28] The result is that "No member of the public has an exclusive right to use the highway", instead "he has merely a right to use it subject to the reasonable user of others, and if that reasonable user causes him to be obstructed he has no legal cause of complaint".[29]

In the context of climate change, we all must use the atmosphere as a space to dispose of greenhouse gases, and that means we must tolerate from others what we expect others to tolerate from us. Public nuisance "is in truth the law of give and take"[30] because those who use the atmosphere must not unreasonably impede others but should expect, and accept, some reasonable and occasional impairment of their use when that is necessary for the use of another. Because not everyone uses the atmosphere in the same way, the question is where and how the line is drawn.

A separate, but related, principle is *de minimis non curat lex*—that the law does not regard trifles[31]—which serves as a policy that the courts "will not allow their processes to be used to pursue a claim unless what is at stake justifies the use of the process".[32] A microscopic scratch on a car door, or a passing brush to the arm while exiting a subway car, do not properly concern the law. The English courts recognised that although the natural flow of a river could not be diverted, the taking of some water, for example for ordinary domestic uses, was *de minimis* such that no right of action flowed in favour of a downstream proprietor.[33]

25 *Soltau v De Held* (1851) Sim (NS) 133, 143 per Kindersley V-C, describing obstruction of a public highway as 'perhaps the most ordinary case of a public nuisance'.

26 *Lingké v Christchurch Corporation* [1912] 3 KB 595 (CA) 602.

27 *Harper v GN Haden & Sons* [1933] Ch 298 (CA) 320.

28 Edmund W Garrett, *The Law of Nuisances* (2nd edn, London, 1897) 32. The fact that a nuisance was only temporary was not, of itself, necessarily fatal to a public nuisance claim, especially if it lasted more than a 'negligible time'. See *Lingké* (n 26) 607, approved in *Wildtree Hotels Ltd v Harrow London Bourgh Council* [2001] 2 AC 1 (HL) 16.

29 *Harper* (n 27) 317.

30 ibid 320.

31 Max L Veech and Charles R Moon, 'De Minimis Non Curat Lex' (1947) 45:5 Michigan Law Review 537, 538. The use of the word 'trifling' is significant. The terms 'minor' and 'de minimis' are not synonymous or interchangeable, see *Rea v Wellington City Council* [2007] NZRMA 449 (HC) [11]. The concept of de minimis is synonymous with 'negligible' (see *Bonnington Castings Ltd v Wardlaw* [1956] 1 All ER 615, 618–19) or 'immaterial' (see *Veba Oil Supply & Trading GmbH v Petrotrade Inc* [2001] EWCA Civ 1832, [2002] 1 All ER 703 [13]).

32 *Rothwell v Chemical & Insulating Co Ltd; Re Pleural Plaques Litigation* [2006] EWCA Civ 27, [2004] 4 All ER 1161 [21].

33 James Kent, *Commentaries on American Law Volume III* (2nd ed, 1832) at 440.

These principles can be used by a court to define a sensible and bounded group of appropriate potential defendants. Not all emissions are necessarily wrong or legally relevant, but some will be. For example, a person emitting at some level reflective of ordinary per capita emissions might be outside the scope of potential legal responsibility—on the basis that we must all tolerate emissions from others to the same extent that we expect our own emissions to be tolerated—but someone who emits substantially more than an ordinary citizen may face potential liability. Precisely where that line is drawn would be a matter for judicial determination in light of evidence.

The causation problem follows from the defendant problem. There are many contributors to greenhouse gas emissions and no single operating cause, such that no one emitter could likely be said to be a cause in fact. This argument was routinely deployed by defendants in water and air pollution public nuisance cases in Victorian England, and it was rejected time and again by the courts. The nature of public rights are such that public nuisances will very often have multiple contributors. In contrast to torts like negligence, the courts did not deploy a causation in fact rule in public nuisance cases; rather, it was sufficient that a defendant was found to be a contributor to the nuisance.[34] Importantly, these cases recognised both that the relevant contribution was to the circumstances amounting to the nuisance, not to any particular harm to the plaintiff, and that a contribution would still be causally relevant as a legal matter even if it was so small as not to be a nuisance in its own right.

The courts were also readily able to resolve with issues of relief, despite public nuisance cases typically raising significant policy questions connected to the harm causing activity being economically or socially beneficial. In *Attorney-General v Birmingham*, the plaintiff sought to restrain the city of Birmingham draining its sewers into the river Tame, upstream of his estate.[35] The city pleaded that such an order would cause a public health catastrophe in the city. The city's pleas were rejected. As Page-Wood V-C saw it, the city had wronged the plaintiff, and so relief had to follow. He observed that it was "a matter of almost absolute indifference whether the decision [would] affect a population of 25[0],000, or a single individual" because it was not for the court to conclude that the benefits of the activity justified the city interfering with the plaintiff's rights. That was a question for the legislature and, as such, if "after all possible experiments, [the defendants] cannot drain Birmingham without invading the Plaintiff's private rights, they must apply to Parliament for power to invade his rights".[36] Or, as he held in a similar case of a sewage pollution nuisance by a city corporation: "The Defendants must either abate the evil—whatever difficulties may be imposed in their way—or they must go to the Legislature; and, no doubt, the Legislature will be ready to afford a remedy if they find the evil is such as is deserving of it".[37]

Unlike some modern courts, which have seen such policy issues as a reason to find tort claims to be non-justiciable,[38] the Victorian courts took a rights-first approach. If they found a wrong, then a remedy would follow. The courts recognised that their granting a remedy might prompt a legislative response—for example, the passing of a statute permitting the nuisance causing activity despite the harms it caused—but this was viewed as an appropriate operation of the separation of powers. Protecting rights according to law was the province of the courts;

[34] See, for example, *Blair v Deakin* (1887) 57 LT 522 (Ch); *Crossley and Sons Ltd v Lightowler* (1867) LR 2 Ch App 478; *Woodyear v Schaefer* 57 Md 1 (1881); *Attorney-General v Ewen* (1895) 3 BCR 468 (BCSC).

[35] (1858) 4 K & J 528, (1858) 70 Eng Rep 220.

[36] ibid 539–42.

[37] *Attorney-General v Leeds Corporation* (1870) 5 Ch App 583, 595.

[38] See, for example, *AEP v Connecticut*, *Sharma*, and the decision of the Court of Appeal of New Zealand in *Smith v Fonterra Co-Operative Group Ltd*, all as discussed below.

policy decisions were for the legislature. Modern judicial invocations of policy as a reason to avoid determining complex tort cases wrongly deny plaintiffs access to justice and involve a judicial pre-emption of policy decisions while simultaneously abrogating the core judicial role of determining rights and providing remedies for wrongs.

A lesson from these cases of the past is that setting the law of tort against legislative regulation is to set up a false dichotomy: The courts develop the common law subject to regulation, and regulation responds to judicial decision-making. It is doubtful that anyone truly believes that tort law applied by the courts in individual cases is a structurally optimal way to address the problem of climate change. But that does not mean tort law cannot, and does not, have a role to play.[39] Judges can be left to judge; policy can be left for the policymakers.

3. A Tentative Present

Despite these strong historical foundations, attempts to apply tort law to the problem of climate change have been fraught. Climate change-related litigation[40] based on private law obligations has been both less prevalent and less successful than constitutional or administrative actions brought against governments connected with exercise of public powers.[41] Most private law climate change claims have been brought in the United States, and none have ultimately succeeded in that jurisdiction.[42]

The "first wave" of private law climate litigation between 2005 and 2015 was characterised by the successive failure of tort cases—on preliminary motions and without trial—on grounds of non-justiciability, displacement, and lack of constitutional standing.[43] Importantly, these cases did not fail on the basis that the elements of the tort causes of action pleaded were not, or could not be, satisfied. Rather, they typically failed on grounds largely peculiar to the political order created by the United States Constitution. However, several significant decisions outside the United States have recently upheld private law claims connected to climate change,[44]

[39] See also Benjamin Ewing and Douglas A Kysar, 'Prods and Pleas: Limited Government in an Era of Unlimited Harm' (2011) 121(2) Yale Law Journal 350.

[40] Climate change-related litigation is generally understood as litigation directly linked to climate changed, including litigation seeking to address greenhouse gas emissions that cause climate change, or adaption to its predicted impacts, but can also encompass a wide penumbra of cases bearing on climate change or on matters that have implications for climate change. See Jacqueline Peel and Hari M Osofsky, *Climate Change Litigation: Regulatory Pathways to Cleaner Energy* (CUP, 2015) 4–8.

[41] The differences between constitutional systems, and between constitutional claims and tortious claims, mean that success in cases like *The State of the Netherlands v Urgenda Foundation*, the Supreme Court of the Netherlands (20 December 2019), case 19/00135 (English translation) do not easily translate to claims in tort in common law jurisdictions. See, Jacqueline Peel, Hari Osofsky, and Anita Foerster, 'Shaping the "Next Generation" of Climate Change Litigation in Australia' [2017] 41 Melbourne University Law Review 793, 805.

[42] Jutta Brunnée and others, 'Overview of Legal Issues Relevant to Climate Change' in Richard Lord and others (eds), *Climate Change Liability: Transnational Law and Practice* (CUP, 2012) 32. There is some recent promise at state level, for example claims by the City and County of Honolulu, including in public nuisance, against energy company Sunoco surviving motions to dismiss in the Supreme Court of the State of Hawai'i (*City & County of Honolulu v Sunoco LP* SCAP-22-0000429, 31 October 2023).

[43] Geetanjali Ganguly, Joana Setzer, and Veerle Heyvaert, 'If at First You Don't Succeed: Suing Corporations for Climate Change' (2018) 38:4 Oxford Journal of Legal Studies 841, 846.

[44] See, for example, *Smith v Fonterra Co-Operative Group Ltd* [2022] NZSC 35; *Sharma v Minster for the Environment* [2021] FCA 560 (holding that the Australian Minister for the Environment owed a duty of care to the plaintiffs not to negligently cause them personal injury, albeit ultimately being overturned on appeal); *Royal Dutch Shell Plc v Vereninging Mileudefensie* ECLI:NL:GHDHA:2024:2100 (12 November 2024) (finding injunctive relief unavailable against the defendant based on the present state

signalling a potential turning point in the so-called second wave of private law climate litigation. In the United States, climate change-related public nuisance actions have increased in recent years at a state level, heralding a reinvigoration of public nuisance litigation in that jurisdiction.[45] However, tort claims connected to climate change remain nascent, with many being dismissed at an interlocutory stage and never reaching trial.

In the United States, early attempts to deploy tort law in cases like *Comer v Murphy Oil*,[46] *American Electric Power Co Inc v Connecticut*,[47] and *Native Village of Kivalina v ExxonMobil*[48] were all met with resounding failure. In *American Electric Power v Connecticut*, for example, the Supreme Court held that the Clean Air Act, and the Environmental Protection Agency (EPA) role authorised by that Act, displaced the tort of public nuisance as a matter of federal law.[49] The Court held that the effect of the Clean Air Act was to permit emissions until the EPA acted, and that what was critical was that Congress had delegated regulatory power to the EPA.[50] Even if the EPA were to decline to regulate emissions altogether, its ongoing power to do so would mean that "the federal courts would have no warrant to employ the federal common law of nuisance to upset the agency's expert determination".[51] The decision in *American Electric Power*, although actually grounded in a peculiarity of United States' constitutional law, appears to have had something of a chilling effect around the world.

Elsewhere in the common law world, the courts have largely proceeded on the basis that tort law and climate change do not mix. In the United Kingdom, for example, public nuisance cases have only succeeded in the climate change context when brought *against* the actions of climate change protesters by polluters looking to restrain protest activity.[52] In Australia, plaintiffs have looked to the tort of negligence rather than public nuisance. In *Sharma v Minister for the Environment*, the Full Court of the Federal Court of Australia rejected a claim brought by a group of Australian children represented by a litigation guardian—a nun—against the Minister for the Environment in negligence concerning administrative decisions connected to expansion of a coal mine.[53] The claim had been allowed at first instance, although the Court has refused to issue the formal injunction sought pending the Minister actually making the decisions at issue.[54] On appeal, the Full Court overturned the decision with the appellate court

of norms regarding private climate responsibility, but not precluding such liability in future cases); *VZW Klimaatzaak v Kingdom of Belgium* 2015/4585/A (17 June 2021) (finding that the defendants had breached Articles 1382 and 1383 of the Belgium Civil Code, which describe negligence-based liability).

[45] Albert C Lin, 'The Second Wave of Climate Change Public Nuisance Litigation' (2019) 51(1) Trends 10.

[46] See discussion of the various iterations of this litigation in, for example, Alex B Rothenberg, 'Decision by Recusal: *Comer v Murphy Oil USA* Lets Naysayers and Disqualified Judges in the Fifth Circuit Determine the Outcome of a Case without a Hearing' (2011) 85(4) Tul L Rev 1131; R Henry Weaver and Douglas A Kysar, 'Courting Disaster: Climate Change and the Adjudication of Catastrophe' (2017) 93 Notre Dame Law Review 295, 324; Richard Lazarus, 'What the Law Supposes Is a Ass' (2010) Environmental Forum 12.

[47] 564 US 410 (2011).

[48] 696 F 3d 849 (9th Cir 2012).

[49] *American Electric Power* (n 47) 424.

[50] ibid 426.

[51] ibid 426.

[52] See *Boyd v Ineos Upstream Limited* [2019] EWCA Civ 515; *Roberts v R* [2018] EWCA Crim 2739; and *R v Brown* [2022] EWCA Crim 6.

[53] [2021] FCA 560. See also Jacqueline Peel and Rebekkah Markey-Towler, 'Recipe for Success? Lessons for Strategic Climate Litigations from the *Sharma*, *Neubauer*, and *Shell* Cases' (2021) 22:8 German Law Journal 1484.

[54] *Sharma* (n 53) [490]–[91].

retreating to a more restrictive application of tort principles.[55] *Sharma* represents an example of the judicial retrenchment cautioned against by Kysar.[56] The Full Court, faced with a bold approach to finding a novel duty of care at first instance,[57] fell back upon well-trodden concerns of lack of coherence, insufficient proximity, indeterminacy, and causation with little effort to develop the tort of negligence or to reimagine doctrine in the face of a novel challenge. The decision was identified as "a major setback for climate litigation applicants globally".[58]

A bastion of hope for tort law and climate change in the common law world has come in the New Zealand case of *Smith v Fonterra Co-operative Group Ltd*.[59] Mike Smith (Ngāpuhi, Ngāti Kahu), a Māori elder and activist, sued seven defendants who either were emitters of greenhouse gases or who supplied products that resulted in the emission of greenhouse gases when consumed.[60] Mr Smith claimed that the defendants' emissions contributed to climate change, which threated customary land in which he had an interest, and other sites of cultural significance. He pleaded claims in public nuisance, negligence, and (what has been called) an "inchoate" tort that sought to hold the defendant strictly liable for knowing contributions to climate change.[61] Mr Smith did not seek damages. Rather, he sought two alternative injunctive remedies:[62] the first, to require the defendants to reduce their emissions over time; and the second, to require the defendants to cease their nuisance creating activities immediately.

The defendants applied to "strike out" Mr Smith's claim, in other words, to have it dismissed before trial on a lack of legal tenability. At first instance the High Court struck out the nuisance and negligence causes of action finding a lack of standing, directness, and causation.[63] However, the Court allowed the "inchoate" tort to proceed to trial on the basis that it was so novel the Court could not conclude the claim might not be established once evidence was heard.[64]

All parties appealed to the Court of Appeal, which dismissed Mr Smith's appeal and allowed the defendants' cross-appeals.[65] The appeal was determined on what was essentially non-justiciability reasoning. The Court held that "the magnitude of the crisis which is climate change simply cannot be appropriately or adequately addressed by common law tort claims pursued through the courts".[66] It held that it was too difficult to define a class of plaintiffs or defendants,[67] that the injunctive relief sought was untenable,[68] and that tort claims in the courts amounted to "an inherently inefficient and ad hoc way of addressing climate change" which was "likely to result in arbitrary outcomes and ongoing litigation that lasts many years".[69] The

55 *Minister for the Environment v Sharma* [2022] FCAFC 35.

56 Kysar (n 1) 48.

57 Jacqueline Peel and Rebekkah Markey-Towler, 'A Duty to Care: The Case of *Sharma v Minister for the Environment* [2021] FCA 560' (2021) 33(3) Journal of Environmental Law 727.

58 Libby Douglas, 'Sharma v Minister for the Environment' (2024) 42(2) Australian Resources & Energy Law Journal 98, 99.

59 *Smith v Fonterra Co-operative Group Ltd* [2020] NZHC 419, [2020] 2 NZLR 394.

60 ibid [6].

61 Maria Hook and others, 'Tort to the Environment: A Stretch Too Far or a Simple Step Forward?' (2021) Journal of Environmental Law 195, 199.

62 *Smith (HC)* (n 59) [12].

63 ibid [73].

64 ibid [103].

65 *Smith (CA)* (n 6).

66 ibid [16].

67 ibid [18]–[19].

68 ibid [20]–[26].

69 ibid [27].

problem of climate change was to be solved, the Court held, by national legislation, and tort litigation was not consistent with the "policy goals and scheme" of New Zealand's emissions reduction legislation.[70] It stated that "private litigation against a small subset of emitters . . . will not be effective to address climate change at a national level, let alone globally. It will be costly and inefficient. And it will be arbitrary in its application and impact".[71] It also considered that a legal inability to establish causation was fatal to the claim, holding that the nature of climate change meant "there is in fact no identifiable group of defendants that can be brought before the Court to stop the pleaded harm", and that an injunction would not prevent the pleaded harm.[72] Finally, the third cause of action, which proposed the creation of a new tort and which had survived strikeout at first instance, was struck out on the basis that although novel, it was a "bare assertion . . . without any attempt to delineate its scope".[73]

The Supreme Court of New Zealand granted leave to appeal,[74] and allowed Mr Smith's appeal.[75] The Supreme Court refused to strike out his claims, holding that in a case founded upon "seriously arguable non-trivial harm . . . the common law should lean towards receipt of the claim, and full evaluation based on evidence and argument over pre-emptive elimination".[76] The Supreme Court also rejected any notion of statutory pre-emption, relying on well-established common law authority that while a statute may displace tort, the courts would be slow to reach that conclusion absent reasonably clear language or necessary implication.[77]

Substantively, the Court recognised that Mr Smith's pleaded claim in public nuisance was legally tenable. First, the Court held that while liability in public nuisance is strict, a defendant will only be liable if the kind of harm suffered was a reasonably foreseeable consequence of the defendant's conduct, meaning there was a real risk of damage.[78] Second, the defendant's act or omission must substantially and unreasonably interfere with public rights, although the Court queried whether an unreasonableness requirement carried any weight.[79] Third, the tort does not depend on any particular person suffering damage, but to have standing a plaintiff must show that they have suffered some damage particular to them.[80] These statements of principle reflected nearly 500 years of Anglo-Commonwealth common law jurisprudence on the law of public nuisance.[81]

70 ibid [33].
71 ibid [33].
72 ibid [92].
73 ibid [124].
74 *Smith v Fonterra Co-Operative Group Ltd* [2022] NZSC 35.
75 *Smith v Fonterra Co-Operative Group Limited* [2024] NZSC 5, [2024] 1 NZLR 134. See also Sam Bookman, '*Smith v Fonterra* and the Climatisation of Tort Law' (2025) 88(1) Modern Law Review 192; David Bullock, 'Climate Change in the Supreme Court of New Zealand: Smith v Fonterra Co-Operative Group Ltd' (2024) 98(7) Australian Law Journal 499.
76 ibid [84]–[85].
77 ibid [97]–[98].
78 ibid [110].
79 ibid [111].
80 ibid [112].
81 See, for example, William L Prosser, 'Private Action for Public Nuisance' (1966) 52 Virginia Law Review 997; Carolyn Sappideen and Prue Vines, *Fleming's The Law of Torts* (10th edn, Thomson Reutrers, 2011) ch 21; John Murphy, *The Law of Nuisance* (OUP, 2010), ch 7; Edwin Peel and James Goudkamp, *Winfield and Jolowicz on Tort* (19th edn, Sweet & Maxwell, 2014), ch 15; Stephen Todd (ed), *Todd on Torts* (8th edn, Thomson Reuters, 2019), ch 10.

Mr Smith's pleading of damage to property was sufficient to ground standing.[82] It also held that pleaded public rights—rights to public health, public safety, public comfort, public convenience, and public peace—were tenable by reference to rights recognised in the leading English authority of *R v Rimmington*[83] and the leading New Zealand authority of *A-G v Abraham and Williams Ltd*.[84] As to causation, the Court held that that while the common law had not previously grappled with a crisis "as all-embracing" as climate change, in the ninteenth and early twentieth centuries it did deal with "another existential crisis, albeit one of lesser scale, when the industrial revolution dramatically enlarged the risk of accidents through the mechanisation of factories, transportation and mining".[85] The Industrial Revolution had also required the common law "to deal with new, widespread risk and damage caused by air and water pollution and the escape of biohazards".[86] It held that existing common law cases where liability was found for water and air pollution involved "a mix of public and private harm and public and private good, and the common law (revised sometimes by statute) has had to mediate liability for the former",[87] and the Court observed that "climate change engages comparable complexities albeit at a quantum leap scale engagement".[88] The Court also recognised the tenability of an aggregate approach to causation in public nuisance cases, holding that it was "certainly arguable that . . . a defendant must take responsibility for its contribution to a common interference with public rights; its responsibility should not be contingent on the absence of co-contribution or be in effect discharged by the equivalent acts of others".[89] However, it held that some degree of line drawing would be required to determine what amounted to a legally relevant contribution, noting that the contributions of those who emit through ordinary domestic activities were *de minimis* and not sufficiently unreasonable to attract liability.[90]

4. New Frontiers of Tort Law and Climate Change

Lessons from the past give us comfort that tort law, and the common law courts, may already have many of the tools needed to grapple with complex collective action problems like climate change. A decision of the present like *Smith v Fonterra* recognises the possibility that existing tort doctrine can engage upon climate change, or that it can develop to do so. It may also be that climate change demands that the common law of torts charts a different course and that it opens itself to new ideas. In meeting the challenges posed by climate change, there is potential for the common law of torts to draw upon different legal ideas—and even legal and philosophical systems—to remain relevant and effective in the age of ecological collapse.

This section focuses on efforts to develop a new climate tort in New Zealand, and the potential influence of Indigenous legal systems and human rights on the future of tort law. My

[82] At [150]–[51]. Reflecting the view expressed in Carolyn Sappideen and Prue Vines (n 81) 211 and Erika Chamberlain and Stephen GA Pitel (eds), *Fridman's The Law of Torts in Canada* (4th edn, Thomson Reuters, 2020) 238.

[83] *R v Rimmington* [2005] UKHL 63; [2006] 1 AC 459.

[84] *Smith (SC)* (75) [145], referring to *Attorney-General v Abraham and Williams Ltd* [1949] NZLR 461 (CA) 484.

[85] ibid [156].

[86] ibid [157].

[87] ibid [157].

[88] ibid [157].

[89] ibid [164].

[90] ibid [168]–[69].

argument here is not that tort law must develop for some freewheeling instrumentalist end or an invocation of legal pluralism as such. Rather, I seek to challenge tort scholars to think critically about how worldviews, especially Eurocentric ones, continue to influence our understanding of the law of obligations, and to question whether perceived constraints on tort law's ability to respond to climate change are driven by something inherent in the law of civil wrongs, or instead by limitations arising from a particular worldview.

To understand the influence of worldview on tort law, it is necessary to first understand a little about Māori, the first people of New Zealand. Māori are descendants of the peoples of Polynesia whose epic ocean-going navigators discovered and then settled New Zealand in the late 1200s and early 1300s CE.[91] Those arriving in New Zealand brought with them sophisticated systems of *tikanga*—laws and customs—of the various Pacific islands and societies from which they departed.[92] Those systems then developed to meet the demands of the larger islands and more temperate climate of New Zealand, resulting in the creation of a new law fit for a new land.[93]

This system of laws and customs, known as *tikanga Māori*, was not homogenous. Rather, as a system designed for small, kin-based village communities, its details varied to meet the history, circumstances, and environment of each particular *iwi* or *hapū*.[94] However, and not wholly unlike the concept of a *common* law that was developing concurrently in England, tikanga Māori was and remains held together by a common set of core principles and values. The "glue" of tikanga Māori is *whanaungatanga*, being the rights and obligations of kinship.[95] Whanaungatanga can be described as "the maintenance of properly tended relationships", but its reach goes beyond the relationships between humans to also encapsulate the human relationship with the physical and spiritual world.[96] Whanaungatanga is closely linked to *whakapapa*, a genealogical concept that describes the connection between all things: animate, inanimate, and spiritual.[97] The unbreakable connections embodied in the ideas of whanaungatanga and whakapapa carry a corresponding obligation of *kaitiakitanga*, a duty to care for one's own. As the Māori worldview, *te ao Māori*, is metaphysically grounded in physical and spiritual interconnectedness, an important manifestation of kaitiakitanga is the duty to care for the environment and natural resources. Combined with concepts of *mana* (the rights and obligations of authority) and *tapu* (the concept and regulation of sacredness), tikanga Māori provided a principled-based system of social order and regulation. There are many ways in te ao Māori to address wrongs. However, a breach of tikanga could result in a *hara* or *take* (a wrong or a right) which required action to be taken or *utu* (meaning reciprocity, which could include the provision of compensation)—or the related concept of *muru* (making good of transgressions of personal or property rights)—to restore *ea* (a state of harmony or balance). A common protective mechanism used when resources or the natural world is out of balance—which may be because of human activity—is a *rāhui* (a prohibition or constraint on certain human activities).

[91] Richard Walter and others, 'Mass Migration and the Polynesian Settlement of New Zealand' (2017) 30 Journal of World Prehistory 351, 371.

[92] Joseph Williams, 'Lex Aotearoa: An Heroic Attempt to Map the Māori Dimension in Modern New Zealand Law' (2013) 21 Waikato Law Review 1, 2.

[93] ibid 2.

[94] ibid 2.

[95] ibid 4.

[96] ibid 4.

[97] ibid 6–7.

Sir Joe Williams, a justice of the Supreme Court of New Zealand and a leading scholar of tikanga Māori, explained extrajudicially that these concepts embodied what might now be called tort law:[98]

> In traditional Māori society, a transgression of another person's personal or possessory rights would see the victim's whānau [immediate family] levying muru on the property of the transgressor's whānau. This would be done with due and public ceremony, demonstrate the support of the hapū [a wider family structure comprising a number of whanau] for the penalty. . . . A particularly egregious wrong, or a particularly important victim, might even ratchet up the level of the muru from usual whānau level action to hapū level. And in the most serious of cases it might even lead to forfeiture of land. The accidental killing of one of my ancestors by a member of the Parawhau of Whangarei led to the latter hapū transferring land to my section of Ngāti Pukenga to *muru* (make good on) the *hara* or wrong. . . . In the 19th century muru was described in English by the settlers as plunder, giving the impression that it was a random act of violent theft. It was of course nothing of the sort. Rather it was a civil/criminal remedy—indeed the primary legal remedy for transgressions of the kind I have described. And it was community sanctioned.

To a tort scholar, the parallels between some of the core values of tikanga Māori and theories of tort law are striking. One can see concepts that might be described as corrective justice, or even civil recourse, underpinning the recognition of, and redress for, wrongs in Māori society. But the differences between tikanga Māori and theories of tort law are just as important. Unlike the highly individualistic philosophies upon which common law theories of tort have historically been based,[99] for Māori, whanaungatanga meant that a wrong was not an individual wrong, even if it was caused by or inflicted upon an individual. Duties, wrongs, and remedies were always a matter of collective responsibility for a kin group: "So muru was not a system of individual to individual compensation or correction as in tort . . . it was an aspect of the whanaungatanga value: it operated kin group to kin group".[100] Recall, too, that whanaungatanga and whakapapa described not only relationships between people, but also a *genealogical* interconnectedness between people and the physical and spiritual world; a wrong to the environment could also be a wrong to people and to the *atua* (gods). These atua to which people can trace their descent lines are manifested and personified in the natural world, including *Ranginui* as the sky father and *Papatūānuku* as the earth mother. The differences between the *Māori law of torts* and *common law of torts* reflected the different settings and worldviews of the people who created those legal orders. While the neighbourhoods of Atkin and Cardozo were collections of people whose relationship with the environment was typically one of instrumentality, conquest, and mastery;[101] for Māori, connection with the environment was immutable and impossible to separate from the human world. The nature and extent of obligations followed accordingly.

Te ao Māori and tikanga Māori give us a familiar, but different, lens through which to view the concepts of obligations, wrongs, and remedies. Duties are owed collectively and extend to

[98] ibid 4–5.

[99] See, for example, Martin A Kotler, 'The Myth of Individualism and the Appeal of Tort Reform' (2007) 59(4) Rutgers Law Review 779.

[100] Williams (n 92) 5.

[101] See, for example, Philipp Pattberg, 'Conquest, Domination and Control: Europe's Mastery of Nature in Historic Perspective' (2007) 14(1) Journal of Political Ecology 1; Sharon R Krause, 'Environmental Domination' (2020) 48(4) Political Theory 443; William Leiss, *The Domination of Nature* (George Braziller, 1972).

a responsibility to care for the world around us because we are not separate from that world. Wrongs are also collective, and so are obligations of remedy. Atomistic ideas of relational proximity and causation in fact are rejected in favour of a holistic view of the world as a necessarily interconnected whole. Māori tort law is not concerned with a "paradigm of harm in which A wrongfully, directly, and exclusively injures B"[102] because that paradigm simply does not reflect the reality of the Māori world or the Māori worldview. Instead, in Māori tort law the paradigm of harm is one in which people, communities, and their environment are recognised as inherently interconnected.

In New Zealand, the courts have moved to recognise tikanga Māori as a fundamental part of the common law of New Zealand.[103] This is not a fusion as such: tikanga Māori and the common law both maintain their identity as separate juridical systems, but it is recognised that tikanga Māori speaks to the common law of New Zealand. In *Ellis v R (Continuance)*, the Supreme Court of New Zealand unanimously recognised that tikanga Māori forms part of the law of New Zealand, and that it will be recognised in the development of the common law where relevant.[104] *Ellis* was consistent with long-standing recognition that Māori customary rights survived the introduction of the common law to New Zealand.[105]

It was in the context of *Ellis*, and a number of other significant decisions on tikanga Māori,[106] that the Supreme Court came to consider the tenability of Mr Smith's claim for recognition of a novel tort.[107] This tort was formulated as a strict liability duty to avoid material contributions to dangerous anthropogenic interference with the climate system,[108] and was said to be an extension of public nuisance and the tort in *Rylands v Fletcher*—infused with principles of tikanga Māori.[109]

The Supreme Court refused to strike out the novel tort, largely on the basis that it had held that the public nuisance claim was legally tenable and that as a trial on that claim would involve the same issues of fact as the claims in negligence and for the novel tort, it was efficient for all claims to be allowed to proceed to trial.[110] However, the Court did offer some insights into how tikanga Māori might shape the future of tort law in New Zealand.

The Court recorded that tikanga Māori had been applied to tort claims in New Zealand for more than 150 years, identifying a claim for conversion of *pounamu* (New Zealand jade/greenstone), and a claim for conversion of a whale carcass, that had both been resolved on the basis of recognition of rights established by tikanga Māori.[111] The Court recognised that a trial on

[102] To use the language of Kysar (n 1) 3.

[103] See, for example, Jacinta Ruru, 'First Laws: Tikanga Māori in/and the Law' (2018) 49 Victoria University of Wellington Law Review 211; Christian Whata, 'Tikanga and the Law: A Model of Recognition' (2023) 4(3) Amicus Curiae 610.

[104] *Ellis v R (Continuance)* [2022] NZSC 114, [2022] 1 NZLR 239.

[105] See, for example, *R v Symonds* (1847) NZPCC 387, 389–90; *Nireaha Tamaki v Baker* (1901) NZPCC 371, 384; *Runanganui o Te Ika Whenua Inc Soc v Attorney-General* [1994] 2 NZLR 20 (CA), 24. This was a general common law principle: *Tijani v Secretary Southern Nigeria* [1921] 2 AC 399.

[106] Including *Trans-Tasman Resources Ltd v Taranaki-Whanganui Conservation Board* [2021] NZSC 127, [2021] 1 NZLR 801.

[107] The pleading of this novel tort recognised that if existing doctrine could not, despite the plaintiff's arguments, engage with an issue like climate change, then it was necessary for the courts to develop tort doctrine such that it could: Douglas A Kysar, 'The Duty of Climate Care' (2024) 73(2) DePaul Law Review 487 at 504.

[108] *Smith (SC)* (n 75) [71].

[109] Others have posed novel tort frameworks in the context of climate change, including the possibility of torts *to* the environment. See Hook et al (n 61).

[110] *Smith (SC)* (n 75) [175].

[111] ibid [183]–[86].

Mr Smith's claims would inevitably engage with tikanga Māori at multiple levels. Mr Smith's interest in land was grounded in tikanga Māori, and he purported to bring the claim not only as a customary landowner, but also as a *kaitiaki* (guardian) on behalf of his family, his descendants, and the land and ocean as distinct entities.[112]

Regardless of whether the common law of New Zealand is willing and able to make this development, or to otherwise infuse principles of tikanga Māori into existing tort structures, these principles provide a basis to question, and to test, prevailing understandings of tort law. They offer recognition that the atomistic ideas of duty, causation, and loss predominant in the Anglo-United States common law are not necessary features of a functional system of civil wrongs, and that an overreliance on such a worldview may unduly constrain tort law's potential and real-world responsiveness.

5. Conclusion

The past tells us that tort law already has doctrinal tools to respond to the harms caused by complex collective action problems. Public nuisance was used, with success, to respond to the problems of water and air pollution in Victorian England, despite these problems having wicked and polycentric overlays, including a multitude of plaintiffs and defendants, challenging issues of causation, and a complex and politically charged statutory and policy context. While not perfect, tort was able to assist addressing the harmful consequences of activities, to provide relief to those suffering the effects of industrialisation, and to drive technological change. The courts proved up to the task and were able to develop tort to meet the demands of the changing society generating the disputes before them. If the courts of Victorian England had known that the invisible harms of the Industrial Revolution—carbon dioxide—were orders of magnitude more devastating than the acrid smoke, putrid odours, lost limbs, and foul water in the cases before them, then surely those courts would have seen an intervention to address the wrongs associated with greenhouse gas emissions as little more than a simple extension of the doctrinal principles they were already applying. As the Supreme Court of New Zealand recognised in *Smith v Fonterra*, "climate change engages comparable complexities" to the challenges faced by the courts during the Industrial Revolution, "albeit at a quantum leap scale enlargement".[113]

Looking to the future presents us with several potential paths for tort law. Tort law may continue its trend of incremental development through the application and extension of established doctrinal principles underpinning long established torts like public nuisance and perhaps negligence. In the Supreme Court's judgment in *Smith v Fonterra*, we see a court moving in this direction, looking to past cases and established doctrine to chart the course ahead, but also with an open mind to the possibility that new ways of thinking about tort may be required. Another path is for the courts to hold tort law back and to relegate it to being a law-of-small-wrongs. As Kysar observes, such a path would involve courts "retrench[ing] even further onto a narrow, classical liberal conception of tort law in the face of the extraordinary conceptual and empirical challenges to that conception posed by climate change. They would do so, however, at the long-term risk of the social relevance and viability of the tort system".[114] Such an approach is epitomised by the Court of Appeal's judgment in *Smith v Fonterra* and its holding that wrongs associated with greenhouse gas emissions and climate change were

112 ibid [188].
113 *Smith (SC)* (n 75) [157].
114 Kysar (n 1) 48.

essentially non-justiciable as a matter of private law because private liability for such matters would be "ineffective and inefficient, and . . . socially unjust".[115]

Perhaps there is also a third way. Climate change might not lead the common law of torts to stasis or incremental development, rather it might lead it to take a quantum leap. The nature of climate change ought to cause tort scholars to critically rethink the theoretical and doctrinal underpinnings of the modern law of torts. A "narrow, classical liberal conception of tort law"[116] grounded in a mix of atomistic, individualistic, and anthropocentric European enlightenment philosophy looks now to be increasingly naïve in a world we know is not only not limitless, but actually at its limits.[117] Human exceptionalism has long since been dispelled by the *science* that grew from the Enlightenment but nevertheless continues to underpin many of our philosophical instincts. The myth of human exceptionality was something Māori already knew. Tikanga Māori developed from a worldview, and a lived experience, that recognised that humans and the natural world were inevitably and inseparably intermeshed. The natural environment was not some separate thing to be conquered or exploited. Rather, tikanga Māori recognised that the use of the environment came with a correlative duty—kaitiakitanga—to protect and to preserve it, not just for further human use but because this was intrinsically important.

This third way, then, might involve the development of a common law of torts responsive to the demands of the Anthropocene—tort law for an age of ecological collapse.[118] Indigenous legal systems, often built from a more environmentally connected worldview, have the potential to reorientate existing legal norms or to generate new ones.[119] Concepts like the core values of tikanga Māori offer an insight into a different starting point for tort law. The "tort law" of tikanga Māori departs from the tort law of Anglo-American scholars primarily by addressing issues at different levels of resolution. It is a system that recognises a world that is interconnected and not atomistic, in which victims and wrongdoers can be communities as well as individuals, and that obligations of stewardship must underpin human interaction with the natural environment. Embracing these ideas would not necessarily fundamentally recast the common law's framing of tort law. The ideas of neighbourhood and proximity might be expanded, or antiquated notions like causation in fact replaced with a more scientific understanding of cause and effect.[120] It might also be that tort law develops to recognise the importance of environmental systems and harms to them, whether through the recognition of a bespoke climate system tort—whereby a certain contribution of harm to the climate system is a wrong—or a more general tort to the environment. The possibilities for the future of the common law of torts are as vast as the challenges it will be called upon to address.

[115] *Smith (CA)* (n 6) [35].

[116] Kysar (n 1) 48.

[117] Jean-Louis Martin, Virginie Maris, and Daniel S Simberloff, 'The need to respect nature and its limits challenges society and conservation science' (2016) 113 (22) Proceedings of the National Academy of Sciences 6105, 6106.

[118] See, for example, Jorge E Viñuales, 'Law and the Anthropocene' (2016) C-EENRG Working Paper 2016-5.

[119] Kathleen Birrell and Daniel Matthews, 'Re-storying Law for the Anthropocene: Rights, Obligations and an Ethics of Encounter' (2020) 31 Law and Critique 275.

[120] For critiques of causation in fact see, for example, Jane Stapleton, 'Unnecessary Causes' (2013) 129 Law Quarterly Review 39; Jane Stapleton, 'An "Extended But-For" Test for Causal Relation in the Law of Obligations' (2015) 35(4) Oxford Journal of Legal Studies 697.

CHAPTER 8

Causation in Tort

MARK A. GEISTFELD AND SANDY STEEL

1. Introduction

In order for a plaintiff, P, to be entitled to compensation from a defendant, D, systems of tort law generally insist that D's conduct, or conduct that can be attributed to D, has been proven to be a cause of harm to P.[1]

Causally connecting D's conduct to P's harm is part of what makes D morally responsible for the harm so as to justify D's being under a duty to compensate P. Absent D's responsibility for causing P's harm, while D might have behaved culpably and could not morally object to incurring a burden for that kind of behaviour, it is unjust to single out D specifically as the source of P's compensation; D can reasonably complain that P's harm is, morally speaking, everyone's problem, rather than D's alone. In this way, causation provides a normatively crucial part of the justification for interpersonal compensatory duties, captured by the conventional characterisation of the relation between D and P as involving an "injurer" and a "victim".[2]

Basing individual responsibility on causal attribution creates two vexing problems for tort litigation over climate change. The first—the *attenuated-causation problem*—stems from the intuitive connection between individual responsibility and having "made a difference" to the occurrence of a harm.[3] This connection is reflected in the centrality of the but-for test for establishing causation in tort cases, which essentially asks whether one phenomenon was necessary for the occurrence of another. When P's harm (stemming from climate change) would have happened anyway without D's conduct (of emitting carbon), there is an obvious respect in which the conduct did not "make a difference" in bringing about the harm.

Although legal systems have rightly recognised that one can cause or causally contribute to an outcome when the but-for test is not satisfied, such situations tend to be categorised as exceptional and are of uncertain scope.[4] The problem is not necessarily that the law adopts, as a default, an overly restrictive concept of cause. As compared to alternative, considerably more complex causal tests, the but-for test may be a defensible default legal heuristic.[5] The problem, rather, is that when a person's conduct is causally connected to another's harm without being necessary for that outcome, those causal attributes may have a justifiable bearing on the extent of liability. For example, this causal problem arises when the plaintiff could have been, and in fact was, tortiously injured by any one of the defendants, but the tortious misconduct of no

[1] See Sandy Steel, *Proof of Causation in Tort Law* (CUP 2015) 1.

[2] On the centrality of causation, see Carolina Sartorio, 'Causation and Responsibility' (2007) 2 Philosophy Compass 749.

[3] See, for example, Boris Kment, 'Causation: Determination and Difference-Making' (2010) 44 Noûs 80, 81 writing that the idea of 'difference-making' is 'undeniably central to our thinking about causation'.

[4] Steel (n 1) ch 1.

[5] We briefly consider some candidates in Section 4.2.

defendant satisfies the but-for test. Although "it would've happened anyway" is not always a good answer to whether one committed a wrong, it can still appropriately limit the extent of one's liability for that wrong.[6]

The attenuated-causation problem, then, refers to the conceptual and normative difficulties of determining whether a person's conduct causally contributes to an outcome despite not satisfying the but-for test, and if so, how such a causal contribution affects the existence and scope of their compensatory duty. This is fundamentally a conceptual and normative problem, rather than an epistemological one, and so is not eliminated by advances in climate attribution science. Even if we have *perfect knowledge* of the causal mechanisms of climate change, it may often still be the case that no particular person's emissions constitute a necessary condition of a particular harm.[7]

Because tort law requires plaintiffs to prove that defendants caused their injuries, another vexing problem occurs when that burden is insurmountable and routinely bars liability. The source of this *causal-proof problem* stems from a higher likelihood that P's harms were caused by background risks under conditions in which it is not possible to discriminate between the causal effect of those background risks and the risk attributable to D's conduct. For instance, if a patient arrives at hospital already seriously ill and likely to die, and then dies while being treated with substandard care, it is often impossible to determine whether their doctor's malpractice made any difference, under both the preponderance-of-the-evidence standard and the higher civilian standard of proof.[8] More likely than not, the preexisting condition would have killed the patient anyway, and yet a blanket denial of liability under the but-for test fails to recognise that such medical malpractice undeniably causes harm in some cases. Inherent uncertainty over causal attribution can foreclose recovery in all cases, effectively negating the duty.[9]

We begin, in Section 2, by explaining why the *attenuated-causation* problem exists in climate change cases. Our overall claim is that if the but-for test is applied in relation to a particular defendant and considers only what would have occurred if the defendant had complied with the tort obligation, then the test will often not be satisfied. This is because (a) substantial wrongful emissions by other persons could produce the harm in any event, (b) prior non-wrongful emissions could mean that the defendant's wrongful emissions would not have made a difference, and (c) the argument is invalid that a collective amount of emissions that is a but-for cause of the plaintiff's harm necessarily implies that a defendant who is part of that group is also a but-for cause of plaintiff's harm or part of it.

In Section 3, we explain the existence of the *causal-proof problem* in climate cases, principally by adverting, again, to the live possibility of a harm being entirely caused by the wrongs of others, by non-wrongful emissions, or otherwise non-tortious background risks.

Section 4 argues that the *attenuated-causation* and *causal-proof problems* can be overcome in a normatively distinctive category of cases. Established doctrines provide a basis for a plaintiff to establish causation by proving that a defendant's wrongful emissions either: (a)

[6] For a general analysis of when and why 'it would have happened anyway' matters in private law, see Sandy Steel, 'Making a Difference: Liability and Necessity' in Kylie Burns and others (eds), *Torts on Three Continents* (OUP 2024).

[7] This is not to deny that developments in attribution science *reduce* the number of situations in which one needs to grapple with the problem, by allowing proof of particularised but-for causation. See Aisha I Saad, 'Attribution for Climate Torts' (2023) 64 Boston College Law Review 867.

[8] For a comparison of the common law and civilian standards of proof, see Steel (n 1) ch 2.

[9] See Mark A Geistfeld, 'Duty-Preserving Tort Rules as an "Old Category" for Justifying the Loss-of-Chance Doctrine in Medical Malpractice Cases' (2024) 73 DePaul Law Review 427.

materially contributed to the plaintiff's harm; or (b) when condition (a) is impossible to demonstrate, the defendant materially increased the risk of the harm, and the harm would not have occurred but-for the combined wrongful conduct of otherwise independent tortfeasors whose wrongful emissions also materially increased the risk of harm. The requirement of causation is a formidable but not insurmountable barrier to recovery for climate-related harms.

2. Individual Carbon Emitters and the Attenuated-Causation Problem

The tort requirement of causation is traditionally broken down into *factual* causation—whether D's conduct actually caused P's harm—and *proximate* or *legal* causation—whether D's conduct had the right type of causal effect on P's harm to hold D justly liable to compensate the harm. In what follows, our focus is on *factual* causation, which is the principal site of the attenuated-causation problem in climate change litigation.

The starting point in assessing factual causation asks a deceptively simple question: If D had complied with the tort obligation, would P's harm not have occurred? If so, then D's breach is a but-for cause of P's harm. As applied to a particular carbon emitter, the answer to this inquiry will often be that their contribution is not a but-for cause of *any* rise in temperature and could not have caused climate-related harms. And even if the emitter's contribution is a but-for cause of increased temperature, that rise may not be a but-for cause of the harm. Other emitters will often provide independently sufficient contributions for the rise in temperature, either because, looking to the future, they would take the place of any emitter already in the market, or looking to the past, the amount of previously released or historical emissions was already enough to cause the harm.[10]

Consider an individual who takes a flight from London to New York that releases 1 tonne of CO2 "per passenger" based on the plane's total CO2 emissions (say 200 tonnes) divided by the number of passengers on the plane (200). Under these conditions, *each passenger* was not a but-for cause of 1 tonne of CO2 emissions. Had any given individual not flown, the plane would in all likelihood still have flown to New York and the CO2 would still have been emitted (perhaps minimally lower, so far as that passenger's weight matters for this purpose). Each passenger contributes to the demand for the flight, and some threshold of aggregate demand will be a but-for cause of the flight being scheduled, but each person's contribution to the aggregate is unlikely to be a but-for cause of this or any other flight. Statements that *you* emitted 1 tonne of CO2 in taking a such a flight are false if they are asserting that you were *a but-for cause* of 1 tonne of CO2 being emitted.

In general terms, a fallacy is commited when a "whole" is a but-for cause of an outcome (the flight causing 200 tonnes of emissions), and it is then inferred that part of this whole (a passenger) *must* also be a but-for cause of the outcome, or a but-for cause of part of the outcome (the 1 tonne of emissions).

Now scale up from an individual to a "carbon major". It has been estimated that if one counterfactually removed the annual carbon emissions of ninety major carbon producers between 1880 and 2010, global mean surface temperature would be 0.4 degrees lower.[11] On this

[10] See Douglas Kysar, 'The Duty of Climate Care' (2024) 73 DePaul Law Review 487, 519–20, describing the 'consequentialist alibi' to the effect that one's contribution makes no difference, and noting that it is 'not without some factual basis'.

[11] B Ekwurzel and others, 'The Rise in Global Atmospheric CO_2, Surface Temperature, and Sea Level from Emissions Traced to Major Carbon Producers' (2017) 144 Climatic Change 579, Section 3.2.

basis, one can conclude that *but-for the group's emissions*, temperature would be lower by 0.4 degrees, and the group's emissions are a but-for cause of any harms attributable to that temperature rise. As should be clear, it does not follow that if any carbon major is responsible for *x per cent* of the total group's emissions, it necessarily is a but-for cause of *x per cent* of all harm caused, let alone *x per cent* of any particular person's harm. There is a logical gap—from the perspective of the but-for test—in any arguments which point to an entity's contribution to the historical cumulative emissions that are a but-for cause of a person's harm, and then infer *from that fact alone* that the entity is liable for the proportionate share of that harm.

Consider in this connection the much-discussed *Lliuya v RWE* case, brought by Luciano Lliuya, a Peruvian farmer and mountain guide, against RWE, a German electricity power company that is assertedly responsible for 0.47% of post-industrial greenhouse gas emissions.[12] Lliuya's land, in Huaraz, is at the foot of the Cordillera Blanca mountain range, which contains glaciers. He claimed that RWE is responsible, under German law, for a share of the approximately 14,000 USD costs he has incurred in taking protective measures (including building a second floor and erecting reinforcements to walls) against the risk of his land being flooded due to overflow from a glacial lake above. Lliuya's claim is based on the concepts of *action taken for another* (*negotiorium gestio*): Essentially, the expenditure incurred was taken on behalf of, by way of discharging its duty, RWE.[13] The OLG Hamm ultimately rejected the claim on the basis that the risk of damage to Lliuya's land was insufficiently "imminent" to establish liability.[14] For our purposes, the court's causal analysis illustrates the general problem under consideration.

There is persuasive evidence that carbon emissions increased the flood risk in Huaraz. Further, but-for the emissions of carbon majors, that risk would be a "medium" risk, rather than a "high" risk, and would not have necessitated the protective measures Lliuya had taken.[15] But even though these industrial carbon emissions were a but-for cause of Lliuya's expenditures, the tort question is whether but-for RWE's emissions, Lliuya would still have needed to spend the money. Without RWE's emissions, global temperature would be *very slightly* lower and Lliuya would still have faced a high glacial flood risk.[16] Lliuya would have needed to take the same protective measures in the absence of the defendant's emissions, and so for tort purposes, there is no but-for causation.[17] Nevertheless, the OLG Hamm simply asserts that the but-for test is satisfied because the defendant's emissions slightly increased the risk.[18] It can be tempting, but wrong, to move from the propositions that (1) some harm would not have occurred without anthropogenic climate change, and (2) a person contributed to anthropogenic climate change, to the conclusion that (3) the person is a but-for cause of the harm (or even a part of the harm).

The but-for test is hard to satisfy in these cases because the threshold at which carbon emissions cause damage by increasing temperature is apparently an instance of what Jane Stapleton calls an "oversubscribed threshold" for which the varied contributions of multiple actors combine to substantially exceed the tipping point.[19] If the threshold at which global carbon

12 For an excellent summary and analysis of the case, see J Schirmer, 'Climate Liability: Causation and Duty Demystified' (2025) 16 Journal of European Tort Law 265.

13 §684 BGB; §1004 BGB. An alternative basis was in unjust enrichment: §812 BGB.

14 OLG Hamm I-5 U 15/17.

15 Schirmer (n 12), citing Rupert Stuart-Smith et al, 'Increased Outburst Flood Hazard from Lake Palcacocha Due to Human-Induced Glacier Retreat' (2021) 14 Nature Geoscience 85.

16 OLG Hamm (n 14) at 42.

17 *Contra* Schirmer (n 15).

18 OLG Hamm (n 14) at 42.

19 Jane Stapleton, 'Unnecessary Causes' (2013) 129 Law Quarterly Review 39.

emissions become harmful is oversubscribed or massively exceeded, then the carbon attributable to any particular emitter would not be necessary for the threshold to be crossed, in which case there is no but-for causation.[20]

Suppose, to illustrate the problem, that there is a threshold of toxicity—1 tonne of pollutant—which results in the death of half of the fish in a river. If there are 3 tonnes of pollutant in the river, all fish die. Suppose one person puts 1 tonne in the river and kills half of the fish. Later, five others simultaneously put 1 tonne each in the river. Under the but-for test, none of these five polluters was a but-for cause of the death of the remaining half of the fish. For each one, their contribution could be removed, and the additional fish would still have died from the remaining 4 tonnes of pollutant the other four polluters added to the river. To the extent that the causal mechanism of climate change is like this—that is, it involves oversubscribed thresholds—then some significant contributions will not be a but-for cause or necessary condition of any harm.[21]

A further difficulty is that the but-for test involves a counterfactual inquiry that will allow for the presence of substantial non-wrongful emissions. The polluted river is typically a static problem in the sense that it would be both feasible and reasonable to cease any further additions of pollution in order to prevent the harms in question. Climate change, by contrast, is a dynamic problem. Carbon emissions cannot instantaneously be shut off across the globe. Historically, it will have been reasonable at the time for large-scale corporate emitters to continue to emit some carbon, and for individuals to do so. Consequently, the but-for counterfactual will only eliminate a particular company's *wrongful* emissions and ask what would have occurred if the emissions were at the pertinent historically lawful level. The likelihood will often be that *some* ongoing emissions are non-tortious and, at the tipping point, would produce the harm in any event.[22]

Nothing we have said shows that the but-for test can never be satisfied in this context. Much depends on the nature of the breach of duty alleged, the type of harm in question, and whether there are principled reasons for grouping emitters into a collective whole that is a but-for cause of the harm. We discuss the latter possibility in Section 4.

For now, consider the type of harm. Suppose it became wrongful for fossil fuel companies to continue to emit at their then-current levels in the early 1990s. If we envisage a counterfactual which removes, say, Chevron's emissions since then, it seems possible to calculate the extent to which its subsequent (wrongful) emissions were a but-for cause of increased temperatures that

[20] The International Panel on Climate Change recognises the existence of 'tipping points' in the climate system, defining them as 'critical thresholds in a system that, when exceeded, can lead to a significant change in the state of the system, often with an understanding that the change is irreversible': Ove Hoegh-Guldberg and others, 'Impacts of 1.5°C Global Warming on Natural and Human Systems', in V Masson-Delmotte and others (eds), *Global Warming of 1.5°C. An IPCC Special Report on the Impacts of Global Warming of 1.5°C Above Pre-industrial Levels and Related Global Greenhouse Gas Emission Pathways, in the Context of Strengthening the Global Response to the Threat of Climate Change, Sustainable Development, and Efforts to Eradicate Poverty* (CUP 2018) 261.

[21] It might be objected that the relevant counterfactual question for the purposes of assessing causation under the but-for test is: *But for the defendant's breach, and all other breaches of duty of a similar kind, would the harm have been avoided in whole or in part?* In other words, the defendant is not permitted to rely, as normative matter, on the breach of duty by others in the but-for counterfactual. As a general proposition, this is not a correct articulation of the but-for test. See Section 4.3.

[22] For an argument that each of us on average causes 6 months of lost life across a lifetime, John Broome, 'How Much Harm Does Each of Us Do?' in M Budolfson, T McPherson, and D Plunkett (eds), *Philosophy and Climate Change* (OUP 2021) 289. Broome's argument does not demonstrate that the subset of wrongful emissions in a person's life is a but-for cause of harm to any specific person.

in turn damaged national economic growth. According to Callahan and Malkin, Chevron's emissions were a but-for cause of $1.98 trillion in damage to the global economy since 1991, and they estimate the loss to particular national economies.[23] As this example illustrates, the more temporally extended the breach (compare the difficulty of showing a but-for effect for emissions during one week to emissions over sixty years), and the more that harms are identified at higher level of generality (say individual effects compared to global impacts), then the more readily demonstrable are but-for causal effects. Scaling down to particular economic losses for even extended periods of individual emissions, as the *Lliuya* case shows, is frequently difficult.

3. Individual Carbon Emitters and the Causal-Proof Problem

It will often be unclear (a) whether a particular harm is causally attributable to climate change at all, rather than to the non-tortious background risk of the harm, and (b) if it is, whether the defendant made a causal contribution to it.

Climate attribution science addresses these issues.[24] "Extreme-event attribution describes a set of scientific methods which calculate the relative increase in the probability of occurrence, or intensity, of a given extreme event. This is done by comparing the defined event's likelihood of occurrence in simulations of the present-day climate with some modelled estimate of a counterfactual climate where some or all anthropogenic influences have been removed."[25] If the analysis shows that anthropogenic influence at least doubled the risk of an extreme weather event, then human carbon emissions, more likely than not, were the cause.

As we noted above, it will not do, for tort liability purposes, to show (on the balance of probabilities), that but-for "some or all anthropogenic influences", a particular harm would not have occurred. The focus, for causation purposes, is upon the counterfactual in which only the *tortfeasor's wrongful emissions* did not occur. Consequently, it may be that a large amount of historic emissions are left in the counterfactual, either because they are not wrongful or because they are not the defendant's. The more emissions left in the counterfactual, the less likely the defendant's conduct will have increased the risk beyond the level required by the balance of probabilities standard of proof (still less likely under higher civilian standards).[26] If the defendant's wrongful emissions did not at least double the risk of an extreme weather event, then the remaining carbon emissions, more likely than not, were the cause. This doubling-of-the-risk requirement can bar liability for individual emitters across all cases, effectively immunising them from tort liability for their wrongful carbon emissions. For example, in relation to an Argentinian heatwave, one study found that the EU's historic emissions (note: not necessarily its *wrongful* emissions) raised the probability of the event from 1 in 15 to 1 in 12—a

[23] Christopher Callahan and Justin Mankin, 'Carbon Majors and the Scientific Case for Climate Liability' (2025) 640 Nature 893, 896. They do not seem to build into their counterfactual simulation the permissibility of *some* continued emissions post-1990. This affects their figures but need not vitiate the possibility of identifying some but-for effect on national economies.

[24] For a recent overview, see Friederike Otte and others, 'Causality and the Fate of Climate Litigation: The Role of the Social Superstructure Narrative' (2022) 13 Global Policy 623.

[25] ibid 742.

[26] For example, when one study took *emissions by specific countries or unions of countries* as the amount to be excised from the counterfactual, to test the increase in risk for a particular instance of heavy rainfall, it found that the 'attributable signal' was 'not significant' with respect to any individual entity or group. ibid 743.

37% increase in risk.[27] More likely than not, then the event would have occurred in any event. Scaling down to a particular emitter, the problem is yet more apparent.

This causal-proof problem might seem to be amenable to an easy and attractive "solution": Accept that P is harmed when D's conduct wrongfully imposes a *risk of damage* upon P. If D's contribution to risk is very small, then D has a trivial compensatory debt to P. This redefinition of the compensable harm seems to solve the attenuated-causation problem by attenuating D's compensatory liability: small risk, small compensatory debt. And while it is often difficult to prove that D's conduct made a difference to the occurrence of physical damage to P, it is much more readily possible to prove that D's conduct *increased the risk* of P's being damaged. Thus, the causal-proof problem is significantly diminished by accepting that risk exposure is a compensable harm.

Defining risk exposure as a compensable harm undoubtedly makes things easier for plaintiffs, but it needs to be shown for independent reason that wrongfully imposing *risk* on another harms that person in such a way as to give rise to a compensatory obligation. Although we cannot fully establish the point here, we think there are at least two formidable difficulties with treating mere risk exposure as a compensable tortious harm.[28]

First, this definition leads to strongly counterintuitive proliferation of "harm": Every time a vehicle passes, you are "harmed" on this view, since there is always some chance the vehicle will crash and cause you bodily injury. Second, once we firmly bring to attention cases of *pure* risk exposure in the absence of other harms such as emotional distress or economic loss, it is not intuitive that being exposed to such a risk is harmful. For instance, suppose that unbeknownst to you, your heart is physically such that a particular set of movements will trigger a heart attack. Miraculously, throughout your life, you never make that set of movements, and the physical condition of your heart never affects your experience of the world, or the duration of your life. Although you have long faced a significant risk of harm, it is not intuitive (to us) that you have actually been harmed—you have never been aware of the risk nor incurred any burdens because of it.

Knowledge of risk exposure can cause other harms, such as anxiety, the economic cost of medically monitoring the risk, or the indignity and upset of having been wrongfully exposed to the risk—but an unknown risk on its own is not a harm. It is unsurprising, then, that when courts have flirted with the idea of treating risk exposure as a compensable harm, they have insisted upon the occurrence of other identifiable harms before countenancing substantial compensatory liability.[29] Liability requires proof showing that the defendant tortiously caused the plaintiff to suffer some compensable harm aside from risk exposure, returning us to the causal-proof problem stemming from the doubling-in-risk requirement for establishing but-for causation in climate change cases.

[27] See Friederike Otte and others, 'Assigning Historic Responsibility for Extreme Weather Events' (2017) 7 Nature Climate Change 759.

[28] See further Adam Slavny and Tom Parr, 'What's Wrong with Risk?' (2019) 8 Thought 76.

[29] See, in English law, *Barker v Corus* [2006] 2 AC 572. For discussion of French cases on this, see Steel (n 1), ch 6. In US law, see, e.g., *Caronia v Phillip Morris USA, Inc.*, 5 N.E.3d 11, 14 (N.Y. 2013) ('A threat of future harm is insufficient to impose liability against a defendant in a tort context. The requirement that a plaintiff sustain physical harm before being able to recover in tort is a fundamental principle of our state's tort system'); *Rozenfeld v Medical Protective Co.*, 73 F.3d 154, 155 (7th Cir. 1996) ('A tort does not occur when the tortfeasor violates his duty of care to the victim, but when the tortfeasor injures the victim'). Once the plaintiff has shown that the defendant tortiously caused some compensable harm, probabilities factor into the calculation of damages for future harms. See Geistfeld (n 9).

4. Meeting the Attenuated-Causation and Causal-Proof Problems

The evidential difficulties of proving causation are not unique to climate change litigation. In confronting these issues in analogous cases, courts have formulated doctrines that might surmount the causal hurdle, depending on the soundness of their underlying rationales.

4.1 Attenuated Causation: Beyond the But-for Test

It is well-known that the but-for test delivers false negatives: It sometimes fails to find a causal link when there is one. As the UK Supreme Court recently explained:

> It has . . . long been recognised that in law as indeed in other areas of life the "but for" test is inadequate, not only because it is over-inclusive, but also because it excludes some cases where one event could or would be regarded as a cause of another event. An example . . . is a case of two fires, started independently of each other, which combine to burn down a property . . . It is natural to regard each fire as a cause of the loss even if either fire would by itself have destroyed the property so that it cannot be said of either fire that, but for that peril, the loss would not have occurred.[30]

Consider the two-fires problem in relation to the tipping-point analysis of catastrophic climate change. Suppose only one of the fires was attributable to the defendant's negligence and the other was naturally occurring. In these cases, some courts have concluded that the defendant's fire was a cause of the harm, even though the other independently sufficient concurrent cause was innocent.[31] This reasoning provides a basis for finding a large carbon emitter causally responsible for climate change at the tipping point, even if non-tortious emissions were also independently sufficient to bring about the same outcome. In these cases, however, a defendant does not necessarily incur any compensatory liability, because the court can still find that the tortious conduct did not cause any compensable *harm*.[32]

This bar to recovery would only apply if the two causal forces were operating simultaneously—if not, an earlier force may have *pre-empted* a later one (suppose one fire destroys the house, and the *later* fire would have fully destroyed it moments afterwards).[33] If we could precisely identify the tipping point for climate change, then the sequencing of emissions rather than their simultaneous occurrence comes into play. Defendants whose wrongful emissions pushed climate change past the tipping point would incur liability for the ensuing harms.

This solution to the causal problem has a troubling implication. Once the threshold has been met, some potentially extensive emissions may be causally redundant, even if they otherwise would be independently sufficient to cause the harm and in that respect are akin to one of

[30] *Financial Conduct Authority v Arch Insurance* [2021] UKSC 1.

[31] See Restatement (Third) of Torts: Physical and Emotional Harm § 27 cmt. d (2010) (adopting this rule).

[32] ibid cmt. d ('When one of multiple sufficient causes is not tortious, the question of damages is a different matter from the causal question. The question of what (if any) damages should be awarded against these tortfeasors properly belongs to the law of damages and is not addressed in this Restatement').

[33] ibid cmt. e.

the two fires. Does it make sense to pin all responsibility on the group of emitters at the tipping point, while absolving some or all of the subsequent emitters from liability altogether?

In light of the massive liability implications, courts are likely to require demanding evidence about the timing of emissions in relation to the tipping point. Whereas we can readily identify the point at which additional water causes a reservoir to burst, the same is not obviously true with respect to additional emissions of carbon into the atmosphere. In the absence of persuasive proof, courts are likely to presume that carbon emissions are simultaneously contributing to the tipping-point around the globe but also find (as in the two-fires case) that the wrongful emissions causally contributed to climate change without having caused any compensable harms—that is, those injuries would have occurred in any event.

The other type of widely recognised problem with the but-for test involves multiple conditions that are individually neither necessary nor sufficient, yet which seem together to produce an outcome (e.g., five people together push a vehicle off a cliff, when three people would have been enough to dislodge it). In these cases, courts have ascribed causal responsibility to a "substantial factor" or "material contribution": Each person materially contributes to pushing the vehicle off a cliff.[34] Courts have adopted this same requirement to evaluate causation in the two-fire cases: Each fire must materially contribute to the destruction of the house in order to count as a cause. Although this test may have originated in public nuisance cases, it is not unique to that tort and is applied to negligence and other claims.[35]

Can large emitters be said to "materially contribute" to, or be "substantial factors" of, climate-related damage? Part of the difficulty is that the words "material contribution" or "substantial factor" are at best a useful label for an intuitively recognisable relation, and at worst a black box for any causal conclusion to be plucked from the air.

4.2 Making a Contribution

The first issue is whether a carbon emitter makes *any* contribution to the existence of climate-harms in an analogous way to the persons who pollute a river, as in the hypothetical in Section 2. Various proposals exist in the literature for modelling the causal problem. Perhaps the most discussed is Richard Wright's NESS (Necessary Element of a Sufficient Set) analysis, according to which, in its original version, B is a cause of A if and only if B is necessary to make a set of existing conditions sufficient for A to occur.[36] In the polluted river problem, each of the five new polluters is necessary for at least one set of conditions sufficient for killing the remaining half of the fish. For example, the original polluter's contribution of 1 tonne can be grouped into a set that includes only 2 tonnes of existing pollutants from the others, thereby triggering the 3 tonne threshold and establishing causation under the NESS test. The same analysis can be

[34] See Steel (n 1) ch 1.

[35] For its application in negligence, see, e.g., *Bailey v Ministry of Defence* [2008] EWCA Civ 883. For discussion of negligence authorities and other torts, Steel (n 1) ch 5. On its application in public nuisance, David Bullock, 'Public Nuisance and Climate Change: The Common Law's Answer to the Plaintiff, Defendant, and Causation Problems' (2022) 85 Modern Law Review 1136, 1159 (cf 1165); Hanoch Dagan and Avihay Dorfman, *Relational Justice* (OUP 2024). For its application as the general rule for determining factual causation in other tort cases, see *Rutherford v Owens-Ill. Inc.*, 941 P.2d 1203, 1214 (Cal. 1997) (explaining that the substantial-factor test applies in all negligence and products liability cases because it is 'a clearer rule of causation—one which subsumes the "but for" test while reaching beyond it to satisfactorily address other situations, such as those involving independent or concurrent causes in fact').

[36] Richard Wright, 'Causation in Tort Law' (1985) 73 California Law Review 1735.

applied to the subsequent five polluters, so that each one's contribution of 1 tonne to an existing amount of 2 tonnes satisfies the amount needed to kill half the fish, making each one a cause of that harm.

Can the NESS test be applied to climate change litigation? As in the case of pollutants emitted into a river, any individual's carbon emissions could potentially be grouped into an actually existing set of just enough carbon so that the individual's incremental contribution exceeds the threshold or tipping point, thereby satisfying the NESS test. However, it is not clear that each person's emissions contribute to the causal mechanism in the same way as the water pollution damages the fish. Assume that D's emissions increase the risk of harm. If the sequencing of emissions is important for the causal mechanism, D's risky emissions can be pre-empted by preexisting carbon emissions, in which case D's risky emissions did not cause any harm. To establish causation under the NESS test, it is not enough for P to prove that D's emissions *increased the risk* of the harm; instead, P must prove that the emissions are implicated in the causal mechanism by which the harm occurred.[37]

Another problem remains. If it is nonetheless assumed that all carbon emissions contribute to damaging climate change, and every person has climate-related tort duties, then everyone is potentially liable in respect of every climate event. Tort law's default position is that each person who materially contributes to an indivisible harm is liable *in full*. Taken to its logical extreme, any person who takes an unnecessary flight would, in principle, be liable in full for every future climate-related harm. If that is the logical implication of accepting the "material contribution" doctrine in climate cases, it will be impossible to accept.

Intuitively, there *is* an important difference as a matter of individual responsibility between different types of causal forces, even holding all else equal. The NESS test does not distinguish between an individual's carbon emissions and those of states or large corporate actors responsible for much larger amounts of emissions—an emission from *any* source, when combined with a set of existing emissions, can be sufficient for causing climate change at a tipping point. However, the causal contributions to climate change are markedly different for different types of emitters and help to explain why it would be unjust to hold a single individual responsible for the entirety of climate change simply because the NESS test permits a finding of causation through the elaborate construction of a tipping point analysis. This kind of causal inquiry fails to register an important difference in the nature of responsibility for different types of factual or necessary causes of a harm.

4.3 Conceptualising a Substantial or Material Contribution

One is either a NESS condition of an outcome or not; it is not a matter of degree, which is why the NESS test can deem a single individual's emissions to "materially contribute" to climate change at the tipping point. This kind of causal analysis does not reflect the law's claim that one can contribute *more or less* to an event.[38] In contrast to the all-or-nothing analytics of the NESS test, tort law draws a distinction between a material causal contribution and one that is

[37] A statement like 'every tonne of carbon makes a difference' is ambiguous. It could mean that 'every tonne of carbon increases the risk of an adverse event', or it could mean that 'every tonne of carbon contributes to the causal mechanism by which a particular harm was produced'. The two are not the same.

[38] See also Jane Stapleton, 'An Extended "But-For" Test for the Law of Obligations' (2015) 35 Oxford Journal of Legal Studies 697.

insubstantial or insignificant. The Third Restatement of Torts adopts this position and relieves trivial causal contributors of liability.[39]

Unfortunately, the existing literature does not provide much assistance in determining what constitutes a "material", "substantial", or "non-trivial" factor. It lacks the conceptual apparatus to register the notion of causation (as opposed to *risk*) being a *scalar* rather than *binary* matter: One is either *necessary* or not, a *necessary* element of a sufficient set *or not*. The Third Restatement simply observes that "[d]etermining whether the contribution of an actor is trivial in comparison to others in the causal set entails a judgment".[40]

Bullock suggests that the question resolves to whether the contribution is "abnormal" or "ordinary".[41] Just as some temporary blocking of the highway may be ordinary, like the smoke temporarily wafting across from one's neighbour's barbecue, so too is the emission of *some* carbon in a lifetime. What is the permissible *de minimis* level that renders one's emissions *ordinary*? That question must be answered before courts can determine whether a defendant emitted an *abnormal* amount of carbon and, therefore, is potentially subject to liability. Bullock's proposal effectively pushes the issue of whether a causal contribution is minimal (or ordinary) into the question of whether the person's conduct is wrongful and fairly subject to liability in the first instance.[42]

It seems plausible, however, that some contributions can be wrongful, and yet it would still be inappropriate to hold a person liable to pay full compensation for all of the ensuing climate harms. For instance, it is doubtful whether flying a private jet for repeated holidays in one year can be justified as a reasonable amount of carbon emissions.[43] This is, in Bullock's sense, *abnormal*. Yet it is still presumably not the case that the unreasonable carbon emissions should render that person liable for *all* climate-related damage indefinitely in the future. If that is correct, some other account is needed whereby a person's contribution, though wrongful, should not attract full liability.[44]

Another suggestion is to think of the *degree* of causal contribution purely in terms of probability-raising.[45] If we consider a causal contribution to an outcome, established by the NESS test or any other one that allows for causality in cases of overdetermination, we can ask how much this contribution increased the probability of the outcome's occurrence. When a defendant's wrongful emissions increased the risk enough to satisfy the but-for test, they made the outcome a legal certainty and are fairly subject to full liability. For cases in which the defendant's contribution is sufficient within the NESS test only because it slightly increased the risk at the tipping point, whereas other large emitters created substantially greater risks at the same time, the relatively minimal degree of causal contribution would subject the defendant as a relatively minor emitter to a relatively minimal amount of compensatory liability.

[39] 'When an actor's negligent conduct constitutes only a trivial contribution to a causal set that is a factual cause of harm under § 27, the harm is not within the scope of the actor's liability': §36.

[40] ibid cmt b.

[41] Bullock (n 34) 1153.

[42] Likewise, the Third Restatement states that the judgment is akin to one of proximate cause, but the issue instead turns on the issue of wrongfulness in the first instance. If a trivial emission is tortious, and the emission is a factual cause of climate change under the NESS test, then liability for the foreseeable harms naturally follows as a matter of proximate cause. Any limitations of liability must instead be based on limiting the duty to exclude trivial emissions, in which case such emissions could not be wrongful.

[43] Compare the rhetorical judicial question concerning liability for using a Landrover in the oral hearing in *Smith v Fonterra Cooperative Group Ltd* [2021] NZCA 552.

[44] It will not help here to speak of '*de minimis*' *harm*, when the harm is indivisible. What is minimal, if anything is likely to be, is the *degree* of causal contribution, not the amount of harm caused.

[45] See Alex Kaiserman, 'Partial Liability' (2017) 23 Legal Theory 1.

In *Lliuya*, the OLG Hamm adopted a variant of this approach.[46] It considered the increase in risk attributable (presumably in a but-for sense) to Lliuya to be *substantial* for the purposes of the German requirement of "adequate" causation (a distinct stage from but-for causation). It did so on the basis that although RWE's emissions increased the absolute risk to Lliuya by a very small amount, the increase in absolute risk was not the only relevant consideration. It was also relevant that among the persons who had also increased the risk of harm, RWE's contribution to the absolute risk was among the highest. Evaluating a substantial contribution in relative rather than absolute terms comports with the Third Restatement's framing of the problem.[47] Thus, although any carbon major increases the risk of harm by only a small amount, the relative increase in risk substantially exceeds the relative contributions of other emitters. This formulation delivers the intuitive result that an ordinary person is not as causally responsible as a carbon major.

This conceptualisation of degrees of causation also provides a way to distinguish material contributions from trivial ones within the NESS test. It provides a basis for exculpating most ordinary individuals from liability for climate change while singling out large carbon emitters as the appropriate locus of causal responsibility. To be clear, there *is* a sense in which many "ordinary" emitters bear a minimal causal responsibility for climate-related harm (assuming each such person contributes to an oversubscribed threshold or "tipping point"). In so far as this minimal responsibility results from wrongful activity, there is in principle no substantive normative objection to their bearing a minimal compensatory debt. The main objection to such claims is simply that the amounts are so small that these compensatory debts would better be enforced by other (aggregate) means rather than litigation. The upshot of this approach places tortious responsibility only on the large carbon emitters.

This approach, however, faces a different problem. When a *material* contribution to an indivisible harm is shown, the default approach in English law and historically in US jurisdictions is to hold the contributor *fully* liable.[48] In US law, a partial analogy is to cases involving asbestosis, a chronic lung disease caused by the prolonged inhalation of asbestos fibres, each of which increasingly but only incrementally impairs breathing capacity. Any defendant responsible for a significant exposure is jointly and severally liable for the entire disablement, which is not otherwise capable of being apportioned into divisible harms attributable to the individual exposures.[49] So, too, if all significant carbon emissions are deemed to be a contributory cause of indivisible climate-related harms, then someone who tortiously emits that amount of carbon could be liable for all of those injuries, despite having contributed only a fraction (albeit significant) of the cumulative emissions. That result may be difficult to accept if the emitter's contribution is very far from being individually necessary or sufficient for the harm in question.

[46] *Lliuya* (n 14) 51–52.

[47] 'When an actor's negligent conduct constitutes only a trivial contribution to a causal set that is a factual cause of harm under § 27, the harm is not within the scope of the actor's liability': §36.

[48] For English law, see *Holmes v Poeton Holdings Ltd* [2023] EWCA Civ 1377, [60], [63], explaining the effect of *Bonnington Castings Ltd v Wardlaw* [1956] AC 613. Tort law in the US recognises this same outcome, but many states have abolished joint and several liability in favour of several liability that can limit the amount of a defendant's liability to its share of comparative responsibility when others also tortiously caused the harm.

[49] For discussion and criticism of this rule, see Jane Stapleton, 'The Two Explosive Proof-of-Causation Doctrines Central to Asbestos Claims' (2009) 74 Brooklyn Law Review 1011, 1013. The analogy is partial since asbestosis is, in principle, divisible, but only evidentially not always so.

4.4 But-For, Again: The No Worse Off Limitation and Causal Grouping

Even if it is established that a particular emitter has *materially contributed* to a particular climate harm, the emitter's not being a necessary condition of the harm can still have legal relevance. If *non-tortious* causes would have caused the harm anyway, there is no duty to compensate, despite the emitter's material contribution.

This is a separate, strictly non-causal stage of the analysis which is generally ignored in discussions of climate change liability.[50] It is, however, important: Even if an emitter is shown to have materially contributed to the cumulative set of emissions triggering the heat-raising mechanisms of climate change, it may still be the case that the causal contribution had no difference-making effect and absolves the defendant from liability. For example, if D's breach damaged P's back in a workplace accident, but P would have succumbed to an unrelated pre-existing spinal disease anyway, D is not liable to pay substantial compensation in relation to P's reduced earnings for the period in which the spinal disease would have rendered D unable to work.[51] Likewise, even if a particular emission could be identified as the "straw that broke the camel's back", it does not follow that the individual emitter is a but-for cause of climate change and subject to compensatory liability under circumstances in which other non-tortious causes would have caused the same harm regardless. In short, the existence of a causal link does not always entail a duty to compensate.

However, if the defendant's breach materially contributed to the outcome, it is widely accepted that D cannot avoid substantial compensatory liability to P by arguing that D's contribution made no difference *because of the actual or hypothetical wrong* of another person. If D wrongfully damages P's leg, but P's leg was also damaged independently by another tortfeasor D2, D cannot point to D2's tort to reduce or eliminate D's liability.[52] This rule has emerged in cases in which D's tort, and D2's tort, are each *independently sufficient* for causing P's damage or part thereof.

This rule requires further justification. Tort law treats each person as an independent agent not ordinarily responsible for the conduct of another, so the but-for test involves a counterfactual in which *only* the defendant behaved non-tortiously while the other(s) engaged in their wrongdoings for which the defendant is not responsible.[53] This inquiry prevents the but-for

50 For discussions of this element of liability, see Richard Wright, 'Causation (Contribution) and the "No Worse Off" Limitation on Liability' (2022) 49 University of Western Australia Law Review 5; Jane Stapleton, 'Unnecessary Causes' (2013) 129 Law Quarterly Review 39.

51 *Jobling v Associated Dairies* [1982] AC 794.

52 *Baker v Willoughby* [1970] AC 467.

53 See David Robertson, 'The Common Sense of Cause in Fact' (1997) 75 Texas Law Review 1765, 1771 (describing the counterfactual inquiry in terms of 'a mental picture of a situation identical to the actual facts of the case in all respects save one: the defendant's wrongful conduct is now "corrected" to the minimal extent necessary to make it conform to the law's requirements'). To see why counterfactual inquiry ordinarily only corrects for the defendant's wrongful conduct and not others as well, suppose D1 and D2 wrongfully fire a bullet at P, and only D1's bullet strikes P, but D2's bullet would have struck P had D1's not done so (imagine that P falls to the ground once struck by D1's bullet). But-for *D1's and D2's* breaches of duty, P's harm would not have occurred. It follows that, on this understanding of the counterfactual, D1 and D2 are both causes of P's harm, even though only D1's bullet struck P. Hence this 'no breach by anyone' counterfactual generates false positives and is not ordinarily the appropriate inquiry for determining factual causation. See Restatement (Third) of Torts: Liability for Physical and Emotional Harm §26 cmt. k (utilising this example to explain why '[a]n act or omission cannot be a factual cause of a harm that has already occurred').

test from assigning causal responsibility to either D or D2 for P's leg injury: If either one acts reasonably while the other continues to act tortiously, P's injury still occurs and so neither defendant is a but-for cause of the harm. To justifiably depart from the normative baseline that treats D and D2 as independent actors responsible only for their own wrongdoing, a tort rule must have a principled reason for grouping the individual misconduct of the defendants. This kind of grouping occurs, for example, when the defendants were acting in concert and agreed to incur responsibility for one another's conduct in pursuit of the collective objective. In the absence of such a principled reason, tort law does not recognise a prima facie justification for grouping defendants like carbon emitters together.

What, then, justifies the above rule that in assessing compensation, the plaintiff can establish but-for causation against the group of defendants? If D and D2 had both complied with their tort obligations, P's leg injury would not have occurred. If each defendant could instead invoke the but-for test to avoid liability because the other's wrongdoing would still have caused the harm, then the multiplicity of their wrongs would be the only reason for denying plaintiff's recovery. None of this evidence contradicts the proof showing that the plaintiff was tortiously injured by one of the defendants. To avoid the injustice of denying the plaintiff's recovery on these uncontested facts, tort law permits plaintiffs to establish compensatory liability against the entire group of defendants whose collective tortious risk contributions were a but-for cause of the injury. This configuration of the evidence normatively distinguishes these cases from those in which tort law refuses to group defendants who were acting independently.[54]

Although individual carbon emitters are not independently sufficient to cause climate change, they can, we suggest, still be subject to this rule. So long as D's contribution meets a threshold of importance (a material or substantial one along the lines conceptualised earlier), it would still be unjust for P to be deprived of compensation simply because of the multiplicity of such contributions from other tortious emitters. Otherwise, each large-scale emitter can argue that it caused *no* loss because of the wrongs of other large emitters, thereby depriving P of any right to compensation in respect of harm that would not have occurred if all these emitters had complied with their tort obligations owing to the plaintiff. If, as this rule allows, it is possible to group together emitters for the purposes of the but-for damages question, matters are reasonably straightforward. As noted, it has been estimated that if one removed the annual carbon emissions of ninety major carbon producers between 1880 and 2010, global mean surface temperature would be 0.4 degrees lower.[55] If this temperature increase is itself a but-for cause of some climate harms, then these ninety producers, *together*, are but-for causes of those harms.

4.5 Meeting the Causal-Proof Problem

So far we outlined one route by which causation and liability may be established: by identifying a substantial causal contribution to the mechanism that caused the harm coupled with the rule that permits a counterfactual but-for inquiry involving no wrongful conduct. However, we noted a difficulty: When the but-for test is not satisfied, it is unclear whether any breach can

[54] Mark A Geistfeld, 'The Doctrinal Unity of Alternative Liability and Market-Share Liability' (2006) 155 University of Pennsylvania Law Review 447; Steel (n 1) ch 4.

[55] Ekwurzel et al (n 11) Section 3.2. The quantative estimates of carbon emissions underlying the estimated increased in temperature derives from Richard Heede, 'Tracing Anthropogenic Carbon Dioxide and Methane Emissions to Fossil Fuel and Cement Producers' (2014) 122 Climate Change 229.

nonetheless be shown to be a causal contribution to the harm, rather than merely a cause of an increased *risk* of the harm.

In some cases, tort law has developed rules that establish a causal connection when all that can be shown is that the defendant is responsible for only a material increase in the tortious risk that might have but probably did not cause the plaintiff's harm. The animating rationale is the same as the one for the grouping counterfactual above: to prevent the elimination of a compensatory right simply due to the multiplicity of wrongs. This kind of rule was recognised as a means of circumventing a causal proof difficulty in *Summers v Tice* and *Cook v Lewis*.[56] In these cases, D1 and D2, as we can dub them, each exposed P to a tortious risk of harm by negligently firing their two guns towards him while on a hunting trip.[57] P was injured by only a single shooter, but it was impossible to demonstrate whether it was D1 or D2. In *Summers* and *Cook*, the US and Canadian courts both held that it was for each wrongful shooter to demonstrate that he did not cause P's injury.

This rule of alternative liability has been widely adopted across the US, with courts justifying it on the ground that "as between two culpable defendants and an innocent plaintiff, it is preferable to put the risk of error on the culpable defendants".[58]

A central reason for doing so inheres in the nature of the evidence before the court. In these cases, the plaintiff proves under the ordinary evidentiary standard that each defendant might have tortiously caused the plaintiff's bodily injury, and one of them did. In light of this evidence, alternative liability rests on the premise that a defendant does not rebut the plaintiff's causal proof by arguing that it is not the probable cause of the harm. All defendants can employ that same argument, with the collective implication that no one tortiously caused the plaintiff's harm—an evidentiary implication the plaintiff's uncontested evidence has already ruled out. Unable to rely on probabilistic evidence to rebut plaintiff's proof of the prima facie case, each defendant within the causal group incurs liability for having jointly caused the plaintiff's physical harm.[59]

In *Sindell v Abbott Laboratories*, the California Supreme Court extended the *Summers* rule when plaintiff's injury was caused by the ingestion of diethylstimbesterol (DES). However, it was impossible to determine which drug company manufactured the drug, due to pharmacist records having been lost or otherwise made irrecoverable during the long latency period of the drug's harmful effect.[60] Several companies had manufactured the generic drug. The California Supreme Court ordered each drug company to pay compensation in proportion to its share of the market at the time of ingestion. A central distinguishing feature of *Sindell*, compared to *Summers*, is that each drug company had manufactured a large number of drugs and had undoubtedly caused harm in a liability-generating way to some indeterminate plaintiffs (whereas one defendant in *Summers* definitely did not cause any harm to anyone). Each defendant manufacturer had a compensatory duty to *someone*, so it could not reasonably rely on a causal argument that would effectively foreclose that obligation in all cases. The *Sindell* court, however, followed *Summers* by restricting application of the rule to cases in which the plaintiff has joined a "substantial share" of the market to the proceedings.[61] Insofar as a "substantial

[56] *Summers v Tice* (1948) 33 Cal 2d 80; *Cook v Lewis* [1951] SCR 830; *Sindell v Abbott Laboratories* (1980) 26 Cal 3d 588.

[57] There are similar cases, with similar results, in several jurisdictions: Steel (n 1) ch 5.

[58] Restatement (Third) of Torts: Physical & Emotional Harm § 28 cmt. g (2010).

[59] For further justifications of this rule, based on the idea that each person is responsible for the deprivation of a compensatory right, even if not the plaintiff's bodily harm, see Steel (n 1) ch 5.

[60] *Sindell v Abbott Laboratories* (1980) 26 Cal 3d 588.

[61] *Sindell*, 937.

share" of the market more likely than not caused the plaintiff's harm, the plaintiff's evidence establishes an entitlement to compensation for the same evidentiary reasons recognised by the *Summers* rule of alternative liability.

This kind of argument was extended, in English law, to the asbestos context in *Fairchild v Glenhaven Funeral Services*.[62] D1, D2, and D3 each wrongfully exposed P to asbestos dust, resulting in P suffering mesothelioma. It was impossible to demonstrate whether D1, D2, or D3 caused P's harm. The House of Lords accepted that a small number of fibres from a single defendant could have caused the mesothelioma (much like only a single bullet caused the plaintiff's injury in *Summers* and *Lewis*). Nonetheless, it held that the defendants' duties of care would be emptied of content if none were held liable. All sources of risk in *Fairchild* were assumed to be wrongful, and so P's mesothelioma would not have occurred if no one had wronged P. Hence P's damages were based on the established fact that the injuries were tortiously caused by any one of the defendants in the causal group. Recovery on this causal basis avoids the injustice of enabling each defendant to avoid liability by relying on the wrongdoing of the other defendants.

This "multiple breach rule" could, in principle, extend to the climate context if two conditions are satisfied. The first is that P's harm would not have occurred, on the balance of probabilities, but-for the wrongful conduct of a group of emitters, thereby satisfying the conditions of either *Summers* (all potential tortious causes) or *Sindell* (a "substantial share" of the potential tortious causes). This is part of the justification of the rule: It protects a person whose right has been violated from losing the protection of the right by virtue of *multiple* wrongs, each of which could have tortiously caused the harm.[63] The second condition is that each member of the causal group must have materially or significantly increased the risk of P's harm in order to incur liability. This is likely to be true in relation to major corporate emitters. In both English and US law, each emitter would then be liable in proportion to the risk to which it exposed A, which limits the liability of each defendant by the extent to which its own carbon emissions contributed to the cumulative emissions that probably caused the injury in question.[64]

However, there are at least four possible disanalogies between the climate context and those in which the multiple breach rule has been applied (shooting accidents, DES cases, and asbestos exposure). First, each person in breach in *Fairchild*, *Summers*, and *Sindell* could have caused the entirety of the outcome on their own: Each is *potentially* individually sufficient for the outcome. A small number of asbestos fibres can cause mesothelioma. Yet, if we accept that a large emitter *individually* increases the probability of climate-related harm, it would seem to follow that the emitter is individually sufficient to cause the outcome in some unidentifiable cases, analogous to the unidentifiable harms the DES manufacturers caused. If an emitter increases the risk of a particular type of harm by 10%, then in 10 of 100 cases we would expect that the harm is due to their emissions. Alternatively, a large emitter might cause an intensification of climate-related harms in general, in which case it is the but-for cause of those enhanced injuries. Under these conditions, the analogy to DES cases is sound in this respect.

But the causal mechanism for climate change might work differently, creating the second potential disanalogy: Whereas not all asbestos fibres contribute to the disease mechanism for mesothelioma, all carbon emissions arguably contribute to the existence of climate-related harms. Asbestos exposure is like roulette with respect to cancer: Each exposure to the fibres

62 [2003] 1 AC 32.

63 'Proof that the group of defendants, more likely than not, caused the harm establishes a prima facie case of liability and identifies the plaintiff as deserving of compensation': Geistfeld (n 54) 491.

64 *Barker* (n 28); *Brown v Superior Court*, 751 P 2d 479 (Cal 1988).

involves a potentially triggering event. The greater the exposure, the more spins of the wheel and the greater the risk. This causal mechanism differs from the example in Section 2 of the pollutant in the river: Each tonne *actually* contributes to the death of the fish and does not simply increase the risk. Tort law differentiates between these two cases. In one (the polluted river case), each person "materially contributes to the damage" and is liable in full. In the other (the asbestos cases), each person merely contributes to the collective risk proven to have injured the plaintiff and incurs partial liability for the injury in proportion to their risk contribution. Although carbon emissions do not unambiguously fall into this latter category, imposing full liability for all climate-related harms on each of the major carbon emitters is problematic for reasons we have identified. That unfairness does not exist for the causal rules under consideration, which require a plaintiff to sue major emitters responsible for a "substantial share" of the wrongful emissions proven to have (collectively) caused the plaintiff's harms. As a member of the collective, each defendant is responsible only for its risk-related proportion of the cumulative wrongful emissions rather than for the entirety of plaintiff's damages.[65]

Third, in all of the cases—asbestos, bullets, and defective drugs—there is a relatively small number of persons who may have causally contributed to the harm. In *Fairchild*, there were three employers in breach of their duty of care to the employee, and at least one of them was causally responsible for his mesothelioma. Even in the DES cases, the number of DES manufacturers was relatively small. By contrast, in the climate change context, if the average Global North individual's lifetime contributions increase the risk of harm to others, then there are potentially hundreds of millions of other risk-creators, and there will be many thousands, if not millions, of victims. The number of relevant defendants would be reduced if there is a threshold at which the risk becomes wrongful. Still, the requirement of a substantial or material increase in risk might permit suit against an enormous number of persons.

In principle, however, the number of persons who contribute to the risk is not itself normatively significant. It is only relevant—apart from the procedural difficulties to which it may give rise—in so far as it bears on the probability that a person causally contributes to harm. In *Summers*, if 10,000 persons had fired simultaneously, the probability that any particular person caused the plaintiff's injury would be very small. In the US, the application of *Summers* requires the plaintiff to join all the potential tortfeasors (as in *Summers* itself). Conceivably, *Summers* would be applied to as to hold each of the 10,000 defendants jointly and severally liable; a more likely result, however, is that each would be held responsible only for its contribution to the risk, limiting the liability of each defendant to 1/10,000 of the plaintiff's injury. Otherwise, each defendant could avoid liability by relying on the wrongful conduct of the other shooters, a result in direct contravention to the underlying rationale for this liability rule. The same logic applies to suits brought against carbon emitters, no matter the number.

Finally, the plaintiffs' injuries in *Summers* and the DES cases were tortiously caused by one of the defendants, even though the plaintiff in each case could not identify which one. Unless all carbon emissions are negligent or otherwise tortious, the mere emission of even large amounts of carbon into the atmosphere is not a tortious act potentially subject to these rules. Grouping the defendants to establish but-for causation does not solve the causal-proof problem stemming from aggregated wrongful emissions that do not at least double the risk of climate-related injury: More likely than not, the background emissions caused the harm, not

[65] This is true for both alternative liability and market-share liability and explains why the California Supreme Court could justifiably conclude that the latter rule is based on the former one: 'When a [defendant] is subject to liability by virtue of its membership in the causal group, [its liability] is appropriately limited by its responsibility as a group member. This responsibility is measured by the likelihood that the [defendant] actually caused the plaintiff's harm'. Geistfeld (n 54) 490.

the collective emissions from the group of defendants. The likelihood that *non-wrongful* background emissions caused the harm can thus pose an obstacle to extending the causal rule in the hunting cases, asbestos cases, and DES cases to climate change.

In these cases, however, there is one further possible basis of liability. Each defendant emitter is known to have wrongfully caused substantial harm to unidentifiable plaintiff(s) in the aggregate, even if the background emissions are the most probable cause of the harm in any given case. Under these conditions, a defendant ought to know that it has a secondary duty to compensate an indeterminate class of persons. Consequently, the defendant cannot reasonably object to being liable up to a total amount of that known secondary duty in relation to persons whom it may have caused harm. This can be achieved, analogously to market share liability, by proportioning liability to the probability of causation in cases in which it is known, on an aggregate basis, that the individual defendant has wrongfully caused harm to a class of indeterminate persons.[66]

5. Conclusion

The discussion in this chapter has explained why a primary difficulty with establishing liability against an individual carbon emitter resides in the inability to demonstrate that its emissions *worsened*, in a but-for sense, a particular right-holder's position (even if it materially contributed to their harm). Drawing on the lessons from the preceding line of analysis provides a path forward.

Recall that the causal analysis is limited to tortious or wrongful carbon emissions and not the total emissions attributable to a particular defendant.[67] In public nuisance, the plaintiff can show that the defendant made a material contribution to the state of affairs constituting the public nuisance.[68] A plaintiff can also establish wrongful emissions as a matter of negligence liability. One relatively clear case could be when carbon emissions attributable to a single actor exceed the required percentage of reductions for the country under international agreements. For example, the Kyoto Protocol (1997) set "binding emissions reduction targets" for industrialised countries to reduce their combined emissions by an average 5.2% below 1990 levels during the first commitment period (2008–2012). One potential implication of this target is that an emitter which neither increased nor reduced its emissions below 1990 levels would have emitted an unreasonable amount of carbon equal to 5.2% of its total emissions, potentially subjecting it to liability for the consequential harms.

A plaintiff will be able to attribute their harm to these kinds of wrongful emissions, we have argued, if:

(1) The emissions materially contributed to the mechanism by which the harm was produced, even if the emissions were not but-for conditions of the harm.

or

(2) The emissions materially increased the risk of the harm, if but-for or material contribution to damage is impossible to prove on the preponderance of the evidence,

and

[66] For a more detailed explanation of this 'secondary duty' justification of proportional liability, see Sandy Steel, 'Justifying Exceptions to Proof of Causation in Tort Law' (2015) 78 Modern Law Review 729.

[67] See Section 3.

[68] See Kysar (n 10), discussing these suits filed so far in the US.

(3) The harm would not have occurred, on the balance of probabilities, but-for the wrongful conduct of *a group* of emitters, of which the defendant is a member.

In principle, any wrongful act that has non-minimally increased the probability of the type of harm suffered is actionable, so long as the harm is attributable, in a but-for sense, to wrongdoing. Since each wrongful act that satisfies (1) or (2)–(3) will not be shown to have been necessary or remotely close to individually sufficient for the outcome, fairness likely demands that liability be apportioned to the degree of causal contribution or degree of material risk increase.[69] In the asbestos context, courts have used rough and ready apportionment techniques, such as by relative length of exposure. In the present context, a carbon major's relative contribution, in terms of emissions output, during the period in which emissions are wrongful for the group, would be an equivalent rough starting point in this context.[70] Major individual wrongful emitters of carbon can be shown to have causally contributed to climate harms and be fairly subject to liability for their proportionate share, even if not always as necessary or sufficient conditions of causing the entirety of a plaintiff's climate-related harms.

[69] For an extended argument in favour of apportionment in cases involving unnecessary and insufficient contributions, Tscahi Keren-Paz and Richard Wright, 'Liability for Mass Sexual Abuse' (2019) 56 American Criminal Law Review 185, 220–23.

[70] This would not be justified on the basis that it reflects the *degree of harm* caused by the wrongful conduct, but rather a very rough and ready approximation of the *degree of risk* or *degree of causal contribution*.

CHAPTER 9

Civil Law Torts

ELBERT R. DE JONG

1. Introduction

AGAINST the backdrop of governmental failures in regulating corporate climate change responsibilities, civil liability law is increasingly invoked for shaping corporate climate change obligations and ultimately for filling regulatory gaps.[1]

A first prominent category of cases in this context are horizontal climate cases where the claimants, for the purpose of preventing hazardous climate change, seek to shape corporate mitigation duties on the basis of national civil liability law, and ask for a court order compelling a corporation to stop or prevent the infringement of this duty. A notable example is provided by the Dutch case of Milieudefensie against Shell, dealing with the obligations of the (former Dutch) carbon major to reduce its scope 1, 2, and 3 greenhouse gas (GHG) emissions.[2] Although the Gerechtshof Den Haag (the Court of Appeal of The Hague) dismissed the claim, among other things because it could not establish a concrete reduction target Shell should adhere to, the court did rule that companies who significantly contribute(d) to climate change, and have it in their power to avoid hazardous climate change, bear an autonomous duty to reduce GHG emissions. This recognition of a private law-based corporate mitigation duty constitutes a worldwide milestone, and the principled, broad, and universal nature of the court's reasoning may serve as a source of inspiration for initiating new corporate climate cases. The case also provides a blueprint for legal reasoning in such cases.

A second prominent category of cases are horizontal climate cases where the claimant is seeking compensation for the (risks of the) impairment of their interests caused by the (alleged) unlawful GHG emissions of a corporation. Here the German case against RWE speaks to the imagination.[3] In that case, Saúl Luciano Lliuya, supported by the NGO German Watch,

[1] See for a recent overview Joana Setzer and Catherine Higham, *Global Trends in Climate Change Litigation: 2025 Snapshot* (Grantham Research Institute on Climate Change and the Environment 2025). See also Karen C Sokol, 'Bringing Courts into Global Governance in a Climate Disrupted World Order' (2023) 108 Minnesota Law Review 163, 29.

[2] Gerechtshof Den Haag, 12 November 2024, ECLI:NL:GHDHA:2024:2099 (*Shell plc v Milieudefensie* et al). For academic commentary, see for example: Douglas A Kysar, 'The Duty of Climate Care' (2024) 73 DePaul Law Review 487; C Voigt and J Udell, 'Duty of Care' in M Wewerinke-Singh and S Mead (eds), *The Cambridge Handbook on Climate Litigation* (CUP 2025); Edward Brans and Mathijs Peters, 'Liability of Non-state Actors for Scope 3 Emissions' in ER de Jong and others (eds), *Corporate Accountability and Liability for Climate Change* (Edward Elgar Publishing 2024).

[3] Oberlandesgericht Hamm, 28 May 2025, Case I-5 u 15/17 (*Saúl Luciano Lliuya v RWE AG*). For a description and discussion of the case see, inter alia, Jan-Erik Schirmer, 'Climate Liability after Lliuya v RWE: Causation and Duty Demystified' (2025) 16 (3) Journal of European Tort Law 265; Will Frank, Christoph Bals, and Julia Grimm, 'The Case of Huaraz: First Climate Lawsuit on Loss and Damage Against an Energy Company Before German Courts' in Reinhard Mechler and others (eds), *Loss and*

sought a court order requiring RWE to make a pro rata contribution to the costs he incurs to safeguard his home against the climate change-induced risks of melting glaciers and the consequential risks of the flooding of the lake situated nearby his residence. He claimed that RWE, one of Germany's largest GHG emitters, should compensate his costs in proportion to the corporation's unlawful GHG emissions. Here the claim ultimately was dismissed. According to the Oberlandesgericht Hamm (the higher regional court of Hamm), the evidence presented to it showed no concrete threat to the property of Lliuya. However, on a principal notion, the court accepted that companies can be held (partially) liable under German law for their contribution to the impact and risks of climate change. And, as in the *Shell* case, this reasoning can offer inspiration and a possible blueprint for similar (compensation) cases.[4]

1.1 Common Features of Liability Law-based Climate Change Litigation

In this chapter, I do not intend to focus on the legal-technical issues of the *Shell* and *RWE* cases (for instance concerning admissibility, unlawfulness, causation, protected interests, and damage). I rather focus on the more fundamental and overarching questions concerning the nature and role of liability law and civil courts that both cases raise. Although there are important differences between them, the two cases exhibit at least three common and interrelated characteristics that underscore their residence at the frontiers of the domain of private law, and that consequently prompt critical questions concerning the domain of private law.

First, questions arise concerning the law-making role of civil courts, and the limits to this role. Crucial in both cases was the acceptance of the courts that they have the competence to engage in further shaping the law. On the one hand, the cases do not operate in a legal vacuum; the legal arguments brought forward by the claimant(s), and the defendants, are rooted in various private law doctrines and established case law, some of which have developed over decades.[5] In *Shell*, Milieudefensie argued that Shell, by failing to sufficiently reduce its GHG emissions, acted in violation of the broadly formulated and open-ended tort provision set out in Article 6:162 of the Dutch Burgerlijk Wetboek (BW). And in the *RWE*, Lliuya argued, among other things, that RWE's emissions constituted an unlawful contribution to the impairment of his property interests protected under Section 1004 of the Bürgerliches Gezetsbuch (BGB). On the other hand, article 6:162 BW and Section 1004 BGB have either not been, or only to a limited extent, applied to similar fact patterns.[6] Ultimately, the claimant asked the

Damage from Climate Change, Climate Risk Management, Policy and Governance (Springer 2019) 475. Reference could also be made to a Swiss horizontal case, brought by four residents of Pari Island (Indonesia) against Holcim AG, a Swiss construction company. They seek compensation for damages caused by floodings induced by rising sea levels, financial support for adaptation measures and a GHG emissions reduction order. In December 2025, the court declared the claim admissible, reasoning that the claim is private law in nature, notwithstanding its political and societal implications. See Kantonsgericht Zug, 17 December 2025, Case A1 2023 9 (*Asmania and others v Holcim AG*).

[4] Paul Grimm and Jan-Erik Schirmer, 'Success Without Victory: Lliuya v RWE Decided' (*Verfassungsblog*, 1 June 2025) <https://verfassungsblog.de/lliuya-rwe-climate-judgment> accessed 7 March 2026. See also Schirmer (n 3).

[5] Gerhard Wagner and Arvid Arntz, 'Liability for Climate Damages under the German Law of Torts' in Wolfgang Kahl and Marc-Philippe Weller (eds), *Climate Change Litigation: A Handbook* (Nomos 2021). The authors ultimately reject civil liability for climate change.

[6] See, for other German mitigation cases against German car manufactures, Sophia Schwemmer and others, *Global Perspectives on Corporate Climate Legal Tactics: Germany National Report* (2nd edn, British Institute of International and Comparative Law 2024). The cases are also addressed in Section 3.1.

court to establish new legal claims whose existence are not readily discernible within the applicable legal framework, thereby explicitly seeking to broaden the scope and substantive content of the law.

A second key commonality is that the claimants essentially rely on the notion of autonomous private law. The basic idea here is that private law constitutes an autonomous legal framework, distinguished from other (public law) legal frameworks, containing theories and concepts of responsibility to prevent the negative effects of corporate activities on public health and the living environment.[7] This framework is characteristically formulated in an open-ended manner and evolves over time, thereby enabling it to adapt to emerging societal challenges. It thus possesses a certain level of adaptability to facilitate the development of new notions of responsibility in relation to climate change.[8] Past examples in which courts have addressed regulatory gaps by developing duties of care for dealing with environmental and health risks, such as in cases involving exposure to hazardous substances and environmental pollution, fuel the idea that the open norms of private law also provide room for accepting new corporate climate obligations.[9] Yet, simultaneously, within the European context corporate climate change responsibility has increasingly been governed by national and European public laws, such as the European Emissions Trading Scheme 1 and 2 (ETS 1 and 2),[10] the Corporate Sustainability Reporting Directive (CSRD),[11] and the Corporate Sustainability Due Diligence Directive (CSDDD).[12] The applicability of these European public laws, and the weakening of it under the current deregulation and simplification agenda of the EU, more specifically the Sustainability Omnibus Directive,[13]raises questions about the room afforded to national private law, and thus also civil courts, to impose (additional) obligations on corporate actors.

Finally, a shared characteristic is the utilisation of liability law by the claimants—in climate change cases, frequently NGOs or claimants supported by them—as a regulatory instrument.[14]

[7] Elbert R de Jong, 'Dutch Climate Change Litigation & The Autonomy of Tort Law' (2024) 3 KlimaRZ 93; Schirmer (n 3).

[8] E.g., Kim Bouwer, 'Lessons from a Distorted Metaphor: The Holy Grail of Climate Litigation' (2020) 9 (2) Transnational Environmental Law 347, 364; Vibe Ulfbeck, 'Climate Change in Tort Law? The New Regulatory and External Effect of Suits against Private Actors', in A Beckers and others (eds), *The Foundations of European Transnational Private Law* (Hart Publishing 2024).

[9] Geetanjali Ganguly, Joana Setzer, and Veerle Heyvaert, 'If at First You Don't Succeed: Suing Corporations for Climate Change' (2018) 38 Oxford Journal of Legal Studies 841.

[10] Directive 2003/87/EC of the European Parliament and of the Council of 13 October 2003 establishing a scheme for GHG emission allowance trading within the Community and amending Council Directive 96/61/EC [2003] OJ L275/32; Regulation (EU) 2023/956 of the European Parliament and of the Council of 10 May 2023 establishing a carbon border adjustment mechanism, [2023] OJ EU L 130/52.

[11] Directive (EU) 2022/2464 of the European Parliament and of the Council of 14 December 2022 amending Regulation (EU) 537/2014, Directive 2004/109/EC, Directive 2006/43/EC, and Directive 2013/34/EU, as regards corporate sustainability reporting [2022] OJ EU L 322/15.

[12] Directive (EU) 2024/1760 of the European Parliament and of the Council of 13 June 2024 on corporate sustainability due diligence and amending Directive (EU) 2019/1937 and Regulation (EU) 2023/2859 [2024] OJ L 202/1. See also Barbara Pozzo, Chapter 29, and Harro van Asselt and Jessica Crow, Chapter 33 of this handbook.

[13] Directive (EU) 2026/470 of the European Parliament and of the Council of 24 February 2026 amending Directives 2006/43/EC, 2013/34/EU, (EU) 2022/2464 and (EU) 2024/1760 as regards certain corporate sustainability reporting requirements and certain corporate sustainability due diligence requirements.

[14] For tort law as a risk regulatory instrument see Elbert R de Jong, 'Tort Law and Judicial Risk Regulation: Bipolar and Multipolar Risk Reasoning in Light of Tort Law's Regulatory Effects' (2018) 9 European Journal of Risk Regulation 14; Hans-W Micklitz, 'Risk, Tort and Liability', in Stefan

Both the *Shell* and the *RWE* cases were brought before court not only to adjudicate the need for legal protection between the litigants, as is typical in civil law proceedings, but also to produce legal and factual effects that extend far beyond the immediate dispute. The underlying rationale, and also the aspiration of the claimants, is that the emergence of such effects serves as an incentive for corporations to adapt their GHG emission policies. And, also due to the polycentric nature of climate change governance, liability law-based litigation inherently produces significant (non-legal) effects that are felt both by the litigants and non-litigants.[15]

With respect to legal regulatory effects, it may be noted that notions of responsibility that are established in a single case can possibly provide fertile soil for the further shaping of corporate climate change obligations in other cases. This dynamic holds true even in cases where the claim is rejected.[16] Illustrative is that Milieudefensie, stimulated by the reasoning and outcome in the first instance ruling in the *Shell* case, where the District Court ordered Shell to reduce its scope 1, 2, and 3 emissions,[17] announced a new mitigation case against ING, a Dutch bank. In that case the NGO demands that ING will substantially reduce its total emissions, require climate change transition plans from major clients, and abandon its financial activities in the oil and gas sector.[18] More importantly, after the ruling on appeal Milieudefensie announced that it will continue to proceed with its case against ING. Furthermore, in 2025 Milieudefensie announced a new mitigation case against Shell, demanding among other things that Shell will cease new investments in oil and gas fields.[19] The seeds for this second case against Shell are largely rooted in the Court of Appeal's reasoning in the first *Shell* case, where the court observed that Shell's new investments in oil and gas fields could constitute a wrongful act.[20] However, the court ruled that the unlawfulness of Shell's investment policies fell outside the scope of the legal issues presented to it, and for that reason it did not address the matter further.

Grundmann, Hans-W Micklitz, and Moritz Renners (eds), *New Private Law Theory: A Pluralist Approach* (CUP 2021); Ulfbeck, 'Climate Change in Tort Law?' See in general on the use of courts as agents for social change Gerald N Rosenberg, 'Courts as Agents of Change' in Lee Epstein and others (eds), *The Oxford Handbook of Comparative Judicial Behaviour* (online edn, Oxford Academic 2023).

[15] See in depth about the effects of climate change litigation Jolene Lin, 'Climate Change and the Court' (2012) 32 Legal Studies 35; Jacqueline Peel and Hari M Osofky, *Climate Change Litigation: Regulatory Pathways to Cleaner Energy* (CUP 2015); Elbert R de Jong, 'Macro Effects in Climate Change Mitigation Cases: Four Empirical Challenges' in Rob A J van Gestel, Jurgen C A de Poorter, and Ed Rubin (eds), *Judicial Policy Making, Empirical Data and Scientific Evidence: Can Courts Manage the Twenty-first Century?* (Edward Elgar Publishing 2026).

[16] E.g., Jacqueline Peel and Rebekkah Markey-Towler, 'Recipe for Success? Lessons for Strategic Climate Litigation from the *Sharma*, *Neubauer*, and *Shell-cases*' (2021) 22 German Law Journal 1484.

[17] Rechtbank Den Haag, 26 May 2021, ECLI:NL:RBDHA:2021:5337.

[18] See the announcement on the website of Milieudefensie, 'Veelgestelde vragen over onze nieuwe Klimaatzaak tegen ING' <https://www.milieudefensie.nl/veelgestelde-vragen-klimaatzaak-ing> accessed 7 March 2026. See for the writ of summons: <https://milieudefensie.nl/klimaatzaak-ing/info/dagvaarding-ing> assessed 7 March 2026. See for the statement of defence <https://ing.com/binaries/content/assets/documents/sustainability/20260217-conclusie-van-antwoord-van-ing-doorzoekbaar-en-zonder-handtekening.pdf> accessed 7 March 2026.

[19] See the announcement on the website of Milieudefensie, 'Nieuwe zaak tegen Shell: stop met aanboren nieuwe olie-en gasvelden—Milieudefensie' <https://milieudefensie.nl/actueel/nieuwe-rechtszaak-tegen-shell-stop-met-aanboren-nieuwe-olie-en-gasvelden?gad_source=1&gad_campaignid=22302667115&gclid=EAIaIQobChMI25b4iZmXjgMVTZmDBx1sJhn3EAAYASAAEgJIefD_BwE> accessed 7 March 2026.

[20] Gerechtshof Den Haag, 12 November 2024, ECLI:NL:GHDHA:2024:2099, paras 7.58–7.62.

The legal regulatory effects of corporate climate change liability also exhibit a distinctly transnational character. Ulfbeck, for instance, notices that "whereas tort law rules may differ from one national legal system to another, tort law systems across the world also display commonalities in terms of the very basic principles of tort law".[21] According to her "this offers an excellent basis for 'cross fertilization' and invites the idea that a concept developed or refined in one legal system can be exported to another legal system".[22] And, with respect to climate change litigation in general, Kysar expresses the hope that inspired by those courts that advance duties of climate care, "other courts [will] join the effort and give rise to a global tapestry of interweaving duties of climate care".[23]

As to the factual regulatory effects, one could think of effects of (the threat of) liability on the availability of energy products and the prices thereof, the economic competitiveness of (national) economies and companies, the availability of jobs, the shift towards renewable energy sources, and others. A specific category of regulatory effects encompasses those that exert both positive and negative impacts on corporate efforts to reduce GHG emissions. For instance, the threat of (successful) compensation claims could lead to an internalisation of (social) climate costs of corporate emissions, with the possibility that these costs will be included in the corporation's climate policies. Injunctions could induce similar preventive effects, for instance because corporations adjust their policies to avoid litigation. Other typical, and often overstated, examples of regulatory effects on emission reduction efforts are carbon leakage effects, substitution effects[24] (e.g., "if one actor is obliged to reduce emissions, others will fill the gap"), or effects related to the behavior of customers (e.g., "if an oil company's obligation to reduce its scope 3 emissions leads to a price increase, customers will get their fuel somewhere else"). Furthermore, one could think of the fact that liability and the threat thereof can influence the social, political, regulatory, and economic conditions that are relevant for a corporation's reduction policies. By way of example,[25] one could think of the possible influence of liability on corporate reputation,[26] or regulatory action taken by governmental actors in response to legal proceedings or in anticipation of it.[27]

These factual regulatory effects notably illustrate that although liability law operates within a bilateral setting, its application yields consequences that extend far beyond that setting, a possibility that ultimately prompts the question whether the possible emergence of such macro-effects should be taken into account when defining the role of liability law in shaping corporate climate change obligations.

21 Ulfbeck, 'Climate Change in Tort Law?' 349.

22 ibid 349.

23 Kysar (n 2) 523.

24 On substitution effects in the context of climate change litigation see, e.g., Guy Dwyer, '"Market Substitution" in the Context of Climate Litigation' (2022) 12 Climate Law 1.

25 In addition to the examples mentioned, one could think of—a lack of—impact of litigation on public and political concern about climate change. See Anna Kovács and others, 'Beyond Courts: Does Strategic Litigation Affect Climate Change Policy Support?' (2024) 79 International Review of Law and Economics 1. One could also think of the fact that litigation can legitimise—or delegitimise—climate science. Hari M Osofsky, 'The Continuing Importance of Climate Change Litigation' (2010) 1 Climate Law 3, 5; Maria Lee, 'The Sources and Challenges of Norm Generation in Tort Law' (2018) 1 European Journal of Risk Regulation 34.

26 See in general Roy Shapira, *Law and Reputation: How the Legal System Shapes Behavior by Producing Information* (CUP 2020).

27 E.g., Brian Preston, 'The Influence of Climate Change Litigation on Governments and the Private Sector' (2011) 2 Climate Law 485.

1.2 Structure of This Chapter

From the characteristics delineated above, three overarching issues emerge concerning the role that liability law, and civil courts, may or may not assume when shaping corporate climate change obligations. These issues, which will be addressed in the following sections, pertain to:

- the institutional competence of civil courts (Section 2);
- the extent to which liability law can function autonomously as a source of corporate climate change obligations (Section 3); and
- the effectiveness, and a possible lack thereof, of liability law as an instrument to reduce (global) GHG emissions (Section 4).

First, various perspectives that may serve as frameworks for addressing these issues are explored. Second, it will be discussed how these perspectives manifest within the literature and case law, with a specific emphasis on the *Shell* case and *RWE* case. From this analysis, different approaches to the role of liability law and civil courts in shaping corporate obligations for climate change are derived (Section 5).

2. Institutional Competence of Civil Courts

Specifically when courts are asked to develop new legal concepts and theories, that is, when they are asked to engage in judicial law making, the question arises whether they are institutionally competent to do so.[28] This question arises even more prominently in civil liability climate change cases due to, on the one hand, the bilateral nature of private law and, on the other, the polycentric nature of issues related to climate change responsibility, the collective action problem inherent in climate change, and the (potentially) significant political and societal implications of imposing civil liability on corporations.

The institutional competence of civil courts can be addressed from a risk regulatory perspective and a legal protection perspective. The risk regulatory perspective emphasises the systemic and multilayered nature of corporate climate governance and tends to view civil courts as ill-suited to assume a regulatory role. In contrast, the legal protection perspective emphasises the courts' role to assess the legal claims presented to it, and to provide effective remedies for the (imminent threat of a) violation of legal obligations. A crucial difference between the perspectives ultimately lies in the weight they assign to the effects of liability law on third-party interests. While the risk regulatory perspective cautions against judicial overreach due to potential significant and unintended consequences for litigants and non-litigants, the legal protection perspective foregrounds the importance of amplifying and upholding legal norms between a claimant and defendant, irrespective of potential significant societal consequences and complex policy trade-offs.

[28] In a legal-technical sense, the institutional competence is further determined by the rules regarding, among other things, admissibility, justiciability (if any) and jurisdiction. See Guy Dwyer, 'Climate Litigation: A Red Herring among Climate Mitigation Tools' in Benoit Mayer and Alexander Zahar (eds), *Debating Climate Law* (CUP 2021), 132–33. As mentioned in section 1.1, this chapter will not deal in depth with the legal technical issues that arise under such doctrines.

2.1 Civil Courts as Risk Regulators

Under the risk regulatory perspective, the institutional competence of civil courts is assessed in terms of their legitimacy and capability to act in a *regulatory* capacity.[29] This regulatory capacity is determined by factors such as the ability of civil courts to:

- coherently regulate the responsibilities and liabilities of multiple corporate emitters, not in the least carbon majors operating across diverse economic sectors and jurisdictions;
- anticipate, assess, and account for the broader implications of their rulings;
- identify, mitigate, and manage potential (and often unforeseen) side effects of judicial decisions on third parties;
- competently engage with complex climate science; and
- ensure the implementation of and compliance with its rulings, which specifically in injunctive relief cases may require ongoing monitoring.

Regarding the position of third parties, it is important to recognise that an adequate regulatory response to climate change requires the regulation of actors who are not parties to the case before the court. However, whether such third-party actors will, in the future, become subjected to judicial scrutiny depends primarily on whether they are challenged in court by individual victims or NGOs. Civil courts lack the competence to initiate cases themselves; they are dependent on the claims brought before them by claimants.[30] From a risk regulatory perspective, this reliance on the claimant's initiative represents a structural limitation on the breadth, timing, and precision of liability law's regulatory functioning.[31] It constrains the court's ability to address systemic or diffuse contributions to climate harm in a comprehensive manner, and may result in a piecemeal approach which can easily (but also falsely as will be discussed below) be seen as a limitation on both the scope and effectiveness of liability law's functioning.[32]

In addition, while national liability law may produce transnational regulatory effects, it remains inherently limited in its capacity to serve as a regulatory instrument for a global problem such as climate change. Private law norm setting occurs on an ad hoc, case-by-case basis in a national setting on the basis of diverging national private laws. On the one hand, this may result in the development of impactful legal precedents potentially catalysing broader behavioral changes across industries and jurisdictions.[33] On the other hand, it could be argued that this use of national liability law leads to a fragmented and inconsistent framework of national corporate climate obligations, creating legal uncertainty and inequality. Such fragmentation may in the end undermine the coherence and effectiveness of global corporate and governmental efforts to reduce corporate GHG emissions and can thus complicate long-term climate change governance.[34]

[29] E.g., Victor E Schwartz, Phil Goldberg and Christopher E Appel, 'Does the Judiciary Have the Tools for Regulating Greenhouse Gas Emissions?' (2011) 46 Valparaiso University Law Review 369.

[30] Peter Cane, 'Tort Law as Regulation', 31 (2002) Common Law World Review 305, 313; Willem H van Boom, *Efficacious Enforcement in Contract and Tort* (Boom juridische uitgevers 2006 47).

[31] See for a discussion of these points also De Jong (n 14).

[32] Dwyer (n 28) 133.

[33] See Section 1.2.

[34] See about this point in relation to Urgenda; Benoit Mayer, The Contribution of Urgenda to the Mitigation of Climate Change' (2023) 33 Journal of Environmental Law 167. See, however, also Monika Hinteregger, 'Civil Liability and the Challenges of Climate Change: A Functional Analysis' (2017) 8 Journal of European Tort Law 238, 246–47, who argues that 'unlike administrative or tax law, the

Elements of a risk regulatory perspective can for instance be found in some of the mitigation cases against German car manufacturers, such as Mercedes-Benz,[35] BMW,[36] and Volkswagen,[37] dealing with their responsibility to switch their production from combustion engine vehicles to climate-friendly vehicles. For instance, in the case against BMW the district court reasoned that the dispute before it was "not a typical bilateral conflict under civil law (between two parties), but deals with complex issues concerning climate neutrality, for which different strategies are conceivable." Determining such strategies requires "fundamental policy and balancing decisions", "which belongs to the core competence of the legislature and the executive".[38] And given the fact that according to the court, they are fulfilling this task adequately, the court did not assume any additional private law obligations (see also Section 3). Similar considerations, dealing with the complexity and policentricity inherent to (private law) issues of climate responsibilities, can be found in the other cases.[39]

Another strong example is provided by the reasoning of the Court of Appeal in *Smith v Fonterra*, which echoes several elements of the risk regulatory perspective. The court emphasised that "the magnitude of the crisis which is climate change simply cannot be appropriately or adequately addressed by common law tort claims pursued through the courts. It is quintessentially a matter that calls for a *sophisticated regulatory* response at a national level supported by international co-ordination".[40] It furthermore considered that "*in effect* Mr. Smith is seeking a court-designed and court-supervised *regulatory regime*".[41] It ultimately concluded that civil courts are insufficiently equipped and legitimised to contribute to the development of such a regime: "[C]ourts do not have the expertise to address the social, economic and distributional implications of different *regulatory design choices*. The court process does not provide all affected stakeholders with an opportunity to be heard, and have their views taken into account. Climate change provides a striking example of a polycentric issue that is not amenable to judicial resolution."[42]

To a certain extent, the Supreme Court of New Zealand dismissed the risk regulatory perspective taken by the Court of Appeal. For instance it held that "it may indeed be beyond the capacity of the common law to resolve climate change in fact, but we are not presently convinced, at this stage of the proceeding, addressing only strike out, that the common law is incapable of addressing *tortious* aspects of climate change".[43] The Supreme Court stipulated that on the basis of previous case law, the claim could be made that the defendants may bear an

functioning of civil liability is not constrained to the territory of one country. Claims for damages can be directly asserted abroad or brought against foreign parties before domestic courts and subsequently enforced abroad. Consequently, civil liability claims, or even the pending threat of such claims, may induce emitters of greenhouse gases to reduce their emissions regardless of the climate protection policy of their state'.

35 Oberlandesgericht Stuttgart, 8 November 2023 12 U 170/22, BeckRS 2023, 31435.

36 Landgericht München, 7 February 2023, O 12581/21, BeckRS 2023, 2861; Oberlandesgericht München, 12 October 2023, 32 U 936/23, BeckRS 2023, 30283.

37 Landgericht Braunschweig, 14 February 2023, 6 O 3931/21, juris, paras 87, 104, 119.

38 Landgericht München, 7 February 2023, O 12581/21, BeckRS 2023, 2861, paras 62 and 70.

39 See Jan-Erik Schirmer, 'Klimahaftung: Überforderung, der Gerichte?', 2024 *Zeitschrift für die gesamte Privatrechtswissenschaft* (2024) 159–80, 162.

40 Court of Appeal of New Zealand 21 October 2021, Smith v Fonterra Co-operative Group Ltd [2021] NZCA 552; [2022] 2 NZLR 284, para 16.

41 ibid para 26.

42 ibid para 26.

43 Supreme Court of New Zealand 7 February 2024, Smith v Fonterra Co-operative Group Ltd, SC 149/2021 [2024] NZSC 5154, para 154.

autonomous duty to reduce emissions, and that the existence of this duty is not contingent on the acts of others.[44] It also held that the legal issues in the case, particularly those in relation to causation, bear resemblance with other situations involving multiple contributors, providing the court with the institutional competence to hear the claim.[45]

Several objections can be made against using the risk regulatory perspective as a yardstick for assessing the institutional competence of civil courts. First, almost any private law dispute inlcudes regulatory aspects which could, seen from a risk regulatory perspective, raise competence issues.[46] Yet, by adhering to this perspective one fails to acknowledge that the core institutional competence of civil courts resides in adjudicating matters of legal protection (see Section 2.2). Second, a significant objection pertains to the determination of the regulatory competence of civil courts, which is often framed as an either/or question regarding who is better positioned to achieve optimal regulation: courts or regulators? While the theoretical answer may be straightforward, experience reveal that public regulators are confronted with various factors—such as scientific uncertainties, short-term economic interests, regulatory capture, a perceived lack of public and political support, inadequate enforcement mechanisms, and so on—which may lead to paralysis at the side of the regulator and ultimately to inadequate regulation.[47] Through the involvement of private law and civil courts, it is to some extent possible to counterbalance these paralyzing factors, thereby *strengthening* the regulatory framework both in terms of norm-setting and enforcement.[48] Within the European context it is precisely this distinctive regulatory potential of private law that has increasingly been recognised. That is because the EU utilises private law as an instrument to achieve European public policy objectives and, consequently, to ensure effective protection of private and public interests. This rise of European regulatory private law has been developing across a range of areas, including competition law, industrial emissions, product safety, privacy law, financial law, and to some extent also in the field of sustainability law.[49] An important nuance to the foregoing is that under the Sustainability Omnibus Directive the role of, inter alia, private law in the area of sustainability law is weakened (see further Section 3).

2.2 Civil Courts as Legal Protectors

Under the second perspective, the institutional competence of civil courts is grounded in the courts' core adjudicative function: to decide the legal claims made by the parties and, where

[44] ibid para 164.

[45] ibid para 157.

[46] Schirmer (n 39) 163.

[47] See, e.g., Patrick Luff, 'The Political Economy of Court-Based Regulation' in Ugo Mattei and John D Haskell (eds), *Research Handbook on Political Economy and Law* (Edward Elgar Publishing 2015) 315, 327–29; Michael G Faure an Roy A Partain, *Environmental Law and Economics. Theory and Practice* (CUP 2019); Claire Stalenhoef, Elbert de Jong, and Michael Faure, 'Licence to Pollute? Revisiting the Regulatory Compliance Defence in Civil Proceedings in Cases of Human Rights Violations' (2025) 37 Journal of Environmental Law 299.

[48] For an analysis of this dynamic in Dutch in relation to the *Urgenda* case, see Liesbeth Enneking and Elbert R de Jong, 'Regulering van onzekere risico's via public interest litigation?' (2014/23) Nederlands Juristenblad 1542–51. See in German about this point Jan-Erik Schirmer, *Nachhaltiges Privatrecht* (Mohr Siebeck 2023) 411.

[49] E.g., Hans-W Micklitz, 'The Visible Hand of European Regulatory Private Law' (2009) 28 Yearbook of European Law 3; Hans-W Micklitz 'European Law of Regulated Industries and Transnational Private Law' in Anna Beckers and others (eds), *The Foundations of European Transnational Private Law* (Hart Publishing 2024).

indicated by the law, to provide legal protection through the application of the available arsenal of private law remedies. In contrast to the risk regulatory perspective, this approach does not derive the court's competence from the broader political, regulatory, or societal dimension of a case. In a way, this perspective thus reflects a more restrained view of the institutional competence of civil courts. However, since the broader societal and regulatory implications of a case are not decisive, this perspective arguably affords civil courts greater leeway to reach outcomes with regulatory implications. That is because the narrower framing of their institutional competence justifies norm-amplification and development as an inherent part of the courts function to provide legal protection, rather than as the court taking on a regulatory role.[50]

In the *Shell* case, Shell essentially argued that liability law does not offer an adequate means for addressing climate change and that given the polycentric nature of the climate crisis and the wide array of third-party interests that are at stake, civil courts lack the competence to impose obligations on a corporation in the context of an individual lawsuit. The District Court and the Court of Appeal rejected this line of reasoning. Illustrative is the reasoning of the District Court that "it does not follow Royal Dutch Shell's argument that the claims of Milieudefensie et al. require decisions which go beyond the lawmaking function of the court. The court must *decide on the claims* of Milieudefensie et al.".[51] Also on appeal, where the admissibility of Milieudefensie was re-examined, the court reflected on the political dimension and societal implications of the case. It held that the political sensitivity or the societal implications of the case do not in themselves deprive the court of its competence to adjudicate the claim, since it is grounded in established private law doctrines, the application of which belong to the core of the court's institutional competence: "[F]or the purpose of cause of action, it is sufficient to establish that Milieudefensie et al. invoke that Shell has a *legal obligation* to reduce its CO_2 emissions. If such a legal obligation can be identified, the fact that *political choices* must be made to combat dangerous climate change and the fact that not everyone will agree on those choices, *do not stand* in the way of the admissibility of the claim."[52]

In the *RWE* case, RWE argued that Lliuya's claim leads to an instrumentalisation of liability law to enforce environmental policy goals, and that this would lead to the courts being overburdened by the enforcement of numerous individual claims.[53] In essence, RWE thus called into question the court's institutional competence given the underlying regulatory goals of the litigation and its potential side-effects (in this case flood gate effects). The court, however, rejected this argument, since it "does not relate to a *legal examination* of the requirements for claims under Section 1004 BGB, but is rather of a *political nature*".[54] In other words, the court must decide on basis of, and within the scope of, the applicable law. The potential (significant) societal and political implications of the case do not alter that fundamental principle. The court also points to its competence to determine whether legal protection must be afforded against the consequences of the emissions of the defendant. The court namely observes: "[T]he defendant's argument that solutions to this conflict can only be implemented at the state and political level is aimed at warding off claims (of emission damage) by affected owners

50 Peter Cane, 'Using Tort Law to Enforce Environmental Regulation?' (2002) 41 Washburn Law Journal 427–68, 466; Douglas A Kysar, 'The Public Life of Private Law: Tort Law as a Risk Regulation Mechanism' (2018) 9 European Journal of Risk Regulation 48.

51 Rechtbank Den Haag, 26 05 2021, ECLI:NL:RBDHA:2021:5337, para 4.1.3.

52 Gerechtshof Den Haag, 12 November 2024, ECLI:NL:GHDHA:2024:2099, para 6.8.

53 Oberlandesgericht Hamm, 28 May 2025, I-5 u 15/17, para 5c.

54 ibid para 5c.

from the outset, without having to enter into a legal examination or even a gathering of evidence on the disputed facts."[55]

Lastly, the court's reasoning in the Swiss *Holcim* case—which draws on comparative legal insights from other horizontal climate cases—also reflects a legal protection perspective. The court, among other things, emphasised that the political dimension of the case, and its potential regulatory and societal effects, does not take away the private law nature of the claims made. The court, while recognising that the application of open-ended private law norms to the matter at hand gives rise to political debate and (could trigger) far reaching precedential and regulatory effects, further held that its task is not to assess or determine climate change policies in general, but to resolve legal disputes that relate to rights, harms and interests falling within the protective scope of the private law provisions invoked by the claimants.[56]

3. Autonomy of Liability Law

The second issue pertaining to the role of liability law, is the extent to which it can function autonomously as a source of corporate climate obligations and, more generally, its relationship with public laws such as the ETS 1 and 2, CSRD, and CSDDD. This relationship between liability law and public law can be understood through the level of autonomy of liability law, which reflects to what extent public law norms are decisive in private law matters. Here, a distinction can be made between a low(er) (Section 3.1) and a high(er) level of autonomy (Section 3.2). Both the *Shell* and *RWE* cases reflect a high degree of autonomy of private law. Moreover, the *Shell* case in particular provides specific grounds for further strengthening this autonomy of private law (Section 3.3).

3.1 A Low Level of Autonomy

In case of a low(er) level of autonomy, public law norms are, as a matter of principle, followed in private law, as private law "merely" plays a subsidiary role in redressing violations of existing public law norms. In so far as actors act in accordance with these public law norms, in principle there is no basis for assuming additional obligations. The justification behind this starting point lies, among other things, in the assumption that public authorities, due to their expertise, democratic legitimacy, and enforcement capabilities, are best positioned to define corporate responsibilities and to weigh competing and divergent interests (i.e., the regulatory perspective described in Section 2.1 resonates here).[57] Moreover, a low level of autonomy is driven by the desire to ensure the unity and coherence of the legal order and to provide legal certainty to those corporations subjected to public regulation.[58] The imposition of additional private law duties by civil courts would accordingly be at odds with, and could even contradict, the public mandate provided to emitting corporations by public law. For this reason, when adhering to a low(er) level of autonomy of private law, emissions that are regulated by public law should not be regarded as unlawful under liability law.[59] In the German mitigation cases

55 ibid para 5c.

56 Kantonsgericht Zug, 17 December 2025, Case A1 2023 9.

57 Eloise Scotford, 'Private Rights and Public Regulation: Civil Liability and the Permit Defence', in Gerd Winter and others (eds), *Property and Environmental Protection in Europe* (Europe Law Publishing 2015) 350.

58 See in the context of German law, with further references, Schwemmer et al 2024 (n 6) 50–52.

59 E.g., Wagner and Arntz (n 5) 69–72.

against Mercedes-Benz,[60] BMW,[61] and Volkswagen,[62] this line of reasoning was reflected in the court's decisions and no additional private law obligations were assumed.[63]

3.2 A High Level of Autonomy

A high(er) level of autonomy implies that even when public law regulation is applicable and complied with by a corporation, additional obligations can still be imposed. Here, public law and private law are primarily seen as communicating vessels. For example, civil courts may partly rely on public law norms when shaping private law obligations. This can occur because a public law norm is not automatically decisive but may serve as an indicative guide in specifying the content and scope of a private law obligation.[64]

Adherence to a high(er) degree of autonomy is, first and foremost, based on the recognition that public and private law embody distinct legal frameworks, both of which are democratically legitimised and pursue their own rationales and objectives. Liability law specifically focuses on the harm that the emission of GHGs may cause in a specific setting to the interests protected by private law, and on the related question whether, and if so how, the defendant in its relation with the claimant can be held liable for this (potential) infringement. In many instances, due to the generic nature of its rules, the substance thereof, and the goals it pursues, public law does not provide clarity on its relevance for harms that can be caused by the acts it governs to interests protected by private law.

Second, and building on this previous point, even when private law has a high level of autonomy, the primacy of public law is acknowledged. In order to determine private law's relationship with public law, it can be examined whether, and to which extent, the public law framework exhaustively regulates the legal issues presented in a liability case and/or excludes any supplementary role for liability law. On the one hand, such an approach recognises that the public law mandate enjoyed by emitting entities is not unconditional or unlimited, but on the other it also recognises that via public law the domain of private law can be defined and restricted, provided that this is explicitly indicated by the regulator.

Third, and last, the strength of this approach ultimately lies in the recognition that the regulatory process is not perfect and can be exposed to various limitations, which may result in regulatory failures (see also Section 2.1). In the case of a low level of autonomy, this would mean that regulatory shortcomings will also have effect in private law. Yet, when applying a high level of autonomy, these shortcomings will not per se be transposed into the domain of liability law, which ensures legal protection for individuals who face (significant) risks as a result of legally allowed emissions.[65]

60 Oberlandesgericht Stuttgart, 8 November 2023 12 U 170/22, BeckRS 2023, 31435, paras 96–105.

61 Landgericht München, 7 February 2023, O 12581/21, BeckRS 2023, 2861, para 71; Oberlandesgericht München, 12 October 2023, 32 U 936/23, BeckRS 2023, 30283paras 79–93.

62 Landgericht Braunschweig, 14 februari 2023, 6 O 3931/21, juris, paras 87, 104, 119.

63 For an extensive description of these cases, see Schwemmer et al 2024 (n 6) 50–52.

64 Schirmer (n 3) 23–24, with further references. Also see Boudewijn de Bruin and Olha Cherednychenko, Chapter 45 of this handbook.

65 See Stalenhoef et al (n 47) with further references.

3.3 The Autonomy of Liability Law in the RWE and Shell Cases

A high(er) degree of autonomy can be observed in both the *RWE* and the *Shell* case. In the *RWE* case, the court held that as a starting point, private law provides the framework for assessing the (un)lawfulness of the harm possibly caused to Lliuya's interests by RWE's emissions, even though these emissions are also subjected to public law norms. According to the court, only when the public law framework governs the private law relationship between RWE and third parties or explicitly excludes the application of private law in that context is there reason to depart from this starting point. Particularly telling is the court's observation that "the fact that greenhouse gases may still be generally compatible with the global climate up to a certain limit says nothing about the specific compatibility for the individual affected—in this case the plaintiff or his property in Huaraz".[66] Ultimately, referring to established case law, the court concludes that the "autonomy of the duties of care under private law" remains, and that for the purpose of protecting individuals "stricter requirements may arise under private law than those applicable under public law".[67]

In the *Shell* case, like the *RWE* case, the Court of Appeal determined the additional scope of liability law primarily by examining whether the imposition of additional corporate climate obligations is excluded by European and national public climate laws. It answers this question in the negative and, implicitly aligning with the primacy of public regulators, finds that governments have even emphasised that companies have their own responsibility to reduce emissions.[68] The court further concludes that the (European) legislator has not explicitly intended to regulate the private law obligations of companies like Shell exhaustively through instruments such as the ETS, the CSRD, and the CSDDD, and thus has not sought to preclude supplementary private law duties of care.[69] At the same time, the court emphasises that in shaping the applicable private law norms, "due regard" must be given to the applicable public law standards (i.e., emphasising that both systems are communicating vessels).[70]

The court specifically addresses the interaction between liability law and the ETS 1 and 2. How this interaction between private law and other public law norms plays out, however, remains unaddressed. Nonetheless, the reasoning reveals at least two potential future pathways.

First, the acceptance of the horizontal applicability of human rights in liability law proceedings—particularly of Articles 2 and 8 of the European Convention on Human Rights (ECHR)—could have significant implications for the relationship between private law and public law. Under Articles 2 and 8 ECHR, and the positive obligations for States to prevent infringements to these provisions, various requirements are imposed on public climate laws.[71]

66 Oberlandesgericht Hamm, 28 May 2025, I-5 u 15/17, para 2d.
67 ibid.
68 Gerechtshof Den Haag, 12 November 2024, ECLI:NL:GHDHA:2024:2099.
69 ibid para 7.53.
70 ibid para 7.54.
71 See Hoge Raad 20 December 2019, ECLI:NL:HR:2019:2006, *NJ* 2020/41 (*Urgenda*) and European Court of Human Rights, 9 April 2024, 53600/20 (*Verein KlimaSeniorinnen and Others v Switzerland*). See recently also Rechtbank Den Haag, 28 January 2026, ECLI:NL:RBDHA:2026:1344 *(Bonaire Climate Case)*, where the District Court ruled that Dutch reduction targets (i.e., 55% reduction by 2030 compared to 1990 and net-zero in 2050) are not in line with Article 8 ECHR. See on this case E.R. de Jong & H. van Asselt, 'The Bonaire Climate Case, State Mitigation Obligations after KlimaSeniorinnen', 9 February 2026, <Verfassungsblog.de, https://verfassungsblog.de/the-bonaire-climate-case/> accessed 7 March 2026.

Applying these requirements in horizontal relationships may mean that compliance with the applicable regulatory framework by a corporation is not sufficient if that regulatory framework itself does not align with Article 2 and 8 ECHR. That is because corporations themselves have an autonomous duty to prevent possible infringements of Article 2 and 8 ECHR.[72] If this indeed is correct, public law regulation only has a safeguarding effect in so far it is in accordance with Article 2 and 8 ECHR.

The second aspect concerns Article 22 of the CSDDD, which in its current form stipulates that corporations must adopt and implement a climate transition plan. This plan aims to ensure, through best efforts, that a company's business model and strategy are compatible with the Paris Agreement goal of limiting global warming to 1.5°C, as well as the European climate goals (particularly climate neutrality by 2050). The transition plan must also include time-bound GHG emissions reduction targets for scope 1, scope 2, and, under certain circumstances, scope 3 emissions. Under the Sustainability Omnibus Directive Article 22 is removed.[73]. The justification behind the removal of Article 22 CSDDD is that the transition plan obligation is "considered disproportionate, particularly due to the administrative burden for companies and supervisory authorities, and could lead to legal uncertainty. These provisions should be repealed to streamline obligations and promote a more targeted and effective implementation of the Directive."[74] Further substantiation, for example regarding the proportionality of a corporate climate transition plan obligation, e.g., in relation to remaining carbon budgets and the costs of a lack of transition planning, is absent. There is also no attention given to how companies would still be expected to assume or fulfil their GHG emission reduction responsibilities. Yet, it is clear that corporations (may) have obligations to further reduce their GHG emissions beyond European public climate laws. Therefore, a result of the Sustainability Omnibus Directive may be that corporations are not obliged to adopt a climate transition plan by statutory law. They still, however, (indirectly) can be held to do so via their duty of care under national tort law. In the Dutch context, the *Shell* ruling then remains decisive. In other jurisdictions, it still needs to be determined whether reduction obligations will be assumed, as well as what those obligations specifically entail. The removal of Article 22 does not, in itself, rule out the adoption of such reduction obligations. However, it may lead to legal inequality and uncertainty regarding reduction obligations under different national private law systems. All in all, abolishing Article 22 CSDDD could paradoxically reinforce exactly what it is meant to prevent: a patchwork of (national) corporate climate obligations and the associate economic uncertainties and administrative burdens.

4. Effectiveness of Liability Law

The third, and last issue, pertains to the effectiveness of liability law, dealing with the question whether, and if so how, effectiveness is relevant in determining the limits to the role of liability law in shaping corporate climate obligations. In addressing this question, a distinction can be made between, what I phrase as "problem-solving effectiveness" (Section 4.1) and "duty-centred effectiveness" (Section 4.2). Since the issue of effectiveness mainly arises in injunctive relief cases aiming at the prevention of future climate harm, I will restrict myself to those cases.

72 See more in detail about this line of reasoning in Stalenhoef et al (n 47).
73 Directive (EU) 2026/470 (Sustainability Omnibus Directive), Article 4 (16).
74 Directive (EU) 2026/470 (Sustainability Omnibus Directive), recital 47.

4.1 Problem-Solving Effectiveness

Problem-solving effectiveness centrers on the extent to which a court ruling contributes to addressing the actual harm or threat against which the claim is directed. For example, in cases seeking a court order obliging a corporation to reduce its GHG emissions, problem-solving effectiveness is determined by the degree to which the mitigation obligation and related court order contribute to the prevention of (global) dangerous climate change. Starting from this notion of problem-solving effectiveness, a major point of criticism regarding liability law-based mitigation cases is that when courts intervene in a single case they may settle the legal dispute between the litigating parties, but they do not solve the underlying issue for which the litigation ultimately is initiated (i.e., a lack of global corporate emissions reductions).[75] This point of criticism highlights that the nature and causes of climate change make it difficult to achieve problem-solving effectiveness through individual liability cases. That is because the extent to which worldwide emissions can be reduced largely depends on the actions of non-litigants. And, as long as those parties do not also reduce their emissions, a mitigation obligation imposed on a single actor or group of actors will not be sufficiently effective.

In *Smith v Fonterra*, the Court of Appeal applied this standard by stating that "bringing proceedings against subsets of emitters is an *inherently inefficient* and ad hoc way of addressing climate change".[76] Yet, as discussed in Section 2.1, the New Zealand Supreme Court's ruling suggests a different perspective on the relevance of problem-solving effectiveness. In the *Shell* case, the Court of Appeal also applies a problem-solving effectiveness standard. In determining the obligations of Shell, as previously discussed, the court ruled that Shell has an autonomous (partial) obligation to reduce its emissions. The existence and content of that legal duty is not contingent on the extent to which compliance with it actually contributes to a global reduction in emissions. Even stronger: The court reasoned that all reductions do matter and that corporations like Shell bear an autonomous obligation to reduce emissions.[77] Yet, strikingly, the court accepted that a lack of problem-solving effectiveness of its ruling is a relevant factor in examining the admissibility of Milieudefensie's claim.

Shell argued that the imposition of a reduction obligation for, in particular, scope 3 emissions caused by the (re)sale of its products, does not make an effective contribution to the reduction of global emissions.[78] In particular, it argued that a reduction in its sales of fossil fuels would merely result in those fossil fuels being sold by another supplier. The court accepted this line of reasoning and held that it had not been established that a reduction in the (re)sale activities of Shell, would lead to a decrease in global GHG emissions. Since according to the court such a reduction in emissions is ultimately precisely what Milieudefensie seeks to achieve through the requested reduction order, the court concluded that such an order would

[75] In relation to *Urgenda*, it was for instance argued that in certain sectors the policies that were implemented to meet the reduction order have led to a slight increase in emissions elsewhere in the world, see Mayer 2023. With respect to the first instance ruling in the *Shell* case, Mayer also argues that the order 'might end up hindering mitigation action, for instance, if a reduced supply of gas hinders the phasing down of coal or forces energy consumers to rely on more carbon-intensive sources of oil and gas'. See Benoit Mayer, 'Judicial Interpretation of Tort Law in Milieudefensie v Shell: A Rejoinder' (2022) 11 Transnational Environmental Law 433, 436.

[76] Court of Appeal of New Zealand 21 October 2021, Smith v Fonterra Co-operative Group Ltd [2021] NZCA 552; [2022] 2 NZLR 284, para 27.

[77] Gerechtshof Den Haag, 12 November 2024, ECLI:NL:GHDHA:2024:2099.

[78] ibid para 7.97.

not be effective.[79] For the court, this conclusion was not altered by potential other effects of a reduction order that may promote a reduction in global corporate GHG emissions, such as the precedent-setting and signalling function it may have, and its possible impact on corporate investment decisions. According to the court these effects are "too speculative" and do not carry legal weight for that reason.[80]

Various objections can be raised against the notion of problem-solving effectiveness as a yardstick for determining the role of liability law in shaping corporate climate obligations. First, the standard appears to be unworkable for empirical reasons and creates the risk that courts may arrive at (empirically) questionable conclusions.[81] For instance, one could question whether courts are capable of making an adequate and comprehensive empirical assessment of the (future) effects and effectiveness of their rulings. One objection is that the court may consider only those effects on global emissions presented by the parties, rather than all relevant effects. For example, in the *Shell* case, the effectiveness debate particularly focused on the occurrence of substitution effects. A possible impact on corporate reputation, public support for climate action, regulatory action, the fact that litigation can serve as a catalyst for new cases, and so on were not exhaustively examined by the court. Even more remarkable in that regard is that the District Court dismissed Shell's argument that a reduction obligation leads to undesirable substitution effects on empirical grounds. It held that "this argument assumes . . . perfect substitution, whereby the place of the Shell group will be taken over one-on-one by other parties. However, it remains to be seen whether this circumstance will transpire".[82]

Moreover, in order to assess the problem-solving effectiveness, courts have to get a *prospective* picture of possible future effects prior to their ruling. To do so in an adequate manner, they will have to work with scenarios that address the relationship between various (possibly) changing societal, economic, and regulatory conditions, on the one hand, and the possible outcomes in the case before the court, on the other hand. Here one problem is that, although there is increasing knowledge about the impact(s) of climate change litigation, there are still significant knowledge gaps about the specific causal relationships between climate change litigation and global corporate GHG emission reductions.[83] This ultimately hinders the possibility of a

79 Remarkably, a procedural aspect seems to be influential for this part of the judgment. Under the first instance ruling, Shell was granted freedom in choosing the measures to meet its scope 3 reduction obligation, without being required to consider market substitution effects. The court of appeal noted that Milieudefensie did not challenge this aspect of the first instance court's decision. Under Dutch appellate procedural law, this means that on appeal this part of the first instance ruling remains intact. In its reasoning the court therefore had to assume that Shell has freedom in determining how to implement the reduction order. The court hints that the outcome *might* have been different if Milieudefensie had asked the court to restrict Shell's choices for implementing the court order. See Gerechtshof Den Haag, 12 November 2024, ECLI:NL:GHDHA:2024:2099, para 7.101.

80 ibid para 7.109.

81 See in general about this point P Cane, 'Consequences in Judicial Reasoning' in J Horder (ed), *Oxford Essays in Jurisprudence* (OUP 2000) 42.

82 Rechtbank Den Haag, 26 May 2021, ECLI:NL:RBDHA:2021:5337, para 4.4.50. Simarly Kantonsgericht Zug, 17 December 2025, Case A1 2023 9, para 5.7.2.

83 See on the state of the art, e.g., Joanna Setzer and Lisa Vanhala, 'Climate Change Litigation: A Review of Research on Courts and Litigants in Climate Governance', *Wiley Interdisciplinary Reviews: Climate Change* 2019, 10:5, e580; Kim Brouwer and Joanna Setzer, 'New Trends in Climate Litigation: What Works?', Working paper, Johns Hopkins University SAIS Europe and European University Institute, 2020; Jacqueline Peel, Alice Palmer, and Rebekkah Markey-Towler, 'Review of Literature on Impacts of Climate Litigation: Report' 2022, <https://www.unimelb.edu.au/data/assets/pdf_file/0008/4238450/Impact-lit-review-report_CIFF_Final27052022> accessed 7 March 2026.

court to make an adequate and comprehensive prospective assessment of the problem-solving effectiveness of its (intended) ruling.[84]

Normative objections can also be raised against the notion of problem-solving effectiveness. The appellate decision in the *Shell* case, for example, illustrates the cynical conclusions to which reliance on it may lead. The core of the court's reasoning is, on the one hand, that Shell and *similar corporations* have an *autonomous duty* to reduce their emissions. On the other hand, the court considers that Milieudefensie lacks sufficient interest in enforcing compliance with this duty because it does not contribute to a global reduction in emissions, which is contingent on the reduction of emissions by other companies. This lack of problem-solving effectiveness is however partly due to the failure of other actors to reduce their emissions, despite as stated by the court their obligation to do so. This reasoning, therefore, partially rests on the assumption that corporations comparable to Shell will not fulfill their obligations, notwithstanding the court's ruling that corporations bear such obligations. This line of reasoning thus legitimises non-compliant behavior by corporations—the opposite, one might think, of the goal of civil adjudication.[85]

4.2 Duty-Centred Effectiveness

From the perspective of duty-centred effectiveness, the question is to what extent liability law is effective in ensuring compliance with the *legal climate obligations* of corporations. To understand how effectiveness is conceptualised under this perspective, it is important to note that liability law operates with both primary and secondary duties. Primary duties express the obligations that actors owe to one another within society. Secondary duties determine the consequences of a failure to fulfill a primary duty; these can also be described as remedial claims. Injunction and compensation are the main remedial claims of liability law. The purpose of remedial claims is to fulfill the primary duty (injunction) or to rectify the consequence(s) of a breach if it occurs (compensation). Thus, the remedial claim is conducive to the realisation of the primary duty and the obligations contained therein, meaning that there is a high level of congruence between primary and secondary duties.[86]

Thus, if it is established that the defendant has a partial responsibility to reduce GHG emissions (the primary duty), then in case of injunctions the secondary duty serves to effectively prevent the violation of that partial responsibility. Given this congruence, the effectiveness of this secondary duty should be assessed by examining the extent to which, and the manner in which, it contributes to the enforcement of the primary duty. For example, it means that when answering the question of whether the actor has a duty to mitigate, if consideration has already been given to the significance of possible substitution effects and these have been dismissed as arguments against accepting such a duty, then these same arguments should not provide the basis for denying the imposition of a secondary (remedial) duty. It is precisely this approach that has been taken by the court in the *Holcim* case[87], where it reasoned that the

[84] See furthermore de Jong (n 15).

[85] See for a similar critique Kysar (n 2). See for a different line of reasoning Kantonsgericht Zug, 17 December 2025, Case A1 2023 9, paras 5.7.1-5.7.2.

[86] See on the previous and the debate on the congruence between primary and secondary duties, inter alia, Hanoch Sheinman, 'Tort Law and Corrective Justice' 22 Law and Philosophy 21 (2003), and John Gardner, 'What is Tort Law For? The Place of Corrective Justice' (2011) 30 Law and Philosophy. See for the debate on this distinction, e.g., Benjamin C Zipursky, 'Rights, Wrongs, and Recourse in the Law of Torts' (1998) 51 Vanderbilt Law Review 1, 73–74.

[87] Kantonsgericht Zug, 17 December 2025, Case A1 2023 9, paras 5.7.1 – 5.7.2.

effective prevention of an imminent proportionate infringement of personality rights is the proper yardstick (instead of the question whether a single case will be effective in addressing climate change in fact). In the *Shell* case, the Court of Appeal fails to appreciate this fundamental point. Another objection to the notion of problem-solving effectiveness is that it disregards that private law allows actors the freedom to decide for themselves whom and when to hold accountable for the violation of a primary duty.[88] Problem-solving effectiveness, one might argue, appeals to the impossibility of linking a secondary duty to multiple violations of an obligation to prevent dangerous climate change through civil liability. This lack of enforcement of the primary duties of non-litigants, however, does not mean that the primary duty of the defendant should not be enforced.[89]

5. Conclusion

It is tempting to assess the role of civil liability law in shaping corporate climate obligations, and the boundaries to that role, from a risk regulatory-oriented perspective, thereby strongly emphasising the political and social dimension of such cases. Applying such a perspective in climate change cases inevitably leads to a very narrow view of private law in general and the role it may play in shaping corporate climate change obligations. This is mainly the case because of a stated lack of institutional regulatory competence on the side of civil courts and the ineffectiveness of liability law in preventing dangerous climate change. However, such a view fails to recognise that civil liability law has its own peculiar autonomous nature, which focuses on the competence of courts to offer legal protection and to ensure effective enforcement of legal obligations. Seen from this perspective, civil liability law could play a valuable autonomous role in shaping corporate climate obligations, which enables it to address gaps in the public regulation of corporate climate change responsibilities.

[88] John C P Goldberg and Benjamin C Zipursky, 'Accidents of the Great Society' (2005) 64 Maryland Law Review 364, 36.

[89] Douglas A Kysar, 'What Climate Change Can Do About Tort Law' (2010) 41 Environmental Law 1, 51.

CHAPTER 10

Products Liability

DOUGLAS A. KYSAR

1. Introduction

HURRICANE Maria in 2017 caused catastrophic loss of life, economic devastation, and widespread suffering throughout Puerto Rico. Official estimates conservatively placed the death toll at 2,975 people.[1] The storm inflicted over $115 billion in damages, making it one of the costliest hurricanes in United States history.[2] Maria destroyed homes, roads, and power lines, leaving the entire island without electricity—some areas remained in the dark for nearly a year. The healthcare system collapsed, exacerbating chronic illnesses and leading to preventable deaths. Businesses shut down, unemployment soared, and thousands of residents were forced to migrate to the US mainland and elsewhere, contributing to significant local population decline and a tangible alteration of the island's identity. The storm also caused severe environmental damage, including deforestation and water contamination, which further hindered recovery efforts. Years later, Maria's ill effects continue to tear at Puerto Rico's social, economic, and ecological fabric.

According to scientists, Hurricane Maria's force and impact were supercharged by human activities that have released greenhouse gases and altered the atmosphere since the Industrial Revolution.[3] It is perhaps not surprising, then, that several impacted Puerto Rico municipalities are seeking legal recourse against major fossil fuel producers, a group of defendants that the municipalities allege are responsible for a substantial share of the accumulated greenhouse gas emissions that cause anthropogenic climate change and exacerbated Maria's devastating effects.[4]

[1] Joshua Hoyos and Alexander Mallin, 'Death Toll in Puerto Rico from Hurricane Maria Officially Raised to 2,975 from 64' (*ABC News*, 29 August 2018) <https://abcnews.go.com/US/death-toll-hurricane-maria-3000-puerto-rico-study/story?id=57179291> accessed 4 June 2025.

[2] National Oceanic and Atmospheric Administration, 'Costliest U.S. Tropical Cyclones' (*NCEI*, 10 January 2025) <https://www.ncei.noaa.gov/access/billions/dcmi.pdf?sort=cost-asc> accessed 4 June 2025.

[3] Research indicates that anthropogenic climate change contributed to higher sea surface temperatures, which fuelled Maria's rapid intensification and extreme rainfall. David Keellings and José J Hernández Ayala, 'Extreme Rainfall Associated with Hurricane Maria Over Puerto Rico and its Connections to Climate Variability and Change' (2019) 46 Geophysical Research Letters 2964.

[4] Complaint for Damages, Municipalities of Puerto Rico v Exxon Mobil, No. 3:22-cv-01550 (DPR 22 Nov. 2022), [5–6]. The territory of Puerto Rico also brought a lawsuit against major oil and gas companies but withdrew its complaint under pressure from the federal government in 2025. See Dharna Noor, 'Puerto Rico Drops Climate Lawsuit After DoJ Sues States to Block Threats to Big Oil' *The Guardian* (London, 2 May 2025) <https://www.theguardian.com/us-news/2025/may/02/puerto-rico-climate-lawsuit-trump> accessed 4 June 2025.

As one among numerous lawsuits brought by US state and local governments against fossil fuel producers,[5] the Puerto Rico municipalities' complaint stands out for multiple reasons. First, the complaint includes highly potent racketeering, conspiracy, and antitrust causes of action, in addition to more familiar theories of liability sounding in tort and consumer protection law. Second, the suit was filed by a prominent claimants-side law firm, heralding perhaps a rise of interest in climate litigation by the sophisticated US plaintiffs' bar that relies on contingency fees and conducts painstaking analysis of the likelihood of any given claim's success. Both of these developments have been taken by observers to reflect a potential maturation of climate accountability lawsuits beyond the initial two waves of such litigation in the US.[6]

More germane to this chapter, the Puerto Rico complaint is also potentially significant for centrering products liability claims among its many theories of defendant responsibility. Apart from a few pioneering treatments,[7] products liability law has not featured prominently in the scholarly literature on climate litigation. Instead, within the private law arena, academics have focused on causes of action relating to public nuisance and deceptive conduct, which appear to offer the most promising—albeit controversial[8]—route to holding major fossil fuel producers responsible for climate-related harms.

Despite this relative lack of academic attention, products liability theories offer their own potential advantages for climate plaintiffs. Most notably, they emerge from an area of law that arguably pioneered the notion of supply chain responsibility. In the US, the EU, and many other jurisdictions, liability for harms caused by defective products typically attaches to any commercial actor who handles a defective product along its chain of distribution. Currently, vanguard laws such as the EU's duty of vigilance directive attempt to impose oversight responsibility on companies for human rights and environmental harms associated with upstream

[5] For overviews of the carbon major lawsuits, see Maximillian Scott Matiauda, 'Rising Tide: The Second Wave of Climate Torts' (2023) 30 University of Miami International & Comparative Law Review 194; Center for Climate Integrity, 'Big Oil Accountability Lawsuits' (4 June 2025) <https://climateintegrity.org/uploads/media/CCI-BigOilAccountabilityLawsuits.pdf> accessed 4 June 2025 (compiling US climate accountability suits).

[6] Korey Silverman-Roati and Maria Antonia Tigre, 'Municipalities of Puerto Rico v. Exxon: A Unique Class Action Against Fossil Fuel Companies Presses for Climate Accountability in the United States' (*Climate Law: A Sabin Center Blog*, 2 December 2022) <https://blogs.law.columbia.edu/climatechange/2022/12/02/municipalities-of-puerto-rico-v-exxon-a-unique-class-action-against-fossil-fuel-companies-presses-for-climate-accountability-in-the-united-states/> accessed 4 June 2025; Tina Casey, 'Big Oil Must Deliver The Goods Under Landmark Climate Litigation Ruling' (*CleanTechnica*, 24 February 2025) <https://cleantechnica.com/2025/02/24/big-oil-must-deliver-the-goods-under-landmark-climate-litigation-ruling/> accessed 4 June 2025.

[7] David A Grossman, 'Warming Up to a Not-So-Radical Idea: Tort-Based Climate Change Litigation' (2003) 28 Columbia Journal of Environmental Law 1, 44–47; David Hunter and James Salzman, 'Negligence in the Air: The Duty of Care in Climate Change Litigation' (2007) 155 University of Pennsylvania Law Review 1741, 1785; Lindsay Leone, 'Putting the Heat on the Fossil Fuel Industry: Using Products Liability in Climate Change Litigation' (2012) 21 Boston University Public International Law Journal 365; Jan-Erik Schirmer, 'Climate Liability: Causation and Duty Demystified' (*SSRN*, 10 April 2025) <https://papers.ssrn.com/sol3/papers.cfm?abstract_id=5153585> accessed 4 June 2025.

[8] For key contributions debating the role of public nuisance in climate change, see Thomas W Merrill, 'Is Public Nuisance a Tort?' (2011) 4 Journal of Tort Law 1; David Bullock, 'Public Nuisance Is a Tort' (2022) 15 Journal of Tort Law 137; David Bullock, 'Public Nuisance and Climate Change: The Common Law's Solutions to the Plaintiff, Defendant and Causation Problems' (2022) 85 Modern Law Review 1136; David Bullock, Chapter 7 of this handbook.

production practices.[9] For decades, the law of products liability has already applied a similarly expansive notion of responsibility to companies for downstream consumption harms.[10]

The difficulty with this notion of supply chain responsibility is that in the climate change context, the conceptual categories demarked by products liability law seem to spill over into one another. Consider, for instance, a livestock farmer whose cows grow and emit methane before being sold and slaughtered to become meat for consumers. In the aggregate, such upstream emissions from the production of meat contribute significantly to anthropogenic climate change,[11] which in turn causes harm throughout the world, including both to the consumers who eat meat and to the farmers whose production practices contribute to climate change. In such a polycentric context, who should be seen as a defendant and who as a plaintiff?[12]

Similarly, consider an individual driver who produces greenhouse gas emissions as they fill their automobile with petroleum and combust the fuel while driving to school, work, home, and elsewhere. Like the livestock farmer, the individual's emissions contribute—in the aggregate—to human-induced climate change. Thus, when a climate-fuelled hurricane subsequently results in the loss of both the consumer's vehicle and the petroleum facility that refined the consumer's fuel, difficult conceptual questions are raised: Who is the polluter and who is the victim? Who is the producer and who is the consumer? And, again, who is the defendant and who is the plaintiff?

This chapter explores the intersection of products liability law and climate change. It asks first what products liability law might do about the climate change crisis, including the drastic need for reduction of greenhouse gas emissions and for acknowledgement and compensation of climate-related harms that already are destined to occur. The chapter then turns the question around to ask how climate change might impact products liability law itself, both narrowly in terms of how the backdrop of climate change might open new arguments within existing products liability doctrine, and more broadly in terms of how judges might reassess the field in a world radically changed by human activity.[13]

9 Christine Godt, 'Climate Protection and Supply Chain Civil Liability' (2023) 10 European Journal of Comparative Law and Governance 330–64.

10 Jaakko Salminen, 'From Product Liability to Production Liability: Modelling a Response to the Liability Deficit of Global Value Chains on Historical Transformations of Production' (2019) 23 Competition & Change 420 (using the history of products liability to analyse emerging regimes of liability for social and environmental harms relating to production within global supply chains).

11 Douglas A Kysar, 'Farm Until It's Gone: Industrial Animal Agriculture and the Limits of Law' (2025) 74 DePaul Law Review 249, 275–79 (reviewing studies that conservatively estimate the contribution of animal agriculture to annual greenhouse gas emissions at 12% to 20% of world totals).

12 Compare Daina Bray and Thomas M Poston, 'The Methane Majors: Climate Change and Animal Agriculture in U.S. Courts' (2024) 49 Columbia Journal of Environmental Law 145, 147 (surveying legal strategies that might be utilised against industrial animal agriculture producers in regard to greenhouse gas emissions) with Luigi Jorio, 'Agriculture Shifts From Climate-Change Culprit To Victim In New Lawsuit' (*Swissinfo.ch*, 28 April 2025) <https://www.swissinfo.ch/eng/climate-solutions/agriculture-shifts-from-climate-change-culprit-to-victim-in-new-lawsuit/89213977#> accessed 4 June 2025 (discussing lawsuit brought by nine farmers and five small agriculture associations against the Swiss government for allegedly not doing enough to combat climate change).

13 Douglas A Kysar, 'What Climate Change Can Do About Tort Law' (2011) 41 Environmental Law 1 (adopting a similar analytical approach to climate tort suits but not discussing products liability law).

2. The Origins and Evolution of Products Liability Law

Over the course of the twentieth century, courts throughout the US developed a distinctive body of law to protect consumers from risks posed by mass-marketed products.[14] These changes—among the most dramatic in the history of the common law—were adopted by courts in response to perceived dysfunctionalities of modern product markets. When simple goods were traded directly between a seller and a buyer, the laws of contract and negligence perhaps seemed adequate to govern the allocation of risk between the parties.[15] As the mass production economy arose, however, legal interventions such as strict products liability law or non-waivable contractual safety warranties came to be seen as necessary to protect consumers from product dangers. Manufacturers were believed to hold exploitative market power over consumers, capable of unilaterally dictating contractual terms in the sale of their wares. Consumers, in turn, were seen as vulnerable to product-caused injuries due to their relative lack of information and understanding regarding health and safety risks posed by increasingly complex goods distributed through increasingly sprawling distribution chains.[16]

Thus, in the US and in many other jurisdictions around the world, modern products liability law developed to impose responsibility on any seller of a product deemed to be in a defective condition. Critically, this liability exists regardless of privity of contract between the seller and the user. Essentially, commercial entities along the entire distribution chain—parts supplier, manufacturer, wholesaler, retailer, and so on—become subject to joint and several liability if the product passes through that entity's hands while containing a defect. To support these major doctrinal shifts, economic theory was mobilised by both scholars and courts: Under a regime of strict seller liability for harms caused by defective products, the thinking went, prices would adjust to reflect the internalised costs of product-caused accidents, providing incentives for the safer design and use of products, as well as a mechanism for spreading the costs of those accidents that could not be avoided.[17] Critically, liability is imposed on sellers as an initial matter, but the ultimate incidence of the cost may be shared by product consumers and other actors depending on a variety of market dynamics.

Whether sounding in tort or contractual warranty law, the crux of the plaintiff's action in any harmful consumer goods case is the concept of a "defective" product. Over time, courts have developed three distinct categories of "defectiveness" with separate doctrinal standards for establishing breach. A "manufacturing defect" occurs when a product departs from the maker's own intended design or quality standard for the product. A "design defect", in contrast, refers to an unreasonably dangerous condition present in a product despite being

[14] James A Henderson Jr., Aaron Twerski, and Douglas A Kysar, *Products Liability: Problems and Process* (9th edn, Aspen Publishers 2021) 3–19.

[15] Alexandra D Lahav, 'A Revisionist History of Products Liability' (2023) 122 Michigan Law Review 509.

[16] George Priest, 'The Invention of Enterprise Liability: A Critical History of the Foundations of Modern Tort Law' (1985) 14 Journal of Legal Studies 461, 517.

[17] Mark Geistfeld, 'Implementing Enterprise Liability: A Comment on Henderson and Twerski' (1992) 67 NYU Law Review 1157, 1160 (1992). Subsequent generations of scholars have largely criticised these early economic arguments in favour of strict products liability. Steven P Croley and Jon D Hanson, 'Rescuing the Revolution: The Revived Case for Enterprise Liability' (1993) 91 Michigan Law Review 683, 713–61 (surveying much of the relevant critical literature and offering new and revitalised arguments in favour of the strict liability approach).

manufactured and distributed as intended by the seller. Finally, a "warning defect" occurs when a product seller fails to provide adequate instructions or warnings regarding the proper use and potential dangers of a product.

Of the three recognised categories of product defectiveness, design defect cases have proven most complex and controversial.[18] Broadly speaking, courts adopt one or more of three different tests for design defect. First, reflecting the contract law lineage of products liability law, some courts hinge design defectiveness on a "consumer expectations test" whereby a product is deemed to be in a defective condition if its dangers exceed what would be expected and considered acceptable to the average or ordinary consumer. Second, reflecting the field's tort law lineage, some courts hinge design defectiveness on a "risk-utility test" whereby "a product is in a defective condition if a 'reasonable person' would conclude that the probability and seriousness of harm caused by the product outweigh the burden or cost of taking precautions".[19] Finally, several courts adopt a narrower version of the risk-utility test whereby a plaintiff must show the existence of an alternative design that would have reduced or avoided the plaintiff's harm in a way that "renders the [actually marketed] product not reasonably safe".[20]

The law of products liability was developed specifically to aid consumers by creating a cause of action focused on the defectiveness of *products* rather than on the unreasonableness of a seller's *conduct*, which was thought to be harder to prove under traditional negligence principles.[21] This focus on products offers conceptual power latent within products liability law that will be returned to in Section 4. For now, it is enough to say that a focus on products over producers does *not* mean that allegedly deceptive or misleading representations are irrelevant under products liability law. Manufacturer promotional conduct, for instance, is "relevant to the foreseeable use of the [product] and the unreasonable danger of the product when used as intended".[22] Whether a court focuses on the content of an ordinary consumer's expectations or the level of risk and utility associated with a product's use, in either case a manufacturer's efforts to shape and influence product awareness and expectations will be relevant to design defectiveness analysis.

Such manufacturer conduct also is relevant to the adequacy of product risk disclosures when considering a warning defect claim. Even a non-defective product warning can become defective if accompanied by manufacturer advertising that undermines the efficacy of the warning. The law of products liability, at least in the US, also incorporates a distinct and expansive cause of action for misrepresentation. While the tort of misrepresentation at common law traditionally required a plaintiff to establish that the defendant intended to mislead,[23] the American Law Institute in 1965 recognised a growing body of case law in support of a cause of action for merely negligent misrepresentation.[24] More recently, the Institute's Third Restatement project went further to make even *innocent* misrepresentations culpable under products liability law:

[18] Douglas A Kysar, 'The Expectations of Consumers' (2003) 103 Columbia Law Review 1700.

[19] *Tincher v Omega Flex Inc* 104 A3d 328, 389 (Pa 2014).

[20] American Law Institute, *Restatement (Third) of Torts: Products Liability* (2007) s 2(b). To complicate matters further, when considering the consumer expectations and risk-utility tests, some jurisdictions have determined that 'a plaintiff may proceed under either theory, or both theories in the alternative'. ibid 408.

[21] *Sullivan v Werner Co* 306 A3d 846, 859 (Pa 2023) (observing that 'the proper focus of a design defect case is on the characteristics of the product and not the conduct of the manufacturer').

[22] *Leichtamer v American Motors Corp* 424 NE2d 568, 579 (Ohio 1981).

[23] *Webster v L Romano Eng'g Corp* 34 P2d 428, 430 (Wash 1934).

[24] American Law Institute, *Restatement (Second) of Torts* (1965) s 311.

> One engaged in the business of selling or otherwise distributing products who, in connection with the sale of a product, makes a fraudulent, negligent, or innocent misrepresentation of material fact concerning the product is subject to liability for harm to persons or property caused by the misrepresentation.[25]

As the next section explains, these various approaches to allegedly deceptive or misleading manufacturer conduct take on special significance in the climate change context.

3. What Products Liability Law Can Do About Climate Change

Could the law of products liability just described be mobilised to hold major emitting entities responsible for the harmful consequences of climate change?[26] This section addresses that question, probing first whether consumer products plausibly could be characterised as defective based on their contribution to climate change and, second, whether plaintiffs could establish a requisite causal connection between those products and climate-related harms. Given space constraints, it does not offer a comprehensive analysis of these questions, but instead highlights some of their most provocative and challenging aspects.

As an initial matter, the cause of action arising from a manufacturing defect would be unavailing for climate change plaintiffs in most cases. This is because greenhouse gas emissions related to the manufacture and use of most consumer products are fully anticipated by sellers, rather than representing a departure from the intended product design. One interesting exception might be natural gas stoves which have been shown to release significant amounts of methane through leakage and incomplete combustion. Using a twenty-year time horizon for converting methane's global warming potential to a CO_2-equivalency, researchers estimate that annual methane leakage from gas stoves in the US exerts a climate impact equivalent to the annual CO_2 emissions from approximately 166,000 gas-powered cars.[27] If this leakage were shown to be the result of unintended flaws in the production of the stoves, then a plausible case for manufacturing defect might be made out. Looking further down the road, if carbon capture and sequestration become widely adopted or even legally mandated features of fossil fuel-based electricity production, then one could imagine manufacturing defect claims premised on unintentional release of greenhouse gases from the sequestration medium—a major concern associated with this method of climate mitigation.

Notwithstanding such possibilities, the more likely causes of action for product-related climate change harms sound in design and warning defect liability. Plaintiff municipalities in Puerto Rico included these counts in their nearly 300-page complaint against major fossil fuel producers and the industry's chief lobbying organisation, the America Petroleum Institute. In early 2025, a federal magistrate judge recommended that each products liability cause of action be dismissed. With respect to design defect, the judge ruled that the plaintiffs' allegations were

[25] American Law Institute, *Restatement (Third) of Torts* (n 20) s 9.

[26] Christina Ross, Evan Mills, and Sean B Hecht, 'Limiting Liability in the Greenhouse: Insurance Risk-Management Strategies in the Context of Global Climate Change' (2007) 26A Stanford Environmental Law Journal 251, 292–93 ('It might be argued that the unnecessary production of large amounts of greenhouse gases was an avoidable power generation and automotive design "defect", which then led to plaintiff's harm from climate change').

[27] Eric D Lebel, Colin J Finnegan, Zutao Ouyang, and Robert B Jackson, 'Methane and NOx Emissions from Natural Gas Stoves, Cooktops, and Ovens in Residential Homes' (2022) 56 Environmental Science & Technology 2529.

"textbook conclusory", as they merely asserted without factual detail that fossil fuel products' risks outweigh their benefits, and did not make any specific allegations with respect to the level of risk an ordinary consumer expects when using such products.[28]

One reading of this opinion is that the plaintiffs had simply not yet devoted time to developing specific facts to support their product defect allegations. But commentators who have more thoroughly examined climate-related design defect claims also have expressed doubt regarding their viability. Jan-Erik Schirmer, for instance, argues that in the case of electricity—which, incidentally, has been held to be a consumer good adequate to trigger the duties of products liability law[29]—plaintiffs would be unable to establish that renewable energy was adequately demonstrated and scalable at the time that most fossil fuel-powered utilities were put into service in order to show the existence of a reasonable alternative design.[30] Factual analysis of that issue is beyond the scope of this chapter, but it is worth noting that as early as 1962, the National Academy of Sciences advised the US government to promote "the maximum utilization of solar energy" in light of the fact that "greatly increasing the use of [] fossil fuels . . . is seriously contaminating the earth's atmosphere with CO_2".[31] Likewise, to assess when historically renewable energy began to qualify as a "cost-effective" alternative,[32] it is important to bear in mind that the uncounted social costs of fossil fuels extend well beyond the climate-related harms that might be raised by plaintiffs. Coal, for instance, is estimated to lead to nearly twenty-five deaths per terawatt-hour through accidents and non-greenhouse gas air pollutants, compared to essentially zero deaths for wind, solar, and nuclear.[33]

Reasonable alternative design analysis for other climate-intensive products is equally complicated. With regard to meat, for instance, plant-based alternatives seem unlikely today to be accepted by the average consumer as a true substitute for the challenged product. Cultivated or lab-grown meat, in turn, has yet to be shown to provide clear climate advantages over conventional meat, despite being potentially more acceptable as a genuine product alternative. In the case of automobiles, plaintiffs could draw on a long and tortured history in the United States of viable transportation alternatives such as the electric car and public transit being overcome by the dominance of private internal combustion passenger vehicles.[34] However, it is unclear how products liability law would grapple with the challenge of comparing entire systems of transportation and industrial existence, rather than merely alternative products within such systems. The demise of street trolleys and other once robust public transport systems in the US was bound up with racial and other kinds of politics that exceed the ordinary bounds of

[28] Municipalities of Bayamon v Exxon Mobil Corp, No CV 22-1550 (SCC)(HRV), 2025 WL 600430 (DPR 20 Feb 2025) [41].

[29] While the American Law Institute's *Restatement (Second) of Torts* fails to provide a concrete definition of 'product', the *Restatement (Third)* defines a product as 'tangible personal property distributed commercially for use or consumption'. American Law Institute, *Restatement (Third) of Torts* (n 20) s 19. This definition encompasses 'other items'—including 'electricity'—when 'the context of their distribution and use is sufficiently analogous to the distribution and use of tangible personal property'. Annotation, 'Products Liability: Electricity' 60 *American Law Reporter 4th* 732 (1988).

[30] Schirmer (n 7). See also Grossman (n 7) 46.

[31] M King Hubbert, *Energy Resources—A Report to the Committee on Natural Resources of the National Academy of Sciences National Research Council* (1962) 96.

[32] Schirmer (n 7) 26.

[33] Our Word in Data, 'Death Rates per Unit of Electricity Production' <https://ourworldindata.org/grapher/death-rates-from-energy-production-per-twh> accessed 4 June 2025.

[34] David A Kirsch, *The Electric Vehicle and the Burden of History* (Rutgers University Press 2000); Nicholas Dagen Bloom, *The Great American Transit Disaster: A Century of Austerity, Auto-Centric Planning, and White Flight* (University of Chicago Press 2023).

products liability analysis.[35] Even the electric vehicle, which is today—more than a century after its first commercial introduction—finally being recognised as a substitute to the internal combustion engine, depends critically on the existence of a charging infrastructure similar to the network of petroleum stations that supports carbon-intensive alternatives.

Another option for climate plaintiffs would be to target jurisdictions that do not hew so tightly to the reasonable alternative design requirement. As noted in Section 3, at least in the US, some jurisdictions apply a looser risk-utility test that does not strictly demand demonstration of a reasonable alternative design. Others adopt an entirely different consumer expectations test for design defect, and still others like Puerto Rico allow plaintiffs to proceed using either test. Under the broader risk-utility test, plaintiffs could make the argument that certain goods like industrially farmed beef are simply on a net basis a social ill, irrespective of whether a superior alternative is presently available. The *Third Restatement* adopts a cautious approach to this theory of design defect liability, calling it the "manifestly unreasonable design" and relegating it to a mere comment in the project's text. In truth, few courts in the United States have utilised this theory of liability and those that do typically have been overruled by legislatures.[36] Still, the category exists, and one wonders whether a product like factory-farmed beef—which causes vast social and environmental externalities while also posing dramatic health risks to consumers and the wider human population[37]—might be usefully analysed through the manifestly unreasonable design lens.

Also of potential value to climate change plaintiffs is the consumer expectations test. Rather than focusing on the risk and utility of a product narrowly construed, this test asks whether a product is "dangerous to an extent beyond that which would be contemplated by the ordinary consumer who purchases it, with the ordinary knowledge common to the community as to its characteristics".[38] For climate-related products, this test invites empirical consideration of whether and to what extent consumers have become aware of the dangers posed by greenhouse-gas intensive products. Importantly, "[w]hether a product is unreasonably dangerous is a question of fact [about which jury members] .... can draw[] their own reasonable conclusions as to the expectations of the ordinary consumer and the knowledge common in the community at large".[39]

Whether the ordinary consumer expects (i.e., understand and accepts) the climate risks of products such as industrial meat is a difficult empirical question. Consider an effort by the Rockefeller Foundation to rigorously quantify and monetise the negative externalities of the US food system, which concluded that although consumers spent $1.1 trillion on food in 2019, the US food system that same year generated $2.1 trillion worth of social and environmental costs.[40] In other words, the economic value of what was harmed by the US food system in

[35] Bloom (n 34).

[36] Kysar, 'The Expectations of Consumers' (n 18).

[37] Kysar, 'Farm Until It's Gone' (n 11) 260–83.

[38] *Giglio v Conn Light & Power Co* 429 A2d 486, 488 (Conn 1980) (citations and internal quotation marks omitted).

[39] ibid 489 (citations and internal quotation marks omitted).

[40] The Rockefeller Foundation, *True Cost of Food: Measuring What Matters to Transform the U.S. Food System* (July 2021) <https://www.rockefellerfoundation.org/wp-content/uploads/2021/07/True-Cost-of-Food-Full-Report-Final.pdf> accessed 4 June 2025. It bears stressing that the Rockefeller report analysed the US food system as a whole, rather than only the industrial animal agriculture sector, and did not limit its analysis to climate-related harms. Evidence specific to the climate impacts of meat, however, reinforces the report's concerns. Maximilian Pieper, Amelie Michalke, and Tobias Gaugler, 'Calculation of External Climate Costs for Food Highlights Inadequate Pricing of Animal Products' (2020) 11 Nature Communications 6117 (finding that if greenhouse gas emissions impacts were incorporated into the price, meat would cost 146% more than at present).

2019 was roughly twice the amount paid for what was created. It is an open question whether consumers actually recognise and accept these costs as a price worth paying for the current food system. Likewise, we do not know whether consumers would have been willing to pay $3.2 trillion for the food they purchased in 2019 in the presence of legally imposed cost internalisation. What seems likely, though, is that the organisation and output of the agriculture sector would be vastly different if the price mechanism incorporated the full social costs of production. In other words, industrial meat products might well be vulnerable to a products liability challenge, at least with regard to the element of defectiveness in a consumer expectations jurisdiction.

As with design defect, climate change plaintiffs also could allege a triable issue of fact with regard to warning defectiveness and misrepresentation. Defendants will contend that the public has long been aware of climate change and its dangers, such that their products pose what the law calls an "open and obvious risk" not subject to disclosure liability. Plaintiffs, in turn, will be able to point to voluminous evidence suggesting that defendants worked actively to subvert public understanding and appreciation of climate change.[41] That evidence might also support theories of liability premised on intentional, negligent, or even innocent product misrepresentation, as noted in the previous section. Even without considering such evidence of alleged misrepresentation, however, a court might well view the facts surrounding the climate impacts of fossil fuels and other greenhouse gas intensive products to be so bound up with scientific expertise as to escape an "open and obvious risk" determination from the vantage point of lay consumers.[42] For all of these reasons, one might think that the most likely outcome of warning defect and misrepresentation claims would be for judges to allow them to proceed to a jury.[43]

Nevertheless, as with the plaintiffs' design defect claims, the magistrate judge in the Puerto Rico municipalities' lawsuit recommended dismissal of the plaintiffs' failure to warn claim, reasoning that "the effects that fossil fuels had on climate change" do not fall within the category of "reasonably foreseeable dangers [] users may encounter using the product".[44] Only the latter type of danger—hazards faced *directly* due to use of the product—triggers a product seller's duty to warn on this view. Was the magistrate judge's vision of products liability law too narrow? After all, important prior decisions have extended a manufacturer's duty to warn well beyond the context of hazards posed immediately to end users themselves.[45] Consider, for

[41] Jessica Wentz and Benjamin Franta, 'Liability for Public Deception: Linking Fossil Fuel Disinformation to Climate Damages' (2022) 52 Environmental Law Reporter 10995 (assessing legal and evidentiary pathways by which courts could infer public reliance on climate disinformation by fossil fuel companies).

[42] *Minnesota v American Petroleum Institute* 62-CV-20-3837 (Minn Dist Ct 14 Feb 2025) [45–46] <https://climatecasechart.com/wp-content/uploads/case-documents/2025/20250214_docket-62-CV-20-3837_memorandum-and-order-1.pdf> accessed 4 June 2025 ('[T]he Court concludes while these allegations discuss an awareness among scientists of the Defendants' products leading to climate change, the Complaint does not plead facts that show that these alleged dangers were obvious to anyone using the product') (internal quotation omitted).

[43] *State ex rel Jennings v BP Am Inc* 2024 WL 98888 (Del Super Ct 2024) [66] (finding that 'the State has stated a claim for failure to warn' by alleging 'that Defendants knew that their products were endangering the environment, and harming their consumers and the State of Delaware (a valid bystander)', but also holding that the question of 'whether the danger was open and obvious', a necessary element for the state's claim, 'is not appropriate for resolution at the dismissal stage').

[44] *Municipalities of Bayamon* (n 28) [41].

[45] *Lawing v Univar USA Inc* 415 SC 209, 224 (2015), reh'g denied (12 Feb 2016) (plaintiffs other than those 'who are injured while handling or operating the dangerous product' may assert strict products liability claims); *In re Methyl Tertiary Butyl Ether (MTBE) Prod Liab Litig* 175 F Supp 2d 593, 625 (SDNY

example, a claim brought by municipal sewage authorities against manufacturers and sellers of "flushable" wipes for failing to warn consumers and users that the wipes could clog the utility's sewers. The court deemed it irrelevant that the utility's injuries were caused by the defendants' failure to warn a large number of product consumers and users rather than the utility itself; the utility could bring a failure-to-warn claim because it was, in the court's view, "a primary and direct victim" of the defendants' failure to warn.[46] Could victims of climate impacts be seen as analogous to the sewage utility, harmed not by widespread use of flushable wipes but by pervasive use of greenhouse gas intensive products?

The climate change context adds a further causal wrinkle in that greenhouse gases do not *themselves* cause harm in the way that the accumulated flushable wipes did. To see why, consider a hypothetical in which the only harm posed by tobacco use was through second-hand smoke and that individual smokers themselves were not directly harmed by smoking. Imagine further that second-hand smoke did not impose harms on individuals in the first instance, but instead globally diffused throughout the atmosphere, intermingled with the exhalations of billions of other smokers which eventually, and collectively, caused harmful effects—not through the smoke itself, but instead through myriad ways in which second-hand smoke disrupts various physical processes occurring throughout the planet. Would courts be comfortable imposing liability on tobacco manufacturer through products liability on those wild facts?

As the thought exercise shows, the main problem for plaintiffs in the products liability context may not be alleging a plausible breach of duty but instead alleging an adequate causal connection between the breach and the plaintiffs' harm. Specifically, plaintiffs must allege causation of the right kind of harm in order to invoke the specialised body of products liability law. It is true that warning defect plaintiffs in many jurisdictions are aided by an evidentiary presumption that adequate warnings would have been heeded by users—a "presumption of proper adherence".[47] But many defendants in climate products liability suits may be able to press the more basic point that plaintiffs' harms are not *product*-caused injuries. Instead, they are injuries caused by the manufacturing processes that generate products or by side effects of product usage that contribute to global physical phenomena that only later result in harms which courts may simply view as too remote to count as product caused.

It is true that products liability law does not require privity of contract between the seller and the consumer or end user to invoke its special regime of liability, but the field does require that the plaintiff's injury results from the defective product's use *as a product*. If the injury is instead caused by the product's manufacturing process[48] or by the cumulative, indirect, and attenuated side effects of the product's usage,[49] then courts might well conclude that the

2001) (manufacturers' duty to warn extends to third parties who are exposed to foreseeable risk from use of products by others); *Hall v Du Pont de Nemours & Co* 345 F Supp 353, 360 (EDNY 1972) ('[M]anufacturers . . . have a duty to users, consumers, and in some circumstances to the general public or portions of it, to produce products with appropriate warnings').

46 *Commissioners of Pub. Works of City of Charleston v Costco Wholesale Corp* No 2:21-CV-42-RMG, 2021 WL 5908758 (DSC 13 Dec 2021) [3–5] (internal quotation omitted).

47 Schirmer (n 7) 30. But see Grossman (n 7) 43 (contending that '[e]ven if warnings about the climate-changing carbon dioxide emissions of defendants' products had been provided, it is likely that most consumers' behavior would not have changed meaningfully').

48 *Schwartz v Accuratus Corp* 7 F Supp 3d 490, 497 (ED Pa 2014).

49 *Mayor and City Council of Baltimore v BP PLC* Case No: 24-C-18-004219 [26] (10 July 2024) (rejecting plaintiffs' claims that defendant oil companies tortiously failed to warn because 'Baltimore does not allege that its injury comes from its own use of or direct exposure to Defendant's fossil fuels but from consumers' decisions to use fossil fuels across the globe for many years').

appropriate causes of action sound in negligence, trespass, nuisance, and other non-products liability registers.

4. What Climate Change Can Do About Products Liability Law

The previous section ended on a deflationary note regarding the potential for products liability law to effectuate meaningful change with regard to humanity's climate trajectory. This does not mean, however, that climate change will not enter into conversation with products liability law in other important ways. As this section argues, climate change is such a pervasive and consequential phenomenon that the law of products liability itself will be altered by climate change, even if judges choose to remain largely on the sidelines with respect to deploying products liability law as an affirmative tool in the quest for decarbonisation.

Most immediately, claimants might take inspiration from the "failure to adapt" theory of liability that has been developed within statutory regimes and other sites of climate contestation.[50] On this approach, rather than trying to establish ultimate responsibility for climate change itself, litigants should instead try to establish a duty to anticipate and guard against the harmful consequences of climate change. In the US, a non-governmental organisation called the Conservation Law Foundation pioneered this theory of liability under the federal Clean Water Act and has used it to significant effect against fossil fuel producers for failing to adequately secure their infrastructure against extreme storm events and other foreseeable consequences of climate change.[51] While the legal claim in these cases does not directly raise the question of responsibility for climate change, the question figures prominently in the background. Most notably, plaintiffs have presented evidence that defendants secured offshore drilling platforms and other financially critical assets while allegedly failing to protect neighbouring communities from risks posed by onshore refinery facilities. Such a disparity suggests both an awareness of climate risks and a willingness to profit from it.[52]

One could easily imagine similar "failure to adapt" reasoning being utilised in the products liability context. The level of risk and utility provided by a product is obviously affected by the environment within which the product is used. When that environment is undergoing dramatic change, the product seller should be expected to monitor and respond accordingly before releasing its wares onto the public.[53] What level of care, for instance, is required of pharmaceutical manufacturers with regard to distributing drugs that require cold storage as humanity enters an era of predictable and frequent electricity blackouts? Should tire manufacturers be expected to take account of the increasing heat of asphalt roadways and the impact of

[50] Dov Waisman, 'Failure-to-Adapt Climate Litigation at 20: An Underutilized Tool?' (2024) 54 Environmental Law Reporter 10960.

[51] Bray and Poston (n 12) 234.

[52] Indeed, plaintiffs allege that defendants have developed detailed engineering and design standards based on a deep understanding of the causes and effects of climate change that create hazards for their critical infrastructure, while leaving often disadvantaged communities adjacent to other industry infrastructure unprotected against those same hazards. *Conservation L Found Inc v ExxonMobil Corp* No 1:16-cv-11950-MLW (Amended Complaint) (D Mass 20 Oct 2017).

[53] Sophie Marjanac and Lindene Patton, 'Extreme Weather Event Attribution Science and Climate Change Litigation: An Essential Step in the Causal Chain?' (2018) 36 Journal of Energy & Natural Resources Law 265, 287–88 ('Advancements in the foreseeability of increased risk of extreme weather and associated losses also have implications for a range of public and private actors who have duties to protect or of trust and loyalty, including public authorities, engineers and company directors').

those changed conditions on tire safety and durability? With hurricanes, wildfires, and other disasters increasing in intensity—and in some cases also in frequency—do manufacturers of windows, doors, and other building materials need to strengthen their products accordingly? Should passenger vehicle manufacturers guard against the risk of harm to children and companion animals who are foreseeably left inside of their products on extreme heat days?

This list of product-related climate adaptation hypotheticals could be expanded ad infinitum. The central point is that product defectiveness does not exist in a vacuum. The environment within which consumer goods are used is undergoing rampant alteration due to the effects of climate change. For products liability law to continue to serve even its narrowly understood role, these contextual changes must be taken into account.

In addition to opening pathways to failure-to-adapt liability, climate change also might prompt deeper questioning of the nature and purpose of products liability law as a field. Like earlier periods of unprecedented injury and loss of life that contributed to significant changes in tort doctrine and practice, the widespread and often devastating impacts of climate change may force a re-evaluation of existing systems for compensating and deterring harm. Just as railroad and workplace carnage forced recognition of new forms of risk in the latter half of the nineteenth century,[54] just as automobile and product-caused accidents revealed extended chains of responsibility in the twentieth century,[55] climate change strains prevailing conceptions of wrongdoing in the twenty-first century. When even the most dystopian climate change scenario fails to register as a responsibility of any actor anywhere, principles of causal and moral responsibility need to be rethought.[56]

Products liability law will not be exempt from this need to evolve in response to suffering that is undeterred, unredressed, and unexplained. Quite the contrary, with its unusual conception and genealogy within the fields of tort and contract law, products liability actually may offer quite valuable resources for the larger effort to instill notions of agency and responsibility into what has been called "the mother of all collective action problems".[57] For the reasons described in the previous section, products liability law remains unlikely in the near term to successfully redress the root causes of climate change. Nevertheless, the presentation of such claims may have edifying effects as they illuminate for judges and other observers new ways of thinking about "limited government in an era of unlimited harm".[58]

One of the most critical aspects of establishing climate accountability, for instance, is the attribution of responsibility for greenhouse gas emissions along complex supply chains. In the context of fossil fuels, producers argue that the vast majority of emissions relating to their products constitute downstream, scope 3 emissions—that is, emissions that occur when an end user combusts the fuel, rather than emissions resulting from actions physically undertaken by producers themselves.[59] Conversely, in the context of climate-intensive animal

[54] John Fabian Witt, *The Accidental Republic: Crippled Workingmen, Destitute Widows, and the Remaking of American Law* (Harvard University Press 2006).

[55] William L Prosser, 'The Assault upon the Citadel (Strict Liability to the Consumer)' (1960) 69 Yale Law Journal 1099; William L Prosser, 'The Fall of the Citadel (Strict Liability to the Consumer)' 50 Minnesota Law Review 791; Nora Freeman Engstrom, 'When Cars Crash: The Automobile's Tort Law Legacy' (2018) 53 Wake Forest Law Review 293.

[56] Douglas A Kysar, *Regulating from Nowhere: Environmental Law and the Search for Objectivity* (Yale University Press 2010).

[57] Douglas A Kysar, 'The Duty of Climate Care' (2024) 73 DePaul Law Review 487, 514.

[58] Benjamin Ewing and Douglas A Kysar, 'Prods and Pleas: Limited Government in an Era of Unlimited Harm' (2011), 121 Yale Law Journal 350.

[59] Kysar, 'The Duty of Climate Care' (n 57) 510.

products like beef, producers argue that the vast majority of emissions occur upstream, when cattle emit methane during the growing phase, prior to ownership and slaughter of the cattle by major meat companies.[60] Given the role of downstream combustors, upstream ranchers, and numerous other actors along the supply chain—including governments that often aggressively subsidise and encourage such climate-harming activities—industries like fossil fuel companies and meat conglomerates question why they should be singled out for sanction.[61]

Products liability law, with its promise of imposing liability jointly and severally along the entirety of a supply chain, seems well designed to lessen, if not entirely overcome this attribution conundrum. The law of products liability invites decision-makers to think in systemic terms, transcending the primitive and highly moralised "A hit B" framing of tort law's genesis. The focus in a products case becomes less on the moral psychological question, "Who did this to me?", and more on the systemic question, "How can this harm be addressed?" A curious feature of products liability law, after all, is the fact that consumer goods *themselves* are described as culpable actors, carrying liability with them along a chain of distribution and spreading it to other product handlers. This depiction is curious because, as Anita Bernstein provocatively queried over three decades ago, "a product cannot be liable, or can it?"[62]

Despite being published only three years after the landmark United Nations Framework Convention on Climate Change 1992, Bernstein's analysis feels remarkably well equipped to grapple with the challenges posed by product-related climate harms. As she notes:

> The one-way vectors of tort and contract theory—"A hit B", "A chose product X", "M manipulated C"—do not begin to describe the network that binds consumers, producers, and observers who select, display, encounter, use, and sell a product. For purposes of products liability, three entities—product, user, and maker—are interrelated agents.[63]

From this more complex and systemic understanding of the nature of consumer product markets, it does not feel odd to describe the goods themselves as "agents"—as Bernstein does—capable of attracting and conveying legal responsibility. Indeed, it would be odd to deny such capacity. To describe the automobile, for instance, as a mere thing is to overlook the profound impact its existence has had on the organisation and expression of human social life wherever it has been introduced. Automobile manufacturers *do* make design choices and consumers *do* make driving decisions, but the vehicle itself drives far more of our existence than is typically recognised or acknowledged.[64]

Thinking in these terms—in terms of actors and networks[65]—affords a simpler, more pragmatic approach to liability assessment than the conventional moralised approach. From this vantage point, major fossil fuel producers and other powerful, concentrated industrial actors can be singled out for liability, not because they stand alone in wrongfully causing harm, but because they are significant nodes in the complex causal chains that lead to greenhouse gas emissions and climate-induced harm. The relevant inquiry is not whether and by how much those producers have specifically and discretely caused climate change through deceptive or other wrongful acts. Instead, from this vantage point, the pertinent question for products

60 Bray and Poston (n 12) 244 (n. 562) ('Most of the animal agriculture industry's emissions are upstream, Scope 3 emissions').

61 Kysar, 'The Duty of Climate Care' (n 57) 509–11.

62 Anita Bernstein, 'How Can a Product Be Liable?' (1995) 45 Duke Law Journal 1, 6.

63 ibid 7 (internal citations omitted).

64 ibid 82 ('Products help to form our selves; products order the lives of human beings long before human beings order the law of products liability').

65 Bruno Latour, *Reassembling the Social: An Introduction to Actor-Network Theory* (OUP 2005).

liability law is whether their location and role in the network affords them efficacy in the effort to reduce the harmful climate impacts of consumer goods. One shifts from an originary and highly moralised tort framing of "A hit B" to a more nuanced framing of how to channel liability to better condition a complex causal network to recognise its own self-induced peril. The public life of private law comes to the fore.[66]

Conceptual advantages accompany such a shift of perspective, notwithstanding arguments that the private law nature of tort claims remains an important perspective when thinking about whether courts should entertain such claims on jurisdictional, procedural, and other preliminary grounds.[67] Speaking of the liability of *the car* serves the goal of promoting systemic rationality in ways that the approach of pointing fingers at governments, producers, and consumers may not. Unlike those other actors, the car travels throughout the network and, as such, is capable of spreading implicit information about the deleterious effects of its use through cost-internalisation. Of course, the car itself is not really made liable, despite the suggestive nomenclature used in products liability law. Plaintiffs still need to identify a defendant with legal personhood who meets not only the requirements for responsibility under products liability in relation to the defective car, but also the more basic requirements for standing as an entity that can be assigned liability at all within the relevant legal system.[68] Nevertheless, focusing on the car as the relevant actor changes the moral register of the analysis.

It is important to note that from this theoretical perspective, consumer-owners could be considered as nodes for liability assessment, just as manufacturers and other commercial handlers presumptively are.[69] After all, from a narrow, materialist perspective, the consumer *is* the actor that causes the release of greenhouse gas emissions when they ignite the engines of their vehicles and the burners of their stoves. Part of the insidious challenge of climate change is the reality that everyone participates every day in such systems of collective self-harm. Why should consumers be exempt from responsibility for their engagement in these collectively calamitous but nonetheless pervasive endeavours?

Despite the field's expansive use of joint and several liability, products liability law has never extended its notion of responsibility to end users themselves, even in the case of consumers whose use of a defective product injures third parties, let alone consumers of greenhouse gas-intensive products whose activities en masse contribute to climate change. Instead, only those actors categorised as "sellers", "manufacturers", or "producers" are subject to the specialised liability regime devised for consumer goods. Non-commercial actors whose product use causes harm to third parties instead must be sued under standard causes of action like negligence or battery.

Such categorical distinctions are troubled by climate change in ways that ultimately might be fruitful both for the effectiveness of the products liability regime and for the larger project of reassessing notions of responsibility in the climate era. Climate accountability litigation in the United States has focused heavily on alleged manipulation and deceit by fossil fuel producers, dialling up the moralised framing of the lawsuits in an attempt to isolate the named defendants

66 Douglas A Kysar, 'The Public Life of Private Law: Tort Law as a Risk Regulation Mechanism' (2018) 9 European Journal of Risk Regulation 48. Also see Aisha Saad, 'Attribution for Climate Torts' (2023) 64 Boston College Law Review 867, 873 (describing ways in which climate change litigation furthers both 'public goals' and 'private goals' of tort law).

67 Ewing and Kysar (n 58).

68 Bernstein (n 62) 3 ('One of the very few defining criteria of a "products liability" case is a person-defendant who engages regularly in a particular business activity').

69 ibid 12 ('The theory of product dynamism recognises the agency and power of the user as well as that of the maker and the product').

from all other actors in the complex causal networks that fuel greenhouse gas emissions.[70] This approach draws support from the experimental finding that moralised tort law framings (e.g., fault-based analyses like negligence) are more psychologically active for decision-makers than more neutral framings (e.g., strict liability).[71] However, the approach also invites moralised counterargument focused on the role of other actors, including plaintiffs themselves.

A US court of appeals panel channelled this concern when it objected to New York City's deception-based lawsuit against carbon major defendants by arguing that "every single person who uses gas and electricity—whether in travelling by bus, cab, Uber, or jitney, or in receiving home deliveries via FedEx, Amazon, or UPS—contributes to global warming".[72] Similarly, during oral argument before the Supreme Court of New Zealand in the *Smith v Fonterra* climate accountability case described by David Bullock in Chapter 7 of this handbook, one justice pointedly asked plaintiff's counsel, "Well, I've got a Land Rover. Sue me! Why don't you sue me?"[73]

Products liability law offers the prospect of dialling down the moral intensity of such climate accountability inquiries. Despite the doctrinal challenges noted in the prior section, fossil fuel producers, electric utilities, and meat conglomerates in theory could be made to bear an initial assessment of liability for the climate impacts of products they market under the motivating principles of products liability law. This could be done *not* because they are deemed to have cynically misled the public and their political representatives—although they may have done this[74]—but simply because they marketed a product that turned out to be defective and harmful to users and other foreseeable victims, and because they represent a sensible location in the product distribution network where liability for those unfortunate harms might initially attach. Conversely, individuals could be excluded from liability for climate-related harms *not* because they are categorically incapable of being seen as harm "producers", as conventional products liability law would have it, but simply because they represent an inconvenient and administratively unworkable node for initial liability assessment.

The shared assumption of both of these conclusions is that *defendants* are not defective—rather, only products are defective. That perspective is critical to the unrealised ambition of products liability law. All of us who participate in systems that depend on greenhouse emissions are prima facie responsible for the harms of climate change, but all of us have recourse to a familiar litany of causal exonerations in our defence.[75] Hence, humanity remains mired within the "mother of all collective action problems". Could a way out of this morass be to focus on the material causes of climate change—the cars, fuel, meat, and other greenhouse

[70] See, for example, *City of Hoboken v Exxon Mobil Corp* No 003179-20 (Amended Complaint) (NJ Super Ct Law Div 21 Apr 2023) [1] (alleging that '[d]efendants have conspired to deceive the world for decades').

[71] Richard L Cupp Jr., and Danielle Polage, 'The Rhetoric of Strict Products Liability Versus Negligence: An Empirical Analysis' (2002) 77 NYU Law Review 874.

[72] *City of New York v Chevron* 993 F3d 81, 86 (2d Cir 2019). See also *Native Vill of Kivalina v ExxonMobil Corp* 663 F Supp 2d 863, 876–77 (ND Cal 2009), aff'd, 696 F3d 849 (9th Cir 2012) ('Though alleging that Defendants are responsible for a "substantial portion" of greenhouse gas emissions . . . Plaintiffs also acknowledge that virtually everyone on Earth is responsible on some level for contributing to such emissions').

[73] Kysar, 'The Duty of Climate Care' (n 57) 511 (quoting Stephen Kós J).

[74] Viveca Morris and Jennifer Jacquet, 'The Animal Agriculture Industry, US Universities, and the Obstruction of Climate Understanding and Policy' (2024) 177 Climatic Change.

[75] For an overview of causation challenges in the causation context, see Mark Geistfeld and Sandy Steele, Chapter 8 of this handbook.

gas-intensive products that have brought humanity to the brink of disaster? If a product can be liable, can it be liable in ways that other actors are not?

5. Conclusion

Over two centuries ago, an English poet concerned with humanity's relationship to nature lamented that the modern worldview had become too immediate and too materialistic:

The world is too much with us; late and soon, Getting and spending, we lay waste our powers;— Little we see in Nature that is ours; We have given our hearts away, a sordid boon![76]

A striking feature of this early nineteenth century passage is its focus on consumption and the role that *individuals* play in giving away their "powers" and their "hearts" in exchange for a "sordid boon". In climate litigation today, we do not see a similar focus on consumers as responsible agents. Defendants instead in these suits are governments, corporations, lobbying organisations, and other collective enterprises. Where do individuals sit within today's "sordid boon" of greenhouse gas intensive items of consumption, other than as passive victims of alleged wrongdoing by entities seen to be more powerful and responsible for the climate crisis?

As Eric Orts notes in Chapter 5 of this handbook, individuals occupy multiple, overlapping social and political roles, and efforts to cordon off acts of consumption from acts of citizenship risk drawing artificial distinctions. Products liability law wants to channel its understanding of consumptive acts in a narrow way, focusing on physical risks posed directly by products to their users and foreseeable bystanders, and somehow containing this interaction within the primitive "A hit B" framework at the heart of tort law's origins. But consumers who purchase products that potentially contribute to harm often understand their acts more expansively. Consumers today frequently demand information regarding the larger impact of goods production on such matters as worker livelihoods, natural resource sustainability, Indigenous rights, and animal welfare, to name but a few examples.[77] Such preferences exceed the narrowly circumscribed range of matters that products liability law presumes to be the province of ordinary consumer expectations for purposes of establishing product defectiveness.

To speak of the level of risk that ordinary consumers expect from pervasive goods like fuel, electricity, and meat opens the question whether everyday acts of necessity and pleasure *must* contribute to cumulative suffering. The consumer who pays a premium to support renewable sources of electricity within their grid can be seen as a sort of micro-producer, attempting through their choices both to expressively signal the collective change they hope to see in the world and to ever so marginally help bring it about. The risk they fear is not the immediate hazard posed by electrons flowing through their walls, such as the risk of shock to curious young fingers or fire from wayward currents. Nor is it even the marginal contribution their individual electricity consumption makes to the global phenomenon of climate change. Instead, the risk they fear is the existential one created by entire *systems* of electricity production that depend on combusting fossil fuels.

From this perspective, using "consumer expectations" as a basis for establishing design defect forces products liability law into far-ranging conversations. To be sure, when many consumers turn on their lights, they may be indifferent whether the electricity that makes their

76 William Wordsworth, *The World is Too Much with Us* (1807).

77 Douglas A Kysar, 'Preferences for Processes: The Process/Product Distinction and the Regulation of Consumer Choice' (2004) 118 Harvard Law Review 525.

illumination possible was fuelled by fossil fuels. Given information and a choice, however, one suspects that many would opt for—that is, they would *expect*—illumination that does not concurrently give rise to existential climate harm. One could attempt to elicit or model the individual's willingness-to-pay for electricity that is less harmful to the global climate, but the nature of the transaction would be awkwardly fit for the stakes at issue. Such hypothetical exercises overlook the profound mismatch between the direct consequences of an individual's choice—real or hypothetical—and the seemingly ordained and disastrous collective outcome. Absent *actual* internalisation of the costs of climate change through products liability law or otherwise, we remain embedded in systems that invite us all to assume nothing we do can make a difference.

For reasons discussed above, products liability law is unlikely to emerge, at least in the near term, as a powerful source of accountability for climate-related harms. However, this area of law—with its peculiar genealogy at the juncture of tort and contract law and its hybrid private/public nature—still may offer unexpected resources for thinking through notions of responsibility against the ruinous backdrop of climate change. For a climate-conscious individual, flipping a light switch powered by fossil fuels is not only a disappointment of *consumer* expectations. It is also a disappointment of expectations regarding *producers* and their obligation to balance private self-interest with social responsibility. It is a disappointment as well regarding the responsibility of *governments* and *citizens* as stewards of collective well-being over time. In short, it is a disappointment of expectations regarding the power of law, both private and public.

Law is not well set up to hear such a messy and multivalent grievance. Complainants instead are asked to come forward as product purchasers, shareholders, competitors, contractors, voters, speakers, religious practitioners, and other such narrowly circumscribed social roles. They are asked to sue under specific causes of action that recognise only certain cognizable injuries. And they are made to challenge only defendants that bear a particular causal and moral relationship to the harm at issue.

The law of products liability is unique in inviting judgment instead of a *thing*, and the role of that thing in causing harm within a system of production. Liability still attaches to actual legal persons, but the focus of the inquiry is not on those persons or their actions. The focus instead is on the thing. Such a detached and systemic perspective might be valuable for a global harm like climate change which has causes that also can be made to appear detached and systemic.

The thing with climate change is . . . we know the things that cause it, but we do not agree on who causes those things and who bears responsibility for them. Perhaps we are having "one thought too many".[78] Perhaps we should focus less on the ultimate moral and legal questions surrounding climate change responsibility and more on the defectiveness of the things that are killing us.

[78] Bernard Williams, *Moral Luck: Philosophical Papers* (CUP 1981) 18.

CHAPTER 11

Consumer Protection

TIFFANIE CHAN, JULIANA VÉLEZ ECHEVERRI, JOANA SETZER, AND CATHERINE HIGHAM

1. Introduction

SINCE the adoption of the Paris Agreement in 2015, there has been a rapid uptake in net-zero pledges from companies.[1] As of June 2025, the Net Zero Tracker database recorded 1,188 publicly listed companies with net-zero targets out of the 2,000 largest companies in the Forbes Global 2000 list.[2] However, despite the proliferation of voluntary standards and guidelines, there remains limited transparency and accountability on whether companies are meeting their targets.[3] Notably, there is insufficient clarity on the extent to which companies are relying on carbon credits to offset their emissions and meet targets.[4] This landscape has contributed to a growing number of cases in which firms overstate their climate efforts or rely on low-integrity carbon credit schemes to claim progress towards net-zero targets—practices that can be described as instances of climate-washing. Such practices have attracted the attention of consumer protection regulators, and an increasing number of consumers have turned to courts for redress.[5] In this context, litigation can help fill regulatory gaps where legislation is absent or is poorly enforced.[6]

This chapter explores the emergence and impact of climate-washing litigation, focusing on climate-washing cases in the Global South and those that challenge the use of carbon credits.[7]

[1] Thomas Hale and others, 'Assessing the Rapidly-Emerging Landscape of Net Zero Targets' (2022) 22 Climate Policy 18.

[2] Net Zero Tracker, 'Data Explorer' (*Net Zero Tracker*) <https://zerotracker.net/> accessed 12 June 2025.

[3] Xiaoyan Jiang, Shawn Kim, and Shirley Lu, 'Limited Accountability and Awareness of Corporate Emissions Target Outcomes' (2025) 15 Nature Climate Change 279.

[4] NewClimate Institute, Oxford Net Zero, Energy and Climate Intelligence Unit, and Data-Driven EnviroLab, 'Net Zero Stocktake 2024' (*Net Zero Tracker*, 2024) <https://zerotracker.net/analysis/net-zero-stocktake-2024> accessed 12 June 2025.

[5] Lisa Benjamin and others, 'Climate-Washing Litigation: Legal Liability for Misleading Climate Communications' (January 2022) <https://cssn.org/wp-content/uploads/2022/01/CSSN-Research-Report-2022-1-Climate-Washing-Litigation-Legal-Liability-for-Misleading-Climate-Communications.pdf> accessed 12 June 2025.

[6] Mikko Rajavuori, Annalisa Savaresi, and Harro van Asselt, 'Mandatory Due Diligence Laws and Climate Change Litigation: Bridging the Corporate Climate Accountability Gap?' (2023) 17 Regulation & Governance 944.

[7] The use of the terms 'Global South' and 'Global North' is contested, subject to interpretation and may be used to distinguish countries based on geographical regions, economic inequalities, and/or socio-economic and historical contexts. We adopt the term 'Global South' in this chapter, recognising that the term connects historical and contemporary patterns of wealth and power and carries an ability to unite communities pursuing climate justice. See Melanie Jean Murcott and Maria Antonia Tigre, 'Developments, Opportunities, and Complexities in Global South Climate Litigation: Introduction to

We argue that climate-washing litigation should not be understood solely as a consumer protection tool but as a broader legal strategy for seeking corporate accountability, advancing climate justice, and reinforcing community rights in the Global South. We analyse three cases where claimants have used litigation to scrutinise the integrity of voluntary carbon markets and contest the exclusion of Indigenous and traditional communities from decision-making processes. These cases illustrate how corporate misrepresentation extends beyond consumer deception and becomes a mechanism for shaping narratives on climate action and legitimises net-zero strategies, even when they directly impact communities' rights to self-determination, land, and participation. They also underscore the need to re-examine the role of public–private boundaries in climate governance and strengthen mechanisms for integrating human rights and environmental protection into private legal frameworks. This discussion contributes to ongoing scholarship on the role of private law in climate governance, illustrating how litigation can confront structural injustices embedded in climate change. We conclude by reflecting on how these cases may reshape legal standards for corporate climate responsibility and influence policy developments in carbon markets.

2. The State of Climate-Washing Litigation

This section summarises the field of climate-washing litigation, to draw out three key points: (1) most climate-washing cases have been filed in the Global North and rely on consumer protection law; (2) a significant proportion of these cases challenge the lack of transparency around using carbon credits to meet climate targets; and (3) studies to date on the impact of climate-washing litigation have primarily focused on remedies awarded in courts or changes to companies' future disclosures. This underestimates the potential for climate-washing litigation to fill accountability gaps in carbon markets.

2.1 Climate-Washing Litigation as a Distinct Legal Phenomenon

Legal scholars broadly agree that climate-washing lawsuits fall within the broader domain of climate litigation.[8] However, it is an ongoing debate whether climate-washing should be categorised as a subtype of greenwashing litigation or as a distinct legal phenomenon. Scholars have traditionally classified greenwashing into two categories: firm-level greenwashing, which consists of misrepresentations about a company's overall environmental impacts, and product-level greenwashing, referring to misleading claims about the environmental benefits or impacts of a specific product.[9] Greenwashing litigation emerged much earlier than

the Special Collection' (2024) 16 Journal of Human Rights Practice 1. In this context, it is a useful lens to understand litigation, which is the focus of this chapter. Our approach is consistent with the increasing prevalence of these terms in climate litigation literature. See, for example, Joana Setzer and Lisa Benjamin, 'Climate Litigation in the Global South: Constraints and Innovations' (2020) 9 Transnational Environmental Law 77; Jolene Lin and Jacqueline Peel, *Litigating Climate Change in the Global South* (2024) (OUP 2024). However, we recognise that these terms risk oversimplifying the diversity and heterogeneity of countries in each group and perpetuating dichotomies based on outdated political and economic divisions.

[8] Benjamin et al (n 5) 4; Jessica Wentz and others, 'Research Priorities for Climate Litigation' (2023) 11 Earth's Future 11.

[9] Magali A Delmas and Vanessa Cuerel Burbano, 'The Drivers of Greenwashing' (2011) 54 California Management Review 64.

climate-washing litigation. During the 1990s, the US Federal Trade Commission brought thirty-seven claims against companies allegedly greenwashing in their marketing, using the Federal Trade Commission Act and the 1992 Green Guides as its basis.[10] We view these cases as distinct from climate-washing litigation, as they did not involve misrepresentations around climate-specific issues, such as companies' efforts to meet their emissions reduction pathways.

Claims made about a company's contribution to mitigating climate change merit separate attention, given the increased complexities around calculating emissions reductions and the science and methodologies behind carbon offsetting.[11] Methodological challenges around companies' emissions and pathways to net zero have implications for how consumers will interpret their disclosures, how policymakers regulate and provide guidance, and how judges interpret existing consumer protection laws that may not have originally been designed to cover climate change. The emergence of climate-washing litigation raises new legal complexities, as it involves not only consumer protection law (often the boundaries of greenwashing lawsuits) but also corporate governance, financial regulation, and due diligence obligations related to climate risk disclosure. If defined narrowly, climate-washing litigation refers only to cases that challenge misleading advertising claims relating to carbon neutrality or net-zero commitments.[12] Broader interpretations of climate-washing litigation include cases against both state and non-state actors that challenge misleading representations about their overall role in addressing climate change and its impacts.[13] For example, this would include where claimants challenge the misalignment between an energy company marketing itself as a "climate-friendly" company while continuing to invest heavily in fossil fuel projects.

In this chapter, we adopt a broad definition of climate-washing litigation, referring to cases that challenge misleading claims about a company's transition and progress towards a just, low-carbon, and climate-resilient future.[14] We align with the Sabin Center for Climate Change Law's Climate Change Litigation Databases' definition for "litigation", which includes both legal proceedings in domestic courts *and* complaints to, or investigations and communications by, quasi-judicial bodies (e.g., advertising standards authorities or competition regulators), OECD National Contact Points, or United Nations Human Rights Council's Special Procedures.

2.2 Climate-Washing Litigation as a Global North Trend

Using this definition and data from the Sabin Center for Climate Change Law's Climate Change Litigation Databases, we identified 161 cases globally between 2015 and 2024 that explicitly raise climate-washing arguments.[15] There are significantly more cases occurring in the

[10] Nick Feinstein, 'Learning from Past Mistakes: Future Regulation to Prevent Greenwashing' (2013) 40 Boston College Environmental Affairs Law Review 229.

[11] Ciara Peacock, 'Misleading Markets: Consumer Protection in the Age of Climate Washing' (2023) 126 West Virginia Law Review 367.

[12] Barbara Ballan and Jason J Czarnezki, 'Disclosure, Greenwashing, and the Future of ESG Litigation' (2024) 81 Washington & Lee Law Review 545.

[13] Benjamin et al (n 5) 4.

[14] Adapted from Joana Setzer and Catherine Higham, 'Global Trends in Climate Change Litigation: 2025 Snapshot' (*Grantham Research Institute on Climate Change and the Environment*, 2025) <www.lse.ac.uk/granthaminstitute/publication/global-trends-in-climate-change-litigation-2025-snapshot> accessed 1 July 2025.

[15] The Sabin Center for Climate Change Law maintains two databases: one contains all climate cases filed in the US before state and federal courts and selected cases before administrative entities. The other is a database of 'global' cases, which includes information on cases filed in all countries *other* than the US and in international and regional courts and tribunals. Using the typology created by Setzer and Higham

Global North, with the highest number of cases in the US (61), Germany (26), UK (24), and Australia (16). Cases have also been recorded in the Netherlands (8), France (5), Canada (4), Italy (3), Switzerland (3), New Zealand (2), Belgium (1), Denmark (1), Poland (1), and Spain (1).[16] The Sabin Center Database contains only three cases from the Global South: Mexico (2) and Brazil (1). Below, we provide an overview of the types of claims with a focus on cases brought against companies, constituting over 90% of the known claims.[17]

Approximately 84% of climate-washing cases base their claim on consumer protection law, both statutory and common law. Many jurisdictions have unfair competition or trade practices legislation (e.g., the German Act against Unfair Competition) or consumer protection-specific legislation (e.g., the California Consumers Legal Remedies Act). In the US cases, additional causes of action include breach of warranties, unjust enrichment, nuisance, deceit, fraud, or misrepresentation. Quasi-judicial cases—often complaints to, or investigations by, consumer protection or competition regulators—are brought under advertising codes (e.g., the UK Code of Non-broadcast Advertising and Direct & Promotional Marketing).

In the US, claims go beyond single advertising campaigns. A group of "climate liability" or "polluter pays" lawsuits filed by state and local governments against the Carbon Majors (big emitters) challenge major disinformation campaigns, arguing that they have misled consumers and the wider public for many years about the harms of their products. It is this alleged deceptive conduct that forms the key legal grounds for these claims, primarily seeking compensation for the government claimants' costs of adapting to climate change impacts. For example, *City of Hoboken v Exxon Mobil Corp* is brought under New Jersey's Consumer Fraud Act, public and private nuisance, trespass, and negligence.[18]

While consumer protection remains the dominant area of law in which climate-washing litigation occurs, similar arguments are emerging to address investors' or shareholders' interests.[19] These cases rely on securities, company, or financial regulation law to challenge misleading communications in relation to a financial product or service. For example, in September 2024, the Federal Court of Australia ordered Vanguard Investments to pay a $12.9 million penalty for making misleading claims about an ESG exclusionary screen applied to investments in their "ethically conscious" bond index fund.[20] "Books and records" cases have also been filed, such as *Abrahams v Commonwealth Bank of Australia*, where claimants sought disclosure of internal documents, which could then potentially be used to show involvement in fossil fuel projects that contradict the firm's ESG commitments and policies.[21] It is possible that the issues raised in "investor" cases may converge with "consumer" cases more and more,

(n 14), we reviewed cases filed since 2015 and identified cases that raised climate-washing arguments. Using data of cases filed up to 31 December 2024 and available on the databases as of 15 May 2025, we identified 161 cases in total.

[16] One case was filed before the International Criminal Court and has been excluded from this country case breakdown.

[17] Eight cases were recorded against government defendants, whereas 153 cases involved corporate defendants.

[18] *City of Hoboken v Exxon Mobil Corp* Civ No 20-3179 NJ Super Ct.

[19] Adam Parr, 'Policy and Law: The Case of Synthetic Nitrogen Fertilizer' (2024) 6 Environmental Research Communications. Parr refers to the *potential* for greenwashing cases to be framed in constitutional and human rights law, but notes that consumer protection, securities, and company law are areas where cases have been litigated.

[20] *Australian Securities and Investments Commission v Vanguard Investments Australia Ltd (No 2)* [2024] FCA 1096.

[21] *Guy Abrahams & Kim Abrahams as trustee for the Guy & Kim Abrahams Family Trust v Commonwealth Bank of Australia* (CBA) NSD864/2021.

to the extent that it becomes increasingly clear that financial interests are contingent on the credibility of a company's commitment to the transition. The focus of this chapter, however, is on consumer protection cases, which have found considerable success in court.[22]

Despite the growing body of literature examining climate-washing litigation, it has largely followed the prevalence of cases in the Global North, and there has been limited attention on how these legal arguments are applied in Global South courts. Although not focused on litigation, an analysis of a large open-pit mining project in Brazil uses the concept of "toxicological climate-washing" to describe false statements on exposure to substances resulting from gold mining, which manufactures doubt about the validity of scientific evidence.[23] The practice of climate-washing is described as a tool that along with corruption and fraudulent reports, has facilitated—according to the authors—ecocide and geocide in Brazil. This suggests an underexplored dimension between climate-washing and environmental justice struggles. This chapter contributes to filling this gap by analysing three Global South cases, as well as commenting on developments elsewhere.

2.3 The Rise of Carbon Credit Climate-Washing Claims

Within climate-washing litigation, there is a rising number of cases challenging carbon credits. Out of the 161 climate-washing cases, we identify over a third (60) that raise arguments specifically about the integrity of carbon credit projects or the use of them to offset emissions. Outside of the US, these claims account for just over 50% of cases.[24] Claimants frequently allege that advertisements lack transparency around the use of credits or that advertisements falsely claim that the purchase of credits can offset the company's impact on climate change.

An example of the former is *Berrin v Delta Air Lines Inc.*[25] The claimant argues that she purchased flights from Delta over other airlines, relying on representations and warranties in advertisements that stated that it was a carbon-neutral airline. However, Delta's carbon neutrality commitment rests on representations that its investments in the voluntary carbon market effectively offset all carbon emissions from its operations. The claimant challenges the assumption that carbon credits can make a company fully "carbon neutral" by raising issues about carbon accounting, additionality (proof that the project would not have occurred without an offsetting purpose and the revenue from the sale of carbon credits), immediacy (the idea that expected emissions reductions will occur over decades), and durability (the degree of permanence of stored carbon). In challenging the methodologies underpinning offsets, these cases raise fundamental questions about the integrity of carbon credits and the role they can play in the transition.

Some cases, such as the *UK Advertising Standards Authority's Ruling on Shell Go+ Campaign*, have a more limited focus on the advertising and information provided to consumers.[26] This case decided that Shell's advertisement did not make clear that "Shell Go+" was a loyalty

[22] Eva Balounová, 'Climate Litigation: Targeting the Aviation Sector' (2023) 7 Chinese Journal of Environment Law 288.

[23] Sergio Ulhoa Dani and others, 'Geocide, Ecocide, and Genocidal Type Outcomes from Large-Scale Open Pit Mountaintop Gold Mining in the Outskirts of Paracatu, Brazil' (2019) 12(3) Environmental Justice.

[24] We identified 50 out of 100 climate-washing cases from the Sabin Center's Global Database (non-US cases) that raised arguments about carbon credits. In the US, we identified 10 out of 61 cases.

[25] *Berrin v Delta Air Lines Inc* 2:23 cv 04150 CD Cal.

[26] *UK Advertising Standards Authority's Ruling on Shell UK Ltd.'s Shell Go+ Campaign* Complaint Ref 20-1049869 Shell UK Ltd.

scheme, which could mislead consumers to believe that they were purchasing a new carbon-neutral fuel, "Shell Go+", rather than participating in a carbon offsetting loyalty scheme. Although principally challenging the lack of disclosure, these cases bring the use of offsetting to the fore, stimulating legal and public debate.

2.4 Impacts of Climate-Washing Litigation

More than half of the 100 climate-washing cases that have reached outcomes have concluded in favour of the claimant.[27] Out of sixty climate-washing cases that raise carbon credit-related arguments, close to 80% have reached an outcome, and for those decided outside of the US, the large majority have been decided in favour of the claimant.[28] However, despite the relatively high levels of success, the impact of such climate-washing cases on emissions reductions remains unclear.[29] The subject of the dispute is usually limited to isolated textual claims in a single ad campaign.[30] Remedies are closely tied to providing redress for these communications, including cease and desist orders, corrective measures, compensatory damages, or penalties if the company fails to remove the advertisement.

Climate litigation can also have indirect effects.[31] Assessing whether climate litigation is effective goes beyond looking at impacts on emissions.[32] Legal scholars have expressed cautious optimism about the role of climate-washing litigation in counteracting misleading corporate practices across multiple sectors, including energy, transportation, finance, and food systems.[33] It has been argued that climate-washing cases have raised media attention and public concern in the aviation sector, as well as pushed for new legislation.[34] Others have referred to the power of litigation and reputational risk in shaping corporate behaviour, noting that "widespread news of private lawsuits against 'beloved companies' seems more likely to force these companies to take action in favour of the environment and consumers than government enforcement".[35] Empirical studies

[27] Setzer and Higham. Following their methodology, the first stage at which a case may be classified as having a given outcome, as opposed to being classed as 'open', is when there is a positive ruling on a procedural issue such as standing or justiciability, even if the case has not proceeded to trial.

[28] In the US, out of the 10 cases that raise arguments related to carbon credits, only five have reached an outcome and one was in favour of the claimant (*Berrin v Delta Air Lines Inc*). This was classified as successful, in favour of the claimant, as the claimant was found to have standing, and the motion to dismiss the case was denied.

[29] Juliana Vélez Echeverri, Catherine Higham, and Joana Setzer, 'Climate-Washing Litigation: Towards Greater Corporate Accountability?' (*Grantham Research Institute on Climate Change and the Environment*, 17 April 2024) <https://www.lse.ac.uk/granthaminstitute/news/climate-washing-litigation-towards-greater-corporate-accountability/> accessed 12 June 2025.

[30] Clemens Kaupa, 'Smoke Gets in Your Eyes: Misleading Fossil Fuel Advertisement in the Climate Crisis' (2021) 10 Journal of European Consumer and Market Law 21.

[31] Jacqueline Peel and Hari M Osofsky, *Climate Change Litigation Regulatory Pathways to Cleaner Energy* (CUP 2015).

[32] Joana Setzer, Nicola Silbert, and Lisa Vanhala, 'The Effectiveness of Climate Change Litigation', in Francesco Sindico, Kate McKenzie, Gastón A Medici-Colombo, and Lennart Wegener (eds), *Research Handbook on Climate Change Litigation* (2024).

[33] Benjamin Franta, 'Corporate Greenwashing: The Lawyers are Coming' (*The European Corporate Governance Institute*, 9 March 2023) <https://www.ecgi.global/publications/blog/corporate-greenwashing-the-lawyers-are-coming?trk=public_post_comment-text> accessed 12 June 2025.

[34] Eva Balounová, 'Climate Litigation: Targeting the Aviation Sector' (n 22).

[35] Claire Fischer, 'Is Twitter the New FTC and EPA? Publicized Private Action as the Anti-Greenwashing Mechanism in Modern Society' (2020) 33 Georgetown Environmental Law Review 315, 318.

provide supporting evidence that litigation risk acts as a deterrent against corporate climate-washing.[36]

In practice, climate-washing litigation is receiving significant attention from the financial sector.[37] In 2021, for example, the Bank of England Biennial Exploratory Scenario included greenwashing litigation as part of its stress testing exercise.[38] EU banking regulators have also referred to climate litigation as a financial risk, recommending prudent risk management.[39] The increased industry awareness of climate-washing litigation has led to concerns about the potential for "greenhushing"—backsliding from transparent communication about corporate climate strategies for fear of accusations of greenwashing.

This chapter contributes to expanding the literature on the impacts of climate-washing litigation by focusing on offsetting claims and exploring the justice dimensions of localised impacts resulting from carbon credit projects. This justice approach has been developed using interdisciplinary research on the social implications and "greenwashing" of green projects in the Global South. In this body of research, the term "greenwashing" is used and framed differently in relation to consumer protection claims—it describes the adverse impact on people of green or sustainable initiatives and the reproduction of environmental injustices through enabling settler colonialism or normalising other systems of inequality.[40] Our analysis below on three Global South cases adapts the approach developed in these studies to understand the underexplored impact of "climate-washing" litigation in Global South contexts.

3. Case Selection

The three Global South climate-washing cases identified in our initial review include the Brazilian case *AMOREMA and AMORETGRAP v Sustainable Carbon and Others* (*AMOREMA*), filed in 2021, and two Mexican cases: *Nuestros Derechos al Futuro y Medio Ambiente Sano and CEMDA v Energy Regulatory Commission* and *Greenpeace v Energy Regulatory Commission*.[41] The two Mexican cases are examples of strategic litigation

[36] Shawn Qu, 'Costs May be a Blessing in Disguise: Litigation Risk and Greenwashing' (2024) 62 Finance Research Letters. This study finds that in China, the growing threat of litigation has curbed misleading ESG claims, signalling that legal accountability mechanisms can influence corporate behaviour even in jurisdictions with limited climate litigation histories.

[37] Network for Greening the Financial System, 'Technical Document: Climate-related Litigation: Raising Awareness About a Growing Source of Risk' (*Network for Greening the Financial System*, 2021) <https://www.ngfs.net/system/files/import/ngfs/medias/documents/climate_related_litigation.pdf> accessed 12 June 2025.

[38] Bank of England, 'Guidance for Participants of the 2021 Biennial Exploratory Scenario: Financial Risks from Climate Change' (*Bank of England*, 2021) <https://www.bankofengland.co.uk/-/media/boe/files/stress-testing/2021/the-2021-biennial-exploratory-scenario-on-the-financial-risks-from-climate-change.pdf> accessed 12 June 2025.

[39] European Banking Authority, 'Guidelines on the Management of Environmental, Social and Governance (ESG) risks' (*European Banking Authority*, 2025) <https://www.eba.europa.eu/publications-and-media/press-releases/eba-publishes-its-final-guidelines-management-esg-risks> accessed 12 June 2025.

[40] For example, Ambreen Tour Ben-Shmuel and Silja Halle, 'Beyond Greenwashing: Prioritizing Environmental Justice in Conflict-Affected Settings' (2023) Environment and Security 209. Other scholars have labelled the process of extracting rights to emit while excluding communities from benefits as 'green extractivim' such as Patricia E Perkins, *Climate Justice and Participatory Research: Building Climate-Resilient Commons* (University of Calgary Press 2023).

[41] *AMOREMA e AMORETGRAP v Sustainable Carbon and others* [2021] ACP 1045416-11.2021.4.01.3900; *Nuestros Derechos al Futuro y Medio Ambiente Sano and CEMDA v Energy Regulatory*

challenging government policy on the grounds that climate considerations have been insufficiently integrated into regulatory decision-making. These cases fall into the relatively rare category of public or administrative law actions that include climate-washing-style arguments. They question the methodology used to determine what qualifies as "clean energy" under Mexico's renewable energy framework and argue that classifying fossil-generated gas as clean energy misleads the public. While these cases raise important issues about misleading climate-related claims at the government level, they do not engage directly with private law and corporate accountability, which is the focus of this chapter.

Our analysis, therefore, focuses on the *AMOREMA* case, which stands out as the sole example in the Sabin Center's Databases of a private law-relevant climate-washing case in the Global South.[42] The claimants argue that the carbon credit project developers misrepresented the nature of these credits, particularly their purported social benefits for the traditional communities living in the areas where the projects were developed. The legal claims extend beyond the project proponents to include corporate buyers of the credits (e.g., Deloitte and Air France), who allegedly misrepresented their sustainability credentials by using the credits without conducting proper due diligence. The transnational nature of this case highlights the increasing legal complexity of transactions in voluntary carbon markets and suggests broader lessons for climate-washing litigation, particularly in jurisdictions where corporate reliance on offsets is central to net-zero strategies.

The *AMOREMA* case shares similarities with a growing number of legal challenges in the Global South that contest the legitimacy and legality of carbon credit projects. This includes two Colombian climate cases that do not explicitly rely on climate-washing arguments, but raise fundamental concerns about the governance of carbon credit projects and the impacts of these projects on local communities. Similarly, a recent judgment issued by the Kenyan Environment and Land Court in January 2025 ruled that the establishment of certain conservancies (land designated for sustainable land uses or wildlife protection) was unconstitutional due to the lack of public participation and violation of the claimants' rights to property, livelihood, and cultural heritage.[43] Like *AMOREMA*, the buyers of credits from this large soil carbon removal project included multinational companies like British Airways and Netflix.[44]

To our knowledge, there has not been a similar climate case in Asia yet. However, the Rimba Raya project in Indonesia, one of the world's largest carbon credit projects, has been subject to ongoing controversy and private disputes.[45] The Ministry of Environment had previously

Commission [2023] Amparo No. 256/2023; *Greenpeace v Energy Regulatory Commission* [2023] Amparo No. 239/2023.

[42] This was identified based on data of cases filed up to 31 December 2024 and available on the databases as of 15 May 2025.

[43] See *Osman & 164 others (Suing on Their Behalf and Behalf of Residents of Merti Sub-County, Chari, and Cherab Wards in Isiolo County) v Northern Rangelands Trust & 8 others* (Petition E006 of 2021) [2025] KEELC 99 (KLR) (24 January 2025).

[44] Joseph Maina, 'Landmark Kenyan Ruling Puts International Carbon Offset Projects into Question' (*The Wave*, 2 April 2025) <https://www.the-wave.net/landmark-kenyan-ruling-international-carbon-offset-projects-question/> accessed 12 June 2025.

[45] Ivy Yin, 'Jakarta Court Voids Revocation of Rimba Raya Carbon Project License: Investor' (*S&P Global*, 16 July 2024) <https://www.spglobal.com/commodity-insights/en/news-research/latest-news/energy-transition/071624-jakarta-court-voids-revocation-of-rimba-raya-carbon-project-license-investor> accessed 12 June 2025. According to Ivy Yin, as of April 2024, 25.7 million credits had been retired and used for emission offsetting claims, accounting for 9.1% of the total retired volume of nature-based avoidance carbon credits (i.e., credits based on emissions that might have existed had a project not been funded), for example, through avoiding deforestation.

revoked the project's forest utilisation business license, allegedly on the basis that local regulations had been violated. Although the State Administrative Court of Jakarta later ruled that the revocation of the license was void and the project may resume operations, this case illustrates how the integrity of carbon credits has important implications for other stakeholders and areas of private law. Following the revocation, investors based outside Indonesia, who had signed purchase and sale agreements with local operators of the project, initiated arbitration proceedings to enforce their rights.[46] Many investors act as intermediaries who sell the credits to further buyers, that is, companies who then rely on credits to meet their emission reduction commitments and make "climate neutrality" claims discussed in Section 2. Noticeably, the voices of local communities affected by the project and the environment itself have not been featured in these legal battles.

As voluntary carbon markets continue to expand and companies face growing scrutiny over the credibility of their sustainability commitments, the use of private law climate-washing arguments may emerge as a significant mechanism for legal accountability. This is particularly relevant in regions where environmental justice concerns intersect with corporate sustainability claims, further complicating the legal and ethical landscape of climate governance. In this chapter, we have chosen to focus on the cases in Brazil and Colombia, providing a regional comparative analysis and a comparison between cases that explicitly include climate-washing arguments and those that do not. This allows us to highlight how climate-washing arguments may help provide an additional legal avenue for communities to challenge the misleading portrayal of carbon credits as unequivocally beneficial climate solutions. This observation underscores the potential for future cases across the Global South to frame their arguments in ways that more explicitly address corporate misrepresentation in the transnational supply chain of carbon credits.

4. Looking Behind Climate Neutrality Claims

The climate-washing cases examined in this chapter present new and complex legal challenges at the intersection of private law (contract and tort claims), public law (environmental and human rights obligations), and transnational corporate accountability frameworks. They reveal a fundamental paradox within carbon markets. While carbon credit schemes rhetorically endorse Indigenous-led conservation, in practice Indigenous and traditional communities who steward the land and natural resources sustainably are often excluded from decision-making processes and denied equitable financial benefits. This exclusion reflects ongoing patterns of climate colonialism, in which Global North actors appropriate land-based climate solutions from the Global South while retaining control over governance structures, financial flows, and economic benefits.[47] The commodification of community-managed lands for carbon offsetting mirrors historical patterns of resource extraction, where environmental benefits are captured by international markets while traditional communities bear the burden of restricted land use, economic marginalisation, and legal exclusion.

The voluntary carbon market exemplifies these inequities. Corporate actors and financial intermediaries from the Global North may partner with governments or third-party certifiers to develop carbon credit projects on communities' lands. These transactions are

[46] ibid.

[47] Nowrin Tabassum, 'Climate Capitalism or Carbon Colonialism? The Critical Features of Climate Change Adaptation and Mitigation Policies' *Handbook of Development Policy* (Edward Elgar Publishing 2021), 313; Laurie Parsons, *Carbon Colonialism: How Rich Countries Export Climate Breakdown* (Manchester University Press 2023).

facilitated by standards such as Verra's Verified Carbon Standard and the Gold Standard, which may not adequately account for Indigenous governance structures.[48] While these initiatives promote the rhetoric of Indigenous inclusion, research has shown that Indigenous communities receive little to no financial compensation, even when their lands are used for offset generation and traded at high prices in international carbon markets.[49] As Graham highlights in Chapter 15 of this handbook, carbon markets, as currently designed, reproduce the logic of dominant legal regimes that have created the conditions of climate change itself.

Beyond financial exclusion, carbon credit projects might violate the internationally recognised rights of Indigenous peoples. Projects may be established without meaningful consultation or adherence to Free, Prior, and Informed Consent (FPIC)—a principle enshrined in the United Nations Declaration on the Rights of Indigenous Peoples.[50] The failure to secure FPIC reflects a broader jurisdictional constraint, as many Indigenous territories lack formal land titles or state-recognised governance structures, further weakening their negotiating power in carbon credit agreements.[51]

The lack of clear land tenure exacerbates structural vulnerabilities, leaving traditional communities susceptible to land grabs, coerced participation in offset schemes, and corporate greenwashing strategies. Private law, including property and contract law, plays a role in perpetuating these structural inequities. For example, disputes in Kenya referred to contracts on conservancies being issued in English, with households unable to read documents prior to signing covenants on their land.[52] Carbon conservation narratives can be strategically deployed to legitimise land dispossession, where companies frame offset projects as essential for climate mitigation while simultaneously displacing traditional land users and restricting their access to natural resources.[53] This dynamic reinforces the inequities embedded in global carbon markets, where credit buyers in the Global North claim environmental benefits at the expense of Indigenous autonomy and livelihoods in the Global South.

The *AMOREMA* case analysed in this chapter exemplifies these injustices, underscoring the need for stronger governance mechanisms to prevent climate-washing in carbon credit projects while addressing historical patterns of environmental exploitation. The case also highlights how litigation can reshape legal norms by demanding greater transparency and accountability. Legal challenges may contribute to the development of new jurisprudence and regulatory frameworks, reinforcing the principle that climate neutrality claims must be linked not only to emissions reductions but also to social equity and justice across corporate value chains.

[48] Connor Joseph Cavanagh and Tor Arve Benjaminsen, 'Political Ecology, Variegated Green Economies, and the Foreclosure of Alternative Sustainabilities' (2017) 24 Journal of Political Ecology 200.

[49] Adam G Bumpas and Diana M Liverman, 'Carbon Colonialism? Offsets, Greenhouse Gas Reductions, and Sustainable Development' in Richard Peet, Paul Robbins, and Michael Watts (eds), *Global Political Ecology* (Routledge 2010); Tracey Osborne, 'Tradeoffs in Carbon Commodification: A Political Ecology of Common Property Forest Governance' (2015) 67 Geoforum 64.

[50] Chunyu Pan and others, 'Key Challenges and Approaches to Addressing Barriers in Forest Carbon Offset Projects' (2022) 33 Journal of Forestry Research 1109.

[51] Katie Patterson, 'Overcoming Barriers to Indigenous Peoples' Participation in Forest Carbon Markets' (2011) 22 Colorado Environmental Law Journal 417.

[52] Maina (n 44).

[53] James Fairhead, Melissa Leach, and Ian Scoones, 'Green Grabbing: A New Appropriation of Nature?' (2012) 39 Journal of Peasant Studies 237.

4.1 The *AMOREMA* Case

AMOREMA and AMORETGRAP v Sustainable Carbon and Others was a class action (*Ação civil Pública* or Public Civil Action) filed in 2021, accusing multiple companies of falsely marketing carbon credits from the Amazon as "social carbon credits" while failing to ensure actual benefits for local communities.[54] The claimants are two associations of residents from the Extractive Reserves of Mapuá (AMOREMA) and Terra Grande-Pracuúba (AMORETGRAP).

In Brazil, Extractive Reserves (*Reservas Extrativistas*, or RESEX) are a category of protected areas for sustainable use, designed to safeguard the livelihoods, territories, and cultures of traditional extractivist communities—such as rubber tappers, Brazil-nut collectors, and small-scale fishers—who rely on the sustainable harvesting of natural resources. The concept of Extractive Reserves emerged from grassroots struggles of these communities in the Amazon, particularly the rubber tappers' movement led by Francisco Alves Mendes Filho, known as Chico Mendes. Mendes became internationally known for organising traditional communities who had opposed the federal development model imposed on the Amazon in the 1970s, which promoted extensive cattle ranching, mining, and logging projects. These policies led to large-scale land concentration, forced displacement of traditional communities, and widespread environmental destruction. Shortly after Mendes's death, the Brazilian federal government created the first Extractive Reserves in 1990. Extractive Reserves are formally recognised under Brazil's National System of Conservation Units (SNUC) and codified by Federal Law No. 9.985/2000. According to the National Register of Conservation Units (CNUC), there are currently ninety-eight Extractive Reserves across the country.[55]

Four key legal issues underpinned the *AMOREMA* case brought by residents of Extractive Reserves. First, the claimants alleged that the defendant companies involved in developing the carbon credit project participated in the illegal takeover of land in a protected Extractive Reserve without providing fair remuneration to the communities. The communities, which hold legal rights to use and manage the land, were excluded from project governance, despite their longstanding role in preserving the environment that formed the basis for the carbon credits.

Second, the claimants argued that the companies that purchased these carbon credits failed to conduct due diligence, acquiring assets of dubious legitimacy. Each transaction involved an unlawful contractual arrangement with the sellers, and the buyers negligently disregarded their duty of care by failing to investigate—or deliberately ignoring—the provenance of the credits, thus committing an unlawful act against traditional communities. Allegedly, even a basic review of the *Ecomapuá* Project would have revealed land tenure conflicts and the presence of over 450 traditional families in the area. Instead, the buyers proceeded with the acquisition of credits covering more than 90,000 hectares in a highly contested region of the Amazon, purchasing them from a company that had previously operated as a logging business. The claimants argued that the buyers' failure to conduct even minimal due diligence—despite promoting their commitment to sustainability—demonstrated gross negligence and underscores their complicity.

[54] *AMOREMA e AMORETGRAP v Sustainable Carbon and others* [2021] ACP 1045416-11.2021.4.01.3900.

[55] National Register of Conservation Units, 'Plataforma oficial de dados do Sistema Nacional de Unidades de Conservação da Natureza' <https://cnuc.mma.gov.br/> accessed 11 July 2025.

Third, the claim is founded on climate-washing arguments. The claimants asserted that the defendant companies systematically misused the name, image, and cultural heritage of traditional communities to promote their carbon credit project as socially responsible. This misrepresentation allowed the defendants to derive financial gains from the reputational and economic value of their fabricated narrative, while the communities received no compensation and were actively misled about the project's impact. The claimants highlighted that multiple corporate defendants, including *Ecomapuá*, Deloitte, and Sustainable Carbon, used the image of these communities in their corporate sustainability campaigns. For instance, Deloitte claimed on its website that the primary goal of the Project is to promote the sustainability of the traditional community—a statement the claimants argued is entirely detached from reality. Sustainable Carbon advertised the project as having supported 450 families while promoting its certification under the Carbon Social Standard. The claimants argued that these statements are misleading, as the communities involved have not received financial benefits nor proper recognition for their role in forest conservation.

Lastly, the claimants alleged that the defendants' actions amounted to carbon credit "land grabbing", where corporations profit from the environmental preservation efforts of traditional communities while denying them rightful compensation. Therefore, the claimants sought compensation for material damages, restitution of profits obtained by the defendants through the sale of carbon credits, and compensation for collective moral damages with amounts to be determined. They also demanded a court order requiring that the defendants cease the sale and purchase of carbon credits originating from the *Mapuá* and *Terra Grande-Pracuúba* Extractive Reserves and cease the unauthorised use of the name and image of the traditional communities.

In December 2023, a legal opinion was prepared on behalf of the claimants, outlining in more detail the question of ownership of the generated carbon credits. It argued that the credits should be attributed to the traditional communities inhabiting these areas, as their environmental conservation efforts enable the creation of these credits. This allegation reflected the wider discussion introduced at the beginning of this section regarding the exclusion of Indigenous communities from carbon market governance and questions about who controls climate finance, how benefits are distributed, and whose knowledge systems shape climate solutions. The submitted legal opinion highlighted violations of property, cultural, and human rights laws and called for the court to hold all companies involved—including buyers in the voluntary carbon market—liable for failing to conduct due diligence, emphasising shared legal responsibility for environmental and social harm.

However, in May 2024, the 9th Federal Environmental and Agrarian Court of Pará dismissed the lawsuits.[56] The Court held that the dispute "was not of an environmental or collective nature" but rather concerned "private patrimonial rights" stemming from contractual arrangements between the communities and the State. The claimants' attempt to frame the case as an environmental matter was rejected. The court found no evidence of environmental harm, noting that the carbon credits were issued through internationally certified voluntary market mechanisms and that the core issue was ownership and commercialisation rights over these credits. As such, the court ruled that the Public Civil Action was procedurally inadequate, as it is intended to protect diffuse or collective interests rather than individual or private economic claims. The case was dismissed without a judgment on the merits.

[56] The decision is available on the Brazilian Climate Litigation Platform maintained by JUMA at the Pontifical Catholic University of Rio de Janeiro (PUC-Rio). <https://litigancia.biobd.inf.puc-rio.br/visualizacao_caso/556/0/> accessed 12 June 2025.

New climate-washing cases relating to carbon credits in Brazil have followed in 2025. Brazil's *Instituto de Defesa do Consumidor* (the consumer protection regulator or IDEC) has taken legal action against *Gol Linhas Aéreas* (*Gol*)[57] and *Localiza*,[58] accusing them of misleading consumers regarding carbon offset programmes. The lawsuits allege that these companies profited from carbon offsetting services without verifying the legitimacy of the projects used for compensation. In *Gol's* case, the airline's offset programme relied on Moss, a fintech company implicated in selling carbon credits from projects suspended by Operation Greenwashing—a large-scale Police investigation into fraudulent carbon credit schemes in Brazil. Similarly, it is alleged that *Localiza*, a car rental company, has engaged in greenwashing by charging an additional fee in the rental contract for "offsetting", without providing information on the origin of the carbon credits, apparent benefits, and the effectiveness of such credits in offsetting emissions. IDEC has also raised that the fee fails to account for key variables such as vehicle type, fuel efficiency, and mileage, casting doubt on its credibility.

4.2 Comparative Analysis to the *Pira Paraná* and *Gran Cumbal* Cases

Alongside the *AMOREMA* case, the *Pira Paraná* and *Gran Cumbal* cases filed in Colombia present a broader picture of due diligence processes in carbon credit projects and the different forms of injustices that communities may face. In July 2022, members of seven Indigenous groups from the *Pira Paraná* territory in the department of *Vaupés* filed a "tutela" action to claim protection for their fundamental rights to the territory, self-determination, and cultural integrity.[59] A few months later, twelve members of the Indigenous community "Gran Cumbal" in the department of Nariño used the same legal action to claim protection for their fundamental rights to FPIC, territory as collective property, self-determination, and participation in decision-making processes.[60] *Tutela* actions are claims for the protection of fundamental constitutional rights provided for under the Constitution of Colombia.

In both Colombian cases, the claimants allege that the companies in charge of developing and verifying the carbon credit project dismiss Indigenous ways of life and self-government structures. They claim that the private companies signed a "mandate contract" with a representative of the Indigenous community without FPIC of the whole community. They also allege a lack of information and economic compensation for the sold carbon credits.

In the *AMOREMA* case, these localised injustices are explicitly tied to the advertising of the project and the buyers of the subsequent credits. While the Colombian cases do not explicitly raise climate-washing arguments in the claim, they broaden our understanding of climate-washing and its interaction with private law, exposing the procedural and distributive justice dimensions of misleading carbon neutrality claims. The cases challenge

57 *Instituto Brasileiro de Defesa do Consumidor (IDEC) v Gol Linhas Aéreas S/A* [2025] Interpelação Judicial 1007633-65.2025.8.26.0100.

58 *Instituto Brasileiro de Defesa do Consumidor (IDEC) v Localiza Rent A CAR S/A* [2025] 1007605-97.2025.8.26.0100.

59 *Pirá Paraná* Indigenous Council and Association of Indigenous Traditional Authorities of river *Pirá Paraná* 'ACAIPI' v Ministry of Environment and Sustainable Development and others [2024] T-9.312.858.

60 Members of Indigenous community 'Gran Cumbal' v SVP Business SAS, Global Consulting and Assessment Services SA, Deutsche Certification Body SAS, COLCX and the Indigenous authority of 'Gran Cumbal' [2023] 2023000095-00.

whether private mechanisms used for developing carbon credit projects ensure a fair climate solution.[61] The Colombian cases directly question the suitability of civil law contracts (known as "mandate contracts" in Colombian law) to transact collective lands of Indigenous peoples. This allows us to examine how contractual obligations and due diligence standards currently intersect with broader public law frameworks, including human rights law.

In both cases, the Constitutional Court found that the projects have impacts on the social, spiritual, and economic lives of Indigenous peoples. The Court established that the projects located on collective lands cannot be developed and implemented without FPIC. In the *Pirá Paraná* case, the Court went further and established that mandate contracts between companies and representatives of Indigenous people do not replace their duty to consult the Indigenous peoples as a collective group. According to the Court, the companies did not apply due diligence standards to respect Indigenous self-government structures, as they were not direct owners of the project and received no remuneration.[62] The Court stated that private law instruments cannot be automatically transferred to ethnic communities and highlighted "the inadequacy of private law instruments to deal with collective rights".[63] The companies failed to adjust legal instruments to the national and international human rights standards.[64] Thus, the Court labelled the lack of an ethnic approach as an "unconstitutional practice". In reaching its decision, the Court recognised the difficulties in determining the ownership of such projects and a lack of state control over the voluntary carbon market and the practices of external actors who participate.[65]

We have limited our analysis in this chapter to known climate litigation in the Sabin Center's Global database as of the end of 2024. However, the legal issues discussed are relevant to many more cases involving carbon credits. Colombia, as an example alone, shows how these cases are likely representative of a wider systemic practice of excluding vulnerable communities from the carbon market. The Colombian Ministry of Environment intervened in the *Pira Paraná* case, opining that their monitoring system reported complaints against half of the carbon projects reviewed by 2022 (75 out of 103 REDD+ projects registered in the National Registry of Greenhouse Emissions Reduction). Most complaints allege a lack of clear information regarding the projects, deficient decision-making processes, and the absence of FPIC for the projects.[66] In 2023, the World Wide Fund for Nature mapped eighty-six REDD+ projects in the Amazon and Pacific regions of Colombia located in collective lands of Indigenous or Black communities.[67]

[61] For further discussion on the effectiveness of carbon offset projects, see Alejandro Guizar-Coutiño and others, 'A Global Evaluation of the Effectiveness of Voluntary REDD+ Projects at Reducing Deforestation and Degradation in the Moist Tropics' (2022) 36 Conservation Biology; Thales AP West and others, 'Overstated Carbon Emission Reductions from Voluntary REDD+ Projects in the Brazilian Amazon' (2020) 117 Proceedings of the National Academy of Sciences.

[62] *Pirá Paraná Indigenous Council and Association of Indigenous Traditional Authorities of river Pirá Paraná 'ACAIPI' v Ministry of Environment and Sustainable Development* [313].

[63] ibid [297].

[64] ibid [274].

[65] ibid [276].

[66] ibid [93].

[67] World Wide Fund For Nature, 'Acuerdos REDD+ justos y equitativos. Una guía para la Amazonía y el Pacífico' (*World Wide Fund For Nature*, 2024) <https://wwflac.awsassets.panda.org/downloads/guia-acuerdos-redd-.pdfhttps://wwflac.awsassets.panda.org/downloads/guia-acuerdos-redd-.pdf> accessed 12 June 2025, 39.

5. Key Implications

In this section, we explore how these three cases contribute to our understanding of the impact and effectiveness of climate-washing litigation in strengthening corporate accountability. We argue that in framing localised violations of human rights using the language and form familiar from climate-washing litigation, claimants can strategically draw the attention of corporate actors, who associate such practices with reputational and financial risk. This framing opens opportunities to target buyers of credits. Second, these cases challenge the dichotomous view between public human rights duties and private actors' responsibilities. In doing so, it strengthens the argument for a "mediation approach" to corporate human rights due diligence, where public and private law remain distinctive empirical fields but are shaped and constructed by each other.[68] We conclude by outlining how this approach may inform future regulation.

5.1 Climate-Washing as a Strategic Framing

The comparative analysis showed how climate-washing arguments were used in *AMOREMA*, but either unintentionally or deliberately avoided, in the Colombian cases, despite building in similar grievances. An important role of frames in litigation is resonance with the targets of mobilisation.[69] Framing choices is a deliberate way of giving meaning to social problems, while assessing the opportunities that using specific frames may create.[70] In the *AMOREMA* case, the strategic use of climate-washing arguments is illustrated by their target defendant choices—multinational companies that buy credits for offsetting emissions along the value chain.

The increased attention from regulators and financial actors around greenwashing might have encouraged *AMOREMA* claimants to use such frames.[71] In Europe, for instance, recognising the growing threat of greenwashing practices, regulatory bodies have started to implement measures to curb misleading environmental claims that rely on carbon offsets. A key example is the European Union's proposed Green Claims Directive, which aims to protect consumers by requiring companies to substantiate their sustainability claims through independent verification. A critical aspect of the Directive is the distinction between emissions reductions achieved through internal company actions versus those offset via carbon credit schemes, bringing much-needed clarity to the term "carbon neutral". Although the Directive has faced political resistance, and many EU member states have supported a scaled-back version that allows companies to conduct internal assessments rather than requiring independent verification, the evolving regulatory discussion has resulted in increased awareness among corporate actors of potential legal risks. A study of twenty European banks found that banks perceive greenwashing litigation, compared to other types of climate litigation, as a top

68 Janne Mende, 'Corporate Human Rights Responsibilities: Rethinking the Public–Private Divide' (2023) 41 Nordic Journal of Human Rights 255.

69 David A Snow and Robert D Benford, 'Ideology, Frame Resonance, and Participant Mobilization' (1988) International Social Movement Research 197.

70 Lasse Lindekilde, 'Discourse and Frame Analysis: In-Depth Analysis of Qualitative Data in Social Movement Research' in Donatella della Porta (ed), *Methodological Practices in Social Movement Research* (OUP 2014).

71 Network for Greening the Financial System (n 37).

concern from a reputational and operational risk perspective.[72] Given that climate-washing arguments might, at present, be more resonant with private actors, bringing this frame into Global South cases can also work instrumentally as a channel to expose human rights violations in carbon credit projects.

Climate-washing framing is also the link that allows litigants to connect the human rights violations to how the credits are being used to meet carbon neutrality claims, challenging the fundamental value chain of credits. According to the Latin American Center for Investigative Journalism and *Mongabay Latam*, after the *Gran Cumbal* project was suspended by the court, Chevron, one of the oil companies that purchased the credits, still exchanged close to 289,000 credits from this project, stating that it was notified too late by the supplier and the credits "mistakenly ended up being part of the offsetting for said period".[73] Tracing the human rights violations to the offsetting purpose may have facilitated litigants to better illustrate how exclusion of Indigenous communities' rights in private contracts can manifest in further violations of consumers' rights elsewhere.

Adding this framing may strengthen litigation's role as a form of "climate consumer collective action" (as defined by Orts in Chapter 5 of this handbook). At present, credits are governed by private contracts between developers, intermediaries, buyers, and others, as well as domestic laws (if there are specific laws in the project jurisdiction concerning the nature of carbon credits). However, credits are traded across national borders and often further commodified into other financial products, forming the basis for other contracts. This legal framework institutionalises information gaps between the creation of the "good" (the carbon credit) and consumers, placing both communities and the climate itself at risk. In highlighting the "washing" element, litigation challenges the opacity in these processes and starkly illustrates the uniqueness, challenges, and urgency of regulating carbon credit supply chains. However, as both the *AMOREMA* and Colombian cases illustrate, private law alone may not be sufficient to protect collective rights. We turn to this question of the public and private law divide below.

5.2 Challenging the Public–Private Divide

Although none of these cases rely explicitly on norms from business and human rights law to bring their claims, the arguments raised nevertheless shed new light on what scholars have referred to as the "double movement" of the private and public in the development of the concept of corporate due diligence and corporate responsibility more broadly.[74] This refers to the privatisation of the transnational governance of human rights, coupled with the subjection of private corporations to new "requirements of publicness"—requirements regarding public participation and transparency to strengthen accountability.[75]

The three cases highlight the limitations of a strict dichotomous approach that relies on corporate voluntarism and self-regulation.[76] They strengthen the case for a "mediation approach"

[72] Agnieszka Smoleńska and others, 'Banks and Climate Litigation Risk: Navigating the Low-Carbon Transition' (June 2025) <https://cetex.org/publications/banks-and-climate-litigation-risk-navigating-the-low-carbon-transition/> accessed 12 June 2025.

[73] Andrés Bermúdez Liévano, 'In Colombia, Chevron Has a Habit of Buying Carbon Credits from Projects Made Behind Indigenous People's Backs' (Latin American Center for Investigative Journalism and Mongabay Latam, 14 May 2025) <https://drilled.media/news/CLIP-Chevron> accessed 12 June 2025.

[74] Antoine Duval, 'Ruggie's Double Movement: Assembling the Private and the Public Through Human Rights due Diligence' (2023) 41 Nordic Journal of Human Rights 279.

[75] ibid.

[76] Mende (n 68).

in the voluntary carbon market, where public regulation and corporate obligations each "(re) produce[] and (in)form[] the scope, logic, and content of the other in such a pervasive way that each is part of the other".[77]

In addition to raising the obligations of suppliers directly engaged in the production and marketing of carbon credits, *AMOREMA* illustrates the legal and conceptual tensions in how carbon credit projects are governed. Although framed by the claimants as an environmental and community rights issue, the Brazilian Federal Court ultimately dismissed the case on the grounds that it involved a private contractual dispute over carbon credit revenues, not a matter of environmental harm or collective interest. The judge explicitly found that the claimants' claims, though presented as a public interest action, concerned purely patrimonial rights stemming from concession contracts with the State and were thus inappropriate for public civil action. This outcome highlights the limitations of relying on private law instruments alone to resolve disputes involving environmental and community rights. It also exposes the difficulty of fitting such cases into conventional legal categories, reinforcing the need for a mediation approach where private and public norms are not treated as separate but mutually constitutive.

The Colombian cases equally illustrate the tension between private and public law, highlighting that private contracts alone may not suffice to protect the interests of the parties directly involved. Going further than the Brazilian court, the Colombian Constitutional Court suspended the project and ruled that "mandate contracts" as a legal instrument fail to address the collective rights of communities. It expressly states that the companies failed to adjust their legal instruments to international and national human rights standards. Having a private law instrument between companies and representatives of Indigenous people did not replace the parties' duty to consult the community as a collective group.

These cases also highlight the limitations of applying existing legal due diligence standards, applicable to transactions of "conventional" goods and services, to carbon credits. Buyer due diligence is a familiar concept to companies in acquisitions of any asset. As a risk mitigation measure, it is part of a balancing exercise by the buyer: What level of due diligence is required to protect shareholders' interests? Having assessed potential risks, the buyer may exercise its commercial leverage and renegotiate contractual terms to account for potential losses. This approach, which relies on companies as voluntary enforcers of human rights in the absence of clear rules and guidance, is particularly problematic in the voluntary carbon market. Consumers and civil society face significant information barriers. There is a lack of transparency on where the credits were bought, what standard of due diligence was conducted on the project, and how credits are then used to make a carbon neutrality claim. Relying on social mobilisation to ensure that communities' rights are protected in or around carbon credit projects is a tall order.

In the Global North context, governmental efforts to address low-integrity carbon credits through climate-washing legislation have been divorced from human rights arguments, representing a missed opportunity for effective action. As Section 2 explained, litigation has emerged as a gap-filler, challenging the lack of transparency creatively through consumer protection litigation. By focusing on the representation of a carbon neutrality claim, claimants can, in parallel, raise underlying doubts about the integrity of carbon credit projects. It is critical not to overlook the possibility of bringing similar but adapted climate-washing cases before Global South courts, which strongly integrate the human rights and justice dimensions of these climate neutrality claims and expand in-court outcomes to suspension of illegitimate projects. The impact of coupling consumer protection climate-washing cases with

[77] ibid [262].

justice-oriented cases can expand how we assess the effectiveness of climate-washing litigation overall.

5.3 Policy Implications Under a Mediation Approach

The cases discussed in this chapter demonstrate the power of litigation in bringing deceptive practices to light. However, litigation alone has limitations—it is often reactive rather than preventive, expensive, and dependent on individual lawsuits to challenge each misleading claim or low-integrity project. While legal actions can set important precedents, they do not provide the systemic oversight needed to ensure corporate climate claims are consistently reliable and verifiable. Carbon market regulation should complement private causes of action to prevent climate-washing at scale.

In voluntary carbon markets, there have been some efforts by states to strengthen oversight and accountability. In Latin America, for example, enforcement actions such as Operation Greenwashing in Brazil illustrate the potential of stringent regulatory oversight. Brazil has also moved towards regulating carbon markets, though concerns remain over gaps in enforcement and exclusions for key polluting sectors such as livestock and agriculture. In Colombia, Decree 1369 of 2014 addresses climate-washing on the consumer end, mandating that all socio-environmental advertising must be truthful, transparent, and verifiable. In the *Pira Paraná* case, the Constitutional Court also ordered the Ministry of Environment to create a protocol that clarifies the requirements for the development of projects in Indigenous peoples and local communities' territories.

Regulatory guidance or binding legislation of this nature can embody a mediation approach and help address both communities' rights and the concerns of private actors along the carbon credit supply chain who are conducting due diligence processes on the integrity of their credits. Private entities involved in carbon credit projects often rely to varying extents on disclosures from host and buyer governments who have signed separate carbon credit agreements under Article 6 of the Paris Agreement. This web of contracts, made between a mix of private and public actors, urgently requires shared and enforceable legal standards on integrity. These standards need to be systematically integrated into the transboundary carbon market supply chain, requiring careful consideration of how statutory third-party rights interact with the common law principle of privity of contract.

Recognising that enforcement actions rely on well-resourced and impartial public actors to identify and address harms associated with poor-integrity carbon credit projects, private litigation by directly affected communities is likely to remain an important tool for holding companies accountable. Without strong regulatory frameworks which also envision a role for private claims, bad faith actors can continue to exploit loopholes, undermining consumer trust and delaying meaningful climate action. Private causes of action, interpreted in line with human rights law, are an important avenue for ensuring that communities have agency in addressing injustices they face.

6. Conclusion

The growing body of climate-washing litigation signals an evolving legal landscape in which companies are increasingly scrutinised for their role in the transition. While much of this litigation has concentrated in the Global North, emerging cases in the Global South demonstrate how arguments related to corporate misrepresentation can challenge the legitimacy of carbon credit projects and their corresponding climate neutrality claims. The three cases analysed expose critical governance gaps in voluntary carbon markets and highlight the intersection of private law, human rights frameworks, and climate justice.

The *AMOREMA* case sheds light on how traditional communities are excluded from decision-making processes, while their identities and conservation efforts are commodified for corporate gain. It also illustrates a key challenge to the dichotomous view between public and private law: The court dismissed the claim, reasoning that it concerned a private contractual dispute rather than environmental harm or a matter of public interest. This outcome underscores the limitations of current legal frameworks and the need to develop regulatory and judicial approaches that better mediate between public and private law in addressing the complex realities of carbon offset projects. Similarly, the Colombian cases expose structural barriers that Indigenous peoples face in asserting control over carbon projects on their lands. The impact of climate-washing litigation extends beyond deterring misleading disclosures and consumer fraud: Cases can challenge the governance, equity, and legitimacy of carbon credit schemes in the regions where they are implemented.

This analysis underscores that climate-washing litigation has potential to be more than a tool for regulating corporate marketing strategies: It can be a mechanism for holding corporations accountable for their role in perpetuating climate injustices. The emergence of climate-washing litigation in the Global South points to the need for transnational legal approaches that recognise the interconnectedness of carbon credit supply chains. As courts increasingly engage with the complexities of climate-related misrepresentations, new legal standards may emerge, setting precedents for corporate responsibility beyond traditional consumer protection frameworks. However, litigation alone is not a substitute for systemic reforms. Ensuring fair and equitable participation of communities will require a combination of legal challenges, regulatory oversight, and inclusive governance mechanisms that counter power asymmetries and prioritise the voices of those most affected.

CHAPTER 12

Unjust Enrichment

MAYTAL GILBOA, YOTAM KAPLAN, AND ROEE SAREL

1. Introduction

CLIMATE litigation in the private law sphere is typically grounded in tort law principles, aiming to establish responsibility for the harm caused by greenhouse gas (GHG) emissions. Scholars and courts increasingly emphasise the limitations of such an approach.[1] First, climate harm is difficult to quantify and prove in court.[2] Second, climate harm is difficult to attribute to specific GHG emitters. As everyone is an emitter, it is nearly impossible to determine which parts of the harm result from the activity of which actors.[3] Third, routine activities contributing to GHG emissions are often difficult to conceptualise as torts or wrongs.

The doctrine of unjust enrichment can supplement tort law as a normative basis for climate litigation and may help avoid some of these hurdles.[4] In particular, a claim in unjust enrichment does not necessarily require proof of harm, a causal link between the harm and the defendant's activity, nor any wrongdoing by the defendant. Rather, the focus of the doctrine of unjust enrichment is on the benefit the defendant has unjustly obtained at the expense of the plaintiff.[5] Thus, unjust enrichment claims can help plaintiffs reorient their strategy: Shift away

[1] Douglas A Kysar, 'What Climate Change Can Do About Tort Law' (2011) 41 Environmental Law 1, 4 ('tort law is unlikely to play a substantial role in the ultimate effort to reduce greenhouse gas emissions'); Tiantian Zhai, 'Double-Faceted Environmental Civil Liability and the Separate-Regulatory Paradigm' (2022) 14 Sustainability 1, 12 ('when the tort system is unequipped or ill-suited to provide a remedy for environmental damage, courts and legislators should understand and respect its limits instead of stubbornly relying on it').

[2] Benjamin Ewing and Douglas A Kysar, 'Prods and Pleas: Limited Government in an Era of Unlimited Harm' (2011) 121 Yale Law Journal 350, 369 ('If the paradigmatic tort is one in which A hits B - a clear, direct, and unlawful action by one actor against another that gives rise to an isolated, retrospective harm - then climate change lies conspicuously far outside the paradigm . . . in many contexts, climate change plaintiffs will want to seek recovery for a present risk of future harm. The circumstances under which courts permit such recovery, however, are quite limited').

[3] Maxine Burkett, 'Litigating Climate Change Adaptation: Theory, Practice and Corrective (Climate) Justice' (2012) 42 Environmental Law Reporter News & Analysis 11144, 11147 ('meeting each element of the tort of negligence-duty, breach, cause, and damages-would be a difficult task for any plaintiff, with establishing the causal link between a defendant's emissions and the alleged harms as the most challenging'); David A Dana, 'The Mismatch Between Public Nuisance Law and Global Warming' (2010) 10 Supreme Court Economic Review 9, 12 ('There is language in a Restatement comment suggesting an unusually broad conception of joint and several liability in the context of environmental public nuisance, but that is slim authority on which to set aside the enormous problems of allocating causal responsibility for global warming').

[4] Maytal Gilboa, Yotam Kaplan, and Roee Sarel 'Climate Change as Unjust Enrichment' (2024) 112 The Georgetwon Law Journal 1039.

[5] See, e.g., Restatement (Third) of Restitution and Unjust Enrichment (American Law Institute 2010) s 1 (Restatement UE) ('A person who is unjustly enriched at the expense of another is subject to liability

from the harmful side of the climate crisis, namely GHG emissions, and focus on its profitable side—fossil fuel extraction. Thus, while nearly everyone is a GHG emitter, the number of significant extractors is small. In fact, a handful of companies are directly responsible for the majority of fossil fuel extraction activities. While these firms are not significant GHG emitters themselves, they play a central role in shaping the current energy market and are profiting immensely from delaying the transition to clean energy.

Naturally, climate litigation based on unjust enrichment law would involve its own challenges, including the need to show that the defendant's enrichment is unjust, and that it comes at the expense of the plaintiff. In this chapter, we develop an argument for establishing the unjust nature of the profits obtained by major fossil fuel extractors, even when the extraction activity in question does not constitute a wrong or a tort. This argument is based on the fact that major fossil fuel extractors deplete the public resource of climate stability while enriching themselves at the expense of the public.

The chapter proceeds as follows. Section 1 explains the need to explore additional normative frameworks to supplement tort law as a conceptual basis for climate litigation. Section 2 delineates the doctrinal framework of liability in unjust enrichment as a basis for climate litigation against major fossil fuel extractors. Section 3 reviews the potential advantages of applying unjust enrichment in this context.

2. The Challenge of Tort-Based Climate Litigation

Tort law is commonly described as either the law of wrongs,[6] for its focus on the defendant's wrongful conduct, or the law of losses, referring to its harm-based approach, aiming to compensate victims for the injuries they suffer.[7] A third central element of any tort claim is that of causation, requiring a claimant to prove a connection between the defendant's alleged wrongdoing and the plaintiff's loss.[8] These three elements are the focal points of tort-based claims

in restitution'). See also Ward Farnsworth, *Restitution: Civil Liability for Unjust Enrichment* (University of Chicago Press 2014) 1–2; Douglas Laycock, 'Scope and Significance of Restitution' (1988) 67 Texas Law Review 1277, 1278. Peter Birks included the availability of a defence as the fourth question in an unjust enrichment claim alongside the elements of enrichment, unjustness, and attainment at the claimant's expense; Peter Birks, *Unjust Enrichment* (2nd ed, OUP 2005) 10.

[6] John C P Goldberg and Benjamin C Zipursky, 'Torts as Wrongs' (2009) 88 Texas Law Review 917; Scott Hershovitz, 'Treating Wrongs as Wrongs: An Expressive Argument for Tort Law' (2018) 10 Journal of Tort Law 405.

[7] The focus on harm is also dominant in the economic analysis of tort law, in which the first aspiration is to minimise the cost of harm and the cost of its prevention. See, e.g., Yotam Kaplan, 'Economic Theory of Tort Law', in Hanoch Dagan and Benjamin C Zipursky (eds), *Research Handbook on Private Law Theory* (Edward Elgar Publishing 2020); Roee Sarel, 'Restraining ChatGPT' (2023) 75 UC Law Journal 115, 136.

[8] See, e.g., Restatement (Third) of Torts: Liability for Physical and Emotional Harm (American Law Institute 2010) s 26 (Restatement Torts), stating that conduct 'is a factual cause of harm when the harm would not have occurred absent the conduct'. Under prevailing tort law, establishing legal liability requires a finding of both factual and proximate causation. While factual causation is viewed as a question of fact—typically determined by the 'but-for' test—proximate causation is considered a matter of legal policy, which limits the defendant's liability for the harm caused. See also Mark Geistfeld and Sandy Steel, Chapter 8 of this handbook.

and the key animating concepts of tort-based litigation. The unique setting of climate litigation poses significant challenges for these core doctrinal concepts.[9]

The harm related to climate change is immense and widespread. Importantly, this harm is universal, generally affecting the entire global population. Temperature changes and sea level rise affect all life on the planet and change the environment in fundamental ways. These deep changes increase the probability of local and regional disasters and extreme weather events in the form of heat waves, forest fires, hurricanes, and droughts.[10] These changes detrimentally affect the habitability of some environments and are harmful to biodiversity. While these are all immense harms, they are difficult to quantify and translate into monetary terms. Much of the harm associated with the climate crisis is future harm, which is difficult to predict accurately. The difficulty in quantifying the harms of the climate crisis, and the abstract nature of this harm, present a significant challenge for tort-based climate litigation.[11] Harm is a core element of any tort claim, and the tort remedy of damages requires the description and measuring of a specific harm.

Tort-based causes of action relevant to climate litigation typically also require some form of wrongful conduct.[12] Such conduct may include gross negligence, violation of existing environmental regulations, or any other conduct that constitutes a "substantial and unreasonable interference with public rights".[13] The requirements of a wrong can be a significant limitation of tort-based actions in the context of climate litigation. The reason for this is that high levels of GHG emissions are not necessarily associated with wrongs, as currently defined under tort law principles. At the same time, any activity that heavily relies on fossil fuels, even when fully compliant with current laws, contributes to global warming and to the climate crisis. The focus on the defendant's wrongful conduct may therefore render many forms of climate related harms unclaimable under a tort-based legal framework.

Lastly, a tort-based claim requires a causal link between the defendant's conduct and the plaintiff's harm.[14] Proof of causation is often a challenge in tort claims.[15] In the context of climate litigation, proof of causation is a particularly daunting task. Global warming is not the outcome of any specific action but is the cumulative result of actions taken over decades by an

[9] For a thorough review of these challenges, see Kysar (n 1).

[10] For a detailed overview of various climate harms, see Gilboa, Kaplan, and Sarel (n 4) 1047–53.

[11] ibid 1049.

[12] On common law and civil law torts, respectively, see David Bullock, Chapter 7, and Elbert de Jong, Chapter 9 of this handbook.

[13] *American Electric Power Co v Connecticut* 564 US 410, 418 (2011).

[14] This is the standard in the United States and other common law countries. See, e.g., Restatement Torts, s 26 ('Tortious conduct must be a factual cause of harm for liability to be imposed'); *Nyang v G4S Care & Justice Services Ltd* [2013] EWHC 3946 (QB); *Snell v Farrell* [1990] 2 SCR 311, para 27; Erik S Knutsen, 'Clarifying Causation in Tort' (2010) 33 Dalhousie Law Journal 153, 156.

[15] See, e.g., Richard W Wright, 'Causation in Tort Law' (1985) 73 California Law Review 1735, 1775 (discussing scenarios familiarly known as overdetermination, whereby two or more defendants act wrongfully and each action alone is sufficient to cause the plaintiff's injury (therefore, none of the defendants' actions can be singled out as the but-for cause of the harm), and proposing the NESS test as a solution); Maytal Gilboa, 'Multiple Reasonable Behaviors Cases: The Problem of Causal Underdetermination in Tort Law' (2019) 25 Legal Theory 77 (examining cases of underdetermination, where the but-for test yields conflicting outcomes—in one scenario, the defendant's negligence is identified as the but-for cause of the plaintiff's injury, while in another, it is not—and proposing a solution based on aggregation of counterfactuals enabling the court to resolve the problem within the framework of a but-for test).

immense number of entities.[16] The number of emitters whose activities directly release GHGs into the atmosphere is vast. Emitters include energy manufacturers such as power plants, varied industries, public transportation, and also private car owners and energy users, among others. Virtually everyone is a GHG emitter. It is, therefore, incredibly difficult to assign liability for harm to any specific actor or to any specific action or decision in this context. The difficulty in linking harm to wrongful conduct means that tort-based climate litigation is always an uphill battle.

These challenges lead scholars to propose reforms, waive some doctrinal requirements, or otherwise simplify the use of tort law as a basis for climate litigation.[17] Below, we explore the possibility of using the law of unjust enrichment as a doctrinal foundation for climate litigation and as a supplement to tort-based litigation.

3. Unjust Enrichment and Climate Litigation

Climate litigation tends to focus on harm, either explicitly utilising tort claims or relying on tort-style logic. This section suggests that climate litigation may benefit from using unjust enrichment as a supplemental normative framework, which introduces a focus on gains rather than losses. We briefly describe the basic concepts animating a claim in unjust enrichment and then demonstrate their applicability to climate litigation.

3.1 Unjust Enrichment: Doctrine and Principles

A claim based on unjust enrichment generally consists of three basic elements: (1) enrichment by the defendant, (2) this enrichment was obtained at the plaintiff's expense, and (3) this enrichment can be described as unjust.[18] The definition of enrichment is broad and encompasses any form of benefit to the defendant, including money, saved expenses, valuable service, or any improvement or increase in their assets. Enrichment must be "at the expense of the plaintiff" in the sense that it corresponds to the plaintiff's loss,[19] or to the violation of the plaintiff's right.[20]

Additionally, to establish liability, the plaintiff must show that the defendant's enrichment is "unjust".[21] Thus, the fact that the defendant was enriched at the expense of the plaintiff does

[16] Gilboa, Kaplan, and Sarel (n 4) 1043.

[17] Kysar (n 1) 44–71.

[18] Restatement UE, s 1.

[19] The notion that the element of 'at the claimant's expense' generally expresses a transfer of value from the defendant to the plaintiff has been noted by Lord Reed in *Investment Trust Companies (in liquidation) v Revenue and Customs Commissioners* [2017] UKSC 29, [2018] AC 275, 342–43. Some scholars articulate an attribution rule based on a counterfactual relationship between the defendant's enrichment and the plaintiff's loss, testing whether the defendant could gain without the plaintiff losing. See, e.g., Eli Ball, *Enrichment at the Claimant's Expense: Attribution Rules in Unjust Enrichment* (Hart, 2016). For a review of the 'at the claimant's expense' element and related quandaries, see, e.g., Graham Virgo, *The Principles of the Law of Restitution* (4th edn, OUP 2024) 120–35.

[20] Daniel Friedmann, 'Restitution of Benefits Obtained Through the Appropriation of Property or the Commission of a Wrong' (1980) 80 Columbia Law Review 504, 548–49, 551. For a proposed causal analysis of the but-for text in this paradigm of cases, see Maytal Gilboa, 'Linking Gains to Wrongs' (2022) 35 Canadian Journal of Law & Jurisprudence 365; Maytal Gilboa, 'Substitute Victims' (2025) 66 Boston College Law Review 97 at 838–40.

[21] Restatement UE, s 1.

not, in itself, justify liability; rather, liability is available only if the defendant's enrichment either lacks juristic reason or is normatively flawed.[22] The requirement for the injustice of the defendant's enrichment is considered the normative core of the law of unjust enrichment and a key mechanism separating meritorious from unmeritorious claims. The nature of this element has been vigorously debated among scholars. Some commentators seek a unifying concept of "unjust" enrichment, which will help distinguish this area of law from other private law fields.[23] Others argue that no such unitary framework exists and that a variety of normative concepts is required in order to explain why the defendant's enrichment is "unjust" in different categories of cases.[24]

One of the controversial issues within this debate concerns the relation between two core categories of gain-based recovery: wrongful enrichment, and unjust enrichment absent a wrong. In the first category, the injustice of the defendant's enrichment is easy to explain, as this enrichment results from wrongful conduct. This category closely follows moral intuition, according to which a wrongdoer should not benefit from their own wrong.[25] This category includes, for example, enrichment obtained by the defendant through copyright infringement,[26] opportunistic breach of contract,[27] or a crime.[28] In the context of climate litigation, this category of cases may include scenarios where polluters violate existing environmental regulations or deceive regulators.[29] In such cases, the resulting profits may be subject to disgorgement.

[22] Below we further elaborate on those two paradigms of gain-based claims, typically viewed as distinct. See n 25–33 and accompanying text.

[23] See, e.g., Ernest J Weinrib, 'Correctively Unjust Enrichment' in Robert Chambers, Charles Mitchel, and James Penner (eds), *Philosophical Foundations of the Law of Unjust Enrichment* (OUP 2009) (providing a theoretical account of unjust enrichment as corrective justice); Maytal Gilboa and Yotam Kaplan, 'The Other Hand Formula' (2022) 26 Lewis & Clark Law Review 883, 892 (proposing 'a simple mathematical criterion explaining the requirement for the injustice of the defendant's gain').

[24] Emily Sherwin, 'Reparations and Unjust Enrichment' (2004) 84 Boston University Law Review 1443, 1452 ('Most of the established grounds for restitution against defendants who are not wrongdoers can be explained by reading the term 'unjust enrichment' to mean enrichment that lacks legal justification, without reference to injustice in a purely moral sense'). See also Robert Stevens, 'The Unjust Enrichment Disaster' (2018) 134 Law Quarterly Review 574, 576 ('The reasons why the courts have held a defendant's enrichment to be unjust vary from one set of cases to another'), as well as his recent book where he develops this view and offers a distinction between the causes of action which give rise to restitution (Robert Stevens, *The Laws of Restitution* (OUP 2023)).

[25] See, e.g., Restatement UE, s 3 ('A person is not permitted to profit by his own wrong').

[26] See generally Pamela Samuelson, John M Golden and Mark P Gergen, 'Recalibrating the Disgorgement Remedy in Intellectual Property Cases' (2020) 100 Boston University Law Review 1999.

[27] See Restatement UE, s 39 ('(1) If a deliberate breach of contract results in profit to the defaulting promisor and the available damage remedy affords inadequate protection to the promisee's contractual entitlement, the promise has a claim to restitution of the profit realized by the promisor as a result of the breach. . . . (2) A case in which damages afford inadequate protection to the promisee's contractual entitlement is ordinarily one in which damages will not permit the promisee to acquire a full equivalent to the promised performance in a substitute transaction. (3) Breach of contract is profitable when it results in gains to the defendant . . . greater than the defendant would have realized from performance of the contract').

[28] A paradigmatic example of such a case is *Riggs v Palmer* 22 NE 188 (NY 1889), where a grandson poisoned his grandfather to inherit the bulk of his estate. Although state law allowed him to inherit, the New York Court of Appeals ruled this constituted unjust enrichment and awarded the inheritance to the grandfather's two aunts to prevent the grandson from benefiting from his crime.

[29] Gilboa, Kaplan, and Sarel (n 4) 1075; Vanessa Cassado-Pérez, and others, 'Climate Lies & Unjust Profits' (2026, forthcoming) Emory Law Journal.

The second core category involves cases where the defendant's enrichment is unjust, despite not being wrongful. These cases include a range of circumstances in which defendants did not commit a wrong but nevertheless obtained a benefit to which they were not entitled. A core example of such form of liability is where a defendant is liable to make restitution of a sum of money transferred to them by mistake.[30] Another example is when a patient received emergency medical treatment while unconscious.[31] A defendant might also be considered unjustly enriched if they derived benefits from a valid court decision—such as a preliminary injunction preventing the plaintiff from commercial activity[32]—that was later reversed.[33] In all these examples, liability does not derive from the defendant's wrongful conduct. Even absent a clearly identifiable wrong, the defendant's enrichment can still be considered unjust. We suggest that liability in unjust enrichment in such cases follows a "property-style" rather than a "tort-style" logic. The defendant's enrichment is "unjust" either because it does not belong to them or because the plaintiff has a superior claim to it. We further develop this point below in applying this theory of liability to the context of climate litigation.

Scholars disagree as to whether these two broad categories of gain-based recovery belong under a united category of "Unjust Enrichment", or whether the category of "wrongful enrichment" is to be considered a subcategory of tort law.[34] For the purposes of the current discussion, we take no position in this ongoing debate. Instead, we find it sufficient to clarify that the aforementioned doctrinal categories function as established grounds of liability, irrespective of the precise nature of their interrelationship or the possibility of integrating them into a unified framework.

3.2 Climate Unjust Enrichment

Contemporary climate litigation tends to focus on the harms associated with climate change. Indeed, the continued use of fossil fuels causes irreversible harm to the global climate system. At the same time, the fossil fuel industry is also extremely profitable.[35] Importantly, this fact

[30] See, e.g, Restatement UE s 57; Andrew Burrows, 'Restitution of Mistaken Enrichments' (2012) 92 Boston University Law Review 767, 767; Birks (n 5) 3.

[31] *Cotnam v Wisdom* 104 SW 164 (Ark 1907) (famously holding that the act of physicians providing medical services to unconscious patients can constitute unjust enrichment).

[32] See *Dass v Tosco Corp 280* F Appx 571, 571 (9th Cir 2008) (affirming the district court's summary judgment, and awarding Tosco Corporation damages in the amount that it could have reasonably made had it not been compelled otherwise by an erroneous injunction that was later revoked).

[33] See, e.g., Laycock (n 5) 1284 (noting that a defendant may be unjustly enriched even without having committed a civil wrong 'by compliance with a judicial order later modified'); see also Ofer Grosskopf and Barak Medina, 'Remedies for Wrongfully-Issued Preliminary Injunctions: The Case for Disgorgement of Profits' (2009) 32 Seattle University Law Review 903, 912.

[34] A different taxonomy used to frame these two approaches of unjust enrichment titles a law of unjust enrichment that includes wrongful enrichment as 'big unjust enrichment', and a law of unjust enrichment that does not include incidents of wrongdoing but rather focuses on the reversal of unjustified transfers between parties as 'small unjust enrichment'. See Lionel Smith, 'Restitution: A New Start?' in Peter Devonshire and Rohan Havelock (eds), *The Impact of Equity and Restitution in Commerce* (Hart 2018) 88–92.

[35] Stanley Reed, 'Oil Companies Ponder Climate Change, but Profits Still Rule' *New York Times* (7 October 2019) >https://www.nytimes.com/2019/10/07/business/energy-environment/oil-companies-climate-change-profits.html> accessed 10 March 2025; Thomas Princen, Jack P Manno, and Pamela Martin, 'Keep Them in the Ground: Ending the Fossil Fuel Era' in Worldwatch Institute (ed), *State of the World 2013* (Island Press/Center for Resource Economics 2013) 161, 163–64 <http://link.springer.com/10.5822/978-1-61091-458-1_14> accessed 10 March 2025 (evaluating the immense profits of the petroleum industry).

explains the perpetuation of the crisis; if the extraction of fossil fuel was not so profitable in the short term, these energy sources would have likely been replaced by cleaner alternatives a long time ago. The high profitability of fossil fuel commerce also explains the regulatory inability to contend with the climate crisis. Regulators are struggling to enforce climate policies on giant multinational corporations, and the political system seems unable to resist the persistent lobbying efforts by these firms,[36] supported through profits that far exceed the budgets of the regulating agencies.

When these firms' commercial activities involve wrongdoing, such as violation of environmental regulations, gross negligence, or deception of regulators, it is easier to identify the firms' enrichment as unjust and subject to disgorgement. However, we argue that the profits of oil giants might constitute unjust enrichment even absent wrongdoing. This mode of liability becomes easier to understand once we view liability in unjust enrichment as following a property-like logic rather than a tort-style form of analysis.

Since antiquity, legal systems have recognised natural resources such as water and breathable air as belonging to the public dominion, or as having some aspect of public ownership.[37] The same holds for resources like air quality,[38] atmospheric balance, and climate stability.[39] These are commons that belong to all people, and not to any group in particular.[40] Even if rights in such assets are not fully delineated, some legal norms do exist in relation to the use and enjoyment of these resources.[41] The common property of climate stability and sustainable environments provides the basic conditions necessary for any other type of activity and

[36] Fossil fuels firms invest heavily in lobbying, and even more so as the climate risk increases (Viktoriya Lantushenko and Carolin Schellhorn, 'The Rising Risks of Fossil Fuel Lobbying' (2023) 56 Global Finance Journal 100829. Fossil industry lobbying factored heavily in failing, delaying, or weakening different federal climate regulations over the years. One prominent example is the failure of the US Senate to take up federal climate legislation after a comprehensive cap on emissions passed the House of Representatives in 2009. See Peter C Frumhoff, Richard Heede, and Naomi Oreskes, 'The Climate Responsibilities of Industrial Carbon Producers' (2015) 132 Climatic Change 157, 162.

[37] The recognition of water and air as commons traces back to Roman law, see The institutes of Justinian s 2.1.1 (533) (Thomas Collet Sanders trans. 1st Am. ed. 1876) ('By the law of nature these things are common to mankind—the air, running water, the sea, and consequently the shores of the sea'). For a general overview of the definition of *res commons* and the law governing it in the roman Justinian code, see Thomas Collett Sandars, *Institutes of Justinian* (1917).

[38] Larry E Erickson and Gary Brase, 'Air Quality as a Common Resource' in Larry E Erickson and Gary Brase (eds), *Reducing Greenhouse Gas Emissions and Improving Air Quality* (CRC Press 2019) 135–48.

[39] See, e.g., Mary Christina Wood and Charles W Woodward, 'Atmospheric Trust Litigation and the Constitutional Right to a Healthy Climate System: Judicial Recognition at Last' (2016) 6 Washington Journal of Environmental Law & Policy 634, 645, 674 (addressing judicial acknowledgement of public trust in the atmosphere and the right to a stable climate system). For the argument that property law should adjust to the anomaly of intertemporal externalities and the problems of overconsumption and overuse by current property holders to protect the rights of future generations, see generally, Yael R Lifshitz, Maytal Gilboa, and Yotam Kaplan, 'The Future of Property' (2023) 44 Cardozo Law Review 1443.

[40] For a general overview of the atmosphere as a global commons, see, e.g., Marvin S Soroos, 'Managing the Atmosphere as a Global Commons' (Fifth Annual Common Property Conference, International Association for the Study of Common Property, Bodo, Norway 1995) <https://dlc.dlib.indiana.edu/dlcrest/api/core/bitstreams/7740f0fa-b416-4a01-a39f-205dda2b1292/content> accessed 4 June 2025.

[41] See, e.g., David Hunter, James Salzman, and Durwood Zaelke, *International Environmental Law and Policy* (5th edn, Foundation Press 2015) 644, 664–65, 901–05 (providing an overviewing of judicial decisions recognising public interest in natural resources including the air and the atmosphere).

thereby underwrite all other rights. These resources are necessary for engaging in any form of life and activity. All people, therefore, have a valid legal interest in them.

The status of these resources as public property carries special meaning for the law of unjust enrichment. In particular, these are resources in which all members of the public have a valid interest. This fact has two important implications for climate litigation and for liability based on unjust enrichment. First, if companies engaged in the extraction of fossil fuels take from this common resource, it would be difficult to define this taking as wrongful enrichment absent some clear violation of a specific legal standard. After all, major extractors, like other members of the public, have a legitimate interest in the common good. Second, if major extractors deplete the resource completely or over-consume it, their enrichment, even if not strictly wrongful, can be construed as unjust. This is so for the same reason that their enrichment is not wrongful: because *all* members of the public have a right to the common resource. Thus, extractors have a right, in principle, to use common resources, and are not wrongdoers; at the same time, when major extractors take from the common resources in such a way that leaves nothing for others, their extraction activity is unjust enrichment because it contradicts others' right to join in benefiting from the common good.

This analysis applies the notion of a corresponding loss, that is, the connection between the defendant's gain and the plaintiff's loss,[42] to the context of climate litigation. This notion is central for establishing liability in unjust enrichment in core categories such as mistaken payments. In such cases, it is easy to show that a sum of money was transferred from the payer to the unintended recipient. In the context of climate litigation, this element is more complex. Instead of pointing out a specific factual relation between a particular defendant and a particular plaintiff, the corresponding loss is based here on the notion that major extractors' profitable use of a shared common resource results in its depletion, and therefore a loss to others.

We argue that this type of enrichment can be considered unjust even if—absent full delineation of rights in the common resource to specific stakeholders—it is difficult to establish a claim akin to a wrongful taking. The example of water sources and water use can illustrate this dynamic. If a water source such as a river or a well is used by the public, all members of the public who have an interest in the resource are considered interest holders or potential beneficiaries. However, if one group decides to pump the well dry and deplete the public resource to its own benefit, this may constitute unjust enrichment at the expense of the public. In the context of climate stability, the resource of carbon pools functions in a similar way. The notion of carbon pools represents the capacity of Earth systems, particularly the atmosphere, to store carbon, thereby regulating temperature changes.[43] Carbon pools are an atmospheric commons belonging to the public, serving as a shared resource essential to maintaining climate stability.[44] The atmospheric carbon pool is a limited resource in terms of its available atmospheric space—there is only so much carbon the atmosphere can hold without destabilising the climate system.[45] This limit is defined and quantified by the concept of the carbon budget.

42 See n 19.

43 Besides the atmosphere, the main carbon pools include oceans, forests, and soils, which compromise the global carbon cycle, see Energy Education, 'Carbon Pool' <https://energyeducation.ca/encyclopedia/Carbon_pool> accessed 22 February 2025.

44 For an overview of different conceptions of the atmospheric commons, see, e.g., Bruce Lankford, 'The Atmospheric Carbon Commons' in Steffen Böhm and Sian Sullivan (eds), *Negotiating Climate Change in Crisis* (Open Book Publishers 2021).

45 This idea was acknowledged more than a decade ago by the chief climate change advisor for the oil giant Shell, see David Hon, 'The Carbon Bubble Reality Check' (3 May 2013) Shell Climate Change <https://blogs.shell.com/2013/05/03/bubble/> accessed 10 March 2025 (explaining the concept that 'there

The problem, represented by the climate crisis, is that this finite storage space is being depleted through the use of fossil fuels.[46]

Current levels of fossil fuel extraction by oil and gas giants already exhaust the carbon budget required to limit temperature changes to levels considered safe to sustain current levels of habitability.[47] If carbon budgets represent a goal to limit emissions to levels equivalent to a maximum increase of 1.5–2 degrees celcius warming,[48] this entails the overall scope of the carbon pool resource available to the *public as a whole*. Equally important, carbon pools are not depleted by the public as a whole; rather, the main beneficiaries of this process are a very small number of firms, global leaders of the fossil fuel industry.[49] This process constitutes unjust enrichment, to the degree it can be shown that a small group of actors is profiting by depleting the public resource of climate stability.

Importantly, such an argument need not assume that the public never benefited from the use of fossil fuels. Of course, the use of fossil fuels entails both costs and benefits to the public. Yet, as scientific consensus on the existence of a climate crisis reflects, for the general public, the continued reliance on fossil fuels is more harmful than it is beneficial. In terms of its net effect, continued extraction activity is most likely not in the interest of the public. Conversely, for fossil fuel giants, continued extraction activity remains net beneficial, and immensely profitable. This is because the harm of the crisis is spread across the population as a whole, but the profits are distributed unevenly.[50] Thus, while the public bears the costs of climate change, the industry obtains immense profits and therefore retains a strong incentive to maintain social dependence on fossil fuels.

Note that concepts like carbon budgets and carbon caps, which limit the level of emissions to maintain climate stability, are not necessarily binding legal norms,[51] and are usually not directly enforced on fossil corporations.[52] Furthermore, when these norms are binding,

is a finite limit to the "atmospheric space" for CO_2 while still ensuring that warming does not rise above 2 °C').

[46] For a scientific explanation of the role of fossil fuels in over-exploitation of the atmospheric carbon pool, see Rattan Lal, 'Sequestration of Atmospheric CO_2 in Global Carbon Pools' (2008)1 Energy & Environmental Science 86.

[47] Studies show that current fossil extractions will inevitably involve the breach of the 1.5 degrees carbon budget, see for example Kelly Trout and others, 'Existing Fossil Fuel Extraction Would Warm the World Beyond 1.5 °C' [2022] 17 Environmental Research Letters, 064010. https://doi.org/10.1088/1748-9326/ac6228. See also Dan Welsby and others, 'Unextractable Fossil Fuels in a 1.5 °C World' (2021) 597 Nature 230.

[48] Current studies show that assuming business as usual, the carbon budget for limiting temperature increase to 1.5 degrees is expected to be exhausted by 2029, see Robin D Lamboll and others, 'Assessing the Size and Uncertainty of Remaining Carbon Budgets' (2023) 13 Nature Climate Change 1360.

[49] According to a recent analysis, 57 actors, almost all of them fossil fuel extractors, are linked to 80% of global emissions since 2015. See Influence Map, 'The Carbon Majors Database: Launch Report 3,4 Carbon Majors (CM)' (2024) <https://carbonmajors.org/briefing/The-Carbon-Majors-Database-26913> accessed 10 March 2025.

[50] For a general formula articulating this idea of disproportionality in terms of unjust climate enrichment, see Gilboa, Kaplan, and Sarel (n 4) 1081.

[51] While countries such as the UK, Germany, and The Netherlands have set a legally binding national carbon budget through climate legislation, it applies to the government, rather than directly to the entities which extract fossil fuels or emit carbon to the atmosphere. See, e.g., UK Parliament, 'What Are Carbon Budgets?' (4 February 2025) <https://commonslibrary.parliament.uk/what-are-carbon-budgets/ > accessed 10 March 2025.

[52] This gap can be demonstrated, for example, by the climate litigation in the Netherlands: While the Hague Court of Appeal ruled that the Dutch government is obliged to a concrete emission reduction

they typically expressly limit only the level of emissions and not the level of extraction.[53] For these reasons, when major extractors extract amounts that exceed the goals represented by carbon budgets, it is difficult to conceptualise their conduct as a basis for a *wrongful* enrichment claim. Yet, in their extraction activity, extractors deplete the public resource, resulting in its corresponding scarcity for other stakeholders. Therefore, the extractors' profits might still be considered unjust.[54]

This type of claim seems plausible as a basis for climate litigation. The global energy market is currently dominated by a small number of giant fossil-fuel corporations, including ExxonMobil, Shell, Chevron, BP, and ConocoPhillips. Currently, twenty-five of these corporations are extracting 60% of global oil and gas production,[55] which entails exploiting 90% of the remaining carbon budget.[56] Current extraction levels represent a depletion of the public resource of the carbon pool and completely exhaust the available carbon emission allowance required to sustain climate stability. Thus, current levels of extraction already exhaust the global carbon budget required to keep global warming below 1.5–2 degrees Celsius.

At the same time, profits for major fossil fuel extractors are immense,[57] putting them at the forefront of global economic powerhouses.[58] Top extractors register profits in the trillions,

target in the *Urgenda* case, it refused at least at present to acknowledge a similar obligation applying to the Oil giant Shell in the subsequent *Milieudefensie* case. Compare: Sabin Center for Climate Change Law, 'Urgenda Foundation v. State of the Netherlands' (2015) Climate Change Litigation Databases <https://climatecasechart.com/non-us-case/urgenda-foundation-v-kingdom-of-the-netherlands/> accessed 10 March 2025, and Sabin Center for Climate Change Law, 'Milieudefensie et al. v. Royal Dutch Shell plc'. (2019) Climate Change Litigation Databases <https://climatecasechart.com/non-us-case/milieudefensie-et-al-v-royal-dutch-shell-plc/> accessed 10 March 2025.

[53] Pietro Andreoni and others, 'Fossil Extraction Bans and Carbon Taxes: Assessing Their Interplay Through Multiple Models' (2023) 26 Science 1 (explaining the problems in current climate policies that do not limit extraction levels, but rather tackle the emissions created further down the supply chain). See also Philippe Le Billon and Berit Kristoffersen, 'Just Cuts for Fossil Fuels? Supply-side Carbon Constraints and Energy Transition' (2019) 52 Environment and Planning A: Economy and Space 1072.

[54] Planned fossil fuel extraction is twice as big as the extraction levels which are consistent with a 1.5 degrees carbon budget, see United Nations Environment Program (UNEP), Production Gap Report 2023 (4th edn, 2023) <https://productiongap.org/wp-content/uploads/2023/11/PGR2023_web_rev.pdf> accessed 10 March 2025.

[55] Nick Ferris, 'Exclusive: How Just 25 Oil Companies Are Set to Blow the World's 1.5°C Carbon Budget' (26 January 2023) Energy Monitor <https://www.energymonitor.ai/sectors/industry/exclusive-how-just-25-oil-companies-are-set-to-blow-the-worlds-1-5c-carbon-budget/?cf-view> accessed 10 March 2025 ('[T]he 25 companies that extracted the most oil and gas in 2021 . . . collectively represented around 60% of global oil and gas production . . . extracting oil and gas from more than 3,700 fields around the world, with a further 300 planned in the immediate future. These fields collectively contain 500 billion barrels of oil and around 2,300 trillion cubic feet of gas').

[56] ibid ('The sum of these emissions (340 billion tons of CO2) represents 90% of the world's entire remaining carbon budget for 1.5°C, which is the volume of carbon emissions scientists estimate we can still emit and avoid the most devastating, irreversible impacts of climate change').

[57] Princen, Manno, and Pamela Martin (n 35) 161, 163–64 ('[T]he petroleum industry is the world's largest, capitalized at $2.3 trillion and accounting for 14.2 percent of all commodity trade. What's more, it is by far the most capital-intensive industry—$3.2 million is invested for every person employed . . . And the petroleum industry is among the most profitable').

[58] Frumhoff, Heede, and Oreskes (n 36) 167 ('[T]he major investor-owned fossil energy producer companies . . . have not only invested in, but sought to guarantee, a future that serves the interests of their shareholders, employees, and executives, but threatens the health, well-being and prosperity of virtually everyone else').

achieving record levels in recent years.[59] These high levels of profitability also explain the willingness of oil and gas corporations to invest heavily in lobbying efforts designed to prevent meaningful climate regulation that might limit extraction levels. In the three years following the Paris Agreement, carbon majors ExxonMobil, Shell, Chevron, BP, and Total collectively spent over $1 billion globally on deceptive climate lobbying and branding efforts designed to protect and expand fossil fuel production.[60] In 2023, the oil and gas industry invested over $133 million on climate lobbying in the US alone; US$3 billion was spent between 1998 and 2023.[61] In 2022, the profits of five leading fossil fuel companies exceeded the US Environmental Protection Agency's annual budget by a factor of twenty, and were five times greater than the yearly climate funding provided by the Inflation Reduction Act.[62] Due to its incredible profitability for a small group of companies, the extraction of fossil fuels is projected to increase at least until 2050.[63]

This dynamic not only explains the structural economic reasons for the climate crisis but also shows why a claim in unjust enrichment might be plausible. A select few are exhausting the public resource of climate stability and making immense profits by depleting the common resources reflected in sustainable carbon budgets and the finite capacity of carbon pools to store emissions.

4. Unjust Enrichment in Climate Litigation: Advantages and Challenges

While tort-based climate litigation has achieved some success, it stands to reason that developing additional strategies is warranted. Introducing unjust enrichment as a supplementary legal mechanism may significantly enhance the effectiveness of climate litigation overall. Focusing on gains rather than harms, the law of unjust enrichment can address a critical element of the climate crisis. It can directly target the incentives of fossil fuel industry leaders to excessively engage in extraction activities for immense profit.

[59] Sam Meredith, 'Big Oil Rakes in Record Profit Haul of Nearly $200 Billion, Fueling Calls for Higher Taxes' (8 February 2023) CNBC <https://www.cnbc.com/2023/02/08/big-oil-rakes-in-record-annual-profit-fueling-calls-for-higher-taxes.html> accessed 10 March 2025 (reporting the upswing profits of the west's Five Big Oil companies, as fossil fuel prices soared following Russia's invasion of Ukraine); Oliver Milman, '"Monster Profits" for Energy Giants Reveal a Self-destructive Fossil Fuel Resurgence' (9 February 2023) Guardian <https://www.theguardian.com/environment/2023/feb/09/profits-energy-fossil-fuel-resurgence-climate-crisis-shell-exxon-bp-chevron-totalenergies> accessed 10 March 2025 ('While 2022 inflicted hardship upon many people around the world due to soaring inflation, climate-driven disasters and war, the year was lucrative on an unprecedented scale for the fossil fuel industry, with the five largest western oil and gas companies alone making a combined $200bn in profits').

[60] InfluenceMap, 'Big Oil's Real Agenda on Climate Change 2019' (March 2019) <https://influencemap.org/report/How-Big-Oil-Continues-to-Oppose-the-Paris-Agreement-38212275958aa21196dae3b76220bddc> accessed 10 March 2025 ('[I]n the three years following the Paris Agreement, the five largest publicly traded oil and gas majors (ExxonMobil, Royal Dutch Shell, Chevron, BP, and Total) have invested over $1Bn of shareholder funds on misleading climate-related branding and lobbying. These efforts are overwhelmingly in conflict with the goals of this landmark global climate accord and designed to maintain the social and legal license to operate and expand fossil fuel operations').

[61] Open Secrets, 'Industry Profile: Oil & Gas' <https://www.opensecrets.org/federal-lobbying/industries/summary?id=E01> accessed 10 March 2025.

[62] Milman (n 59).

[63] United Nations Environment Program (UNEP), 'Production Gap Report 2023' (4th edn, 2023) <https://productiongap.org/wp-content/uploads/2023/11/PGR2023_web_rev.pdf> accessed 10 March 2025

Harm-based climate litigation is always an uphill battle because of the elusive nature of proving particular climate harms. One of the key advantages of an unjust enrichment cause of action in the context of climate litigation lies in its potential ability to circumvent some of the significant evidentiary burdens associated with proof of harm required in tort claims. Harm resulting from GHG emissions largely consists of non-monetary future harm, spread across whole populations.[64] Such harm is difficult to identify and quantify. More importantly, the exact measure of such harm is even more difficult to prove in court due to its diffusion across both space and time. The difficulty in proving the full scope of harm in court leads to a clear risk of under-compensation in harm-based climate litigation. Many claims might be rejected as plaintiffs are unable to prove their harm; in other cases, compensation will be too low compared to the actual (and yet impossible to preponderantly prove) scope of harm. Considering the high profitability of the fossil fuel industry, this outcome can lead to a problem of severe underdeterrence of key fossil fuel extractors. Extraction remains profitable to oil and gas giants simply because their profits are so incredibly high, and the full cost of their harmful activity is not captured under the framework of tort-based litigation.

Gain-based litigation can help mitigate these concerns. The gains of oil industry leaders are present monetary gains, concentrated in the hands of a small number of firms. Though the exercise of proving and measuring these gains may not always prove trivial, it seems to be typically much easier compared to the difficulty of proving and measuring the scope of long-term widespread environmental harm, which is not directly manifested in monetary sums. Unlike harm, which must be translated into monetary terms, the gains obtained by extractors are already monetary in nature. Restitutionary recovery is, therefore, straightforward and less reliant on speculative or uncertain calculations.[65] More specifically, to distinguish extractors' legitimate gains from their unjust profits, courts can utilise the notion of carbon budgets. Thus, any gain obtained through extraction activity that necessarily overwhelms national or global carbon budgets may be considered unjust enrichment. Conversely, profits obtained from extraction levels under the carbon budget would be considered legitimate. Importantly, measuring recovery based on the gains of oil giants carries clear advantages in terms of inducing deterrence. Once fossil fuel extraction ceases to be so highly profitable for a select few, it is more likely that a transition away from these energy sources will finally become feasible.

Another possible advantage of gain-based climate litigation relates to the causal chain behind the process of global warming. The harm of the climate crisis includes phenomena such as extreme heat waves,[66] increases in infectious diseases,[67] droughts,[68] tropical

[64] See Gilboa, Kaplan, and Sarel (n 4).

[65] Gilboa, 'Linking Gains to Wrongs' (n 20) 367 ('[W]hereas in [tort] cases focusing on the plaintiff's harm, the but-for result must ultimately be translated into monetary terms to determine the recovery amount, in gain-based damages cases, the but-for result reflects both the difference that the defendant's wrongfulness has made and the sum of recovery').

[66] Susana Clusella-Trullas, 'The Point of No Return for Species Facing Heatwaves' (2022) 611 Nature 39, 39); Jian Cheng and others, 'Cardiorespiratory Effects of Heatwaves: A Systematic Review and Meta-Analysis of Global Epidemiological Evidence' (2019) 177 Environmental Research 1 (finding a significant association between heatwaves and cardiovascular and respiratory morbidities); Zhiwei Xu and others, 'Impact of Heatwave on Mortality under Different Heatwave Definitions: A Systematic Review and Meta-analysis' (2016) 89 Environmental International 193, 193.

[67] See, e.g., IPCC, 'Climate Change 2022: Impacts, Adaptation and Vulnerability: Summary for Policymakers' (2022), 9–11 <https://report.ipcc.ch/ar6/wg2/IPCC_AR6_WGII_FullReport.pdf> accessed 10 March 2025; Daune J Gubler and others, 'Climate Variability and Change in the United States: Potential Impacts on Vector and Rodent-borne Diseases' (2001) 109 Environmental Health Perspectives 223, 223–31.

[68] IPCC, Impacts (n 67) 18 (noting the connection between increasing heat and drought); US Environmental Protection Agency (EPA), 'Climate Change Indicators: Weather and Climate' <https://

storms,[69] floods,[70] and fires.[71] Such disasters cause loss of life, injuries, health risks, and the destruction of infrastructure.[72] These harms are the result of broader climate changes, mainly the rise in temperature and changes in sea level.[73] Those global changes, in turn, are caused by GHG emissions of an incredibly large number of emitters. Finally, the activity of emitters is made possible by, and is therefore the outcome of extraction activity. This means that extractors and extraction activity are very difficult to link to climate harm. Extraction activity is several steps removed from ultimate climate harm, with many intervening actors operating in between extraction and harm. Extractors, therefore, find it easy to argue that the causal link between their activity and climate harm, and therefore also their responsibility for harm, is significantly interrupted by the intervening actions and choices of emitters.

While proving causation along this chain might be possible,[74] it proves extremely difficult within the traditional framework of tort litigation. This harm-based analysis seems more suitable for establishing the liability of emitters rather than extractors. Thus, along the causal chain described above, emitters are much closer to actual harm compared to extractors, who appear further away from the harm on the causal chain. This is problematic since the number of emitters, as opposed to extractors, is immense. If emitters are responsible for the harms associated with the climate crisis, this outcome is near-meaningless in the legal sense, as everyone is an emitter to some extent. The task of distinguishing between emitters in terms of responsibility for the climate crisis is fraught with conceptual and practical hurdles, and the large number of emitters entails great difficulties in attributing specific harms to specific emitters in terms of the but-for test of causation.[75]

It is therefore important to find legal mechanisms that would allow litigation efforts to focus on extractors rather than emitters. The number of key extractors (as opposed to emitters) is

www.epa.gov/climate-indicators/weather-climate> accessed 4 June 2025 (describing the connection between changes in temperature and vulnerability to drought).

[69] Joshua Studholme and others, 'Poleward Expansion of Tropical Cyclone Latitudes in Warming Climates' (2022) 15 Nature Geoscience (describing the connection between greenhouse gas emissions and tropical cyclones, which pose 'profound risks to the planet's most populous regions'); Tom Matthews, Robert Wilby, and Conor Murphy, 'An Emerging Tropical Cyclone-Deadly Heat Compound Hazard' (2019) 9 Nature Climate Change 602, 603 (describing the threat of more common tropical cyclones).

[70] IPCC, 'The Physical Science Basis: Chapter 11: Weather and Climate Extreme Events in a Changing Climate' (2021) 1518 <https://www.ipcc.ch/report/ar6/wg1/downloads/report/IPCC_AR6_WGI_SPM.pdf> accessed 10 March 2025 ('The projected increase in the intensity of extreme precipitation translates to an increase in the frequency and magnitude of pluvial floods').

[71] Gensuo Jia and others, 'Land–Climate Interactions', *Climate Change and Land: An IPCC Special Report on Climate Change, Desertification, Land Degradation, Sustainable Land Management, Food Security, and Greenhouse Gas Fluxes in Terrestrial Ecosystems* (P R Shukla and others eds., 2019) 133 ('future climate variability expected to enhance the risk and severity of wildfires').

[72] Press Release, IPCC, 'Climate Change: A Threat to Human Wellbeing and Health of the Planet, Taking Action Now Can Secure Our Future' (28 February 2022), <https://www.ipcc.ch/site/assets/uploads/2022/02/PR_WGII_AR6_english.pdf> accessed 10 March 2025) ('To avoid mounting loss of life, biodiversity and infrastructure, ambitious, accelerated action is required to adapt to climate change, at the same time as making rapid, deep cuts in greenhouse gas emissions').

[73] Scott A Kulp and Benjamin H Strauss, 'New Elevation Data Triple Estimates of Global Vulnerability to Sea-level Rise and Coastal Flooding' (2019) 10 Nature Communications 1, 2.

[74] See, e.g., Christopher W Callahan and Justin S Mankin, 'Carbon Majors and the Scientific Case for Climate Liability' (2025) 640 *Nature* 893.

[75] See n 16.

small, and their influence over long-term processes in the energy market is great.[76] For these reasons, they are far more appropriate candidates to be defendants in climate litigation. In a tort-style, harm-based legal framework, establishing the responsibility of extractors might be possible, but it is extremely challenging evidentially and conceptually. Extractors are further away on the causal chain from the harm compared to emitters and are not significant emitters themselves. A key advantage of a gain-based approach to climate litigation is that it can more naturally focus on extractors rather than emitters. Extractors are the profit centre in the energy market and immensely benefit from extraction activity that involves the complete depletion of public resources.

Of course, climate litigation based on unjust enrichment is not a panacea, and would require plaintiffs to convince courts that defendants are enriched at their expense and that this unjust enrichment can be measured and distinguished from defendants' legitimate profits.[77] Despite such challenges, unjust enrichment law is a useful addition to the litigation toolkit, and can offer significant advantages as a supplement to the existing tort-based framework. The basic concepts presented here would have to be further developed by courts on a case-by-case basis, depending on the specifics of the evidence presented before the court. While there is no guarantee that courts will accept such claims, potential advantages over tort-based litigation are apparent. These pertain mainly to the ability to shift the focus more easily from emitters to extractors, and to the relative ease of proving monetary gains as opposed to abstract, non-monetary losses.

5. Conclusion

This chapter explored the potential of the law of unjust enrichment to complement existing tort-based approaches in climate litigation. While tort law continues to play a vital role in addressing climate-related harm, its inherent limitations—particularly regarding proof of harm, causation, and wrongdoing—suggest the need for additional legal tools. Unjust enrichment offers several distinct advantages that make it a promising addition to the existing climate litigation toolbox.

The fundamental insight driving this analysis is that the climate crisis is not merely a story of harm, but also one of concentrated profit. A small number of fossil fuel corporations have achieved unprecedented levels of profitability through activities that deplete the public resource of climate stability. This depletion occurs via the exhaustion of carbon pools—a common resource that, like water or air, belongs to the public. In this chapter, we suggest that the fact that these corporations derive immense profits from depleting this shared resource can provide the foundation for unjust enrichment claims, even in cases where traditional tort-based wrongdoing is difficult to establish.

The practical advantages of this approach are significant. First, by focusing on gain rather than harm, unjust enrichment claims can potentially circumvent some of the evidentiary challenges that plague tort-based climate litigation. While climate harm is often future-oriented, difficult to quantify, and spread across populations, the profits of fossil fuel corporations are present, monetary, and concentrated. This shift in focus from speculative future damages to concrete present gains not only simplifies the measurement of recovery but also potentially enhances the deterrent effect of climate litigation.

[76] Cassado-Pérez et al (n 29).

[77] Gilboa, Kaplan, and Sarel (n 4) 1081–94.

Second, unjust enrichment doctrine naturally directs attention towards extractors rather than emitters. This is crucial because while the number of significant emitters is too large to make litigation against them practically meaningful, the number of major extractors is small and their market power is substantial. By targeting these key players, unjust enrichment claims can potentially address the structural economic incentives that drive the climate crisis.

More broadly, the analysis in this chapter highlights the importance of developing legal tools that can effectively target the economic structures driving environmental degradation. The immense profitability of fossil fuel extraction has created powerful incentives against the transition to cleaner energy sources and enabled industry leaders to resist meaningful regulation through extensive lobbying efforts. By providing a mechanism to directly address gains from fossil fuel extraction, unjust enrichment law might help alter the underlying incentive structure that perpetuates the climate crisis.

CHAPTER 13

Fiduciary Law

SETH DAVIS AND GREGORY SHAFFER

1. Introduction

ONE remarkable fact about climate change is how disproportionately a few agents contribute to causing it. In 2023, Oxfam reported on global "carbon billionaires"—125 of them—each of whom "are responsible for emitting an average of 3 million carbon tons each year".[1] Their responsibility is bound up with that of legal persons: corporations and states. Between 1988 and 2017, a mere twenty-five firms were ultimately responsible for over 50% of global industrial emissions.[2] In 2023, more than half of humankind's CO_2 emissions from fossil fuels and cement could be traced to thirty-six corporations. The five largest emitters were state-owned enterprises (SOEs) from just four states: Saudi Arabia, India, China, and Iran. The five largest privately-owned emitters were incorporated in just three states: the United States, the United Kingdom, and France.[3] These firms enjoy the benefits of states' corporate laws, state subsidies, and policies that support fossil fuel use.[4] Thus, human beings have created what we might call "superagents" that are wasting our most important resource, the climate that sustains our lives on our only home.[5] If only there were a legal tool to change the operating instructions of these superagents to make them responsible stewards of the Earth's climate.

Climate activists, attorneys, and international organisations have looked to fiduciary law to incorporate the climate into the mandates of corporations and states. Their efforts, we argue, are about (re)coding "the code of capital". As the legal scholar Katharina Pistor has defined it, capital is an asset plus its legal coding.[6] Land, debt, and even persons have been coded as assets by the law of capital at various times in history. Today, corporate lawyers spend many billable

[1] Oxfam, 'Who Is Responsible for Climate Change?' (3 December 2023) <https://perma.cc/KX8V-F2ZT> accessed 29 June 2025.

[2] Tess Riley, 'Just 100 Companies Responsible for 71% of Global Emissions, Study Says' *The Guardian* (10 July 2017) <https://perma.cc/KPD6-FHKJ>.

[3] CarbonMajors, '2023 Data Update' (March 2025) <https://perma.cc/UEU3-8LJE> accessed 29 June 2025. See also Damian Carrington, 'Half of World's CO_2 Emissions Come from 36 Fossil Fuel Firms, Study Shows' *The Guardian* (5 March 2025) <https://perma.cc/2J6P-HKXN>.

[4] The member states of the EU and 19 other nation-states were responsible for more than 80% of annual carbon emissions in 2022. Laura Paddison and Annette Choi, 'As Climate Chaos Accelerates, Which Countries are Polluting the Most?' *CNN* (2 January 2024) <https://perma.cc/LYD5-S4KS>. Historically, 23 rich, developed countries are responsible for half of emissions. Nadja Popovich and Brad Plumer, 'Who Has the Most Historical Responsibility for Climate Change?' *New York Times* (12 November 2021) <https://perma.cc/RDW9-4UTJ>.

[5] On corporations and states as 'superagents', see David Runciman, *The Handover: How We Gave Control of Our Lives to Corporations, States and AIs* (W. W. Norton 2023).

[6] Katharina Pistor, The Code of Capital: How Law Creates Wealth and Inequality (Princeton University Press 2019) 2.

hours working to minimise legal regulation while maintaining the "endorsement by state law" of an asset's status as capital.[7] Paradigmatic fiduciary relationships include those between trustees and their beneficiaries and between corporate managers and shareholders. Trust law, Pistor writes, is an "ingenious module[] for coding capital".[8] It provides a tool for the wealthy to shield capital from creditors, including private creditors and tax authorities. Corporate law, which includes the fiduciary duties of directors and officers, provides a code for the management of corporate assets.[9]

The idea of recoding capital is that corporate managers owe fiduciary duties that require (or at least permit) them to consider climate risks, and that state actors, as public trustees, are required to protect the atmosphere for current and future generations. These duties would apply to directors of business corporations (including, but not limited, to energy companies); institutional investors, such as pension funds and asset managers (including Vanguard, State Street, and BlackRock, or the "Big Three"); and nation-state and sub-state governments as well as SOEs. Within the US, critics have attacked this fiduciary approach and linked it to "cultural Marxism" as part of a backlash against Environmental, Social, and Governance (ESG) investing. But the turn to fiduciary law is not radical. Rather, it works within the code of capital even as it has pitted different elites within capitalist economies against one another (such as asset managers versus fossil fuel firms in the US).

In this chapter, we aim to understand contests over the fiduciary code of capital and climate change. Drawing upon the theory of transnational legal ordering (TLO),[10] we focus upon the recursive development of fiduciary norms, charting the interplay between efforts to make climate stewardship a settled fiduciary norm and corporate and state efforts to thwart such a normative settlement. We explain why fiduciary law, which crosses the boundary between private law and public law, is a promising source of norms to constrain corporate managers and state actors. The challenge for proponents is to trigger positive interactions between private law, public law, and international law to embed climate concerns in fiduciary law transnationally. Opponents try to use fiduciary law for the opposite end, exploiting indeterminacy and ideological contradictions to launch a legal attack backed with populist rhetoric about the legitimacy of the courts, institutional investors, and international organisations associated with the fiduciary response to climate change. Thus, there are formidable barriers to creating a TLO that encodes within capital an obligation to account for climate change. To illustrate these points, we contrast developments in the EU, where a TLO involving fiduciary law may be emerging, with those in the US, where political backlash has stalled—and may even reverse—the use of fiduciary law to address climate change.

2. Four Features of Fiduciary Law

Climate activists, attorneys, investors, and international organisations have framed corporate and state responsibility for climate change in fiduciary terms. If corporate directors and officers, institutional investors, and state governments are fiduciaries, and if climate impacts and risks are encompassed within their fiduciary mandates, then they abuse the authority entrusted to them by ignoring climate change and its effects. Four features of fiduciary law make

[7] ibid 210–11.

[8] ibid 42.

[9] ibid 48.

[10] Terence C Halliday and Gregory Shaffer, 'Transnational Legal Orders' in Terence C Halliday and Gregory Shaffer (eds), *Transnational Legal Orders* (CUP 2015) 3.

it uniquely promising as a source of norms to encode climate concerns into the management of capital.

2.1 A Common Code for Capital Across Common and Civil Law Jurisdictions

To begin, fiduciary law is part of the code of capital that states provide across jurisdictions, and it thus can be used to advance climate change mitigation goals globally. The quintessential fiduciary duty is the duty of loyalty. Fiduciaries must act on behalf of their beneficiaries, however those beneficiaries are defined. This means that fiduciaries violate their duty of loyalty when they pursue their own interests or the interests of a third party rather than their beneficiaries' interests. In addition, fiduciary mandates may be oriented to purposes, in which case fiduciaries must faithfully pursue those purposes and not others. Fiduciaries owe duties of care when working to fulfil their mandates.

Both common law and civil law jurisdictions have fiduciary norms and institutions, which helps make cross-jurisdictional convergence possible. In 2019, Principles for Responsible Investment (PRI) and the United Nations Environment Programme (UNEP) issued *Fiduciary Duty in the 21st Century*, which began with functional comparisons between common law and civil law jurisdictions' treatment of fiduciary duties.[11] In common law countries, "fiduciary duties are the key framework governing the discretion of investment decision makers".[12] In civil law jurisdictions (such as Brazil, China, the EU, France, Germany, and Japan), the codes specify fiduciary obligations that are functionally equivalent to the common law duties of loyalty and care.[13] The German Civil Code, for instance, provides for the mandate contract (*Auftrag*), which is "the foundation for the development of a functional equivalent to fiduciary duties in the common law world".[14] These include an investment decision-maker's "[d]uty to act conscientiously in the interests of beneficiaries", and not in their own interest—in other words, the duty of loyalty.[15]

2.2 Fiduciary Mandates

The second promising feature of fiduciary law is its manner of regulating the behaviour of corporate officers, institutional investors, and other fiduciaries. Fiduciary law's architecture is built around fiduciary mandates. The fiduciary's mandate defines the fiduciary's office, scope of authority, and responsibilities. This is why, for instance, lawyers have labelled the public trust doctrine the "law's DNA"—it is, in other words, a code that constitutes the existence, authority, and responsibility of states.[16]

[11] United Nations Environment Programme Finance Initiative, 'Fiduciary Duty in the Twenty-First Century: Final Report' (October 2019) <https://perma.cc/6N4R-SFCJ> accessed 29 June 2025.

[12] ibid 11.

[13] ibid.

[14] Thilo Kuntz, 'Transnational Fiduciary Law: Spaces and Elements' in Seth Davis, Thilo Kuntz, and Gregory Shaffer (eds), *Transnational Fiduciary Law* (CUP 2023) 37, 49.

[15] United Nations Environment Programme Finance Initiative (n 11) 11.

[16] Gerald Torres and Nathan Bellinger, 'The Public Trust: The Law's DNA' (2014) 4 Wake Forest Journal of Law & Policy 281, 283.

All fiduciaries have mandates that are constitutive of the fiduciary's authority. Fiduciaries have legal powers to be exercised for an "other-regarding mission".[17] Within common law countries, "[i]t is a fundamental principle of equity that a fiduciary power may be exercised only for a purpose for which the power has been conferred".[18] As Lionel Smith has pointed out, this is a general principle of fiduciary law present in civil law jurisdictions too.[19]

Fiduciary powers and fiduciary liabilities, at bottom, are defined by the fiduciary's mandate to serve either persons or purposes. Fiduciary service mandates, as defined by Paul Miller and Andrew Gold, constitute a legal relationship in which the fiduciary has authority to act on behalf of specific persons, the beneficiaries.[20] In a private donative trust, for example, trustees have a mandate to manage the trust property on behalf of a specified class of persons, the trust beneficiaries.[21] Fiduciary governance mandates, by contrast, constitute a legal relationship in which the fiduciary has authority to act in pursuit of specified purposes, rather than specific persons.[22] The public trust doctrine is an example; as a public trustee, the state has the authority, as well as a duty, to steward public resources for the public interest. In the climate context, at the international level, principle 3 of the Rio Declaration of 1992 provides that governments must account for not only the living but also for future generations.[23] This obligation has been a central reference for youth activists in lawsuits against governments around the world for their failure to take climate action.[24]

Fiduciary law, then, provides a vehicle for incorporating climate concerns into the "other-regarding mission" of corporations and states. Corporate directors and officers owe fiduciary duties of loyalty and care to the company and (at least) its shareholders. Those duties may encompass consideration of climate risks at least (but not necessarily limited to) when those risks are relevant to shareholder value.[25] Corporate directors have a duty to disclose climate risks to the business. And they have a duty of oversight with respect to the corporation's compliance with law, including climate-related legal rules.[26] Pension funds and asset managers also have

[17] Lionel Smith, 'The Cough Drops of Loyalty' in Evan Fox-Decent, John CP Goldberg, and Lionel Smith (eds), *Understanding Private Law: Essays in Honour of Stephen A Smith* (Bloomsbury 2025) 289, 295.

[18] Grand View Private Trust Co. v Wong (No 2) [2022] UKPA 47 [1]. See also Smith (n 17) 294–95 (explaining, in Hohfeldian terms, that this principle 'relates to the exercise of a legal power, and the remedy is that the exercise of the power is liable to be set aside').

[19] Smith (n 17) 295.

[20] Paul Miller and Andrew S. Gold, 'Fiduciary Governance' (2015) 57 William & Mary Law Review 513, 519.

[21] ibid 522.

[22] ibid 523–24.

[23] UN Conference on Environment and Development, *Rio Declaration on Environment and Development*, UN Doc. A/CONF.151/26/Rev.1 (Vol. I), annex I (Aug. 12, 1992) ('The right to development must be fulfilled so as to equitably meet developmental and environmental needs of present and future generations').

[24] Larissa Parker and others, 'When the Kids Put Climate Change on Trial: Youth-Focused Rights-Based Climate Litigation Around the World' (2022) 13 Journal of Human Rights and the Environment 64.

[25] Stavros Gadinis and Amelia Miazad, 'Corporate Law and Social Risk' (2020) 73 Vanderbilt Law Review 1401. On the fiduciary duty of investors, see Maurits Dolmans and Andreas Wildner, 'Sustainable Fiduciary Duties for Investors—How Fiduciary Duties Can Be the Key to Escape the Climate Prisoner's Dilemma' <http://dx.doi.org/10.2139/ssrn.4962416> accessed 12 January 2025.

[26] Thilo Kuntz, 'How ESG is Weakening the Business Judgment Rule' in Thilo Kuntz (ed), *Research Handbook on Environmental, Social and Corporate Governance* (Edward Elgar Publishing 2024) (hereinafter, *ESG Handbook*) 64, 67; William J Moon, 'Transnational Corporate Law Litigation' (2025) 74 Duke Law Journal 901, 926, 942–50.

fiduciary duties that may require (or at least permit) them to consider climate impacts. These institutional investors may play a uniquely important role in regulating corporate behaviour by demanding that corporate managers factor climate concerns into corporate governance. Finally, national and sub-state governments are trustees for the public, with fiduciary duties to preserve common resources like the climate for current and future generations, including through regulating corporate behaviour and operating SOEs sustainably.[27]

2.3 Fiduciary Law's Regulation of Corporations and States

Fiduciary law's third attribute is that it traverses the boundaries between private law and public law and between corporate responsibility and state responsibility. Climate change is a problem that crosses the boundary between private law and public law, and fiduciary law regulates both corporations and states in ways that can be mutually reinforcing in response to climate change.

Fiduciary law provides tools to prompt increased state regulation. Chief among them, at least in common law countries, is the public trust doctrine, which has been the basis for litigation to force regulatory action by the political branches of domestic governments. The public trust doctrine holds that waterways and other resources are entrusted to the stewardship of state actors, who must manage and preserve them in the public interest.[28]

As the climate movement has grown, some of its participants have turned to the public trust idea to develop a "common global platform" for litigation in domestic courts that aims to hold government actors to a fiduciary duty to preserve the climate for current and future generations.[29] Organisations such as Our Children's Trust have spearheaded multi-jurisdiction strategies, which include litigation in national and subnational courts with trust-based arguments tailored to local law.[30]

This state-focused strategy has scored some victories in domestic courts while government actors continue to resist judicial implementation of a public fiduciary duty to preserve the climate. Courts in various jurisdictions, including India, Pakistan, and the US, have recognised the public trust doctrine's applicability to a broad range of environmental issues, including

[27] For discussion of both private firms and state-owned enterprises, see Ernest Lim, 'Fiduciary Duty and Corporate Externalities: Rethinking Directors' Climate Obligations' (30 April 2025), European Corporate Governance Institute—Law Working Paper No. 842/2025 <http://dx.doi.org/10.2139/ssrn.5250589>. See also Ernest Lim, 'The Government Controlling Shareholder as a Fiduciary: Implications for Climate Change Management and Litigation' (2024) 35 European Business Law Review 311.

[28] Joseph L Sax, 'The Public Trust Doctrine in Natural Resource Law: Effective Judicial Intervention' (1970) 68 Michigan Law Review 471.

[29] Mary Christina Wood and Gordon Levitt, 'The Public Trust Doctrine in Environmental Decision Making' in LeRoy C Paddock, Robert L Glicksman, and Nicholas S Bryner (eds), *Decision Making in Environmental Law* (Edward Elgar 2016) 73, 77, 82.

[30] Our Children's Trust, 'Global Legal Actions' <https://perma.cc/P8CF-RJFN> accessed 29 June 2025. One of us (Davis) filed an *amicus* brief on behalf of Members of the US Congress in support of the *Juliana v United States* litigation, one of the suits brought by Our Children's Trust attorneys. On July 23, 2025, after the final version of this Chapter was completed, the International Court of Justice gave its Advisory Opinion on the obligations of states regarding climate change, which concluded that climate change treaties and customary international law oblige states to ensure protection of the climate system from anthropogenic greenhouse gas emissions. *Obligations of States in respect of Climate Change*, Advisory Opinion, 2025 ICJ Rep No 187 (July 23). This landmark decision, which refers to due diligence obligations, may support future climate litigation that concretizes states' obligations as climate trustees, but as of now, that remains to be seen.

climate-related policymaking.[31] But the institutional legitimacy of these judicial decisions remains contested, with governments successfully raising jurisdictional and procedural objections to judicial recognition and enforcement of public fiduciary obligations to address climate change.[32]

Successful litigation against governments' actions can feed into the progressive development of private law constraints on corporate actors. Corporate directors' fiduciary duties include exercising due care to ensure that the corporation complies with law, including regulatory law requiring corporations to address climate change. This dynamic creates the potential for mutually reinforcing normative development, as we shall discuss below.

2.4 Investment Fiduciaries and Capital Flows

Fourth, and perhaps most important, fiduciary law provides a tool for targeting investment decisions and capital markets—targeting, in other words, capital flows and access to capital that support (or undermine) emission reduction goals, and thus the problem at its source. Fiduciary law bears directly on capital flows through its rules regulating investments by fiduciaries. With the rise of ESG commitments, lawyers have argued that institutional investors' fiduciary duties encompass climate concerns. Former Chief Justice of the Delaware Supreme Court Leo Strine maintained that "[f]iduciary duties must impose additional accountability upon institutional investors and free them to consider their beneficiaries' interests as human beings who are not just investors, but workers, parents, breathers of air, and citizens".[33] As BlackRock, one of the Big Three asset managers, once put it, "[s]ustainability is no longer something that can be addressed after strategic investment decisions have been made; it is indispensable to making investment decisions".[34]

Institutional investors, such as asset managers and pension funds, can function as regulators of corporate behaviour through their decisions about portfolio risk and return and their setting of standards for investment decisions that consider firms' climate impacts. Investors, both private firms and SOEs, are coordinating responses to climate change through "investor climate alliances" such as Climate Action 100+.[35] The management of ESG funds became a big business;[36] at one time, the Climate Action 100+ alliance included 600 investors managing, in the aggregate, $68 trillion in assets.[37] The alliance's members include private firms, sovereign wealth funds, and pension funds, not to mention nonprofit organisations, which aim together to steer investments in a climate-sensitive direction.[38] The alliance aims to be a vehicle for coordinating capital investment with international public law to "deliver[] net zero

[31] Seth Davis, 'The Public Trust as Transnational Law' in *Transnational Fiduciary Law* (n 14) 146, 148, 153.

[32] ibid 165–66.

[33] Leo E Strine Jr., 'Toward Fair and Sustainable Capitalism' (August 2020) 15 <https://perma.cc/2PTR-HA2U> accessed 29 June 2025.

[34] BlackRock Investment Institute, 'Launching Climate-Aware Return Assumptions' (February 2021) <https://perma.cc/8PEU-PPMM> accessed 29 June 2025.

[35] Amelia Miazad, 'Investor Climate Alliances' (2025) 102 Washington University Law Review 797, 797–99. See also Climate Action 100+, 'See About Climate Action 100+' <https://perma.cc/PXK7-Q4N4> accessed 29 June 2025.

[36] Seth Davis, 'ESG, the Alien Tort Statute, and Private Regulation's Legitimacy Trap' in *ESG Handbook* (n 26) 179, 196–201 (describing the turn against ESG investing in the US).

[37] Miazad (n 35), at 810.

[38] ibid.

GHG emissions by 2050, in line with the goals of the Paris Agreement to pursue efforts to limit warming to 1.5°C".[39]

3. The Potential for a TLO

PRI/UNEP's *Fiduciary Duty in the 21st Century* report suggested that there is already a settled TLO around the incorporation of climate risks and other ESG concerns into investment decisions, backed by legal enforcement of "investors' fiduciary duties".[40] But, as the high-profile departures of the largest asset managers from the Climate Action 100+ alliance suggest,[41] this conclusion was premature at best. Key corporations and government actors have mobilised against these efforts. In the US, for example, members of Congress have challenged Climate Action 100+ and twenty-six states have enacted anti-ESG laws.[42] These developments raise the question: What would a settled TLO look like?

TLO theory provides a framework for evaluating normative settlement around a fiduciary solution to the climate change problem. Where there is concordance across the local, national, and transnational levels in terms of law and practice, a transnational legal order or TLO has emerged. Halliday and Shaffer define a TLO as an ideal type: "a collection of formalized legal norms and associated organizations and actors that authoritatively order the understanding and practice of law across national jurisdictions".[43] A TLO arises from the social construction of a problem (such as climate change) and the legal tools to address it. Such a legal order may develop, or fail to develop, through the dynamic interaction of actors and institutions that frame social problems, including their framing as *legal* problems, and work to shape the content, enforcement, and everyday practice of law at the transnational, national, and local levels. That is, TLO "may expand or recede as actors construct competing conceptions of social 'problems' and seek to develop, import, and export norms across jurisdictional boundaries".[44] This may occur not just across the boundaries between nation-states, but also across those between the private and public spheres of action as both corporations and states are subjected to, and resist, the application of fiduciary norms to hold them accountable for climate impacts.

Normative settlement would mean a new normal in terms of expectations and practices as to what fiduciary law requires of corporations and states. From the vantage of proponents of these efforts, the climate must be within the operating instructions—the code—of capital. Considering climate risks would be a component of good corporate governance, necessary for investment fiduciaries, and part of the public trust that states, as providers of the code of capital, and investors in their own right, are obliged to fulfil.

Such a TLO would arise from dynamic interactions of private and public institutions across the local, national, and international levels. In practice, advocates have addressed different institutions and levels. Their efforts suggest the outlines of a global TLO that would combine private regulation, national law and judicial enforcement, and international organisations.

Some efforts have targeted private actors and private regulation with at least temporary success. Several years ago, it seemed that there was a consensus among global institutional

[39] Climate Action 100+, 'The Three Goals' <https://perma.cc/5DAM-MB8Q> accessed 29 June 2025.

[40] United Nations Environment Programme Finance Initiative (n 11) 8 ('Globally, there are over 730 hard and soft-law policy revisions, across some 500 policy instruments, that support, encourage or require investors to consider long-term value drivers, including ESG issues').

[41] Miazad (n 35) 853.

[42] ibid 837.

[43] Halliday and Shaffer (n 10) 3.

[44] ibid 18.

investors and asset managers that fiduciary duties required or at least permitted consideration of climate-related risks. Advocates pressed the Big Three asset managers to require emission reductions from firms in which they invest.[45] Other private regulatory mechanisms could mobilise companies that provide liability insurance to corporate directors and officers.[46]

To the extent that normative development in private institutions has lasting success, which remains to be seen, it could support normative settlement at the level of state regulation by reducing resistance from powerful firms who have developed green energy alternatives in ways that provide them with an advantage in relation to competitors. This dynamic led to the replacement of ozone depleting substances and the tightening of national and international regulation under the 1987 Montreal Protocol on Substances that Deplete the Ozone Layer. Divisions within business, in other words, can enhance prospects for meaningful state regulation.[47]

Advocates may also target state actors at the national level. The public trust doctrine, which norm entrepreneurs have mobilised through domestic litigation, may be a legal tool to force greater state regulation to address climate risks. Forcing states to act may in turn feed into the progressive development of a private law of fiduciary obligations related to the climate. Normative settlement at the national level would also implicate SOEs, which, as we have noted, are major contributors to climate change.[48]

International organisations have pushed states and corporations to take account of their contributions to climate change. The United Nations has been one of the key actors advocating for corporations, asset managers, and institutional investors to (re)code fiduciary norms to account for climate risks, including with the *Fiduciary Duty in the 21st Century* report, which was drafted in partnership with representatives of private investment firms.[49] Other examples of international action include the Paris Agreement, which can be glossed in fiduciary terms,[50] the United Nations Guiding Principles on Business and Human Rights (UNGPs) and Sustainable Development Goals (SDGs), the OECD Guidelines for Multinational Enterprises on Responsible Business Conduct, and the EU's comprehensive ESG regulations, which include the Sustainable Finance Disclosure Regulation (SFDR),[51] Corporate Sustainability Reporting Directive (CSRD),[52] and Corporate Sustainability Due Diligence Directive (CS3D),[53] all of which build upon (and in someways alter) the architecture of corporate law and fiduciary norms at the national and local levels.

[45] Dorothy S Lund, 'Asset Managers as Regulators' (2022) 171 University of Pennsylvania Law Review 77, 82.

[46] Amelia Miazad, 'D&O Insurers as Climate Governance Monitors' (2024) 104 Boston University Law Review 1181, 1185.

[47] Robert Falkner, 'The Business of Ozone Layer Protection: Corporate Power in Regime Evolution' in David L Levy and Peter J Newell (eds.), *The Business of Global Environmental Governance* (MIT Press 2004).

[48] Lim (n 27).

[49] United Nations Environment Programme Finance Initiative (n 11) 8.

[50] Davis (n 31) 163–64 (citing Paris Agreement to the United Nations Framework Convention on Climate Change (Dec. 12, 2015), in force 4 November 2016) <https://perma.cc/CBC5-ER9A>).

[51] Regulation (EU) 2019/2088 of 27 November 2019 on sustainability-related disclosures in the financial services sector [2019], OJ L 317/1.

[52] Directive (EU) 2022/2464 of the European Parliament and of the Council of 14 December 2022 amending Regulation (EU) No 537/2014, Directive 2004/109/EC, Directive 2006/43/EC, and Directive 2013/34/EU [2022], OJ L 322/15 (CSRD).

[53] Directive (EU) 2024/1760 of the European Parliament and of the Council of 13 June 2024 on corporate sustainability due diligence and amending Directive (EU) 2019/1937 and Regulation (EU) 2023/2859 [2024], OJ L 2024/1760 (CS3D). For detailed discussion of these various EU Directives as

4. Barriers to Normative Settlement

There are fundamental challenges to establishing climate-related fiduciary responsibilities in the code of capital across countries through private law, public law, international law, and their combination. First, the "sword-and-shield problem", where actors can use fiduciary law not only to advance, but also to thwart climate action, arises from legal indeterminacy and ideological contradictions within fiduciary law. Second, the *legitimacy trap* results from the fiduciary solution's association with courts, institutional investors, and international organisations, which makes it susceptible to populist attacks, particularly though not exclusively in the US. Third, the *interface problem* arises from the interface between fiduciary norms that involve equitable standards such as ESG investing and other forms of legal ordering, as this plays out across norm adoption and implementation. These thus remain formidable barriers to creating a TLO that encodes within capital an obligation to account for climate change.

4.1 Four Drivers of Recursive Change within Law

TLO theory posits four drivers (and potential obstructers) of recursive legal change. By "recursive legal change", we mean legal change dynamically driven to address the social and political construction of a problem, including in response to the failure of (or challenges confronting) earlier efforts.

First, addressing a social problem effectively depends on relative consensus regarding the nature of the problem and its resolution. In the area of climate change, legal development and practice face the problem that many key actors deny that climate change is a problem, or where they accept it is a problem, they prioritise other concerns, such as economic growth or individual freedom. This dispute about priorities, as we shall see, is central to contests about fiduciary duties of corporate and state actors. The development of the law often involves contests over problem definition and diagnostics that remain ongoing, such as at the level of implementation.

Second, law often involves compromise among different factions, leaving unresolved tensions and ideological contradictions. As Halliday and Shaffer explain, legal norms may be internally contradictory "because lawmakers draw variably from unresolved ideological clashes in order to reach a negotiated outcome".[54] These contradictions and tensions can drive the law's dynamic development, or they can trigger stalemate as actors contest over the resolution of these contradictions and tensions over time. The area of fiduciary law, for example, has both libertarian and communitarian roots. Communitarians stress the other-regarding nature of fiduciary duties. Libertarians, in contrast, stress fiduciary law's private ordering aspects that enable individuals to create trusts and other instruments to shield against claims on assets.

Third, legal rules vary in clarity, which provides opportunities for actors to advance certain interpretive propositions over others. In the area of climate change, for example, climate activists press corporations and governments to take climate change into account as part of their private global warming is a public good. Opponents, in contrast, use fiduciary law to focus corporate mandates on immediate financial returns.

they relate to private law and climate change, see Harro van Asselt and Jessica Crow, Chapter 33 of this handbook.

[54] Halliday and Shaffer (n 10) 38–39.

Finally, implementation of the law often confronts a mismatch between the creators of legal norms and those who implement them. As Halliday and Shaffer write, "*actor mismatch* occurs when those actors who wield power in the national and local implementation of transnational legal norms are not represented, or otherwise do not prevail, in international and transnational negotiations".[55] Those who adopt transnational norms, such as at the international level, are quite different than those who implement them at the state and local levels. This mismatch includes that between transnational norm developers, such as at the UN, the EU, and other international and supranational bodies, and national implementers. It can also involve a mismatch between national legislators or courts and local administrators and businesses.

4.2 Barriers to Implementing Fiduciary Law to Address Climate Change

These four drivers and obstructers of legal change—contestations over the understanding and diagnostics of a problem, ideological contradictions within law resulting from ongoing struggle, the legal indeterminacy of norms, and actor mismatch between those who enact law and those who implement it—are reflected in three barriers to implementing fiduciary law to address climate change.

4.2.1 The Sword-and-Shield Problem

Fiduciary norms can be a sword to force corporate and state actors to consider climate risks. But they can also shield them from such concerns, raising the sword-and-shield problem. Activists aim to use private law as a sword to advance climate action. But climate sceptics and those focused on short-term profit maximisation can marshal fiduciary law as a shield against forcing the incorporation of climate concerns into corporate and investor decision-making. They may be supported by scholars who believe that climate change activists are stretching fiduciary concepts beyond their traditionally accepted boundaries.

The sword-and-shield problem is a problem of legal indeterminacy,[56] one that implicates (and stems, at least in part, from) ideological tensions within fiduciary law and ongoing contests over the nature and impact of the climate problem. At the corporate level, there remains debate about whether and to what extent climate risks are consistent with fiduciary duties. The duty of loyalty is indeterminate. The shareholder primacy model limits the fiduciary mandate to shareholder value maximisation—a service mandate. Yet other models conceive of the corporate directors' mandate in governance terms. Consider, for example, the idea that their mandate entails a "duty of societal responsibility".[57] Importantly, this model has been offered as a corrective to stakeholder models, which, while broader than shareholder primacy models, nevertheless have been criticised as too limited in the context of climate change.[58]

Fiduciary norms are also indeterminate as applied to state action. At a fundamental level, contestation remains over whether and to what extent state officials are fiduciaries. Even the public trust doctrine, which imposes some fiduciary duties on states, is contested in its scope and the level of deference to be paid to political actors. Public trust doctrine, as currently

[55] ibid.

[56] For more on the sword-and-shield problem, see Seth Davis, 'The False Promise of Fiduciary Government' (2014) 89 Notre Dame Law Review 1145.

[57] Jaap Winter, 'Addressing the Crisis of the Modern Corporation: The Duty of Societal Responsibility of the Board', in Gregor Bachmann and others (eds), *Festschrift für Christine Windbichler zum 70. Geburtstag am 8. Dezember 2020* (De Gruyter 2021).

[58] ibid.

applied, varies by jurisdiction and does not clearly answer the basic question whether the climate is a protected public trust resource. Even if government conduct is viewed in fiduciary terms, conservatives stress the importance of economic growth over climate change as a government priority, questioning the fundamental diagnosis and prioritisation of climate change as a problem.

4.2.2 The Legitimacy Trap

Second, advocates of fiduciary duties regarding the climate face a legitimacy trap. Public actors contend that defining and addressing climate change is the responsibility of democratically elected governments, not courts. They thus contend that it is illegitimate to force private corporations to reduce emissions through fiduciary law claims without a democratic mandate.

Ideological contradictions in the fiduciary law field contribute to such legitimacy traps.[59] As noted earlier, advocates for stronger responses to climate change articulate a communitarian vision of fiduciary law, which stands for an ideal of regard for others. But fiduciary law also encompasses libertarian visions of personal liberty to control capital. These visions are reflected in accounts of fiduciary law as a contractarian enterprise, which enables capital to create trusts and other structures. Pistor highlights this libertarian aspect in her work, where capital creates private trusts and other tools to avoid claims on assets.[60]

This ideological tension at the heart of the field expresses itself in different ways when it comes to climate change. One of the very strategies for incorporating climate concerns into investment and management decisions partially reflects a libertarian stance. In focusing on private regulation, some reject the idea that the state has the capacity or legitimacy to address complex issues such as climate change through public regulation.[61]

Another version of the legitimacy trap arises in public trust litigation before US federal courts. Here, the opposition argues that public trust litigation is an attempt by special interest groups to enlist the courts in forcing anti-democratic regulation on fossil fuel producers and other corporations. In this area, they stress that any regulatory initiative must remain with legislators and agencies.[62] In short, the challenge of the legitimacy trap highlights both ideological tensions within the field and ongoing struggles over the diagnosis and prioritisation of the problem of climate change.

4.2.3 The Interface Problem

The successful use of fiduciary law also confronts an *interface problem*. This problem is doctrinal and institutional and will be familiar to students of the law/equity divide in common law countries, which historically was both doctrinal and institutional, with the common law courts on one side and the Court of Chancery on the other.[63]

[59] Davis (n 36).

[60] Pistor (n 6). This tension is also explored in Carla Spivak, Chapter 17 of this handbook.

[61] Jonathan R Macey, 'ESG Investing: Why Here? Why Now?' (2022) 19 Berkeley Business Law Journal 258, 262, 265 (contending that ESG's rise is a 'remarkable libertarian turn in the history of American law').

[62] Donald J Kochan, 'State Courts are No Place for Climate Lawsuits' (*The Hill* 7 April 2023) <https://perma.cc/6CC4-TFTV> accessed 15 July 2025. See also Laura Burgers, 'Should Judges Make Climate Change Law?' (2020) 9 Transnat'l Envt. L. 55, 60 (discussing debate and arguing that 'the climate litigation trend is likely to influence the democratic legitimacy of judicial decisions on climate change').

[63] On the modern 'fusion' (or lack thereof) of law and equity, see Andrew Burrows, 'We Do This at Common Law but That in Equity' (2002) 22 Oxford Journal of Legal Studies 1.

The doctrinal dimension concerns the interface between standards and rules in the regulation of fiduciaries. The fiduciary duties of loyalty and care are open-ended, moralistic, and sweeping in their potential applications. These equitable standards may overlap with legal rules, and thus have the potential to "swallow up the law", and create their own risks of opportunistic and manipulative misuse.[64] To keep equity in its (proper) place, courts have developed various doctrines, such as the business judgment rule in corporate law, that "cordon[] off the more expansive attributes of fiduciary law" or otherwise manage the interface between equitable standards and legal rules.[65]

Another dimension of the problem arises from the interfaces between legal institutions. Private, public, and international law all interact. They potentially can do so in ways that advance climate action through fiduciary law. But they also can raise challenges in the ways that they interface. Because of the indeterminacy and ideological tensions within fiduciary norms, on the one hand, and actor mismatch, on the other hand, an interface problem arises among and within transnational, national, and local institutions, law, and legal practice. The enactment of rules and their interpretation by courts may encounter significant challenges in translating them into actual state and corporate practice, as we will see from divergent developments in the US and EU.

These barriers—the sword-and-shield problem, the legitimacy trap, and the interface problem—raise significant challenges to any normative settlement around fiduciary law as an effective response to climate change. Yet they nonetheless also can spur recursive change in the law in which fiduciary law eventually incorporates climate change into the code of capital.

5. Divergent Developments: The US and the EU

The use of fiduciary law to advance climate initiatives is flagging in the US, while a normative settlement may be emerging in Europe that develops fiduciary norms to address climate change. Within the US, the sword-and-shield problem and the legitimacy trap have been significant barriers to normative settlement in national and local law, leaving proponents to hope that business imperatives and private regulation will suffice to incorporate climate change into corporate decision-making, notwithstanding political backlash and the use of public institutions to attack such practices. Within the EU, the picture is different: There is growing concordance across the supranational, national, and local levels that climate change is an important consideration for fiduciaries. Even so, the interface problem remains an important challenge for the success of a TLO, and a successful populist attack on these efforts remains imaginable.

5.1 The US

The backlash in the US against so-called woke ESG investing, including the enactment of anti-ESG laws by twenty-six states,[66] and the Trump administration's rollback of Biden-era

[64] Andrew S Gold and Henry E Smith, 'The Equity in Corporate Law' (2025) 100 Notre Dame Law Review 789, 803.

[65] ibid 803; see also ibid 837 (analogising ESG to equity).

[66] Daniel Wiessner, 'Republican-led US States Appeal Ruling Allowing Biden ESG Investing Rule' *Reuters* (26 October 2023) <https://www.reuters.com/legal/republican-led-us-states-appeal-ruling-allow

regulatory efforts, illustrates the barriers to normative settlement.[67] The opposition and relative failure at the federal level to use public trust litigation to force the federal government as a public trustee to regulate in response to climate change further reflects such challenges. But these gloomy signs are tempered by the persistence of climate concerns among many fiduciaries who believe such concerns are important under a shareholder-value model of corporate officers' fiduciary duties. Moreover, there have been some successes at the state level to implement pro-ESG legislation and to use public trust litigation, although the practical impact of both has been minimal.[68]

Prior to the second Trump administration, multiple developments suggested that the shareholder primacy model might lose out, at least if it was viewed as *prohibiting* consideration of climate risks. Wall Street's Big Three index managers—BlackRock, Vanguard, and State Street Global Advisors—advocated taking climate risks into account, and they were poised to wield significant influence in corporate decision-making. At the national level during the Biden administration, the Department of Labor promulgated a regulation under the Employee Retirement Income Security Act (ERISA) permitting fiduciaries of employee benefit plans to engage in ESG investing[69] while the Securities and Exchange Commission (SEC) adopted rules[70] to standardise public companies' climate-related disclosures. These developments linked with broader international and transnational developments, including those within the EU addressed below.

But the progress sparked a backlash, and it faces complete unravelling under the second Trump administration. The backlash assumed a populist rhetoric, attacking elites, although the backlash itself was supported by elite institutions like the Heritage Foundation. Heritage Action's ESG Hurts campaign provided model legislation governing the fiduciary duties of state fund managers, and model legislation that bars state entities from doing business with companies that have ESG commitments.[71] The anti-ESG campaigns pitted fossil fuel companies and fossil fuel states like Texas against Wall Street institutions.

Conservative states targeted BlackRock and other large index managers for their ESG investment policies. Nine states withdrew almost $13.3 billion in funds from BlackRock alone, and Florida banned state pension fund investment in BlackRock's sustainable investment funds.[72] Eleven states enacted state pension fiduciary acts defining the fiduciary duties of state asset managers to exclude ESG concerns.[73] In this way, they strove to undermine efforts

ing-biden-esg-investing-rule-2023-10-26> accessed 12 June 2025. For in-depth examination of state-level anti-ESG laws, see John Dernbach, Chapter 35 of this handbook.

[67] US Envtl. Prot. Agency, 'EPA Launches Biggest Deregulatory Action in U.S. History' (12 March 2025) <https://perma.cc/9G9G-ZMHN> accessed 29 June 2025.

[68] Dernbach (n 66) (detailing pro-ESG legislation in US states and concluding that it will only marginally impact the global trajectory of ESG); *Held v State* 560 P 3d 1235 (MT 2024) (holding that Montana Environmental Protection Act violated Montana Constitution insofar as it precluded consideration of greenhouse gas emissions and climate change during environmental reviews).

[69] US Dep't of Labor, Final Rule, Prudence and Loyalty in Selecting Plan Investments and Exercising Shareholder Rights, 87 FR 73822 (1 December 2022).

[70] US Securities and Exchange Comm'n, The Enhancement and Standardization of Climate-Related Disclosures for Investors, 89 FR 21668 (28 March 2024).

[71] Heritage Action for America, 'Model Legislation' (ESG Hurts 2025) <https://perma.cc/3RWT-H5HU> accessed 29 June 2025. See generally Chris Crews, 'The Far Right Culture War on ESG' (2023) 14 Religions 1257 (describing Heritage Action's ESG Hurts campaign).

[72] Dernbach (n 66).

[73] ibid.

by transnational networks such as Climate Action 100+ to develop a transnational order for climate change through private governance.[74] In response, institutional investors such as BlackRock tempered their commitment to ESG, and some withdrew their membership in alliances such as Climate Action 100+.[75]

The Trump administration, in parallel, rolled back national regulations and worked to undermine efforts in international organisations. At the national level, the administration decided not to defend the SEC's climate-related disclosure rule against a lawsuit brought by Republican state attorneys general and other litigants, and the SEC took steps to rescind the rule. Internationally, the US purportedly called on the OECD to remove references to climate change from its guidelines on business and human rights.

This backlash illustrates the indeterminacy and ideological tensions within fiduciary law that have enabled opponents to use fiduciary norms to push back on climate change initiatives. While advocates deploy a more expansive conception of fiduciary law that is communitarian in its other-regarding outlook, opponents assert a shareholder primacy norm that has strong libertarian roots, as we earlier noted, arguing that pursuing shareholder value and factoring in environmental concerns conflict. Recent doctrinal developments in Delaware, which rejected the idea of a fiduciary duty to diversified investors (and thus investors' interests in the broader economy), tempered the case that corporate managers must consider the broader societal impacts of their decisions.[76]

The backlash against ESG investing in the US also illustrates the legitimacy trap. In the face of failed government responses, many of them due to ideological opposition by conservatives, climate activists turned to private regulation through ESG as another regulatory solution. The response from conservatives was to object to private regulation on democratic grounds. Republican members of Congress and state attorneys general, for example, argued that ESG is a "cartel" without democratic accountability which seeks to force a "woke" agenda on corporations.[77]

The question for the short term is whether ESG has become a settled enough norm within companies that they will still pursue it as part of corporate directors' fiduciary duties. Some are sanguine and believe this will happen. We are more sceptical because of the many levels within government that can thwart such developments. Only after BlackRock backed off of its ESG commitments did Texas agree to allow it to do business again with the state government.[78]

Moreover, even where corporations and large index fund managers incorporate ESG, it can reflect greenwashing and be used to forestall state regulation. ESG standards are notoriously varied and vague, and in this way resemble equitable standards generally. Reliance on disclosure obligations and ESG metrics can result in opportunistic behaviour in which corporations maintain that they are taking action so that there is no need for public

[74] Miazad (n 35) 853.

[75] ibid 799, 803, 853.

[76] *McRitchie v Zuckerberg* 315 A 3d 518, 529 (Del. Ch. 2024) ('It is not reasonably conceivable that Delaware corporate law currently operates on a diversified-investor model'). For discussion of the academic literature and activist shareholder movement behind the diversified-investor model, see Ernest Lim, Chapter 18 of this handbook.

[77] Davis (n 36) 196–201.

[78] Jack Pitcher, 'BlackRock Is Off Texas' Blacklist. Where the ESG Battle Stands Now' *Wall Street Journal* (4 June 2025) <https://www.wsj.com/finance/blackrock-is-off-texas-blacklist-where-the-esg-battle-stands-now-1cc1f958#> accessed 12 July 2025.

regulation[79]—another way in which fiduciary law may function as a shield against real action on climate change.[80]

Nonetheless, the picture is complex across US states. It is conceivable that state efforts in places like Texas may fail to halt the transformation of fiduciary law in accounting for climate change over time. States also are divided. California, which is among the top seven US states in terms of oil and gas production, has supported enhanced state and corporate action to address climate change. California's massive state pensions (such as CalPERS and CalSTRS) continue to take a leading role in incorporating ESG and climate-oriented fiduciary mandates into investment decisions. In addition, many US companies will be subject to legal orders abroad. These include EU directives that impose climate-related reporting and disclosure duties. These duties, in turn, may feed into US corporate directors' fiduciary obligation to oversee the company's operations and compliance with law.[81] Much will depend on the impact of the Trump administration's efforts to embed itself and its followers in power over time.

5.2 The EU

The EU has a long tradition, stretching back to the Maastricht Treaty, of recognising sustainability as a responsibility of its member states.[82] National traditions within Europe, in parallel, have been more open to a stakeholder model of corporate governance, building from the incorporation of employee voice in corporate decision-making as reflected in the German and Dutch corporate models. These stakeholder traditions create greater opportunity for integrating ESG-related duties of care into corporate management. European courts have similarly taken a lead in recognising the fiduciary duties of both governments and corporations regarding climate change. As a result, fiduciary law is recursively developing in Europe through the interaction of legislative action at different levels of government, judicial decisions, and private ordering, thus shaping fiduciary duties to account for climate change.

Through this combination of supranational, national, and private law developments, a TLO could be forming in the EU in which fiduciary norms, as reflected in ESG disclosure duties, play an important role. This process has worked vertically, as national laws and litigation provide support for EU interventions, and EU directives reciprocally help to drive national change. It also has worked horizontally across national public and private law systems.[83] EU directives and regulations have built upon fiduciary standards in national law and created significant new rules. Litigation before national courts has challenged government and corporations, raising arguments that include fiduciary norms and European human rights law,

[79] See Barbara Ballan and Jason J Czarnezki, 'Disclosure, Greenwashing, and the Future of ESG Litigation' (2024) 81 Washington & Lee Law Review 545, 548 nn 7–11 (citing examples).

[80] The problem of symbolic action also besets government initiatives. Governments may aim to signal to the public that action is being taken, but with the knowledge that in practice it will create few constraints on capital. See Murray Edelman, *The Symbolic Uses of Politics* (1967 edn, University of Illinois Press 1985). National governments, for example, may engage in such behaviour when they make international pledges to address climate change.

[81] For background law, see *Stone v Ritter*, 911 A 2d 362 (Del. 2006); *In re Caremark Int'l Inc Derivative Litig*, 698 A. 2d 959 (Del. Ch. 1996). For analysis of the potential influence of ESG directives on corporate law, see Luca Enriques, Matteo Gatti, and Roy Shapira, 'How the EU Sustainability Due Diligence Directive Could Reshape Corporate America' European Corporate Governance Institute' Law Working Paper No. 817/2025 (27 May 2025) <http://dx.doi.org/10.2139/ssrn.5083571> accessed June 12, 2025.

[82] Treaty on European Union (Maastricht Treaty) (signed 7 February 1992, entered into force 1 November 1993) [1992] OJ C191/1, art. 2.

[83] Barbara Pozzo, Chapter 29 of this handbook.

with some courts giving European human rights instruments horizontal effect within national private law.[84]

The European Commission created Action Programmes from the 2000s onwards that addressed private law instruments to guide business behaviour on sustainable development. EU member states also took independent action. Notably, in 2017, France adopted the Duty of Vigilance Act, which creates liability for companies that fail to identify, prioritise, and assess risks, or "prevent serious harm to human rights and fundamental freedoms, the health and safety of persons and the environment".[85] Such liability includes failures "resulting from the activities of the company and from the companies it controls, directly or indirectly, as well as the activities of subcontractors or suppliers with whom an established business relationship is maintained".[86] In 2021 Germany, in turn, adopted the Supply Chain Due Diligence Act that subjects companies of a defined size to administrative fines for failure to comply with the act's requirements.[87] Although these laws reference company obligations, they inescapably affect the duties and mandates of corporate officeholders.

The EU then followed these developments with two directives that aim to harmonise and standardise due diligence obligations on companies across the EU's twenty-seven member states. In 2022, it adopted the CSRD, which creates a double materiality standard pursuant to which an enterprise must report not only regarding the impact of sustainability on its financial situation, but also the sustainability impact of its operations on people and the environment over the short, medium, and long term, thus pressing corporations to account for other stakeholders.[88] The CSRD can be considered extraterritorial in its reach as it covers not only large EU businesses of a defined size, and small and medium-sized EU undertakings operating in the "public interest", but also third country enterprises having EU annual revenues of at least 150 million Euros.[89]

In 2024, the EU followed with the CS3D, which further expanded transparency obligations and incorporated new conduct rules for companies.[90] The CS3D addresses both EU member states and companies, requiring states to incorporate into national laws requirements that companies address human rights violations and environmental impacts over their entire value chains, both within *and* outside of Europe. Companies are to adopt a strategy that is in line with the Paris Agreement's goal of limiting global warming to 1.5 degrees Celsius.[91] They are subject to civil liability for compliance failures, including those of their business partners in their value chains. Although such civil liability of a corporation engages tort law, it also implicitly entails duties on corporate management to uphold the law as part of their duty to take steps to ensure that the corporation complies with the law.

[84] Olha O Cherednychenko and Boudewijn de Bruin, Chapter 45 of this handbook.

[85] The liability is up to 30 million Euros for companies with over 5,000 employees in France or 10,000 employees globally. Article 1 of the Duty of Vigilance Law, codified in Article L. 225-102-4 of the French Commercial Code (authors' translation). See Loi no 2017-399 du 27 mars 2017 relative au devoir de vigilance des sociétés mères et des entreprises donneuses d'ordre, JORF no 0074 du 28 mars 2017.

[86] ibid.

[87] The fines are up to 8 million euros or up to 2% of annual global turnover. Gesetz über die unternehmerischen Sorgfaltspflichten zur Vermeidung von Menschenrechtsverletzungen in Lieferketten (Lieferkettensorgfaltspflichtengesetz - LkSG), 16.07.2021, BGBl. I 2021, Nr. 46 vom 22.07.2021, S. 2959.

[88] CSRD (n 52).

[89] ibid.

[90] CS3D (n 53).

[91] ibid art 22.

Litigation before European national courts has developed as well. Litigants in civil law jurisdictions have repeatedly relied upon national law, including tort law, as well as international human rights law and EU directives, to develop arguments that states and corporations have duties of care to address climate risks. Among scholars, the relationship between tort law and fiduciary law is a contested one. Some have argued that several European court decisions, which cite a wide variety of legal instruments from both private law and public law, confirm that corporate managers' fiduciary duties include societal responsibilities,[92] that responsible investment strategies must include sustainability concerns,[93] and that state actors are trustees of the climate.[94]

Well-known examples from the Dutch courts illustrate these points concerning what might be termed a "duty of climate care"[95] that may be grounded in civil law tort provisions with implications for fiduciary law in both civil law and common law countries. The Dutch Civil Code defines a tortious act broadly to include consideration of both written law as well as "what according to unwritten law has to be regarded as proper social conduct".[96] This broad norm of the unwritten standard of care was cited by the litigants in two landmark cases involving the Dutch government and Royal Dutch Shell LLP. Dutch law has a tradition of a stakeholder conception of corporate governance, one that some Dutch lawyers have argued encompasses sustainability concerns.

In the *Urgenda* litigation, which was brought by a Dutch environmental organisation (the Urgenda Foundation) and 900 Dutch citizens, the District Court of the Hague applied public principles under Dutch law's duty of care to force the Dutch government to take affirmative steps to reduce greenhouse gas emissions.[97] The court held that the Dutch government had a duty of care to the Dutch people that entailed a specific and significant obligation: By 2020, the government had to lower greenhouse gas emissions 25% below 1990 levels. The court synthesised multiple sources, including Dutch constitutional law, EU law, principles of international environmental law, and principles from the European Convention on Human Rights (ECHR). Its decision was upheld on appeal by both the Hague Court of Appeals and the Supreme Court of the Netherlands, which pointed to a duty of care under Articles 2 and 8 of the ECHR, respectively concerning the right to life and the right to private life.[98] This duty, which the Supreme Court labelled one of "due diligence" and "good governance", entailed "positive obligations" to reduce the country's greenhouse gas emissions by at least 25% by 2020.[99]

In 2021, in the case *Milieudefensie et al. v Royal Dutch Shell plc* in the Hague, a court ruled for the first time that a company—Royal Dutch Shell LLP—breached its duty of care in relation

[92] Eric W Orts, 'Is There Really a Fiduciary Duty to Destroy the Climate' (17 March 2025) The CLS Blue Sky Blog <https://perma.cc/NPP8-79Z8> accessed 29 June 2025.

[93] CIEL, 'Trillion Dollar Transformation: Fiduciary Duty, Divestment, and Fossil Fuels in an Era of Climate Risk' (December 2016) <https://perma.cc/5ZN5-RBAF> accessed 29 June 2025.

[94] Erin Ryan, 'Public Trust Principles and Environmental Rights: The Hidden Duality of Climate Advocacy and the Atmospheric Trust' (2025) 49 Harvard Environmental Law Review 225.

[95] Douglas A Kysar, 'Duty of Climate Care' (2024) 73 DePaul Law Review 487.

[96] Dutch Civ Code Art. 6:162(2).

[97] Case C/09/456689/HA ZA 13-1396, *Urgenda Foundation v Netherlands* (District Court of the Hague), ECLI:NL:RBDHA:2015:7196 (14 June 2015).

[98] Case 19/00135, *Netherlands v Urgenda Foundation* (Supreme Court of the Netherlands), ECLI:NL:HR:2019:2007 (20 December 2019).

[99] ibid paras 6.5, 7.3.6, 7.5.1.

to its climate strategies.[100] The Hague Court of Appeal affirmed that there exists a duty of care under Dutch law for companies to mitigate climate change, although it gave discretion to the company to decide how it should do so.[101] Synthesising tort law, EU law, international human rights law, and international environmental law, the Dutch courts held that Shell had a duty of care to reduce its climate impacts.

Some argue that the developments in the EU should be viewed as the *replacement* of a private corporate governance fiduciary legal order with a substituted rules-based regulatory order.[102] Yet, these developments also can be viewed in terms of the interaction of public and private law that gives rise, to borrow from Jens-Hinrich Binder, to "functional fiduciary law".[103] As Thilo Kurtz has argued, they involve a recursive development of EU and European national law through which ESG rules harness obligations involving existing fiduciary duties and trigger changes in fiduciary law itself, leading to further duties on corporate officers, including their compliance with due diligence laws as part of a duty of care.[104] Although EU directives apply to corporations directly, and not to corporate managers as fiduciaries, they shape directors' and officers' fiduciary duties to ensure that the company complies with these directives as part of their duty of care, and thus of due diligence. In the process, they shape actors' understandings of fiduciary duties, constituting the law-in-action.

The impact of EU developments on actual practice nonetheless remains a challenge, as contests between corporations and environmental stakeholders play out. Corporations have lobbied the European Commission to pare back commitments. In 2025, the European Commission proposed to the European Council and European Parliament a package that would reduce the burden on companies under the CSRD and CS3D.[105] The proposed changes to the CSRD would, among other things, simplify reporting standards and limit the information that must be requested and reported up the value chain. With respect to the CS3D, its effective date would be delayed until July 2028, the scope of the due diligence obligation would generally be limited to a corporation's operations, its subsidiaries' operations, and direct business partners, the duty to terminate relationships with suppliers would be eliminated, and the duty to engage with stakeholders would be limited as well. This proposal to reduce burdens resembles the recurring feature of fiduciary law where equitable standards are cabined by legal rules. In common law countries, attempts to manage the indeterminacy of equitable standards are a driver of legal change in the relationship between equity and law. In the EU, the push and pull over the ESG-related directives resembles this dynamic with the proposed changes to cabin the scope of the CSRD and CS3D.

[100] Case C/09/571932, *Milieudefensie* et al *v Royal Dutch Shell plc* (District Court of the Hague), ECLI:NL:RBDHA:2021:5339, paras 4.4.17, 5.1–5.9 (26 May 2021).

[101] Case 200.302.332/01, *Shell plc v Milieudefensie* et al (Hague Court of Appeal), RBDHA, C/09/571932, ECLI:NL:GHDHA:2024:2100, paras 7.24–7.27, 7.63–7.66, 7.81, 7.96, 7.111.

[102] Sebastiaan Niels Hooghiemstra, 'EU "Rule-Based" ESG Duties for Investment Funds and Their Managers Under the European "Green Deal"', in *ESG Handbook* (n 26) 203, 204.

[103] Jens-Hinrich Binder, 'Transnational Fiduciary Law in Financial Intermediation: Are We There Yet? A Case Study in the Emergence of Transnational Legal Ordering', in *Transnational Fiduciary Law* (n 14) 98, 108–09.

[104] Supra nn 25–26 and accompanying text.

[105] Proposal for a Directive of the European Parliament and of the Council amending Directives (EU) 2022/2464 and (EU) 2024/1760 as regards the dates from which Member States are to apply certain corporate sustainability reporting and due diligence requirements, COM(2025) 80 final 2025/0044 (COD); Proposal for a Directive of the European Parliament and of the Council amending Directives 2006/43/EC, 2013/34/EU, (EU) 2022/2464, and (EU) 2024/1760 as regards certain corporate sustainability reporting and due diligence requirements, COM(2025) 81 final 2025/0045 (COD).

At the national level, challenges have also arisen to the implementation of due-diligence, equitable standards. While France adopted its Duty of Vigilance Act in 2017, it has yet to adopt administrative decrees to implement it as of this writing in 2025.[106] These developments illustrate ongoing contestation and challenges of actor mismatch within Europe. While legislatures may act, administrative bodies might not. And where administrative bodies act, implementation that affects outcomes may remain a challenge.

The challenges of actor mismatch involving the interface problem played out as well in the touted *Urgenda* litigation before the Dutch courts. The Dutch judgments are rightly viewed as a landmark, showing promise for a transnational litigation strategy based on applying fiduciary principles against governments. However, some find that the Dutch government, in response, took actions that technically complied with the court order, but may have slightly *increased* global emissions overall by simply displacing emissions to other countries.[107] Such an outcome again illustrates the interface problem between international commitments and implementation by national bureaucracies. In this case, the interface problem was between international law and Dutch government pledges, on the one hand, and judicial decisions and national executive action, on the other. Moreover, corporate actors have also successfully used private law as a shield elsewhere in Europe, arguing that their responsibility to shareholders is to maximise shareholder returns and that activists' demands interfere with their ability to do so. In the UK, an English court rejected activists' climate claims under fiduciary law in the case of *ClientEarth v Shell* in 2023.[108] Royal Dutch Shell had moved its corporate seat to the UK for multiple reasons, notably following the Hague District Court ruling.

6. Conclusion

Fiduciary law offers significant promise for shaping the code of capital through private, public, and international fiduciary law norms so that capital takes account of climate change. It cuts across both common and civil law countries. It targets the source of the problem in investment and capital flows through creating fiduciary mandates that apply both to persons and to purposes. The developments we have traced in the US and Europe are playing out in jurisdictions around the world as part of transnational legal ordering processes.[109]

However, fiduciary law's promise faces serious challenges at the level of law-in-action, especially given political developments in the US. The challenges involve ongoing contests over the diagnostics of the problem and responsibilities for it; ideological tensions within fiduciary law; legal indeterminacy in its interpretation; and actor mismatch between norm adoption and implementation. While fiduciary law offers promise for addressing climate change, it also provides tools for opponents to thwart that promise. Climate advocates must overcome this sword-and-shield problem within fiduciary law, as well as legitimacy traps and interface challenges, if they are to be successful in encoding duties within capital to account for climate change and safeguard the future of life on this small, vulnerable planet.

106 See Begüm Kilimcioğlu, 'The French Duty of Vigilance Law: A Reference Guide for the Transposition of the Corporate Sustainability Due Diligence Directive' (2025) 48 Netherlands Quarterly of Human Rights 31, 34 (noting that a decree from the Council of State (Conseil d'Etat) has not been issued).

107 Benoit Mayer, 'The Contribution of *Urgenda* to the Mitigation of Climate Change' (2022) 35 Journal of Environmental Law 167, 169.

108 *ClientEarth v Shell Plc* [2023] EWHC 1897, [94] (Ch) (24 July 2023) (appeal taken from Eng.).

109 See generally *ESG Handbook* (n 26).

PART III

Property

CHAPTER 14

Property Law

J. B. RUHL AND JIM ROSSI

1. Introduction

PROPERTY law and nature have had a complex relationship for millennia. Some of the earliest and most bedrock property law doctrines that persist to this day were designed eons ago to manage the curveballs nature throws at humans and their property. For example, the doctrine of avulsion—that the boundaries of a property remain the same even if the land has been moved or submerged by sudden natural causes, such as a storm or flood—dates back to Roman law.[1] In the other direction, property law is brimming with doctrines designed to manage how humans dominate and extract resources from nature. From wild foxes to groundwater to oil and natural gas, the "rule of capture" has also proved influential since Roman law in designing doctrines from the trivial to those of great significance.[2] Indeed, property law's rule of capture facilitated the unlocking of fossil fuels from the Earth that led to the modern climate change predicament and its egregious insult to nature.[3] There also are property doctrines designed to address instances in which one person intervenes in or manipulates nature to secure some benefit, but in so doing puts another person in harm's way. Altering the natural flow of water across one's property has long been a property "no-no" if it injures another's property, for example.[4]

Property doctrines like these have evolved over time to respond to "changed circumstances or new knowledge" regarding nature.[5] Examples of changed circumstances fuelling doctrinal change in property law have generally involved some kind of innovation humans have initiated regarding how we access and extract resources from nature. The introduction of increasingly intensive subsurface mineral extraction, for example, necessitated doctrinal adjustments to the relationship between surface and mineral estate owners.[6] As an example of new knowledge

1 Joseph L Sax, 'The Accretion/Avulsion Puzzle: Its Past Revealed, Its Future Proposed' (2010) 23 Tulane Environmental Law Journal 305.

2 Michael C Blumm and Lucus Ritchie, 'The Pioneer Spirit and the Public Trust: The American Rule of Capture and State Ownership of Wildlife' (2005) 35 Environmental Law 101.

3 Jack Whiteley, 'Property's Climate' (unpublished draft on file with authors) (thoroughly detailing how 'property law in the United States has facilitated greenhouse gas emissions').

4 John Rood, 'The Rights and Remedies on Permitting, Diverting, Increasing and Obstructing the Natural Flow' (1908) 6 Michigan Law Review 448.

5 *Lucas v South Carolina Coastal Council* 505 U.S. 1003 (1992). For numerous doctrinal examples, see Michael C Blumm and J B Ruhl, 'Background Principles, Takings, and Libertarian Property: A Reply to Professor Huffman' (2010) 37 Ecology Law Quarterly 805.

6 KK DuVivier, 'Animal, Vegetable, Mineral—Wind? The Severed Wind Power Rights Conundrum' (2009) 49 Washburn Law Journal 69 (describing severance doctrine's history in ancient Greek mining royalties and English mining law, before recounting early US justifications for severable mineral estates due to gold, coal, and other precious mineral mining expeditions, especially in the West).

driving doctrinal change, scientific advancements in the past seventy-five years revealing the ecological and economic benefits of wetlands, once deemed nuisances due to their foul odours and undesirable wildlife (such as mosquitoes), have profoundly changed their status in property law.[7] In short, much of the history of doctrinal change in property law has been attributable to humans either changing how they engage with nature or learning something they did not know about nature.

Through those millennia of doctrinal change in property law, however, there has been one constant: the Earth system. The Earth system is not to be confused with nature. The Earth system is, in the simplest of terms, how the Earth operates at planetary scales.[8] Nature is a representation of local conditions of the Earth system at any given point in time. Humans have been mucking around with nature since *homo sapiens* appeared on the planet roughly 300,000 years ago. Humans have hunted and then domesticated animals, removed nature to make way for vast cities and highways, introduced species to ecosystems with naively good intentions and disastrous results, and done much more to change nature.[9] Until recently in our species' timespan, however, none of our transgressions on *nature* had much lasting effect on the *Earth system*—on how the Earth system works to produce the nature of the time. That has changed.

The Earth system has transformed many times in the history of our planet, but never before this much because of humans.[10] The emission of greenhouse gases (GHG) from burning of fossil fuels—fuels produced from resource extraction governed by property's rule of capture—is now changing the Earth's climate system. Left unchecked, and amplified by other stressors such as pollution and biodiversity loss, those changes will trigger changes in other Earth systems, such as ocean circulation systems, nutrient transport systems, wildfire regimes, and others, which in turn will cascade to trigger change in yet other Earth systems.[11] As the Earth system as a whole changes, nature—the Earth system representation at any given time—will also necessarily change. This disruption has already become so severe in magnitude and global in scale, that many scientists argue humans have pushed the Earth system from the Holocene into a new geological epoch—the Anthropocene.[12] In short, the impact of humans on the Eath system since the Industrial Revolution is extreme, unprecedented, and potentially irreversible.

What has this got to do with modern property law? Put simply, as much as property law has co-evolved around its relationship with nature, it has never before had to co-evolve with *Earth system change*. Property law did not even exist before the last era of Earth system change. Like everything else in human existence since then, therefore, property law has evolved in a state of Earth system "stationarity".[13] The Anthropocene, however, will be anything but stationary. A planetary future of "non-stationarity" does not portend well for the safety and security of hundreds of millions of humans, leading many public and private institutions to call for policies supporting

[7] Blumm and Ruhl (n 5).

[8] Will Steffen and others, 'Trajectories of the Earth System in the Anthropocene' (2018) 115 Proceedings of the National Academy of Sciences 8252 <https://www.pnas.org/doi/10.1073/pnas.1810141115> accessed 30 June 2025 (discussing actions in different fields needed to ensure climate stabilisation).

[9] Peter Vitousek and others, 'Human Domination of Earth Ecosystems' (1997) 277 Science 494.

[10] Thomas F Stocker, 'Surprises for Climate Stability' (2020) 367 Science 1425.

[11] Timothy M Lenton and others, 'Climate Tipping Points—Too Risky to Bet Against' (2019) 575 Nature 592 < https://www.nature.com/articles/d41586-019-03595-0> accessed 7 July 2025 (discussing different tipping point thresholds and the drastic consequences of failing to avoid them).

[12] Steffen et al (n 8).

[13] Robin Kundis Craig, 'Stationarity Is Dead-Long Live Transformation: Five Principles for Climate Change Adaptation Law' (2010) 34 Harvard Environmental Law Review 9.

preventive "mitigation" of climate change to avoid and reduce impacts,[14] and advancing preparatory "adaptation" to respond to the impacts of climate change we cannot mitigate.[15]

Given the role property law has played in giving rise to climate change,[16] it stands to reason that it should have a role in advancing both mitigation to slow or reverse climate change, and adaptation to help manage climate change impacts. Those roles are unlikely to be fulfilled if property law itself does not change. In this chapter, therefore, we first broadly conceptualise how Earth system nonstationary and property law intersect, then we examine specific mitigation and adaptation contexts in which property law is likely to be pressed into service, in many instances through doctrinal change.[17]

2. Earth System Non-Stationarity and Property Law

It seems intuitive that climate disruption will disrupt private interests and relationships—that is a premise behind the need for climate change mitigation and adaptation. All fields of private law thus will be touched by climate disruptions, but property law is distinct in one profound aspect—the Earth's climate system disruptions change and are changed by property. That is, the actual object of property doctrine—physical real property—directly contributes to, and is directly disrupted by, climate change. The question we tackle in this chapter, therefore, is whether and how private law property doctrines will need to evolve to reduce and manage those disruptions. Some background on the scope and scale of climate disruption thus is useful to frame the question.

Although the Earth system has changed dramatically over billions of years, for the past 8,000 years—and certainly for as long as the common law has been at work—our climate system has been remarkably stable.[18] To be sure, variability in weather patterns has led to severe droughts, hurricanes, wildfires, and other natural disaster events requiring public and private law responses.[19] But the upper and lower bounds of temperature, rainfall, floods, storm intensity, and other such events were relatively stable over millennial time scales. This "idea that natural systems fluctuate within an unchanging envelope of variability"—known as stationarity—became a foundational premise in the planning, design, financing, and operation of the world's infrastructure, agriculture, energy industry, and all other sectors.[20]

[14] Intergovernmental Panel on Climate Change, Priyadarshi R Shukla and others (eds), *Climate Change 2022: Mitigation of Climate Change* (*Working Group III contribution to the Sixth Assessment Report of the Intergovernmental Panel*, 2022) <https://www.ipcc.ch/report/ar6/wg3/downloads/report/IPCC_AR6_WGIII_SPM.pdf> accessed 5 July 2025.

[15] Intergovernmental Panel on Climate Change, Hans-Otto Pörtner and others (eds), *Climate Change 2022: Impacts, Adaptation and Vulnerability* (*Working Group II contribution to the Sixth Assessment Report of the Intergovernmental Panel*, 2022) <https://www.ipcc.ch/report/ar6/wg2/downloads/report/IPCC_AR6_WGII_SummaryForPolicymakers.pdf> accessed 5 July 2025.

[16] Whiteley (n 3).

[17] The scope of our discussion is on property doctrine within the domain of private law. We do not address regulatory takings, zoning and other public land use regulation regimes, or governmental management of publicly owned property.

[18] Stocker (n 10) (discussing the relative climate stability of the past eight thousand years compared to the preceding ice age).

[19] Daniel A Farber, *Disaster Law and Policy, Second Edition 2nd* (Aspen Publishers) (examining legal ramifications of disasters in public and private sectors).

[20] PCD Milly and others, 'Climate Change. Stationarity Is Dead: Whither Water Management?' (2008) 319 Science 573.

With climate change already well underway, the scientific consensus is that the Earth's climate system has entered a long era of non-stationarity of climate averages, climate variances, and relationships between different climate components.[21] As a consequence, everything driving and affected by climate faces a nonstationary future as well, including infectious diseases, wildfires, ecosystem integrity, infrastructure, agriculture, and so on.[22] This does not mean that climate is random or arbitrary, though it does mean that predictions cannot rely solely on the past to plan the future around simple linear extrapolations.[23] Rather, the assumption of stationarity for any mitigation or adaptation policy purpose must be replaced with the expectation of non-stationarity and what has been called a "no-analogue future".[24]

It is implausible that such novel changes will affect only nature. Importantly for our purposes, the systemic nature of these impacts and risks means that public and private actors will take actions (or not) with respect to their uses of property that will have consequences not only for themselves but for others within the scope of what we call (and describe in more detail below) their property "mitigation footprint" and "adaptation footprint". The mitigation footprint of property use is not the same as the carbon footprint's measure of GHG emissions. Rather, it is defined by how one's asserted use of property affects the capacity *of others* to mitigate climate change. The adaptation footprint is defined by the question of who could be harmed by an actor's uses of property in the face of climate change impacts, whether that be through a failure to adapt or through taking of maladaptive measures.

Climate mitigation and adaptation are relatively new initiatives for public and private entities. While there has been considerable discussion of policy strategies for mitigation and adaptation, not much thought has been given to their property use footprints. These new footprints of property use may be substantially different from, say, footprints of noise, pollution, and other harms that are the traditional fodder of property law and regulation. To complicate matters further, as non-stationarity progresses—as the averages, variances, and relationships of the climate system continue to shift—one's mitigation and adaptation footprints could change in scope and form in unexpected, even novel ways. Sorting out impacts of property uses is inevitably complicated under those conditions. Indeed, it is fair to say that the property law system has *never* processed doctrinal design under those kinds of dynamic planetary conditions and their impacts on social systems. It stands to reason that the answers to property ownership design and dispute resolution may come out differently than they have in the long period of predictable stationarity. At the very least, that possibility should not be ignored.

That prospect leads to the question central to the evolution of property doctrine: What do we want property law to do, if anything, to actively shape the way private actors operate in their mitigation and adaption footprints? It seems inevitable from the foregoing descriptions of climate change impacts that climate change mitigation and adaptation will become fodder for

[21] Bernard Cazelles and Simon Hales, 'Infectious Diseases, Climate Influences, and Nonstationarity' (2006) 3 PLoS Medicine e328.

[22] Bueno de Mesquita and others, 'Taking Climate Change into Account: Non-stationarity in Climate Drivers of Ecological Response (2021) 109 Journal of Ecology, 1491 (ecosystems and infectious diseases); Jeremy S Littell and others, 'Climate Change and Future Wildfire in the Western United States: An Ecological Approach to Nonstationarity' (2018) 6 Earth's Future 1097 (wildfires); Milly (n 20) (infrastructure).

[23] Steffen et al (n 8) (discussing the unprecedent impacts on planetary processes caused by human activities).

[24] The term was popularised in Douglas Fox, 'Ecology. Back to the No-Analog Future?' (2007) 316 Science 823 ('These odd communities [are] called "no analogue" ecosystems because no modern counterparts for them exist').

property disputes—indeed, they already have—and that private law will be asked to evolve in response. As guideposts for directing that evolution, there are several possible collective goals the private law of property could use as a framework for evaluating the efficacy of possible doctrinal changes: (1) preserving the stability of property law, to help promote more stable private investments and to encourage planning around an increasingly uncertain set of natural conditions; (2) promoting efficient, or at least cost-effective and non-wasteful, investments in both mitigation and adaptation; (3) advancing socially just mitigation and adaptation, which must be fair and equitable, especially to the least well off segments of society; and (4) prioritising precautionary mitigation and adaptation.[25]

These policy guideposts are not necessarily mutually exclusive or at sharp odds, but neither are they necessarily always harmonious or synergistic. In looking to the various guideposts, therefore, courts applying property law doctrine in contexts of climate change mitigation and adaptation need to be attentive to tensions between the goals and strike a balance, rather than fixate on one guidepost to the exclusion of others. We offer suggestions below in this regard, first for mitigation and then for adaptation. We believe that this ultimately has important implications for the footprint of private property law, so to speak, and how the relationships and remedies it provides will be defined to address a future where Earth system non-stationarity is the new normal.

3. Property Law for Mitigation

Climate change mitigation pursues the broad objective of reducing atmospheric GHG concentrations primarily by (1) directly reducing GHG emissions and (2) expanding GHG sinks. Mitigation policy is dominated by complex decisions over whether and how to promote new forms of low-carbon energy production, adoption of more efficient technologies for society such as the electrification of transportation, and significant deployment of carbon capture and sequestration technology. As is well discussed, at the state and local level alike, public mitigation policies span from housing to transportation, energy, water, and taxation.[26] Less examined is how all of these mitigation policies present profound and unresolved questions for property law. We divide these issues into three buckets: (1) ownership design, (2) use restrictions, and (3) novel property disputes. Managing these buckets of property law issues surrounding mitigation will require keeping a careful eye on how they influence overall carbon emissions, demonstrating the importance of how private law, properly conceived, will play an important role in helping to reduce carbon emissions in a manner that also provides opportunities to advance other social benefits.

3.1 Ownership Design

Mitigation policy has led to a quest for decarbonisation through development of renewable energy resources and for sequestration of greenhouse gasses to increase sinks. In both cases, novel ownership design questions are arising on top of settled doctrines distributing ownership rights in subsurface and other resources. These "square peg-round hole" questions do not

25 We present, and elaborate upon, similar guideposts for evaluating private law in light of climate adaptation in a separate article. Jim Rossi and JB Ruhl, 'Adapting Private Law for Climate Change Adaptation' (2023) 76 Vanderbilt Law Review 827.

26 Frank W Geels and others, 'Sociotechnical Transitions for Deep Decarbonization' (2017) 357 Science 1242; Frank W Geels and others, 'The Socio-Technical Dynamics of Low-Carbon Transitions' (2017) 1 Joule 463.

necessarily require new doctrines, but finding the right fit will require applying settled statutory and contract terms to new contexts. This section applies our guideposts to some key private property ownership issues at the centre of climate mitigation policy.

3.1.1 Solar Rights

For centuries, property law has been central to disputes surrounding the access to sunlight by conflicting uses of property, including for purposes of solar energy production. Under the doctrine of ancient lights (a longstanding principle in English common and statutory law), a property owner receiving sunlight across adjoining property was granted a negative prescriptive easement to keep an adjacent landowner from interfering with that sunlight. The scope of the ancient lights doctrine was always defined narrowly (historically, it protected light for purposes like reading, not for energy protection), but as solar energy production gives rises to a need for uninterrupted access to sunlight, property disputes have given this old doctrine a new life.

Despite efforts to define a first in time doctrine for access to sunlight, most American courts have rejected the doctrine of ancient lights, instead addressing conflicts between property owners related to access to sunlight through basic principles related to trespass and nuisance. There is little doubt that as a general proposition, ownership of land includes ownership of the energy potential of that land.[27] Resort to nuisance and trespass can help to resolve interference with solar rights, much as these doctrines were used to address early conflicts surrounding flooding from mill development.

Just as state Mill Acts expanded eminent domain for purposes of hydro development, many states have adopted solar right and solar easement laws, helping to define the scope of solar access for energy production. While these laws may authorise solar easements, the implementation of these easements depends on private voluntary arrangements. As Sarah Bronin has observed, an unfortunate lack of clarity continues to plague solar rights, in many instances making the development of solar energy more complicated and uncertain than it needs to be.[28] Moreover, just as the rule of capture can promote wasteful development of common pool resources such as oil and gas, a property regime that ignores basic ownership issues related to solar rights can unintentionally promote uses of solar energy that do not maximise societal benefits, including climate mitigation.[29]

3.1.2 Wind Rights

In a similar manner, securing the public benefit of increased wind power resource availability has led to a growing conversation among property law scholars and practitioners over the prospect of a severable wind estate as a way to define wind rights.[30] A wind power facility,

[27] If energy potential is central to a property right in land, a related issue, which we do not discuss here, is whether a landowner has a property right to interconnect its land to the energy grid in order to allow for the development and sale of that energy potential to others in society. Jon Wellinghoff and Steven Weissman, 'The Right to Self-Generate as a Grid-Connected Customer' (2015) 36 Energy Law Journal 305.

[28] Sara C Bronin, 'Solar Rights' (2009) 89 Boston University Law Review 1217 (exploring the history of access to sunlight).

[29] Sara C Bronin, 'Modern Lights' (2009) 80 University of Colorado Law Review 881 (advocating, in the case of disputes over entitlement to the sun's rays, awarding rights 'to the property owner whose use of sunlight will most benefit society').

[30] Thomas Boyd, 'Who Owns the Texas Sky? An Analysis of Wind Rights in Texas' (2015) 45 Environmental Law Reporter 10426 (comparing severable wind estates to severable mineral estates, arguing they accord with Texas contract law and property law); Cameron K Rivers, 'Change in the Wind: Severance of the Wind Estate in Texas' (2019) 14 Texas Journal of Oil, Gas and Energy Law 91('[T]he

obviously, does not generate its own wind; rather, it requires a continued flow across the windshed landscape to the wind turbines. Although leases and easements also could serve as means for establishing wind flows across the relevant properties, the arguments in favour of a severable wind estate stress the greater certainty such an estate interest would provide wind power developers in securing a stable wind supply.[31] On the other hand, any new divisions to the unified fee will present new sources of ambiguity and of friction between the respective sub-estate owners, which has led some scholars to caution against severability and favour the lease or easement form.[32] As it stands, some US states have moved in favour of allowing severed wind estates, while several others have adapted wind leases and wind easements as ways to secure wind flows.[33]

3.1.3 Subsurface Rights

Climate mitigation policies also see a central role for carbon sequestration as a form of carbon sink. Much as with solar and wind, the success of carbon sequestration policies depends on how property rights regarding geological storage facilities are approached. Consider "pore space"—the open spaces between particles of soil, sand, and rock underground. Pore space has long been used for purposes of mineral storage and extraction (including natural gas fracturing), but it is also critical for promoting low carbon energy technologies, including

severability of the wind estate is already supported by existing laws and public policy objectives, the most important of which are that people are already severing the wind estate, severance promotes certainty and stability in the energy sector, and a severed estate—unlike a lease—can be passed down or sold'); Shanisha Y Smith, 'What Lies Beneath Above: Mineral, Wind, and Groundwater Estates in Texas and The Severance Implications' (*Issuu, 2021*) <https://issuu.com/leosur/docs/thl_janfeb21_6e0a4b8ce97191/s/12123728> accessed 30 June 2025 ('Property ownership theories support the severance of the wind estate'); Rachel Givens, 'Pecos Bill's Turbines in the Tumbleweeds: Extending the Texas Property Code to Permit Severance of Wind Rights Through Testate and Intestate Succession' (2022) 14 Estate Planning & Community Property Law Journal 579 ('The Texas legislature should create legislation that recognizes wind as a private property interest and allows landowners to sever the wind estate from surface ownership, including testate and intestate succession method').

31 Rivers (n 30) 103 ('Recognizing a wind severance as valid would assuage the costs and uncertainty wind developers now face'); Givens (n 30) 600 ('One major reason for having clear legislation within this area of wind law is that legislation may greatly reduce the number of complaints filed in opposition to wind farm development').

32 DuVivier (n 6) ('[W]hile property law may permit the severance of wind rights, the traditional rationales for mineral severance do not support severance as the most effective method for encouraging the development of wind power'); Troy A Rule, 'Wind Rights under Property Law: Answers Still Blowing in the Wind' (2012) 26 Probate and Property 56 (describing novel questions related to wind rights, including takings of severed wind estates and dispute resolution between surface owners and wind estate owners).

33 For severed wind estate developments, see, e.g., Abby Roughton, 'Contra Costa Water District v. Vaquero Farms, Inc., 58 Cal. App. 4th 883 (1997): Case Brief Summary' (*Quimbee*) <https://www.quimbee.com/cases/contra-costa-water-district-v-vaquero-farms-inc> accessed 30 June 2025. ('[O]ne may have a right to use wind power rights without owning any interest in the land . . . . Windpower rights clearly are "substantial" rights and thus may be condemned, or excluded from condemnation, despite their factual novelty under present law'); *Ridge Renewables LLC v Hale Cnty. Wind Farm LLC* No. A43616-2012 (64th Dist. Ct., Hale County, Tex. 11 May 2023) (court recognised a severed wind property interest); Wyoming Statutes, ss 34-1-151(e) (acknowledging potential severance of the wind estate from the surface estate in requiring its disclosure in certain circumstances). For wind easements, see, e.g., Minnesota Statutes, s 500.30 (granting wind easement rights); North Dakota Century Code, s 17-04-03 (2005) (granting wind easement rights); South Dakota Codified Laws, s 43-13-17 (1996) (granting wind easement rights); Montana Code, s 70-17-403 (2011) (granting wind easement rights).

storing carbon dioxide through carbon capture and storage (CCS) technology, where captured CO_2 is injected into these spaces to be permanently sequestered. Pore space can also be used to store hydrogen gas in underground formations.[34]

Under the *ad coelum* doctrine in US law, the surface owner owns property from the heavens to the core of the earth. Hard minerals, such as limestone, shale, coal, and similar minerals, and fugacious minerals, such as oil and gas, are thus owned by the surface owner. Surface owners may, however—and often do—sever off portions of their property (their "estate"). As with wind rights, this subsurface severance creates a separate mineral and surface estate called a "split estate". When severance of the mineral and surface estates occurs, this raises the question of who owns the pore space.

Ownership of pore space can be complex and varies by location. When it comes to private ownership of pore space, two distinct rules apply, depending on the jurisdiction. Under the American rule, which most states tend to follow, the surface owner owns pore space unless it is expressly granted to a mineral estate holder. Under the English rule, adopted by a minority of states, pore space is owned by the mineral estate owner.[35]

These rules, however, do not always clearly resolve issues related to pore space. Some jurisdictions, for example, do not have a history with the use of subsurface property for energy protection and, as a result, have not clearly adopted any approach at all.[36] Even when one approach has clearly been adopted, is not always clear when pore space rights "vest", nor is there a universally accepted approach to resolving ambiguities in deeds related to core space. The American rule would make it clear that unless a deed expressly says otherwise, pore space rights that are unrelated to mineral right production default to the surface owner, unless clearly reserved to the mineral holder. But what if the creation and availability of pore space is dependent upon the removal of minerals, such as gas or petroleum? After all, a surface owner cannot possess full rights in the pore space until the mineral owner has extracted the minerals. So, when exactly does pore space become "pore space"? And would a deed conveying mineral extraction rights include the use of pore space by the mineral owner for activities related to mineral rights extraction?

In some jurisdictions, deeds allowing subsurface rights for natural gas production have been interpreted broadly to allow the mineral estate owner to engage in injection activities related to hydraulic fracturing.[37] But if the use of pore space for gas production techniques such as fracturing is considered to be a part of the mineral estate, then might this also allow the use of pore space for CCS aimed at mitigating the carbon impacts of natural gas production or use from those same mineral rights? If so, then can it also be used for hydrogen storage aimed to offset the climate impacts of those same carbon-intensive minerals, or does the surface owner always retain control over this?

While mineral rights holders frequently argue for the application of a rule of capture to storage activities that are concurrent with oil and gas production, most states do not appear to allow the mineral holder to use pore space for storage of fossil fuels produced off site.[38] The

[34] The specific geological requirements and technical challenges for hydrogen storage differ somewhat from CO_2 storage, an issue that is beyond the scope of the discussion in this chapter.

[35] Jean Feriancek, 'Resolving Ownership of Pore Space' (2011) 26 Natural Resources & Environment 49 ('[O]wnership of pore space by the surface owner is considered the majority view in the United States').

[36] Abigail M Jones, 'Pore Space: The Final Frontier' (2024) 38 Natural Resources & Environment 55.

[37] Hannah Wiseman, 'Defining Pore Space Ownership and Related Issues: A Summary' (2022) <https://celp.psu.edu/wp-content/uploads/2022/12/Definition-of-pore-space-and-related-issues_Summary-for-posting.pdf> accessed 5 July 2025.

[38] ibid.

rights to pore space for storage, including carbon storage such as CCS or hydrogen storage, should typically default to the surface owner. As has been observed by others, applying a strong rule of capture to pore space in these kinds of contexts can result in wasteful and inefficient use, coordination problems, and statutory schemes that would eventually require regulatory or statutory solutions.[39]

In the context of sunlight, wind, and sequestration pore space, similar principles seem important for allowing private law solutions to promote mitigation strategies. Recognition of severable estates for solar, wind, and pore space provides a mechanism to allow property law to begin to manage these resources for low-cost carbon production, in a manner that helps to incentivise the use of these resources for climate mitigation while also providing some mechanisms to help minimise waste.

Such doctrines will be particularly important as new low-carbon forms of energy are developed. Recent discoveries of large reservoirs of pure natural hydrogen trapped below impermeable subsurface geologic formations have spurred interest in exploring for and extracting from reservoirs of this so-called gold hydrogen.[40] With extensive reserves believed to be present in the US,[41] the question arises, as with pore space, as to who owns gold hydrogen when the mineral estate has been severed. Although the extraction process could be adapted from techniques used for petroleum and natural gas, hydrogen is formed in different ways and areas than those resources and may even be renewable.[42] As with CCS, encouraging the use of pore space for the development of such resources will require clear definition of a severable estate. The American rule provides a mechanism to ensure that development of the low carbon fuel will be incentivised without promoting needless waste.

Complicating matters even further, obtaining a contiguous block of pore space rights at the scale necessary for commercial CCS or hydrogen storage projects is challenging. Pore space that is usable for commercial energy storage typically extends over a number of separately owned surface parcels. In the context of oil and gas law, private law and regulatory approaches have developed to address this coordination challenge, including approaches such as unitisation, that can compel pooling of subsurface pore rights where a certain threshold of property owners (typically a significant supermajority) agree. With pore space, however, only around a quarter of states have adopted unitisation statutes, allowing the use of pore space (along with equitable compensation) once a threshold percentage of surface owners agree.[43] In most states, therefore traditional private law remedies, such as trespass and nuisance, will remain vital to ensuring that the pore space owner's property interests are protected, and that pore space is not used in a wasteful manner that fails to reduce aggregate carbon emissions.

[39] Joseph Schremmer, 'Pore Space Property' (2021) Utah Law Review 1, 14, 47.

[40] Laurent Truche and others, 'A Deep Reservoir for Hydrogen Drives Intense Degassing in the Bulqizë Ophiolite' (2024) 383 Science 618; Rafael Ortiz Cebolla and Carlos Navas, 'Supporting Hydrogen Technologies Deployment in EU Regions and Member States: The Smart Specialisation Platform on Energy (S3PEnergy)' (2019) 44 International Journal of Hydrogen Energy 19067.

[41] US Geological Survey, 'Geologic Hydrogen Prospectivity Map Explorer and Data Release for Prospectivity Mapping for Geologic Hydrogen' (*USGS*, 16 January 2025) <https://certmapper.cr.usgs.gov/data/apps/hydrogen/> accessed 5 July 2025.

[42] US Geological Survey, 'The Potential for Geologic Hydrogen for Next-Generation Energy' (*USGS*, 13 April 2023) <https://www.usgs.gov/news/featured-story/potential-geologic-hydrogen-next-generation-energy> accessed 5 July 2025.

[43] Madeline Lewis, 'Core Space Unitization for Geologic Sequestration of Carbon Dioxide' (*Great Plains Institute, Center for Energy Regulation and Policy Analysis, School of Energy Resources, University of Wyoming* 2024) <https://carboncaptureready.betterenergy.org/wp-content/uploads/2024/07/SER-Unitization-Analysis_FINAL.pdf> accessed 5 July 2025.

3.2 Use Restrictions

To put it bluntly, decarbonising the economy will require extensive behavioural change, including by private property owners. Public law, of course, is one legal mechanism for forcing changes in practices, from requiring greater housing density to driving electric vehicles. But private climate governance is increasingly playing a role as well and could leverage various tools of property law.

3.2.1 Homeowner Associations

More than half of new residential homes in the US are members of homeowner associations (HOAs). Most HOAs attach restrictions to their member's property deeds. While some of these are considered voluntary, HOA members are typically required to follow recorded neighbourhood restrictions and rules in addition to any applicable local zoning laws that restrict property use.

HOA use restrictions routinely produce public goods for the community and could readily promote climate mitigation. For example, an HOA could prohibit the use of combustion engines for lawn maintenance. More often, however, HOA deed restrictions likely serve as a barrier to reducing carbon emissions. For example, even though more dense housing would reduce carbon impacts related to housing and transportation, it is not uncommon for HOA restrictions to require a minimum size for residential homes, to limit how many homes can be constructed on a single subdivision lot, and to prohibit future subdivision of property. These kinds of HOA use restrictions can contribute to urban sprawl and impose restrictions on alternative uses of property that would reduce carbon emissions.

While the language of some deeds restricting property use may be clear (for example, a minimum lot size recorded on a deed that prohibits future subdivision of property), the language in HOA deed restrictions is often unclear. For example, an HOA covenant prohibiting the use of metallic roofing materials or vague language limiting any modification to a home that is visible from the street could potentially be applied to keep some residential homes from installing solar panels. In Raleigh, North Carolina, an HOA required a homeowner to remove solar panels that were visible from the street, subjecting the homeowner to more than $50,000 in fines for violation of the HOA's architectural review standards.[44]

For purposes of encouraging carbon mitigation, we think it important that any ambiguity in HOA use restrictions be construed to favour sustainable practices that would promote carbon mitigation. Thus, absent an express use restriction (such as a clear prohibition on the placement of solar panels on a home), our guideposts would suggest that courts should not enforce the use of ambiguous HOA covenants or vague architectural review standards to prohibit a homeowner from installing energy efficient equipment, such as solar panels or EV charging stations. Consistent with this approach, the North Carolina Supreme Court ultimately rejected the HOA's decision to restrict the installation of solar panels that are visible from the street, although the court left open the possibility that an HOA could impose reasonable restrictions on use that do not effectively prohibit the use of solar panels.[45]

Even if an HOA covenant were to use clear language (rather than unwritten architectural standards) to limit the placement of solar panels on property, state or local laws requiring

[44] Elizabeth Ouzts, 'North Carolina Supreme Court to Review How Much Power HOAs Have Over Solar' (Canary Media, 4 April 2022) <https://www.canarymedia.com/articles/enn/n-c-supreme-court-to-rule-on-how-much-power-hoas-have-over-solar> accessed 5 July 2025.

[45] *Belmont Association Inc. v Farwig* 381 N.C. 306, 873 S.E.2d 486 (N.C. 2022).

access to solar may still pre-empt the HOA use restriction.[46] Our guideposts promoting carbon mitigation and considering the potential equities and unfairness to residents would favour broad reading of such laws to only allow reasonable limitations on use rather than outright prohibitions on residential carbon mitigation investments—thus favouring private resident carbon mitigation over unprincipled or arbitrary enforcement of HOA restrictions that would effectively prohibit residential installation of solar panels.

Just as much as HOA use restrictions can, if not approached carefully, hobble private property owner carbon mitigation efforts, HOAs present an important opportunity to encourage collective climate mitigation. Elinor Ostrom's pioneering work identified how voluntary local communities can overcome many of the collective action barriers to promoting sustainability for common pool resources.[47] Similarly, HOAs are local communities responsible for coordinating neighbouring properties and managing shared resources. In this sense, we think that there are untapped opportunities for HOAs to use their covenants to promote carbon reduction through shared resources such as the installation of solar panels, microgrids, and EV charging stations in common spaces. Our guideposts would also suggest that HOA covenants presumptively not be read to prohibit these kinds of voluntary carbon mitigation arrangements between neighbours.

3.2.2 Conservation Easements

Similarly, consider conservation easements as a potential opportunity for private carbon reduction. Landowners can promote carbon storage by their property resources through avoided deforestation (i.e., leaving the land to evolve under its natural ecological conditions) or by making new investments in reforestation, afforestation, or other carbon reductions. Conservation easements often restrict land use to preserve its natural state. A conservation easement represents a commitment not to develop land, but if a conservation easement is read too broadly to limit carbon offsets or future use of land to produce carbon reduction or storage activities, this could hobble socially beneficial private carbon reduction activities. For this reason, our guideposts favour flexibility in interpreting conservation easements to encourage private carbon reduction investments. Conservation easements should limit property use and development, consistent with the expectations of the original easement grant. However, absent a clear easement to the contrary, the ultimate touchstone for determining when carbon credits can be used or new investments in carbon reduction can be made on property operating under a conservation easement should not be whether there is any change in the natural state of the property. Rather, the focus should be on whether, consistent with the original easement grant, an easement produces a net reduction in carbon producing activities.[48]

[46] Kristina Caffrey, 'The House of the Rising Sun: Homeowners' Associations, Restrictive Covenants, Solar Panels, and the Contract Clause' (2010) 50(3) Natural Resources Journal 721; Edwin Kisiel, 'Solar Panels in Condominium Communities' (2020) 8 LSU Journal of Energy Law and Resources 9; Evan J Rosenthal, 'Letting the Sunshine In: Protecting Residential Access to Solar Energy in Common Interest Developments' (2013) 40 Florida State University Law Review.

[47] Elinor Ostrom, *Governing the Commons: The Evolution of Institutions for Collective Action* (CUP 1990); Elinor Ostrom, 'Collective Action and the Evolution of Social Norms' 14 Journal of Economic Perspectives 137 (2000). See also Michael P Vandenbergh and Paul Stern, Chapter 31 of this handbook.

[48] Isaac Lunt, 'Toward Distributed Nature: The Afforestation Easement and a Regenerative Land Ethic' (2024) 124 Columbia Law Review 1081.

3.3 Novel Property Disputes

Liability for the harms and risks presented by carbon mitigation, such as CCS projects, is a complex issue with a range of legal and regulatory considerations. An effective liability framework for dealing with the harms created by various carbon mitigation measures will need to balance the need to protect the public and the environment with the need to encourage investment in carbon mitigation technologies. Given that CCS requires the capture, transport, and underground storage of carbon for centuries into the future, the potential for extreme event disasters or ongoing leakage causing harm to humans or their environment is significant. Thus, from the perspective of human health and safety, CCS will likely not only require common law remedies but will also require some kind of comprehensive regulatory and insurance framework (far beyond the scope of this chapter).

The common law of property, however, can provide important background principles to help resolve conflicts between property owners regarding CCS activities, especially where these conflicts cause harm to property value or business losses.[49] Subsurface invasions, such as escaped liquid or gas associated with CCS activities, could be said to constitute a "trespass" to the extent that it constitutes a physical invasion to another's property. At the same time, trespass is typically limited to a one-time invasion and, even then, effective remedies for trespass can require some clear interference with another's use of their property. To the extent that trespass can help to resolve these kinds of disputes, it will likely be limited to those situations where subsurface property rights are fully articulated and—again even then—it is unlikely to provide a sufficient legal remedy for ongoing harms or risks presented by CCS.

Much like conflicts between property owners regarding wind and solar projects, conflicts regarding carbon mitigation activities such as CCS are more likely to be resolved under nuisance-like principles. With nuisance, courts are required not simply to determine whether there has been an invasion of a preexisting property right but to balance the reasonableness of the ongoing interference with other uses of property. In striking this balance courts will typically consider factors such as the nature and the severity of the harm, the usefulness of the activity and the character of the surrounding area. A nuisance approach to liability for activities such as CCS has many advantages over focusing on trespass or treating liability for CCS under strict liability principles—because it allows for the recognition of the value of carbon mitigation from the activity, as well as the flexibility to take into account considerations that will encourage carbon mitigation activities in areas where the risks of harm are least likely. It will also recognise how the standard of care for an activity such as CCS can evolve with time and experience, allowing for heightened liability standards in the future as more is learned about risk management in the future.

4. Property Law for Adaptation

Legal and policy discourse around the goal of climate change adaptation was initially resisted for fear of leading to complacency undermining mitigation policy.[50] As it became increasingly evident that mitigation policy would not avoid substantial climate change impacts, adaptation

[49] Joseph A Schremmer, 'Getting Past Possession: Subsurface Property Disputes as Nuisances' (2020) 95 Washington Law Review 315.

[50] J B Ruhl, 'Climate Change Adaptation and the Structural Transformation of Environmental Law' (2010) 40 Environmental Law 363, 433.

necessarily had to be recognised as an essential component of climate policy.[51] Legal scholars also were quick to observe that climate change impacts and adapting to them would likely require doctrinal responses in property law.[52] Perhaps out of confidence that mitigation policy would gain traction, these early commentaries predicted that "climate adaptation requires more tinkering with property rights, but not necessarily wholesale rethinking".[53]

Tinkering has long been a feature of doctrinal evolution. Property law has recognised that the human-nature social-ecological system presents risks distributed across social relationships that change along with changes in other systems, such as technology, and has built-in mechanisms for adapting to those relationships. As wildfire became an increasing risk in Western US states, for example, courts accommodated demand for protective housing materials (such as replacing wood shingles on homes with fire resistant shingles) even when prohibited by HOA covenants.[54]

Since then, however, it has become clear that the goals of the Paris Agreement—to contain global rise in average temperatures to no more than 2°C, and ideally to no more than 1.5°C—are unlikely to be achieved and that extreme events will be more frequent and increasingly more extreme as Earth system tipping points loom.[55] While we may not be at the point of "wholesale rethinking" of property law, this new reality suggests that more than "tinkering" will be required. Whether we call it rewiring, upgrading, or remodelling, what does the future of property law look like?

The concept of the adaptation footprint serves as a conceptual model for imagining answers to that question. Consider two owners of adjacent parcels, Ann and Bob. Any action Ann takes on her property has a footprint of potential effects on Bob's parcel. In wildfire-urban interface zones, for example, how Ann manages brush on her property can increase or decrease Bob's exposure to risk of wildfires. Put simply, the adaptation footprint concept accounts for the ways in which climate change is altering the risk footprints Ann and Bob pose to each other, and to others. In general, many risks in the adaptation footprint will be amplified and more widely distributed than before climate change began altering the Earth system, and some risks will be entirely novel. Moreover, as climate change continues to alter the Earth system, the adaptation footprint itself will not be static. Like the Earth system, one's adaptation footprint will evolve in a context of non-stationarity.

To be sure, public law (zoning, environmental law, building codes) has played a large role in managing private risk footprints, and surely will weigh in as the adaptation footprints of private actors become increasingly salient and unstable. But so has private law weighed in as risks change, and it is unlikely that private law will remain static as our adaptation footprints take hold and dynamically evolve.

[51] Victor B Flatt, 'Unsettled: How Climate Change Challenges a Foundation of Our Legal System, and Adapting the Legal State' (2016) Brigham Young University Law Review 1397 (arguing that legal doctrines will become less settled as 'the world on which our system is based becomes less settled'); R Henry Weaver and Douglas A Kysar, 'Courting Disaster: Climate Change and the Adjudication of Catastrophe' (2017) 93 Notre Dame Law Review 295 (asking 'how long can . . . [courts' previous] conservative approach hold up under a barrage of catastrophic harms?'); Craig (n 13); John G Sprankling, 'Property Law for the Anthropocene Era' (2017) 59 Arizona Law Review 737.

[52] Holly Doremus, 'Climate Change and the Evolution of Property Rights' (2011) 1 UC Irvine Law Review 1091.

[53] ibid 1115.

[54] *Fink v Miller* (1995) 896 P.2d 649.

[55] Timothy M Lenton and others, 'Tipping Elements in the Earth's Climate System' (2008) 105 Proceedings of the National Academy of Sciences 1786 <https://www.pnas.org/doi/10.1073/pnas.0705414105> accessed 7 July 2025; Lenton et al (n 11).

We see three roles for property law in that respect. One is to apply—through tinkering if necessary—existing doctrines to account for the amplification and broadened distribution of risks already addressed in property law, such as flooding and wildfires. A second role is to craft new doctrinal responses for cases in which either such risks overwhelm the adaptive capacity of existing doctrines, or entirely novel risks are presented (such as impacts of sea-level rise) for which no existing doctrine could effectively be adapted to manage. The third role is to manage private adaptation initiatives, including those taken in response to public climate change adaptation policy.

In order for property law to adapt coherently and effectively in each of these roles, we propose that it (and thus property owners) must not only embrace the concept of the adaptation footprint, but also its non-stationarity. This means that to the extent property law, like other private law realms, incorporates "reasonable actor" standards, those standards should impose a duty to reasonably foresee non-stationarity and a corresponding duty to anticipate the consequences of actions in the evolving adaptation footprint. To be sure, this goes beyond tinkering and into the realm of rewiring, but simple observation of the world around us today (such as the increasing intensity and frequency of major storms) would inform any reasonable person that the changing Earth system is presenting an entirely new risk profile to humans. Property law (and private law generally) now operates in a context in which it must be assumed by all actors that this year's record storm event or flood will soon be exceeded by another record-setter, and that virtually all features of nature are in flux. The absolving power of the refrain "I didn't see that coming" is as dead as is stationarity itself. In short, property law must adapt to require that we all are held responsible to "see that coming". Below we suggest how that new standard of reasonability plays out in the three roles we outline for the property law of climate change adaptation, with consideration of how our guideposts suggest property law should steer in each role.

4.1 Adapting to Evolving Risks

The theme of climate change adaptation in one word is "more"—as in more extreme, more frequent, more devastating. Yet, to some extent it is also more of the same, as many property doctrines have developed to manage injuries that climate change is exacerbating but not fundamentally changing beyond more. In these contexts, the adaptation footprint is expanding, and with it the foreseeability of non-stationarity. Tinkering with property doctrines may be needed to adjust accordingly in such cases, and our proposed guideposts can inform how much and for what purpose.

Nuisance law, for example, mediates between conflicting uses of property when harm from one to the other is unreasonable. The basic framework of nuisance law can easily accommodate the principle of the fundamental foreseeability of nonstationary and expanding adaptation footprints in its calculus. Nuisance doctrine thus would incorporate the duty to reasonably foresee non-stationarity and a corresponding duty to anticipate the consequences of actions in the evolving adaptation footprint.[56] Any user of private property thus should be held accountable for both in determining whether they have caused nuisance to another property—for example, from the effects of a poorly designed seawall or the removal of coastal dunes. Similarly, the doctrine of waste could incorporate harsher conditions resulting from climate change to impose a heightened duty of maintenance to avoid permissive waste.[57] And the same conditions could provide reason to adjust the relationship between dominant and

[56] Craig (n 13).

[57] Samuel Niiro, 'An Injury to the Inheritance: Locating an Affirmative Obligation to Climate Adaption in the Law of Waste' (2019) 52 Columbia Journal of Law and Social Problems 653; Tara K

servient estates in servitudes law (such as maintenance of an easement) and landlord-tenant law (such as habitability of premises).

The doctrinal adjustments just described reveal a core difference between climate change mitigation and adaptation, and how our proposed guideposts might apply. Because carbon dioxide emitted anywhere has the same effect on climate, mitigation goals can be advanced largely without regard to physical location. In other words, a reduction in emissions (or an increase in sinks) from a given doctrinal adjustment in property law in Texas has the same impact on climate as it would if performed in Maine or Canada or Australia. Climate change adaptation, by contrast, is highly localised in terms of the threats posed and the effectiveness of measures in response. The adaptation profiles for Phoenix and Madrid, for example, are largely driven by heat whereas, for coastal cities, sea-level rise is a more significant threat. At the local scale, moreover, the distributional effects of a particular doctrinal reform will matter in terms of our guideposts of stability, efficiency, equity, and precaution. To the extent a nation's property law is shaped at subnational jurisdiction scales—for example, in the US, where it is largely the domain of state and local law—these localised variations in adaptation threats and responses are likely to steer different jurisdictions towards different goals.

With these characteristics in mind, our working thesis is that for adaptation to incremental climate impacts, property doctrine tinkering is best suited to promote effective adaptation consistent with the goals of pre-existing doctrine, with stability of legal doctrine as the overarching goal. The doctrine of waste, for example, promotes efficient use of property as between the relevant interests (such as present and future estates; landlord and tenant). For the kind of incrementally evolving climate risks that affect property, that goal should remain the driving principle. Likewise, nuisance law's balancing of the utility of the defendant's conduct versus the gravity of the plaintiff's harm should remain the efficiency-driven guidepost but should take into account how the expanding adaptation footprint and nonstationary effects of climate change factor into the balancing (most likely by increasing the harm side of the assessment). Public nuisance doctrine in particular may find the harm side to be increasing in weight. In short, there is good reason to believe that existing property doctrines, and the policies that have shaped them for centuries, can absorb climate change adaptation with only minor tinkering, and that stability of the doctrines and the policies in place should be the default guidepost going forward.

4.2 Adapting to Excessive and Novel Risks

At some point, more may simply amount to too much, overwhelming the ability of property doctrine to adapt through mere tinkering and with a goal of stability foremost in mind. If "no-analogue" truly means no-analogue for a future on the other side of climate extremes and tipping points, then novel forms of risk are likely to arise for which we also have no analogue existing in property doctrine with which to tinker. In particular, there is increasing concern among prominent climate scientists that cascade failures could spread widely through infrastructure and other social and economic systems with potentially catastrophic impacts, further expanding the adaptation risk footprints associated with uses of property.[58]

A prominent example is sea-level rise. Accretion, avulsion, and related doctrines for managing change along dynamic littoral property lines evolved long before sea-level rise appeared in modern times. Can sea-level rise be integrated into that body of law, or will it so

Righetti and Joseph A Schremmer, 'Waste and the Governance of Private and Public Property' (2022) 93 University of Colorado Law Review 609 (proposing a renewed and strengthened application of waste doctrine across a variety of resources and applications).

[58] Emily N Bondank and Mikhail V Chester, 'Infrastructure Interdependency Failures From Extreme Weather Events as a Complex Process' (2020) 2 Frontiers in Water 1.

fundamentally change how the coastline behaves that a new doctrinal principle is needed?[59] True enough, on a year-to-year basis sea-level rise is incremental and nearly imperceptible, but over decades—particularly in flat coastal areas—the physical effects can be extreme, even to the point of submerging entire parcels. New (and controversial) doctrines, such as rolling easements, have already begun to be explored and tested.[60]

Similarly, nuisance, waste, and other property doctrines, even with concerted tinkering, may not be sufficient to fill in coverage of the entire adaptation footprint. Can we envision a more general "maladapation" property/tort doctrine that borrows from nuisance and negligence? The Intergovernmental Panel on Climate Change (IPCC) has defined "maladaptation" as "*actions* that may lead to increased risk of adverse climate-related outcomes, including via increased greenhouse gas emissions, increased or shifted vulnerability to climate change, more inequitable outcomes, or diminished welfare, now or in the future".[61] Failure to adapt may itself be a form of maladaptation.[62]

A more methodical way of envisioning how property law could evolve under extreme conditions is to stress test existing doctrine against predicted physical risk scenarios at extreme global temperature models (such as 2°C, 3°C, or even 4°C).[63] The first level of such an exercise is to envision the impacts to property uses (such as how does sea-level rise affect coastal properties and how does extreme heat affect wildfire regimes). Our inquiry would then go to the next level, exploring how such changed conditions alter the adaptation footprint relationship and the impacts of one's use of property on others.

Where such an exercise builds reason to anticipate extreme and novel impacts requiring new approaches to property law, how should our guideposts anticipate and steer doctrinal evolution? Here we see the opposite approach from the one suggested above for incremental change. That is, stability is likely an unrealistic goal, and pursuing efficiency would require more knowledge than will be available given the extreme nonstationary. Rather than building on existing doctrine, truly novel doctrinal change will involve testing for results before stabilising new doctrine and promoting efficiency going forward. Under those conditions, equity and precaution may serve as more judicially prudent guideposts, to minimise the potential that doctrinal evolution could have unintended negative consequences.

4.3 Adapting to Adaptation

Adaptation to climate change will require extensive public law responses, such as through planning, building codes and zoning, and infrastructure development. Private actors also will have an interest implementing private adaptation measures *and* in responding to public

[59] Alyson Flournoy, 'Beach Law Cleanup: How Sea-Level Rise Has Eroded the Ambulatory Boundaries Legal Framework' (2017) 42 Vermont Law Review 89; Sax (n 1) 355–56 ('Any effort to characterize today's rising sea levels as avulsive or accretive is empty of meaning. . . . The old categories don't fit the contemporary reality').

[60] Katherine Meek, 'Rolling Easements as a Viable Tool to Address Rising Sea Levels in US Coastal Communities' (2023) 41 UCLA Journal of Environmental Law and Policy 99; Courtney B Johnson and Steven R Schell, 'Adapting to Climate Change on the Oregon Coast: Lines in the Sand and Rolling Easements' (2013) 28 Journal of Environmental Law and Litigation 447.

[61] IPCC, Impacts (n 15), 7 (emphasis added).

[62] Lisa Schipper, 'Maladaptation: When Adaptation to Climate Change Goes Very Wrong' (2020) 3 One Earth 409 (including no response as a form of maladaptation).

[63] J B Ruhl and Robin K Craig, '4°C' (2021) 106 Minnesota Law Review 191 (stress testing for public law adaptation).

adaptation regulatory measures. How can property law develop and innovate doctrines to facilitate private adaptation initiatives and respond to public adaptation regulation?

As for mitigation, property mechanisms such as HOA covenants and conservation easements could also be directed at adaptation. For example, an HOA in a wildfire zone might include provisions regarding brush maintenance, or a conservation easement might have coastal adaptation foremost in mind through provisions requiring maintenance of dune vegetation. Standard easement and other servitude arrangements could also be adapted for climate adaptation, such as to establish wildfire buffers and floodway easements, with built-in flexibility to adapt as climate change impacts continue to evolve.

We anticipate that our suggested guideposts for such private adaptation measures would play out the same as we suggest for their mitigation counterparts. That is, covenant provisions should be interpreted as between the parties so as to maximise the adaptation goals consistent with other governing provisions, but also to minimise interference with public adaptation policies such as building codes. Likewise, public law regulating HOA and similar private arrangements should be applied to minimise interference with desirable adaptation measures and to pre-empt maladaptive measures.

5. Conclusion

There is much work ahead to direct property law's future in response to climate change, both for mitigation and for adaptation. We believe the field is up to the challenge. Not only that, we believe that property law will be an essential complement to public law in achieving societal mitigation and adaptation policies. This is not to say public and private law will necessarily always be harmonious going forward. We allude above to instances in which public law might pre-empt private law arrangements if deemed contrary to public goals, and we have not delved into how public law initiatives, such as aggressive zoning or application of public trust principles, could bump up against regulatory takings claims.[64] Those prospects loom regardless of whether property law doctrine evolves in response to climate change and may inform how doctrine evolves, but should not be overriding or even significant drivers—those questions will sort out over time. Rather, property law innovation for climate change mitigation and adaptation should be most mindful of when and how it should promote stability, efficiency, equity, and precaution and—above all else—how property law should grapple with the foreseeability of non-stationarity and the dynamically changing mitigation and adaptation footprints of property uses. With foundations initiated by other legal scholars, we have endeavoured in this chapter to holistically outline some core principles and illustrative examples in those directions, with the hope that our treatment can serve as a foundation for yet more engagement by scholars, practitioners, and the courts.

[64] Robin Willscheidt and Robin Kundis Craig, 'Sea Level Rise and Takings Liability' (2024) 16 George Washington Journal of Energy and Environmental Law 47; Margaret E Peloso and Margaret R Caldwell, 'Dynamic Property Rights: The Public Trust Doctrine and Takings in a Changing Climate' (2011) 30 Stanford Environmental Law Journal 51.

CHAPTER 15

Cultures of Land Use and Ownership

NICOLE GRAHAM

1. Introduction

LAND laws are grounded in culturally specific ontologies, epistemologies, and languages of place and human-environment relations. They emerge from and reinforce paradigms regarding the significance of land, and the roles of human and more-than-human actors in sustaining cultural and biophysical life. This chapter compares two different kinds of legal regimes or cultures regulating land use and ownership—those of First Peoples and those of settler colonial states—and explores how they shape both the production of climate vulnerability and potentially transformative responses.

In settler colonial jurisdictions, the coexistence of multiple legal orders—those of First Peoples and of colonists—renders visible the cultural specificity and historical contingency of now dominant property regimes.[1] This legal plurality, and the continuing legacies of colonisation, offer a critical vantage point from which to interrogate the entanglement of land laws with the material conditions of climate change. The temporal and spatial dimensions of legal ordering—how laws emerge in relation to diverse ecologies over time—are fundamental to understanding how different legal cultures negotiate and adapt to environmental change. The capacity of legal orders to recognise and respond to dynamic climatological and ecological contexts is central to their long-term viability and sustainability.

The climate crisis demands not only a deep and critical evaluation of the adaptability of the legal orders of First Peoples and settler colonial states to various dynamic material contexts, but importantly also the application of these lessons to the status quo. The challenge is not merely technical—it is cultural. Laws are capable of developing and stretching to accommodate new and different contexts in which they must function, but their plasticity is determined, in part, by the legal cultures in which they are embedded. These cultures structure what counts as lawful, valuable, or possible, and thereby enable or constrain societal responses to ecological crises and climate change.

Property law, of course, regulates the distribution of the goods of life both within and beyond a human society. While some property laws come and go, others endure over very long periods of time. What are the elements of property regimes that have successfully adapted to numerous and various material challenges, including previous climate changes? The legal cultures of land use and ownership are the focus of this chapter.

The laws and legal cultures of First Peoples are diverse and highly specific to particular places. Although a pan-Indigenous legal order and legal culture does not exist, it is frequently

[1] Brian Tamanaha, 'Understanding Legal Pluralism: Past to Present, Local to Global' (2008) 30 Sydney Law Review 392; Margaret Davies, 'Decolonising (and) Legal Pluralism' (2025) 52(3) Journal of Law and Society 1.

observed that place-based laws and legal cultures foreground the importance of obligation, reciprocity, interdependence, and kinship with the more-than-human cohabitants of, and from, a place.[2] Place-based land laws are also frequently articulated through languages characterised by place-attachment[3] and place-based socio-legal identities and relations.[4]

Colonial settler legal cultures, while also internally variegated, derive from a shared colonial genealogy in which land is dephysicalised, atomised, and rendered culturally legible and valuable only as a suite of commodities and assets. Reproduced through atopic European legal imaginaries and naïve economic models, colonial settler property law is premised on the absence of place[5] and any metabolic and affective connection to it. This ontological orientation has facilitated and legitimated "ecological overshoot": economic and ecological activities that have "overwhelmed the regenerative and assimilative capacities" of the planet.[6]

Climate change is therefore not *the* problem as much as it is *a* problem and a "co-symptom"[7] of culturally specific economic and regulatory dysfunction. Degenerative landscape change, biodiversity loss, and dangerously disruptive weather events at the global scale are not anthropogenic—they are sociogenic, in that they emerge from the norms, structures, and institutions of particular societies, rather than from humanity as a whole.[8] Human societies, and the economies and legal regimes that have supported their existence, have flourished across time and place for very long periods. The forced removal of peoples from places, the rejection of place-based knowledges and laws, and the prohibition of place-based cultures, kinship systems, and languages are clearly and deeply implicated in decision-making of the kind that erodes the material bases of human societies.

Focusing on the cultural specificity and material agency of land use and ownership in different legal regimes, we can see that laws manifest a society's ecological sensitivity and economic viability. Learning lessons from longstanding place-based legal regimes, it is imperative to recognise and acknowledge that the dominant placeless legal regime is a barrier to adaptation to climate change. Without rapid transformations towards entirely new legal regimes grounded in place-based ontologies of land use and ownership, the effects of many "so-called

2 See for example John Borrows, *Recovering Canada: The Resurgence of Indigenous Law* (University of Toronto Press 2002); Kirsten Anker, 'Land' in Alexandra Popovici and Lionel Smith (eds), *McGill Companion to Law* (Paul-André Crépeau Centre for Private and Comparative Law, 2012) <https://www.mcgill.ca/companion/list/land> accessed 23 July 2025; Mary Graham, 'Some Thoughts on the Philosophical Underpinnings of Aboriginal Worldviews' (2008) 45 Australian Humanities Review 181. See also Sam Bookman, Chapter 46 of this handbook.

3 David Seamon, 'Place Attachment and Phenomenology: The Dynamic Complexity of Place' in Lynne Manzo and Patrick Devine-Wright (eds), *Place Attachment: Advances in Theory, Methods and Applications* (Routledge, 2nd edn, 2020).

4 Irene Watson, 'Aboriginal Relationships to the Natural World: Colonial "Protection" of Human Rights and the Environment' (2018) 9(2) Journal of Human Rights and the Environment 119; Catherine Laudine, *Aboriginal Environmental Knowledge: Rational Reverence* (Routledge, 2016); Deborah Bird Rose, *Nourishing Terrains: Australian Aboriginal Views of Landscape and Wilderness* (Australian Heritage Commission, 1996).

5 Nicole Graham, *Lawscape: Property, Environment, Law* (Routledge 2011).

6 William E Rees, 'What's the Real Problem? And Can We Do Anything About It?' *Desert Report* (13 January 2025) <http://desertreport.org> accessed 9 July 2025.

7 ibid.

8 See for example, Dipesh Chakrabarty, 'Postcolonial Studies and the Challenge of Climate Change' (2012) 43 New Literary History 1; Peipei Tian and others, 'Keeping the Global Consumption within Planetary Boundaries' (2024) 365 Nature 625.

environmental problems"[9] including climate change, will critically damage organised human societies.[10]

2. The Bonds Between Land Use and Ownership, and Planetary Health

Legal regimes define and distribute the access to, control of, responsibility for, and cultural significance of land.[11] Through land laws in particular, legal regimes generate and enforce the materially consequential bonds between land use and land ownership. These bonds are foundational to the ways landscapes are nurtured or exhausted and how habitats are sustained or disrupted. The bonds between land use and land ownership are inextricable and determine the metabolic functionality of human societies.[12]

For over 160 years, substantial research from multiple disciplinary methods and perspectives has demonstrated that there are perverse and catastrophic consequences of disrupting the metabolism of life cycles. The uncoupling of sites of consumption and waste has depleted soil health,[13] diminished water quality and security, and dispossessed and/or discounted the lands of place-based communities for the purposes of food production and waste disposal. The creation of "ghost acres", "phantom lands", and "shadow ecologies" for and by these entirely dysfunctional economies displaces and conceals the costs and consequences of naïve and placeless legal regimes from its beneficiaries. Placeless legal regimes and cultures of land use and ownership are "little more than imaginative balloons untethered from reality. They contain no reference to anything outside themselves".[14] So much for the ideas of reason and human exceptionalism that underpin European and colonial settler epistemologies and ontologies.

The climate crisis is not only a consequence of economic overreach—it is also a result of the legal architecture that has upscaled the problem of placelessness to all the places via the technologies of colonisation and globalisation. Placeless legal regimes have dispossessed human communities, displaced them from their lands, discounted the value of their lands, and mandated certain land use practices in favour of distant consumers and wasters. The current climate crisis would not have emerged without a sustained history of physically removing people from the places in which they had lived for centuries and millennia. Their dislocation undermined existing non-transplantable legal regimes that derived from and regulated complex

9 Rees (n 6). 'So-called' because the problem lies with the societal practices generating harmful ecological effects rather than with the environments experiencing them.

10 Jem Bendell, 'Deep Adaptation: A Map for Navigating Climate Tragedy, *IFLAS Occasional Paper 2* (2nd edition, 2020) <www.iflas.info> accessed 23 July 2025.

11 Nicole Graham, 'Property, and Environment' in *The Wiley-AAG International Encyclopaedia of Geography: People, the Earth, Environment, and Technology* (Wiley-Blackwell 2017); Tania Murray Li, 'What is Land? Assembling a Resource for Global Investment' (2014) 39 Transactions of the Institute of British Geographers 589.

12 Metabolism in this sense refers to the life cycles of the goods of life on which human societies depend. See: Nicole Graham, 'Dephysicalised Property and Shadow Places' in Robyn Bartel and Jennifer Carter (eds), *Handbook of Space, Place and Law* (Edward Elgar Publishing 2021).

13 See John Bellamy Foster, 'Robbing the Earth of its Capital Stock: An Introduction to George Waring's "Agricultural Features of the Census of the United States for 1850"' (1999) 12 (3) Organisation and Environment 293.

14 Rees (n 6).

people–place relations.[15] Without the place-based knowledge that generated the laws of local communities, and without the observance of local laws by those communities, landscapes were misread, neglected, cleared, deforested, dammed, extracted, and damaged by the placeless newcomers.[16]

Urban development, deforestation, industrial agriculture, land financialisation, and the extraction and combustion of fossil fuels at scales to power economic and ecological activities that exceed planetary boundaries are not legally neutral acts. Each of these practices require legal mechanisms to legitimate land ownership and permissible uses. Legal regimes incentivise and mainstream these land use practices while rendering others—such as agroecology, common lands, farming polycultures, and food sovereignty movements—marginal, illegal, or invisible.[17]

The cumulative effect of facilitating these land use practices is a form of regulatory myopia: Legal regimes continue to legitimate and protect the very practices that drive climate instability. However, not all legal regimes function in this way. Across the world and for millennia, numerous First Peoples' legal systems have developed sophisticated and adaptive frameworks for land use and ownership that are deeply embedded in specific place-based knowledge and responsive to local material conditions. As this chapter will go on to suggest, such legal systems offer critically helpful insights into the possibilities for legal adaptation to the climate crisis.

To understand why some legal regimes have proven more ecologically and climatically adaptable than others, it is necessary to examine the legal-cultural assumptions that structure the bond between land use and land ownership. These assumptions are often implicit, embedded in doctrinal form, institutional design, and the language of law itself. A legal regime that enshrines the alienability of land and its exclusive possession constructs a fundamentally different material reality than one that manifests the sanctity of land through kinship obligations, reciprocity, intrinsic relationality, and care. The impacts of these differences are now apparent not only in terms of social significance but in the condition of the Earth's atmosphere.

3. The Significance of Legal Cultures

Legal regimes are more than rules and conventions—they are cultural constructs, embedded in distinct worldviews, social practices, economic activities, and institutional histories. Understanding law in terms of culture helps explain how different societies come to conceptualise and practise law differently. What is law? What is it for, and what should it do—particularly with respect to land and the more-than-human world? Roger Cotterrell observed, "everything about law's institutions and conceptual character needs to be understood in relation to the social conditions which have given rise to it. In this sense law is indeed an

[15] Jon Altman and Sean Kerins (eds), *People on Country: Vital Landscapes, Indigenous Futures* (Federation Press 2012); Bill Gammage, *The Biggest Estate on Earth: How Aborigines Made Australia* (Allen and Unwin 2011); Laudine (n 4).

[16] Alfred Crosby, *Ecological Imperialism: The Biological Expansion of Europe, 900–1900* (CUP 2004); Thomas Dunlap, *Nature and the English Diaspora: Environment and History in the United States, Canada, Australia and New Zealand* (CUP 1999); Cameron Muir, *The Broken Promise of Agricultural Progress: An Environmental History* (Routledge 2014); John Weaver, *The Great Land Rush and the Making of the Modern World 1650–1900* (McGill-Queens University Press 2003).

[17] Philip McMichael, 'Global Land Grabs, Food and Power' in Nicole Graham, Margaret Davies and Lee Godden (eds), *The Routledge Handbook of Property, Law and Society* (Routledge 2023) 252.

expression of culture".[18] Laws governing land use and ownership are expressions of cultural beliefs about "proper or right conduct"[19] in relation to land broadly conceived. Laws of land use and ownership are thus neither universal nor abstract even though they pertain to fundamental and often theoretical questions.

Legal culture research across fields including legal history, legal anthropology, sociology of law, legal geography, and political science focuses not only on the content of legal rules, but on how law is generated, expressed, used, and experienced in different societies and at different times. Sally Merry identified four aspects of legal culture: legal practices, legal attitudes, legal mobilisation, and legal consciousness.[20] Legal consciousness and legal attitudes refer to the ways people understand and accept law, and their beliefs about its role in social life. These cultural orientations are central to the operation of legal regimes. For example, "legal consciousness may be expressed as a positive rejection of the authority of law [whereby] law may lack legitimacy and so be powerless to prevent maladaptive practices".[21] Legal attitudes also influence the "potential effectiveness of adaptation strategies that rely on the use of law",[22] especially where deeply entrenched norms of property ownership resist environmental law reforms, for example in relation to private agricultural land.[23]

Legal culture research is important and relevant to questions about climate change adaptation because it makes clear that cultures of law can work to "neutralise the promise of law in bringing about social change".[24] We will examine the reasons for this in considering two different kinds of legal cultures of land use and ownership in the following sections. It is important, before moving to those examples, to appreciate that effective strategies to adapt human societies to the climate crisis therefore demand more than technological innovation and policy reform; they require a critical analysis of the relevant, dominant legal culture.

Reckoning with and dismantling the anthroparchic (i.e., humans as apex species for whose sole benefit the natural world exists) foundations and commitments of dominant legal cultures of land use and ownership in affluent societies is key to fulfilling the "promise of law" to facilitate and regulate adaptation to the climate crisis. However, as individual choices and behaviours are shaped by culturally available expectations, and since, subsequently, no democratic government is running on a platform of reducing consumption and waste (i.e., contracting economies), radical intervention is necessary. The obvious intervention is often articulated in terms of the sociogenic ingredients of climate change: possessive individualism, unlimited economic growth, private wealth, libertarianism, unfettered consumption, cheap nature/extractivism, invisible waste, and small government.

[18] Roger Cotterell *The Sociology of Law* (1984) cited in Susan S Silbey, 'Legal Culture and Cultures of Legality' in John Hall, Ming-Cheng Lo, and Laura Grindstaff (eds), *Routledge Handbook of Cultural Sociology* (Routledge 2019) 426, 428.

[19] Mary Graham, 'The Law of Obligation, Aboriginal Ethics' (2023) 37 Parrhesia 1, 2.

[20] Sally Merry, 'What is Legal Culture—An Anthropological Perspective' (2010) 5 Journal of Comparative Law 40.

[21] Eric Hoddy and others, 'Legal Culture and Climate Change Adaptation: An Agenda for Research' (2023) 14 WIREs Climate Change e825, 8.

[22] ibid 11.

[23] Nicole Graham, 'Land Clearing Laws Bring out Worrying Libertarian Streak' (*The Conversation*, 4 August 2014) < https://theconversation.com/land-clearing-laws-bring-out-worrying-libertarian-streak-29978> accessed 23 July 2025; Robyn Bartel and Nicole Graham, 'Property and Place Attachment: A Legal Geographical Analysis of Biodiversity Law Reform in New South Wales' (2016) 54 Geographical Research 267.

[24] Hoddy et al (n 21) 10.

The paradigmatic dichotomies of private and public interests, and gain and loss, are expressly identified in reflections on the cultural barriers to implementing adaptive strategies to the climate crisis. Controversial English geographer Jem Bendell asked, "what do we need to let go of in order to not make matters worse?"[25] American legal scholar Eric Biber wrote:

> The dramatic increase in human impairments to global systems will trigger an increase in government intrusion in individual lives and decision-making . . . test[ing] a range of legal doctrines intended to protect individual rights against government overreach.[26]

Canadian human ecologist and economist William Rees wrote:

> The world's wealthy "haves" are not about to transition *en masse* to the lifestyles that would be required to sustain even half the present global population. Sharing cumulative wealth and income is not a defining characteristic of modern societies.[27]

American novelist Jonathan Franzen wrote:

> Overwhelming numbers of human beings need to accept higher taxes and severe curtailment of their familiar lifestyles without revolting. They must accept the reality of climate change and have faith in the extreme measures taken to combat it. They have to make sacrifices for distant threatened nations and distant future generations.[28]

The affective theme of a necessary intervention is a predominantly negative one—"intrusion", "sharing" wealth, higher taxes, and "sacrifice". Foregrounding loss in conceptualisations of climate crisis adaptation is important, because, for individuals in affluent societies—or affluent individuals in "economically developing" societies, such loss may be tangible and deeply felt. Yet, while candid engagement with this reality is essential to leading transformative change, there remains a critical question: Does this emphasis risk framing necessary transformation as an insurmountable challenge? Can the recalibration of people-place relations be conceptualised and experienced beyond the prevailing discourse of loss?

Rather than framing necessary transformations in terms of sacrificing private interests for the sake of collective exigencies or the public good, these questions invite us to consider whether frameworks rooted in reconnection and responsibilities might better capture the possibilities of adaptive futures. Reframing adaptation in terms that centre learning, continuity, relationality, and justice—rather than absence, loss, and decline—opens space for stronger narratives, particularly those grounded in place-based ontologies, where connection to land is sustained through reciprocal responsibilities.

Critically interrogating the boundaries between private and public interests, and moving beyond the naïveté of unsustainable, individualistic modes of living, are essential steps towards urgently needed adaptation to the climate crisis. Understanding the relationship between law and culture, especially the significance of legal consciousness and legal attitudes, can collectively underpin broader social fidelity to law. Education about the climate crisis is essential for fostering meaningful cultural transformation, as it provides the knowledge about the material conditions of mainstream lifestyles that are necessary to shape and shift consciousness and attitudes—knowledge that has historically been rejected, excluded, and marginalised within

25 Bendell (n 10) 22.

26 Eric Biber, 'Law in the Anthropocene Epoch' (2017) 106 Georgetown Law Journal 1, 5.

27 Rees (n 6).

28 Jonathan Franzen, 'What If We Stopped Pretending the Climate Apocalypse Can Be Stopped?' (*New Yorker*, 8 September 2019) <https://www.newyorker.com/culture/cultural-comment/what-if-we-stopped-pretending> accessed 23 July 2025.

Western education systems and epistemologies. The following two sections explore the climate crisis through the lens of two distinct legal cultures.

4. Place-Based Legal Cultures

The legal regimes of First Peoples across the world exhibit substantial diversity, as they are generated by the distinct geographies, ecologies, economies, and cultural histories of their respective societies. However, many of these legal regimes have similar ontological and epistemological foundations, and are often characterised by long-standing resilience to challenges, which distinguishes them from settler colonial legal orders. Several interrelated features emerge from such foundations and characteristics to constitute various but distinctively place-based legal cultures.

Place-based legal cultures are grounded in the ontological premise that place is, itself, a sentient and often sacred being, brought into being by ancestral or life-giving spirits. Place is not understood as a collection of discrete landscape features or as the jurisdiction or territory of a polity, but as a dynamic and heterogeneous living whole. Thus, neither the metaphysical nor physical qualities of place are static, silent, or passive. For example, in Australia, what Anglo-Australian law refers to as "land" is referred to in Aboriginal-Australian laws as "Country", which is "an Aboriginal English word that encompasses the seas, waters, rocks, animals, winds, and everything that exists in and makes up a place, including humans".[29]

Complementing an holistic understanding of land as place, or Country, is the ontological positioning of human beings as existing only because of, and always within and part of, a community of life that is sustained by a specific place. What it means to be human is determined relationally rather than solipsistically. "All beings—human, animal, plant, process, thing and affect—[are] vital and sapient, with their own knowledge and Law."[30] Relational ontology discourages the model of individuated human subjectivity associated with "unreflective" possessiveness. Rather than denying early tendencies towards possessive individualism in human development, it conceptualises the process of becoming fully human as a maturation: a movement from the early developmental orientation of me/my/I towards a consciously embraced ethic of we/our/us. This ethic is often expressed through languages of care, reciprocity and co-dependence with other human and non-human beings who are understood to belong to, and with, that place.

> Possessiveness precedes altruism and it therefore takes a higher order of abilities to maintain sharing behaviour . . . the effect of this transcendence of ego is to inculcate a sense of communal identity and, most importantly, to encourage reflective engagement in all activities. [This is] what it means to be human.[31]

Relational ontologies that are often foundational to place-based legal regimes are also often expressed through complex and sophisticated kinship systems, which formalise legal identities and responsibilities within a network of human and more-than-human relations.[32] Kombumerri and Wakka Wakka philosopher Mary Graham writes that relational ontologies

[29] Bawaka Country, 'Caring as Country: Singing Up Sovereignties' in Nicole Graham, Margaret Davies, Lee Godden (eds), *The Routledge Handbook of Property, Law and Society* (Routledge 2023) 16.

[30] ibid 17.

[31] Mary Graham (n 2) 188.

[32] Kirsten Anker, 'Ecological Jurisprudence and Indigenous Relational Ontologies: Beyond the "Ecological Indian"?' in Kirsten Anker, Peter Burdon, Geoffrey Garver, Michelle Maloney, Carla Sbert (eds), *From Environmental to Ecological Law* (Routledge 2020).

are premised on the fact that "we are not alone in the world . . . people are not discrete entities".[33] Kinship systems are culturally specific, and in the legal regimes of some First Nations, unlike in European traditions, kinship is not confined to relationships among humans alone.

Place-based legal regimes are often characterised by kinship systems which describe legally binding relationships and responsibilities between human and the more-than-human members of a place, for example, through moieties.[34] In the Yolŋu culture of communities in far northern Australia, the "all-encompassing matrix of kinship-identity that gives every element of reality a defined position in relation to all others . . . is a form of metaphysical DNA".[35] Kinship relationships may be affective but they may also be economic. Whereas Western knowledge systems taxonomise life at the species level, "the unit of survival in the real biological world is *organism* plus *environment*. The organism may need the family line to reproduce but . . . the family line or species cannot survive without its particular environment".[36]

The epistemological foundations of place-based legal regimes are also place-based and are closely linked to kinship rules. Knowledge can be reproduced and generated through cultural activities including song, dance, art, and formal education at specific places at specific points in time, about those places and times. From a young age, individuals learn different lessons and forms of knowledge according to their kinship roles and responsibilities. In some First Nations societies, land—conceived as place or Country—is regarded as the origin and guardian of knowledge. As Elders explain, Country "guides us and teaches us . . . it knows".[37]

Graham foregrounds the importance of what she terms "reflective engagement in all activities" in relation to the acquisition and application of knowledge "which in Western culture culminates in science".[38] Developing deeply reflective capabilities is critical, she says, to understanding ethics, or how to *be* and how to engage in lawful or "right" conduct. "Reflection is not a narcissistic reflection of a fixed self, but rather, as part of the development of human beings arising from Place."[39] This conceptualisation of knowledge is "not a static set of information that is handed down with little change from one generation to the next",[40] or mere capacity for reasoning; rather, it is understood as an ongoing process of learning and behaving—an embodied practice.

Kirsten Anker notes that such "[k]nowledge is not limited to how it is expressed in representational form, but includes how it is learned, enacted and negotiated in situ".[41] Engaging "reflectively" in place-based cultures thus happens physically as well as cognitively, through multiple and sensory methods including listening, smelling, seeing, tasting, and touching. Just as scientific knowledge is not a sum of data but a method of learning about something, knowledge in First Nations' societies is also a "dynamic system of understanding" that is "based on in-depth knowledge and continuous interaction with the land" which supports strong

[33] Mary Graham (n 19) 9.

[34] Lauren Dousset, *Australian Aboriginal Kinship* (Pacific Credo Publications, 2011).

[35] *Yolŋu Power: The Art of Yirrkala* (Art Gallery of NSW 2025).

[36] Laudine (n 4) 106.

[37] Gay'wu Group of Women, *Songspirals: Sharing Women's Wisdom of Country through Songlines* (Allen & Unwin 2019) xxii.

[38] Mary Graham (n 19) 8–9.

[39] ibid 3.

[40] Douglas Nakashima, Jennifer Rubis, and Igor Krupnik, 'Introduction' in Douglas Nakashima, Jennifer Rubis, and Igor Krupnik (eds), *Indigenous Knowledge for Climate Change Assessment and Adaptation* (CUP 2018) 11.

[41] Anker (n 32) 113.

sensitivity to environmental changes both expected and unexpected.[42] Indeed, First Nations' societies are renowned for their resilience to change for these reasons.

Relational ontologies, and reflective and material epistemologies thus form the foundation of place-based legal regimes. These foundations are overlaid with legal obligations to land and kin, including both ancestors and future generations. Legal obligations take precedence over individual entitlements to, or benefits from, Country. Laws grounded in relationality synthesise the agency of land as place, the interdependence of humans with other life forms, and the necessity of reflective engagement with the world. A relational foundation fosters responsibility to and accountability for place, which Graham terms a "custodial ethic".[43]

As noted at the outset of this section, place-based legal regimes take distinct forms across different First Nations societies. These systems are "complex and particular rather than one-size-fits-all".[44] Conflating diverse legal principles and practices is therefore both inaccurate and counterproductive, as it risks missing or obscuring the unique features and internal coherence of each regime. The contextual and holistic nature of place-based laws is typically integral to their economic and ecological sustainability. Place-based laws are not intuited; they are developed through long-term experience, learning, and practice within specific environments and climates. As Irene Watson notes, the knowledge of place "comes from the living of it".[45]

Analyses of place-based legal regimes should take care not to reproduce reductive or essentialising assumptions that "collapse" First Nations' peoples into the landscape.[46] Such approaches can romanticise First Nations' cultures in ways that perpetuate a racialised narrative and obscure the complexity, diversity, and dynamism of their legal regimes.[47] As scholars have long cautioned, the portrayal of First Nations' peoples as inherently living "in harmony" with nature—whether in general terms or in relation to specific environments—reflects a "primitivist fallacy". This fallacy underpins uncritical claims that "traditional" societies are innately conservationist, possess the "remedies for the ills of industrial capitalism", and/or provide ideal models "for human survival".[48]

As Anker observes, the critiques of racist and ahistorical tropes, such as the "noble savage" and the "ecological Indian", are essential when analysing legal cultures, particularly because such stereotypes set an "impossible ideal against which Indigenous peoples are judged as either corrupted or inauthentic".[49] Reductive narratives about place-based legal regimes hinder serious progress towards climate change adaptation by obscuring "individual specificities and eras[ing] Indigenous voices and their heterogeneity".[50] The effectiveness of land use and ownership laws does not rest on whether they are inherently and universally "right", but on whether they meaningfully and practically describe, explain, and regulate land use in response to dynamic, local material conditions.[51] Laws that extend beyond the material contexts from

[42] Nakashima et al (n 40) 11.

[43] Mary Graham (n 19) 3.

[44] Nicole Graham (n 5) 198.

[45] Irene Watson, 'Buried Alive' (2002) 13 Law and Critique 255.

[46] Jessica Weir, *Murray River Country: An Ecological Dialogue with Traditional Owners* (Aboriginal Studies Press 2009) 23.

[47] Anker (n 32) 111; see also: Kirsten Anker and Mark Antaki 'The Super-Factual Anthropocene and Encounters with Indigenous Law' in Peter Burdon and James Martel (eds), *The Routledge Handbook of Law and the Anthropocene* (Routledge 2023).

[48] Fred Cahir, Ian D Clark and Philip A Clarke, *Aboriginal Biocultural Knowledge in South-Eastern Australia: perspectives of early colonists* (CSIRO Publishing, 2018) xv–xvi.

[49] Anker (n 32) 110.

[50] ibid 112.

[51] Nicole Graham (n 5) 199.

which they derive their authority are likely to falter because the economies they facilitate and protect cannot be sustained when detached from the realities of place.

While place-based legal regimes may share certain ontological and epistemological foundations, their economic and ecological materialities vary significantly—both from one another and from the abstract, decontextualised forms of placeless legal regimes. It is therefore neither appropriate nor feasible to isolate and appropriate a legal practice or principle from a First Nations society free of its specific place-based context and authority. As Anker says, "Indigenous knowledge comes attached to Indigenous peoples and all their relatives" which "might make for messy negotiations at times".[52]

Caution is also warranted before dismissing arguments for considering place-based models of land-use and ownership laws as "deterministic" if such critiques are unfounded or foreclose research that "can significantly add to our understanding of human cultural variability, within sound theoretical frameworks for evidence-based enquiry",[53] especially in the context of climate crisis adaptation. Rejecting the trope of the " 'ecological Indian' takes us away from the idea of timeless Indigeneity conserving static nature, but not the ecological character of Indigenous law".[54]

In the context of the climate crisis, a critically important and urgent question concerns the intrinsic connection between ways of being and knowing and adaptive capacity. While it is vital to explore how First Nations' Elders and lawyers can inform and shape the development of effective climate adaptation policies and practices,[55] an even more pressing research priority for non-Indigenous legal scholars is to cultivate greater cultural intelligence regarding their own legal systems—particularly in interrogating how the foundational paradigms of those systems enable and constrain adaptive capacity.

5. Placeless Legal Cultures

Prior to the enclosure of the commons and the colonisation of foreign lands and peoples, land use and ownership in Britain were governed by a myriad of highly variable and locally specific laws, referred to as "customs" by increasingly centralised and nationalising law-makers.[56] As legal historians have observed, land in English law previously had a "greater significance than the sum of its economic production and use value".[57] But with the economic and cultural "transition from feudalism to capitalism . . . land was increasingly regarded as an object of property",[58] that facilitated the dispossession of peasants in England, Wales, Scotland, and Ireland,

[52] Anker (n 32) 114.

[53] Alan Outram and Amy Bogaard, *Subsistence and Society in Prehistory: New Directions in Economic Archaeology* (CUP 2019) 49.

[54] Anker (n 32) 105.

[55] Tashi Dorji and others, 'Understanding How Indigenous Knowledge Contributes to Climate Change Adaptation and Resilience: A Systematic Literature Review' (2024) 74 Environmental Management 1101, 1116.

[56] See for example: E P Thompson, *Customs in Common* (Merlin Press 1991); Peter Fitzpatrick, *The Mythology of Modern Law* (Routledge 1992); Jeanette Neeson, *Commoners: Common Right, Enclosure and Social Change in England, 1700–1820* (CUP 1993); Laura Brace, *The Idea of Property in Seventeenth Century England* (Manchester University Press 1998); Peter Karsten, *Between Law and Custom: 'high' and 'low' legal cultures in the lands of the British Diaspora—the United States, Canada, Australia and New Zealand 1600–1900* (CUP 2002).

[57] David Seipp, 'The Concept of Property in the Early Common Law' (1994) 12 (1) Law and History Review 46.

[58] Nicole Graham (n 12) 281.

and of First Nations' peoples across the world.[59] Sustained periods of violent land-taking were rationalised by the notion of "improvement" of both those peoples and their lands, into "cultured" people and "cultivated" landscapes.[60]

The forced removal of First Nations' peoples from their lands and the dismissal, rejection, and prohibition of their laws and languages, brought about profound transformations in land use and ownership in those places. These disruptions fractured bonds between land use and ownership and often resulted in the suppression or loss of place-based knowledge systems. "Land had to be free from customs and rights which interfered in the most productive land use."[61] Diverse, localised forms of land tenure and land use practices were gradually homogenised into dominant national and imperial property regimes, characterised by abstract and universalising notions of ownership. Within property theory, this shift is described as the "dephysicalisation of property"[62]—the reconfiguration of land as an abstract relation between a "person" and a "thing"[63] detached from material contexts.

The dephysicalised model of interhuman relations is expressed in terms of abstract legal rights through which a person or legal entity holds a legal interest in relation to commodifiable resources or assets which are devoid of family, kinship, or community obligations or prohibitions.[64] Wesley Hohfeld criticised society's "unfortunate tendency to confuse and blend" physical things, such as land, with abstract property rights.[65] The abstractness of rights later led to observations that modern property could "include all legal relations"[66] and was a "vacant concept" so meaningless that it could be regarded as "an illusion".[67]

Importantly, dephysicalised property "is not just a theory—it is a practice".[68] Structured around abstraction and individuated rights, the dephysicalised model of property functioned to enable the alienability of land and its fragmentation into discrete, fungible units, supporting the development of national and global markets through which wealth was created and accumulated.[69] Today, the dephysicalised model of land use and ownership is deeply entrenched and uncritically accepted in mainstream cultural, economic and legal discourses. It

[59] Weaver (n 16); Onur Ulas Ince, 'Between Equal Rights: Primitive Accumulation and Capital's Violence' (2018) 46 (6) Political Theory 885; Henry Jones, 'Property, Territory, and Colonisation: An International Legal History of Enclosure' (2019) 39 (2) Legal Studies 187.

[60] Paul Langford *Polite and Commercial People: England 1727–1783* (Clarendon Press 1989); Andrew McRae, 'Husbandry Manuals and the Language of Agrarian Improvement' in Leslie and Raylor (eds), *Culture and Cultivation in Early Modern England: Writing and the Land* (Leicester University Press 1992) 35; Dunlap (n 16); John Gascoigne *The Enlightenment and the Origins of European Australia* (CUP 2002); Lynn Hollen Lees *Planting Empire, Cultivating Subjects: British Malaya 1786–1941* (CUP 2017).

[61] Jones (n 59) 189.

[62] Nicole Graham (n 12).

[63] Nicole Graham (n 5) 43.

[64] Margaret Davies, 'Persons, Property, and Community' (2012) 2 (2) feminists@law 1.

[65] Wesley Newcomb Hohfeld, 'Some Fundamental Legal Conceptions as Applied in Legal Reasoning' (1913) 23 (1) Yale Law Journal 16, 20.

[66] Kenneth Vandervelde, 'The New Property of the Nineteenth Century: The Development of the Modern Concept of Property' (1980) 29 (2) Buffalo Law Review 325, 362.

[67] Kevin Gray, 'Property in Thin Air' (1991) 50 Cambridge Law Journal 252, 252.

[68] Nicole Graham (n 12) 283.

[69] Michael Burger and Paul Frymer, 'Property Law and American Empire' (2012) 34 University of Hawai'i Law Review 471; K-Sue Park, 'The History Wars and Property Law: Conquest and Slavery as Foundational to the Field' (2021) 131 Yale Law Journal 1062; Jessica Shoemaker, 'Papering Over Place: When Land Becomes Asset Class' in Bram Akkermans (ed), *Research Agenda in Property Law* (Edward Elgar Publishing 2024).

has entirely erased the legal significance of place, reshaped human societies, and transformed people-place relations around the world into placeless legal cultures.

Placeless legal cultures have historically undermined non-transferable place-based legal regimes that derive from and regulate complex people-place relationships.[70] Placeless laws continue to do so today as part of continuing "regimes of dispossession"[71] and the financialisation of property.[72] As Jessica Shoemaker observes, "across many landscapes . . . we see aggressive use of property strategies to commodify, concentrate, and increase absentee ownership in both rural and urban environments".[73] The shift from place-based, land-oriented legal regimes to frameworks abstracted from physical contexts and local land-use cultures remains one of the most significant obstacles to the effective implementation of environmental law in Anglophone jurisdictions.[74]

The recognised role of placeless legal regimes in producing the sociogenic conditions of the climate crisis[75] underscores the urgent need to critically evaluate and disrupt them.[76] Yet the dominance of these regimes has entrenched a myopic orthodoxy of property rights, such that their expansion is now framed as a solution to serious environmental problems and global heating through environmental markets, carbon trading, and offset schemes. The effectiveness of these rights-based mechanisms "is limited by the fragility of the scientific-technical apparatus and assumptions on which the identity of new objects of property are founded".[77]

The atomisation of land into tradeable commodities—formulated variously as property interests that are transacted as rights—constitutes the foundational logic of placeless legal regimes. Rights-based market instruments cannot offer effective solutions to the climate crisis precisely because it is this very logic that produced the crisis to begin with. As Thomas Kuhn observed, "revolutions are inaugurated by a growing sense . . . that existing institutions have ceased adequately to meet the problems posed by an environment that they have in part created".[78]

Critiques of the notion of the "Anthropocene" have corrected the misattribution of climate change to "the human species as an undifferentiated whole" by observing that it is actually the consequence of "the operation of a specific economic system promoted by a global

70 Altman and Kerins (n 15); Gammage (n 15); Laudine (n 4).

71 Michael Levien, 'Regimes of Dispossession' in Nicole Graham, Margaret Davies, and Lee Godden (eds), *Routledge Handbook of Property, Law and Society* (Routledge 2023).

72 Lisa Adkins, Melinda Cooper, and Martijn Konings, *The Asset Economy: Property Ownership and the New Logic if Inequality* (Polity Press 2020); Murray Li (n 11).

73 Shoemaker (n 69) 128.

74 Joseph Sax, 'Environmental Law Forty Years Later: Looking Back and Looking Ahead', in Michael Jeffery, Jeremy Firestone, and Karen Bubna-Litic (eds), *Biodiversity Conservation, Law and Livelihoods* (CUP 2008).

75 Jan McDonald, 'Mapping the Legal Landscape of Climate Change Adaptation', in Tim Bonyhady, Andrew Macintosh, and Jan McDonald (eds), *Adaptation to Climate Change: Law and Policy* (Federation Press 2010) 1–37; Shalanda Baker, 'Adaptive Law in the Anthropocene' (2015) 90 (2) Chicago-Kent Law Review 563; Eric Biber (n 26); Lynda Butler, 'Property, Climate Change, and Accountability' in Nicole Graham, Margaret Davies, and Lee Godden (eds), *Routledge Handbook of Property, Law and Society* (Routledge 2023) 287.

76 Shoemaker (n 69).

77 Bonnie Holligan, 'Property and Environmental Markets' in Nicole Graham, Margaret Davies, and Lee Godden (eds), *Routledge Handbook of Property, Law and Society* (Routledge 2023) 264, 273; see also Rohini Pande, 'Can the Market in Voluntary Carbon Credits Help Reduce Global Emissions in Line with Paris Agreement Targets?' (*Science*, 9 May 2024) < https://www.science.org/doi/10.1126/science.adp5223 > accessed 24 July 2025.

78 Thomas Kuhn, *The Structure of Scientific Revolutions* (3rd edn, University of Chicago Press 1996) 92.

minority".[79] Analysis of trade, GDP, and GHG emissions data confirm a strong correlation between affluence and climate change through the "appropriation (of labour and land)" and its "displacement (of work and environmental loads)".[80] There are "considerable variations in the contribution to [planetary boundary] transgression among different expenditure (income) groups across countries"[81] which invalidate the perpetuation of the species-centric account of climate change.

Given the "disproportionate responsibility of affluent groups in both developed and developing countries . . . [showing that] considerable environmental pressures are caused by overconsumption",[82] there are clearly no solutions to the climate crisis available to us by reproducing the logic and mechanisms of placeless legal regimes and economies "born in colonial Britain".[83] Despite the dominance of placeless legal regimes, it is important to remember that they are self-referencing and self-reproducing elements of a broader culture whose primary purpose is unlimited growth of production and consumption, "which is fundamentally re-organising the flows in the Earths' life-support system".[84]

Although placeless legal regimes are a relatively recent development in human history, the urgency of climate adaptation constrains opportunities for their critical reassessment, despite mounting evidence of their inadequacy. There is a pressing need to move beyond these frameworks and explore alternative legal approaches. For a long time, place-based cultures of land use and ownership have been treated as relics of the past, juxtaposed to both present and imagined legal futures. Engaging with place-based legal regimes has often been viewed as irrelevant to contemporary legal problem-solving at best, and as nostalgically impractical or romantic at worst. As Lesley Head observed:

> Modernity's relentless growth-oriented track to the future has created a situation where stepping off that track is construed as going backwards. It is important to cut across this linear conflation of sustainability with backwardness and a romanticised localism. Some "backward" steps are in fact entirely sensible and forward-thinking.[85]

In the context of the climate crisis, legal research that is truly "sensible and forward-thinking" requires deep cultural intelligence about the dominant legal regime. Legal scholars, particularly in the field of private law, must recognise that the climate crisis is not external to the legal cultures and mechanisms of private law itself. Placeless legal cultures are at the heart of the problem because they fracture and break the bonds between land use and ownership. Acknowledging the problem, however, is no longer sufficient; let us remember that "the significance of crises is the indication they provide that an occasion for retooling has arrived".[86]

[79] Alf Hornborg, 'Colonialism in the Anthropocene: The Political Ecology of the Money-Energy-Technology Complex' (2019) 10(1) Journal of Human Rights and the Environment 7, 8. See also Donna Haraway, 'Anthropocene, Capitalocene, Plantationocene, Chthulucene: Making Kin' (2015) 6(1) Environmental Humanities 159.

[80] Hornborg (n 79) 18.

[81] Tian et al (n 8) 625.

[82] Tian et al (n 8) 630.

[83] Hornborg (n 79) 8.

[84] Hans-Peter Plag, 'Modern Climate Change: A Symptom of a Single-Species High-Energy Pulse' in Dale E Miller and Ben Eggleston (eds), *Moral Theory and Climate Change* (Routledge 2020) 6–34, 9.

[85] Lesley Head and Chris Gibson, 'Becoming Differently Modern: Geographic Contributions to a Generative Climate Politics' (2012) 36 (6) Progress in Human Geography 699, 709.

[86] Kuhn (n 78) 76.

6. Conclusion

Legal regimes determine legitimate interests in land and are thus contingent features of planetary health because they incentivise and prohibit materially significant land use practices. Laws creates a bond between land use and land ownership, and there is substantial variation between different legal regimes as to the effects of these bonds on planetary health. This variation is due to the cultural specificity of the paradigms, languages, and kinship systems pertaining to humans and the more-than-human world that underpin a legal regime.

The legal plurality of colonised jurisdictions foregrounds the cultural specificity of land use and ownership laws and provides important analytical opportunities to evaluate the relationship between climate change and property law. The significance of time, and the relevance of the diverse material conditions and limits of the places in which human societies develop their laws, are fundamental to these analyses. Adaptation to such dynamic contexts is key to the long-term viability of property regimes. But beyond evaluative reflections on the adaptation of the laws of First Peoples and settler colonial states to various dynamic material contexts, there is the more important application of these lessons to the status quo.

The regulatory agility required to adapt the status quo to the existential challenge of climate change is imperative, but is it possible? The plasticity of law underpins the survival of human societies across the world and over millennia. The enablers and barriers to adaptation are more than technical—they are embedded in legal cultures. "The future of climate change will be shaped in part by whether and how we reflexively come to terms with its cultural instantiations."[87] It is therefore important to understand both the dominant legal culture and the legal cultures that have successfully adapted to numerous and various material challenges (including previous climate changes).

Legal obligations generating affective and reciprocal people-place relations underpin longstanding regimes. In the first Aboriginal land rights case in Australian law, Justice Blackburn conceded that:

> The evidence shows a subtle and elaborate system highly adapted to the country in which people led their lives, which provided a stable order of society and was remarkably free from the vagaries of personal whim or influence. If ever a system could be called "a government of laws, and not of men", it is that shown in the evidence before me.[88]

His Honour's jurisprudential humility and honesty exemplify the kind of epistemic openness needed to engage with the complex cultural challenges of the climate crisis. Such an approach corrects "the Western imaginary that there was a legal vacuum pre-dating colonisation across the world and that the colonial world brought law as well as other so-called 'improvements'".[89]

Cultural intelligence reveals that beyond the "extractive mindset"[90] of the dominant dephysicalised and placeless model of property, "care is the guiding principle" in place-based legal regimes.[91] "In caring for Country, humans are stewards or custodians" who attend and

[87] Zeke Baker, 'Three Propositions toward a Cultural Sociology of Climate Change' in John Hall, Ming-Cheng Lo, and Laura Grindstaff (eds), *Routledge Handbook of Cultural Sociology* (Routledge 2019) 95–103, 101.

[88] *Milirrpum v Nabalco* (1971) 17 FLR 141, at 267.

[89] Davies (n 1) 2.

[90] Richie Howitt and Sandie Suchet-Pearson, 'Rethinking the Building Blocks: Ontological Pluralism and the Idea of "Management"' (2006) 88(3) Geografiska Annaler: Series B 323.

[91] Bawaka Country (n 29) 19.

respond "to the messages of non-human beings who are respected kin, family members."[92] Such legal regimes oblige humans to situate their land use practices within relevant geographical and ecological conditions and limits at a scale beyond a single species and a single human lifetime.

Current attention to carbon markets and the "mineral-paved road to net zero"[93] reproduce the logic and mechanisms of placeless legal cultures and may well involve further degradation of lands and waters. The urgency and gravity of the climate crisis calls for a substantial deepening of cultural intelligence and meaningful collaboration with the enduring authority, intellectual rigour, and practical success of First Nations' societies. Such engagement is essential to addressing the jurisdictional and jurisprudential vulnerabilities that arise from culturally myopic approaches to law.

As noted earlier, however, place-based knowledge is inherently inseparable from the specific places and communities from which they emerge and is also "embedded in a web of relationships defining who may use it, when it may be used, appropriate uses, and the rituals, words or practices that must accompany its use".[94] The point is not to "borrow" or "appropriate" elements from place-based legal regimes, but to develop and enhance critical reflections on the dominant placeless legal regime by understanding the nature of legal change, resilience and adaptation from the place-based legal regimes that endure today.[95] To conclude, recall Merry's thesis about legal culture that they endure because legal consciousness and legal attitudes in the community recognise the authority of law, to which I would add that they also endure because the material conditions support that society. As Val Napoleon has observed:

> One of the most important things to understand about any law is how it changes. And it has to change in order to be an effective part of governance—it has to be appropriate to new contexts and circumstances or it simply will not work. It also has to be appropriate to the experiences of the people or it will have no meaning or legitimacy.[96]

[92] ibid.

[93] Pip Abbott, 'Where Do We Stop for First Nations Culture Heritage on the Critical Mineral-Paved Road to Net Zero in Australia?' (2025) 28 Asia Pacific Journal of Environmental Law (in press).

[94] Terry Williams and Preston Hardison, 'Culture, Law, Risk and Governance: Contexts of Traditional Knowledge in Climate Change Adaptation' (2013) 120 Climate Change 531, 534.

[95] Bendell (n 10) 16.

[96] Val Napoleon, 'Thinking about Indigenous Legal Orders' in Rene Provost and Colleen Sheppard (eds), *Dialogues on Human Rights and Legal Pluralism* (Springer 2013) 139.

CHAPTER 16

Intellectual Property

GRAHAM REYNOLDS

1. Introduction

A wide range of scholarly commentary has considered the intersection of intellectual property (IP) and climate change.[1] Some commentary has proposed ways through which patent regimes can be modified to incentivise the development of "green", environmentally friendly, or environmentally sound technologies (EST).[2] Other works have engaged with the question of how best to facilitate the transfer of ESTs both within countries and globally, including through waivers of IP rights and licensing (either compulsory or voluntary).[3] A third category

[1] See, for instance, Peter Drahos, 'Bargaining over the Climate: Lessons from Intellectual Property Negotiations' (2011) 2 Climate Law 1; Peter S Menell and Sarah M Tran (eds), *Intellectual Property, Innovation and the Environment* (Edward Elgar Publishing 2014); Joshua D Sarnoff ed., *Research Handbook on Intellectual Property and Climate Change* (Edward Elgar Publishing 2018); Matthew Rimmer (ed), *Intellectual Property and Clean Energy: The Paris Agreement and Climate Justice* (Springer 2018); Abbe E L Brown, *Intellectual Property, Climate Change and Technology: Managing National Legal Intersections, Relationships and Conflicts* (Edward Elgar Publishing 2019); Matthew Rimmer, 'Beyond the Paris Agreement: Intellectual Property, Innovation Policy, and Climate Justice' (2019) 8 Laws 2; William Nordhaus, 'The Challenge of Green Innovation' in Walter G Park (ed), *Handbook of Innovation and Intellectual Property Rights* (Edward Elgar Publishing 2024); Bita Amani, Caroline B Ncube, and Matthew Rimmer (eds), *The Elgar Companion to Intellectual Property and the Sustainable Development Goals* (Edward Elgar Publishing 2024); Jacques de Werra (ed), *Intellectual Property & Sustainable Development* (Schulthess 2024).

[2] Ofer Tur-Sinai, 'Patents and Climate Change: A Skeptic's View' (2018) 48 Environmental Law 211; Jesse L Reynolds, Jorge L Contreras, and Joshua D Sarnoff, 'Intellectual Property Policies for Solar Geoengineering' (2018) 9(2) WIREs Climate Change e512; Mahatab Uddin and Saleemul Huq, 'Protecting Soft Adaptation Technologies under Intellectual Property Rights Systems' (2020) 25 Intellectual Property and Technology Law Journal 19; Matthew Rimmer, 'Carbon Capture and Storage: Intellectual Property, Innovation Policy and Climate Change' in Hirdan Katarina de Medeiros Costa and Carolina Arlota (eds), *Carbon Capture and Storage in International Energy Policy and Law* (Elsevier 2021); Modupe O Oyebanj and others, 'Patents on Environmental Technologies and Environmental Sustainability in Spain' (2022) 14(11) Sustainability 6670; Reto M Hilty and Pedro Henrique D Batista, 'Potential and Limits of Patent Law to Address Climate Change' (2023) 72 GRUR International 821; Elham Ghaffarian, Mark Perry, and Siva Barathi (Sharl), 'Intellectual Property Supporting a Green Framework for Sustainability' in Siva Barathi (Sharl) Marimuthu and Anu Lähteenmäki-Uutela (eds), *The Changing Food Law Landscape* (Routledge 2024); Lodewijk Van Dycke, 'Why Patents on Climate Technologies Must Be Cut Short' (2024) 73(4) GRUR International 717; Mihaela Onofrei and others, 'The Effects of Environmental Patents on Renewable Energy Consumption' (2024) 6(4) Green Finance 630.

[3] Ahmed Abdel-Latif, 'The Rise of Public–Private Partnerships in Green Technologies and the Role of Intellectual Property Rights' in Margaret Chon, Pedro Poffe, and Ahmed Abdel-Latif (eds), *The Cambridge Handbook of Public–Private Partnerships, Intellectual Property Governance, and Sustainable Development* (CUP 2018); Stefano Angelucci, F Javier Hurtado-Albir, and Alessia Volpe, 'Supporting Global Initiatives on Climate Change: The EPO's "Y02–Y04S" Tagging Scheme' (2018) 54 World Patent

of works has focused on how IP reforms could help advance climate mitigation and adaptation efforts in ways other than through modifications to the patent system, such as through amendments to copyright or trademark legislation.[4]

Some of the ideas explored in these works have been put into action. For instance, a number of countries have implemented fast-track programmes that expedite examination of patent applications for EST inventions.[5] In addition, in an attempt to increase the transfer and

Information S85; Buzz Hardin, 'Compulsory Licensing of Climate Engineering Patents: How Embracing Technology and Researching-Sharing Strategies Brings Us One Step Closer to Solving Climate Change' (2020) 73 Arkansas Law Review 611; Dalindyebo B Shabalala, 'Climate Change, Technology Transfer and Intellectual Property: A 'Modest Proposal' for an IP Enforcement Moratorium' (2020) 31(1) Fordham Environmental Law Review; Caoimhe Ring, 'Patent Law and Climate Change: Innovation Policy for a Climate in Crisis' (2021) 35 Harvard Journal of Law and Technology 373; Mahatab Uddin, *Climate Change Law, Technology Transfer and Sustainable Development* (Routledge 2021); Jayne Piana, 'Diffusion of Green Technology: Patents, Licenses, and Incentives' (2022) 52 Texas Environmental Law Journal 37; Matthew Rimmer, 'Open for Climate Justice: Intellectual Property, Human Rights, and Climate Change' (18 October 2022) <https://ssrn.com/abstract=4258718> accessed 3 June 2025; Ankit Singh and Yogendra Srivastava, *Patent Law, Green Technology and Innovation* (Routledge 2022); Suma Athreye and others, 'Intellectual Property Rights and the International Transfer of Climate Change Mitigating Technologies' (2023) 52 Research Policy 104819; Juana Bustamante and others, 'Resolving the Patents Paradox in the Era of COVID-19 and Climate Change: Towards a Patents Taxonomy' (2023) 52 Research Policy 104850; Matthew Rimmer, 'Promethean Dreams: Intellectual Property and Climate Change in the Anthropocene' in Alexandar Zahar and Leonie Reins (eds), *Climate Technology and Law in the Anthropocene* (University of Bristol Press 2024); Aayush Bhardwaj and Heena Parveen, 'Intellectual Property in the Age of Climate Change: Balancing Innovation and Sustainability through Green Technology' (2024) The Academic 672; Remi Saidane, 'Balancing Obligations to Develop Climate Change Technologies with IP and Trade Objectives: An Evaluation of the Systemic Integration of the Paris Agreement into TRIPS' (2024) 55 International Review of Intellectual Property and Competition Law 1055; Francisco H Fernandez, 'Technology Transfer under the TRIPS Agreement: A Comeback to Address Global Crises' in Jelena Bäumler and others (eds), *European Yearbook of International Economic Law* (Springer 2025).

[4] See, for instance, Leslyn Lewis, 'Evergreening Through Trade Secrets as an Impediment to Green Technology Transfer to the Developing World' (2018) 18 Asper Review of International Business and Trade Law 23; Margaret Chon, 'Trademark Goodwill and Green Global Value Networks' in Matthew Rimmer (ed), *Intellectual Property and Clean Energy: The Paris Agreement and Climate Justice* (Springer 2018) 275; Claudia Nyarko Mensah and others, 'Innovation and CO2 Emissions: The Complimentary Role of Eco-patent and Trademark in the OECD Economies' (2019) 26 Environmental Science and Pollution Research 22878; Samuel E Cayton, 'The "Green Patent Paradox" and Fair Use: The Intellectual Property Solution to Fight Climate Change' (2020) 11 Seattle Journal of Technology, Environmental & Innovation Law 214; Jean Dryden, 'Climate Change, Copyright and Archives' (2021) 2 Comma 387; Lisa Benjamin, 'Intellectual Property' in Lavanya Rajamani and Jacqueline Peel (eds), *The Oxford Handbook of International Environmental Law* (2nd edn, OUP 2021); Graham J Reynolds, 'Of Lock-Breaking and Stock Taking: IP, Climate Change, and the Right to Repair in Canada' (2023) 101 Compensation & Benefits Review 31; Anthony C K Kakooza, 'Innovations in Climate Adaption: Lessons from Uganda's National Agricultural Research Organization (Naro)' (2024) 12 South African Intellectual Property Law Journal 134; Roxana Blasetti, 'The Development of Distinctive Signs for Collective Use: A Latin American Perspective' in Andrea Zappalaglio and Enrico Bonadio (eds), *The Future of Geographical Indications* (Springer 2025).

[5] See, for instance, Antoine Dechezleprêtre and Eric Lane, 'Fast-Tracking Green Patent Applications' (*WIPO Magazine*, 3 June 2013) <https://www.wipo.int/web/wipo-magazine/articles/fast-tracking-green-patent-applications-38465> accessed 2 June 2025; Instituto Nacional da Propriedade Industrial, 'Green Patents' (*Ministério do Desenvolvimento, Indústria, Comércio e Serviços*, 16 November 2020) <https://www.gov.br/inpi/en/services/patents/prioritized-examination/pilot-projects/green-patents> accessed 2 June 2025; Government of Canada, 'Advanced Examination for Green Technologies' (*Government of*

take-up of ESTs, the World Intellectual Property Organization (WIPO) created the WIPO GREEN online platform to "connect[] providers and seekers of environmentally friendly technologies".[6] Another example of an initiative relating to IP and climate change is the Eco-Patent Commons, which was developed by IBM along with a number of other industrial firms as an "effort to pool patents for the promotion of green/clean technologies".[7]

Despite these efforts (among others), climate change has continued to accelerate, resulting in a number of negative impacts on individuals and communities.[8] Many have drawn attention to the negative impacts of climate change on human rights including rights to life, food, health, housing, and the right to a safe, clean, and healthy environment.[9] While these impacts are being experienced everywhere, they are being felt particularly severely by both developing countries and by vulnerable groups within both developed and developing countries.[10]

Can IP regimes do more to address the human rights impacts of climate change, and if so, how? While there exists a considerable literature on climate change and IP,[11] as well as climate change and human rights,[12] relatively few works have considered these three areas together.[13] This chapter seeks to contribute to this understudied intersection.

Canada, 1 October 2024) <https://ised-isde.canada.ca/site/canadian-intellectual-property-office/en/patents/patent-applications-examination-and-patents/advanced-examination-green-technologies> accessed 2 June 2025; Intellectual Property Office (UK), 'Patents: Accelerated Processing' <https://www.gov.uk/guidance/patents-accelerated-processing> accessed 2 June 2025.

[6] World Intellectual Property Organization (WIPO), 'WIPO GREEN' (WIPO) <www3.wipo.int/wipogreen/en/> accessed 2 June 2025.

[7] See Jorge J Contreras, Bronwyn H Hall, Christian Helmers, 'Pledging Patents for the Public Good: Rise and Fall of the Eco-Patent Commons' (2019) 57 Houston Law Review 61.

[8] James E Hansen and others, 'Global Warming Has Accelerated: Are the United Nations and the Public Well-Informed?' (2025) 67(1) Environment: Science and Policy for Sustainable Development 6.

[9] See, for instance, OHCHR, *Report of the Office of the United Nations High Commissioner for Human Rights on the Relationship Between Climate Change and Human Rights*, UN Doc A/HRC/10/1 (15 January 2009); Stephen Humphreys (ed), *Human Rights and Climate Change* (CUP 2010); UNHRC Res 41/21 (2019) UN Doc A/HRC/RES/41/21; Kuan-Wei Chen, Hoda Asgarian, 'Climate change is a human rights issue' (*The Conversation*, 20 May 2024) <https://theconversation.com/climate-change-is-a-human-rights-issue-228156> accessed 2 June 2025.

[10] UNHRC Res 41/21 (2019) UN Doc A/HRC/RES/41/21.

[11] For literature at the intersection of climate change and IP, see nn 1–4.

[12] See, for instance, Stephen Humprheys (ed), *Human Rights and Climate Change* (CUP 2010); Siobhán McInerney-Lankford, Mac Darrow, and Lavanya Rajamani, *Human Rights and Climate Change: A Review of the International Legal Dimensions* (World Bank 2011); Sumudu Atapattu, *Human Rights Approaches to Climate Change* (Routledge 2015); Ottavio Quirico and Mouloud Boumghar (eds), *Climate Change and Human Rights* (Routledge 2015); Bridget Lewis, *Environmental Human Rights and Climate Change* (Springer, 2018); Sébastien Duyck, Sébastien Jodoin, and Alyssa Johl (eds), *Routledge Handbook of Human Rights and Climate Governance* (Routledge 2018); Mary Robinson and Caitríona Palmer, *Climate Justice: Hope, Resilience, and the Fight for a Sustainable Future* (Bloomsbury 2019); Margaretha Wewerinke-Singh, *State Responsibility, Climate Change and Human Rights Under International Law* (Bloomsbury 2019); James R May and Erin Daly, *Human Rights and the Environment* (Edward Elgar Publishing 2019); Linnéa Nordlander, *Human Rights and Climate Change: The Law on Loss and Damage* (Routledge 2023).

[13] See, for instance, Kavita Kapur, 'Climate Change, Intellectual Property, and the Scope of Human Rights Obligations' (2011) 11 Sustainable Development Law & Policy 58; Alexandra Phelan, 'Climate Change and Human Rights: Intellectual Property Challenges and Opportunities' in Matthew Rimmer (ed), *Intellectual Property and Clean Energy: The Paris Agreement and Climate Change* (Springer 2018); Matthew Rimmer, 'Open for Climate Justice: Intellectual Property, Human Rights, and Climate Change' <https://papers.ssrn.com/sol3/papers.cfm?abstract_id=4258718> (18 October 2022) accessed 2 June 2025; Chelsea Bodimeade and Felicity Deane, 'Evolving Theory of IP Rights: Promoting Human

Drawing from the work of the United Nations Office of the High Commissioner of Human Rights (OHCHR), which "aims . . . to promote a human rights-based approach to climate action", this chapter argues that when considering further reforms to the IP system in relation to climate change, scholars, courts, policymakers, and legislators should adopt a human rights-based approach.[14] By a human rights-based approach, I am referring to one that is "shape[d] and guide[d]" by "human rights norms, standards, considerations, and obligations";[15] that is "firmly grounded in the human rights principles of substantive equality and non-discrimination, participation and empowerment, accountability and access to justice, transparency and the rule of law";[16] and that aims to strengthen capacity as a core goal.[17]

In addition to being called for by the OHCHR, such an approach is also supported by the UN's 2030 Agenda for Sustainable Development[18] and by the Paris Agreement, which provides that when taking action to address climate change, countries should do so in a manner that considers, promotes, and respects their human rights obligations.[19]

The adoption of a human rights-based approach to IP and climate change could result in a number of outcomes including a new set of possibilities for substantive IP reform drawn from human rights doctrine, as well as the incorporation within IP regimes of a different set of principles and values that are generally associated with IP law (namely those associated with human rights). The adoption of such an approach could also help to highlight where IP reforms are likely to be ineffective in achieving improved outcomes for those individuals and communities whose human rights are most negatively impacted by climate change, resulting

Rights in the Agreement on Trade-Related Aspects of Intellectual Property Rights' (2023) 18(8) Journal of Intellectual Property Law & Practice 603; Elena Izyumenko, 'Intellectual Property in the Age of the Environmental Crisis: How Trademarks and Copyright Challenge the Human Right to a Healthy Environment' (2024) 55 International Review of Intellectual Property and Competition Law 864. Other works that reference human rights in the context of IP and climate change include Abbe E L Brown, 'Intellectual Property and Climate Change' in Rochelle C Dreyfuss and Justine Pila (eds), *The Oxford Handbook of Intellectual Property Law* (OUP 2018); Joshua D Sarnoff and Margaret Chon, 'Innovation Law and Policy Choices for Climate-Change Related Public–Private Partnerships' in Margaret Chon, Pedro Roffe, and Ahmed Abdel-Latif (eds), *The Cambridge Handbook of Public–Private Partnerships, Intellectual Property Governance, and Sustainable Development* (CUP 2018). See also the work of Matthew Rimmer and others at the intersection of IP and climate justice, including Matthew Rimmer (ed), *Intellectual Property and Clean Energy: The Paris Agreement and Climate Justice* (Springer 2018); Matthew Rimmer, 'Beyond the Paris Agreement: Intellectual Property, Innovation Policy and Climate Justice' (2019) 8(1) Laws 7; and Lívia Regina Batista-Pritchard, 'Climate Justice in the Intersection between the CBDR&RC Principle and Intellectual Property Rights: A Critical Reading of International Cooperation' (2024) 20 Journal of Global Ethics 179.

[14] UNCHR, 'OHCHR and Climate Change' (UNCHR) <https://www.ohchr.org/en/climate-change> accessed 2 June 2025.

[15] UNGA 'Report of the Secretary-General' (2024) UN Doc A/HRC/57/30 <https://docs.un.org/en/A/hrc/57/30> accessed 2 June 2025.

[16] UN Committee on the Elimination of Discrimination against Women, 'General Recommendation No. 37 (2018) on the Gender-Related Dimensions of Disaster Risk Reduction in the Context of Climate Change' (2018) UN Doc CEDAW/C/GC/37 <https://digitallibrary.un.org/record/1626306?ln=en&v=pdf> accessed 2 June 2025.

[17] ibid.

[18] UN Sustainable Development Group, '2030 Agenda and the Sustainable Development Goals' (2025) <https://unsdg.un.org/2030-agenda> accessed 14 June 2025.

[19] Paris Agreement, being an Annex to the Report of the Conference of the Parties on its Twenty-First Session, 12 December 2015, UN Doc FCCC/CP/2015/10/Add.1, 55 ILM 740 [Paris Agreement].

in the redirection of attention towards other initiatives that show greater promise for the achievement of this goal.[20]

It is not possible in the context of this chapter to fully describe the impact that a human rights-based approach, if widely applied, might have on the intersection of IP and climate change. Rather, the goal of this chapter is to provide an introduction to the idea of a human rights-based approach to climate change and IP, to help ground further discussion in this area. This chapter also seeks to act as a call to action for others to join in considering how the adoption of a human rights-based approach can contribute to a reshaping of IP law, both with respect to climate change and more generally.

This chapter will proceed in four parts. Section 1 is this introduction. Section 2 will set out what I am referring to as a human rights-based approach to climate change and IP. Section 3 will discuss several possible outcomes flowing from the adoption of a human rights-based approach to IP and climate change. This section will also discuss the limits of IP rights as mechanisms through which to advance human rights. Section 4 is the conclusion.

2. IP, Human Rights, and Climate Change

2.1 Climate Change and Human Rights

The Intergovernmental Panel on Climate Change (IPCC), in its Sixth Assessment Report (AR6), found that "[i]t is unequivocal that human influence has warmed the atmosphere, ocean and land".[21] Noting that "[h]uman-induced climate change is already affecting many weather and climate extremes in every region across the globe", the IPCC stated that "[e]vidence of observed changes in extremes such as heatwaves, heavy precipitation, droughts, and tropical cyclones, and, in particular, their attribution to human influence, has strengthened since AR5 [the IPCC's Fifth Assessment Report]".[22]

The IPCC concluded that climate change has resulted in "widespread adverse impacts and related losses and damages to nature and people".[23] Consistent with this conclusion, the UN Human Rights Council (UNHRC), in a study on the impact of loss and damage from climate change on human rights, writes that "[e]stimates of the annual economic cost of loss and damage in developing countries alone amounted to at least $435 billion in 2020, a figure that is expected to rise to at least $580 billion by 2030, excluding non-economic losses and damages".[24]

In addition to economic losses, climate change has also had significant negative impacts on human rights. The UNHRC notes that these impacts are "both direct and indirect, with cascading implications for different interconnected rights".[25] Human rights impacted by climate

[20] See, for instance, Jayne Piana, 'Diffusion of Green Technology: Patents, Licenses, and Incentives' (2022) 52 Texas Environmental Law Journal 37; Titilayo Adebola, 'Governing Climate Adaptation Innovation in Africa: A Case Study of Nigeria' (2024) 12 South African Intellectual Property Law Journal 81; William Nordhaus, 'The Challenge of Green Innovation' in Walter G Park (ed), *Handbook of Innovation and Intellectual Property Rights* (Edward Elgar Publishing 2024).

[21] Intergovernmental Panel on Climate Change (IPCC), '2023: Summary for Policymakers' in *Climate Change 2023: Synthesis Report.* Contribution of Working Groups I, II and III to the Sixth Assessment Report of the Intergovernmental Panel on Climate Change [Core Writing Team, H Lee and J Romero (eds.)]. IPCC, Geneva, Switzerland, 1–34, doi: 10.59327/IPCC/AR6-9789291691647.001, 5.

[22] ibid.

[23] ibid.

[24] UNGA 'Report of the Secretary-General' (n 15).

[25] ibid.

change have been said to include "the right to life, the right to adequate food, the right to the enjoyment of highest attainable standard of physical and mental health, the right to adequate housing, the right to self-determination, the rights to safe drinking water and sanitation, the right to work and the right to development".[26]

With respect to the right to food, for instance, the UN Secretary-General, in a 2023 report, wrote that "[c]limate change poses a serious threat and is increasingly becoming an obstacle to the full and effective realisation of the right to food".[27] This report notes that climate change "affects the four components of the right to food—namely, its physical and economic accessibility, availability, adequacy and sustainability—in different and related ways".[28] The food supplies of vulnerable regions are particularly at risk.[29]

With respect to the right to health, the UN Office of the High Commissioner for Human Rights (UNCHR) notes that

> [t]he World Health Organization (WHO) maintains that climate change is affecting health now, and will do so in the future . . . describ[ing] the main health risks posed by climate change as more intense heatwaves and fires; increased prevalence of food-, water- and vector-borne diseases; increased likelihood of undernutrition; and lost work capacity in vulnerable populations.[30]

The UNCHR also states that "[c]limate change is expected to widen existing health inequalities, both between and within populations".[31]

With respect to the right to housing, in 2022, the Special Rapporteur on Adequate Housing as a Component of the Right to an Adequate Standard of Living, and on the Right to Non-Discrimination in this Context, Balakrishnan Rajagopal, wrote in a Report that "[t]he climate crisis is also a housing crisis", and that "global warming . . . has . . . severely threaten[ed] the realization of the right to housing around the world", with impacts that "are disproportionately affecting people in countries that are particularly vulnerable to the adverse effects of climate change and people in vulnerable situations deepening existing inequalities and having a disproportionate impact on those who contribute least to climate change".[32]

With respect to the right to water, Special Rapporteur on the Human Rights to Safe Drinking Water and Sanitation, Pedro Arrojo Agudo, has argued that "the main socio-economic impacts [of climate change] are generated around water", and therefore, "adaptation strategies must be based on a hydrological transition that strengthens environmental and social resilience in the face of climate change".[33]

[26] UNHRC Res 41/21 (2019) UN Doc A/HRC/RES/41/21.

[27] UNGA 'Report of the Secretary General on the Adverse Impact of Climate Change on the Full Realization of the Right to Food' UNHRC 53rd Session UHN Doc A/HRC/53/47 (2023).

[28] ibid.

[29] ibid.

[30] UN High Commissioner for Human Rights, 'Frequently Asked Questions on Human Rights and Climate Change' (2021) <https://www.ohchr.org/sites/default/files/Documents/Publications/FSheet38_FAQ_HR_CC_EN.pdf>, accessed 2 June 2025.

[31] ibid.

[32] UNCHR, 'Report by Special Rapporteur Balakrishnan Rajagopal' (2022) UN Doc A/HRC/52/28 <https://www.ohchr.org/en/documents/thematic-reports/ahrc5228-towards-just-transformation-climate-crisis-and-right-housing> accessed 2 June 2025.

[33] UNCHR, 'Special Thematic Report by Special Rapporteur Petro Arrojo Agudo on Climate Change and the Human Rights to Water and Sanitation' (2022) <https://www.ohchr.org/en/documents/thematic-reports/special-thematic-report-climate-change-and-human-rights-water-and> accessed 2 June 2025.

With respect to the right to self-determination, climate change has been described as a significant threat to the self-determination of groups. As noted in a report produced by the Australian Institute of International Affairs:

> In 2009, the United Nations Human Rights Council recognised self-determination as one of the human rights most affected by climate change. Climate change will inevitably displace individuals, limiting their ability to practice their culture and freely engage in economic, social, and cultural development. Although the effects of climate change on the right to self-determination concerns all groups around the world, certain groups, including Small Island Developing States (SIDS) and Indigenous peoples, are particularly at risk.[34]

Climate change is also resulting in significant negative impacts on the right to a safe, clean, healthy, and sustainable environment. As stated in a report for Canada's Library of Parliament, "[c]limate change affects the air we breathe, the availability of food and water, and the rate and intensity of extreme weather events, such as floods, droughts and storms that have great potential to cause harm to human populations".[35]

While climate change impacts everyone, not everyone is impacted equally. As summarised by the UN Human Rights Council, climate change impacts are unequally distributed, with the poorest and most vulnerable populations bearing the greatest burden of losses and damages.[36] Historical emissions driving modern climate change were linked to exploitative economic models, colonialism, and structural racism, while ongoing inequities—particularly affecting Indigenous peoples and local communities—continue to heighten vulnerability.[37] Countries that contributed least to industrial emissions often lack the resources needed to protect their populations and environments from climate effects.[38]

As I argued in a previous work, countries have both legal and moral obligations to take action to address climate change.[39] These obligations flow from a number of different sources, including from international treaties focused on climate change or human rights that these countries have signed and ratified.[40]

This chapter builds on this work by arguing that in taking actions to fulfill these commitments in the context of IP, a human rights-based approach should be adopted. The idea that

[34] Jasmin L'Green and Zara Bendit-Rosser, 'The Impact of Climate Change on the Right to Self-Determination' (*Australian Institute of International Affairs*, 2022) <https://www.internationalaffairs.org.au/australianoutlook/the-impact-of-climate-change-on-the-right-to-self-determination/> accessed 2 June 2025.

[35] Robert Mason, 'Climate Change and the Right to a Healthy Environment: International and Canadian Developments' (*Library of Parliament*, 2023) <https://lop.parl.ca/sites/PublicWebsite/default/en_CA/ResearchPublications/202312E> accessed 2 June 2025.

[36] UNGA 'Report of the Secretary-General' (n 15).

[37] UNGA 'Report of the Secretary-General' (n 15).

[38] UNGA 'Report of the Secretary-General' (n 15).

[39] Reynolds (n 4).

[40] See, for instance, International Covenant on Economic, Social and Cultural Rights, 16 December 1966, 993 UNTS 3 [ICESCR]; International Covenant on Civil and Political Rights, 19 December 1966, 999 UNTS 171 [ICCPR]; United Nations Framework Convention on Climate Change, 9 May 1992, 1771 UNTS 107 (entered into force 21 March 1994) [UNFCCC]; Kyoto Protocol to the United Nations Framework Convention on Climate Change, 11 December 1997, 2303 UNTS 162 (entered into force 16 February 2005); Amendment to the list in Annex I to the United Nation Framework Convention on Climate Change, 26 October 2010, 2707 UNTS (entered into force 26 October 2010) [Copenhagen Accord]; Paris Agreement, 12 December 2015, 3156 UNTS (entered into force 4 November 2016) [Paris Agreement].

"human rights norms, standards, considerations and obligations should shape and guide all climate action" was articulated by the Secretary-General of the UN Human Rights Council in a report published in 2024.[41] This statement is grounded in part in the Paris Agreement, which provides in the Preamble that:

> Acknowledging that climate change is a common concern of humankind, Parties should, when taking action to address climate change, respect, promote and consider their respective obligations on human rights, the right to health, the rights of indigenous peoples, local communities, migrants, children, persons with disabilities and people in vulnerable situations and the right to development, as well as gender equality, empowerment of women and intergenerational equity.[42]

The idea that actions taken to address climate change should be consistent with human rights values and obligations also finds support in General Recommendation No. 37 (2018) on the Elimination of Discrimination against Women. This recommendation, which focuses on "gender-related dimensions of disaster risk reduction in the context of climate change", provides that:

> Any steps taken by States parties to prevent, mitigate and respond to climate change and disasters within their own jurisdictions or extraterritorially must be firmly grounded in the human rights principles of substantive equality and non-discrimination, participation and empowerment, accountability and access to justice, transparency and the rule of law.[43]

2.2 The Relationship Between IP and Human Rights

In the previous section, I discussed the relationship between climate change and human rights. I also argued that countries considering further action related to IP and climate change should adopt a human rights-based approach. That is to say, when taking action to address climate change, countries should do so in a way that considers, respects, and promotes their human rights obligations, and that is consistent with human rights principles and values. In the next part of this chapter, I will describe what a human rights-based approach to climate action might look like in the context of IP. Before doing so, it is important to first describe, in general terms, the relationship between IP and human rights.

[41] UNGA 'Report of the Secretary-General' (n 15).

[42] Paris Agreement (n 19).

[43] General Recommendation No. 37 (2018) (n 16). For more information on human rights-based approaches, see, for instance, Joel E Oestreich, *Power and Principle: Human Rights Programming in International Organizations* (Georgetown University Press 2007); Jakob Kirkemann Boesen and Tomas Martin, 'Applying a Rights-Based Approach' (*The Danish Institute for Human Rights*, 2007) <https://www.humanrights.dk/files/media/migrated/applying-a-rights-based-approach-2007-an-inspirational-guide-for-civil-society.pdf> accessed 14 June 2025; Damilola S Olawuyi, *The Human Rights-Based Approach to Carbon Finance* (CUP 2016); Government of Canada, 'Human Rights-based Approach' (May 2017) <https://www.international.gc.ca/world-monde/issues_development-enjeux_developpement/priorities-priorites/human_rights-droits_personne.aspx?lang=eng> accessed 14 June 2025; European Commission, 'Human Rights Based Approach' (May 2025) <https://wikis.ec.europa.eu/spaces/ExactExternalWiki/pages/50108948/Human+Rights+Based+Approach> accessed 14 June 2025; UN Sustainable Development Group, 'Human Rights-Based Approach' (2025) <https://unsdg.un.org/2030-agenda/universal-values/human-rights-based-approach> accessed 14 June 2025.

Widespread consideration of the relationship between IP and human rights is a somewhat recent phenomenon.[44] While some works engaged with this intersection in the period prior to the 1980s and 1990s, interest in this area (particularly by scholars based in the West) increased significantly in response to the development and introduction of the Agreement of Trade-Related Aspects of Intellectual Property Rights (TRIPS Agreement).[45] The TRIPS Agreement outlines a minimum set of standards for IP protections that all countries that are WTO members must meet. For many developing and least developed countries, signing on to the TRIPS Agreement required them to take steps to strengthen intellectual property protections in ways that—in the view of some—created conflict with human rights including the rights to health, education, food, and freedom of expression.

Another development that has led to greater consideration of the intersection of IP and human rights is the emergence and widespread use of the internet and other digital network technologies. Concerns raised by stakeholders with respect to the impact of the internet on the rights of both copyright owners and users have led to a number of legislative reforms. These reforms include the addition, to copyright legislation, of provisions that make it an infringing act to circumvent technological protection measures (TPM) in specific circumstances.[46] This reform has been criticised on human rights grounds, including with respect to the rights of persons with disabilities and the right to freedom of expression.[47]

One motivation cited by scholars for engaging with human rights arguments in the context of IP is the hope that such engagement can help push back against what some view as the inappropriate expansion of IP law, including in response to the legislative reforms noted above. These scholars argue that consideration of human rights in the context of IP can lead to a rebalancing between IP rights and other rights or interests in ways that ultimately help improve individual or community well-being.[48]

Several examples from both the international and domestic spheres can be seen as providing support for this position. At the international level, one example of an initiative that is strongly linked to human rights is the WIPO administered Marrakesh Treaty to Facilitate Access to Published Works for Persons Who Are Blind, Visually Impaired, or Otherwise Print

44 Works engaging with the intersection of IP and human rights include Rosemary J Coombe, 'Intellectual Property, Human Rights and Sovereignty: New Dilemmas in International Law Posed by the Recognition of Indigenous Knowledge and the Conservation of Biodiversity' (1998) 6 Indiana Journal of Global Legal Studies 59; Willem Grosheide, *Intellectual Property and Human Rights: A Paradox* (Edward Elgar Publishing 2010); Laurence R Helfer and Graeme W Austin, *Human Rights and Intellectual Property: Mapping the Global Interface* (CUP 2011); Duncan Matthews, *Intellectual Property, Human Rights and Development* (Edward Elgar Publishing 2011); Christophe Geiger (ed), *Research Handbook on Human Rights and Intellectual Property* (Edward Elgar Publishing 2015); Peter K Yu, 'Intellectual Property and Human Rights 2.0' (2019) 53 University of Richmond Law Review 1375; Paul L C Torremans, *Intellectual Property and Human Rights* (4th edn, Kluwer Law International 2020).

45 Agreement on Trade-Related Aspects of Intellectual Property Rights, 15 April 1994, Marrakesh Agreement Establishing the World Trade Organization, Annex 1C, 1869 UNTS 299, 33 ILM 1197 (1994) [TRIPS Agreement].

46 See for instance Canada's *Copyright Act*, RSC 1985, c C-42 ss 41–42.22.

47 See, for instance, Ian R Kerr, Alana Maurushat, and Christian S Tacit, 'Technical Protection Measures: Tilting at Copyright's Windmill' (2002–2003) 34 Ottawa Law Review 7; Patricia Akester, 'The Political Dimension of the Digital Challenge: Copyright and Free Speech Restrictions in the Digital Age' (2006) 1 Intellectual Property Quaterly 16; Jingyi Li and Niloufer Selvadurai, 'Facilitating Access to Published Works for Persons with a Print Disability: Amending Australian Copyright Laws to Ensure Compliance with the Marrakesh Treaty' (2017) Monash University Law Review 619.

48 See, for instance, Yu (n 45) 1424.

Disabled.[49] The first global IP treaty to focus on exceptions or limitations to copyright infringement, this agreement aims to increase access to accessible versions of books for individuals who are blind, visually impaired, or who have print disabilities, by requiring countries that ratify it to remove copyright barriers to the creation and distribution of such works.[50] Adopted in 2013, it entered into force in 2016.[51] A second example of an initiative linked to both IP and human rights at the international level is the Doha Declaration on the TRIPS Agreement and Public Health, which affirms that the TRIPS Agreement "can and should be interpreted and implemented in a manner supportive of WTO members' right to protect public health and, in particular, to promote access to medicines for all".[52]

At the domestic level, courts in several jurisdictions have taken steps to acknowledge the connection between IP and human rights, including by affirming that the rights of copyright owners must be balanced with freedom of expression considerations. In *Eldred v Ashcroft*, for instance, Ginsburg J., who delivered the opinion of the Supreme Court of the United States, referred to fair use as a "built-in First Amendment accommodation[]", and a "traditional First Amendment safeguard[]".[53] To give an example from Canada, Bennett J., in her majority decision for the British Columbia Court of Appeal in a 2017 decision entitled *Vancouver Aquarium Marine Science Centre v Charbonneau*, confirmed that in determining whether injunctive relief should be granted in an interlocutory injunction proceeding concerning copyright issues, the impact of any injunction on the *Charter* value of freedom of expression may be a relevant factor for courts to consider.[54]

Despite these examples, however, some scholars argue that human rights arguments have largely been unsuccessful in reshaping global intellectual property law in more progressive ways.[55] While a number of reasons have been offered to explain this lack of impact, Okediji attributes the failure of human rights to reshape IP to "the narrow vision of human rights—one that excludes economic, social and cultural rights—that has dominated the IP/human rights interface".[56] She states that "[t]he result is that the human rights/IP framework has largely

[49] World Intellectual Property Organization, 'Marrakesh Treaty to Facilitate Access to Published Works for Persons Who Are Blind, Visually Impaired or Otherwise Print Disabled', 27 June 2013, 3162 UNTS [Marrakesh Treaty].

[50] World Intellectual Property Organization, 'The Marrakesh Treaty: Helping to End the Global Book Famine' (WIPO 2016) <https://www.wipo.int/edocs/pubdocs/en/wipo_pub_marrakesh_overview.pdf> accessed 2 June 2025.

[51] ibid.

[52] World Trade Organization, 'Ministerial Declaration of 14 November 2021', WTO Doc WT/MIN(01)/DEC/1, 41 ILM 746 (2002) [hereinafter Doha Declaration] s 4.

[53] *Eldred v Ashcroft*, 537 US 186 (2003) 190.

[54] *Vancouver Aquarium Marine Science Centre v Charbonneau*, 2017 BCCA 395 [72]. For cases from Europe, see, for instance, *Ashby Donald and others v France*, ECHR 36769/08 [5th section], 10 January 2013; *Neij and Sunde Kolmisoppi v Sweden*, App no 4037/12, IHRL 2038 (ECHR 2013), 19 February 2013; *Case C-401/19 Poland v Parliament and Council*, CJEU ECLI:EU:C:2022:297.

[55] See, for instance, Ruth L Okediji, 'Intellectual Property in the Image of Human Rights: A Critical Review' in Rochelle Cooper Dreyfuss and Elizabeth Siew-Kuan Ng (eds), *Framing Intellectual Property in the 21st Century* (CUP 2018); Ruth L Okediji, 'Does Intellectual Property Need Human Rights' (2018) 50 New York University Journal of International Law and Politics 1; Ahmed Abdel-Latif and Pedro Roffe, 'The Interface Between Intellectual Property and Sustainable Development' in Irene Calboli and Maria Lillà Montagnani (eds), *Handbook of Intellectual Property Research: Lenses, Methods, and Perspectives* (OUP 2021); Martin Senftleben, 'The Unproductive 'Overconstitutionalization' of EU Copyright and Trademark Law: Fundamental Rights, Rhetoric and Reality in CJEU Jurisprudence' (2024) 55 International Review of Intellectual Property and Competition Law 1471.

[56] Ruth L Okediji, 'Does Intellectual Property Need Human Rights' (2018) 50 International Review of Intellectual Property and Competition Law 1, 5.

operated as a justification for the core architecture of the international IP system, with human rights considerations channeled through doctrines already hard-wired in contemporary IP jurisprudence".[57]

Rather than abandon consideration of this intersection, however, Okediji instead argues that we need to approach it differently. She offers several ways in which this could occur, including by "embrac[ing] possibilities for IP reform that could emerge from a serious engagement with the panoply of economic, social, cultural, and group rights";[58] by adopting an approach to IP and human rights that focuses on empowering developing countries and on capacity development;[59] and by being aware of the ways in which human rights and IP frames are grounded in specific knowledge systems, cultural approaches, and ways of knowing, and by taking steps to challenge the biases inherent in these frames.[60] This articulation of the human rights/IP interface is consistent with the human rights-based approach to IP proposed in this chapter. Rather than helping to justify or reinforce the international IP system as structured, it offers the potential for transformative reform.

3. Applying a Human Rights-based Approach to the Intersection of Climate Change and IP

3.1 Climate Change and IP

As noted above, many works have engaged with the intersection of climate change and IP. Consistent with the widely held view that technological innovation can help advance both climate mitigation and adaptation efforts, a number of these works have focused on ways through which to modify the patent system to encourage the development of ESTs. Reforms canvassed in these works include creating fast-track processes for patent applications for EST inventions,[61] modifying the term of patent protection for ESTs,[62] developing a wild card patent system through which innovation in one area (for instance ESTs) will result in a patent bonus that can be applied to a different invention,[63] expanding the scope of the research exception to patent infringement to increase research activity relating to ESTs,[64] rejecting patents for

57 ibid 20.

58 ibid 9.

59 ibid 67.

60 ibid. This latter argument draws in critical approaches to intellectual property law, such as those outlined by Margaret Chon and Carys Craig. See Margaret Chon, 'Intellectual Property Research and Critical Studies' in Irene Calboli and Maria Lillà Montagnani (eds), *Handbook of Intellectual Property Research* (OUP 2021); and Carys J Craig, 'Critical Copyright Law and the Politics of "IP"' in Emilios Christodoulidis, Ruth Dukes and Marco Goldoni (eds), *Research Handbook on Critical Legal Theory* (Edward Elgar Publishing 2021).

61 See, for instance, Matthew Rimmer, 'Intellectual Property and Global Warming: Fossil Fuels and Climate Justice,' in Matthew David and Debora Halbert (eds), *The SAGE Handbook of Intellectual Property* (Sage 2014); Abbe E L Brown, 'Intellectual Property and Climate Change,' in Rochelle C Dreyfuss and Justine Pila (eds), *The Oxford Handbook of Intellectual Property Law* (OUP 2018); Jayne Piana, 'Diffusion of Green Technology: Patents, Licenses, and Incentives,' (2022) 52 Texas Environmental Law Journal 37.

62 See for instance Estelle Derclaye, 'Should Patent Law Help Cool the Planet? An Inquiry from the Point of View of Environmental Law: Part II' (2009) 31 European Intellectual Property Review 227, 230.

63 See for instance Keith Maskus, 'Differentiated Intellectual Property Regimes for Environmental and Climate Technologies' (*OECD Environment Working Papers*, 2010) <https://doi.org/10.1787/5kmfwjvc83vk-en> accessed 2 June 2025.

64 See for instance Hilty and Batista (n 2).

"environmentally damaging technologies",[65] and making it easier for parties to apply for compulsory licenses for certain EST inventions.[66]

A second category of works has focused on how best to increase access to ESTs, including through the transfer of ESTs between countries. Among other proposals, these works have discussed different institutional mechanisms through which to encourage or facilitate the transfer of technologies,[67] considered the impact of waivers of IP rights on transfers,[68] and analysed the role that could be played by compulsory licenses in increasing access to ESTs in developing and least-developed countries.[69]

A third category of works has focused on how reforms to IP could help address the negative impacts of climate change in ways other than through amendments to patent legislation. Trademark-focused works have examined questions relating to greenwashing, eco-labelling, and the use of collective or certification marks to signal where products either promote climate goals or are particularly polluting.[70] Works that engage with copyright have considered a range of issues related to climate change including the impact of TPM provisions on the right to repair,[71] whether existing defences to copyright infringement are sufficient to permit the kinds of uses that could help in addressing climate change;[72] and the link between upcycling, copyright infringement, and climate change.[73] Several pieces consider the impact of trade secret protection on climate change efforts.[74]

In addition to these scholarly works, this chapter has also noted several initiatives relating to IP and climate change adopted by countries, companies, or institutions, including the creation

[65] See for instance Abbe EL Brown, 'Intellectual Property and Climate Change' in Rochelle Dreyfuss and Justine Pila (eds), *The Oxford Handbook of Intellectual Property Law* (OUP 2018), 979; Benjamin, Lisa, 'Intellectual Property' in Lavanya Rajamani and Jacqueline Peel (eds), *The Oxford Handbook of International Environmental Law* (2nd edn, OUP 2021).

[66] See for instance Hilty and Batista (n 2).

[67] See for instance Emma Perot, 'Technology Transfer, Climate Change and the Developing Countries: The Difficulties posed by Green Patents' (2023) 18(5) Journal of Intellectual Property Law & Practice 397.

[68] See for instance Su Jung Jee and others, 'Making Intellectual Property Rights Work for Climate Technology Transfer and Innovation in Developing Countries' (*University of Oxford*, 3 September 2024) <https://oms inet.files.svdcdn.com/production/files/Making_IPR_work_Sep_2024_WP-combined.pdf?dm=1725443682> accessed 2 June 2025.

[69] See for instance Rohan Cherian Thomas, 'A Legal Analysis of Transfer and Compulsory Licensing of Green Technology in India to Mitigate Climate Change' (2023) 8 Environmental Law and Practice Review 60.

[70] See for instance Rimmer, Matthew, *Intellectual Property and Clean Energy: The Paris Agreement and Climate Justice* (Springer 2018); Alexandra Mogyoros, 'Improving Eco-labels: Are Green Certification Marks Up to the Task' (2023) Journal of Intellectual Property Law & Practice 367; Jacques de Werra (ed), *Propriété intellectuelle et développement durable/Intellectual Property & Sustainable Development* (Schulthess 2024).

[71] See for instance Reynolds (n 4).

[72] See for instance Estelle Derclaye, 'The Role of Copyright in the Protection of the Environment and the Fight Against Climate Change: Is the Current Copyright System Accurate?' in Joshua Sarnoff (ed), *Research Handbook on Intellectual Property and Climate Change* (Edward Elgar Publishing 2016).

[73] Elena Izyumenko, 'Intellectual Property in the Age of the Environmental Crisis: How Trademarks and Copyright Challenge the Human Right to a Healthy Environment' (2024) 55 International Review of Intellectual Property and Competition Law 864.

[74] See for instance Leslyn Lewis, 'Evergreening through Trade Secrets as an Impediment to Green Technology Transfer to the Developing World,' (2018) 18 Asper Review of International Business and Trade Law 23.

of fast-track patent application processes for EST inventions, the development of the WIPO GREEN online platform, and the introduction of the Eco-Patent patent pool initiative.[75]

The scholarly works and initiatives canvassed above would—if successfully implemented—result in human rights benefits. However, actions or initiatives taken under a human rights-based approach would result in a different range of possibilities for reform at the intersection of IP and climate change, as well as a different set of outcomes. The following section will discuss, in more detail, outcomes that might flow from the adoption of a human rights-based approach to IP and climate change.

3.2 The Impact of a Human Rights-based Approach on the Intersection of Climate Change and IP

I have described earlier how climate change negatively impacts a range of human rights including rights to life, food, health, housing, water, self-determination, and the right to a safe, clean, and healthy environment.[76] States are obligated to act to respond to human rights violations. These obligations flow from a number of sources, both international and domestic. International commitments include those provided for in international human rights instruments that countries have signed and either acceded to or ratified. At the domestic level, commitments to protect human rights are provided for in bills of rights both constitutional or otherwise, in legislation, and at common law.

Earlier in this chapter, I defined a human rights-based approach as one that is shaped by human rights obligations; that is informed by human rights values and principles; that aims to strengthen the capacities of vulnerable groups within and outside of one's jurisdiction; and—drawing from Okediji's critique of the existing human rights/IP interface—that engages deeply with economic, social, and cultural rights and is "attentive to the distributive justice elements and inherent biases" of both human rights and IP frames.[77]

At least three types of outcomes might flow from the adoption of a human rights-based approach to climate change and IP. First, the application of a human rights-based approach could lead to a different set of reform proposals than are generally considered by lawmakers seeking to address the negative effects of climate change through IP reform. Second, the application of a human rights-based approach could lead to consideration of a different set of principles and values than has traditionally been the case in the context of IP law. Third, the application of a human rights-based approach could help identify those circumstances where IP reforms may not be as effective as other mechanisms in seeking to achieve improved outcomes for those individuals and communities whose human rights are most negatively impacted by climate change.

One example of an application of a human rights-based approach to the intersection of climate change and IP, in which the first two outcomes are evident, relates to the right to food. In a 2024 report of the UN High Commissioner for Human Rights, entitled "Measures for Minimizing the Adverse Impact of Climate Change on the Full Realization of the Right to Food", it is stated that "[p]olicies regarding intellectual property should not harm, but rather should support, the protection and fulfilment of the right to food, including in terms of

[75] See nn 5–7.

[76] See nn 9–10.

[77] Ruth Okediji, 'Does Intellectual Property Need Human Rights' (2018) 50 NYU Journal of International Law and Politics 1, 67.

biodiversity, access, affordability and human rights pertaining to seeds and plant varieties".[78] The report cites the Committee on Economic, Social and Cultural Rights' general comment No. 17 (2005), which states that "intellectual property . . . has a social function" and which notes that "States parties thus have a duty to prevent unreasonably high costs for access to essential medicines, plant seeds or other means of food production, or for schoolbooks and learning materials, from undermining the rights of large segments of the population to health, food and education".[79] While acknowledging the incentive function of intellectual property rights and the possibility that this can lead to additional investment in "climate-resilient agriculture", the report quickly pivots to highlighting the "concerns . . . raised that the benefits of scientific progress are not being equitably shared and that intellectual property rights are hampering rather than helping the realization of the right to food".[80] The report specifically references the Special Rapporteur on the Right to Food's concern that international IP law may limit farmers' rights to save, use, and exchange seeds, and notes the "critical need to take measures to protect food-related rights and knowledge, which includes the knowledge of Indigenous Peoples, peasants, local communities and other people living in rural areas", in a manner consistent with a number of international human rights declarations.[81]

One can imagine, then, that IP reforms undertaken under a human rights-based approach and directed towards addressing the impact of climate change on the right to food might foreground the social function of IP law; require evidence prior to expanding rights; ensure that mechanisms are in place to share the benefits of discoveries equitably; provide protection for the rights of farmers to save, use, and exchange seeds; and protect the rights and knowledge of Indigenous peoples (among other groups). Furthermore, rather than highlighting the incentive function of IP rights, a human rights-based approach to IP and the right to food could instead highlight how the reforms proposed above might enhance values of dignity and equity.

Similarly, in considering possible IP reforms, the goal of which is to address the negative impacts of climate change on the right to health, a human rights-based approach might focus on reforms that seek to strengthen the position of vulnerable groups both within and outside of one's jurisdiction. These reforms could include an expanded research exception to patent infringement specifically relating to health risks faced by vulnerable populations; additional incentives to encourage further research into climate-related health risks faced by vulnerable populations; programmes that help to facilitate the transfer of medication across national borders for the benefit of vulnerable populations; and modifications to both copyright and patent laws, the goal of which is to enhance capacity in relation to health-related expression and inventions.

In the same way, when considering how to modify IP laws in order to respond to the ways in which the right to self-determination is threatened by climate change, a human rights-based approach could direct policymakers towards reforms rooted in Indigenous legal traditions,

[78] UN High Commissioner for Human Rights (UNCHR), 'Measures for Minimizing the Adverse Impact of Climate Change on the Full Realization of the Right to Food: Report of the United Nations High Commissioner for Human Rights' (*United Nations*, 1 February 2024) <https://digitallibrary.un.org/record/4038900?ln=en&v=pdf> accessed 2 June 2025.

[79] UN Committee on Economic, Social and Cultural Rights (35th sess.: 2005), 'General Comment No. 17 (2005), The Right of Everyone to Benefit from the Protection of the Moral and Material Interests Resulting from Any Scientific, Literary or Artistic Production of Which He or She Is the Author (article 15, paragraph 1c, of the Covenant)' (*United Nations*, 12 January 2026) <https://digitallibrary.un.org/record/566430?ln=en&v=pdf> accessed 2 June 2025.

[80] ibid.

[81] ibid.

in the United Nations Declaration on the Rights of Indigenous Peoples (UNDRIP), or in domestic legislation the purpose of which is to ratify UNDRIP. These reforms could include ceding authority to Indigenous groups to control how their knowledge relating to climate change is used or commercialised, among other IP reforms.[82]

In addition to helping direct policymakers to a set of substantive proposals, principles, or values different to those generally considered in the context of IP and climate change, the adoption of a human rights-based approach to the intersection of IP and climate change can also help to highlight the limits of IP reform in seeking to improve the well-being of individuals and communities most negatively impacted by climate change. For instance, while expansions in IP protection might encourage the development of technologies that could be useful in supporting climate mitigation or adaptation efforts, to what extent will vulnerable communities see the benefits of these technologies? Depending on the circumstances, it could be the case that non-IP based interventions including direct government support are needed either instead of IP reforms or as a supplement to them, to ensure that the benefits of technological innovation flow to those individuals and communities most vulnerable to the negative impacts of climate change.

The question of the limits of IP is central to a 2024 working paper by Jee and others.[83] In this paper, the authors engage in the debate over the impact of IP rights on the question of whether developing countries can "meet[] their technological needs" in relation to climate change.[84] This paper asks "[a]re existing technology transfer mechanisms and the current TRIPS framework suitable for promoting the diffusion of climate change technologies? If so, how and when do they work? If not, what reforms can make national and international policy work better?"[85]

While this working paper does not explicitly engage with human rights, elements of its methodology are in alignment with a human rights-based approach to IP and climate change, including its focus on participation, empowerment, and capacity development. The paper concludes that the call to "expand[] TRIPS waivers to climate technologies" is "unlikely to facilitate" international technology transfer and could result in negative consequences.[86] Rather, Jee and others highlight "environmental regulation and financial incentives", along with other "demand-focused policies" as potential solutions, while at the same time noting that "scarce public budgets remain a barrier to fiscal support in poor countries".[87] Jee and others' work also highlights capacity development as a critical piece of any plan to support developing countries in meeting their technological needs relating to climate change. The authors argue that building technical expertise and ensuring the availability of financing for local entrepreneurs is essential and should be prioritised.[88] In contrast, they describe weakening intellectual

[82] See for instance Gordon Christie, 'Aboriginal Rights, Aboriginal Culture, and Protection' (1998) 36 Osgoode Hall Law Journal 447; Val Napoleon and others, *Indigenous Intellectual Property: An Interrupted Intergenerational Conversation* (University of Toronto Press 2025); Johnny Mack and Graham J Reynolds, 'Thinking Differently: Creating Spaces of Autonomy for the Revitalization of Indigenous Legal Traditions in the Context of Copyright' in Graham J Reynolds, Alexandra Mogyoros, and Teshager Dagne (eds), *Intellectual Property Futures: Exploring the Global Landscape of IP Law and Policy* (University of Ottawa Press 2025).

[83] Su Jung Jee and others, 'Making Intellectual Property Rights Work for Climate Technology Transfer and Innovation in Developing Countries' (University of Oxford, 3 September 2024) <https://oms-inet.files.svdcdn.com/production/files/Making_IPR_work_Sep_2024_WP-combined.pdf?dm=1725443682> accessed 2 June 2025.

[84] ibid 1.

[85] ibid 1.

[86] ibid 18.

[87] ibid 19.

[88] ibid 19.

property rights as a "cynical minimalist approach".[89] In the authors' view, measures that would be particularly meaningful include the provision of "funding to implement simple but impactful solutions", along with "formalised systems for targeted knowledge transfer".[90]

Although not in the climate change context, Gold's work on COVID-19 vaccines also highlights the limits of IP in both driving innovation and facilitating access to technology for individuals in developing countries. Gold concludes that "[d]uring the pandemic, intellectual property (IP) was not a significant driver of innovation; instead, it contributed to limiting and then delaying global access to vaccines and drugs".[91] According to Gold, it was procurement contracts (largely from government) that led to vaccine development, with patents playing a "more significant role once the first vaccines and antivirals have made it to market".[92]

With respect to access, Gold argues that "[d]ifferent vaccine and drug companies exercised their patents and trade secrets to control knowledge flows and threaten independent organizations—such as the World Health Organization's South African hub—from developing them, thus delaying access".[93] Gold notes how the World Health Organization as well as other experts have highlighted the need for additional "manufacturing facilities either domestically or nearby [in order] to ensure access".[94] These facilities could be funded either privately or through government support.

In a similar manner, the adoption of a human rights-based approach to IP and climate change allows for consideration of a broader range of policy solutions than do works that focus more squarely on climate change through an IP lens. Rather than ask what IP reforms may help to address the negative impacts of climate change, a human rights-based approach to IP and climate change focuses first on the climate-related needs of vulnerable individuals and communities and asks what reforms—IP or otherwise—are best suited to addressing these needs. While the answer may be IP reform, this is only one of a number of possibilities. As described above, these additional possibilities include the development and introduction of financial incentives, capacity building programmes, knowledge transfer systems, procurement contracts, and manufacturing facilities.

This section has discussed the possible application of a human rights-based approach to the intersection of IP and climate change. As described above, the application of such an approach could result in a number of outcomes, including the identification of a different set of proposals for reform than are usually considered in the context of IP, as well as a broader range of principles and values than is often the case in IP matters (through the inclusion of principles and values rooted in human rights). The application of such an approach can also help determine which reforms to prioritise on the basis of their impact on those individuals and groups that are most at risk from the negative effects of climate change.

4. Conclusion

One of the great challenges facing societies today is how to respond to climate change. What role does IP law play in relation to this challenge? What role can it play? Thus far, IP reforms relating to climate change have focused on ways through which to fast-track innovation relating

89 ibid 19.

90 ibid 19.

91 E Richard Gold, 'What the COVID-19 Pandemic Revealed About Intellectual Property' (2022) 40 Nature Biotech 1428.

92 ibid.

93 ibid.

94 ibid.

to ESTs, as well as attempts to bring together interested parties in order to facilitate technology transfer.

One area in which IP regimes can do more in relation to climate change is in helping to address the negative effects of climate change on human rights. This chapter has argued that one way to do so is through the adoption of a human rights-based approach to the intersection of IP and climate change. As outlined above, such an approach is guided by human rights obligations, is grounded in human rights principles, focuses on strengthening capacity, and—building on the work of Okediji—is attentive to the ways in which both human rights and IP are structured, as well as their inherent biases.

The application of this approach offers new opportunities for the intersection of climate change and IP. Rather than focusing on how to calibrate IP's rules to encourage the development of technological innovations, it draws our attention instead to the impacts of IP's rules on human rights. In particular, it asks us to consider the impact of IP on the human rights of those individuals and groups most vulnerable to the negative effects of climate change. This shift in perspective may lead to a different set of options for reform, namely those grounded in human rights norms and obligations. In addition, by considering human rights values and principles including substantive equality, participation, and empowerment alongside values traditionally associated with IP like incentivising and encouraging creativity and innovation, new possibilities are created for legislative action. Lastly, a human rights-based approach to the intersection of IP and climate change can also help identify where IP reforms may not be as effective as other measures in supporting the rights of vulnerable individuals or groups. It could be the case, for instance, that rather than increasing IP protection (or waiving it), the most effective way to address the negative impacts of climate change on vulnerable individuals or groups could be for governments to partner with these groups in capacity building.

As noted above, this chapter is intended as an introduction to the idea of a human rights-based approach to the intersection of IP and climate change. It seeks to outline both what this approach consists of, as well the outcomes that might result from the application of such an approach. It is also meant as a call to action for others to further consider how such an approach might be applied in specific circumstances.

Ultimately, the application of a human rights-based approach to the intersection of IP and climate change could lead to a reimagining of the IP system in light of human rights obligations and values, and in a way that centres and empowers vulnerable individuals and communities. In addition to helping ensure that IP-related climate mitigation and adaptation efforts benefit those who are most at risk from the negative effects of climate change, such a reimagining could also help address other societal challenges at the intersection of IP and human rights, including how to ensure equitable access to medicines, or how to guarantee access to works of expression for persons with disabilities. In this way, the application of such an approach could be truly transformative.

CHAPTER 17

Trusts

CARLA SPIVACK

1. Introduction

THE idea of the Earth as held in trust for future generations is older than the law itself. The world's three major religions all treat the preservation of the environment for future generations as a moral imperative. According to the Book of Genesis, God gave the Earth to His people and their offspring "as an everlasting possession", to be cared for and passed on to each generation.[1] Islamic law holds the Earth to be God's bounty to be preserved and passed on to future generations.[2] Indigenous and tribal religions also express the belief in holding the Earth in trust for the future.[3] Some modern writers have approached the issue as one of intergenerational equity, expressing a similar "preservation as trust" concept in different terms. John Rawls, for example, argued for the preservation of cultural and institutional culture, as well as undefined "capital", for future generations, urging that no generation should be left in a worse position than preceding generations.[4]

The fundamental concepts underlying the trust do, indeed, seem well-suited to addressing the unprecedented problem of climate change, at least its legal aspects. Most importantly, the trust is defined by split title, meaning that one party manages assets for the beneficial use of other people, the beneficiaries—often, but not necessarily, members of future generations. The point is not that split title itself contains the idea of future beneficiaries; that idea is contained in the idea of environmental preservation itself. Rather, split title uniquely strips physical possession of beneficial use. This split is the unique contribution of the trust. It strips the legal possessor of the ability to exploit or deplete the asset, imposing on that person or entity the duty to preserve or manage it for someone else.[5] This structure seems ideally suited to environmental conservation, which is based on the idea of preserving, rather than exploiting, the environment, for the beneficial use of others. The idea of conservation, and climate change amelioration, in turn, seems to supply a multigenerational paradigm. And of course, any trust can be drafted to benefit future generations; most today are, for tax reasons if nothing else. My only point here is that the split title offers an ownership structure that uniquely fits the needs of environmental preservation.

[1] Genesis 1:26–31, 17:7–8.

[2] Siraj Hait and Hilary Lim, *Land, Law, and Islam: Property and Human Rights in the Muslim World* (Zed Books 2006) 25.

[3] Edith Brown Weiss, *In Fairness to Future Generations: International Law, Common Patrimony, and Intergenerational Equity* (Transnational Publishers 2006) 18.

[4] John Rawls, *A Theory of Justice* (Harvard University Press 1971) 285.

[5] Of course, a person could be a trustee as well as a beneficiary. But in her role as trustee, her title would not include beneficial enjoyment.

Thinking about the trust in the context of climate change, however, also amply illustrates the device's double-edged (in that context) nature. As Austin Wakeman Scott pointed out a century ago, the trust has always wobbled on the line between law reform and evasion.[6] While "much of the progress of English law is due to the doctrines of the law of uses and trusts", Scott concedes that the trust has "often served as a means of evading the law".[7] Indeed, paradoxically, "the evasion which in the long run proves successful is usually a reform".[8] In this article, Scott goes on to credit the trust with undermining English feudalism, "revolutionizing" the law of conveyancing, and enabling business organisations, among much else.[9] Further on, Scott identifies some asset protection features of the trust on the "evasion" side of the line.[10] If the trust can achieve these radical changes in the law, it may be well-suited to pushing the legal system towards the revolutionary changes climate change demands. On the other hand, as I will show, its evasive capabilities may—and do, in fact—also undermine those very efforts.

This legal ambiguity of the trust is due to its nature as an instrument of private law. The goal of private law is to effectuate individual aims to the extent law and public policy allow. The trust is an empty vessel, ready to be filled with whatever content the settlor wishes. On the one hand, the trust form offers flexibility as a form of real property ownership that because of split title, makes it a useful device for conservation, preservation, and environmental protection with future generations in mind. More broadly, the trust's ability to push the law to evolve to meet changing circumstances seems useful in addressing an unprecedented existential threat like climate change. On the other hand, this same flexibility and innovative capacity have also led to the trust's extensive use as a mechanism for tax avoidance and the consolidation of dynastic wealth, and make the trust form a driver of wealth inequality and climate harm. All of these outcomes are negatively associated with both the acceleration of climate change and the harshness and disparate impact of its effects. This paradox, however, is inherent in a private law ownership form that exists to effectuate individual goals. Thus, the trust raises the question of whether private law is an appropriate arena in which to seek solutions to collective problems like climate change. This chapter will explore both the climate preservation uses of the trust form and its uses that hinder those goals by enabling private goals like wealth accumulation, tax avoidance, and fossil fuel use.

In discussing the various roles the trust form plays and can play in the context of climate change, this chapter deploys a very general definition of a trust as any relationship whereby a party holds and manages property for the benefit of someone else—usually some kind of beneficiary. Where trusts are designed to ameliorate climate change and its effects, the beneficiary is usually the general public and its future generations. When trusts are used in ways that have a pernicious effect on the climate and on governments' ability to address climate change effects, they are more often traditional trust forms, like dynastic trusts and land trusts devised to avoid externalities and hide ownership.

This chapter proceeds as follows: Section 2 explores uses of the trust to ameliorate climate change, as well as criticism that has been raised about some of these forms. Current uses of the trust to ameliorate climate change predominantly involve two forms: the public trust, a doctrine as old as Roman law and the common law, that potentially places the sovereign as trustee of property that belongs to the citizenry, such as the sea, the shore, and some types of land, like

6 Austin Wakeman Scott, 'The Trust as an Instrument of Law Reform' (1922) 31 Yale Law Journal 457, 457–58.

7 ibid 458.

8 ibid.

9 ibid.

10 ibid.

forests and wilderness. Second, there has been a proliferation of various forms of conservation trusts over the past two or three decades. This is a general term covering a variety of ownership forms that have in common the preservation of the environment for future generations. Some combine public and private ownership, but some are purely private; some involve management of easements, while some involve title ownership. This section will also discuss the role of Native Peoples in performing trust stewardship of the environment and proposed, unprecedented, uses of the trust form in the context of climate change. These include proposals to hold the global atmosphere and the Earth's oceans in trust. Finally, Section 2 will survey the uses of trust-like devices and relationships in civil law countries to steward the environment.

Section 3 turns to trusts that impede climate amelioration. Here, I locate the heart of the problem of the trust as private law instrument in the context of public problems: the role of the trustee. I discuss the role of the traditional trustee in managing and investing trust assets and raise the question of whether his or her duties under conventional financial profit models should be modified to include the duty to preserve the planet for the future trust beneficiaries, as some have argued.

Section 4 turns to what we might call, in the context of climate amelioration, the "dark side" of the trusts. This section explains the ways trusts hinder governments' response to climate change and increase the impact of those governments and climate change on the world's poor and marginalised. This section focuses on multigenerational dynastic trusts that amplify the problem of climate change in at least three related ways. First, these trusts avoid paying taxes in significant amounts, thus depriving the public fisc of the funds necessary to combat the progression and effects of climate change. Second, these trusts contribute to world wealth inequality, thus skewing the impact and costs of climate change towards those on the low-wealth end of the spectrum. Finally, the wealth accumulation these trusts enable allows the 1% to create an outsize carbon footprint. The chapter concludes by noting that both the ameliorative and climate-harmful effects of the trust are inherent in its nature as an instrument of private law and by returning to the broader question of whether private law can address climate change on the necessary scale.

2. Trusts to Ameliorate Climate Change

This section explores the use of the public trust doctrine and the use of conservation trusts to fight the effects and progress of climate change. The public trust, an ancient doctrine in both the common and civil law, seems to offer a ready-made device to protect public resources from the depredation caused by climate change; as this section will show, however, there are limits embedded within the doctrine that may undermine this usefulness. Another trust variant, the "conservation trust", already plays a significant role in environmental preservation and climate amelioration. Conservation trusts, according to one author, "represent the first time, perhaps, that a conservation ethic manifests itself in private property law".[11] Finally, the trust-related doctrine of waste has been offered as way of addressing climate change in this context.[12]

[11] Mary Christina Wood and Zachary Welcker, 'Tribes as Trustees Again (Part 1): The Emerging Tribal Role in the Conservation Trust Movement' (2008) 32 Harvard Environmental Law Journal 373, 428.

[12] Anthony L I Moffa, 'Wasting the Planet: What A Storied Doctrine of Property Brings to Bear on Environmental Law and Climate Change' (2012) 27 Journal of Environmental Law and Litigation 459, 460.

2.1 The Public Trust Doctrine

The public trust doctrine, as noted, arguably traces its roots to Roman law. Justinian's Institutes provide that the "air, running water, the sea, and consequently the seashore" were "common to all" and thus open to the use of the public at large.[13] The Institutes further provide:

> Again, the public use of the sea-shore, as of the sea itself, is part of the law of nations; consequently everyone is free to build a cottage upon it for purposes of retreat, as well as to dry his nets and haul them up from the sea. But they cannot be said to belong to any one as private property, but rather are subject to the same law as the sea itself, with the soil or sand which lies beneath it.[14]

Further, individuals could freely use these common resources and even build on them, provided that the improvements were consistent with the resources' public use. No private person could appropriate these resources for exclusive private use.[15] According to Joseph Sax, the doctrine of public use declined after the fall of the Roman Empire in Europe, and was later doctrinally reinvigorated to some extent by Magna Carta.[16] Cited in particular in this respect are clauses 33 and 47.[17] Clause 33 states that "all fish weirs on the Thames and on the Medway and all through England are to be entirely dismantled, save on the seacoast".[18] This provision, however, may have less to do with the waterways as public trust property than with competition between the king's fishing rights and the competing fishing and navigation rights claimed by other powerful players in the feudal land system, namely, feudal lords and abbeys.[19] The public trust doctrine was later expanded by the common law, likely beyond the intended scope of Magna Carta—or, for that matter, Justinian.[20] This has led some to question its doctrinal existence entirely, and to call it a legal "fable".[21] Perhaps the best response to this in the context of climate change is Helen Babcock's argument that the alleged "legal fiction" of the public trust is, quoting Lon Fuller, "the growing pains of the language of the law"—that is, a "way of adjusting old rules to new facts to lessen the impact of legal change . . . where new social and business practices are necessitating a reconstruction of legal doctrine".[22]

To varying degrees, the idea that certain natural resources were held in common for the use of everyone seems to appear in the early common law, although English law does not recognise the public trust doctrine as such, and there is controversy about the exact meaning of the record.[23] For example, the Charter of the Forest of 1217 recognised a public right in the

13 Samuel Ruddy, 'Finding A Constitutional Home for the Public Trust Doctrine' (2020) Environs: Environmental Law & Policy Journal 139, 143.

14 Joseph Sax, 'The Public Trust in Tidal Areas: A Sometime Submerged Traditional Doctrine' (1970) 79 Yale Law Journal 762, 763–64, quoting Justinian Institutes 2.1.1–2.1.6.

15 Ruddy (n 13) 143.

16 Sax (n 14) 765.

17 ibid 766–67.

18 ibid at 766, quoting Magna Carta 23.

19 Ruddy (n 13) 144.

20 For arguments on both sides of this legal history, cf James L Huffman, 'Speaking of Inconvenient Truths—A History of the Public Trust Doctrine' (2007) 18 Duke Environmental Law & Policy Forum 1, 14; Patrick Deveney, 'Jus Publicum and The Public Trust Doctrine: A Historical Analysis' (1978) 1 Sea Grant Law Journal 13.

21 ibid.

22 Hope M Babcock, 'The Public Trust Doctrine: What a Tall Tale They Tell' (2009) 61 South Carolina Law Review 393, 400, citing Lon L Fuller, *Legal Fictions* (Stanford University Press 1967) 29.

23 Ruddy (n 13) 143.

land's natural resources, in that case, a public right to hunt.[24] From the thirteenth to the nineteenth century, recognition of public access rights to natural resources developed further in the English common law, as treatises and courts expanded on its recognition. The American Constitution inherited this doctrine. From the beginning, shoreline states incorporated it into their law, eventually including a "wide range of resources, including beaches, seashore amenities (like public bathhouses), parklands, historical landmarks, wildlife, air, and even downtown areas".[25]

Early on, the United States Supreme Court recognised the public trust doctrine as well: In the 1842 case, *Martin v Lessee of Waddell*, it ruled that sovereignty imposed public trust duties on state governments, in this case, the State of New Jersey, which held "the shores, and rivers and bays and arms of the sea, and the land under them . . . as a public trust for the benefit of the whole community to be freely used by all for navigation and fishery".[26] In 1892, the Supreme Court decided *Illinois Central Railroad v Illinois*, an iconic public trust case, holding that Illinois' public trust duties barred it from selling a large portion of the bed of Lake Michigan to a private railroad.[27]

American public trust doctrine has been understood by the legislative and executive branches to mean that natural resources should be preserved for future generations. As far back as 1965, the White House report, "Restoring the Quality of Our Environment", stated: "[T]he land, air, water, and living things of the United States are heritage of the whole nation. They need to be protected for the benefit of all Americans, both now and in the future".[28] Even more explicitly, Congress declared in 1968 that the federal government has an obligation to "fulfil the responsibilities of each generation as trustee of the environment for succeeding generations".[29]

Based on this history, the public trust doctrine seems like a logical starting point for a discussion of trusts in relation to climate change. The cases, however, exhibit the problem of using a form that was invented to achieve private goals to achieve public outcomes. Over the past fifteen years or so, climate plaintiffs have filed a series of cases that represent an evolving endeavour to apply the public trust doctrine to the needs posed by climate change. The primary doctrinal obstacles they have encountered in these attempts have been the jurisdictional (that is, is the public trust a state doctrine), definitional (specifically, does the public trust include the atmosphere[30]), and the question of whether the public trust doctrine incorporates all of the aspects of trust in private law, in particular, an affirmative fiduciary duty to preserve the environment rather than a mere duty to keep it undeveloped and available to the public.

In 2011, the plaintiffs in *Alec L. v Jackson* sued several heads of government agencies for failing in their fiduciary duty to protect the atmosphere, as a public trust resource, from the effects of climate change.[31]

[24] ibid.

[25] ibid.

[26] 41 US 367 (1842).

[27] Ruddy (n 13) 143.

[28] Trial Pleading, *Juliana v United States*, 2015 WL 4747094 (OR 2015). See also 1 William H Rodgers Jr., *Environmental Law: Air and Water* (West Publishing Company 1986) 155 (describing the public trust doctrine); Alexandra B Klass, 'Modern Public Trust Principles: Recognizing Rights and Integrating Standards' (2006) 82 Notre Dame Law Review 699, 702 (same); *Kelley v 1250 Oceanside Partners* 140 P.3d 985 (Haw. 2006) (same).

[29] Trial Pleading, *Juliana v United States* (n 28) [264].

[30] Thomas Boudreau, 'The Earth's Atmosphere as a Global Trust: Establishing Proportionate State Responsibility to Maintain, Restore, and Sustain the Global Atmosphere' (2017) 7 Barry University Environmental and Earth Law Journal 39.

[31] *Alec L. v Jackson*, 863 F. Supp. 2d 11 (D.C. 2012).

The plaintiffs sought a declaration that the atmosphere was encompassed by the public trust doctrine, that the government had a fiduciary duty to preserve it for future generations by reducing carbon emissions, and that the government had breached that duty.[32] The court ruled that public trust was a matter of state, not federal, law, and that the remedy the plaintiffs sought (directing government agencies to limit the amount of carbon allowably discharged into the atmosphere) would encroach on the decision-making authority and competence of federal agencies.[33] In a 2013 case, the Arizona Court of Appeals left open the possibility of the public trust including the atmosphere, and asserted that it was up to state courts to determine what fell within the doctrine.[34] A 2012 Texas case also held out the possibility that the state public trust encompassed the atmosphere.[35]

The two most prominent climate cases making arguments premised on the public trust are *Julianna v United States*[36] and *Chernaik v Brown*.[37] First, in the federal case of *Julianna v United States*,[38] a group of young plaintiffs sued the US government for breaching its public trust duty and violating the Constitution's Fifth Amendment's property and due process guarantees by continuing to consume fossil fuels and support greenhouse gas-producing industries.[39] The Ninth Circuit, in its words, "reluctantly" dismissed the case for lack of standing, ruling that ordering the government to prevent climate change was a matter for the political branches, and that the plaintiffs lacked constitutional standing to bring the case.[40] The Ninth Circuit also dismissed an amended complaint in 2024, and the Supreme Court denied cert in 2025.[41] Dissenting to the dismissal, Judge Aiken found a right to climate protection under a federal public trust doctrine, rights that "both predated the Constitution and are secured by it".[42] There is indeed a line of Supreme Court cases that do seem to acknowledge a federal public trust of the public lands in the United States.[43]

In a similar case, *Chernaik v Brown*,[44] plaintiffs sued the state of Oregon for failing in its fiduciary duty to protect all the natural resources held in public trust, which the plaintiffs asserted included the atmosphere, the state's waters, wildlife, and fish.[45] The plaintiffs also sought a declaration that the public trust doctrine encompassed a fiduciary duty to affirmatively act to protect these natural resources for the public as beneficiary. The Oregon Supreme Court held that the public trust doctrine encompassed only the "navigable waters and the

[32] ibid 13–14.

[33] ibid 16–17 (explaining that the plaintiffs are asking the court to make determinations on what constitutes an acceptable amount of atmospheric carbon dioxide and that those 'determinations . . . are best left to the federal agencies').

[34] *Butler v Brewer*, 2013 WL 1091209 (Ariz App 14 March 2013) (dismissing for failure to raise a constitutional violation or challenge a state statute).

[35] *Bonser-Lain v Texas Commission on Environmental Quality*, 2012 WL 3164561 (Texas District Court August 2, 2012).

[36] *Juliana v United States*, 217 F Supp 3d 1224 (D Or 2016).

[37] *Chernaik v Brown*, 475 P 3d 68, 72 (OR 2019).

[38] *Juliana* (n 36).

[39] ibid.

[40] ibid 1165 ('Reluctantly, we conclude that such relief is beyond our constitutional power. Rather, the plaintiffs' impressive case for redress must be presented to the political branches of government').

[41] *Juliana v United States*, 145 S Ct 1428 (2025).

[42] *Juliana* (n 36) 1250.

[43] For discussion of these cases, see generally Zachary Berliner 'What About Uncle Sam? Carving a New Place for the Federal Public Trust Doctrine in Federal Climate Litigation' (2018) 21 University of Pennsylvania Journal of Law and Social Change 339.

[44] *Chernaik* (n 37).

[45] ibid 72.

submerged and submersible lands underlying those waters", and, though it allowed that the "public trust is capable of expanding to include more natural resources", it declined to expand it "at this time".[46] While acknowledging that it had expanded the doctrine in past decisions, as the plaintiffs urged, it observed that the expansion of the doctrine in those cases "all resulted from disputes involving a specific body of water and furthered the primary purpose of the doctrine—protecting the public's right to use navigable waters for fishing and navigation".[47] Here, the plaintiffs argued that the doctrine extended to the atmosphere and all fish and wildlife, which the court rejected as beyond the core purpose of the historical public trust. In doing so, the court declined to apply the test the plaintiffs proposed, which would have defined resources subject to the public trust as those that "(1) are not easily held or improved and (2) are of great value to the public for uses such as commerce, navigation, hunting, and fisheries". While the court agreed that these factors were relevant, it deemed the test "so broad that it is difficult to conceive of a natural resource that would not satisfy it".[48]

It also held that the state's public trust duties did not extend to affirmative action to protect and preserve resources, but rather were merely to preserve them for public use.[49] It also refused to impose an affirmative fiduciary duty on the state, stating that the case law "cannot be read to conclude that all common-law principles of private trust law govern the public trust doctrine".[50]

Public trust-based climate change lawsuits continue to struggle in state courts. In *Aronow v Minnesota*, a twenty-five-year-old Minnesota resident, sued the state for failing to protect the atmosphere from greenhouse gas emissions and thus to protect the atmosphere for future generations.[51] The court granted the state's motion to dismiss on the grounds that the state's public trust law applied only to navigable waters, and the Minnesota Court of Appeals affirmed.[52]

As these cases suggest, the public trust doctrine faces a number of doctrinal impediments as a cause of action in the context of climate change. First, it varies significantly from state to state, leading to potentially inconsistent outcomes.[53] This inconsistency in state outcomes can lead to paradoxical results from a climate change perspective: At the state level, opponents of various renewable energy projects like large-scale wind and solar farms have brought suit based on the state's public trust doctrine.[54] More importantly, while most commentators agree that the doctrine covers bodies of water, shoreline, and underwater land, there's much less agreement that it extends to the atmosphere as a whole. Further, it may not impose all of the affirmative duties of a private trustee. Because of these limitations, it may not be well-suited to use by the courts in addressing climate change, although doing so would likely be within the ambit of permissible legislative action. Finally, whether or not there is a federal common law public trust doctrine is subject to debate.

[46] ibid.

[47] ibid 80.

[48] ibid 82.

[49] ibid 82–83.

[50] ibid 83.

[51] *Aronow v Minnesota*, 2012 WL 4476642 (2012).

[52] ibid.

[53] Thomas W Merrill, 'The Public Trust Doctrine: Some Jurisprudential Variations and Their Implications' (2016) 38 U Hawai'i Law Review 261, 266 (but noting that even varying as it is, the doctrine does require the state to devote a 'set of resources . . . identified as public').

[54] See, e.g., *Alliance to Protect Nantucket Sound v Energy Facilities Siting Board*, 932 NE 2d 787 (Mass 2010).

2.2 Conservation Trusts

"Conservation trust" is a general term with broad meaning. It usually refers to the holding of land or conservation easements in a trust like form for the purposes of conservation, a legal arrangement that has become widespread over the past few decades.[55] They are usually community-based trusteeship of land with the public as the beneficiaries.[56] As trust-like devices, they are governed by the rules of fiduciary duties like prudent management, obedience, and loyalty to the beneficiary.

Conservation trusts arose as a response to so-called debt-for-nature trades, in which a country's foreign debt would be forgiven in exchange for a commitment to domestic conservation investment.[57] These exchanges proved problematic because they tended to flood the country's domestic market with currency, which in turn destabilised local economies.[58] These efforts also fell short for lack of long-term funding.[59] In 1993, Congress enacted legislation allowing NGOs to establish conservation endowments with dollars allocated to the US Agency for International Development (USAID).[60] The pilot country for this type of fund was Bhutan, because of its environmental diversity, geographical location, and conservation-minded government.[61] Due to success there, conservation trust funds based on this model became widespread.[62]

Within the US, conservation trust funds have evolved as overall attitudes towards government and land management have changed. Increasing frustration with perceived government inefficiency and incompetence has gradually undermined long-accepted Progressive Era notions of land management through governmental agencies.[63] These concepts have given way over the past two or three decades to organisations well-suited to trust principles such as cooperatives, public–private partnerships, government-private partnerships, and others.[64] These organisations also take a less binary approach to land management than earlier models. Instead of strict public–private categories of land, they treat land as "an integrated mosaic" based more on ecological processes than clearly delineated parcels.[65] One author refers to this process as "devolution and dispersion" of land management.[66]

The trust form has proved appealing to both private and public actors in this new landscape. Businesspeople appreciate the trust form's focus on achieving specific goals and using a standard of prudence to handle resources; for public and nonprofit sector actors, the trust offers clarity for court oversight and enforcement.[67] The trust form is appealing to everyone involved for its long-established body of law.

55 Sally K Fairfax and Darla Guenzler, *Conservation Trusts* (University Press of Kansas 2001) 6–13.

56 ibid 204.

57 Marianne Guerin-McManus, 'Conservation Trust Funds' (2001) 20 UCLA Journal of Environmental Law & Policy 1, 6.

58 ibid.

59 ibid.

60 ibid.

61 ibid.

62 ibid.

63 ibid 7.

64 ibid 6.

65 ibid 7.

66 ibid 6.

67 ibid 12.

The conservation trust can take different forms. A conservation easement can be held by a trust; an environmental group can buy land outright to hold in trust; a government-private partnership can hold land in trust for conservation. Waterways can also be held in trust. Use of these trust forms has grown by leaps and bounds over the past few decades.[68]

Many of the trusts used for climate protection purposes in the US today serve to protect the environment and threatened resources.[69] There are several notable examples of the trust form used for environmental protection today in the US. The Platt River Whooping Crane Preservation Trust, which was formed in 1978 as a resolution to litigation, continues to function as an effective environmental organisation.[70] Its purpose is to "finance programs and activities to protect and maintain the physical, hydrological and biological integrity of the Big Bend area . . . as a life support system for . . . migratory bird species that use it".[71] The beneficiary is the public at large.[72] The property of the trust was supplied by a large payment from one of the parties to the litigation. The trustees are appointed by the three major parties to the litigation.[73] Accountability is supplied by the ongoing involvement of the framers of the trust and the attorney general.[74]

Another way the trust is used for environmental purposes is through what might be called a "governmental trust". This term loosely embodies a range of trust-like organisations made up of government agencies, whose boards consist of appointees from various state and federal agencies to carry out a specific mission; some are actually government agencies themselves. The resources they administer are overseen by multiple government agencies. Using the trust form instead of the usual agency format for decision-making gives them flexibility to respond to local conditions and changes. Three examples of this kind of trust—a mitigation bank to preserve wetlands in Dade County, Florida, The Exxon Valdez Oil Spill Trustee Council, and the Department of Hawaiian Homelands—exhibit a range of possibilities for the formation and uses of such trusts.[75] The Dade County wetlands mitigation project administers funds paid on an ongoing basis as fines by companies who destroy wetlands to preserve and reestablish other wetlands in the county.[76] The Exxon Valdez Oil Spill Trustee Council uses the investment income of the 900 million dollar civil settlement in the wake of the disaster to replace or restore the natural resources destroyed by the spill.[77] The Department of Hawaiian Homelands is an established trust fund that grants its beneficiaries—those with at least 50% Hawaiian blood—land and housing where they can own homes and pursue native traditions of land cultivation.[78] The DHHL has been plagued with problems, however, such as producing

[68] Zachary Bray, 'Reconciling Development and Natural Beauty: The Promise and Dilemma of Conservation Easements' (2010) 34 Harv Environmental L Rev 119, 123.

[69] Fairfax (n 55) 35.

[70] ibid 38.

[71] ibid 43.

[72] ibid.

[73] ibid.

[74] ibid.

[75] ibid 55–59.

[76] ibid.

[77] See 'Exxon Valdez Oil Spill Trustee Council,' *Alaska Department of Fish and Game* <https://www.adfg.alaska.gov/index.cfm?adfg=divisions.evosmission> accessed 21 July2025.

[78] 'About,' *Department of Hawaiian Home Lands* <https://dhhl.hawaii.gov/> accessed 21 July 2025. *See also* 'Hawaiian Home Lands Trust,' *United States Department of the Interior* <https://www.usccr.gov/files/historical/1991/91-011.pdf> accessed 21 July 2025.

substandard housing and failing to serve its beneficiaries, thousands of whom can remain on wait lists for decades.[79]

These organisations have had varying degrees of success with the trust form, partly because, due to their close affiliation with government agencies, they replicate it less closely than other forms of environmental trust. This has raised concern about accountability: While all three of these trusts produce detailed and extensive financial disclosures, their accountability has been more questionable—and questioned. For example, because the Dade County wetland preservation trust was run wholly through government agencies, there was very little transparency and accountability.[80]

These trust forms have drawn criticism on a number of grounds. First, they may pose problems of permanence and "lock in".[81] The permanence required by the tax code or terms of the trust may impose restrictions on owners in the future when the restrictions have become "obsolete or injurious".[82] Another worry is popular perception that wealthy people are using overvalued conservation easements to get inflated tax breaks.[83] In fact, critics have raised distributional concerns, noting that "[b]ecause most of the owners of land burdened by conservation easements are affluent, or even rich, the prospect of such a giveaway [through the federal tax deduction] raises serious distributional concerns".[84] In fact, these concerns have solid foundation: As Adam Looney of the Brookings Institution has shown, the tax deduction for conservation easements "has become a lucrative way for real estate developers in expensive resort destinations to finance development projects—depriving the government of billions of dollars of revenue and in some cases doing little to advance environmental protection".[85] Taxpayers either take deductions based on grossly inflated property values, or developers sell the right to take the deductions to taxpayers, then use the funds to buy the land and develop part of it, enabling a higher valuation on the remaining property. Total deductions for conservation easements totalled US$3.2 billion in 2014.[86] Looney enumerates ways to address this exploitation of the system, but they seem unlikely to be enacted.

2.3 The Trust Role of Native People

Native American Tribes have a special cultural connection to the idea of a trustee relationship with the Earth and are beginning to assimilate that philosophy and conservation trusts into their sovereignty efforts.[87] As Sam Bookman notes in Chapter 46 of this handbook,

[79] 'A BROKEN TRUST: The Hawaiian Homelands Program: Seventy Years of Failure of the Federal and State Governments to Protect the Civil Rights of Native Hawaiians,' *Hawaii Advisory Committee to the United States Commission on Civil Rights* < https://www.usccr.gov/files/historical/1991/91-011.pdf> accessed 21 July 2025.

[80] Fairfax (n 55) 55–59.

[81] Bray (n 68) 137.

[82] ibid.

[83] ibid 147.

[84] Julia D Mahoney, 'Perpetual Restrictions on Land and the Problem of the Future' (2002) 88 Viriginia Law Review 739, 750–51.

[85] Adam Looney, 'Charitable Contributions of Conservation Easements,' *Brookings Institution* (2017) <https://www.brookings.edu/wp-content/uploads/2017/05/looney_conservationeasements.pdf> accessed 28 June 2025.

[86] ibid.

[87] Mary Christina Wood and Matthew O'Brien, 'Tribes as Trustees Again (Part II): Evaluating Four Models of Tribal Participation in the Conservation Trust Movement' (2008) 27 Stanford Environmental Law Journal 477, 484.

"Indigenous people play an outsize role in global climate governance".[88] Many tribes and nations see the Earth as a gift of the Creator, entrusted to them for care and preservation for future generations.[89] For example, Bookman quotes the Navajo Tribal Code as imposing a duty on Tribe members to "respect, preserve and protect all that was provided for we were designated as the steward" for future generations.[90] Nicole Graham also discusses aspects of Indigenous cultures that stand in juxtaposition to colonialist regimes of extraction that have led to the climate crisis.[91] These aspects of Indigenous culture dovetail with the conservation trust movement, and some have called for native harnessing of that movement to restore sovereignty over aboriginal lands. Traditional Native land and resource management lends itself to trust concepts. As Bookman notes, the US has at least twenty-five Native conservation trusts, encompassing both cultural access and conservation easements. Native management ethics include "temperance in the use of resources" as a conscious strategy not to exhaust natural resources.[92] Pacific Northwest Tribes' traditions of fishing salmon exemplify this approach: Singing and ceremonies welcome the arrival of salmon in the spring, and fishing must wait until there is ritual expression of reverence and gratitude for the harvest.[93]

Traditional tribal knowledge of ecosystems, passed down through the centuries, is also crucial in reviving damaged ecosystems. An example of this is the use of Native ecological knowledge in reviving the salmon population in the Columbia River Basin by using a "gravel to gravel" holistic approach rather than the traditional approach, which involved compartmentalising the ecosystem into separate components like water temperature, toxins, harvest, and so on.[94]

There are also Native traditions of restorative manipulation of nature, such as controlled burns and thinning of dense stands of trees that grew in the aftermath of industrial logging.[95] Finally, tribal law, interwoven with spiritual commitments and practices, calls for the preservation of the natural world for future generations of beneficiaries.

One legal entry point for tribes in the conservation trust landscape is the granting of easements. As early as 1905, the Supreme Court held in *United States v Winans* that treaty language reserved easements on land acquired by the government.[96] The Court has also read treaties to give Tribes water rights in after-acquired land, rights that give these Tribes power in negotiating over the use of these lands.[97] A number of groundbreaking projects illustrate ways native tribes and nations can play a conservation role through trust-like devices.

There are four basic models for this approach. First, in the Tribal Holder model, a tribe can hold full title to conservation land or a conservation easement. These usually involve some kind of external legal mechanism—an easement or a covenant—that would mandate the land's conservation. An example of the latter is the Yainix Ranch, a 788 acre parcel in the Upper Klamath Basin of Southern Oregon, where land that had been severely degraded by overgrazing was bought by a couple who then gave the Klamath Tribe a conservation easement over the land.[98] The Tribe, through the easement, became responsible for restoring the

88 See Sam Bookman, Chapter 46 of this handbook.
89 Wood and O'Brien (n 87) 484.
90 Bookman (n 88).
91 Nichole Graham, Chapter 16 of this handbook.
92 Wood and Welcker (n 11) 380.
93 ibid.
94 ibid 383.
95 ibid 384.
96 *Unites States v Winans*, 198 US 371 (1905).
97 *Winters v Unites States*, 207 US (1954).
98 Wood and Welcker (n 11) 380.

land, while the couple who own the land manage it in compliance with an ecological restoration plan monitored by the easement holder. In the case of the Quinault Indian Reservation, which holds land in fee subject to a conservation easement, the Tribe practices sustainable timber harvesting, fish habitat restoration, and wildlife management.[99] Tribes also form their own land trusts to hold conservation title. An example of this is the Intertribal Council of the Sinkyone region of California.[100] Finally, there is a model where non-native groups acquire land to employ programmes that protect tribal environmental interests.[101]

As in the case of the various non-native forms of conservation trust, the trust device has unique legal features that make it possible for tribes to greatly increase their role in conservation beyond their fee and trust lands. Because of the trust's split title of ownership, it allows for some degree of undoing the harms of conquest: It allows tribes and nations to control and manage lands taken by conquest in the first century of Western expansion. The trust allows for the expansion of native land management beyond today's tribal lands. To an extent, the trust also allows for some rectification of the fragmentation caused by the Bureau of Indian Affairs' management of trust lands.

Many Native American Tribes and Nations have a traditional trust-like relationship with the environment, and this heritage has led them to play a role in the conservation trust movement. Many Native people have a governing mandate that calls on them to act as stewards of the land.[102] As one author has noted, "For Indian Tribes, who generally interpreted their relationship with the land as holistic, cyclical and permanent, sustainability was the natural result, if not the conscious goal, of deeply rooted environmental ethics and traditional land based economies."[103] Tribes are beginning to participate in the conservation trust movement. One author calls for tribes to "reassert environmental sovereignty over aboriginal lands and resources through trust tools", either as landholders or easement holders.[104] As this section has shown, several examples of this already exist.

The literature also contains many suggested ways to use the trust form to fight climate change.

2.4 Waste

Finally, a doctrine related to trusts, the doctrine of waste, has been put forward as a legal mechanism for preserving the environment.[105] According to the doctrine of waste, a life tenant may not deplete or destroy—"waste"—property destined to vest in a remainder beneficiary.[106] By this logic, the Earth is in trust to us, its life tenants, and we are bound by the life tenancy doctrine of waste.[107] This argument has never formed the basis for a climate change based cause of action, and it is not clear how helpful it would be. For one thing, there's no remainder beneficiary in whom the property would vest—the trust arguments about climate change are based on the idea that every generation holds the Earth in trust for the next generation; there is no

[99] ibid 380.
[100] ibid.
[101] ibid.
[102] ibid 374.
[103] Rebecca Tsosie, 'Tribal Environmental Policy in an Era of Self-Determination: The Role of Ethics, Economics, and Traditional Ecological Knowledge' (1996) 21 Vermont Law Review 225, 286–87.
[104] Wood and Welcker (n 11) 398.
[105] Moffa (n 12) 459, 460.
[106] Jesse Dukeminier and Robert Sitkoff, *Property* (10th edn, Wolters Kluwer 2022) 291–93.
[107] ibid. See also Moffa (n 12) 470–81.

ultimate owner. Moreover, a life tenant may exploit the resources of the property and use it for her benefit, as long as its value is not depleted. Again, this seems like a clumsy fit for the contours of climate change litigation.

2.5 Environmental Trusts in the Civil Law World

Outside of the common law world, there are legal concepts similar to the public trust that have provided the basis for climate change litigation. For example, Article 225 of the Brazilian Constitution states "all have the right to an ecologically balanced environment, which is an asset of common use and essential to a healthy quality of life, and both the Government and the community shall have the duty to defend and preserve it for present and future generations".[108]

In 2022, four Brazilian political parties filed a Direct Action of Unconstitutionality for Omission against the Federal Union, asserting that the national government had failed to maintain its obligation to the Climate Fund under the Paris Agreement.[109] The parties claimed the government's inaction towards climate change violated its Article 225 duty to preserve ecology and manage protected territories, flora, and fauna.[110] The Supreme Federal Court ruled in favour of the plaintiffs, finding a violation of Article 225 in the government's failure to maintain international climate change obligations.[111] The Court's decision links a constitutional duty to preserve entrusted resources to international action on climate change:

> [T]he issue pertaining to climate change is a constitutional matter. Along these lines, Article 225 . . . of the Constitution expressly establishes the right to an ecologically balanced environment, imposing on the Public Power the duty to defend, preserve and restore it for present and future generations. Therefore, environmental protection is not part of the Chief Executive's political judgment of convenience and opportunity. It is an obligation which the Chief Executive is bound to fulfil.[112]

Uganda has also expanded its public trust doctrine over the past few years to the constitutional level. The doctrine was first articulated in a Supreme Court opinion imposing a duty on the government as trustee to obtain consent from local communities when altering existing environmental protections.[113] At the time, a public trust was codified and enforceable against the state through its constitution.[114] Following a series of statutory and constitutional revisions, the Ugandan public trust was expanded to encompass a variety of natural resources.[115] Article 237 of its constitution today states "the Government or a local government as determined by Parliament by law, shall hold in trust for the people and protect, natural lakes, rivers,

[108] Constituição Federal [Constitution] art. 225 1988 (Brazil). See Danielle de Andrade Moreira, Chapter 41 of this handbook.

[109] 'PSB et al. v. Brazil (on Climate Fund)' *Sabin Center for Climate Change Law* <http://climatecasechart.com/non-us-case/psb-et-al-v-federal-union/> accessed 22 December 2022 (providing a summary of the Brazilian case and an unofficial English translation of the court's decision).

[110] ibid.

[111] ibid.

[112] ibid.

[113] See generally Erin Ryan, Holly Curry, and Hayes Rule, 'Environmental Rights for the 21st Century: A Comprehensive Analysis of the Public Trust Doctrine and Rights of Nature Movement' (2021) 42 Cardozo Law Review 2490 (providing an overview of recent public trust developments in a variety of regions, including Africa and Latin America).

[114] ibid.

[115] ibid.

wetlands, forest reserves, game reserves, national parks and any land to be reserved for ecological and touristic purposes for the common good of all citizens".[116]

3. Trusts Inimical to Climate Preservation (I)

The central reason private trusts can and do work against climate amelioration is the operation of the fiduciary duty rule. The Uniform Prudent Investor Act states this rule as: "A trustee shall invest and manage the trust assets solely in the interest of the beneficiaries."[117] Thus, the rule prevents the trustee from pursuing any goals in trust management other than the interests of the beneficiaries, as defined by the settlor. Since most private trusts are set up to support the beneficiaries financially, those interests usually consist solely of maximising return on investments. Thus, the rule seems to bar any kind of socially—or environmentally—conscious investing unless such investing is stated as part of the purpose of the trust. Lest there be any doubt, the Comment to Section 5 makes it clear:

> No form of so-called "social investing" is consistent with the duty of loyalty if the investment activity entails sacrificing the interests of trust beneficiaries—for example, by accepting below-market returns—in favor of the interests of the persons supposedly benefitted by pursuing the particular social cause.[118]

This comment is directed at ESG investing, that is, environmental, social, and governance investing, a strategy that bases investment decisions on how they manage risks and opportunities related to their environmental and social impact, and governance structures of their investments.[119] Professionals who work with private trusts have inherited a strict focus on financial growth as the only measure of the best interest of the beneficiaries. Susan Gary and others have argued, however, that ESG investing need not impair financial outcomes; several studies Gary cites support this assertion.[120]

Despite the rules governing trustee investing, the current generation of trust beneficiaries may be more interested in climate-conscious and ESG investing than their parents and grandparents, the settlors of their trusts. This generational split raises the question of whether intergenerational equity supports these beneficiaries being able to change the terms of their trusts to accommodate climate concerns. This, in turn, raises the question of whether the Claflin Doctrine should be revisited. The Claflin Doctrine is an American development that broke with English precedent regarding modifying and terminating trusts. Unlike the English *Saunders v Vautier*[121] rule, which allows for beneficiaries to change the terms of a trust after the death of the settlor, the *Claflin v Claflin* case states that the beneficiaries of a trust may change the terms of the trust after the settlor's death only if the proposed changes do not violate the settlor's material purpose in creating the trust.[122] This doctrine has the effect of prioritising the settlor's intent over the wishes of the beneficiaries, even if the settlor has long been dead.

[116] Constitution art 237 2010 (Uganda) (emphasis added).

[117] Uniform Prudent Investor Act, Section 5.

[118] Uniform Prudent Investor Act, Comment to Section 5.

[119] See, e.g., John H Langbein and Richard Posner, 'Social Investing and the Law of Trusts' (1980) 79 Michigan Law Review 72, 96–97 (collecting authority). For pension trust assets, see generally Ian D Lanoff, 'The Social Investment of Private Pension Plan Assets: May it Be Done Lawfully under ERISA?' 31 Labor Law Journal 387 (1980).

[120] Susan N Gary, 'Best Interests in the Long Term: Fiduciary Duties and ESG Integration' (2019) 90 University of Colorado Law Review 731, 750.

[121] *Saunders v Vautier* [1841] EWHC Ch J82, (1841) 4 Beav 115 (1841) 49 ER 282.

[122] *Claflin v Claflin* [1889] 20 NE 454.

What constitutes the material purpose of the trust has been broadly construed. It can include protecting assets from the beneficiary's creditors, distributing assets to beneficiaries at certain ages or achievements, providing for the beneficiaries' education, and so on. In the *Claflin* case itself, the trust was to terminate and distribute the assets to the beneficiary when he turned thirty. Before reaching thirty, the sole beneficiary sued to terminate the trust early, pointing out that there were no other beneficiaries to be harmed. The court refused, however, because the settlor had intended the property to be held in trust until the beneficiary turned thirty, and his intent should be carried out unless it contravened some positive rule of law or public policy.[123] This is still the law in most jurisdictions in the US today, although there is limited leeway in the doctrine of equitable deviation. Later cases, in fact, have expanded the doctrine so that even drastic changes in circumstances cannot justify a trust's termination.

The English rule for modifying trust terms is different. The 1841 case of *Saunders v Vautier* ruled that beneficiaries who have full legal capacity and who collectively have a vested and indefeasible interest in the trust may override provisions in the trust that postpone the transfer of the assets to them. Unlike the *Claflin* court's adherence to the letter of the settlor's intent, the *Saunders* court leaned more towards the meaning of beneficial property ownership—that is, someone who has a right to property may do with it as he or she pleases. If the trust gives an absolute right to property, limited only by a time constraint, the beneficial owner has a right to that property. This rule, of course, does not apply to discretionary trusts, since the beneficiary's right to the property is not absolute, but limited by the trustee's discretion.

I make this foray into trust deviation as background to the suggestion that intergenerational equity may offer a path for re-examination of *Claflin*. Trusts settled by a generation less or not at all concerned with climate change may have funded trusts with assets now understood by a new generation of beneficiaries as harmful to the planet. These beneficiaries might argue that they should be able to seek changes in investment directions in the trust instrument that put money into fossil fuels and redirect those investments to energy sources that are not carbon based, or towards other industries that mitigate climate change.

Another trust doctrine that might also allow for changes of this kind is that of equitable deviation. This doctrine allows a court to order changes in the terms of the trust if unforeseen circumstances are such that leaving the trust terms in place will frustrate the settlor's purpose. This doctrine does not concern itself with the best interests of the beneficiaries; its focus is on achieving the original intent of the settlor in the face of circumstances that the person could not have foreseen at the time he or she had the trust drafted. The original intent, presumably, consisted of financial support for the beneficiaries. Thus, it is a conservative doctrine that does not really allow for changes in the trust terms that respond to a need for changing goals and outcomes. Rather, it looks back at the settlor's goals for the trust and seeks to achieve them in light of changing external factors. Because of its essentially conservative nature, the doctrine of equitable deviation does not seem to be a useful tool for changing trust terms to address climate change.

Another possibility is that the Prudent Investor Rule can be read to require climate-conscious investing. Gary argues that fiduciary duty requires a long-term investment time horizon, increasing the need to take ESG information into consideration. It follows that a prudent fiduciary investor not only may, but should, use ESG information in "developing financial policy and decisions".[124]

Of course, a settlor of a private trust could direct the trustee to make investments in assets and industries that reduce or address the risk of climate change in some way. Or, a settlor could

[123] ibid.
[124] Gary (n 120) 732.

give the trustee leeway to make investment decisions that would improve the beneficiary's future, broadly defined to include investments ameliorative of climate change if they were also financially beneficial to them. But given the long life of today's trusts, the settlor may have acted before climate change became the widespread concern that it is today or may simply not have cared to direct investments in this way. In Chapter 13 of this handbook, Davis and Shaffer argue for "encoding" climate concerns into the management of such trust structures as business corporations, institutional investors, and asset managers.[125] In other words, they argue that such investors should consider climate impacts in making investment decisions and that in fact, the fiduciary duty should be redefined to require such considerations. As my discussion in this section indicates, this is problematic in light of current fiduciary law. In fact, a corporate board member or asset manager who elevated climate concerns over investment returns would be liable for breach of his or her fiduciary duty. Such considerations would violate the very definition of fiduciary duty. Nonetheless, as Davis and Shaffer show, fossil fuel investing is a serious impediment to climate progress. This seems to raise a question at the heart of this entire handbook: Can private law, driven as it is by the purpose of achieving primarily private wishes and goals, solve massive public problems?

4. Trusts Inimical to Climate Preservation (II)

The private trusts of the wealthy are implicated in climate change in many related ways: They enable tax avoidance that robs the public fisc of the funds to fight climate change; they increase wealth inequality, which in turn creates disparate climate impacts among rich and poor; and the wealth they create enables massive and disproportionate carbon consumption.[126]

Trusts' earliest use in England was driven by, among other things, the desire to avoid feudal dues—in today's terms, taxes. They served other purposes, however, like protecting the vulnerable and providing for family members, that do not depend on their tax avoidance features. The tax avoidance features, however, have taken on great force in American financial planning over the past few decades. Because of their depletion of the public fisc, they threaten publicly funded efforts to mitigate the effects of climate change in the US.

They also increase wealth inequality by skewing the tax burden towards low- and middle-income taxpayers and by using investment vehicles that contribute little to job creation and wealth circulation. This wealth inequality, in turn, increases the impact of the harmful effects of climate change on vulnerable and marginalised groups. Finally, evidence suggests that wealth inequality itself can help increase greenhouse gas emissions, driven by the carbon intensity of many items of luxury consumption such as air travel and vacation home ownership.[127]

With respect to the estate tax, in the US, the combination of the revision or overturning of the Rule Against Perpetuities and the Generation Skipping Tax (GST) exclusion amount has deprived the government of significant tax revenue. The GST was originally passed to prevent donors from putting money into trust to benefit generations like grandchildren and those further removed. This eliminated a taxable event by avoiding the transfer to the next generation, who likely did not need the money. In response to this manoeuvre, Congress passed the GST, which taxes wealth transfers to "skipped" generations. The exclusion amount for the GST tax, however, has risen to, as of 2025, US$14 million per person (so almost US$30 million per

[125] See Davis and Shaffer, Chapter 13 of this handbook.

[126] Douglas Kysar, 'Ways Not to Think About Climate Change' (*Social Science Research Network* 1 May 2024) 35–36 <https://papers.ssrn.com/sol3/papers.cfm?abstract_id=4921823> accessed 23 July 2025.

[127] Clinton G Wallace and Shelley Welton, 'Taxing Luxury Emissions' (2024) 109 Cornell Law Review 1153.

couple). This allows a couple, for example, to transfer almost US$30 million to a trust and have it grow tax-free for generations.

Avoiding climate change and addressing its impacts cost money—government money. It is difficult to put a final conclusive number on current and future costs of climate change and climate change amelioration but estimates exist for costs within individual sectors. For example, costs of coastal damage from climate-change related storms in the US are estimated to reach US$5 trillion by 2100 in the absence of emissions reductions.[128] As early as 2014, a survey of adaptation needs across several sectors concluded that for the US "adaptation cost could be as high as tens or hundreds of billions of dollars per year by the middle of this century".[129]

Addressing these losses and meeting these adaptation needs will require money generated by tax revenues. The trusts described above avoid taxes in multiple ways and strip the government's ability to protect all its citizens from the effects of climate change. Government funding fights climate change in ways that benefit everyone: It provides billions in Climate Pollution Reduction Grants to state and local governments, tribes, and territories to develop and implement plans to reduce greenhouse gas emissions; it invests in renewable energy sources through grants and research projects; it builds green infrastructure projects like public walkways, cycleways, and electric car infrastructure; it invests in adapting to climate change by building seawalls and improving water management; and it offers subsidies and tax rebates for green projects, among many other actions.

Yet, tax evasion trusts rob the public fisc of the resources it needs to accomplish these responses that the government is uniquely suited to carry out. On the other side of the coin, the wealthy who benefit from these trusts can, due to their tax-free wealth, engage in highly anti-social forms of adaptation, like building underground compounds, "seasteading" (i.e., building artificial cities at sea), or buying vast tracts of "climate-proof" land in the middle of the country and placing it in trust so title is impossible to trace.

5. Conclusion

It is nearly impossible to think about climate change without invoking, at least implicitly, the notion of a trust relationship with the Earth. Indeed, the idea of preserving the environment for future generations, that is, preserving it, leaving it thriving, and not committing waste, are essential trust concepts. Thus, it is not surprising that many religious, moral, and philosophical arguments for climate preservation and intergenerational equity appear as concepts of trusteeship. It's also clear that some notion of trusteeship, rather than extraction and exhaustion, of resources, must drive efforts to mitigate climate change. The problem is that trusts are instruments of private law. They were devised to achieve individual, private goals. Thus, they are inevitably and by definition also instruments of wealth concentration and tax avoidance, both of which impede efforts to slow and mitigate environmental disaster. Trusts are empty vessels that contain the settlor's wishes. As such, they will always serve both socially beneficial and socially harmful ends. Though their worst excesses can be contained by legislation, they ultimately raise the question of whether the instruments of private law can help solve the public problem of climate change, or whether public law must intervene.

[128] US Environmental Protection Agency, *Climate Change in the United States: Benefits of Global Action* (2015) 7 <https://19january2017snapshot.epa.gov/sites/production/files/2015-06/documents/cirareport.pdf> accessed 23 July 2025.

[129] Fran Sussman and others, 'Climate Change Adaptation Cost in the US: What Do We Know?' (2014) 14 Climate Policy 242.

PART IV

Corporate and Commercial Law

CHAPTER 18

Corporate Law and Governance

ERNEST LIM

1. Introduction

A key issue in the field of directors' duties and climate change is whether directors are required to consider climate-related risks and opportunities as part of their legal duties, particularly when these affect the company's long-term interests, often equated with financial materiality.[1] Significant progress has been made on this front.[2] A related issue is the enforcement of these duties, an area where less progress has been made due to courts' general reluctance to second-guess board decisions.[3] These two issues constitute what I call "the internal dimension of directors' duties".

However, a third important issue concerns what I call "the external dimension of directors' duties". This dimension asks whether directors of a limited liability company can and should consider the adverse impacts of the company's operations on climate change, the economy, nature, or society, even if doing so is not necessarily tied to, or may even adversely affect, the financial interests of the firm-specific shareholders, at least in the short term. This external dimension is the primary subject of analysis in the chapter, which focuses on Anglo-American and Chinese corporate governance.

While there has been extensive discussion on investor stewardship, stakeholderism, and corporate purpose,[4] the issue of the external dimension of directors' duties has received relatively less attention in Anglo-American literature, despite deserving scrutiny given fresh challenges and renewed motivations. Three such motivations are identified and evaluated. The first is the timeliness of the universal ownership argument and the 2024 Delaware Court of

[1] Ravi Bansal, Marcelo Ochoa, and Dana Kiku, 'Climate Change and Growth Risks' (2016) National Bureau of Economic Research Working Paper No 23009 <https://www.nber.org/papers/w23009> accessed 15 March 2025; Edith Ginglinger and Quentin Moreau, 'Climate Risk and Capital Structure' (2023) 69 Management Science 7492; Patrick Bolton and Marcin Kacperczyk, 'Do Investors Care About Carbon Risk?' (2021) 142 Journal of Financial Economics 517.

[2] Commonwealth Climate and Law Initiative (CCLI) and Climate Governance Initiative (CGI), 'Directors' Duties Navigator: Climate Risk and Sustainability Disclosures' (26 September 2024) < https://commonwealthclimatelaw.org/directors-duties-navigator-climate-risk-and-sustainability-disclosures-fourth-edition-2024> accessed 13 June 2025.

[3] *ClientEarth v Shell plc* [2023] EWHC 1137 (Ch); Ernest Lim and Umakanth Varottil, 'Climate Risk: Enforcement of Corporate and Securities Law in Common Law Asia' (2022) 22 Journal of Corporate Law Studies 391.

[4] See, e.g., Lucian Bebchuk and Roberto Tallarita, 'The Illusory Promise of Stakeholder Governance' (2020) 106 Cornell Law Review 91; Zohar Goshen and Assaf Hamdani, 'Will Systematic Stewardship Save the Planet?' (2023) European Corporate Governance Institute: Law Working Paper No 739/2023 < https://www.ecgi.global/sites/default/files/working_papers/documents/willsystematicstewardshipsavetheplanet_o.pdf> accessed 13 June 2025.

Chancery decision in *McRitchie v Zuckerberg*.[5] Although the court held that directors do not owe duties to diversified investors, only to the company and its firm-specific investors, the decision is important for clarifying when directors can still internalise corporate negative externalities even if not tied to firm-specific shareholders' financial interests.

The second motivation stems from recent regulations with extra-territorial effects, such as the 2024 European Union Corporate Sustainability Due Diligence Directive (CSDDD),[6] which requires companies to address adverse impacts on human rights and the environment, and the 2023 EU Corporate Sustainability Reporting Directive (CSRD),[7] requiring reporting on a double materiality basis.[8] These regulations make it inevitable that responsible boards of in-scope EU and non-EU companies must consider how internalising and reporting on adverse impacts is permitted or required by their fiduciary duties.

Finally, there is overwhelming evidence that state-owned enterprises (SOEs)[9] are among the world's largest greenhouse gas (GHG) emitters. SOEs typically have multiple purposes, including promoting environmental, economic, and social objectives, in addition to generating profit.[10] This raises a question of legal significance and practical interest: Whether directors of SOEs can and should address climate-related or systemic considerations that are not necessarily tied to firm-specific shareholders' financial interests.

I critically analyse two legal arguments in favour of the external dimension of directors' duties and advance a third one.

The first argument is the incorporation of nature-related provisions into the corporate constitution by limited liability companies in the UK.[11] While these provisions permit boards to address systemic considerations, they have limitations in theory and practice as they operate within an enlightened shareholder primacy model.

The second argument, popularised by Hart and Zingales, is that directors can and should cater to shareholders' non-financial preferences.[12] I consider four mechanisms for doing so, but I conclude that this argument is unpersuasive, as most studies show that shareholders pressure boards for financial reasons.[13]

The third and novel argument that I advance and endorse is that in the context of SOEs, directors' fiduciary duties can align with those of the controlling shareholder and the asset owner.[14] This is because in each of these duties the fiduciary is permitted, and potentially required, to consider the impacts of the SOE's operations on climate change, the economy, or

[5] 315 A.3d 518 (Del Ch 2024).

[6] Directive (EU) 2024/1760 of the European Parliament and of the Council of 13 June 2024 on corporate sustainability due diligence and amending Directive (EU) 2019/1937 and Regulation (EU) 2023/2859 [2024] OJ L2024/1760.

[7] Directive (EU) 2022/2464 of the European Parliament and of the Council of 14 December 2022 amending Regulation (EU) No 537/2014, Directive 2004/109/EC, Directive 2006/43/EC and Directive 2013/34/EU, as regards corporate sustainability reporting [2022] OJ L 322/15.

[8] See Section 3.1.2.2 of this chapter.

[9] The OECD acknowledges that definitions of SOEs vary across countries but adopts a broad approach, defining them as 'any corporate entity recognized by national law as an enterprise in which the state exercises ownership': OECD, *OECD Guidelines on Corporate Governance of State-Owned Enterprises* (2023) 14.

[10] See Section 3.1.3 of this chapter.

[11] See Section 3.2.1 of this chapter.

[12] Oliver Hart and Luigi Zingales, 'Companies Should Maximize Shareholder Welfare not Market Value' (2017) 2 Journal of Law, Finance, and Accounting 247.

[13] See Section 3.2.2 of this chapter.

[14] See Section 3.2.3 of this chapter.

society, even if doing so is not necessarily tied to the financial returns of the firm-specific shareholders. This argument is illustrated by SOEs in China. The analysis suggests directors of coal-fired power plant Chinese SOEs can prioritise broader economic considerations above firm-specific shareholder returns. This analysis of SOEs yields at least three lessons for the US and global corporate governance discourse on climate change.

I discuss the internal dimension in Section 2, analyse the three motivations for addressing the external dimension in Section 3.1, evaluate the three arguments in support in Section 3.2, and conclude with potential lessons in Section 4.

2. The Internal Dimension: Directors' Duties to Consider Climate-Related Risks and Opportunities and the Enforcement of These Duties

2.1 The Internal Dimension of Directors' Duties

Under the laws of Delaware, the UK, and many other common and civil law jurisdictions, it is well-established that directors' duties to the company include acting in good faith in the company's best interests, exercising reasonable care, skill, and diligence, avoiding unauthorised conflicts of interest and unauthorised receipt of profits, and considering all relevant factors while excluding irrelevant ones in decision-making.[15]

Climate-related risks and opportunities are considered relevant factors because they materially affect the company's financial interests, especially in certain sectors.[16] Therefore, it is widely accepted that the board, acting in the company's best interests and exercising reasonable care, skill, and diligence, must address material climate risks and opportunities in its decision-making process, as these impact the company's long-term interests.[17] This may necessitate implementing appropriate systems and processes, such as transition plans, internal carbon pricing mechanisms, and scenario analysis to assess and quantify climate risk.[18] Mainstreaming climate change into board decisions is largely uncontroversial, especially with the widespread adoption of frameworks like the International Sustainability Standards Board disclosure framework by regulators and stock exchanges.[19] Legal opinions and analyses on directors' duties regarding climate risks across numerous jurisdictions attest to the ongoing relevance of the internal dimension.[20]

[15] See, e.g., John Armour and others, 'The Basic Governance Structure: The Interests of Shareholders as a Class' in Reiner Kraakman and others (eds), *The Anatomy of Corporate Law: A Comparative and Functional Approach* (3rd edn, OUP 2017) 69–70.

[16] See the literature cited in (n 1).

[17] See CCLI and CGI, Directors' Duties Navigator (n 2).

[18] Task Force on Climate-related Financial Disclosures, 'Recommendations of the Task Force on Climate-related Financial Disclosures' (June 2017) <https://assets.bbhub.io/company/sites/60/2021/10/FINAL-2017-TCFD-Report.pdf> accessed 15 March 2025.

[19] 'Increasing Global Adoption of ISSB Standards' (*Debevoise and Plimpton*, 19 February 2025) < https://www.debevoise.com/insights/publications/2025/02/increasing-global-adoption-of-issb-standards> accessed 15 March 2025.

[20] See CCLI and CGI, Directors' Duties Navigator (n 2).

2.2 Enforcement

A more challenging issue than whether directors must consider climate-related factors is the enforceability of these duties by courts. The English High Court decision in *ClientEarth v Shell Plc*[21] provides a key example. ClientEarth, a minority shareholder and charity, brought a derivative action against Shell's directors, alleging breach of duties (to exercise reasonable care and to promote the company's success under UK law) as they failed to implement adequate measures for net-zero emissions goals, specifically regarding Scope 3 emissions.

Mr Justice Trower denied permission, rejecting the claim primarily on two grounds. First, because there was no universally accepted methodology for achieving the company's set reductions, directors could not be said to have made a decision that no reasonable director would make. Second, directors are required to balance addressing climate risks with other commercial considerations.

However, the first ground rests on a non sequitur: the absence of a universal methodology does not mean there can be no breach of duty, and it is surprising to insist on unanimity on a credible transition plan before assessing a breach. The second ground is also a non sequitur: Recognising that directors must balance competing considerations does not justify automatic judicial deference.

The duty to exercise reasonable care, skill, and diligence requires directors to consider relevant information. The scope should include directors familiarising themselves with material scientific and economic evidence on climate change, as a reasonable director in the same sector would. Courts should carefully examine whether directors have discharged this duty instead of giving absolute deference. For instance, boards could potentially use outdated or questionable climate scenario analyses.[22] For fossil fuel companies like Shell, valuation depends on future profitability based on energy scenarios and management assumptions.[23] If a company uses outdated scenarios in its baseline analysis,[24] it raises questions about whether directors considered irrelevant factors or failed to consider relevant ones, potentially breaching their duties to exercise reasonable care and to act in the company's best interests.

3. The External Dimension: Directors' Consideration of Corporate Impact on Climate Change, the Economy, or Society

While directors addressing climate-related or systemic considerations as part of their legal duties and the enforcement thereof falls under the internal dimension, the external dimension concerns the contested issue of whether directors can and should address the detrimental effects of the company's operations on the environment, economy, or society, known as negative

[21] [2023] EWHC 1897 (Ch).

[22] Madison Condon, 'Corporate Scenarios: Drawing Lessons from History' (2025) 48 Seattle University Law Review 277, 279, 294.

[23] TA Hansen, 'Stranded Assets and Reduced Profits: Analysing the Economic Underpinnings of the Fossil Fuel Industry's Resistance to Climate Stabilization' (2022) 158 Renewable and Sustainable Energy Reviews 112, 144; Madison Condon, 'Market Myopia's Climate Bubble' (2022) Utah Law Review 63.

[24] Outdated scenarios include Shared Economic Pathway and IPCC's RCP8.5: see Zeke Hausfather and Glen P Peters, 'Emissions—the "Business as Usual" Story is Misleading' (2020) 577 Nature 618; Emily Ho and others, 'Not all Carbon Dioxide Emissions Scenarios Are Equally Likely: A Subjective Expert Assessment' (2019) 155 Climate Change 545.

externalities. This view posits that directors must consider these considerations, even if they are not necessarily tied to, or even adversely affect, the financial returns of firm-specific shareholders. In essence, directors need to consider both the effects of climate change on the enterprise value (financial materiality—the internal dimension) and the effects of the company's operations on climate change, the economy, or society (impact materiality[25]—the external dimension).

3.1 Importance of Addressing the External Dimension of Directors' Duties

There is compelling evidence that companies are significant contributors to climate change and impose negative externalities. The 2024 Carbon Majors Database reported that fifty-seven companies were linked to 80% of global fossil CO_2 emissions since 2016.[26] Among the largest historical polluters, SOEs constitute a significant portion, and many privately held and SOE companies have increased fossil fuel operations since 2016.[27] This data calls into question the notion that maximising shareholder returns inevitably leads to pro-environmental or pro-social behaviour.[28] In the context of climate change, continuing fossil fuel operations may be more profitable in the short to medium term than decarbonising.[29] The intense lobbying by petrostates and fossil fuel companies against phasing out fossil fuels at COP28 supports this.[30] Furthermore, the idea of a necessary alignment between promoting environmental or social good and profit maximisation ("win-win") lacks widespread empirical support.[31] To the contrary, one study suggests that pollution can maximise shareholder value, particularly at the expense of community well-being.[32]

This does not mean corporate law should abandon promoting environmentally or socially responsible behaviour or that shareholder value maximisation is the only valid path for directors.[33] Rather, it implies that trade-offs between environmental/social good and profit maximisation exist, and corporate law should consider whether boards are legally permitted

[25] Chiara Mio, Marisa Agostini, and Francesco Scarpa, *Sustainability Reporting: Conception, International Approaches and Double Materiality in Action* (Palgrave Macmillan 2024).

[26] Carbon Majors <https://carbonmajors.org/index.html> accessed 15 March 2025.

[27] ibid.

[28] See, e.g., Stephen M Bainbridge, *The Profit Motive: Defending Shareholder Value Maximization* (CUP 2023); Frank Easterbrook and Daniel R Fischel, The Economic Structure of Corporate Law (Harvard University Press 1991) 37–39.

[29] Hansen (n 23).

[30] COP28 refers to the 28th session of the Conference of the Parties to the United Nations Framework Convention on Climate Change that was held in Dubai, United Arab Emirates, from 30 November to 12 December 2023. Damian Carrington, 'OPEC Rails Against Fossil Fuel Phase-Out at COP28 In Leaked Letters' *The Guardian* (London, 8 December 2023); Damian Carrington, 'COP28 Failed to Halt Fossil Fuels' Deadly Expansion Plans—So What Now?' *The Guardian* (London, 14 December 2023).

[31] See, e.g., Luca Berchicci and Andrew A King, 'Material Sustainability and Stock Return: Faith is Not Enough' (2022) 7 Journal of Financial Reporting 41; Andrew A King and Kenneth P Pucker, 'The Dangerous Allure of Win-Win Strategies' (2021) 19 Stanford Social Innovation Review 34; Martin Oehmke and Marcus M Opp, 'A Theory of Socially Responsible Investment' (2024) Review of Economic Studies 1.

[32] Roy Shapira and Luigi Zingales, 'Is Pollution Value-Maximizing? The DuPont Case' European Corporate Governance Institute Law Working Paper No 723/2023723/2023 <https://www.ecgi.global/sites/default/files/working_papers/documents/ispollutionvaluemaximizing.pdf> accessed 20 March 2025.

[33] See, e.g., Bainbridge (n 28) 166–68.

or required to address climate or systemic risks even if they conflict with firm-specific shareholder returns. This question has gained significance for at least three reasons: the rise of the universal ownership movement and *McRitchie v Zuckerberg*,[34] recent EU regulations requiring disclosure of impact materiality and addressing adverse impacts, and the fact that SOEs are major GHG emitters with multiple objectives beyond profit-making.

3.1.1 Universal Ownership and *McRitchie v Zuckerberg*

Large institutional investors, such as pension funds, mutual funds, and insurance companies (including asset managers and asset owners), are known as universal owners because they hold diversified portfolios across the economy.[35] Their portfolio performance is dependent on systemic considerations like the economy, market, and geopolitics. Universal owners may be willing to sacrifice financial returns from one company in their portfolio because the negative externalities it produces (like GHG emissions) will affect other companies in their portfolio, thereby impacting overall portfolio returns. This in turn affects the long-term risk-adjusted returns for their beneficiaries, to whom asset owners owe fiduciary duties. The universal ownership argument is supported by both intellectual discourse[36] and adoption by asset owners[37] and international organisations.[38]

In *McRitchie v Zuckerberg*,[39] a shareholder sued Meta's directors, officers, and the controlling shareholder for allegedly breaching fiduciary duties by maximising financial interests without considering the adverse impact of the company's products (such as misinformation and mental health harms) on the broader economy and society, which harmed diversified investors' interests. The plaintiff argued directors owed duties to diversified investors and were required to reduce firm-specific negative externalities (at Meta) to improve returns for diversified investors' portfolios.

Vice Chancellor Travis Laster of the Delaware Court of Chancery rejected this claim, holding that under Delaware law, directors owe duties only to the company and its shareholders, not to diversified investors. He stated directors are not legally required to consider the effects of the company's operations on the economy, climate change, or society (stakeholders) that are not tied to firm-specific shareholders' financial interests, emphasising that Delaware law follows a firm-specific model, not a diversified-investor model.

However, it is crucial to distinguish between breach of duties by directors if (a) they fail to consider diversified investors' interests (the claimant's argument) or (b) they do consider these interests. The latter breach is unlikely to occur in practice due to the business judgment rule in some jurisdictions;[40] courts are unlikely to hold directors liable for considering diversified investor or other stakeholder interests if doing so is not inconsistent with the company's

34 *McRitchie* (n 5).

35 See, e.g., Madison Condon, 'Externalities and the Common Owner' (2020) 95 Washington Law Review 1.

36 See, e.g., James Hawley and Andrew Williams, 'The Emergence of Universal Owners: Some Implications of Institutional Equity Ownership' (2000) 43 Challenge 43.

37 See, e.g., Norges Bank Investment Management, '2025 Climate Action Plan' (*Norges Bank Investment Management*, 2025) <https://www.nbim.no/en/responsible-investment/2025-climate-action-plan/>/> accessed 13 June 2025.

38 See, e.g., Principles for Responsible Investment, 'Active Ownership 2.0' (2019) <https://www.unpri.org/investment-tools/stewardship/active-ownership-20> accessed 13 June 2025.

39 *McRitchie* (n 5).

40 Armour et al (n 15) [3.4.1].

interests, unless it causes significant financial detriment to firm-specific shareholders. This is likely to be the position under Delaware and UK law.

3.1.1.1 *When Must Directors Internalise Negative Externalities?*

An important qualification from *McRitchie* is that Vice Chancellor Laster held that directors *must* consider risks to the broader economy if their decisions "consistently or profoundly harm the broader economy because such harm would prevent creating durable long-term value for firm-specific stockholders".[41] This is significant because companies, particularly in fossil fuel sectors, are major contributors to GHG emissions, which drive global temperature increases and cause economic harm that ultimately affects shareholders' interests. This raises the question of whether companies can continue externalising costs while delivering high shareholder returns.

Empirical studies highlight the severe potential adverse financial impact of climate change on shareholders' returns and global asset valuation. Estimates include a 40% potential loss of net present value of future losses if current mitigation actions are maintained.[42] One study forecasts a 50% destruction of GDP between 2070 and 2090.[43] Another study reports that each 1°C rise in global temperature persistently reduces global GDP by 12%, implying substantial welfare loss and a high social cost of carbon.[44] These effects are compared to "experiencing the 1929 Great Depression, forever".[45] In light of this evidence, directors may not be complying with their fiduciary duties to promote the company's long-term interests if they do not address corporate adverse impacts on climate change, given that these will inevitably affect the company's interests.

However, it can be argued that demonstrating climate change's adverse impact on the economy is distinct from proving it will lead to adverse impacts on a company's assets (including shares). This distinction is partly due to the reliance on contestable and varied climate scenario analyses used by companies for valuation. Asset prices also depend on assumptions about how transition risks are priced, future damages, effectiveness of renewables, carbon capture deployment, policy speed, shifts in consumer and investor sentiment, and market resilience.

Despite these complexities in quantifying climate change's financial risks on a company, they do not negate the argument that corporate law should regulate negative externalities generated by companies. Evidence shows these externalities will harm the company's interests; for example, companies causing adverse impacts on nature (including climate change) have faced lawsuits or permit rejections, leading to reduced market valuations and credit ratings.[46]

41 *McRitchie* (n 5) 74.

42 Riccardo Rebonato, Dherminder Kainth, and Lionel Melin, 'How Does Climate Risk Affect Global Equity Valuations?' (*EDHEC Risk Climate Impact Institute*, 2024) <https://climateinstitute.edhec.edu/publications/how-does-climate-risk-affect-global-equity-valuations-novel-approach> accessed 24 March 2025.

43 Sandy Trust and others, 'The Emperor's New Climate Scenarios: Limitations and Assumptions of Commonly Used Climate-change Scenarios in Financial Services' (*Institute and Faculty of Actuaries*, 2023) 26 <https://actuaries.org.uk/media/qeydewmk/the-emperor-s-new-climate-scenarios.pdf> accessed 24 March 2025.

44 Adrien Bilal and Diego R Känzig, 'The Macroeconomic Impact of Climate Change' (2024) National Bureau of Economic Research Working Paper No 32450 <https://www.nber.org/system/files/working_papers/w32450/w32450.pdf> accessed 24 March 2025.

45 ibid.

46 Sir Partha Dasgupta, HM Treasury, Government of UK, 'Final Report: The Economics of Biodiversity: The Dasgupta Review' (2021) <https://www.gov.uk/government/publications/final-report-the-economics-of-biodiversity-the-dasgupta-review> accessed 24 March 2025.

3.1.1.2 *When Can Directors Address Negative Externalities?*

Another key issue from *McRitchie* is whether directors *can* address the effects of the company's operations on climate change, the economy, or society, or consider diversified investors' interests, even if not tied to firm-specific shareholders' financial interests. Vice Chancellor Laster held that under Delaware law, directors are legally permitted to do so if shareholders agree to insert or amend specific provisions in the corporate charter. These provisions could pertain to the company's purpose, for whom it is managed, and the board's powers.[47] This position is likely applicable under UK law as well.[48]

3.1.2 Regulatory Requirements: EU CSDDD

The EU Corporate Sustainability Due Diligence Directive (CSDDD),[49] in force since July 2024, requires EU Member States to mandate EU and non-EU companies that are subject to the CSDDD to identify, prevent, and end adverse human rights and environmental impacts in their operations, subsidiaries, and chain of activities. It also permits national supervisory authorities to impose financial penalties limited to three percent of the entity's net worldwide turnover.

While the CSDDD does not mandate specific outcomes, required measures include implementing prevention action plans, seeking contractual assurances from business partners with verification, changing operational processes or infrastructures, and modifying business plans/strategies/operations.[50] Sanctions by member state authorities can include orders to cease conduct or perform actions.

However, recent proposals by the European Commission, whose provisional agreement was approved by the European Parliament in December 2025, aim to simplify the CSDDD. Changes include narrowing the scope of companies subject to the legislation and limiting due diligence to companies' operations, their subsidiaries, and direct business partners in the chain of activities.[51] Another change removed the requirement for companies to put into effect a climate transition plan.[52] Scholars argue this watering down may lead to more litigation.[53] The proposal also eliminated private civil suits.[54]

3.1.2.1 *EU CSRD*

Complementing the CSDDD, the EU Corporate Sustainability Reporting Directive (CSRD), in force since January 2023, requires EU and non EU companies to report on how sustainability issues (including climate change) affect their financial performance (financial materiality) *and* on the impacts of company activities on sustainability matters (impact materiality).

47 *McRitchie* (n 5) 93–95.

48 UK Companies Act, s 172(2); *BTI 2014 LLC v Sequana SA* [2022] UKSC 25.

49 CSDDD (n 6).

50 ibid Recital 38.

51 Proposal for a Directive of the European Parliament and of the Council amending Directives 2006/43/EC, 2013/34/EU, (EU) 2022/2464, and (EU) 2024/1760 as regards certain corporate sustainability reporting and due diligence requirements, COM(2025) 81 final 2025/0045 (COD) 18.

52 ibid 19.

53 Concerns Regarding Potential Re-Opening of Article 22 CSDDD (Letter to President Ursula von der Leyen and Commissioner Valdis Dombrovskis) <https://media.business-humanrights.org/media/documents/Concerns_regarding_potential_re-opening_of_Article_22_CSDDD_-_17-02-25_1.pdf> accessed 15 March 2025.

54 CSDDD Omnibus Proposal (n 51) 20.

This "double materiality" disclosure is a key aspect.[55] In-scope companies must describe principal actual or potential adverse impacts in their operations and value chain, actions taken to prevent, mitigate, remediate, end impacts, and the results. Thus, while CSDDD imposes obligations to address negative externalities, CSRD imposes obligations to report on measures taken. At least 10,000 non-EU companies may be subject to CSRD.[56] Recent Commission proposals include extending reporting timelines and reducing entities subject to CSRD,[57] but importantly, the double materiality requirement has been reaffirmed.[58]

3.1.2.2 *Commentary on CSDDD, CSRD, and Directors' Duties*

Undertaking a detailed evaluation of CSDDD or CSRD is beyond the scope of this chapter,[59] but it is clear that neither regulation specifically imposes duties on directors to address climate or systemic risks or consider non-shareholder interests; the duties are imposed on the companies. It could even be argued that directors' duties do not require them to consider corporate adverse impacts on climate or the economy. This is because a provision in the original CSDDD version—requiring directors, as part of acting in the company's best interests, to consider consequences for sustainability matters—was removed from the final version.[60] This removal was due to concerns about inappropriate interference with national laws on directors' duties and potential director liability.[61] The rationales for including the provision initially were to harmonise laws and promote certainty, as divergent regulations could distort competition.[62]

But the spectre of directors' liability is exaggerated and often used to deter regulatory intervention. Requiring directors to address negative externalities as part of their duties is distinct from courts imposing liability for breaching these duties. Courts are generally reluctant to second-guess directors unless there is bad faith, illegality, fraud, or conflicts of interest, with many jurisdictions having a business judgment rule or equivalent.[63]

Although the provision was removed, directors of in-scope companies must still ensure their company complies with CSDDD and CSRD. These regulations can influence how a

55 For a critical analysis of impact materiality, see Felix E Mezzanotte, 'Corporate Sustainability Reporting: Double Materiality, Impacts, and Legal Risk' (2023) 23 Journal of Corporate Law Studies 633, 645–55.

56 Dieter Holger, 'At Least 10,000 Foreign Companies to Be Hit by European Rules' (*Wall Street Journal*, 5 April 2023) <https://www.wsj.com/articles/at-least-10-000-foreign-companies-to-be-hit-by-eu-sustainability-rules-307a1406> accessed 26 March 2025. But this figure may be less in light of the provisional agreement amending the CSRD which restricts the scope of companies subject to it.

57 Proposal for a Directive of the European Parliament and of the Council amending Directives (EU) 2022/2464 and (EU) 2024/1760 as regards the dates from which Member States are to apply certain corporate sustainability reporting and due diligence requirements, COM (2025) 80 final 2025/0044 (COD).

58 CSDDD Omnibus Proposal (n 51) 5.

59 See Barbara Pozzo, Chapter 29 and Harro van Asselt and Jessica Crow, Chapter 33 of this handbook.

60 European Commission, 'Proposal for a Directive of the European Parliament and the Council on Corporate Sustainability Due Diligence and Amending Directive (EU) 2019/1937' COM (2022) 71 final, art 25.

61 Council of the European Union, 'Proposal for a Directive of the European Parliament and of the Council on Corporate Sustainability Due Diligence and Amending Directive (EU) 2019/1937: General Approach' (30 November 2022) No 15024/1/22 Rev 1, para 31; Steen Thomsen 'Sustainable Corporate Governance and the Road to Stagnation' (*Oxford Business Law Blog*, 14 April 2022) <https://blogs.law.ox.ac.uk/business-law-blog/blog/2022/04/sustainable-corporate-governance-and-road-stagnation> accessed 13 June 2025.

62 CSDDD (Original) (n 61).

63 Armour et al (n 15).

company's "best interests" and the standard of reasonable care expected of directors are interpreted and enforced. An EU commentator notes that despite the removal, directors within the directive's scope have a "new compass" or standard for decision-making that can "profoundly change their fiduciary duty towards the firm".[64] As Lord Sales of the UK Supreme Court emphasised, directors' legal obligations are shaped by the "general environment of expectation created by initiatives by regulators and in civil society".[65] Thus, a minimum effect of CSDDD and CSRD is that directors of in-scope companies will find it difficult to argue they are not permitted or ought not to consider the impact of operations on climate change, environment, or human rights in their decisions, even if not tied to shareholder returns.

Some commentators make a stronger claim for US companies subject to CSDDD, arguing that their directors could breach *Caremark*[66] oversight duties if CSDDD-related risks are central and they fail to establish oversight systems, disregard red flags, or approve non-compliant plans.[67] Importantly, a *Caremark* breach is independent of whether directorial conduct or corporate impact is tied to shareholder value. In the UK, a prominent scholar argues that directors who fail to give adequate attention to risk and control functions run a greater risk of breaching the duty of care and facing considerable potential for personal liability.[68]

3.1.3 SOEs

Two key features of SOEs are relevant. First, SOEs are notorious and recalcitrant contributors to climate change. Data show that SOEs account for a significant portion of global GHG emissions and own/manage large percentages of fossil fuel assets.[69] Many of the largest historical polluters among SOEs have increased emissions since the Paris Agreement.[70] However, SOEs also play a crucial role in decarbonisation, accounting for over 50% of planned renewable energy investments.[71] Some studies indicate SOEs perform better than non-SOEs in areas like CO_2 emissions and renewable investments, particularly in emerging countries.[72]

Second, SOEs generally do not have profit maximisation or promoting shareholders' financial interests as their sole or primary purpose. They pursue diverse, public-oriented socio-economic objectives including poverty alleviation, employment creation, environmental

[64] Jens-Hinrich Binder, 'Leading Wherever They Want? CSR, ESG and Directors' Duties' in Jens-Hinrich Binder, Klaus Hopt, and Thilo Kuntz (eds), *Corporate Purpose, CSR, and ESG* (OUP 2024).

[65] Lord Sales, 'Directors' Duties and Climate Change: Keeping Pace with Environmental Challenges' (Speech Anglo-Australasian Law Society, Sydney, 27 August 2019) <https://supremecourt.uk/speeches/lord-sales-at-the-anglo-australasian-law-society-sydney> accessed 15 March 2025.

[66] Caremark, 698 A.2d 959, adopted by Stone, 911 A.2d 362, 365.

[67] Luca Enriques, Matteo Gatti, and Roy Shapiro, 'How the EU's Sustainability Due Diligence Directive Could Reshape Corporate America' 78 Stanford Law Review (forthcoming).

[68] Eilis Ferran and Pedro Schilling de Carvalho, 'Reconciling Shareholder Primacy and the Interests of People and Planet' (2025) L.Q.R. (forthcoming).

[69] Carbon Majors, 'Carbon Majors: 2023 Data Update' (*Carbon* Majors, March 2025) <https://carbonmajors.org/briefing/The-Carbon-Majors-Database-2023-Update-31397> accessed 15 March 2025.

[70] Jonathan Watts, 'Just 57 Companies Linked to 80% of Greenhouse Gas Emissions Since 2016' *The Guardian* (London, 4 April 2024) < https://www.theguardian.com/environment/2024/apr/04/just-57-companies-linked-to-80-of-greenhouse-gas-emissions-since-2016> accessed 15 March 2025.

[71] Alexander Pfeiffer and others, '"The '2°C Capital Stock" for Electricity Generation: Committed Cumulative Carbon Emissions from the Electricity Generation Sector and the Transition to a Green Economy' (2016) 179 Applied Energy 1395.

[72] Po-Hsuan Hsu, Hao Liang, and Pedro Matos, 'Leviathan Inc. and Corporate Environmental Engagement' (2023) 69 Management Science 7719.

protection, industrial development, and fiscal stability.[73] They control key energy systems and infrastructure. The OECD regards SOEs as a primary channel for states to act as economic actors.[74] SOEs can thus facilitate government implementation of net-zero targets, with countries incorporating climate objectives into state ownership policies.[75] Examples include Sweden requiring SOEs to align with government net-zero targets and China requiring SOEs to formulate emissions reduction and energy conservation plans.[76]

Given their multiple purposes, some explicitly climate-related, directors of SOEs must consider the adverse impacts of operations on climate change and the environment. Because of these multiple objectives, SOE directors can consider issues normally outside the scope of directors of profit-maximising companies focused on financial returns. These issues include intergenerational equity[77] and non-financial benefits like community health impacts. In short, directors of SOEs can, and in certain circumstances, must consider both financial and impact materiality.

3.2 Three Arguments in Favour of Directors Addressing the Impacts of the Company's Operations on Climate Change, the Economy, or Society

There are at least three legal arguments supporting the claim that directors can and should address the impacts of the company's operations on climate change, the economy, or society (the external dimension), even if unrelated to or adversely impacting firm-specific shareholders' financial interests. These arguments also support considering the interests of diversified investors or universal owners. The arguments include incorporating nature-related provisions into corporate constitutions, catering to shareholders' preferences, and aligning fiduciary duties in the context of SOEs.

3.2.1 Incorporating Nature into the Corporate Constitution

The enlightened shareholder primacy model, exemplified by Section 172 of the UK Companies Act 2006, requires directors to promote the company's success for shareholders' benefit while having regard to non-shareholder interests, including community and environmental impacts.[78] This implies directors are not required to consider non-shareholder interests if doing so does not benefit shareholders. However, Section 172(2) permits shareholders to modify the corporate constitution to legally require directors to promote the company's success for stakeholders, the environment, or other entities, in addition to benefitting the members.

Since 2022, at least three UK limited liability companies have incorporated "nature" into their corporate governance by amending their articles of association.[79] These amendments are

73 Luc Bernier, Massimo Florio, and Philippe Bance (eds), *The Routledge Handbook of State-Owned Enterprises* (Routledge 2020).

74 OECD, *State-Owned Enterprises and Corruption: What are the Risks and What can be Done?* (OECD Publishing 2018), 11.

75 OECD, *Implementing the OECD Guidelines on Corporate Governance of State-Owned Enterprises: Review of Recent Developments* (OECD Publishing 2020).

76 Annette I De Kleine Feige, 'State-Owned Enterprises and Climate Action' (World Bank Group 2021) 9.

77 Gareth Davies, 'Climate Change and Reversed Intergenerational Equity: The Problem of Costs Now, for Benefits Later' (2020) 10 Climate Law 266.

78 *BTI 2014 LLC v Sequana SA* [2022] UKSC 25.

79 Faith in Nature Ltd; House of Hackney Group Ltd; Betternotstop Ltd. See Isabella Kaminski 'Eco Beauty Company "Appoints Nature" to its Board of Directors' *The Guardian* (London, 22

part of a broader UK movement for nature-positive corporate governance. The amendments are innovative because none require linking the prescribed or permissible conduct to shareholders' financial interests, contrasting with the UK Companies Act's default position.

The amendments include five types of provisions. The first is a corporate object clause requiring the promotion of corporate success for shareholders' benefit and the use of best endeavours to have a positive or to minimise negative impact on nature (defined as the natural world and non-human species).[80] One company also requires regard for the interest of future generations.[81]

The second is a directors' duties clause specifically requiring directors to act in good faith to promote company success in achieving the corporate objectives, reiterating the need to have regard for the impact on nature and future generations.[82] A separate clause states that directors need not prioritise any particular stakeholder, including shareholders and nature.[83]

Third, there is a clause requiring the appointment of a "nature guardian" to the board, tasked with ensuring that the board considers the environmental or nature impact of its decisions.[84] This guardian, who is a director, may have voting rights.[85]

Fourth, the board is required to provide written, recorded reasons if a decision on "nature reserved matters" is not in accordance with the nature guardian's advice.[86]

Finally, shareholders are entitled to an annual report explaining the company's environmental impact, and the nature guardian must be satisfied with the report's contents.[87]

These clauses are noteworthy as they legally obligate directors to effectuate corporate objects that expressly include having positive and avoiding negative impacts on nature. This effectively requires directors to give effect to double materiality.

However, the efficacy of these pro-nature clauses is questionable as the shareholder primacy model remains fundamentally unchallenged. There are at least five problems with these clauses.

First, it is unclear whose interests should be prioritised when they conflict, such as when investing in renewables will benefit nature but may affect shareholders' short-term financial

September 2022) <https://www.theguardian.com/environment/2022/sep/22/eco-beauty-company-faith-in-nature-board-directors> accessed 15 March 2025; House of Hackney, 'Taking Their Seat at the Table' <https://www.houseofhackney.com/en-intl/pages/nature-our-director?srsltid=AfmBOorPfgn6flgb8nrKkEVOn121L3Gzp7qYupiujYRowAdBpsPFtYBG> accessed 15 March 2025; Catherine Sellars, 'Appointing Nature to the Board—Can it be Done?' (*Stevens & Bolton*, 29 February 2024) <https://www.stevens-bolton.com/site/insights/articles/appointing-nature-to-the-board-storm-in-a-teacup> accessed 13 June 2025.

80 Articles of Association of Faith in Nature Ltd (SC068493) (adopted by special resolution passed on 15 August 2023). Article 3.1.2.1, 1.1 <https://find-and-update.company-information.service.gov.uk/company/SC068493/filing-historyhttps://find-and-update.company-information.service.gov.uk/company/SC068493/filing-history> accessed 15 March 2025. It appears that the definition of nature encompasses climate and the environment but is broader than them.

81 Articles of Association of House of Hackney Group Ltd (10696709) (dated 27 Aug 2024), Article 3.1<https://find-and-update.company-information.service.gov.uk/company/10696709/filing-history> accessed 15 March 2025. 'Future generations' is defined in art 2.1 as '7 generations of humans, plants, and animals on earth from today's date', i.e., 27 August 2024.

82 Faith in Nature (n 80) art 3.2; House of Hackney Group (n 81) art 3.2.

83 Faith in Nature (n 80) art 3.3; House of Hackney Group (n 81) art 3.3.

84 Faith in Nature (n 80) art 3.2, 1.1; House of Hackney Group (n 81) art 3.2, 2.1.

85 Faith in Nature (n 80) arts 5.4, 6.1.

86 ibid art 8.2; House of Hackney Group (n 81) art 4.2.6. Nature Reserved Matters refer to matters related to nature and designated as such by the board.

87 Faith in Nature (n 80) art 10; House of Hackney Group (n 81) art 25.

interests. The constitution offers no guidance, and stating that no interests will be prioritised is unhelpful. The ambiguity of the clauses and the discretion afforded to directors make it difficult to hold them liable. If the company is serious about protecting nature, the constitution should explicitly require prioritising nature's interests unless it will cause significant shareholder detriment or it is contrary to explicit shareholder instructions.

Second, only members, not the nature guardian or stakeholders, can enforce the constitution. Under UK law, members can only enforce clauses affecting them *as members*,[88] making it difficult for a member to enforce a pro-nature objects clause, as protecting nature does not necessarily benefit them in that capacity. It is suggested that members or the nature guardian should be permitted to enforce specific provisions to bypass the "qua member" rule.

Third, the right to sue directors for breach of duty in a derivative action rests solely with members. The nature guardian or stakeholders lack such a right. It is suggested that the nature guardian should be allowed to bring a derivative action, perhaps by issuing them a nominal share for this purpose.

Fourth, the nature guardian can be removed by a simple majority of shareholders. To prevent removal by shareholders prioritising profit, it is suggested requiring an extraordinary resolution for removal and restricting share transfers to shareholders who subscribe to the corporate purpose.

Finally, the pro-nature clauses can be removed or weakened by a special resolution. While current shareholders may be committed, future shareholders providing fresh capital could gain a majority and remove the clauses if they prioritise profit. It is suggested the clauses should be entrenched by requiring a higher threshold (e.g., 90%) for removal.

Delaware law allows similar amendments to corporate charters, but the same problems identified for UK companies would likely apply. As *McRitchie* noted, shareholders can amend the constitution to specify the company's purpose, a requirement that the company shall be managed for the benefit of certain constituencies, and limitations on directors' powers to promote those interests.

3.2.2 Directors Catering to Shareholders' Preferences

The second argument supporting directors' consideration of the effects of corporate operations on climate change or the economy, even if inconsistent with shareholders' financial interests, is that directors should give effect to shareholders' preferences if permitted by the corporate constitution and the law. Companies face significant pressure from shareholders and stakeholders on various ESG and LGBTQ+ issues.[89] Hart and Zingales argue that the Delaware shareholder primacy model does not equate solely to maximising share price; what is required is for directors to act in the company's interests for shareholders' benefit, and this benefit can encompass giving effect to shareholders' preferences, including for social, ethical, or environmental causes not necessarily tied to financial returns.[90] Thus, boards are not precluded from considering institutional shareholders' environmental and social preferences. Some empirical studies suggest investors are willing to sacrifice financial returns for environmental or social agendas.[91]

88 UK Companies Act 2006, s 33; *Hickman v Kent or Romney Marsh Sheep-Breeders' Association* [1915] 1 Ch 881.

89 Tom C W Lin, *The Capitalist and the Activist: Corporate Social Activism and the New Business of Change* (Berrett-Koehler Publishers 2022).

90 Hart and Zingales (n 12).

91 Brad M Barker, Adair Morse, and Ayako Yasuda, 'Impact Investing' (2021) 139 Journal of Financial Economics 162; Scott Hirst, Kobi Kastiel, and Tamar Kricheli-Katz, 'How Much Do Investors Care About Social Responsibility?' (2023) Wisconsin Law Review 977.

However, challenges exist in accurately and fairly reflecting the preferences of a company's shareholders. Shareholders have diverse preferences and intensities, ranging from pure profit maximisers to those prioritising strong environmental or social performance. Ascertaining specific preferred actions is difficult. Asset owners also face difficulty determining their beneficiaries' preferences.

For pro-ESG minority shareholders, coordinating to influence votes requires significant cost and effort.[92] It is difficult to identify shareholders genuinely interested in climate action versus those paying lip service. One study found that US signatories to the Principles for Responsible Investment did not have better portfolio ESG scores and showed no evidence of improving portfolio companies' scores.[93] A 2024 study in Europe and the UK revealed that the four largest asset managers were the least supportive of ESG resolutions, blocking proposals for improved environmental and/or labour practices, thereby questioning their public commitments.[94] Coordination efforts also risk potential competition law violations, though this can be addressed.[95]

Despite these challenges, empirical studies show investors have successfully pressured boards through different engagement strategies. There are at least four mechanisms shareholders can use to influence boards. The first is via executive compensation. Institutional investors have pressured boards to link executive compensation to shareholders' ESG preferences. One study shows executive compensation linked to investor preferences (via say on pay votes) correlated with a 10% improvement in ESG performance and adoption of environmentally friendly policies.[96] A global survey found ESG metrics in 81% of executive incentive plans,[97] with a tenfold increase in linking CEO pay to ESG metrics between 2018 and 2021.[98]

The second is via shareholder proposals. Shareholders can submit proposals for general meeting agendas. Statutory restrictions exist,[99] but studies suggest proposals can be effective, even if withdrawn, in improving environmental or social performance.[100]

92 Thilo Kuntz, 'ESG Demand-Side Regulation: Governing the Shareholders' in Jens-Hinrich Binder, Klaus Hopt, and Thilo Kuntz (eds), *Corporate Purpose, CSR, and ESG* (OUP 2024).

93 Rajna Gibson Brandon and others, 'Do Responsible Investors Invest Responsibly?' (2022) 26 Review of Finance 1389.

94 ShareAction, 'Voting Matters 2024: Are Asset Managers Using Their Proxy Votes for Action on Environmental and Social Issues?' (ShareAction 2025) 15. The four largest asset managers are BlackRock, Vanguard, Fidelity, and State Street.

95 See Julian Nowag and Thomas Cheng, Chapter 21 of this handbook.

96 Mary Ellen Carter, Andrea Pawliczek, and Rong Irene Zhong, 'Say on ESG: The Adoption of Say-on-Pay Laws, ESG Contracting, and Firm ESG Performance' (2022) European Corporate Governance Institute: Finance Working Paper No 886/2023 <https://www.ecgi.global/sites/default/files/working_papers/documents/sayonesg.pdf> accessed 27 March 2025; Shira Cohen and others, 'Executive Compensation Tied to ESG Performance: International Evidence' (2023) 61 Journal of Accounting Research 805.

97 Shai Ganu and others, 'Global Report on ESG Metrics in Incentive Plans 2023' (*WTW*, 23 January 2024) < https://www.wtwco.com/en-in/insights/2024/01/global-report-on-esg-metrics-in-incentive-plans-2023> 13 June 2025.

98 Edna Twumwaa Frimpong, 'The Growing Influence of ESG in Executive Compensation' (*Reward & Employee Benefits Association*, 22 September 2021) <https://reba.global/resource/the-growing-influence-of-esg-in-executive-compensation.html> accessed 13 June 2025.

99 ClientEarth, 'Know Your Rights: A Guide for Institutional Investors to the Law on Climate-Related Shareholder Resolutions' (ClientEarth 2021) <https://www.clientearth.org/latest/documents/know-your-rights-a-guide-for-institutional-investors-to-the-law-on-climate-related-shareholder-resolutions/> accessed 27 March 2025.

100 Alexander Dyck and others, 'Do Institutional Investors Drive Corporate Social Responsibility? International Evidence' (2019) 131 Journal of Financial Economics 693.

The third is via private communication. Engaging privately, often through closed-door meetings, has been argued to be the most effective activism.[101] Studies find a causal link between reduced carbon emissions and increased share percentage held by large index funds, suggesting more engagement via calls and meetings when these funds own more shares in high-emitting firms.[102] Meetings with boards are reported as the majority of successful engagements, with shareholder proposals used mainly to increase bargaining power.[103]

The final mechanism is via shareholder-company contracts. Pro-environmental/social controlling shareholders may enter agreements with the company (as permitted by Section 122(18) of the Delaware Corporate Law) requiring or prohibiting certain actions, provided these agreements do not violate the corporate constitution or law.

However, the majority of empirical studies on institutional investor pressure for ESG inclusion suggest the motivation is primarily financial,[104] as climate-related risks are financially material in many sectors. Many studies show that incorporating ESG preferences led to increased long-term shareholder returns.[105] Consistent with this, a survey of portfolio managers found most investors, including sustainable funds, would not voluntarily sacrifice even one basis point of return for environmental/social goals, citing fiduciary duty to clients.[106]

Thus, the majority of studies do not seem to support the idea that boards should sacrifice firm-specific financial returns to address climate change or other systemic risks, rendering it challenging to support the external dimension of directors' duties. Boards should be cautious using catering to shareholder preferences as justification for addressing risks not linked to or adversely impacting shareholders' returns, as only a handful of studies show shareholders willing to sacrifice returns for environmental or social agendas. Furthermore, the ability and willingness of US shareholders to submit ESG proposals is hindered by the rising anti-ESG movement[107] and companies threatening lawsuits.[108]

101 Marco Becht and others, 'Returns to Shareholder Activism: Evidence from a Clinical Study of the Hermes UK Focus Fund' (2009) 22 Review of Financial Studies 3093.

102 Jose Azar and others, 'The Big Three and Corporate Carbon Emissions Around the World' (2021) 142 Journal of Financial Economics 674.

103 Alexander Dyck and others, 'Do Institutional Investors Drive Corporate Social Responsibility? International Evidence' (2019) 131 Journal of Financial Economics 693.

104 Elroy Dimson, Oguzhan Karakas, and Xi Li, 'Active Ownership' (2015) 28 The Review of Financial Studies 3225; Elroy Dimson, Oguzhan Karakas, and Xi Li, 'Coordinated Engagements' (2018) European Corporate Governance Institute: Finance Working Paper No 721/2021 < https://www.ecgi.global/sites/default/files/working_papers/documents/coordinatedengagements_0.pdf> accessed 27 March 2025; Steven Johnson, 'ESG Fund Outflows Hit Record as a Sustainable Investing Backlash Grows' *Financial Times* (London, 25 April 2025).

105 Tamas Barko, Martijin Cremers, and Luc Renneboog, 'Shareholder Engagement on Social, Environmental, and Governance Issues' (2022) 180 Journal of Business Ethics 777.

106 Alex Edmans, Tom Gosling, and Dirk Jenter, 'Sustainability Investing: Evidence from the Field' (2024) European Corporate Governance Institute: Finance Working Paper No 1028/2024 < https://www.icpmnetwork.com/wp-content/uploads/2024/08/RI-Survey-20240715P.pdf> accessed 27 March 2025.

107 See, e.g., Taylor Nchako and Lisa Benjamin, 'ESG Backlash in the United States—Investor Concerns or "Red Scare"?' (*SSRN*, 10 September 2024) <https://ssrn.com/abstract=5003794> accessed 27 March 2025.

108 See, e.g., *Exxon Mobil Corporation v Arjuna Capital LLC and others* (No. 4:24-cv-00069-P) (17 June 2024).

3.2.3 SOEs: Aligning Directors' Fiduciary Duties with the Fiduciary Duties of the Controlling Shareholder and the Asset Owner: Fiduciary Duties of Directors, the State Controlling Shareholder, and the State Asset Owner of SOEs

Discussions on directors' and investors' duties regarding climate change or ESG typically assume a conventional profit-maximising company and large private institutional investors. However, SOEs are significant GHG contributors. Importantly, SOEs are established with multiple commercial and non-commercial objectives, including promoting social and economic development, creating employment, and providing goods or services like affordable energy. The government (or its controlled entity) is often both the controlling shareholder and a key asset owner with a diversified portfolio.

Three important implications follow. First, as SOEs pursue both commercial and non-commercial purposes, what constitutes the "best interests of the company" for directors' fiduciary duty cannot be determined primarily or exclusively by shareholders' financial interests. For example, state-owned power companies exist to provide low-cost electricity and allow government control of strategic sectors.[109] Therefore, in discharging their duty to act in good faith in the SOE's best interests, directors are permitted, and potentially required, to consider the effects of corporate actions on climate change, the economy, or society, even if it reduces the SOE's financial returns, provided the corporate constitution or legislation does not preclude them. This analysis is consistent with the firm-specific model emphasised in *McRitchie*, as the SOEs have been established to consider these broader considerations. Directors are unlikely to breach their duty of reasonable care by internalising negative externalities, as the standard of care is influenced by the company's nature, size, industry norms, and applicable regulations.

Second, given that an SOE's best interests involve balancing commercial and non-commercial considerations, the state (or its controlled entity) as a controlling shareholder, if subject to fiduciary duties,[110] can legitimately sacrifice its financial returns from the SOE to address broader climate/economy considerations, particularly if the government has issued climate-related legislation. The state, acting in the public interest,[111] must balance financial and non-financial considerations to promote the common good, not just narrow financial returns. The state as controller can pressure directors to align with its demands,[112] potentially removing those who defy its wishes or appointing those who are aligned. In systems with strong political oversight, directors appointed by the controller are likely to heed the controller's preferences.[113] Consequently, how directors discharge their duties can align with the controlling shareholder's preferences, facilitating consideration of climate or economic impacts not solely tied to financial returns.

[109] Bernier (n 73).

[110] In China, Delaware, and Germany, for example, controlling shareholders are subject to fiduciary duties (or duty of loyalty) under certain circumstances: PRC 2024 Company Law, Section 180, 192; *Jones v H.F. Ahmanson & Co* 460 P.2d 464 (Cal. 1969); *In re Sears Hometown and Outlet Stores, Inc. Stockholder Litigation*, 2024 WL 262322 (Del. Ch. Jan. 24, 2024); BGH 1.2.1988, II ZR 75/87: see C Gerner-Beuerle and M A Schillig, *Comparative Company Law* (OUP 2019) 626–30.

[111] Ernest Lim, 'The Government Controlling Shareholder as a Fiduciary: Implications for Climate Change Management and Litigation' (2024) 35 European Business Law Review 311.

[112] Arjuna Dibley, 'When Does "Leviathan" Innovate? A Legal Theory of Clean Technological Change at State-Owned Electric Utilities' (2023) 47 Harvard Environmental Law Review 135, 151–58.

[113] Lauren Yu-Hsin Lin and Curtis J Milhaupt, 'Party Building or Noisy Signalling? The Contours of Political Conformity in Chinese Corporate Governance' (2021) 50 Journal of Legal Studies 187.

The final implication is that the state (or its controlled entity) is often an asset owner, holding a diversified portfolio including that specific SOE, other SOEs, and non-SOEs. The state, as an asset owner, owes fiduciary duties to its beneficiaries (such as the pensioners in a public pension fund), not the individual SOE.[114] Thus, while the SOE's corporate purposes do not define the asset owner's duty (as they do for the directors' and controller's duty), the state asset owner is permitted to and should address climate or systemic considerations if they materially impact the long-term risk-adjusted returns of its beneficiaries. As climate risks and opportunities are material to the balancing of returns against risks, state asset owners should consider these at the asset, portfolio, and whole-economy levels.[115] The government, as both asset owner and diversified investor, is fundamentally concerned with overall economic performance as it impacts portfolio returns. Thus, the asset owner is incentivised to internalise the negative externalities of one SOE in its portfolio if failing to do so adversely impacts overall economic performance and its portfolio. The asset owner would be willing to sacrifice returns from a specific company to enhance overall portfolio returns. Conversely, they would be disincentivised from causing one company to internalise externalities if they outweigh the financial benefits to the overall portfolio.

That the asset owner is a state supports the alignment of directors' duties with the asset owner's duties, as both are likely to take a long-term approach. Because companies are usually formed to last indefinitely, directors must promote the company's long-term interests. While funds can have varied time horizons, a state asset owner is likely to take a long-term approach to beneficiaries' interests. This long-term perspective means SOE directors should not be pressured solely to maximise short-term shareholder returns, and state asset owners should not be pressured to maximise short-term returns for beneficiaries. More importantly, this long-term perspective allows directors to consider broader, long-term considerations like climate change impacts, intergenerational equity, community health, and socio-economic inequality. The state asset owner can and should consider these insofar as they impact long-term risk-adjusted returns.

For all these reasons, the fiduciary duties of the director, the state as controlling shareholder, and the state as asset owner can align because all three are permitted to consider the impacts of corporate operations on climate change or the economy, even if not tied to or potentially adversely affecting firm-specific shareholder returns. However, the grounds for doing so differ: Directors or controllers act in the SOE's best interests (balancing financial/non-financial); and the asset owner acts in beneficiaries' best interests (considering material impacts on long-term risk-adjusted returns). The significance of considering climate or systemic issues even at the expense of shareholder returns can be illustrated with Chinese SOEs.

3.2.3.1 *Chinese SOEs*

Chinaistheworld'slargestGHGemitter[116]andsecond-largesteconomy,[117]withnet-zeropledgesfor 2060.[118] Chinese SOEs are crucial as both emitters and renewable energy producers. SOEs

114 The beneficiaries (or someone who is authorised to act on their behalf in a representative capacity) can enforce these duties against the asset owner (or another applicable fiduciary) for breach of duties.

115 Financial Markets Law Committee, 'Pension Fund Trustees and Fiduciary Duties: Decision-Making in. the Context of Sustainability and the Subject of Climate Change' (Financial Markets Law Committee, 2024) [6.6].

116 IEA, 'The Changing Landscape of Global Emissions' (*IEA*, March 2024) <https://www.iea.org/reports/co2-emissions-in-2023/the-changing-landscape-of-global-emissions> accessed 15 March 2025.

117 World Bank Group, 'GDP Ranking' (*World Bank Group*, 18 December 2024) <https://datacatalog.worldbank.org/search/dataset/0038130> accessed 15 March 2025.

118 'China Headed Towards Carbon Neutrality by 2060; President Xi Jinping Vows to Halt New Coal Plants Abroad' (UN News, 21 September 2021) <https://news.un.org/en/story/2021/09/1100642#:~:text=

account for 50% of China's CO_2 emissions[119] and are the largest fossil fuel producers,[120] dominating global coal production[121] and electricity generation emissions.[122] Yet, they are also leaders in renewable energy,[123] accounting for a large share of new wind capacity,[124] and investing significantly in low-carbon energy.[125] SOEs are thus critical to China's decarbonisation policy.[126] Unlike shareholders in typical profit-maximising companies, the Chinese government (via the State-owned Assets Supervision and Administration Commission of the State Council) as controlling shareholder has goals beyond financial returns, including affordable energy, social development, and economic growth.[127]

The case of coal-fired power plant SOEs is illustrative. They provide bulk electric power vital for China's development,[128] are the dirtiest fossil fuel source, and represent two-thirds of the global total coal capacity.[129] Interestingly, China continues to build coal plants despite net-zero targets, accounting for 95% of new global coal construction in 2023.[130]

The Chinese government is both the controlling shareholder and asset owner of the coal-fired power plant SOE and related SOEs like the state-owned bank (that provides financing to the coal-fired power plant SOE), the construction company (which is hired by the coal-fired power plant SOE), and the grid purchaser (with which the coal-fired power plant SOE does business). The government builds these plants not just for financial gain but also to provide

"China%20will%20strive%20to%20peak,coal%2Dfired%20power%20projects%20abroad> accessed 25 March 2025.

119 John Lin and Philippe Benoit, 'China's State-Owned Enterprises Hold Keys to Carbon Neutrality' (*Alliance Bernstein*, 14 September 2022) <https://www.alliancebernstein.com/corporate/en/insights/esg-in-action/esg-in-action-chinas-state-owned-enterprises-hold-keys-to-carbon-neutrality.html> accessed 25 March 2025.

120 Michael R Davidson, 'Low-Carbon Transition Planning in China's Coal and Power Soes: Case of China Energy' (SSRN, 31 May 2022) <https://ssrn.com/abstract=4124504> accessed 15 March 2025.

121 Enerdata, 'Coal and Lignite Production' (Enerdata, 2023) <https://yearbook.enerdata.net/coal-lignite/coal-production-data.html> accessed 15 March 2025.

122 TRT World, 'China's Giant State-Owned Firms Pollute More Than Entire Nations' (*TRT World*, 2021) <https://www.trtworld.com/asia/china-s-giant-state-owned-firms-pollute-more-than-entire-nations-51309> accessed 15 March 2025.

123 Edward White, 'China's "Dinosaur" State-Owned Enterprises Make a Green Pivot' *The Financial Times* (London, 3 January 2024).

124 Fang Zhang, 'Leaders and Followers in Finance Mobilization for Renewable Energy in Germany and China' (2020) 37 Environmental Innovation and Societal Transitions 203.

125 'Huaneng Power International Makes New Strides in Green Energy' (*GreenergyDaily.com*, 6 June 2019) <https://hxny.com/nd-41695-0-17.html> accessed 15 March 2025.

126 Zhang Fang and Zuo Jialu, 'State-Owned Enterprises' Responses to China's Carbon Neutrality Goals and Implications for Foreign Investors' (*Georgetown Journal of International Affairs*, 15 February 2023) <https://gjia.georgetown.edu/2023/02/15/state-owned-enterprises-responses-to-chinas-carbon-neutrality-goals-and-implications-for-foreign-investors/> accessed 25 March 2025.

127 Benoit Mayer, Mikko Rajavuori, and Mandy Meng Fang, 'The Contribution of State-Owned Enterprises to Climate Change Mitigation in China' (2017) 7 Climate Law 97.

128 Chi Zhang and others, 'On Electricity Consumption and Economic Growth in China' (2017) 76 Renewable and Sustainable Energy Reviews 353.

129 'Global Coal Fleet Inches Up as Retirements Drop, Construction Starts Seesaw' (*Global Energy Monitor*, 10 April 2024) <https://globalenergymonitor.org/press-release/global-coal-fleet-inches-up-as-retirements-drop-construction-starts-seesaw/> accessed 15 March 2025.

130 Molly Lempriere, 'China Responsible For 95% of New Coal Power Construction in 2023, Report Says' (*CarbonBrief*, 4 November 2024) <https://www.carbonbrief.org/china-responsible-for-95-of-new-coal-power-construction-in-2023-report-says/> accessed 15 March 2025.

affordable, accessible energy to consumers and businesses, while aiming for profitability.[131] The government is also an asset owner/diversified investor with a portfolio of SOEs and non-SOEs.[132]

Two points are emphasised. First, for directors and the controlling shareholder of a coal-fired power plant SOE, pursuing only that specific SOE's shareholder returns is overly simplistic. The SOE is part of a system of other SOEs controlled by the same government, which is also a diversified asset owner. Thus, directors and the controlling shareholder cannot be solely concerned with maximising the SOE's specific returns. They should consider the externalities produced, such as health or environmental harms, on households, businesses, and state-owned banks providing financing. They must also consider just transition issues,[133] balancing phasing down coal plants (thus causing unemployment) with the availability and affordability of clean energy alternatives. These are complex trade-offs beyond maximising shareholder returns. Directors and the controlling shareholder must balance economic gains from coal with the state's net-zero ambitions.

Second, and interestingly, a key reason for continued investment and construction of coal plants in China despite net-zero targets is the government's likely view that the broader economic benefits currently outweigh the costs.[134] These broader economic considerations differ from and go beyond firm-specific financial returns. A standard profit-maximising company would focus on firm-level financial analysis, considering climate risks primarily because assets might become stranded, severely impacting financial interests and shareholder returns. Stranded assets increase capital costs, deplete cash flow, and escalate insurance premiums.[135] Studies predict significant stranding in the global power sector[136] and coal assets.[137]

It is puzzling that Chinese SOEs build more coal plants if they face severe stranding risks. The insight from Clark, Benoit, and Walters is that the Chinese government likely prioritises broader economic benefits.[138] This implies directors and the controlling shareholder of SOEs likely considered broader economic considerations at the country level, not just firm-specific profitability. Had they adopted a narrow financial analysis, they would have phased down or out coal fleets due to unprofitability; instead, they built more.

The authors show the difference between broader economic and firm-specific financial considerations.[139] Economic cost-benefit analysis extends across the value chain to consumers, calculated by their willingness to pay after-delivery costs. Firm-level financial analysis is restricted to profits from electricity sales after construction and delivery costs. Valuation

[131] ibid.

[132] Pangyue Cheng, 'Institutional Investors in China: Problems and Prospects' (2022) 2 Columbia Business Law Review 664, 672–83.

[133] Gang He and others, 'Enabling a Rapid and Just Transition Away from Coal in China' (2020) 3 One Earth 187.

[134] Alex Clark, Philippe Benoit, and Jonathan Walters, 'Government Shareholders, Wasted Resources and Climate Ambitions: Why is China Still Building New Coal-Fired Power Plants?' (2023) 23 Climate Policy 25.

[135] Weirong Zhang and others, 'Quantifying Stranded Assets of the Coal-Fired Power in China Under the Paris Agreement Target' (2023) 23 Climate Policy 11.

[136] Deger Saygin and others, 'Power Sector Asset Stranding Effects of Climate Policies' (2019) 14 Energy Sources, Part B: Economics, Planning and Policy 99.

[137] Haonan Zhang, Xingping Zhang, and Jiahai Yuan, 'Transition of China's Power Sector Consistent with Paris Agreement into 2050: Pathways and Challenges' (2020) 132 Renewable and Sustainable Energy Reviews 110102.

[138] Clark et al (n 134).

[139] ibid 29–30.

techniques differ: Financial valuation uses a private discount rate (company's weighted average cost of capital), while economic valuation uses a social discount rate. An economic country-level analysis might show Chinese coal plants breaking even after seven years, generating net economic value before 2030. This contrasts with a firm-level financial analysis showing shareholders receiving returns twenty-one years after operation. This partly explains the continued and increased coal operations.

However, the authors conclude that planned coal plants may never generate positive economic returns assuming shadow carbon pricing rises from US\$15 to US\$30/tCO_2 from 2026 to 2041.[140] A more ambitious shadow carbon price increase to US\$60/tCO_2 in 2041 could lead to economic losses. An important implication is that directors and the controlling shareholder acting in the SOE's best interests (including broader economic considerations) should not build more coal plants, contrary to the current situation in China.

3.2.3.2 *Summary*

Two points emerged. First, the analysis of SOE directors' fiduciary duties, along with the state's duties as controlling shareholder and asset owner, shows these duties can align. All three fiduciaries can and should consider climate change or other systemic considerations (like the broader economy) not tied to firm-specific shareholders' financial returns. Second, findings from Chinese coal-fired SOEs suggest the Chinese government (as controller and asset owner) invests in/constructs coal plants because it likely prioritises broader economic considerations over firm-specific financial ones in SOE transition plans. The risk is that the social cost of carbon may eventually exceed the net economic benefits.

To be clear, the Chinese SOE case study is not intended to show that directors are internalising negative externalities or mitigating adverse impacts. Instead, its importance lies in supporting the claim regarding the external dimension of directors' duties. In Chinese SOEs, directors do consider broader economic considerations not linked to SOE shareholders' financial returns. This aligns with SOE purposes and can align with the fiduciary duties of the state as the controlling shareholder and asset owner. This decision-making process is not unique to Chinese SOEs; government-owned utilities in the US show similar processes.[141] Furthermore, the case study is consistent with the claim that directors of Chinese renewable energy SOEs address negative impacts and social costs, even if they affect short or medium-term financial returns due to high financing costs.

4. Conclusion

A primary justification for requiring directors to address climate-related risks/opportunities or systemic considerations is their impact on the company's interests, often linked to financial materiality or firm-specific shareholder returns. This justification also underpins requirements for companies to report on climate risk impacts on them. However, an exclusive or predominant focus on financial materiality may have inadvertently hindered accountability for corporate negative externalities and provided arguments to those who believe corporate law is not the appropriate tool for addressing negative externalities. This chapter addresses

[140] ibid 33. These shadow carbon prices are based on the Chinese government's own stated objective of phasing out coal, which reflects the preferences of the state as the controlling shareholder.

[141] Dibley (n 112) 191–93.

this unsatisfactory situation.[142] It explains why analysing the external dimension of directors' duties is crucial and evaluates arguments supporting it.

The key argument is that the external dimension of directors' duties finds compelling support in SOEs. Directors of SOEs do and should consider the company's impacts on climate change, the economy, or society, even if doing so is not tied to SOE-specific shareholder returns. This is because SOEs have multiple purposes, and the state, as the controlling shareholder and asset owner, considers climate and other systemic factors, allowing the fiduciary duties of directors, the controller, and the asset owner to align. Analysing director duties in SOEs, as I mentioned earlier, is critical because SOEs and their state owners are major contributors to climate change and facilitators of decarbonisation, yet debates often focus on non-SOEs and the US institutional investors. This analysis offers several lessons for US and global corporate law discourse on climate change.

First, the external dimension of directors' duties is relevant to corporate governance discussions of government-owned utility companies, both in the US (where approximately 2,000 such utilities account for more than 15% of US production capacity)[143] and globally (representing over 60% of the world's electricity capacity).[144] This calls into question the argument by some US scholars that directors risk breaching their duties if shareholders pressure them to sacrifice firm-specific returns by addressing climate change or other systemic matters.[145] This is because the duties of SOE directors can align with those of the state as controller and asset owner. The external dimension, as illustrated by the Chinese SOEs, also helps us to understand the corporate governance of other top ten largest GHG emitters, including India and Indonesia. The SOEs in these countries have accelerated coal plant production, contrary to net-zero ambitions, a striking finding of the 2024 Carbon Majors Database.[146]

Second, the universal ownership argument can cut both ways. While proponents argue that it supports mitigating climate change, as reducing the negative externalities in one company will improve overall portfolio returns, the reverse is equally true. The universal owner (like the Chinese government, which controls SOEs and is concerned with the whole economy) is unlikely to reduce the carbon emissions in one company if it is not outweighed by long-term returns to the remainder of its portfolio. The Chinese government has ramped up coal-fired power operations because it concludes broader economic gains for China outweigh externality costs. Carbon-intensive activities of one or more SOEs contribute to overall economic gains for the state as asset owner, providing little incentive to reduce negative externalities. This partly explains the significant increase in emissions from Asian coal plant expansion

[142] To be clear, directors must not do away with material financial considerations, otherwise the company will become financially unviable which will lead to its demise: Stephen Beer, 'ESG Must Learn from the Tech Bubble—Returns Matter: Investors Must Not Forget about Profits, Even as They Focus on Wider Criteria' *Financial Times* (London, 17 August 2021).

[143] US Energy Information and Administration, 'Investor-Owned Utilities Served 72% of U.S. Electricity Customers in 2017' (Today in Energy, 15 August 2019) <https://www.eia.gov/todayinenergy/detail.php?id=40913> accessed 15 March 2025.

[144] Andrew Prag, Dirk Röttgers, and Ivo Scherrer, '*State-Owned Enterprises and the Low-Carbon* Transition' OECD Environment Working Papers No 129 (OECD Publishing, 2023), 8.

[145] Goshen and Hamdani (n 4); Marcel Kahan and Edward B Rock, 'Systematic Stewardship with Tradeoffs' (2023) 48 J. Corp. Law 497. For a critique of the corporate governance of US public utilities, see Aneil Kovvali and Joshua C Macey, 'The Corporate Governance of Public Utilities' (2023) 40 Yale J Reg 569.

[146] Carbon Majors (n 26).

noted in the 2024 Carbon Majors Database, alongside other factors such as geopolitical risks and energy security concerns.[147]

Finally, the external dimension, as seen in Chinese SOEs, demonstrates the conflict between the broader economic benefits of carbon-intensive SOEs and the negative externalities they cause. A key question for corporate law is whether directors' and investors' fiduciary duties can be used to reduce this conflict and what incentives[148] or capabilities they have. Directors of carbon-intensive SOEs must balance diverse goals: the country's broader economic goals, just transition issues (considering coal generated over 2.7 million jobs in China in 2021),[149] shareholders' returns, and negative externalities. One suggestion is to link shadow carbon pricing[150] (incorporating environmental and social costs or benefits) with executive compensation contracts and promotion systems for SOE directors and managers. This aligns with the multiple purposes of SOEs, which involve weighing, balancing, and giving effect to environmental protection, social benefits, and economic growth.

[147] David Sandalow and others, 'Guide to Chinese Climate Policy 2022' (Oxford Institute of Energy Studies 2022).

[148] The current incentive structure seems to reward the continuation of coal-intensive activities because the promotion of the local government officials depends to a certain extent on meeting short-term GDP growth targets: Bas Heerma van Voss and Ryan Rafaty, 'Sensitive Intervention Points in China's Coal Phaseout' (2022) 163 Energy Policy 112797.

[149] Alex Clark and Weirong Zhang, 'Estimating the Employment and Fiscal Consequences of Thermal Coal Phase-Out in China' (2022) 15 Energies 800.

[150] Kshama Harpankar, 'Internal Carbon Pricing: Rationale, Promise and Limitations' (2019) 10 Carbon Management 219; Lixin Cui and others, 'How Policy Preferences Affect the Carbon Shadow Price in the OECD' (2022) 311 Applied Energy 118686; World Bank Group, 'The Shadow Price of Carbon in Economic Analysis: 2024 Guidance Note' (*World Bank Group*, 2024) <https://documents1.worldbank.org/curated/en/099553203142424068/pdf/IDU1c94753bb1819e14c7818312155800606 75b1.pdf> accessed 15 March 2025.

CHAPTER 19

Climate Disclosure in the Global South

MARIA EDUARDA LESSA AND MARIANA PARGENDLER

1. Introduction

The climate emergency has increasingly impacted various areas of public and private law. In a short period, climate change has become a mainstream concern for corporate law and governance around the world. Recent debates and initiatives in this field have focused on a wide range of legal strategies, including disclosure obligations, fiduciary duties, due diligence requirements, shareholder proposals, and the definition of corporate purpose.[1]

Arguably the most conspicuous regulatory development in this "green turn" of corporate governance is the rise of corporate climate-related disclosure.[2] The last decade has witnessed the proliferation and consolidation of global standards for sustainability and climate reporting driven by international and nonprofit organisations.[3] This chapter examines the evolution

[1] See, e.g., Madison Condon, '"Green" Corporate Governance' in Jeffrey N Gordon and Wolf-Georg Ringe (eds), *Oxford Handbook of Corporate Law and Governance* (2nd edn, OUP 2025); Stavros Gadinis, 'Dissonance in Climate Disclosure: the SEC, EU, California, and ISSB Regimes' (2024) Working Paper <https://ssrn.com/abstract=4828188> accessed 1 July 2025; George S Georgiev, 'The Market Essential Role of Corporate Climate Disclosure' (2023) 56 UC Davis Law Review 2105–35; Cynthia A Williams, 'Fiduciary Duties and Corporate Climate Responsibility' (2021) 74 Vanderbilt Law Review 1875–[ii]; Ernest Lim, 'Sustainability and Corporate Mechanisms in Asia' (CUP 2020); Dan W Puchniak and Umakanth Varottil, 'Climate-Related Shareholder Activism as Corporate Democracy: A Call to Reform "Acting in Concert" Rules' (2025) 50 Journal of Corporation Law 617; OECD, Climate Change and Corporate Governance (OECD Publishing 2022) 43–49; Tim Bowley and Jennifer G Hill, 'The Global ESG Stewardship Ecosystem' (2024) 25 European Business Organization Law Review 229–68; Virginia Harper Ho, 'Stakeholders & The Dawn of Corporate Climate Governance' (2025) Working Paper <https://ssrn.com/abstract=5124607> accessed 1 July 2025; Jeffrey N Gordon, 'Unbundling Climate Change Risk from ESG' Columbia Law and Economics Working Paper No. 667 (2024) <https://ssrn.com/abstract=4547679> accessed 1 July 2025.

[2] Maria Eduarda Lessa, 'The Green Turn of Corporate Law' (2025) 6.1 Corporate and Business Law Journal 27.

[3] 'The Proliferation of Sustainability Accounting Standards Comes with Costs' (*The Economist*, 3 October 2020) < https://www.economist.com/business/2020/10/03/the-proliferation-of-sustainability-accounting-standards-comes-with-costs > accessed 2 July 2025. For consolidation efforts, see 'IFRS Foundation Announces International Sustainability Standards Board, Consolidation with CDSB and VRF, and Publication of Prototype Disclosure Requirements' (*IFRS Foundation*, 3 November 2021); IFRS Foundation, *Progress on Corporate Climate-related Disclosures—2024 Report* (November 2024) 108 (in 2024, jurisdictions with 'approximately 57% of global gross domestic product, more than 40% of the global market capitalisation and more than half of global GHG emissions' progressed towards ISSB adoption or use). On the role of nonprofits in developing climate disclosure standards and pushing

of climate disclosure as a window into the impact of climate change on corporate law and governance.[4]

Given the global scale of climate change, a key question is whether and how the legal systems of different jurisdictions have adopted climate disclosure requirements, and, if so, based on which standards. The existing literature has primarily focused on legal developments in the Global North, particularly in the EU and US.[5] Relatively few studies have addressed climate-related initiatives in the Global South from a comparative perspective.[6]

However, the North–South divide has been historically central in debates over environmental sustainability and climate change. This divide has been a key theme in the international and environmental law literature on climate change.[7] A prevalent perspective suggests that the Global South does and should resist climate change mitigation efforts in the absence of compensation.[8] According to the principle of "common but differentiated responsibilities", Global North countries, being wealthier and historically larger emitters of greenhouse gases (GHG), bear the responsibility to lead the climate transition, while Global South economies, with limited resources, should have the opportunity to prioritise development.[9] The Global South has played a pivotal role in linking environmental issues—including climate change—with development matters in international climate negotiations.[10] From this standpoint, a

for their adoption, see Mariana Pargendler and Elizabeth Pollman, 'Engines of External Corporate Governance' (2026) Working Paper (on file with authors).

[4] Disclosure requirements may also have significant implications for related corporate governance issues. See Virginia Harper Ho, 'Corporate Climate Governance' (2024) ECGI Law Working Paper No. 804/2024 <https://ssrn.com/abstract=4934244> accessed 1 July 2025.

[5] See, for works exploring US and EU climate disclosures, Gadinis (n 1) 15; Gordon (n 1) 2. See also John Armour, Luca Enriques, and Thom Wetzer, 'Mandatory Corporate Climate Disclosures: Now, But How?' (2021) 3 Columbia Business Law Review 1085–1146 (criticising the lack of mandatory standardisation of climate reporting).

[6] We use the terms 'Global North' and 'Global South' to refer to economies traditionally classified as developed and developing countries, respectively. For a discussion of different terminologies, see Mariana Pargendler, 'The Global South in Comparative Corporate Governance' in Jeffrey N Gordon and Wolf-Georg Ringe (eds), *Oxford Handbook of Corporate Law and Governance* (2nd edn, OUP 2025) <https://ssrn.com/abstract=4699188> accessed 1 July 2025. For studies including Global South jurisdictions, see Virginia Harper Ho, 'China & Transnational Green Finance: Diverse Influences in an Unsettled Field' (2024) Working Paper <https://ssrn.com/abstract=4945150> accessed 1 July 2025; Virginia Harper Ho and Stephen Kim Park, 'ESG Disclosure in Comparative Perspective: Optimizing Private Ordering in Public Reporting' (2019) 41(2) University of Pennsylvania Journal of International Law 249–328 (addressing ESG disclosures in South Africa, Brazil, and China).

[7] See, e.g., Michael Grubb, 'Seeking Fair Weather? Ethics and the International Debate on Climate Change' (1995) 71 International Affairs 462; Joyeeta Gupta, *The Climate Change Convention and Developing Countries: From Conflict to Consensus?* (Springer 1997); Lavanya Rajamani, *Differential Treatment in International Environmental Law* (OUP 2012); Shawkat Alam and others (eds), *International Environmental Law and the Global South* (CUP 2015).

[8] See, e.g., Stephen M Gardiner, 'Ethics and Global Climate Change' (2004) 114 Ethics and Global Climate Change 578–83; Cass R Sunstein, *Climate Justice: What Rich Nations Owe the World—and the Future* (MIT Press 2025).

[9] The principle was first adopted in the United Nations Framework Convention on Climate Change (1992). See, for a description, Christopher D Stone, 'Common but Differentiated Responsibilities in International Law' (2004) 98 American Journal of International Law 276; Lavanya Rajamani, 'The Principle of Common but Differentiated Responsibility and the Balance of Commitments under the Climate Regime' (2022) 9 Review of European, Comparative & International Environmental Law 120.

[10] Sakiko Fukuda-Parr and Bhumika Muchhala, 'The Southern Origins of Sustainable Development Goals: Ideas, Actors, Aspirations' (2020) 126 World Development 104706; Marc Williams, 'The

combination of limited state capacity and national development concerns has positioned the Global South in a narrow and often adversarial role within global climate governance.[11]

This traditional view of the Global South in global climate governance has influenced emerging scholarship on corporate governance. Scholars have depicted the Global South—particularly China—as resistant to the climate agenda championed by the Global North, especially by the EU.[12] Moreover, the "focus on development first and respect for national sovereignty" has led to the assumption that the Global South would be less supportive of global climate standards.[13]

Conversely, other characteristics of Global South countries and their legal systems may make them more receptive to the incorporation of climate change considerations through private law. Recent scholarship has highlighted how Global South jurisdictions may embrace "legal heterodoxy" in private law, adopting doctrinal approaches that are innovative relative to the Global North by incorporating broader public policy and distributional objectives.[14] Global South countries have pioneered distinct and often bolder forms of "heterodox stakeholderism" in corporate law, including parent company liability for environmental obligations, mandatory corporate social responsibility (CSR) requirements, and racial diversity policies for corporate ownership and management.[15] In the realm of climate change litigation, these jurisdictions have similarly innovated by linking climate change with human rights to protect vulnerable populations.[16] Moreover, North–South disparities may drive the Global South to combat climate change because of its heightened vulnerability to physical and transition risks due to factors such as geography, social inequality, and resource scarcity.[17]

Third World and Global Environmental Negotiations: Interests, Institutions and Ideas' (2005) 5 Global Environmental Politics 48, 56; Jens Marquardt, Anna Fünfgeld, and Joshua Philipp Elsasser, 'Institutionalizing Climate Change Mitigation in the Global South: Current Trends and Future Research' (2023) 15 Earth System Governance 100163.

[11] Andrew Hurrell and Sandeep Sengupta, 'Emerging Powers, North–South Relations and Global Climate Politics' (2012) 88(3) International Affairs 463–84, 467 (noting that 'the picture of emerging economies as the "great irresponsibles" has become embedded').

[12] Roza Nurgozhayeva and Dan W Puchniak, 'Corporate Purpose Beyond Borders: A Key to Saving Our Planet or Colonialism Repackaged?' (2023) ECGI Law Working Paper No. 744/2023 <https://ssrn.com/abstract=4652012> accessed 1 July 2025.

[13] ibid 53.

[14] Kevin E Davis and Mariana Pargendler (eds), *Legal Heterodoxy in the Global South* (CUP, 2025). See also Mariana Pargendler, 'How Universal Is the Corporate Form? Reflections on the Dwindling of Corporate Attributes in Brazil' (2019) 58 Columbia Journal of Transnational Law 1; Kevin E Davis, Mariana Pargendler, and Maria Eduarda Lessa, 'Legal Heterodoxy in the Global South: Priority of Workers versus Secured Creditors in Insolvency' (2025) ECGI Law Working Paper No. 843/2025 <https://ssrn.com/abstract=5250599> accessed 1 July 2025; Mariana Pargendler and Olivia Pasqualeto, 'Overcoming Corporate Separateness: The Early Origins and Evolution of Group Liability for Workers and Beyond' American Journal of Comparative Law (forthcoming) (on file with authors).

[15] Mariana Pargendler, 'Corporate Law in the Global South: Heterodox Stakeholderism' (2024) 47 Seattle University Law Review 535–79.

[16] Joana Setzer and Lisa Benjamin, 'Climate Litigation in the Global South: Constraints and Innovations' (2019) 9 Transnational Environmental Law 77-101, 85 (noting that in contrast to Global North litigation, Global South litigants 'use existing legislative tools and human rights discourses to highlight the vulnerability of their populations to climate change and protect their valuable ecosystems'). See also Jacqueline Peel and Jolene Lin, 'Transnational Climate Litigation: The Contribution of the Global South' (2019) 113(4) American Journal of International Law 679–726.

[17] Barry S Levy and Jonathan A Patz, 'Climate Change, Human Rights, and Social Justice' (2015) 81 Annals of Global Health 310; Glenn Althor, James E M Watson, and Richard A Fuller, 'Global Mismatch Between Greenhouse Gas Emissions and the Burden of Climate Change' (2016) 6 Nature: Scientific

Additionally, a third possibility is that Global South jurisdictions may be more susceptible to the influence of international climate standards and to pressures to conform with them.[18]

This chapter explores these competing views by examining how core jurisdictions in the Global South—Brazil, India, China, and South Africa (BICS)—have engaged with, or resisted, the global agenda on corporate climate disclosure, or have promoted innovations of their own. The BICS comprise the leading three Global South nations by GDP as of 2024, plus South Africa, a country noted for its legal innovations in public and private law and its unusually large stock markets relative to GDP.[19] These jurisdictions have also exhibited greater levels of stock market capitalisation as a percentage of GDP compared to the four largest economies in the Global North.[20]

Contrary to predictions of strong resistance to the climate agenda, the BICS were either early adopters of international disclosure frameworks or pioneers in tying the environmental and climate agenda to local concerns. Brazil was the first jurisdiction to adopt International Sustainability Standards Board (ISSB) standards globally in 2023, while China has expanded on ISSB standards to include a double materiality approach. Although South Africa and India have not yet adopted international climate disclosure standards, they were global pioneers in corporate sustainability reporting. South Africa has incorporated impact dimensions into corporate sustainability disclosures since 2002. India, in turn, innovated by requiring stakeholder-inclusive mandatory business responsibility reporting encompassing climate disclosures for large, listed companies in 2012. This move preceded the adoption of climate disclosures in the largest Global North economies (the US, EU, Germany, Japan, the UK, and France), though the Indian climate disclosure framework subsequently fell short of corresponding Global North rules.[21] Rather than invariably opposing or simply importing international climate disclosure standards, these findings suggest significant Global South agency in this domain.

Secondly, this chapter maps the adoption of climate disclosure frameworks in the largest economies in each of the Global South and Global North.[22] We find that Global North disclosures are generally broader and more comprehensive than Global South disclosures. This is consistent with traditional assumptions of Global South inertia towards climate change and with weaker securities regulation. The EU has famously pioneered the strongest climate disclosure requirements. There is, however, significant variation in disclosure frameworks within the Global North and Global South blocs, with some Global South jurisdictions outperforming non-EU Global North counterparts and vice versa.

Admittedly, our analysis concentrates on disclosure requirements "on the books", without assessing their effectiveness or enforcement levels, which are predicted to be weaker in the

Reports 20281 (finding that '20 of the 36 highest emitting countries are among the least vulnerable' to climate change).

[18] Pargendler (n 6) (describing traditional views concerning foreign influence on corporate laws in the Global South).

[19] ibid. See also World Bank Group, 'GDP (Current US$)' (World Bank Open Data 2026).

[20] Pargendler (n 6).

[21] See Section 4 of this chapter.

[22] We used 2024 World Bank data on GDP to define the largest economies. We selected Global South jurisdictions following the criteria adopted by Pargendler (n 15) 570, which cover the jurisdictions that are both classified as developing countries by the United Nations Conference on Trade and Development (UNCTAD) and as low- or middle-income countries by the World Bank. This results in the selection of the US, Germany, Japan, the UK, and France in the Global North, and China, India, Brazil, Mexico, and Indonesia in the Global South. See (n 19).

Global South.[23] We cannot rule out the phenomenon of "cosmetic compliance" with international norms.[24] Furthermore, most existing requirements are still not fully effective and, like the global climate agenda more generally, are subject to backlash.

The remainder of this chapter is structured as follows. Section 2 examines the emergence of international standards for corporate climate disclosure. Section 3 describes the adoption of corporate climate disclosure standards in the BICS jurisdictions. Section 4 compares the adoption of corporate climate disclosure standards in the largest Global North and Global South economies. Section 5 examines how the observed patterns fit existing views about the regulatory tendencies in the Global South. Section 6 concludes.

2. The Emergence of International Standards on Corporate Climate Disclosure

Following earlier experiments with international standards for voluntary sustainability reporting, most notably the Global Reporting Initiative (GRI) launched in 1997,[25] the last couple of decades have witnessed the emergence and growing standardisation of global standards focused on climate disclosure. In 2001, the GHG Protocol, developed by the World Resources Institute and the World Business Council for Sustainable Development, introduced a methodology for emissions measurement that is widely recognised as the gold standard in carbon accounting.[26] The Protocol breaks down emissions into Scopes 1, 2, and 3. Scope 1 refers to direct GHG emissions from sources that are owned or controlled by the company. Scope 2 accounts for indirect emissions from purchased energy. Scope 3 emissions, which have been among the most contentious issues in climate disclosure,[27] encompass all other indirect emissions throughout the company's value chain. This carbon disclosure framework laid the foundation for the standardisation of corporate climate reporting.[28]

In 2015, the G20 prompted the Financial Stability Board (FSB) to address climate risk, leading to the formation of the Task Force on Climate-Related Financial Disclosures (TCFD).[29] This industry-led initiative was tasked with creating guidelines for corporate climate disclosure. Released in 2017, the TCFD guidance focuses on disclosure of climate-related risks and opportunities.[30] These risks and opportunities should be identified by the company, integrated into its strategy, assessed through metrics and targets, and overseen by management. TCFD recommends disclosure of Scopes 1, 2, and, if appropriate, Scope 3 emissions. The International

[23] See the literature cited in (n 14).

[24] Hyoung-Kyu Chey, 'Explaining Cosmetic Compliance with International Regulatory Regimes: The Implementation of the Basel Accord in Japan, 1998–2003' (2006) 11 New Political Economy 271; Gen Goto, Alan K Koh, and Dan W Puchniak, 'Diversity of Shareholder Stewardship in Asia: Faux Convergence' (2020) 58 Vanderbilt Journal of Transnational Law 829, 874–76.

[25] 'Our Mission and History' (*Global Reporting Initiative*) <https://www.globalreporting.org/about-gri/mission-history/> accessed 1 July 2025.

[26] The Greenhouse Gas Protocol, *A Corporate Accounting and Reporting Standard (rev edn)* 2004 25.

[27] See generally Gadinis (n 1) (for a description of regulatory approaches to Scope 3 reporting).

[28] Lynn M LoPucki, 'Corporate Greenhouse Gas Disclosures' (2022) 56 UC Davis Law Review 405, 425.

[29] 'About' (*Task-Force on Climate-related Financial Disclosures*) <https://www.fsb-tcfd.org/about/> accessed 1 July 2025. See, for a description, Mariana Pargendler, 'The Rise of International Corporate Law' (2021) 98 Washington University Law Review 1765–1820.

[30] *Task Force on Climate-related Financial Disclosures: Overview* (*Task-Force on Climate-related Financial Disclosures*, December 2022) 12 <https://www.fsb-tcfd.org/publications/> accessed 1 July 2025.

Monetary Fund and the United Nations' Special Envoy for Climate Change and Finance have advocated for mandatory implementation of TCFD reporting standards, which were adopted by various jurisdictions and paved the way for climate disclosure harmonisation.[31]

In 2021, the International Financial Reporting Standards (IFRS) Foundation, a global standard-setting organisation, established the International Sustainability Standards Board (ISSB) to develop global baseline standards for sustainability reporting.[32] Described as "a culmination of the work of the TCFD", ISSB succeeded it after the task-force was disbanded by the FSB in 2023.[33] ISSB published general sustainability reporting standards (IFRS S1) and specific standards for climate change disclosure (IFRS S2) in 2023.[34] The standards "fully incorporate"[35] TCFD recommendations and further extend disclosure requirements to material Scope 3 emissions.[36] In 2023, the International Organization of Securities Commissions (IOSCO) urged its members to consider implementing ISSB,[37] which has since been adopted by dozens of jurisdictions around the world.[38] Both TCFD and ISSB approach climate disclosure from a financial materiality perspective, which focuses on the impact of climate-related risks and opportunities on the company's financial performance for an investor audience.[39] This contrasts with GRI's impact materiality, which emphasises reporting of corporate sustainability impacts for a broader multi-stakeholder audience.[40]

In 2023, the European Commission introduced the European Sustainability Reporting Standards (ESRS) for purposes of reporting under the Corporate Sustainability Reporting Directive (CSRD).[41] Under this framework, Scopes 1, 2, and 3 emissions disclosures are

31 Brandon D Stewart, 'Shining Some Light on Mandatory Corporate Climate-Related Disclosure' (2020) 17 McGill Journal of Sustainable Development Law 34.

32 'International Sustainability Standards Board: About the International Sustainability Standards Board' (*IFRS Foundation*) <https://www.ifrs.org/groups/international-sustainability-standards-board> accessed 1 July 2025.

33 FSB, 'FSB Plenary Meets in Frankfurt' (*FSB Press Release*, 6 July 2023). See also 'ISSB and TCFD' (*IFRS Foundation*) <https://www.ifrs.org/sustainability/tcfd> accessed 1 July 2025.

34 'ISSB Issues Inaugural Global Sustainability Disclosure Standards' (*IFRS Foundation*, 26 June 2023) <https://www.ifrs.org/news-and-events/news/2023/06/issb-issues-ifrs-s1-ifrs-s2/> accessed 1 July 2025.

35 FSB Plenary Press Release (n 33).

36 IFRS Sustainability, *Comparison: IFRS S2 Climate-related Disclosures with the TCFD Recommendations* (November 2024). See also Veronica Poole and Neil Stevenson, 'Comparing Climate-Related Disclosure Requirements' (*Global Association of Risk Professionals*, 11 September 2024) ('While TCFD recommends that companies consider disclosing scope 3 GHG emissions in addition to disclosure of scopes 1 and 2, this is mandated by the ISSB (subject to materiality)').

37 IOSCO, 'IOSCO Endorses the ISSB's Sustainability-Related Financial Disclosures Standards' (*Media Release IOSCO/MR/19/2023*, 25 July 2023) (calling on member jurisdictions to 'consider ways in which they might adopt, apply or otherwise be informed by the ISSB Standards').

38 See, for a comprehensive list of jurisdictions, IFRS Foundation (n 3).

39 Climate Disclosure Standards Board, *Materiality and climate-related financial disclosures* (2018) 6; IFRS Foundation, 'ISSB: Frequently Asked Questions' <https://www.ifrs.org/groups/international-sustainability-standards-board/issb-frequently-asked-questions/> accessed 1 July 2025.

40 Global Reporting Initiative, 'The Materiality Madness: Why Definitions Matter' (*The GRI Perspective*, 22 February 2022) 3 <https://www.globalreporting.org/media/r200jx53/gri-perspective-the-materiality-madness.pdf> accessed 1 July 2025.

41 Commission Delegated Regulation (EU) 2023/2772 of 31 July 2023 supplementing Directive 2013/34/EU of the European Parliament and of the Council as regards sustainability reporting standards [2023] OJ L2023/2772 (ESRS); Directive (EU) 2022/2464 of 14 December 2022 amending Regulation (EU) No 537/2014, Directive 2004/109/EC, Directive 2006/43/EC and Directive 2013/34/EU, as regards corporate sustainability reporting [2022] OJ L322/15.

mandatory regardless of materiality. ESRS combines elements of ISSB and GRI standards.[42] The European standard is based on a "double materiality" threshold, which combines both financial and impact materiality.[43] Stakeholders include traditional constituencies such as workers, consumers, and local communities, as well as nature as "a silent stakeholder".[44] ESRS requires disclosure of any negative impact that initiatives to address climate-related risks and opportunities may have on other sustainability issues.[45] These features have led scholars to assert that ESRS provides for the "highest degree of stakeholder integration in corporate governance".[46]

3. The Evolution of Corporate Climate Disclosure in the BICS

This section addresses the evolution of climate disclosure frameworks in the BICS jurisdictions. Our analysis suggests Global South agency and innovation in climate disclosure. We start with Brazil's early adoption of ISSB, followed by India's pioneering climate disclosure in stakeholder-oriented corporate responsibility reports. Next, we examine China's recent embrace and modification of international disclosure standards, before concluding with South Africa's voluntary standards and early adherence to impact materiality.

3.1 Brazil

In October 2023, Brazil became the first jurisdiction to adopt ISSB reporting standards (IFRS S1 and S2).[47] These standards were implemented on a voluntary basis starting in 2024 and became mandatory in 2026.[48] The new disclosure requirements, enacted through a resolution by Brazil's Securities Commission (Comissão de Valores Mobiliários or CVM), apply to listed companies, investment funds, and insurance companies. Notably, CVM chose to waive the usual public consultation and regulatory impact analysis before adopting ISSB standards, emphasising the goal of "maintain[ing] convergence with international standards".[49] During

42 Directorate-General for Financial Stability, Financial Services and Capital Markets Union, 'The Commission adopts the European Sustainability Reporting Standards' (*European Commission*, 31 July 2023) <https://finance.ec.europa.eu/news/commission-adopts-european-sustainability-reporting-standards-2023-07-31_en> accessed 1 July 2025; European Commission Questions and Answers on the Adoption of European Sustainability Reporting Standards (31 July 2023).

43 ESRS (n 41) paras 14, 21.

44 ESRS (n 41) AR 6–7.

45 ibid para 53.

46 Harper Ho (n 4) 23.

47 Michael Kapor, 'Brazil Becomes First Country to Adopt Global ESG Reporting Rules' (*Bloomberg Law* 20 October 2023) <https://news.bloomberglaw.com/esg/brazil-becomes-first-country-to-adopt-global-esg-reporting-rules> accessed 1 July 2025.

48 Comissão de Valores Mobiliários (CVM), Resolução CVM nº 193 (20 October 2023) art 1.

49 CVM, Decisão do Colegiado no Processo nº 19957.003419/2023-47, Relatora: Superintendência de Normas Contábeis e de Auditoria (11 October 2023). A regulatory impact analysis is a mandatory 'prior assessment' before the issuance of regulatory acts, which includes analysis of regulatory costs, alternative solutions, and their respective costs. The CVM decision relied on a waiver for regulatory acts seeking to maintain convergence with international standards. Decreto nº 10.411 de 30 de junho de 2020 (D.O.U. 01/07/2020 p. 35) arts 2(I), art 4(VI), and 6(VI)-(VII). CVM launched consultations and approved Brazilian ISSB standards in 2024, again without a regulatory impact analysis noting that it aimed exclusively 'to update or repeal norms considered obsolete, without changing their merit'. See CVM, Edital de Consulta Pública SNC nº 02/2024 (13 May 2024); CVM, Edital de Consulta Pública SNC nº 03/2024 (13 May 2024).

the approval process, the opinion of the Specialised Office of the Federal Attorney General, requested by CVM, cited IOSCO's endorsement of the standards and described alignment with multilateral agreements as "essential to fulfil[ling] one of this agency's most important strategic objectives: to promote and ensure the efficient functioning of the regulated sector".[50] These developments defy earlier sceptical predictions about future progress on sustainability issues in Brazil given the significant political clout and resistance from the agribusiness sector.[51]

While CVM has required the disclosure of environmental risks since 2009 and social risks since 2014,[52] it first mandated disclosure of climate risk factors and of the role of management in overseeing climate risks and opportunities in 2021. This was part of a broader expansion of ESG disclosure by Resolution 59, which also required companies to report, on a comply-or-explain basis, whether they considered TCFD or other international climate standards and adopted a GHG emissions inventory.[53] The Resolution sought to "meet the growing demand of investors for environmental, social, and governance (ESG) information and to align Brazilian regulation with the advances in all developed markets".[54] CVM characterised the new regulation as disaggregating the existing "socio-environmental" reporting requirements into "separate items for social, environmental, and climate issues".[55] A pre-consultation with the Financial Innovation Laboratory (Laboratório de Inovação Financeira), a multi-sector forum on sustainability co-founded by the Inter-American Development Bank, the Brazilian Development Association, and CVM,[56] considered the existing frameworks in the US and the EU, as well as global reporting standards such as GRI, Sustainability Accounting Standards Board (SASB), and International Integrated Reporting Council.[57]

Earlier voluntary initiatives by Brazil's stock exchange (B3) paved the way for the adoption of mandatory climate disclosure in the country. In 2011, as part of a partnership with the GRI, B3 began recommending that listed companies disclose whether they published sustainability reports or explain why they did not.[58] This recommendation was overtly inspired by the 2010 listing requirement of the Johannesburg Stock Exchange (JSE) and mandatory requirements for state-owned enterprises in France, Denmark, and Sweden since 2007.[59] In 2017, B3 expanded its earlier recommendation to mention consideration of Sustainable Development Goals (SDGs) in sustainability or integrated reports.[60] However, B3's proposal to require companies listed on Novo Mercado, the country's premium corporate governance segment,

[50] Advocacia-Geral da União, Procuradoria Federal Especializada junto à Comissão de Valores Mobiliários, *Parecer n. 00073/2023/GJU - 2/PFE-CVM/PGF/AGU* (1 September 2023) 2, 4.

[51] Luciana Dias, 'Corporate Governance and Sustainability in Brazil' in Beate Sjåfjell and Christopher M Bruner (eds), *The Cambridge Handbook of Corporate Law, Corporate Governance and Sustainability* (CUP 2019) 345.

[52] CVM, Resolução CVM nº 480 (7 December 2009); CVM, Resolução CVM nº 552 (9 October 2014) (amending Resolução CVM nº 480).

[53] CVM, Resolução CVM nº 59 (22 December 2021) Annex 24, ss. 1.9, 4.1, 7.1.

[54] CVM, Public Consultation Notice SDM nº 9/2020 (2020) 2.

[55] ibid 10.

[56] 'Quem Somos' (*Laboratório de Inovação Financeira*) <https://labinovacaofinanceira.com/quem-somos/>.

[57] Laboratório de Inovação Financeira and B3, Documento submetido em pré-consulta pública de Proposição de Revisão da ICVM 480 (2020). See also Public Consultation Notice SDM nº 9/2020 (n 54).

[58] BM&FBOVESPA, Comunicado Externo, 'Proposta de adoção ao modelo "Relate ou Explique" para Relatórios de Sustentabilidade ou Similares para Empresas Listadas' 23 December 2011.

[59] ibid 2.

[60] B3, Comunicado Externo, 'Proposta de adoção ao modelo "Relate ou Explique para os Objetivos de Desenvolvimento Sustentável para Empresas Listadas' 12 April 2017.

to publish a social and environmental report prepared according to international standards failed due to rejection by a majority of member firms.[61] These voluntary and softer initiatives follow Brazil's well-known tradition of using voluntary standards as a strategy to mitigate opposition to capital market reforms.[62]

3.2 India

In 2009, the Ministry of Corporate Affairs (MCA) published the Corporate Social Responsibility Voluntary Guidelines (CSR Guidelines),[63] a series of voluntary principles described as a "regulatory nudge" for business responsibility by Indian companies.[64] The preamble highlighted the twenty-first century's focus on "the desire for inclusive development and the imperatives of climate change".[65] Among the core elements, the CSR Guidelines encouraged companies to "proactively respond to the challenges of climate change" by adopting "cleaner production methods", "efficient use of energy", and "environment-friendly technologies".[66] In 2011, new National Voluntary Guidelines (NVGs)[67] were introduced to integrate "learnings from various international and national good practices" with a "distinctively 'Indian' approach" tailored to its "many unique requirements".[68] Principle 6, dedicated to environmental protection, emphasised how "environmental issues are interconnected at the local, regional and global levels", stressing the importance of addressing "global warming, biodiversity conservation and climate change in a comprehensive and systematic manner".[69]

In 2012, the Securities and Exchange Board of India (SEBI) introduced the mandatory Business Responsibility Report (BRR), based on the principles set out in the NVGs,[70] for the top 100 listed entities in India by market capitalisation.[71] When enacting the BRR, SEBI emphasised that companies are "accountable not merely to their shareholders" but also to "the larger society which is also its stakeholder".[72] SEBI subsequently expanded BRR's reach to India's top 500 and 1,000 listed entities based on market capitalisation in 2015 and 2019, respectively.[73] The Indian regulator provided a suggested framework for BRR, which included

[61] Dias (n 51) 351 (finding that from the 129 Novo Mercado firms required to approve the change by a 2/3 majority, 50 voted against it, 49 voted in favour and 29 abstained).

[62] Ronald J Gilson, Henry Hansmann, and Mariana Pargendler, 'Regulatory Dualism as a Development Strategy: Corporate Reform in Brazil, the U.S., and the EU' (2011) 63 Stanford Law Review 475.

[63] Ministry of Corporate Affairs, *Corporate Social Responsibility Voluntary Guidelines* (December 2009) (CSR Guidelines).

[64] Ministry of Corporate Affairs, *Report of the Committee on Business Responsibility Reporting* (2020) 22.

[65] CSR Guidelines (n 63) 9.

[66] ibid 12.

[67] Ministry of Corporate Affairs, *National Voluntary Guidelines on Social, Environmental and Economic Responsibilities of Business* (July 2011).

[68] ibid 4.

[69] ibid 19.

[70] Securities and Exchange Board of India (SEBI), *Business Responsibility Reports* (Circular CIR/CFD/DIL/8/2012, 13 August 2012) (BRR Circular) Annexure II.

[71] ibid 1.

[72] ibid.

[73] Securities and Exchange Board of India (Listing Obligations and Disclosure Requirements) (Amendment) Regulations, 2015 (22 December 2015); Securities and Exchange Board of India (Listing Obligations and Disclosure Requirements) (Fifth Amendment) Regulations, 2019 (26 December 2019).

the company's strategies and initiatives to address global environmental issues such as climate change and Clean Development Mechanism projects.[74] A 2017 survey found that 60% of the top 100 listed companies in India adopted the suggested framework, while 97% reported on initiatives to address environmental risks.[75] However, only 46% disclosed or commented on strategies to address climate change.[76] By 2020, the MCA noted that "sustainability reporting in India [was] still in its infancy".[77]

In 2021, SEBI replaced the BRR with the Business Responsibility and Sustainability Report (BRSR).[78] The development of the BRSR involved a public consultation that considered sustainability disclosure frameworks from Denmark, South Africa, China, Malaysia, the Philippines, and the EU, and engaged a variety of local stakeholders, international organisations, and global standard setters.[79] The new standards, which apply to the top 1,000 listed entities in India by market capitalisation,[80] are divided into essential (mandatory) and leadership (voluntary) indicators. Mandatory disclosures encompass Scopes 1 and 2 GHG emissions as well as mitigation projects. Scope 3 emissions disclosure remains voluntary. The BRSR also mandates disclosure of policies to implement the National Guidelines on Responsible Business Conduct, which updated the NVGs in 2018 and cover climate-related initiatives, including goals, targets and performance, board approval and management oversight, and independent assessment of existing policies.

SEBI's chairman emphasised that Indian regulators "kept [their] ground realities in mind" when conceiving the BRSR,[81] highlighting that "for a country like India social factors are as relevant and important as climate related factors".[82] He elaborated on how SEBI deliberately embraced a "climate plus approach", extending beyond environmental metrics to include quantitative social metrics such as workforce diversity, employee health and safety, employee engagement and welfare, social impact assessments of projects, procurement from marginalised and vulnerable groups, CSR spending in aspirational districts, and beneficiaries of CSR projects.[83]

While the BRR framework was pioneering in 2012, India's climate disclosure has not yet reached the granularity and comprehensiveness of those in other jurisdictions. Current Indian requirements do not meet the standards set by global climate reporting frameworks adopted in the Global North and in other Global South jurisdictions.

[74] BRR Circular (n 70) Annexure I.

[75] KPMG, 'Business Responsibility Reporting: An Analysis of Top 100 BSE and NSE Listed Companies' (July 2017) 4.

[76] ibid 19.

[77] Ministry of Corporate Affairs (n 64) 23.

[78] SEBI, *Business Responsibility and Sustainability Reporting by Listed Entities* (Circular SEBI/HO/CFD/CMD-2/P/CIR/2021/562, 10 May 2021) (BRSR Circular).

[79] Ministry of Corporate Affairs (n 64) 21. It also cites Australia, Mexico, the US, and France. ibid 22. The revision sought to align the NVGs with the SDGs and the United Nations Guiding Principles on Business and Human Rights. ibid 5. Global standards assessed include the United Nations Global Compact, Global Reporting Initiative, Integrated Reporting, Carbon Disclosure Project (CDP), ISO 26000, and SASB. ibid 19–20.

[80] BRSR Circular (n 78) 2.

[81] Federation of Indian Chambers of Commerce & Industry, 'Driving Climate Action through Disclosures: BRSR as Bedrock for ESG Action in India' (10 November 2021), para 16.

[82] ibid.

[83] ibid.

3.3 China

The year 2024 gained recognition as the "year for disclosure" in China.[84] In April, Chinese stock exchanges implemented climate disclosure aligned with international standards for listed companies.[85] By May 2024, the Chinese government published draft sustainability disclosures based on ISSB IFRS S1 for public comment.[86] By the end of the year, China had issued its first unified sustainability disclosure framework for voluntary adoption.[87] These measures highlight China's efforts to align domestic disclosure requirements with global reporting standards for climate-related information, even if full convergence remains elusive. The evolution of climate disclosure in China closely aligns with the party-state's regulatory priorities to achieve climate neutrality, reflecting its leverage as "owner-regulator-financier" in shaping sustainability reporting.[88]

China has a mixed regime of voluntary and mandatory requirements, based on international disclosure standards, issued by the Ministry of Ecology and Environment (MEE), the China Securities Regulatory Commission (CSRC), the State-Owned Assets Supervision and Administration Commission of the State Council (SASAC), and Chinese stock exchanges.[89] Virginia Harper Ho has labelled China as an "adaptive importer" of sustainability disclosures.[90] While earlier initiatives seemed relatively more endogenous, Chinese climate reporting is increasingly influenced and shaped by international policies and frameworks.[91]

84 'China Embarks on a Journey of ESG Disclosure: 2024 Progress and Focus for 2025' (*United Nations Environment Programme*, 7 January 2025) <https://www.unepfi.org/industries/banking/china-embarks-on-a-journey-of-esg-disclosure/> accessed 1 July 2025.

85 Shanghai Stock Exchange (SSE), *Guidelines No. 14 of Shanghai Stock Exchange for Self-Regulation of Listed Companies—Sustainability Report (Trial)* (12 April 2024) (SSE Guidelines); Beijing Stock Exchange (BSE), *Continuous Supervisory Guidelines No. 11 for Companies Listed on Beijing Stock Exchange—Sustainability Report (Trial)* (12 April 2024) (BSE Guidelines); PwC, 'Guidelines on Self-Regulation of Listed Companies—Sustainability Report (Trial) of the People's Republic of China' (18 April 2024) <https://www.pwccn.com/en/services/audit-and-assurance/capabilities/publications/guidelines-self-regulation-listed-companies-apr2024.html#:~:text=April%202024,ending%20on%2031%20December%202025> accessed 1 July 2025.

86 Giulia Interesse, 'China Releases ESG Reporting Standards for Businesses' (*China Briefing*, 20 June 2024) <https://www.china-briefing.com/news/china-releases-esg-reporting-standards-for-businesses/> accessed 1 July 2025.

87 Giulia Interesse, 'China Unveils Its First Set of Basic Standards for Corporate Sustainability (ESG) Disclosure' (*China Briefing*, 23 December 2024) <https://www.china-briefing.com/news/china-unveils-basic-standards-for-corporate-sustainability-esg-disclosure/> accessed 1 July 2025.

88 Edmund Downie, Erica Downs, and Yushan Lou, 'China's Climate Disclosure Regime: How Regulations, Politics, and Investors Shape Corporate Climate Reporting (Columbia University CGEP 2023) 10. See also Helen Hong Yang and Alan Farley, 'Convergence or Divergence? Corporate Climate-change Reporting in China' (2016) 24 International Journal of Accounting & Information Management 391, 395–97 (describing the role of the Chinese government in fostering climate disclosure).

89 Downie, Downs, and Lou (n 88) 34–35 (describing the roles of MEE, SASAC and CSRC in the Chinese disclosure framework); Harper Ho, China & Transnational Green Finance (n 6) 21–22.

90 Harper Ho, China & Transnational Green Finance (n 6) 20–21 (noting that adaptation may be found in CSRC rules encouraging poverty alleviation and rural development disclosure).

91 In 2011, a report by the International Finance Corporation noted that '[m]ost domestic sustainability guidelines feature local characteristics while also being in line with international guidelines'. International Finance Corporation, 'Sustainability Reporting Guidelines: Mapping & Gap Analyses for Shanghai Stock Exchange' (*International Finance Corporation*, June 2011) 22 < https://documents1.worldbank.org/curated/en/939331468012023031/pdf/626360PUB0Suso0B0x0361488B0PUBLIC0.pdf> accessed 1 July 2025. In 2016, Yang and Farley concluded that there was 'a significant overlap'

The MEE imposes mandatory emissions disclosures on companies identified by the government as high polluting based on violations of environmental obligations since 2003,[92] a requirement that was expanded over time.[93] Starting in 2021, the CSRC listing rules have encouraged voluntary disclosure of measures to reduce carbon emissions by listed companies.[94] The CSRC also encourages the disclosure of efforts related to the active fulfilment of social responsibilities, poverty alleviation, and rural revitalisation.[95]

Under the guidance of the CSRC, the Shenzhen Stock Exchange (SZSE) issued voluntary CSR guidelines in 2006,[96] and the Shanghai Stock Exchange (SSE) introduced environmental disclosures guidelines in 2008.[97] The CSR guidelines recommended disclosure of environmental protection policies, including reduction of raw materials and fuel consumption, minimisation of negative environmental impacts, and actions supporting sustainable development.[98] They also encouraged listed companies to adopt low pollutant emissions equipment and processes.[99] At the same time, SASAC guidelines urged state-owned enterprises to fulfil their social responsibility.[100] These initiatives "drew strongly on the CPC's [Communist Party of China] political ideology", which sought to "model international best practice in corporate reporting".[101] While sustainability reporting by Chinese companies experienced "rapid growth" at the time,[102] the absence of comprehensive guidelines resulted in low comparability and reliability of disclosures.[103]

As previously noted, SSE and SZSE—which are fully owned by the government—established mandatory sustainability reporting requirements for Chinese listed companies in 2024.[104] Since 2026, Shanghai and Shenzhen apply the sustainability requirements to top listed domestic companies and dual-listed companies.[105] The climate disclosure framework, aligned

between Chinese and international guidelines, but the latter 'tend to be more general'. They also found 'disclosure items that are unique to the Chinese context'. Yang and Farley (n 88) 392. In 2024, Harper Ho affirmed that China has been 'an importer rather than an exporter, reflecting the increased settling of transnational TCFD-based corporate reporting standards'. Harper Ho, China & Transnational Green Finance (n 6) 23.

92 The Reporting Exchange, 'An Overview of Sustainability and Corporate Reporting in China' (Climate Disclosures Standards Board and World Business Council for Sustainable Development 2018) 7 <https://www.wbcsd.org/wp-content/uploads/2023/12/The-Reporting-Exchange-An-overview-of-sustainability-and-corporate-reporting-in-China.pdf> accessed 1 July 2025.

93 Downie, Downs, and Lou (n 88) 33–34.

94 Harper Ho, China & Transnational Green Finance (n 6) 20.

95 ibid.

96 SZSE, *Shenzhen Stock Exchange Social Responsibility Instructions to Listed Companies* (25 September 2006) (SZSE CSR Guidelines).

97 Yang and Farley (n 88) 397; The Reporting Exchange (n 92) 7.

98 SZSE CSR Guidelines (n 96) arts 27–28.

99 ibid art 29.

100 Yang and Farley (n 88) 397.

101 ibid 396.

102 International Finance Corporation (n 91) 9.

103 ibid 2–3.

104 SSE Guidelines (n 85); BSE Guidelines (n 85); PwC (n 85). The stock exchanges also published implementation guides for the reporting requirements. See Shanghai Stock Exchange, 'SSE Releases Sustainability Reporting Guidance to Drive High-Quality ESG reporting by Listed Companies' 17 January 2025.

105 SSE 2024 Guidelines (n 85) art 3; PwC (n 85). The Beijing Stock Exchange, which lists primarily small and medium entities, adopted voluntary reporting standards for listed companies. BSE Guidelines (n 85) art 3.

with ISSB standards, includes reporting on climate risks and opportunities, as well as their impact on the company's business model, operations, development strategy, financial positions, operational results, cash flows, and financing methods and costs.[106] Companies must also report on climate-related transition plans, indicators, and targets.[107] Disclosure is mandatory for Scope 1 and 2 emissions and voluntary for Scope 3 emissions.[108] Moreover, reporting entities must describe technologies, products, and services that contribute to decarbonisation and carbon neutrality.[109]

The government also introduced unified sustainability reporting standards for Chinese companies in 2024, the Corporate Sustainability Disclosure Standards—Basic Standards (Trial) (CSDS). These standards draw explicitly from IFRS S1,[110] but depart from ISSB's single materiality standard to embrace double materiality.[111] The disclosures, which cover climate, environmental, social, and governance-related topics,[112] remain voluntary. Chinese authorities have announced plans to establish mandatory sustainability and climate-related disclosure standards by 2027 and implement an ISSB-aligned disclosure framework for all Chinese companies by 2030.[113]

3.4 South Africa

Hailed as a "global leader in sustainable corporate governance",[114] South Africa was a pioneer in requiring integrated reporting for listed companies in 2010.[115] However, it still lacks a mandatory framework for climate-related disclosures within corporate law or securities regulation. Corporate climate disclosure remains voluntary in South Africa through a combination of standards by the King Code and the JSE,[116] which require integrated reporting on an apply and explain basis.[117]

Although the King Code does not explicitly address climate-related disclosure, the King IV Guidance Paper on the Responsibilities of Governing Bodies in Responding to Climate Change, issued in 2021, recommends disclosure of the impacts of climate-related risks on governance, strategy, risk management, and performance.[118] It also advises boards to report on

106 SSE Guidelines (n 85) arts 21–22; BSE Guidelines (n 85) arts 21–22.

107 SSE 2024 Guidelines (n 85) art 23; BSE 2024 Guidelines (n 85) art 23; PwC (n 85).

108 SSE 2024 Guidelines (n 85) art 24; BSE 2024 Guidelines (n 85) art 24; PwC (n 85).

109 SSE 2024 Guidelines (n 85) art 28; BSE 2024 Guidelines (n 85) art 28; PwC (n 85).

110 Interesse (n 86).

111 Lake Wang, 'China's New ESG Reporting Standard Leaves Room for Local Elements' (*Asian Corporate Governance Association*, 24 June 2024) <https://www.acga-asia.org/blog-detail.php?id=86> accessed 1 July 2025.

112 'China Takes Steps Towards Unified National Sustainability Disclosure Regime' (*Climate Cooperation China*, 24 January 2025) <https://climatecooperation.cn/climate/china-takes-steps-towards-aunified-national-sustainability-disclosure-regime/> accessed 1 July 2025.

113 Interesse (n 86).

114 Christopher M Bruner, *The Corporation as Technology: Re-Calibrating Corporate Governance for a Sustainable Future* (OUP 2022) 227.

115 JSE Limited Listing Requirements (Service Issue 13); Robert G Eccles, George Serafeim, and Pippa Armbrester, 'Integrated Reporting in South Africa' 3 (*Harvard Business School Case No. 9-413-038*, September 2012) (rev November 2012) 1.

116 See, for a description, Harper Ho and Park (n 6) 295.

117 Institute of Directors in Southern Africa *King IV Report on Corporate Governance for South Africa* (2016) 28; Johannesburg Stock Exchange, *JSE Limited Listing Requirements, Service Issue 31* (January 2024) item 7.F.

118 Institute of Directors in South Africa *King IV Guidance Paper: Responsibilities of Governing Bodies in Responding to Climate Change* (2021) 17.

the entity's commitment to respond to climate change and mitigation actions.[119] The Guidance Paper supports the double materiality standard for climate disclosure.[120]

In 2022, the JSE issued voluntary Sustainability Disclosure Guidance and Climate Disclosure Guidance, which are informed by global standards while encouraging a "stakeholder-inclusive" approach.[121] The primary objective of the Climate Disclosure Guidance is to support alignment of JSE-listed companies' disclosure with ISSB and the King IV Guidance Paper.[122] The CEO of JSE Group explained that the sustainability reporting guidance aims to "help companies navigate the landscape of reporting standards" while "provid[ing] explicitly for the South African context".[123]

Although the structure and requirements almost entirely reproduce ISSB standards, the JSE goes beyond them by incorporating a double materiality approach.[124] The Climate Disclosure Guidance includes stakeholder-related disclosures for each of the four climate disclosure pillars of ISSB—governance, strategy, risk, and metrics and targets. These disclosures encompass monitoring of affected stakeholders' views, the company's stakeholder engagement processes, impacts of the business strategy on people, the environment, and the economy, transition plans' commitment to stakeholder engagement with workers, and communities.[125] They also cover steps taken to access a variety of internal and external perspectives in management risk identification, as well as metrics on stakeholder engagement with workers and communities on transition plans.[126] The EU's CSRD and ESRS, enacted in 2022 and 2023, respectively, mandate similar disclosures.[127]

The JSE attributes the concept of double materiality to the European Commission.[128] However, inspired by GRI guidelines, South African voluntary sustainability reporting has embodied stakeholder concerns into the materiality assessment for sustainability reporting since 2002.[129] Scholars have considered South Africa a "prominent" and "innovative" player in sustainability and integrated reporting, which is partly credited to the country's "political history and transition from apartheid to multi-racial democracy".[130]

In 1994, King I provided for a "board duty" to "present a balanced and understandable assessment of the company's position in reporting to stakeholders", including "material matters of [their] significant interest and concern".[131] In 2002, King II introduced a specific section

[119] ibid 18.

[120] ibid 17.

[121] Johannesburg Stock Exchange *JSE Climate Disclosure Guidance* (2022) (JSE Climate Guidance); Johannesburg Stock Exchange, *JSE Sustainability Disclosure Guidance* (2022) (JSE Sustainability Guidance).

[122] JSE Climate Guidance (n 121) 14.

[123] JSE Sustainability Guidance (n 121) 3.

[124] JSE Climate Guidance (n 121) 16.

[125] ibid 26–28.

[126] ibid 31–33.

[127] See (n 41).

[128] JSE Climate Guidance (n 121) 16.

[129] Institute of Directors in Southern Africa *King II Report on Corporate Governance for South Africa* (2002) 290, 339 ('The level of stakeholder interest in a given aspect or indicator is the key determinant of its significance, or materiality, to a sustainability report').

[130] Alexandra F Clayton, Jayne M Rogerson, and Isaac Rampedi, 'Integrated Reporting vs. Sustainability Reporting for Corporate Responsibility in South Africa' (2015) 29 Bulletin of Geography: Socio-Economic Series 7, 10.

[131] Institute of Directors in Southern Africa, *King Report on Corporate Governance* (1994) (King I) Principles 9.1–9.3, 33; King II (n 129) para 4 ('Unlike its counterparts in other countries at the time . . . the King Committee in 1994 successfully formalised the need for companies to recognise that they no longer act independently from the societies and the environment in which they operate'); G J Rossouw,

on "integrated sustainability reporting", which included a description of the company's "social, transformation, ethical, safety, health and environmental management policies and practices".[132] However, companies were left to develop their own materiality standards while having regard for "international models and guidelines, as well as national statutory definitions".[133] The Code linked sustainability reporting to the African philosophy of "Ubuntu", noting that "[i]nternational experience . . . is a wake-up call to Africans not to abandon their cultures when they become part of the business sector, but to import and infuse these practices into the corporate world".[134]

In 2009, King III further clarified South Africa's conception of an "integrated report", explaining that sustainability reporting should not "be a matter of collating information and reporting at the end of the year", but "integrated with other aspects of the business process and managed throughout the year".[135] In 2016, King IV reproduced this reporting framework anchored on the notions of corporate citizenship, stakeholder inclusivity, and sustainable development.[136] While previous versions applied on a comply or explain basis, King IV established an "apply or explain" framework.[137] These developments are consistent with Global South values and needs favouring the embrace of broader objectives in private law.[138]

4. Climate Disclosure Requirements in the Global North and Global South

This section compares the corporate climate disclosure frameworks of the five largest economies in each of the Global North (the US, Germany, Japan, UK, and France) and Global South (China, India, Brazil, Indonesia, and Mexico) as of June 2025.[139] In the US, we consider both Securities and Exchange Commission (SEC) and California climate disclosure frameworks due to the state's pioneering approach to climate disclosure and significant economic importance.[140] Before proceeding, a caveat is in order: There is major variation in the size of capital markets, measured by market capitalisation, of the jurisdictions examined, which may hinder comparability. The total market capitalisation of Global North jurisdictions is about four times larger than the total market capitalisation of Global South jurisdictions. The US alone represents 75.99% of the total market capitalisation of the largest Global North economies and

A van der Watt, and D P Malan, 'Corporate Governance in South Africa' (2002) 37 Journal of Business Ethics 289, 300 (describing King I as the 'first report on corporate governance' to adopt an 'integrated approach').

[132] King II (n 129) Principle 5.1.1.

[133] ibid Principle 5.1.3.

[134] ibid 99.

[135] Institute of Directors in Southern Africa, *King III Report on Governance for South Africa* (2016) (King III) 110.

[136] King IV (n 117) 23.

[137] King IV (n 117) 7. The 'apply or explain' approach was described as 'the original intellectual thinking of the King Committee'. See also Parmi Natesan and Prieur du Plessis, 'Why King IV's "Apply and Explain" Is So Important' (*Institute of Directors in South Africa*, 20 February 2019) (noting that it 'decisively moves away from a compliance-based approach').

[138] Davis and Pargendler (n 14).

[139] For selection criteria, see (n 22). See also Table 19.2.

[140] Loyti Cheng, David A Zilberberg, and Emily Roberts, 'California Enacts Major Climate-related Disclosure Laws' (*Harvard Forum on Corporate Governance*, 22 October 2023) ('It is estimated that S.B. 253 and S.B. 261 will cover over 5,000 and 10,000 companies, respectively'); Dani Anguiano, 'California's Economy Surpasses Japan's as it Becomes Fourth Largest in World' (*The Guardian*, 24 April 2025).

TABLE 19.1 Total Equity Market Capitalisation of the Largest Economies in the Global North and South in USD (2022)

Global North		Global South	
Jurisdiction	*Market capitalisation*	*Jurisdiction*	*Market capitalisation*
US	40,297,980.32	China	11,469,346.09
Japan	5,380,475.46	India	3,603,482.44
UK	3,095,983.43	Brazil	794,417.90
France	2,365,950.24	Indonesia	610,288.39
Germany	1,889,663.94	Mexico	454,370.43
Total	**53,030,053.39**	**Total**	**16,931,905.25**

Source: World Bank Group, 'Market Capitalization of Listed Domestic Companies (Current US$)' (*World Bank Open Data*, 2025) <https://data.worldbank.org/indicator/CM.MKT.LCAP.CD>.

57.6% of the combined North and South market capitalisation of the jurisdictions examined. Similarly, China and India together account for 89% of Global South market capitalisation and 21.54% of the total North and South market capitalisation—while Mexico, which has the smallest capital market in our sample, only represents 2.68% of the market capitalisation of the jurisdictions examined. This context is important as significantly smaller levels of capital market development reduce the scope of application and practical relevance of corporate climate disclosure rules.

Notably, we find significant recent convergence in the adoption of mandatory climate disclosure standards in the last decade: All the largest economies in the Global North and South have imposed some form of climate reporting requirement on public companies. Since the 2025 decision by the US SEC to end its defence of the climate disclosure rule, the United States stands out as an outlier among the largest Global North and Global South economies in lacking corporate climate disclosure requirements at the federal level.[141]

The rapid growth of mandatory climate disclosure was significantly influenced by the emergence of international climate disclosure standards as a product of "international corporate law".[142] The disclosure schemes of all Global North jurisdictions and three Global South jurisdictions are explicitly based on the main international climate reporting frameworks (TCFD, ISSB, or ESRS). These frameworks can be described as "legal implants" as they were first conceived at the supranational level with the aim of international adoption—unlike traditional "legal transplants" that reflect the transpositions of legal solutions originating in a given jurisdiction to a foreign context.[143] Except for Germany and France, which follow the more demanding ESRS, all of the largest Global North jurisdictions have adopted TCFD-based standards. Interestingly, the Global South was faster to adopt—even if occasionally slower to implement—ISSB, TCFD's cutting-edge successor, which has been embraced by Brazil and

141 'SEC Votes to End Defense of Climate Disclosure Rules' (*SEC Press Release*, 27 March 2025).
142 On 'international corporate law', see Pargendler, Rise of International Corporate Law (n 29).
143 On 'legal implants', see ibid 1774–76.

Mexico. In China, regulators developed specific standards for Chinese companies, which also present a "high level of interoperability" with ISSB and GRI.[144] Like the EU, China has diverged from TCFD and ISSB standards, which are based on single materiality, by adopting double materiality.

International influence, even if less explicit, cannot be ruled out in India and Indonesia. Indian regulators consulted "on a one to one basis" with the SASB, GRI, and World Bank before introducing the current regime for sustainability disclosure,[145] whose preparatory reports also took account of developments in the international sphere.[146] Likewise, GRI was "one of the guidelines" used by regulators in developing the Indonesian sustainability report,[147] which was established as part of the country's Sustainable Finance Plan—a national framework for sustainable development formulated with input from a wide range of national and international organisations and foreign governments.[148] Although neither India nor Indonesia explicitly prescribe a materiality approach for sustainability reporting, both frameworks hint at elements of impact materiality.[149]

Despite high-level convergence in the adoption of mandatory corporate climate disclosure frameworks, there are differences with respect to the scope and content of mandatory rules, which are generally more expansive in the Global North jurisdictions examined. Four out of five jurisdictions examined in the Global North, but only two out of five in the Global South, have some form of Scope 3 disclosure requirement in place. In the Global North, EU jurisdictions have mandatory Scope 3 emissions disclosure and the UK imposes Scope 3 disclosure related to business travel for large unquoted companies and LLPs, but all other Scope 3 emissions remain voluntary.[150] California's state-level statutory disclosure also covers Scope 3 emissions, though federal-level SEC rules limited emissions reporting to Scopes 1 and 2.

[144] KPMG, 'China Stock Exchanges Finalised Mandatory Sustainability Reporting Requirements for Larger Listed Entities' (2024) 7; Kazuma Osaki and Di Tang, 'China's Sustainability Reporting for Listed Companies' *PRI Policy Briefing* (November 2024) 3.

[145] Securities and Exchange Board of India, 'Memorandum on Business Responsibility and Sustainability Reporting by listed entities' 4.

[146] See (n 79).

[147] Otoritas Jasa Keuangan, *Roadmap for Sustainable Finance in Indonesia 2015–2019* (December 2014) 3–4.

[148] ibid 5–6. OJK held consultations with the International Finance Corporation (IFC)-World Bank, Swiss State Secretariat for Economic Affairs, US Agency for International Development, and multiple government entities and branches.

[149] Indonesian companies must disclose their impact on society and the environment. Otoritas Jasa Keuangan, OJK Regulation No. 51/POJK.03/2017 (27 July 2017) arts. 1(13), 10(1)-(3), and 12. See, concluding that Indonesia adopts a double materiality approach, 'The Future of Business: Evolving Through ESG and Climate Reporting: Indonesia' (*RSM*, 9 January 2025); 'ESG in APAC: Indonesia by SSEK Law Firm' (*Slaughter and May*, 2024). Indian companies must report 'material responsible business conduct and sustainability issues' that 'present a risk or an opportunity'. BRSR Circular (n 78) Annexure I. We found sources indicating that the country follows a double materiality approach and others suggesting that it adheres to single materiality. Compare 'ESG in APAC: India by Khaitan & Co' (*Slaughter and May*, 2024) with KPMG, *Business responsibility and sustainability reporting: the new dimension of ESG reporting* (2021) 3. See also Sugandha Yadav, 'Beyond materiality: Materiality in ESG disclosures under securities regulations in India' (2023) Working Paper <https://ssrn.com/abstract=4793785> (concluding that India's materiality approach for sustainability reporting is unclear).

[150] HM Government, *Environmental Reporting Guidelines: Including Streamlined Energy and Carbon Reporting Guidance* (March 2019) 50.

Only Japan has adopted Scope 1 and 2 disclosures for Prime Market listed companies under TCFD on a comply-or-explain, rather than on a strictly mandatory basis.[151] A survey indicates that 84% of the top 225 listed companies in the country—the Nikkei 225—disclosed such emissions in 2024.[152] All Japanese listed companies must report on climate risks, but disclosure of metrics and targets—which includes emissions—remains voluntary.[153] In the Global South, Brazil and Mexico require disclosure of material Scope 3 emissions under ISSB, but China and India limit GHG reporting to Scopes 1 and 2 emissions. Indonesia requires emissions disclosure by type, without following the GHG Protocol,[154] standing out as the only jurisdiction in our sample that does not adhere to the Protocol's standards for emissions reporting.

In terms of scope of application, three Global North jurisdictions require disclosure from non-listed entities, but no Global South jurisdiction does so. EU standards are again the most rigorous in covering listed and non-listed companies, as well as small and medium entities. Under the Omnibus proposal, however, the scope of the CSRD may be "reduced by about 80%" with exclusion of large undertakings with up to 1,000 employees and small and medium entities.[155] Standards in both the UK and California go beyond listed companies to include large private entities exceeding certain size thresholds.[156] The exceptions in the Global North are the US (federal level) and Japan, which confine climate disclosure to listed companies.

5. Regulatory Tendencies in the Global South

This section examines the adoption of corporate climate disclosure by the five largest Global South jurisdictions and South Africa in light of three perspectives on their regulatory tendencies: The resistance view, the foreign influence view, and the legal heterodoxy view.

Exemplifying legal heterodoxy in the Global South, both India and South Africa were pioneers in sustainability disclosure initiatives with an emphasis on social and environmental impact—though not using the language of double materiality and without a targeted focus on climate disclosure. Introduced in 2012, India's BRR preceded climate reporting initiatives in Global North jurisdictions often considered pioneers, such as the UK, the EU, and France, although the latter subsequently adopted more stringent standards. In the UK, all listed companies are required to disclose GHG emissions since 2013.[157] It was not until 2014 that the EU

[151] Tokyo Stock Exchange, Securities Listing Regulations (1 April 2024) 3.1.3.

[152] KPMG Sustainable Value Services Japan, *Survey of Corporate Reports in Japan 2024: Towards Corporate Reporting for Sustainable Value* (April 2025) 40–41S.

[153] Financial Services Agency, *Publication of the Finalized Amendments to the 'Cabinet Office Order on Disclosure of Corporate Affairs' and Other Relevant and Applicable Cabinet Office Orders after Public Consultation* (*FSA Weekly Review No.* 524, 9 February 2023).

[154] OJK (n 149); Otoritas Jasa Keuangan, OJK Circular Letter No. 16/SEOJK.04/2021 (29 June 2021).

[155] Commission, 'Proposal for a Directive of the European Parliament and of the Council Amending Directives (EU) 2022/2464 and (EU) 2024/1760 as Regards the Dates from Which Member States Are to Apply Certain Corporate Sustainability Reporting and Due Diligence Requirements' COM (2025) 80 final 3–4.

[156] HM Government, *Environmental Reporting Guidelines: Including Streamlined Energy and Carbon Reporting Guidance* (March 2019) 50; S.B. 253, 2022–2023 Leg., Reg. Sess. (Cal. 2023) (all business entities doing business in California with annual revenue over USD 1,000,000,000); S.B. 261, 2022–2023 Leg., Reg. Sess. (Cal. 2023) (all business entities doing business in California with annual revenue over USD 500,000,000).

[157] The Companies Act 2006 (Strategic Report and Directors' Report) Regulations 2013, SI 2013/1970, pt. 7, 15, 20 (UK). In the context of ESG disclosure, see Harper Ho and Park (n 6) 306 (describing the UK as a 'global leader in the promotion of non-financial reporting').

introduced the Non-Financial Reporting Directive (NFRD), which requires disclosure of development, performance, position, and impact of the company on "environmental, social and employee matters, respect for human rights, anti-corruption and bribery matters".[158] In 2015, France's Energy Transition Law introduced comply-or-explain disclosure of climate financial risks, measures to mitigate them, the consequences of the company's activities and the use of the goods and services it produces on climate change.[159] France has been described as an "early mover"[160] and "pioneer" that "launche[d] an international movement",[161] despite similar Indian disclosures being in place three years earlier. Similarly, South Africa's King Code incorporated impact materiality for sustainability reporting twelve years before the EU adopted this approach in the 2014 NFRD.[162]

Foreign influence has also played a key role in the Global South, as it has in the Global North. None of the jurisdictions examined have escaped the global diffusion of international disclosure standards. Some Global South jurisdictions, such as Brazil and Mexico, have strictly adhered to ISSB standards.

At the same time, there is only limited evidence of resistance to the climate disclosure agenda in the Global South. On the one hand, despite their early roles in sustainability disclosure, South Africa still lacks mandatory climate disclosure requirements, while India's framework currently falls short of the standards set by global climate reporting frameworks. On the other hand, Brazil, China, and Mexico have embraced broader requirements compared to the US and Japan, falling behind only EU jurisdictions and California, which contradicts a strong version of the climate resistance view in this area.

6. Conclusion

In recent years, there has been a remarkable rise in corporate climate disclosure both in the largest Global North and Global South economies. We observe the influence of international standards in the Global South and Global North, as well as Global South legal heterodoxy. Brazil was the first jurisdiction to adopt ISSB standards, which is consistent with the foreign influence view. India and South Africa pioneered distinct stakeholder-oriented approaches to sustainability disclosure, which exemplify legal heterodoxy in the Global South. The scope of climate disclosure obligations in the largest Global South economies is generally more limited than that in the largest Global North economies given the EU's leadership in this area but exceeds that of other jurisdictions such as the US and Japan.

[158] Directive (EU) 2014/95 of 22 October 2014 amending Directive 2013/34/EU as regards disclosure of non-financial and diversity information by certain large undertakings and groups [2014] OJ L330/1.

[159] Loi n° 2015–992 du 17 août 2015 relative à la transition énergétique pour la croissance verte (amending Code de commerce, Art. L225-37 and Art. L225-102-1), Art. 173. See also Principles for Responsible Investment (2016) 'French Energy Transition Law: Global Investor Briefing' 7–8. Earlier versions of the Commercial Code already required listed companies and non-listed companies meeting certain thresholds to report the ways in which they consider the social and environmental consequences of their activity and societal commitments in favour of sustainable development. Code de commerce, Article L225-102-1 as amended by Loi n° 2001-420 du 15 mai 2001, art. 116 (V) and Article L225-102-1, as amended by Loi n° 2010-788 du 12 juillet 2010, art. 225.

[160] Armour, Enriques, and Wetzer (n 5) 1111.

[161] Forum pour l'Investissement Responsable, 'Article 173-VI: Understanding the French Regulation on Investor Climate Reporting' (2016) 6.

[162] Milena Mitrovic, 'Materiality Concept(s) in the EU Sustainability (Non-Financial) Reporting' (2024) 62 (4) *Pravo i privreda* 603, 617.

This complex landscape defies conventional narratives of strong Global South resistance to North-led climate initiatives. There is significant variation both within the Global South and the Global North. Since the abandonment of the SEC Climate Rule in 2025, the US is the only large economy in our sample lacking substantial climate disclosure standards at the federal level. Once hailed as an influential leader in global corporate governance developments, the US is a clear laggard in this global trend—and the strongest exemplar of resistance in our sample. However, it remains to be seen whether the rapid and sweeping embrace of corporate climate disclosure around the world will survive the nationalistic and industry-led backlash that fuelled the US retreat.

TABLE 19.2 Corporate Climate Disclosure Frameworks: Global North (2025)

Jurisdiction	*Disclosure type*	*Standards*	*Adopted*	*Effective*	*Scope*	*Materiality*	*GHG emissions*
US	Mandatory	TCFD	2024	2025 - suspended	Listed companies	Single materiality	Scopes 1 and 2
California	Mandatory	TCFD	2023	2026	Large companies	Single materiality	Scopes 1, 2 and 3
Japan	Mandatory	TCFD	2023	2023	Listed companies	Single materiality	N/A
Germany	Mandatory	ESRS	N/A	2024*	Listed and non-listed companies	Double materiality	Scopes 1, 2 and 3
UK	Mandatory	TCFD	2018	2019	Listed and non-listed companies	Single materiality	Scopes 1, 2 and 3 (business travel)
France	Mandatory	ESRS	2023	2024*	Listed and non-listed companies	Double materiality	Scopes 1, 2 and 3

Corporate Climate Disclosure Frameworks: Global South (2025)

Jurisdiction	*Disclosure type*	*Standards*	*Year adopted*	*1st year effective*	*Scope*	*Materiality*	*GHG emissions*
China	Mandatory	Modified ISSB/ESRS	2024	2025	Large listed companies	Double materiality	Scopes 1 and 2
India	Mandatory	Bespoke (incl. GRI)	2021	2022	Large listed companies	?	Scopes 1 and 2
Brazil	Mandatory	ISSB	2023	2026	Listed companies	Single materiality	Scopes 1, 2 and 3
Mexico	Mandatory	ISSB	2025	2025	Listed companies	Single materiality	Scopes 1, 2 and 3
Indonesia	Mandatory	Bespoke (incl. GRI)	2017	2020*	Listed companies	?	Scopes 1, 2 and 3

* Implementation phased in for different categories of companies with extended deadlines for non-listed entities and small and medium enterprises.

CHAPTER 20

Finance

ARJUNA DIBLEY

1. Introduction

THE international climate regime has sought to mobilise public financial flows to climate activities for decades.[1] But these public financial flows have fallen short. The Climate Policy Initiative estimates that the gap between current financial flows and those needed to meet the goals of the Paris Agreement—to limit the global temperature increase to 1.5°C above pre-industrial levels—stands at US$5.93 trillion annually.[2] While public financial flows have been increasing over the years—a trend that almost certainly looks to be reversed at the time of writing[3]—the climate regime has gradually expanded its sources. Indeed, one of the Paris Agreement's central objectives is to make "finance flows consistent with a pathway towards low greenhouse gas emissions and climate-resilient development".[4] This broad "climate alignment" goal is intended to capture private sources of finance.[5] To be sure, private climate financing has increased in recent years, but a closer look at the data reveal that much of this growth comes from households in relation to domestic investment, rather than financial institutions.[6] As such, private finance flows by institutions

[1] Public finance has been a part of the climate regime since the 1992 United Nations Framework Convention on Climate Change, see Section 2 of this chapter.

[2] Baysa Naran and others, 'Global Landscape of Climate Finance 2024: Insights for COP29' (Climate Policy Initiative October 2024) 9, 43.

[3] At the time of writing, several donor countries have announced reduction in their foreign aid commitments, see, for example, 'Putting America First In International Environmental Agreements' (*The White House*, 20 January 2025) <https://www.whitehouse.gov/presidential-actions/2025/01/putting-america-first-in-international-environmental-agreements/> accessed 25 March 2025; 'Reevaluating And Realigning United States Foreign Aid' (*The White House*, 21 January 2025) <https://www.whitehouse.gov/presidential-actions/2025/01/reevaluating-and-realigning-united-states-foreign-aid/> accessed 25 March 2025; and Philip Loft and Philip Brien, 'UK to Reduce Aid to 0.3% of Gross National Income from 2025' (*UK Parliament*, 28 February 2025) <https://commonslibrary.parliament.uk/uk-to-reduce-aid-to-0-3-of-gross-national-income-from-2027/> accessed 26 March 2025.

[4] United Nations Framework Convention on Climate Change (UNFCCC), Decision 1/CP.21, 'Adoption of the Paris Agreement' (UN Doc FCCC/CP/2015/10/Add.1, 29 January 2016) Art 2.1(c) (Paris Agreement).

[5] The term 'climate alignment' is increasingly being used in policy documents and discussions to refer to Paris Agreement Art 2.1(c), see for example: OECD, *OECD Review on Aligning Finance with Climate Goals: Assessing Progress to Net Zero and Preventing Greenwashing* (OECD Publishing 2024) <https://www.oecd.org/en/publications/oecd-review-on-aligning-finance-with-climate-goals_b9b7ce49-en.html> accessed 1 April 2025.

[6] Naran et al (n 2) 28, 40; Barbara Buchner and others, 'Global Landscape of Climate Finance 2023' (Climate Policy Initiative November 2023) 19.

and other non-household actors in advanced economies will need to increase to meet this need.[7]

On its face, an increase in climate investment and climate risk management is in the interest of private financial system actors, at least over the long term. Not only is there money to be made from investing in some of the new green technologies which will underpin transitions to the economy as a result of climate change, but ongoing investment in high emitting technologies is contributing to climate-related physical, transition, and liability risks. Dirty investment drives up emissions, which in turn, are leading to increasing severity of climate impacts, higher levels of vulnerability in the real economy, and climate-related financial risks for financial actors.[8] Under any of the "long-tail" damages scenarios estimated by climate economic models, this could well lead to large-scale financial system shocks and losses.[9] Despite this, the financial system is plagued by market and regulatory failures that undermine the ability of financial actors to coordinate, act over longer time periods, and account for public goods. Hence the need for the climate-alignment goal, in the first place.

National policymakers, regulators, and investors have started to try and address the barriers to climate-aligned financial flows, but not under the banner of the Paris Agreement. Instead, under the guise of the so-called sustainable finance or environment, social, and governance (ESG) investment agenda, which has long had a "climate-first" focus, governments have widely adopted climate disclosure laws,[10] sustainability taxonomies, green bond standards, and regulatory tools like climate risk stress tests. These regulatory instruments are all largely aimed at correcting information deficits and asymmetries among firms, investors, and regulators in public financial markets. The regulatory interventions rest on the assumption that if market actors are provided with more complete and comparable climate-related information, they will efficiently allocate capital and avoid climate risks in a way which align the financial system more closely to the Paris Agreement goals.

Regulatory measures to date have addressed the genuine and much needed information gaps about climate change within financial markets. However, such measures are also producing unintended outcomes which are at odds with the Paris Agreement goals. Rational financial decision-making is not just resulting in firms and investors reducing carbon liabilities and climate risks. Instead, actors are also increasingly shifting high-carbon assets and climate-related risks to entities outside of the emerging climate-information ecosystem, including to actors who have the least capacity to respond to such liabilities and risks. This "leakage" of carbon liabilities and climate risks offends a fundamental notion under international climate law to address the distributional inequities arising because of climate change.

Achieving climate alignment requires broad reforms across domestic and international private law, which is an endeavour beyond this chapter's scope but addressed elsewhere in this handbook. Here, I focus on how private lawyers can confront the leakage arising from the climate information regime, which is a necessary condition if financial markets are to support climate alignment meaningfully. Drawing on emerging literature in corporate law, contract, and financial regulation, I show that existing legal tools primarily aim to deter firms from shifting carbon liability and climate risk. This chapter extends that conversation on "risk-shifters", exploring how law might also incentivise these firms to retire dirty assets. Because firms cannot

[7] Buchner et al (n 6) 19–20.

[8] Madison Condon, 'Market Myopia's Climate Bubble' (2022) 2022 Utah Law Review 63.

[9] See generally, Gernot Wagner and Martin L Weitzman, *Climate Shock: The Economic Consequences of a Hotter Planet* (Princeton University Press 2015).

[10] See Virginia Harper Ho, Chapter 23 of this handbook; Maria Eduardo Lessa and Mariana Pargendler, Chapter 19 of this handbook.

easily capture the public gains of closing high-emissions assets or reducing systemic climate risks, they underinvest in these positive externalities. I suggest that targeted instruments such as tax credits or transferable credits could help correct this misalignment.

I also consider how private law can shape the incentives of carbon and climate risk "recipients". All parties—risk-shifters, recipients, and governments—stand to gain from avoiding this transfer. To improve coordination, I argue for more transparent disclosure of climate risk-shifting and suggest that performance-based contracts, including sustainability-linked insurance contracts, could help to reduce climate risks in a smoother way that reduces the inequities of sharp finance withdrawal.

These mechanisms are not sufficient to achieve full climate alignment on their own. However, if information-based financial markets are to contribute meaningfully to climate goals, correcting these distortions is a necessary starting point.

The remainder of the chapter is set out as follows. Section 2 discusses the climate-alignment objective of the Paris Agreement and the key private law mechanisms advanced towards this end under the guise of the sustainable finance agenda. I highlight how these private-law instruments have predominantly focused on addressing information-based market failures. In Section 3, I argue that this narrow focus on information has created perverse incentives for investors to shift, rather than reduce, carbon liabilities and climate risks leading to leakage. In Section 4, I build on the existing legal scholarship and propose mechanisms that limit carbon and climate risk leakage, before concluding in Section 5.

2. How the Private Law Response to Climate Alignment Has Been Shaped by the Sustainable Finance Agenda

Finance as a theme has been central to the international climate regime since the 1992 United Nations Framework Convention on Climate Change (UNFCCC), the first global treaty to focus on the emerging threat of global warming. However, in its early development, finance was primarily considered within the domain of public-to-public transfers.[11] It was not until the late 2000s that the Conference of the Parties (COP) of the UNFCCC started to explicitly call for the provision of non-public sources of finance.[12] This call crystalised in the US$100 billion finance goal which included a request for finance from a "variety of sources, public and private, bilateral and multilateral, including alternative sources".[13] The COP decisions reflect the

[11] The UNFCCC requires its developed country parties to supply 'new and additional financial resources' for developing countries to formulate and implement climate-related policies. It further requires developed countries to 'assist the developing country Parties that are particularly vulnerable' in meeting the costs of adapting to the adverse effects of climate change. UNFCCC (9 May 1992) 1771 UNTS 107 arts 4.3 and 4.4.

[12] The Bali Action Plan called for '[i]mproved access to adequate, predictable and sustainable financial resources and financial and technical support, and the provision of new and additional resources, including official and concessional funding for developing country Parties'. UNFCCC, 'Report of the Conference of the Parties on its Thirteenth Session, Held in Bali from 3 to 15 December 2007: Action Taken by the Conference of the Parties' at its Thirteenth Session' (Addendum, FCCC/CP/2007/6/Add.1, United Nations 14 March 2008) 5.

[13] UNFCCC, 'Report of the Conference of the Parties on its Seventeenth Session, Held in Durban from 28 November to 11 December 2011: Action Taken by the Conference of the Parties at its Seventeenth Session' (Addendum, FCCC/CP/2011/9/Add.1, United Nations 15 March 2012) 23, [130].

historical emphasis of the UNFCCC framework, which points to public and private finance as a way of compensating parties for the distributional inequalities of climate change.

2.1 The Paris Climate-Alignment Goal

The Paris Agreement codified these COP decisions into a treaty calling for ongoing support to developing countries from a "wide variety of sources".[14] Indeed, the New Collective Quantified Goal agreed pursuant to the Paris Agreement at COP 29 in 2024 explicitly calls for mobilising at least US$1.3 trillion per year by 2035,[15] with developed countries "taking the lead, of [providing finance to developing countries of] at least USD 300 billion per year by 2035".[16]

Importantly, aside from these historical quantified finance provisions in the UNFCCC regime, the Paris Agreement also includes an overarching goal in Article 2.1(c): to make "finance flows consistent with a pathway towards low greenhouse gas emissions and climate-resilient development".[17] Sitting in the objective clause of the Agreement, the "climate-alignment" goal is puzzling. It refers neither to the standard terms used in historical climate finance provisions, nor to its providers and recipients. Instead, it adopts new terminology such as finance "flows", "consistent", and "pathway" that is not further defined. The way the climate-alignment objective interacts with other provisions, particularly Article 9, of the Paris Agreement has been the subject of some (although surprisingly limited) academic discussion.[18]

There are two opposing views in the literature on the climate-alignment objective. On the one hand, some argue that the objective clause is subjugated to other articles—particularly Articles 4 and 9—and can only refer to aligning finance flows from developed to developing countries.[19] Others suggest that the chapeau in the clause, which refers to all parties, would suggest that it is meant to apply more broadly than just developed to developing finance flows.[20] The latter broader interpretation seems to be confirmed by historical analysis of negotiating texts, and qualitative interviews with negotiators who suggest that the purpose of the clause is "to make all finance flows (and capital stocks) consistent with the agreement's mitigation and adaptation objectives".[21] This implies that the article is "not only about the provision of finance but also about advancing regulation such as for fixing market imperfections, setting directions and creating enabling environments".[22] This view seems to also be supported by ongoing discussions at the UNFCCC at the time of writing.[23]

14 Paris Agreement (n 4), art 9.3.

15 UNFCCC, 'Decision -/CMA.6: New Collective Quantified Goal on Climate Change' (advance unedited version) [7].

16 ibid [8].

17 Paris Agreement (n 4) art 2(1)(c).

18 Alexander Zahar, 'The Paris Agreement and the Gradual Development of a Law on Climate Finance' (2016) 6 Climate Law 75; Luis H Zamarioli and others, 'The Climate Consistency Goal and the Transformation of Global Finance' (2021) 11 Nature Climate Change 578; Megan Bowman, 'Polaris and Pluralism: Presenting a Legal Analytical Framework for Climate Finance' (2023) 17 Carbon & Climate Law Review 3.

19 Zahar (n 18).

20 Bowman (n 18); Zamarioli et al (n 18); Shelagh Whitley and others, 'Making Finance Consistent with Climate Goals: Insights for Operationalising Article 2.1c of the UNFCCC Paris Agreement' (ODI, WRI, RMI, E3G 2018).

21 Zamarioli et al (n 18).

22 ibid 581.

23 'First Workshop under the Sharm El-Sheikh Dialogue on Article 2, Paragraph 1(c) of the Paris Agreement and Its Complementarity with Article 9' (*United Nations Climate Change*) <https://unfccc.int/event/first-workshop-under-the-sharm-el-sheikh-dialogue-on-article-2-paragr

In sum, Article 2.1(c) of the Paris Agreement calls for a holistic approach to financial flows, to better attract climate finance beyond traditional public sector actors, and including, among others, private actors. Parties call for such flows to support vulnerable and developing countries. To do this effectively requires efforts on the part of governments and private actors to better align their incentives for climate-related investment activities.

2.2 Sustainable Finance and Information-based Market Failures

Governments and private actors have already taken some steps to try and address the incentive problems related to climate alignment. But their motivation for doing so has not only been driven by the UNFCCC process, but also by longer running efforts to realign the financial system in a way that accounts for the sustainable development agenda; what has come to be known more colloquially as the ESG investing or sustainable finance agenda. It is important to understand the origins of these sustainable finance efforts, as these have shaped the focus and direction of most private law climate-alignment efforts to date, at least in liberal market economies.

The concept of ESG, the forerunner to sustainable finance, emerged in the early 2000s.[24] During this era, and under the leadership of then-Secretary General Kofi Annan, the United Nations (UN) sought to build stronger relationships with investors, which they saw as pivotal for delivering the UN's Sustainable Development Goals—the social and economic development goals then guiding the UN's agenda. In 2003, the UN Environment Programme had established a Finance Initiative (UNEP-FI) that formed a working group of twelve asset management firms to explore the materiality of "Social, Environmental, and Corporate Governance Issues" for equity pricing.[25] And in 2005, the UN Global Compact published a report which captured some of the work of the UNEP-FI working group titled "Who Cares Wins", in which the ESG moniker was first used and through which the term came to reach a mass audience.[26]

This link between sustainable investments and a reduction in risks—or, in the language of the report, the "contribut[ion] to more stable and predictable markets"—was a hallmark of

aph-1c-of-the-paris-agreement> accessed 27 March 2025; UNFCCC, 'First Work in 2024 Under the Sherm el-Sheikh Dialogue on the Scope of Article 2, paragraph 1(c), of the Paris Agreement and its Complementarity with Article 9, of the Paris Agreement (Summary Report, SES/2024/WA1/SummaryReport, United Nations 9 August 2024) [27]–[29].

[24] Elizabeth Pollman, 'The Making and Meaning of ESG' (2024) 14 Harvard Business Law Review 403; 414; Elliot Wilson, 'The United Nations Free-Thinkers Who Coined the Term "ESG" and Changed the World' (*Euromoney*, 1 October 2021) <https://www.euromoney.com/article/294dqz2h1pqywgbyh3zls/esg/the-united-nations-free-thinkers-who-coined-the-term-esg-and-changed-the-world> accessed 27 March 2025; Thierry Roncalli, *Handbook of Sustainable Finance* (2022).

[25] United Nations Environment Programme Finance Initiative, 'The Materiality of Social, Environmental and Corporate Governance Issues to Equity Pricing' (CEO Briefing, August 2004) 2.

[26] In the words of the report, 'Ultimately, successful investment depends on a vibrant economy, which depends on a healthy civil society, which is ultimately dependent on a sustainable planet. In the long term, therefore, investment markets have a clear self-interest in contributing to better management of environmental and social impacts in a way that contributes to the sustainable development of global society. A better inclusion of environmental, social, and corporate governance (ESG) factors in investment decisions will ultimately contribute to more stable and predictable markets, which is in the interest of all market actors.' United Nations Global Compact, 'Who Cares Wins: Connecting Financial Markets to a Changing World' (Final Report, 2005), 3.

the sustainable investing movement that followed.[27] To operationalise the Who Cares Wins report, the UN Principles of Responsible Investment (UN-PRI) network was formed in 2005, promoting six mutually agreed principles, such as: "Principle 1: We will incorporate ESG issues into investment analysis and decision-making processes . . . Principle 3: We will seek appropriate disclosure on ESG issues by the entities in which we invest".[28]

As these principles make clear, the focus of sustainable investing was about creating standardised approaches for market participants to disclose sustainability information with a view to allow such participants to incorporate the information into their investment decision-making. In this way, the movement was built on top of orthodox thinking about the "informational efficiency" of the capital markets.[29]

In the informational efficiency view of the capital markets, rational investors, acting in their own self-interest, quickly absorb new information about financial assets and this drives their buying and selling activity.[30] But to enable these efficient financial markets, material information that could affect the price of assets should not be held back by misplaced incentive structures of investors or firms.[31] To this end, a legitimate source of intervention in the capital markets is to address information asymmetries, where one party in a transaction has more or better information than the other, or informational deficiencies, which can limit the efficient pricing of financial assets and thus the efficiency of the market.[32]

The sustainable finance agenda thus focuses heavily on correcting the informational shortcomings of financial markets. The foundational approach to ESG investing was for investors and companies to voluntarily provide sustainability information to each other. The movement's founders deliberately eschewed discussion of reforming financial institutions themselves, as this might have been unpopular with the founders and undermined their "insider" strategy.[33] This proved to be a sound strategic choice. Although the sustainable finance agenda and ESG have recently faced a significant backlash, at its peak it was a more than US$120 trillion industry, with more than half of all the world's institutional capital managed by investors committed to the UN PRI principles.[34]

Given this level of industry endorsement, the principles became the cornerstone of sustainable finance regulations. And the growth of such regulation has been significant. The UN PRI

[27] Pollman (n 24) 417–23.

[28] 'What Are the Principles for Responsible Investment?' (*Principles for Responsible Investment*) <https://www.unpri.org/about-us/what-are-the-principles-for-responsible-investment> accessed 26 March 2025.

[29] This 'efficient capital market hypothesis' is most famously explained in Eugene F Fama, 'Efficient Capital Markets: A Review of Theory and Empirical Work' (1970) 25 Journal of Finance 383.

[30] ibid.

[31] Ronald J Gilson and Reinier H Kraakman, 'The Mechanisms of Market Efficiency' (1984) 70 Vanderbilt Law Review 549.

[32] See, for example, Joseph E Stiglitz and Andrew Weiss, 'Credit Rationing in Markets with Imperfect Information' (1981) 71 American Economic Review 393.

[33] One of the key architects of ESG, James Gifford, characterised his strategy as a 'get more bees with honey' strategy: Elliot Wilson (n 24); see also James Marlay, 'From the Wilderness to the UN: How One Australian Influence the World of Investing' (*Livewire*, 24 May 2022) <https://www.livewiremarkets.com/wires/from-the-wilderness-to-the-un-how-one-australian-influenced-the-world-of-investing>.

[34] Principles for Responsible Investment, 'Principles for Responsible Investment: Annual Report 2024' (Annual Report, 2024) 5.

estimates that there are over 1,000 sustainable finance regulations enacted by governments, a more than ten-fold increase over twenty years.[35] This includes instruments such as:

- Mandatory or Voluntary Climate Risk Disclosure: Climate disclosure instruments require or encourage companies or investors to correct information asymmetries or deficiencies by analysing and then disclosing to the market details on their climate-related transition risk and physical risk exposures.[36] While some scholars argue that financial markets already price in these types of risks and thus no additional government intervention is justified,[37] many scholars in law and finance have argued that—through mandatory and standardised climate risk metrics—markets will be better able to price climate risks efficiently, mitigating the mispricing that can result from hidden information.[38]
- Sustainable Finance Taxonomies: A taxonomy acts as a legal "dictionary" that defines whether financial instruments qualify as environmentally sustainable.[39] By establishing clear technical criteria for what counts as "green" (e.g., significant contribution to climate mitigation, no significant harm to other objectives), they reduce ambiguity about sustainability definitions.[40] This provides a floor on the quality of green financial products, but is also used to prevent "greenwashing"—ensuring that only projects meeting transparent standards can be marketed as sustainable.[41]

[35] Hazell Ransome, 'Regulation Database Update: The Unstoppable Rise of RI Policy' (*Principles for Responsible Investment*, 17 March 2021) <https://www.unpri.org/pri-blog/regulation-database-update-the-unstoppable-rise-of-ri-policy/7352.article> accessed 27 March 2025. See also Virginia Harper Ho, Chapter 23 of this handbook.

[36] Madison Condon and others, 'Mandating Disclosure of Climate-Related Financial Risk' (2020) 23 New York University Journal of Legislation and Public Policy 745. See, for example, *Treasury Laws Amendment (Financial Market Infrastructure and Other Measures) Act 2024* (Cth) (Aus); The Enhancement and Standardization of Climate-Related Disclosures for Investors, 89 Fed Reg 21668 (March 6, 2024) (US); Companies (Strategic Report) (Climate-related Financial Disclosure) Regulations 2022 (UK); Hong Kong Exchange, *Rules and Guidance*, Appendix C1 (HK); 'Sustainability Reporting—Singapore Exchange (SGX)' <https://www.sgx.com/sustainable-finance/sustainability-reporting> accessed 26 March 2025 (SG).

[37] Paul G Mahoney and Julia D Mahoney, 'The New Separation of Ownership and Control: Institutional Investors and ESG' (2021) 2021 Columbia Business Law Review <https://journals.library.columbia.edu/index.php/CBLR/article/view/8639> accessed 25 March 2025.

[38] Condon et al (n 36); John Armour, Luca Enriques, and Thom Wetzer, 'Mandatory Corporate Climate Disclosures: Now, But How?' (2021) 2021 Columbia Business Law Review <https://journals.library.columbia.edu/index.php/CBLR/article/view/9106> accessed 9 June 2025.

[39] Nathan de Arriba-Sellier, 'Sustainable Finance: Green Taxonomies as Instruments of System Change?' in Josephine van Zeben and Chris Hilson (eds), *A Research Agenda for Environmental* (2025) <https://www.elgaronline.com/edcollchap-oa/book/9781035324408/book-part-9781035324408-19.xml> accessed 20 February 2025. Most countries are still in the process of developing their taxonomy, see, for example, Australian Sustainable Finance Institute and Australian Government, *Developing an Australian Sustainable Finance Taxonomy: Initial Phase* (Grant Report for Treasury, 30 June 2024) (Aus); HM Treasury, *UK Green Taxonomy* (Consultation, November 2024) (UK); Monetary Authority of Singapore, *Singapore-Asia Taxonomy for Sustainable Finance: 2023 Edition)* December 2023) (SG); Hong Kong Monetary Authority, *Hong Kong Taxonomy for Sustainable Finance* (3 May 2024) (HK).

[40] Arriba-Sellier (n 39).

[41] Amanda Shanor and Sarah E Light, 'Greenwashing and the First Amendment' (2022) 122 Columbia Business Law Review 2033; Sebastian Steuer and Tobias H Tröger, 'The Role of Disclosure in Green Finance' (2022) 8 Journal of Financial Regulation 1.

- Green Labels and Certifications: Regulators and industry bodies have also developed green labelling schemes to convey ESG information in a simple, credible manner.[42] Labels for financial products like green bonds and sustainable investment funds serve as shorthand indicators that a product meets certain ESG standards, helping to bridge the information gap between product providers and investors. In theory, a green label reduces search costs and uncertainty for investors who want to allocate capital to sustainable assets—they can rely on the label rather than performing complex due diligence on each product's ESG attributes.[43]

Governments around the world are starting to adopt these information-correcting regulatory approaches. Recent data suggest that around half of the sustainable finance regulatory instruments now on the books of governments around the world are focused on corporations or investors making sustainability and climate disclosures to the market.[44] Governments—at least developed countries—are also using these regulatory instruments to demonstrate their commitment to climate alignment under the Paris Agreement. For example, under the Paris Agreement, developed countries are required to submit biennial communications under Article 9.5, outlining projected levels of climate finance they intend to provide or which they have "mobilised".[45] Such reports, although not directly focused on Article 2.1 (c), often include references to it, and include references to climate disclosure obligations, green taxonomies, and labelling rules, among others.[46]

To be sure, not all sustainable finance regulation and regulatory actions to date have been in the form of capital markets regulation seeking to correct information-based market failures. Central banks and prudential regulators, for instance, have also played an increasingly important role in sustainable finance regulatory architecture.[47] Climate stress tests, for instance, serve to reveal the sensitivity of financial institutions' portfolios to plausible climate scenarios,

[42] See, for example, Australian Treasury and the Australian Office of Financial Management, *Australian Government Green Bond Framework* (December 2023) (Aus); Regulation (EU) 2023/2631 of the European Green Bonds and optional disclosures for bonds marketed as environmentally sustainable and for sustainability-linked bonds [2023] OJ L (EU); Ministry of Finance Singapore, *Singapore Green Bond Framework* (January 2025) (SG).

[43] Michael Eckhart, 'Financial Regulations and ESG Investing: Looking Back and Forward' in Daniel C Esty and Todd Cort (eds), *Values at Work: Sustainable Investing and ESG Reporting* (Palgrave Macmillan 2021) 220.

[44] Ransome (n 35); see also Emma Lecavalier and others, '2024 Oxford Climate Policy Monitor' (University of Oxford 2025) 18.

[45] Paris Agreement (n 4) art 9.5 requires biennial reporting of progress towards arts 9.1 and 9.3.

[46] Countries mostly report public law steps towards climate alignment in these reports, such as fossil fuel subsidy removal. But some report on steps towards climate alignment. See for example, Government of Canada, *Canada's Biennial Communication on Climate Finance 2024* (UNFCCC 2024) 4–5, 9–10 <https://unfccc.int/sites/default/files/resource/Canada_BC9.5_2024_EN.pdf> accessed 1 April 2025 (discusses sustainable finance efforts, including the establishment of the Sustainable Finance Action Council and support for climate-related financial disclosures (see esp. paras 17–18, 39–41); and Council of the European Union, *European Union Biennial Communication on Climate Finance 2024* (UNFCCC 2024) 8–9, 13 <https://unfccc.int/sites/default/files/resource/EU_BC9.5_2024.pdf> accessed 1 April 2025 (describes implementation of the EU Sustainable Finance Disclosure Regulation (SFDR) and its relevance to Article 2.1(c) alignment (see paras 21–24, 37)).

[47] Christina Skinner, 'Central Banks and Climate Change' (2021) 74 Vanderbilt Law Review 1301; Mercy Berman DeMenno, 'Environmental Sustainability and Financial Stability: Can Macroprudential Stress Testing Measure and Mitigate Climate-Related Systemic Financial Risk?' (2023) 24 Journal of Banking Regulation 445.

allowing regulators to understand the concentration and amplification of climate risk across the financial system, an issue unlikely to be detected by decentralised market actors. In this way, these measures are about protecting financial stability by producing ex-ante information for regulators about future climate risk at the level of financial systems.

Some financial regulatory measures move beyond mere information sharing between market participants and regulators. Central banks, for example, can actively seek to incentivise financial actors to make more green investments: The European Central Bank announced in 2022 that it would incorporate climate change considerations into the Eurosystem's purchases of corporate sector securities. To this end, the Eurosystem tilted its corporate bond purchases to favour green bonds in its primary market bidding behaviour.[48] Also, in some rare cases, governments have signalled that they are willing to directly address the barriers to increased sustainability-related investment arising from the way financial institutions themselves are regulated.[49] Indeed, sustainable finance regulatory efforts outside of liberal market economies do sometimes have a greater willingness to focus on addressing other market failures. For example, in 2022, the China Banking and Insurance Regulatory Commission issued guidelines requiring banks and insurance institutions to be guided by the state's pollution prevention and carbon neutrality goals, to ensure a gradual and orderly reduction in the carbon intensity of their asset portfolios, with the eventual aim of achieving carbon neutrality.[50]

Clearly, not all efforts towards climate alignment to date are focused on correcting information-based market failures. However, my claim in this section is that the balance of regulatory efforts, at least in liberal market economies, has been towards this end. This emphasis on information correction as the regulatory "tool of choice" is significant, because such approaches are having unintended consequences which could make the Paris Agreement climate-alignment goal harder to achieve.

3. How Information Correcting Regulation Can Undermine Climate Alignment Through Leakage

Private law scholars are not blind to the limits of information as a means of achieving climate alignment. Indeed, scholars have argued that the organisational structure of financial intermediaries,[51] the incentives of "green gatekeepers",[52] and the limits of shareholder lawsuits,[53]

[48] European Central Bank, 'Frequently Asked Questions on Incorporating Climate Change Considerations into Corporate Bond Purchases' (8 January 2025) <https://www.ecb.europa.eu/mopo/implement/app/html/ecb.faq_cspp_climate_change.en.html> accessed 26 March 2025.

[49] Australian Treasury, *Sustainable Finance Strategy* (Consultation Paper, November 2023) 28–30.

[50] China Banking and Insurance Regulatory Commission [2022] No 15 (Notice of the China Banking and Insurance Regulatory Commission on Printing and Distributing Green Finance Guidelines for the Banking and Insurance Industry) arts 12, 16.

[51] Roberto Tallarita, 'The Limits of Portfolio Primacy' (2023) 76 Vand L Rev 511; Tom Gosling, 'Universal Owners and Climate Change' (2025) 11 Journal of Financial Regulation 1.

[52] Luca Enriques, Alessandro Romano, and Andrew Tuch, 'Green Gatekeepers' (2024) 109 Minnesota Law Review 1.

[53] John Armour, Luca Enriques, and Thom Wetzer, 'Green Pills: Making Corporate Climate Commitments Credible' (2023) 65 Arizona Law Review 285, 312. See also Diane Strauss and Aisha I Saad, 'Can Investors Rely on Corporate Sustainability Commitments?' in Daniel C Esty and Todd Cort (eds), *Values at Work: Sustainable Investing and ESG Reporting* (Palgrave Macmillan 2020) 195–96.

among others, limit the extent to which information can result in more climate-supporting action in the economy. Part of the reason is that climate change is not just a financial markets problem, and does not only derive from information failures, but instead from collective action problems and other incentive problems at multiple levels which lead to unpriced negative externalities.[54] This range of problems and potential legal solutions are addressed in other chapters of this handbook; in this chapter, I focus on addressing the emerging problems in relation to the climate information system. I contend that as the growing climate information regulatory systems start to expand, these are also leading to leakage of carbon and climate risks which undermine the purpose of the climate-alignment goal.

There are two interrelated firm behaviours arising from the climate information measures to date which lead to leakage: namely, carbon and climate risk-shifting. What I refer to as carbon liability shifting is given various names in the extant legal scholarship: "brown-spinning",[55] "carbon shedding",[56] or "climate-driven asset partitioning".[57] This refers to a range of corporate law strategies to divest direct ownership—but not necessarily control—over an asset that has high emissions, usually in an attempt to evade requests for climate information or carbon prices imposed by an investor or regulator or partner. Where carbon liability shifting relates to responsibility for emissions, climate risk-shifting refers to the responsibility that firms have for climate-related financial risks. Climate risk-shifting arises where firms divest themselves from assets due to their exposure to physical or transition risks. In some cases, firms may divest themselves of carbon intensive assets to avoid transition risks, in which case they may be pursuing both carbon liability and climate risk-shifting. But often, climate risk-shifting occurs where financial institutions increase the costs of capital or retreat from a market, owing to rising climate risks. I discuss both processes in turn.

3.1 Carbon Liability Shifting

One of the primary pathways through which climate information might result in climate alignment is by investors stewarding high emissions companies towards a lower emissions pathway through shareholder engagement or litigation. The problem with the logic of this pathway is that companies presently have options available to them other than disclosing their high emissions; namely, they can shift their emissions from entities within the emerging climate-information system, to those outside it, such as state-owned enterprises (SOEs), private unlisted companies, or subsidiaries which are not caught by the system.[58] For instance, ConocoPhillips, a prominent high emissions firm in the United States, documented a substantial reduction of approximately 22% in its emissions during the year 2017. The primary driver of this decline was attributed to ConocoPhillips divesting certain oil and gas assets to Hilcorp Energy, which has been identified

54 Nadia Ameli and others, 'Climate Finance and Disclosure for Institutional Investors: Why Transparency Is Not Enough' (2020) 160 Climatic Change 565.

55 Alperen A Gözlügöl and Wolf-Georg Ringe, 'Net-Zero Transition and Divestments of Carbon-Intensive Assets' (2022) 56 UC Davis Law Review 1963.

56 Tracy D Hester, 'Spinning Off Carbon: Corporate Restructuring in a Climate Bankrupt World' 32 New York University Environmental Law Journal 339.

57 John Armour, Luca Enriques, and Thom Wetzer, 'Dark and Dirty Assets: Greening Climate-Driven Asset Partitioning' (14 June 2022) <https://blogs.law.ox.ac.uk/business-law-blog/blog/2022/06/dark-and-dirty-assets-greening-climate-driven-asset-partitioning> accessed 28 March 2025.

58 Gözlügöl and Ringe, 'Net-Zero Transition and Divestments of Carbon-Intensive Assets' (n 55).

as the preeminent methane emitter in the United States and is supported by the considerable resources of the private equity firm, Carlyle.[59]

The problem arises because the climate financial information system, which is being developed, and which focuses primarily on publicly traded companies, is exceedingly narrow. The world's most emissions-intensive firms operate outside the boundaries of the public financial markets and the accompanying climate information system.[60] Notably, SOEs, in which governments are controlling shareholders, are the most significant firms when it comes to fossil fuel supply, owning most of the world's oil, gas, and coal supply, and they play a significant role on the demand side of the energy system too.[61] However, SOEs often sit outside the ambit of disclosure requirements.[62] In other words, one of the most important firm types from a climate perspective is not captured by the climate information system.

The effect of this omission is that climate information requirements and investor action have contributed to carbon asset shifting, rather than writing off or phasing down such assets. I come back to approaches to respond to this behaviour below. But before doing so, it is important to consider how this phenomenon also applies with respect to climate risks.

3.2 Climate Risk-Shifting

Investors are reacting to the new information environment also by shifting climate risk, not just carbon liabilities, off their balance sheet. Often, this risk-shifting pushes climate risks from financial institutions, with greater bargaining power in a contract, to their former customers.[63] The private law literature highlights at least two arenas where such climate risk-shifting is already occurring in financial markets.[64]

First, in respect of commercial housing insurance markets, as the climate risk information environment becomes richer, insurers are better able to understand the risk exposure of their insured assets, and in some cases this is leading to what Nevitt and Pappas refer to as "insurance retreat".[65] While the authors do not claim that this retreat flows directly from

[59] Alperen Gözlügöl and Wolf-Georg Ringe, 'Private Companies, Brown-Spinning, and Climate-Related Disclosures in the U.S.' (*The Harvard Law School Forum on Corporate Governance*, 14 April 2022) <https://corpgov.law.harvard.edu/2022/04/14/private-companies-brown-spinning-and-climate-related-disclosures-in-the-u-s/> accessed 29 March 2025.

[60] Roberto Tallarita, 'The Limits of Portfolio Primacy' (2023) 76 Vanderbilt Law Review 511.

[61] Arjuna Dibley, 'When Does "Leviathan" Innovate? A Legal Theory of Clean Technological Change at Government-Owned Electric Utilities' (2023) 47 Harvard Environmental Law Review 135; see also Ernest Lim, Chapter 18 of this handbook.

[62] Of course, some SOEs are connected to capital markets, see, for example, Arjuna Dibley, 'Confronting Carbon in the State Sector: Why Engaging SOEs Is Critical for the Climate Challenge' (*ECGI Blog*, 20 June 2023) <https://www.ecgi.global/publications/blog/confronting-carbon-in-the-state-sector-why-engaging-soes-is-critical-for-the> accessed 2 March 2025.

[63] Annie Brett, 'Rethinking Environmental Disclosure' (2024) 112 California Law Review 1535, 1583.

[64] As the climate information environment becomes more developed, it is likely that this type of climate risk-shifting and financial retreat will appear in other parts of the financial system, such as housing mortgage markets. See, for example, Adele Fontana and others, 'From Flood to Fire: Is Physical Climate Risk Taken into Account in Banks' Residential Mortgage Rates?' (2025) European Central Bank Research Paper Series No. 2025/3036 <https://papers.ssrn.com/sol3/papers.cfm?abstract_id=5176497> accessed 31 March 2025.

[65] Mark Nevitt and Michael Pappas, 'Climate Risk, Insurance Retreat, and State Response' (2024) 58 Georgia Law Review 1603; Belinda Storey and others, 'Insurance Retreat in Residential Properties from

disclosure regulation, they do highlight how it is a consequence of insurance firms calculating physical risk impacts and removing insurance from areas where risks are too widespread and significant to allow risk pooling to effectively work. In a sense, this is exactly the benefit of insurance—to act as a risk transfer mechanism and send price signals to change incentives of those that are lifting premiums up for the pool. However, because global warming is a trend change to the climatic system (rather than a cyclical change) with wide impacts, it is leading to insurers removing insurance coverage entirely. The effect is that the climate risk previously carried by insurers is shifted to pre-existing property owners who either face "increased risk of disaster losses or financial losses from exiting the market".[66]

Similarly, existing research has demonstrated how climate risk information is resulting in risk-shifting in sovereign lending markets. A small group of mostly large institutional investors lend money to countries through the acquisition of country issued bonds and notes. There has been a precipitous increase in sovereign lending over the past decade, particularly after the COVID-19 pandemic, as economically depressed countries looked to the debt market to fund social programmes during periods of low economic activity and thus reduced tax revenue collection.[67] While sovereign issuers initially did not appear to be accounting for climate risks when issuing such debt,[68] credit rating agencies and investors subject to climate risk information ecosystems started to price in climate risks.[69] More recently, this has led to sovereign climate risk accounting approaches that perhaps inadvertently penalise developing countries, as they favour the structure of high-income countries which have lower "emissions intensity" than lower-income countries.[70] The effect is that sovereign climate risk information is creating incentives for investors to remove or penalise developing countries through higher debt capital costs and "financing retreat" right at a time when they need more finance to pay for climate risks.[71]

These emerging carbon liability and climate risk-shifting behaviours undermine the very objectives of the climate information system that is being developed. They also undermine the climate-alignment goal in other significant ways. By encouraging high carbon assets to move outside the financial system in which they may be managed, carbon liability shifting undermines the overarching Paris Agreement goal to reduce emissions. Similarly, the climate risk avoidance approaches discussed above in relation to insurance and sovereign markets exacerbate distributional conflicts and adaptation outcomes for the most vulnerable, including developing countries, and in this way undermine the fundamental adaptation objectives of the Paris Agreement.

Future Sea Level Rise in Aotearoa New Zealand' (2022) CESifo Working Paper No. 10017 <https://papers.ssrn.com/sol3/papers.cfm?abstract_id=4257216> accessed 31 March 2025; Robert R M Verchick and Lynsey Johnson, 'When Retreat is the Best Option: Flood Insurance after Biggert-Waters and Other Climate Change Puzzles' (2014) 47 John Marshall Law Review 695.

66 Nevitt and Pappas (n 65) 1618.

67 Asian Development Bank, *Climate Change and Sovereign Risk* (2020) <https://www.adb.org/publications/climate-change-and-sovereign-risk> accessed 23 June 2025.

68 Arjuna Dibley, Thom Wetzer, and Cameron Hepburn, 'National COVID Debts: Climate Change Imperils Countries' Ability to Repay' (2021) 592 Nature 184.

69 Gerhard Kling and others, 'The Impact of Climate Vulnerability on Firms' Cost of Capital and Access to Finance' (2021) 137 World Development 105131.

70 Arjuna Dibley and others, 'Biases in "Sustainable Finance" Metrics Could Hinder Lending to Those That Need It Most' (2024) 634 Nature 294.

71 ibid.

3.3 Addressing the Problems Related to, Not Abandoning, Climate Information

Despite the criticisms levelled towards the climate information system and its ability to effectively further the Paris Agreement goals, it is too early to suggest that the approach be abandoned. There is some evidence to suggest that capital markets are starting to price in climate risks in a limited way, correlating with the rise of—even if not caused by—information disclosure rules.[72]

Additionally, information failures about carbon and climate related risks continue to abound in the financial system, despite the extent of existing efforts.[73] Existing climate information may not account for the full extent of climate risk, leading to its underestimation.[74] For example, Condon highlights how fundamental simplifications in the process of integrated assessment models (IAMs), which are used by financial system actors, may be leading to underestimation of climate impacts.[75] There are also circumstances where relevant climate risk information is lacking altogether, leading to mispricing of climate risk by financial actors. For instance, in my own work with colleagues, we show how financial risks associated with climate change litigation and liability create potentially material financial risks, which remain systematically under analysed and reported and potentially under accounted in asset pricing.[76]

The fact that investors may be starting to respond to climate risk information, and the presence of ongoing informational gaps, suggest that it would be prudent to allow climate information systems to mature further. For these reasons, even legal and financial scholarship that is critical of the information-first approach also tends to suggest improving the system rather than abandoning it.[77] For example, Brett's analysis of a broad range of environmental disclosure regimes in the US argues that disclosure alone is often not impactful at driving behaviour change.[78] But information regimes are not inherently ineffective; what is needed are legal tools alongside information disclosure that change the incentives of regulated entities themselves—the theme of the next section of this chapter.[79]

[72] Patrick Bolton and Marcin Kacperczyk, 'Do Investors Care about Carbon Risk?' (National Bureau of Economic Research, April 2020) <https://www.nber.org/papers/w26968> accessed 5 July 2024.

[73] S Kreibiehl and others, 'Chapter 15: Investment and Finance', *IPCC, 2022: Climate Change 2022: Mitigation of Climate Change. Contribution of Working Group III to the Sixth Assessment Report of the Intergovernmental Panel on Climate Change* (CUP 2023) 1580 <https://www.ipcc.ch/report/ar6/wg3/chapter/chapter-15/> accessed 19 March 2025.

[74] Irene Monasterolo and Luca de Angelis, 'Blind to Carbon Risk? An Analysis of Stock Market Reaction to the Paris Agreement' (2020) 170 Ecological Economics 106571.

[75] Madison Condon, 'Market Myopia's Climate Bubble' (2022) 2022 Utah Law Review 63. This is a point which has also been echoed by prominent climate economists, such as in Nicholas Stern, Joseph E Stiglitz, and Charlotte Taylor, 'The Economics of Immense Risk, Urgent Action and Radical Change: Towards New Approaches to the Economics of Climate Change' (National Bureau of Economic Research, February 2021) <https://www.nber.org/papers/w28472> accessed 19 March 2025.

[76] Thom Wetzer, Rupert Stuart-Smith, and Arjuna Dibley, 'Climate Risk Assessments Must Engage with the Law' (2024) 383 Science 152.

[77] Steuer and Tröger (n 41); Roberta Di Marco and others, 'Symbol or Substance? Scrutinizing the "Risk Transparency Premise" in Marketized Sustainable Finance: The Case of TCFD Reporting' (2023) 32 Business Strategy and the Environment 3027; Brett (n 63); Ameli et al (n 54).

[78] Brett (n 63) 1585.

[79] ibid 1589.

4. Addressing Carbon Liability and Climate Risk-Shifting by Moving Beyond Information-based Market Failures

The previous section described how the emergence of climate-information regulation is driving some entities to engage in carbon liability and climate risk-shifting behaviour. This behaviour allows carbon liabilities and the financial risks of climate impacts to leak out of the regulated financial system and onto other actors. This leakage is happening in areas where firms have the strongest incentives to shift their liabilities, either because they are facing immediate costs associated with high emissions assets or liabilities from already materialising financial risks, and relatively easy or low-cost pathways to offload such assets and liabilities. This section considers the legal reforms that might increase the costs of this behaviour for both the shifting and the recipient entities.

4.1 Carbon Liabilities

Existing scholarship has considered interventions to address the incentives of both shifting entities and, to a lesser extent, the recipient side, that might reduce carbon liability shifting.

With respect to the shifting entity, scholars have suggested making amendments to US corporate law to make it more challenging for entities to shift carbon liabilities. Hester, for instance, proposes that corporate regulators should develop a transparency framework which captures corporate restructuring activities related to carbon liabilities.[80] Practically, this means corporations would need to regularly disclose details of any spinoffs, bankruptcies, or asset transfers that relate to their carbon-intensive operations, giving regulators, investors and the public better knowledge about carbon transfers, and enabling the possibility of private or public law suits using existing law to prevent such transfers.[81]

In addition to transparency regimes, Hester also recommends amendments to legal frameworks to disincentivise carbon transfers. Drawing on the example of New Jersey's Industrial Site Recovery Act, where companies must either declare no hazardous discharges before transferring an asset or submit a cleanup plan with a bond, Hester suggests a similar approach with respect to carbon. That is, if a corporation falls within a carbon intensive sector, it would need to notify a regulator of its intent to dispose of an asset, and would be required to meet certain thresholds to show it can address carbon liability or it would need to post a bond to cover such liabilities.[82] In other words, the original owning company would be required to retain the carbon liability of its asset transfer.

Sidestepping Hester and others' politically contentious step of corporate law reform, Armour and colleagues make a similar suggestion but using existing law and contracts.[83] They suggest that a climate concerned investor could use securities laws which require shareholder approval of certain transactions such as the Class 1 transactions rules in the UK. In the case of a firm seeking to dispose of a high carbon asset, the authors suggest that the climate conscious shareholder approve the transfer only with so-called green pill covenants or dual class share

[80] Hester (n 56) 378.
[81] ibid 378–85.
[82] ibid 389–90.
[83] Armour et al, 'Dark and Dirty Assets: Greening Climate-Driven Asset Partitioning' (n 57).

structures.[84] In both cases, the climate conscious investor can compel the shifting company to retain control over the high emissions asset and ultimately dispose of it.[85] Such "green pills" also have the effect of increasing transparency about firm commitment to climate goals.

These corporate and contractual proposals focus on encouraging the shifting firm to retain responsibility over the high carbon asset. The logic being that the shifting firm will come under pressure to phase down the asset from an investor or other source. However, these proposals do not consider what would enable or incentivise shifting firms to phase down or phase out such high carbon assets themselves. If shifting firms are not incentivised to deal with the high carbon asset themselves, then it is possible that those firms might use other strategic behaviour to escape their carbon liabilities, as coal firms have done in relation to their environmental liabilities in the US.[86]

Legal frameworks must evolve to enable firms to capture the positive externalities associated with the early retirement of carbon-intensive assets. In other words, legal mechanisms are needed to allow firms and investors to internalise the broader public benefits of emissions reductions. This is particularly important because under prevailing corporate governance norms, firms are unlikely to retire productive assets—regardless of their emissions intensity—unless such action can be justified as advancing the financial interests of the company.[87] By structuring returns to reflect the public climate value of asset retirement, legal tools may help align emissions-reducing actions with fiduciary obligations.

Policymakers have begun to grapple with this challenge, though existing proposals remain contested. Consider, for example, the efforts underway to support the phaseout of coal-fired power plants (CFPPs). In some instances, replacing CFPPs with renewable energy can improve a firm's financial outlook over the medium to long term. In such cases, innovative contractual structures have been used to attract climate-focused investors willing to absorb near-term losses in exchange for longer-term gains.[88] Some electric utilities have issued low-cost bonds, backed by future electricity tariffs, to finance the early closure of coal plants.[89] However, these strategies often rely on investors who are comfortable receiving short-term returns from coal generation and tend to be more viable when the asset is already approaching the end of its useful life. They are significantly less effective for assets with substantial remaining productive capacity.

To address this gap, several governments—particularly in the US and Asia—have proposed the development of carbon offset crediting mechanisms to monetise the avoided emissions associated with early CFPP retirement.[90] These proposals involve the issuance of credits

[84] Described more completely here: Armour et al, 'Green Pills: Making Corporate Climate Commitments Credible' (n 53).

[85] Armour et al, 'Dark and Dirty Assets: Greening Climate-Driven Asset Partitioning' (n 57).

[86] Joshua Macey and Jackson Salovaara, 'Bankruptcy as Bailout: Coal Company Insolvency and the Erosion of Federal Law' (2019) 71 Stanford Law Review 879.

[87] Marcel Kahan and Edward Rock, 'Systemic Stewardship with Tradeoffs' (2023) 48 Journal of Corporations Law 498.

[88] Shravan Bhat, Whitney Mann, and Alex Murray, 'Financing Mechanisms to Accelerate Managed Coal Power Phaseout' (Rocky Mountains Institute 2023) Working Paper <https://rmi.org/insight/metrics-and-mechanisms-to-finance-managed-coal-phaseout/>.

[89] ibid.

[90] US State Department, Bezos Earth Fund, and The Rockerfeller Foundation, 'Energy Transition Accelerator: Core Framework' (Energy Transition Accelerator 2023) <https://www.etaccelerator.org/_files/ugd/17314c_ce8fabc2fce04e8cb29bdd3cc85f0f37.pdf> accessed 1 April 2025; Monetary Authority of Singapore (MAS), 'Transition Credits' <https://www.mas.gov.sg/development/sustainable-finance/transition-credits> accessed 2 April 2025.

for so-called Scope 4 emissions—emissions that would have occurred in the absence of an intervention—either at the project or jurisdictional level. Yet such approaches are fraught with difficulty. Counterfactual baselines are often speculative and inconsistent, emissions leakage can be hard to control, and the prospect of rewarding firms for closing assets they arguably might be required to close anyway raises significant moral hazard concerns.[91]

Despite, or perhaps because of, the problems in this area, this remains a promising area for further legal and policy innovation. Private law scholars could play a vital role in designing mechanisms that enable firms to exit carbon-intensive investments while satisfying legal and financial constraints. One potential avenue is the development of methodologies to quantify the avoided social cost of carbon and to link this to tax incentives for asset retirement.[92] Similarly, governments or third parties could establish clear, credible approaches to valuing the public benefits of emissions reductions to attract impact investors.[93] These early ideas remain underdeveloped and merit deeper theoretical and empirical investigation.

Looking beyond shifting firms, scholars have also proposed steps to disincentivise recipient firms from receiving carbon assets. That is, they have proposed mechanisms which might disincentivise companies or investors from receiving high carbon assets. The literature primarily recommends doing so through more disclosure. Gözlugöl and Ringe and Phang and Chia respectively recommend that private companies and SOEs that receive dirty assets should be subject to equivalent climate-related disclosures as publicly listed firms and investors.[94] In fact, some efforts are already underway in practice to try and increase disclosures for both firm types.[95] The effect of these measures would be to "expand" the climate information regulatory space.

The idea behind expanding climate information requirements outside the incumbent system is that this might disincentivise recipient firms from taking on dirty assets. It may indeed be the case that such disclosures create disincentives for a select number of these firms, but it is not clear that the logic of disclosure, which was created based on publicly traded and competitive financial markets, easily translates to SOEs and privately held firms, which tend to be dominated by (government) block holders.

Consider an SOE, for instance. If it is wholly government owned, the decision to take on the dirty asset is likely to be influenced by the interests of its government controlling shareholder.[96]

[91] Kaya Axelsson, Claire Wigg and Matilda Becker, 'Is Impact out of Scope? A Call for Innovation in Climate Standards to Inspire Action across Companies' Spheres of Influence' (2024) 15 Carbon Management 2382995.

[92] There have been some macroeconomic analyses which have estimated significant savings from coal phase out and replacement with renewables when accounting for the social cost of carbon. See for example, Tobias Adrian, Patrick Bolton, and Alissa M Kleinnijenhuis, 'The Great Carbon Arbitrage' (2022) WP/22/107 <https://www.imf.org/en/Publications/WP/Issues/2022/05/31/The-Great-Carbon-Arbitrage-518464> accessed 2 April 2025.

[93] Gosling (n 51).

[94] Gözlugöl and Ringe, 'Net-Zero Transition and Divestments of Carbon-Intensive Assets' (n 55); Rachel Phang and Yaru Chia, 'Sustainability and the Sunlight of Disclosure: ESG Disclosure in Three Asian Financial Centres' (2024) 33 Review of European, Comparative & International Environmental Law 209.

[95] See, for example, OECD, *Corporate Governance of State-Owned Enterprises* (Report, 2024), and IPSASB, Climate Related Disclosures (Website, 2025) <https://www.ipsasb.org/consultations-projects/sustainability-climate-related-disclosures> accessed 12 March 2025; Institutional Investors Group on Climate Change, *Paris Aligned Investment Initiative: Net Zero Investment Framework for the Private Debt Industry* (Report, 23 March 2024).

[96] See Ernest Lim, Chapter 18 of this handbook.

If the government block holder is less concerned about climate change, or is pursuing other geopolitical or energy security interests, they can often use corporate governance mechanisms to shape the decision of the firm about the acquisition of new assets, including through the board, direct reporting on firm strategy, and public financing, among others.[97] In this context, it is not clear that climate information will dissuade the block holder to change its interests on climate change. If the firm were partially privatised, or had significant exposure to the debt market, and such investors were climate conscious, then a disclosure obligation may allow these investors to shape the decision to take on the asset, but this is likely to be the exceptional case, and not the rule.

It is worth noting here that the question of why private firms and SOEs are willing and able to take on dirty assets, and how ownership affects such a decision, is an area where more research is needed. However, it is likely that in firms where there is a government or private block holder, more disclosure will not act as a meaningful disincentive for the firm to take on a dirty asset. What is needed are reforms that shape the block holders' interests, not that of the firm. For example, with respect to SOEs, this might involve more targeted approaches to get the agencies or ministries with the legal mandate to act as shareholder for the state to understand the total portfolio climate risks of its SOEs, and how such risks pass back to the balance sheet of the government.[98] As credit ratings agencies increasingly incorporate climate risk analysis into how they set sovereign and corporate ratings, equipping governments with an understanding of their climate risk exposure can incentivise them to shift how they manage their SOEs.

4.2 Climate Risk-Shifting

While the literature on legal responses to carbon liability shifting is growing, there has been comparatively less focus on managing climate risk-shifting. Yet the need for effective legal tools in this area is equally important. Existing proposals in the literature tend to concentrate on financial institutions—the entities most actively shifting risk—and, in particular, on mechanisms to compel or incentivise them to continue providing financial services to climate-exposed communities despite growing hazards.

As climate risks intensify with rising emissions, financial institutions are increasingly equipped with sophisticated tools for identifying and managing their exposure.[99] In response, many have begun to rely on existing contractual mechanisms to withdraw from high-risk markets. This retreat is largely voluntary, reflecting the foundational structure of private law, which is built on the principle of consensual participation. The challenge therefore lies in using legal mechanisms to counteract a process that is itself legally permitted, if not encouraged from a financial risk management point of view.

[97] Dibley, 'When Does "Leviathan" Innovate? A Legal Theory of Clean Technological Change at Government-Owned Electric Utilities' (n 61).

[98] There have been some steps in practice to this end. For example, analysis done in Colombia has shown how SOEs transition risk exposure creates significant financial liabilities in aggregate at the national level. Willis Tower Watson and Universidad de Los Andes, 'Understanding the Impact of a Low Carbon Transition on Colombia' (2023) <https://www.wtwco.com/en-gb/insights/2023/08/understanding-the-impact-of-a-low-carbon-transition-on-colombia> accessed 1 April 2025.

[99] Madison Condon, 'Climate Services: The Business of Physical Risk' (2023) 55 Arizona State Law Journal 147.

With this financial risk management perspective in mind, some scholars argue that financial institutions may be more likely to continue to provide financial services to high risk areas if some portion of their climate risk exposure is absorbed by the public sector—particularly in relation to ongoing products such as insurance.[100] Others go further, contending that the financial sector's retreat from climate-exposed areas will have significant distributional consequences, disproportionately affecting already vulnerable communities. This has led to the concept of "blue lining"—a form of exclusionary financial practice in which communities are effectively excluded on the basis of climate vulnerability.[101] To address this, some scholars propose mandatory obligations akin to fair lending laws in the US. For instance, Fenlock and colleagues suggest imposing a legal duty on insurers to provide equitable access to financial services in high-risk areas.[102]

While normatively compelling, these proposals raise difficult practical and legal questions. It is not clear, for example, if insurers should be required to remain in one market if doing so would require substantial premium increases in another market. More fundamentally, forcing financial institutions to remain engaged in high-risk areas may concentrate systemic climate risk within certain market segments, ultimately creating the potential for public spillovers that threaten financial stability. Thus, while short-term regulatory mandates may provide temporary relief, there is a longer-term need for legal instruments that reshape the incentives and behaviours of both financial risk-shifters and recipients.

One possible approach that is being trialled by governments lies in promoting coordination between financial institutions, their clients, and governments.[103] Consider real estate insurance, for example. Insurance companies are retreating from high climate risk areas because the climate information regime is partially creating pressure for them to reduce their exposure to climate financial risks. In some cases, insurers may be able to reduce their risk profile if their clients' risk exposure was reduced—such as through investments in flood-proofing or fire-resilient infrastructure. In other cases, meaningful risk reduction would require government intervention or support in addition to steps that real estate owners could take.

While such approaches require a combination of public and private law mechanisms, private laws could be used to manage the relationship between insurer and client. Drawing on a model like a sustainability linked bond, a sustainability linked insurance contract could adjust premiums by conditioning favourable premium terms on measurable adaptation actions.[104] Indeed, at the time of this chapter's writing, the first sustainability linked insurance contract had just been issued.[105] This approach would allow financial institutions to remain engaged

[100] Nevitt and Pappas (n 65).

[101] Brooklyn Montgomery and Monica Palmeira, 'Bluelining: Climate Financial Discrimination on the Horizon' (The Greenlining Institute 2023).

[102] Maria Frausto, 'Is Bluelining the "New" Redlining? How Insurance Discrimination Deepens Climate Disparities' (*Center for International Environmental Law*, 9 August 2024) <https://www.ciel.org/bluelining-insurance-discrimination-climate-crisis/> accessed 31 March 2025.

[103] The Australian Government's National Emergency Management Agency launched a Hazards Insurance Partnership in 2023, based on this logic. See, National Emergency Management Agency, 'Hazards Insurance Partnership' (8 Sept 2024) <https://www.nema.gov.au/our-work/resilience/hazards-insurance-partnership> accessed 23 June 2025.

[104] Massimo Mariani and others, 'Sustainability-Linked Bonds, Corporate Commitment and the Cost of Debt' (2025) 74 Research in International Business and Finance 102658.

[105] 'Swiss Captive Pilots First Sustainability-Linked Insurance' (*Commercial Risk*, 22 November 2024) <https://www.commercialriskonline.com/swiss-captive-sbb-pilots-first-ever-sustainability-linked-insurance-contract/> accessed 2 April 2025.

while encouraging recipients to reduce their own exposure to physical climate risks. However, there are natural limits to such a model. It may not work well in areas where real estate owners have limited access to finance. Also, once the recipient has done all that is reasonably within their control, continued exposure may remain high due to structural or geographic vulnerabilities. However, a contract of this nature may at least provide time before the financial institution retreats, allowing asset owners greater time to transition.

5. Conclusion

This chapter has argued that the predominant approach that governments are taking for addressing climate alignment in financial markets has been to address climate-related information deficits and asymmetries. However, because investors are still faced with a range of other market and regulatory failures limiting their ability to pursue climate alignment, this chapter shows that in some cases financial institutions are not minimising carbon liabilities and climate risks. Instead, they appear to be pushing such liabilities and risks beyond the reach of the emerging climate-information regulatory perimeter. The effect of some of these actions, is that climate liabilities and risks are leaking off the balance sheets of private firms and into the hands of the public, including in developing countries and communities, offending the basic distributional goals of the Paris Agreement.

This chapter has put forward some ways that private law can respond to these immediate emerging consequences of carbon and climate risk-shifting, including corporate law and contractual and regulatory instruments. While these approaches alone will not result in climate alignment, they are necessary preconditions to prevent financial market actors from cheating the climate information system that is being developed. In the long term, to get closer to achieving climate alignment, scholars and practitioners need to deepen their focus beyond addressing information-based market failures in financial markets and focus more on how to tackle financial institution and corporate incentives which are limiting climate investment and risk management. Only then can financial flows begin to support, rather than frustrate, the broader aims of the climate regime.

CHAPTER 21

Competition Law

JULIAN NOWAG AND THOMAS CHENG

1. Introduction

THE relationship between climate change and antitrust has been fraught with controversy. The issue came to the fore in the US with its fight against "woke capitalism"[1] and the lawsuit against investors, such as BlackRock and others. They have been accused of violating antitrust rules by having jointly committed to reducing CO_2 emissions of the companies that they have invested in.[2] However, this specific issue also takes place within the broader debate about the relationship between sustainability and antitrust. On the one hand, there are antitrust purists who argue that antitrust should concentrate exclusively on economic considerations such as economic efficiency and consumer welfare. An expansion of focus to non-economic matters, such as sustainability or climate changes, stretches antitrust beyond its capability and invites enforcement officials and judges to make policy decisions which they are ill-equipped to make. These purists argue that sustainability and climate change concerns are irreconcilable with the consumer welfare paradigm that has dominated modern antitrust. They suggest that incorporating such concerns will require a weighing of incommensurable qualities such as consumer harm against sustainability or climate benefits.

On the other hand, climate change advocates believe that the insistence on purism is misguided and that in the face of the existential crisis of climate change, humanity can spare no effort and must utilise all levers at its disposal to slow down climate change. In Europe, a number of competition authorities have issued guidelines singling out agreements that pursue sustainability and climate benefits, otherwise known as sustainability agreements, for special consideration. For instance, the Competition and Markets Authority in the UK issued its Green Agreements Guidance on 23 October 2023, in which it indicated a more permissive approach to what are known as "Climate Change Agreements".[3] To climate change advocates, the question is not whether but *how* antitrust should accommodate sustainability concerns.

[1] See, e.g., James Surowiecki, 'The War on "Woke Capitalism" Is Backfiring' *The Atlantic* (31 January 2024) <www.theatlantic.com/ideas/archive/2024/01/republicans-wokecapital-esg-investment/677294/> accessed 23 December 2024.

[2] See Complaint in *Texas et al. v BlackRock, Inc. et al.* Docket No. 6:24-cv-00437 (E.D. Tex. 27 November 2024). For a discussion with regard to antitrust law see Maurits Dolmans, Wanjie Lin, and Jessica Hollis, 'Sustainability and Net Zero Climate Agreements: A Transatlantic Antitrust Perspective' (8 September 2023) <https://ssrn.com/abstract=4571804> accessed 9 June 2025.

[3] Competition and Markets Authority, 'CMA 185 Green Agreements Guidance: Guidance on the Application of the Chapter I Prohibition in the Competition Act 1998 to Environmental Sustainability Agreements' (2023) <https://assets.publishing.service.gov.uk/media/6526b81b244f8e000d8e742c/Green_agreements_guidance_.pdf> accessed 25 June 2025.

This chapter will wade into this debate by adopting an intermediate position. It argues that it is indeed possible to adapt the consumer welfare standard to incorporate sustainability and climate change considerations with some adjustments. Some of them are minor, while some of them may be more far-reaching and may cause discomfort for the antitrust purists. But we believe that the adjustments we propose are consistent with the underlying rationale and spirit of consumer welfare. In fact, we argue that in some instances, the interests of antitrust and climate change are aligned and antitrust enforcement concomitantly advances climate change goals. Ultimately, we want to bridge the gap between antitrust and climate change and show that it is possible for the two to work together to advance the interests of humanity. This chapter, like the debate around sustainability and climate change in competition law, focuses on agreements. It thus leaves out questions of abuse of dominance,[4] mergers,[5] and enforcement.[6] The chapter first provides a brief overview of the relevant rules of EU and US antitrust law. Then, it highlights how antitrust enforcement can foster climate change goals. Finally, it explores the vexed discussion of how agreements should be treated under the relevant antitrust rules that appear to restrict competition but provide climate benefits. However, before delving into the details, a clarification of terminology is in order. This chapter uses the term "sustainability" to refer to environmental sustainability, specifically climate change concerns, which is the theme of this handbook. "Sustainability" is the term most commonly used by the antitrust community to refer to climate change considerations. This admittedly betrays a lack of precision as sustainability is not limited to environmental sustainability and can encompass social sustainability such as fair wages for workers and fair trade prices for farmers to ensure the sustainability of farming communities. In fact, sustainability can be understood to refer to the Sustainable Development Goals promulgated by the United Nations,[7] which consist of seventeen primary objectives including access to education, basic nutrition, and adequate healthcare, among others. Nonetheless, this chapter will adopt the conventional usage in the antitrust community and use sustainability to refer to environmental sustainability and more specifically climate change.

2. A Quick Overview of EU Competition Law and US Antitrust Law

While competition law in both the EU and the US (or antitrust as the field is known in the US[8]) have many common features, their legal set-up and operation differ. Both regimes prohibit anticompetitive concerted action. In general, the EU's approach to concerted action follows a two-step analysis. The first step consists of two sub-steps. Under the first sub-step, concerted action as defined by Article 101, TFEU needs to be established. Under the second

[4] On dominance see, e.g., Marios Iacovides and Valentin Mauboussin, 'Unilateral Conduct and Sustainability under EU Competition Law' in Julian Nowag (ed), *Research Handbook on Sustainability and Competition Law* (Edward Elgar Publishing 2024) 352–74.

[5] See, e.g., Elias Deutscher and Stavros Makris, 'Making Sustainability Visible: A New Framework and Operationalisation Tests for Merger Control' in Julian Nowag (ed), *Research Handbook on Sustainability and Competition Law* (Edward Elgar Publishing 2024) 375–411.

[6] Julian Nowag, *Global Antitrust and Sustainability: Law, Economics, Enforcement* (OUP 2025), ch 5; Giorgio Monti, 'Implementing a Sustainability Agenda in Competition Law and Policy' in Julian Nowag (ed), *Research Handbook on Sustainability and Competition Law* (Edward Elgar Publishing 2024) 249–63.

[7] For an overview of the Sustainable Development Goals, see https://sdgs.un.org/goals.

[8] We use the terms 'antitrust' and 'competition law' interchangeably, referring to the body of law that regulates anticompetitive concerted action or collusion, unilateral conduct, and mergers.

sub-step, competitive harm of the concerted action must be shown. More precisely, the authority or claimant has to show that the action has the object or the effect of restricting competition as defined by Article 101(1), TFEU. In this assessment, a possible sliding scale regarding the burden of proof can be observed: By-object restrictions, which allow an anticompetitive practice to be condemned without a detailed analysis of effects, ease the burden of proof on the authority or claimant while demonstrating effects is a more resource- and evidence-intensive exercise.[9] Once an anticompetitive concerted action is established, the burden shifts to the defendant to show that the conditions of Article 101(3), TFEU are fulfilled. Article 101(3), TFEU requires the defendant to show that its conduct produces positive effects and that these effects outweigh the competitive harm ascertained under Article 101(1), TFEU.

US antitrust law functions similarly to EU competition law in many ways, but there are also important differences. The main operative statutory provisions in US antitrust in this context is Section 1 of the Sherman Act. It is concerned with multi-firm conduct. While Article 101, TFEU distinguishes between different types of multi-firm interaction such as agreements and concerted practices, the invocation of Section 1 is premised on an agreement. Despite the language in Section 1 referring to contracts, combinations, and conspiracies in restraint of trade, these distinct terms have been collapsed into one single concept known as a Section 1 agreement.[10] Once an agreement is established, which is not always straightforward, the court proceeds to assess its competitive effects.

As the US Supreme Court noted in the *California Dental Association* case, there is a sliding scale of legal standards that can be applied: "What is required, rather, is an enquiry meet for the case, looking to the circumstances, details, and logic of a restraint."[11] On one end of the spectrum is the per se rule, under which an inquiry into competitive effects is entirely obviated. All that is required is proof that the alleged conduct took place. The rationale behind the per se rule is that "there are certain agreements or practices which because of their pernicious effect on competition and lack of redeeming virtue are conclusively presumed to be unreasonable and therefore illegal without elaborate inquiry as to the precise harm they have caused or the business excuse for their use".[12] Some practices are so likely to be anticompetitive that a *de novo* inquiry into competitive effects in every case is deemed unnecessary. The per se rule is similar to by-object restriction under EU law, except that under the per se rule, no justification for the business practice is entertained, whereas, at least in theory, the exemption under Article 101(3), TFEU remains available even for a by-object restriction. There was a time when the per se rule applied to a wide range of conduct, including most vertical restraints.[13] That has slowly changed over the last five decades and only hardcore cartel conduct and certain kinds of group boycott remain subject to the per se rule.

On the other end of the spectrum is the Rule of Reason, under which the Court will conduct a plenary analysis of competitive effects, taking into account the market environment and the likely or actual effects of the conduct at issue. In the *Chicago Board of Trade* case, the US Supreme Court describes the Rule of Reason as follows: "To determine [the legality of a business practice] the court must ordinarily consider the facts peculiar to the business to which

[9] See Maria Ioanidou and Julian Nowag, 'Can Two Wrongs Make a Right? Reconsidering Minimum Resale Price Maintenance in the Light of *Allianz Hungária*' (2015) 11(2–3) European Competition Journal 340.

[10] Sherman Antitrust Act 1890 (US).

[11] *California Dental Association v Federal Trade Commission* 526 U.S. 766, 781 (1999).

[12] *Northern Pacific Railway Co. v United States* 356 U.S. 1, 5 (1958).

[13] Herbert Hovenkamp, *Federal Antitrust Policy: The Law of Competition and its Practice* (4th edn, West Publishing 2011) 490–91.

the restraint is applied, its condition before and after the restraint is imposed; the nature of the restraint and its effect, actual or probable."[14] The Rule of Reason is similar to the by-effect restriction under Article 101(1). One main difference between the two is that under Article 101, TFEU, the prohibition and justification steps are bifurcated whereas under the Rule of Reason, the anticompetitive effects and the procompetitive justifications are considered together, albeit in a process of sequential analysis as highlighted by the United States Court of Appeals for the DC Circuit in the *Microsoft* case.[15] Article 101(3), TFEU clearly delineates the requirements.[16] In comparison, the justification process under the Rule of Reason is relatively open-ended and unstructured.[17]

In between the per se rule and the Rule of Reason is what is known as the quick look analysis, which is applied to business practices that are facially anticompetitive but for which the Court is willing to entertain some initial justifications. If the justification is accepted, the case will be analysed under the Rule of Reason, as in the *California Dental Association* case. If the justification is rejected, which the Court did in the *Professional Engineers* case,[18] and the *NCAA* case,[19] the practice will be summarily condemned. The quick look analysis is usually applied to business practices that amount to a direct restriction of competition for which the main remaining question is whether there exists an acceptable justification for it. The quick look analysis could be relevant to sustainability and climate change agreements that directly restrict output, which can only be justified if the Court is persuaded by its sustainability or climate change benefits.

Consumer welfare is an important parameter of analysis under both EU competition law and US antitrust law. While the consumer welfare standard has come under pressure in the US in recent years,[20] and has never been the sole goal of EU competition law,[21] it is still an important leitmotiv for both jurisdictions. In fact, there are some who would argue that

[14] *Board of Trade of City of Chicago v United States* 246 U.S. 231, 238 (1918).

[15] *United States v Microsoft Corp* 253 F.3d 34, 58–59 (D.C. Cir. 2001).

[16] There are four conditions for establishing a justification under Article 101(3), TFEU, for an agreement prohibited under Article 101(1), TFEU.

[17] Roger D Blair and D Daniel Sokol, 'The Rule of Reason and the Goals of Antitrust: An Economic Approach' (2012) 78 Antitrust Law Journal 471, 472.

[18] *National Society of Professional Engineers v United States* 435 U.S. 679 (1978).

[19] *National Collegiate Athletic Association v Board of Regents of the University of Oklahoma* 468 U.S. 85 (1984).

[20] See, e.g., Tim Wu, *The Curse of Bigness: Antitrust in the New Gilded Age* (2018 Columbia Global Reports); Mark Glick, 'How Chicago Economics Distorts 'Consumer Welfare' (2019) 64:4 Antitrust Bulletin 495–513; Sandeep Vaheesan, 'The Profound Nonsense of Consumer Welfare Antitrust' (2019) 64:4 Antitrust Bulletin 479–94; Steven C Salop, 'Question: What Is the Real and Proper Antitrust Welfare Standard? Answer: The True Consumer Welfare Standard' (2020) 22 Loyola Consumer Law Review 336; Barak Y Orbach, 'The Antitrust Consumer Welfare Paradox' (2011) 7(1) Journal of Competition Law & Economics 133–64; Robert W Crandall and Winston Clifford, 'Does Antitrust Policy Improve Consumer Welfare? Assessing the Evidence' (2003) 17(4) Journal of Economic Perspectives 3–26; Herbert Hovenkamp, 'Is Antitrust's Consumer Welfare Principle Imperiled?' (2019) 45 Journal of Corporation Law 101–30; Roger D Blair and Daniel D Sokol, 'Welfare Standards in U.S. and EU Antitrust Enforcement' (2013) 81 Fordham Law Review 2497–2541; Kati Cseres, 'The Controversies of the Consumer Welfare Standard' (2006) 3(2) Competition Law Review 121–73; Cristina Caffarra, "Consumer Welfare Is Dead': What Do We Do Instead? A Perspective from Europe' (*ProMarket*, 27 April 2023) <www.promarket.org/2023/04/27/consumer-welfare-is-dead-what-do-we-do-instead-a-perspective-from-europe/> accessed 23 December 2024.

[21] See, e.g., K Stylianou and M Iacovides, 'The Goals of EU Competition Law: A Comprehensive Empirical Investigation' (2022) 42(4) Legal Studies 620–48.

protecting consumer welfare should be the sole objective of antitrust law. Under the consumer welfare standard, the benchmark for legality is whether consumer welfare is augmented or diminished by a particular activity.

We will explore the interface between antitrust and climate changes goals from a consumer welfare perspective. The debate is often framed as a conflict between the public interest of climate change goals and consumer welfare, more specifically, whether a public interest exception should be made for climate change agreements. Some jurisdictions have in place specific rules that allow for the balancing between competitive harms and the public interest. For example, Article 8 of the Swiss Cartel Act is titled "Exceptional authorisation for compelling public interest reasons".[22] Similarly, where "a benefit to the public" exists, Part VII, Division 1 of the Australian Competition and Consumer Act 2010, provides for an authorisation by the Competition Commission.[23]

In this chapter, however, we focus on two regimes that do not explicitly allow public interest exceptions, the EU and the US. We argue that sustainability considerations need not be addressed through a public interest exception and can be effectively accommodated under a consumer welfare standard. The consumer welfare standard need not be jettisoned to pursue sustainability. The focus of this chapter will be on environmental sustainability in the context of concerted action/collusion, which is chosen as it has been the main focus of the competition-sustainability debate. The discussion, however, will also be pertinent to the context of social sustainability.[24] The chapter will proceed by first examining how the authorities can use antitrust law to act as a guardian of sustainability by using the law as a sword[25] against unsustainable business practices. It will then explore how antitrust can be applied to enable private sustainability efforts by allowing sustainability to act as a shield against charges of anticompetitive conduct. Both sections will explore how this can be done within the consumer welfare framework that applies a consumer welfare calculus. The chapter will conclude with a brief discussion of the competition-sustainability interface in the context of unilateral conduct and mergers.

3. Fostering Climate Change Goals Through Cartel Enforcement

In this section, we explore efforts by competition agencies to use antitrust to protect climate change goals that are entirely consistent with the consumer welfare standard. Such efforts can contribute to the pursuit of a more sustainable world, help fight against environmental degradation, or help reduce emissions. These efforts may entail an orthodox application of antitrust

[22] Swiss Cartel Act (CartA) 6 October 1995, art 8.

[23] Competition and Consumer Act 2010 (Cth) pt VII div 1, s 90.

[24] On the issue of environmental and social sustainability see Torsten Krause, 'Environmental Sustainability' in Julian Nowag, *Research Handbook on Sustainability and Competition Law* (Edward Elgar Publishing 2024) 12–31; Torsten Krause, 'Social Sustainability' in Julian Nowag, *Research Handbook on Sustainability and Competition Law* 32–48.

[25] On this terminology see Julian Nowag, *Global Antitrust and Sustainability: Law, Economics, Enforcement* (OUP 2025); Simon Holmes, 'Climate Change, Sustainability and Competition Law' (2020) 8 Journal of Antitrust *Enforcement* 355. This builds on the basic distinction as developed in Julian Nowag, *Environmental Integration in Competition and Free-Movement Laws* (OUP 2017) 1–12 and Julian Nowag 'Competition Law's Sustainability Gap? Tools for an Examination and a Brief Overview' (2022) Nordic Journal of European Law 150–52.

focused purely on price or the invocation of sustainability-related parameters to uphold competition and thereby foster climate change goals.

Conventional application of antitrust can contribute to climate change matters through enforcement against cartels. In particular, competition authorities guided by a consumer welfare standard can make a contribution by targeting cartels that restrict competition on sustainability or climate change relevant parameters. For example, the French competition authority brought a case against firms producing PVC and linoleum floor covering for agreeing not to compete on the environmental dimensions of their product.[26] The agency highlighted that

> the effect of this agreement was to eliminate "competitive marketing practices based on environmental characteristics" and "avoid unnecessary controversy relating to particular products and adopt a consistent marketing approach" in order to prevent "reckless green marketing". . . . Tradesmen, retailers and consumers, increasingly sensitive to the debate surrounding the impact of air quality on human health, specifically as a result of releases from PVC floor coverings, could not receive the standard of information that might have prevailed in the absence of this agreement, and might have enlightened their purchasing decisions.[27]

In another case, the French authority fined a cartel whose members agreed not to compete on the inclusion in their food container products of a problematic but legal substance,[28] thereby depriving consumer choice and preventing competition from facilitating the phasing out of a harmful substance. A similar approach can be taken where a cartel would ensure that companies do not disclose their emissions to consumers thereby preventing competition on emissions (or emission targets).

There is a clear parallel between these recent cases in the EU and a much older US case that concerned competition between car manufacturers on emission cleaning devices. In the 1960s, a cartel case under Section 1 of the Sherman Act was initiated against the four largest automobile manufacturers and their trade association. They were accused of hindering the adoption of pollution control technology, which led to millions of vehicles operating without effective emission control devices, thereby contributing to air pollution.[29] The case was resolved through a consent decree requiring the defendants to cease their action without any admission of guilt.[30]

The consumer welfare standard can also contribute to climate change goals by promoting competition for climate-relevant innovation. Antitrust enforcement can propel firms to produce products with better environmental and climate attributes that are valued by consumers. Another car emission related case that highlights this point is the EU's recent AdBlue case.[31] The case concerned the biggest German car makers, which the European Commission found to have colluded to limit competition in the development of emission cleaning technology

[26] Autorite de la Concurrence, Décision 17-D-20 relative à des pratiques mises en œuvre dans le secteur des revêtements de sols résilients (18 October 2017) <www.autoritedelaconcurrence.fr/fr/decision/relative-des-pratiques-mises-en-oeuvre-dans-le-secteur-des-revetements-de-sols-resilients> accessed 17 January 2025.

[27] ibid.

[28] The substance is Bisphenol A. Although it is authorised for use in the manufacturing of food containers, there are studies that suggest detrimental effects on human beings.

[29] *United States v Automobile Manufacturers Association*, 307 F. Supp. 617 (C.D. Cal. 1970).

[30] For more details on the US emission case, see also Sarah E Light, 'The Law of the Corporation as Environmental Law' (2019) 79 Stanford Law Review 171–75, who portrays it as an important development in the control of vehicle emissions.

[31] Case AT.40178—Car Emissions (COMP.G.4/ GM (8 July 2021, Brussels) <https://ec.europa.eu/competition/antitrust/cases1/202146/AT_40178_8022302_3050_5.pdf>accessed 18 January 2025.

from 2006 to 2014. The technology at issue was selective catalytic reduction, which is essential for diesel engines in passenger cars to meet EU emissions standards. The parties exchanged information to ensure that they would not compete to develop technology that would exceed the regulatory requirements for emissions ("over fulfilment") for passenger cars.[32]

The case was novel in the unique approach it adopted to examine innovation effects, particularly those related to environmental protection. It was the first instance where a competition authority treated a restriction of competition on (environmental) innovation as a by-object restriction.[33] This classification as a by-object restriction affirmed the inherently anticompetitive nature of the conduct. As a cartel, it constituted a most serious violation of EU competition law. It also marked a departure from the more orthodox assessment of innovation harm, as the European Commission did not attempt to quantify the innovation harm. The case translated the environmental harm into consumer welfare terms, asserting that environmental performance is a significant factor in competition, especially in the context of car purchases and even more so for premium cars. A point that equally applies to greenhouse gas emissions.

Overall, these cases demonstrate that climate benefits and consumer harm need not share a conflicting relationship. The two could coincide and enforcement against consumer harm resulting from cartels can foster climate goals.

4. Cooperation Under a (Sustainable) Consumer Welfare Standard

After having explored situations where the same conduct harms both the consumers and the climate and how enforcement against such conduct furthers consumer welfare and climate goals simultaneously, this section turns to scenarios where firms cooperate to pursue sustainability or climate objectives, thereby attracting antitrust scrutiny. The first part of this section delves into cases where the conduct may appear to be anticompetitive at first sight but turns out to be innocuous upon closer scrutiny. The second part explores the antitrust treatment of standard setting, which is particularly relevant in the climate context as it pertains to procompetitive (emission) standards. The final part discusses how climate change-related cooperation can be assessed under the consumer welfare standard and suggests adjustments to prevent the standard from unduly obstructing collaborative efforts to foster climate change goals.

4.1 Why a Closer Look Is Mostly Necessary

The question of the legal treatment of climate change agreements or agreements that purport to pursue climate benefits does not lend itself to a simple answer. Instead, a closer look is often necessary. In the EU, the first step is to assess whether such an arrangement is considered a by-object restriction or whether a resource-intensive assessment of effects should be conducted. In the US, the same question is framed in different terms: whether the per se rule or the Rule of Reason is applicable to a sustainability agreement.

However, this broad distinction only provides the general categories. A closer inspection is needed to determine whether and which of these should apply to the climate change

[32] The case also involved legitimate collaboration, so the Commission took the unusual step of issuing also an accompanying comfort letter that highlights the boundaries of permissible cooperation.

[33] On the object or effect distinction, see also Section 4.1 of this chapter.

agreement in question. In the EU, the new horizontal guidelines[34] of the Commission set out a number of sustainability agreements that are *unlikely* to restrict competition. In other words, such agreements may not even be within the scope of Article 101, TFEU and do not fall into either of these categories. These agreements that are *unlikely* to restrict competition are those that "ensure compliance with sufficiently precise requirements or prohibitions in legally binding international treaties, agreements or convention".[35] Equally unlikely are agreements that do not concern "the economic activity of undertakings, but their internal corporate conduct [such as commitments to] to eliminate single-use plastics from their business premises",[36] agreements to exchange information for example via a database regarding "(un)sustainable business practices in supply chains",[37] and agreements to start industrywide campaigns to increase the awareness of consumers of the impact of their consumption.[38] Beyond these categories of agreements, the general assessment of whether the agreement restricts competition by object or effect is conducted.

By-object restrictions are concerted behaviours that can be seen as restricting competition "by its very nature".[39] For such restrictions, the actual or potential effects on the market need not be examined.[40] Restrictions may be classified as by-object restrictions, either because of robust and reliable experience indicating that the agreement is inherently harmful[41] or because the specific features of the agreement in question suggest its particular harmfulness to competition.[42] In any case, interpreted strictly, the concept of by-object restrictions applies only to agreements which

> in themselves and having regard to the content of their provisions, their objectives, and the economic and legal context of which they form part, [result in] a sufficient degree of harm to competition, [and thus] . . . it is not necessary to assess their effects, since some forms of coordination between undertakings can be regarded, by their very nature, as being harmful to the proper functioning of normal competition in themselves.[43]

Thus, the assessment of the legal and economic context is crucial. In this assessment, it is necessary to examine the nature of the product as well as the structure and actual functioning of the market(s).[44] Any pro-competitive argument raised by the parties must also be taken into account as part of this context, in particular where such arguments can call into question the inherently harmful nature of the agreement.[45] At the same time, the focus on the legal and

[34] European Commission, 'Guidelines on the Applicability of Article 101 of the Treaty on the Functioning of the European Union to Horizontal Co-operation Agreements' (2023) Official Journal of the European Union, C series 259, 21 July 2023, 1–125.

[35] ibid para 528.

[36] ibid para 529.

[37] ibid para 530, where the agreement only concerns the sharing of this information but leaves it to the individual company whether or not such suppliers will be excluded.

[38] ibid para 531.

[39] Case C-67/13P *Card Bancaire v Commission* EU:C:2014:2204 paras 49–50.

[40] Case, C-501/06P, C-513/06P, C-515/06P and C-519/06P *GlaxoSmithKline* EU: C:2009:610 para 55; Case C-209/07 *BIDS* EU:C:2008:643 para 16; Case C-8/08 *T-Mobile Netherlands and Others* EU:C:2009:343 para 29.

[41] Case C-228/18 *Budapest Bank Nyrt. and Others* EU:C:2020:265 paras 76 and 79.

[42] Case C-591/16P *Lundbeck*, P, EU:C:2021:243 paras 130–31.

[43] Case C-307/18 *Generics (UK) Ltd and Others* EU:C:2020:52 para 67 and cases cited therein.

[44] Case C-67/13P *Card Bancaire v Commission* EU:C:2014:2204 para 53.

[45] Case C-307/18 *Generics (UK) Ltd and Others* EU:C:2020:52 paras 103–07; Case C-883/19P *HSBC v Commission* EU:C:2023:11 para 139. But those pro-competitive effects must be relevant, related to the specific agreement, sufficiently significant and demonstrated, see *Generics (UK) Ltd* para 107.

economic context means that it not necessary to show a direct link between the restriction and price increases to establish a by-object restriction.[46] And while the parties' intention can be taken into account, it is not a necessary element of the analysis.[47]

This means that for agreements that genuinely pursue climate change objectives, their aims need to be considered as part of the legal and economic context. It will have a substantial influence in assessing whether a restriction by-object exists.[48] The Commission in footnote 371 of the Horizontal Cooperation Guidelines suggests that where a such genuine aim exists, it would "justify a reasonable doubt as to the anti-competitive object of the agreement".[49] Thus, for such climate change agreements, the effect of competition would have to be shown rather than assumed. As part of this assessment of the effect on competition under Article 101(1), TFEU, options exist to incorporate their climate benefits outside the consumer welfare framework.[50] Within this framework, however, it needs to be established whether the sustainability agreement creates competitive harm[51] and if so, whether the pro-competitive effects outweigh these negative effects.[52]

A different distinction is drawn under US antitrust law, that is, between the per se rule and the Rule of Reason, with the former very much the exception rather than the rule in modern antitrust. From a time when most vertical agreements, tying arrangements, cartel agreements such as price fixing and market allocation, and most group boycotts were per se illegal in the 1960s and 1970s, the evolution of antitrust over the last five decades has been one of the gradual abandonment of the per se rule in favour of the Rule of Reason. Today, only hardcore cartel agreements and certain kinds of group boycotts remain subject to the per se rule under the *Socony-Vaccuum Oil* case[53] and the *Northwest Wholesale Stationers* case.[54]

A few other US Supreme Court cases are also relevant to sustainability and climate change agreements. First, in the *BMI* case,[55] the Supreme Court rejected the per se rule in favour of the Rule of Reason when analysing the competitive effects of an agreement which the Court acknowledged could constitute a price fixing agreement in the literal sense, but which was

[46] As Article 101, TFEU is designed to protect not only the immediate interests of consumers but also the structure of the market and thus competition as such, see Case C-8/08 *T-Mobile Netherlands and Others* EU:C:2009:343 paras 38–39.

[47] See Case C-228/18 *Budapest Bank Nyrt. and Others* EU:C:2020:265 para 37; Case C-67/13P *Card Bancaire v Commission* EU:C:2014:2204 para 54; Case C-286/13P *Dole Food and Dole Fresh Fruit Europe v Commission* EU:C:2015:184 para 118.

[48] European Commission (n 33) paras 533–34.

[49] Pointing further out that this should be '[i]n principle' and that '[t]he pursuit of the sustainability objective should not however be uncertain. See by analogy Case C-307/18 *Generics (UK)* EU:C:2020:52 paras 107–08.

[50] For example, it can be argued that the *Albany* exception for collective bargaining established in Case C-67/96 *Albany International* EU:C:1999:430 should be applied in the context of sustainability (see in this regard, e.g., Holmes (n 24) 370). Another route is the *Wouters* route which applies an objective necessity to legitimate objectives which sustainability might be, see Julian Nowag, *Environmental Integration in Competition and Free-Movement Laws* (OUP 2017) 217–21; Sandra Marco Colino, 'Antitrust's Environmental Footprint: Redefining the Boundaries of Green Antitrust' (2024) 103 North Carolina Law Review 135.

[51] See in this regard the next Section 4.2 of this chapter, on sustainability standards.

[52] See in this regard Section 4.3 of this chapter.

[53] *United States v Socony-Vacuum Oil Co.* 310 U.S. 150 (1940).

[54] *Northwest Wholesale Stationers v Pacific Stationery & Printing Co.* 472 U.S. 284 (1985). There is some debate as to whether qualified per se rule which applies to tying falls within the same category, *Jefferson Parish Hospital District No. 2 v Hyde* 466 U.S. 2, 33–35 (1984).

[55] *Broadcast Music v Columbia Broadcasting System 441* U.S. 1 (1979).

indispensable for the creation of a vastly superior and economically efficient product, the blanket license for copyrighted music.

Second, despite arguments by some commentators to the contrary,[56] it is strictly speaking not true that the Court has never entertained non-economic justifications for an agreement. In the *NCAA* case,[57] the Supreme Court withheld the application of the per se rule in favour of what is known as a quick look analysis to an agreement which most certainly constituted price fixing and output restriction on the ground that the agreement may help to preserve the venerable tradition of intercollegiate athletics. Although the agreement was ultimately condemned under the quick look analysis, the *NCAA* case calls into question the assertion that non-economic arguments have no place in US antitrust.

A further example of this is *U.S. v Brown University*,[58] where the United States Court of Appeal for the Third Circuit applied the Rule of Reason to the Overlap agreement, under which certain Ivy League universities coordinated their financial aid packages to individual applicants on the grounds that ensuring diversity in the student body improved the quality of higher education. Those who object to such a characterisation of the case may argue that student diversity was not treated as a public interest justification overriding consumer welfare but as a dimension of product quality and as such the case was ultimately still decided on consumer welfare terms. If that is indeed the case, the same logic can equally apply to sustainability and climate agreements where climate benefits are deemed to be a product attribute. Although it must also be noted that in the *Professional Engineers* case,[59] the Supreme Court refused to entertain the defendant's argument that excessive competition could lead to substandard engineering services, jeopardising public safety.

The implications of the foregoing for the legal treatment of climate change agreements under US antitrust law are the following. First, the Rule of Reason should apply to bona fide climate agreements. Unless an agreement is in fact a hardcore cartel agreement dressed up with fabricated sustainability or climate benefits, which is sometimes referred to as greenwashing, the Rule of Reason should apply. This is in keeping with the general trend of US antitrust law in favour of the Rule of Reason for non-cartel horizontal cooperation agreements. Second, standardisation agreements not accompanied by hardcore restrictions, which often emerge in the environmental context, should also be analysed under the Rule of Reason. Third, if horizontal cooperation is necessary for the emergence of an economically efficient arrangement or a new climate friendly product, an agreement would remain subject to the Rule of Reason even if it entails hardcore restrictions.

Finally, although the Supreme Court has never explicitly ruled on the permissibility of sustainability or climate justifications for an otherwise anticompetitive agreement, the door remains open for non-economic justifications. The *National Engineers* case can be distinguished on the ground that the Court's objection in that case was not so much an outright rejection of the public safety justification. Instead, the Court rejected the argument that competition will not incentivise engineers to provide safer engineering services. The Court seemed to be suggesting that a restriction of competition was not necessary because competition would also generate the desired public safety benefits.

56 Colino (n 49) 144.

57 *National Collegiate Athletic Association v Board of Regents of the University of Oklahoma* 468 U.S. 85 (1984).

58 *United States v Brown University* 5 F.3d 658 (3d Cir 1993).

59 *National Society of Professional Engineers v United States* 435 U.S. 679 (1978).

4.2 Procompetitive Sustainability Standards

There are numerous standards in the sustainability or climate change field, either privately set for specific products or situations[60] or promulgated by standardisation bodies such as the International Standard Organisation (ISO). For example, the ISO has issued ISO 14020:2000 that covers "Environmental Labels and Declarations—General Principles". ISO 14024:2018 bears the title "Environmental Labels and Declarations—Type I environmental labelling—Principle". It sets out the principles for formulating the requirements for environmental labels using a life cycle approach and the principles for awarding labels that certify compliance. Even the UN is involved in this field. It has promoted the United Nations Forum on Sustainability Standards.[61] Equally, the UN Conference on Trade and Development has adopted an assessment tool kit for evaluating the impacts of voluntary sustainability standards.[62]

Overall, technical and quality standards often receive a lenient treatment because they are presumed to facilitate innovation.[63] In the US, in the *Allied Tube* case,[64] the Supreme Court noted that if standard-setting bodies "promulgate . . . standards based on the merits of objective expert judgments and through procedures that prevent the standard-setting process from being biased by members with economic interests in stifling product competition . . . those private standards can have significant procompetitive advantages".[65] Where a standard-setting agreement is not accompanied by price fixing, a group boycott, or other hardcore cartel conduct, the Rule of Reason generally applies.

Moreover, the Standards Development Organization Act of 2004 amended the National Cooperative Research and Production Act and extended Rule of Reason treatment to standard-setting activities by standards development organisations. In fact, the American Bar Association went so far as stating that where "participation criteria are transparent, access to the standard is on the basis of reasonable and non-discriminatory criteria, and certification is awarded objectively",[66] the sustainability or climate benefits of an agreement should outweigh its competitive harm, and hence the agreement should be deemed legal under the Rule of Reason. At the very least, the consensus is that absent hardcore cartel conduct, the Rule of Reason should apply to standard-setting activities where participation is voluntary and where the standard is set objectively, absent manipulation by members.

Thus, it can be said that under US antitrust law, standard-setting agreements that do not involve hardcore restrictions, which may emerge in the environmental and climate change context, should also be analysed under the Rule of Reason.[67] Some difficulties remain here as voluntary standards devoid of an enforcement mechanism may be of questionable effectiveness. Attempts to bolster the effectiveness of a privately set standard through coercive measures may invite harsher antitrust scrutiny. As far as standard setting goes, the state of the law is still not entirely satisfactory.

60 Such as private labels for sustainability matters.

61 Which is a joint initiative of FAO, ITC, UNCTAD, UN Environment, and UNIDO.

62 See UNCTAD, *Framework for the Voluntary Sustainability Standards Assessment Toolkit* (2020) UNCTAD/DITC/TAB/INF/2020/5 <https://unctad.org/system/files/official-document/ditctabinf2020d5_en.pdf> accessed 22 January 2025.

63 See for example European Commission (n 33) para 257, 263.

64 *Allied Tube v Indian Head, Incorporated* 486 U.S. 492 (1988).

65 ibid 501.

66 American Bar Association, Antitrust Law Section, 'Sustainability and Competition Law—Report of the International Developments and Comments Task Force' (2021) 9.

67 For more details see in the next section.

In its latest push to address sustainability initiatives by firms, the EU has set out in detail the principles applicable to sustainability and climate standards. In general, it treats standard setting differently from other horizontal cooperation and uses a more lenient approach for its assessment because standards are generally seen as pro-competitive.[68] In the new horizontal guidelines, the Commission specifically addresses sustainability and climate change standards and explains how it would assess such standards. The Commission sets out a "soft safe harbour" within which such standards escape further antitrust scrutiny.[69] The Commission sees such standards as a tool that can be used for a variety or aims, including "to phase out, withdraw, or, in some cases, replace non-sustainable products (e.g., fossil fuels such as oil and coal, plastics) and processes (for example, coal-fired steel production) with sustainable ones".[70]

The Commission explains that where a number of conditions are fulfilled, the "soft safe harbour" applies and the standardisation agreement will most likely fall outside the scope of the Article 101(1), TFEU prohibition as it is "unlikely to produce appreciable negative effects on competition".[71] Where the standard does not meet these conditions, it will have to be examined more closely.[72] The conditions that need to be fulfilled in order to benefit from the "soft safe harbour" include transparent development procedures, absence of obligations on non-participating undertakings, absence of binding maximum standards, absence of exchange of commercially sensitive information not objectively necessary for the standard, effective and non-discriminatory access to the standard, absence of significant anticompetitive effects or a combined market share in excess of 20% for the participating undertakings.[73]

Similar to the rules in the US, these conditions are primarily intended to prevent possible price coordination between participants, foreclosure of alternatives (in particular alternative standards), and discrimination or exclusion of competitors.

Overall, a large number of agreements that aim to reduce greenhouse gases, such as agreements to phase out greenhouse gas-emitting production processes could benefit from this carve-out from Article 101(1), TFEU.

4.3 Assessing Other Climate Collaborations

This section examines how and to what extent climate sustainability benefits can be incorporated into antitrust assessments when anticompetitive effects are present. It discusses how to balance the anticompetitive effects and the positive climate effects within a consumer welfare framework. It explicitly eschews a societal or total welfare standard. It begins by explaining how harms and benefits are generally balanced in the EU competition law. It then discusses the new approach that updates the existing measurement tools for assessing consumer benefits of sustainability and climate agreements. This is followed by an overview of how sustainability benefits could be integrated within the Rule of Reason under a consumer welfare standard. The section concludes with suggestions for further improvement on how to incorporate sustainability benefits within the consumer welfare framework.

[68] European Commission (n 33) paras 439; 475–778 which also applies to sustainability standards, sees para 545.

[69] ibid para 549.

[70] ibid para 538.

[71] ibid para 549.

[72] It will then have to be assessed whether the standardisation agreement has the object or effect of restricting competition, see Section 4.3 of this chapter and if so whether the benefits outweigh the harm, see Section 4.4 of this chapter.

[73] ibid para 549 (footnotes omitted).

In the EU, Article 101, TFEU furnishes the framework for balancing anticompetitive effects and pro-competitive benefits. Where an agreement is considered to restrict competition within the meaning of Article 101(1), TFEU, it needs to be assessed whether any redeeming features fulfil the conditions of Article 101(3), TFEU. According to Article 101(3), TFEU, the agreement must provide for an improvement of "production or distribution of goods" or promote "technical or economic progress" while benefiting consumers. At the same time, the restriction of competition must be necessary to achieve the benefits, and competition cannot be eliminated in its entirety. The Commission interprets this test in a consumer welfare manner as meaning that *consumers* in the *relevant market* must at least be compensated for any loss. In other words, those that are affected by the restriction of competition (and thus are possibly paying a higher price) cannot be worse off after the net effect of the harms and benefits of the agreement are weighed.[74] This interpretation is a consumer-welfare-centric approach. It is restrictive because benefits cannot be considered if they either do not benefit *consumers* or—even if there are consumer benefits—the benefits accrue to consumers outside the *relevant market*. For climate change benefits, in particular for greenhouse gas emissions, this creates problems as this narrow interpretation of the EU antitrust rules means that such reductions must be shown to benefit the affected consumers.[75]

While broader approaches have been suggested for climate change matters,[76] the focus of the European Commission has been on consumer welfare and in economics terms, this assessment can be said to be guided by Pareto efficiency, since those consumers affected by the anticompetitive action cannot be made worse-off, even if that would benefit others. The benefits to consumers considered within this consumer welfare framework typically encompass cost savings but can extend to quality improvements and innovation. Cost savings may only be occasionally relevant in the sustainability context and quality improvements and sustainable innovation are likely to feature more prominently. The assessment of quality and innovation is traditionally focused on the user experience directly resulting from the product. One critical issue is the value that redounds to consumers, measured typically by their willingness to pay.[77]

In the latest version of its horizontal cooperation guidelines, the European Commission has explained how it will apply these principles in the context of sustainability and climate agreements.[78] It suggests an update to the tools for measuring consumer benefits and sets out three

[74] See, e.g., European Commission (n 33) para 18.

[75] The restriction of competition can, for example, affect the consumers by increasing the price of the goods in question.

[76] The UK and Austria adopted a different approach. The UK in its Green Guidance explained that its competition authority 'therefore considers it appropriate, in the case of climate change agreements, to depart from the general approach' and consider climate benefits more broadly: see CMA 185 Guidance (n 3). In Austria, this led to a change in the law, which otherwise mirrors the conditions of Article 101(3), TFEU. The legislature there added another paragraph to their Article 101(3), TFEU equivalent, i.e., Section 2 (1) of the Federal Act against Cartels and other Restraints of Competition (Cartel Act 2005—KartG 2005) (Austria) (as amended, effective 10 September 2021). This addition reads as follows: 'Consumers shall also be deemed to enjoy a fair share of the benefits which result from improvements to the production or distribution of goods or the promotion of technical or economic progress if those benefits contribute substantially to an ecologically sustainable or climate-neutral economy.'

[77] On quality assessment in competition law, see, e.g., OECD, 'The Role and Measurement of Quality in Competition Analysis: Key Findings, Summary and Notes' (2013) OECD Roundtables on Competition Policy Papers No 141 <doi.org/10.1787/46db870b-en> accessed 13 June 2025.

[78] On the development of these guidelines compared to the previous situation see also Julian Nowag and Wolf Sauter, 'The European Commission's New Horizontal Guidelines: A Great Reset for Competition Law and Sustainability?' (2023) 2 Competition Law & Policy Debate 57–62.

metrics under which the Commission will measure the consumer welfare gains. These are: "individual use value benefits", "individual non-use value benefits", and "collective benefits". The "individual use benefit" seems closest to the standard measurement as it measures the benefit that consumers derive from the direct use of the improved good. "Individual non-use value benefits" and "collective benefits" measure matters that have previously not been considered as such. Between the two, the "individual non-use value benefits" are more akin to more traditional measurements. It captures quality improvement by ascertaining consumers' willingness to pay for a more sustainable product. Consumers may deem the product superior due to its general societal benefits, even though these benefits are not enjoyed by them directly.[79]

The final form of benefits, "collective benefits", moves away from a reliance on willingness to pay as a means of quantification and sits more awkwardly within a consumer welfare framework. The Esuropean Commission explains that "collective benefits" are objective benefits that the consumers receive irrespective of individual appreciation.[80] This contrasts with individual non-use benefits, which are more subjective in nature. For example, increases in life expectancy can be measured and taken into account irrespective of the value an individual attaches to increased longevity due to reduced pollution. To align this approach with the consumer welfare framework, the Commission adopts a somewhat unusual restriction when considering such benefits. It limits the extent to which these "collective benefits" can be taken into account.[81] They may only be considered insofar as they reach the consumers that are affected by the restriction of competition.[82] In the context of greenhouse gas emissions, one would have to first calculate the total value of the emission reductions. The value of X would be divided by the number of affected people to obtain the individual value of the reduced emissions. This value could then be multiplied by the number of affected consumers to calculate the overall "collective benefits" of the affected consumers that can be taken into account. It is also worth noting that any of the benefits (use/non-use/collective benefits) individually or combined are considered when assessing the benefit for the consumers,[83] and that future benefits can be accounted for, but that a discount rate will be applied.[84]

In the US, the courts balance the anticompetitive effects of a business practice against its procompetitive benefits under the Rule of Reason. In the *Microsoft case*, court laid down the following four-step process for a Rule of Reason analysis.[85] First, the plaintiff must demonstrate the anticompetitive effect of the defendant's conduct, which must harm the competitive process and thereby harm consumers. This reference to consumer harm is a nod to the consumer welfare standard. Second, upon a showing of anticompetitive effects, the burden shifts to the defendant to proffer a procompetitive justification. Third, the burden shifts back to the plaintiff to rebut the proffered procompetitive justification. Finally, if the justification remains unrebutted, the plaintiff must demonstrate that the anticompetitive effects outweigh the procompetitive benefits. Despite this reference to balancing, however, few US courts have

[79] European Commission (n 33) para 575. In other words, 'voluntary (altruistic) choices of individual consumers', para 582; an example could be a forest close to someone's home. The person even though never directly 'uses' the frost may still be willing to pay for to having it maintained or protected.

[80] ibid para 582. The term 'objective benefits' stems from the Court's case law, see, e.g., Joined Cases 56 and 58–64 *Consten and Grundig v Commission*, ECLI:EU:C:1966:41, 348.

[81] E.g., European Commission (n 33) paras 583–85.

[82] See also ibid para 587. In this paragraph, the Commission explain how companies would have to go about to prove these benefits.

[83] ibid para 590.

[84] ibid para 591.

[85] *United States v Microsoft Corp* 253 F.3d 34, 58–59 (D.C. Cir. 2001).

engaged in a direct or even quantitative balancing of competitive harm and benefits in a Rule of Reason case. The degree of precision of the Rule of Reason is often said to be grossly overstated.[86] In the *Microsoft* case itself, the DC Circuit did not conduct any direct balancing, either due to the defendant's failure to offer a procompetitive justification or the plaintiff's failure to rebut the proffered justification.

Compared to the EU, there is considerably less guidance under US antitrust law regarding the incorporation of sustainability benefits under the Rule of Reason. Professor Sandra Marco Colino has noted that as of February 2024, there had been no US case in which the court accepted on sustainability grounds what otherwise would constitute a per se violation.[87] The discussion of explicit balancing of competitive harm and sustainability benefits, and the detailed classification of various kinds of sustainability benefits contained in the Commission Guidelines are absent in the US case law. There has been no guidance from the US Supreme Court so far on whether sustainability benefits will be considered under the Rule of Reason. Some have argued that case law such as the *Professional Engineers* case established that non-economic considerations are beyond the purview of US antitrust.[88] As previously argued, this interpretation is not undisputed, and the *NCAA* case represented an instance where the Supreme Court gave weight to a non-economic justification.[89] The question remains open as to whether sustainability benefits can be considered under Rule of Reason.

Commentators of the Chicago School persuasion tend to characterise sustainability as a non-economic objective and hence contend that it should be kept out of antitrust.[90] The extent to which this is true depends on whether and the extent to which sustainability benefits can be subsumed under the consumer welfare framework. Benefits that have been described as "individual use benefits" in the Commission Guidelines would most readily lend themselves to incorporation in a consumer welfare analysis. Many of them can be attributed to product quality or something which consumers can enjoy directly through the consumption of the product. Such benefits are clearly relevant under a consumer welfare standard.

Whether individual non-use value benefits should be considered under Rule of Reason would depend on the availability of evidence on consumer valuation of such benefits. To the extent there is concrete evidence of the consumer valuation of such benefits, there is no reason why such benefits should be excluded. After all, there is nothing inherent in the concept of consumer welfare that limits its consideration solely to utility that consumers derive directly from the consumption of the product. Any value that consumers derive from the production and existence of the product is relevant. It is similar to the value that consumers allegedly derive from the amateur status of the NCAA in the *NCAA* case. This is not something that benefits consumers directly, but it is something that the Supreme Court apparently believed to be important to consumers. In fact, it is noteworthy that the Supreme Court seemed to take that consumer preference for granted without requiring any empirical evidence. If the Court

86 Maurice E Stucke, 'Does the Rule of Reason Violate the Rule of Law?' (2009) 42 UC Davis Law Review 1375.

87 Sandra Marco Colino, 'Antitrust's Environmental Footprint: Redefining the Boundaries of Green Antitrust' (2024) 103 North Carolina Law Review 135, 145.

88 *National Society of Professional Engineers v United States* 435 US 679 (1978).

89 *National Collegiate Athletic Association v Board of Regents of the University of Oklahoma* 468 U.S. 85 (1984).

90 Alexander Raskovich and others, *Colluding to Go Green: Global Antitrust Institute Comments on the Austrian Federal Competition Authority's Draft Guidelines to Exempt 'Sustainability Agreements'* (2022) George Mason Law & Economics Research Paper No 22–29 <https://ssrn.com/abstract=4144191> accessed 25 June 2025.

believes that consumers demonstrate such a self-evident preference for sustainability benefits, the need for quantitative proof or empirical evidence for consumer valuation could be likewise obviated.

"Collective benefits" probably present the greatest analytical difficulty. Its distinct categorisation from individual non-use benefits is an implicit concession of consumer indifference towards them. Can the consumer welfare standard incorporate something to which consumers attach little value? One way to justify the inclusion of collective benefits under the consumer welfare standard is to expand the standard beyond consumer subjective valuation to objective benefits. For example, there are those who are against vaccination. Objectively, however, it is impossible to deny the benefit of herd immunity against an infectious disease, regardless of the subjective valuation of individual consumers. Similarly, the scientific consensus is that a temperature increase of two degrees Celsius higher than the pre-Industrial Revolution norm will bring devastating consequences and few would prefer that. The aversion to catastrophic natural disasters in the future is indisputably beneficial, also to the economy, in the long run, regardless of the myopic preference of some current consumers. The consumer welfare standard can be extended to incorporate such benefits.

Another way to justify the inclusion of collective benefits is to hypothesise future consumers. Again, future consumers would clearly prefer a world devoid of devastating natural disasters caused by climate change. These consumers do not yet exist. But there is no reason why their preferences should be disregarded. Relying on future effects to justify a present business conduct is not as novel or unprecedented in antitrust as it may initially seem. Antitrust regularly attaches weight to innovation which could be highly uncertain, and to which present and future consumers may attach little value. Investments in R&D may produce no innovation at all, or the innovation produced may not be deemed useful or valuable by future consumers. But that has not stopped antitrust from attaching weight to dynamic efficiency considerations in its analysis of patent exploitation practices, which implicate innovation incentives. By the same logic, there is no reason why antitrust cannot consider the future effects of current business practices on climate change when evaluating their legality. This argument is no doubt controversial, but it is one worth exploring. It echoes Professor Amelia Miazad's proposal of the universal consumer standard to allow antitrust to take into account the effects of a business practice on future consumers.[91]

Aside from the uncertainty and long-term nature of sustainability benefits, another stumbling block for the incorporation of these benefits into a consumer welfare framework is how benefits outside the affected market, and in particular those occurring in the future, can be considered.[92] Regarding the incorporation of out-of-market benefits, the difficulty can be partially addressed by adopting the "closely related or connected" markets approach.[93] The EU Court, for example, has suggested such an approach in the *Mastercard* case and other cases.[94] A similar approach was also taken in the *American Express* case in the US.[95] This approach suffers from some limitation in that most of these cases concerned two-sided markets and it is not clear whether the same rationale would apply outside of this context. One further

[91] Amelia Miazad, 'Prosocial Antitrust' (2022) 73 Hastings Law Journal 1637.

[92] See Julian Nowag, 'Sustainability and Competition' (2020) *OECD Roundtables on Competition Policy Papers*, No. 262 <https://doi.org/10.1787/18e2061c-en> accessed 25 June 2025.

[93] See Julian Nowag, *Environmental Integration in Competition and Free-Movement Laws* (OUP 2017) 234–38.

[94] Case C-382/12 P MasterCard and Others v Commission ECLI:EU:C:2014:2201 and Case C-238/05 *Asnef-Equifax, Servicios de Información sobre Solvencia y Crédito SL* ECLI:EU:C:2006:734.

[95] *Ohio v American Express Co.* 585 U.S. 529 (2018).

complication is that many sustainability benefits can be found in completely unrelated or disconnected markets. For these benefits, even the closely related or connected markets approach will be of no avail.

The analogy to innovation may be of some help. Take the example of innovation in the pharmaceutical industry. It is often argued that potentially anticompetitive practices in the industry may be justified on innovation incentive grounds.[96] Put simply, the additional revenue generated by a potentially anticompetitive practice can be used to fund further research and development, which will generate more innovation in the future. Under this logic, it is never expected or required that the future innovation be found in the same market in which present consumers are harmed. There is no requirement that the relevant consumers suffer no net harm when innovation incentives are used to justify potentially anticompetitive practices. Innovation can emerge in completely unrelated markets, and that has not rendered the innovation incentives thus generated irrelevant. This is particularly pertinent in the context of the pharmaceutical industry as drugs are often put to off-label use or may be put to completely unintended uses. Ozempic and other weight loss drugs that were originally developed to treat diabetes is an apt illustration of this. If we are willing to consider out-of-market pharmaceutical innovations to justify potentially anticompetitive practices, there is no immediately apparent reason to treat sustainability benefits differently.

Finally, as in innovation cases, a discount rate has to be applied to calculate the present value of future benefits. The European Commission suggests in its guidelines that it would apply a discount rate to future benefits.[97] The question as in many innovation cases will be what the appropriate discount rate is. This will need to be determined on a case-by-case basis.

5. Conclusion

This chapter explored how antitrust can use the established consumer welfare framework to incorporate climate change goals. The chapter focused on agreements that are addressed by Article 101, TFEU and Section 1 of the Sherman Act. These areas have traditionally been the centre of antitrust discourse, especially where consumer welfare is concerned, and have equally been at the forefront in the climate change and antitrust debate. After outlining the relevant legal frameworks in the EU and the US, the chapter examined how antitrust enforcement can be aligned with climate objectives and how enforcement against cartels can foster climate goals. It then turned to joint private initiatives aimed at addressing climate change, highlighting that many of these climate change agreements may fall outside the scope of antitrust prohibitions altogether. Furthermore, it analysed how climate-focused standard-setting can yield procompetitive outcomes and generally receives favourable treatment under antitrust law. Finally, the chapter considered agreements that do restrict competition but may nonetheless be justified under Article 101(3), TFEU or the Rule of Reason. It showed how many climate benefits can be considered within the current antitrust framework as they can be framed as improving consumer welfare, although important limitations remain.

In this regard, the chapter represents an initial attempt to bridge the divide between antitrust purists, who want to keep non-economic considerations out of antitrust analysis, and advocates, who believe that antitrust has an unavoidable responsibility to contribute to the efforts to combat climate change. While this is by no means the last word on the subject, we

[96] Patricia M Danzon and Adrian Towse, 'Pharmaceutical Innovation: Incentives and Regulation' (2016) 35 Health Affairs 798.

[97] European Commission (n 33), para 591.

believe it is a necessary beginning. Contrary to the antitrust purists who see this conversation as misguided or futile, we believe that it is incumbent upon commentators like us to help antitrust find a way to reconcile consumer welfare with sustainability and climate change. Climate change is too critical a threat to the future of humanity for anyone to ignore. Although this chapter is focused on agreements, the analytical approach based on consumer welfare developed here can also be extended to other areas of antitrust, including unilateral conduct[98] and merger control.[99]

[98] See, e.g., Catherine Ellwanger and others, 'EU Green Mergers & Acquisitions Deals: How Merger Control Contributes to a Sustainable Future' (2023/2) Competition Merger Brief <https://competition-policy.ec.europa.eu/system/files/2023-09/kdal23002enn_mergers_brief_2023_2.pdf> accessed 18 January 2025.

[99] See, e.g., Marios Iacovides and Valentin Mauboussin. 'Unilateral Conduct and Sustainability under EU Competition Law' in Julian Nowag, *Research Handbook on Sustainability and Competition Law* (Edward Elgar Publishing 2024) 352–74.

CHAPTER 22

Insurance Law

FRANZISKA ARNOLD-DWYER

1. Introduction

CLIMATE change threatens human well-being and planetary health.[1] The wildfires following consecutive periods of heavy rainfall and severe drought in Los Angeles (January 2025) and the widespread flooding following extreme rainfall in the South of Spain (October 2024) are just two recent examples of extreme weather-related events linked to climate change.[2]

Extreme weather-related events devastate lives, livelihoods, homes, and business and communal property, while also interrupting public services and business activities. Clean-up costs and lost economic activities during the reconstruction period generate additional costs. In 2024, natural catastrophes are estimated to have caused economic losses of USD 320 billion,[3] as well as non-economic consequences, including negative impacts on people's physical and mental health and loss of biodiversity. Urban areas are particularly exposed to natural catastrophes because they are densely populated and contain a high concentration of housing, commercial property, infrastructure, and public services.[4] Vulnerability increases in countries and regions with high levels of poverty, governance challenges, limited access to basic services and resources, violent conflict, and high levels of climate-sensitive livelihoods.[5] Where natural disasters interact with high vulnerability in the least developed and developing countries, they can escalate into humanitarian crises and increase those countries' debt burden further.[6]

Too often the risk of natural disasters is inadequately addressed until the disaster strikes. The European Commission's recent preparedness strategy paper identified several reasons why crisis management tends to be mostly reactive, rather than proactive: (1) there may be insufficient use of strategic foresight, an absence of awareness and anticipation, and a lack of early warning tools; (2) responsibility for preparedness may be fragmented between different authorities and stakeholders, and as a result there may be no holistic approach to preparedness and prevention; and (3) it may not be clear who should pay for ex ante measures and what resources are available.[7]

[1] Core Writing Team, Hoesung Lee, and José Romero (eds), 'Climate Change 2023 Synthesis Report: Summary for Policymakers' (IPCC, 2023) C.1.

[2] ibid A.2.1 and Figure SPM 1(b).

[3] Munich Re, 'Climate Change is Showing its Claws: The World is Getting Hotter, Resulting in Severe Hurricanes, Thunderstorms and Floods' (9 January 2025) <http://munichre.com/en/company/media-relations/media-information-and-corporate-news/media-information/2025/natural-disaster-figures-2024.html> accessed 20 January 2026.

[4] Hans-Otto Pörtnerand others, Climate Change 2022: Impacts, Adaptation and Vulnerability (CUP 2021) B.2.

[5] ibid.

[6] ibid.

[7] European Commission and the High Representative of the Union For Foreign Affairs and Security Policy, 'Joint Communication to the European Parliament, the European Council, the Council, the

The Paris Agreement[8] aims to strengthen the global response to the of threat climate change through mitigation, adaptation, and finance.[9] Climate change adaptation—the process of adjustment to actual or expected climate change and its effects in order to moderate harm or exploit beneficial opportunities—encapsulates notions of loss prevention and preparedness. While the Paris Agreement binds only the current signatory countries, financial institutions from the private sector are expected to contribute to climate financing solutions.[10]

Insurance is a private sector post-disaster solution. Over recent years, the insurance industry has positioned itself to contribute to the fight against climate change and the transition to a low carbon economy by insuring property against climate-related weather risks and by "de-risking the transition"—that is, providing insurance for new climate technologies and infrastructure projects that are needed to achieve industrial decarbonisation.[11] But can insurers also play an ex ante role by engaging with (prospective) policyholders and society in loss prevention and by fostering preparedness through their products and services? In this chapter, it is argued that they could and should play this role because the climate emergency demands it and because it makes business sense. This chapter examines to what extent insurance law could facilitate bottom-up solutions at the individual contract level by (1) knowledge-sharing on loss prevention and preparedness, and (2) financing of loss prevention measures by insurers, with reference to existing principles of insurance contract law and contractual provisions in insurance contracts. It addresses a research gap on the private law framework and contractual solutions for using insurance for loss prevention and preparedness for natural disasters in a nascent body of legal and business management literature on insurance and climate change.[12]

This chapter is structured as follows: After dealing with scope and definitional matters in the remainder of Section 1, Section 2 explains how insurance against natural hazard risk operates and examines the interlinked issues of insurability and protection gaps. Section 3 considers the limitations of the traditional insurance model in addressing protection gaps and the (un)suitability of conventional contractual tools for incentivising loss prevention. Section 4 discusses the societal, macro-economic, and business justifications for why insurers should engage with policyholders to implement loss prevention measures. Section 5 examines the legal implications of knowledge-sharing on loss prevention and the financing of loss prevention measures

European Economic and Social Committee and the Committee of the Regions on the European Preparedness Union Strategy' JOIN (2025) 130 final.

[8] Paris Agreement under the United Nations Framework Convention on Climate Change (adopted 12 December 2015, entered into force 4 November 2016) TIAS 16-1104.

[9] Paris Agreement, art 2(1).

[10] UN Framework Convention on Climate Change ("UNFCCC"), 'Matters relating to the global stocktake under the Paris Agreement' (13 December 2023) Decision -/CMA.5 paras 63, 113, 158.

[11] See, e.g., OECD, 'Enhancing the insurance sector's contribution to climate adaptation' (OECD Publishing 2023) 5; The Geneva Association, 'Climate Tech for Industrial Decarbonisation: What role for insurers?' (The Geneva Association 2024); Howden and BCG, 'The Bigger Picture' (*Howden Group*, 2024) <https://www.howdengroup.com/sites/huk.howdenprod.com/files/2024-06/the-bigger-picture-whitepaper.pdf> accessed 20 January 2026; Swiss Re, 'Climate Change' <https://www.swissre.com/risk-knowledge/mitigating-climate-risk/climate-change.html> accessed 20 January 2026.

[12] Paula Jarzabkowski, and others, *Disaster Insurance Reimagined* (OUP 2023); Franziska Arnold-Dwyer, *Insurance, Climate Change and the Law* (Routledge 2024); Carlo Pugnetti and others, 'Leading the Green Insurance Revolution' (2022) ZHAW School of Management and Law, Working Paper No. 1 <https://digitalcollection.zhaw.ch/server/api/core/bitstreams/4dcdb470-956d-4726-8a6a-a884a266da33/content> accessed 20 January 2026.

by insurers, and makes proposals for a tailored loss prevention clause for property insurance contracts.

Although some natural catastrophes have not been conclusively scientifically linked to climate change, I will use "natural catastrophes" and "natural hazards" as a shorthand for those which have increased in frequency and severity, or have been amplified, due to climate change (primarily windstorms, flooding, and wildfires). "Natural catastrophes" or "nat cat" is the risk terminology used by the insurance industry, but the United Nations Office for Disaster Risk Reduction (UNDRR) encourages the use of "natural hazard/s" instead to highlight the significant role that human decisions and actions play in creating vulnerability and shaping the scale and impact of these events.[13] "Loss prevention" means prophylactic actions taken to reduce the risk of future losses occurring. This could either be done by reducing the risk of the occurrence of the insured event (better described as "risk prevention"), or by mitigating the impact of the loss or damage if the insured event occurs ("loss prevention" in the narrow sense). We can slow down and (possibly still) reverse climate change through climate change mitigation measures, but we have little evidence as to when and to what extent this would decrease the frequency and severity of those natural hazards. In insurance actuarial terms it is more difficult to attribute risk prevention measures to a measurable risk reduction within the twelve-month time frame of a typical insurance policy and the twelve-month horizon relevant to insurers' capital requirements.[14] This chapter is therefore focused on loss prevention in the narrow sense which aligns with the Paris Agreement climate change adaptation goal of reducing the harmful impacts of climate change effects that we are already experiencing. In the insurance context, this means taking pre-disaster measures that reduce the exposure and vulnerability to natural hazard risks.[15] "Preparedness" requires developing resilience strategies and implementing procedures to deal with the impacts of disasters when they strike and to make it easier for people and businesses to resume their social and economic activities as soon as possible. "Policyholder" and "insured" are used interchangeably as the context requires.

As the theme of the book is climate change and private law, public disaster preparedness and response solutions and community-based insurance solutions[16] are outside the scope of this chapter, and insurance public–private partnerships have been excluded for space limitation reasons. Unless otherwise indicated, cases and legislation cited are from English and UK law.

2. Insuring Against Natural Hazards: The Issues

The insurance sector plays a critical role in absorbing the financial risk of loss from natural hazards. Insurance is a private contractual arrangement whereby the insured transfers the risk of a loss caused by a specified event to the insurer in return for the payment of a premium

[13] UNDRR, '#NoNaturalDisasters' <https://www.preventionweb.net/organization/nonaturaldisasters> accessed 14 May 2025.

[14] PRA Rulebook, Solvency II Firms, Minimum Capital Requirement, 3.1 and Solvency Capital Requirement—General Provisions, 3.3.

[15] National Association of Insurance Commissioners, 'National climate resilience strategy for insurance' (March 2024) <https://content.naic.org/sites/default/files/draft-naic-national-climate-resilience-strategy-12-1-2023-updated.pdf> accessed 20 January 2026.

[16] For community-based solutions, see, e.g., 'resilience bonds' discussed in Franziska Arnold-Dwyer and Julian Enoizi, 'The Need for a Sea Change in Climate-related Insurance' (*Guy Carpenter*, 6 June 2023) <https://www.guycarp.com/content/dam/guycarp-rebrand/insights-images/2023/06/2023-5-The-Need-for-a-Sea-Change-in-Climate-Change-Insurance_Published.pdf> accessed 20 January 2026.

by the insured. The focus of the discussion in this chapter will be on insurance for property damage, including homes, business premises, and personal property. Property insurance is a form of indemnity insurance where the insurer undertakes to hold the insured harmless in respect of a loss or damage caused to the insured's interest in the property by an insured event in return for the payment of a premium by the insured.[17]

The economic basis of property insurance is that a risk averse person can transform his or her risk of a large financial loss resulting from the loss of, or damage to, property into the certainty of losing a relatively small amount through premium payments. In return for paying premiums, the insured gains peace of mind that in the event of a loss covered by the insurance contract, it will be indemnified for that loss by the insurer.[18] The insurer can absorb the risk more efficiently because of risk spreading: The individual risks transferred from a large number of policyholders are pooled in a way that reduces the risk to everyone in the pool.[19] Insurers can also manage risks more effectively because they can (1) diversify their portfolios with different risks (different assets, time horizons, locations, insured perils), (2) pass on risk through reinsurance, and (3) invest the premium income more profitably compared to an individual or business investing the premium savings it would make by not buying insurance.[20]

2.1 Insurability

Not all risks are insurable. Insurable risks share common attributes: Losses must be accidental, definite, and calculable; exposure to catastrophic losses must be limited; premiums must be affordable; and there must be no legal and public policy restrictions on insuring.[21] Conversely, uninsurable risks display characteristics that make them unacceptable, unsuitable, or economically unviable for insurance. Chronic physical risks associated with climate change—such as sea level rises, coastal erosion, and temperature increase—are not insurable as they happen gradually over a longer time horizon, and therefore lack in definition and fortuity. But even acute physical risks (such as windstorms, flooding, or wildfires) have already become uninsurable in some regions, and are on the verge of uninsurability in others, because of their (1) increased frequency and severity leading to a steep rise in claims costs and (2) potentially catastrophic effects, exacerbated by regional vulnerabilities and exposure. In 2024, insurers' estimated natural catastrophe losses reached US$135 billion, which is above the previous ten-year average of US$98 billion.[22] At least two-thirds of these insured losses were in the US.[23]

As underwriting processes become more technologically sophisticated and data-driven, insurers will become less likely to accept risks further down the insurability scale, such as properties with certain building characteristics located in floodplains and in wildfire areas. The cross-subsidising effect of pooling different risks will become increasingly undermined.[24]

[17] *Sky UK Ltd v Riverstone Managing Agency Ltd* [2024] EWCA Civ 1567, at [43] per Lord Justice Popplewell.

[18] See further Tom Baker, Kyle Logue, and Chaim Saiman, 'Insurance Law and Policy' (5th edn, Aspen, 2021), Ch. 1 III.

[19] ibid.

[20] Eric A Posner and E Glen Weyl, 'An FDA for Financial Innovation: Applying the Insurable Interest Doctrine to the 21st Century Financial Markets' (2013) 107 Northwestern University Law Review 1307, 1314.

[21] Baruch Berliner, 'Large Risks and Limits of Insurability' (1985) 10 The Geneva Papers on Risk and Insurance: Issues and Practice, 313, 325.

[22] Munich Re (n.3).

[23] ibid.

[24] Jarzabkowski (n.12), Ch. 2.

Insurers will compete for the prime risks, while excluding cover for less desirable (less insurable) risks or charging premium at levels that make insurance cover for those risks unaffordable.[25] Moreover, insurability is threatened as the "peril regions" method of risk spreading is becoming unsuitable due to the compounding and cascading effect of natural hazards that traverses sectoral and regional boundaries.[26] Studies and real life examples from different regions show the increase in property uninsurability due to growing exposure to natural catastrophe risk.[27]

2.2 Protection Gaps

Increasingly unaffordable premiums, and the reduction, limitation, or withdrawal of coverage create new and exacerbate existing protection gaps. "Insurance protection gaps" have been defined as the difference between the amount of insurance that is economically beneficial and the amount of coverage actually purchased, whereas "risk protection gaps" are defined as the difference between total economic losses and insured losses.[28] In 2024, over 55% of global total economic losses from natural catastrophes were uninsured, leaving a protection gap of around US$180 billion.[29] In the EU, approximately a quarter of the losses incurred from natural catastrophe events are insured (in some EU countries lower than 5%).[30]

Natural hazard protection gaps can result in a significant financial burden for affected individuals and businesses. Without insurance, they are less likely to have the financial resilience to withstand a negative shock to their assets and income, and to absorb increased expenditure. Where protection gaps lead to hardship and have cascading effects on economic activities, supply chains, and the performance of loans and investments across the financial system,[31]

[25] Fred Hawke, 'The Big Wind Blows: On Northern Australia' in Bariş Soyer and Özlem Gürses (eds), *Insurability of Emerging Risk: Law, Theory and Practice*' (Hart 2025), 161, at 179–80.

[26] Nicholas Simpson and others, 'A Framework for Complex Climate Change Risk Assessment' (2021) 4(4) One Earth 489.

[27] See, e.g., European Central Bank (ECB) and European Insurance and Occupational Pensions Authority (EIOPA), 'Towards a European system for natural catastrophe risk management' (EIOPA 2024) 10; Canada: Climate Council, 'One In 25 Australian Homes Uninsurable by 2030: Climate Council Launches Cutting Edge Digital Climate-Risk Map' (press release 3 May 2022) <https://www.climatecouncil.org.au/resources/australian-homes-uninsurable-2030-climate-risk-map/> accessed 20 January 2026; California: Leyland Cecco, 'The Uninsurables: How Storms and Rising Seas Are Making Coastlines Unlivable' (*The Guardian*, 13 October 2022, Matthew Sellers, 'State Farm to Pull Out of 72,000 California Insurance Policies' *(Insurance Business Magazine*, 20 March 2024) <https://www.insurancebusinessmag.com/us/news/breaking-news/state-farm-to-pull-out-of-72000-california-insurance-policies-482069.aspx> accessed 20 January 2026; Eliyahu Kamisher, 'California Insurance Chief Backs 22% State Farm Rate Hike' (*Bloomberg*, 18 March 2025) <https://www.bloomberg.com/news/articles/2025-03-14/california-insurance-chief-backs-22-state-farm-rate-increase> accessed 20 January 2026; Europe: Max Tesselaar, WJ Wouter Botzen, and Jeroen CJH Aerts, 'Impacts of Climate Change and Remote Natural Catastrophes on EU Flood Insurance Markets: An Analysis of Soft and Hard Reinsurance Markets for Flood Coverage' (2020) 11 Atmosphere 146.

[28] The Geneva Association, 'Understanding and Addressing Global Insurance Protection Gaps' (The Geneva Association 2018) 8.

[29] Munich Re (n.3).

[30] ECB, 'The Climate Insurance Protection Gap' <https://www.ecb.europa.eu/ecb/climate/climate/html/index.en.html#:~:text=While%20the%20effects%20of%20such,5%25%20(see%20chart).> accessed 20 January 2026.

[31] International Association of Insurance Supervisors, 'A Call to Action: the Role of Insurance Supervisors in Addressing Natural Catastrophe Protection Gaps' (IAIS 2023) 14.

governments will be under pressure to step in to offer financial relief ultimately resulting in higher taxation,[32] negative impacts on GDP, and prolonged recovery pathways.[33]

3. Limitations of Traditional Insurance

To what extent can private law—specifically insurance law—support natural hazard loss prevention? There is a growing body of insurance and sociology literature that sees insurance as a governance tool to manage and control risk: Insurers can perform quasi-governmental functions regulating their policyholders' behaviour and achieve specific outcomes to mitigate the risk insured and prevent loss through price signalling, coverage exclusions, policy limits, and risk mitigation terms.[34] Nevertheless, several legal hurdles and practical limitations to using a traditional insurance contract as an instrument for loss prevention exist.[35]

3.1 Price-Signalling, Coverage Exclusions, Deductibles, and Limits

Premium pricing, coverage exclusions (contractual terms excluding specified risks from the insurance coverage), deductibles, and limits can send important signals to (prospective) policyholders about their exposure to high levels of risk. Confronted with a high premium or coverage exclusions, prospective policyholders will be incentivised to make positive risk adjustments to secure insurance cover at better rates and more comprehensive terms. However, these contractual tools may not operate as intended if they do not support policyholders in taking loss prevention measures. Rather, policyholders could be faced with unaffordable premium levels, coverage exclusions, and limited coverage for the very risks for which protection is most urgently needed. As noted in Section 2.3, unaffordable premiums and coverage withdrawal (whether in total, by exclusion, or by limitations) create coverage gaps rather than reducing them.

3.2 Risk Mitigation Terms

Risk mitigation terms (including insurance warranties, conditions, and innominate terms)[36] are contractual terms requiring the insured to do or refrain from doing something during the insurance policy period to maintain or reduce the level of risk. One such term is a so-called reasonable precautions clause, which requires the insured to take all reasonable precautions for the protection of the insured property. This type of clause tends to be interpreted narrowly so as not to extend to (ordinary) negligence of the insured as otherwise the insurer would be entitled to decline liability if negligence of the insured is established, which is usually the very

[32] ECB and EIOPA, 'Policy Options to Reduce the Climate Insurance Protection Gap: Discussion Paper' (EIOPA 2023) paras 1.1–1.3.

[33] ibid.

[34] Richard V Ericson, Aaron Doyle, and Dean Barry, *Insurance as Governance* (University of Toronto Press 2003); Tom Baker and Jonathan Simon, 'Embracing Risk' in Tom Baker and Jonathan Simon (eds), *Embracing Risk—The Changing Culture of Insurance and Insurability* (University of Chicago Press 2002).

[35] For a detailed consideration, see Arnold-Dwyer (n 12), chs 3 and 7.

[36] For the identification and classification of insurance contract terms and the consequences of their breach, see further John Birds, Ben Lynch,Simon Paul and others, *MacGillivray on Insurance Law* (16th edn, Sweet & Maxwell 20225) ch 10.

conduct which the policy is designed to cover.[37] Other risk mitigation terms may require more specific measures to mitigate loss—such as a promissory warranty in a homeowner policy that doors must be kept locked with a three-lever mortice lock; or an electrical installation inspection warranty in a business premises policy. While risk mitigation terms can be used to regulate risk by contractually requiring the insured to take risk mitigation or loss prevention measures, their performance can be onerous and the consequences of breaches can be draconian.[38] Insurers tend not to provide any advice to their policyholders on how they can comply with risk mitigation terms. For consumer policyholders, legal boundaries exist on what the insurer could fairly request them to do,[39] and there are commercial limits as to what insurers can ask any type of policyholder to do. Therefore, many risk mitigation terms aim only for the status quo, so that the risk the insurer has already assumed and for which the policyholder has already paid for coverage, does not worsen during the policy period, but they do not prescribe affirmative loss prevention measures. The costs of complying with risk mitigation terms are always borne by the insured. Instead, behavioural control terms, rather than being coercive, could be drafted as "nudge terms" that reward loss preventative behaviour,[40] and I will return to this in Section 5.

3.3 **Post-Event Claims Payments**

Claims payments are triggered by an insured event and require proof of loss—conventional property insurance never pays out in advance of a loss occurring. Therefore, insurance funds tend not to be available for ex ante loss prevention measures. Frequently, there is a formal process requiring the insured to give "notice of loss", following which the insurer will first assess the validity and quantum of the claim before making any payment. This process can take several weeks or even months. Insurers are bound by a statutory implied term to pay any sums due in respect of a valid claim within a reasonable time, but that time does not start running until the insurer has had a reasonable time to investigate and assess the claim.[41] This time lag in claims payments can be particularly problematic for natural hazard claims where insurance pay-out will be most needed immediately after the event (such as for alternative accommodation and basic provisions).

Claims payments could be used to "build-back-better"—that is, to reinstate property to a standard that is more resilient to prevailing natural hazards. This may be more expensive than building back to the same standard as before. The indemnity principle limits the insured's claim to his or her loss; the insured cannot recover more.[42] The default rules for the calculation of a loss are that (1) if property is destroyed completely, the measure of indemnity is calculated with reference to the value of the property at the date of the loss; and (2) if the

[37] See, e.g., *Beauchamp v National Mutual Indemnity Insurance Co* [1937] 3 All E.R. 19 at 27 per Finlay J; *Woolfall and Rimmer v Moyle* [1942] 1 K.B. 66.

[38] A breach of warranty or a non-compliance with a condition precedent could entitle the insurer to decline liability. See Insurance Act 2015, ss 10 and 11.

[39] These limits include the Consumer Rights Act 2015, s62 (unfair terms in consumer contracts are not binding on the consumer) and the Financial Conduct Authority Consumer Duty (FCA Handbook PRIN 2.1.1R Prin 12, regulated financial services firms are required to act to deliver good outcomes for retail customers).

[40] Applying Thaler and Sunstein's Nudge Theory (see: Richard H Thaler and Cass R Sunstein, *Nudge: Improving Decisions About Health, Wealth and Happiness* (Penguin 2012)) to insurance policy terms; see Arnold-Dwyer (n 12), sec 7.6.2.

[41] IA 2015, s.13A.

[42] *Castellain v Preston* (1883) 11 QBD 380 (CA) 386.

property is damaged, the measure of indemnity is calculated by reference to the reasonable cost of the repairs.[43] The principle of betterment requires the insured to account for the profit made following the effecting of repairs or replacement by the insurers that leave the insured better off after the loss than before.[44] In *Sartex Quilts and Textiles Ltd v Endurance Corporate Capital Ltd*, the English Court of Appeal held that betterment only applies where the insured derives real pecuniary advantage from reinstatement but not where the rebuilding results in improvements that are incidental and unavoidable. If building codes and regulations require rebuilding to a better standard, this is regarded as "unavoidable" and there should be no deduction for betterment.[45] Similarly, in *Medical Assurance Society New Zealand Ltd v East*, the New Zealand Court of Appeal held that the insurer's obligation to restore a building "to a condition substantially the same as new, so far as modern materials allow" meant the property had to be rebuilt in accordance with contemporary planning consent requirements, notwithstanding that this would lead to improvements in the property.[46]

Property insurance policies often contain "basis of settlement" clauses which provide for the reinstatement or repair of property that has been damaged, or the replacement of lost items. The measure of indemnity is then determined by reference to the cost of reinstatement of the property even if reinstatement costs are more than the pre-loss value of the property.[47] "Betterment" does not apply if the principle has been excluded on the true construction of the basis of settlement clause. The drafting of these clauses could be adjusted to provide for "resilient reinstatement" so that buildings are rebuilt to higher safety standards with features designed to prevent or reduce natural hazard damage. This is already happening: For example, in Australia, Suncorp Insurance's homeowner policies offer reinstatement with additional recommended resilience options to help protect against severe weather up to AU$5,000–$10,000.[48] Under the UK Flood Re "Build Back Better" scheme, homeowners can install property flood resilience measures up to the value of £10,000 when repairing their properties after a flood loss.[49]

Overall, insurance cannot prevent the peril's occurrence, it does not pay out in advance of a loss occurring, and it usually does not cover the costs of pre-emptive loss prevention measures. Post-event claims payments do not cover additional costs to meet build-back-better standards in the absence of specific policy terms.

4. Justifications for Loss Prevention

Driven by insurance supervisors, there is growing awareness of the need for loss prevention. The International Association of Insurance Supervisors (IAIS) notes that addressing protection gaps is essential to support financial stability and policyholder protection, and to ensure

[43] See the Marine Insurance Act 1906, ss 67 and 69, and for a more detailed discussion: MacGillivray (n 36) ch 19, sec. 3.

[44] Betterment is only broadly applied in the non-marine context; see *Reynolds and Anderson v Phoenix Insurance Co* [1978] 2 Lloyd's Rep. 440. For marine insurance, see MIA 1906, s.69(1).

[45] [2019] EWHC 1103, [90]–[96] per Leggatt LJ.

[46] [2015] NZCA 250.

[47] Robert Merkin, *Colinvaux's Law of Insurance* (13th edn, Sweet & Maxwell 2022) para 11–161.

[48] 'How can Suncorp Insurance help Build it Back Better™?' (*Suncorp Insurance*) <https://www.suncorp.com.au/insurance/home/build-it-back-better.html> accessed 29 June 2025

[49] 'Build Back Better' (*Flood Re*) <https://www.floodre.co.uk/buildbackbetter/> accessed 20 January 2026.

fair, safe, and stable insurance markets.[50] The IAIS further notes that loss prevention is a key action to reduce natural catastrophe protection gaps.[51]

Supervisory "interest" may harden into guidance and rules in due course as insurance supervisors are concerned about the spill-over effects to the rest of the financial system and to the real economy if protection gaps are left unaddressed.[52] For the reasons explained in Section 2.2, governments and NGOs are becoming concerned about protection gaps that will widen unless addressed with solutions that include loss prevention.[53]

It is not suggested that the insurance industry is responsible for safeguarding the stability of the financial system and humanitarian interests. Nevertheless, businesses are called upon to align their strategies and operations to "support a precautionary approach to environmental challenges" and "undertake initiatives to promote greater environmental responsibility".[54] Insurers who subscribe to the UN Principles for Sustainable Insurance should, among other things, aim to:

- develop products and services which reduce risk and encourage better risk management,
- develop or support literacy programmes on risk, and
- integrate ESG issues into repairs, replacements, and other claims services.[55]

There are economic arguments and business reasons for insurers to support risk prevention by sharing expertise and supporting funding. Unmitigated climate risk is a risk factor for insurers that can impact financial results through mounting claims and elevated regulatory capital levels.[56] The proverb that prevention is better than the cure has become a fundamental principle in healthcare where it means that proactive awareness and preventative interventions are more effective than later remedial action. This is also reflected in health insurance where costs for health check-ups and diagnostic tests are often covered regardless of whether they reveal any medical conditions. Similarly, risk reduction and loss prevention are also widely practiced under the banner "cyber hygiene" in the technology risk space where the insurance industry supports corporate policyholders with cyber risk assessments, cybersecurity tools, and monitoring services as part of the coverage package.[57]

[50] IAIS (n 31) para 2.1.

[51] ibid para 3.3. Also see, EIOPA's work on protection gaps and loss prevention (EIOPA, 'Report on Non-Life Underwriting and Pricing in Light of Climate Change' (2021) EIOPA-BoS-21/259 01); ECB and EIOA (n 27 and n 32); and NAIC (n 15) in which 'pre-disaster mitigation' is a key action to manage climate risk and close protection gaps.

[52] IAIS (n 31) para 2.1; and IAIS, Bank for International Settlements: Financial Stability Institute and Swiss Financial Market Supervisory Authority, 'Mind the Climate-Related Protection Gap: Reinsurance Pricing and Underwriting Considerations' (March 2025) para 98 <https://www.iais.org/2025/03/fsi-insights-note-published-on-climate-related-protection-gaps-from-a-reinsurance-perspective/> accessed 14 May 2025.

[53] High-Level Panel on Closing the Protection Gap, 'Crisis Protection 2.0: Future-Proofing Our World' (Centre for Disaster protection 2025) 5; G7 Italia 2024 Finance Ministers and Central Bank Governors' Meeting, 'High-Level Framework for Public–Private Insurance Programmes against Natural Hazards' (G7 Italia 2024) 2. See also Section 2.3.

[54] UN Global Compact, 'The Ten Principles of the UN Global Compact' Principles 7 and 8 <https://unglobalcompact.org/what-is-gc/mission/principles> accessed 20 January 2026.

[55] United Nations Environment Programme Finance Initiative, 'Principles for Sustainable Insurance' Principle 1 <https://www.unepfi.org/insurance/insurance/the-principles/> accessed 20 January 2026.

[56] PRA, 'Supervisory Statement 5/25–Enhancing Banks' and Insurers Approaches to Managing Climate Risk' (December 2025), section 2.

[57] See, e.g., AIG, 'Why Choose AIG for Cyber Insurance?' <https://www.aig.co.uk/home/risk-solutions/business/cyber> accessed 20 January 2026.

A recent US Chamber of Commerce report, using twenty-five natural disaster scenarios as examples, shows that each US$1 of investment in resilience and disaster preparedness reduces a community's economic costs after an event by US$7.[58] Loss prevention and preparedness measures can reduce the number of lost lives and homes, reduce the impact on business profits, and—with fewer jobs lost—maintain labor force numbers and economic production, thereby ensuring income flows from continuing economic activities.[59] Given that insurers will pay for at least some of these losses, they would benefit from contributing their risk management expertise and financial resources to loss prevention and preparedness.

Moreover, insurers' current response of raising premiums and withdrawing coverage leads to loss of business. By adding loss prevention and preparedness services to their products, insurers can tackle the underlying insurability issue, regain business, and buy reinsurance at better rates, as well as (re)building trust, relevance, and goodwill among their customer base. It ensures long-term commercial viability in the face of climate-related uninsurablity scenarios. Engaging in loss prevention can reduce an insurer's exposure to reputational damage and "green" litigation risk.[60] Sustainability-related disclosure frameworks will enhance transparency as to which insurers do and do not support loss prevention.[61] It is an opportunity for insurers to transform their traditional business model into an innovative combined model where they act as risk carriers and promote loss prevention through existing transmission channels.

Ultimately, what is not insurable is not investable:

> Risk cannot be transferred (no insurance), risk cannot be absorbed (no public capacity), and risk cannot be adapted to (physical limits exceeded). That means no more mortgages, no new real estate development, no long-term investment, no financial stability. The financial sector as we know it ceases to function. And with it, capitalism as we know it ceases to be viable.[62]

To summarise, there are societal and macro-economic justifications, and also strong business reasons, for insurers to engage with policyholders to implement loss prevention measures in order to maintain the insurability of natural catastrophe risks and reduce protection gaps.

5. Insurance Law and Loss Prevention

The decision-making power to implement loss prevention measures at the individual household or business property level is ultimately with the owner. Due to information gaps and

[58] US Chamber of Commerce, Allstate, and the US Chamber of Commerce Foundation, 'The Preparedness Payoff: The Economic Benefits of Investing in Climate Resilience' (*US Chamber of Commerce*, 2024).

[59] ibid.

[60] See Erik Knutsen, 'Insurance and 'Green' Liability: How Liability Insurers Can Propel Climate Change Action' in Cherie Metcalf and Stephanie Stern (eds) *Institutions and Effective Climate Action* ((University of Toronto Press, forthcoming).

[61] See UK: Companies Act 2006 ss 414CA and FCA Handbook, UK Listing Rules r 6.6.9; EU: Sustainability-related Disclosures in the Financial Sector Regulation (EU) 2019/2088; Corporate Sustainability Reporting Directive (EU) 2022/2464; European Sustainability Reporting Standards (ESRS 1 General Requirements, ESRS 2 General Disclosures ESRS E1 Climate Change); International: IFRS International Sustainability Disclosure Standards IFRS S2.

[62] Günther Thallinger (board member of global insurer Allianz), 'Climate, Risk, Insurance: The Future of Capitalism' (*LinkedIn*, 25 March 2025) <https://www.linkedin.com/pulse/climate-risk-insurance-future-capitalism-g%C3%BCnther-thallinger-smw5f/?trackingId=009VHzX5olB7Lqb%2FOqesiw%3D%3D> accessed 14 May 2024.

cognitive biases,[63] consumers and businesses alike frequently fail to appreciate that their property is vulnerable to natural hazards.[64] Even if they do, they may not know what they should do to reduce the risk of loss or damage to their property. Moreover, loss prevention measures can be expensive[65] and policyholders may not have the inclination or the financial means to invest in them. Consumers in particular may also expect the state to provide financial support when a natural disaster occurs.[66] Nudge theory suggests that people's choices and decision-making can be influenced by incentives coupled with information about why a particular choice is advantageous to them.[67] Using behavioural economics techniques, insurers can address challenges posed by lack of risk awareness and lack of funding by leveraging their pre-contractual engagement with prospective policyholders and their contractual relationship with policyholders using their expertise and financial incentives. In this section, I will examine two bottom-up solutions at the individual contract level: (1) loss prevention knowledge-sharing, and (2) loss prevention financing by insurers, with reference to existing principles of insurance contract law and established terms in insurance contracts.

5.1 Knowledge Sharing

The insurance industry holds vast amounts of data on the occurrence and impacts of natural catastrophe events. To manage its own exposure, the industry has developed advanced expertise in climate and natural catastrophe risk assessment and risk management.[68] This expertise could be leveraged by making climate risk information available in order to build awareness about exposure to natural hazards, and by sharing knowledge and expertise on potential loss prevention measures that the policyholder could take.[69] This is already happening to some extent at the public level where insurance data feeds into publicly run early warning systems that alert affected communities of impending natural catastrophe events, allowing for timely evacuations and preventive measures. In a 2023 report, the Organisation for Economic Co-operation and Development (OECD) suggested that insurers could also share information with their policyholders directly, among others, on the following:

1. local climate-related risk exposures and corresponding socio-economic consequences;
2. information indicating how policyholders' premiums might be impacted in the future by a changing climate;
3. loss prevention measures that policyholders could take, based on current as well as future climate conditions;
4. specific information on available premium discounts for loss prevention, including any conditions that must be met to receive those discounts;

63 Mariusz Fras, Dariusz Pauch, and Damian Walczak, 'Determinants of the Behaviour of Entities on the Insurance Market in the Light of Changes Introduced by the IDD Directive' (2024) 47 Journal of Consumer Policy 533 541; and more generally see: Daniel Kahneman, *Thinking, Fast and Slow* (Penguin 2012).

64 EIOPA, 'Impact Underwriting: Report on the Implementation of Climate-Related Adaptation Measures in Non-Life Underwriting Practices' (EIOPA 2023) 57.

65 E.g., EUR 3,000 for a flood-proof door; GBP 70/sqm for green-roofing.

66 ECB and EIOPA (n 32) 10.

67 Thaler (n 40) chs 2 and 14.

68 OECD (n 11) 5–8.

69 Jarzabkowski (n 12).

5. information on potential sources of funding or financing for investing in loss prevention measures (such as from government grants, as discussed in Section 5.2.3); and
6. information on trusted contractors to implement loss prevention measures.[70]

By way of shorthand, I will refer to this information in the aggregate as "loss prevention information". Insurers have regulatory information duties relating to their organisation and their insurance products,[71] but these duties do not extend to loss prevention information. Does insurance contract law require the insurer to disclose loss prevention information to a (prospective) policyholder?

5.1.1 Pre-Contractual Information Duties

The statutory pre-contractual duty to give a fair presentation of the risk only applies to the insured, but not the insurer.[72] However, courts have long recognised the existence of a common law pre-contractual duty of disclosure on the part of the insurer, arising under the principle of utmost good faith.[73] Nos. 1 and 4 from the list in Section 5.1 may well be information that a prudent prospective policyholder would like to know in deciding whether or not to purchase insurance and on what premium terms. No. 2 is immaterial to the placement of the current risk, as it relates to premium rates under future insurance contracts. No. 3 may be material to the extent that a prospective policyholder may not want to buy insurance at all if, by implementing the loss prevention measures, the risk of loss can be minimised to zero or to an amount where the prospective policyholder would not want to buy insurance. No. 3 could also be material if premium discounts are available for specified loss prevention measures—this is the No. 4 situation. Nos. 5 and 6 are extraneous to the placement of the insurance and would therefore not fall within the insurer's pre-contractual duty.

Another issue with the insurer's pre-contractual duty is that there is considerable uncertainty about whether any remedy is available upon its breach. For marine insurance, the mutually applicable principle of utmost good faith was codified in s.17 of the Marine Insurance Act (MIA) 1906 and has since been regarded as declaratory of the common law as it applies to non-marine insurance. Until its partial deletion by s.14(3) of the Insurance Act 2015, s.17 of the MIA 1906 provided that the consequence of a breach of the principle of utmost good faith by either party would entitle the other party to avoid the contract. From that the courts had extrapolated that avoidance would be the only remedy available to parties, with no action in damages.[74] Following the deletion of the remedy of avoidance from s.17 which leaves the principle of good faith intact, it is unclear if there is now no remedy at all for a breach of the insurer's duty of disclosure,[75] or if this has opened up the possibility for a remedy in damages.[76]

70 OECD (n 11) 21–22.

71 FCA Handbook, 'Insurance Conduct of Business Sourcebook' (ICOBS) chs 4 and 6.

72 IA 2015, s.3(1). In relation to consumer insureds, the duty is duty to take reasonable care not to make a misrepresentation to the insurer; see Consumer Insurance (Disclosure and Representations) Act 2012, s 2(2).

73 *Carter v Boehm* (1766) 3 Burr. 1905, 1909 per Lord Mansfield; *Banque Keyser Ullmann SA v Skandia (UK) Insurance Co Ltd* [1990] 1 Q.B. 665, 772 per Slade LJ; accepted on this point by the House of Lords in [1991] 2 A.C. 249, 268 per Lord Bridge, and 280 per Lord Templeman.

74 ibid 280 per Lord Templeman.

75 IA 2015, Explanatory Notes, para 116.

76 Terry O'Neill and Franziska Arnold-Dwyer, *The Law of Reinsurance in England and Bermuda* (6th edn, Sweet & Maxwell 2024) para 6–125.

5.1.2 Contractual Information Duties

Whether the insurer has any contractual duties to provide loss prevention information is a matter of contractual interpretation. In the first instance, the court would look to the express terms of the policy. An express term to that effect would be highly unusual in a standard consumer or commercial policy, although it could be part of an individually negotiated insurance contract. It is unlikely that the courts would be minded to imply a term to that effect as it is not necessary to give business efficacy to the insurance contract.[77] Moreover, the courts have given the post-formation (continuing) duty to observe good faith a limited scope whereby "the content of the obligation . . . has a different application and content in different situations" during the performance of the insurance contract.[78] Apart from contract variation situations, the courts have been reluctant to find that post-formation, the continuing duty of good faith requires the provision of information.

On balance, although insurance contract law is not averse to information requirements, the parties cannot rely on it as the sole basis for insurers to provide loss prevention information. Instead, insurers could consider offering loss prevention information as an additional service for specific insurance products. Generic loss prevention information could be produced cost-efficiently based on insurers' existing know-how and data and be provided alongside the product information that insurers are already required to give to a (prospective) policyholder.[79] More tailored advice could be part of a risk assessment that the insurer shares with the policyholder or could be a stand-alone separately chargeable service. Insurers could harness technology to control the costs of preparing and distributing tailored loss prevention information. For example, the Zurich Risk Advisor app, available to corporate policyholders of globalinsurer Zurich, enables users to carry out a risk self-assessment on the basis of which the app then offers actionable risk management and loss prevention insights and can connect the user to Zurich professionals who can carry out a more in-depth remote risk assessment.[80] With the advance of AI, models could be trained to analyse property-specific data in combination with data on local climate-related risks and their potential impacts more accurately, and to suggest tailored loss prevention measures.

There are concerns that the provision of loss prevention information could contravene the restriction on insurers not to carry on any commercial business other than insurance business and activities directly arising from that business,[81] but these are overstated precisely because loss prevention arises directly from insurance business. The risk of tort liability has also been used as an argument against informational engagement by insurers with policyholders.[82] There could be a risk of negligent advice liability in respect of No. 3, whereas Nos. 4–6 are purely factual, and No. 2 is more likely to be regarded as statement of opinion (see Section 5.1). Among other elements, the insured would have to show that it relied on the negligent advice to succeed in an action for damages. There are measures that insurers could take to protect themselves, such as verifying any information against government and scientific advice and

[77] For the business efficacy test see: *Marks & Spencer Plc v BNP Paribas Securities Services Trust Co (Jersey) Ltd* [2015] UKSC 72, at [15]–[27] per Lord Neuberger (PSC).

[78] *The Star Sea* [2001] UKHL 1, [48] per Lord Hobhouse.

[79] ICOBS (n 71).

[80] Zurich, 'Zurich Risk Advisor' <https://www.zurich.com/commercial-insurance/tools/zurich-risk-advisor> accessed 20 January 2026.

[81] PRA Rulebook, Solvency II Firms, General Conditions Governing Business, 9.1.

[82] Kyle D Logue, 'Encouraging Insurers to Regulate: The Role (If Any) for Tort Law' (2015) 5(6) UC Irvine L Rev 1355; and Kenneth Abraham and Daniel Schwarcz 'The Limits of Regulation by Insurance' (2022) 98 Indiana Law Journal 215, 237–41.

using disclaimer language. Overall, for the provision of loss prevention information to be a contract feature rather than a voluntary service rendered by the insurer, the insurance contract should contain express provisions that detail what information the insurer will provide and when (and whether there is an obligation to provide updated information during the policy period), and whether there will be a charge in addition to the premium.

5.2 Financing Loss Prevention

Costs are a significant barrier to loss prevention measures at the household level. Could insurers indemnify a policyholder for prevention costs incurred, or even make advance payments before a natural catastrophe event occurs? In answering this question, I will focus on the "hold harmless" obligation and indemnity principle, the marine insurance duty to sue and labour, the duty to mitigate, and the doctrine of subrogation, but leave aside the potential implications that this would have on consumer protection, reinsurance arrangements, accounting, and regulatory capital.

5.2.1 Hold Harmless and Indemnity Principle

In property insurance, the indemnity principle limits the insured's claim to his or her loss caused by an insured peril.[83] Ergo, the indemnity principle does not extend to payments that are not compensating loss or to payments made in advance of the insured peril. And yet, in *Sky UK Ltd v Riverstone Managing Agency Ltd*, the Court of Appeal reconfirmed the orthodoxy under English law that underlying the principle of indemnity is the insurer's primary obligation to hold the insured harmless:

> A contract of insurance against damage to property is a contract of indemnity, which is often described as a contract to hold someone harmless . . . The promise is to hold the assured harmless in the sense that the insurer promises that the assured will not suffer the insured damage. It is in the nature of a warranty that the insured damage will not occur . . . That promise represents the insurer's primary obligation under the contract of insurance.[84]

It could be argued that performance of the hold harmless obligation should—as *Sky* suggests—require the insurer to take steps to prevent the loss from occurring and that this, by extension, should give rise to a right to recover costs from the insurer, should the insured itself implement suitable loss prevention measures. However, the courts have stopped short of taking the "hold harmless" obligation to the logical but unrealistic conclusion that the insurer must (take steps to) prevent the loss. Generally speaking, English contract law does not compel specific performance and regards damages as an adequate remedy. Regarding property insurance contracts, no one expects insurers to prevent the loss from occurring, and in many instances an absolute obligation to prevent loss would be outside the insurers' control and likely impossible to perform. Rather it is the layperson's perception that the insurer's obligation is to pay compensation for losses incurred—which corresponds to the insurer's secondary obligation to pay damages (in the form of a claims payment) if the insured peril occurs and causes loss to the insured.[85] The *Sky* decision is subject to an application for appeal to the Supreme Court, and it remains to be seen whether the Supreme Court will consider the meaning of the insurer's "hold harmless" obligation. While the indemnity principle provides no or limited support

[83] *Castellain v Preston* (1883) 11 QBD 380 (CA) 386.
[84] [2024] EWCA Civ 156, [43] per Lord Justice Popplewell.
[85] ibid.

for insurers being obligated to fund loss prevention measures, the "hold harmless" obligation serves as a "moral reminder" to insurers about what they promised to do.

5.2.2 Sue and Labour Costs and Mitigation Damages

A sue and labour clause usually requires (1) the insured to take such measures as may be reasonable for the purpose of averting or minimising a loss, and (2) the insurer to pay to the insured any expenses properly incurred pursuant to the clause in addition to any indemnity payable.[86] The insurer's liability for sue and labour costs is in addition to the indemnity under the insurance contract.[87] Sue and labour costs are recoverable if they are extraordinary expenses reasonably incurred for the purpose of preserving the property from loss by an insured peril.[88] The insured's duty to sue and labour and its right to recover sue and labour costs is activated when the peril has arisen or is imminent.[89]

Could sue and labour clauses be a blueprint for insurers to contribute to loss prevention costs in relation to natural catastrophes? There are several considerations. First, the courts have been skeptical towards any attempt to recover such costs from the insurer in the absence of a sue and labour clause or similar provisions.[90] Such provisions are not common in non-marine insurance contracts and there is no non-marine equivalent to the MIA 1906, s.78.

In general contract law, mitigation requires the injured party to take all reasonable steps to avoid the consequences of the breach of contract. Accordingly, (1) there is no recovery for loss which should reasonably have been avoided, (2) there is recovery for costs incurred in taking reasonable mitigating steps, even if such steps end up increasing the loss, and (3) if the loss is successfully reduced by the taking of reasonable mitigating steps then the party in breach is entitled to the benefit of that.[91] The case law does not speak with a consistent voice as to whether an insured can recover expenses incurred to prevent or minimise loss as "mitigation damages" under general contract law principles in the absence of a sue and labour clause or similar provision:

- In *Yorkshire Water Services Limited v Sun Alliance London Insurance Plc*, the Court of Appeal commented *obiter dicta* that in the absence of policy provisions, the insured has no duty to mitigate its loss and the insurer has no duty to reimburse mitigation expenses, and there is no basis for implying a term to that effect.[92] The insured under a liability policy had undertaken flood alleviation works costing over £4 million to avoid incurring liability to neighbouring businesses but was unable to recover these loss mitigation costs because the policy required the insured at his own expense to prevent further damage. In

[86] See MIA 1906, s 78(4) and (1) which codified the sue and labour clause contained in the old S.G.Form policy. Even without a sue and labour clause, the insured under a marine insurance contract is under a duty to sue and labour (s 78(4)).

[87] *Kuwait Airways Corp v Kuwait Insurance Co SAK No.1)* [1999] 1 Lloyd's Rep. 803, 816 per Lord Hobhouse.

[88] *Royal Boskalis Westminster NV v Mountain* [1999] QB 674.

[89] *National Oilwell (UK) Ltd v Davy Offshore Ltd* [1993] 2 Lloyd's Rep 582, at 618 per Judge Coleman.

[90] See, e.g., *Seele Austria GmbH & Co v Tokio Marine Europe Insurance Ltd* [2007] EWHC 1411 and the discussion in Mark Templeman, Claire Blanchard, Philippa Hopkins and others, *Arnould: Law of Marine Insurance and Average* (21st edn, Sweet & Maxwell 2024) [25–36] and [25–37]; *Yorkshire Water Services Ltd v Sun Alliance and London Insurance Plc* [1997] 2 Lloyd's Rep 21.

[91] These rules of mitigation were most recently reaffirmed by the Supreme Court in *Sharp Corp Ltd v Viterra BV* [2024] UKSC 14, [85] per Lord Hamblen.

[92] *Yorkshire Water Services Limited v Sun Alliance London Insurance Plc* [1997] C.L.C. 213.

any event, alleviation works carried out before the insured event occurred could not be recovered as mitigation damages because no breach had occurred at this point.[93]

- More recently, the Court of Appeal considered mitigation damages in *Sky UK Ltd v Riverstone Managing Agency Ltd.*[94] Two of the issues in the case were whether the insured under a construction all risks policy could recover (1) access damage, being damage deliberately caused in order to assist in remedying insured damage, and (2) investigation costs incurred in evaluating the extent and nature of the damage the project caused by water ingress. In respect of (1) the Court of Appeal applied the general contract law mitigation rules to an insurance contract without discussing the preceding insurance case law on this point. The Court of Appeal noted that access damage is recoverable as mitigation damages but, on the facts, no mitigation steps had been taken.[95] In respect of (2) the Court of Appeal held that they would either be recoverable as an insured loss under the policy if a loss was discovered, or as mitigation damages in the event no (insured) damage was discovered.[96] The decision is being appealed by the insurers.

Academic opinions (prior to *Sky*) are divided too.[97]

I suggest that loss mitigation is consistent with the duty of utmost good faith, aligns with the practice of using express risk mitigation terms (see Section 3.2), and constrains the moral hazard that invites the insured to act imprudently in the knowledge that it has insurance. It is further suggested that a duty to mitigate can be reconciled with insurance cover for negligence for three reasons: (1) an error of judgment or negligence in respect of mitigation is unlikely to constitute a new intervening cause unless it is so significant as to displace the operation of the insured peril;[98] (2) as a matter of interpretation, the standard of care for mitigation could be set to be consistent with negligence cover, so that only gross negligence and intentional failure to mitigate would constitute a breach;[99] and (3) they minimally overlap in time: Negligence cover is relevant up to and including the time of loss, whereas the duty to mitigate arises from the time of the (anticipated) breach (see later in this section below). Moreover, if the loss prevention measure is based on loss prevention information provided by the insurer (as suggested in Section 5.1.2), the risk of failing to take appropriate loss prevention measures can be reduced practically, as well as reducing legal risk via a potential contributory negligence defence.[100] Allowing the insured to recover mitigation damages recognises that mitigation of loss benefits the insurer whose liability would be reduced if the mitigation steps taken are successful.

Reimbursement for mitigation damages is available in other jurisdictions, for example, under the German Insurance Contact Law Act (Versicherungsvertragsgesetz, §82), the Swiss Insurance Contract Act (Versicherungsvertragsgesetz, Art. 38c I), and the Principles of

[93] ibid at 221–22, per Lord Justice Stuart-Smith.

[94] *Sky UK Ltd v Riverstone Managing Agency Ltd* [2024] EWCA Civ 156.

[95] ibid [83]–[85], per Lord Justice Popplewell.

[96] ibid [89], per Lord Justice Popplewell.

[97] No duty to mitigate: Colinvaux (n 47) paras [11–298] and [11–299]; Maggie Hemsworth, *The Law of Insurance Contracts* (Service Issue 61, Informa 2024); there should be duty to mitigate: Peter MacDonald Eggers, 'Sue and Labour and Beyond: The Duty to Mitigate Insured Loss' [1998] Lloyd's Maritime and Commercial Law Quarterly 228, 233.

[98] This proposition was accepted by the courts in respect of the duty to sue and labour: see *Netherlands v Youell* [1998] 1 Lloyd's Rep. 236; and *Delos Shipholding SA v Allianz Global Corporate and Specialty SE* [2024] EWHC 719 (Comm).

[99] By analogy, see cases in n 37.

[100] Law Reform (Contributory Negligence) Act 1945, s 1(1).

European Insurance Contract Law (Art. 9:102). Moreover, the "bailee clause", a standard clause in international cargo insurance, which requires the insured to preserve rights against third parties,[101] is an example of a contractual term that imposes mitigation duties that precede the loss and allows for the recovery of mitigation costs.

Secondly, for sue and labour costs to be recoverable, the insured peril must be imminent or operative. The case law offers differing analyses on the necessary temporal link between the sue and labour steps and the insured peril and probability of insured loss:

- "the subject-matter of insurance is brought into such danger that without unusual or extraordinary labour or expense a loss will very probably fall on the underwriters";
- when a vessel (= insured asset) is "in the grip of a peril";[102]
- "once an insured peril has begun to take effect";[103]
- when "in all the circumstances the assured has acted reasonably to avert a loss when there was a risk that insurers might have to bear it";[104] and
- "where a peril has begun to operate, but also where it threatens to do so".[105]

While the occurrence of extreme weather-related events is becoming ever more probable, they are not necessarily imminent in time and, when they occur, they do not necessarily cause recoverable insured loss. Based on current case law it is unlikely that the courts would allow the recovery of costs for prophylactic loss prevention measures as sue and labour costs for future natural catastrophes when there is no existing or imminent threat to the insured property. Nevertheless, the notion of imminence is sufficiently flexible to stretch its temporal scope as data analytics and new technologies enable early detection of impending natural hazards.

As regards mitigation under general contract law principles, there is no duty on a party to mitigate before there has been a breach.[106] In insurance contracts the breach occurs when the insured suffers a loss caused by an insured peril. Taking the "hold harmless" analysis in insurance contracts one step further, it could be argued that the insurer who has no intention or ability to prevent natural catastrophe losses from occurring commits an anticipatory breach. The insured, as the innocent party, is entitled to ignore the anticipatory breach and to perform its side of the bargain.[107] In the instance of an anticipatory repudiation, the editors of *Chitty on Contracts* suggest that a duty of mitigation would arise from the point in time when the anticipatory breach is accepted by the innocent party.[108] As a corollary, the reasonably incurred loss prevention costs from that point in time should be recoverable as mitigation damages.

[101] Lloyd's Market Association, 'JCC Cargo Clauses' Clause A 1/1/09 cl 16.2 <https://www.lmalloyds.com/lma/underwriting/marine/JCC/JCC_Clauses_Project/Cargo_Clauses.aspx> accessed 20 January 2026.

[102] *Linelevel Ltd v Powszechny Zaklad Ubezpieczen SA (the Nore Challenger)* [2005] 2 Lloyd's Rep. 534, [82] per Cooke J.

[103] *Noble Resources and Unirise Development v George Albert Greenwood (The Vasso)* [1993] 2 Lloyd's Rep. 309.

[104] *Integrated Container Service v British Traders Insurance Co* [1984] 1 Lloyd's Rep. 154, 158–59 per Lord Justice Eveleigh.

[105] *Royal Boskalis Westminster NV v Mountain* [1997] L.R.L.R. 523, 606–08 per Rix J. This point was not challenged on appeal: *Royal Boskalis Westminster NV v Mountain* [1999] QB 674.

[106] *RTI Ltd v Mur Shipping BV* [2024] UKSC 18, [2024] 2 W.L.R. 1350 at [86] per Lord Hamblen and Lord Burrows.

[107] *White & Carter (Councils) Ltd v McGregor* [1962] A.C. 413.

[108] Hugh Beale (ed), *Chitty on Contracts* (35th edn, Sweet & Maxwell 2023) paras 30–106 and 30–111.

Thirdly, under a sue and labour clause, the insured is reimbursed for expenses it has already incurred, rather than obtaining advance payment. Similarly, mitigation loss needs to be incurred before it can be recovered. Consumer policyholders and small businesses may not have the resources to pay for loss prevention measures up-front. On the other hand, large investments in loss prevention measures by insurers—whether upfront or by way of reimbursement—may be disproportionate to the annual premium they charge (see Section 5.2.3).

As the law stands, the duty to sue and labour, the duty to mitigate, and the corollary rights to recover sue and labour/mitigation costs, provide no firm doctrinal basis for insurers to be required to finance loss prevention measures, although there are a number of authorities that would be supportive towards developing a wider right of recovery in respect of loss prevention measures in a natural catastrophe context. The insurer's primary "hold harmless" obligation could be performed by implementing or paying for the implementation of loss prevention measures. Perhaps most importantly, the case law informs how an express sue and labour-inspired loss prevention clause could be drafted. It should:

- Set out the scope of the insured's duty by specifying which specific loss prevention measures the insured is required to undertake. This should tie in with any contractual provisions in respect of the insurer providing loss prevention information—see Section 5.1);
- specify the trigger or timing when the duty becomes operative. This could be done by using parametric insurance techniques of setting triggers that relate to early warning signs that a natural catastrophe is probable to occur;
- provide for the recoverability of reasonably incurred costs in discharging the duty as a disbursement that is separate to any claims payments;
- if advance payment is to be made by the insurer, there needs to be control and accountability mechanisms to ensure that the funds are spent appropriately for the pre-agreed loss prevention measures; and
- limit liability for breach to instances of gross negligence that break the chain of causation.

It is likely that the combined dynamics of (1) the need for tackling protection gaps, (2) advances in science and technologies that will make early warning systems more widespread, more accurate, and able to predict natural catastrophe and impacts ever sooner, and (3) the development of better and more cost-effective loss prevention tools at household level, will make contractual loss prevention arrangements an emerging feature in property policy drafting.

5.2.3 Subrogation

Loss prevention measures can be costly. While they benefit the insured and the wider community in the short, medium, and long term, the insurer may only benefit fractionally for the time it is on risk for the property insured. Insurance companies are not charities but commercial enterprises that are first and foremost accountable to their shareholders and are bound by a risk-based prudential regulatory framework. At a policy level, consideration must therefore be given to the allocation of cost between the insured, the insurer, other asset stakeholders (such as mortgage banks), and wider society (through taxpayers' funds) that reflects the benefits that accrue to different stakeholders, on different timescales, and with different degrees of impact and probability. Private law cannot answer policy-based distributional questions but it can provide the mechanisms for the allocation of costs and payments.

Insurance contract law also offers avenues for insurers to make recoveries in respect of payments made. An insurer is entitled to exercise rights of subrogation if the insurer has made an indemnity payment to the insured in respect of the insured loss.[109] Subrogation may come into play where the insurer has paid (post-event) claims but would not be applicable to stand-alone reimbursements of sue and labour/mitigation costs.

Insofar as the insured has been indemnified, the insurer becomes subrogated to all rights and remedies of the insured in and in respect of the insured subject-matter insured,[110] principally being rights of action against third parties and rights to recoveries. Rights of actions against third parties have not been available in respect of natural catastrophe—as acts of God, there would be no defendant to sue. This may be changing as attribution science advances and legal concepts such as causation and remoteness of loss evolve so that claimants can raise allegations that the defendant's activities have contributed to climate change and seek damages because of climate harm manifesting in natural hazards.[111] In the UK, where insurers have paid claims that include "build-back-better" elements for which government grants or subsidies are available, insurers may also be able to exercise subrogation rights against those grants/subsidies. In *Stonegate Pub Co Ltd v MS Amlin Corporate Member Ltd*[112] and in *Gatwick Investment Ltd v Liberty Mutual Insurance Europe SE*[113] the courts held that insureds claiming under their business interruption insurance for COVID-related business closures must give credit for government grants received under the Coronavirus Job Retention Scheme (CJRS). It was immaterial that the government had not given any thought to the position of insurers and their potential subrogation rights, provided that the government had not intended the CJRS to operate to the exclusion of insurers.[114] Taking advantage of recoveries, where available, is essential to keeping insurers' claims costs down.

Overall, the parties to an insurance contract cannot exclusively rely on the insurance and contract law default regime to support bottom-up loss prevention solutions at the individual contract level. But legal duties and principles in the default regime—such as the insurer's pre-contractual duty of disclosure, the insurer's "hold harmless" obligation, the duty to sue and labour and its corresponding right to reimbursement for sue and labour costs, and the doctrine of subrogation—point the way for tailored contractual terms that could provide such solutions which, over time, could harden into standard contract terms.

6. Conclusion

As extreme weather-related events are increasing in their frequency and severity, insurers' capacity for absorbing losses is reaching its limits. Natural hazard protection requires interlinked solutions at public, public–private, and private levels. Moving the dial even just a little from the insurance paradigm of post-event compensation towards loss prevention and preparedness requires difficult policy decisions around individual and collective responsibilities for implementing loss prevention measures and the allocation of costs between individuals, insurers, the state (= taxpayers), and other stakeholders. In addition to contributing to

[109] *John Edwards and Co v Motor Union Insurance Co Ltd* [1922] 2 KB 249, at 254–55 per Judge McCardie.

[110] MIA 1906, s.79(2). For further discussion see: MacGillivray (n 37) ch 24.

[111] See, e.g., *Luciano Lliuya v RWE AG* Case number 5 U 15/17 OLG Hamm (Germany) <https://www.olg-hamm.nrw.de/behoerde/presse/Pressemitteilungen/14_26_PE_OLG_VT-Lliuya_RWE/index.php> accessed 20 January 2026.

[112] *Stonegate Pub Co Ltd v MS Amlin Corporate Member Ltd* [2022] EWHC 2548.

[113] *Gatwick Investment Ltd v Liberty Mutual Insurance Europe SE* [2024] EWHC 124 (Comm).

[114] *Stonegate Pub Co Ltd v MS Amlin Corporate Member Ltd* [2022] EWHC 2548, [284] per Judge Butcher.

insurance public private partnerships, insurers can leverage their contractual relationships with policyholders to support loss prevention efforts by knowledge-sharing on loss prevention and preparedness, and by contributing to the financing of household-level loss prevention measures. With their risk management expertise, access to data, and ability to leverage new technologies, insurers can expand their products and services into natural hazard loss prevention while pursuing long-term business growth. This could create a growing virtuous circle of loss prevention leading to captured loss prevention data leading to enhanced insurability leading to reduced protection gaps leading to business growth leading to more loss prevention leading to more loss prevention data leading to greater insurability of more assets in more natural hazard affected regions leading to further closing of protection gaps leading to long-term business growth, and so on. Existing insurance law doctrines and principles are naturally shaped around the traditional post-event compensation model but need not stand in the way of loss prevention. Tailored loss prevention clauses may have a whiff of insurance heresy right now but are likely to become standard contract terms in property insurance policies in the not-too-distant future as a means of tackling protection gaps and creating transformative business opportunities. Prevention is better than cure (insurance claims) and untreated injuries (uninsured losses).

CHAPTER 23

Securities Regulation

VIRGINIA HARPER HO

1. Introduction

CLIMATE change has already had a dramatic impact on the evolution of securities law and regulation in many jurisdictions. Indeed, the integration of climate considerations and other sustainability, or environmental, social, and governance (ESG) factors, into securities regulation has accelerated in recent years as the physical effects of climate change have become more apparent. These trends reflect a growing awareness of the significant financial risks that climate change presents to companies, investors, capital markets, and economies worldwide.[1] At the same time, securities regulation itself plays a critical role in facilitating market pricing of climate risk, which can, in theory, help investors direct capital towards sustainable uses and a post-carbon transition.[2] Indirectly, through market regulation, and more directly through its impact on corporate governance, securities regulation also has the potential to encourage climate action by firms and their investors.

This chapter traces these developments and considers where securities regulation may have force in driving companies to reduce climate externalities that are the primary source of anthropogenic climate change. It argues that while securities regulation alone cannot compel companies to mitigate climate externalities, it can support the market mechanisms that may incentivise investors, market intermediaries, and companies themselves to change how they approach climate risk. Whether it does so and to what extent varies widely across capital markets. This chapter therefore concludes by exploring factors that are contributing to the

[1] Financial Stability Board (FSB), 'Assessment of Climate-related Vulnerabilities: Analytical Framework and Toolkit' (January 2025) <https://www.fsb.org/2025/01/assessment-of-climate-related-vulnerabilities-analytical-framework-and-toolkit/> accessed 1 July 2025; Basel Commission on Banking Supervision (BCBS), 'Core Principles for Effective Banking Supervision' (April 2024) <https://www.bis.org/bcbs/publ/d573.pdf> accessed 1 July 2025; BCBS, 'Principles for the Effective Management and Supervision of Climate-Related Financial Risks' (June 2022) <www.bis.org/bcbs/publ/d532.pdf> accessed 1 July 2025; Financial Stability Oversight Council (FSOC), 'Report on Climate-Related Financial Risk; (October 2021) <home.treasury.gov/system/files/261/FSOC-Climate-Report.pdf> accessed 1 July 2025; Commodity Futures Trading Commission (CFTC), 'Managing Climate Risk in the U.S. Financial System' (September 2020) <https://www.cftc.gov/sites/default/files/2020-09/9-9-20%20Report%20of%20the%20Subcommittee%20on%20Climate-Related%20Market%20Risk%20-%20Managing%20Climate%20Risk%20in%20the%20U.S.%20Financial%20System%20for%20posting.pdf> accessed 1 July 2025.

[2] Sebastian Steuer and Tobias H Tröger, 'The Role of Disclosure in Green Finance' (2022) 8 Journal of Financial Regulation 1 (examining its potential impact). Evidence of actual impact is currently modest. See Alex Edmans, Tom Gosling, and Dirk Jenter, 'Sustainable Investing in Practice: Objectives, Constraints, and Limits to Impact' (European Corporate Governance Institute: Finance Working Paper No. 1028/2024) (20 September 2024), http://dx.doi.org/10.2139/ssrn.4963062, accessed 11 July 2025.

simultaneous harmonisation and divergence currently observed in the role securities regulation plays in the post-carbon transition.

To make clear the scope of this discussion, "securities regulation" is defined here to include the law and regulation governing financial products and investment activities, the securities markets themselves, and the obligations of corporate issuers, investors, and market intermediaries.[3] Securities regulation is also an area of law characterised by regulatory hybridity between public and private domains, since it encompasses the oversight of standard-setting and enforcement activities by self-regulatory organisations, such as stock exchanges, and by other private actors who support the function of the capital markets and may serve as gatekeepers. At the same time, it is no doubt apparent to readers that while securities regulation, like corporate law, commercial law, and other areas of business law, focuses on market activity and may therefore be referred to as "private law",[4] it is also a species of public law. Specifically, securities regulation facilitates capital raising, remedies information asymmetries between issuers and investors, and provides mechanisms for public and private enforcement.[5] Many of these dimensions have evolved in response to the climate crisis and may offer tools to respond to it. Finally, it should be noted that this chapter focuses primarily on the rules and mechanisms that are available under US law. However, it also explores key reforms led by the EU and by international standard setters that are more strongly influencing how capital market regulation globally responds to the climate crisis.

2. Climate Change and the Evolution of Securities Regulation

From its inception, securities regulation as a field has responded to pressures that affect the real economy as well as those that impact investors and the capital markets themselves. Indeed, securities regulation was born out of a financial crisis—the Great Depression.[6] Similarly, in the wake of the 2008 global financial crisis, international financial regulators began to focus on climate risk as a potential threat to the stability of the capital markets. These efforts were led by the G20's Financial Stability Board and its Task Force on Climate-related Financial Disclosure (TCFD), which ultimately identified climate change as a source of financial risk for firms and investors whose nature and magnitude vary across sectors.[7] The TCFD also established internationally accepted definitions of climate risk that include the physical effects of climate

[3] International Organization of Security Commissions (IOSCO), 'Objectives and Principles of Securities Regulation (May 2017) <https://www.iosco.org/library/pubdocs/pdf/IOSCOPD561.pdf.> accessed 1 July 2025.

[4] Thomas W Merrill, 'Private and Public Law,' in Andrew Gold and others (eds), *Oxford Handbook of the New Private Law* (OUP 2020), 589–90 (explaining that the influence of law and economics scholarship on these fields has diminished public–private distinctions).

[5] Securities regulation shares the core features of public law domains, namely, the presence of a public regulator and a governing statutory regime rather than reliance on private contract, custom, or the common law, and a functional focus on producing public goods, such as information disclosure. ibid 577 (identifying these features with public law fields).

[6] More recent crises such as the collapse of Enron, Worldcom, and Parmalat led to major reforms under the Sarbanes-Oxley Act, and the global financial crisis of 2008 led to further sweeping reforms under the Dodd-Frank Act—all of which have had ripple effects on regulation internationally. See n 33.

[7] Task Force on Climate-Related Financial Disclosures (TCFD), 'Final Report: Recommendations of the Task Force on Climate-related Financial Disclosures' (2017) <https://www.fsb.org/2017/06/recommendations-of-the-task-force-on-climate-related-financial-discl osures-2/.> accessed 2 July 2025.

change ("physical risk") and the legal, operational, reputational, and market risks arising from rapidly changing regulatory and market environments ("transition risk").[8] However, the TCFD concluded that financial institutions, operating firms, investors, and regulators lacked comparable, reliable information on the potential *financial* effects of climate change.[9] This led to the development of the voluntary TCFD framework for reporting climate-related financial risk, which is now the basis of all international climate reporting mandates worldwide.

The TCFD framework and other green finance reforms respond to growing investor attention to the financial impacts of climate change and rising investor demand for information on its risks and impacts.[10] Investment strategies that integrate climate risk and other ESG factors because of their financial materiality have also gone mainstream, adding to global demand for socially responsible investments or, alternatively, sustainable, responsible, and impact (SRI) investment products and services.[11] Rising demand has raised concerns about ESG greenwashing, which has also spurred regulatory efforts to set standards for sustainable investment products and services.[12] As Section 3 explains, these market trends also have corporate governance effects, since institutional investors and other shareholders now engage companies on climate concerns in addition to other ESG matters.[13]

However, what has put climate change risks and impacts on the agenda of securities regulators more explicitly are governments' commitments under the Paris Agreement to support climate change adaptation and mitigation and to align global capital and investment flows towards a post-carbon transition.[14] The Paris Agreement is also the basis of rising climate litigation and investor engagement with portfolio firms around their climate resilience, transparency, and level of climate action.[15]

[8] With the formation of the International Accounting Standards Board (IASB), the TCFD framework and its definitions and guidance have been incorporated into the IASB's international climate and sustainability reporting standards.

[9] TCFD (n 7) 1–3, 8 (discussing the limits of publicly disclosed information and the 'lack of focus on financial impacts' in pre-existing voluntary frameworks).

[10] Phillipp Krueger, Zacharias Sautner, and Laura T Starks, 'The Importance of Climate Risks for Institutional Investors' (2020) 33 Review of Finance Studies 1067; Florencio Lopez-de-Silanes, Joseph A McCahery, and Paul C Pudschedl, 'Institutional Investors and ESG Preferences' (2024) 32 Corporate Governance: An International Review 1060. See also Arjuna Dibley, Chapter 20 of this handbook.

[11] IOSCO, 'Recommendations on Sustainability-Related Practices, Policies, Procedures and Disclosure in Asset Management' FR08/21 (June 2021) <https://www.iosco.org/library/pubdocs/pdf/IOSCOPD679.pdf> 8 accessed 1 July 2025 (discussing rising investor demand); see also Virginia Harper Ho, '*Sustainable Finance & the Public Turn in Corporate Law,' in A Research Agenda for Corporate Law*, Christopher Bruner and Marc Moore eds (Edward Elgar Publishing 2023) 121–39.

[12] On these measures, see Section 2.2.

[13] Koemas Papadopoulos, Jun Frank and Pinak Parikh, 'U.S. Shareholder Proposals: A Decade in Motion' (October 2024) <https://www.iss-corporate.com/library/us-shareholder-proposals-a-decade-in-motion/> accessed 1 July 2025.

[14] The Paris Agreement itself provides that its aim is 'to strengthen the global response to the threat of climate change . . . including by [limiting temperature rise] and making finance flows consistent with a pathway towards low greenhouse gas emissions and climate-resilient development'. Paris Agreement to the United Nations Framework Convention on Climate Change art 2(1)(c), 12 December 2015, TIAS no. 16-1104.

[15] On developments in climate litigation against corporations and governments, see Maria A Tigre and Margaret Barry, 'Climate Change in the Courts: A 2024 Retrospective' (Sabin Center for Climate Change Law, January 2025) <https://scholarship.law.columbia.edu/sabin_climate_change/240/> accessed 1 July 2025.

In response, regulators in most leading capital markets have moved rapidly over the past decade to mandate climate and sustainability disclosures. As discussed below, they have also set common standards for defining green investment activities, mandated climate-related competencies for regulated financial institutions and investment professionals and cracked down on greenwashing and other forms of investment fraud.

The US remains a laggard in the green finance transition and in its regulatory response to climate change. Although the US Securities and Exchange Commission (SEC) was the first regulator globally to introduce guidance for issuers on climate-risk materiality and encourage more robust climate-risk disclosures,[16] recent policy debates, legal battles, and even pronouncements from the SEC itself have questioned the agency's authority to address climate-related risks and the need for it to do so.[17] However, climate-related financial risks clearly implicate several dimensions of the SEC's traditional mission to "protect investors, maintain fair, orderly and efficient markets, and promote capital formation".[18] As the International Organization of Securities Commissioners (IOSCO) has recognised, these matters also lie within the statutory mission of regulators in other jurisdictions as well.[19]

2.1 Climate Disclosure Mandates

To begin, a core function of securities regulation is to ensure that investors and the capital markets have access to reliable information regarding companies that issue securities to the public.[20] Over several decades at least, a vast patchwork of voluntary standards and frameworks for corporate reporting on climate and other ESG factors has developed, in addition to regulatory guidance. However, investors and regulators alike have found voluntary standards and existing rules on risk disclosure ineffective in generating investment-grade information on climate risk.[21] This has led to the development of international climate and sustainability disclosure standards by the International Sustainability Standards Board (ISSB), the EU, and the US SEC, and to the uptake of international standards by the state of California, among others.[22] All of these standards are TCFD-based and build on decades of work by private

[16] US Securities and Exchange Commission (SEC), Commission Guidance Regarding Disclosure Related to Climate Change, 75 Federal Register 6,290 (8 February 2010).

[17] See, for example, Mark T Uyeda, 'Statement by Acting Chair Uyeda on Climate-related Disclosure Rules' (*SEC*, 11 February 2025) <https://www.sec.gov/newsroom/speeches-statements/uyeda-statement-climate-change-021025> accessed 1 July 2025.

[18] See SEC, 'Enhancement and Standardization of Climate-Related Disclosures for Investors', 89 Federal Register 21,668, 21,671, 21,683 (28 March 2024) (to be codified at 17 CFR parts 210, 229, 239, 249) (referencing relevant sections of the Securities Act of 1933 and the Securities Exchange Act of 1934).

[19] See IOSCO (n 3) 3 (defining the purpose of securities regulation as protecting investors, ensuring that markets are 'fair, efficient, and transparent', and reducing systemic risk); IOSCO, 'Sustainable Finance and the Role of Securities Regulators and IOSCO' FR04/2020 (April 2020) <https://www.iosco.org/library/pubdocs/pdf/IOSCOPD652.pdf.> accessed 1 July 2025 (surveying international initiatives by securities regulators).

[20] IOSCO (n 3); John Coffee, 'Market Failures and the Economic Case for a Mandatory Disclosure System' (1984) 70 Virginia Law Review 717.

[21] IOSCO (2020) (n 19) 23–26 (discussing these limitations); IOSCO, 'Report on Sustainability-Related Issuer Disclosures' FR04/21 (June 2021) <https://www.iosco.org/library/pubdocs/pdf/IOSCOPD678.pdf> accessed 1 July 2025 (same). See also Hans B Christensen, Luzi Hail, and Christian Leuz, 'Mandatory CSR and Sustainability Reporting: Economic Analysis and Literature Review' (2021) 26 Review of Accounting Studies 1176.

[22] International Sustainability Standards Board (ISSB), 'IFRS S1 General Requirements for Disclosure of Sustainability-Related Financial Information' (June 2023) <www.ifrs.org/issued-standards/ifrs-sus

standard-setters like the Sustainability Accounting Standards Board (SASB), the Climate Disclosure Standards Board (CDSB), and the Carbon Disclosure Project, and all are intended to standardise how material information on climate and sustainability risks reaches the capital markets. Since 2023, regulators in over thirty jurisdictions, accounting for over 40% of global market capitalisation, have taken steps to adopt mandatory climate and sustainability reporting requirements aligned with the ISSB.[23] In sum, one of the most visible impacts of climate change on securities regulation is the expansion and "hardening" of international climate disclosure mandates.

There are also links between direct climate regulation outside of the securities laws and the scope and impact of climate disclosure mandates. First, the materiality of climate transition risk, which determines whether it must be reported or not, depends on the perceived costs and legal and regulatory risks of corporate climate inaction. When climate regulation becomes more stringent or more strictly enforced, climate risk is more likely to be material; similarly, lax regulation and enforcement reduce climate risk materiality. By making reliable corporate climate information more readily available, the introduction of climate disclosure mandates may also lower plaintiffs' costs of pursuing climate litigation against corporate defendants, which should increase the materiality of climate transition risk. At the same time, deregulation and legal challenges against corporate or government climate responses may increase the reputational and legal risks associated with taking climate action. The climate transition risk assessments of transnational companies will therefore be affected by the shifting regulatory and enforcement landscapes in different jurisdictions.[24]

2.2 Anti-Fraud Regulation, Fund Labelling, and Taxonomies

Securities regulators worldwide have also taken steps to protect investors from fraud with regard to investment products that claim to integrate climate and other ESG factors or to promote certain climate, environmental, or societal goals. A key source of market confusion is the absence of standardised definitions for green, sustainable, or ESG investment products or services, which has left fund managers and other market actors free to use such terms in ways that are inconsistent and may mislead investors.

In response, financial regulators in the EU, China, ASEAN, and other global capital markets have developed common standards or taxonomies for investment products and activities.[25]

tainability-standards-navigator/> accessed 1 July 2025; ISSB, 'IFRS S2 Climate-Related Disclosures' (June 2023) www.ifrs.org/issued-standards/ifrs-sustainability-standards-navigator/. The European Sustainability Reporting Standards (ESRS) implement Directive (EU) 2022/2464 of the European Parliament and of the Council of 14 December 2022 amending Regulation (EU) No 537/2014, Directive 2004/109/EC, Directive 2006/43/EC, and Directive 2013/34/EU, as regards corporate sustainability reporting [2022] (OJ L322, 16 December 2022) ('CSRD'). Mandatory TCFD- or ISSB-aligned disclosure rules are pending in California and have been proposed in New York and other states. See Virginia E Harper Ho, 'Corporate Climate Governance' (2026) 51 Journal of Corporation Law (forthcoming) (discussing these developments).

[23] IFRS Foundation, 'Progress on Corporate Climate-Related Disclosures: 2024 Report' (November 2024) <https://www.ifrs.org/content/dam/ifrs/supporting-implementation/issb-standards/progress-climate-related-disclosures-2024.pdf> accessed 1 July 2025.

[24] Tigre and Barry (n 15) (identifying climate litigation challenging corporate and government climate action, as well as cases pushing them to do more).

[25] The EU has established a multilateral platform for taxonomy alignment. 'International Platform on Sustainable Finance (IPSF)' <https://finance.ec.europa.eu/sustainable-finance/international-platform-sustainable-finance_en> accessed 1 July 2025.

Another approach, adopted by the US SEC, is to create labelling rules for climate-related or ESG-integrated investments and for those that claim to promote certain environmental or societal impacts.[26] Still others require direct registration with the regulator before an ESG or climate-focused fund may be marketed to retail investors.[27] All of these measures reflect traditional investor protection concerns and the need to prevent the dissemination of fraudulent and misleading information to the market.

Currently, efforts are ongoing to align and simplify these taxonomies and expand their use, but taxonomy criteria and scope still vary across markets.[28] In addition, standards for many green investment products, including green bonds, climate bonds, transition bonds, and other climate-linked debt instruments, remain based on private industry standards.[29]

2.3 Oversight of Intermediaries and Gatekeepers

Another important dimension of securities and financial regulation is the oversight responsibility that regulators exercise over stock exchanges and other private actors who shape corporate incentives to monitor and respond to climate risk.[30] These include investment intermediaries, such as asset managers and investment advisers, as well as auditors, rating agencies, and proxy advisory firms. In this regard, securities regulation is an important source of "gatekeeper" regulation.[31] As demand for climate disclosure assurance, ESG ratings, and related advisory services rises, calls for regulators to develop new oversight regimes have risen as well.[32] These oversight functions align with the traditional anti-fraud and investor protection goals of securities regulation, and in the US, have also been extended by congressional authorisation over time.[33]

[26] Investment Company Names, 88 Federal Register 70436 (11 October 2023) (codified at 17 CFR parts 230, 232, 239, 270, 274) (amending Rule 35d-1 of the Investment Company Act).

[27] For instance, in Hong Kong, the regulator authorises funds meeting regulatory criteria as ESG funds. Securities and Futures Commission (Hong Kong), 'List of ESG Funds' <https://www.sfc.hk/en/Regulatory-functions/Products/List-of-ESG-funds> accessed 1 July 2025.

[28] European Commission, 'Commission Simplifies Rules on Sustainability and EU Investments, Delivering Over €6 billion in Administrative Relief' (26 February 2025) <https://finance.ec.europa.eu/publications/commission-simplifies-rules-sustainability-and-eu-investments-delivering-over-eu6-billion_en> accessed 1 July 2025.

[29] See Christoph Kumpan, 'Green Bonds and Their New Regulation in the EU' in Jens-Hinrich Binder, Klaus J Hopt, and Thilo Kuntz (eds), *Corporate Purpose, CSR, and ESG: A Trans-Atlantic Perspective* (OUP 2024), 301–18 (placing the EU Green Bonds Regulation in the context of the widely referenced voluntary standards of the International Capital Market Association (ICMA) and the Climate Bonds Initiative's Climate Bonds Standard).

[30] On the SEC's oversight of stock exchanges, see Geeyoung Min and Kwon-Yong Jin, 'Relational Enforcement of Stock Exchange Rules' (2021) 47 BYU Law Review 149, 158–63.

[31] Dorothy S Lund, 'Asset Managers as Regulators' 171 University of Pennsylvania Law Review 77; Kenneth W Abbot, David Levi-Faur and Duncan Snidal, 'Theorizing Regulatory Intermediaries: the RIT Model' (2017) 670 Annals of the American Academy of Political and Social Science 14; John C Coffee Jr, *Gatekeepers: The Professions and Corporate Governance* (OUP 2006); Reinier H Kraakman, 'Gatekeepers: The Anatomy of a Third-party Enforcement Strategy' (1986), 2 Journal of Law, Economics, and Organization 53.

[32] See for example, IOSCO, 'Supervisory Practices to Address Greenwashing' FR12/23 (December 2023) <https://www.iosco.org/library/pubdocs/pdf/IOSCOPD750.pdf> accessed 1 July 2025 (reviewing initiatives for oversight of asset managers, ESG ratings and data products providers).

[33] For example, the Sarbanes-Oxley Act of 2002 created the Public Company Accounting Oversight Board (PCAOB) and placed it under SEC oversight. Sarbanes-Oxley Act of 2002, Pub L 107-204, 116 Stat 745 (codified throughout Sections 11, 15, 18, 28, and 29 U.S.C.A. (2003)); see also Dodd-Frank Wall Street

2.4 Systemic Risk and Market Stability

Financial regulators also recognise that the global scale and rapid pace of climate change pose systemic risks to entire economies.[34] The concern is that climate blindness may lead to sudden instability among financial institutions and across the economy when these risks materialise.[35] Reducing systemic risk is within the purview of securities regulators' mission to protect investors and maintain fair, stable, and efficient markets.[36] Reliable information is also essential if central banks and other regulators are to monitor systemic climate risks and safeguard the resilience of financial systems over time.[37] For this reason, international climate disclosure standards encourage or require companies to conduct climate resilience testing and to develop and report progress against climate transition plans.[38] As many commentators have observed, the systemic risk effects of climate change also elevate the materiality of climate risk as compared to other ESG risks that may not pose economy-wide threats .[39]

3. The Potential Impact of Securities Regulation on Climate Change

Although historically, securities regulation is a field that has been seen as isolated from climate-risk concerns, this discussion has shown that many aspects of securities regulation are rapidly evolving to address climate-related financial risks and impacts. Securities regulation is also foundational to global climate change responses. The impact will depend heavily on how investors and markets respond to climate-risk information, as well as on the direction of domestic climate change policy and regulation in different jurisdictions. Nonetheless, some of the mechanisms discussed above are already influencing global climate change action.

3.1 Disclosure Regulation and Climate Externalities

Disclosure regulation is the most visible area in which securities regulation is reshaping incentives for the largest firms and their investors to address climate risks and impacts. In many jurisdictions, ISSB-aligned climate reporting and corporate governance mandates are being introduced by stock exchanges, which bodes well for implementation by listed firms.[40] The

Reform and Consumer Protection Act, Pub. L. No. 111 - 203, § 929-Z, 124 Stat. 1376, 1871 (2010) (codified at 15 U.S.C. § 78o) (instituting sweeping reforms in response to global financial crisis of 2008).

[34] See sources cited (n 1).

[35] On its underlying sources, see Madison Condon, 'Market Myopia's Climate Bubble' [2022] Utah Law Review 63.

[36] IOSCO, 'Mitigating Systemic Risk: A Role for Securities Regulators' 19–20, 39-53 (February 2011) <https://www.iosco.org/library/pubdocs/pdf/ioscopd347.pdf> accessed 1 July 2025 (discussing securities regulators' role in promoting financial stability); see Hilary J Allen, 'The SEC as Financial Stability Regulator,' (2017) 43 Journal of Corporation Law 715.

[37] TCFD (n 7) 2.

[38] On these measures, see Harper Ho (n 22).

[39] See Jeffrey N Gordon, 'Unbundling Climate Change Risk from ESG' Columbia Law and Economics Working Paper No 667 <https://papers.ssrn.com/sol3/papers.cfm?abstract_id=4547679> accessed 1 July 2025.

[40] Compliance with stock exchange listing rules is generally high despite exchanges' heavy reliance on reputational sanctions and voluntary compliance. Min and Jin (n 30). On corporate disclosure in the Global South, see Maria Eduarda Lessa and Mariana Pargendler, Chapter 19 of this handbook.

expectation is that the "greening" of the capital markets can enable investors to direct capital towards low-carbon or sustainable investments.[41] In addition, under the EU's "double-materiality" reporting standard, companies are expected to mitigate corporate externalities.[42] The implementation of these corporate climate reporting mandates is an essential prerequisite to asset managers' compliance with requirements in the EU, UK, and elsewhere (though not in the US) for them to monitor portfolio and entity-level climate and sustainability integration.[43]

Of course, investment-grade information is a necessary but not sufficient condition for markets to steer corporate climate action, reward low-carbon and climate-positive investments, and direct capital over time away from investments with higher climate risks or impacts. Investor willingness to push firms towards credible climate action commitments appears to ebb and flow in the US and elsewhere in response to shifting market and policy winds. As other commentators have observed, it is therefore unlikely that disclosure alone will motivate companies to take positive climate action on a scale that can address climate externalities without support from climate regulation and alignment with market incentives for investors.[44] Nonetheless, for those signals to work, markets must efficiently and reliably incorporate climate risk information. It appears that markets are increasingly pricing climate risk, but how efficiently markets do so and the financial effects of climate risk remain open empirical questions as the quantity and quality of public climate risk information continue to rise.[45]

It is too early to assess the real-world impact of climate reporting mandates, since implementation is only in its early stages. However, empirical studies have shown that earlier mandatory risk factor disclosures and greenhouse gas (GHG) emissions reporting in some jurisdictions have had informational and real (i.e., behavioural) effects.[46] These results may be due to the reputational and peer effects of transparency on managers and to the fact that companies "manage what [they] measure".[47] Since the ISSB and other TCFD-based standards emphasise quantitative measures and clear metrics and targets for climate risk management and climate action, the effect of these mandates on firm behaviour should be stronger.

There are, nonetheless, limits to relying on disclosure as a form of soft regulation. More information may not translate into greater transparency or greater corporate accountability if it contributes to information "overload" and "box-checking".[48] Higher reporting costs may also

[41] See sources referenced (n 2) (examining this question theoretically and empirically).

[42] European Financial Reporting Advisory Group (EFRAG), ESRS 1 General Requirements (November 2025), <https://www.efrag.org/en/draft-simplified-esrs> para 58. See also Harro van Asselt and Jessica Crow, Chapter 33 of this handbook.

[43] See discussion in Section 3.2.2.

[44] Robert G Eccles, Vanessa Havard-Williams, and Mark Manning, 'The Limits of Reporting on Sustainability Impacts in Changing Corporate Behaviour' [2024] European Business Law Review 527, 546; Edmans et al (n 2).

[45] Shaojun Zhang, 'Carbon Returns Across the Globe' (2025) 80 Journal of Finance 615; Stefano Giglio, Bryan Kelly, and Johannes Stroebel, 'Climate Finance' (2021) 13 Annual Review of Financial Economics 15.

[46] Phillipp Krueger and others, 'The Effects of Mandatory ESG Disclosure Around the World' (2024) 62 Journal of Accounting Research 1795; Benedikt Downar and others, 'The Impact of Carbon Disclosure Mandates on Emissions and Financial Operating Performance' (2021) 26 Review of Accounting Studies 1137 (studying mandatory GHG reporting effects in the UK).

[47] Louis Lowenstein, 'Financial Transparency and Corporate Governance: You Manage What You Measure' (1996) 96 Columbia Law Review 1335, 1342–45.

[48] TSC Industries, Inc v Northway, Inc, 426 US 438, 448–49 (1976) (identifying the potential for disclosure overload).

discourage capital formation through the public markets and weaken their competitiveness if other markets have less burdensome rules. These concerns have come to the fore in the US debate over the SEC's climate disclosure rules and have put pressure on Europe to streamline climate disclosure regulation as the US halts its disclosure mandates.[49]

3.2 Corporate Climate Governance

As I have explained elsewhere, the introduction of corporate climate and sustainability disclosure mandates is also likely to have significant indirect effects on corporate governance and therefore on corporate climate strategy and operational decisions, even though these frameworks do not alter corporate fiduciary duties or the powers of corporate directors, shareholders, or stakeholders under corporate or company law in any given jurisdiction.[50] Specifically, international climate disclosure standards encourage firms to monitor and manage their own climate risk and, under the European standards, to reduce their climate impacts as well.[51] Equally important is the extent to which securities law mechanisms support or discourage climate risk oversight by shareholders and other investors, as discussed below.

3.2.1 Disclosure-Driven Climate Governance

To begin, all of the TCFD-based international disclosure mandates require corporate reporting on corporate governance matters, either directly or on a comply-or-explain basis. The ISSB and European standards require companies to implement climate risk management and oversight mechanisms in much the same way as earlier reforms under the Sarbanes-Oxley and Dodd-Frank Acts, required companies to report on, and therefore to implement, independent boards, internal financial controls, and risk governance.[52] International climate disclosure rules now require covered companies to measure GHG emissions, develop climate-resilient strategies, and exercise climate risk oversight and risk management.[53] Under the European standards, reporting companies must also adopt transition plans, implement due diligence systems, and report progress against Paris-aligned climate action targets.[54] Existing climate governance rules introduced by stock exchanges in many markets already require listed firm boards to have access to climate expertise, aligning with international climate reporting standards.[55] Even in the US, which has not implemented mandatory climate disclosure, there is evidence that many US companies have voluntarily implemented at least some of the internal climate governance mechanisms recommended by TCFD-based disclosure regimes.[56]

49 On European reforms to consolidate and narrow climate reporting obligations, see European Commission (n 28).

50 Harper Ho (n 22) 13–18 (comparing the TCFD-based standards). On directors' fiduciary duties, see Ernest Lim, Chapter 18 of this handbook.

51 Harper Ho, ibid 15–19 (discussing relevant provisions of the ISSB standards and the ESRS 2).

52 On these earlier reforms, see n 6.

53 Although the Trump administration is not supporting the defence of the federal rules adopted by the SEC in 2024, state TCFD-based climate disclosure mandates have similar effects. See Harper Ho (n 22).

54 Harper Ho (n 22) 17–18.

55 The ISSB requires reporting of an assessment of board-level expertise or access to it, while the ESRS includes an affirmative requirement. ibid 46 (discussing IFRS S2, para 6, and EFRAG, ESRS 2 General Disclosures (November 2025), https://www.efrag.org/sites/default/files/media/document/2025-12/November_2025_ESRS_2.pdf, par 12(b)).

56 Papadopoulos et al (n 13) 4 (reporting that 'approximately 96% [of S&P 500 companies] disclose some form of climate change strategy, while 88% have established quantitative GHG emissions reduction targets').

Empirical studies give cause to expect that mandatory climate governance disclosure will affect managerial incentives and advance corporate climate governance.[57] Commentators from different jurisdictions have also observed that climate-related corporate governance codes, climate disclosure mandates, climate litigation, and investor pressure around climate and other ESG issues are shifting the standard of conduct that is reasonably expected of corporate directors and officers under existing corporate fiduciary duties in the US and elsewhere.[58] Corporate directors and officers may therefore already have affirmative duties to address climate externalities, a question taken up elsewhere in this handbook.[59] The key observation here, however, is simply that the integration of climate risk factors into securities regulation will have ripple effects on corporate governance, as has been the case with other major securities law reforms in the past.

3.2.2 Shareholder Governance Rights and Climate Change

Moreover, securities regulation establishes mechanisms for the exercise of shareholder governance rights for large firms in ways that can support or discourage corporate climate change responses. These rules determine whether institutional investors can make investment, voting, and engagement decisions on the basis of information about the climate and sustainability risks of portfolio firms, coordinate their exercise of "voice", and take account of beneficial owner interests and preferences.[60] Although the mechanisms themselves are generally content-neutral and can facilitate both pro-climate and anti-climate action, they have been widely used by pro-social shareholders and have already had a strong influence on companies' perception of climate risk materiality in the US and in other capital markets.

3.2.2.1 *Shareholder Engagement*

First, securities regulation prescribes the scope for direct shareholder engagement around climate concerns, including through the use of shareholder proposals. Shareholder proposals filed at public companies in the US on climate and other ESG issues continue to rise and draw strong support despite a rise in anti-ESG proposals.[61] However, the SEC's use of its no-action review process influences whether certain proposals must appear on the corporate proxy or may be excluded by the company and not reach a shareholder vote. Of particular relevance to ESG and climate-related shareholder proposals is the SEC's shifting interpretation of which proposals touch upon the "ordinary business" of the company but may still go to a vote because they concern significant social policy issues.[62] In 2025, the SEC under the Trump

[57] See authorities cited (n 46).

[58] See Cynthia A Williams, 'Fiduciary Duties and Corporate Climate Responsibility' (2021) 74 Vanderbilt Law Review 1875; Ernest Lim and Umakanth Varottil, 'Climate Risk: Enforcement of Corporate and Securities Law in Common Law Asia' (2022) 22 Journal of Corporate Law Studies 391. For related legal opinions from common law jurisdictions, see Commonwealth Climate and Law Initiative <https://commonwealthclimatelaw.org/publication/> accessed 1 July 2025.

[59] Ernest Lim, Chapter 18 of this handbook.

[60] These potential levers have been widely identified in the literature on stakeholder governance. See for example Alessio M Pacces, 'Sustainable Corporate Governance: The Role of the Law' in Danny Busch, Guido Ferrarini and Seraina Grünewald(eds), *Sustainable Finance in Europe: Corporate Governance, Financial Stability and Financial Markets* (2nd edn, Springer 2024); Thilo Kuntz, 'ESG Demand-side Regulation: Governing the Shareholders' in Binder et al (n 29) 319–56.

[61] Papadopoulos et al (n 13) 7 (reporting a 30% rise in pro-ESG proposals filed at US companies annually). See also John Dernbach, Chapter 35 of this handbook.

[62] 17 CFR 240.14a-8(i)(7) (2024). On the earlier and current interpretive guidance, see SEC Division of Corporate Finance, Shareholder Proposals: Staff Legal Bulletin No 14M (CF) (12 February 2025)

administration quickly reversed the Biden administration's position on these matters and restored an earlier interpretation that allows companies to more easily exclude climate-related proposals if they impermissibly interfere with management discretion.[63]

3.2.2.2 *Shareholder Voting Rights*

Shareholders also have other governance rights that depending on the jurisdiction, include the right to nominate or approve directors and to express a view on executive compensation ("say on pay"). Some companies may also voluntarily extend voting rights to shareholders on their climate strategy ("say on climate").[64] For all of these matters, securities regulation establishes the mechanisms and information disclosures for proxy solicitation and voting. As international disclosure rules elevate climate risk oversight to the board level and encourage companies to link climate and sustainability measures to executive compensation, the scope and implementation of these rules will affect investors' ability to change how corporate boards and officers approach climate risk. The degree to which regulators require transparency on the voting records of mutual funds and investment intermediation also affects the extent to which beneficial owners' preferences for corporate climate action will be taken into account,[65] which some scholars have suggested would advance climate action and other pro-social goals.[66]

3.2.2.3 *Shareholder Collective Action Problems*

In addition, securities law can either reduce or amplify strong collective action problems and market disincentives that discourage shareholder engagement with portfolio firms.[67] Specifically, securities regulation defines the rules for communications among shareholders with respect to corporate governance actions. Together with antitrust regulation,[68] it also sets the permitted bounds of coordinated shareholder engagements that could have a greater impact on how listed companies deal with carbon emissions, biodiversity impacts, and other climate externalities.[69] While securities law could facilitate coordinated investor engagement towards climate-positive goals,[70] US rules in this regard are more restrictive than in other

<https://www.sec.gov/about/shareholder-proposals-staff-legal-bulletin-no-14m-cf?> accessed 1 July 2025.

63 ibid.

64 Say-on-climate resolutions, more common among European companies, have declined worldwide recently. Forum pour L'Investissement Responsible, 'European Say on Climate Report' (2024) <https://www.frenchsif.org/isr_esg/wp-content/uploads/SayOnClimate-Report2024-EN_13.09.pdf> accessed 1 July 2025; Harlan Tufford and others, 'Is Say-on-Climate Losing Steam?' (*MSCI*, 17 April 2024) <https://www.msci.com/www/quick-take/is-say-on-climate-losing-steam/04562255050> accessed 1 July 2025.

65 Kuntz (n 60) 319, 348–53 (referring to these as 'indirect demand-side regulation'); Pacces (n 60) 161.

66 Oliver Hart and Luigi Zingales, 'The New Corporate Governance' (2022) 1 The University of Chicago Business Law Review 195; Oliver Hart and Luigi Zingales, 'Companies Should Maximize Shareholder Welfare Not Market Value' (2017) 2 Journal of Law, Finance, Accounting 217. On constraints, see sources cited at n 44.

67 On the disincentives, see Ronald J Gilson and Jeffrey N Gordon, 'The Agency Costs of Agency Capitalism: Activist Investors and the Revaluation of Governance Rights' (2013) 113 Columbia Law Review 863; Roberto Tallarita, 'The Limits of Portfolio Primacy' (2023) 76 Vanderbilt Law Review 511.

68 See Julian Nowag and Thomas Cheng, Chapter 21 of this handbook.

69 On the antitrust challenge and possible responses, see Amelia Miazad, 'Investor Climate Alliances' (2025) 102 Washington University Law Review 797; Amelia Miazad, 'Prosocial Antitrust' (2022) 73 UC Hastings Law Journal 1637.

70 See Wolf-Georg Ringe, 'Investor-Led Sustainability in Corporate Governance' (2022) 7 Annals of Corporate Governance 93.

jurisdictions,[71] and SEC guidance on beneficial ownership reporting issued in 2025 may further limit shareholders' ability to influence corporate climate strategy and undertake coordinated engagements of the sort contemplated by the United Nations' Principles for Responsible Investment (UNPRI) and other voluntary investor climate commitments.[72]

3.2.2.4 *Mandatory ESG Integration*

Finally, securities regulation in many jurisdictions establishes obligations for investment advisers and institutional investors to take account of beneficial owners' ESG preferences and to incorporate climate risk information and other financially relevant ESG factors into investment analysis and voting and engagement policies.[73] Most prominent among these are the EU's Sustainable Finance Disclosure Regulation (SFDR) and the UK's Sustainability Disclosure Requirements (SDR).[74] With some variation, the EU and the UK rules include entity and product-level disclosures, which require covered financial services providers to report on how sustainability is integrated into investment and engagement decisions, and in the case of the SFDR, on how negative externalities associated with the investment strategy (i.e., principal adverse impacts or PAIs) are integrated into due diligence policies.[75] These measures should reduce greenwashing and will require certain asset managers to monitor portfolio firms and consider climate risks and externalities. In contrast, the lack of consistent federal policies or rules in the US permitting, much less requiring, institutional investors to do so presents a continued barrier to climate-informed investment there.[76]

3.3 Gatekeeper Regulation

As observed above, securities regulators also influence market actors' incentives to address climate risks and impacts through their regulatory oversight over financial intermediaries and other gatekeepers in the capital markets.[77] Many of these actors, such as proxy advisors, ESG rating agencies, auditors, and assurance providers, adopt policies and provide services that

[71] See John D Morley, 'Too Big to Be Activist' (2019) 92 Southern California Law Review 1407.

[72] See Patrick Temple-West, Amelia Pollard, and Eric Platt, 'BlackRock and Vanguard Halt Meetings with Companies After SEC Cracks Down on ESG' *Financial Times* (London, 20 February 2025); Ross Kerber, 'Trump's SEC Leader Shifts Power from Investors to Boardrooms' (*Reuters*, 18 February 2025) <https://www.reuters.com/business/trumps-sec-leader-shifts-power-investors-boardrooms-2025-02-18/> accessed 1 July 2025.

[73] See sources (n 65). See also Freshfields, 'A Legal Framework for Impact: Sustainability Impact in Investor Decision-Making' (July 2021) <https://www.freshfields.com/globalassets/our-thinking/campaigns/a-legal-framework-for-impact/a-legal-framework-for-impact.pdf> accessed 2 July 2025 (surveying relevant rules in 11 major investment markets).

[74] Regulation (EU) 2019/2088 of 27 November 2019 on Sustainability-related Disclosures in the Financial Services Sector [2019] OJ L317/1. https://eur-lex.europa.eu/legal-content/EN/TXT/?uri=CELEX%3A02019R2088-20240109 [SFDR]; FCA, 'Sustainability Disclosure Requirements (SDR) and Investment Labels' *Policy Statement PS23/16* (November 2023) <https://www.fca.org.uk/publication/policy/ps23-16.pdf> accessed 1 July 2025; FCA, 'Sustainability Disclosure Requirements (SDR) and Investment Labels' *Policy Statement PS23/16* (November 2023) <https://www.fca.org.uk/publication/policy/ps23-16.pdf> accessed 1 July 2025 (introducing final rules).

[75] On the SFDR, see Kuntz (n 60) 334–37.

[76] See Max Schanzenbach and Robert Sitkoff, 'Reconciling Fiduciary Duty and Social Conscience: The Law and Economics of ESG Investing by a Trustee' (2020) 74 Stanford Law Review 381. On the policy shifts, see Virginia Harper Ho, 'US ESG Regulation in Transnational Context' in Binder et al (n 29) 89–90.

[77] See notes and discussion (n 31).

inform corporate and investor decision-making. They may also directly support corporate and investor efforts to measure and monitor carbon emissions and climate risk.

Most are self-regulatory organisations or follow voluntary industry guidance, but in the case of proxy advisory firms and ESG rating agencies, some regulators have taken steps to exercise greater oversight in order to address potential conflicts of interest, set standards of conduct and expertise, and introduce accountability mechanisms to "monitor the monitors".[78] These measures can constrain, but can also build the emerging ecosystems of sustainable finance that are needed to support corporate climate governance and disclosure and to advance the investor protection goals of the securities laws.

3.4 Standardisation, Coordination, and Harmonisation

Perhaps the most important way in which securities regulation can impact climate change is through the standardisation, coordination, and harmonisation of capital market regulation, and it is here that securities law offers comparative advantages over other sources of law and norms. First, climate disclosure and any corporate governance mechanisms adopted by stock exchanges or under the securities laws apply to firms on a consolidated basis and are therefore not limited to a single entity. Under international climate disclosure standards, they also reach the reporting company's "value chain".[79] This offers greater potential to combat climate blindness and reduce climate risk across a corporate enterprise transnationally.

Also, in contrast to corporate law, which prioritises shareholder interests, securities regulation's investor protection mission extends across asset classes and can support better external climate monitoring by bondholders, investment trustees, and other creditors. The highly intermediated nature of enforcement mechanisms for debt instruments and the prevalence of securitisation makes oversight challenging, but bondholders and other creditors often invest over longer time horizons that increases the exposure of the underlying assets to climate risk, potentially incentivizing risk oversight.[80] At the same time, green bonds and other forms of debt financing are essential to meeting the capital demands of the post-carbon transition, and as Section 2 observed, they also require clear standards to prevent greenwashing.

Securities regulators and stock exchanges are also highly integrated into transnational networks that engage their peers and other market participants.[81] IOSCO and the World Federation of Exchanges are among the "network hubs" that facilitate transnational alignment of climate disclosure standards and dialogue across these networks to promote climate

[78] See for example EU Parliament and EU Council, 'Regulation (EU) 2024/3005 of the European Parliament and of the Council of 27 November 2024 on the Transparency and Integrity of Environmental, Social and Governance (ESG) Rating Activities, and Amending Regulations (EU) 2019/2088 and (EU) 2023/2859 (Text with EEA Relevance)' Official Journal of the European Union, L series, 2024/2005 (12 December 2024); IOSCO, ESG Ratings and Data Products Providers (21 November 2021) <https://www.iosco.org/library/pubdocs/pdf/IOSCOPD690.pdf> accessed 1 July 2025.

[79] On the definition of "value chain", see IFRS S1 (n 22) app A and ESRS 1 (n 42) app A.

[80] See, for example, UNPRI, 'Responsible Investment in Securitized Debt: A Technical Guide' (10 June 2025) <https://www.unpri.org/securitised-debt/responsible-investment-in-securitised-debt-a-technical-guide/13272.article> last visited 12 July 2025.

[81] On private networks for corporate reporting and networks for securities regulation and enforcement facilitated by IOSCO, see Stavros Gadinis, 'Three Pathways to Global Standards: Private, Regulator, and Ministry Networks' (2015) 109 American Journal of International Law 1.

resilience across capital markets.[82] Since climate risks are global in scope and impact, standardisation and coordination across capital markets should lower the compliance costs of companies and the costs to investors associated with integrating climate-related information into investment and governance decisions. Standardisation should also lower the regulatory costs of transitioning financial markets so that they can efficiently price climate risk.

At the same time, securities regulators and stock exchanges are highly sensitive to market shifts and competitive effects.[83] Whether capital markets will face stronger incentives to compete on their green credentials in response to interexchange competition and the Brussels effect, as has been the case for Singapore and Hong Kong,[84] or whether deregulatory pressures will discourage sustainable finance reforms and depress climate action over the long term remains to be seen. These questions implicate long-standing debates in securities regulation about the market for listings, the preconditions for strong capital markets, and regulatory arbitrage, among others.

3.5 Public and Private Enforcement

Finally, public enforcement by securities regulators plays an essential role in the post-carbon transition by policing greenwashing and other forms of fraud in the securities markets. For example, under the Biden administration, the US SEC established an ESG Task Force that pursued enforcement actions against ESG funds and asset managers.[85] If maintained over time, similar efforts could improve the credibility of green product claims, issuer climate disclosures, and voluntary climate commitments by firms and their investors.

Depending on the jurisdiction, private enforcement, market demand from investors, and pressure from industry peers is also important in pushing companies to comply with climate disclosure mandates and adopt climate governance measures, such as transition plans and resilience strategies and targets. Private securities fraud actions may also be relatively easier to bring in many jurisdictions as compared to shareholder derivative litigation challenging climate inaction under domestic corporate law.[86]

However, there are several factors that weigh in favour of more modest expectations. First, mandatory climate risk monitoring and reporting is everywhere in its infancy, with opposition to climate regulation in the US and calls to reduce regulatory burdens in Europe. Even under the more robust international regimes, the need for reasonable transition measures such as phase-ins and exemptions means that most will not take full effect for many years. In the US, whether private enforcement can push forward better climate reporting and more robust climate action in the face of unsupportive federal policies and even policy opposition is doubtful. Second, forward-looking climate risk information and new disclosure requirements may be

[82] See Virginia Harper Ho, 'Beyond Transplant: A Network Innovation Model of Transnational Regulatory Change' (2024) 71 American Journal of Comparative Law 513, 520–21 (discussing international organisations as network hubs).

[83] John C Coffee Jr, 'Racing Towards the Top: The Impact of Cross-listing and Stock Market Competition on International Corporate Governance' (2002) 102 Columbia Law Review 1757; Amir N Licht, 'International Diversity in Securities Regulation: Roadblocks on the Way to Convergence' (1989) 20 Cardozo Law Review 227.

[84] On the Brussels effect, see Anu Bradford, *The Brussels Effect: How the European Union Rules the World* (OUP 2020).

[85] SEC, 'SEC Announces Enforcement Task Force Focused on Climate and ESG Issues' (4 March 2021), https://www.sec.gov/newsroom/press-releases/2021-42.

[86] See Lim and Varottil (n 58) (making this argument with respect to several Asian common law jurisdictions).

covered by litigation safe harbours that temporarily limit the space for private enforcement.[87] In the US, where private enforcement plays a relatively greater role in combatting securities fraud, claims alleging material omissions of climate risk information have also been made more difficult under recent Supreme Court precedent.[88] Private enforcement of emerging climate reporting mandates is likely to remain weak in the EU as well.[89] Indeed, both common and civil law systems already rely more heavily on public enforcement of securities laws.[90] For all these reasons, whether companies take their climate disclosure obligations seriously will continue to depend on the strength of public enforcement, especially in the early implementation stages.

Nonetheless, private enforcement and public enforcement are also mutually reinforcing. For instance, private securities fraud litigation (and indeed corporate fiduciary litigation alleging risk oversight breaches by directors) has often followed on the heels of SEC investigations.[91] In addition, investor protection through public enforcement of the securities law aligns with the work of consumer protection authorities and also with civil litigation against false advertising of securities and corporate green commitments alike.[92] If companies come under pressure from investors and regulators to produce more consistent and precise climate-related information, both private securities fraud litigation and public enforcement should be expected to rise.

4. Taking Stock: Does Securities Regulation Matter?

Climate change is a chronic global crisis. Therefore, while there are grounds to expect both markets and law to play important roles, the literatures on transnational regulatory change, institutional change, and the interaction of public and private responses to climate change suggest that it will be difficult to assess the impact of any one area of law on private actors and market systems in isolation.[93] Much will depend on institutional path

[87] These are available in the US for forward-looking information under the Private Securities Litigation Reform Act of 1995 (PSLRA) and were extended in the US final climate disclosure rules. SEC (n 18) Item 1507.

[88] See *Macquarie Infrastructure Corporation et al v Moab Partners, LP*, 144 S Ct 885 (2024) (concluding that liability cannot be imposed under Rule 10b-5(b) for 'pure omissions' even in the face of an affirmative disclosure requirement). See also John C Coffee Jr and Joshua Mitts, 'Can Section 11 Be Saved? "Tracing" a Path to Its Survival' (2025) 15 Harvard Business Law Review 1 (observing the practical challenges imposed by *Slack Techs, LLC v Pirani*, 598 US 759 (2023) to claims of misleading statements or omissions in registration statements).

[89] See Tania Pantazi, 'The Introduction of Mandatory Corporate Sustainability Reporting in the EU and the Question of Enforcement' (2024) 25 European Business Organization Law Review 509.

[90] Howell E Jackson and Mark J Roe, 'Public and Private Enforcement of Securities Laws: Resource-based Evidence' (2009) 93 Journal of Financial Economics 207, 207–10, 230–33.

[91] ibid 206, 210 (citing authorities on public enforcement as precursor to civil securities litigation). On the 'piggy-backing' of corporate fiduciary duty litigation in the US on public enforcement, see Roy Shapira, 'A New Caremark Era: Causes and Consequences' (2021) 98 Washington University Law Review 1857, 1885.

[92] On the growing role of federal securities class actions and other private climate litigation against companies in the US and Europe, see Tigre and Barry (n 15) 20–21.

[93] Joanna Vince and others, 'Understanding Policy Integration Through an Integrative Capacity Framework' (2024) 43 Policy and Society 381.

dependencies,[94] the policy mix in particular jurisdictions,[95] the presence of exogenous shocks,[96] and the recursive interactions of investors, gatekeepers, and regulators themselves over time.[97]

At present, there is evidence of increasing but incomplete harmonisation and convergence in some areas of securities regulation, such as climate disclosure standardisation. There is also fundamental divergence in the regulatory reach, substantive scope, and strength of commitment among securities regulators globally concerning climate-related rulemaking and enforcement. These differences have been amplified by anti-ESG backlash in the US and elsewhere, which has brought to light continued scepticism among the public and some governments about the materiality of climate risk to companies and the severity of the climate change threat. As this section explains, several factors appear to determine how actively securities regulators respond to the climate crisis and the scope and impact of their efforts: (1) the level of comfort with market mechanisms or top-down regulation in the jurisdiction, (2) the strength of national and regional climate commitments; and (3) regulators' scope of authority.

4.1 Regulatory—or Market-Driven—Approaches

One source of variation is that in much of Europe and Asia, mandatory climate disclosure and other green finance initiatives have been led by securities and financial regulators, whereas in the US, private initiatives have played a larger role. Examples include private standard-setting, shareholder engagement around climate disclosure and board composition, and corporate voluntary commitments to reduce emissions. Other markets, such as the UK, fall somewhere in the middle.[98] These differences can be traced to local variations in regulatory approach, market conditions, and the mechanisms for investor influence that are unfortunately beyond the scope of this chapter. However, it is likely that some degree of regulatory steering is needed to address transnational threats such as climate change that require rapid, coordinated responses and have cross-border implications.

4.2 Policy Support for Climate Action

As the above discussion shows, the ultimate impact of securities regulation on climate action depends heavily on the degree of domestic and international policy support. In this regard, the EU is widely recognised as the leader in green finance regulation, building on extensive legal

94 See Johannes Gerschewski, 'Explanations of Institutional Change: Reflecting on a "Missing Diagonal" (2024) 115 American Political Science Review 218 (observing the importance to institutional change of path dependencies and gradual change on the one hand, and policy shocks on the other).

95 Andrea Migone and Michael Howlett, 'The Purpose of Policy Portfolios: Design, Intention, and Logic' (2024) 44(4) Journal of Public Policy 809–25; Cristina Peñasco, Laura D Anadón, and Elena Verdolini, 'Systematic Review of the Outcomes and Trade-offs of Ten Types of Decarbonization Policy Instruments' (2021) 11 Nature Climate Change 257; Karoline S Rogge and Kristin Reichardt, 'Policy Mixes for Sustainability Transitions: An Extended Concept and Framework for Analysis' (2016) 45 Research Policy 1620.

96 See Gerschewski (n 94) (citing authorities).

97 On the dynamism and recursivity of transnational regulatory change see Terence C Halliday and Gregory Shaffer (eds), *Transnational Legal Orders* (CUP 2015); Harper Ho (n 82) 522–26.

98 See Irene-marié Esser and Iain MacNeil, 'ESG Regulation, CSR, and Corporate Purpose: A UK Perspective,' in Binder et al (n 29), 141–60.

and policy frameworks, including the European Green Deal, the EU Action Plan, and the EU Climate Law, that have been developed by the EU and its member states. In addition, international efforts by regulators and investors to standardise climate change reporting and encourage corporate climate action and risk oversight all draw support ultimately from national climate action commitments under the Paris Agreement.

Lack of consistent public policy support for climate action domestically or internationally reduces the incentives for private actors to respond to climate risk. This is because public policies affect the visibility and business "salience" of climate and environmental concerns to companies and their management, informing how they assess climate risk materiality and the costs and benefits of stronger climate action.[99] While climate inaction by governments reduces transition-related climate risk for companies, it increases the probability and magnitude of future physical climate risk impacts on firms and on the planet. Prior research also suggests that climate ambivalence or hostility by powerful states like the US can weaken the implementation of climate initiatives elsewhere and encourage regulatory arbitrage—the proverbial "race to the bottom".[100] The shifting priorities of the SEC under the Biden and Trump administrations therefore present real challenges—witness Biden's "whole of government" commitment to climate action followed by Trump's abandonment of the Paris Agreement.[101] Weak public policy support for climate action in the US may therefore affect the resolve of climate-forward governments elsewhere and of companies and their investors as well.

4.3 The Standard Setter and Its Remit

Prior literature has also found that who the standard-setter or enforcer is can affect the ultimate impact of policy or rulemaking initiatives and their harmonisation (or divergence) transnationally.[102] For example, writing on sources of corporate governance rules, Chan and Lim observe that whether rules or standards are set by legislators, regulators, or private standard setters will affect the standards' legitimacy, the standard-setting pace and process, and implementation and enforcement.[103] Standard-setting by securities regulators and other administrative agencies is inherently more nimble and more bounded in scope, as compared to legislation. However, attempts at rapid implementation of climate-related agency rules and legislation have both met resistance. Policy unpredictability is itself costly to companies and can weaken compliance incentives, since companies may opt to challenge climate regulation, evade enforcement, or simply stall and wait for the political winds to shift. Examples in the

[99] 'Stakeholder salience' is widely discussed in the management literature on corporate social responsibility (CSR). See Donna J Wood and others, 'Stakeholder Identification and Salience after 20 Years: Progress, Problems, and Prospects' (2021) 60 Business and Society 196–245.

[100] See Stavros Gadinis, 'The Politics of Competition in International Financial Regulation' (2008) 49 Harvard International Law Journal 447 (finding that regulatory convergence and harmonisation in standard-setting are most strongly influenced by peer states and that the political dominance of powerful states heavily influences whether regulatory innovations are adopted by financial regulators elsewhere).

[101] Compare Trump's Executive Order 'Putting America First in International Environmental Agreements' (*White House*, 20 January 2025) <https://www.whitehouse.gov/presidential-actions/2025/01/putting-america-first-in-international-environmental-agreements/> accessed 1 July 2025, and Biden's 'Executive Order on Tackling the Climate Crisis at Home and Abroad' (*Perma*, 27 January 2021) <https://perma.cc/T3TU-EJ27> accessed 1 July 2025.

[102] For example, Gadinis (n 81) (examining various private, regulatory, and 'ministry' standard setters in financial regulation).

[103] Jonathan Chan and Ernest Lim, 'How It Matters Who Makes Corporate Rules' (2024) 25 European Business Organization Law Review 655.

US context discussed above include the pendulum swing of the rules governing whether pension fund fiduciaries in the US are permitted to integrate ESG factors into investment and voting decisions, and the SEC's shifting positions on the permissibility of shareholder proposals under Rule 14a-8(i)(7).[104]

Securities regulators are also bound by the scope of their statutory authority, which is affected by whether the regulator is positioned at the national level, the subnational level (as in Canada and Australia), or the regional level (as in the EU), and by the ability of securities regulators to coordinate their efforts with financial and environmental regulators.[105] For example, regulatory silos may prevent securities regulators from extending climate reporting rules to certain investors, such as pension funds or banks, that are under the remit of other regulators. Another dimension is the question of which firms are under the relevant regulatory authority, for instance, whether the regulator's authority extends only to listed firms and whether multiple regulators are engaged, as in the UK and the EU, in extending climate risk monitoring to large private firms across the entire market.[106]

A related and more fundamental difference among jurisdictions is the degree of discretion the regulator has to adopt climate change rules within the scope of its statutory authority. Historically, the remit of securities regulators has not been understood to encompass climate and environmental matters, even though, as we saw earlier, climate change implicates many aspects of their core mission concerning investor protection and, depending on the jurisdiction, oversight of market intermediaries. As the above discussion shows, the EU and its member states have adopted extensive frameworks, legislation, and regulations to support a green finance transition and to require companies to reduce their climate externalities.[107] In contrast, the authority of securities regulators and stock exchanges in the US to advance climate disclosure or any new rulemaking, much less climate-related corporate governance, has been significantly constrained in recent years and will likely be narrowed further.[108] The SEC's final climate rules were immediately challenged in 2024, and SEC commissioners under the Trump administration ceased to defend the rules in court.[109] This weakening of the regulatory authority of US administrative agencies is

[104] See text accompanying nn 61–63.

[105] On variations across common law jurisdictions, see Christopher M Bruner, *Corporate Governance in the Common-Law World: The Political Foundations of Shareholder Power* (OUP 2013) 78 and fig 3–4.

[106] HM Government (UK), 'Sustainability Disclosure Requirements: Implementation Update 2024,' (2024) <https://assets.publishing.service.gov.uk/media/66505ba9adfc6a4843fe04e5/Sustainability_Disclosure_Requirements__SDR__Implementation_Update_2024.pdf> accessed 1 July 2025. The UK, for example, is adopting sustainability reporting standards for non-listed firms that lie beyond the authority of the FCA, and its Companies Act 2006 already extends certain ESG disclosure obligations to all firms. ibid.

[107] For the legal foundations of the EU climate and sustainability disclosure rules, see Appendix A to ESRS 2 (n 55).

[108] The US Supreme Court's decision in *Loper Bright Enterprises v Raimondo*, 603 US 369 (2024) abandoned the long-standing doctrine of *Chevron* deference to administrative agency interpretations of regulation. The Supreme Court's earlier decisions in West Virginia v EPA, 142 S Ct 2587 (2022) (articulating the 'major questions' doctrine) and National Federation of Independent Business v Department of Labor, 595 US 109 (2022), as well as a range of cases challenging climate regulation in the lower courts, make clear that administrative agencies' power to act under their authorising statutes will be quite narrowly construed. Tigre and Barry (n 15) 16–19 (surveying climate deregulation cases). See also SEC v Jarskey, 608 US (2024) (preventing the SEC from relying on administrative hearings in securities fraud cases involving civil penalties); and Alliance for Fair Board Recruitment v SEC, 21-60626 (5th Cir 2024) (striking down the NASDAQ's board diversity rules).

[109] SEC, 'SEC Votes to End Defense of Climate Disclosure Rules' (*SEC*, 27 March 2025) <https://www.sec.gov/newsroom/press-releases/2025-58> accessed 2 July 2025.

unprecedented and stands in stark contrast to the role of securities and financial regulators nearly everywhere else.

The extent to which securities regulators may directly or indirectly regulate business conduct also varies.[110] Most jurisdictions recognise that securities regulation should, at minimum, align with other bodies of public law, such as environmental law and direct climate-related regulation, that directly target corporate climate externalities. For instance, the EU's 2014 non-financial reporting directive (NFRD) and the more recent Corporate Sustainability Reporting Directive (CSRD) and Corporate Sustainability Due Diligence Directive (CSDDD), even in their scaled-back forms, are intended to cause companies to become more climate resilient, mitigate climate impacts, and conduct environmental and human rights due diligence. In contrast, the SEC sought to avoid imposing any conduct requirements on covered firms in its final climate disclosure rules, presumably due to the uncertain scope of its general statutory authority with regard to issuer conduct without relying on specific Congressional mandate.

5. Conclusion

As the above discussion shows, securities regulation can support but not displace direct regulation of climate externalities. Much depends on investors' ability and willingness to monitor climate risks and reward climate-resilient firms. Given the many disincentives to investor engagement, it is far from clear that greater corporate transparency around material climate risks will motivate investors to push for corporate climate action, especially in the absence of imminent and tangible costs to climate laggards.

The proper conclusion to draw from this, however, is not that securities regulation is irrelevant to global climate change responses, but that it is pivotal. Only reforms to securities and financial regulation can enhance market institutions and infrastructures so that markets can better price climate risk, become climate resilient, and support climate-informed capital allocation and corporate climate governance. Even without consistent investor support, securities regulation outside the US is already pushing regulated entities and large firms, both public and private, to strengthen climate risk management and oversight. On the other hand, when securities regulation is neutral or hostile to climate risk integration and investor climate action, it weakens companies' incentives to monitor climate risk, increasing the likelihood of a disruptive post-carbon transition. Securities regulation can therefore either support and align with, or conversely frustrate, the stronger tools for corporate climate action that direct climate legislation and other bodies of public law may provide. In a very real sense, then, how securities regulators respond to the climate crisis may determine how easy or difficult it will be for companies and, perhaps more importantly, their investors to do so.

Despite the high uncertainty surrounding these questions, transnational regulatory change is an iterative process shaped by the continued interactions of public and private actors over time.[111] We may therefore expect that the increasing risks to companies and their investors from climate change will only make clearer the urgent need for a truly global green finance transition, and that positive corporate and investor climate action and the greening of securities regulation will continue to be mutually reinforcing.

110 The SEC has at times engaged in rulemaking with corporate governance effects but has also faced legal challenge for exceeding its statutory authority even when such rulemaking was undertaken at the behest of Congress. See Virginia Harper Ho, 'Modernizing ESG Disclosure' (2022) University of Illinois Law Review 277, 303, 346–47 (citing examples).

111 Halliday and Shaffer (n 97).

CHAPTER 24

Bankruptcy Law

JOSHUA C. MACEY

1. Introduction

WHEN creditors fear that a distressed firm's assets are insufficient to fully satisfy their claims, they can be expected to race to the courthouse to secure repayment before other creditors. While individually rational, this behaviour can result in the dismemberment of firms that still have substantial going-concern value, ultimately leaving investors and other stakeholders worse off than they would be if the firm continued to operate.

Bankruptcy law has long served as a mechanism to solve this collective action problem.[1] Its central provisions—especially the automatic stay, the absolute priority rule, and the prohibition on fraudulent transfers—all serve to coordinate creditor actions, ensuring that individual creditors cannot precipitate the unnecessary dissolution of valuable corporate enterprises when they pursue recoveries in their individual capacities.

As I and others have argued, however, many of the provisions that are designed to coordinate creditor actions can work at cross-purposes with environmental laws.[2] That is because bankruptcy doctrines that are designed to address the collective action problems can also put debtors with substantial but unpaid environmental obligations in a position to hold up environmental regulators.

Consider two examples. First, regulators are often reluctant to bring enforcement actions against financially distressed firms, especially when enforcement would leave taxpayers responsible for significant remediation costs. Of course, deferring enforcement can ultimately lead to even higher cleanup costs as continued operations generate new environmental harms. Still, regulators have strong incentives to kick the proverbial can down the road, since deferring enforcement can plausibly induce other regulatory bodies to intervene, foist responsibility for environmental remediation onto future policymakers, or generate new revenue that can be used to remediate past environmental damage. Regulators will therefore sometimes postpone enforcement in the hope that some future source of revenue will emerge that can pay for environmental harms that should have been borne by the firm, leaving firms with

[1] Thomas H Jackson, *The Logic and Limits of Bankruptcy Law* (Harvard University Press 1986); Thomas H Jackson, 'Bankruptcy, Non-Bankruptcy Entitlements, and the Creditors' Bargain' (1982) 91 Yale Law Journal 857; Douglas G Baird, 'A World Without Bankruptcy' (1987) 50 Law & Contemporary Problems 173.

[2] Joshua C Macey and Jackson Salovaara, 'Bankruptcy as Bailout: Coal Company Insolvency and the Erosion of Federal Law' (2019) 71 Stanford Law Review 879; Terra Baer, Pranjal Drall, and Joshua Macey, 'Too Liable to Regulate: The Hidden Costs of Fossil Fuel Decommissioning and Remediation' 115 California Law Review (2027) (forthcoming); Martin Lockman, 'Environmental Repair in the Energy Transition' (2026) 114 California Law Review (forthcoming) <https://papers.ssrn.com/sol3/papers.cfm?abstract_id=5087880>.

significant unpaid or underfunded environmental liabilities in a relatively strong position to push for regulatory forbearance.

Second, bankruptcy can pit the interests of past environmental claimants against the interests of future environmental claimants. If environmental claimants cannot be paid out of existing funds, they may push for a reorganisation so that the firm can continue to operate and generate income that will increase firm value in the future and thus increase the recoveries available to them in bankruptcy. Victims of past pollution thus rationally prefer the firm to continue to operate to generate money to satisfy their claims. By giving existing claimants voting and other governance rights, bankruptcy empowers stakeholders who are likely to favour reorganisation even when liquidation would be preferable from society's perspective. Doing so prioritises—perhaps with good reason, perhaps not—the efficient resolution of existing cases and controversies over broader policy objectives such as deterrence, the articulation of social values, or the development of new legal doctrines.[3] Regardless of whether or not this is justified, bankruptcy's "continuation bias" can result in substantial new environmental harms that are unlikely to be satisfied, particularly in the context of ambitious national decarbonisation policies that that can be met only if large fossil fuel companies eventually liquidate.

In theory, bankruptcy law could be tweaked to address these issues by giving non-adjusting creditors such as tort and environmental claimants a super priority claim, making it easier to bring fraudulent transfer claims, and strengthening protections for future claimants who are unable to participate in the bankruptcy proceeding. In practice, however, cross-border insolvency proceedings, perhaps especially for multinational fossil fuel companies, create opportunities for strategic behaviour by firms and states that limit the effectiveness of bankruptcy-specific reforms. For example, if one country adopts ambitious environmental laws, firms may spin off risky assets to reduce or eliminate their exposure to individual countries' decarbonisation policies. Alternatively, countries may push firms to file domestically in the hope that they can increase recoveries for creditors in their jurisdictions. That dynamic could lead to inequities as residents and communities in some countries receive an outsize recovery from corporate reorganisations, and it could also lead to a new, global race to the courthouse as countries try to recover whatever value they can before the firm liquidates. Global forum shopping thus appears inevitable as firms look for sympathetic jurisdictions that either prefer reorganisation or that protect local economic interests.[4]

[3] cf Abbe R Gluck, Elizabeth Chamblee Burch, and Adam S Zimmerman, 'Against Bankruptcy: Public Litigation Values Versus the Endless Quest for Global Peace in Mass Litigation' (2024) Yale Law Journal Forum 525; Anthony J Casey and Joshua C Macey, 'Bankruptcy by Another Name' (2024) Yale Law Journal Forum 1016.

[4] This has long been a challenge domestically in the US. See Jared A Ellias, 'What Drives Bankruptcy Forum Shopping? Evidence from Market Data' (2018) 47 Journal of Legal Studies 119; Barry E Adler and Henry N Butler, 'On the "Delawarization of Bankruptcy" Debate' (2003) 52 Emory Law Journal 1309; David A Skeel Jr, 'What's So Bad About Delaware?' (2001) 54 Vanderbilt Law Review 309; Anthony J Casey and Joshua C Macey, 'Bankruptcy Shopping: Domestic Venue Races and Global Forum Wars' (2001) 37 Emory Bankruptcy Developments Journal 436; Lynn M LoPucki, *Courting Failure: How Competition for Big Cases Is Corrupting the Bankruptcy Courts* (University of Michigan Press 2006); Laura Napoli Coordes, 'The Geography of Bankruptcy' (2015) 68 Vanderbilt Law Review 381; Samir D Parikh, 'Modern Forum Shopping in Bankruptcy' (2013) 46 Connecticut Law Review 159; Lynn M LoPucki and Sara D Kalin, 'The Failure of Public Company Bankruptcies in Delaware and New York: Empirical Evidence of a "Race to the Bottom"' (2001) 54 Vanderbilt Law Review 231; Theodore Eisenberg and Lynn M LoPucki, 'Shopping for Judges: An Empirical Analysis of Venue Choice in Large Chapter 11 Reorganizations' (1999) 84 Cornell Law Review 967.

This chapter considers how bankruptcy law creates tension between environmental law, which often favours reorganisation, and decarbonisation efforts, which in many cases are better served by liquidation. It further examines how cross-border insolvencies can exacerbate this tension by creating opportunities for strategic behaviour by firms and states. Ultimately, the chapter argues that because state-level bankruptcy reforms are vulnerable to strategic behaviour, more effective pathways to managing the orderly decline of multinational fossil fuel companies lie outside the bankruptcy system—particularly reforms to environmental laws and managed government interventions. It concludes by proposing bankruptcy and non-bankruptcy reforms that would curb opportunism and strategic behaviour, making it easier for countries to wind down large firms without leaving past tort and environmental claimants out to pasture.

2. The Purpose of Bankruptcy Law

Bankruptcy scholars have long debated why countries adopt a unified, national bankruptcy system and the rules that should govern that system. Although there is persistent disagreement about how far to extend bankruptcy protections, scholars have generally coalesced around the view that bankruptcy is designed to address a particular collective action problem that arises when firms become financially distressed.[5] If creditors are concerned that a firm will be unable to meet its obligations, they will race to the courthouse, seek a judgment, and try to collect whatever value they can. Although this race to the courthouse may be in the interest of individual creditors, it can lead to the dismemberment of firms that have greater value as going concerns.

Although the particulars differ by country, bankruptcy law's core provisions—the automatic stay, preference rules, the absolute priority rule, and channelling injunctions that prevent creditors from pursuing recovery in other forums—provide, at least in theory, an orderly process for reorganising firms in order to maximise the value of the estate. The reorganisation occurs in a single forum. Creditors cannot pursue recovery elsewhere. After the reorganisation plan is confirmed, creditors can only recover if they participated in the bankruptcy proceeding. This system should benefit all creditors, including tort and environmental claimants,[6] as it increases the total pool of assets available and prevents the dismemberment of firms that have value as a going concern.

Another benefit of the bankruptcy process is that it provides a forum for renegotiating a firm's financial obligations.[7] Bankruptcy law, both in the US and elsewhere, typically divides creditors into classes and creates voting rules, overseen by a judge or other government official, that allow interested parties to negotiate the terms of the reorganisation plan. Creditors whose financial interests are impaired can participate in this voting process. These creditors vote against a background of rules such as the absolute priority rule that determine each classes' legal entitlements. Creditors have an incentive to participate in the process, since failure to do so risks losing the ability to bring a claim against the debtor. And they have an interest in reaching an agreement with other creditors, since they are negotiating against the backdrop of coercive rules that allow a subset of creditors to force the confirmation of a reorganisation plan—even if some creditors object—so long as the plan meets certain criteria. In many

[5] Baird (n 1).

[6] Anthony J Casey and Joshua C Macey, 'In Defense of Chapter 11 for Mass Torts' (2023) 90 University of Chicago Law Review 973

[7] Anthony J Casey, 'Chapter 11's Renegotiation Framework and the Purpose of Corporate Bankruptcy' (2020) 120 Columbia Law Review 1709.

respects, therefore, the bankruptcy process provides a forum in which parties that contracted with the debtor can renegotiate among themselves about how to reorganise or sell firm assets to maximise value for investors and other stakeholders.

3. The Challenge of Non-Adjusting Creditors

But certain creditors are poorly situated to participate in the bankruptcy process or take measures to protect their interests once firms become distressed. Unlike financial creditors—who negotiate with the firm ex ante and can account for risks by charging higher interest rates, requiring that the debtor post collateral, insisting on restrictive covenants in debt agreements, or refusing to lend to the debtor altogether—tort victims and environmental claimants have less ability to take such measures. They did not choose to contract with the debtor or accept the risk that they would be exposed to harm, but instead find that they have a claim against the debtor by virtue of the fact that the debtor engaged in risk-taking or misconduct that caused tort or environmental harm. These claimants therefore lack many of the contractual tools that are available to other creditors to limit exposure to firms' financial distress; hence the term "non-adjusting creditors".

For this reason, tort and environmental claimants are unusually vulnerable to strategic behaviour by debtors and other corporate stakeholders. One key challenge is that in many jurisdictions, involuntary creditors do not hold priority claims in bankruptcy. As a result, they must compete with other unsecured creditors for whatever value remains after secured and priority creditors are paid.[8] This vulnerability is compounded by the fact that non-adjusting creditors are also vulnerable to strategic measures firms take to partition liability, either by shifting liability to underfunded subsidiaries or spinning off assets that have accrued or are likely to accrue an unmanageable level of liability. While fraudulent transfer is designed to address this challenge, administrative and evidentiary hurdles often limit its effectiveness.

On the classic account, non-adjusting creditors such as tort and environmental claimants should be given stronger protections in bankruptcy law to increase the likelihood that they are compensated for harms arising from corporate misconduct or corporate risk-taking.[9] Common proposals include giving these creditors a priority or super priority claim and strengthening fraudulent transfer law. Additional reforms could expand their power within bankruptcy—by, for example, giving them a unilateral right to propose or veto the reorganisation plan. Alternatively, or perhaps in conjunction with these measures, regulators could impose bonding or insurance requirements that guarantee that funds are allocated to and available for tort and environmental claimants. A more radical approach would be to pierce the corporate veil such that shareholders face unlimited lability for certain corporate harms.[10] Note that besides the veil-piercing proposal, these reforms operate within the bankruptcy framework by increasing the likelihood that non-adjusting creditors can recover by participating in the bankruptcy proceeding.

[8] This is not universally true. In the US, for example, some environmental laws require that the firm post a bond to cover cleanup, and when environmental claims are considered an administrative expense, they receive priority treatment.

[9] Lindsey D Simon, 'Bankruptcy Grifters' (2022) 131 Yale Law Journal 1154; Vince Buccola and Joshua Macey, 'Claim Durability and Bankruptcy's Tort Problem' (2021) 38 Yale Journal on Regulation 766; Judson Boomhower, 'Drilling Like There's No Tomorrow: Bankruptcy, Insurance, and Environmental Risk' (2019) 109 American Economic Review 391.

[10] Henry Hansmann and Reinier Kraakman, 'Toward Unlimited Liability for Corporate Torts' (1990) 100 Yale Law Journal 1879.

4. Environmental Liability Creates Incentives to Reorganise, Not Liquidate

A less well-studied challenge is that large environmental claims can create incentives for firms to reorganise even when it would be preferable from society's perspective for the firm to liquidate. That is both because bankruptcy itself favours reorganisation, and because liquidation will often reduce funds available to pay environmental claimants or used to remediate past environmental harms. That, in turn, gives regulators and environmental claimants an incentive to use their governance rights to push for reorganisation to increase the likelihood that there are funds to remediate past harms and pay for cleanup.

In some respects, non-adjusting creditors' interests do not align with the interests of other creditors. One of the reasons to impose liability for tort and environmental mismanagement is to compensate victims of corporate risk-taking. Another is that liability creates pressure for firms to mitigate the risks they pose to third parties and the environment. Note that these two goals are in tension when a firm is in financial distress. Ex post, environmental law's remedial goal of restoring damaged ecosystems is more likely to be served if the firm continues operating so that it can continue to generate new income to fund remediation. By contrast, ex ante, environmental law's deterrent function of discouraging environmentally harmful conduct is better served when firms that cannot meet their environmental obligations are forced to liquidate. Firms are of course more likely to avoid liquidation—and thus generate future revenue that can be used to repay its existing creditors, including environmental and tort claimants—if they reorganise and continue producing. As a result, tort and environmental claimants can increase recoveries by pushing for a reorganisation, even if the reorganisation will lead to significant future environmental harms.

Bankruptcy law's preference for reorganisation—sometimes known as the continuation bias—implicitly privileges environmental law's remedial goal over deterrence. Although tort and environmental claimants often do not choose to contract with the firm, bankruptcy allows them to influence the reorganisation plan by giving them voting rights and allowing them to challenge proposed reorganisation plans. Claimants who have suffered significant harm will rationally—and rightly, in my view—support a reorganisation plan that increases their financial recovery. They can for that reason be expected to vote to confirm a reorganisation plan that will maximise firm value, even if doing so can be expected to exacerbate future environmental degradation.

To put this issue concretely, victims of past environmental harms and tortious conduct may push for a reorganisation plan that does not take adequate precautions to mitigate the risk that the firm will engage in excessive tortious conduct or environmental mismanagement in the future, hoping that they will receive a larger payout if the firm underinvests in mitigating future environmental and tort risks. In extreme cases, non-adjusting creditors may have an incentive to push for reorganisation plans that produce judgment proof companies that will be unable to pay future non-adjusting creditors.

A related challenge is that liquidation can impose significant political costs on the regulators and policymakers charged with enforcing environmental compliance. As I have documented elsewhere, regulators have tolerated asset transfers from large, relatively well-capitalised companies to underfunded firms, seemingly because they did not want to force liquidation or acknowledge that coal mines and onshore gas wells were idle or orphaned.[11] A particular

[11] See, e.g., Macey and Salovaara (n 2); Baer et al (n 2).

difficulty for regulators has been that aggressive enforcement of reclamation, remediation, and decommissioning laws would reveal that the firms had not set aside sufficient funds to cover the full costs of decommissioning coal mines and gas wells. When large coal mining companies have filed for bankruptcy, for example, regulators have authorised (or declined to block) asset transfers to highly undercapitalised firms.[12] Relatedly, in the context of onshore gas drilling, environmental regulators have been reluctant to bring enforcement action against companies that acquire idle gas wells, seemingly out of concern that aggressive enforcement would force the firm to liquidate, leaving regulators and taxpayers responsible for potentially billions of dollars of abandoned gas wells decommissioning costs.[13]

This is a predictable and understandable political calculus. Aggressive enforcement of environmental laws can trigger liquidation, forcing taxpayers to pay for environmental remediation or leaving idle and abandoned mines and wells that pose significant environmental hazards. By foregoing enforcement, regulators and policymakers can postpone a decision that could have grave political consequences. It is possible, of course, that the market will rebound, generating funds that can later be used to pay for cleanup, and regulators who decline to fully enforce environmental laws may simply be crossing their fingers and hoping that market conditions improve for fossil resources.

It is also possible, however, that regulators are themselves playing a game of chicken. In the US, state regulators are often responsible for overseeing specific environmental statutes. If corporations cannot afford to remediate environmental harms, the federal government may (and often has) stepped in to provide financial support for burdened communities. This has some environmental benefits, since it funds cleanup in the state, but it also has significant downsides, since it creates moral hazard for state regulators, who may intentionally under enforce state environmental laws to create further pressure for the federal government to intervene.

5. Challenges in the Global Context

Many of the problems described in the previous section become more difficult to manage in the context of cross-border insolvencies, largely because effective cross-border insolvency requires that debtors and other sovereigns voluntarily accept that sovereign's insolvency process. If one country develops bankruptcy procedures that would force fossil fuel companies to liquidate, it would reduce other sovereigns' incentives to accept that bankruptcy process and would encourage debtors to file elsewhere or engage in other forms of strategic behaviour to shield their assets from the reach of the environmentally friendly country.

Cross-border insolvency law deals with insolvency cases involving entities that operate or have assets and liabilities in multiple countries. Because insolvency laws differ significantly between jurisdictions, cross-border insolvency has long struggled to develop a process that provides an efficient reorganisation process while respecting each country's substantive laws.

There are three particular challenges: first, jurisdictional tensions create uncertainty about which country should oversee the proceeding and which substantive laws should apply; second, when assets are located in different countries, the court administering the insolvency proceeding (or the debtor's estate) must be able to collect, oversee, and distribute assets to creditors; and third, the possibility of forum shopping allows debtors to file strategically in jurisdictions that will offer favourable legal outcomes.[14]

[12] See, e.g., Macey and Salovaara (n 2).

[13] Baer et al (n 2).

[14] Anthony J Casey and Joshua C Macey, 'Bankruptcy Shopping: Domestic Venue Races and Global Forum Wars' (2001) 37 Emory Bankruptcy Developments Journal 436; Anthony J Casey, Aurelio

Largely in response to these issues, many countries—including the US—have adopted the United Nations Commission on International Trade Law (UNCITRAL) Model Law on Cross-Border Insolvency.[15] The Model Law establishes an international framework that is designed to promote cooperation between courts in different countries, legal certainty for creditors, investors, and debtors, and the fair and efficient management of cross-border insolvencies.[16]

The Model Law proposes that debtors initiate a single main proceeding—known at the Center of Main Interest (COMI)—in one jurisdiction while non-main proceedings that affect the main proceeding can be opened in other jurisdictions. The COMI is supposed to refer to the jurisdiction in which the debtor primarily conducts business, manages operations, and makes key decisions, though there is considerable latitude for forum shopping. The designation of a COMI and recognition by other countries triggers core bankruptcy procedural protections. For example, in the US, if the foreign proceeding is deemed a "foreign main proceeding" (meaning it is pending in the debtor's COMI), then the automatic stay prevents creditors from pursuing claims against the debtor in the US.

The US adopted the Model Law approach in the Bankruptcy Abuse Prevention and Consumer Protection Act of 2005, which created Chapter 15 of the Bankruptcy Code to address cases involving foreign insolvency proceedings seeking assistance from US courts.[17] Once a foreign proceeding has been initiated, a foreign court will designate a representative to request recognition by a US bankruptcy court.[18] If the US bankruptcy court recognises the foreign proceeding as a main proceeding, Chapter 15 automatically imposes a stay similar to Chapter 11 that pauses litigation, enforcement actions, and asset seizures in the US.[19] The purpose of recognition of the foreign proceeding is to allow foreign representatives to control or safeguard assets that are located in the US to maximise recoveries for creditors. Chapter 15 also explicitly promotes communication and cooperation between US courts and foreign courts. Importantly, relief under Chapter 15 may be denied if granting it would be "manifestly contrary" to US public policy.[20]

The Model Law is often thought to endorse something called "modified universalism". Universalism advocates for a single insolvency forum for resolving cross-border insolvencies (the continued role of non-main proceedings is responsible for the "modified" moniker). This differs from the historical approach, known as "localism", in which "the courts in each national jurisdiction seize the property physically within their control and distribute it according to local rules".[21] Localism risks creating a global race to the courthouse.

Importantly, the Model Law approach has two challenges that make it difficult for bankruptcy law to ensure the orderly wind-down of multinational firms responsible for significant carbon emissions: first, it requires voluntary buy-in from different jurisdictions, and second, it struggles to prevent debtors from shopping for favourable forums. This makes it extremely

Gurrea-Martínez, and Robert K Rasmussen, 'A Commitment Rule for Insolvency Forum' (2025) 4 University of Chicago Business Law Review 51; Robert K Rasmussen, 'Resolving Transnational Insolvencies Through Private Ordering' (2000) 98 Michigan Law Review 2252.

[15] *UNCITRAL Model Law on Cross-Border Insolvency* (1997).

[16] *In re ABC Learning Centres Ltd* 728 F3d 301, 306 (3rd Cir 2013).

[17] 11 United States Code s 1504, 1509, 1515, 1517.

[18] 11 United States Code s 101(24).

[19] 11 United States Code s 1509(b)(2).

[20] 11 United States Code s 1506; *In re Toft* 453 BR 186 (Bankr SDNY 2011); *In re Gold & Honey Ltd* 410 BR 357 (Bankr EDNY 2009).

[21] Andrew T Guzman, 'International Bankruptcy: In Defense of Universalism' (2000) 98 Michigan Law Review 2177, 2179.

difficult for a single country to increase the stringency of bankruptcy law to encourage the liquidation of companies that own and operate infrastructure responsible for significant carbon emissions.

One problem is that when one country introduces stringent environmental regulations aimed at aggressive decarbonisation, multinational corporations may attempt to strategically restructure their assets to minimise the impact of these policies and reorganise elsewhere to limit their exposure to that country's laws. A firm could isolate environmentally risky assets, such as fossil fuel production plants or aging industrial facilities, by spinning them off into undercapitalised subsidiaries or separate entities. It would not be surprising, for example, if large energy firms with significant European operations initiated asset transfers or created subsidiaries to shield parent companies from extensive cleanup liabilities or compliance costs resulting from new environmental mandates in countries like Germany or the Netherlands.

Of course, those countries that want to increase the pace of decarbonisation could strengthen fraudulent transfer law, but doing so might encourage the companies to liquidate and sell their assets to firms that operate primarily outside of Europe. Alternatively, the firm may file in a country that does not accept these fraudulent transfer rules, leading to inconsistent substantive laws and a global race to the bottom. For these reasons, attempts to prevent asset transfers could trigger liquidations that still result in the assets being transferred, thus perversely exacerbating precisely the problem they are trying to address.

A related challenge is that as different sovereigns embrace different climate priorities, countries themselves may encourage or even pressure firms to file domestically rather than abroad. This tactic would be employed in hopes of enhancing recoveries for local creditors, employees, and affected communities. Countries naturally think that domestic insolvency proceedings will prove more sympathetic to local interests, and the struggle to reach a consensus about how to create a universal cross-border insolvency mechanism is largely due to the fact that countries are reluctant to cede control over restructuring proceedings that have significant local effects.

Moreover, if a few countries adopt bankruptcy-specific reforms that are far more protective of the environment or more favourable to local interests, other countries may respond by refusing to recognise proceedings in that country. In other words, the existence of a foreign main proceeding today is based on a delicate equilibrium in which countries recognise that it is efficient and mutually beneficial for the reorganisation to occur primarily in a single jurisdiction, but that equilibrium could quickly change if countries seek to amend their insolvency laws to pursue decarbonisation policies. Such behaviour could spark a global competition, effectively creating the race to the courthouse in which jurisdictions rush to secure as much value as possible from distressed firms before eventual liquidation. That is precisely the race to the courthouse that bankruptcy is designed to prevent, and it is becoming more likely as countries develop plausible alternatives to the US bankruptcy process.[22]

Ultimately, these two dynamics could encourage global forum shopping of the worst sort, with firms actively seeking jurisdictions sympathetic to their interests—either those favouring reorganisation due to economic incentives or those prioritising local economic stability over rigorous environmental enforcement. The tension between environmental law and decarbonisation thus interacts in perverse ways with the collective action problems created by cross-border insolvencies. To the extent that increasingly stringent climate obligations drive firms to relocate to other jurisdictions, they allow firms to file in jurisdictions that are sceptical of

[22] Oscar Couwenberg and Stephen J Lubben, 'Good Old Chapter 11 in a Pre-Insolvency World: The Growth of Global Reorganization Options' (2021) 46 North Carolina Journal of International Law 353.

attempts to force a firm into liquidation. As a result, the availability of multiple international bankruptcy venues grants debtors even more power to engage in strategic insolvency manoeuvres, complicating regulators' efforts to hold firms accountable for environmental obligations and undermining global decarbonisation efforts.

6. Solutions

Perhaps the upshot of this analysis is that an orderly wind-down of fossil fuel companies is highly unlikely to occur through bankruptcy, and that non-bankruptcy reforms are needed to manage the decline of fossil infrastructure. Of course, none of these proposals is a panacea. They all entail trade-offs and can prompt strategic behaviour. The goal is simply to identify reforms that are likely to result in meaningful environmental stewardship.

Bankruptcy-specific reforms are, of course, important and worthwhile. For example, countries should amend their domestic insolvency laws to give environmental claimants a priority claim in bankruptcy. Doing so would both increase the likelihood that debtors pay the full costs of remediating environmental damage and reduce past environmental claimants' incentives to push for reorganisation. Countries should also strengthen fraudulent transfer law to facilitate recovery when firms have spun off assets to try to shield them from environmental regulators and environmental claimants. Equally important, countries should clarify that they will not recognise main proceedings if those proceedings subordinate environmental liabilities or use overly lenient fraudulent transfer claims.

This final suggestion—that countries refuse to recognise foreign proceedings that do not respect their environmental policies—is delicate, since it could contribute to precisely the kinds of collective action problems I have described in Section 5. Debtors could respond by moving assets and businesses abroad, and countries that do not share one country's decarbonisation policies may retaliate by refusing to recognise the environmentally friendly country's insolvency proceedings.

As should by now be clear, it is important to recognise that non-bankruptcy reforms can leave countries much less vulnerable to strategic behaviour ex post by regulating pre-bankruptcy conduct to make it more difficult to escape environmental obligations when they come due and thus reduce the stakes of the bankruptcy process. First, and perhaps most importantly, countries should require a full cash bond to guarantee that firms are capable of complying with environmental laws that require environmental remediation. Because firms spin off assets and liabilities before filing for bankruptcy protection, and because some jurisdictions could make it difficult to pursue the spin-offs, it is important to ensure that the firm has set aside assets to guarantee that it can remediate environmental harms that it has caused. The best way to do this is to insist that the firm has set aside enough money to fully fund its environmental obligations. Unfortunately, because countries have not required a full-cost bond in the past, it is likely to be politically difficult to shift to full cost bonding, since any attempt to do so could precipitate liquidations or spin offs that are politically unpalatable.

A second-best option is to mandate insurance or a surety bond. The benefit of this approach is that a third-party will have skin in the game and thus an incentive to monitor the debtor to make sure that it is able to meet its environmental obligations. The downside is that distressed firms and industries often struggle to procure insurance. In some cases, such as the coal mining industry in the US, it appears that distressed coal mining companies have begun to procure insurance from firms that are themselves unlikely to be able to meet environmental obligations that they insure. This, too, is a predictable consequence of an industry that is becoming judgment proof. Why would a well-capitalised insurance company want to underwrite environmental obligations of a company that is unlikely to be able to meet those obligations?

For these reasons, insurance creates its own set of risks, especially in industries that can expect to contract significantly as the world decarbonises. This moral hazard problem means that it will become increasingly difficult for firms to obtain high-quality insurance at precisely the moment it is most needed.

The last, and perhaps inevitable, option is for countries to develop an investment fund that can manage the orderly liquidation of fossil industries.[23] Given that significant cleanup and remediation obligations are likely to fall to the public, environmentally friendly regulators should develop lending authorities that oversee the orderly liquidation of fossil infrastructure. The idea would be to offer an incentive for firms to liquidate in environmentally responsible ways. The government would set up a dedicated authority (akin to existing sovereign wealth funds, infrastructure banks, or environmental trust funds). The fund could be capitalised through various methods such as direct government investment, contributions from industry (levies or fees on fossil-fuel operations), and green bonds or other sustainable investment instruments. Fossil fuel companies facing insolvency or unmanageable cleanup obligations could voluntarily apply for support from the fund. Eligibility criteria would include financial distress, willingness to commit to an environmentally responsible liquidation, and agreement to transparent oversight.

As an incentive to participate, the fund would offer loans, bridge financing, or grants with favourable terms (low-interest or interest-free, longer repayment periods, or partial forgiveness). These incentives would specifically target activities like decommissioning fossil fuel facilities responsibly, environmental remediation of polluted sites, proper capping and abandonment of oil and gas wells, and worker transition programmes, including retraining and relocation assistance. These provisions would hopefully reduce the incentive of workers, tort claimants, and environmental claimants to push for reorganisation, since they would receive substantial benefits through liquidation.

Participating companies would submit comprehensive liquidation plans detailing environmental measures, cleanup methods, timelines, and independent verification mechanisms. In order to receive funds, the firm would be required to meet clearly defined environmental and social criteria. The authority could oversee performance through regular audits, inspections, and transparent reporting standards. Ideally, the fund would be able to recover at least partial value from liquidated assets, for example through the sale or repurposing of infrastructure and rehabilitated lands.

7. Conclusion

In short, because bankruptcy, especially cross-border bankruptcies that involve assets and subsidiaries in many different countries, is vulnerable to strategic behaviour and abuse, it is important for governments to intervene early and aggressively so that they can wind down fossil infrastructure while securing buy-in from local communities and other interests that are likely to be harmed by the liquidation of large fossil fuel companies. Although targeted reforms to bankruptcy and non-bankruptcy law could be useful, the optimal solution appears to be an investment authority that encourages financially distressed companies to choose responsible liquidation over abandonment or strategic insolvency manoeuvres. This approach would proactively manage environmental risks, minimise public liability for costly cleanups, and ease the economic transition for affected workers and communities.

[23] For one approach, see Saule T Omarova and Brian Richardson, 'Public Investment as Constitutional Power and Accountability Challenge' (2025) 92 University of Chicago Law Review 461.

CHAPTER 25

International Commercial Arbitration

YING ZHU

1. Introduction

INTERNATIONAL commercial arbitration is a method of resolving international commercial disputes through arbitral tribunals, rather than national courts.[1] Parties commonly include an arbitration clause in a commercial contract, stating that any future dispute arising out of or in relation to the contract will be determined by an arbitral tribunal whose constitution and operation will be subject to procedures provided in the arbitration clause (ad hoc arbitration) or be administered by an arbitration institution (institutional arbitration).[2] In the absence of a pre-dispute arbitration agreement, parties can also agree to submit an existing dispute to arbitration through a submission agreement.

As compared to litigation, international commercial arbitration as a dispute resolution mechanism has several unique features. It offers parties more flexibility in choosing procedural rules that govern the disputes. The arbitration proceedings can be confidential at the parties' discretion. The neutrality of the proceedings is particularly appealing when one of the disputing parties is a state or state entity where the other disputing party may seek to avoid litigation in the court of that state. Besides, the enforceability of international commercial arbitration awards is supported by the Convention on the Recognition and Enforcement of Foreign Arbitral Awards (New York Convention), which facilitates the recognition and enforcement of awards rendered in one jurisdiction by the courts of other Contracting Parties.[3]

Nonetheless, commercial arbitration as a mechanism for resolving climate-related disputes has received inadequate attention in the literature. Most research on the intersection of arbitration and climate change has primarily focused on investor–state arbitration rather than on commercial arbitration. However, in practice, there is an increasing number of commercial

[1] Gary B Born, *International Commercial Arbitration*, vol 1 (3rd edn, Kluwer Law International 2021) 67; Alan Redfern and Martin Hunter, *Law and Practice of International Commercial Arbitration* (4th edn, Sweet & Maxwell 2004) 1.

[2] There are two types of commercial arbitration: ad hoc arbitration and institutional arbitration. For institutional arbitration, the parties choose a specific arbitration institution to administer the arbitration proceedings. On the other hand, parties may also opt for ad hoc arbitration which is not conducted under the auspice of an arbitral institution. For ad hoc arbitrations, the parties may choose non-institutional rules such as the UNCITRAL Arbitration Rules to govern the procedures of arbitration. W Michael Reisman, W Laurence Craig, William W Park and Jan Paulsson, *International Commercial Arbitration: Cases, Materials, and Notes on the Resolution of International Business Disputes* (2nd edn, Foundation Press 2015) 89.

[3] The Convention on the Recognition and Enforcement of Foreign Arbitral Awards (New York Convention), 21 U.S.T. 2517, 330 U.N.T.S. 3 (10 June 1958).

arbitration cases that address environmental and, in particular, climate-related interests. The 2025 International Arbitration Survey conducted by Queen Mary University of London and White & Case LLP, which surveyed over 2,400 respondents, indicates that one third of respondents have encountered public interest issues in their investment and commercial arbitrations over the past five years, and that "commercial arbitration is the type of arbitration in which public interest issues are most frequently encountered".[4] Among these cases, environmental issues account for 30% of disputes involving public interest concerns.[5]

This chapter examines the opportunities and challenges of using commercial arbitration to resolve climate-related disputes. It evaluates whether commercial arbitration is appropriate for addressing climate issues and explores potential reform strategies. The chapter proceeds as follows: Section 2 introduces the emerging trend of resolving climate disputes in international commercial arbitration. Section 3 discusses the advantages of international commercial arbitration as a regime for solving climate-related commercial disputes. It also assesses the limitations of the existing international commercial arbitration regime in balancing private and public interests, its impacts on resolving climate-related disputes, and potential reforms to be made. Section 4 draws a conclusion.

2. International Commercial Arbitration and Climate-Related Disputes

The interaction between climate change and international commercial arbitration encompasses multiple dimensions. Broadly speaking, it can be categorised into two aspects: (1) dispute-based, where arbitration is used to resolve climate-related disputes, and (2) sector-based, where arbitration addresses conflicts in specific sectors aimed at achieving climate goals.

First, from a dispute-based perspective, climate change gives rise to various types of commercial disputes to be resolved through international commercial arbitration. Today, international transactions face increasing climate-related risks, including physical and transition risks. *Physical* risks result from the direct impacts of climate change, such as floods, wildfires and sea level rise, which may lead to property damages or supply chain disruptions.[6] Disputes arising from physical climate impacts can be resolved via arbitration. For instance, a company that suffers property damage caused by a wildfire may pursue compensation from its insurance provider, and when a dispute arises, it is resolved through arbitration if the insurance contract includes an arbitration clause.

In addition to physical risks, climate transition also generates commercial disputes. *Transition* risks refer to the risks arising from the shift to a low-carbon economy, including regulatory changes, technological advancements, and evolving consumer preferences.[7] For instance, some jurisdictions have adopted mandatory requirements for companies to disclose climate information. When a supplier company fails to accurately disclose its greenhouse gas

[4] Queen Mary University of London School of International Arbitration and White & Case LLP, *2025 International Arbitration Survey: The Path Forward: Realities and Opportunities in Arbitration* (Final report, June 2025), 21 <https://www.qmul.ac.uk/arbitration/media/arbitration/docs/White-Case-QMUL-2025-International-Arbitration-Survey-report.pdf> accessed 26 June 2025.

[5] ibid.

[6] Stefano Giglio, Bryan Kelly, and Johannes Stroebel, 'Climate Finance' (2021) 13 Annual Review of Financial Economics 15, 17.

[7] ibid.

emissions, it may breach the warranties and representations in the contract and result in disputes with other parties in the supply chain who rely on accurate environmental information to meet their own legal obligations. Such disputes are resolved through arbitration when the contract includes an arbitration agreement.

Second, from a sector-based perspective, international commercial arbitration has been extensively utilised to resolve disputes arising from both traditional industries critical to the climate transition and emerging sectors related to climate mitigation and adaptation. On the one hand, arbitration has been widely used to address disputes in key economic sectors such as energy, infrastructure, and finance, which are essential for combating climate change. On the other hand, climate change also opens up a broad spectrum of new business opportunities related to climate mitigation and adaptation, such as renewable energy, sustainable transportation, and climate-resilient infrastructure and agriculture. When disputes emerge from transactions within these sectors, international commercial arbitration can serve as a dispute resolution mechanism which offers a neutral forum for parties to solve their disputes.

Given the extensive interactions between international commercial arbitration and climate change, the ICC Commission on Arbitration and Alternative Dispute Resolution (ADR) adopts a broad definition of climate-related commercial arbitration "to include any dispute arising out of or in relation to the effect of climate change and climate change policy, the United Nations Framework Convention on Climate Change ("UNFCCC") and the Paris Agreement".[8] In particular, the ICC identified three categories of climate-related disputes: (1) "contracts relating to the implementation of energy or other systems transition, mitigation or adaptation"; (2) "contracts without any specific climate related purpose or subject-matter but where a dispute involves or gives rise to a climate or related environmental issue"; and (3) "submission or other specific agreements entered into to resolve existing climate change or related environmental disputes, potentially involving impacted groups or populations".[9]

The following paragraphs illustrate three specific scenarios where international commercial arbitration has been used to solve climate-related disputes in practice. First, as climate adaptation and mitigation projects grow, the contracts for these projects often include arbitration clauses to resolve any future disputes. Second, even if a contract is not directly about climate action, it might include climate-related terms—such as climate disclosures or climate risk allocation—that could lead to disputes resolved through international commercial arbitration. Third, a dispute that involves climate interests of third parties may be solved through international commercial arbitration.

2.1 Disputes Arising from Climate-Related Projects

International commercial arbitration plays a critical role in solving disputes arising from climate mitigation and adaptation projects. A prominent example is carbon market disputes. Voluntary Carbon Markets facilitate climate transition by allowing private parties to voluntarily buy and sell carbon credits to meet carbon mitigation goals. Disputes may arise from breaches of contract, such as misrepresentation of credit value by the seller or non-payment by the purchaser. While some carbon market disputes are solved through litigation,[10] commercial

[8] ICC, 'Resolving Climate Change Related Disputes through Arbitration and ADR' (November 2019), para 2.1 <https://iccwbo.org/wp-content/uploads/sites/3/2019/11/icc-arbitration-adr-commission-report-on-resolving-climate-change-related-disputes-english-version.pdf> accessed 26 June 2025.

[9] ibid para 2.3.

[10] Carbon credits disputes have been filed in domestic courts. For instance, in *Carbonext Tecnologia em Soluções Ambientais Ltda. v Amazon Imóveis*, the Claimant Carbonext is a company that specialises

arbitration proceedings have been used to solve disputes arising from carbon credit transactions, particularly those involving cross-border transactions.

For instance, in 2024, Canadian company Carbon Streaming initiated an arbitration claim against Hong Kong-based project development company Infinite-Earth and its shareholders.[11] The dispute concerns the Rimba Raya project in Indonesian Borneo, one of the world's largest carbon-offsetting initiatives.[12] Carbon Streaming alleged that Infinite-Earth had violated several agreements related to the project, including the purchase and sale agreement (PSA) between the two companies, the strategic alliance agreement (SAA) with Infinite-Earth Limited's shareholders, and other associated contracts.[13]

There are also a growing number of commercial arbitration cases arising from the Kyoto Protocol administered by the Permanent Court of Arbitration (PCA) and the Arbitration Institute of the Stockholm Chamber of Commerce (SCC).[14] These disputes mainly concern flexibility mechanism transactions including the Clean Development Mechanism and the Joint Implementation Mechanism.[15]

The International Emission Trading Association (IETA) is promoting the use of commercial arbitration in addressing carbon credit disputes. In recent years, the IETA has published a list of standardised emission trading agreements which adopt arbitration as their dispute resolution mechanisms. In 2023, the IETA published a set of standardised Emission Reduction Purchase Agreements (ERPAs) to facilitate trading in Verified Carbon Credits. Article 27.14 of the ERPAs provides:

> Any dispute arising out of or connected with this Agreement, including a dispute as to the existence, validity or termination of this Agreement or this Clause 27.14 or any non-contractual obligation arising out of or in connection with this Agreement, shall be resolved by arbitration in London, England conducted in English by a single arbitrator pursuant to the rules of the London Court of International Arbitration, save that, unless the Parties agree otherwise, neither Party shall be required to give general discovery of documents, but may be required only to produce specific, identified documents which are relevant to the dispute.[16]

on the preservation of the Amazon by developing carbon credit projects like REDD+ to reduce greenhouse gas emissions and prevent deforestation. Carbonext signed a contract with Amazon Imóveis for the purchase of carbon credits, where Amazon Imóveis agreed to transfer 331,080 credits. When Amazon Imóveis failed to transfer the credits, Carbonext filed a lawsuit in a state court in Brazil to enforce its contractual rights. *Carbonext Tecnologia em Soluções Ambientais Ltda. v Amazon Imóveis* (Voluntary Carbon Market), 1072768-63.2021.8.26.0100, Decision (1 July 2021) <https://climatecasechart.com/non-us-case/carbonext-tecnologia-em-solucoes-ambientais-ltda-v-amazon-imoveis-voluntary-carbon-market/> accessed 26 June 2025.

[11] Carbon Streaming, 'Carbon Streaming Initiates Claims in Connection with the Rimba Raya Project' <https://www.carbonstreaming.com/news/carbon-streaming-initiates-claims-in-connection-with-the-rimba-raya-project/> accessed 26 June 2025. See also Jack Ballantyne, 'Canadian Entity Launches Claim Over Carbon-Offset Project' <https://globalarbitrationreview.com/article/canadian-entity-launches-claim-over-carbon-offset-project> accessed 26 June 2025.

[12] ibid.

[13] ibid.

[14] Lucia Bizikova, 'On Route to Climate Justice: The Greta Effect on International Commercial Arbitration' (2022) 39 Journal of International Arbitration 79, 95–96.

[15] ibid. See also Chester Brown, 'International, Mixed, and Private Disputes Arising Under the Kyoto Protocol' (2010) 1(2) Journal of International Dispute Settlement 447, 467–71.

[16] IETA, Emissions Reduction or Removal Purchase Agreement (Version 1.0) (February 2023), art. 27.14 <https://ieta.b-cdn.net/wp-content/uploads/2023/09/IETA_TradingDocuments_PrimaryERPA_v1.0.pdf> accessed 26 June 2025.

The IETA has also adopted arbitration as an alternative dispute resolution mechanism (in addition to court litigation) for its Emission Allowances Single Trade Agreement (STA) designed for the EU emissions trading system. It provides a template for an arbitration clause:

> [*Any dispute arising under, out of or in connection with this Agreement shall be resolved by arbitration. The language of arbitration shall be [*insert detail (e.g., English)]. The appointing authority shall be the [*insert detail (e.g., Secretary General of the Permanent Court of Arbitration)]. The number of arbitrators shall be [*insert detail (e.g., three)]. The place of arbitration shall be [*insert detail (e.g., London)], and the applicable rules of arbitration shall be [*insert detail (e.g., the Optional Rules for Arbitration of Disputes Relating to Natural Resources and/or the Environment of the Permanent Court of Arbitration)].[17]

2.2 Disputes Over Climate-Related Clauses in Contracts

The second type of climate-related commercial arbitration involves disputes over climate-related clauses in contracts. As companies face increasing physical and regulatory climate risks, industries like energy, mining, supply chain management, and construction may adopt contractual clauses that allocate these risks.

For instance, contracts commonly include force majeure clauses that exempt parties from liability if non-performance results from unforeseeable events beyond their control, such as extreme weather conditions like storms and floods.[18] Moreover, a contract may include environmental indemnity clauses, requiring one party to compensate the other for environmental damages or liabilities.[19] For example, the 2019 Model Mine Development Agreement (MMDA), developed by the International Bar Association (IBA) as a template for agreements between host States and mining companies, contains sample indemnification provisions that allocate environmental liabilities.[20] The MMDA stipulates that the mining company shall indemnify the State against all losses resulting from environmental damages caused by the company or its violations of environmental laws, while the State shall indemnify the company for historical environmental pollution for which the company bears no responsibility.[21] Disputes arising from breaches of these clauses can be solved through international commercial arbitration if the parties agree.

Besides, failure to meet climate disclosure obligations may lead to disputes under the representations and warranties clauses to be resolved through international commercial arbitration. For example, disputes can arise from mergers and acquisitions (M&A) when a target company has not disclosed climate-related risks—such as undisclosed emissions or regulatory violations.

[17] IETA, Emission Allowances Single Trade Agreement for Phase IV of The EU ETS (Version 6.0) (IETA, 2019), art. 10.1 <https://ieta.b-cdn.net/wp-content/uploads/2023/09/IETA_TradingDocuments_STA_v6.0.pdf> accessed 26 June 2025.

[18] Martin Dietrich Brauch, Perrine Toledano, and Cody Aceveda, 'Allocation of Climate-Related Risks in Investor–State Mining Contracts' (June 2022) <https://scholarship.law.columbia.edu/sustainable_investment_staffpubs/224> accessed 26 June 2025 (assessing the clauses allocating climate-related risks in investor–state contracts in the mining sector, including force majeure, indemnification, insurance, stabilisation, periodic review, warranties and representation, step-in rights, and termination).

[19] ibid.

[20] International Bar Association, 'Model Mine Development Agreement: A Template for Negotiation and Drafting' (4 April 2011), art. 37.6 <https://www.mmdaproject.org/presentations/MMDA1_0_110404Bookletv3.pdf> accessed 26 June 2025.

[21] ibid.

The *Solvay v Edison* case concerns legal disputes arising from environmental misrepresentation during the M&A process. In this case, Solvay, a Belgium chemical company, filed a commercial arbitration claim administered by the ICC against an Italian utility Edison over breaches of environmental representations and warranties in the sales agreement during the acquisition of two industrial plants.[22] The environmental misrepresentation includes a failure to disclose historical contamination at the sites which subsequently resulted in various administrative and criminal proceedings.[23] Solvay alleged that Edison was liable for misrepresentations during the sale.[24] The arbitral tribunal upheld claims by Solvay, finding that there existed "deliberate misrepresentations" in environmental guarantees in the sales agreement.[25]

2.3 Disputes Involving Climate Interests of Third Parties

In a broader sense, the interplay between commercial arbitration and climate disputes also includes cases where disputes have wider impacts on the climate interests of third parties, such as local communities.

In a recent case, an Italian company Bonatti Group and its subsidiary brought an arbitration claim in the ICC against a Canadian company Coastal GasLink (operated by TC Energy) for alleged wrongful termination of the construction contract of a natural gas pipeline.[26] The amount of the claim was estimated to be up to US$1.2 billion.[27] The construction of the project was delayed because of the COVID-19 restrictions as well as the protests from Indigenous communities since the pipeline runs through Indigenous lands.[28] The Bonatti entities claimed that the Coastal GasLink had failed to control protests against the pipeline project, caused repeat destruction of the construction equipment, and left workers exposed to threats.[29]

3. Solving Climate-Related Disputes in International Commercial Arbitration: Opportunities and Challenges

International commercial arbitration is designed to provide a flexible, efficient, and confidential mechanism of solving commercial disputes between private parties. It offers disputing parties a broad autonomy to choose applicable law, arbitration rules and forum, with a confidential dispute settlement procedure and a pro-enforcement mechanism to limit states' second look at the arbitral awards. These features offer several advantages for resolving climate-related commercial disputes.

[22] Jack Ballantyne, 'Italian Utility Liable for Breaching Environmental Guarantees' (*Global Arbitration Review*, 23 July 2021) <https://globalarbitrationreview.com/italian-utility-liable-breaching-environmental-guarantees> accessed 27 June 2025.

[23] Sebastian Perry, 'Edison Pays Award Over Environmental Breaches' (*Global Arbitration Review*, 15 February 2023) <https://globalarbitrationreview.com/article/edison-pays-award-over-environmental-breaches> accessed 27 June 2025.

[24] ibid.

[25] Ballantyne, Italian Utility (n 22).

[26] Jack Ballantyne, 'ICC to Hear Canadian Pipeline Row' (*Global Arbitration Review*, 14 December 2023) <https://globalarbitrationreview.com/article/icc-hear-canadian-pipeline-row> accessed 27 June 2025.

[27] ibid.

[28] ibid.

[29] ibid.

First, given the urgency of addressing climate change, it is crucial to have an efficient mechanism to solve climate-related commercial disputes, especially for sectors such as renewable energy and climate adaptation. Arbitration offers advantages in this regard, as parties have greater flexibility to choose procedures that facilitate a speedy resolution of disputes. For instance, the ICC has various procedural rules in commercial arbitration that can be used for expediting the resolution of climate-related disputes, including case management techniques as well as choices of expedited and emergency arbitration.[30] The PCA has adopted Optional Rules for Arbitration of Disputes Relating to Natural Resources and/or the Environment in 2001 (Environmental Rules).[31] To ensure timely response to environmental issues, the Environmental Rules adopt various innovations to shorten the arbitration procedures, including shorter time periods for appointment procedures and submissions.[32] It also includes a fall-back appointment procedure, which provides that when there is a failure to appoint arbitrators by parties or their appointing authorities, the Secretary-General of the PCA will act as the appointing authority to ensure a rapid constitution of a panel.[33]

Moreover, international commercial arbitration provides a greater degree of procedural flexibility. Unlike litigation, where parties have limited control over the appointment of judges, arbitration allows parties to select arbitrators based on their specific expertise and experience. Besides, most arbitration rules permit parties to appoint experts to provide technical evidence and allow tribunals to appoint experts for opinions relevant to the disputes.[34] Those expert opinions will facilitate the resolution of climate-related disputes, particularly in cases involving complex scientific or professional issues beyond the expertise of the arbitrators. The PCA's Environmental Rules have introduced innovative measures for appointing arbitrators and experts by establishing two panels: one comprising arbitrators with expertise in environmental and natural resources law, and the other consisting of environmental science experts.[35] Disputing parties also have the freedom to choose arbitrators who are not listed in these designated panels.[36]

Finally, when climate-related disputes involve multiple jurisdictions, the enforcement of arbitral award is more reliable compared to litigation, due to the existence of the New York Convention. The New York Convention was made in 1958 to facilitate recognition and enforcement of foreign arbitral awards.[37] It imposes an obligation on Contracting Parties to recognise and enforce foreign awards excepted for several exhaustive grounds. These grounds for denying recognition or enforcement of foreign awards by a contracting party include the invalidity of the arbitration agreement, violations of due process, awards exceeding the scope of the submission, the composition of the arbitral tribunal or procedures not in accordance with the parties' agreement or the law of the arbitration seat, or awards not yet binding, set aside, or suspended.[38] Besides, a country may refuse enforcement if the subject matter is not arbitrable

[30] ICC, Resolving Climate Change (n 8) para 5.25–5.37.

[31] For a comprehensive analysis, see Dane P Ratliff, 'The PCA Optional Rules for Arbitration of Disputes Relating to Natural Resources and/or the Environment' (2001) 14 Leiden Journal of International Law 887.

[32] The PCA Optional Rules for Arbitration of Disputes Relating to the Environment and/or Natural Resources ('The Environmental Rules'), arts. 6(2) and 23.

[33] ibid arts. 6(2) and 7(2)(b).

[34] See, e.g., ICC Arbitration Rules (2021), arts. 25(2) and (3); UNCITRAL Arbitration Rules (2021), arts. 27(2) and 29; the LCIA Arbitration Rules (2020), arts. 20(1) and 21.

[35] The Environmental Rules (n 32), arts. 8(3) and 27(5).

[36] ibid.

[37] New York Convention (n 3).

[38] ibid art. V(1).

under its law or if enforcement would violate its public policy.[39] This pro-enforcement stance, supported by the broad ratification of the Convention by over 170 countries, provides a significant advantage in ensuring the worldwide enforceability of arbitral awards.

However, some features of international commercial arbitration—such as respecting party autonomy, safeguarding privacy and confidentiality, and supporting the enforcement of arbitral awards—also impose limitations on the protection of public interests. When climate-related issues are involved, a key challenge is how to balance public and private interests in the arbitration proceedings. The following paragraphs propose three approaches to balancing public and private interests in climate-related international commercial arbitration.

3.1 Clarifying the Arbitrability of Climate Disputes Under International Commercial Arbitration

The "arbitrability" of a dispute refers to whether the dispute is capable of settlement by arbitration.[40] Arbitrability serves as a safeguard that shields certain public issues from being decided by arbitration. An underexplored question is: Are all climate-related commercial disputes arbitrable under international commercial arbitration, or are there certain disputes of such importance to public intersts that they should be exclusively adjudicated by courts?

There is no universal answer, as the arbitrability of a dispute is determined by national law. In the past decades, there has been a trend towards broadening the scope of arbitrability to encompass private disputes with public implications, with some exceptions such as intellectual property, bankruptcy, employment, antitrust, and corruption.[41] Generally, environmental or climate-relate disptues are not considered non-arbitrable matters. In practice, courts have tended to interpret non-arbitrable matters narrowly and have shown a preference for a pro-arbitration approach in line with the New York Convention.[42] This shift has been viewed as a "collapse" of the non-arbitrability doctrine, which leads to an expansion of the scope of arbitration where the arbitrators are increasingly making decisions that impact public interests.[43] Disputes arising from public–private contracts, such as government procurement agreements, concession contracts, and contracts for public services like energy and education, are increasingly being solved through commercial arbitration.[44] According to a report by the ICC, 19%

[39] ibid art. V(2).

[40] International commercial arbitration practice and literature distinguish between "subjective arbitrability" and "objective arbitrability". Both conditions must be satisfied for a dispute to be considered arbitrable. Subjective arbitrability pertains to the parties' agreement to resolve a dispute through arbitration, while objective arbitrability requires that the applicable law permits the dispute to be settled by arbitration. In this chapter, the term "arbitrability" refers to objective arbitrability.

[41] Klára Drličková, 'Arbitrability And Public Interest In International Commercial Arbitration' (2017) 17 Interantional and Comparative Law Review 55, 58; Karim A Youssef, 'Part I Fundamental Observations and Applicable Law, Chapter 3: The Death of Inarbitrability' in Loukas A Mistelis and Stavros Brekoulakis (eds), *Arbitrability: International and Comparative Perspectives, International Arbitration Law Library*, Volume 19 (Kluwer Law International 2009) 50, 52-55.

[42] UNCITRAL Secretariat Guide on the Convention on the Recognition and Enforcement of Foreign Arbitral Awards (2016) 234–36.

[43] Stavros Brekoulakis and Margaret Devaney, 'Public–Private Arbitration and the Public Interest under English Law' (2017) 80 Modern Law Review 22, 23.

[44] Stavros Brekoulakis, 'The Public Interest in Arbitration' (2023) 39 Arbitration International 203, 203; Chester Brown, 'Chapter 15: States as Participants in International Arbitration' in Stefan M Kröll, Andrea Kay Bjorklund, and Franco Ferrari (eds), *Cambridge Compendium of International Commercial and Investment Arbitration* (CUP 2023), 424–38.

of its cases in 2024 involved states or state entities as disputing parties, involving 45 states and 143 state-owned entities.[45] For instance, in 2017, the Austrian OMV Group brought a commercial arbitration claim against Romanian Ministry of Environment at the ICC.[46] The Claimant argued that Romania had breached the privatisation contract by failing to make payments for environmental remediation.[47] In 2020, the arbitral tribunal decided in favour of the Claimant, finding that Romania should pay the claimant €59 million in damages.[48]

This has raised questions on how to protect public interests in commercial arbitration, and how to consider arbitration's interaction with society at large.[49] Some countries have adopted special rules governing public–private arbitrations, such as requiring public–private arbitration to be reviewed by administrative courts or requiring the transparency of public–private arbitration by subjecting such arbitration to the principle of publicity.[50] In the context of investment arbitration, there have been reform proposals of carving out climate-related disputes from investment arbitration. For example, the modernisation of the Energy Charter Treaty (ECT) excludes certain fossil fuel projects from treaty protection.[51] While a blanket exclusion of climate disputes from commercial arbitration may not be feasible or desirable, countries have the authority to reject the arbitrability of disputes involving the interpretation of particular climate-related legislation if they deem arbitration unsuitable for resolving such disputes.

Another option is to develop a set of commercial arbitration rules designed specifically for solving climate-related disputes. As an analogy, the Hague Rules on Business and Human Rights Arbitration (the Hague Rules) was developed by a group of experts and practitioners under the auspices of the Centre for International Legal Cooperation.[52] The rules were adopted to promote the use of arbitration to solve human right claims against companies.[53] The Hague Rules were built on the United Nations Commission for International Trade Law's Arbitration Rules, with adjustments to facilitate resolving human right-related disputes.[54] Moreover, as noted above, the PCA has developed the Environmental Rules for resolving commercial disputes related to environment and natural resources.[55] A similar initiative can be adopted for climate-related commercial arbitration, whose arbitration rules may be adjusted to suit the special features of disputes related to climate change.

[45] ICC, 'ICC Dispute Resolution Statistics: 2024' (*International Chamber of Commerce*, 24 June 2025) < https://iccwbo.org/news-publications/news/icc-dispute-resolution-statistics-2024/#top> accessed 3 Feburary 2026.

[46] Lacey Yong, 'Romania Faces Environmental Claim at ICC' (*Global Arbitration Review*, 25 April 2017) <https://globalarbitrationreview.com/article/romania-faces-environmental-claim-icc> accessed 27 June 2025.

[47] ibid.

[48] ibid.

[49] William W Park, 'Private Disputes and the Public Good: Explaining Arbitration Law' (2004) 20 American University International Law Review 903, 903.

[50] The former approach has been adopted by France and the latter by Brazil, see Brekoulakis (n 45).

[51] ibid. Agreement in Principle on the Modernization of the Energy Charter Treaty (24 June 2022), CC 750 Rev Annex NI, Section B <https://www.bilaterals.org/IMG/pdf/reformed_ect_text.pdf> accessed 27 June 2025.

[52] The Hague Rules on Business and Human Rights Arbitration (2019) <https://docs.pca-cpa.org/2019/12/The-Hague-Rules-on-Business-and-Human-Rights-Arbitration.pdf> accessed 27 June 2025.

[53] ibid.

[54] Bruno Simma and Giorgia Sangiuolo, 'The Hague Rules on Business and Human Rights Arbitration: Some Challenges and Responses' (2022) 28 Southwestern Journal of International Law 401.

[55] The Environmental Rules (n 32).

3.2 Balancing Party Autonomy with Public Policies

International commercial arbitration respects party autonomy in choosing the applicable law and the forum for dispute resolution. Such autonomy is reflected in the arbitration agreement which specifies the procedural and substantive laws governing the arbitration process. Parties may choose their preferred procedural rules to govern the arbitration: they can opt for ad hoc arbitration, allowing them to tailor procedural rules to their specific needs; or they may select institutional arbitration, choosing from a variety of arbitration institutions and adopting their established rules and services.[56] Moreover, parties are also free to select the law or principles (such as *lex mercatoria*) that will govern the substance of their dispute. For example, the UNCITRAL Arbitration Rules specify that "[t]he arbitral tribunal shall apply the rules of law designated by the parties as applicable to the substance of the dispute".[57] Similarly, the ICC Rules state that "[t]he parties shall be free to agree upon the rules of law to be applied by the arbitral tribunal to the merits of the dispute".[58] The arbitration agreement may include a specific choice of law clause that governs the interpretation and validity of the arbitration agreement itself, alongside the choice of law applicable to the substantive contract.

Parties also have the freedom to select the seat of arbitration (*locus arbitri*). The choice of seat is crucial for the conduct of arbitration and the enforcement of awards. Parties tend to select a jurisdiction known for its supportive arbitration laws.[59] They also prefer countries that are parties to the New York Convention to facilitate the recognition and enforcement of arbitral awards. Moreover, under the New York Convention, if an award is set aside at the seat of arbitration, this can serve as grounds for other jurisdictions to refuse recognition and enforcement of that award.[60] Therefore, selecting the seat requires strategic consideration, including an assessment of the public policies of that jurisdiction to ensure favourable arbitration and enforcement conditions.

The fragmented nature of global climate governance can give rise to regulatory arbitrage, where parties select applicable laws or arbitration seats that are most favourable to their interests.[61] For example, parties may consider the strictness of climate standards—such as disclosure obligations and emissions regulations—when choosing the applicable law to the substantive contract. They might also evaluate whether the arbitration seat has mandatory rules on climate regulation that could potentially lead to arbitral awards being set aside due to conflicts with such rules. A similar trend has been observed in commercial disputes involving economic sanctions, where companies have changed their choice of arbitration seat to avoid jurisdictions with stringent sanctions regulations.[62]

[56] Mia Louise Livingstone, 'Party Autonomy in International Commercial Arbitration: Popular Fallacy or Proven Fact?' (2008) 25(5) Journal of International Arbitration 529, 530.

[57] UNCITRAL Arbitration Rules (2021), art. 35(1).

[58] ICC Arbitration Rules (2021), art. 21(1).

[59] A recent survey shows that the five most preferred seats of arbitration are London, Singapore, Hong Kong, Beijing, and Paris. Queen Mary University of London School of International Arbitration and White & Case LLP (n 4) 2.

[60] The New York Convention (n 3) art. V(1)(e).

[61] 'Regulatory arbitrage' is defined as a phenomenon where private parties can choose a more favourable law or jurisdiction to govern their business transactions to circumvent less favourable laws or jurisdictions. Jan Kleinheisterkamp, 'Overriding Mandatory Laws in International Arbitration' (2018) 67 International and Comparative Law Quarterly 903, 909–10.

[62] Queen Mary University of London School of International Arbitration and White & Case LLP (n 5) 10–11 (the survey illustrates that '30% of respondents who answered the question [on the impact of sanctions on their arbitration proceedings] said they chose a different seat to ensure that their dispute

In turn, private parties' forum-shopping behaviours can also shape countries' regulatory approaches. On the one hand, such tactics may lead to negative normative competition among countries, potentially resulting in a race to the bottom by discouraging the adoption of stronger climate regulations. On the other hand, regulatory arbitrage could foster a positive form of competition—sometimes described as a race to the top—in specific climate-friendly sectors such as renewable energy, electric vehicles, and adaptation projects. In these areas, countries might compete to establish reliable and advantageous legal frameworks that promote and attract sustainable commercial activities.

Nonetheless, party autonomy is not without limits. Arbitral tribunals can—and sometimes should—consider public policy concerns.[63] First, in cases where parties have not specified the applicable law, arbitral tribunals usually have discretion to determine the appropriate law to apply. For example, the UNCITRAL Arbitration Rules allow tribunals, in the absence of a designated applicable law by the parties, to apply "the law which it determines to be appropriate".[64] This enables arbitral tribunals to apply climate legislation or regulation in disputes related to climate issues if they deem it applicable. The PCA Environmental Rules takes a step further by requiring tribunals to apply "the national and/or international law and rules of law it determines to be appropriate" in the absence of the parties' consent on the applicable law.[65] This provision accords tribunals the discretion to apply international treaties (such as climate treaties) in the arbitration proceedings.

Second, tribunals cannot disregard the mandatory laws of the seat, since a failure to comply with these rules may lead to the annulment of the award.[66] Besides the chosen law and the seat's law, the tribunal may also take into account the laws of a third country when rendering an award, especially if it is foreseeable that enforcement of the award may be in that country (e.g., where assets are located). Disregarding the mandatory laws of that country may result in a refusal of award enforcement by its courts. If climate law is considered part of mandatory rules, the tribunal should apply it regardless of parties' chosen law.[67]

Another related question is whether courts can refuse to recognise or enforce an international commercial arbitration award due to its conflict with public policy related to climate change. The New York Convention provides that one ground for denying recognition

could be arbitrated. Many interviewees highlighted Dubai, Hong Kong and Singapore as increasingly preferred arbitral seats for disputes impacted by sanctions. Some also cited difficulties in arbitrating such disputes in popular European and US seats in particular, such as challenges related to banking restrictions, non-responsive respondents and the potential for anti-suit injunctions being acquired in sanctioned jurisdictions by adverse parties').

63 According to Blessing, arbitral tribunals operate in a middle ground, striking a balance between public and private interests: 'On the one hand, the international arbitrator is not the guardian of the interests of foreign States which sometimes show a kind of arrogance in seeking to impose their national laws, perceptions and interests on others. On the other hand, the international arbitrator is not simply the "obedient servant" of the parties.' Marc Blessing, 'Mandatory Rules of Law versus Party Autonomy in International Arbitration' (1997) 14(4) Journal of International Arbitration 23, 40.

64 UNCITRAL Arbitration Rules (2021), art. 35(1).

65 The Environmental Rules (n 32) art. 33.

66 George A Bermann, 'Introduction: Mandatory Rules of law in International Arbitration' (2007) 18 American Review of International Arbitration 1, 1–2.

67 Nonetheless, there is still a lack of consensus in academia and practice regarding the definition of mandatory rules, as well as regarding when and how arbitral tribunals should apply mandatory rules of law against party autonomy. Ibrahim Shehata, 'Application of Overriding Mandatory Rules in International Commercial Arbitration: An Empirical Analysis' (2017) 11(4) World Arbitration & Mediation Review 391.

or enforcement of a foreign arbitral award is "[t]he recognition or enforcement of the award would be contrary to the public policy of that country".[68] This public policy exception serves as a "safety-valve" enabling countries to prevent the recognition or enforcement of awards they deem incompatible with their legal regimes.[69]

However, the New York Convention does not provide a definition of public policy, allowing each country to determine the scope and content of its own domestic public policies that may justify denying the recognition and enforcement of an award. The term "of that country" in Article V(2)(b) of the New York Convention indicates that public policy refers to the public policy of the country where recognition and enforcement is sought. Therefore, the standard of public policy is a "national standard". In practice, courts in different countries have adopted diverse interpretations of public policy, but they generally adopt a narrow interpretation to include only those "fundamental principles pertaining to justice or morality" as public policies that can be a ground for refusing the enforcement of arbitral awards.[70] For instance, in the United States, courts may refuse enforcement only when the enforcement "would violate the forum state's most basic notions of morality and justice".[71]

Despite the lack of existing case law, it is possible that a country's domestic court views climate justice as a fundamental moral principle falling within the public policy exception under the New York Convention. Moreover, legislators, courts and scholars have taken efforts to seek a more uniform "international public policy" or "transnational public policy".[72] Some commentators have argued that when considering whether a principle is sufficiently fundamental to justify refusing enforcement, a considerable factor is international conventions, including human rights agreements.[73] Following this rationale, a country's court could refuse to enforce an arbitral award if it deems climate treaty obligations as international public policies falling within the public policy exception under the New York Convention.

3.3 Promoting Transparency and Third-Party Participation

International commercial arbitration is characterised by its private and confidential nature. The privacy of arbitration means that third parties, absent the consent of the disputing parties, are generally excluded from the arbitration proceedings. The confidentiality of arbitration requires that the information related to the arbitration be kept confidential and not disclosed to third parties. These features of privacy and confidentiality are often considered as key reasons why private parties prefer arbitration over traditional litigation, as they allow dispute resolution to be shielded from public scrutiny and sensitive commercial information to be protected.

However, when climate disputes are resolved through international commercial arbitration, these same features pose challenges. The private and confidential nature of arbitration makes it unlikely for the public to access information about the proceedings or participate in the decision-making process without the consent of the disputing parties. In many cases, the

[68] The New York Convention (n 3) art V(2)(b).

[69] Reinmar Wolff, *New York Convention: Convention on the Recognition and Enforcement of Foreign Arbitral Awards of June 10 1958: Article-by-Article Commentary* (2nd edn, CH Beck 2019).

[70] ibid.

[71] *Parsons & Whittemore Overseas Co. v Societe Generale de L'Industrie du Papier* (RAKTA), 508 F.2d 969, 974 (2d Cir. 1974) and other cases.

[72] Wolff (n 77).

[73] P Mayer and A Sheppard, 'Final ILA Report on Public Policy as a Bar to Enforcement of International Arbitral Awards' (2003) 19 Arbitration International 249.

public is even unaware of the existence of such arbitration proceedings—even when they involve public interests, such as environmental protection or climate change.[74]

It is noteworthy that there is no general binding rule that international commercial arbitration proceedings must be confidential.[75] The duty of confidentiality arises from two sources: the agreement between the parties concerning confidentiality, and the applicable law or arbitration rules that impose a confidentiality obligation.[76] The nature and scope of confidentiality vary among jurisdictions. Some legal systems recognise an implied duty of confidentiality, meaning confidentiality is presumed unless explicitly waived, while others require an express agreement to establish a duty of confidentiality.[77] Certain jurisdictions, such as England and France, have statutory regulations that govern confidentiality in arbitration proceedings; conversely, jurisdictions like the United States and Australia generally leave the question of confidentiality to the courts.[78]

Arbitration rules also contain varying provisions regarding confidentiality. Some rules establish a general duty of confidentiality unless the parties agree otherwise. For example, the London Court of International Arbitration (LCIA) Rules provide that "[t]he parties undertake as a general principle to keep confidential all awards in the arbitration, together with all materials in the arbitration created for the purpose of the arbitration and all other documents produced by another party in the proceedings not otherwise in the public domain, save and to the extent that disclosure may be required of a party by legal duty, to protect or pursue a legal right, or to enforce or challenge an award in legal proceedings before a state court or other legal authority".[79] The Rules also provide that "the LCIA does not publish any award or any part of an award without the prior written consent of all parties and the Arbitral Tribunal".[80] Similarly, the Arbitration Rules of the SCC under Article 3 provide that unless otherwise agreed by the parties, "the SCC, the Arbitral Tribunal and any administrative secretary of the Arbitral Tribunal shall maintain the confidentiality of the arbitration and the award".[81] The Hong Kong International Arbitration Centre (HKIAC) Administered Arbitration Rules also specify that "[u]nless otherwise agreed by the parties, no party or party representative may publish, disclose, or communicate any information relating to: (a) the arbitration under the arbitration agreement; or (b) an award or Emergency Decision made in the arbitration",[82] and that this confidentiality obligation also "applies to the arbitral tribunal, any emergency arbitrator, expert, witness, tribunal secretary, and HKIAC".[83] The Singapore International Arbitration Centre (SIAC) Arbitration Rules stipulate "a continuing obligation to treat all matters relating to the proceedings as confidential" unless otherwise agreed by the parties.[84]

[74] Kirsten Odynski and Héloïse Broc, 'Commercial Arbitration' in Edgardo Sobenes, Sarah Mead, and Benjamin Samson (eds), *The Environment Through the Lens of International Courts and Tribunals*, 370 (TMC Asser Press 2022).

[75] Weixia Gu, 'Confidentiality Revisited: Blessing or Curse in International Commercial Arbitration?' (2006) 15 American Review of International Arbitration 607, 612.

[76] ibid.

[77] Avinash Poorooye and Ronan Feehily, 'Confidentiality and Transparency in International Commercial Arbitration: Finding the Right Balance' (2016) 22 Harvard Negotiation Law Review 275, 286–98.

[78] ibid.

[79] The LCIA Arbitration Rules (2020), art 30.1.

[80] ibid art 30.3.

[81] The SCC Arbitration Rules (2023), art 3.

[82] The HKIAC Arbitration Rules (2024), art 45.1.

[83] ibid art 45.2.

[84] The SIAC Arbitration Rules (2025), art 59.1.

In contrast, the ICC Rules do not treat confidentiality as a default requirement. Instead, they provide that "[u]pon the request of any party, the arbitral tribunal may make orders concerning the confidentiality of the arbitration proceedings or of any other matters in connection with the arbitration and may take measures for protecting trade secrets and confidential information".[85] The UNCITRAL Arbitration Rules do not include a specific confidentiality clause but provide that "[a]n award may be made public with the consent of all parties or where and to the extent disclosure is required of a party by legal duty, to protect or pursue a legal right or in relation to legal proceedings before a court or other competent authority".[86]

Recent years have seen a reform of investment arbitration rules to enhance transparency in the case of investor–state disputes. The reform includes the UNCITRAL Rules of Transparency in Treaty-Based Investor–State Arbitration (UNCITRAL Transparency Rules), which was adopted and came into effect in 2014, and the United Nations Convention on Transparency in Treaty-Based Investor–State Arbitration (the Mauritius Convention), adopted in 2014 and entered into force in 2017.[87] These Rules are concluded to promote transparency of investment arbitration, providing for obligations of publication of documents,[88] third-party participation,[89] and open hearings.[90] They also specify the scope of confidential or protected information as exceptions for transparency, including confidential business information and other protected information.[91]

Some scholars have discussed the possibility of extending the principles of the UNCITRAL Transparency Rules to the realm of commercial arbitration.[92] However, such a reform is unlikely to be widely accepted by private parties, for whom confidentiality is often a core interest in arbitration proceedings.[93] Similarly, arbitration institutions are unlikely to pursue significant revisions aimed at increasing transparency if such changes conflict with the preferences of private parties.

A potential approach to enhancing the transparency of climate-related commercial arbitration is to consider such arbitration as subject to the disclosure obligations applicable to listed companies. Even when parties have explicit confidentiality agreements, arbitration rules generally permit disclosure of arbitration proceedings when necessary to pursue or enforce a legal right or claim, or to comply with laws, regulations, or court orders.[94] When one or both disputing parties are listed companies, the confidentiality of international commercial arbitration should be balanced against the companies' obligations to disclose inside information to the public. Specifically, a listed company may be required to disclose the existence

[85] The ICC Arbitration Rules (2021), art 22(3).

[86] The UNCITRAL Arbitration Rules (2021), art 34(5).

[87] The Mauritius Convention was concluded to allow states to apply UNCITRAL Transparency Rules to investment treaties concluded before the conclusion of the UNCITRAL Transparency Rules. The United Nations Convention on Transparency in Treaty-Based Investor–State Arbitration, Preamble.

[88] UNCITRAL Rules on Transparency in Treaty-based Investor–State Arbitration, art 3.

[89] ibid art 4 and art 5.

[90] ibid art 6.

[91] ibid art 7.

[92] Poorooye and Feehily (n 85) 286–98; Matthew Carmody, 'Overturning the Presumption of Confidentiality: Should the UNCITRAL Rules on Transparency Be Applied to International Commercial Arbitration' (2016) 19 International Trade and Business Law Review 96. Mary Zhao, 'Transparency in International Commercial Arbitration: Adopting A Balanced Approach' (2019) 59 Virginia Journal of International Law 175.

[93] Poorooye and Feehily (n 85) 315–16.

[94] Alexis C Brown, 'Presumption Meets Reality: An Exploration of the Confidentiality Obligation in International Commercial Arbitration' (2001) 16 American University International Law Review 969.

of arbitration if such a dispute is likely to have a "significant" or "material" impact on the company's share value.[95]

However, the criteria for determining when an arbitration is likely to cause such a significant or material impact remain uncertain. For instance, under the Hong Kong Arbitration Ordinance, there is a general prohibition on disclosing information related to arbitration proceedings or awards. Nonetheless, under the Hong Kong Securities and Futures Ordinance (SFO), listed companies are required to disclose "inside information", which is defined as specific information that is not generally known but would likely have a material effect on the price of the listed securities.[96] Therefore, a company may need to disclose arbitration if it is deemed likely to materially affect its share price. In practice, many companies disclose ongoing litigation or potential disputes in their annual reports, and such disclosures are generally not considered breaches of confidentiality when they merely note the existence of arbitration proceedings.[97] For example, the Hong Kong Arbitration Ordinance permits parties to disclose information to government or regulatory bodies when legally obliged to do so.[98] Nonetheless, it remains uncertain whether listed companies should disclose more than just the existence of arbitration proceedings, raising questions about the scope of disclosure obligations in the context of climate-related disputes.

Besides, a country can amend its arbitration law to introduce a mandatory transparency requirement for commercial arbitration cases involving public entities or related to public interests. For example, in 2015, Brazil amended its arbitration law to allow public administrators to participate in arbitration, while explicitly requiring that such arbitration adhere to the principle of publicity.[99] This amendment was made to address the accountability issue in public–private arbitration.[100] But it is noteworthy that in the absence of an international consensus, mandatory transparency reforms in one jurisdiction may be circumvented by parties simply choosing to arbitrate in other jurisdictions with more lenient transparency requirements.[101]

In addition to the lack of transparency, the private nature of international commercial arbitration is also in tension with the principle of public participation for resolving environmental disputes. Climate-related disputes usually involve public interests beyond the commercial interests of private parties. For instance, failure to fulfil a construction contract for climate adaptation projects—such as building dams or flood defences—may impact interests of local communities. However, in cases where environmental disputes are resolved through commercial arbitration, it is unlikely that the disputing parties would invite NGOs or other interested third parties to participate in the proceedings.[102]

Arbitration institutions can revise their arbitration rules to facilitate multi-party arbitration in resolving climate-relates disputes. For instance, the PCA Environmental Rules allow multiparty arbitration which encompasses states and non-state disputing parties, including

[95] Valéry Denoix de Saint Marc, 'Confidentiality of Arbitration and the Obligation to Disclose Information on Listed Companies or During Due Diligence Investigations' (2003) 20(2) Journal of International Arbitration 211, 215.

[96] The Hong Kong Securities and Futures Ordinance, Section 307A(1).

[97] De Saint Marc (n 103) 214.

[98] The Hong Kong Arbitration Ordinance, s 18(2).

[99] Brazilian Arbitration Act 2015 (Law 13,129/2015), 26 May 2015, arts 1(1) and 2(3).

[100] Laura Carneiro de Mello Senra, 'Arbitrating Disputes between Public Servants and Public Entities under Brazilian Law' (2019)16 Brazilian Journal of Alternative Dispute Resolution 7, 20.

[101] Poorooye and Feehily (n 85) 286–98; See also Catherine A Rogers, 'Transparency in International Commercial Arbitration' (2006) 54 University of Kansas Law Review 1301, 1327.

[102] Odynski and Broc (n 82), at 373.

companies, non-governmental organisations, intergovernmental organisations, and private parties.[103] Nonetheless, a balance must be maintained between allowing the participation of non-disputing parties and the protection of the substantive and procedural rights of disputing parties, as permitting third parties to interfere in the arbitration proceedigns could impact the equal treatment of disputing parties, as well as due process and the efficiency of the proceedings.[104] This requires an appropriate procedure governing the scope of participation of third parties, including the attendance of hearings, access to documents, and submission of briefs.

4. Conclusion

The urgent timeline for climate transition necessitates the facilitation and promotion of global capital flows for climate mitigation and adaptation. This requires not only substantive laws that ensure a fair allocation of rights and obligations in climate-related commercial activities but also an effective and efficient dispute resolution system for solving climate-related disputes. In comparison to litigation, international commercial arbitration offers several advantages. It provides a neutral and flexible dispute resolution mechanism, granting parties wide autonomy in choosing the applicable law and arbitration seat. Moreover, parties have the opportunity to appoint arbitrators with expertise in climate-related sectors or relevant scientific knowledge. The enforceability of arbitration awards under the New York Convention provides another unique advantage when the climate-related business transactions involve multiple jurisdictions. However, a balance must be struck between ensuring reliable dispute settlement through an efficient and neutral mechanism and safeguarding public interests in commercial disputes. As discussed in this chapter, achieving this balance involves clarifying the arbitrability of climate disputes, balancing party autonomy with public policies, and promoting transparency and inclusivity in arbitration proceedings.

103 The Environmental Rules (n 32), Introduction.

104 For a policy debate on third-party participation in investment arbitration, see Kyla Tienhaara, 'Third Party Participation in Investment-Environment Disputes: Recent Developments' 16(2) Review of European Community & International Environmental Law 230, 239–41.

CHAPTER 26

Labour Law

FRANCES FLANAGAN

1. Introduction

> Translating the human person into the commodity "labour power" is an act of institutional creation on par with the parallel process of converting the earth into "land."[1]

MODERN labour law emerged from, and is constitutive of, industrial society. As the domain of law which sets the terms by which human activity is translated into labour power, it has been critical to the fossil fuel-based industrial systems that are responsible for climate change. It is also crucial to enabling the essential work of reproducing human and non-human life in modern societies—activities such as caretaking, domestic work, cleaning, subsistence agriculture and fishing, cleaning, land remediation—to be performed in ways that are secure and life-enhancing. Labour law has a deep political texture and plays an important role in structuring the expectations of the future for households, enterprises, and societies. Its purposes are multiple and contradictory as it simultaneously secures capital accumulation on the one hand and a legitimate social order on the other.[2]

The traditional justifications for labour law as a body of law that is distinct from the law of contract are expressed in universal terms that do not acknowledge the existence or importance of ecological systems and non-human forms of life. The first of these is the idea that labour is not a commodity and that labour relationships necessarily involve an inequality of bargaining power between the parties. It expresses the notion that people are not objects to be bought and sold according to the laws of commerce but are rather relational beings inherently deserving of respect and dignity.[3] Another key justification concerns the centrality of labour law to democracy, because the potency of workers as democratic and political subjects is diminished when they are subject to despotic power at work. According to this idea, the rebalancing of power relations between employees and employers in workplace bargaining permeates the wider democratic project of rebalancing power in society: Democracy at work and democracy in

[1] Simon Deakin, 'Anthropogenic Labour Law: The Coevolution of Law and Work' in Guy Davidov, Brian Langille, and Gillian Lester (eds), *The Oxford Handbook of the Law of Work* (OUP 2024).

[2] Ruth Dukes and Wolfgang Streeck, *Democracy at Work: Contract, Status and Post-Industrial Justice* (Polity 2022) iii–ix (emphasis in original).

[3] The idea that 'labour is not a commodity' and the related concept that there is an inequality of bargaining power between employers and employees have been described as the 'basic instinct' of labour law. 'Labour is not a commodity' is an expression enshrined in the US 1914 Clayton Antitrust Act ('The labor of a human being is not a commodity or article of commerce'); and in the first principle of the revised constitution of the International Labour Organization in 1944.

society both involve skills of political agency, responsibility, and compromise, as well as the capacity for solidarity over self-interested action.[4] Both ideas have enduring importance in a climate changed world that is rife with sacrifice zones[5] and infrastructural collapse, and where the eco-social systems necessary for human flourishing (including the opportunity to express views democratically) are being undermined from many directions.[6]

Notwithstanding labour law's historic contributions to social justice, its present and future role in mitigating climate change is not self-evident. Despite the rise of just transition discourse and the welcome recognition that the "jobs versus environment" binary is a political construction rather than a syllogism, there are examples across the world of the institutions and instruments of labour law being used to delay fossil fuel phase-out (see Section 2.2.2 of this chapter), in spite of the scientific recognition that the majority of fossil fuel resources must be left *in situ* for there to be a sustainable and secure basis for the sustenance of life.[7] Labour law exhibits significant limitations in its capacity to protect and secure many forms of work which are directly associated with maintaining systems of social and ecological reproduction, such as the care for people suffering ill-health and starvation due to the breakdown of air, water and soil biome breakdown, atmospheric heat changes, pandemics, and vector-bone and other infectious diseases. Labour law's protective gaze is a highly partial one. It is heavily structured by the concept of the contract of employment which functionally limits its application to many forms of work which do not readily fit an industrial paradigm and excludes many environmental issues from the scope of collective bargaining.

Understanding labour law's current and potential role in climate stabilisation requires attention to the structural limitations in its ambit that flow from private law and a sensitivity to the imprint of anthropocentric ideas from the nineteenth and twentieth centuries concerning the role of law in limiting the harms engendered by industrial capitalism. In particular, it is crucial to grapple with the fact that the foundational theories of labour law were premised on a positive nexus that was drawn between the expansion and security of coal-based industry (including mining, railways, factories, ports, and shipping) and the expansion and security of collective human capacity. This assumption silently informed both the outer "gaze" of protection in the contract of employment and the shape and nature of labour law's procedural interventions that situated the law of work within a wider social institutional order. Similar historically specific ideas that are central to labour law that are being challenged by current conditions include:

- The idea that there is an isomorphic relationship between the well-being and stability of the worker and household, industry, and society.
- The notion that legal interventions to enhance well-being that are directed at the household level will "organically" flow up and across to other sectors and society in general.

4 Ruth Dukes, *The Labour Constitution: The Enduring Idea of Labour Law* (OUP 2014).

5 The term 'sacrifice zone' has reflected the concerns of different kinds of environmentalism since the 1970s, but generally denotes 'a specific geographic location where socioecological life is rendered dispensable by and for those with more power than those impacted.' Annabel Ipsen and Amanda McMillan Lequieu, 'From Rationalized Exploitation to Supra Sacrifice Zones: Tracing Sacrifice Zones as a Keyword of Environmental Sociology' (2024) Environmental Sociology 1.

6 Chiara Armeni and Maria Lee, 'Participation in a Time of Climate Crisis' (2021) 48 Journal of Law and Society 549.

7 Dan Welsby and others, 'Unextractable Fossil Fuels in a 1.5C World' (2021) 597 Nature 230; Lorenzo Pellegrini and others, 'Institutional Mechanisms to Keep Unburnable Fossil Fuel Reserves in the Soil' (2021) 149 Energy Policy 112029.

- The assumption that the primary reference points for nation-states regulating the just terms of industrial activity are the interests of living citizens within their own borders, rather than human rights obligations owed to people beyond them and also to future generations.
- The notion that the primary threat to societal stability and well-being is industrial action rather than fires, floods, drought, disease, temperature changes, food systems, and/or the breakdown of socioecological and infrastructural systems without organisation or human planning.

Viewing the law of work in tandem with changing understandings of the relationship between fossil fuel industrial processes and human well-being is a crucial, if under-explored, dimension of the obligation to understand the law of work in its historic context.[8]

This chapter is organised in three sections. The first section outlines the way in which labour law's "grammar" as a kind of "call and response" between private and public law has engendered different kinds of omissions and affordances for mitigating climate change harms.[9] The second section explains the role that the key theoretical justifications advanced for labour law in the late nineteenth and twentieth centuries have played in shaping labour law's relationship to fossil fuel-dependent industrial processes and mentalities concerning rights, democratic power, and social stability. The third section examines the legacies of those frameworks in terms of the capacity of labour law to respond to environmental crises today. The chapter concludes with a discussion of the potential pathways for making labour law more eco-socially responsive and responsible.

2. Public and Private Dimensions of Labour Law and the Climate Crisis

The modern contract of employment emerged at the end of the nineteenth century. Its key features include the fact that it does not refer to status distinctions of gender, race, or class. It countenances reciprocal and continuing obligations between individuals and employers. It incorporates embedded constitutional statutory and customary standards alongside those negotiated by the parties. Its enforcement is vested in civil rather than criminal courts. It is also hierarchical, in the sense that it subordinates employees to employers and validates the managerial authority of the employer.[10] In other words, employers can issue commands to workers over what they must do and, if such commands are lawful and reasonable, employees have a duty to obey them.[11]

Langille has described labour law as a kind of "call and response" between private and public law, in which public law is called upon to address the undesirable results of private law.[12] In place of commercial terms that maximise profitability such as, for example, extremely low

[8] Zoe Adams and Simon Deakin, 'Institutional Solutions to Precariousness and Inequality in Labour Markets: Institutional Solutions to Precariousness and Inequality' (2014) 52 British Journal of Industrial Relations 779.

[9] Brian Langille, 'The Contractual Lens' in Guy Davidov, Brian Langille, and Gillian Lester (eds), *The Oxford Handbook of the Law of Work* (OUP 2024) 44.

[10] Deakin (n 1) 14.

[11] Joellen Riley Munton, 'The Managerial Prerogative and Variation of the Employment Contract' in Guy Davidov, Brian Langille, and Gillian Lester (eds), *The Oxford Handbook of the Law of Work* (OUP 2024) 265.

[12] Langille (n 10) 44.

wages, long hours, and/or dangerous conditions, labour law intervenes to impose requirements such as minimum wage rates, leave, and rest entitlements. It also imposes procedural requirements that enable employees to engage in the freedom to associate, organise, and collectively bargain over the terms and conditions of their employment.[13]

There is scholarly debate over whether labour law should be viewed as "internal" to private law (because it is animated by the same values of relational justice that are intrinsic to contract law),[14] or "external" to it.[15] It is not necessary to intervene in those debates here, other than to make the basic observation that on either theory, labour law's concern is with harms to and vulnerabilities of persons, rather than places or things. Even if existing labour law can be successfully theorised as internal to private law, the effects created by its public or social law dimensions, in the form of statutory regulation, are nevertheless quite different in terms of their bearing on climate change. For that reason, this section discusses the private and public law dimensions in sequence.

2.1 Limitations to Climate Change Mitigation that Derive from Private Law

The contract of employment is a bilateral relationship between the employee and employer. This basic legal "grammar" of the law of work[16] has a number of consequences in terms of how labour law constructs and allocates responsibility for ecosocial harms and to whom it extends protection.

Labour law applies to employees and not independent contractors, with the exception of work health and safety law. Employees are persons who work for the benefit of another, for remuneration, in a contractual relationship and do not delegate their work to others. Courts have developed multi-factor tests to assess whether someone is an employee. These commonly consider a range of matters that are indicia of the degree of control that the employer has over the worker and the extent to which the worker is subordinated to the employer.[17]

In inquiring whether a worker is an employee, labour law is interested in responding to a particular kind of vulnerability only, that which emerges from the worker's relationship with the employer. The law's gaze, in this respect, is dyadic. It is not concerned with intervening to protect workers who are vulnerable in a general sense (i.e., because they live in a sacrifice zone or are without shelter), nor does it inquire about the purpose of the work in terms of its contribution to the vulnerability of others. Labour law is largely indifferent to the purpose of different kinds of work: Its principles operate on the same terms, whether the work in question involves transporting sandbags to protect a hospital from flooding or financing coal seam gas exploration. Managerial prerogative allocates responsibility for any climate harms generated by the enterprise to the employer; they do not flow through to the employee via the contract of employment. Occupational health and safety laws may oblige employers

13 Brian Langille, 'Human Development: A Way out of Labour Law's Fly Bottle' in Hugh Collins, Gillian Lester and Virginia Mantouvalou (eds), *Philosophical Foundations of Labour Law* (OUP 2018).

14 Hanoch Dagan and Michael Heller, 'Can Contract Emancipate? Contract Theory and the Law of Work' (2023) 24 Theoretical Inquiries in Law 49.

15 Cynthia Estlund, 'Is Labor Law Internal or External to Private Law? The View from Cedar Point—ProQuest' (2023) 24 Theoretical Inquiries in Law 124, 126.

16 Hugh Collins, 'The Many Ideas of Labour Law' in Guy Davidov, Brian Langille, and Gillian Lester (eds), *The Oxford Handbook of the Law of Work* (OUP 2024) 157.

17 Guy Davidov and Lester, 'The Concept of "Employee"' in Guy Davidov, Brian Langille, and Gillian Lester (eds), *The Oxford Handbook of the Law of Work* (OUP 2024).

to make a workplace environmentally safe (see Section 2.2.1), but they do not prevent them from undertaking lawful businesses that make society in general less safe, such as fossil fuel extraction.

One consequence of the centrality of the contract of employment to labour law is that it excludes the majority of the world's workers from protection, due to their informal or "atypical" status,[18] because they work without a formal agreement, and/or are in triangular labour relationships.[19] This includes a great deal of labour required for climate change adaptation, which is the maintenance and repair of social and physical infrastructures necessary for the flourishing of human beings and other living species in the present and future.[20]

The striking disjuncture between labour law's discursive commitment to protection and its functional exclusion of most workers has long historical roots which may be traced to John Locke's *Two Treatises of Government*, which justified private property based on the idea that value was created when a person mixed labour with natural resources to produce an object. Locke's definition of labour, which was reproduced by Smith, Marx, and Hegel, excluded every kind of service: servants, carers, coachmen, maids, gardeners, carers for children and the elderly, shepherds, nurses, cooks, cleaners, and more. Not only were these activities performed by the majority of workers; they were (and remain) essential preconditions to the possibility of industrial manufacturing.[21] To the extent that these forms of work have come to be latterly protected by labour law, it has commonly been on terms that are distinctly inferior to other sectors. In the US, for example, the category of healthcare and social assistance is both the largest sector of employment and occupies the bottom quintile of the American wage structure.[22] Paid care work occurring under "zero-hours" (casual) contracts functionally excludes workers from protection from unfair dismissal, parental leave, and other entitlements because of the need for continuous hours to be performed as qualification; it is also associated with reduced opportunities for unionisation due its prevalent performance in private homes and part-time status.[23] As several scholars have observed, there is a sense in which legal protection for such work falls within the normative concept of "sustainability", since a society which fails to nurture the capabilities of its essential workforce cannot be regarded as meaningfully durable.[24]

[18] Supriya Routh, 'Postcolonialism and Labour Law' in Guy Davidov, Brian Langille, and Gillian Lester (eds), *The Oxford Handbook of the Law of Work* (OUP 2024) 53.

[19] Diamond Ashiagbor, 'Race and Colonialism in the Construction of Labour Markets and Precarity' (2021) 50 Industrial Law Journal 506, 526.

[20] Supriya Routh, 'Embedding Work in Nature: The Anthropocene and Legal Imagination of Work as Human Activity Work Regulation and Environmental Sustainability' (2018) 40 Comparative Labor Law & Policy Journal 29; Anil Verma, Ana Gomes, and Dieric Guimares, 'Life With Rights: Inclusive Labour Law and Decent Work for Wastepickers in Brazil' (2023) 39 International Journal of Comparative Labour Law and Industrial Relations 359; Chantel Carr, 'Repair and Care: Locating the Work of Climate Crisis' (2023) 30 Dialogues in Human Geography 221.

[21] Axel Honneth, *The Working Sovereign: Labour and Democratic Citizenship* (Polity 2024) 97.

[22] Gabriel Winant, 'The Baby and the Bathwater: Class Analysis and Class Formation after Deindustrialisation' [2024] Historical Materialism 1, 7.

[23] Sandra Fredman and Judy Fudge, 'The Contract of Employment and Gendered Work' in Mark Freedland and others (eds), *The Contract of Employment* (OUP 2016) 234.

[24] Tonia Novitz, 'Sustainability as a Guide for the Future Development of International Labour Law?', in Brian Langille and Anne Trebilcock (eds), *Social Justice and the World of Work: Possible Global Futures* (Hart Publishing 2023); Paolo Tomassetti, 'Labor Law and Environmental Sustainability Work Regulation and Environmental Sustainability' (2018) 40 Comparative Labor Law & Policy Journal 61.

2.2 Public Law Dimensions of Labour Law that Bear Upon Climate Change

2.2.1 Substantive Entitlements

For workers able to meet the test of employment, labour law provides a range of substantive protections such as minimum wages, sick and parental leave, protections against unfair dismissal, and occupational health and safety standards. Each of these entitlements predated the acceleration of climate change in the postwar period. Parental leave, for example, emerged from the goals of equality and non-discrimination based on gender; and occupational health and safety from moral concerns over women and children in factories in the nineteenth century. But all are of major importance as measures for making labour sustainable, available, and resilient during times of climate change adaptation. As employees will necessarily have to take more time away from work to attend to their own and the illnesses of family members, deal with collapsing infrastructures, and respond to acute emergencies such as fires and floods, labour law will play a critical role in ameliorating the fear and experience of unemployment and economic security that would exacerbate these predicaments.[25]

Work health and safety law also offers crucial protection to workers in a climate change context, particularly as it is not limited by the requirements of employment status. Researchers have identified the ways in which the climate crisis has expanded the positive obligations on employers to take "reasonably practical" measures to adapt through investment in infrastructural measures in buildings, air conditioning, misting systems, and ventilation for indoor workers; for outdoor workers air-conditioned cabins, flexible working hours, working rotation, changes to dress codes, shade canopies, the implementation of monitoring programmes, and "buddy systems" and regular breaks.[26] In some European states, laws provide compensation for the loss of income experienced by households as the result of extreme temperatures.[27] These measures are valuable, even if their enterprise-specific nature means that they cannot adequately respond to disruption which is generalised, chronic, involves multiple kinds of infrastructure breakdown, and/or requires the wholesale relocation of people dwelling in an entire region. Nor can they address climate change's primary causes, since the imperative to leave fossil fuels in the ground would necessitate the winding down of fossil fuel enterprises themselves—a matter unlikely to be judged as "reasonably practical" from the perspective of the employer.

Substantive labour law protections are also important in securing the preconditions for the development of political subjectivities required to support climate change policies. As Honneth has observed, a lack of economic independence makes it difficult to form independent political opinions. Long hours make political engagement difficult. If someone has their work and perspectives chronically devalued and ignored at work, it can become difficult to develop confidence in the validity and value of political views. The capacity to participate in democratic will formation is undermined by being forced to perform work that is unstimulating and monotonous or so insecure that it fosters an acute fear of unemployment.[28]

[25] Gabrielle Golding, Phillipa McCormack, and Kerryn Brent, 'The Changing Climate of Australian Employment Law' (2023) 46 University of New South Wales Law Journal 1284, 1298.

[26] International Labour Organization, 'Working on a Warmer Planet: The Impact of Heat Stress on Labour Productivity and Decent Work' (2019) 79–80; Elizabeth Humphrys, 'Inertia in Transformed Times: Work Health and Safety amid Climate Change' (2024) 66 Journal of Industrial Relations 685.

[27] ibid 77.

[28] Honneth (n 22) 38.

Leave entitlements and limitations on working time can also be understood as providing time-spaces for "non-productivist" activities and mentalities which might underwrite non- and post-capitalist social formations.[29]

2.2.2 Procedural Entitlements

Given the systemic nature of climate change, provision for collective, as well as individual responses to the climate threat are essential in a work context. Freedom of association emerged in the eighteenth and nineteenth centuries through the winding back of criminal liabilities for conspiracy, combination, and penal master and servant laws.[30] In the twentieth century, an extensive body of statutory law emerged that regulated collective labour law, concerning the operation and rules for trade unions, collective bargaining, and strike action.[31] These laws enabled the regulated operation of unions, whose activities acted to redistribute income and deepen social ties, and provided a vehicle for the aggregation of workers' political voices. In some jurisdictions, these mechanisms were also accompanied by works councils which participate in the strategic decisions of businesses over a wide range of issues.[32]

The place of environmental concerns in the history of the working class communities and trade unions has a history too extensive to comprehensively survey here.[33] In Australia, for example, the Builders Labourers Federation, in alliance with progressive movements and resident activists, placed bans on destructive urban developments based on the notion that there was a "social responsibility of labour" to create buildings that were socially beneficial to the community at large.[34] In the late 1970s, the Australian Council of Trade Unions (ACTU) robustly debated the question of whether Australia should continue to engage in uranium mining and exports in light of the existential threat posed by nuclear weapons, arguing for a moratorium on all new uranium mining and a national referendum to decide the issue.[35] More recently, the ACTU has jointly published research reports on green jobs in industry and developed demands for emissions targets and increased investment in clean export and manufacturing industries, rapid electrification, and renewables.[36] Some unions have articulated demands for democratic control and ownership of energy systems as a basis for addressing the climate crisis through the global networks such as "Trade Unions for Energy Democracy".[37] Others have been active supporters of Indigenous traditional owners resisting

[29] Elise Dermine, 'Towards a Sustainable Social Law. What Role for Legal Scholars?' (2023) 39 International Journal of Comparative Labour Law and Industrial Relations 320.

[30] Ewan McGaughey, 'Competition and Labour Law in the United Kingdom: History, Theory and Practice' in Ewan McGaughey, Sanjukta Paul, and Shae McCrystal (eds), *The Cambridge Handbook of Labor in Competition Law* (CUP 2022).

[31] Alan Bogg, 'Freedom of Association', *The Oxford Handbook of the Law of Work* (OUP 2024) 425–26.

[32] Collins (n 17) 165.

[33] Victor Silverman, 'Sustainable Alliances: The Origins of International Labor Environmentalism' (2004) 66 International Labor and Working-Class History 118; Stefania Barca, 'Laboring the Earth: Transnational Reflections on the Environmental History of Work' (2014) 19 Environmental History 3; Jedediah Purdy, 'The Long Environmental Justice Movement' (2018) 44 Ecology Law Quarterly 809.

[34] Kurt Iveson, 'Building a City For "The People": The Politics of Alliance-Building in the Sydney Green Ban Movement' (2014) 46(4) Antipode 992.

[35] Clifford B Donn, *The Australian Trade Union Movement and Uranium Mining* (North Ryde, 1978) 3.

[36] Frank Stilwell, 'From Green Jobs to Green New Deal: What Are the Questions?' (2021) 32 The Economic and Labour Relations Review 155.

[37] Sean Sweeney, 'Beyond Recovery: The Global Green New Deal and Public Ownership of Energy', Trade Unions for Energy Democracy (TUED Working Paper #16, 31 August 2023) <https://www.tuedglobal.org/bulletins/beyond-recovery-the-global-green-new-deal-and-public-ownership-of-energy> accessed 25 June 2025. See Trade Unions for Energy Democracy <https://www.tuedglobal.org/>.

the exploitation of their land for fracking.[38] The International Trade Union Confederation (ITUC) and the International Transport Federation recently submitted written comments to the International Court of Justice regarding the request for an Advisory Opinion on the obligations of states with respect to climate change.[39]

The scope for lawfully applying industrial power in support of environmental concerns under labour law, however, is more limited. Collective bargaining over matters related to the environment is possible in some jurisdictions (so called "green bargaining"), particularly if there is a clear nexus with job security, wages, hours, or leave entitlements. Climate issues without a direct connection to the employment relationship, such as energy-efficiency and waste management measures; planning for net zero; emissions targets and governance and corporate accountability for employer's environmental impact (including in relation to investment decisions) may not be supported, however.[40] In Australia, restrictions on the scope of green bargaining flow from the early twentieth century, when bargaining was limited to issues directly affecting work done and excluding indirect matters affecting work such as the opening hours of a business, financing arrangements, supply of raw materials, and (by implication) environmental matters.[41] The Australian system also imposes a structural bias towards enterprise bargaining, making industry- or supply-chain level collective negotiation (which are the most logical and effective approaches in tackling root causes of climate change) unavailable.

Consultation, rather than bargaining over enforceable conditions backed by the threat of industrial action, has been the dominant mechanism for negotiating climate change measures under labour law.[42] The European Green Deal, for instance (which encompasses a Just Transition Mechanism, Social Climate Fund, and the EU Fair Transition Recommendation) aims to encourage employee participation in corporate restructuring through consultation only.[43] The model clause put forward by the ACTU for enterprise bargaining agreements is also framed in terms of consultation and co-operation, via mechanisms of information and consultation embedded in workplace environment and sustainability committees.[44] These

[38] 'Huge Union Delegation Supports Gomeroi Rights against Santos's First Nations and Environmental Destruction', Maritime Union of Australia (Media Release, 7 November 2022) <https://www.mua.org.au/news/huge-union-delegation-supports-gomeroi-rights-against-santoss-first-nations-and-environmental> accessed 25 June 2025.

[39] International Trade Union Confederation, 'ITUC/ITF Submission to the ICJ: Request for an Advisory Opinion on the Obligations of States with Respect to Climate Change' (22 March 2024) <https://www.ituc-csi.org/ituc-itf-submission-to-the-icj> accessed 25 June 2025.

[40] An empirical study of enterprise agreements in Australia, for instance, found that only 7% of agreements had an environmental clause. Of those that did, 40% of them placed obligations to protect the environment on employees rather than employers, 8% linked environmental issues to disciplinary procedures (including summary dismissal) and only 3% of clauses linked sustainability to climate change. Raymond Markey and Joseph McIvor, 'Environmental Bargaining in Australia' (2019) 61 Journal of Industrial Relations 79.

[41] *Clancy v Butchers' Shop Employees Union* (1904) 1 CLR 181. Victoria Lambropoulos, 'Greening Australian Workplaces: Workers and the Environment' (2009) 34 Alternative Law Journal 189; Eugene Schofield-Georgeson, 'Legal Obstacles and Possibilities for Environmental Bargaining in Australia' (2023) 65 Journal of Industrial Relations 297.

[42] Ben Crawford and David Whyte, 'Workers on the Front Line of Climate Change: Re-Politicizing Trade Union Climate Action' (2025) 164 International Labour Review.

[43] Sergio Canalda, 'The European Green Deal: A Useful Framework for Anticipating Change in Companies?' (2023) 39 International Journal of Comparative Labour Law and Industrial Relations, 419.

[44] ACTU, 'Industrial Work on Bushfires, Natural Disasters Etc: Draft Model Clause' <https://www.actu.org.au/wp-content/uploads/2023/08/sample-model-clause-for-ea-bargaining-bushfires-and-natural-disasters-20200219.pdf> accessed 23 May 2025.

measures are different in kind to the form of collective bargaining over an enterprise's impact on the environment in general that has been recommended by the European Economic and Social Committee.[45] They also fall short of measures that would support the ambition of organisations which seek to reorient control over energy production and consumption on a public basis.[46]

Arguably the most critical contribution made by collective labour law to the climate crisis has been a negative one: the pattern of opposition to timely fossil fuel phase out policies on the part of fossil fuel unions. This opposition has taken multiple forms, and commonly coexists with (or is articulated through) just transition policies that ostensibly acknowledge the societal urgency of addressing climate change and reaching net zero by 2050.[47] In Nigeria, for example, unions have opposed the removal of fossil fuel subsidies.[48] In Norway, unions have legitimised oil extraction on the grounds of comparative "cleanness" of the Norwegian petroleum industry and energy demands.[49] In Germany, unions have argued that a just transition is a "slow" transition that preserves the status quo for as long as possible.[50] In Australia, unions have argued for carbon capture and storage and increased gas expansion as critical dimensions of climate policy, and have advocated just transition processes that exclude coal exports—Australia's greatest contribution to climate change—from their ambit.[51] In the UK, the GMB Union has argued for "plans not bans" in opposition to the UK Labour Party's proposal to ban new oil and gas exploration in the North Sea.[52] In Ecuador, unions have opposed the 2023 referendum to leave oil reserves in the ground in Yasuni National Park in the Amazon region.[53] In Columbia, trade union representatives "believe in a green transition that does not halt oil and gas production".[54]

[45] European Economic and Social Committee, *Green Collective Bargaining* (Opinion SOC/747-EESC-2022, adopted 14 June 2023) <https://www.eesc.europa.eu/en/our-work/opinions-information-reports/opinions/green-collective-bargaining> accessed 23 June 2025.

[46] Paolo Tomassetti, 'Energy Transition: A Labour Law Retrospective' [2022] Industrial Law Journal.

[47] Steven J Harry, Tomas Maltby, and Kacper Szulecki, 'Contesting Just Transitions: Climate Delay and the Contradictions of Labour Environmentalism' (2024) 112 Political Geography 103114; Frances Flanagan, 'Just Cessation: How Might the Climate Imperative to Phase Out Fossil Fuel Extraction Reshape the Concept of Just Transition?' (2023) 39 International Journal of Comparative Labour Law and Industrial Relations 393.

[48] Camilla Houeland, 'The Social Contract and Industrial Citizenship: Nigerian Trade Unions' Role in the Recurring Fuel Subsidy Protests' (2022) 92 Africa 860.

[49] Andreas Ytterstad, Camilla Houeland, and David C Jordhus-Lier, 'Heroes of the Day After Tomorrow: "The Oil Worker" in Norwegian Climate Coverage 2017–2021' (2021) 2021 Journalism Practice; David C Jordhus-Lier, Camilla Houeland, and Tale Hammero Ellingvag, 'Alienating Assemblages: Working the Carbonscape in Times of Transformation' [2021] Progress in Human Geography 1. Camilla Houeland, David C Jordhus-Lier, and Frida Hambro Angell, 'Solidarity Tested: The Case of the Norwegian Confederation of Trade Unions (LO-Norway) and Its Contradictory Climate Change Policies' (2021) 53 Area 413, 416.

[50] Tobias Kalt, 'Jobs vs. Climate Justice? Contentious Narratives of Labor and Climate Movements in the Coal Transition in Germany' (2021) 30 Environmental Politics 1135, 1143.

[51] Flanagan (n 48). AWU, 'Future Gas Strategy' (2023) 1 <https://awu.net.au/wp-content/uploads/2024/02/231113-Future-Gas-Strategy-AWU-submission.pdf> accessed 18 June 2024.

[52] GMB Union, 'UK Energy Needs "Plans Not Bans"' (6 June 2023) <https://www.gmb.org.uk/news/uk-energy-needs-plans-not-bans> accessed 3 March 2025.

[53] Pedro Alarcón, 'What Next for Supply-Side Policy in the South: Emerging Lessons from Ecuador's Yasuní Initiative' (2024) 24 International Environmental Agreements: Politics, Law and Economics 75.

[54] Camilo Andrés Garzón, 'Petro-Politics Camilo Andrés Garzón' (*Phenomenal World*, 18 September 2024) <https://www.phenomenalworld.org/interviews/cesar-loza/> accessed 4 March 2025.

These positions are not representative of all unions, or even all unions entangled with the fossil fuel industry.[55] Nevertheless, given that 90% of all known fossil fuel reserves and resources held by companies must stay in the ground to limit global warming to 1.5 degrees, and that governments, in aggregate, still plan to produce more than double the amount of fossil fuels in 2030 than is consistent with that target, understanding labour law's role in enabling opposition to just cessation policies is crucial. Even in circumstances where social and economic entitlements for transitioning fossil fuel workers are comparatively strong, research suggests that employee resistance to climate policies is shaped by wider failures in labour law to adequately respond to austerity politics, wealth inequality, and the dualisation of the labour market.[56]

3. Theoretical Justifications for Labour Law

As the analysis above indicates, the private and public law dimensions of labour law bear upon climate change mitigation differently. To grasp why, it is necessary to historicise the theoretical justifications advanced for labour law in terms of the relationship that is assumed to exist between continuity in fossil fuel-based industrialisation, on the one hand, and democracy, social progress, and stability, on the other.

3.1 "Labour Is Not a Commodity" and the Inequality of Bargaining Power

Irish economist Dr John Kells Ingram was the first to use the expression that "labour is not a commodity" in a speech delivered to the British Trades Union Congress meeting in Dublin in 1880.[57] His argument heavily emphasised the importance of understanding the regulation of wages in employment as something that concerned the social body as a whole and its secure reproduction. The purpose of the wage was "the indispensable means of keeping [the worker] in such a state of physical health, material security, and moral quietude that he may be able to continue his service to society, and to prepare a new generation for the same service". Ingram argued that employers were under a moral responsibility to see themselves not as self-maximising individuals or entities but rather as associates of workers in "the execution of a great social function . . . [and in doing so] they render possible the continuation, under equitable conditions, of the common work of society".[58]

Ingram's formulation is striking in its grandeur and the holistic nature of its vision, which yoked together material, moral, spiritual, and intellectual elements with an overall concern for the secure reproduction of society. The regulation of wages was one facet of the general social

[55] One study explored how a manufacturing union operating in a coal heartland used its associational power to encourage other workers and community members to support a regional just transition plan: see Caleb Goods and Bradon Ellem, 'An Improbable Driver of "Just Transitions"? Union Power in the Coal Heartland of Western Australia's Energy Shift' (2024) 117 Energy Research & Social Science 103721. See also Nicole Kleinheisterkamp-González, 'Agencies of Transition: Why German Coal Workers Are Not Accepting an Energy Transition despite Social Provisions' (2025) 2 Environmental Research: Energy 015005.

[56] Kleinheisterkamp-González (n 56) 11.

[57] Paul O'Higgins, '"Labour Is Not a Commodity": An Irish Contribution to International Labour Law' (1997) 26 Industrial Law Journal 225, 226.

[58] John Ingram, *Work and the Workman: Being an Address to the Trades' Union Congress in Dublin* (Ponsonby, 1884) 5.

problem of "how to subordinate all social forces to the highest permanent well-being of the entire community".[59] He spoke against Adam's Smith's economistic and utilitarian formulation of the minimum wage—"it is but equity that they who feed, clothe, and lodge the whole body of the people, should have such a share of the produce of their labour as to be themselves tolerably well fed, clothed and lodged"—as treating working men as social functionaries. For Ingram, secure wages and trade union membership were the means to education, sympathies between working people, a "new spirit of independence and self-respect", moral elevation, reduced strikes, and a secure family life:

> A life of work and nothing but work is no life for a man, who must be degraded into a mere instrument of production. An Irish poet has claimed for the working classes—'leisure to live, leisure to live, leisure to taste their freedom' and the demand is a just one.[60]

A similarly holistic perspective infused the theory of Henry Bournes Higgins, who famously applied the recognition of unequal bargaining power in the employment relationship to justify an enforceable living wage in Australian federal labour law. Law was required to counter "the usual, but unequal, contest, the higgling of the market for labour, with the pressure for bread on one side, and the pressure for profits on the other".[61] Like Ingram, Higgins viewed law through a conceptual prism oriented to securing the general moral and social improvement of the whole society, which subordinated freedom of contract to the public good.[62] He saw the Arbitration Court as representative of "the public as a third party" with the task to "prefer the general good to private gain" and look to "the diffusion among the masses of such benefits as Nature and civilization afford". "No parts of the body social can be really healthy", he argued, "unless all parts are healthy".[63]

Unlike Ingram, Higgins was explicitly concerned with crafting a framework for labour law that prevented interruption to industrial production. The first object of the Commonwealth Conciliation and Arbitration Act 1904 was "to prevent lockouts and strikes".[64] This imperative was in keeping with Imperial anxieties to ensure that the new Australian nation was economically productive, "civilised", and white, and that the catastrophic strikes in the maritime, mining, and shearing industries in the 1890s were not repeated. As Higgins wrote in 1919:

> It is the prevention of stoppages in operations required by the public that is the object of the power given by the Constitution. The work of the country must be carried on. The community requires that what it needs shall be continuously supplied . . . above all the needs of those who are dearest to us, as the most helpless,—the children. Their constitution and the future of the race must not suffer by privation.[65]

Securing the uninterrupted production of mining was, for Higgins, of "the greatest importance".[66] Like Ingram, Higgins understood the regulation of labour as a precondition for the moral and spiritual elevation of the populace (as well as a material matter), while also viewing

[59] ibid 4.

[60] ibid 14.

[61] *Ex parte H.V. McKay* (1907) 2 CAR 1

[62] PS Callaghan, 'Idealism and Arbitration in H.B. Higgins' New Province for Law and Order' (1983) 7 Journal of Australian Studies 56, 58.

[63] ibid 62–63.

[64] Conciliation and Arbitration Act 1904 (Cth), s 2.

[65] Henry Bournes Higgins, 'A New Province for Law and Order. II' (1919) 32 Harvard Law Review 189, 204.

[66] 'MR. H. B. Higgins' *Western Mail* (Perth, Western Australia, 31 January 1903) 16.

it as a "catastrophe" and a "calamity" for a mine to close down.[67] Labour protections were thus explicitly anchored in legal mechanisms designed to ensure that fossil fuel-dependent industrial production was uninterrupted.

3.2 Democracy

A concern with continuity in coal mining, in particular, was an explicit feature of Beatrice and Sidney Webb's theoretical justifications for labour law. Their 1897 book *Industrial Democracy* characterised trade unions as democracies due to their internal constitutions based on the principle of "government of the people by the people for the people".[68] The Webbs emphasised the spontaneity of unions' emergence: "These thousands of working-class democracies, spontaneously growing up at different times and places [are] perpetually recasting their constitutions to meet new and varying conditions".[69] The unions' pursuit of continuity of employment was central to their function. They quoted the *Rules and Regulation of the Amalgamated Society of Engineers* (London, 1851) on this point:

> There is a fear always prominent on the mind of him who thinks of the future that it may not continue, that tomorrow may see him out of employment, his nicely arranged matters for domestic comfort overthrown.... How much is contained in that word continuance, and how necessary to make it a leading principle of our association![70]

They also praised the vast scale of organisation within and between different coal unions, describing meetings of the Miners' Federation of Great Britain as a "Miner's Parliament" and "the most important assembly in the Trade Union world".[71] Its jurisdiction encompassed both very local technical grievances all the way up to societal matters such as the nationalisation of mines and the making of Saturday a regular whole-day holiday.[72] They quoted British statistician George Richardson Porter's 1847 text *The Progress of the Nation* to describe the critical role occupied by the coal industry to the wider prosperity of society. Porter described coal mines as the source of the greatest riches, without which "our iron mines must long ceased to be worked, and nearly every important branch of manufacture which we now possess must have been rendered impracticable.... Without the labour of the 118 233 persons employed in the coal mines of Great Britain, how many of the hands employed in factories must have been idle, or turned to other pursuits?"[73] Coal mining, and the security of its performance, thus existed as a kind of blueprint for their theorisation of industrial democracy, as it did for the German labour law theorist Hugo Sinzheimer.[74]

[67] *The Barrier Branch of the Amalgamated Miners' Association of Broken Hill v The Broken Hill Proprietary Company Limited* (1909) 3 CAR 1 34.

[68] Beatrice and Sidney Webb, *Industrial Democracy v.1.* (Longmans, Green and Co., Paternoster Row, London, 1879), P.vi.

[69] ibid.

[70] ibid 145–46.

[71] ibid 44–45.

[72] ibid.

[73] George Richardson Porter, *The Progress of the Nation: In Its Various Social and Economical Relations, from the Beginning of the Nineteenth Century* (John Murray 1847) 276, 78.

[74] In ways that bore similarities to Higgins, Sinzheimer argued that the outer boundaries of permitted economic activity were to be set by the public interest, although offering a more detailed theorisation about the regulation of the economy by a group of 'economic organisations' including unions, works councils, employers and employer associations. See Dukes (n 5). The cartelisation of coal mines in 1919 into a National Coal Council (consisting of labourers and employees, as well as employers

3.3 The Legacies of Traditional Labour Law Theory for Climate Responsibility

Although Ingram, Higgins, and the Webbs came from differing intellectual traditions, they each saw the imperative to regulate labour with a holistic and societal perspective rather than a dyadic and transactional one. They shared a commitment to theorising the regulation of labour as a matter for generalised societal improvement, as well as the moral, spiritual, and reproductive capacities of individual workers. They also located these imperatives in the context of modern industrial systems that served the public good by being in a state of continual, and not interrupted, operation. Their perspectives thus reflected an awareness of the interdependence of individuals, households, industries, technologies, and society, albeit within the context of the age of empire and coal-based industrialisation.[75] This section discusses how this context for labour law has shaped its ability to respond to climate change.

3.3.1 The Presumption of Alignment Between Industrial and Societal Interests

The grand societal project articulated by Webbs, Ingram, and Higgins assumed an alignment between the expression of industrial interests at the workplace level and societal interests in general. Each looked on trade unions and trade union confederations as linking institutions between the different scales and as maintaining, as a virtue, the ability to move between highly localised issues of concern and large, society-level problems. The capability of moving between industrial and societal concerns without any necessary contradiction reflected assumptions about unions as class-based organisations. In 1977, the Secretary of the ACTU expressed the notion in these terms:

> For the workers, the union is not merely an expression of their dissatisfaction with the terms of employment, but also the form of protest against their disfranchised position in the community as a whole . . . the trade union is . . . not exclusively the worker's answer to his position in the plant, though specific complaints facilitate expansion of the organization. It is primarily an expression of the workers' needs in this society.[76]

The alignment between advocacy concerning the societal and industrial interests was always, in reality, partial: It generally did not apply to women, non-white workers, and those who worked outside the Fordist paradigm of twentieth-century mass industrial production. The necessity for fossil fuel phase down in the interests of socioecological stability represents an acute manifestation of a divergence between societal interest and the industrial interests of

and consumers) served as a model for his more general theory. Knut Wolfgang Noor, 'Economic Constitution: On the Roots of a Legal Concept Symposium in Honor of Judge T. Noonan Jr.' (1994) 11 Journal of Law and Religion 343, 350.

[75] Eric Hobsbawm, *The Age of Empire* (Weidenfeld and Nicolson 1987). The period from 1875 to the First World War has been referred to as an 'age of empire', a time of colonisation, urbanisation, increased flow of carbon-based industrialisation, and rising democratic political forces. Metropolitan populations in industrialised countries were highly dependent on coal energy sources following the introduction of electricity in the 1880s. The introduction of iron rails, bridges, and rail networks connected the coalface to cities, ports, and sites of manufacturing and electrical power generation, a system that required large volumes of concentrated energy to flow along narrow channels maintained by specialist bodies of workers. Timothy Mitchell, *Carbon Democracy: Political Power in the Age of Oil* (Verso 2011) 19.

[76] D W Rawson, 'The Law and the Objects of Federal Unions' (1981) 23 Journal of Industrial Relations 295, 299.

unions in fossil fuel industries. The latter remain, as they did in the mid-nineteenth century, bound by rules that require them to pursue the continuity of their industry and improvement of the industrial and social interests of their membership who are defined with reference to their industries of employment.[77] Societal advocacy for legislation and regulation that preserves the industrial and social interests of their membership, such as support for ongoing issuing of fossil fuel licenses, accompanied by carbon-capture "technofixes" are all consistent with such rules.

Societal advocacy for rapid fossil fuel phase out, by contrast, is not. Unions attempting to undertake such activities would face a range of practical, political, and legal obstacles. In the 1970s, a union attempting to exercise industrial power for environmental purposes was deregistered. While recognising the social desirability of environmental issues, the court found that protecting them was "the business of government" and not the union, and that the union had breached its own rules that required it to act in the interests of its members as builders only, and not in their capacity as citizens.[78] A union that did not meet the requirements for lawful strike action today (which would include pursuit of demands outside the matters permitted by the Fair Work Act) would lose its immunities from losses attendant on industrial action, would be subject to orders to cease the action, and would be vulnerable to the imposition of penalties in the Federal Court.[79]

Labour law's "industrial interests as trumps" dynamic also plays out in debates within trade union confederations over climate change. LO-Norway, the national trade union confederation, in 2017, for example, decided to support the continuation of the offshore Norwegian petroleum oil exploration despite opposition from the majority of delegates (193 of 315) and their largest affiliate, *Fagforbundet*, the Norwegian Union of Municipal and General Employees. The union representing members in the petroleum and process industry, Industri Energi, had policies for the continuation and expansion of the gas industry. LO-Norway followed a principle of "issue ownership", which was not a formal rule but a norm where affiliate unions do not voice strong opinions about sectors where they do not have members. As one of that union's advisors explained:

> The principle of issue ownership states concretely that if you unionise a sector, *your sector determines*. But on the issue of oil and gas, it is also a question of climate. Our argument is that this to an extent affects our members, [as well as being] an overarching problem, a societal problem.[80]

The determinative compromise position that was reached stopped short of cessation and reinforced the principle that the union representing workers directly involved in the sector had priority over unions representing workers' "societal" interests.

[77] The objects of the main union responsible for coal exports in Australia, the Queensland Mining and Energy Union, require the union to 'endeavour, by all lawful means . . . to carry on, or participate directly or indirectly and alone or with others the carrying on of any mining or prospecting operation and related activities thereto' and to 'watch over, improve, foster and protect the industrial and social interests of the membership', who are defined as employees (inter alia) of the coal, shale, oil and gas industries. Fair Work Commission, 'Rules of the Mining and Energy Union and its District Branches' (2023) <https://www.fwc.gov.au/documents/sites/ballot-withdrawal-cfmmeu-d2022-10/d2022-10-final-further-amended-annexure-5-meu-2023-08-23.pdf> accessed 12 April 2026.

[78] *Master Builders' Association (NSW) v Australian Building Construction Employees and Builders Labourers Federation* (1974) 23 FLR 356.

[79] Shae McCrystal, 'Why Is It So Hard to Take Lawful Strike Action in Australia?' (2019) 61 Journal of Industrial Relations 129, 138.

[80] Houeland et al (n 50) 417.

3.3.2 Limits on the Redistribution of Industrial Citizenship Between Sectors

As a consequence of the pre-eminent status of industrial sectors associated with carbon flows (such as mining, railways, factories, and ports), industrial power is not evenly distributed across the labour market. There are favourable "rules of recruitment" for fossil fuel-linked industrial sectors.[81] Sectors historically categorised as "non-industrial" or "non-productive", due to their service-based nature, experience relatively lower wages and conditions due to a combination of minimal or second-class protections and the reduced capacity to bring industrial action and bargain.[82] Differentials between sectors vary by jurisdiction, but in Australia are particularly stark by virtue of the operation of compulsory conciliation and arbitration system which provided for "wage justice" adjustments between sectors based on a yardstick of the industrial fitter and turner.[83] Mining employees currently earn more than one and a half times the average weekly earnings of employees in healthcare and social assistance.[84] In some offshore oil and gas facilities, unions claim to have a membership of 98%,[85] in contrast to 2.3% in accommodation and food services in 2024.[86] Clean energy sectors lag behind the pay and conditions available in fossil fuel sectors.[87]

As postcolonial scholars have long observed, it is critical to develop both counternarratives and constructive legal tools to enable the experiences and agency of historically marginalised peoples to be recognised and supported.[88] Labour law's current ability to make adjustments to wage relativities of this kind is highly constrained, notwithstanding the obvious role that wage differentials play in making particular forms of eco-socially valuable employment less attractive and vice versa. Significant adjustments have been made in Australia based on arguments concerning the undervaluation of sectors based on discriminatory concepts of gender, with aged care workers receiving raises in minimal pay rates of up to 28.5%.[89] However, such mechanisms are currently largely confined to instances where historic undervaluation can be positively demonstrated based on gender.

[81] Jedediah Purdy, 'People as Resources: Recruitment and Reciprocity in the Freedom-Promoting Approach to Property' (2007) 56 Duke Law Journal 1047.

[82] Winant (n 23) 26.

[83] Brett Heino, 'The Engine of Antipodean Fordism: Australia's Metal Trades Award, 1947–63' (2019) 6 Australia and New Zealand Law and History, 143.

[84] Australian Bureau of Statistics, 'Average Weekly Ordinary Time Earnings, Full-Time Adults by Industry' (2025) <https://www.abs.gov.au/statistics/labour/earnings-and-working-conditions/average-weekly-earnings-australia/latest-release> accessed 8 July 2025.

[85] David Marlin-Guzman, 'LNG Exports at Risk as Woodside and Chevron Strikes Loom' *Financial Review* (2023) <https://www.afr.com/work-and-careers/workplace/lng-exports-at-risk-as-woodside-and-chevron-strikes-loom-20230809-p5dv3n> accessed 17 June 2025.

[86] Australian Bureau of Statistics, 'Trade Union Membership, Australia' (2024) <https://www.abs.gov.au/statistics/labour/earnings-and-working-conditions/trade-union-membership/latest-release> accessed 17 June 2025.

[87] Australian Government, 'The Clean Energy Generation: Workforce Needs for a Net Zero Economy' (2023) 11 <https://www.jobsandskills.gov.au/sites/default/files/2023-10/The%20Clean%20Energy%20Generation_0.pdf> accessed 20 May 2025.

[88] Routh (n 19) 50.

[89] Aged Care Award 2010; Nurses Award 2020; Social, Community, Home Care and Disability Services Industry Award 2010, Fair Work Commission [2022] FWCFB 200 (4 November 2022).

4. Conclusion

This chapter has outlined some of the ways in which labour law simultaneously supports, ignores, and undermines climate change mitigation and adaptation. It has argued that labour law's private law grammar leads labour law to exclude a large proportion of the global workforce from protection, while allocating responsibility for climate harms to employers under systems where employees have a largely consultative role. Its public law dimension has functioned to enhance the terms of recruitment and industrial citizenship of workers in fossil fuel related industries relative to other workers, enabling them to exercise societal and industrial power to oppose, slow down, or modify policies for rapid fossil fuel phase-out. This power emerged, in part, from the fact that the theoretical justifications advanced for labour law co-developed with concepts of democracy and societal well-being that were entwined with notions of progress based on carbon-intensive industrialisation. For all of these limitations, the substantive and procedural protections of labour law remain critical for democratising societies and enabling the necessary work that reproduces life to take place on secure, just, and sustainable terms.

The ambivalent contribution of labour law to the climate crisis sketched in this chapter is somewhat at odds with many of the current dominant scholarly debates in the field concerning labour law's relevance and underlying rationale.[90] These are dominated by questions of how labour might extend (and re-extend) its scope, depth, and enforceability to workers who labour outside the contract of employment or on its margins.[91] Rather than argue for a particular rationale for labour law (based on, for example, a capabilities approach, human rights, or anti-subordination), this chapter has instead endeavoured to locate some of labour law's well known justifications in their historic contexts. Nor does it entirely conform with postcolonial approaches to labour law which emphasise pluralism and multiplicity,[92] or approaches that characterise labour law itself as a form of sustainability[93] to the extent that it centres urgent fossil fuel cessation as high priority for collective well-being.

According to the perspective pressed here, it is necessary to critically attend simultaneously to private law's *failures* (in scope) and public law's *successes* (in embedding a particular, carbon-reliant version of interdependency) to enable labour law to become climate-responsive. In terms of the first part, the analysis suggests an agenda for the expansion of protections to the majority of workers which is not unfamiliar: the need for laws that extend freedom of association to ensure workers can take collective action against any organisation that wields power over them as workers; obligations on employers to provide safe working conditions and spaces to organise; widened protections for workers from unfair dismissal; and leave provisions that take account of climate impacts.[94]

[90] Guy Brian Davidov and Brian Langille, *The Idea of Labour Law* (OUP 2011).

[91] M Freedland and N Kountouris, 'Towards a Comparative Theory of the Contractual Construction of Personal Work Relations in Europe' (2008) 37 Industrial Law Journal 49; Simon Deakin, 'What Exactly Is Happening to the Contract of Employment? Reflections on Mark Freedland and Nicola Kountouris's Legal Construction of Personal Work Relations' (2013) 7 Jerusalem Review of Legal Studies 135; Alain Supiot, *Beyond Employment: Changes in Work and the Future of Labour Law in Europe* (OUP 2001).

[92] Routh (n 19) 56.

[93] Tomassetti (n 25); Tonia Novitz, 'Collective Labour Rights for Working People: The Legal Framework Established by the International Labour Organization' in Sanjukta Paul, Shae McCrystal, and Ewan McGaughey (eds), *The Cambridge Handbook of Labor in Competition Law* (CUP 2022).

[94] Ruth Dukes and Wolfgang Streeck, 'Labour Law after Neoliberalism?' (2023) 50 Journal of Law and Society 165, 182.

The latter aspect—attending to the climate problems created by public law's successes—invites new and challenging thinking. What would it practically mean to "return" to the holistic stabilisation of an independent society, reconceived in ecological terms, as a theoretical justification for labour law? A comprehensive analysis is not possible here, but one starting point may be to enlarge the objects of labour law statutes to acknowledge state obligations to advance an effective response to climate change based on the best available scientific knowledge and international law obligations, and with them the permitted terms of collective bargaining and industrial action.

What would a normative commitment to securing societal stability mean for labour law's grammar in the law of contract, with its inherent assumption that parties are free to meet and agree on terms over lawful matters, including employment in fossil fuel extractive industries? The imperative of cessation, even "just cessation", is ostensibly at odds with a core dimension of labour law as it pertains to particular sectors.[95] The legacy of the past may not be helpful, as there are no straightforward historical analogues for the normative urgency of "stranding" fossil fuel resources.[96]

What is clear is that as has always been the case with labour law, much depends on the governance of society in general, and the collective willingness to restrain private interests of all kinds (financial, technological, communicative, and energy actors) in the public interest. Even though labour law does bear upon democratic capacity, ultimate decision-making power over fossil fuel extraction resides outside the scope of labour law. Other key institutions that co-evolved with labour law have changed in fundamental ways since the mid-twentieth century, including the welfare state, vertically integrated firms, and industrial trade unions with large memberships.[97] The reckoning of labour law with climate will also take place in parallel with evolving mechanisms of environmental and climate governance, involving both public and private law.

[95] Flanagan (n 48).

[96] Peter Newell and Angela Carter, 'Understanding Supply-Side Climate Policies: Towards an Interdisciplinary Framework' (2024) 24 International Environmental Agreements: Politics, Law and Economics 7, 9.

[97] Adams and Deakin (n 9).

CHAPTER 27

Maritime Law

MARTIN DAVIES

1. Introduction

International commercial shipping accounts for about 3% of global greenhouse gas (GHG) emissions.[1] Reducing to zero the GHG emissions from the shipping industry would obviously make only a small overall contribution to the global climate change crisis, but nevertheless, the maritime sector is presently implementing profound emission-reduction measures that are transforming the way that all commercial ships operate. As this chapter will show, ships are already subject to some of the first internationally uniform, legally enforceable regulations requiring gradually more stringent reductions in carbon emissions with the goal of reaching net zero by 2050.

Carbon emission regulations promulgated by the International Maritime Organization (IMO) came into force on 1 January 2023; they apply to all ships throughout the world of gross registered tonnage more than 400 tonnes.[2] Compliance with the regulations requires ship operators to make present-day operational changes and to engage immediately in long-term planning for the use of alternative fuels and different ship designs. Amendments to the original IMO regulations have already been made, in April 2025, although implementation of those regulations has been delayed as a result of opposition by the United States. It is expected that more modifications will be made in the future in order to achieve the IMO's stated goal of achieving net-zero carbon emissions from the global shipping industry by 2050.

The shipping industry has also been made part of the European Union's Emissions Trading System (ETS) since January of 2024.[3] The details of how the ETS carbon market works and how it relates to private law are considered elsewhere in this handbook,[4] but for present purposes it suffices to say that the ETS creates a second layer of carbon emission regulation for operators whose ships trade into or within ports in the European Union, over and above the requirements of the IMO scheme. Efforts are being made to harmonise the two schemes, but

[1] International Maritime Organization (IMO), *Fourth Greenhouse Gas Study 2020* <https://www.imo.org/en/ourwork/Environment/Pages/Fourth-IMO-Greenhouse-Gas-Study-2020.aspx> accessed 25 April 2025.

[2] The gross registered tonnage of a ship is the weight of steel and other materials making up the fabric of the ship itself. Even the smallest commercial cargo ships weigh thousands of gross registered tonnes. To give readers a frame of reference, a 400-grt vessel is about the size of a harbour tug. The ship's deadweight tonnage, which is also used as an important measure in the IMO regulations is very different: it is explained below (n 30).

[3] Regulation (EU) 2015/757 of the European Parliament and of the Council of 29 April 2015 (as amended) <https://eur-lex.europa.eu/legal-content/EN/TXT/PDF/?uri=CELEX:02015R0757-20240101> accessed 31 October 2025.

[4] See Harro van Asselt and Jessica Crow, Chapter 33 of this handbook.

it should be obvious that compliance with both sets of regulations demands a great deal of focused attention by ship operators. To describe decarbonisation of the shipping industry as a hot topic at the moment is a gross understatement. It seems likely to produce as fundamental a transformation of global shipping practice as the shift from sailing ships to steamships did in the late nineteenth century.

Sections 2 and 3 of this chapter describes how the IMO regulations have binding force on almost all ships in the world. Section 4 considers how the regulations are to be enforced. Section 5 describes the evolving IMO strategies and the details of how the regulations work. Section 6 gives a brief description of the effect of the European Union's ETS on the shipping industry.

2. IMO, MARPOL, and Pollution Prevention Regulations

The IMO is a specialised agency of the United Nations, with responsibility for the safety and security of shipping and the prevention of marine and atmospheric pollution by ships.[5] There are presently 176 countries that are Member States of IMO and three Associate Members.[6]

As part of the restructuring of international organisations that occurred after the Second World War, a diplomatic conference in Geneva in 1948 made provision for the creation of a body named the Inter-Governmental Maritime Consultative Organization, or IMCO, with one of its aims being: "To provide machinery for co-operation among governments in the field of governmental regulation and practices relating to technical matters of all kinds affecting shipping engaged in international trade, and to encourage the general adoption of the highest practicable standards in matters concerning maritime safety and efficiency of navigation".[7] Unlike the other international organisations created at this time,[8] such as the World Bank and the International Monetary Fund, IMCO did not come into existence until 1958, largely because some countries were reluctant to adopt the founding Convention as they felt that the text had been written by and for the benefit of the handful of countries that dominated world shipping at that time.[9]

In the interim between 1948 and 1958, before IMCO's founding convention came into force, another diplomatic conference adopted the International Convention for Prevention of Pollution by Oil 1954[10] (known as OILPOL 54), which agreed that pollution prevention would become the responsibility of IMCO once the new organisation was established, even though the original 1948 convention made no reference to marine pollution or the environment.

[5] International Maritime Organization, *Introduction to IMO* <https://www.imo.org/en/About/Pages/Default.aspx> accessed 31 October 2025.

[6] International Maritime Organization, *Member States* <https://www.imo.org/en/OurWork/ERO/Pages/MemberStates.aspx> accessed 31 October 2025.

[7] International Maritime Organization, *Brief History of IMO* <https://www.imo.org/en/About/HistoryOfIMO/Pages/Default.aspx> accessed 31 October 2025.

[8] A notable exception is the proposed International Trade Organization (ITO), which did not finally come into existence as the World Trade Organization (WTO) until 1995.

[9] International Maritime Organization (IMO), *Convention on the International Maritime Organization* <https://www.imo.org/en/About/Conventions/Pages/Convention-on-the-International-Maritime-Organization.aspx> accessed 31 October 2025 (hereafter 'IMO Convention').

[10] International Convention for Prevention of Pollution by Oil, 12 May 1954, 327 UNTS No 4714 (1959).

The focus of IMCO changed significantly after a major oil spill from the tanker *Torrey Canyon* in 1967,[11] which highlighted dramatically both the possibility of enormous environmental damage from oil tanker accidents, and also the considerable deficiencies in the international system for assessing liability and compensation for oil spill damage. In a not exactly speedy response, IMCO adopted a new convention in 1973 to succeed and replace OILPOL 54, entitled the International Convention for the Prevention of Pollution from Ships[12] (known as MARPOL), and in 1975, it established both a Marine Environment Protection Committee (MEPC) and a Legal Committee.[13] The 1975 amendments to the 1948 convention also changed the name of the organisation to the IMO and amended Article 1 by adding to the list of purposes "the prevention and control of marine pollution from ships, and to deal with legal matters related to the purposes set out in this Article".[14] (The 1975 amendments, and thus the name change, did not come into force until 1982.)

MARPOL was substantially amended by Protocol in 1978 in response to a spate of oil tanker accidents in 1976 and 1977, although the original 1973 text had not yet then come into force. The combined instrument, known as MARPOL 73/78,[15] came into force on 2 October 1983. It is now one of the most widely adopted international conventions governing private law, with 161 countries party to the Convention as amended by the 1978 Protocol, the combined merchant fleets of which constitute approximately 98.89% of the world's merchant fleet.[16]

MARPOL 73/78 contains regulations aimed at preventing and minimising pollution from ships, both accidental and from routine operations. The comprehensive and highly technical regulations are contained in six Annexes, which affect the design and structure of all ships—not just oil tankers—as well as requirements for their operation. Annexes I to V govern oil pollution (Annex I, which came into force in 1983); pollution by noxious liquid substances (Annex II, which came into force in 1987); pollution by harmful packaged substances (Annex III, which came into force in 1992); pollution by sewage (Annex IV, which came into force in 2003); and pollution by garbage (Annex V, which came into force in 1988). Annexes I and II are mandatory; Annexes III, IV, and V are optional, in the sense that countries party to MARPOL 73/78 must separately adopt the relevant instruments before they come into force for that country.

Annex VI, which entered into force in 2005, is concerned with air pollution from ships. It is Annex VI that contains the new regulations governing carbon emissions from ships. More than 100 of the 161 countries party to MARPOL 73/78 have adopted Annex VI, representing 96.95% of world merchant shipping by tonnage.[17]

[11] For a contemporary account, see T Gill, F Booker, and F Spoer, *The Wreck of the Torrey Canyon* (David & Charles, 1967).

[12] The Final Act and text of the original 1973 version of MARPOL can be read at <https://wwwcdn.imo.org/localresources/en/KnowledgeCentre/ConferencesMeetings/Documents/MARPOL%201973%20-%20Final%20Act%20and%20Convention.pdf> accessed 31 October 2025.

[13] IMO Convention (n 9).

[14] ibid.

[15] Protocol of 1978 relating to the International Convention for the prevention of pollution from ships 1973, 17 February 1978, 1340 UNTS No 22484 (1983) (hereafter MARPOL 73/78).

[16] International Maritime Organization, *Status of IMO Treaties (20 November 2024)* <https://wwwcdn.imo.org/localresources/en/About/Conventions/StatusOfConventions/Status%202024.pdf> 127 accessed 31 October 2025 (hereafter 'Status of Treaties').

[17] The Status of Treaties document (n 16) lists countries party to optional Annexes III, IV and V, but does not (yet) list countries party to Annex VI. However, see International Maritime Organization, *100th State Joins Ship Air Pollution and Emissions Treaty* (8 June 2021) <https://www.imo.org/en/MediaCentre/PressBriefings/pages/MARPOL100State.aspx> accessed 31 October 2025 (acknowledging Argentina's ratification of Annex VI) (hereafter '100th State').

3. MARPOL Annex VI

Annex VI of MARPOL 73/78 was initially designed to deal with emissions of sulphur oxides (SOx), nitrogen oxides (NOx) and particulate matter (PM) from ships. It established a sliding downward scale of permitted emissions of these pollutants from year to year, and defined several sulphur control emission areas (SECAs), which are sea areas where even stricter emission controls apply.[18] The global limit on sulphur in ships' fuel oil (i.e., the limit applicable throughout the world outside the SECAs) was reduced substantially with effect from 1 January 2020, from 3.5% to 0.5%.[19] Predictably, this has led to the widespread use of low-sulphur fuel oil (LSFO) by ships, which was already common among ships trading into any of the SECAs.

SOx, NOx, and PM are not greenhouse gases, although they can indirectly contribute to global heating as a result of aerosolisation. The initial concern of Annex VI was thus on airbourne pollutants that can directly affect human health. However, Annex VI was the obvious place for the IMO to introduce new regulations governing carbon emissions from ships, which indirectly affect human health by damaging the environment.

The other significant reason for IMO using Annex VI as the vehicle for implementing its decarbonisation strategy was that enforceable regulations with worldwide effect could be introduced fairly promptly and easily, without the need for a diplomatic conference, a new international convention, or an amending protocol, and the correspondingly long delays that usually attend formal diplomatic procedures such as these. Fairly unusually for an international convention, MARPOL 73/78 may be amended by a procedure known informally as "tacit acceptance".[20] If a two-thirds majority of the MEPC adopts a proposed amendment to an Annex to MARPOL 73/78 (including, obviously, Annex VI), the amendment is communicated to all countries party to the Convention and then is deemed to be accepted unless a country party informs the IMO that its express approval is necessary before the amendment enters into force for that country.[21] Amendments to an appendix to an annex are deemed to have been accepted ten months after circulation to countries party to the Convention, unless not less than one-third of countries party, or countries party representing more than 50% of the world's gross tonnage, object.[22]

Importantly, the requisite two-thirds majority at MEPC is only of those countries present and voting, provided that they represent at least 50% of the gross tonnage of the world's merchant fleet.[23] All countries party to the Convention are entitled to participate in the proceedings of the appropriate body (in this case, the MEPC),[24] but not all do, of course.

In short, Annex VI can effectively be amended by resolution of the IMO's MEPC, which is therefore, in practical terms, the regulator of carbon emissions from almost all ships

[18] The four initial SECAs were the Baltic Sea, the North Sea, the North American area (covering designated coastal areas of the United States and Canada), and the US Caribbean Sea (around Puerto Rico and the US Virgin Islands). The fifth, covering the Mediterranean Sea, was created with effect from 1 May 2025.

[19] International Maritime Organization, *IMO 2020—Cleaner Shipping for Cleaner Air* < https://www.imo.org/en/MediaCentre/PressBriefings/pages/34-IMO-2020-sulphur-limit-.aspx> accessed 31 October 2025.

[20] MARPOL 73/78 (n 15), art 16(2).

[21] ibid art 16(2)(f)(ii)

[22] ibid art 16(2)(f)(iii).

[23] ibid art 16(2)(d), (f)(i).

[24] ibid art 16(2)(c).

everywhere in the world.[25] Any regulations amended by MEPC that are subsequently accepted by "tacit acceptance" take effect for almost all of the world's ships, given that over 96.95% of the world's merchant ships are registered in countries party to Annex VI.[26] (Ironically, this seems effectively to be the fruition of some countries' initial concerns about the 1948 proposals for IMCO, namely that the countries that dominate world shipping can legislate for everyone else. That concern seems to belong to a bygone era, however.)

4. Enforcement of Annex VI: Flag State Control, Classification Societies, and Port State Control

4.1 Flag State Control

As explained in more detail in the next section, all ship operators must now record the quantity of carbon emissions from their ships and, in particular, must calculate the ship's carbon intensity indicator (CII), which reflects not only the total quantity of carbon emissions, but also the intensity of those emissions relative to the size of the ship and the quantity of the cargo it can carry. (If a small ship and a large ship emit the same total quantity of carbon, the small ship's CII is greater than the larger ship's CII.) The ship's CII performance against the targets set by the IMO regulations is graded at the end of each calendar year, on a scale from A to E. Grading of a ship's performance is the responsibility of the flag state—that is, the country in which the ship is registered.

Many commercial ships are registered in what are politely called "open register" countries, where the requirement stated by Article 91(1) of the UN Convention on the Law of the Sea (UNCLOS) that there be a "genuine link" between a ship and the country purporting to confer its nationality upon that ship[27] is satisfied simply by the shipowner's desire (usually for commercial reasons) to register the ship in that country, whether or not the shipowner itself has any connection with the country. (A less polite, but perhaps better known, term for open register countries is "flags of convenience" states. However, because many countries now operate "second registers" for international users as well as their own national registries,[28] the more pejorative term "flag of convenience" is now regarded as outmoded; it has been described by an influential text as an "historic reputation without foundation, based on prejudice rather than fact".)[29]

Many "open register" countries do not have the resources to comply with what is now their annual MARPOL Annex VI obligation to grade the CII performance of every ship registered

[25] *See* the lengthy list of the MEPC's amendments and interpretive documents in relation to Annex VI at International Maritime Organization, *Index of MEPC Resolutions and Guidelines related to MARPOL Annex VI* <https://www.imo.org/en/OurWork/Environment/Pages/Index-of-MEPC-Resolutions-and-Guidelines-related-to-MARPOL-Annex-VI.aspx#1> accessed 31 October 2025.

[26] See '100th State' (n 17).

[27] United Nations Convention on the Law of the Sea, 10 December 1982, 1833 UNTS 3163 (hereafter UNCLOS), art 91(1).

[28] Australia is an example of a country with both a General Register and an International Register: see Shipping Registration Act 1981 (Cth) ss 15A, 56(1),(2); Martin Davies and Anthony Dickey, *Shipping Law* (5th edn, ThomsonReuters 2024) [3.20], [3.320], [3.330].

[29] Edward Watt and Richard Coles, *Ship Registration: Law and Practice* (3rd edn, Informa 2019) [4.01].

in that country. To give a simple example, the world's third-largest ship registry by measure of deadweight tonnage[30] is presently the Marshall Islands.[31] As of 1 January 2025 there were 4,254 ships registered in the Marshall Islands, with a deadweight capacity of about 12.5% of the world's total.[32] The United Nations estimated that the population of the country on 28 October 2025 was 37,806,[33] or an average of 8.41 members of the entire population per registered ship. Obviously, the Marshall Islands can only comply with its MARPOL Annex VI obligations by subcontracting the task to an entity with significantly more resources than the country itself could possibly have. As is the case with many other flag state obligations for smaller countries, the task is often delegated to a recognised classification society.

4.2 Classification Societies

Classification societies are private organisations that publish (in the form of rules) minimum technical requirements for the design, construction, maintenance, and survey of ships and other marine facilities, and certify whether those requirements have been met.[34] For ships, classification societies verify compliance with their published standards both during construction and periodically during the ship's service life.

Classification societies are independent of shipowners, shipbuilders, insurers, or others engaged commercially in the business of shipping. Twelve of the most reputable classification societies have formed the International Association of Classification Societies (IACS) to provide what it describes as "an assurance of professional integrity and maintenance of high professional standards".[35]

Certification by a reputable classification society is of crucial importance for shipbuilders, shipowners, insurers, and flag states. It is no exaggeration to say that classification society certification is indispensable for the commercial operation of any ship. For example, shipbuilding contracts typically contain "class clauses", which make the builder's compliance with the designated classification society's rules a condition of the shipbuilding contract and thus of the buyer's obligation to pay the purchase price for the newly built ship. Standard form ship sale contracts also typically make classification society certification a condition of sale of second-hand ships. First-party hull and machinery insurance policies make continued classification society certification of the ship a condition of insurance. Similarly, the indemnity insurance cover provided by Protection and Indemnity Associations (P&I Clubs) against liabilities

[30] The deadweight tonnage of a ship is the quantity of cargo it can carry, not the weight of the ship itself, which is the ship's gross tonnage (see n 2). For many ships, deadweight tonnage far exceeds gross tonnage, meaning that many ships can carry much more than their own weight.

[31] United Nations Conference on Trade and Development (UNCTAD), *Review of Maritime Transport 2025* 51, Table II.2 <https://unctad.org/system/files/official-document/rmt2025_en.pdf> accessed 31 October 2025.

[32] ibid.

[33] World Population Review, *Marshall Islands Population 2024 (Live)* <https://worldpopulationreview.com/countries/marshall-islands> accessed 31 October 2025.

[34] *See generally* Felix Goebel, *Classification Societies: Competition and Regulation of Maritime Information Intermediaries* (Zurich 2017); International Association of Classification Societies (IACS), *Classification Societies: What, Why and How?'* <https://iacs.s3.af-south-1.amazonaws.com/wp-content/uploads/2022/06/15153229/Classification-what-why-how.pdf> accessed 31 October 2025.

[35] International Association of Classification Societies (IACS), *About Us* <https://iacs.org.uk/about-us/> accessed 31 October 2025.

incurred by shipowners is dependent on continued classification society certification of the entered ship.[36]

The International Convention for the Safety of Life at Sea 1974 (SOLAS)[37] requires that a ship must be certified by a recognised classification society before a SOLAS certificate can be issued to it. Regulation 3-1 of Part A-1 of Chapter II-1 of SOLAS 1974 provides: "[S]hips shall be designed, constructed and maintained in compliance with the structural, mechanical and electrical requirements of a classification society which is recognized by the Administration [of the flag state's government]." Without a SOLAS certificate, it is virtually impossible for a ship to be entered on the register of ships in any country, even those with "open registers", because virtually all countries are party to the SOLAS Convention. One hundred and sixty-eight countries, representing approximately 98.91% of the gross tonnage[38] of the world's merchant fleet, are Contracting States to SOLAS.[39]

In short, for many ships the principal overseer of their compliance with the many and varied regulations in international conventions such as SOLAS and MARPOL (including Annex VI) is, in practice, a classification society rather than a governmental authority such as the US Coast Guard. Indeed, even the US Coast Guard subcontracts some regulatory oversight to classification societies.[40]

4.3 Port State Control

Even with widespread subcontracting by smaller flag states to large professional overseers such as classification societies, it remains true to say that some countries are less rigorous in their enforcement of international shipping regulations than others, and thus are closer to earning the pejorative description "flags of convenience".[41] Although it is difficult for IMO to acknowledge this openly for obvious political reasons (all flag states are formally regarded as equal members of IMO), the IMO is keenly aware that enforcement of Annex VI of MARPOL will be uneven (to put it politely) if reliance is based solely on compliance by flag states with their oversight obligations. For that reason, it is expected that port state control will play a significant role in practice in enforcing the carbon emission regulations in Annex VI. The IMO describes port state control as "a backup to flag state implementation, a second line of defence against substandard shipping".[42]

[36] P&I Clubs operate as insurers of a very broad range of ships' liabilities. They are mutual self-insurance associations of participating shipowners. Twelve Clubs form the International Group of P&I Clubs, which between them provide liability cover for 90% of the world's oceangoing tonnage: see International Group of P&I Clubs <https://www.igpandi.org/> accessed 31 October 2025. Because each Club's rulebook (its multiparty contract between participating members) contains a 'pay to be paid' clause, the Clubs are, technically, indemnity insurers rather than liability insurers.

[37] International Convention for the Safety of Life at Sea, 1 November 1974, 1184 UNTS No 18961 (1980).

[38] See n 30.

[39] Status of Treaties (n 16) 19.

[40] United States Coast Guard, *Flag State Control Division: Classification Society Authorizations (CG-CVC-4)* <https://www.dco.uscg.mil/Our-Organization/Assistant-Commandant-for-Prevention-Policy-CG-5P/Inspections-Compliance-CG-5PC-/Commercial-Vessel-Compliance/Flag-State-Control-Division/ClassSocAuth/> accessed 31 October 2025.

[41] See n 29.

[42] International Maritime Organization, *Port State Control* <https://www.imo.org/en/OurWork/IIIS/Pages/Port%20State%20Control.aspx> accessed 31 October 2025.

"Port state control" is the generic term used for measures of many different kinds imposed on trading ships by the countries that those ships visit.[43] It occupies a sometimes-sensitive position in international law terms because it is the imposition of legal action by one country on ships registered in another country, bringing with it possible issues of concern for international relations. *Coastal* states have only limited power to regulate the activities of foreign-flagged ships in their coastal waters because the right of innocent passage enshrined in UNCLOS (and in customary international law) entitles ships of all countries, whether coastal or landlocked, to be unhampered by legal interference from the coastal state except in limited (and defined) circumstances designed to protect the peace, good order, or security of the coastal state.[44] *Port* states, on the other hand, are entitled to exercise more far-reaching regulatory powers over visiting ships because the right of innocent passage ends when a ship voluntarily completes its voyage in port. Articles 218 and 219 of UNCLOS authorise port states to undertake investigations and, if warranted by the evidence, to institute proceedings in respect of polluting discharges from any ship in violation of applicable international rules, including discharges occurring on the high seas beyond the port state's territorial sea or exclusive economic zone, and to prevent the ship from sailing if it threatens damage to the marine environment.[45] This authority is plainly broad enough to encompass port state activity in relation to the carbon emission regulations in Annex VI; what is not yet so clear is how that may actually be done.

In practice, many port state control activities begin with the inspection of foreign-flagged ships arriving in port to ensure that they have the appropriate documentation certifying their compliance with SOLAS and MARPOL requirements of various kinds, and that the condition of the ship is consistent with that documentary certification. It would be extremely inconvenient for any globally trading ship to have to undergo a thorough port state inspection every time it visits a different country, so port states have cooperated with one another to share information gleaned from an inspection in order to obviate the need for other port states to conduct repetitive successive inspections.

The first such cooperative agreement was made in 1982 by fourteen European countries that established the *Paris Memorandum of Understanding on Port State Control* (the Paris MoU).[46] There are now twenty-eight countries party to the Paris MoU (not all of them European).[47] Pursuant to an IMO resolution in 1991,[48] similar MoUs have been created for the Pacific region (Tokyo MoU; twenty-two countries),[49] South

[43] See generally George Kasoulides, *Port State Control and Jurisdiction: Evolution of the Port State Regime* (Martinus Nijhoff, Dordrecht, 1993); Oya Özçayir, *Port State Control* (2nd edn, Routledge, London, 2004). With particular reference to Annex VI of MARPOL, *see* Jesper Jarl Fanø, *Enforcing International Maritime Legislation of Air Pollution through UNCLOS* Ch 4 (Bloomsbury 2009).

[44] UNCLOS (n 27) arts 17, 19(1), 21, 24.

[45] UNCLOS (n 27) arts 218, 219.

[46] Paris MoU on Port State Control, *History* <https://parismou.org/about-us/history> accessed 31 October 2025.

[47] Paris MoU on Port State Control, *Organisation* <https://parismou.org/about-us/organisation> accessed 31 October 2025. The countries are Belgium, Bulgaria, Canada, Croatia, Cyprus, Denmark, Estonia, Finland, France, Germany, Greece, Iceland, Ireland, Italy, Latvia, Lithuania, Malta, Montenegro, the Netherlands, Norway, Poland, Portugal, Romania, the Russian Federation, Slovenia, Spain, Sweden, and the United Kingdom.

[48] IMO Resolution A.682.17 (1991).

[49] Asia-Pacific PSC, Tokyo MoU, *Welcome to Tokyo MoU* <https://www.tokyo-mou.org/> accessed 31 October 2025.

and Central America (Acuerdo de Viña del Mar; sixteen countries),[50] the Caribbean (twenty countries),[51] the Mediterranean (eleven countries),[52] the Indian Ocean (twenty countries),[53] the Atlantic coast of Africa (Abuja MoU; twenty-two countries),[54] the Black Sea (six countries),[55] and the Persian Gulf (Riyadh MoU; six countries).[56]

The global network of regional port state control MoUs is designed to share information about substandard ships that have been found to be in violation of regulations that require a particular standard of performance. The Annex VI carbon emission regulations do not penalise failure to comply with particular standards of performance, but rather merely require rating of the level of a ship's performance against required standards, so it is not yet clear how port state control will or can have an impact on compliance. What is clear, however, is that the IMO does expect port states to be active participants in the task of reducing greenhouse gas emissions, as evidenced by a resolution of the MEPC on 16 December 2022, entitled "Invitation to Member States to Encourage Voluntary Cooperation between the Port and Shipping Sectors to Contribute to Reducing GHG Emissions from Ships".[57]

It is conceivable, for example, that port states might in the future refuse access to ships graded below a certain level with regard to their carbon intensity (see Section 5.1), or impose different levels of port charges for differently graded ships. It is, at present, too early to tell. Plainly, however, port states will have some role to play in encouraging ships to maintain high grades in their effort to reduce carbon emissions.

5. The IMO Strategies and Regulations

5.1 The 2023 Regulations

The initial IMO GHG strategy was adopted in 2018; it proposed the goal of reducing total carbon emissions from ships by at least 50% by 2050 as compared to 2008 levels, using the regulatory and enforcement mechanisms described above.[58] Although the IMO proposed what were perhaps the first mandatory carbon-reduction measures to be legally enforceable on an international basis, it was criticised for being insufficiently adventurous in its goals,

50 AVM Acuerdo de Viña del Mar, *Acuerdo Latinoamericano sobre Control de Buques por el Estado rector del Puerto* <https://alvm.prefecturanaval.gob.ar/> accessed 31 October 2025.

51 CMOU Caribbean Memorandum of Understanding on Port State Control, *About Us* < https://www.caribbeanmou.org/content/about > accessed 31 October 2025.

52 Mediterranean MoU on Port State Control <https://www.medmou.org/Home.aspx> accessed 31 October 2025.

53 Indian Ocean Memorandum of Understanding on Port State Control, *About IOMOU: History* <https://www.iomou.nic.in/wtLf6Ozlo3JH21oyfoUCiYdSkIrPZsQlinM3ZjRqsYkThj7mnSeRf2nqoNORoeVbz3C7rtiDH6M3+1LD25LGXLtlwJLKQ1ag==&l2=/g==.> accessed 24 April 2025.

54 Abuja MoU on Port State Control, *About Us* <https://abujamou.org/en/about/> accessed 31 October 2025.

55 Black Sea MoU, *About Us* <https://bsmou.org/about/> accessed 24 April 2025.

56 Riyadh Memorandum of Understanding on Port State Control <https://riyadhmou.org/members/> accessed 31 October 2025.

57 MEPC Resolution.366(79), 16 December 2022, MEPC <HOMEPAGE/history.php?l1=9w==&main=9MRxvdnUArYi3c7MhauhAySs1dzcT2rBWqs+YCGRYETunszTiM6sxMr5N9e8xFbFj+79.15.Add.1>.

58 International Maritime Organization (IMO), *Initial IMO GHG Strategy* <https://www.imo.org/en/MediaCentre/HotTopics/pages/reducing-greenhouse-gas-emissions-from-ships.aspx> accessed 24 April 2025.

particularly after the United Nations Framework Convention on Climate Change Conference of 2021 in Glasgow (COP26). In particular, the initial IMO strategy of at least a 50% reduction by 2050 seemed relatively timid in comparison with the EU's Emission Trading Scheme (ETS), with its stated goal of a reduction to zero emissions by 2050. In November 2021, almost immediately after the end of COP26, the IMO's MEPC resolved (at its meeting MEPC 77) to "strengthen the ambition" of the original strategy.[59] As a result, although the IMO went ahead with introducing the initially proposed carbon emission regulations for all ships with effect from 1 January 2023, it also produced a revised strategy in 2023, with the goal of net-zero emissions by 2050, and it now describes the 2023 regulations as "mid-term measures".[60] In April 2025, it proposed modified regulations intended to come into force in 2027; these are described in Section 5.2.

A complete description of the 2023 regulations would be out of place in a book such as this, as they are complex and technical, even for those familiar with ship operations. In brief, every ship of more than 400 gross tonnes must now have a Ship Energy Efficiency Management Plan (SEEMP) designed to improve energy efficiency and to collect fuel consumption data, and an Energy Efficiency Existing Ship Index (EEXI) that sets up its carbon intensity indicator (CII). The CII is the ratio of the total carbon dioxide emissions from the ship per deadweight tonne[61] per (nautical) mile[62] that the ship travels. The EEXI is assessed only once, but the annual operational CII is reviewed every year by the ship's flag state (or its classification society subcontractor; see Section 4.2) and the ship is then given a rating from A to E. Poor ratings must be corrected, and the expected CII for each ship is gradually reduced from year to year. The regulations are "performance based", which means that they stipulate the result that must be achieved, rather than the means by which that result must be achieved. Shipowners can achieve the desired results by switching to alternative, low-, or non-carbon fuels, and/or by using operational measures such as "slow steaming" (i.e., sailing more slowly, which itself uses less fuel per nautical mile travelled and so produces fewer carbon emissions) in order to reduce wasteful time spent waiting for a berth at the port of destination, and/or by other technical measures such as hull coatings that reduce friction and thus improve engine efficiency. There are many other options: Shipowners are now implementing many different ways of reducing the CII of their ships, and they will continue to have to improve their CII as the years go by.

What is not yet clear is how, in practice, low annual grades will affect a ship's commercial operations. International shipping is an often ruthlessly efficient market, and the assumption behind the IMO's regulations is that the market will reward good grades and punish bad grades. Will a B-rated ship be cheaper or more expensive than an A-rated ship? Will the ship's rating restrict its geographical operation if port state control becomes a significant indirect enforcer of the regulations, for example, if a port state begins denying access to ships with a C or D rating? None of this is yet known. What is also not yet clear is how the significant extra costs of compliance will be shared among commercial operators. In whatever way the shipping market

[59] International Maritime Organization (IMO), *Maritime Environment Protection Committee (MEPC) 77, 22–26 November 2021* <https://www.imo.org/en/MediaCentre/MeetingSummaries/Pages/MEPC77.aspx> accessed 31 October 2025.

[60] International Maritime Organization (IMO), *2023 IMO Strategy on Reduction of GHG Emissions from Ships* <https://www.imo.org/en/OurWork/Environment/Pages/2023-IMO-Strategy-on-Reduction-of-GHG-Emissions-from-Ships.aspx> accessed 31 October 2025.

[61] The deadweight tonnage of the ship is how much cargo it can carry: see n 30.

[62] A nautical mile is 1.15 land-measured miles. It is based on the length of one minute of latitude of the Earth's surface.

ends up resolving these questions, one thing is certain: The landed cost of goods carried by sea will become incrementally more expensive as the commercial operators pass on the significant extra costs to the ultimate consumers of the goods that they carry. More than 80% of tangible goods in international trade are carried by sea,[63] all of which will henceforth have to incorporate into their price to the consumer a small portion of the cost of shipping's compliance with the regulations. In short, it will be almost impossible for anyone to avoid the indirect economic impact of the regulations.

5.2 The 2025 proposed revisions to the Regulations[64]

The IMO's MEPC met from 7 to 11 April 2025 (MEPC 83) to consider modifications to the existing regulations, which are now described as "medium-term" measures. The modifications are described as the IMO Net-Zero Framework.

Before describing the measures themselves, it is important to note that they were not adopted by the IMO's preferred tacit acceptance procedure, described above,[65] which was used to implement the original 2023 regulations. Because the amendments proposed to MEPC were opposed by several participating countries, they were put to a formal vote at MEPC, a very rare occurrence. The vote in the Committee was positive—63 countries (79%) in favour, and 19 opposed (21%)—but the unusual procedural posture meant that the proposed amendments were not circulated for tacit acceptance. Instead, an Extraordinary Session of MEPC (only the second of its kind) was held from 14 to 17 October 2025 with the aim of producing an affirmative majority for the proposed measures. Following intense political pressure by the United States, which "unequivocally rejects" the Net-Zero Framework, the Extraordinary Session voted by a narrow majority to adjourn discussion of adoption of the modified regulations for 12 months until October 2026.[66] In a joint statement issued just days before the Extraordinary Session, US Secretary of State Marco Rubio, US Secretary of Energy Chris Wright and US Secretary of Transportation Sean Duffy urged countries to reject the proposed measures and threatened retaliatory action against any country that supported the measures.[67] Faced with this threat, some countries that had supported the measures in April 2025 abstained or changed their votes at the Extraordinary Session. At the time of writing,[68] it is unclear whether the Net-Zero Framework will ever come into force. If it does, it will not do so until 2028; if not, the 2023 regulations will continue to apply.

63 United Nations Conference on Trade and Development (UNCTAD), *Review of Maritime Transport 2025* < https://unctad.org/system/files/official-document/rmt2025_en.pdf> accessed 31 October 2025.

64 Much of this section is drawn from an excellent report produced by Lloyd's Register, *IMO Marine Environment Protection Committee (MEPC 83): Summary Report* (April 2025) <https://maritime.lr.org/MEPC-83-Summary-Report> accessed 31 October 2025.

65 See (nn 20 to 23).

66 International Maritime Organization (IMO), *IMO Net-Zero Shipping Talks to Resume in 2026* <https://www.imo.org/en/mediacentre/pressbriefings/pages/imo-net-zero-shipping-talks-to-resume-in-2026.aspx> accessed 31 October 2025.

67 US Department of State, *Taking Action to Defend America from the UN's First Global Carbon Tax – the International Maritime Organization's IMO "Net-Zero Framework"* <https://www.state.gov/releases/office-of-the-spokesperson/2025/10/taking-action-to-defend-america-from-the-uns-first-global-carbon-tax-the-international-maritime-organizations-imo-net-zero-framework-nzf> accessed 31 October 2025.

68 31 October 2025.

Much as expected before MEPC 83, the proposed new regulations incorporate some market-based features similar to those in the EU's carbon emission reduction regime (see Section 6), while preserving the essential data-collection-assessment-verification-certification qualities of the IMO's original 2023 regulations. Whereas the CII concept described in the previous section measures outputs, the new regulations are designed, in effect, to measure inputs.

The proposed new regulations create a new standard called the GHG fuel intensity (GFI), which measures the energy intensity of the fuel (generically known as bunkers) that the ship uses, and other emission capture measures used by the ship. In broad terms, the GFI is the carbon dioxide equivalent in grams per megajoule of energy the fuel or energy source provides. Each ship is required to calculate its annual GFI. Each energy source used by a ship is assessed and certified by an IMO-recognised Sustainable Fuel Certification Scheme that measures the energy source's "well to wake" GHG emissions. Well to wake standards measure not only the carbon footprint of the ship's consumption of a particular fuel, but also the entire carbon footprint associated with the production and transportation of the energy source before it is used by the ship. In the same way that the 2023 regulations require a ship's CII to reduce progressively, so also its GFI will be required to decrease in successive years.

Assessment of compliance is measured by a market-based process using a concept known as the direct compliance target (DCT). Each ship is given an annual DCT for its GFI. Its compliance balance is the difference between its DCT and its actual attained GFI, multiplied by the total amount of energy used. Thus, the more energy a ship uses, the larger its compliance balance will be if its actual attained GFI does not meet its DCT.

If the ship has a positive compliance balance—that is, if its actual attained GFI is less than its DCT—then the ship is considered compliant and need take no further action to receive certification. The ship will then be issued credits in the form of surplus units, which it may then sell to other shipowners, or bank for future use, or simply cancel voluntarily. If the ship has a negative compliance balance, it must buy surplus units from compliant shipowners. If a ship ends up in compliance deficit, it must buy remedial units at a sliding scale of expense beginning at $100 per tonne of CO_2 equivalent, at least until 2030, when the prices will be reviewed.

6. The European Union's Emission Trading Scheme (ETS) as It Applies to Shipping

The European Commission announced on 14 July 2021 that shipping would gradually be introduced into the EU's Emissions Trading System (ETS). As explained elsewhere in this handbook,[69] the ETS is a carbon market that operates in relation to all industries in all EU countries with the aim of achieving climate neutrality by 2050. Since January 2024, the ETS has been extended to cover CO_2 emissions from all cargo and passenger ships of 5,000 gross tonnage or above[70] entering or leaving EU ports, regardless of the flag that they fly.[71] The inclusion of shipping into the ETS is to be phased in, with 40% of emissions to be reported for 2025, 70% for 2026, and 100% from 2027 onwards.[72]

[69] Harro van Asselt and Jessica Crow, Chapter 33 of this handbook.

[70] Note that this threshold is higher than the 400-grt threshold for the IMO regulations: see n 2. Nevertheless, a 5,000-grt cargo ship is still a fairly small ship.

[71] European Commission, *Reducing Emissions from the Shipping Sector* <https://climate.ec.europa.eu/eu-action/transport/reducing-emissions-shipping-sector_en> accessed 31 October 2025.

[72] ibid.

From 1 January 2025, all ships entering or leaving EU ports are subject to monitoring, reporting, and verification (MRV) requirements that require completion, and independent verification, of both a monitoring plan and an annual emissions report, both of which are to submitted to the European Commission by 31 March of the following year.[73] Once the Verified Emissions Report (VER) has been accepted by the European Commission, a Document of Compliance is issued, which must then be carried on board the ship in question. Predictably, the process of independent verification of monitoring plans and emissions reports relies heavily on the services of classification societies.[74]

As with all other industry participants subject to the EU ETS, all ships subject to the scheme are granted a number of EU allowances (EUAs), each of which represents the right to emit the GHG equivalent of one metric tonne of carbon dioxide. The "cap-and-trade" nature of the scheme means that participants can trade unused EUAs and must buy extra EUAs if they are not compliant or face a fine of €100 per tonne of excess carbon dioxide emitted.[75]

The combined effect of the IMO regulations and the phasing in of the EU ETS scheme in relation to shipping is that shipowners trading into or between EU ports must now comply with two rather different regimes designed to reduce carbon emissions. Although the means of complying with both regimes are obviously similar—recording emissions, implementing measures to reduce them, and so on—the administrative cost of satisfying the requirements of two regulatory regimes is obviously onerous, despite the fact that the IMO's proposed Net-Zero Framework intends to introduce market-based measures that emulate, at least to some extent, the EU's market-based approach.

7. Conclusion

Many, if not most, of the present measures aimed at reducing global carbon emissions are implementations at a national or regional level of undertakings that countries have given at an international level. They are aspirational at best, in the sense that countries face no sanctions, other than international opprobrium, for failing to do what they have said they would do. In stark contrast, and with little or no attention being paid by anyone outside of those directly interested or affected, an agency of the United Nations has imposed internationally uniform, legally enforceable measures that require concrete steps to be taken by private actors in an industry with global significance—private actors who have a vital, indispensable role to play in the conduct of international trade. Successful compliance with these new measures may not reduce the total amount of global GHG emissions by much, but it will certainly affect the price of internationally traded goods. It may thus, perhaps, act as a canary in the coalmine for how the costs of saving the planet from the unmitigated effects of global warming might be passed on to individuals throughout the world in the price of the products that they buy and use every day.

[73] European Commission, *Monitoring, Reporting and Verification* <https://climate.ec.europa.eu/eu-action/eu-emissions-trading-system-eu-ets/monitoring-reporting-and-verification_en> accessed 31 October 2025. Although the UK is no longer a member of the European Union, the MRV requirements apply to the UK, too: see Merchant Shipping (Monitoring, Reporting and Verification of Carbon Dioxide Emissions) (Amendment) (EU Exit) Regulations 2018 (UK).

[74] See, for example, Det Norske Veritas (DNV), *MRV: Monitoring, Reporting and Verification (EU and UK)* <https://www.dnv.com/maritime/insights/topics/mrv/> accessed 31 October 2025.

[75] ibid. See also Harro van Asselt and Jessica Crow, Chapter 33 of this handbook.

CHAPTER 28

Investor–State Disputes

KYLA TIENHAARA

1. Introduction

INVESTOR–STATE dispute settlement (ISDS), the main enforcement mechanism for thousands of international investment treaties, was once considered an arcane practice, with very few people outside of a small community of arbitrators and lawyers even aware of its existence. Although the public remains largely ignorant of the inner workings of ISDS, the consequences of arbitral decisions are now more broadly understood, and in those countries where arbitral awards have exceeded the annual budget of major government ministries, ISDS has left deep scars.[1] Nobel prize winning economist Joseph Stiglitz has referred to ISDS as "legal terrorism".[2]

ISDS first emerged in bilateral investment treaties (BITs) signed in the late 1960s and early 1970s alongside the more traditional mechanism of state–state dispute settlement. Procedurally, ISDS was modelled off the system of international commercial arbitration between private entities and has been characterised by many as an essentially *private* system of law.[3] Some disagree with this designation, but what is indisputable is that ISDS panels adjudicate matters of *public* concern, such as the protection of human health and the environment and, increasingly, efforts to mitigate and adapt to climate change.

Much of the literature critiquing ISDS has focused on environmental policy disputes and the potential for the threat of an investor claim to chill environmental policy development.[4] It is only in the last decade that concern about climate policy has come to the forefront of discussions about ISDS. This development is largely the result of several high-profile ISDS cases in Europe and the decision of the EU and many of its member states to withdraw from the Energy Charter Treaty (ECT)—the treaty most frequently invoked in ISDS—because it is not aligned with the objectives of the Paris Agreement and the EU Green Deal.[5] Concerns about the potential conflict between investment regimes and the Paris Agreement have also been recognised by the Intergovernmental Panel on Climate Change (IPCC), and raised in discussions

[1] Toby Landau KC, 'International Investment Arbitration and the Search for Depoliticisation' (2023) Alexander Lecture 2023: Chartered Institute of Arbitrators <www.youtube.com/watch?v=2ql6AlR6xec&t=3s> accessed 7 June 2025.

[2] Joeseph Stiglitz, 'Allowing Foreign Firms to Sue Governments for Lost Profits Is Legal Terrorism—It Must End', *The Guardian* (London, 7 March 2023).

[3] Catharine Titi, 'Investment Treaty Arbitration Caught in The Public–Private Law Divide' (2024) 45 Michigan Journal of International Law 441.

[4] Jorge E Viñuales, *Foreign Investment and the Environment in International Law* (CUP 2012); Kyla Tienhaara, 'Regulatory Chill in a Warming World: The Threat to Climate Policy Posed by Investor–State Dispute Settlement' (2018) 7 Transnational Environmental Law 229.

[5] Lukas Schaugg, 'Why the Energy Charter Treaty Modernization Doesn't Deliver for Climate' (*IISD Explainer*, 12 December 2024) <www.iisd.org/articles/explainer/modernized-ect-doesnt-deliver-for-climate> accessed 7 June 2025.

at the Organisation for Economic Cooperation and Development (OECD) and stakeholder engagements conducted by the United Nations Framework Convention on Climate Change (UNFCCC) Standing Committee on Finance.[6]

This chapter first outlines some basics of international investment law to set the scene for how investors can use ISDS to challenge climate policy measures. It then delves into a series of cases brought by coal investors in four countries. The chapter concludes with consideration of the potential of various proposals to reform the investment regime to bring it into alignment with the Paris Agreement.

2. Investment Law and Climate Policy: The Basics

2.1 The Basis for Claims

More than 2500 BITs and plurilateral trade and investment agreements were in force as of early 2025.[7] A majority (70%) of these treaties are more than twenty years old. While treaty drafting practice has changed over time, with many of the more recently signed agreements being much more carefully worded, research has indicated that tribunals interpret these "modern" treaties in much the same way as older ones.[8] For this reason, and because old agreements dominate the treaty landscape, this section will refer generally to the types of provisions that are most frequently deployed by investor claimants and not to the text of specific treaties.

The substantive protections that are of greatest relevance in climate policy cases are state commitments to non-discrimination (national treatment and most-favoured nation treatment), to provide fair and equitable treatment (FET), and to not (indirectly) expropriate investments without compensation. Tribunals have interpreted these protections in diverging ways and there is no system of precedent or an appellate body that might help to bring consistency to the jurisprudence.[9] Sunset clauses will also be briefly reviewed given their relevance to reform discussions.

2.1.1 Non-Discrimination

At first glance, provisions on non-discrimination appear unlikely to cause concern from a climate policy perspective. So long as climate mitigation and adaptation measures are not designed to benefit domestic firms while harming foreign ones, or to give preference to firms from specific countries over others, one would assume that there could be no basis for a claim of discrimination. This is, unfortunately, not the case. Investors frequently argue that broadly

[6] IPCC, 'Climate Change 2022: Mitigation of Climate Change. Contribution of Working Group III to the Sixth Assessment Report of the Intergovernmental Panel on Climate Change' [P R Shukla and others (eds)] (CUP 2022); David Gaukrodger, 'The Alignment of Finance Flows under the Paris Agreement' (Organisation for Economic Co-operation and Development 2022); UNFCCC Standing Committee on Finance, 'Report of the Standing Committee on Finance, Addendum: Synthesis of views regarding ways to achieve Article 2, paragraph 1(c), of the Paris Agreement', FCCC/CP/2023/2/Add.3–FCCC/PA/CMA/2023/8/Add.3 (UNFCCC 2023).

[7] Based on data from UNCTAD, 'International Investment Agreement Navigator' <https://investmentpolicy.unctad.org/international-investment-agreements> accessed 10 February 2025.

[8] Wolfgang Alschner, *Investment Arbitration and State-Driven Reform: New Treaties, Old Outcomes* (OUP 2022).

[9] N Jansen Calamita, 'The (In)Compatibility of Appellate Mechanisms with Existing Instruments of the Investment Treaty Regime' (2017) 18 Journal of World Investment and Trade 585.

applied public interest measures are discriminatory or that their projects have been denied permits because of their nationality. Such claims are possible because tribunals have interpreted non-discrimination provisions broadly to include protection against de facto discrimination, meaning that no evidence is required that the government *intended* to discriminate.[10]

The potential is quite high for climate policy disputes to emerge based on de facto discrimination claims. As noted by VanDuzer, it is common for climate policies to treat "businesses engaged in carbon-intensive activities . . . differently from those with less carbon-intensive operations".[11] Whether such claims are successful will depend, in large part, on what tribunals believe is an appropriate comparator. Some tribunals have used a "competitive test" to determine if two investors are in "like circumstances".[12] For example, a tribunal could find that the treatment of a foreign owner of a coal power station should be compared with a domestic owner of a hydro power station because they are competitors in the electricity market. If such an approach is taken, a coal power phase-out may be in breach of the national treatment standard.[13] However, a tribunal may instead only compare investors in exactly the same circumstances (such as coal power investors) or consider arguments from the host state about the legitimate public purpose of differentiating economic activities based on their carbon emissions.[14]

2.1.2 FET

The FET standard is the most frequently invoked provision in ISDS cases and the basis for most successful investor claims.[15] There is a significant amount of ambiguity in the wording of FET clauses which creates uncertainty about the scope of protection provided. Tribunals have differed substantially on the extent to which they have interpreted the standard as requiring the stabilisation of the legal conditions concerning the investment at the time the investment is made and fulfillment of the investor's "legitimate expectations".[16] Tribunals that do not accept that FET "freezes" the applicable regulatory regime for the duration of the investment have still diverged on what kind of changes are acceptable. Some focus on the degree of the change

[10] Andrea Kay Bjorklund, 'The National Treatment Obligation' in Katia Yannaca-Small (ed), *Arbitration Under International Investment Agreements: A Guide to the Key Issues* (2nd edn, OUP 2018).

[11] J Anthony VanDuzer, 'The Complex Relationship between International Investment Law and Climate Change Initiatives: Exploring the Tension' in Panagiotis Delimatsis (ed), *Research Handbook on Climate Change and Trade Law* (Edward Elgar Publishing 2016) 443.

[12] Anne van Aaken and Tomer Broude, 'Ways of Reforming International Investment Agreements to Make them More Compatible with Climate Change Goals' in *OECD Public Consultation on Investment Treaties and Climate Change: Compilation of Submissions* <www.oecd.org/content/dam/oecd/en/topics/policy-sub-issues/investment-treaties/climate-alignment/2022-04%20Climate%20change%20consultation%20-%20compilation%20of%20submissions.pdf> accessed 7 June 2025.

[13] Fiona Marshall, Aaron Cosbey, and Deborah Murphy, 'Climate Change and International Investment Agreements: Obstacles or Opportunities?' (International Institute for Sustainable Development 2010).

[14] Valentina Vadi, 'Beyond Known Worlds: Climate Change Governance by Arbitral Tribunals?' (2015) 48 Vanderbelt Journal of Transnational Law 1285.

[15] Katia Yannaca-Small, 'Fair and Equitable Treatment: Have Its Contours Fully Evolved?' in Katia Yannaca-Small (ed), *Arbitration Under International Investment Agreements: A Guide to the Key Issues* (2nd edn, OUP 2018).

[16] Chen Yu, 'Disentangling Legal Stability from Legitimate Expectations: Towards Greater Deference to Regulatory Changes in Renewable Energy Transition Policies in Investment Arbitration' (2025) 24 World Trade Review 101.

only (such as was it "drastic" or "fundamental") while others question whether the change was "reasonable" or "proportionate" to the public policy objectives.[17]

Given that many proposed climate measures could be considered radical changes from the status quo, especially when viewed from the perspective of investors, there is potential for successful FET claims.[18] As noted by one arbitrator:

> [I]n an era where radical reforms in the energy sector are not only desirable but necessary for the sustainability of human life on Earth, it seems incongruous now to be interpreting the FET standard as requiring States to buy back their right to implement those reforms at the highest price . . . The regulatory chill that inevitably accompanies this approach will be no consolation to a warming planet.[19]

2.1.3 (Indirect) Expropriation

Historically, particularly in the immediate post-colonial period, the direct taking of property by a state through nationalisation or direct expropriation was a major problem for foreign investors. Such cases are now rare, although it is notable that the tribunal in *Rockhopper v Italy* found that a ban on offshore oil development constituted a direct expropriation.[20] Nevertheless, so-called indirect expropriation is now widely considered to be a more significant issue for investors and for policymakers. When considering whether a public policy measure amounts to an indirect expropriation, some tribunals have focused solely on the impact of the measure on the investor while others have weighed the impact against the purpose of the measure, considering the broad "police powers" held by states.[21]

Expropriation, whether direct or indirect, is lawful under investment treaties provided that several key conditions have been met. These are that the (indirect) expropriation is for a public purpose, is carried out with due process, is non-discriminatory, and is accompanied by the payment of compensation.[22]

2.1.4 Sunset Clauses

Sunset (or "survival") clauses are common in investment treaties and allow for investments already established at the time of termination to continue to benefit from the provisions in the agreement for a further five to twenty years.[23] For example, oil exploration company Rockhopper successfully sued Italy after the country had withdrawn from the ECT.[24] Sunset

[17] Federico Ortino, 'The Obligation of Regulatory Stability in the Fair and Equitable Treatment Standard: How Far Have We Come?' (2018) 21 Journal of International Economic Law 845.

[18] Manish Aggarwal and Ridhi Kabra, 'Regulating for Climate Change Without Breaching Investment Treaties' in Annette Magnusson and Anja Ipp (eds), *Investment Arbitration and Climate Change* (Kluwer Law International 2023).

[19] *Mathias Kruck, Frank Schumm, Joachim Kruck, Jürgen Reiss and others v Kingdom of Spain* [2022], ICSID Case No. ARB/15/23, Partial Dissenting Opinion of Zachary Douglas [54–57].

[20] Alessandra Arcuri, 'On How the ECT Fuels the Fossil Fuel Economy: Rockhopper v Italy as a Case Study' (2023) 7 Europe & the World: A law review 1.

[21] Aggarwal and Kabra (n 18).

[22] M Sornarajah, *The International Law on Foreign Investment* (CUP 2004).

[23] Arthur Lauvaux, 'Towards a Bumpy Ride into the Sunset: On the Mutual Termination of IIAs and their Sunset Clauses' (2022) 38 Arbitration International 203.

[24] Alessandra Arcuri, Kyla Tienhaara, and Lorenzo Pellegrini, 'Investment Law v. Supply-Side Climate Policies: Insights from *Rockhopper v. Italy* and *Lone Pine v. Canada*' (2024) 24 International Environmental Agreements: Politics, Law and Economics 193.

clauses are relevant to discussions around the reform of the investment regime in a timeframe consistent with the need for urgent climate action (see further Section 4).

2.2 The Process

ISDS is an ad hoc process whereby a panel of three arbitrators (one chosen by the state, one by the investor, and the third either agreed to by both parties, or appointed by an arbitral institution) determines whether a treaty has been breached and, if so, determines how much monetary compensation to award the investor. The procedural rules that govern disputes are most commonly those developed by the International Centre for the Settlement of Investment Disputes (ICSID) or the UN Commission on International Trade Law (UNCITRAL).

As noted in the introduction, ISDS was modelled on commercial arbitration where confidentiality and closed proceedings are considered critical to protecting business interests, in contrast with public legal forums where transparency and accessibility are important principles. While improvements have been made in the ICSID and UNCITRAL rules over time, it is still the case that not all ISDS proceedings are open to the public, not all awards are published, and the ability of third parties to participate is extremely limited.[25]

A separate set of concerns about the ISDS process relates to arbitrators, who have broad discretion to interpret investment treaties. Several studies have examined the incentive structure produced by the party-appointment system for arbitration and concerns that it may reduce arbitrator impartiality.[26] The practice of double-hatting—when an individual acts as legal representative for an investor in one ISDS case, while acting as an arbitrator in another—also raises serious concerns about conflicts of interest.[27] Other studies have highlighted the lack of diversity in the "pool" of commonly selected arbitrators, which might introduce cognitive biases in the system.[28] Expertise on climate science or policy is not a pre-requisite for appointment in a climate-relevant ISDS case.

[25] Nicolás Perrone, 'Investment Treaty Law and Matters of Recognition: Locating the Concerns of Local Communities' (2023) 24 Journal of World Investment and Trade 437; Ladan Mehranvar, 'How the International Investment Law Regime Undermines Access to Justice for Investment-Affected Stakeholders' (Columbia Center on Sustainable Investment, 2024) <https://scholarship.law.columbia.edu/sustainable_investment/29/> accessed 7 June 2025.

[26] Julian Donaubauer, Eric Neumayer, and Peter Nunnenkamp, 'Winning or Losing in Investor-to-State Dispute Resolution: The Role of Arbitrator Bias and Experience' (2018) 26 Review of International Economics 892; Daniel Behn and others, 'Evidence-Guided Reform: Surveying the Empirical Research on Arbitrator Bias and Diversity in Investor–State Arbitration' in Manfred Elsig, Rodrigo Polanco, and Peter van den Bossche (eds), *International Economic Dispute Settlement: Demise or Transformation?* (CUP 2021); Malcolm Langford, Daniel Behn, and Maria Chiara Malaguti, 'The Quadrilemma: Appointing Adjudicators in Future Investor–State Dispute Settlement' (2023) 14 Journal of International Dispute Settlement 149; Stavros Brekoulakis and Anna Howard, 'Impartiality and the Construction of Trust in Investor–State Dispute Settlement' (2023) 38 ICSID Review - Foreign Investment Law Journal 644.

[27] Malcolm Langford, Daniel Behn, and Runar Hilleren Lie, 'The Ethics and Empirics of Double Hatting' (2018) 6 European Society of International Law Reflection 7. While such conflicts can be challenged by a party to the dispute under the applicable arbitral rules, most challenges are dismissed (see Behn et al n 26). While these issues are of concern regardless of the subject of an ISDS case, it is worth noting that in a 2022 survey of the arbitration industry, 41% of respondents agreed that 'arbitrator bias and issue conflicts would present a major challenge' for resolving climate change related disputes; see 'Future of International Energy Arbitration Survey Report: 2022' (*Queen Mary University London*, 20 January 2023) <https://www.qmul.ac.uk/arbitration/media/arbitration/docs/Future-of-International-Energy-Arbitration-Survey-Report.pdf> accessed 7 June 2025.

[28] Mavluda Sattorova, *The Impact of Investment Treaty Law on Host States* (Bloomsbury 2018).

2.3 The Outcome

The outcome of an ISDS case is referred to as an award. If a tribunal finds that an investment treaty has been breached, the award will typically direct the state to pay monetary damages to compensate the investor. If a state fails to pay an arbitral award, the investor can have courts in countries that are signatories to the ICSID Convention or New York Convention—also known as the Convention on the Recognition and Enforcement of Foreign Arbitral Awards—enforce it through asset seizure. Tribunals have substantial leeway when it comes to determining the amount of compensation to award an investor as treaties typically provide little or no guidance on this subject. Monetary awards are therefore "dependent on the assumptions and philosophy of the adjudicating tribunal".[29] As noted by Dimopoulos, "the vast majority of tribunals consider that public policy, including environmental justifications, are irrelevant for the determination of the quantum of compensation".[30]

Many tribunals choose to award compensation based on what the income of a project might have been if it had proceeded without the interference from the government that was found to breach the investment treaty.[31] Using the discounted cash flow (DCF) method of valuation to assess this is particularly popular among arbitrators. This approach is especially problematic when used to evaluate projects that have yet to be built or to commence operation, because they have no history of profitability on which to base future projections. Arbitrators, who are trained in law rather than economics, have little understanding of DCF and must rely on expert reports submitted by the parties that may be deliberately misleading.[32] There have been concerns raised in a number of arbitrations about potential conflicts of interest between valuation experts and arbitrators.[33] The valuation will also be very sensitive to the discount rate that is applied and there is no standard that tribunals must follow in this regard.[34]

As a result of the use of DCF, there has been an increasing number of very large ISDS awards.[35] The average award over the last decade was US$385 million pre-interest, whereas it was only US$98 million in the period 2004–2013.[36] For cases involving oil and gas or mining

[29] Jason Pan, 'Valuation Standards for Calculating ICSID Awards' (2014) 14 Pepperdine Dispute Resolution Law Journal 355, 356.

[30] Angelos Dimopoulos, 'Climate Change and Investor–State Dispute Settlement: Identifying the Linkages' in Panagiotis Delimatsis (ed), *Research Handbook on Climate Change and Trade Law* (Edward Elgar Publishing 2016) 425.

[31] Jonathan Bonnitcha and Sarah Brewin, 'Compensation Under Investment Treaties' (International Institute for Sustainable Development 2020) <www.iisd.org/sites/default/files/publications/compensation-treaties-best-practicies-en.pdf> accessed 7 June 2025.

[32] Juan Carlos Boué, '"Lying with Numbers" in International Arbitration Against States' (2024) 15 Journal of International Dispute Settlement, 5.

[33] Jonathan Bonnitcha and others, 'Damages and ISDS Reform: Between Procedure and Substance' (2023) 14 Journal of International Dispute Settlement, 213.

[34] Boué (n 32); George Kahale, 'Submission to the OECD's Public Consultation on Investment Treaties and Climate Change' in *OECD Public Consultation on Investment Treaties and Climate Change: Compilation of Submissions* (2022) <www.oecd.org/content/dam/oecd/en/topics/policy-sub-issues/investment-treaties/climate-alignment/2022-04%20Climate%20change%20consultation%20-%20compilation%20of%20submissions.pdf> accessed 7 June 2025.

[35] Bonnitcha and Brewin (n 31).

[36] UNCTAD, 'Facts and Figures on Investor–State Dispute Settlement Cases' (IIA Issues Note 3/2024) <https://unctad.org/system/files/official-document/diaepcbinf2024d5_en.pdf> accessed 7 June 2025.; UNCTAD, 'Compensation and Damages in Investor–State Dispute Settlement Proceedings' (IIA Issues Note 1/2024) <https://unctad.org/publication/compensation-and-damages-investor-state-dispute-settlement-proceedings> accessed 7 June 2025.

investments, the average was US$609 million and US$527 million respectively (in the period 1990–2022).[37] Importantly, there is potential for the payment of ISDS awards to be "crippling" for some states.[38] For example, in 2019, just after receiving a US$6 billion loan from the International Monetary Fund (IMF) to deal with an economic crisis, Pakistan was ordered by an arbitral tribunal to pay mining investors US$5.8 billion in damages after they lost their ability to develop a copper and gold deposit.[39] The award was more than two times what the country spends per year on healthcare.[40] In addition to being crippling for the state, it was clearly a windfall for the investors. The award was more than twenty-five times the sunk costs of the investors (US$220 million)[41] and was almost twenty times the price recorded in an arm's-length transaction for the proposed mine.[42] The award against Pakistan, which has been aptly described as "a travesty",[43] could be viewed as an extreme case of arbitrator discretion gone awry. However, it must be noted that even smaller awards can be considered excessive if they are not grounded in a realistic assessment of what an investment is worth.[44] Furthermore, they can also be crippling, particularly if investors pile on, bringing multiple ISDS cases over one policy decision.[45]

2.4 Types of Climate-Relevant Claims

There is no consensus on how to categorise climate-relevant ISDS cases. This chapter is primarily concerned with what Fermeglia and others refer to as "stranded asset claims" that involve "claims for compensation following the *introduction* of climate justified policy measures which reduce the value of existing investments".[46] Notably, such claims can arise as a result of the introduction of either mitigation or adaptation measures.[47] These are distinguishable from cases concerning the *modification* of existing policies, such as a reduction in incentives for renewable energy investment or changes to rules around carbon markets.[48]

[37] Ian Clemence and Saleema Damji, 'PwC International Arbitration Damages Research 2023 Update' (*PwC*, 2023) <www.pwc.co.za/en/assets/pdf/international-arbitration-damages-study-2023.pdf> accessed 7 June 2025.

[38] Martins Paparinskis, 'Crippling Compensation in the International Law Commission and Investor–State Arbitration' (2022) 37 ICSID Review - Foreign Investment Law Journal 1.

[39] Bonnitcha and Brewin (n 31); Paparinskis (n 38).

[40] Jeffrey Sachs, 'How World Bank Arbitrators Mugged Pakistan' (*Project Syndicate*, 26 November 2019) <www.project-syndicate.org/commentary/world-bank-corrupt-arbitration-ruling-against-pakistan-by-jeffrey-d-sachs-2019-11> accessed 7 June 2025.

[41] Asif Shazad, 'Pakistan in Talks with Tethyan Copper to Resolve $5.8 Billion Dispute: Sources' (*Reuters*, 12 November 2020) <www.reuters.com/article/pakistan-mining-tethyan-idUSKBN27S2N7> accessed 7 June 2025.

[42] Juan Carlos Boué, 'The Investor–State Dispute Settlement Damages Playbook: To Infinity and Beyond' (2023) 24 Journal of World Investment and Trade 372.

[43] Boué (n 32).

[44] ibid.

[45] See, e.g., discussion of renewable energy cases brought against Spain in Section 2.4.

[46] Matteo Fermeglia and others, 'Mapping Climate-Related Investment Arbitrations' (2024) 21 Transnational Dispute Management 21, 8 (emphasis added).

[47] On the latter, see *Eco Oro Minerals Corp v Republic of Colombia* [2021] ICSID Case No. ARB/16/41, Decision on Jurisdiction, Liability and Directions on Quantum.

[48] Ladan Mehranvar and Sunayana Sasmal, 'The Role of Investment Treaties and Investor–State Dispute Settlement in Renewable Energy Investments' (Columbia Center for Sustainable Investment 2022); Paul Barker and Marisa Martin, 'Carbon Markets, Emissions Trading, and Investor–State Disputes' in Annette Magnusson and Anja Ipp (eds), *Investment Arbitration and Climate Change* (Kluwer Law International 2023).

Cases concerning the modification of climate policies are not discussed in any detail in this chapter.[49] However, it is worth briefly addressing the argument made by some observers that cases of this nature (particularly if they involve renewable energy investors) should be considered "positive" from a climate policy perspective. There is also an associated argument that ISDS is necessary for the energy transition because it will help to facilitate flows of foreign direct investment (FDI) in green sectors.[50] Two points in response merit consideration. First, available evidence does not support the conclusion that investment treaties are a useful mechanism to facilitate FDI in renewable energy, whereas there are other mechanisms (such as political risk insurance) that are proven to be effective.[51] Second, the fact that an ISDS case involves a renewable investor does not mean that the outcome of that case will be positive from a climate policy perspective. Governments need flexibility to experiment with policies and adapt them to changing economic conditions.[52] For example, Spain, when faced with a global economic crisis, adjusted its feed-in-tariff for renewable energy because it had become fiscally unsustainable. This led to more than fifty ISDS claims and over US $ 1.4 billion in liability by 2023.[53] As a consequence, public money that could have been directed to climate mitigation measures is instead being spent on compensating private actors, even though their investments continued to operate and make a profit.[54] This experience has no doubt contributed to the conclusion drawn by the Spanish government that ISDS will have a chilling impact on climate policy.[55] Recent cases arising in Honduras also highlight that renewable energy investors are not inherently more public-minded than investors in other sectors; solar investors are challenging the efforts of the current democratic government to alter contracts that were

[49] The author has addressed this issue in: Kyla Tienhaara and Christian Downie, 'Risky Business? The Energy Charter Treaty, Renewable Energy, and Investor–State Disputes' (2018) 24 Global Governance 451; Kyla Tienhaara, 'Does the Green Economy Need Investor–State Dispute Settlement?' in Kate Miles (ed), *Research Handbook on Environment and Investment Law* (Edward Elgar Publishing 2019).

[50] Guillermo Garcia-Perrote and Ella Wisniewski, 'Time for a Clean Energy Charter Treaty? Examining the Role of ISDS in Promoting and Protecting Renewable Energy Investments' in Alan M Anderson and Ben Beaumont (eds), *The Investor–State Dispute Settlement System: Reform, Replace or Status Quo?* (Kluwer Law International 2020).

[51] Josef C Brada, Zdenek Drabek, and Ichiro Iwasaki, 'Does Investor Protection Increase Foreign Direct Investment? A Meta-Analysis' (2021) 35 Journal of Economic Surveys 34; Mehranvar and Sasmal (n 48); Wolfgang Alschner, 'To Transform the International Investment Regime, Look to Political Risk Insurance and Not (Only) to Investment Treaties' (*Investment Treaty News*, 27 January 2025) <www.iisd.org/itn/2025/01/27/transform-international-investment-regime-political-risk-insurance-wolfgang-alschner/> accessed 7 June 2025.

[52] UNCTAD, 'Treaty-Based Investor–State Dispute Settlement Cases and Climate Action' (Issues Note 4/2022, September 2022) <https://unctad.org/system/files/official-document/diaepcbinf2022d7_en.pdf> accessed 7 June 2025.

[53] Debevoise and Plimpton, 'Courts Grapple with State Immunity as Spain Resists Enforcement of Arbitral Awards' (*Debevoise in Depth*, 7 September 2023) <www.debevoise.com/-/media/files/insights/publications/2023/09/07_courts-grapple-with-state-immunity-as-spain.pdf?rev=c13192b077af490d99157899e137be94&hash=45EE9F9368A9D165FBA49501BEE7E0AD> accessed 7 June 2025.

[54] Ladan Mehranvar and Lisa E Sachs, 'The Role and Relevance of Investment Treaties in Promoting Renewable Energy Investments' in Annette Magnusson and Anja Ipp (eds), *Investment Arbitration and Climate Change* (Kluwer Law International 2023).

[55] David Boyd 'Paying Polluters: The Catastrophic Consequences of Investor–State Dispute Settlement for Climate and Environment Action and Human Rights' Report of the Special Rapporteur on the Issue of Human Rights Obligations Relating to the Enjoyment of a Safe, Clean, Healthy and Sustainable Environment' (United Nations General Assembly 2023 A/78/168) <https://documents-dds-ny.un.org/doc/UNDOC/GEN/N23/205/29/PDF/N2320529.pdf?OpenElement> accessed 7 June 2025.

made under an authoritarian regime under improper procedures.[56] Mehranvar and Sachs conclude that the likely reason why proponents of ISDS contend that it is an important tool for the energy transition is that they are trying "to preserve the traditional investment regime in the face of shattering public trust".[57] In other words, they are deploying greenwashing tactics in an attempt to legitimise a deeply problematic and unpopular system.

Finally, in addition to claims that directly concern the introduction or modification of climate policies, there are a large number of ISDS cases that could be considered climate-relevant because they involve carbon intensive investments.[58] An example is the *Rockhopper* case where the government introduced a ban on offshore oil production in response to public pressure.[59] Public concern was largely focused on the potential for an oil spill to damage the local economy and environment, not the climate crisis per se. Nevertheless, the outcome of the case is highly relevant to climate policy in two key respects. First, Rockhopper's success may encourage other investors to challenge bans on fossil fuel development that are adopted to further climate mitigation goals and could dissuade governments from adopting or implementing such bans. Notably, the former Climate Minister of New Zealand has said that when the government was designing the country's ban on oil and gas exploration, they were cognisant of the rising number of ISDS cases targeting environmental regulations, and that the risk of litigation was repeatedly raised and discussed in cabinet. In response to this risk, the government did not implement a full ban on exploration (limiting it to offshore) and did not revoke any existing licences.[60] Second, the monetary awards that investors receive—which as discussed in Section 2.3 can go far beyond the amount invested in a project—can facilitate further fossil fuel developments that are incompatible with a 1.5 or 2°C pathway. This is what happened in the *Rockhopper* case where the investor was awarded over €250 million in damages and costs when it had only invested around €36 million in exploration.[61] Following the issuance of the award, the firm quickly announced that it would direct its winnings to oil exploration activities in the Falkland Islands.[62] To date, there have been at least 349 ISDS cases related to fossil fuel investments resulting in compensation of US$82.8 billion paid to the industry.[63]

3. ISDS and the Phase-Out of Coal

Coal has long been identified as the "dirtiest" fossil fuel and the first in line to be phased out. Coal-fired power plants are the single largest source of carbon emissions.[64] The IEA Net Zero

56 Luciana Ghiotto and others, 'The Corporate Assault on Honduras: Mafia-Style Investments and the Honduran People's Struggle for Democracy and Dignity' (Institute for Policy Studies 2024).

57 Mehranvar and Sachs (n 54).

58 UNCTAD (n 52) [2] also includes cases relating to other types of environmental policy measures as 'related to measures or sectors that are of direct relevance to climate action'.

59 *Rockhopper Italia S.p.A., Rockhopper Mediterranean Ltd, and Rockhopper Exploration Plc v Italian Republic*, ICSID Case No. ARB/17/14, Final Award (23 August 2022); Arcuri (n 20).

60 Phoebe Weston and Patrick Greenfield, 'Why fear of billion-dollar lawsuits stops countries phasing out fossil fuels' *The Guardian* (London, 6 March 2025).

61 Arcuri et al (n 24).

62 Rockhopper Exploration, 'Arbitration Award' (24 August 2023) <https://rockhopperexploration.co.uk/2022/08/successful-arbitration-outcome/> accessed 7 June 2025.

63 Lea Di Salvatore and others, 'Investor–State Dispute Settlements: A Hidden Handbrake on Climate Action' (International Institute for Environment and Development and Columbia Center on Sustainable Investment 2023) <www.iied.org/21971iied> accessed 7 June 2025.

64 Fatih Birol and David Malpass, 'It's Critical to Tackle Coal Emissions' (IEA, 8 October 2021) <www.iea.org/commentaries/it-s-critical-to-tackle-coal-emissions> accessed 7 June 2025.

by 2050 transition pathway requires that all unabated coal plants be retired by 2040 at the latest.[65] Sixty countries had committed by the end of 2024 to the Powering Past Coal Alliance which aims to phase out existing unabated coal power generation and end the development of new coal power stations without operational carbon capture and storage (CCS).[66] A number of Just Energy Transition Partnerships (JETPs) have been developed to help countries in the Global South finance the phase-out of coal power.[67]

Governments seeking to accelerate the phase-out of coal can either increase the cost of operations (such as through carbon pricing) or mandate plant closures. In some cases, both mechanisms may be deployed (such as carbon pricing being introduced, but if market forces do not act quickly enough then a mandated phase-out follows). The introduction of a carbon pricing scheme has not been a central issue in any ISDS cases to date. The regulatory shutdown approach has, in contrast, resulted in several claims.

3.1 The Netherlands

In December 2019, the Dutch Coal Ban Act entered into force.[68] The Act requires coal plants that have less than 44% efficiency to cease production by 1 January 2025. Newer, more efficient plants would have until 1 January 2030 to close or convert to alternative fuels.[69] The period between 20 December 2019 and 1 January 2030 when newer plants are permitted to continue operating without any new restrictions is referred to as a "transition period" and was created to allow companies to recover their initial investments. Monetary compensation would only be provided if a power plant operator is disproportionally affected by the ban and compensation to the operator would not be considered unlawful state aid under EU rules.[70]

Two German companies—RWE and Uniper—separately challenged the Coal Ban Act in ISDS claims launched under the ECT in 2021.[71] Both companies had recently built power plants that would have to be retired early. RWE's 1560 MW plant (Eemshaven) started operation in 2015, and the company claims it could operate "until 2055 or beyond".[72] Uniper's 1070 MW plant (Maasvlakte Power Plant 3) started operation in 2016, and the company claims that

[65] IEA, 'Net Zero by 2050' (IEA 2021) <www.iea.org/reports/net-zero-by-2050> accessed 7 June 2025.

[66] Powering Past Coal Alliance, 'Our Work' <https://poweringpastcoal.org/our-work/> accessed 7 June 2025.

[67] Jose A Ordonez and others, 'Just Energy Transition Partnerships and the future of coal' (2024) 14 Nature Climate Change 1026.

[68] IEA, 'Coal Ban Act' <www.iea.org/policies/18112-coal-ban-act> accessed 7 June 2025.

[69] RWE argued that conversion to 100% biomass is not viable, but this claim is undermined by the fact that RWE has another plant in the Netherlands that it has since converted to 100% biomass. See RWE, 'Amercentrale' <https://benelux.rwe.com/en/locations-and-projects/amer-power-plant/> accessed 7 June 2025.

[70] Bart-Jaap Verbeek, 'Compensation for stranded assets? German energy giants claim billions in public funds for loss-making Dutch coal-fired power plants' (*SOMO*, 28 April 2021) <www.somo.nl/compensation-for-stranded-assets> accessed 7 June 2025.

[71] In parallel with the ISDS claims, RWE and Uniper also launched claims in the Dutch courts under the European Convention on Human Rights. In November 2022, the claims were rejected by the Hague District Court, which found that the coal phase-out was foreseeable and that the companies had promised but failed to deliver substantial emissions reductions using biomass and CCS. See Yulia Levashova, 'Climate Litigation and Responsible Business Conduct in the Dutch District Court' (*Daily Jus*, 13 June 2023) <https://dailyjus.com/world/2023/06/climate-litigation-and-responsible-business-conduct-in-the-dutch-district-court> accessed 7 June 2025.

[72] *RWE AG and RWE Eemshaven Holding II BV v Kingdom of the Netherlands* (ICSID Case No ARB/21/4) Claimant's Memorial (18 December 2021).

in the absence of the ban, it could operate "until 2056 or beyond".[73] The companies describe the Coal Ban Act as a radical and fundamental change of policy that they could not have anticipated at the time of their investment, in breach of the articles on expropriation and FET in the ECT. The exact amount of compensation that each company claimed it was owed is redacted from their Memorials (i.e., the submissions that they made to the tribunals). However, RWE mentions more than once that the damages inflicted by the Netherlands "exceed EUR 1.4 billion, excluding interest"[74] and media reports suggest that Uniper was seeking €1 billion.[75]

Both the *RWE* and *Uniper* cases have been discontinued for different reasons. RWE dropped its case following a decision of a German court that it was contrary to EU law for a dispute between a European firm and an EU Member State to be resolved in investment arbitration.[76] A requirement for Uniper to withdraw its claim was included in a financial bail-out package from the German government.[77]

3.2 Germany

In 2020, Germany introduced a coal ban with two separate phase-out plans for hard coal and lignite and an overall objective of having all plants closed by 2038.[78] For the lignite industry, an agreement was negotiated that sets out the dates by which each plant is to be shut down. A compensation package of €4.35 billion accompanied the agreement. Under this agreement, companies waived their rights to bring ISDS claims over the phase-out.[79] The German government has, so far, not disclosed how the amounts of compensation paid to lignite operators were calculated and which assumptions they were based on, but has admitted that the waiver for ISDS claims was a factor that influenced the amount of compensation paid.[80] Several experts have suggested that the overall amount is excessive,[81] especially in light of the economic

73 *Uniper SE, Uniper Benelux Holding BV and Uniper Benelux NV v Kingdom of the Netherlands* (ICSID Case No. ARB/21/22), Claimant's Memorial (20 May 2022).

74 RWE (n 72).

75 Megan Darby, 'Coal Generator Uses Investment Treaty to Fight Netherlands Coal Phaseout' (*Climate Home News*, 21 May 2020) <www.climatechangenews.com/2020/05/21/uniper-uses-investment-treaty-fight-netherlands-coal-phaseout/> accessed 7 June 2025.

76 *RWE AG and RWE Eemshaven Holding II BV v Kingdom of the Netherlands* (ICSID Case No ARB/21/4) Order of the Tribunal Taking Note of the Discontinuance of the Proceeding and Decision on Costs (12 January 2024).

77 Sabin Center for Climate Law, 'Uniper v. the Netherlands' <https://climatecasechart.com/non-us-case/uniper-v-netherlands/> accessed 7 June 2025.

78 Hard coal, also known as black coal or anthracite, has the highest energy density of all types of coal and produces less CO_2 emissions per unit of energy produced than lignite, also known as brown coal. See USGS, 'What Are the Types of Coal?' <www.usgs.gov/faqs/what-are-types-coal> accessed 7 June 2025.

79 Amandine Van Den Berghe and Ida Westphal, 'The German Lignite Phase-Out Contract and Investment Arbitration' (*ClientEarth Briefing*, September 2020) <www.clientearth.org/media/vu5amwng/the-german-lignite-phase-out-contract-and-investment-arbitration-isds-ce-en.pdf> accessed 7 June 2025.

80 Nico Schmidt, 'Wie Schiedsgerichte Europas Klimaziele Bedrohen' (BuzzFeed News, 15 June 2023) <www.buzzfeed.de/recherchen/energiecharta-vertrag-schiedsgerichte-europa-klimaziele-90214917.html> accessed 7 June 2025 (translated using Google Translate).

81 Library of Congress, 'Germany: Law on Phasing-Out Coal-Powered Energy by 2038 Enters into Force' (31 August 2020) <www.loc.gov/item/global-legal-monitor/2020-08-31/germany-law-on-phasing-out-coal-powered-energy-by-2038-enters-into-force/> accessed 7 June 2025; Climate Action Network Europe and European Environmental Bureau, 'Money for Nothing? Commission Set to Release First Findingson Golden Handshake to German Lignite' <https://eeb.org/wp-content/uploads/2021/

difficulties that lignite power plants have faced in recent years.[82] For the hard coal sector, plants are to be shut down based on age with the opportunity for operators to receive an incentive payment if they voluntarily shut down earlier. The incentives are provided through a reverse-auction system. In this system, powerplant operators who are willing to close early make bids for compensation and the government accepts the lowest bids.[83] Those that do not bid, or do not have their bids accepted, are forced to close after a specific date with no compensation.

In 2023, Azienda Elettrica Ticinese (AET), a legal entity wholly owned by the Swiss Canton of Ticino and a shareholder in the Lünen hard coal power plant, filed an ISDS claim against the German government under the ECT. The shareholders of the plant, which other than AET are primarily German, opted not to participate in the reverse-auction system. AET complains that it has not been compensated for measures that will cause the Lünen Plant, which commenced operation in 2013, to be shut down in 2031, twenty years before the end of its economic life. AET argues that the closure will occur before they "will have even repaid the loans taken on for its construction".[84] AET argues that the coal ban breaches several provisions of the ECT, including those on non-discrimination, FET, and expropriation. On non-discrimination, AET emphasises the more favourable treatment received by lignite power plants as well as older hard coal power plants which can reasonably expect to recoup their investment costs prior to closure.

The damages requested by AET are calculated using the DCF method and amount to €85.5 million plus interest for an alleged €23 million investment in a plant that has recorded losses every year since it began operations.[85] This claim was pending at the time of writing.

3.3 Canada

In 2015, the government of the Province of Alberta launched a Climate Leadership Plan, which included a carbon pricing mechanism and a phase out of coal-fired electricity generation by 2030. At the time there were eighteen coal-fired generating plants, twelve of which were scheduled to close prior to 2030. The remaining six would have to convert to other fuel sources or technologies to remain open. Alberta made "Off-Coal Agreements" with the three owners of these six plants and provided Transition Payments, based on the book value of each plant. The total amount paid out was CAD$1.36 billion. The payments were conditioned on commitments from the companies to continue to participate in Alberta's electricity market (such as by switching to gas fired power production or renewable energy).[86]

04/Media-advisory-_State-aid-for-German-lignite_-CANE_EEB_April_2021_final.pdf> accessed 7 June 2025.

82 David Jones, 'The Cash Cow Has Stopped Giving: Are Germany's Lignite Plants Now Worthless?' (Sandbag 2019) <https://thecoalhub.com/wp-content/uploads/2019/08/2019-Cash-Cow-report-1.3.pdf> accessed 7 June 2025.

83 Raam Tambe, 'Investor State Dispute Settlement and Net Zero Initiatives: Case Study of Germany's Coal Exit Auctions' (2024) 25 Chicago Journal of International Law 301.

84 *Azienda Elettrica Ticinese v Federal Republic of Germany* (ICSID Case. No. ARB/23/47), Claimant's Memorial (26 July 2024) [12].

85 Fabian Flues, 'Dangerous Precedent: How an Arbitration Claim is Jeopardising Germany's Coal Phase-Out' (Powershift, April 2025) <https://power-shift.de/wp-content/uploads/2025/05/AET-ISDS-arbitraton-Germany-coal-exit-energy-charter_web.pdf> accessed 7 June 2025.

86 Lauren Vriens, 'The End of Coal: Alberta's Coal Phase-Out" (IISD 2018) <www.iisd.org/publications/report/end-coal-albertas-coal-phase-out> accessed 7 June 2025.

At the time, Westmoreland Coal Company was the owner of three mine-mouth coal mines in Alberta. Mine-mouth coal operations are mines developed near a power plant for the purpose of supplying coal to the plant. Two of Westmoreland's mines were adjacent to coal plants that were directly impacted by the phase-out. The coal power phase-out was a de facto coal mining phase-out given the logistical challenge of exporting coal from Alberta (which is landlocked) to a viable market as well as the low prices globally for the commodity. In addition, according to Westmoreland, carbon pricing measures had the effect of accelerating the phase-out. By June 2024, coal-powered electricity had been completely phased-out in Alberta, more than five years ahead of schedule.[87]

Westmoreland Coal Company filed an ISDS claim in 2018.[88] This case was withdrawn by the company in 2019, because it had filed for bankruptcy in the US and was going through restructuring. A second case was filed by a different corporate entity (Westmoreland Mining Holdings) in the same year. This case was dismissed at the jurisdictional phase with the tribunal finding that the company had not been the investor at the time that the dispute arose.[89] In 2022, the original corporate entity (Westmoreland Coal Company) filed a new claim which was also dismissed at the jurisdictional stage for technical reasons.[90]

The company sought damages exceeding CAD$470 million in its first two claims but did not quantify them in its third. In each case, the company argued that through Alberta's coal-fired power phase out, Canada had breached articles on national treatment and FET. In its 2022 claim, the company added a claim of expropriation. With respect to national treatment, the company focused on the fact that the power companies that had received transition payments were all Canadian, whereas it, an American firm, had not received any compensation.

3.4 Australia

In 2020, Waratah Coal, an Australian mining company owned by billionaire and former Australian politician Clive Palmer, had its applications for a mining lease and environmental approval for a coal project in the Galilee Basin referred to the Land Court of Queensland. In 2022, in a historic decision, the Court recommended that these applications should be refused.[91] The decision was partially grounded on the basis that coal from the mine would generate significant carbon emissions (1.58 billion tonnes), which in turn would exacerbate climate change and thereby undermine human rights, including the rights of Indigenous peoples and children. The Queensland government was not bound by this ruling but choose to follow the court's recommendation and refused to issue the necessary permits for the mine.

In October 2023, Zeph Investments (a company registered in Singapore) filed an ISDS claim under the Singapore-Australia Free Trade Agreement. Zeph Investments had acquired (in 2019) 100% of the shares in Mineralogy Canada Acquisition Corp., which in turn owned

[87] Government of Canada, 'Powering Past Coal Alliance: Phasing Out Coal' <www.canada.ca/en/services/environment/weather/climatechange/canada-international-action/coal-phase-out.html> accessed 7 June 2025.

[88] Government of Canada, 'Westmoreland Coal Company v. Government of Canada (2018)' <www.international.gc.ca/trade-agreements-accords-commerciaux/topics-domaines/disp-diff/westmoreland-02.aspx?lang=eng> accessed 7 June 2025.

[89] *Westmoreland Mining Holdings, LLC v Canada* (ICSID Case No. UNCT/20/3) Award (31 January 2022).

[90] *Westmoreland Coal Company v Government of Canada* (ICSID Case No. UNCT/23/2) Award (17 December 2024).

[91] *Waratah Coal Pty Ltd v Youth Verdict Ltd & Ors (No 6)* [2022] QLC 21.

Waratah Coal. The company is seeking AUD$69 billion in compensation for the rejection of its applications for its proposed mine. The Notice of Intent claims that Australia has breached the FET standard and has expropriated Zeph's investment. The Notice criticises the Land Court decision and characterises the judge, who is regarded as a highly distinguished jurist and expert in environmental law,[92] "as a political appointee with an anti-coal, pro-climate change activist agenda . . . [who has] publicly expressed her support for the extremist climate change action organisation 'Extinction Rebellion'".[93]

Zeph appears to now be pursuing this claim, along with two other ones, under a different treaty: the Association of Southeast Asian Nations (ASEAN)-Australia-New Zealand Free Trade Agreement (AANZFTA). In one case, Zeph is seeking approximately AUD$41 billion in damages. Because the Notice of Arbitration has not been made public, it is difficult to ascertain the precise nature of the claims in this case. However, it has been revealed in a procedural order that the complaint concerns a decision by the Government of Queensland to grant another company an environmental offset in an area where Waratah Coal had mineral exploration licences.[94] The final claim under AANZFTA relates to the refusal of the Queensland Government to approve the development of a 1.4GW coal-fired power station on a cattle property near the town of Alpha in the Galilee Basin. This plant would have sourced coal from the mine that was rejected. Zeph has estimated the value of the project at approximately AUD$10.1 billion. All three claims are pending.[95]

3.5 Analysis

One observation that can be drawn from these cases is that different models of phase-out plans do not appear to insulate governments from investor claims. The Dutch government provided a transition period and an opportunity to change the fuel used in power plants and was sued for not providing monetary compensation. The German government utilised a reverse-auction system, which experts have suggested could reduce the risk of legal action,[96] and was sued for not providing adequate monetary compensation. The government of Alberta provided monetary compensation to power plants but was nevertheless sued by a coal mining firm. The

[92] Stephen Long, 'Who Knew Queensland's Richest Man is a Foreign Investor?' (*Australia Institute*, 24 November 2023) <https://australiainstitute.org.au/post/who-knew-queenslands-richest-man-is-a-foreign-investor/> accessed 7 June 2025.

[93] Zeph Investments, 'Notice of Intent to Commence Arbitration' (20 October 2023) <www.ag.gov.au/sites/default/files/2023-10/notice-of-intention-to-commence-arbitration-zeph-20-october-2023.pdf> accessed 7 June 2025, 5.

[94] Environmental offsetting is utilised in Australia as a mechanism to reduce the impact of economic activities such as mining on threatened ecosystems and species (see further: Government of Australia, 'Environmental Offsets Under the EPBC Act' <https://www.dcceew.gov.au/environment/epbc/approvals/offsets, accessed 7 June 2025).

[95] These three claims are distinct from a fourth case brought by Zeph Investments over an iron-ore project in West Australia. In November 2024, the parties agreed to temporarily suspend proceedings in the three coal-related arbitrations until a jurisdictional ruling is made by the tribunal in the iron-ore case. Australia's jurisdictional objection in the iron-ore case, which would equally apply in the others, is that Zeph Investments is a 'form of corporate façade with no substantive business operations of its own in Singapore'. *Zeph Investments Pte Ltd v Commonwealth of Australia*, Australia's Statement on Preliminary Objections (22 January 2024); See also: Government of Australia, 'International Trade and Investment Law'<www.ag.gov.au/international-relations/international-law/international-trade-and-investment-law> accessed 7 June 2025.

[96] Silvana Tiedemann and Finn Müller-Hansen, 'Auctions to Phase Out Coal Power: Lessons Learned from Germany' (2023) 174 Energy Policy 113387, 11.

Queensland government rejected a coal mine and a power plant on climate grounds before either had commenced construction (thus preventing the assets from becoming stranded in the transition away from coal) and was sued. The only mechanism adopted in these countries that has not been challenged in arbitration is the payment of compensation to lignite power plants in Germany, where the government negotiated an ISDS waiver with plant owners. As these payments have been viewed by many as overly generous, a concern that arises from the German experience is that the best way to avoid ISDS is to commit to large payments to foreign investors. This diverts public money from better uses and creates moral hazard.

Several further patterns emerge in the pleadings of the parties in these cases.

3.5.1 The Right to Compensation versus the Right to Regulate

Investors in the cases reviewed are quick to point out that they are not challenging the existence of climate change or the need to address it. Instead, they frame their claims as being about a right to compensation. For example, in nearly identical wording to RWE's Memorial in its case against the Netherlands (they employed the same law firm), AET argues in its case against Germany that:

> The dispute is neither about the existence of climate change and its consequences, nor is it about contesting the need to reduce CO2 emissions or even a State's right—in principle—to prohibit the firing of coal. It is instead about a very simple issue: if a State forces an investor to sacrifice its lawful investment for the public benefit, then the State has to pay compensation. This is a tenet not only of the Energy Charter Treaty (ECT), but of investment protection in general.[97]

While investors frame the right to compensation as straightforward, a duty to compensate is only mentioned in international investment treaties in provisions on expropriation. Furthermore, even with expropriation, many argue that there are exceptions for measures that fall within a state's police powers, which the respondents in the cases reviewed highlight. Germany goes even further to argue that a "measure that implements obligations under the Paris Agreement cannot trigger compensation duties. Otherwise, the risk of liability may create a chilling effect".[98]

Respondent states also detail their reasons for not providing compensation or for limiting it to certain groups. For example, in the Netherlands, the decision not to provide monetary compensation was explained as follows:

> In view of the foreseeability of CO_2 reduction measures for the power plants as early as 2005, the "polluter pays" principle, the possibility for the owners of the power plants to continue generating electricity using fuels other than coal and the generous transition periods offered by this bill, the cabinet believes that there is a "fair balance" between the public interest served by this ban and the interest of the owners of the power plants affected by the regulation of their property. This bill therefore does not a priori provide for additional detriment compensation beyond the transitional periods already offered.[99]

In Germany, the government notes that it had a duty to avoid unnecessary public spending and furthermore wanted to avoid setting a precedent for unwarranted compensation that might be

[97] *AET* Memorial (n 84) [6].

[98] *Azienda Elettrica Ticinese v Federal Republic of Germany* (ICSID Case. No. ARB/23/47), Respondent's Counter-Memorial (26 March 2025) [419].

[99] *RWE AG and RWE Eemshaven Holding II BV v Kingdom of the Netherlands* (ICSID Case No ARB/21/4) Claimant's Memorial (18 December 2021) [303].

invoked in other regulated industries in the future.[100] Germany also argues that the legislator "had to undertake a complex balancing exercise" which included not only consideration of reducing emissions but also "the security of energy supply as well as jobs and social peace" to explain why lignite investors were provided with a negotiated compensation package.[101] Similarly, Canada stressed that Alberta's goal in providing power plants with payments was to maintain reliable electricity provision through the transition.[102]

3.5.1.1 *Neoliberal Ideology*

Several of the claims made by investors in these cases reflect a neoliberal approach to climate policy which emphasises the importance of efficiency (i.e., promoting the cheapest policy option rather than one that will be most effective in quickly driving down emissions or that will be the most equitable in terms of the distribution of costs and benefits) and relies on technological optimism and the promise of carbon markets.[103] It appears that investors are attempting to frame their claims in a way that would avoid them being categorised as climate deniers. In other words, they are not claiming that legislators do not have a reason to act. Instead, they are putting forward an argument for *how* they should act.

In terms of technology, several investors bemoan in their pleadings that governments did not provide more subsidies for CCS to allow coal power plants to continue operating. This is nothing new; companies have been relying on the prospect of CCS to try to persuade governments that coal can be "clean" for close to two decades.[104] Indeed, it is worth noting that the Netherlands and Germany point out that a significant factor in the decision to allow new coal plants to be built in the 2010s was the expectation (reinforced through lobbying) that CCS would allow them to remain viable in a carbon-constrained world.

With respect to carbon markets, RWE, Uniper, and AET all argue that the Netherlands and Germany respectively should reduce emissions through the EU Emissions Trading Scheme, rather than mandating the closure of coal plants. Germany counters this argument by indicating that the country never promised to address climate change solely through market measures, which "would only reach so far to limit global warming".[105] Westmoreland is the only investor that directly challenges carbon pricing in its claim, presumably because in this case the policy was effective in accelerating the phase-out of coal power in Alberta.

From a public policy perspective, it is questionable for arbitrators—with no expertise in climate policy and no accountability to the public—to be deliberating on the most effective/efficient/equitable mechanisms for governments to deploy in response to the climate crisis. Furthermore, investors should not be able to use investment treaties to lock-in neoliberal approaches, which may have been adopted following lobbying efforts by industry (to stave off stricter forms of regulation), in the face of increasing evidence that those approaches are significantly limited in their effectiveness in addressing climate change.[106]

[100] *AET* Counter-Memorial (n 98) [211].
[101] ibid [4].
[102] Vriens (n 86).
[103] See further Peter Newell and Matthew Paterson, *Climate Capitalism: Global Warming and the Transformation of the Global Economy* (CUP 2010).
[104] Richard Conniff, 'The Myth of Clean Coal' (*Yale Environment 360*, 2 June 2008) <https://e360.yale.edu/features/the_myth_of_clean_coal> accessed 7 June 2025.
[105] *AET* Counter-Memorial (n 98) [73].
[106] For further discussion of how investors create the conditions for investment (through lobbying and (dis)information campaigns) that they then seek to have stabilised through investment law, see Kyla Tienhaara and Fergus Green, 'Climate Obstruction and Capital Accumulation by Feigned Victimization: TC Energy and the Political Economy of Investor–State Dispute Settlement' (2025) Business & Politics 1.

3.5.5.2 *Speculative Futures*

The speculative nature of each of the claims reviewed is notable. The coal plants in Canada, the Netherlands, and Germany had not yet been shut down by phase-out policies when the cases were launched. This adds a new dimension to the "crystal ball" critique of arbitration.[107] Typically, tribunals look into the future to speculate about lost profits. However, in the cases reviewed, the tribunals are tasked with looking into the future to first assess the more fundamental question of whether the treaty *will be breached* and then applying that finding to determine state liability in the present. For example, the Netherlands argued that any ISDS claim from a coal plant owner should be commenced in 2030 when "assessment can be made based on fact rather than assumption".[108] If tribunals are prepared to speculate about future breaches of treaties, this overreach of authority will have significant implications for climate policy and the energy transition. The purpose of having a *transition* is to ensure that change is gradual to minimise economic disruption and to allow for careful planning and sound investment decisions. Investor claims that challenge long-term planning could have a chilling effect on such efforts.

The speculative aspect of these claims is even more pronounced when one considers market factors. Each of the projects, including the coal mines in Canada and Australia,[109] had the potential to become uneconomic in the absence of government efforts to phase out coal. Indeed, the plants in the Netherlands and Germany had recorded losses in the years leading up to the phase-outs in those countries.[110] Other policy measures, particularly carbon pricing, may be playing some role in the economics of the investments in question, but it is also the case that the cost of alternative sources of energy has drastically fallen in recent years and developing a new renewable energy project is now cheaper than running an existing coal plant in most parts of the world.[111] What these cases demonstrate is that having an unprofitable investment does not lessen an investor's willingness to make a claim for compensation, it may even increase it. ISDS is, perhaps, viewed by investors as an eleventh-hour option to squeeze some final profits out of a dying industry.

[107] George Kahale, 'Keynote Address' (8th Investment Treaty Arbitration Conference, Prague, 23 October 2018) <www.bilaterals.org/IMG/pdf/keynote_address_by_george_kahale_iii.pdf> accessed 7 June 2025.

[108] *RWE AG and RWE Eemshaven Holding II BV v Kingdom of the Netherlands* (ICSID Case No ARB/21/4) Respondent's Counter-Memorial (5 September 2022) [22].

[109] Waratah Coal's own expert witness in the Land Court case assessed potential revenue from the project at AUD$25.5 billion and noted that after capital and operating costs, the project could be a loss maker. See BIS Oxford Economics, 'Galilee Coal Project: Cost-Benefit and CGE Analysis' (2022) <https://australiainstitute.org.au/wp-content/uploads/2023/01/Tessler-2022-Galilee-Coal-Project-Cost-Benefit-and-CGE-Analysis-BIS-Oxford-Economics-March-2022.pdf> accessed 7 June 2025; *Westmoreland Mining Holdings, LLC v Canada* (ICSID Case No. UNCT/20/3) Statement of Defence (26 June 2020).

[110] Verbeek (n 70); Sarah Brown, 'German State Awards €317 Million To Loss-Making Coal Plants' (*Ember*, 8 December 2020) <https://ember-energy.org/latest-insights/german-state-awards-e317-million-to-loss-making-coal-plants/#:~:text=Eleven%20hard%20coal%20plants%20will,in%20the%20last%20two%20years> accessed 7 June 2025.

[111] Matt Gray, 'How to Waste Over Half a Trillion Dollars: The Economic Implications of Deflationary Renewable Energy for Coal Power Investments' (*CarbonTracker*, 12 March 2020) <https://carbontracker.org/reports/how-to-waste-over-half-a-trillion-dollars/> accessed 7 June 2025.

4. Conclusion

Government measures to phase out coal have been challenged in four different countries. These early examples of the clash between climate policy and investment law are the "canary in the coalmine"; we can expect many more disputes of this nature as the energy transition proceeds. To be clear, all the claims reviewed in this chapter may be (or might have been, if the cases had not been discontinued) rejected on the merits by a tribunal. However, even if states "win" coal phase-out cases, it will be important to examine the tribunals' reasoning carefully. If tribunals determine that the coal assets in question were effectively worthless even in the absence of a phase-out policy, and refuse to award compensation on that basis, then this will not signal to states that they have the policy space to phase-out other, more valuable, carbon-intensive investments. What is needed from tribunals, to prevent regulatory chill, is crystal clear statements that asset holders do not have a right to compensation when their assets are stranded by climate policies. Even then, the lack of a system of precedent in arbitration will leave policymakers with significant uncertainty.

This leads logically to the conclusion that the investment regime needs to be either radically reformed or phased out to protect climate policy space. Incremental reforms have already been adopted and found wanting. For example, some countries have introduced clarifying language and exceptions clauses in new treaties which aim to limit the ability of arbitrators to creatively interpret provisions in ways that benefit investors and circumscribe the policy space of governments.[112] Unfortunately, this approach neglects to address the main source of ISDS cases which is the large stock of "old" investment treaties.[113] Furthermore, changes in wording do not appear to have had a significant impact on arbitral interpretations of key provisions.[114]

One option for more substantial reform under discussion at the OECD and elsewhere is to introduce carve-outs of climate policy and/or the fossil fuel sector from the scope of investment treaty coverage.[115] Carve-outs have already been deployed in investment treaties to remove protection for other harmful investments and to protect state sovereignty in sensitive areas (such as tobacco control and tax policy). For states interested in pursuing the modification of existing treaties to introduce climate carve-outs, it would be most efficient to negotiate a multilateral or plurilateral agreement, rather than in many separate bilateral talks.[116]

Another option is to carve out ISDS from investment treaties. When the North American Free Trade Agreement (NAFTA) was renegotiated, Canada and the US excised ISDS from their reciprocal relationship. Other countries have effectively achieved an ISDS carve-out through

112 UNCTAD, 'The International Investment Treaty Regime and Climate Action' (2022) IIA Issues Note 3/2022 <https://unctad.org/system/files/official-document/diaepcbinf2022d6_en.pdf> accessed 7 June 2025.

113 Lauge Poulsen and Geoffrey Gertz, 'Reforming the Investment Treaty Regime: A 'Backward-Looking' Approach' (Chatham House, The Royal Institute of International Affairs, 2021).

114 Alschner (n 8).

115 Joshua Paine and Elizabeth Sheargold, 'A Climate Change Carve-Out for Investment Treaties' (2023) 26 Journal of International Economic Law 285; Ana Novik and David Gaukrodger, 'Future of Investment Treaties Track 1: Investment Treaties and Climate Change: Methods to Align Investment Treaty Benefits for Energy Investment with the Paris Agreement and Net Zero' (OECD 2024).

116 Helionor de Anzizu and Nikki Reisch, 'Overcoming International Investment Agreements as a Barrier to Climate Action: A Toolkit to Safeguard Fossil Fuel Measures from Investment Treaty Claims' (Center for International Environmental Law 2024) <www.ciel.org/wp-content/uploads/2024/02/Overcoming-International-Investment-Agreements-as-a-Barrier-to-Climate-Action.pdf> accessed 7 June 2025.

side letters with treaty partners; for example, this is the approach taken by New Zealand in the Comprehensive and Progressive Agreement for a Trans-Pacific Partnership and other regional treaties. Removing ISDS leaves the investment provisions in treaties enforceable through state–state dispute settlement, which is not ideal but is preferable to the status quo because states are more publicly accountable than corporations and most have made clear commitments to address climate change under the Paris Agreement.

Finally, there is the option for states to terminate or withdraw from investment treaties. For example, both Germany and the Netherlands (along with many other EU members) have withdrawn from the ECT. Sunset clauses can limit the impact of termination, but it is possible to negotiate the nullification of these clauses. This was the approach taken in an Intra-EU BIT Termination Agreement that was developed in the EU following a court ruling that BITs are incompatible with EU law.[117] There are now similar proposals to neutralise the sunset clause among countries withdrawing from the ECT.[118]

While these examples demonstrate promise, radical reform and termination efforts are currently being approached in a piecemeal fashion and, too often, countries in the Global North are acting in a defensive manner to preserve their own policy space without consideration of the needs of the Global South. The future of humanity depends upon *all* governments acting with urgency to direct their economies on a path of rapid transformation. As we travel down this path, it is imperative that investment law gets out of the way.

117 ibid.

118 Lukas Schaugg and Suzy Nikièma, 'Model Inter Se Agreement to Neutralize the Survival Clause of the Energy Charter Treaty Between the EU and Other non-EU Contracting Parties' (IISD, 2024) <www.iisd.org/publications/brief/energy-charter-treaty-survival-clause> accessed 7 June 2025.

CHAPTER 29

Corporate Sustainability and the European Union

BARBARA POZZO

1. Introduction

TODAY, European legislation on corporate sustainability consists of a large and complex body of regulations that is broken down into technical rules in various sectors and has developed gradually over time. To understand the deep roots of this evolution we have to go back in time, to the beginning of this story.

In 1957, the Treaty establishing the European Economic Community did not provide for any specific community competence in environmental matters, which was only introduced in 1987 with the Single European Act.[1]

With the Maastricht Treaty (Treaty),[2] the foundation treaty of the EU in 1992, the principle of sustainable development was introduced in Article 2: "The Community has the task of promoting . . . a harmonious and balanced development of economic activities throughout the Community, sustainable, non-inflationary and environmentally friendly growth."

Today, the Treaty presents the principle of sustainable development in various provisions. Beyond its mention in the Preamble, Article 3 establishes this principle in relation to both the internal market and Europe's international role in promoting sustainable development worldwide. Article 21 also states that sustainable development will play a key role in the EU's external activities. In particular, the EU must define and pursue common policies and actions and work towards a high degree of cooperation in all fields of international relations. The primary objective is to promote sustainable economic, social, and environmental development in developing countries, with the goal of eradicating poverty. Additionally, the EU must contribute to developing international measures that preserve and improve environmental quality and ensure sustainable management of global natural resources.

The principle of sustainable development is further emphasised in Article 37 of the Charter of Fundamental Rights, which is dedicated to the environment, and which states: "A high level of environmental protection and the improvement of the quality of the environment must be integrated into the policies of the Union and ensured in accordance with the principle of sustainable development." It is no coincidence that starting from these years, the protection of the environment and the principle of sustainable development also entered the Constitutions of the Member States, thus taking root as a value superior to ordinary laws.[3]

[1] Single European Act [1987] OJ L 169, 1.

[2] Consolidated Version of the Treaty on European Union [2008] OJ C115/13, 1.

[3] Barbara Pozzo, 'La tutela dell'ambiente nelle Costituzioni. Profili di diritto comparato alla luce dei nuovi principi introdotti dalla Carta di Nizza', Barbara Pozzo and Mauro Renna (eds), *L'ambiente nel nuovo Titolo V della Costituzione* (Giuffrè 2004), 6.

The idea behind the principle of sustainable development seems simple in theory: It is about leaving future generations with at least the same level of opportunities that we had. As stated in the Brundtland Report: "Sustainable development is development that meets the needs of the present without compromising the ability of future generations to meet their own needs."[4] On the other hand, it is more difficult to determine which legislative measures should be adopted and what is the right mix of legal instruments (between public and private law) to achieve this magical point of equilibrium between today's and tomorrow's needs.[5] To give consistency to this principle, the EU has integrated sustainable development into its policies and legislation. In 2001,[6] it implemented a specific EU Strategy for Sustainable Development, in which the European Commission (Commission) stated that economic growth, social cohesion, and environmental protection must go hand in hand. The strategy called for better coordination among policies addressing the economic, environmental, and social dimensions of sustainability, while launching the global role of the EU in this field.

The EU 2020 Strategy[7] was published in the aftermath of the economic crisis of 2008, focusing on three priorities for the development to 2020: (1) smart growth, with the aim of developing an economy based on knowledge and innovation; (2) sustainable growth, with a focus on promoting a more resource efficient, greener and more competitive economy; and (3) inclusive growth, with the target of fostering a high-employment economy delivering economic, social and territorial cohesion.

Finally, in 2019, the EU's Better Regulation Agenda[8] was published. The introduction of better regulation principles had its origins in the desire for better European governance, and for anchoring sustainable development in the EU's policymaking by looking at economic, social, and environmental impacts together.

2. A Strategic Turn: From Command-and-Control to Market-Based Instruments

As far as the tools for achieving sustainable growth are concerned, it is worth remembering that at the end of the last century there was an important turning point.

Since the early 1990s, the Commission has adopted a revised approach, stemming from an investigation conducted by the European Environment Agency entitled "Environment in the European Union at the turn of the century".[9] This investigation showed that the large number of environmental directives that had come into force up to that point had not achieved the

[4] Gro Brundtland, *Our Common Future* (OUP 1987).

[5] Edith Brown-Weiss, *Fairness to Future Generation: International Law, common patrimony and intergenerational Equity* (Transnational Publishers 1989); Daniel A Farber and Paul A Hemmersbaugh, 'The Shadow of the Future: Discount Rates, Later Generations, and the Environment' [1993] 46 Vanderbilt Law Review 267.

[6] European Commission, *Communication from the Commission: A Sustainable Europe for a Better World: A European Union Strategy for Sustainable Development* (Brussels, 15 May 2001) COM (2001) 264 final.

[7] Communication from the Commission, 'Europe 2020: A strategy for smart, sustainable and inclusive growth' Brussels, 3.3.2010 COM (2010) 2020.

[8] 'Better Regulation: Taking Stock and Sustaining Our Commitment', European Commission, 15 April 2019.

[9] European Environment Agency, *Environment in the European Union at the Turn of the Century* (Environmental Assessment Report No 2/1999, Luxembourg, 20 June 1999) <http://www.eea.europa.eu/publications/92-9157-202-0> accessed 29 June 2025.

desired results in terms of environmental protection. The reasons provided in this regard by the report were many: the limited national implementation of European standards, the limited application of these standards, and the limited enforceability of environmental protection standards by citizens.

Faced with this situation, the Commission has over time developed new environmental policy instruments and has become more inclined to evaluate the potential of private law in this sector, in the various Action Programmes that have followed one another to date.

With the Fifth Environmental Action Programme adopted in 1992 entitled "Towards Sustainability" (Fifth Action Programme), the Commission considered the expansion of the range of policy instruments.[10] To guide the change in the approach to environmental problems and encourage a spirit of "shared responsibility", the Commission has emphasised the need to propose a wider range of tools that can enable companies to participate more in a process of raising awareness of environmental issues.[11]

It is worthwhile mentioning that since then, the Commission has adopted an approach that "reflects the growing realisation in industry and in the business world that not only is industry a significant part of the (environmental) problem but it must also be part of the solution".[12]

The traditional instruments of environmental policy—those based on the command-and-control model—were supplemented by so-called market instruments, that seek to address the market failure of "environmental externalities" either by incorporating the external cost of production or consumption activities through taxes or charges on processes or products, or by creating property rights and facilitating the establishment of a proxy market for the use of environmental services.

In assessing the Fifth Action Programme, the Commission referred explicitly to taxes, charges, specific environmental incentives, trading systems, eco-labelling and environmental accounting programmes, regulations governing liability for damage caused to the environment, and finally, environmental agreements.[13]

The Sixth Environment Action Programme launched new strategies for the period 2002–2010.[14] The Commission announced that one of the objectives of environmental policy was to make the market work in favour of the environment, through better co-operation with businesses, introducing incentive systems for companies with the best environmental

[10] [1993] OJ C 138/5.

[11] Fifth European Community Environment Programme: Towards Sustainability, European Commission, [1993] OJ C 138/70, 7.

[12] ibid 19.

[13] Commission of the European Communities, Communication from the Commission, Europe's Environment: What Directions for the Future? The Global Assessment of the European Community Programme of Policy and Action in relation to the Environment and Sustainable Development, 'Towards Sustainability' COM (1999) 543 final. In the following Communication, entitled: Europe's environment: What directions for the future?, which offered an intermediate report on the application of the programme, the Commission noted that the previous five years had seen the implication of many new initiatives in the Member States to incentivise the use of market instruments, recognising that the new policies had achieved the desired results.

[14] European Commission, Communication from the Commission to the Council, the European Parliament, the Economic and Social Committee and the Committee of the Regions on the Sixth Environment Action Programme of the European Community 'Environment 2010: Our Future, Our Choice': The Sixth Environment Action Programme, COM (2001) 31 final. See also European Commission, Decision No 1600/2002/EC of the European Parliament and of the Council of 22 July 2002 laying down the Sixth Community Environment Action Programme: 'Environment 2010: Our future, Our choice' [2022] OJ EC L 242/1.

performance, promoting the transition towards more environmentally friendly products and processes, and encouraging the adoption of eco-labels to allow consumers to compare similar products on the basis of their environmental performance. This integrated strategic approach would incorporate new ways of working with markets, engaging citizens, businesses, and stakeholders to change harmful production and consumption patterns.[15]

In 2007, the Commission published a Green Paper on market-based instruments,[16] further investigating these tools and emphasised that market-based instruments would be crucial for achieving real change by altering incentives for businesses and consumers.

In the Seventh General Union Environment Action Programme, entitled "Living Well, within the Limits of Our Planet" (Seventh Action Programme),[17] the Commission defined the guidelines up to 2020, bringing together—within the context of a renewed concept of well-being in which the economic prosperity and well-being of the EU are closely related to its natural capital—environmental concerns and market dynamics.[18]

The Seventh Action Programme reflects the EU's commitment to transforming itself into an inclusive green economy capable of guaranteeing growth and development, protecting human health and well-being, creating decent jobs, reducing inequalities, and investing in biodiversity.[19]

To achieve these ambitious objectives, the Commission underlined the need to have "an appropriate mix of policy instruments"[20] in order to enable businesses and consumers to improve their understanding of the impact of their activities on the environment and to manage that impact. These policy tools are realised through a broad examination of legal instruments, public law, and private law, including economic incentives, market instruments, and information requirements, as well as voluntary measures and instruments that engage stakeholders at various levels, to complement legislative frameworks.[21]

Finally, with the Eighth Action Programme,[22] co-operation with companies is increasingly becoming a key issue. The Commission aims to optimise environmental taxation, market-based instruments, and green budgeting tools while ensuring socially equitable transitions and supporting businesses in developing standardised natural capital accounting practices.[23] To achieve this goal, the programme identifies specific business-focused tools: promoting sustainable corporate governance through mandatory EU-level due diligence requirements, and encouraging responsible business practices in the EU's external policies, including trade policy.[24]

In light of these positions taken by the Commission in the various action programmes, and analysing European legislation from the 2000s onwards, it can be seen that private law instruments have been chosen to guide the behaviour of companies in various sectors, such as

[15] ibid recital 6.

[16] European Commission, *Green Paper on Market-based Instruments for Environment and Related Policy Purposes* COM (2007) 140 final.

[17] Decision No 1386/2013/EU of the European Parliament and of the Council of 20 November 2013 on a General Union Environment Action Programme to 2020 [2013] OJ L 354/171.

[18] ibid pt 17.

[19] ibid pt 10.

[20] ibid recital 33.

[21] ibid.

[22] Decision (EU) 2022/591 of the European Parliament and of the Council of 6 April 2022 on a General Union Environment Action Programme to 2030 [2022] OJ L 114/22.

[23] ibid 33 (v).

[24] ibid 34 (ah) (ii).

environmental liability, to implement mitigation tools against climate change and, finally, to increase collaboration with companies on the basis of voluntary agreements.

2.1 Liability for Environmental Damage

Environmental liability has been presented by various parties as a powerful tool for guiding the behaviour of companies,[25] as a deterrent against activities considered harmful to the environment, and as an effective tool for obtaining the internalisation of negative environmental externalities.[26]

A comparative analysis shows how civil liability can be a valid tool in this sector,[27] provided that several conditions are met. Specifically, civil liability requires clear definitions of environmental damage, identification of liable parties, well-defined standing to sue with proper incentives for quick action, liability regimes tailored to environmental damage characteristics, and established compensation criteria that enable insurance coverage.

The various EU initiatives that have emerged in this area[28] resulted in the adoption of Directive 2004/35 on environmental liability with regard to the prevention and remedying of environmental damage.[29]

2.2 Tradable Pollution Rights to Fight Climate Change

Among market-based instruments, tradable pollution rights are used to provide an incentive to corporations to use resources in a sustainable manner. Tradable pollution rights were introduced at the end of the 1960s[30] in the US in response to the need to limit emissions required under US legislation on atmospheric pollution, without thereby halting economic growth. The Clean Air Act provided for maximum concentrations of specific polluting substances for each area, which gave rise to the problem as to how to ensure that economic growth would continue also in the regions in which the concentration thresholds had already been reached or exceeded.[31] The idea underlying tradable pollution rights is that environmental degradation is

25 Donald Dewees, 'Tort Law and the Deterrence of Environmental Pollution' in Tom Tietenberg (ed), *Innovation in Environmental Policy* (Edward Elgar Publishing 1992) 139–64; Michael Faure, 'Environmental Liability' in Michael Faure (ed), *Tort Law and Economics* (Edward Elgar Publishing 2009) 247–86.

26 The Green Paper on remedying environmental damage examined the usefulness of civil liability as a means for the prevention and remediation of environmental harm. European Commission, Communication from the Commission to the Council and Parliament and the Economic and Social Committee: *Green Paper on Remedying Environmental Damage* COM (1993) 47 final. The Commission analysed civil liability as an instrument for imposing standards of behaviour and therefore achieving a preventive effect, and as a concretisation of the polluter pays principle, introduced at European level by the 'First Action Program on the environment', dating back to 22 November 1973.

27 Barbara Pozzo, *Danno ambientale ed imputazione della responsabilità: Esperienze giuridiche a confronto* (Giuffrè, 1996).

28 After the Green Paper on Remedying Environmental Damage (n 26), the White Paper on Environmental Liability, discussed possible approaches to implementing options (directive and recommendation) to achieve a harmonised regime on environmental liability. European Commission, *White Paper on Environmental Liability* COM (2000) 66 final.

29 Council Directive 2004/35/CE of 21 April 2004 on Environmental Liability with regard to the Prevention and Remedying of Environmental Damage [2004] OJ EC L 143/56.

30 John H Dales, *Pollution, Property and Prices* (University of Toronto Press 1968).

31 Richard Schmalensee and Robert N Stavins, 'Policy Evolution Under the Clean Air Act' [2019] Journal of Economic Perspectives 33, 27.

the result of the incomplete allocation of proprietary rights over the use of natural resources. For many environmental goods and services, there are no markets, or only incomplete markets, and this shortcoming is a source of economic inefficiency. Supporters of the instruments in question consider that there is a strong tendency to exploit and degrade resources that are commonly owned.[32]

With tradable pollution rights, companies are given a legal right to pollute a certain amount per fixed time span. Firms that pollute less can then sell their leftover pollution permits to firms that pollute more. The freedom to trade pollution "entitlements" gives an incentive for polluters to consider abatement (since they can sell their surplus quotas) while others face the cost of having to purchase permits.[33]

Tradable pollution rights have been taken into consideration by the EU only later, in the process of adopting the Kyoto Protocol. The Kyoto Protocol[34] in fact had recourse to market instruments to guarantee the achievement of targets, including international emission trading (IET), joint implementation (JI), and the clean development mechanism (CDM).[35]

In March 2000, the Commission adopted a Green Paper on greenhouse gas emissions trading within the EU,[36] which was followed by the adoption of Directive 2003/87/EC of 13 October 2003[37] establishing a scheme for greenhouse gas emission allowance trading within the Community, thereby providing for the first implementation within Europe of one of the mechanisms provided for under the Kyoto Protocol. Directive 2003/87/EC regulates the trading of emissions rights with a view to achieving emissions reductions throughout the Community where their cost is less high.

2.3 Voluntary Agreements

In an attempt to involve companies more and more in the dynamics of ecological policies, so-called voluntary agreements between companies and public administration have been introduced to achieve specific objectives in the field of environmental protection. During the 1980s and 1990s, voluntary agreements have been regarded as "an element of a distinctly 'German' policy mix",[38] while the Netherlands too, made extensive use of such environmental agreements.[39]

[32] Barbara Pozzo, 'Private Law and Sustainability' in M Santos Silva and others (eds), *Routledge Handbook of Private Law and Sustainability* (Routledge 2024) 5–45.

[33] Daniel H Cole D H, 'From Local to Global Property: Privatizing the Global Environment? Clearing the Air: Four Propositions about Property Rights and Environmental Protection' [1999] Duke Environmental Law & Policy Forum, 10, 103.

[34] Kyoto Protocol to the United Nations Framework Convention on Climate Change (adopted 11 December 1997, entered into force 16 February 2005) 2303 UNTS 148.

[35] Jonas Meckling and Steffen Jenner, 'Varieties of Market-based Policy: Instrument Choice in Climate Policy' (2016) Environmental Politics, 5, 25, 853.

[36] European Commission, *Green Paper on Greenhouse Gas Emissions Trading within the European Union* COM (2000) 87 final.

[37] Council Directive 2003/87/EC of 13 October 2003 establishing a Scheme for Greenhouse Gas Emission Allowance Trading within the Community and amending Council Directive 96/61/EC (Text with EEA relevance) [2003] OJ L 275, 32.

[38] Charles Lees, 'Environmental Policy in the United Kingdom and Germany' [2007] German Politics 16, 164.

[39] Ellis Immerzeel-Brand, 'Assessing the Performance of Negotiated Environmental Agreements in the Netherlands' in Patrick ten Brink (ed), *Voluntary Environmental Agreements. Process, Practice and Future Use* (Greenleaf Publishing 2002).

At the EU level, the Commission published in 1996 a Communication to the Council and the Parliament on environmental agreements.[40] The Communication acknowledges that environmental agreements have a range of potential benefits, including incentivising a more participatory approach by industry, the possibility to create tailor-made and cost-effective solutions, and finally the quicker fulfilment of environmental objectives.

The most well-known examples of Community agreements developed in relation to the environment are those from the associations of European, Japanese, and Korean car producers on the reduction of CO_2 emissions produced by cars. These agreements have been recognised in other Commission recommendations.[41] The Decision of the European Parliament and of the Council established a scheme to monitor the average specific emissions of CO_2 from new passenger cars,[42] supplementing such agreements.

An exhaustive inquiry into the use of this instrument was carried out by the Organisation for Economic Co-operation and Development (OECD) in a report published in 1999,[43] in which it was concluded that environmental agreements are more effective if they are used as part of a *policy mix* in conjunction with economic and legislative instruments.

Environmental agreements can come from a variety of sources. Firstly, they can be purely spontaneous decisions initiated by stakeholders in a broad range of areas in which the Commission has neither proposed legislation nor expressed an intention to do so. The Commission encourages stakeholders to be proactive in developing such agreements. Secondly, they can be a response by stakeholders to an expressed intention of the Commission to legislate. Thirdly, they can be initiated by the Commission. The assessment criteria and procedural requirements for handling environmental agreements will depend in part on the source of the initiative.

Policymakers have shown an increasing interest in environmental agreements in recent years. The potential of such agreements between stakeholders—often representative associations of business—to contribute to environmental policy objectives is widely recognised. Member States and the Community have already gained some experience with environmental agreements, and the results so far are encouraging. While such agreements are not an environmental panacea, nor will they be the optimal instrument in all circumstances, they have a potentially valuable role to play in complementing—but not replacing—other policy instruments, notably legislation.

Subsequently, in 2002, the Commission published a new Communication on environmental agreements[44] in which "voluntary environmental agreements" are presented as instruments that are best suited to the new requirements resulting from the Fifth Programme onwards.

[40] Communication from the Commission to the Council and the European Parliament on Environmental Agreements, Brussels, 27.11.1996 COM (96) 561 final.

[41] Commission Recommendation 1999/125/EC of 5 February 1999 on the reduction of CO2 emissions from passenger cars (notified under document number C(1999) 107) (Text with EEA relevance) [1999] OJ L 40; and Commission Recommendation 2000/304/EC of 13 April 2000 on the reduction of CO2 emissions from passenger cars (JAMA) (notified under document number C(2000) 803) (Text with EEA relevance) [2000] OJ L 100.

[42] Council Decision No 1753/2000/EC of 22 June 2000 establishing a scheme to monitor the average specific emissions of CO2 from new passenger cars [2000] OJ L 202, 1.

[43] OECD, *Voluntary Approaches for Environmental Policy—an Assessment* (OECD 1999).

[44] Communication from the Commission to the European Parliament, the Council, the Economic and Social Committee and the Committee of the Regions: Environmental Agreements at Community Level: Within the Framework of the Action Plan on the Simplification and Improvement of the Regulatory Environment COM (2002) 412 final.

The consensus-based approach of environmental agreements aims to help resolve the traditional conflict between environmental protection and economic development, transforming industry's role from problem creator to solution provider.

3. From Linear to Green and Circular Economy

The involvement of the market and business in environmental policies has been at the centre of the various initiatives that the EU has launched in the transition from a linear economy to a green economy.

When we talk about a *green economy*, we start from the assumption that the economy that has developed according to the parameters of neoclassical theories has not duly taken into account the value of the environment that was used in production processes or, on the contrary, was destroyed or impoverished by them.[45] *Green economy* moves away from *linear economy*, which refers to the straight progression that a product can follow, with a beginning, a middle, and an end, without recycling or reuse and producing high level of wastes.[46] By not considering the value of environmental resources when calculating business costs, this linear economy led to a development that was not sustainable from an environmental point of view.

A green economy, on the other hand, is one in which costs deriving from the degradation of ecosystems in production processes are internalised and recycling and reuse become important.[47] The model adopted by the green economy therefore analyses not only the economic benefits of a given production system, which results in an increase in the gross domestic product, but also the impact and damage that this system has on environmental resources. In a way, the green economy debate is a concrete expression of the principle of sustainable development, since it is based on the conviction that the present well-being and that of future generations strongly depends on environmental risks and ecological scarcity of goods.[48]

In preparation for the UN Rio Summit that took take place in 2012, the Commission prepared a Communication[49] where green economy is presented as a key target for the EU. Green economy is defined as "an economy that can secure growth and development, while at the same time improving human well-being, providing decent jobs, reducing inequalities, tackling poverty and preserving the natural capital upon which we all depend".[50] The Commission acknowledges that business participation is crucial for effectiveness. Building on existing

[45] Morris Altman, 'When Green isn't Mean: Economic Theory and the Heuristics of the Impact of Environmental Regulations on Competitiveness and Opportunity Cost' (2001) Ecological Economics 36, 31.

[46] Eleonore Loiseau and others, 'Green Economy and Related Concepts: An Overview' (2016) 36 Journal of Cleaner Production, 139, 361.

[47] Achim Steiner, 'Focusing on the Good or the Bad: What Can International Environmental Law Do to Accelerate the Transition Towards a Green Economy?' (2010) 103 American University International Law Review 25, 843.

[48] Ireneusz Miciuła and others, 'The Current Picture of the Transition to a Green Economy in the EU: Trends in Climate and Energy Policy versus State Security' (2021) 14(23) Energies 8181; Armand Kasztelan, 'On the Road to a Green Economy: How Do European Union Countries 'Do Their Homework'?' (2021) 14(23) Energies 5941.

[49] Communication from the Commission to the European Parliament, the Council, the European economic and social committee and the committee of the regions, *Rio+20: Towards the Green Economy and Better Governance* COM (2011) 363 final.

[50] ibid 5.

green commitments in industries like food, beverage, and chemicals, progress requires enhanced public–private partnerships, business networks, and financing facilities to drive green innovation and practices.[51]

To develop a sustainable, low-carbon, resource-efficient, and competitive economy, the EU has further supported the transition to a more circular economy, as part of the green economy strategy,[52] where the value of products, materials, and resources is maintained in the economy for as long as possible, and the generation of waste minimised.[53] According to the Action Plan launched in 2015, the transition to a circular economy will encourage sustainability and competitiveness in the long term. The Commission put under scrutiny the production process and the production design, to promote reparability, upgradability, durability, and recyclability of products, by developing product requirements relevant to the circular economy in its future decision to amend the *Ecodesign Directive*[54] and the *Waste Directive*[55] to bring them into line with the aims of the circular economy.[56]

In March 2020, the Commission adopted the new Circular Economy Action Plan,[57] which envisages collaboration with businesses to create a framework for sustainable products that will offer new opportunities in the EU and beyond. The Commission emphasises that this is a progressive but irreversible transition towards a sustainable economic system that represents an indispensable part of the new EU industrial strategy.[58]

4. The EU Strategy for Corporate Social Responsibility

Another important aspect of the European policies that were taking shape regarding the role of businesses in addressing the risks associated with the environment and climate change concerned corporate social responsibility.

The European Union officially began to concern itself with social responsibility following the Lisbon European Council of March 2000, during which an appeal was made to companies' sense of responsibility regarding good practices related to education, continuous training, work organisation, social inclusion, and equal opportunities, as well as the environment.[59]

[51] ibid 10.

[52] Marco Migliorelli, Philippe Dessertine (eds), *The Rise of Green Finance in Europe, Opportunities and Challenges for Issuers, Investors and Marketplaces* (Palgrave Macmillan 2019).

[53] Communication from the Commission to the European Parliament, the Council, the European Economic and Social Committee and the Committee of the Regions, *Closing the Loop: An EU action plan for the Circular Economy* COM (2015) 614 final.

[54] Regulation (EU) 2024/1781 of the European Parliament and of the Council of 13 June 2024 establishing a Framework for the setting of Ecodesign Requirements for Sustainable Products, amending Directive (EU) 2020/1828 and Regulation (EU) 2023/1542 and repealing Directive 2009/125/EC [2024] OJ L 2024/1781.

[55] In 2023 the Commission presented a *Proposal for a Directive of the European Parliament and of The Council amending Directive 2008/98/EC on waste* COM (2023) 420 final.

[56] EU Action Plan for Circular Economy (n 53) 4.

[57] Communication from the Commission to the European Parliament, the Council, the European Economic and Social Committee and the Committee of the Regions, *A new Circular Economy Action Plan For a cleaner and more competitive Europe* COM/2020/98 final.

[58] ibid 2.

[59] Lisbon European Council 23 and 24 March 2000, Presidency Conclusions, 39 <https://www.europarl.europa.eu/summits/lis1_en.htm> accessed 30 June 2025.

Interest in these issues and the phenomenon of Codes of Ethics had grown steadily since the mid-80s and really boomed in the 90s, when about 90% of US companies had such codes, while in Europe the percentage was around 40%.

The Green Paper on Corporate Social Responsibility published in 2001 aimed to "raise awareness and encourage discussion on new forms of promoting corporate social responsibility",[60] thus initiating a debate on how the EU could promote corporate social responsibility, utilise existing experiences, and introduce innovative practices.

With the Green Paper, the Commission launched a real awareness campaign on environmental issues, arguing that the EU and the Member States could play an important role in helping businesses identify market opportunities and make investments that could be beneficial for both the companies and the environment.

In the renewed EU Strategy 2011–14 for Corporate Social Responsibility,[61] the Commission underlined that corporate social responsibility offers a set of values on which to base the transition to a sustainable economic system.[62] In this context, disclosure of social and environmental information, including climate-related information, was considered a tool that could facilitate stakeholder engagement and the identification of material sustainability risks. In addition, the Commission emphasised that disclosure obligations could become an important element of accountability, helping to strengthen public trust in companies.[63]

The Commission's intention to involve companies more and more in environmental and climate-related policies seems increasingly clear, even if it will still take some time before the objectives outlined in the Commission's Green Papers are transformed into binding objectives.[64]

5. The Green Deal

The Green Deal,[65] adopted in 2019, sets the blueprint for the transformational change to turn the EU into the first climate-neutral continent by 2050. All twenty-seven EU Member States are committed to reducing emissions by at least 55% by 2030, compared to the 1990 levels.[66]

To achieve these objectives, the Green Deal proposes a series of measures, including investments in renewable energy, energy efficiency, and sustainable transport, as well as reforms in agricultural and forestry practices and measures to promote a circular economy.

[60] European Commission, *Green Paper Promoting a European framework for Corporate Social Responsibility*, Brussels COM (2001) 366 def.

[61] Communication from the Commission to the European Parliament, the Council, the European Economic and Social Committee and the Committee of the Regions, *A renewed EU strategy 2011–14 for corporate social responsibility* COM (2011) 681 final.

[62] ibid 3.

[63] ibid 11.

[64] Pall A Davidsson, 'Legal Enforcement of Corporate Social Responsibility within the EU' (2002) Columbia Journal of European Law 8, 529; Sorcha MacLeod, 'Corporate Social Responsibility within the European Union Framework' (2005) Wisconsin International Law Journal 23, 541.

[65] Communication from the Commission to the European Parliament, the European Council, the Council, the European Economic and Social Committee and the Committee of the Regions: *The European Green Deal* COM/2019/640 final.

[66] Hugo-Maria Schally, 'The EU Green Deal and the Sustainability of Corporate Activities' in M Santos Silva and others (eds), *Routledge Handbook of Private Law and Sustainability* (Routledge 2024), 517.

Among other things, the Green Deal emphasised that the private sector will be fundamental in financing the green transition. For this reason, it was necessary to send long-term signals to direct financial flows and capital towards green investments and avoid stranded assets.[67]

In this context, the Commission announced the launch of a renewed sustainable finance strategy aiming at strengthening the foundations for sustainable investment. As a first measure, the Green Deal was requiring the European Parliament and Council to adopt a taxonomy for classifying environmentally sustainable activities. Sustainability should have been further integrated into the corporate governance framework, as it was highlighted that many companies still focus too much on short-term financial results rather than on long-term development and sustainability aspects.[68] In order to increase companies' disclosure of climate and environmental data to render investors fully informed about the sustainability of their investments, the Green Deal required—among others—the review of the Non-Financial Reporting Directive.[69] The objective was also to offer greater opportunities to investors and companies, making it easier for them to identify sustainable investments and guaranteeing their credibility. With this objective in mind, clear labels for retail investment products and the development of an EU standard for green bonds were planned, in order to facilitate sustainable investments in the most convenient way.

Finally, the Green Deal stated that climate and environmental risks must be managed and integrated into the financial system. This should have involved better integrating these risks into the EU prudential framework and assessing the adequacy of existing capital requirements for green assets.

In line with the European Green Deal, the European Climate Law[70] came into force in July 2021, requiring Member States to achieve net-zero greenhouse gas emissions by 2050. It further states that the Commission will promote a new green business model,[71] while fostering dialogue with business community.[72]

6. The Rise of Green Finance

The 2015 Paris Agreement on Climate Change and the adoption of the Sustainable Development Goals (SDGs) by the United Nations in 2015 marked a turning point in societal awareness of the challenges of climate change and sustainable development.[73]

A new wave of reforms started in December 2016 through the establishment by the Commission of a High-Level Experts Group (HLEG), formed by twenty seniors from the

[67] The European Green Deal (n 65) 16.

[68] Green Paper, Corporate Social Responsibility (n 60) 17.

[69] Council Directive 2014/95/EU of 22 October 2014 amending Directive 2013/34/EU as regards disclosure of non-financial and diversity information by certain large undertakings and groups [2014] OJ L 330, 1–9.

[70] Council Regulation (EU) 2021/1119 of 30 June 2021 establishing the framework for achieving climate neutrality and amending Regulations (EC) No 401/2009 and (EU) 2018/1999 [2021] OJ L 243/1 (European Climate Law).

[71] ibid recital 22.

[72] ibid art 9.

[73] Danny Busch, Guido Ferrarini and Seraina Grünewald (eds), *Sustainable Finance in Europe: Corporate Governance, Financial Stability and Financial Markets* (Palgrave Macmillan 2021); Marco Migliorelli and Philippe Dessertine (eds), *The Rise of Green Finance in Europe: Opportunities and Challenges for Issuers, Investors and Marketplaces* (Palgrave Macmillan 2019); Katrin Hummel and Dominik Jobst, 'An Overview of Corporate Sustainability Reporting Legislation in the European Union' (2024) Accounting in Europe, 21, 320.

financial community. The HLEG published the EU Strategy on Sustainable Finance interim report in July 2017 and the final report in January 2018.

In March 2018, the Commission issued the European Commission Action Plan on Financing Sustainable Growth (Action Plan),[74] stating that as the financial sector acts as an intermediary between users and providers of capital, it has a key role to play in this green transition. This Action Plan needs to be considered an integral part of the Capital Markets Union (CMU) Action Plan and must also be seen in conjunction with the broader European climate plans: the Green Deal and the European Climate Law[75] that forms part of it. The Action Plan identifies three main objectives:

(1) reorienting capital flows towards sustainable investment, in order to achieve sustainable and inclusive growth;

(2) managing financial risks stemming from climate change, environmental degradation, and social issues; and

(3) fostering transparency and long-termism in financial and economic activity.

The Action Plan envisions ten key actions introducing definitions of sustainable economic activities and sustainable investments, labels, disclosure, organizational, and conduct duties of financial intermediaries, in relation to sustainability risks and factors, as well as sustainability disclosures by companies and corporate due diligence duties in relation to sustainability.[76]

The implementation of such Action Plan relies on the technical work of a Technical Experts Group (TEG, composed of thirty-five experts from the financial community), supported by a Member States Experts Group (MSEG), which was created in April 2018.

The MSEG gathers financial market and environmental experts from Member States to allow effective coordination of sustainable finance initiatives at European and national levels, and to assist the Commission in implementing EU legislation and policies related to sustainable finance.

6.1 The EU Taxonomy Regulation

As pointed out by the Action Plan in 2018, a shift of capital flows towards more sustainable economic activities must be underpinned by a shared understanding of what "sustainable" means. That is why, a unified EU classification system—or taxonomy—is necessary to provide clarity on which activities can be considered sustainable. This is also due to the risk of confusing terminology and deliberate deception, where activities are presented as more environmentally friendly than they actually are—a phenomenon known as greenwashing.

[74] Communication from the Commission: *Action Plan, Financing Sustainable Growth* COM (2018) 97 final.

[75] European Climate Law (n 70) 1.

[76] Eugenia Macchiavello and Michele Siri, 'Sustainable Finance and Fintech: Can Technology Contribute to Achieving Environmental Goals? A Preliminary Assessment of Green Fintech' (2020) European Banking Institute Working Paper Series <https://ssrn.com/abstract=3672989> accessed 29 June 2025; Michele Siri and Shanshan Zhu, 'Will the EU Commission Successfully Integrate Sustainability Risks and Factors in the Investor Protection Regime? A Research Agenda' (2019) 11(22) Sustainability, 6292; Danny Busch, 'Sustainable Finance Disclosure', EU Financial Sector EBI Working Paper Series 2020 No. 70 <https://papers.ssrn.com/sol3/papers.cfm?abstract_id=3650407> accessed 29 June 2025.

The EU Taxonomy Regulation,[77] which entered into force on 12 July 2020, and the following delegated acts,[78] set the criteria to identify an environmentally sustainable economic activity. According to the EU Taxonomy Regulation, an economic activity qualifies as "environmentally sustainable" where that economic activity contributes substantially to at least one of six environmental objectives—climate change mitigation, climate change adaptation, sustainable use and protection of water and marine resources, transition to a circular economy, pollution prevention and control, or the protection and restoration of biodiversity and ecosystems. It may also qualify by enabling other activities to contribute to these objectives. Additionally, the activity must not significantly harm any of the other objectives and must comply with minimum social safeguards. These safeguards require alignment with the OECD Guidelines for Multinational Enterprises, the UN Guiding Principles on Business and Human Rights, the International Labour Organization's core conventions, and the International Bill of Human Rights.

In order for an economic activity to qualify as an environmentally sustainable activity, it is in addition required that the activity concerned complies with detailed technical screening criteria. Supported by the Sustainable Finance Platform's dialogue on technical standards implementation, the delegated acts established criteria—adapted for technical and scientific progress—to determine whether economic activities significantly contribute to at least one of six environmental objectives without causing significant harm to the others.

Specifically, two Delegated Regulations published during 2021, the first of which is known as the Climate Delegated Act, sets out the technical screening criteria for certain industrial sectors, such as energy, construction, manufacturing, and transport, in order to determine under which conditions a given economic activity makes a substantial contribution to the first two sustainability objectives, that is, climate change mitigation or adaptation.[79]

The second Delegated Regulation complements the EU Green Taxonomy Regulation by clarifying the content and presentation of non-financial information.[80] In particular, companies subject to sustainability reporting requirements must include in the non-financial statement information on how and to what extent the company's activities are linked to economic activities that are considered environmentally sustainable according to the classification of the Taxonomy Regulation. The Delegated Regulation therefore identifies the environmental impact key performance indicators (KPIs) that are useful for measuring the degree of environmental sustainability of an economic activity, and therefore of an investment, taking into account the sector and size of the companies subject to the disclosure requirements.

[77] Council Regulation (EU) 2020/852 of 18 June 2020, on the establishment of a framework to facilitate sustainable investment and amending Regulation (EU) 2019/2088.

[78] C/2021/2800 final Commission Delegated Regulation (EU) supplementing Regulation (EU) 2020/852 (EU Climate Taxonomy) [2021] OJ C (2021) 2800 final.

[79] Commission Delegated Regulation (EU) 2021/2139 of 4 June 2021 supplementing Regulation (EU) 2020/852 of the European Parliament and of the Council by establishing the technical screening criteria for determining the conditions under which an economic activity qualifies as contributing substantially to climate change mitigation or climate change adaptation and for determining whether that economic activity causes no significant harm to any of the other environmental objectives [2021] OJ L 442, 1–349.

[80] Commission Delegated Regulation (EU) 2021/2178 of 6 July 2021 supplementing Regulation (EU) 2020/852 of the European Parliament and of the Council by specifying the content and presentation of information to be disclosed by undertakings subject to Articles 19a or 29a of Directive 2013/34/EU concerning environmentally sustainable economic activities, and specifying the methodology to comply with that disclosure obligation [2021] OJ L 443, 9–67.

In 2022, a new Commission's Delegated Regulation[81] was adopted, adding to the list of economic activities in the European taxonomy specific activities related to the nuclear and gas energy sectors, in order to promote the green transition and the reduction of the use of solid or liquid fossil fuels.

Two other Delegated Regulations were adopted in 2023: Delegated Regulation (EU) 2023/2485[82] and Delegated Regulation No. 2023/2486.[83] The latter aimed to define the technical screening criteria to determine the conditions under which a given economic activity makes a substantial contribution to the remaining four taxonomic objectives, namely the sustainable use and protection of water and marine resources, the transition to a circular economy, the prevention and reduction of pollution, and the protection and restoration of biodiversity and ecosystems, without significantly harming any other environmental objective. Finally, the EU Delegated Regulation No. 2023/2485 amended the technical screening criteria for climate objectives contained in Del. Reg. 2021/2139 by including additional economic activities that contribute significantly to climate change mitigation and adaptation (mainly services for prevention of and response to disasters and climate emergencies).[84]

6.2 The Sustainable Financial Disclosure Regulation

Another key pillar of the Commission's Action Plan on Sustainable Finance launched in 2018 is the Sustainable Financial Disclosure Regulation.[85]

After having defined what can be considered ecologically sustainable, the next step undertaken by the Commission was to arrange for financial intermediaries to integrate sustainability considerations into their investment policy and advice, while providing transparency to the investing public about the extent to which they do this.

In practice, many financial intermediaries were already doing this to a greater or lesser extent, because there has been a significant demand for sustainable investments for some time, but there were no harmonised rules at European level. This was changed by the Sustainable Financial Disclosure Regulation (SFDR), which came into force in March 2021.

[81] Commission Delegated Regulation (EU) 2022/1214 of 9 March 2022 amending Delegated Regulation (EU) 2021/2139 as regards economic activities in certain energy sectors and Delegated Regulation (EU) 2021/2178 as regards specific public disclosures for those economic activities, C/2022/631 [2022] OJ L 188, 1–45.

[82] Commission Delegated Regulation (EU) 2023/2485 of 27 June 2023 amending Delegated Regulation (EU) 2021/2139 establishing additional technical screening criteria for determining the conditions under which certain economic activities qualify as contributing substantially to climate change mitigation or climate change adaptation and for determining whether those activities cause no significant harm to any of the other environmental objectives, C/2023/3850 [2023] OJ L 2023/2485.

[83] Commission Delegated Regulation (EU) 2023/2486 of 27 June 2023 supplementing Regulation (EU) 2020/852 of the European Parliament and of the Council by establishing the technical screening criteria for determining the conditions under which an economic activity qualifies as contributing substantially to the sustainable use and protection of water and marine resources, to the transition to a circular economy, to pollution prevention and control, or to the protection and restoration of biodiversity and ecosystems and for determining whether that economic activity causes no significant harm to any of the other environmental objectives and amending Commission Delegated Regulation (EU) 2021/2178 as regards specific public disclosures for those economic activities, C/2023/3851 [2023] OJ L 2023/2486.

[84] Ilaria Ceriana, 'The EU Green Taxonomy' in Eugenia Macchiavello and Michele Siri (eds), *Sustainable Finance and Financial Education: A Snapshot* (Giappichelli 2024) 90.

[85] Regulation (EU) 2019/2088 of the European Parliament and of the Council of 27 November 2019 on sustainability-related disclosures in the financial services sector [2019] OJ L 317, 1.

This new Regulation imposes on financial market participants and financial advisors certain disclosure obligations related to sustainable risks and factors.[86] Information for end investors about sustainability risk integration, adverse sustainability impacts, and environmental or social characteristics in investment decisions and advisory processes is insufficiently developed due to the lack of harmonised requirements. To address this gap, the Commission is introducing specific criteria through the SFDR.[87] In particular, the Regulation aims to reduce information asymmetries in principal-agent relationships with regard to the integration of sustainability risks, the consideration of adverse sustainability impacts, the promotion of environmental or social characteristics, and sustainable investment; the Regulation seeks to do so by requiring financial market participants and financial advisers to make precontractual and ongoing disclosures to end investors when they act as agents of those end investors.[88]

Article 2, point (17) defines "sustainable investment" as investment in economic activities contributing to environmental objectives (measured by resource efficiency, emissions, biodiversity, and circular economy indicators) or social objectives (including inequality reduction, social cohesion, labour relations, human capital development, and support for disadvantaged communities), provided such investments avoid significant harm to other objectives and ensure investee companies maintain good governance practices regarding management, employee relations, compensation, and tax compliance.[89]

The goal of this Regulation is to provide transparency: The SFDR is intended to enable investors to compare information in the investment process of investment firms not only about specific products they offer "at product level", but also about their respective firm as a whole, that is, "at entity level". It is connected to the Taxonomy Regulation as it tends to avoid greenwashing, defined by the same Taxonomy Regulation in the 11th Recital as the "practice of gaining an unfair competitive advantage by marketing a financial product as environmentally friendly, when in fact basic environmental standards have not been met". In this regard, the SFDR does not force investment funds to consider environmental, social, and governance (ESG) criteria when investing, but it sets out rules that require them to justify the sustainability claims that they make about their financial products.

6.3 The Corporate Sustainability Reporting Directive

While the SFDR requires asset managers to disclose how they address sustainability risks in their investment policies and the potential impact of these risks on returns, the Corporate Sustainability Reporting Directive (CSRD),[90] adopted on 22 October 2022, deals more

[86] Danny Busch, 'EU Sustainable Finance Disclosure Regulation' (2023) Capital Markets Law Journal 18.3.303; Chiara Cremasco and Leonardo Boni, 'Is the European Union (EU) Sustainable Finance Disclosure Regulation (SFDR) Effective in Shaping Sustainability Objectives? An Analysis of Investment Funds' Behaviour' (2024) 14 (4) Journal of Sustainable Finance & Investment 1018–36.

[87] Sustainable Financial Disclosure Regulation (n 85) recital 5.

[88] ibid recital 10.

[89] ibid art 2(17).

[90] Council Directive (EU) 2022/2464 of 14 December 2022 amending Regulation (EU) No 537/2014, Directive 2004/109/EC, Directive 2006/43/EC and Directive 2013/34/EU, as regards corporate sustainability reporting [2022] OJ L 322, 15–80.

generally with sustainability information to be disclosed by companies. The new CSRD aims to cope with the rapid growth of a market for sustainability information, expanding the scope of the previous Non-Financial Reporting Directive (NFRD).[91]

The NFRD introduced into European law for the first time the duty to disclose non-financial information for large undertakings that meet specific requirements. Although it was considered a key step in the EU's efforts to enhance ESG transparency, requiring large companies to disclose how they manage ESG challenges, the NFRD soon faced criticism for its limited disclosure requirements and scope. Companies falling under the scope of the NFRD had to disclose details of their policies relating to five key factors in their annual reports: environmental protection; social responsibility and treatment of employees; respect for human rights; company board diversity regarding gender, age, education, and profession; and finally, anti-corruption and bribery.[92]

The NFDR allowed companies to choose from various International, European, or national frameworks. These frameworks included, among others, the OECD Guidelines for Multinational Enterprises, the ISO 26000 for Social Responsibility, or the Commissions' guidelines to help companies disclose environmental and social information.[93]

The NFRD aimed to fulfil two core objectives: providing investors and stakeholders with essential information on a company's non-financial activities and encouraging companies to adopt stronger social and environmental practices. This approach, known as "double materiality",[94] refers to the analysis and evaluation of how ESG issues influence the financial performance of a company (financial materiality) and, at the same time, how company activities impact social and environmental issues (impact materiality).[95]

According to the new approach adopted by the CSRD, the increased demand for corporate sustainability information results from changing business risks and greater investor awareness of their financial consequences, particularly for climate-related risks.[96]

To this end, the CSRD is now providing the obligation to disclose a sustainability report which is standardised in content and format. The Commission has in fact adopted the European Sustainability Reporting Standards (ESRS)[97] that cover the full range of ESG issues, including climate change, biodiversity, and human rights, providing information for investors to understand the sustainability impact of the companies in which they invest.

[91] Council Directive 2014/95/EU of 22 October 2014 amending Directive 2013/34/EU as regards disclosure of non-financial and diversity information by certain large undertakings and groups [2013] OJ L 330, 1–9.

[92] ibid recital 6.

[93] ibid recital 9.

[94] Nathan de Arriba-Sellier and Arnaud Van Caenegem, 'Sustainability-Related Materiality in the SFDR' in Kern Alexander, Matteo Gargantini, and Michele Siri (eds), *The Cambridge Handbook of EU Sustainable Finance* (CUP 2025) 251.

[95] Josef Baumüller and Karina Sopp, 'Double Materiality and the shift from Non-financial to European Sustainability Reporting: Review, Outlook and Implications' (2022) 23(1) Journal of Applied Accounting Research.

[96] CSRD (n 90) recital 11.

[97] Commission Delegated Regulation (EU) 2023/2772 of 31 July 2023 supplementing Directive 2013/34/EU of the European Parliament and of the Council as regards sustainability reporting standards, C/2023/5303 [2023] OJ L 2023/2772.

Further, under the CSRD, all large European companies[98] and those listed on EU-regulated markets[99] will need to prepare the sustainability statements in a human-readable format and a machine-readable format that meet the requirements of the European Single Electronic Format (ESEF),[100] in order to render the availability of information standardised.

Following the NFDR, the CSRD further builds on the concept of double materiality as a foundational reporting principle, requiring companies to assess both financial materiality and impact materiality more rigorously. Information on material impacts has to be included within the sustainability report with regard to the undertaking's own operations as well as the operations with its value chain, including its products and services, and its business relationships. Information about the undertaking's whole value chain may also include that of third parties, if the undertaking's value chain extends outside the Union.

In comparison with the NFDR, the CSRD has extended its scope from approximately 12,000 to 49,000 companies. The new Directive now applies to the following entities:

- EU large undertakings: these include every undertaking established in the EU that meet the requirement of Directive 2013/34/EU.
- EU small and medium undertakings of public interest: these include small and medium undertakings established in the EU that are of public interest according to the Directive 2013/34/EU.
- Third-country undertakings: these include third-country undertakings with annual EU revenues of at least €150 million in the most recent two years, which also own:
    - o a large EU-based undertaking, or
    - o an EU-based subsidiary with securities listed on an EU-regulated market exchange, or
    - o an EU branch office with at least €40 million in net turnover.

Under the NFRD companies were not required to provide external assurance for their sustainability information, in contrast to financial information which needed to be assured by their statutory auditor. On the contrary, the goal of the CSRD is to guarantee an equal level of reliability to financial reporting and sustainability reporting.

To this end, the EU has adopted a progressive approach, introducing a limited assurance review regime for sustainability reports, with the possibility of moving to a reasonable assurance requirement at a later stage. The Directive itself explains the difference between the two regimes:[101] The conclusion of a limited assurance engagement is usually provided in a negative form of expression by stating that no matter has been identified by the practitioner to conclude that the subject matter is materially misstated. In a limited assurance engagement, the auditor performs fewer tests than in a reasonable assurance engagement. The amount of work for a limited assurance engagement is therefore less than for a reasonable assurance engagement. The amount of work in a reasonable assurance engagement entails extensive procedures including consideration of internal controls of the reporting undertaking and substantive testing and is therefore significantly greater than in a limited assurance engagement.

[98] Large companies are those that on the balance sheet date for two consecutive financial years, exceed two of the following three criteria (including EU and non-EU subsidiaries): 250 employees, net revenue of €50 million or total assets of €25 million.

[99] These are EU and non-EU companies with debt or equity securities listed on an EU regulated market, excluding micro undertakings.

[100] European Securities and Markets Authority (ESMA), Electronic Reporting <https://www.esma.europa.eu/issuer-disclosure/electronic-reporting> accessed 15 July 2025.

[101] CSRD (n 90) recital 60.

6.4 The Corporate Sustainability Due Diligence Directive

The Corporate Sustainability Due Diligence Directive (CSDDD)[102] adopted on 13 June 2024 marks the transition from transparency obligations to rules of conduct for companies.[103] After the endorsement of the United Nations Guiding Principles on Business and Human Rights (UNGPs), several European countries adopted legislation on mandatory due diligence.[104] The CSDDD aims to harmonise due diligence requirements across EU Member States and standardise responsible business conduct, building on previous national and EU-level regulations[105] like France's Duty of Vigilance Act of 2017[106] and Germany's Supply Chain Due Diligence Act of 2021.[107]

The starting point of the new directive is that the behaviour of companies in all sectors of the economy is crucial for the success of the Union's sustainability objectives, as Union companies, especially the large ones, rely on global value chains.[108] The Directive applies to very large EU companies employing more than 1,000 employees and generating a net worldwide annual turnover of €450 million, regardless of the sector in which they operate.[109]

This Directive sets ambitious goals, aiming to ensure that companies operating in the internal market contribute to sustainable development by identifying, prioritising, preventing, mitigating, ending, minimising, and remediating actual or potential adverse human rights and environmental impacts from their operations, subsidiaries, and business partners throughout their value chains, while ensuring access to justice for those affected by failures to meet these duties.[110]

To achieve these ambitious goals, the CSDDD expects the due diligence process to cover the six steps defined by the Guide for responsible business conduct, which includes due diligence measures for companies to identify and address negative impacts on human rights and the environment. That process encompasses the following steps:

(1) integrating due diligence into policies and management systems;[111]
(2) identifying and assessing adverse human rights and environmental impacts;
(3) preventing, ceasing or minimising actual and potential adverse human rights and environmental impacts;[112]

[102] Council Directive (EU) 2024/1760 of 13 June 2024 on corporate sustainability due diligence and amending Directive (EU) 2019/1937 and Regulation (EU) 2023/2859 [2024] OJ L 2024/1760.

[103] Josef Baumüller and Stefan O Grbenic, 'Moving from Non-Financial to Sustainability Reporting: Analyzing the EU Commission's Proposal for a Corporate Sustainability Reporting Directive (CSRD)' (2021) 18(4) Facta Universitatis: Economics and Organization 369–81.

[104] Nicolas Bueno and others, 'The EU Directive on Corporate Sustainability Due Diligence (CSDDD): the Final Political Compromise' (2024) 9(2) Business and Human Rights Journal, 294–300.

[105] Christopher Patz, 'The EU's Draft Corporate Sustainability Due Diligence Directive: A First Assessment' (2022) Business and Human Rights Journal 291.

[106] *Loi no 2017-399 du 27 mars 2017 relative au devoir de vigilance des sociétés mères et des entreprises donneuses d'ordre, JORF no 0074 du 28 mars 2017.*

[107] Gesetz über die unternehmerischen Sorgfaltspflichten zur Vermeidung von Menschenrechtsverletzungen in Lieferketten (Lieferkettensorgfaltspflichtengesetz, LkSG), 16.07.2021, BGBl. I 2021, Nr. 46 vom 22.07.2021, S. 2959.

[108] CSDDD (n 102) recital 4.

[109] ibid art 2.

[110] ibid recital 16.

[111] ibid art 7.

[112] ibid art 10, 11.

(4) monitoring and assessing the effectiveness of measures;[113]
(5) communicating;[114] and
(6) providing remediation.[115]

According to the Directive, the process of due diligence will include the entire value chain inside and outside Europe. Therefore, the CSDDD will have extraterritorial implications, including the promotion of changes in the policies and practices of companies along the value chains. In order to maintain and further develop their business relationships with companies falling within the scope of the directive, foreign companies will have to adapt to the new human rights and environmental standards.

Moreover, companies will also have to adopt a plan to ensure that the business model and strategy of the company are compatible with the transition to a sustainable economy and with the limiting of global warming to 1.5 °C in line with the Paris Agreement (i.e., a transition plan).[116]

The most innovative dispositions introduced by the CSDDD are the ones that provide civil liability for companies and the right to full compensation should a negative impact occur and cause damage.[117]

Companies subject to the Directive will be liable for the damages resulting from adverse environmental or human rights impacts that occur in three contexts: (1) in the company's own operations; (2) in the company's subsidiaries; and (3) in the operations of direct or indirect business partners in the value chain.

In order to be held liable for damage caused to a natural or legal person (a) the company must intentionally or negligently fail to comply with the obligations of preventing potential adverse impact and bringing actual adverse impacts to an end, and (b) as a result of this failure, damage is caused to the natural or legal person's legal interests, that are protected under national law.[118] According to Article 37, Member States would have had to transpose the Directive by 26 July 2026.

6.5 The Future Ahead

On 26 February 2025, the Commission adopted two Proposals[119] aimed at reducing the complexity of EU requirements for all companies, in particular small and medium enterprises (SMEs) and small mid-cap companies. The directive postponing the application dates ("stop-the-clock") was then approved as Directive (EU) 2025/794 of the European parliament and of the council of 14 April 2025 amending Directives (EU) 2022/2464 and (EU) 2024/1760 as regards the dates from which Member States are to apply certain corporate sustainability reporting and due diligence requirements.[120]

113 ibid art 15.
114 ibid art 16.
115 ibid art 12.
116 ibid art 22.
117 ibid art 29.
118 ibid art 29, 1 (a) and (b)9.
119 Proposal postponing the application of some reporting requirements in the CSRD and the transposition deadline and application of the CSDDD: Omnibus I: COM (2025)80; Proposal for a Directive amending the Directives: Accounting, Audit, CSRD and CSDDD: Omnibus I: COM (2025) 81.
120 OJ L, 2025/794, 16.4.2025

The new Directive focuses on the regulatory framework on larger companies, which are likely to have a greater impact on the climate and the environment, while enabling companies to access sustainable financing for their clean transition.

More specifically, the main amendments to the CSRD aim to streamline and refocus sustainability reporting obligations. Key changes include removing approximately 80% of companies from its scope, concentrating requirements on larger firms with greater environmental and social impact. The amendments seek to avoid placing reporting burdens on smaller companies within the value chains of larger ones and postpone reporting requirements for some companies by two years, until 2028. They also reduce the scope of EU Taxonomy reporting, limiting it to the largest companies while allowing others to report voluntarily. Additional changes introduce the option to report partially aligned activities to support a gradual sustainability transition, apply a financial materiality threshold, and cut reporting templates by about 70%. Simplifications are also made to complex criteria, such as "do no significant harm" regarding chemical use. Lastly, adjustments are made to the green asset ratio (GAR) for banks, allowing them to exclude exposures to companies outside the revised CSRD scope from the calculation.

On the other side, the most significant changes to the CSDDD focus on simplifying requirements to reduce complexity and costs for companies within its scope. Key amendments include limiting systematic due diligence to direct business partners and reducing the frequency of monitoring from annually to every five years, with additional assessments as needed. The changes also aim to lessen the burden on SMEs and small mid-cap companies by restricting the information large companies can request during value chain mapping. Further harmonisation of due diligence rules across the EU is introduced to ensure a level playing field. While EU civil liability conditions are removed, victims retain the right to full compensation, and companies are protected from excessive liability in line with national legal systems. Additionally, companies are granted more time to prepare, with the application of due diligence requirements for large firms postponed to 26 July 2028, and the adoption of implementation guidelines advanced to July 2026.

Needless to say, these important requests for changes to the two directives undermine the very backbone of the ecological transition that was to be achieved through green finance. The two Proposals are now submitted for consideration and adoption by the European Parliament and the Council and will come into force once an agreement is reached, the evaluation of which remains to be seen.

7. Conclusion

To date, the legislative texts examined are complemented by several others aimed at reducing greenwashing and improving disclosures such as the EU Climate Benchmarks Regulation,[121] the Standard for European Green Bonds (EuGB),[122] and the Proposal for a Green Claims Directive.[123] Another set of reforms has been introduced, through a series of amendments to

[121] Regulation (EU) 2019/2089 of the European Parliament and of the Council of 27 November 2019 amending Regulation (EU) 2016/1011 as regards EU Climate Transition Benchmarks, EU Paris-aligned Benchmarks and sustainability-related disclosures for benchmarks OJ [2019] L 317/17.

[122] Regulation of the European Parliament and of the Council (EU) 2023/2631 of 22 November 2023 on European Green Bonds and optional disclosures for bonds marketed as environmentally sustainable and for sustainability-linked bonds [2023] OJ L 2023/2631.

[123] Proposal for a directive of the European Parliament and of the Council on substantiation and communication of explicit environmental claims (Green Claims Directive) COM/2023/166 final.

six delegated Regulations[124] of the MiFID II,[125] IDD,[126] UCITS,[127] AIFM,[128] and Solvency II Directives,[129] that outline the organisational and conduct duties of financial advisors and portfolio managers in relation to sustainability, such as collecting sustainability preferences of investors andoffering of products in line with such preferences.

In conclusion, the EU has made substantial efforts to systematically integrate sustainability into economic decision-making, mobilise private finance, and incentivise the real economy to adopt responsible business practice throughout global supply chain. While the resulting regulatory framework may appear complex and difficult to navigate,[130] the trajectory that has led from the incorporation of the principle of sustainability into the Treaties in 1992 to the detailed regulations of recent years is clearly irreversible.

Although the amendments proposed in 2025 slow the practical implementation of the directives on sustainability reporting and sustainability due diligence, the EU is expected to continue advancing in this direction with increasing attention to human rights across the supply

[124] Commission Delegated Directive No 2021/1270 of 21 April 2021 amending Directive 2010/43/EU as regards the sustainability risks and sustainability factors to be taken into account for Undertakings for Collective Investment in Transferable Securities (UCITS); Commission Delegated Regulation No 2021/1255 of 21 April 2021 amending Delegated Regulation (EU) No 231/2013 as regards the sustainability risks and sustainability factors to be taken into account by Alternative Investment Fund Managers (AIFM); Commission Delegated Regulation (EU) 2021/1257 of April 2021 amending Delegated Regulations (EU) 2017/2358 and (EU) 2017/2359 (IDD) as regards the integration of sustainability factors, risks and preferences into the product oversight and governance requirements for insurance undertakings and insurance distributors and into the rules on conduct of business and investment advice for insurance-based investment products; Commission Delegated Directive (EU) 2021/1269 of 21 April 2021 amending Delegated Directive (EU) 2017/593 (MiFID II) as regards the integration of sustainability factors into the product governance obligations; Commission Delegated Regulation (EU) 2021/1256 of 21 April 2021 amending Delegated Regulation (EU) 2015/35 (Solvency II) as regards the integration of sustainability risks in the governance of insurance and reinsurance undertakings; Commission Delegated Regulation (EU) 2021/1253 of 21 April 2021 amending Delegated Regulation (EU) 2017/565 (MiFID II) as regards the integration of sustainability factors, risks and preferences into certain organisational requirements and operating conditions for investment firms.

[125] MIFID: Markets in financial instruments directive, refers to Directive 2014/65/EU of the European Parliament and of the Council of 15 May 2014 on markets in financial instruments and amending Directive 2002/92/EC and Directive 2011/61/EU (recast) Text with EEA relevance [2014] OJ L 173, 349–496.

[126] IDD: Insurance distribution Directive, refers to Council Directive (EU) 2016/97 of 20 January 2016 on insurance distribution (recast) [2016] OJ L 26 19–59.

[127] UCITS: Undertakings for Collective Investment in Transferable Securities, refers to European Union Directive 85/611/EEC that establishes the terms for the placement in member countries of funds with domicile in one of these. The UCITS regulation aims to simplify and make the rules for the sale of funds within the EU more transparent. Council Directive 85/611/EEC of 20 December 1985 on the coordination of laws, regulations and administrative provisions relating to undertakings for collective investment in transferable securities [1985] OJ L 375, 3–18.

[128] AIFMD: Alternative Investment Fund Managers Directive, refers to Directive 2011/61/EU of the European Parliament and of the Council of 8 June 2011 on Alternative Investment Fund Managers and amending Directives 2003/41/EC and 2009/65/EC and Regulations (EC) No 1060/2009 and (EU) No 1095/2010 (Text with EEA relevance) [2011] OJ L 174, 1–73.

[129] Council Directive 2009/138/EC of 25 November 2009 on the taking-up and pursuit of the business of Insurance and Reinsurance (Solvency II) (recast) [2009] OJ L 335, 1–155.

[130] Charlotte Villiers, 'New Directions in the European Union's Regulatory Framework for Corporate Reporting, Due Diligence and Accountability: The Challenge of Complexity' (2022) 13European Journal of Risk Regulation 548.

chains, environmental protection, and the mitigation of the adverse impacts that corporate activities may have on climate change.

The principle of sustainability in Europe has entered into constitutions, civil codes, and even schoolbooks. It is an integral part of a culture and a mentality that has been established in the new generations. What needs to be rethought is the model that we want to impose on companies that currently feel hamstrung by excessive and hyper-technical regulations that they have to endure without being able to fully benefit from them—not the values underlying the model.

CHAPTER 30

Non-Governmental Organisations and Private Standard Setting

CYNTHIA A. WILLIAMS

1. Introduction

THIS chapter describes and analyses private standard setting as a partial solution to the challenges of climate change. Section 2 describes some of the more influential private climate standard setting initiatives, those developed by accountants, investors, and industry coalitions, particularly with respect to climate disclosure. It also describes some technical initiatives informing investors and markets. These categories are porous, since many of the standard setters overlap and/or collaborate with each other. The goal of Section 2 is to set out some influential actors and the standards they have produced. To put the materials in context, some brief discussion of private standard setting generally is provided.

As a caveat to Section 2, though, the construct of "private" standard setting needs to be understood as potentially misleading, since private standard setters are often intertwined with governments, government actors, and/or multilateral organisations that also incorporate government actors. As Stepan Wood has argued, governments are often intertwined with private standard setting in various ways; in his work he has identified eight distinct roles for governments in private standard setting.[1] Related to this point, Lisa Fairfax has most recently shown that the voluntary nature of many such standards, particularly investor-focused disclosure standards, belies market and consumer forces causing firms to treat these standards as effectively mandatory.[2] The implications of this integration of governments and private standard setters, and blurring distinctions between mandatory and voluntary standards, point to the

[1] Stepan Wood, 'Environmental Management Systems and Public Authority in Canada: Rethinking Environmental Governance' (2003) 10(1) Buffalo Environmental Law Journal 129, 131. Wood describes the eight roles as follows: 'Steering (influencing the development, use or content of voluntary initiatives through official policy pronouncements, participation in standards development or creation of legal ground rules or backstops for voluntary initiatives); Self-discipline (applying voluntary initiatives to government operations or agreeing to international trade rules that turn voluntary standards into constraints on regulatory authority); Knowledge production (generating and disseminating ideas, information and expertise about the design, use or value of voluntary initiatives); Reward (providing material incentives for adherence to voluntary initiatives through regulatory relief programs, financial incentives or green procurement policies); Command (issuing legally binding requirements to adhere to voluntary initiatives through court orders or legislation); Benchmarking (using voluntary initiatives as standards for 'reasonableness' in civil actions or 'due diligence' in regulatory prosecutions); Challenge (challenging firms or other organisations to adhere to voluntary initiatives); and Borrowing (incorporating voluntary initiatives into legal instruments such as statutes and regulations)'.

[2] Lisa M Fairfax, 'Dynamic Disclosure: An Exposé on the Mythical Divide between Voluntary and Mandatory ESG Disclosure' (2022) 101 Texas Law Review 273.

importance of this topic for regulatory design in addressing climate change and motivating the necessary transition to a low-carbon future. Since governments may often adopt private standards, and this adoption may be a way to shape regulation, we might particularly want to ask what is missing from the private standards and best practices so far.

I will then take up two analytic questions in Sections 3 and 4. First, this description of private climate standards suggests that unlike many other areas of private standard setting, investors and investor-focused NGOs have developed the most significant standards. Other writers have come to a similar conclusion.[3] If that is correct, what are the implications? Does this investors' role suggest limits to the power of these standards, or is it a point of leverage to be further developed?

Second, observing that many private climate disclosure standards have become globally influential, such as those from the Taskforce on Climate-Related Financial Disclosures (TCFD), which have been incorporated into the International Sustainability Standards Board (ISSB)'s climate disclosure standards, while some celebrated substantive standards, such as the Glasgow Financial Alliance for Net Zero (GFANZ), which required divesting from coal, are disintegrating, what implications can be drawn? I will argue that market-enhancing standards such as expanded disclosure or those developing new markets and financial opportunities, such as the Climate Bond Initiative (CBI)'s sector standards for selling a new class of bonds, can become globally significant and effective within their remit. In contrast, I argue market-limiting standards are unlikely to develop such power. Observing this distinction, my conclusion is that if private substantive standards are to be a powerful tool in establishing limits to new financing or insuring of oil or coal, incentives within firms would need to be realigned, perhaps through the structure of executive compensation. Otherwise, it is unrealistic in a competitive, modern capitalist economy to think that even in coalition, market-limiting standards will thrive. Section 5 concludes the chapter.

2. Private Standard Setting and Climate Change

2.1 Private Standards and Corporate Accountability

Private and quasi-private standards have been a feature of economic relationships since the earliest days of trade. Accounting standards are an ubiquitous example of private standard setting. For instance, there is evidence of accounting standards being used in ancient Athens to audit government accounts starting in 500 to 300 BC.[4] Today, the most widely used global accounting standards are International Financial Reporting Standards (IFRS), developed by a private entity, the International Accounting Standards Board (IASB). As those standards became influential, governments were given an oversight function as part of IASB's governance

[3] Daniel C Esty and Nathan de Arriba-Sellier, 'Zeroing in on Net-Zero: From Soft Law to Hard Law in Corporate Climate Change Pledges' (2023) 94 Colorado Law Review 435, 442 (stating that companies net-zero pledges are 'largely defined and enforced, not by governments, but rather by interested stakeholders, most notably from the finance and investment worlds').

[4] Margaret Blair, Cynthia A Williams, and Liwen Lin, 'The Roles of Standardization, Certification, and Assurance Services in Global Commerce' in Lorenzo Sacconi and others (eds), *Corporate Social Responsibility and Corporate Governance: The Contribution of Economic Theory and Related Disciplines* (Palgrave Press 2011), citing George J Costouros, *Auditing in the Athenian State of the Golden Age (500–300 B.C.)* (eGrove 1978).

structure, but the standards are still developed separately from governments.[5] In 2021, at COP 26 in Glasgow, the IFRS Foundation announced the establishment of the ISSB with a remit to develop sustainability disclosure standards. These standards will be discussed below.

As global trade expanded after World War II, the International Organisation for Standardization (ISO), a non-governmental organisation, was founded, in 1946.[6] Over the next forty years, ISO developed thousands of technical standards for product specifications and quality, reducing transaction costs in negotiating contracts and allowing global trade to flourish. Then, "in 1987, the ISO embarked on a significant new path when it adopted the ISO 9000 standards of quality management", applicable to the management systems firms use rather than to specific product specifications.[7] These standards by which processes within firms and manufacturing plants could be certified—thus providing information unable to be determined by inspecting the quality of products—have had great influence. The number of firms and manufacturing facilities certified to the ISO 9000 standards grew rapidly, "from 27,816 in 48 countries in 1993, to 670,399 in 154 countries by 2004 (ISO Survey)".[8]

During the same period that ISO 9000 was being developed (work had begun in 1980), private standard setting for other industries began, and standards began to incorporate social and environmental factors as well as safety and health. One of the first industry-specific sets of standards was the Responsible Care Initiative in chemicals manufacturing, begun in Canada in 1983 but accelerated in response to the tragedy in 1984 in which 15,000–20,000 people in Bhopal, India died and another 500,000 people were injured by the escape of methyl isocyanate from an insecticide plant owned by Union Carbide.[9] Over the past three decades such standards have been developed by multilateral organisations; public/private partnerships; multi-stakeholder negotiation processes; industries and companies; institutional investors; functional groups such as accountancy firms and social assurance consulting groups (many of which did not exist more than twenty years ago); NGOs; and non-financial ratings agencies.[10] Privately developed standards for responsible business conduct now exist in virtually every industry and service.[11]

These industry and regulatory developments did not exist in a vacuum, and for the most part were not initiated by companies themselves (unlike in the chemical industry) but were reactions to the multifaceted corporate accountability movement begun in the 1970s. In a 1999 paper written for the World Wildlife Fund (WWF) and the World Resources Institute (WRI), Broad and Cavanagh developed a matrix to describe and analyse this movement.[12] They include descriptions of the (1) strategic goals of the various actors (such as environmental or

[5] International Financial Reporting Standards Foundation, 'About Us' <www.ifrs.org/about-us/our-structure/> accessed 23 May 2025.

[6] International Organization for Standardization, 'About' <www.iso.org/about> accessed 23 May 2025.

[7] Blair et al (n 4) 3.

[8] ibid (citing ISO Survey 2004).

[9] Jean M Belanger, 'Responsible Care in Canada: The Evolution of an Ethic and a Commitment,' (2005) 27 (Mar–Apr) Chemistry International 2.

[10] Julia Black, 'Decentering Regulation: Understanding the Role of Regulation and Self-Regulation in a 'Post-Regulatory' World,' (2001) 54(1) Current Legal Problems 103.

[11] See, e.g., Cynthia A Williams, 'Corporate Responsibility and Corporate Governance' in Jeffrey Gordon and Georg Ringe (eds), *Oxford Handbook of Corporate Law and Governance* (2nd edn, OUP 2025) (describing the trend of private corporate responsibility standards with examples across a range of industries).

[12] Robin Broad and John Cavanagh, 'The Corporate Accountability Movement: Lessons and Opportunities' (1999) 23(2) Fletcher Forum of World Affairs 151. For a more comprehensive description

labour rights activists); (2) the targets of the campaigns (individual companies such as Nestle or Nike versus whole industries); (3) the methods being used; and (4) the geographic focus. Among methods described were company or industry codes of conduct (private standards, in our nomenclature); efforts to include labour or environmental clauses in trade agreements; direct action; ethical consumption efforts; consumer campaigns generally; litigation; shareholder resolutions and actions; and dialogue and engagement with companies directly.[13] The role of expanded social and environmental disclosure was discussed briefly as part of shareholder methodologies, in that some socially responsible investors (SRI), also an outgrowth of the corporate accountability movement, were starting to ask for such disclosure. Climate change as a corporate accountability issue is not mentioned in this 1999 report.

2.2 Private Standards Specific to Climate Change

Private standard development specific to climate change has emphasised global frameworks for disclosure of emissions; corporate climate governance and risk management; systems for measuring emissions; and technical climate standards and assessment tools. Investor and corporate coalitions have been key to each of these developments.

2.2.1 Measuring Greenhouse Gas Emissions

Measuring greenhouse gas (GHG) emissions and allocating them to different aspects of a company's productive processes is the earliest private climate standard this author's investigations have uncovered. A collaboration begun in late 1997 by WRI and the World Business Council for Sustainable Development (WBCSD) created the Greenhouse Gas Protocol.[14] As the GHG Protocol describes the initial process, WRI and WBCSD "convened a core steering group comprised of members from environmental groups (such as WWF, Pew Center on Global Climate Change, The Energy Research Institute) and industry (such as Norsk Hydro, Tokyo Electric, Shell) to guide the multi-stakeholder standard development process".[15] The GHG Protocol defines the following three categories of emissions: Scope 1, emissions from the company or other entity's operations; Scope 2, emissions from purchased energy; and Scope 3, emissions from the entity's supply and distribution chains, thus the entity's entire value chain. According to the GHG Protocol, in 2023, 97% of S&P 500 companies that are disclosing information to CDP used its standards.[16] It is currently developing "standards, tools, and on-line training" to help countries and cities track their progress in meeting their goals to reduce GHG emissions pursuant to the Paris Agreement from December 2015.[17]

A newer initiative to measure "financed emissions", those enabled by financial institutions' lending, underwriting and investments, is now underway, called the Partnership for Carbon

of many of the people who launched the corporate accountability movement in the US, some significant proportion of whom lived and worked in Boston, see Sandra Waddock, *The Difference Makers: How Social and Institutional Entrepreneurs Created the Corporate Responsibility Movement* (Greenleaf Publishing 2008). Sandra Waddock is a business school professor who was an early observer and contributor to the analysis of corporate social responsibility within the business academic literature.

[13] ibid 154–60.

[14] Greenhouse Gas Protocol, 'History of GHG Protocol' <https://ghgprotocol.org/about-us> accessed 23 May 2025.

[15] ibid.

[16] ibid.

[17] ibid.

Accounting Financials (PCAF). PCAF was started by fourteen Dutch banks in 2015, and by today has created the Global GHG Accounting and Reporting Standard for the Financial Industry.[18] PCAF is a collaboration supported by over 500 financial institutions committed to disclosing emissions associated with their financial activities, that is, their Scope 3 emissions.[19] PCAF is working with the Carbon Disclosure Project (CDP) (discussed below) to clarify and systematise these "financed emissions" standards.[20] This work is undoubtedly accelerated by the GFANZ commitments by financial institutions with over $130 trillion in invested capital committing to be net zero 2050 in their portfolios of investments and lending. These financial institutions thus need metrics to track their progress. As discussed below, many US and Canadian banks and asset managers have pulled out of GFANZ, and the status of their net-zero commitments is ambiguous.

2.2.2 Climate Risk and Governance Disclosure

One method of promoting corporate accountability that has become central in climate accountability is expanded ESG (environmental, social, and governance) disclosure. In fact, disclosure is the major private standards regulatory mechanism being used to address climate change. One early, significant contributor was (and still is) CDP. Beginning in 2000, and supported then by thirty-five investors, CDP sends short annual surveys to companies around the world about their GHG emissions and targets, if any, for reducing emissions. By today, over 740 financial institutions support the CDP surveys, representing US$130 trillion in invested assets, and companies in 130 countries and about two/thirds of global market capitalisation report through CDP.[21] At one point CDP created the CDP Standards Board and developed private standards for climate disclosure, which standards have now been folded into the ISSB's Sustainability Disclosure and Climate Disclosure Standards,[22] as discussed below.

In 1997, the Coalition for Environmentally Responsible Economies (CERES) and the Tellus Institute, established the Global Reporting Initiative (GRI) to provide standards for corporate sustainability disclosure. In 2002, GRI was spun off as an independent entity in the Netherlands.[23] GRI disclosure has not been focused on climate risk disclosure, but its voluntary, multi-stakeholder framework for sustainability reporting has been widely adopted. Sixty-eight percent of reporting companies worldwide and 78% of the Global 250 use GRI as the basis for their corporate sustainability reporting.[24] After four iterations of its guidelines for "impact reporting on economy, environment, and people", GRI produced a set of general standards in 2016 for sustainability reporting, including disclosure of energy use as its "climate" disclosure, and subsequently it issued various specialised standards for different industries and topics that

[18] Partnership for Carbon Accounting Financials (PCAF), 'The History of PCAF' <https://carbonaccountingfinancials.com/en/about#about-pcaf> accessed 23 May 2025.

[19] PCAF, <https://carbonaccountingfinancials.com/> accessed 23 May 2025.

[20] CDP, 'PCAF and CDP Align Data Quality Systems' <https://www.cdp.net/en/insights/pcaf-and-cdp-align-data-quality-systems-to-support-standardization> accessed 14 June 2025.

[21] CDP, <https://www.cdp.net/en> accessed 14 June 2025.

[22] IFRS, 'Climate Disclosure Standards Board' <www.ifrs.org/sustainability/climate-disclosure-standards-board/> accessed 23 May 2025. See Esty et al (n 3); Blair et al (n 4); International Financial Reporting Standards Foundation (n 5).

[23] CERES, 'About Us: History' <www.CERES.org/about> accessed 23 May 2025.

[24] Global Reporting Initiative (GRI), 'Our Position in the Reporting Landscape' <www.globalreporting.org/public-policy-partnerships/the-reporting-landscape/> accessed 23 May 2025.

include energy use.[25] As of 2023, GRI has started further work on standards for climate change disclosure.[26]

Other sustainability disclosure standards that have been broadly adopted include those created by the Sustainability Accounting Standards Board (SASB), based in the US, with a focus on key sustainability challenges that may have material financial impacts within industries and subindustries;[27] the International Framework (Integrated Reporting), developed by the International Integrated Reporting Council (IIRC), focusing on strategy, governance, performance, and prospects of companies' use of six kinds of capital (financial, manufactured, intellectual, human, social and relationship, and natural);[28] and the Carbon Disclosure Standards Board (CDSB)'s framework for reporting environmental and climate information in required corporate reports such as the annual report[29] that was an offshoot of the CDP.[30]

The most clearly influential disclosure standards specific to climate are those promulgated by the TCFD. Created by the multilateral entity the Financial Stability Board (FSB) on then-Governor Mark Carney's request, the TCFD released its voluntary standards for the disclosure of companies' climate governance, strategy, risk management, and metrics and targets in 2017.[31] Chaired by Michael Bloomberg, founder of Bloomberg L. P., and co-chaired by Mary Schapiro, former Chair of the US Securities and Exchange Commission (SEC), the TCFD disclosure standards had been adopted by 4,000 organisations from more than 100 countries by November 2022, with a combined market capitalisation of US$27 trillion. The TCFD standards are also the basis for a number of significant regulatory proposals and enacted laws, such as in law enacted by New Zealand and the UK and in the US Securities and Exchange Commission's (now doomed) climate disclosure proposal. As of October 2023, the TCFD has disbanded, stating that it has "fulfilled its remit", and has asked the ISSB to take over progress on monitoring climate disclosure.[32]

Given the maturing of the voluntary sustainability reporting field, a consolidation process is underway. Each of the investor-oriented entities just mentioned (CDP, CDSB, SASB, and the IIRC) is working with the accounting industry through the IFRS (International Financial Reporting Standards) Foundation's newly established ISSB to create integrated sustainability reporting standards.[33] Announced at COP26 in Glasgow in November 2021,[34] the ISSB initiative shows the blurred lines between voluntary and governmental action. The IFRS Foundation (described above)[35] is an independent non-profit incorporated in Delaware, with its main headquarters in London and its standard-setting for international accounting

[25] GRI, <www.globalreporting.org> accessed 23 May 2025.

[26] GRI, 'Project for Climate Change Standards' <www.globalreporting.org/standards/standards-development/project-for-climate-change-standards/> accessed 23 May 2025.

[27] Sustainability Accounting Standards Board, <https://sasb.ifrs.org/> accessed 23 May 2025.

[28] International Integrated Reporting Framework, <www.integratedreporting.org> accessed 23 May 2025.

[29] Climate Disclosure Standards Board, <https://www.cdsb.net> accessed 23 May 2025.

[30] CDP (n 21).

[31] Task Force on Climate-Related Financial Disclosures (TCFD), <https://www.fsb-tcfd.org/> accessed 23 May 2025.

[32] ibid.

[33] International Sustainability Standards Board (ISSB), <www.ifrs.org/groups/international-sustainability-standards-board/> accessed 23 May 2025.

[34] ibid.

[35] See text accompanying Blair et al (n 4).

standards accomplished through the IASB.[36] The creation of the ISSB was supported by powerful multilateral organisations such as the G7, the G20, the FSB, and the International Organization of Securities Commissions, African Finance Ministers, and Finance Ministers and Central Bank Governors from more than forty jurisdictions.[37] (Such blurring is not new, but may be accelerating, as mentioned in the introduction to this chapter and in the work of Lisa Fairfax.)[38] The GRI, which has an explicit stakeholder focus rather than an investor focus, is working alongside the ISSB to "ensure complementary and interoperable standards".[39]

In 2023, ISSB released its general sustainability disclosure standard (S1), as well as a climate disclosure standard (S2).[40] Since these standards were developed within ISSB by consolidating the output of most of the significant sustainability and climate disclosure standards setters into its process, including SASB, TCFD, the Value Reporting Framework,[41] and the CDP's Sustainability Disclosure Framework,[42] today, the ISSB is the most significant private standard setter for climate disclosure. In parallel, the IFRS published an exposure draft in July 2024 with examples of how climate-related uncertainties should be disclosed in the company's financial statements.[43] In June 2025, the IASB tentatively decided to publish most of the examples, subject to its members' approval.[44] Both the ISSB and the IFRS/IASB's work suggest a direction of travel that may eventually require companies to price climate risk and the negative externalities of production and require those prices and costs to be incorporated into companies' annual, audited financial reports.

TCFD and ISSB are two of three global initiatives to develop standards for sustainability and climate disclosure that have emerged within the last decade. In addition, in 2020, a biodiversity disclosure initiative was launched, the Taskforce on Nature-related Financial Disclosures (TNFD). This initiative was motivated by World Economic Forum (WEF) research conducted together with Price Waterhouse Coopers showing that US$44 trillion "of economic value generation—over half the world's total GDP—is moderately or highly dependent on nature and its services".[45] TNFD's framework for understanding and accounting for nature-related

[36] International Accounting Standards Board, 'About' <www.ifrs.org/groups/international-accounting-standards-board/> accessed 23 May 2025.

[37] ibid.

[38] Black (n 10) 103–47 (for an early analysis of the phenomenon of the blurring of government and voluntary standard-setting).

[39] GRI, 'GRI welcomes first two IFRS Sustainability Disclosure Standards' <www.globalreporting.org/news/news-center/progress-towards-a-strengthened-sustainability-reporting-system/> accessed 23 May 2025.

[40] ISSB, 'Standards Navigator' <www.ifrs.org/issued-standards/ifrs-sustainability-standards-navigator/> accessed 23 May 2025.

[41] TCFD (n 31) (stating that as of 2023 TCFD has been disbanded and its work transferred to the IFRS Foundation).

[42] ISSB, 'Climate Disclosure Standards Board' <www.ifrs.org/sustainability/climate-disclosure-standards-board> accessed 23 May 2025.

[43] IFRS, 'Exposure Draft: Climate-Related and Other Uncertainties in the Financial Statements: Proposed Illustrative Examples',https://www.ifrs.org/content/dam/ifrs/project/climate-related-other-uncertainties-fs/iasb-ed-2024-6-climate-uncertainties-fs.pdf> accessed 22 July 2025.

[44] IFRS, 'Climate-Related and Other Uncertainties in the Financial Statements' <https://www.ifrs.org/projects/work-plan/climate-related-risks-in-the-financial-statements/> accessed 22 July 2025 (discussing June 2025 IASB meeting where the tentative decision was taken).

[45] 'Nature Risk Rising: Why the Crisis Engulfing Nature Matters for Business and the Economy' (World Economic Forum, 19 January 2020) <www.weforum.org/publications/nature-risk-rising-why-the-crisis-engulfing-nature-matters-for-business-and-the-economy/> accessed 23 May 2025.

dependencies, risks, and opportunities was published in September of 2023, and is in use by over 500 firms and organisations with US$17 trillion of assets under management.[46] Underlying its disclosure framework is a process suggested to firms to "understand, identify and assess nature-related dependencies, impacts, risks and opportunities".[47]

2.2.3 Technical Climate Standards and Assessment

Many organisations have developed technical standards to support and evaluate the transition to a low-carbon economy. This summary is by necessity partial, given the proliferation of such initiatives. It provides a brief introduction to some of the most highly visible technical standard setters and also offers some indication of the way that assessment tools are being developed to judge emissions reductions and net-zero transition strategies. These technical standards go beyond disclosure by developing substantive standards for transition initiatives across multiple sectors.

One organisation that has developed standards for transition and climate aligned projects and bonds to support those projects is the Climate Bonds Initiative (CBI), which created the idea of certified climate and green bonds and has substantially helped to grow that market.[48] Established in 2010, currently there are US$3.656 trillion of climate and green bonds issued and certified to CBI or comparable green bond standards.[49] CBI has created twenty-two technical standards for projects able to be certified as appropriate for the issuance of climate bonds, from agriculture to cement to shipping to steel to wind energy.[50] CBI's process for developing its technical standards involves scientific experts and industry specialists comprising technical working groups in each of the twenty-two areas where standards have been developed, but the actual approval of the standards is by a governance body that includes major environmental organisations (such as the Natural Resources Defense Council (NRDC)) and climate change focused investor coalitions such as Institutional Investor Group on Climate Change (IIGCC) and CERES.[51] It has also developed a taxonomy of climate aligned criteria for projects, which criteria were incorporated into the EU Sustainable Finance Taxonomy.[52]

Another entity developing standards for companies to use to set GHG emissions reduction targets consistent with 1.5° C goals and measure their performance according to those targets is the Science Based Targets Initiative (SBTi), which is another project of WRI. Incorporated as a charity in the United Kingdom in 2023, SBTi was formed as a collaboration between WRI, WWF, CDP, and the United Nations Global Compact.[53] It states that by the end of 2023, over 4,000 companies and financial institutions were setting emissions reduction targets consistent

[46] TNFD, 'TNFD Adopters' <https://tnfd.global/engage/tnfd-adopters/> accessed 14 June 2025.

[47] TNFD, 'Additional Guidance' <https://tnfd.global/publication/additional-guidance-on-assessment-of-nature-related-issues-the-leap-approach/> accessed 23 May 2025.

[48] Climate Bonds Initiative, <https://climatebonds.net> accessed 23 May 2025. This author is not an objective observer of CBI, having been involved in the organisation from its earliest inception, in weekly discussions with three other co-founders over the course of a year before it was incorporated as a charity in the UK, and having been a trustee on its board for ten years.

[49] ibid.

[50] CBI, 'Standard: Sector Criteria' <www.climatebonds.net/standard/sector-criteria> accessed 23 May 2025.

[51] CBI, 'Governance: Standards Board' <www.climatebonds.net/standard/governance/board> accessed 23 May 2025.

[52] CBI, 'Climate Bonds Taxonomy' <www.climatebonds.net/standard/taxonomy> accessed 23 May 2025.

[53] Science Based Targets Initiative (SBTi), <www.wri.org/initiatives/science-based-targets> accessed 23 May 2025.

with SBTi, and having their targets validated by the SBTi.[54] It has now begun the consultation process on a second version of its transition standards, a process that was prolonged by debates within the organisation over the proper role—if any—of carbon offsets in a science based transition plan.[55]

An investor-led assessment initiative is the Transition Pathway Initiative (TPI), which was established in 2017 to assess companies' and countries' transition plans and governance against benchmarks developed by other entities, including the SBTi.[56] In June of 2022, it established an academic research centre at the London School of Economics and Political Science (LSE) Grantham Research Institute on Climate Change and the Environment to develop standards by which it will evaluate companies' and countries' carbon performance and management of the transition to a low-carbon economy.[57] As an example of its standards and assessments, in 2024 the TPI published an assessment of the climate transition strategies and targets of twenty-six global banks, ten additional US banks with large cross-regional business, and two custodian banks.[58] The assessment evaluated banks' net-zero transition ambitions against the Net Zero Banking Assessment Framework (NZBAF) that the TPI Research Centre had developed, which is an "investor-led framework developed in consultation with IIGCC and CERES evaluating banks on seventy-two sub-indicators across ten areas, such as their decarbonisation strategy, climate governance, or exposure and emissions disclosure".[59] The TPI also performed more in-depth quantitative assessment of the banks' transition strategies and metrics, paying attention to which sectors and business activities each bank included in their transition strategies.[60] Each of its assessments to date—of companies in twenty-four sectors, banks, bond underwriters in oil and gas and utilities, and countries—are meant to inform investors about the seriousness with which these entities are addressing the transition to a low-carbon economy.

One policy initiative that is not setting its own standards, but synthesising sector-specific emissions reductions benchmarks from other UN, investor, and NGO initiatives, as well as from the scientific literature, is the Berlin-based New Climate Institute.[61] Its sector-specific industry standards are meant to provide scientifically sound emissions targets for companies to use in developing their transition plans through to 2050, and for investors to use to assess those plans.[62] The targets have been developed in reliance on the UN Framework Convention on Climate Change assessments, the UN High-Level Expert Group standards (2022), ISO's Net Zero Guidelines (ISO 2022), the SBTi Corporate Net Zero Standard (SBTi 2024), and the

[54] ibid.

[55] These debates were well publicised. The draft standard 2.0 published in 2025 focusses primarily on companies reducing their emissions and reduces the scope for companies to purchase offsets while maintaining SBTi certification. Kenza Bryan, 'Top Climate Standard-Setter Responds to Carbon Credit Backlash' *Financial Times Moral Money* (London, 21 March 2025) <https://www.ft.com/content/cfc30f35-f525-462b-8321-38233a1a7046> assessed 15 June 2025.

[56] Transition Pathway Initiative, <https://www.transitionpathwayinitiative.org/overview> assessed 15 June 2025.

[57] ibid.

[58] ibid.

[59] Transition Pathway Initiative, <https://www.transitionpathwayinitiative.org/banks> assessed 15 June 2025.

[60] ibid.

[61] New Climate Institute, < https://newclimate.org/> assessed 15 June 2025.

[62] New Climate Institute, <https://newclimate.org/sites/default/files/2024-04/NewClimate_CorporateBenchmarksRepository_April2024.pdf> assessed 15 June 2025.

UNFCC Race to Zero Starting Line and Leadership Practices 3.0 criteria (Race to Zero 2022).[63] Sectors included are automotive manufacturers, energy utilities, fashion retailing, food and agriculture, oil and gas, international aviation, supermarket retail, steel, cement, electronics, information and communications technology, international shipping, industrial corporations, pulp and paper, chemical manufacturing, construction, and real estate.[64] This Institute also assesses the German and EU governments' policies and international diplomacy for consistency with the European Green Deal and the Paris Agreement, which may eventually provide data for further standard setting.

One final project that seeks, ultimately, to inform science-based targets for standard setting primarily for cities and companies is the Lancet Planetary Health Commission, an academic collaboration among sixty-five scientists across thirty-nine universities around the world.[65] This Commission report is based on but goes beyond the biophysical Planetary Boundaries work of the Potsdam Institute for Climate Impact Research, the UN 2030 Agenda and associated Sustainable Development Goals (SDGs), and the "doughnut economics" work that used planetary boundaries and added social indicators to define a "safe and just operating space" for humanity.[66] The Lancet Planetary Health Commission explicitly adds justice and distributional elements to those frameworks to describe "safe and just Earth-system Boundaries (ESBs)" necessary to create "a safe and just corridor that is essential to ensuring sustainable and resilient human and planetary health and thriving in the Anthropocene".[67] It then identifies principles for "translating" these justice-expanded ESBs into science-based targets, especially for cities and businesses "because both are responsible for large shares of environmental pressures across all ESBs",[68] while recognising the substantial challenges of "downscaling" to individual industry sectors and then companies.[69] What is striking to this author about the underlying analytic work informing this project and its arguments for science-based targets is its clear recognition that "ensuring Earth-system stability and resilience requires addressing issues of social justice, underlying drivers and pressures, and distributions and technical aspects of how resources are produced, distributed, and consumed".[70]

2.2.4 Investor Coalitions

Over the past three to four decades, coalitions of investors recognising the importance of responsible business conduct and sharing best practices to advance responsible business conduct have proliferated. One example is the United Nations' Principles for Responsible Investment (PRI), established in 2006. By 2022, institutions managing US$121 trillion of invested capital have committed to the PRI, which requires investors to incorporate ESG data into investment practices across their asset classes. PRI has not been a standard setter on climate, but since 2018 has worked with outside advisors on what it calls the Inevitable Policy Response (IPR)

[63] ibid.

[64] ibid.

[65] The Lancet Planetary Health Commission, 'A Just World on a Safe Plante: a *Lancet Planetary Health*-Earth Commission Report on Earth-system Boundaries, Translations, and Transformations' (2024) 8:e813-73 Planetary Health <https://www.thelancet.com/action/showPdf?pii=S2542-5196%2824%2900042-1> accessed 15 June 2025. The corresponding author is Dr. Juan C Rocha at the Stockholm Resilience Centre, Stockholm University.

[66] ibid 4.

[67] ibid 1.

[68] ibid 34.

[69] ibid.

[70] ibid 3.

to climate change and to share best practices for investors on how to avoid sharp corrections through such policy responses.[71]

Among shareholder entities, the Broad and Cavanagh analysis discussed above points to the Interfaith Center on Corporate Responsibility (ICCR), started in 1984 and still a leading advocate and organiser of social and environmental shareholder resolutions; and then known as CERES, which has played a prominent role in developing investor coalitions to promote corporate and financial understanding of climate change financial risks and opportunities.[72] In 2002, CERES issued a highly influential report setting out the case that climate risk is financial risk, and in 2003 it launched the Investors' Network on Climate Risk together with the United Nations' Environment Programme (UNEP).[73] CERES leadership regarding investors and climate risk has been extremely important, including by initiating Climate Action 100+ , a global consortium of over 600 investors engaging with 169 of the top emitting companies worldwide.[74] This investor engagement is directed at obtaining what it describes as three clear commitments from companies: (1) to reduce their GHG emissions; (2) to improve climate governance at the board level; and (3) to improve climate disclosure consistent with the TCFD framework and to strengthen transition plans, including seeking certification consistent with the SBTi.[75] These goals are stated to be "in order to create shareholder value",[76] consistent with the stated purpose of the initiative: "Climate Action 100+ is an investor-led initiative to ensure the world's largest corporate greenhouse gas emitters take appropriate action on climate change in order to mitigate financial risk and to maximise the long-term value of assets".[77] CERES has not been a standard setter itself, so far as this author is aware, but has provided consistent, long-term leadership among investors seeking better climate data and strong climate commitments.

3. Investor Leadership in Standard Setting: Benefits and Limitations

Institutional investor leadership is evident throughout the private standard-setting process, which this analysis emphasises. Climate Action 100+ is a coalition of five investor groups: the Asia Investor Group on Climate Change (AIGCC), CERES, the Investor Group on Climate Change (IGCC), IIGCC, and PRI. Similarly, CDP and SBTi are investor-backed, while SASB, ISSB, TCFD and TNRD are each designed to inform investors. However, investors are not the only entities shaping these private standards. The substantive, technical standards of CBI and SBTi, as well as the disclosure standards of SASB, ISSB, TCFD and TNRD, are informed by technical advisory groups that include NGOs such as CDP, corporate participants, accounting firms, and (for SBTi)

71 United Nations Principles for Responsible Investment, 'Inevitable Policy Response Project' <www.unpri.org/inevitable-policy-response/what-is-the-inevitable-policy-response/4787.article> accessed 23 May 2025.

72 Broad and Cavanagh (n 12) 158 (ICCR); 153–54 (quoting CERES co-chair Joan Bavaria); 158 (CERES engagement with companies). For CERES role in developing climate coalitions, see Climate Action 100+ (n 74).

73 CERES, 'About: 2002 and 2003' <www.CERES.org/about> accessed 23 May 2025.

74 Climate Action 100+, 'Global Investors Driving Business Transition' <www.climateaction100.org/> accessed 23 May 2025.

75 ibid 'The Three Goals' <www.climateaction100.org/the-three-goals/> accessed 23 May 2025.

76 ibid.

77 Climate Action 100+ (n 74).

the UN through the UN Global Compact. Nevertheless, institutional investor leadership has been highly significant in having climate change recognised as a material financial risk and in developing standards for greater disclosure of companies' actions to address that risk.

Institutional investor leadership has some obvious advantages in a market economy. First, large accumulations of invested capital are respected and, more often than not, the views of those managing such accumulations are treated seriously, particularly if they are coming from "the mainstream". When Larry Fink of BlackRock stated in his 2020 letter to CEOs that we are "on the edge of a fundamental reshaping of finance" to incorporate sustainability and climate change, it was widely reported on in the press and spurred debate.[78] Indeed, when these kind of statements were followed in 2021 by institutional investors with US$130 trillion of invested capital signing onto the GFANZ, debate turned to political resistance and ultimately litigation in the US—indicating that the views of GFANZ signatories were being taken seriously.[79]

Second, there is a legitimacy to investors' requests for disclosure of more and better climate data. It is presumed that the request is based on sophisticated understandings of climate change and nature loss as material financial risks. In addition, the expertise investors and particularly industry participants contribute to private standard setting is important to potentially ground the standards in feasible best practices and achievable ambitions, which are other aspects of legitimacy.[80] This legitimacy from corporate involvement in private standard setting includes the risks of insufficiently protective standards being adopted, as the debate over carbon offsets within SBTi exemplifies.[81] Yet insights from corporate actors in standard setting in the transition economy are encouraged, since innovation and learning from within corporate enterprises and their supply chains could improve industry-sector transition standards as they are promulgated and revised.

Third, large accumulations of invested capital can have power, including the power to meet with companies for their climate engagement. Climate Action 100+ states that 90% of the companies with which it engages now have board committees for climate change governance, and 80% now have net-zero commitments.[82] These data suggest that the highly emitting companies that Climate Action 100+ is targeting are treating the requests of these large investors seriously. As new private standard setters SBTi and TPI develop scientifically informed substantive standards by which companies' transition plans can be judged or certified, a virtuous cycle could develop in which exaggerated claims about net-zero plans are reduced, and the ambitions of climate leaders within industry sectors are more clearly recognised and rewarded by institutional investors.

Last, private standard setting does not exist in a regulatory vacuum but is informed by and informs public regulation.[83] Benjamin Cashore and others propose an analytic framework for evaluating the relationships between private and public regulation that is based on identifying

[78] See, e.g., Andrew Ross Sorkin, 'New Lodestar for BlackRock: Climate Crisis' *New York Times* (New York, 14 Jan 2020) B1.

[79] Cynthia A Williams, 'Private Climate Governance of Finance: "Net Zero" Prospects and Politics' (2024) 26 University of Pennsylvania Journal of Business Law 1195 (for discussion of these developments in the US).

[80] Steven Bernstein and Benjamin Cashore, 'Can Non-State Global Governance be Legitimate? An Analytic Framework' (2007) 1 Regulation & Governance 347.

[81] (n 55). This risk has long been understood by private governance scholars. See Julia Black, 'Constructing and Contesting Legitimacy and Accountability in Polycentric Regulatory Regimes (2008) 2 Regulation & Governance 137.

[82] Climate Action 100+ (n 75).

[83] Wood et al (n 1).

the "governance sphere" that regulation is addressing, defining a governance sphere as "all efforts to address a common problem".[84] Building on an emerging literature, Cashore and others identify different relationships between private and public governance, generally identifying relationships of complementarity, competition, or coexistence.[85] Moreover, they emphasise that competition over the definition of a problem is an important aspect of private standard setting that can be observed both within multi-stakeholder private standard-setting initiatives and between such initiatives and government.[86]

As an example of the importance of this competition over the problem definition, we can look to the global climate disclosure standards. Within the common problems of climate change and sustainability, the disclosure framework developed by TCFD has informed the IFRS Sustainability Disclosure Standards 1 and 2, and both have informed disclosure regulations in thirty jurisdictions as of December 2024.[87] Investors could provide more serious support for overcoming the political economy problems that led to private standard setting, namely, government failures to regulate climate change as strenuously and effectively as the scale of the challenge requires.[88] Yet investors may also align with corporations in defining the problems to be overcome narrowly,[89] such as information asymmetries regarding emissions or a lack of standardised data. In contrast, a more expansive definition of the problems to be addressed may focus on business models that depend on consumerism or constant economic growth without frameworks to require internalising the negative externalities from those business practices.[90] As with the expertise and legitimacy points discussed previously, investor-focussed and corporate multi-stakeholder private standard setting has power to affect public regulation, but that power will understandably be exercised within the limits of existing business models. It is to the limitations of the private standards set by and for investors that this analysis now turns.

First, the world has approximately US$450 trillion of investment capital to deploy.[91] Even if PRI's members, or GFANZ coalition's initial members, both comprising US$130 trillion of investment capital, were all serious about investing consistent with climate change parameters—and they are presumably not all serious—that would still leave close to three-quarters of investment capital potentially misaligned.

Second, investors will go where there is money to be made. For years oil and gas stock values were lower than the S&P 500 benchmark, until 2022 when Russia invaded Ukraine. Then, investors poured into oil and gas stocks, which surged in value.[92] That reflects rational (albeit

[84] Benjamin Cashore and others, 'Private Authority and Public Policy Interactions in Global Contexts: Governance Spheres for Problem Solving' (2021) 15(4) Regulation & Governance 1166, 1170.

[85] ibid.

[86] ibid.

[87] Deloitte, 'Adoption of IFRS Sustainability Disclosure Standards by Jurisdiction' (*IAS Plus*, 19 December 2024) <https://www.iasplus.com/content/7f753e89-0775-4cef-8338-86a49618796f> accessed 7 July 2025.

[88] Daniel C Esty, 'Mastering the Labyrinth of Sustainability: Toward a New Foundation for the Market Economy' (2022) 4 Revue Europeenne Du Droit 118 (arguing for regulatory systems to require, at a minimum, that companies internalise all negative externalities in order to advance sustainable capitalism based upon the polluter pays principle).

[89] cf Cashore et al (n 84), 1177 (discussing the under-theorised importance of how public and private actors define the problem to be solved by any regulations or private standards being proposed).

[90] Esty (n 88).

[91] Jens Beckert, *How We Sold Our Future: The Failure to Fight Climate Change* (Polity 2025) 133.

[92] Jakhongir Kakhkharov and others, 'Global Evidence on the Russia-Ukraine Conflict and Energy Stock Returns' [2024] 93 International Review of Economics & Finance 413.

unfortunate in this context) economic behaviour, as we would expect and in many circumstances demand of investors. Empirical work by Bolton and Kacperczyk contributes a number of important findings to the question of what can be expected of investors in their paper *Do Investors Care About Carbon Risk?*[93] First, some investors, such as asset managers, pension funds, and insurance companies, are limiting their exposure to industries with high scope 1 emissions, such as oil and gas, utilities and transportation, while other investors "loaded up" on those stocks.[94] Second, the stock of companies with high CO_2 exposure earns higher returns than others, showing that investors are demanding compensation for the perceived risks of such exposure.[95] Depending on an investor's time frame for investment, however, it may want to take the higher risk/higher returns today and hedge against tomorrow. This point suggests limits to investors' motivations to produce fundamental change in companies' strategies (until the higher returns companies need to pay substantially affects their blended cost of capital).

Third, by relying on investors, companies and accounting firms to develop private standards, and lead on advocacy for adoption, either for disclosure or substantive limits, almost all arguments for taking action get filtered through the language of financial risk. As we have seen, these arguments can be undermined and/or bogged down in arguments over appropriate discount rates and future uncertainties.[96] Moreover, even if it is clearly shown that climate change portends systemic financial risk, it has been difficult in many instances to translate that risk into specific financial risks to individual companies, sectors, and industries. Clearly not impossible, but difficult and expensive. These difficulties are compounded by the lack of standardised, required, quantitative metrics for measuring financial risks to individual companies from climate change (and nature and biodiversity loss),[97] although progress is being made here. The welter of seemingly competing sustainability metrics can lead to companies' boards being unwilling or unable to agree on mitigation policies given uncertain financial analyses of future risks. This uncoordinated (although becoming consolidated) landscape can also provide the opportunity for greenwashing through positive "cherry picking", and the disclosure of unreliable data.[98]

Fourth, investor standard setting and investor focused advocacy take moral arguments off the table because of the perceived need to filter all arguments through the language of finance and financial risk. The contrast with the Lancet Planetary Health Commission's work is striking. Other than the GRI framework for triple-bottom line disclosure, which derives from a corporate accountability foundation, the investor-oriented private climate standards that predominate today lack either a social justice orientation or an underlying analysis of

[93] Patrick Bolton and Marcin Kacperczyk, 'Do Investors Care about Carbon Risk?' (2021) 142(2) Journal of Financial Economics 517–49.

[94] ibid 544–47.

[95] ibid 519, 544.

[96] Dirk Schoenmaker and Willem Schramade, 'Which Discount Rate for Sustainability?' (2024) Journal of Sustainable Finance and Accounting 100010 <https://doi.org/10.1016/j.josfa.2024.100010> accessed 15 July 2025 (summarising debate as between Nordhaus' 4.3% discount rate to evaluate investments in climate mitigation and adaptation versus Stern's 1.4% rate and discussing more recent debates over the proper social discount rate to apply).

[97] Esty (n 8) 124–25 (describing problems of multiple metrics for the task of requiring companies to internalise the negative externalities of their operations).

[98] ibid.

distributional harm from today's investment approaches. Rather, these standards focus more narrowly on emissions reductions, corporate climate governance, and corporate disclosure.

This author is well aware of the "least common denominator" phenomenon in developing collaborative approaches to difficult problems. Moreover, emissions reductions are difficult undertakings to achieve at a global scale, and thus the ambitions of these standards and actors should be recognised and applauded. Yet the emphasis on maintaining and expanding high net worth individuals' and wealthy countries' financial assets and protecting them from future harm suggests significant limitations from a justice and morality perspective. Should the US$68 trillion of invested capital of Climate Action 100+ or the US$130 trillion of PRI be challenged to more directly confront the extent to which their approaches to investment are contributing to making vulnerable peoples' lives worse? Does the investment community have a moral obligation to address "Northern" climate contributions to "Southern" harm, or at least to recognise the implications of their biases in investment?[99] Truly addressing these issues, as in the Lancet Planetary Health Commission analysis, would require significant changes in public pension funds' understandings of their fiduciary obligations, for instance, and may need changes in the law to require duties to the public good of future generations as an aspect of those obligations.[100] The point here is to assert that climate-aware investors' emphasis on protecting asset values and creating shareholder wealth for the world's wealthiest citizens strikes a morally hollow note.

Fifth, and finally, it is unclear that the ambition of these standards, focused so heavily on disclosure, is equal to the task of shaping the future we need. It is likely unrealistic to think that these standards alone could be equal to that task, since we need "all hands on deck" collaborations, including with governments, to produce frameworks that will motivate GHG reductions at scale. Mandatory disclosure of scope 1 emissions under some US and UK regimes has shown a 7% to 10% reduction in GHG emissions by the disclosing entities.[101] It is not clear that voluntary quantitative GHG disclosure will have the same effect, however, even given all the pressures on the largest companies to disclose, and it is unlikely that voluntary qualitative governance disclosure will, except more slowly and indirectly.[102]

It may be that as assessment standards increasingly turn to transition plans and net-zero strategies, both of companies and of finance, as discussed above, ambitions will develop that are more protective of global planetary health. This effect of the private transition plan assessment standards will likely be enhanced by EU Directives—in particular, the Corporate Sustainability Reporting Directive and the Corporate Sustainability Due Diligence Directive—that may soon require the largest EU and global companies doing business in the EU to report on their transition plans and actions taken to implement them.[103] Yet, as discussed in the

[99] Roland Mees, *Sustainable Action and Motivation: Pathways for Individuals, Institutions and Humanity* (Routledge 2019) (discussing the moral obligations of individuals and institutions, including financial institutions, regarding sustainability and climate change, and the motivational problems that limit action on those obligations).

[100] Seth Davis and Gregory Shaffer, Chapter 13 of this handbook; Ernest Lim, Chapter 18 of this handbook.

[101] Cynthia A Williams, 'Does Climate Disclosure Work to Reduce Greenhouse Gas Emissions? Emerging Evidence Suggests Cautious Optimism' (2025) 48(2) Seattle University Law Review 571 (analysing existing empirical evidence).

[102] ibid.

[103] The precise requirements for transition plans and disclosure about them are not finalised as of July 2025, when this chapter was written because the EU Commission is cutting back on the requirements in its prior sustainability Directives. It published an Omnibus Proposal in February

Lancet Planetary Health Commission report, reducing carbon emissions is just one part of the transition necessary to produce a stable, just Earth-system, as is necessary for future generations to flourish.[104]

4. What Is Reasonable to Expect of Private Standards?

The limitations just discussed give rise to a more fundamental question: What is reasonable to expect of private standards generally with respect to climate change, given the scope of the climate change problem and the interacting elements of the transitions needed? Observing the difference between how the TCFD disclosure standards were received in the commercial world and its continuing influence on regulation globally, versus the disintegration of the GFANZ, this authors suggests that market-enhancing private standards such as disclosure can reasonably be expected to become influential, while market-limiting standards will struggle to be influential in a competitive market economy. Some facts about GFANZ are sketched out here in order to further define and explore this suggestion.

In April 2021, in the lead up to the COP26 climate negotiations in Glasgow, GFANZ was announced with over US$70 trillion of assets under management within banks, asset managers, and asset owners.[105] These financial institutions pledged to, among other things, "establish credible net zero commitments covering all financed activities in all sectors of the financial system".[106] By the time of the COP26 meetings in November, more than US$130 trillion of assets under management among banks, asset managers, asset owners, and insurance companies had pledged to be net zero by 2050.[107] These pledges were tied to a commitment to align the entities' financial activities with the substantive standards of the UN Race to Zero, which include limiting financing of new oil and gas, and excluding new coal financing altogether.[108] Led by former UK Bank of England Governor Mark Carney, who is now Canada's prime minister, GFANZ seemed to have some promise as a voluntary industry standard for the constituent entities to reduce the carbon emissions of their "financed emissions".

2025, to 'make sustainability reporting more accessible and efficient; simplify due diligence to support responsible business practices; strengthen the carbon border adjustment mechanism for a fairer trade; and unlock opportunities in European investment programmes'. EU Commission Director-General for Communication, 'Commission Proposes to Cut Red Tape and Simplify Business Environment' Commission Europa EU News and Media, 26 Feb. 2025 < https://commission.europa.eu/news-and-media/news/commission-proposes-cut-red-tape-and-simplify-business-environment-2025-02-26_en> accessed 15 July 2025. See also Barbara Pozzo, Chapter 29, and Harro van Asselt and Jessica Crow, Chapter 33 of this handbook.

[104] Lancet Planetary Health Commission report (n 65).

[105] United Nations Climate Change, 'New Financial Alliance for Net Zero Emissions Launches' (2021) <https://unfccc.int/news/new-financial-alliance-for-net-zero-emissions-launches> accessed 15 June 2025.

[106] ibid.

[107] Simon Jessop and Andrea Shalal, 'CCOP 26 Coalition Worth $130 trillion Vows to Put Climate at the Heart of Finance' (*Reuters*, 3 November 2021) <https://www.reuters.com/business/cop/wrapup-politicians-exit-cop26-130tn-worth-financiers-take-stage-2021-11-03/> accessed 15 June 2025.

[108] Mark Segal, 'Mark Carney-Led GFANZ Drops Requirement for Race to Zero Commitment for Members' (*ESG Today*, 28 Oct 2022) <https://www.esgtoday.com/mark-carney-led-gfanz-drops-requirement-for-race-to-zero-commitment/> accessed 15 June 2025.

By 2025, the Alliance is in disarray. Efforts to align GFANZ with the substantive standards of the UN's Race to Zero collapsed. Membership criteria were loosened, and were untethered from promises to meet the Race to Zero standards, in an effort, ultimately unsuccessful, to keep the coalition intact.[109] Asset manager Vanguard and insurance companies Zurich Insurance Company and Munich Re left GFANZ in an early wave of defections (late 2022 and early 2023).[110] By January 2025, GFANZ has lost American banks and asset managers Goldman Sachs, Wells Fargo, Citigroup, Bank of America, Morgan Stanley, and JPMorgan Chase.[111] Canada's largest banks soon followed suit, with Bank of Montreal (BMO), TD Bank Group, CIBC, and National Bank leaving before Pres. Trump's 2025 inauguration,[112] and RBC leaving soon after.[113] Goldman Sach's departure led the Net Zero Asset Managers, part of GFANZ, to suspend operations while it undertook a review of the initiative.[114]

What do these developments say, if anything, about the limits of private climate standards? We might not have seen these defections if anti-ESG politics had not emerged so energetically in the US in 2022.[115] Those anti-ESG political activities became focussed on GFANZ. Members of GFANZ such as BlackRock, JPMorgan Chase, Citigroup, and Bank of America were targeted with requests for information from nineteen state attorneys general in the US for their participation, with claims of alleged antitrust violations and breaches of fiduciary duties.[116] Those allegations were followed closely by legislative efforts in oil and gas producing states to exclude state business with, or pension fund investment in, these and other listed banks for their "fossil fuel boycotts". Yet, the earliest defectors included re-insurers from the EU, not targeted US firms.[117] Moreover, and more significant: It is precisely because these standards suggested limiting financing new oil and gas, and pulling out of coal financing, that they became politically controversial. The economic interests of the affected industries caused those interests and aligned politicians to take the private standards seriously and attack them in multiple venues. Presumably any other serious climate private standards with substantive, market-limiting potential, would produce similar political pushback.

Expanded voluntary climate disclosure standards, as in TCFD, or CBI's twenty-two technical standards for bond issuance in different sectors, are market supporting. The TCFD

109 ibid.

110 Ross Kerber and Noor Zainab Hussain, 'Vanguard Quits Net Zero Climate Effort, Citing Need for Independence' (*Reuters*, 7 December 2022) <https://www.reuters.com/business/sustainable-business/vanguard-quits-net-zero-climate-alliance-2022-12-07/> accessed 15 July 2025; Andrew Putwain, 'Why Are Massive Re/insurers Leaving Net Zero Groups?' (*Insurance Investor*, 13 April 2023) <https://insuranceinvestor.com/articles/why-are-massive-reinsurers-leaving-net-zero-groups/> accessed 15 July 2025.

111 Saijel Kishan and Natasha White, 'Wall Street's Top Banks Just Quit a Popular Net-zero Alliance' (*Bloomberg Standard*, 6 January 2025) <https://www.bloomberg.com/news/articles/2025-01-04/wall-street-banks-keep-quitting-major-climate-alliance> accessed 15 July 2025.

112 Nivedita Balu, 'Top Canadia Banks Quit Global Climate Coalition Ahead of Trump Inauguration' (*Reuters*, 17 January 2025) <https://www.reuters.com/business/finance/bmo-becomes-first-canadian-bank-withdraw-net-zero-banking-alliance-2025-01-17/> accessed 7 July 2025.

113 Jeffrey Jones, 'Climate Alliance Loses Last Big Canadian Bank as RBC Withdraws' (*Globe and Mail*, Toronto, 31 Jan. 2025) <https://www.theglobeandmail.com/business/article-climate-alliance-loses-last-big-canadian-bank-as-rbc-withdraws> accessed 7 July 2025.

114 Net Zero Asset Managers Initiative, 'Update from Net Zero Asset Managers' Initiative' <https://www.netzeroassetmanagers.org/update-from-the-net-zero-asset-managers-initiative> accessed 7 July 2025.

115 John Dernbach, Chapter 35 of this handbook; see also Williams (n 79).

116 Williams (n 79).

117 See text accompanying (n 110).

disclosure informs investors, consumers, and employees, while burnishing the reputations of participating firms, even as the disclosure does not require changes in business strategies or operations. The disclosure can be, and often is, cheap talk, and yet it can attract new investors, consumers, and even employees. CBI's standards helped to create an entirely new market in "climate bonds" and "green bonds", for which there was great market demand and a small "greenium" in early years (a few basis points shaved off the promised interest, which saves the issuing entity money).[118]

In contrast, voluntary substantive standards, either on climate or corporate responsibility, will often be market limiting, and certainly were expected to be in the GFANZ example: Firms committed to stop financing new coal production, for instance, and to limit oil and gas funding. Exploring the distinction between "market supporting" and "market limiting" private standards may yield useful insights into what is reasonable to expect from private climate governance standards. This author concludes, at least at this stage, that if market limiting substantive requirements are to be enacted, they will need to be enacted by governments, or in coalitions of governments and private standard setters, not by private standard setters alone, with all of the political economy difficulties that engaging governments entails.

A number of caveats are in order. First, the categories "market supporting" and "market limiting" may overlap, and in individual cases would need further exploration. For instance, if a bank—let us assume Bank of America—vows as part of GFANZ not to fund new oil or gas projects, and not to fund coal generally, that is market limiting for its lending, underwriting and arranging in those industries. But might it be market supporting, as disclosure often is, in encouraging new customers to open bank accounts, or new investors or expanded investment from SRI funds? Clearly such an announcement could be argued to be both market supporting and market limiting. For the distinction to be useful, it would be necessary to evaluate the standard's dominant implications within the given sector. Would the projected new deposits and investment outweigh the lost income from reduced fossil fuel lending? Likely not, so that announcement would be understood to be part of a market limiting standard.

Second, perhaps a better way of understanding the distinction being suggested is to ask if a private standard is consistent with the usual market logic in the identified sector, or whether it pushes against the usual market logic. The more a private standard challenges the usual market logic, the more likely it is to be difficult to maintain. That contextual evaluation will be a matter of degree, since both substantive and disclosure standards will create costs for the firm during the first year of implementation and potentially without corresponding increases in revenue (unlike, for instance, rolling out a new marketing campaign). But presumably the degree of challenge will play a role in the take up and efficacy of private standards. It may generally be that market limiting standards are more of an "irritant" to market logics than those that are market supporting, such as disclosure, but this generalisation would need further examination.

Third, the degree of competition in a sector likely plays a significant role in the uptake and sustainability of market-limiting standards such as those in GFANZ. Money is not entirely fungible, given that the terms of lending and underwriting will vary between finance firms and their clients. If one GFANZ bank does not fund new coal, however, there will be many other non-GFANZ banks to fill the gap. It could be that finance is just too competitive a sector, with

118 Opinion Lex, 'Green Bonds: The Disappearing Greenium is a Welcome Development' (*Financial Times*, 2 January 2023) <https://www.ft.com/content/915d12e7-1ff4-48c3-87c2-76b2904d03ce> accessed 15 June 2025.

too many willing "interlopers", and an almost-fungible product, to expect that voluntary limitations on what to finance could be successful.

It is suggested here that this distinction could provide some analytic power to answer the question of why TCFD and similar disclosure initiatives have been successful, globally, while GFANZ has collapsed. Yet further research is necessary. Perhaps the real distinction that is driving this example of "take up versus collapse" is the difference between private standards for disclosure versus private substantive standards. If that distinction holds across governance spheres, with private disclosure standards being more generally implemented and socialised versus private substantive standards, that would be a significant limit on the power of private standard setting.

5. Conclusion

This chapter has described many of the NGO private standards being developed and utilised to address climate change, most of which operate through developing standards for expanded climate disclosure. Very recently we are also starting to see initiatives such as SBTi and TPI developing standards by which to judge companies' and countries' transition plans. Investors have been key participants in these processes, which have given the standards credibility with business partners and a serious degree of global acceptance.

Yet, this chapter has identified a number of limitations to the apparent power of these private standards to address the underlying problem of climate change. As Cashore and others observed of private standard setting regarding sustainability, "[m]any of the large-scale [negative] trends that private governance was created to address are accelerating".[119] At the least, we need to better understand what can—and cannot—be accomplished by private standard setting, what kinds of problems are amenable to private solutions, and how private standard setting can best motivate other parties, including governments, to act.

119 Cashore et al (n 84) 1173.

CHAPTER 31

Private Environmental Governance

MICHAEL P. VANDENBERGH AND PAUL C. STERN

1. Introduction

For roughly five decades, lawyers have been taught that environmental law occurs when governments protect the environment and manage natural resources. Not surprisingly, the most popular learning supplement for environmental law and policy students begins by stating that "[t]he simplest definition of 'environmental law and policy' might read: 'the use of public authority to protect the natural environment and human health from the impacts of pollution and development' ".[1] In this view, governments are the actors who address climate change and other environmental or natural resource problems, and the available public governance instruments include international agreements, national and subnational laws and regulations, and government financial incentives.

This is the dominant view of environmental law, and it leads students, scholars, and policymakers to ask, "What can government do?" when confronting climate change and other environmental problems. This approach generated substantial gains in environmental quality and resource management over the last fifty years despite a more than doubling in global population and economic activity. But in an era in which the federal government and roughly half of the states in the US are actively opposing decarbonisation—and many other national and subnational governments around the world are moving slowly, if at all—this mental model is a principal barrier to reducing climate risk, because it excludes much of the most important global and US climate mitigation activity.

The better question to ask is, "What can any organisation do?" When asked in this way, a multitude of new answers emerge that fill gaps in public governance and buy time for the severity of the problem to stimulate more successful government action. These private governance institutions and activities are not the product of top-down processes, often following deductive theories. Instead, they are the result of bottom-up processes in which a wide range of advocates have developed climate mitigation responses—often in the face of government inaction and theory-driven resistance to private sector action.

Elinor Ostrom was awarded the 2009 Nobel Memorial Prize in Economic Sciences for her decades of work,[2] developing a complementary approach to governance. Her work draws on

[1] James Salzman and Barton H Thompson Jr., *Environmental Law and Policy* (4th edn, Foundation Press 2014); Michael P Vandenbergh, Sarah E Light, and James Salzman, *Private Environmental Governance* (Foundation Press 2023) (presenting the private governance perspective in the companion publication in the same Foundation Press series).

[2] See, for example, Elinor Ostrom, *Governing the Commons: The Evolution of Institutions for Collective Action* (CUP 1990); Elinor Ostrom and others, *The Drama of the Commons* (National Academy Press, 2002); Thomas Dietz, Elinor Ostrom, and Paul C Stern, 'The Struggle to Govern the Commons' (2003) 302 Science 1907–12.

studies of how bottom-up institutions developed by resource users have emerged—sometimes over many generations—to manage a wide range of challenging "common-pool" natural resources, that is, ones in which the self-interested actions of individual users lead to resource depletion. She and her colleagues identified design principles for these private ordering institutions. On the surface, this approach, which often relies on iterative relationships among small groups working at a local level, does not appear relevant to a global commons problem like climate change. The small groups with iterative relationships at the core of Ostrom's private ordering often do not exist in the settings most responsible for large carbon emissions.

Ostrom also said, however, that what works in practice can also work in theory.[3] This chapter explores the emergence of nonstate or private environmental governance institutions that are functioning not only at the local small group level, but also at the global, national, and subnational levels. These institutions have important weaknesses and are not a substitute for government action, but they are filling gaps in government climate mitigation efforts and reducing carbon emissions by billions of tons per year. The authors explore the boundaries of private and public climate governance, the motivations for nongovernmental actors to reduce carbon emissions, the effects of private climate governance initiatives on carbon emissions, the efforts to discourage private climate governance initiatives, the spillover effects of private governance on public governance, and how private environmental governance initiatives can be assessed and their effectiveness enhanced.

2. Private Environmental Governance Defined

We begin by defining private environmental governance (PEG). We eschew terms that are drawn from the extensive US and European political science and sociological literatures in favour of a simple, functional approach that can be understood by a broad climate law and policy audience. A simple definition also avoids the jargon and ambiguation that can arise from terms commonly used within disciplinary silos. By PEG, we refer to actions in which actors other than governments perform the traditional governmental functions of pollution reduction, common pool resource management, and efforts to equitably allocate environmental amenities.

In our review of PEG climate initiatives, we neither favour nor disfavour private versus public actors. We simply use the term "private" to identify actors who can perform environmental governance functions without drawing on or being limited by the constraints on adoption and implementation of government laws, policies, and programmes. The actors engaged in PEG include for-profit organisations, trade associations, advocacy-focused nonprofit organisations, coordinating or non-advocacy focused nonprofit organisations, religious organisations, and civic and cultural organisations. Examples of PEG include the Marine Stewardship Council's (MSC's) fisheries standards, which were formed by a leading advocacy group and a leading company and now apply to roughly 20% of all the fish caught for human consumption around the world; the use of environmental requirements in supply chain contracts by many of the largest corporations in the world; the Equator Principles, which promote environmental disclosure akin to the landmark US National Environmental Policy Act and have been adopted by banks representing over 70% of all global project finance funding; and

[3] See Lee Ann Fennell, 'Ostrom's Law: Property Rights in the Commons' (February 2011) 5 International Journal of the Commons 9, 9–27 (describing Ostrom's Law as 'a resource arrangement that works in practice can work in theory').

the CDP (formerly the Carbon Disclosure Project) carbon disclosure system, through which more than 10,000 companies report their carbon emissions under pressure from investors with more than US$100 trillion in assets under management.[4]

PEG can easily be confused with other concepts that do not play the same gap-filling roles regarding climate change, and our vocabulary can constrain our ability to see important differences among these concepts. For instance, we typically refer to PEG initiatives as global rather than international because they do not involve nation-states. The term "transnational governance" is a step in the right direction but remains anchored in the concept of nation-states. Other terms, such as nonstate market-driven governance organisations, transgovernmental networks, and private transnational regulatory organisations, are valuable, but all embed more specific assumptions about these institutions. For instance, are they always market-driven, and does the term "regulatory" capture the way they function or obscure the difference between government and private enforcement tools?[5] We seek to avoid these questions with our use of the general term "private environmental governance". The term "non-state actor" on the surface captures many PEG institutions, but it often includes subnational governments, and they are subject to many of the same constraints as national and international governmental organisations that hinder their gap-filling role regarding climate change.[6]

As we use the term, "PEG" does not refer to privatisation of government functions because privatisation requires actions by governments, and an essential feature of PEG is that it does not require new governmental actions. PEG initiatives often perform governmental functions, but they do not involve government transferring governmental functions to private actors. For the same reason, PEG also does not involve government delegation of public authority to private actors to establish standards.[7] Similarly, PEG does not involve the use of government market mechanisms such as cap-and-trade systems, carbon taxes, or subsidies. These programmes harness private markets to reduce pollution, but they rely on government action, which is increasingly unlikely regarding climate change in the US and many other countries. For climate change, PEG institutions include nongovernmental actors that play a coordinating role regarding the actions of other nongovernmental actors and the actions of nation-states.[8]

[4] See Michael P Vandenbergh and Patricia Moore, 'Environmental Governance by Contract: The Growth of Environmental Supply Chain Contracting' (2022) 12 Michigan Journal of Environmental and Admin Law 1; Louis G Leonard, 'Under the Radar: A Coherent System of Climate Governance, Driven by Business' (2020) 60 Environmental Law Reporter 10546–72; E W Orts, 'Climate Contracts' (2011) Virginia Environmental Law Journal 29, 198; Sarah E Light and Eric W Orts, 'Parallels in Public and Private Environmental Governance'(2015) Michigan Journal of Environmental & Adminministrative Law, 5, 1; Vandenbergh, Light, and Salzman (n 1). See also Cynthia Williams, Chapter 30 of this handbook.

[5] See Steven Bernstein and Benjamin Cashore, 'Can Non-State Global Governance Be Legitimate? An Analytical Framework' (2007) 1(4) Regulation and Governance 347, 349–50; Kenneth W Abbott, Jessica F Green, and Robert O Keohane, 'Organisational Ecology and Institutional Change in Global Governance' (2016) 70(2) International Organisation 247–77.

[6] See, for example, United Nations Environment Programme, 'Emissions Gap Report 2024' (24 October 2024) <https://www.unep.org/resources/emissions-gap-report-2024> accessed 18 March 2025.

[7] See Peter L Strauss, 'Private Standards Organisations and Public Law' (2013) 22 William & Mary Bill of Rights Journal 497 (examining delegation of federal standard-setting); Nina A Mendelson, 'Private Control over Access to Public Law: The Perplexing Federal Regulatory Use of Private Standards' (2014) 112 Michigan Law Review 737; Jessica Green, *Rethinking Private Authority: Agents and Entrepreneurs in Global Environmental Governance* (Princeton University Press 2013) (discussing delegation of authority on climate change).

[8] See, for example, Robert O Keohane and David G Victor, 'The Regime Complex for Climate Change' (2011) 9 Perspectives on Politics (7), 7; Matt Potoski and Aseem Prakash, 'Green Clubs: Collective Action and Voluntary Environmental Programs' (2013) 16 Annual Review of Political Science 399.

Many scholars draw a bright line between mandatory or regulatory programmes and "voluntary" programmes, and they include PEG initiatives in the voluntary category.[9] We do not draw such a stark dichotomy. The leading research on compliance with federal environmental regulatory requirements suggests that material noncompliance rates of roughly 25% are common, so full compliance is not the norm with so-called mandatory government programmes that have civil and criminal enforcement tools.[10] Greenwashing and noncompliance with PEG requirements are common and present a challenge to private governance just as they do to public governance.[11] But it is important to understand that the absence of government enforcement tools and enforcing agencies does not mean that private standards lack influence or, conversely, that mandatory regulations are always fully enforced.

Private environmental investigations are common elements of governance, even though they are rarely discussed in public fora or produce public documents. For instance, Michael Gerrard concluded that roughly US$500 million is spent each year on private environmental investigations in connection with corporate real estate, merger and acquisition, financing, and other transactions—more than than the entire federal Environmental Protection Agency (EPA) enforcement budget of roughly US$300 million.[12] Similarly, although private actors lack the civil and criminal environmental law enforcement tools of government agencies, they often can enforce the environmental provisions in supply chain contracts, commercial loan covenants, and other agreements. Although a criminal indictment is perhaps the most powerful enforcement tool—and is only available to governments—a call from a loan officer threatening to declare an act of default or from a procurement officer threatening to prohibit a company from bidding on a contract because it cannot meet the carbon emissions policy of the buying company can create substantial pressure for compliance.

3. The Climate Change Response: Private Ordering at a Global Scale

Research led by Ostrom developed principles for the design of institutions that can manage common pool resources in the absence of government action. For the management of locally bounded common pool resources, this research identified a wide range of successful informal, bottom-up institutions. This research suggests that the principal governance requirements are the ability to provide (1) accurate, trustworthy information about the state of the resource and related human-environment interactions, uncertainty in the system, and users' values; (2) effective conflict resolution mechanisms, including some that function outside of court systems

[9] See, for example, Cary Coglianese and Jennifer Nash, 'Motivating Without Mandates: The Role of Voluntary Programs in Environmental Governance' in Lee Paddock, Robert Glicksman, and Nicholas S Bryner (eds), *Decision Making in Environmental Law* (Edward Elgar Publishing 2016) (describing PEG initiatives as voluntary programmes).

[10] See Wesley A Magat and W Kip Viscusi, 'Effectiveness of the EPA's Regulatory Enforcement: The Case of Industrial Effluent Standards' (Oct., 1990) 33(2) Journal of Law & Economics 331–60.

[11] Shelley Welton, 'Neutralizing the Atmosphere' (October 2022) Yale Law Journal 325; Amanda Shanor and Sarah E Light, 'Greenwashing & the First Amendment' (2022) Columbia Law Review.

[12] See Michael B Gerrard, 'A Proposal to Use Transactions to Leverage Environmental Disclosure and Compliance' 420, 422 in Jody Freeman and Charles D Kolstad (eds), *Moving to Markets in Environmental Regulation: Lessons from Twenty Years of Experience* (2007) (noting the amount spent on private environmental assessments); see also Michael P Vandenbergh, 'The Private Life of Public Law' (2005) 105 Columbia Law Review 2029, 2049 (noting the size of the enforcement budget of the federal Environmental Protection Agency).

or other governmental institutions; (3) sanction systems to induce compliance, often in the form of informal and graduated sanctions; (4) support for coordination and rule enforcement through technological and physical infrastructure; and (5) the ability to adapt institutional designs over time.[13]

To apply the lessons of this private ordering work to global commons, researchers have identified the value of (1) investing in science to understand the resource and its interactions with the interested and affected parties; (2) independent monitoring of the resource; (3) participation of the parties in framing scientific questions for analysis as well as assessing scientific results and developing rules; (4) integrating scientific analysis with broadly based deliberation; (5) identifying norms for the use of the outputs of these efforts and determining enforcement mechanisms, ensuring participation of higher- and lower-level actors; (6) connecting institutions from the local to the global levels in the processes of developing rules as well as monitoring and sanctioning; and (7) embedding flexibility for institutional adaptation and change.[14]

3.1 The Climate Challenge

The global nature of the climate change problem poses a fundamental challenge for private ordering systems that rely on iterative relationships and informal sanctioning to induce behaviour change. In the face of this global threat—and with the widespread assumption that environmental law and policy is the exercise of public authority—it is not surprising that climate scholars have focused for the last three decades principally on the development of international agreements implemented by nation-states. And given the attractive features of pricing carbon, it is not surprising that the public law instrument of choice during this period has been a carbon tax or cap-and-trade system.

This approach has failed, however. Global carbon emissions are increasing, the 1.5°C aspiration for global average temperature established in the Paris Agreement has largely been abandoned, the 2°C target seems increasingly likely to share the same fate, the prospects for an effective post-Paris international agreement are mixed at best, and the US for at least the next four years from the time of writing will be encouraging fossil fuel use rather than decarbonisation. Research suggests that if all nations had complied with all Paris Agreement commitments through 2025, the pathway would result in a 2.6° to 3.1°C future,[15] but the international and national processes have not produced that level of compliance. In short, if the goal is something close to 1.5°C, 2°C, or even 3°C, both common sense and the research on common pool resource management call for the development of complementary institutional forms. The need for multiple approaches may be especially critical because time is of the essence. The longer humanity delays in reducing its impact on the global climate system, the sharper the changes that will be needed to achieve a particular target level of climate change.

[13] See Thomas Dietz, Elinor Ostrom, and Paul C Stern, 'The Struggle to Govern the Commons' (2003) 302 Science 1907–12.

[14] Paul C Stern, 'Design Principles for Global Commons: Natural Resources and Emerging Technologies' (2011) 5 International Journal of the Commons 213, 224–25; Paul C Stern, Kimberly S Wolske, and Thomas Dietz, 'Design Principles for Climate Change Decisions' (2021) 52 Current Opinion in Environmental Sustainability 9–18.

[15] Joeri Rogelj and others, 'Paris Agreement Climate Proposals Need a Boost to Keep Warming Well Below 2°C' (2016) 534(7609) Nature 631–39.

Moreover, the focus on public governance likely has had negative spillover effects on the development of other, more feasible options.[16] The focus on international agreements and national laws has displaced alternatives that avoid what John Gibbons, President Clinton's science advisor, called "Disney's Law"—the idea that wishing will make it so.[17] And, as Stanford economist Larry Goulder has noted, the theoretical appeal of specific government instruments, such as a carbon tax, has discouraged the pursuit of less ideal but more feasible governance options.[18] The political polarisation and gridlock in the US induced the Biden administration to shift from a polluter pays approach to a beneficiary pays approach in the Infrastructure Investment and Jobs Act (IIJA) and the Inflation Reduction Act (IRA), and this appeared to be a valuable shift in the period after this legislation was adopted. But within weeks after the Trump administration took office it became clear that many of the decarbonisation subsidies in the IIJA and IRA would not endure.

Simply put, if the goal is 2°C, or even 3°C, common sense and the common pool resource management research suggest the value of understanding and expanding complementary governance institutions. Climate scientists have identified feedback effects and tipping points in the climate system that suggest the need for large, urgent emissions reductions to avoid locking in harms for many generations. Development of feasible, effective governance options, even if they conflict with existing mental models of environmental law and policy and pose risks, is essential.

3.2 The Private Environmental Governance Response to Climate Change: Private Ordering Beyond Small Groups

Although Ostrom focused principally on management of common pool resources in small group settings in which iterative relationships facilitate informal sanctions and rewards, she was aware of the value of exploring private ordering for global problems such as climate change and was open to adapting the lessons of local private ordering to address these problems.[19] As we noted at the outset, Ostrom emphasised the importance of inductive theory, suggesting that theory should adapt to reflect—not reject—the institutional arrangements that emerge to address a problem.

As to climate change, private organisations have emerged to fulfill many of the core environmental functions typically assigned to governments and have followed design principles similar to those Ostrom developed for local commons. Informational regulation is a starting point for governance, and private governance institutions have emerged to develop

[16] For a discussion of positive and negative spillover effects, see Heather B Truelove and others, 'Positive and Negative Spillover of Pro-environmental Behavior: An Integrative Review and Theoretical Framework' (2014) 29 Global Environmental Change 127–38.

[17] See Paul C Stern, Thomas Dietz, and Michael P Vandenbergh, 'The Science of Mitigation: Closing the Gap Between Potential and Actual Reduction of Environmental Threats' (Sept. 2022) 91 Energy Research & Social Science 102735 (citing John Gibbons, 'Sustainable Growth: Fantasy or Vision?' (26 January 2016) <https://www.youtube.com/watch?v=YzD2733svt8> accessed 21 March 2025).

[18] Lawrence H Goulder, 'Timing Is Everything: How Economists Can Better Address the Urgency of Stronger Climate Policy' (2020) 14 Review of Environmental Economics and Policy (1) 143–56.

[19] See, for example, Thomas Dietz, Elinor Ostrom, and Paul C Stern, 'The Struggle to Govern the Commons' (2003) 302 Science 1907–12 (asking, 'Is it possible to govern such critical commons as the oceans and the climate? We remain guardedly optimistic'); Elinor Ostrom, Marco A Janssen, and John M Anderies, 'Going Beyond Panaceas' (2007) 104 Proceedings of the National Academy of Sciences 15176–78 (noting the opportunity for global-level private governance).

and disclose climate information at the product, corporate, and project levels.[20] The dominant accounting system for carbon emissions around the world is the World Resources Institute/World Business Council on Sustainable Development Greenhouse Gas Standard. Multiple private systems have emerged to provide product carbon labelling, and some of these systems appear to be driving important behaviour change by the firms making labelled products.[21] The dominant disclosure system for corporate carbon emissions is the CDP disclosure standard, which, as we mentioned at the outset, uses the pressure of investors with more than US$100 trillion in assets to induce more than 10,000 companies and other organisations to disclose emissions. Although the European Union has adopted disclosure requirements, the US Securities and Exchange Commission has withdrawn its climate change disclosure rule and the California state disclosure rules are subject to a court challenge, leaving the CDP disclosure standard as likely the most influential carbon disclosure standard for many US companies and other organisations.[22] In the US, the dominant project-specific environmental disclosure system for over five decades has been the National Environmental Policy Act (NEPA), but its regulatory enforcement is being curtailed by the Trump administration and its application to climate change is being curtailed by the US Supreme Court. The Equator Principles are a private NEPA analogue that requires disclosure of carbon emissions and climate risks, and they have been adopted by banks providing over 70% of the project finance funding around the world.

Private institutions also have emerged to provide a form of private regulation that extends across companies and across international boundaries. A recent study concluded that 80% of the ten largest firms in seven global sectors include environmental requirements in supply chain contracts.[23] These supply chain contracting requirements often include carbon emissions reduction requirements. For example, Walmart worked with the Environmental Defense Fund and other advocacy groups to commit to and achieve a billion tons of carbon emissions reductions, an amount roughly equal to Germany or Japan eliminating all carbon emissions for a year. These reductions were achieved largely through Walmart's roughly 100,000 suppliers worldwide—and did not require an international agreement. These companies operate in many countries that do not have active climate mitigation efforts underway.

Another form of emissions regulation has emerged through the Science Based Targets initiative (SBTi). Although SBTi has been subject to internal disputes arising out of concerns about the role of carbon offsets and has suffered a recent loss of funding, it is remarkably similar to a carbon emissions regulatory programme that the EPA might develop if it were authorised by legislation to establish an economy-wide emissions reduction programme.[24] The SBTi induces companies to commit to an emissions pathway consistent with a global 1.5°C goal, reviews their plans to achieve the goal, requires emissions disclosure, and updates the required steps to the extent an organisation is off-track.

Climate mitigation also has been driven by private and public–private initiatives that involve investors, lenders, and insurers. Initiatives by Climate Action 100+ and other private organisations have combined advocacy groups and investors to pressure companies to disclose

[20] Stern, Wolske, and Dietz (n 14) 9–18.

[21] Khan M R Taufique and others, 'Revisiting the Promise of Carbon Labeling' (2022) 12 Nature Climate Change 132–40.

[22] Oren Perez and Michael P Vandenbergh, 'Making Climate Pledges Stick: A Private Ordering Mechanism for Climate Commitments' (2023) 50 Ecology Law Quarterly 683–25.

[23] Vandenbergh and Moore (n 4) 1.

[24] Sally Fisk, Michael Mahoney, and Michael Vandenbergh 'Moving in Synch' (May/June 2022) Environmental Forum 40–47.

and reduce emissions. Roughly two-thirds of the Standard and Poor's 500 firms have made major climate commitments,[25] and although the extent to which they will achieve those commitments remains unclear, there is no comparable government requirement. Similarly, initiatives involving lenders and insurers have induced corporate climate commitments. These investor, lender, and insurer initiatives and commitments have been attacked on antitrust grounds and fiduciary duty grounds, and some firms have pulled out of initiatives such as the Net-Zero Banking Alliance, a hybrid United Nations-private initiative, but there is little evidence of a fundamental pullback in core climate commitments.

Although most climate governance attention is directed at corporations, other organisations are also major carbon emitters, and some participate in PEG climate initiatives. For instance, our research suggests that the organisations affiliated with the Catholic Church would be one of the fifty largest emitting countries if they were a country.[26] Similarly, colleges and universities emit substantial amounts of carbon through their medical centres, facility heating and cooling, staff commuting, faculty and student travel, and other activities. Participants in CDP reporting, SBTi, and carbon commitment organisations often include these types of religious, educational, and civic and cultural organisations.

4. A Model of Private Environmental Governance

To the extent theoretical developments often lead to and precede practical applications, PEG has bucked the trend. The emergence of PEG climate institutions was not predicted by scholars writing decades ago, but the limitations of international, national, and subnational governance suggest that focusing only on arrangements that square with the dominant public authority-based mental model of environmental governance is unlikely to lead to adequate climate mitigation. Instead, we suggest that a better approach for an urgent, irreversible problem like climate change is to follow Ostrom's suggestion and work inductively to develop a theoretical framework that reflects the institutional arrangements that have emerged in practice. To do so, we explore the motivations for the actors who engage in PEG and the ways in which PEG is—or is not—reflecting the private ordering principles developed by scholars who study small group management of common pool resources.

Using the term "private politics", David Baron and colleagues noted more than a decade ago the importance of market and non-market reactions to public governance.[27] As suggested by Figure 31.1, this approach started with the traditional understanding of organised and unorganised interests inducing government to regulate, and it captured the importance of corporate reactions to government environmental regulatory actions and to the influence of boycotts and litigation.

Government responses to climate change and other environmental issues have been limited, however, and in the US only one major pollution control or polluter pays statute has

[25] Jean Eaglesham, 'Climate Promises by Businesses Face New Scrutiny' (*Wall Street Journal*, 5 November 2021) <https://www.wsj.com/articles/climate-promises-by-businesses-face-new-scrutiny-11636104600> accessed 15 July 2025.

[26] See Michael P Vandenbergh and Jonathan M Gilligan, *Beyond Politics The Private Governance Response to Climate Change* (CUP 2017) ch 8.

[27] See David P Baron, 'Private Politics, Corporate Social Responsibility, and Integrated Strategy' (2001) 7(9) Journal of Economic and Management Strategy 7–45.

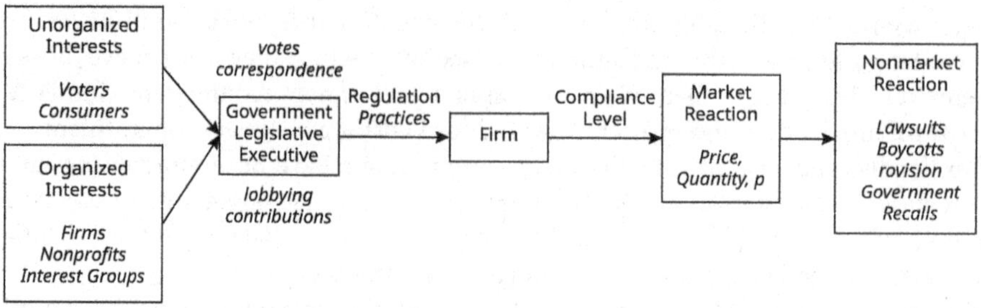

FIGURE 31.1 Accounting for market and non-market reactions

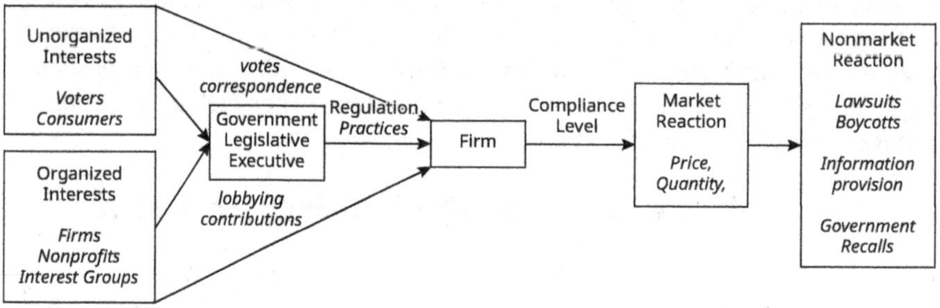

FIGURE 31.2 Accounting for private environmental governance pressure

been adopted since 1990.[28] Congress has been able to pass beneficiary pays or subsidy statutes, but not statutes pricing pollution or enabling new regulatory regimes, and the durability of the subsidies from the IIJA and IRA are uncertain at best. In recent years, unorganised and organised interests have sought to achieve their preferences for environmental protection not only through the traditional options of voting and lobbying legislators and government officials, but also through bypassing government in favour of pressuring corporations and other private institutions directly. As suggested by Figure 31.2, an updated model should reflect not only the importance of corporate reactions to government environmental regulatory actions and to boycotts and litigation, but also corporate reactions to the direct pressure applied by customers, employees, local community members, and others who have preferences for environmental protection unmet by governments and the supply chain contractors, investors, lenders, and insurers who also respond to those direct pressures.

Assessments of PEG often assume that firms are principally motivated by direct retail consumer purchasing behaviour and that because willingness to pay more for green goods in the US is limited, much of the claimed climate mitigation activity must be greenwashing.[29] Roughly 60% of the American public expresses concern about climate change and support for climate mitigation,[30] however, and levels of support are higher in many other countries, so unless firms cater only or primarily to a subset of the population, they operate against the backdrop of a consumer base that supports action on climate change. In addition, although

[28] Michael P Vandenbergh, 'Private Environmental Governance' (2013) 99 Cornell Law Review 129.

[29] Welton (n 11) 325; Shanor and Light (n 11) 2043–45.

[30] See, for example, Yale Climate Communication Project (2024) <https://climatecommunication.yale.edu> accessed 21 March 2025 (reporting on survey results regarding climate beliefs and policy support). See also Eric Orts, Chapter 5 of this handbook.

direct consumer retail purchasing behaviour is important, it is just one of many ways that consumers can induce corporate PEG actions. For instance, although boycotts and direct losses of retail sales are important, many companies may be less concerned about a direct loss of sales of a particular product than the effects of general brand or reputation damage that can occur through social media campaigns. Brand or reputation effects also may influence how potential future regulators perceive the firm.

Employee recruitment and retention is essential to many firms as well. On balance, firms can assume that the same support for climate mitigation that exists among consumers also exists among potential and current employees. The 60% figure is even higher for those firms that rely on recent graduates from college, professional, or graduate schools in many fields, again assuming that general population survey data can be translated to the employment context.

Efficiency also may be a driver of PEG climate initiatives. Research suggests that when pressed to disclose the carbon footprint of products, companies often identify efficiencies that reduce costs.[31] These efficiencies can arise from the company or from its suppliers, and the ability to achieve supply chain efficiencies may explain Walmart's willingness to commit to Project Gigaton, the billion-ton reduction programme from its supply chains described in Section 3.2.

Other firms also may create pressure on companies to engage in PEG climate activities. Perhaps the most important driver arising from firm-to-firm interactions is pressure from supply chain contracting requirements. A firm may have customer, employee, efficiency, or other incentives to reduce its carbon emissions. Research suggests that potential customers, employees, and community members are likely to hold a firm accountable not only for its own emissions, but also for the emissions of its tier one and tier two suppliers.[32] Not surprisingly, given this broad perceived moral boundary of the firm, as discussed above roughly 80% of the large firms in a recent study included environmental requirements in their supply chain contracting.[33] In turn, supply chain contracting may be a particularly important part of global climate mitigation because supply chain requirements bypass national and subnational boundaries and extend carbon emissions reduction pressure to company facilities in countries whose governments are not adopting laws designed to reduce emissions. Independent monitoring, one of the design principles enumerated above, is probably essential for preventing greenwashing as a strategy for meeting supply chain requirements.

In 2021, more than a third of retail investors globally reported that they had invested with environmental, social, and governance (ESG) factors in mind, and another 39% said they had considered it, and although some state attorneys general and private litigants have increased the pressure on investment firms to back off of ESG initiatives—and caused many firms to tone down the rhetoric—investment firms continue to support climate mitigation initiatives.[34] The same is true for many of the largest commercial lenders and insurers. These firms decline to lend to or insure certain carbon-heavy companies and projects, and they create pressure on the companies they work with to reduce emissions.

31 Taufique and others (n 21) 137–39.

32 Michael P Vandenbergh and others, 'The Moral Boundary of the Firm' (2025) 110 Iowa L Rev <https://ssrn.com/abstract=5045216> accessed 21 March 2025.

33 Vandenbergh and Moore (n 4) 1.

34 GlobeScan Radar 2021, 'Retail Investors' Views of ESG 4' (December 2021) <https://globescan.com/wp-content/uploads/2021/12/GlobeScan-Radar-2021-Retail_Investors_Views_of_ESG-Full-Report.pdf> accessed 15 July 2025; John Dernbach, Chapter 35 of this handbook.

Within the decisional space provided by the business judgment rule, the values and norms of corporate managers also may affect their decisions regarding firm commitments and actions. Although they are legally obligated to pursue the interests of the companies they serve, the business judgment rule provides opportunities to pursue climate mitigation activities that are in the long-term interests of the firm. For those firms that will face physical or transition risks from climate change, a wide range of actions may be well within the managers' decisional space.[35]

The mix of motivations for firms to participate in PEG climate initiatives likely differs from firm to firm and across various types of individual and collective actions. But the important insight is that no one driver of firm behaviour is likely to function alone. Instead, a mix of motivations is likely necessary to explain the widespread activity underway in the US and around the world.

4.1 Private Ordering Beyond Small Groups

Ostrom identified successful private ordering institutions for commons management that emerged from small groups and identified what she called design principles for effective institutions. The examples of PEG climate initiatives discussed above often exist at regional and global levels, however, and only rarely function through small group interactions. Understanding how private ordering can emerge in these larger settings can provide insights into the potential for PEG climate initiatives to continue filling gaps in public climate governance. Some of Ostrom's design principles are applicable at higher levels of social organisation and are evident in the institutional arrangements described above.[36] This section lists and discusses several Ostrom-inspired principles for PEG climate initiatives:

(1) Provide accurate, trustworthy information about the state of the resource and related human-environment interactions, uncertainty in the system, and users' values, particularly at points of decision.

Much of the information about the carbon emissions and other climate-relevant aspects of corporate behaviour is uncertain, but many of the most important PEG climate institutions fill this role by increasing the accuracy and availability of information about emissions, including institutions such as the World Research Institute and World Business Council for Sustainable Development Greenhouse Gas Protocol, the CDP disclosure system, the International Sustainability Standards Board. Advocacy groups play a watchdog role, either collaboratively or in adversarial relationships with corporations. Social media then makes information sharing something that can occur on a global level rather than just among participants in a small group.

(2) Establish independent monitoring and accountability systems that hold monitors accountable to the parties and protect the parties from violation of agreed rules, for example by greenwashing efforts.

[35] Ernest Lim, Chapter 18 of this handbook.

[36] For reviews of design principles, see, Stern (n 14) 213–14; Paul C Stern and others, 'Design Principles for Carbon Emissions Reduction Programs' (2010) 44 Environmental Science and Technology 4847, 4847–48; Robert O Keohane and David G Victor, 'The Regime Complex for Climate Change' (2011) 9.1 Perspectives on Politics, 17–23.

For instance, the investors of many large companies require suppliers to report to Ecovadis.[37] Ecovadis also assesses the accuracy of corporate disclosures using a comprehensive scorecard for environmental, social, and governance issues. In addition, businesses have formed to play a "monitor of monitors" role.[38]

(3) Implement effective conflict resolution mechanisms, including some that function outside of court systems or other governmental institutions.

Extensive conflict resolution mechanisms exist in PEG collaborative institutions ranging from the MSC seafood standards to the CDP disclosure and SBTi carbon emissions reduction programme. In addition, supply chain contracts, finance agreements, commercial loans, and insurance agreements often include conflict resolution provisions that enable the parties to resolve disputes without going to court.[39]

(4) Establish sanction systems to induce compliance, often in the form of informal and graduated sanctions.

Many PEG climate institutions lack formal sanction systems, but economic drivers enable supply chain contracting, investing, lending, and insuring to create pressure for compliance through formal mechanisms, like enforcement of covenants and other provisions in agreements, and informal mechanisms, like exclusion from contracts, lending, investments, and insurance opportunities. In addition, naming and shaming by advocacy groups can drive compliance with corporate commitments and programmes.[40] The economic benefits of efficiency and positive brand or reputation effects with customers, employees, and local community members also provide motivations for carbon emissions reductions even though they may not function as sanctions.

(5) Support monitoring, coordination, and rule enforcement through technological and physical infrastructure.

Philanthropic organisations often provide important early support, and in some cases provide ongoing support, to enable organisations to acquire the technological expertise and equipment and build the institutional structures necessary to enable them to enforce their commitments.[41] Social media platforms enable the rapid, global flow of information. "Deep green" organisations conduct boycotts and naming-and-shaming campaigns that drive companies to engage in more cooperative expertise and information-sharing relationships with "light green" organisations.[42]

[37] See, for example, Ecovadis, 'Enterprise Solutions for Sustainable Supply Chains' <https://ecovadis.com/lp/2025-02-en-sem-enterprise/?utm_source=google+ads&utm_medium=paid&utm_campaign=2025-02-Brand-US-Google+Ads> accessed 21 March 2025 (providing reporting and accountability services to corporations and investors). In addition, the United Nations has developed an international investor-led organisation that tracks the progress of corporate signatories. See United Nations Principles for Responsible Investment, <https://www.unpri.org> accessed 15 July 2025.

[38] An example is the firm led by Bill Baue, Ralph Thurm, and Mark McElroy, 'Redesign, Resilience, Regeneration', R3.0. <https://www.r3-0.org/> accessed 21 March 2025.

[39] See Ying Zhu, Chapter 25 of this handbook.

[40] See Vandenbergh et al (n 1) 160–62 (discussing role of naming and shaming in motivating corporate private environmental governance actions).

[41] See, for example, Angel Hsu, 'NAZCA: Track Climate Pledges of Cities and Companies' (2016) 532 Nature 303, 303 (discussing mechanisms for monitoring and enforcement).

[42] See, for example, Andrew J Hoffman, 'Shades of Green' (Spring 2009) 40 Stanford Social Innovation Review (distinguishing between bright green and deep green environmental non-profit organisations).

(6) Design institutions for adaptability over time in response to changing environmental and political conditions, technological possibilities, and the parties' objectives and targets.

A number of PEG climate institutions have adapted over time in response to criticisms and changing conditions. Examples include efforts by CDP to account for supply chain emissions and SBTi to account for deep differences among participants in the role that carbon offsets should play in achieving compliance. The extent to which institutional designs will be able to adapt to the increasing need to fill gaps in public climate governance, however, is unclear, as is the ability of the initiatives to maintain momentum in the US in the face of active resistance by the federal government and many states.

4.2 Effects on Climate Mitigation

Calculating the carbon emissions reductions attributable to PEG climate initiatives is difficult and involves not only measurement issues but also assumptions about the additionality of emissions reductions. The best current estimate is that corporate climate commitments, if achieved, will yield in the range of 3.2 to 4.2 billion tons of global annual carbon emissions reductions by 2030.[43] Reductions in this range would be greater than the annual emissions of India, the third-highest emitting country. Corporate climate commitments at the global level for 2050 are subject to greater uncertainty, but they are much larger than the 2030 commitments.[44] In the United States, the voluntary green power market is a significant part of the private climate governance landscape and is an indicator of what has been achieved so far in one country. In 2023, roughly 9.7 million customers procured 319 million megawatt-hours (MWh) of renewable electricity in the voluntary green power market, representing 44% of non-hydro renewable energy generation and 8% of US retail electricity sales.[45] Based on current data on the fuel mix of electricity production in the US, these renewable energy purchases equate to over 190 million tons of carbon emissions reductions, an amount roughly equivalent to the annual emissions of Iraq.[46]

4.3 Effects on Public Governance

A common concern about PEG climate initiatives is that they have negative spillover effects on public climate governance. This could occur if they induce the public to believe that climate

[43] Lois Guthrie and Luke Blower, 'Corporate Climate Disclosure Schemes in G20 Countries After Cop 21' (*OECD*, 3 July 2017) 15 <https://www.oecd.org/environment/cc/g20-climate/collapsecontents/Climate-Disclosure-Standards-Board-climate-disclosure.pdf> accessed 28 December 2023. For data on corporate climate commitments, see Institute for Carbon Removal Law & Policy, *Carbon Removal Corporate Action Tracker*, <https://docs.google.com/spreadsheets/d/1vf—uXsf6fo7MuNpPya2Kz82DxteohHgtOXimgpRA3c/edit#gid=0> accessed 28 December 2023.

[44] 'Climate Action Note: Data You Need to Know' (*UNEP*, 9 November 2021) <https://www.unep.org/explore-topics/climate-action/what-we-do/climate-action-note/state-of-climate.html?gclid=Cj0KCQjw4s-kBhDqARIsAN-ipH0RvEgYH-4PS7TProgdIw9MF3J2hGoKnCyFlYNqb8TSX3cSusUomXsaAr2_EALw_wcB> accessed 22 June 2023; *see* Institute for Carbon Removal Law & Policy (n 43).

[45] Eric O'Shaughnessy, 'The State of the U.S. Voluntary Green Power Market (2023 Data)' (*NREL*, 18 September 2024) slide 2 <https://www.nrel.gov/analysis/green-power.html> accessed 31 July 2025.

[46] US Energy Information Administration, 'How Much of U.S. Carbon Dioxide Emissions Are Associated with Electricity Generation?' (11 December 2024) <https://www.eia.gov/tools/faqs/faq.php?id=74&t=11> accessed 31 July 2025.

problems have been addressed and reduce public demand for government legislation or regulations. Although these concerns seem misplaced in an era in which the US federal government and roughly half the states are actively resisting decarbonisation, it is important to acknowledge that concern about greenwashing and its effects on public support for government action are widespread.

For several reasons, the effects on public governance also could be positive. Companies and other private organisations that commit to private climate initiatives have incentives to support government regulatory programmes that will raise noncompliant rivals' costs and ensure that their emissions reductions will be supplemented by emissions reductions arising from government regulatory requirements. Similarly, companies that have reduced emissions will bear lower costs from a carbon tax and can be expected to be less resistant to federal or state carbon tax legislation.

Private climate institutions also can provide models for public governance. The Environmental Defense Fund describes its private governance activities as providing "proof of concept" for public governance, and there are numerous examples of this phenomenon. For instance, in the US, the Biden administration federal procurement standards would have required CDP carbon emissions disclosure by many federal contractors, a requirement that could not have been adopted and made effective in the absence of pre-existing private disclosure standards and monitoring mechanisms.[47]

Research has demonstrated that solution aversion drives resistance to climate mitigation.[48] When conservatives learn that a carbon tax or regulations are the likely response to climate change, they become less accepting of climate science and less supportive of climate mitigation. Learning about private sector action, however, can bypass some of this solution aversion, thereby offering political flexibility in an otherwise dramatically polarised policy space.

4.4 Limitations

Although PEG climate initiatives can play a gap-filling role, private sector action is not a panacea. A principal barrier lies in political science theory, which is strongly focused on public policy and much less on policy development and implementation by the private and nonprofit sectors. Related to this is a conceptual barrier—a failure to recognise that devoting the research, policy development, and implementation resources necessary to exploit the PEG opportunity could yield major global carbon emissions reductions without undermining public governance. The panacea bias, which leads decision-makers to pursue comprehensive solutions, even if they are infeasible, is one conceptual barrier. A related barrier arises from the perspectives, staffing, and funding of advocacy groups. Although some groups have made substantial strides in developing private climate governance programmes, such as CDP, the World Wildlife Fund, and the World Resources Institute, or in advocacy that induces corporations to

[47] For a discussion of the Biden administration's climate-related federal procurement requirements and how they incorporated private standards, see Michael P Vandenbergh and Patricia Moore, 'Environmental Governance by Contract: The Growth of Environmental Supply Chain Contracting,' (2022) 12 Michigan Journal of Environmental & Administrative Law 1, 13 n 54.

[48] See Troy H Campbell and Aaron C Kay, 'Solution Aversion: On the Relation Between Ideology and Motivated Disbelief' (2014) 107 Journal of Personality and Social Psychology 809; Ash Gillis and others, 'Convincing Conservatives: Private Sector Action Can Bolster Support for Climate Change Mitigation in the United States' (2021) 73 Energy Research & Social Science 101947; see also Jennifer C Cole and others, 'Social Psychological Perspectives on Political Polarization: Insights and Implications for Climate Change' (2023) 18 Perspectives on Psychological Science 1–27.

participate in or form private climate initiatives, such as the Environmental Defense Fund, the Natural Resources Defense Council, and Greenpeace, much of the resources in many of these organisations and nearly all of the resources in other potentially important non-governmental organisations (NGOs) are devoted to government advocacy. And of course, opposition to developing both public and private institutions for mitigating climate change will continue to come from organisations with an interest in continuing exploitation of fossil fuels.

Efforts by federal and state officials to discourage ESG investing and collaborative PEG initiatives appear to be having some effect. The use of fiduciary duty suits, antitrust actions, and decisions about where to invest state funds, and which companies to contract with, all increase the economic and social pressure on firms that are attempting to engage in climate mitigation.

As with the classic small group private ordering studied by Ostrom, when the pressure on the resource becomes too great, private systems break down. The most recent example is the major growth in projected electricity demand arising from artificial intelligence AI-driven data centres. In the face of major increases in electricity demand, some major AI firms have reframed or backed away from climate commitments, although they still appear to be doing more than they are required to by government regulatory requirements in many cases.[49]

Greenwashing is widespread, and widely discussed research has concluded that many firms only had plans in place to achieve roughly a quarter of their emissions reduction commitments.[50] Naming and shaming can reduce greenwashing risks but a committed greenwasher is unlikely to be deterred by naming and shaming alone. Independent monitoring systems can also provide a deterrent though implementing them, even if developed privately, may prove difficult in the presence of determined greenwashers. AI can also provide opportunities for identifying and disclosing greenwashing, and advocacy groups may be able to take advantage of the insights from the social science-based tax compliance literature, which has found that it is important not to create the impression that noncompliance is widespread. In other words, a successful naming and shaming approach will call out bad actors without creating the impression that bad actors are common and without discouraging corporate managers from making commitments.[51]

5. Next Steps

The emergence of PEG climate institutions can be explained if governance theory accounts for the effects of the gap in public responses to climate change. A transition has occurred from public preferences for climate mitigation being directed almost exclusively towards government agencies and legislatures to a combination of government and private sector approaches. Development of a theory to reflect the emergence of PEG climate institutions requires understanding the large mix of motivations that drive private sector action and the interactions among not only governments and corporations, but also corporations, advocacy groups, customers, employees, local communities, supply chain purchasers, investors, lenders, and

[49] See Jan-Erik Schirmer, Chapter 44 of this handbook. For a discussion of the stress placed on corporate carbon emissions by projected growth in data centre energy use, see for example Lynne Kiesling, 'Data Center Electricity Use IV: Unrealistic Emissions Targets?' (Center for Science, Technology & Energy 22 August 2024) <https://ctse.aei.org/data-center-electricity-use-iv-unrealistic-emissions-targets/> accessed 15 July 2025.

[50] See Eric J Johnson and others, 'Widespread Misestimates of Greenhouse Gas Emissions Suggest Low Carbon Competence' (2024) 14 Nature Climate Change 707.

[51] See, for example Michael P Vandenbergh, 'Beyond Elegance: A Testable Typology of Social Norms in Corporate Environmental Compliace' (2003) 22 Stanford Environmental Law Journal 55.

insurers. Whether PEG continues to play an important role, and whether it can expand as some governments backtrack, will be affected by whether philanthropic organisations understand the value of gap-filling; the success of independent monitoring; the often skeptical and sometimes downright dismissive attitudes towards private governance of academics and NGOs; whether NGOs refocus their efforts on applying direct pressure and supplying expertise to the private sector; the motivations of the private sector in the face of NGO pressure for climate action and government resistance; whether NGOs understand the balance between naming and shaming bad actors and rewarding good actors; whether AI can increase incentives to make and comply with climate commitments; and whether scholars and advocates can gain a better understanding of the spillover effects of private governance on public governance and how to increase the likelihood of positive effects.

6. Conclusion

The top-down, government-focused approach to environmental protection that emerged in the 1960s and 1970s in the US and many other countries generated substantial gains in environmental quality and resource management. This occurred despite a more than doubling in global population and economic activity. But polarisation and collective action problems in the US and other countries have hobbled the ability of international, national, and subnational government laws and policies to respond to climate change and other emerging environmental threats. In the last few decades, private institutions have emerged to address climate mitigation. These new institutions reflect many of the design principles that Elinor Ostrom identified in her path-breaking work on private ordering. However, because these institutions function at regional and global levels removed from the small groups that dominated the early work on private ordering, those principles need modification on the basis of experience with higher levels of social organisation and governance of global commons.

CHAPTER 32

Private International Law

EKATERINA ARISTOVA AND UGLJEŠA GRUŠIĆ

1. Introduction

THIS chapter explores private international law (PIL) issues arising in climate change litigation. This focus naturally limits the scope of our analysis to (1) climate change cases, (2) based on private law, and (3) of a transnational nature.

The definition of *climate change litigation* is widely debated.[1] For the purposes of this chapter, we adopt the definition used by the Sabin Center for Climate Change Law at Columbia University, which identifies cases for inclusion in its climate change litigation databases based on two criteria: "cases must generally be brought before judicial bodies" and "climate change law, policy, or science must be a material issue of law or fact in the case".[2]

Our analysis is limited to climate change cases *based on private law*. As this handbook demonstrates, private law offers numerous causes of action where climate change law, policy, or science is a material issue. The diversity across fields of private law, especially from a comparative perspective, is striking. A comprehensive study of climate change in PIL would engage with all such fields, but that exceeds the possibilities of a single contribution to an edited collection. We therefore focus further on PIL issues arising in climate change cases that have *actually* been brought before courts. With this goal in sight, Section 2 surveys transnational climate change cases based on private law with an emphasis on key case studies, which justifies a focus on tort litigation, broadly defined to include tort or delict claims and civil enforcement of statutes like duty of vigilance/due diligence legislation.

That said, we acknowledge that climate change litigation is evolving rapidly.[3] Factors like advances in attribution science, the development of international jurisprudence linking climate change and human rights and the emergence of innovative legal arguments influence its trajectory. Writing on this subject is challenging due to the fluidity of the legal landscape. Accordingly, Section 2 presents key case studies as illustrative examples rather than an exhaustive list.

In one sense, all climate change litigation is *transnational*, given the global nature of the problem. However, not all climate change cases based on private law raise PIL issues. For the

[1] Kate McKenzie and others, 'Climate Change Litigation: One Definition to Rule Them All . . . ?' in Francesco Sindico and others (eds), *Research Handbook on Climate Change Litigation* (Edward Elgar 2024) 1.

[2] Climate Litigation Database, Sabin Center for Climate Change Law, Columbia University, 'About' <https://climatecasechart.com/about/> accessed 2 July 2025.

[3] The evolution of climate change litigation is captured in annual reports published by the Grantham Research Institute on Climate Change and the Environment at the London School of Economics and Political Science. Joana Setzer and Catherine Higham, *Global Trends in Climate Change Litigation: 2025 Snapshot* (Grantham Research Institute, LSE 2025).

purposes of this chapter, we define transnational climate change litigation as that which does or could raise PIL issues because an international element is present, such as the foreign location of one or both parties, conduct, or damage.

PIL is not international law. While legal instruments like the 2019 Hague Judgments Convention[4] and any future business and human rights treaty[5] may affect climate change litigation, most of the law in this field is domestic or regional (i.e., EU). However, existing literature largely focuses on EU PIL.[6] In this chapter, we go beyond this by adopting a broader comparative perspective. Nonetheless, we acknowledge that most transnational climate change cases based on private law have been brought in Continental Europe. The European experiences, discussed in Section 2, inform our discussion of other PIL traditions.

Our main argument is that PIL is important for climate change litigation because it can either facilitate or restrict access to remedy by opening or closing the jurisdiction of particular courts and the application of particular law(s) and by regulating the cross-border effectiveness of remedies. In a world where some courts and laws are more receptive to climate change arguments than others, this function of PIL matters. In this sense, PIL can respond, to an extent, to the drivers and impacts of climate change and may itself be impacted by climate change in addition to being called to address it. Accordingly, our analysis of the intersection of climate change and PIL contributes to a growing discourse on PIL and sustainability,[7] the role of PIL in global governance,[8] and the use of PIL as a regulatory tool.[9]

At the same time, we caution against overstating the importance of PIL. The practical experience we have with transnational climate change litigation does not reflect lively academic debates. Compared to the related phenomenon of business and human rights and environmental (BHRE) litigation, understood in a narrow sense (i.e., excluding climate change litigation), the gap between theory and practice is glaring.[10]

4 Convention of 2 July 2019 on the Recognition and Enforcement of Foreign Judgments in Civil or Commercial Matters, entered into force 1 September 2023.

5 UN Human Rights Council, 'Open-Ended Intergovernmental Working Group on Transnational Corporations and Other Business Enterprises with Respect to Human Rights' (OHCHR) <https://www.ohchr.org/en/hr-bodies/hrc/wg-trans-corp/igwg-on-tnc> accessed 7 July 2025.

6 For an overview, see Uglješa Grušić, 'Climate Change Litigation and EU Private International Law' in Ekaterina Aristova and Justin Lim (eds), *Climate Litigation in Europe Unleashed: Catalysing Action against States and Corporations* (*Bonavero Institute of Human Rights, Bonavero Reports 2/2024*, 5 March 2024) <https://www.law.ox.ac.uk/sites/default/files/2024-07/Climate%20Litigation%20in%20Europe%20Unleashed_Catalysing%20Action%20against%20States%20and%20Corporations.pdf> accessed 2 July 2025.

7 Eduardo Álvarez-Armas, 'SDG 13: Climate Action' in Ralf Michaels, Verónica Ruiz Abou-Nigm, and Hans Van Loon (eds), *The Private Side of Transforming Our World: UN Sustainable Development Goals 2030 and the Role of Private International Law* (Intersentia 2021) 409; Ralf Michaels and Samuel Zeh, 'Sustainability and Private International Law' in Marta Santos Silva and others (eds), *Routledge Handbook of Private Law and Sustainability* (Routledge 2024) 479.

8 Horatia Muir Watt, 'Private International Law beyond the Schism' (2011) 2 Transnational Legal Theory 347; Horatia Muir Watt and Diego Fernández Arroyo (eds), *Private International Law and Global Governance* (OUP 2014).

9 Robert Wai, 'Transnational Liftoff and Juridical Touchdown: The Regulatory Function of Private International Law in an Era of Globalization' (2002) 40 Columbia Journal of Transnational Law 209; Uglješa Grušić, 'International Environmental Litigation in EU Courts: A Regulatory Perspective' (2016) 35 Yearbook of European Law 180.

10 Ekaterina Aristova, *Tort Litigation against Transnational Corporations: The Challenge of Jurisdiction in English Courts* (OUP 2024).

This argument is advanced as follows. Section 2 provides an overview of transnational climate change cases based on private law with a focus on key case studies. Its aim is to inform discussion of PIL issues arising in climate change litigation. Section 3 considers jurisdiction. Section 4 examines applicable law, while Section 5 addresses the recognition and enforcement of foreign judgments. These three sections adopt a comparative perspective. Section 5 concludes.

2. Transnational Climate Change Litigation: Current Trends and Case Studies

At the time of writing this chapter, the Sabin Center maintained two databases: one for climate change litigation in the US, categorised by claim type,[11] and one distinguishing cases against governments, corporations, and individuals outside the US (Global Database).[12] However, neither records transnational cases as a distinct category. Identifying such cases requires consulting secondary sources.[13] Climate change litigation in the US has a longer history and has distinct features, warranting separate discussion from other jurisdictions.

2.1 US Case Studies

The US was among the first jurisdictions where climate change litigation against corporations emerged. In the early 2000s, a small number of cases were brought against oil, gas, and electric companies, but they were unsuccessful due to challenges related to standing, proof of harm, and causation.[14]

However, over the past decade, a growing wave of so-called climate deception cases have gained momentum. These cases are commonly brought by US states and municipalities against fossil fuel companies for allegedly misleading the public about the risks of global warming and the defendants' role in the climate crisis. Claimants argue that fossil fuel companies knew about the link between their products and climate change but concealed this information from consumers. They seek remediation for the costs of increasing flooding, forest fires, and heatwaves. These cases are based on a variety of causes of action, including product liability, negligence, and public and private nuisance.

As of September 2024, at least twenty-six climate deception cases have been brought in the US against some of the world's largest oil, gas, and coal corporations.[15] Some cases raise PIL

[11] Global Climate Change Litigation Database, Sabin Center for Climate Change Law, Columbia University, 'U.S. Climate Change Litigation' <https://climatecasechart.com/us-climate-change-litigation/> accessed 2 July 2025.

[12] Global Climate Change Litigation Database, Sabin Center for Climate Change Law, Columbia University, 'Non-U.S. Climate Change Litigation' <https://climatecasechart.com/non-us-climate-change-litigation/> accessed 2 July 2025.

[13] See for example César Rodríguez-Garavito (ed), *Litigating the Climate Emergency: How Human Rights, Courts, and Legal Mobilization Can Bolster Climate Action* (CUP 2022); Michael Burger and Maria Antonia Tigre, *Global Climate Litigation Report: 2023 Status Review* (Sabin Center and United Nations Environment Programme 2023); Geetanjali Ganguly, 'Breaking New Ground in Private Climate Litigation' in Sindico and others (n 1) 123; Setzer and Higham (n 3).

[14] Geetanjali Ganguly, Joana Setzer, and Veerle Heyvaert, 'If at First You Don't Succeed: Suing Corporations for Climate Change' (2018) 38 Oxford Journal of Legal Studies 841, 846–49.

[15] Zero Carbon Analytics, 'Big Oil in Court: The Latest Trends in Climate Litigation against Fossil Fuel Companies' (11 September 2024) <https://zerocarbon-analytics.org/archives/energy/latest-trends-in-climate-litigation-against-fossil-fuel-companies> accessed 2 July 2025.

issues, such as personal jurisdiction over non-US defendants[16] and territorial scope of US laws.[17] None have yet proceeded to trial.

2.2 Non-US Case Studies

As of 16 June 2025, the Global Database recorded 243 cases against corporations. These include proceedings in domestic courts across nearly thirty countries, as well as cases before non-judicial and quasi-judicial bodies, such as OECD National Contact Points. Court proceedings are a smaller subset, but cover a wide range, including administrative challenges to fossil fuel projects, claims for false or misleading advertising, shareholder lawsuits on climate-related financial risks, and challenges to carbon credit schemes. Most climate change cases against corporations are purely domestic, raising no PIL issues. Only a small number are transnational and can be categorised into three groups based on the remedy sought.

2.2.1 Reduction in Greenhouse Gas Emissions

The first category includes cases against fossil fuel companies for failing to set and implement greenhouse gas (GHG) emission reduction targets aligned with the 2015 Paris Agreement.[18] These cases are forward-looking. Claimants seek injunctions ordering corporations to adjust their business models to reduce GHG emissions. Even though these cases are commonly brought by local claimants against a locally domiciled company, they are transnational because claimants request a reduction of GHG across the defendants' global operations covering Scope 1–3 emissions, that is direct and indirect emissions, including those occurring in the value chain.

The most prominent case in this category is *Milieudefensie v Royal Dutch Shell Plc* in the Netherlands. It was brought in 2019 by seven civil society organisations (CSOs) and 17,379 individuals against Royal Dutch Shell (Shell), the parent company of a global energy and petrochemical group. The claimants alleged that Shell had a duty under the unwritten standard of care pursuant to Article 6:162 of the Dutch Civil Code to contribute to the prevention of dangerous climate change through its group policies. The jurisdiction of Dutch courts was sought under the Brussels I *bis* Regulation[19] on two alternative bases: Shell's domicile in the Netherlands under Article 4(1) and the place of the event giving rise to the damage (the adoption of the group policies) in the Netherlands under Article 7(2).

On 26 May 2021, the Hague District Court famously ordered Shell to reduce the carbon dioxide emissions resulting from its global operations by at least 45% by 2030, compared with 2019.[20] Two issues of importance for PIL were decided. First, the court denied standing to a CSO seeking to represent foreign victims of climate change, thus focusing the litigation on damage suffered by Dutch residents.[21] Second, the court found that Dutch law was applicable on the basis of Article 7 of Rome II Regulation[22] as either the *lex loci actus* (i.e., the law of the

[16] *In re Fuel Industry Climate Cases* (Sup Ct Cal, 8 October 2024).

[17] *City of Oakland v BP Plc*, 325 F Supp 3d 1017 (ND Cal 2018).

[18] Paris Agreement of 12 December 2015 to the UN Framework Convention on Climate Change, entered into force 4 November 2016.

[19] Regulation (EU) No 1215/2012 of 12 December 2012 on jurisdiction and the recognition and enforcement of judgments in civil and commercial matters (recast) [2012] OJ L 351/1 (Brussels I *bis*).

[20] *Milieudefensie v Royal Dutch Shell Plc*, the Hague District Court, 26 May 2021, English translation ECLI:NL:RBDHA:2021:5339.

[21] ibid [4.2.5].

[22] Regulation (EC) No 864/2007 of 11 July 2007 on the law applicable to non-contractual obligations (Rome II) [2007] OJ L 199/40.

country where the event giving rise to the damage—the adoption of group policies by Shell—occurred) or the *lex loci damni* (i.e., the law of the country where the damage occurred).[23]

The judgment was appealed, but not with respect to these two issues. On 12 November 2024, the Hague Court of Appeal allowed the appeal and refused to impose a specific emission reduction target.[24] An appeal is currently pending before the Dutch Supreme Court.

Similar cases replicating the Milieudefensie legal strategy have been brought in other jurisdictions, including Germany, Italy, and Japan, but to the best of our knowledge and based on publicly available sources, the parties and courts in these cases have not invoked PIL arguments.

2.2.2 Remediation of Climate Change Damage

The second category includes cases seeking damages or adaptation measures for past and/or future losses caused by the defendants' GHG emissions. These claims rely on attribution science tracing the historical accumulation of GHG in the atmosphere to a specific company.[25]

The leading case in this category is *Lliuya v RWE AG* in Germany.[26] It started in 2015, when Saúl Luciano Lliuya, a Peruvian from Huaraz, with the support of the CSO Germanwatch, filed a civil claim against RWE, Germany's largest electricity producer. The claim is pursued under Article 1004 of the German Civil Code and alleges that RWE, having knowingly contributed to climate change through significant GHG emissions, shares responsibility for the melting of mountain glaciers near Huaraz and should bear a proportional share of the cost of flood protection measures. The claimant sought the jurisdiction of German courts under Article 4(1) of Brussels I *bis* and German law was pleaded as applicable under Article 7 of Rome II.

On 15 December 2016, the Essen District Court rejected the claim, finding no provable causal link between the GHG emissions of a single emitter and specific climate change impacts. However, the Hamm Higher Regional Court allowed the appeal on 30 November 2017, establishing the admissibility of the claim and advancing it to the evidentiary phase. On 28 May 2025, the court ultimately dismissed the claim but affirmed an important legal principle. Companies can, in principle, be held legally liable under German law for damage caused by their contribution to climate change.[27] The judgment is likely to support ongoing and future cases against major corporate emitters. The court confirmed its jurisdiction under Article 4(1) of Brussels I *bis*[28] and recorded the parties' agreement on the application of German law under Article 14 of Rome II, while noting that the claimant could unilaterally choose German law as the *lex loci actus* (the law of the place where the emissions occurred and policies were adopted) under Article 7.[29]

In Switzerland, four residents of the Indonesian island of Pari, supported by several CSOs, have sued Holcim, a Swiss-based global building materials manufacturer.[30] The claimants

[23] *Shell* District Court Judgment (n 20) [4.3].

[24] *Milieudefensie v Shell Plc*, the Hague Court of Appeal, 12 November 2024, English Translation ECLI:NL:GHDHA:2024:2100.

[25] Rupert F Stuart-Smith and others, 'Filling the Evidentiary Gap in Climate Litigation' (2021) 11 Nature Climate Change 651.

[26] 'Luciano Lliuya v RWE AG' (*Global Climate Change Litigation Database*, 2015) <https://climatecasechart.com/non-us-case/lliuya-v-rwe-ag/> accessed 2 July 2025.

[27] For an unofficial English translation, see *Luciano Lliuya v RWE AG* <https://rwe.climatecase.org/sites/default/files/2025-06/Judgement%20OLG%2028_05_2025.pdf> accessed 2 July 2025.

[28] ibid 23.

[29] ibid 29–30.

[30] 'Asmania and others v Holcim' (*Global Climate Change Litigation Database*, 2022) <https://climatecasechart.com/non-us-case/four-islanders-of-pari-v-holcim/> accessed 2 July 2025.

allege a violation of their personality rights under Article 28 of the Swiss Civil Code, resulting from Holcim's past, ongoing, and future excessive GHG emissions, which have led and will lead to damage on the island to be redressed under Article 41 of the Code of Obligations (Part 5 of the Swiss Civil Code). The claimants have requested the following remedies: (1) proportional compensation of climate change damage; (2) a reduction of Holcim's GHG emissions by 43% by 2030 and by 69% by 2040, compared with 2019; and (3) financial contribution to adaptation measures on the island. The case notably combines elements of the *Shell* and *Lliuya* cases (i.e., reduction in GHG emissions and remediation of climate change damage). Based on publicly available sources, PIL arguments have not been elaborated upon by either the parties or the courts. However, it is reasonable to assume two things: first, that the jurisdiction of Swiss courts is sought under Article 2(1) of the Lugano Convention[31] (which is identical to Article 4(1) of Brussels I *bis*); and second, that Swiss law is pleaded as applicable under Article 138 of the Swiss PIL Act, which lays down a rule similar to Article 7 of Rome II for claims for injuries from emissions, Article 133, the choice-of-law rule for torts in the absence of party autonomy, or the general exception clause under Article 15.

A similar case is being pursued in Belgium, where Hugues Falys, a Belgian farmer, along with several CSOs, has sued Total Energies, a French-based global energy and petroleum group.[32] Falys's farm experienced extreme weather events, including heatwaves and droughts. The claimants seek to hold TotalEnergies liable under Belgium's extracontractual civil liability provisions, requesting compensation and an immediate cessation of investments in new fossil fuel projects. The jurisdiction of Belgian courts is sought on the ground of the place of damage in Belgium under Article 7(2) of Brussels I *bis*, while Belgian law is pleaded as applicable under Article 7 of Rome II. At the time of writing, the case is still in an early procedural stage with a hearing scheduled for November 2025.

2.2.3 Breach of Statutory Duty of Vigilance/Due Diligence

The third category includes cases commenced in France under the 2017 Duty of Vigilance Law (Vigilance Law),[33] which obliges large French companies to establish and effectively implement vigilance plans to identify and prevent human rights abuses and environmental damage. It provides for a two-fold enforcement mechanism. If a company fails to comply with the Vigilance Law, a party with standing can serve the company with a three-month formal notice for breach of its obligations, irrespective of whether actual harm has occurred. Upon expiration of the notice period and in the event of continued non-compliance, the party can seek an injunction with a potential periodic penalty payment. The Vigilance Law also establishes a remediation mechanism allowing individuals to file a civil liability claim if a breach of the vigilance obligations caused otherwise-preventable damage.

The enforcement of the Vigilance Law has so far led to several formal notices, some of which have been followed by court summonses seeking injunctions and civil liability claims.[34] The Global Database records at least two transnational climate change cases brought under this

[31] Convention of 30 October 2007 on jurisdiction and the recognition and enforcement of judgments in civil and commercial matters, entered into force 1 January 2010.

[32] 'Hugues Falys, FIAN, Greenpeace, Ligue des droits humains v TotalEnergies (The Farmer Case)' (*Global Climate Change Litigation Database*, 2024) <https://climatecasechart.com/non-us-case/hugues-falys-fian-greenpeace-ligue-des-droits-humains-v-totalenergies-the-farmer-case/> accessed 2 July 2025.

[33] *Loi no. 2017-399 du 27 Mars 2017 relative au devoir de vigilance des sociétés mères et des entreprises donneuses d'ordre.*

[34] Duty of Vigilance Radar, 'Cases' <https://vigilance-plan.org/court-cases-under-the-duty-of-vigilance-law/> accessed 2 July 2025.

law. The first is a civil liability claim against the French supermarket giant Casino, alleging that its involvement in the cattle industry in Brazil and Colombia contributed to environmental damage, including deforestation that destroyed carbon sinks essential for climate regulation.[35] The second case targets Total over an oil project in Uganda and Tanzania.[36] The Global Database also records two cases against BNP Paribas concerning the climate risks of its activities[37] and financing of businesses allegedly responsible for the deforestation of Amazon,[38] although it is not clear from the publicly available sources if these cases fall within the definition of transnational climate change litigation as defined in Section 1.

PIL issues have not been central to the enforcement of the Vigilance Law, with discussions largely limited to scholarly and policy debates.[39] Nevertheless, lessons from the Vigilance Law are relevant for the EU Corporate Sustainability Due Diligence Directive (CSDDD).[40] The CSDDD introduces human rights and environmental due diligence obligations for certain EU and non-EU companies. Although a recent proposal by the European Commission envisages the removal of the harmonised EU-wide civil liability regime for the breach of its obligations,[41] national laws will fill this gap and thus establish civil liability regimes as one of the enforcement mechanisms. The CSDDD's interaction with PIL rules is a topic of ongoing debates.[42]

2.3 **Reflections**

The case studies lead us to draw three conclusions.

First, transnational climate change cases based on private law remain relatively uncommon. A few factors may explain this finding. While cases against corporations have increased since 2020,[43] most litigation focuses on enforcing state duties under international and domestic public law. Few legal instruments address direct corporate obligations in the context of climate change, so private law claims often rely on innovative arguments still being tested in courts, as seen in cases like *Shell* and *Lliuya*.

[35] 'Envol Vert and Others v Casino' (*Global Climate Change Litigation Database*, 2021) <https://climatecasechart.com/non-us-case/envol-vert-et-al-v-casino/> accessed 2 July 2025.

[36] 'AFIEGO and Others v Total' (*Global Climate Change Litigation Database*, 2023) <https://climatecasechart.com/non-us-case/afiego-et-al-v-total/> accessed 2 July 2025.

[37] 'Notre Affaire à Tous Les Amis de la Terre, and Oxfam France v BNP Paribas' (*Global Climate Change Litigation Database*, 2023) <https://climatecasechart.com/non-us-case/notre-affaire-a-tous-les-amis-de-la-terre-and-oxfam-france-v-bnp-paribas/> accessed 2 July 2025.

[38] 'Comissão Pastoral da Terra and Notre Affaire à Tous v BNP Paribas' (*Global Climate Change Litigation Database*, 2023) <https://climatecasechart.com/non-us-case/comissao-pastoral-da-terra-and-notre-affaire-a-tous-v-bnp-paribas/> accessed 2 July 2025.

[39] Klaas Hendrik Eller, 'Private International Law and the Many Faces of Corporate Due Diligence: Lessons from the French Loi de vigilance' (*BHRJ Blog*, 11 December 2024) <https://bhrj.blog/2024/12/11/private-international-law-and-the-many-faces-of-corporate-due-diligence-lessons-from-the-french-loi-de-vigilance/> accessed 2 July 2025.

[40] Directive (EU) 2024/1760 of 13 June 2024 on corporate sustainability due diligence and amending Directive (EU) 2019/1937 and Regulation (EU) 2023/2859 OJ L 2024/1760 (CSDDD).

[41] European Commission, 'Proposal for a Directive amending CSDDD' COM(2025) 81 final (26 February 2025), art 5.

[42] European Group of PIL, 'Recommendation of 8 October 2021' <https://gedip-egpil.eu/wp-content/uploads/2021/02/Recommandation-GEDIP-Recommendation-EGPIL-final-1.pdf>; 'Recommendation of 11 September 2022' <https://gedip-egpil.eu/wp-content/uploads/2022/07/Recommendation-GEDIP2022E.pdf> accessed 2 July 2025.

[43] Joana Setzer and Rebecca Byrnes, *Global Trends in Climate Change Litigation: 2020 Snapshot* (Grantham Research Institute, LSE 2020) 18–19.

Moreover, transnational climate change litigation is inherently difficult to frame. On the one hand, purely domestic and transnational cases face similar procedural and substantive challenges, including funding, standing, justiciability, and causation.[44] On the other hand, transnational cases face additional obstacles, including complex questions of jurisdiction, applicable law, and enforcement. These barriers may help explain why the US District Court for the Northern District of California in *City of Oakland v BP Plc* dismissed the relevance of transnational litigation altogether, ruling that global warming should be addressed by political branches.[45]

Our second finding is that transnational climate change cases based on private law have emerged in a small number of jurisdictions, notably the US and a few Continental European countries. Some scholars attribute this to the benefits of litigating in these countries.[46]

However, other factors may also influence the choice of forum. The nature of claims and the types of arguments advanced result in climate change litigation being targeted against specific corporations, commonly referred to as the "carbon majors" (i.e., some of the world's largest fossil fuel and building materials producers), which have historically had a significant and measurable impact on climate change. Richard Heede's study on carbon majors revealed that nearly two-thirds of major industrial GHG emissions (from fossil fuel use, methane leaks, and cement manufacture) originated in just ninety companies around the world.[47] According to the Carbon Majors database, a database of historical production data that spans back to 1854, the 104 investor-owned emitters covered by the database come from the following countries: Australia (4), Austria (1), Brazil (1), Canada (7), China (4), Czechia (2) France (1), Germany (3), India (2), Indonesia (2), Ireland (1), Italy (1), Japan (3), Kazakhstan (1), Luxembourg (2), Mexico (1), Poland (1), Russia (18), South Africa (3), Spain (1), Switzerland (2), Thailand (1), Ukraine (2), the UK (6), and the US (34).[48] In much of the world, all or the majority of carbon majors are state-owned,[49] making litigation against them significantly more challenging.[50]

Finally, PIL has not yet played a major role in climate change litigation, which may seem surprising at first glance, given the global nature of the problem and the fact that PIL regulates private law relationships with an international element. At the same time, this may reflect how cases are currently framed. In contrast to BHRE litigation, which focuses on the allocation of liability within the legal entities of a multinational enterprise domiciled in multiple jurisdictions, transnational climate change litigation typically targets the parent company as the sole defendant, simplifying cross-border considerations. Nonetheless, climate change litigation is evolving rapidly and PIL issues may yet attract more attention.

[44] See generally Douglas A Kysar, 'The Duty of Climate Care' (2024) 73 DePaul Law Review 487.

[45] *City of Oakland* (n 17).

[46] Álvarez-Armas (n 7) 424; Judith Spiegel, 'Forum Shopping in the EU: A Useful Strategy in Corporate Climate Change Litigation?' (2024) 8 Católica Law Review 177, 179.

[47] Richard Heede, 'Tracing Anthropogenic Carbon Dioxide and Methane Emissions to Fossil Fuel and Cement Producers, 1854–2010' (2014) 122 Climatic Change 229.

[48] Carbon Majors, 'Entities' <https://carbonmajors.org/Entities> accessed 2 July 2025.

[49] The database lists 70 state-owned emitters from 33 countries.

[50] Further discussion of specific issues arising in climate change litigation against state-owned carbon majors is outside the scope of this chapter.

3. Jurisdiction

PIL concerns adjudicative jurisdiction, that is, the rules and principles determining when a court can hear and decide a case with cross-border elements.[51] Therefore, this chapter does not address subject-matter jurisdiction or federal-question and diversity jurisdiction in the US. Nor do we examine the allocation of jurisdiction within federal states, although the federal context in which some jurisdictional rules operate is, as will be seen, crucial.

Our focus is on tort litigation, broadly defined to include tort or delict claims and civil enforcement of statutes like duty of vigilance/due diligence legislation. The practical experience we have with transnational climate change litigation shows that particularly important in this context are rules of general jurisdiction based on the defendant's connections with the forum country and rules of special/specific jurisdiction based on connections between the tort and the forum country. If a court has general jurisdiction over a defendant, it can hear and decide all claims against the defendant, including those concerning foreign conduct and damage. If a court has special/specific jurisdiction over a defendant based on conduct/damage occurring within the territory of the court, it can hear and decide only claims arising out of that conduct/damage. Since, as mentioned earlier, transnational climate change litigation typically targets the parent company as the sole defendant, jurisdictional rules based on connections between claims against local and foreign defendants are not of great importance, unlike in transnational BHRE litigation.

There is no treaty regulating direct jurisdiction in civil and commercial matters in general or tort matters in particular at a global level. Consequently, the jurisdiction of courts to hear and decide climate change cases depends on domestic law and, in the case of EU Member States and the European Free Trade Area (EFTA) states, Brussels I *bis* and the Lugano Convention.

To enable a meaningful comparison of jurisdictional laws, two preliminary remarks are necessary. First, jurisdiction is regulated at three different levels.[52] The first level sets the outer limits of jurisdiction. Constitutional law limits, particularly those developed under the Fifth and Fourteenth Amendments of the US Constitution,[53] represent significant jurisdictional restraints. The second level of regulation provides bases of jurisdiction, that is, specific rules on which jurisdiction can actually be based. The third level concerns judicial discretion for the individual case.

Second, a comprehensive global comparison of jurisdictional rules is neither feasible nor necessary here. As mentioned earlier, transnational climate change cases based on private law have so far targeted investor-owned carbon majors, based in a limited number of countries. Consequently, it is the rules of general jurisdiction in the laws of these countries that matter. On the other hand, the rules of special/specific jurisdiction in tort matters from all countries are potentially relevant because emissions occur in many places and climate change damage can be suffered anywhere. Furthermore, Michaels usefully frames different approaches to jurisdiction in terms of two paradigms: "Continental European law stands for the first, US law stands for the second. Traditional English law stands, in many regards, somewhere between both paradigms".[54]

[51] Ralf Michaels, 'Jurisdiction, Foundations', *Max Planck Encyclopedia of Private International Law* (2017) 1042.

[52] ibid 1043–45.

[53] *International Shoe Co v State of Washington*, 326 US 310 (1945).

[54] Ralf Michaels, 'Two Paradigms of Jurisdiction' (2006) 27 Michigan Journal of International Law 1003; Michaels (n 51) 1048.

3.1 General Jurisdiction

A rule giving general jurisdiction to the courts of the defendant's home country enjoys a wide international acceptance. Under Brussels I *bis*, the courts of the defendant's domicile have general jurisdiction over the defendant.[55] A legal person is domiciled where it has its statutory seat, central administration, or principal place of business.[56] Claimants expressly relied on this jurisdictional rule in the *Shell* and *Lliuya* cases.

US law has a similar rule of general jurisdiction.[57] It is based on contacts between the defendant and the forum state that are so constant and pervasive as to render the defendant essentially at home in the forum state. Paradigmatic examples include the place of incorporation or principal place of business of a corporation. The assumption of general jurisdiction on a broader basis is unconstitutional in the US. Thus, in *In re Fuel Industry Climate Cases*, the defendants who had their principal places of business in California did not contest the jurisdiction of Californian courts.[58]

In England, the claimant may serve a claim form as of right on companies incorporated, registered, or having a place of business in England.[59] The claimant may serve a claim form out of the jurisdiction with the permission of the court where the defendant is domiciled in England.[60] Jurisdiction assumed on this basis is general and the *Moçambique* rule that excludes the jurisdiction of English courts in proceedings that concern foreign property[61] does not exclude climate change litigation that concerns foreign emissions.[62]

A rule giving general jurisdiction to the courts of the defendant's home country also exists in all other countries from which major investor-owned emitters come.[63]

55 Brussels I *bis* (n 19) art 4(1).

56 ibid art 63(1) and (2).

57 *Milliken v Meyer*, 311 US 457 (1940); *Goodyear Dunlop Tires Operations SA v Brown*, 564 U.S. 915 (2011); *Daimler AG v Bauman*, 571 US 117 (2014).

58 *In re Fuel Industry Climate Cases* (n 16) fn 1.

59 Civil Procedure Rules, r 6.9(2); Companies Act 2006, s 1139(1); *Adams v Cape Industries Plc* [1990] 1 Ch 433 (CA).

60 Civil Procedure Rules Practice Direction 6B, para 3.1(1). Domicile is defined in Civil Jurisdiction and Judgments Act 1982, s 42(4).

61 *British South Africa Co v Companhia de Moçambique* [1893] AC 602 (HL); *Hesperides Hotels Ltd v Aegean Turkish Holidays* [1979] AC 508 (HL).

62 Civil Jurisdiction and Judgments Act 1982, s 30. See, generally, Guillaume Laganière, 'Local Polluters, Foreign Land and Climate Change: The Myth of the Local Action Rule in Canada' (2020) 16 Journal of Private International Law 390.

63 For Australia, see, for example, Federal Court Rules 2011 (Cth), r 10.42(g); Uniform Civil Procedure Rules 2005 (NSW) Sch 6 (g). For Canada, see, for example, Uniform Court Jurisdiction and Proceedings Transfer Act 2021, r 3(d); Rules of Civil Procedure (Ontario), RRO 1990, Reg 194, r 17.02(p); Quebec Civil Code, arts 3134, 3148(1). For Brazil, India, Russia, and South Africa, see Stellina Jolly and Saloni Khanderia, 'Reflecting Remarks' in Stellina Jolly and Saloni Khanderia (eds), *Private International Law in BRICS: Convergence, Divergence and Reciprocal Lessons* (Bloomsbury 2024) 119, 132–33. For China, Indonesia, Japan, and Thailand, see Wilson Lui and Anselmo Reyes, 'Introduction' in Anselmo Reyes and Wilson Lui (eds), *Direct Jurisdiction: Asian Perspectives* (Bloomsbury 2021) 1, 9. For Kazakhstan, see Civil Procedure Code, art 29. For Mexico, see National Code of Civil and Family Procedure, art 1117; Code of Civil Procedure for the Federal District, art 156(IV). For Switzerland, see Lugano Convention, arts 2(1), 60. For Ukraine, see Law on Private International Law, art 76(1)(2).

3.2 Special/Specific Jurisdiction

Generally speaking, rules of jurisdiction in tort matters can give jurisdiction to the courts for the place of conduct and/or the place of damage. Despite an opinion to the contrary,[64] claimants do not need to prove a causal link between the defendant's conduct and damage when relying on a rule of special/specific jurisdiction for torts.[65] Since a rule of jurisdiction based on the place of conduct often overlaps with widely available jurisdictional bases, such as rules giving general jurisdiction to the courts of the defendant's home country or special/specific jurisdiction to the courts for the place of a branch, agency, or other establishment, a rule of jurisdiction based on the place of damage is arguably of greater importance in transnational climate change litigation.

A rule giving special/specific jurisdiction to the courts for the place of conduct enjoys a wide international acceptance. Under Brussels I *bis*, a person domiciled in a Member State may be sued in another Member State, in matters relating to tort, delict, or quasi-delict, in the courts for the place of the event giving rise to the damage.[66] The meaning of this concept in climate change litigation is controversial and is discussed below where we present the equivalent concept used in Article 7 of Rome II.

US law allows specific jurisdiction where there is a link between both the facts of the claim and the defendant and the forum state, in the sense that the defendant performs some act by which it "purposefully avails itself of the privilege of conducting activities within the forum State, thus invoking the benefits and protections of its laws".[67] In *In re Fuel Industry Climate Cases*,[68] the court held that Californian courts had specific jurisdiction over the foreign defendants. The court found that the defendants had purposefully availed themselves of the privilege of doing business in California, and that the plaintiffs' claims arose out of or related to the defendants' extensive contacts with California. These contacts included the defendants' sale and promotion of fossil fuel products in California, their allegedly deceptive statements regarding climate change, and the alleged injuries the plaintiffs' suffered in California.[69]

In England, the claimant may serve a claim form out of the jurisdiction with the permission of the court where a claim is made in tort and damage which has been or will be sustained results from a "substantial and efficacious" act[70] committed, or likely to be committed, within the jurisdiction.[71]

The wide international acceptance of the rule giving special/specific jurisdiction to the courts for the place of conduct is reflected in the 2019 Hague Judgments Convention, which

[64] Fanny Giansetto, 'Le droit international privé à l'épreuve des nouveaux contentieux en matière de responsabilité climatique' (2018) 145 Journal du droit international 507.

[65] *In re Fuel Industry Climate Cases* (n 16), referring to *Ford Motor Co v Montana Eighth Judicial District Court* 592 U.S. 351, 343 (2021); Olivera Boskovic, 'Le contexte transnational en matière de responsabilité climatique' in Mathilde Hautereau-Boutonnet and Stéphanie Porchy-Simon, *Le changement climatique, quel rôle pour le droit privé?* (Dalloz 2019) 193, 198–99.

[66] Brussels I *bis* (n 19) art 7(2); Case 21-76 *Handelskwekerij G J Bier BV v Mines de potasse d'Alsace SA* ECLI:EU:C:1976:166.

[67] *Hanson v Denckla*, 357 US 235, 253 (1958).

[68] *In re Fuel Industry Climate Cases* (n 16).

[69] See ibid 11–13 for references to similar cases from Hawaii, Connecticut, Colorado, Delaware, and Massachusetts.

[70] *Metall und Rohstoff AG v Donaldson Lufkin & Jenrette Inc* [1990] 1 QB 391 (CA), 437.

[71] Civil Procedure Rules Practice Direction 6B, para 3.1(9)(b).

recognises acts or omission in the state of origin directly causing death, physical injury, and damage to or loss of tangible property as a basis of indirect jurisdiction.[72]

On the other hand, a rule giving jurisdiction to the courts for the place of damage is controversial. For example, such a rule is unconstitutional in the US, where specific jurisdiction requires a link between the defendant and the forum state.[73] The occurrence of damage in the forum state is not enough, regardless of its foreseeability.[74]

Under Brussels I *bis*, a person domiciled in a Member State may be sued in another Member State, in matters relating to tort, delict, or quasi-delict, in the courts for the place of direct damage.[75] This jurisdictional rule is relied on in the *Farmer* case in Belgium. It has been criticised as being too uncertain and there are calls to limit jurisdictionally relevant damage to foreseeable damage. This issue is further discussed below where we present the equivalent concept used in Article 7 of Rome II.

The equivalent jurisdictional rule in English law is much broader. The claimant may serve a claim form out of the jurisdiction with the permission of the court where a claim is made in tort and damage was sustained, or will be sustained, within the jurisdiction.[76] Damage for this purpose seems to be interpreted broadly to cover both direct and indirect damage.[77]

A rule giving jurisdiction to the courts for the place of damage is accepted in much of the rest of the world, sometimes with a foreseeability proviso,[78] although not universally.[79]

The rule of special jurisdiction in tort matters of Brussels I *bis* allocates jurisdiction on a so-called mosaic basis. If the defendant's conduct/damage occurs in more than one country, the courts that have jurisdiction on the basis that some of the conduct/damage occurred within their territory have jurisdiction solely over claims for the consequences of the conduct/damage occurring within their territory.[80] The "mosaic principle" limits the power of the courts of EU Member States to holistically deal with climate change claims. On the other hand, English law has recently introduced a useful jurisdictional basis to consolidate complex transnational disputes. If an English court has jurisdiction on any basis (including on the basis of conduct or damage within the jurisdiction), it can permit service of the claim form for all related claims.[81]

[72] 2019 Hague Judgments Convention (n 4) art 5(1)(j).

[73] *Hanson v Denckla* (n 67).

[74] ibid; *Asahi Metal Industry Co v Superior Court of California*, 480 US 102 (1987); *J McIntyre Machinery Ltd v Nicastro*, 564 US 873 (2011); *Walden v Fiore*, 571 US 277 (2014); *Bristol-Myers Squibb Co v Superior Court of California*, 582 US 255 (2017).

[75] Brussels I *bis* (n 19) art 7(2); *Bier* (n 66); Case C-220/88 *Dumez France SA v Hessische Landesbank* ECLI:EU:C:1990:8; Case C-364/93 *Marinari v Lloyds Bank Plc* ECLI:EU:C:1995:289.

[76] Civil Procedure Rules Practice Direction 6B, para 3.1(9)(a). The *Moçambique* rule does not exclude climate change litigation that concerns foreign emissions: (n 62).

[77] *FS Cairo (Nile Plaza) LLC v Brownlie* [2021] UKSC 45; *Fong Chak Kwan v Ascentic Ltd* [2022] HKCFA 12.

[78] For BRICS, see Jolly and Khanderia (n 63) 134. For East Asian jurisdictions, see the entries for China, Hong Kong, Japan (which adopts a foreseeability proviso), Malaysia, Singapore, South Korea, Taiwan, and Vietnam in Lui and Reyes (n 63) 26, 44–45, 95, 162, 137, 117, 69 and 192, respectively. For the domestic laws of EU Member States, see Arnaud Nuyts, 'Study on Residual Jurisdiction: General Report' (3 September 2007) 32–34; Tobias Lutzi, Ennio Piovesani, and Dora Zgrabljić Rotar, 'Comparative Report' in Tobias Lutzi, Ennio Piovesani, and Dora Zgrabljić Rotar (eds), *Jurisdiction over Non-EU Defendants: Should the Brussels Ia Regulation Be Extended?* (Bloomsbury 2023) 3, 21–22.

[79] In addition to US law, this jurisdictional rule is questionable in Canada: *Club Resorts Ltd v Van Breda* 2012 SCC 17; cf Guillaume Laganière, *Liability for Transboundary Pollution at the Intersection of Public and Private International Law* (Bloomsbury 2022) 125–34.

[80] Case C-68/93 *Shevill v Presse Alliance SA* ECLI:EU:C:1995:61.

[81] Civil Procedure Rules Practice Direction 6B, para 3.1(4A)(c).

3.3 Judicial Discretion

Laws also differ in their approach to judicial discretion for the individual case. EU law adopts the strictest approach. A court with jurisdiction under a jurisdictional rule of Brussels I *bis* cannot refuse to exercise it on the basis of the *forum non conveniens* doctrine,[82] although it can, under certain conditions, refuse to hear and decide a case where a parallel or related action is pending in another state.[83]

However, US and English law adopt *forum non conveniens*, which gives their courts discretion to refuse to hear and decide a case. The US and English approaches differ in some significant aspects. For instance, US courts can take public interest factors into account[84] and discriminate against foreign claimants.[85] *Forum non conveniens* is a general feature in most common law countries.[86] It is also available in some civil law, particularly East Asian, countries.[87] The *forum non conveniens* tests in these countries differ, but it is considered that the Australian version is the most favourable for claimants in transnational BHRE and climate change litigation. The Australian version allows dismissal or stay only where an available foreign tribunal is the natural or more appropriate forum and the local tribunal is clearly inappropriate.[88] At the moment, none of the factors to be taken into account under the different versions of *forum non conveniens* specifically relates to these kinds of litigation. Nevertheless, a proposal has been made recently that English law should be modified to ensure that jurisdictional decisions by the English courts take into account their environmental impact, that is, the environmental impact of the selection of a particular forum.[89]

Rules on parallel and related actions and *forum non conveniens* have the potential to restrict access to remedy. Furthermore, *forum non conveniens* is likely to play an important role when climate change litigation is commenced by foreign individuals and communities, even where a wrongdoing in the forum state is alleged. *Forum non conveniens* challenges are thus likely to reflect the Global North/Global South asymmetries of power and injustices embedded in climate change. As there are no cases where rules on parallel and related actions or *forum non conveniens* have been an issue in climate change litigation, it is difficult to estimate their role in this context. However, there is a new claim in English courts related to environmental damage

[82] Case C-281/02 *Owusu v N B Jackson, trading as 'Villa Holidays Bal-Inn Villas'* ECLI:EU:C:2005:120.

[83] Brussels I *bis* (n 19) arts 29–34. For a discussion of Article 30, see Eduardo Álvarez-Armas, 'Climate Change Litigation through the Prism of Private International Law' (2024) 28 Spanish Yearbook of International Law 343, 357–58.

[84] Compare *Gulf Oil Corp v Gilbert*, 330 US 501, 508–09 (1945) and *Lubbe v Cape Plc* [2000] 1 WLR 1545 (HL), 1566–67.

[85] Compare *Piper Aircraft Co v Reyno*, 454 US 235, 255–56 (1981) and *Lubbe v Cape* (n 84) 1566–67.

[86] *Voth v Manildra Flour Mills Pty Ltd* (1990) 171 CLR 538 (Australia); *Van Breda* (n 79) (Canada); *Fong* (n 77) (Hong Kong); *Mayar (HK) Ltd v Owners and Parties, Vessels MV Fortune Ltd AIR* [2006] SC 1828 (India); *American Express Bank Ltd v Mohamed Toufic Al-Ozeir* [1995] 1 MLJ 160 (SC) (Malaysia); *Rappo v Accent Delight International Ltd* [2017] 2 SLR 265 (Singapore). See also the entry for Myanmar in Lui and Reyes (n 63) 223–24. It does not exist in Sri Lanka, although there is inherent power to stay proceedings in cases of *lis pendens*: Lui and Reyes (n 63) 287. Query whether it exists in South Arica (a mixed system): see Jolly and Khanderia (n 63) 115.

[87] See the entries for China, Indonesia, Japan, Philippines, South Korea, and Taiwan in Lui and Reyes (n 63) 19–20, 250–51, 89, 233–34, 114–15 and 64, respectively.

[88] *Voth* (n 86).

[89] Alex Mills, 'Sustainability and Jurisdiction in the International Civil Litigation Market' (2024) 20 Journal of Private International Law 1.

following a storm and flooding, which has a climate change element,[90] which might shed more light on this matter.

4. Applicable Law

PIL also addresses the determination of the applicable law. There are two basic approaches to determining the applicable law in general, including in transnational climate change litigation: multilateralism, which employs multilateral or bilateral choice-of-law rules to "refer the decision of the dispute, depending on the facts of the case, to either the law of the forum or to the law of a foreign jurisdiction";[91] and unilateralism, which relies either on unilateral choice-of-law rules, with "the sole function of designating the *lex fori*",[92] or on rules for determining the territorial scope of a specific set of provisions and overriding mandatory rules.[93]

There is a strong link between jurisdiction and applicable law. If a court has general jurisdiction over a defendant (see the *Shell*, *Lliuya*, *Holcim*, and Vigilance Law cases), it can hear and decide all claims against the defendant, including those concerning foreign conduct and damage. If a court has special/specific jurisdiction over a defendant based on conduct occurring within the territory of the court, it can hear and decide claims for that conduct, including claims for consequent foreign damage. In these two kinds of cases, it may be important to establish whether the claimant should plead their case under the *lex fori* or one or more foreign laws. If a court has special/specific jurisdiction over a defendant based on damage occurring within the territory of the court (see the *Farmer* case, as well as the *Shell* case), it can hear and decide only claims for that damage (with the exception of laws, such as English law, which contain a rule of jurisdiction over related claims). In such cases, again, it may be important to establish whether the claimant should plead their case under the *lex fori* or foreign law. If litigation occurs under a law other than the law of the place of emissions, the question of the effectiveness of any enabling rules of, or administrative authorisations issued in, the place of emissions arises. Furthermore, the place of litigation matters because a court can always apply its overriding mandatory rules to situations falling within their scope, which is particularly important in the US, where the key question has been the territorial scope of US laws.

4.1 Choice of Law

In the EU and the UK, the law applicable to non-contractual obligations in civil and commercial matters is determined by Rome II, which applies to events giving rise to damage which occur after 11 January 2009.[94] Since climate change litigation concerns environmental

[90] 'Malawian Villagers Take Legal Action against Primark Owner Associated British Foods After Flooding Destroyed Their Village and Left Seven People Dead' (4 May 2025) <https://www.leighday.co.uk/news/news/2025-news/malawian-villagers-take-legal-action-against-primark-owner-associated-british-foods-after-flooding-destroyed-their-village-and-left-seven-people-dead/> accessed 2 July 2025.

[91] Jürgen Basedow, 'Choice of Law', *Max Planck Encyclopedia of Private International Law* (2017) 311, 314.

[92] Stéphanie Francq, 'Unilateralism', *Max Planck Encyclopedia of Private International Law* (2017) 1779, 1787.

[93] ibid 1787–89.

[94] Rome II (n 22) arts 1, 2, 31, 32; Case C-412/10 *Deo Antoine Homawoo v GMF Assurances SA* ECLI:EU:C:2011:747.

damage,[95] Article 7 comes into play. It empowers the claimant to select either the law of the place where the direct damage occurred (*lex loci damni*) or the law of the place where the event giving rise to the damage occurred (*lex loci actus*). The parties can agree on the applicable law under Article 14. Furthermore, Article 17 permits a court to take into account, as a matter of fact and insofar as is appropriate, the rules of safety and conduct which were in force at the place and time of the event giving rise to the liability in assessing the conduct of the person claimed to be liable.

There are lively debates in the field of choice of law concerning the interpretation of the event giving rise to the damage and the relevant damage.[96] For example, Petersen Weiner and Weller[97] outline four main approaches regarding the *lex loci actus* under Article 7: (1) applying the law of the place of the business decision; (2) applying the law of the place of the emitting plant(s); (3) applying the law of the place leading to the damage in the most predominant way (a focal point approach); and (4) the choice by the victim approach. They propose their own approach, which differentiates between claims for compensation/adaptation and claims for mitigation. In compensation/adaptation claims, Petersen Weiner and Weller's approach involves applying the law of the place of the emitting plant(s) on a "mosaic" basis as the starting point, granting the courts discretion to estimate the proportion of each plant's GHG emissions, a fall-back rule in favour of the law of the central place of emissions and a last-resort rule in favour of the law of the place of the business decision at the real seat of the company. In mitigation claims, the *lex loci actus* should be interpreted as the law of the place of the business decision.

Lehmann and Eichel[98] adopt the premise that the determination of the *lex loci damni* should be limited to avoid the potential application of the law of every country in the world. They propose tempering Article 7 by an analogous application of the foreseeability proviso in the second paragraph of Article 5(1) of Rome II, which deals with product liability. Van Loon[99] and Nishitani[100] also advocate incorporating a foreseeability requirement in determining the *lex loci damni*. Álvarez-Armas[101] and Kieninger[102] oppose the foreseeability requirement.

[95] *Shell* District Court Judgment (n 20) [4.3.2.]; *Lliuya* Hamm Higher Regional Court Judgment of 28 May 2025 (n 27) 30.

[96] There are identical debates in the field of jurisdiction under Article 7(2) of Brussels I *bis* (n 19). However, stakes differ in the field of choice of law. While the law of jurisdiction accepts and sometimes even promotes concurrent jurisdiction, Rome II only allows the application of a single law to one issue. Moreover, under Rome II, the applicable law can be the law of any country in the world (Article 3). These differences could lead to different interpretations of seemingly identical connecting factors in these two fields.

[97] Madeliene Petersen Weiner and Marc-Philippe Weller, 'The "Event Giving Rise to the Damage" under Art. 7 Rome II Regulation in CO2 Reduction Claims' (2021/2022) XXIII Yearbook of Private International Law 261; 'Corporate Climate Liability in Private International Law' (2024) 26 Japanese Yearbook of International Law 2, 12–15.

[98] Matthias Lehmann and Florian Eichel, 'Globaler Klimawandel und Internationales Privatrecht: Zuständigkeit und anzuwendendes Recht für transnationale Klagen wegen klimawandelbedingter Individualschäden' (2019) 83 Rabel Journal of Comparative and International Private Law *(RabelsZ)* 77.

[99] Hans van Loon, 'Principles and Building Blocks for a Global Legal Framework for Transnational Civil Litigation in Environmental Matters' (2018) 23 Uniform Law Review 298, 316.

[100] Yuko Nishitani, 'Localisation of Damage in Private International Law and Challenges of Climate Change Litigation' (2022) 6 International Business Law Journal 707, 716–17.

[101] Álvarez-Armas (n 83) 358–61.

[102] Eva-Maria Kieninger, 'Conflicts of Jurisdiction and the Applicable Law in Domestic Courts' Proceedings' in Wolfgang Kahl and Marc-Philippe Weller (eds), *Climate Change Litigation: A Handbook* (Beck 2021) 119, 130–31, 144–45.

Laganière[103] adopts a related position, arguing against a foreseeability requirement, but in favour of a directness of damage requirement.

While there is disagreement in the literature regarding foreseeability and directness of damage, there is a large degree of consensus that both the *lex loci actus* and the *lex loci damni* apply on a "mosaic" basis. The "mosaic principle" can therefore limit the power of the courts of EU Member States and UK courts to holistically deal with climate change claims.

Another point of disagreement revolves around the application of Article 17. The question arises whether this article enables a court seised of a climate change litigation where the applicable law is not the place of emissions to decide in favour of the defendant based on the argument that its conduct complied with the rules of, or authorisations issued in, that place. On the one hand, the objectives of environmental law support limiting the transnational effect of the rules of, or authorisations issued in, the place of emissions. On the other hand, the fact that GHG emissions are lawful and legitimate in the places where they occur can influence legal reasoning.

Weller and co-authors[104] argue that the courts can scrutinise the substance of authorisations, as well as the regulatory objectives of the provisions on which they are based, if provided for by the law designated as applicable by Article 7. Taking a more assertive stance, Lehmann and Eichel[105] connect the application of the *lex loci damni* with Article 17. They propose that the *lex loci damni* should only be applied to liability where an authorisation does not exist, was obviously invalid, obtained by fraud, or consciously transgressed. Conversely, Boskovic,[106] Álvarez-Armas,[107] Kieninger,[108] and Michaels and Zeh[109] advocate limiting defendants' access to Article 17. Offering an alternative perspective, Pasqua[110] argues that the Emissions Directive[111] contains a unilateral rule, allowing a Member State court to take into account an authorisation issued by a Member State whose law is neither the law of the forum nor the law designated as applicable by Article 7.

These debates are only partially reflected in existing case law. In *Shell*, the Hague District Court relied on the objectives of environmental law underlying Article 7. The court held that the event giving rise to the damage encompassed the adoption of a group policy at the defendant's Dutch headquarters as an independent cause of the damage.[112] It also found that Dutch law could apply as the *lex loci damni*.[113] Finally, while the court took administrative authorisations into account, it held that they did not prevent the claims from proceeding.[114] The Hague Court of Appeal did not discuss choice of law in its judgment allowing the appeal because Shell did not maintain its challenge to the application of Dutch law. In the *Lliyua* and *Farmer* cases, the claimants invoked Article 7 to plead the application of German and Belgian

103 Laganière (n 79) 179.

104 Marc-Philippe Weller and Mai-Lan Tran, 'Climate Litigation against Companies' (2022) 1 Climate Action 1, 10–11; Petersen Weiner and Weller, 'Corporate Climate Liability' (n 97) 15–17.

105 Lehmann and Eichel (n 98).

106 Boskovic (n 65) 202–03.

107 Álvarez-Armas (n 83) 353–55.

108 Kieninger (n 102) 142–44.

109 Michaels and Zeh (n 7) 485.

110 Marco Pasqua, 'Authorisations to Emit Greenhouse Gases: A Conflict-of-Laws Perspective' (2023) 3 Italian Review of International and Comparative Law 409.

111 Directive 2003/87/EC of 13 October 2003 establishing a scheme for greenhouse gas emission allowance trading within the Community and amending Council Directive 96/61/EC [2003] OJ L 275/32.

112 *Shell* District Court Judgment (n 20) [4.3.2.]–[4.3.6].

113 ibid [4.3.7].

114 ibid [4.4.44]–[4.4.48].

law, respectively. The Hamm Higher Regional Court in the *Lliuya* case merely recorded in its 2025 judgment the parties' agreement on the application of German law under Article 14 of Rome II.[115]

As there appears to be no climate change litigation outside the EU that has given rise to choice-of-law issues and there is a limited academic scholarship on this subject,[116] it will suffice to mention key choice-of-law patterns outside the EU. Symeonides's comparative study of seventy-three choice-of-law codifications enacted in the last fifty years around the world shows that the special choice-of-law rule for environmental damage from Article 7 of Rome II has not been influential internationally.[117] The vast majority of codifications continue to follow the *lex loci delicti* rule as the basic rule for tort conflicts and subject it to express exceptions.[118] While about a dozen codifications define the *locus delicti* as the place of conduct and an equal number as the place of injury,[119] thirty codifications have an intentionally flexible definition of the *locus delicti*, which authorises the application of either the *lex loci actus* or the *lex loci damni*, whichever favours the victim (*favor laesi*).[120] The application of the *lex loci damni* sometimes comes with a foreseeability proviso.[121] Exceptions to the *lex loci delicti* rule include common-domicile, closer-connection, and pre-existing-relationship exceptions.[122] Twenty-seven codifications provide that if a state other than the state of conduct governs the tort, the court should nevertheless "take into account", or apply, the rules of "safety and conduct" of the state of conduct.[123] The debates concerning the interpretation of the connecting factors used in Article 7 of Rome II, as well as the application of Article 17 to climate change litigation, are of relevance in this context given the widespread use of the *locus delicti* as the basic rule, the *favor laesi* principle, and the "safety and conduct" rules.

Many countries, especially common law ones, do not have codifications. In some common law systems, including India, Hong Kong, and Singapore, choice-of-law rules for torts are derived from English common law.[124] Under these rules, domestic torts are governed by domestic law,[125] whereas foreign torts are subject to the double-actionability rule, which stipulates that a claim in tort can succeed only if it is actionable as a tort according to the *lex fori* and the law of the place of the tort imposes civil liability.[126] The double-actionability rule is

115 *Lliyua* (n 27) 29.

116 For exceptions, see Nishitani (n 100) (Japan), Guillaume Laganière, 'Choice of Law Issues in Tort-Based Climate Change Litigation' (2023) 74 University of New Brunswick Law Journal 33 (Canada), and commentators discussing how US choice-of-law rules would apply to climate change litigation: Michael Byers, Kelsey Franks, and Andrew Gage, 'The Internationalization of Climate Damages Litigation' (2017) 7 Washington Journal of Environmental Law and Policy 264, 292–95; Kieninger (n 102) 146–47; Spiegel (n 46) 189–90.

117 Only Albania has adopted it: Symeon Symeonides, *Codifying Choice of Law Around the World: An International Comparative Analysis* (OUP 2014) 62. Switzerland has a similar rule for injuries from emissions in Article 138 of its PIL Act.

118 ibid 52–53.

119 ibid 59.

120 ibid 53.

121 ibid 60–62.

122 ibid 53, 58.

123 ibid 58.

124 Saloni Khanderia, 'India' in Jolly and Saloni (n 63), 313, 331–32, referring to *Kotah Transport Ltd v Jhalawar Transport Services Ltd*, AIR 1960 Raj 224 and *Sona Devi v Anil Kumar* [2011] 3 TAC 552; *Red Sea Insurance Co Ltd v Bouygues SA* [1995] 1 AC 190 (PC, appeal from Hong Kong); *Rickshaw Investments Ltd v Nicolai Baron von Uexkull* [2006] SGCA 39.

125 *Szalatnay-Stacho v Fink* [1947] KB 1 (CA).

126 *Phillips v Eyre* (1870) LR 6 QB 1; *Chaplin v Boys* [1971] AC 356 (HL); *Red Sea Insurance* (n 124). The double-actionability rule is put on a statutory footing in 15 codifications: Symeonides (n 117) 58.

particularly unsuitable for climate change litigation, as it is, in a way, the polar opposite of Article 7 of Rome II and, as such, unfavourable to claimants. Because of the deficiencies of the double-actionability rule, many common law countries have created new common law rules. Australian law, for example, provides for a strict *lex loci delicti* rule for both interstate and international cases,[127] whereas Canadian common law lays down a flexible *lex loci delicti* rule for international cases.[128] It is not entirely clear if these rules point to the place of conduct or the place of injury as the *lex loci delicti*,[129] although a strong argument has been made in favour of the law of the place of injury for Canadian law.[130] The debates concerning the interpretation of the event giving rise to the damage and the relevant damage in Article 7 of Rome II are therefore also of relevance in this context.

Some US courts still follow the first conflicts Restatement of 1933, which provides for the application of the *lex loci damni*.[131] Although US courts that joined the US "choice-of-law revolution" adopt diverse and malleable approaches,[132] Symeonides has identified several trends.[133] Courts continue to apply the law of the state in which both the conduct and the injury occurred, if that state is also the domicile of either the tortfeasor or the victim. In cross-border torts in which the parties are not domiciled in the same state or states with identical laws, courts apply the law of either the state of conduct or the state of injury, whichever favours the claimant. In common-domicile cases, the law of the common domicile applies to issues of loss distribution and the law of the state of conduct and injury applies to issues of conduct regulation. Curiously, however, in the few US climate change cases where PIL issues have actually arisen, courts have not applied choice-of-law rules. Instead, they have approached the issue of applicable law as one of territorial scope of US laws.

4.2 Territorial Scope

States frequently extend their prescriptive jurisdiction to persons and activities beyond their borders, a practice commonly referred to as "extraterritorial" regulation. This approach is increasingly recognised as a useful tool for addressing global challenges, including climate change.[134]

A notable example is the Vigilance Law. While this law directly obliges large French companies to establish and effectively implement vigilance plans, it applies to human rights and environmental risks across their global supply chains, including subsidiaries, subcontractors, and suppliers with whom they have an established commercial relationship. In this way, this law reaches beyond French borders. The French legislator intended the Vigilance Law to have an overriding mandatory application, adopting a unilateral approach to its enforcement.[135] One issue remains unresolved. The Vigilance Law relies on general civil law for the imposition

127 *John Pfeiffer Pty Ltd v Rogerson* [2000] HCA 36; *Regie National des Usines Renault SA v Zhang* [2002] HCA 10.

128 *Tolofson v Jensen* [1994] 3 SCR 1022.

129 ibid 1050; *Pfeiffer* (n 127) [81].

130 Laganière (n 116).

131 American Law Institute, *Restatement of the Law, Conflict of Laws* (1934) s 377.

132 American Law Institute, *Restatement (Second) of Conflict of Laws* (1971) ss 6(2) and 145.

133 Symeonides (n 117) 50–52.

134 Hanna L Buxbaum, 'Extraterritoriality in Comparative Context: Defining the Scope of State Law in a Global Era' in Hannah L Buxbaum (ed), *Extraterritoriality in Comparative Perspective* (Brill | Nijhoff 2025) 3, 30.

135 Eller (n 39).

of liability for the breach of its provisions. It is, however, unclear if the relevant rules of the French Civil Code apply on an overriding basis or whether the civil liability rules of the law designated as applicable under the choice-of-law rules of Rome II apply.

Similarly, the CSDDD introduces due diligence obligations for large EU companies, as well as non-EU companies that generate a significant net turnover in the EU. As mentioned above, the original text of the directive provided a harmonised EU-wide civil liability regime for the breach of its obligations. It additionally provided that the laws of Member States transposing its liability regime would be of overriding mandatory application.[136] However, a recent proposal by the European Commission envisages the removal of this regime, although it also states that this removal does not restrict the possibility for Member States to provide that any domestic liability regimes are of overriding mandatory application.[137]

In the US, the presumption against extraterritoriality limits the reach of federal statutes beyond US borders.[138] The principle has played an important role in transnational BHRE litigation commenced under the Alien Tort Statute (ATS).[139] Its relevance has also been considered in transnational climate change litigation. For example, in *City of Oakland v BP PLC*, Oakland and San Francisco brought public nuisance claims against five fossil fuel companies for contributing to climate change and rising sea levels. The District Court held that to the extent that the claims were based on foreign emissions, they ran counter to the presumption against extraterritoriality and the principle of "judicial caution" applied in ATS cases.[140] The Court of Appeal for the Ninth Circuit did not revisit this aspect of the case.[141] Nonetheless, the decision of the district court has been heavily criticised for erroneously applying the presumption against extraterritoriality, a principle of *statutory construction*, to limit the territorial reach of federal *common law* rules, whose application should have been determined by choice-of-law rules.[142]

5. Foreign Judgments

The preceding discussion highlights at least four points of relevance for the recognition and enforcement of foreign judgments. First, in some cases, local authorities have acted as claimants. Does the rule in common law countries prohibiting the enforcement of foreign public law preclude the enforcement of such judgments? Second, in many cases, claimants have sought injunctions. Does the rule—which exists in some common law countries—that only judgments for a fixed sum of money are enforceable bar the enforcement of such judgments? Third, indirect jurisdiction requirements may pose challenges, particularly when the defendant was not domiciled in the country of origin. Finally, since most transnational climate change cases are still in their early stages or have been dismissed on various grounds, the cross-border effectiveness of judgments has not yet become an issue. We will therefore only focus

136 CSDDD (n 40) art 29(7).

137 EU Proposal (n 41) Recital 28.

138 *Morrison v National Australia Bank*, 561 U.S. 247 (2010); *RJR Nabisco v European Community*, 579 U.S. ___ (2016). Some state laws have similar presumptions that apply to state statutes.

139 *Sosa v Alvarez-Machain*, 542 U.S. 692 (2004); *Kiobel v Royal Dutch Petroleum Co*, 569 U.S. 108 (2013).

140 *City of Oakland* (n 17) 1025. See also *City of New York v BP Plc*, 325 F Supp 3d 466 (SDNY 2018).

141 *City of Oakland v BP Plc*, 969 F 3d 895 (9th Cir 2020).

142 William S Dodge, 'Misusing the Presumption against Extraterritoriality in Climate Change Litigation' (2019) 1 Courts & Justice Law Journal 118; Aaron B Rudyan, 'Extraterritoriality in Common Law Climate Actions: Judicial Restraint or Judicial Error?' (2019) 37 Pace Environmental Law Review 177.

on the issues raised by the specific points mentioned above and leave aside issues like natural justice and public policy, while noting that they may also have a role to play.

The rule prohibiting the enforcement of foreign public law applies only to judgments based on claims involving an act of a sovereign character, the exercise or enforcement of a sovereign right, or the vindication of sovereign power.[143] Private law claims that can be brought equally by public authorities and private parties do not fall within this category and their cross-border enforcement should not be problematic.[144]

The rule that only judgments for a fixed sum of money are enforceable exists in some common law countries, most notably England, where it precludes the enforcement of foreign injunctions.[145] This rule has been abandoned in some common law countries.[146] However, even where it remains in force, it may be effectively circumvented by commencing local proceedings for an injunction and seeking to have the foreign judgment recognised as *res iudicata*.[147] Accordingly, this rule is of limited practical significance.

Indirect jurisdiction requirements may pose an insurmountable obstacle. Where the defendant was domiciled in the country of origin, such requirements are unlikely to be problematic. However, if the court of origin assumed jurisdiction on another basis, such as the place of conduct or the place of damage, the enforcement of the judgment may be precluded in countries that recognise the jurisdiction of foreign courts on narrower bases. English law, for example, recognises only the defendant's presence within the territory of the court of origin and submission as bases of indirect jurisdiction.[148]

There are international instruments that provide a harmonised regime for the recognition and enforcement of foreign judgments. The best known among them are Brussels I *bis* and the 2019 Hague Convention. Brussels I *bis* enables the free movement, within the EU, of both money and non-money judgments given by the courts of Member States in civil and commercial matters. It imposes indirect jurisdiction requirements only in cases involving exclusive jurisdiction and in insurance, consumer and employment matters.[149] The Lugano Convention extends this regime to EFTA States. The 2019 Hague Convention, currently binding on thirty-three Contracting Parties, governs the recognition and enforcement of both money and non-money judgments in civil and commercial matters.[150] It imposes indirect jurisdiction requirements. Importantly, it permits recognition and enforcement of judgments given by the courts of the defendant's habitual residence.[151] It also covers judgments from courts where the defendant's branch, agency, or other establishment is located, for claims arising from that establishment's activities.[152] Finally, it includes judgments from courts where an act or omission directly caused harm, for claims based on non-contractual obligations arising from death, physical injury, or damage to or loss of tangible property.[153] These bases of indirect jurisdiction are particularly useful when proceedings in the court of origin were commenced against a

143 *Skatteforvaltningen v Solo Capital Partners LLP* [2023] UKSC 40.

144 *United States of America v Ivey* 30 OR (3d) 370, 139 DLR (4th) 570.

145 *Airbus Industrie GIE v Patel* [1999] 1 AC 119 (HL).

146 *Pro-Swing Inc v Elta Golf Inc* [2006] 2 SCR 612 (Canada); *Brunei Investment Agency v Fidelis Nominees Ltd* [2008] Jersey LR 337 (Jersey); Reciprocal Enforcement of Foreign Judgments Act (Chapter 265), s 4(4) (Singapore).

147 *Pattni v Ali* [2006] UKPC 51.

148 *Adams v Cape Industries* (n 59).

149 Brussels I *bis* (n 19) arts 1, 2(a), 45(1)(e), 45(2), 45(3).

150 2019 Hague Judgments Convention (n 4), arts 1, 2, 3(1)(b).

151 ibid arts 5(1)(a), 3(2).

152 ibid art 5(1)(d).

153 ibid art 5(1)(j).

defendant domiciled there or when the defendant's conduct occurred there. However, if the court of origin assumed jurisdiction based solely on the place of damage, recognition and enforcement of the judgment under the Convention may be problematic.

6. Conclusion

Transnational climate change cases based on private law remain limited but increasing in number, with rules of general jurisdiction playing a critical role to date. Courts commonly assert jurisdiction over claims against parent companies domiciled in the forum for conduct occurring within the territory of the forum, which has enabled landmark cases including *Shell* and *Lliuya*. However, special/specific jurisdiction in tort matters is increasingly relevant, particularly where damage occurs within the forum.

Jurisdiction is important for several reasons. Since conduct and damage are relevant connecting factors for both jurisdiction and applicable law, courts usually apply the law of the forum in transnational climate change cases. Bringing a claim in a country that adopts *forum non conveniens* may complicate access to remedy. As some jurisdictional bases are more widely accepted than others, choice of forum may affect the cross-border recognition and enforcement of the resulting judgment. Jurisdiction also decisively influences procedural matters such as funding, collective redress, justiciability, and evidentiary matters.

In the EU, Article 7 of Rome II has proven particularly influential, offering claimants the flexibility to invoke either the law of the place of damage or the law of the place of the event giving rise to the damage. Article 17, despite its uncertain and potentially problematic interaction with Article 7, has not presented an obstacle to the claimant's choice of law so far. This choice is crucial in navigating the temporal and geographical complexities of climate harm, where decision-making, emissions, and the resulting impacts occur over time and often span multiple jurisdictions. In other regions, similar flexibility in choice-of-law rules may be lacking.

Normatively, transnational climate litigation raises fundamental yet difficult questions. Should PIL doctrines adapt to accommodate transboundary, systemic, diffuse, and cumulative conduct and damage? Should territorial links provided by the location of policymaking, emissions, and damage be equally relevant? Should foreseeability of damage play a role? While a dedicated PIL regime for climate litigation may not be necessary, the European experiences show that existing rules, if interpreted adaptively, can respond to the unique challenges of climate change litigation. Nonetheless, a readiness to evolve remains essential to ensure PIL contributes meaningfully to climate justice.

PART V

Area Perspectives

CHAPTER 33

The European Union

HARRO VAN ASSELT AND JESSICA CROW

1. Introduction

THIS chapter considers the European Union as a pertinent site to study the application of private law to the climate crisis. The EU is a key region to consider for several reasons. Historically, Europe can be seen as the cradle of industrialisation, and to this day European countries remain some of the largest historical greenhouse gas emitters.[1] The region is also home to several of the world's largest economies, including G20 countries such as France, Germany, and Italy. Moreover, the sheer size of the EU's single market means that the EU can exert significant market power, influencing rules and practices in other jurisdictions through the "Brussels effect".[2] The EU is also a region where new approaches to climate change law have been pioneered, from the launch of the world's first transnational emissions trading system (ETS) in 2005,[3] to the adoption of a regulatory mechanism that addresses the emissions embedded in imports into the region in 2023.[4] Moreover, the EU has for several decades sought to play a leadership role in the development of international climate policy.[5]

Against this backdrop, this chapter examines the role of private law in responding to climate change in the EU as well as its Member States. In doing so, the chapter complements existing literature that has focused primarily on the ways in which European public law has sought to address climate change, including through passing framework climate laws,[6] adopting climate plans,[7] setting renewable energy

[1] Simon Evans, 'Analysis: Which Countries Are Historically Responsible for Climate Change?' (*Carbon Brief*, 5 October 2021) <https://www.carbonbrief.org/analysis-which-countries-are-historically-responsible-for-climate-change/> accessed 28 June 2025.

[2] Anu Bradford, *The Brussels Effect: How the European Union Rules the World* (OUP 2021).

[3] Directive 2003/87/EC of 13 October 2003 Establishing a Scheme for Greenhouse Gas Emission Allowance Trading within the Community and Amending Council Directive 96/61/EC [2003] OJ L275/32.

[4] Regulation 2023/956/EU of 10 May 2023 Establishing a Carbon Border Adjustment Mechanism [2023] OJ L130/52 (CBAM Regulation).

[5] Andrew Jordan and others, 'Understanding the Paradoxes of Multilevel Governing: Climate Change Policy in the European Union' (2012) 12(2) Global Environmental Politics 43, 52.

[6] Kati Kulovesi and others, 'The European Climate Law: Strengthening EU Procedural Climate Governance?' (2024) 36(1) Journal of Environmental Law 23; Thomas L Muinzer (ed), *National Climate Change Acts: The Emergence, Form and Nature of National Framework Climate Legislation* (Bloomsbury 2020).

[7] Orla Kelleher and Clodagh Daly, 'Litigating the Fit for 55 Package: Statutory and Rights-based Challenges to National Energy and Climate Plans as a Means of Implementing and/or Enhancing the Ambition of the EU's Fit for 55 Package' (2025) 34(1) Review of European, Comparative & International Environmental Law 49.

targets,[8] and regulating the fuel efficiency of cars.[9] The European public law framework offers an important backdrop for the development of European private law and, as we shall see in this chapter, directly interacts with the application of private law to climate change. At the same time, the EU and its Member States are also at the forefront of developments at the interface of private law and climate change. This is evident from the development of dedicated legislation regulating how private actors must address climate change, including mandatory due diligence legislation[10] and anti-greenwashing legislation.[11] Even more so, the EU and its Member States are playing a prominent role in the development of private law on climate change through the judiciary. Not only is the EU home to some of the leading cases in climate change litigation,[12] several of these cases have been grounded in private law.

The remainder of the chapter is structured as follows. Section 2 discusses several key features of EU (public) climate law that may impinge on the application of private law to climate change. Section 3 turns to the development of private law in Europe, pointing to the common foundations of the various private law systems in the EU. The next two sections examine the development of European private law in relation to climate change, with Section 4 focusing on legislative responses and Section 5 analysing the role of courts. Section 6 concludes.

2. EU Climate Law

Since its inception in the early 1990s, the European legal framework for climate change has grown to become both comprehensive and highly complex.[13] Here we do not seek to offer a chronological or exhaustive overview of the development of EU climate law. Instead, we identify several key features of the European climate law that are also relevant for private law responses to climate change, namely: (1) EU climate law's market orientation, (2) a strong reliance on target-setting, (3) a focus on promoting the EU's international competitiveness, and (4) a growing number of challenges of climate policy ambition and implementation in national and European courts.

[8] Alessandro Monti and Beatriz Martinez Romera, 'Fifty Shades of Binding: Appraising the Enforcement Toolkit for the EU's 2030 Renewable Energy Targets' (2020) 29(2) Review of European, Comparative & International Environmental Law 221.

[9] Nicolas de Sadeleer, 'Light-Vehicles Emissions Standards Under EU Law in the Wake of the 'Dieselgate'' in Marjan Peeters and Mariolina Eliantonio (eds), *Research Handbook on EU Environmental Law* (Edward Elgar Publishing 2020) 379.

[10] See, e.g., Directive (EU) 2024/1760 of 13 June 2024 on Corporate Sustainability Due Diligence and Amending Directive (EU) 2019/1937 and Regulation (EU) 2023/2859 [2024] OJ L2024/1760 (CSDDD); *Loi no. 2017-399 du 27 Mars 2017 relative au devoir de vigilance des sociétés mères et des entreprises donneuses d'ordre* (Duty of Vigilance Law). See also Barbara Pozzo, Chapter 29 of this handbook.

[11] See, e.g., Directive (EU) 2024/825 of 28 February 2024 amending Directives 2005/29/EC and 2011/83/EU as Regards Empowering Consumers for the Green Transition through Better Protection against Unfair Practices and through Better Information [2024] OJ L2024/825; European Commission, 'Proposal for a Directive of the European Parliament and of the Council on Substantiation and Communication of Explicit Environmental Claims (Green Claims Directive)' COM(2023) 166 final, 22 March 2023 (Green Claims Directive proposal). See also Tiffanie Chan, Juliana Vélez Echeverri, Catherine Higham, and Joana Setzer, Chapter 11 of this handbook.

[12] Joana Setzer and others, 'Climate Litigation in Europe' (Grantham Research Institute on Climate Change and the Environment, London School of Economics and Political Science (GRI-LSE, 2022) <https://www.lse.ac.uk/granthaminstitute/wp-content/uploads/2022/12/Climate-litigation-in-Europe_A-summary-report-for-the-EU-Forum-of-Judges-for-the-Environment.pdf> accessed 28 June 2025.

[13] Marjan Peeters, 'EU Climate Law: Largely Uncharted Legal Territory' (2019) 9(1–2) Climate Law 137.

At its inception, the European project was primarily concerned with economic cooperation rather than environmental protection. The 1957 Treaty of Rome established a common (now "internal") market where goods, people, services, and capital could freely move across borders.[14] Nevertheless, the goals of European cooperation gradually came to encompass a variety of political goals, including environmental protection.[15] However, the goals of European environmental laws and policies were often still linked to the functioning of the bloc's internal market. Specifically, the harmonisation of environmental standards was deemed desirable not just to protect the environment but also to avoid competitive distortions among Member States.

The EU's market orientation is also reflected in the development of European climate law. Among the first EU-wide climate policies were energy efficiency labels for a range of household appliances, adopted with a view to harmonising emerging standards in Member States.[16] An initial attempt in 1992 by the European Commission to adopt a market-based instrument in the form of an EU-wide carbon and energy tax failed due to the requirement that fiscal measures be adopted by unanimity.[17] However, when the EU sought to demonstrate international climate leadership following the adoption of the Kyoto Protocol in 1997, the EU again turned to a market-based instrument, this time securing internal agreement.[18] Over time, the EU ETS has become the centrepiece of EU climate change law, covering 40% of European emissions, including the power sector, energy-intensive industries, and shipping. Although other sectors, including agriculture, buildings, and road transport, have been covered by separate "effort-sharing" instruments that set differentiated targets for EU Member States,[19] some of these sectors will participate in a separate trading system, dubbed "ETS2", from 2027 onwards.[20]

Although EU climate law thus significantly relies on market-based instruments for its implementation, it is also characterised by a form of traditional regulation, namely the setting of targets.[21] This began with the Kyoto Protocol's target of reducing greenhouse gas emissions by 8% by 2008–2012 (compared to 1990 levels),[22] followed by targets for 2020 (-20%),[23] 2030

[14] Friedl Weiss and Clemens Kaupa, *European Union Internal Market Law* (CUP 2014) 3–7.

[15] See Suzanne Kingston, Veerle Heyvaert, and Aleksandra Čavoški, *European Environmental Law* (CUP 2017) 2–4.

[16] See, e.g., Council Directive 92/75/EEC of 22 September 1992 on the Indication by Labelling and Standard Product Information of the Consumption of Energy and Other Resources by Household Appliances [1992] OJ L297/16, art 1.

[17] Andrew Jordan and Tim Rayner, 'The Evolution of Climate Policy in the European Union: An Historical Overview' in Andrew Jordan and others (eds), *Climate Change Policy in the European Union: Confronting the Dilemmas of Mitigation and Adaptation?* (CUP 2010) 52, 59–60.

[18] Harro van Asselt, 'Emissions Trading: The Enthusiastic Adoption of an 'Alien' Instrument?' in Andrew Jordan and others (eds), *Climate Change Policy in the European Union: Confronting the Dilemmas of Mitigation and Adaptation?* (CUP 2010) 125.

[19] See Marjan Peeters and Natassa Athanasiadou, 'The Continued Effort Sharing Approach in EU Climate Law: Binding Targets, Challenging Enforcement?' (2020) 29(2) Review of European, Comparative & International Environmental Law 201.

[20] Directive 2023/959/EU Amending Directive 2003/87/EC Establishing a System for Greenhouse Gas Emission Allowance Trading within the Union and Decision (EU) 2015/1814 Concerning the Establishment and Operation of a Market Stability Reserve for the Union Greenhouse Gas Emission Trading System [2023] OJ L130/134.

[21] Claire Dupont and others, 'Three Decades of EU Climate Policy: Racing toward Climate Neutrality?' (2023) 15 WIREs: Climate Change e863, 3.

[22] Kyoto Protocol to the United Nations Framework Convention on Climate Change (adopted 11 December 1997, entered into force 16 February 2005) 37 ILM 22, Annex B.

[23] European Council, 'Presidency Conclusions, Brussels, 8–9 March 2007' <https://www.consilium.europa.eu/ueDocs/cms_Data/docs/pressData/en/ec/93135.pdf> accessed 28 June 2025.

(-55%),[24] and 2050 (climate neutrality).[25] These emissions targets have been accompanied by other types of targets, including for renewable energy[26] and energy efficiency.[27] The importance of target-setting in the EU has grown with the adoption of framework climate laws in many European countries. By the end of 2024, seventeen out of twenty-seven Member States had adopted such laws.[28] In addition, the EU itself has adopted such legislation in the form of the European Climate Law. Through these laws, targets can—and, in some cases, have—become legally binding and enforceable through domestic courts (which, as we highlight below, has indeed happened in several EU Member States).[29]

Another feature, aligned with the market orientation of EU climate law, is the consistent focus on safeguarding the competitiveness of European industry. This emphasis was apparent in the early years of the EU ETS, when trade-exposed companies successfully lobbied for protection against the impacts of a European carbon price that their third-country competitors would not be burdened with. They initially received this protection in the form of freely distributed emissions allowances to protect against carbon leakage.[30] Following the 2019 European Green Deal, a new form of protection was introduced in the form of a Carbon Border Adjustment Mechanism, which requires importers into the EU to pay a charge reflecting the carbon costs of the imported product.[31] In addition, following the adoption of the Inflation Reduction Act in the United States, which created major incentives to boost American green industries, the EU adopted a range of laws and policies to boost its own competitiveness, including the Net Zero Industry Act[32] and the Critical Raw Materials Act.[33] The competitiveness imperative also emerged from the influential 2024 Draghi Report, which

[24] Regulation 2021/1119 of 30 June 2021 Establishing the Framework for Achieving Climate Neutrality and Amending Regulations (EC) No 401/2009 and (EU) 2018/1999 (European Climate Law) [2021] OJ L243/1 (European Climate Law), art 4(1).

[25] ibid art 2. The European Climate Law does not set a 2040 target, but it sets out the process to do so. Following this process, the European Commission proposed a target of -90% by 2040. European Commission, 'Securing our Future: Europe's 2040 Climate Target and Path to Climate Neutrality by 2050 Building a Sustainable, Just and Prosperous Society' COM(2024)63 final, 6 February 2024. This target was agreed by the European Parliament and Member States in December 2025, albeit with the possibility for the EU to achieve up to 5% of the target through using high-quality international carbon credits. European Commission, 'EU Agrees on a 2040 Climate Target that Sets a Clear Path towards a Decarbonised and Competitive Economy', Press Release (10 December 2025).

[26] Directive (EU) 2023/2413 of 18 October 2023 Amending Directive (EU) 2018/2001, Regulation (EU) 2018/1999 and Directive 98/70/EC as Regards the Promotion of Energy from Renewable Sources, and Repealing Council Directive (EU) 2015/652 [2023] OJ L2023/2413, art 1(2)(a).

[27] Directive (EU) 2023/1791 of 13 September 2023 on Energy Efficiency and Amending Regulation (EU) 2023/955 (Recast) [2023] OJ L231/1, art 4(1).

[28] Ecologic Institute, 'Climate Framework Laws Info-Matrix' (2024) <https://www.ecologic.eu/19320> accessed 28 June 2025.

[29] See Chris Hilson, 'Hitting the Target? Analysing the Use of Targets in Climate Law' (2020) 32(2) Journal of Environmental Law 195.

[30] Directive 2009/29/EC of 23 April 2009 Amending Directive 2003/87/EC so as to Improve and Extend the Greenhouse Gas Emission Allowance Trading Scheme of the Community [2009] OJ L140/63, art 10a.

[31] CBAM Regulation (n 4).

[32] Regulation (EU) 2024/1735 of 13 June 2024 on Establishing a Framework of Measures for Strengthening Europe's Net-Zero Technology Manufacturing Ecosystem and Amending Regulation (EU) 2018/1724 [2024] OJ L2024/1735.

[33] Regulation (EU) 2024/1252 of 11 April 2024 Establishing a Framework for Ensuring a Secure and Sustainable Supply of Critical Raw Materials and Emending Regulations (EU) No 168/2013, (EU) 2018/858, (EU) 2018/1724 and (EU) 2019/1020 [2024] OJ L2024/1252.

specifically called for coordinated industrial policy in the EU.[34] Following this report, the European Commission adopted a set of new measures, including a Competitiveness Compass setting out the EU's vision and priorities in this area,[35] a Clean Industrial Deal outlining plans to help decarbonise emitting sectors such as steel and cement,[36] and "Omnibus" proposals to "cut red tape and simplify EU rules for citizens and business",[37] some of which were adopted in December 2025.[38]

Lastly, a prominent feature of climate law in the EU is that it has become a hotbed for "strategic"[39] or "framework"[40] litigation against both states and companies.[41] Among other claims, such litigation has challenged the ambition of climate targets. Although litigation challenging the ambition of the EU's climate targets has failed due to the EU's stringent standing requirements,[42] litigation at the Member State level has had a major impact. In the landmark *Urgenda* case in the Netherlands, the Dutch government was ordered to increase its 2020 target to 25%, with the courts drawing on provisions in Dutch tort law as well as human rights law.[43] And in *Neubauer*, the German Constitutional Court ruled that the target set in the German Climate Protection Act was insufficient as the target unduly shifted the burden of climate action to future generations.[44] The implementation of framework climate laws has also been challenged, for instance in Ireland, where non-governmental organisations successfully challenged the plan devised by the Irish government pursuant to its Climate Action and Low Carbon Development Act.[45] Strategic litigation has also been directed at companies, most notably in the *Milieudefensie v Shell* case in the Netherlands (see Section 5 of this chapter).

This brief overview of some key features of European climate law has served to not only introduce key aspects of the European public law framework for addressing climate change, but also to identify possible intersections between public and private law responses to climate law on the continent. Before we move on to discuss the private law responses, however, we first briefly discuss the concept and development of European private law.

[34] European Commission, 'The Draghi Report on EU Competitiveness' (2024) <https://commission.europa.eu/topics/eu-competitiveness/draghi-report_en#paragraph_47059> accessed 28 June 2025.

[35] European Commission, 'A Competitiveness Compass for the EU' COM(2025) 30 final, 29 January 2025.

[36] European Commission, 'The Clean Industrial Deal: A Joint Roadmap for Competitiveness and Decarbonisation' COM(2025) 85 final, 26 February 2025.

[37] European Commission, 'Commission Proposes to Cut Red Tape and Simplify Business Environment' (26 February 2025) <https://commission.europa.eu/news/commission-proposes-cut-red-tape-and-simplify-business-environment-2025-02-26_en> accessed 28 June 2025.

[38] See European Commission, 'Prosperity and Competitiveness – Implementation Tracker' <https://commission.europa.eu/priorities-2024-2029/competitiveness/implementation-tracker_en> accessed 29 January 2026.

[39] Jacqueline Peel and Rebekkah Markey-Towler, 'Recipe for Success? Lessons for Strategic Climate Litigation from the Sharma, Neubauer, and Shell Cases' (2021) 22(8) German Law Journal 1484.

[40] Joana Setzer and Catherine Higham, 'Global Trends in Climate Change Litigation: 2025 Snapshot' (GRI-LSE 2025) <https://www.lse.ac.uk/granthaminstitute/publication/global-trends-in-climate-change-litigation-2025-snapshot/> accessed 29 January 2026.

[41] Setzer et al (n 12).

[42] CJEU, Case T-330/18, *Carvalho and Others v Parliament and Council*, ECLI:EU:T:2019:324; Case C-565/19 P, *Carvalho and Others v Parliament and Council*, ECLI:EU:C:2021:252.

[43] *State of the Netherlands v Urgenda Foundation* (20 December 2019) Netherlands Supreme Court, ECLI:NL:HR:2019:2007. See Elbert de Jong, Chapter 9 of this handbook.

[44] BVerfG, *Neubauer v Germany*, 1 BvR 2656/18 (24 March 2021).

[45] *Friends of the Irish Environment v Government of Ireland* [2020] IESC 49.

3. EU Private Law

European private law can refer to both the European common law (*ius commune*) that underpins different national legal systems in Europe and to private law laid down in the EU's *acquis communautaire*.[46]

The idea of a European *ius commune* emerged in the twelfth century, with Roman legal texts (e.g., the *Corpus Juris Civilis*) becoming influential among legal scholars in Europe. Although this did not mean that the same law applied across Europe, it meant that there was a common way in which the law was taught and discussed.[47] In the nineteenth century, the onset of nation-states and a trend of codification[48] led to the breaking down of this notion of a *ius commune* but, to this day, Roman law still influences the private law systems in many European countries. For instance, due diligence duties that can be found in various EU Member States can be traced back to the Roman law under which a "wrongdoer would be held liable for acts of negligence if he or she had failed to comply with the standard of conduct which would have been exercised in the circumstances by the diligent *paterfamilias* (i.e. prudent father of family/head of the household)".[49] Since the late twentieth century—and also since the ascendance of the EU—there has been a revival of the idea of a *ius commune*, with academics and policymakers showing renewed interest in uncovering the common foundations of private law in different parts of Europe, including through projects aimed at identifying relevant principles and rules.[50] However, notwithstanding calls from EU institutions[51] and academics,[52] a European Civil Code remains a distant prospect.

At the same time, however, the EU has gradually developed its own body of private law, even though its competences in this area are not explicitly circumscribed in its founding treaties.[53] EU private law includes consumer protection laws, unfair trading laws, financial services laws, product and environmental liability laws, and other legislation developed in the service of the internal market.[54] In addition, primary EU law also has come to cover private law, for instance

[46] Nils Jansen, 'European Private Law' in Jürgen Basedow and others (eds), *Max Planck Encyclopedia of European Private Law* <https://max-eup2012.mpipriv.de/index.php/European_Private_Law> accessed 28 June 2025.

[47] Dirk Heirbaut and Matthias E Storme, 'The Historical Evolution of European Private Law' in Christian Twigg-Flessner (ed), *The Cambridge Companion to European Union Private Law* (CUP 2010) 20.

[48] Civil codes were adopted in Prussia (1794), France (1804), and Austria (1811). Cees van Dam, *European Tort Law* (2nd edn, OUP 2013) 127.

[49] Lise Smit and others, 'Study on Due Diligence Requirements through the Supply Chain. Final Report' (European Commission 2020) 158.

[50] See, e.g., Study Group on a European Civil Code and the Research Group on EC Private Law (Acquis Group), *Principles, Definitions and Model Rules of European Private Law. Draft Common Frame of Reference (DCFR)* (Sellier 2009).

[51] European Parliament, 'Resolution on Action to Bring into Line the Private Law of the Member States' [1989] C158/400, para 2 (calling for a European Code of Private Law).

[52] Hugh Collins, 'Why Europe Needs a Civil Code' (2013) 21(4) European Review of Private Law 907.

[53] Stephen Weatherill, 'Competence and European Private Law' in Christian Twigg-Flessner (ed), *The Cambridge Companion to European Union Private Law* (CUP 2010) 58, 58.

[54] As noted by Cherednychenko, the distinction between private and public law in these laws can be blurred: Some of these laws 'not only regulate the conduct of businesses vis-à-vis private parties and/or liability for damage caused by their products or activities, but also clearly confer individual rights and remedies on such parties', whereas 'other EU measures limit themselves to the former aspect, focusing primarily on the public enforcement of harmonised rules'. Olha O Cherednychenko, 'Rediscovering the Public/Private Divide in EU Private Law' (2019) 26(1–2) European Law Journal 27, 29–30.

in the field of competition law.[55] This fragmented and limited body of law falls short of a comprehensive EU private law system, and national laws in EU Member States continue to play a major role. However, the application of those national laws is governed by a common set of EU regulations to determine the choice of law (Rome II) and which court has jurisdiction (Brussels I *bis*),[56] which results in limited divergences between national laws as "these conflict rules have the effect of referring a given case to the same national law".[57]

The upshot of this concise discussion is that to understand the relevance of EU private law for climate change, it is important to examine legal developments at both the EU level and the Member State level. Accordingly, the following sections will look at both levels, though we will by no means be comprehensive in our treatment of Member State legislative and judicial developments.

4. EU Private Law and Climate Change: Legislative Approaches

This section examines the development of legislation in the EU and some of its Member States in various areas of private law, focusing on financial law, company law, and consumer law. The discussion shows that climate change considerations are increasingly integrated in relevant legislation, either through new legislation, amendment of existing legislation, or the development of delegated regulation. Although relevant Member State developments will be discussed, given the overall importance of the EU legal framework, the emphasis will be on EU-wide legal instruments.

4.1 Financial Law

A first area in which the EU has developed climate-related legislation is financial law, which includes climate-related reporting requirements and the development of guidance concerning the sustainability of investments. Initial corporate social responsibility reporting requirements were introduced through the Accounts Modernisation Directive in 2003.[58] However, the implementation of the vague requirements varied across Member States, with some Member States still convinced that such reporting should be voluntary.[59] Addressing these problems, the EU adopted the Non-Financial Reporting Directive (NFRD) in 2014.[60] The NFRD did not

[55] Christian Twigg-Flessner, 'Introduction: Key Features of European Union Private Law' in Christian Twigg-Flessner (ed), *The Cambridge Companion to European Union Private Law* (CUP 2010) 1, 2.

[56] Regulation (EC) No 864/2007 of the European Parliament and of the Council of 11 July 2007 on the Law Applicable to Non-contractual Obligations (Rome II) [2007] OJ L199/40; Regulation (EU) No 1215/2012 of 12 December 2012 on Jurisdiction and the Recognition and Enforcement of Judgments in Civil and Commercial Matters (Recast) [2012] OJ L351/1.

[57] Jürgen Basedow, 'EU Private Law' in Jürgen Basedow and others (eds), *Max Planck Encyclopedia of European Private Law* <https://max-eup2012.mpipriv.de/index.php/EU_Private_Law> accessed 28 June 2025. See also Ekaterina Aristova and Ugljesa Grusic, Chapter 32 of this handbook.

[58] Directive 2003/51/EC of 18 June 2003 Amending Directives 78/660/EEC, 83/349/EEC, 86/635/EEC and 91/674/EEC on the Annual and Consolidated Accounts of Certain Types of Companies, Banks and Other Financial Institutions and Insurance Undertakings [2003] OJ L178/16.

[59] Daniel Gergely Szabó and Karsten Engsig Sørensen, 'New EU Directive on the Disclosure of Non-Financial Information (CSR)' (2015) 12(3) European Company and Financial Law Review 307, 312–13.

[60] Directive 2014/95/EU of 22 October 2014 amending Directive 2013/34/EU as Regards Disclosure of Non-Financial and Diversity Information by Certain Large Undertakings and Groups [2014] OJ L330/1.

explicitly specify that covered companies (with more than 500 employees) must report on climate-related risks in their non-financial statements. Instead, the NFRD broadly referred to "environmental" matters,[61] and subsequent voluntary guidelines by the Commission included numerous examples of how companies could report on climate risks.[62] However, the NFRD exhibited several weaknesses. The reported information was not useful to appraise the impacts of sustainability issues on companies (single materiality) as well as companies' impacts on sustainability (double materiality). Moreover, companies were faced with a complex and at times diverging set of reporting requirements from the EU as well as other organisations (e.g., the Global Reporting Initiative).[63]

The Corporate Sustainability Reporting Directive (CSRD) seeks to overcome these weaknesses, thereby "radically chang[ing] the manner in which greenhouse gas emissions are reported" in the EU.[64] The CSRD requires covered companies to report, among others, on their climate plans that need to ensure that their "business model and strategy are compatible with the transition to a sustainable economy and with the limiting of global warming to 1.5°C in line with the Paris Agreement . . . and the objective of achieving climate neutrality by 2050 as established in [the European Climate Law] and, where relevant, the exposure of the undertaking to coal-, oil- and gas-related activities".[65] Importantly, the CSRD also integrates the European Sustainability Reporting Standards (ESRS) in its architecture.[66] The ESRS include detailed climate-specific standards (ESRS E1),[67] which require CSRD-covered companies to report, among others, on emissions along the value chain.[68] The standards also provide further details related to the reporting of companies' climate transition plans.[69]

Several other, yet related, EU regulatory instruments seek to provide information to investors and other decision-makers concerning the environmental credentials of companies and their products. First, the Sustainable Finance Disclosure Regulation establishes disclosure requirements for specific financial market participants and financial products.[70] Second, the Taxonomy Regulation introduces standards for what economic activities can be considered to contribute to sustainability and requires covered companies to report on alignment with

[61] ibid arts 1(1) and 1(3), introducing arts 19a and 29a to Directive 2013/34/EU.

[62] European Commission, 'Guidelines on Non-Financial Reporting (Methodology for Reporting Non-Financial Information)' [2019] OJ C215/1.

[63] Nora Hahnkamper-Vandenbulcke, 'Non-Financial Reporting Directive' (European Parliamentary Research Service 2021) 2.

[64] Marloes Brans, Ronnie Bloemberg, and Felix Felder, 'Reporting under the "E" of the CSRD. An Overview of Legal Requirements and a Comparison with Existing Obligations under Environmental Law, Focussing on the Netherlands' (2024) 33(5) European Energy and Environmental Law Review 232, 235.

[65] Directive (EU) 2022/2464 of 14 December 2022 Amending Regulation (EU) No 537/2014, Directive 2004/109/EC, Directive 2006/43/EC and Directive 2013/34/EU, as Regards Corporate Sustainability Reporting [2022] OJ L322/15, arts 1(4) and 1(7), introducing arts 19a and 29a to Directive 2013/34/EU.

[66] ibid art 1(8)), introducing art 29b to Directive 2013/34/EU.

[67] EFRAG, 'Draft European Sustainability Reporting Standards. ESRS E1: Climate Change' (2022) <https://www.efrag.org/sites/default/files/sites/webpublishing/SiteAssets/08%20Draft%20ESRS%20E1%20Climate%20Change%20November%202022.pdf> accessed 28 June 2025.

[68] ibid paras 41–49.

[69] ibid paras 13–16.

[70] Regulation (EU) 2019/2088 of 27 November 2019 on Sustainability-Related Disclosures in the Financial Services Sector [2019] OJ L317/1 (SFDR).

those standards,[71] with two delegated regulations spelling out the criteria for the contribution to climate change mitigation and adaptation.[72] Third, the EU set minimum standards for two new low-carbon benchmarks—the EU Climate Transition Benchmarks and the more ambitious EU Paris-aligned Benchmarks—for administrators and users of financial benchmarks.[73] Fourth, the EU Green Bonds Regulation sets out rules for bond issuers that want to use the voluntary European Green Bond (or EuGB) label.[74]

The various EU sustainable finance legal instruments are closely intertwined. For instance, the Taxonomy Regulation requires CSRD-covered companies to report on the extent to which their activities are associated with environmentally sustainable economic activities under the Regulation;[75] managers of financial products covered by the SFDR need to report on how their activities align with the Taxonomy Regulation; the SFDR requires sustainable investment products aimed at reducing carbon emissions to follow EU Paris-aligned and Climate Transition Benchmarks;[76] and at least 85% of the proceeds of European green bonds are to be allocated to taxonomy-aligned activities.[77]

Although the EU has developed a sophisticated and ambitious set of regulations on climate-related financial disclosure and the climate contribution of investments, the broader EU agenda of boosting competitiveness is likely to limit the scope and effects of these regulations. With the adoption of the Omnibus proposals in December 2025, the European institutions have significantly curtailed the scope (cutting the number of companies covered by 80%) of the CSRD.[78] Meanwhile, an amendment to the Taxonomy Regulation limited what companies had

[71] Regulation (EU) 2020/852 of 18 June 2020 on the Establishment of a Framework to Facilitate Sustainable Investment, and Amending Regulation (EU) 2019/2088 [2020] OJ L198/13 (Taxonomy Regulation). See Barbara Pozzo, Chapter 29 of this handbook.

[72] Commission Delegated Regulation (EU) 2021/2139 of 4 June 2021 Supplementing Regulation (EU) 2020/852 of the European Parliament and of the Council by Establishing the Technical Screening Criteria for Determining the Conditions under Which an Economic Activity Qualifies as Contributing Substantially to Climate Change Mitigation or Climate Change Adaptation and for Determining Whether that Economic Activity Causes no Significant Harm to any of the Other Environmental Objectives [2021] OJ L442/1; Commission Delegated Regulation (EU) 2022/1214 of 9 March 2022 amending Delegated Regulation (EU) 2021/2139 as Regards Economic Activities in Certain Energy Sectors and Delegated Regulation (EU) 2021/2178 as Regards Specific Public Disclosures for Those Economic Activities [2022] OJ L188/1.

[73] Regulation (EU) 2019/2089 of 27 November 2019 amending Regulation (EU) 2016/1011 as Regards EU Climate Transition Benchmarks, EU Paris-Aligned Benchmarks and Sustainability-Related Disclosures for Benchmarks [2019] OJ L317/17; Commission Delegated Regulation (EU) 2020/1818 of 17 July 2020 Supplementing Regulation (EU) 2016/1011 of the European Parliament and of the Council as Regards Minimum Standards for EU Climate Transition Benchmarks and EU Paris-Aligned Benchmarks [2020] OJ L406/17.

[74] Regulation (EU) 2023/2631 of the European Parliament and of the Council of 22 November 2023 on European Green Bonds and Optional Disclosures for Bonds Marketed as Environmentally Sustainable and for Sustainability-linked Bonds [2023] OJ L2023/2631 (Green Bonds Regulation).

[75] Taxonomy Regulation (n 71) art 8.

[76] SFDR (n 70) art 9(3). See Enrico Partiti, 'Addressing the Flaws of the Sustainable Finance Disclosure Regulation: Moving from Disclosures to Labelling and Sustainability Due Diligence (2024) 25 European Business Organization Law Review 299, 321.

[77] Green Bonds Regulation (n 74) art 4 and Annex I.

[78] Latham & Watkins LLP, 'European Institutions Reach Agreement on Sustainability Omnibus' (18 December 2025) <https://www.lw.com/en/insights/european-institutions-reach-agreement-on-sustainability-omnibus> accessed 29 January 2026.

to report.[79] While these reforms have been presented as simplifications by the Commission, critics argue that they amount to deregulation to the detriment of EU climate action.[80]

4.2 Company Law

Closely related to the emerging web of regulations on financial law, the EU and its Member States have also deployed company law in the fight against climate change, notably through mandatory due diligence legislation.[81] Such legislation generally requires companies above a certain threshold (e.g., related to turnover or number of employees) to carry out due diligence to identify, assess, monitor, prevent, and mitigate adverse environmental and human rights impacts across their supply chain.[82]

This type of legislation has been adopted in France and Germany, with further legislation being proposed in several other EU Member States.[83] However, while the German Supply Chain Act covers environmental issues, it only applies to a limited set of environmental risks related to human health and does not mention climate change.[84] The French Duty of Vigilance Law also does not refer to climate change specifically but its broad reference to "environmental damage"[85] can be read to encompass climate change impacts and, accordingly, the law has been used as a basis for climate litigation (see Section 5 of this chapter). Although other Member States (e.g., Austria, Belgium, the Netherlands) have been in the process of developing their own due diligence legislation, these developments were overtaken by the adoption in 2024 of the EU Corporate Sustainability Due Diligence Directive (CSDDD).

[79] Commission Delegated Regulation (EU) 2026/73 of 4 July 2025 amending Delegated Regulation (EU) 2021/2178 as Regards the Simplification of the Content and Presentation of Information to Be Disclosed Concerning Environmentally Sustainable Activities and Delegated Regulations (EU) 2021/2139 and (EU) 2023/2486 as Regards Simplification of Certain Technical Screening Criteria for Determining Whether Economic Activities Cause No Significant Harm to Environmental Objectives [2026] OJ L2026/73.

[80] 'The Big EU Deregulation: Disastrous Omnibus Proposal Erodes EU's Corporate Accountability Commitments and Slashes Human Rights and Environmental Protections' (*Greenpeace*, 24 March 2025) <https://www.greenpeace.org/static/planet4-eu-unit-stateless/2025/03/24b1894e-joint-cso-statement-reacting-to-omnibus-publication.pdf> accessed 28 June 2025. Following an initial legal challenge, the EU Ombudsman found that the way in which the Omnibus proposals were prepared by the Commission amounted to 'maladministration'. European Ombudsman, 'Recommendation on the European Commission's Compliance with "Better Regulation" Rules and Other Procedural Requirements in Preparing Legislative Proposals That It Considered to Be Urgent (983/2025/MAS - the "Omnibus" Case, 2031/2024/VB - the "Migration" Case, and 1379/2024/MIK - the "CAP" case)' (25 November 2025).

[81] Mikko Rajavuori, Annalisa Savaresi, and Harro van Asselt, 'Mandatory Due Diligence Laws and Climate Change Litigation: Bridging the Corporate Climate Accountability Gap?' (2023) 17(4) Regulation & Governance 944.

[82] Jonathan Bonnitcha Robert McCorquodale, 'The Concept of "Due Diligence" in the UN Guiding Principles on Business and Human Rights' (2017) 28(3) European Journal of International Law 899.

[83] Business and Human Rights Resource Centre, 'National & Regional Movements for Mandatory Human Rights & Environmental Due Diligence in Europe' (6 March 2024) <https://www.business-humanrights.org/en/latest-news/national-regional-movements-for-mandatory-human-rights-environmental-due-diligence-in-europe/> accessed 28 June 2025.

[84] Act on Corporate Due Diligence Obligations in Supply Chains (*Lieferkettensorgfaltspflichtengesetz*) of 16 July 2021 (BGBl. I p 2959) s 2(3).

[85] Duty of Vigilance Law (n 10) art 1.

The CSDDD's general due diligence obligations do not directly apply to climate change.[86] However, the CSDDD initially required covered companies to "adopt and put into effect" a climate transition plan aligned with the Paris Agreement and the European Climate Law.[87] This plan needed to include (1) time-bound targets for 2030 and in five-year steps up to 2050; (2) a description of decarbonisation levers and actions planned, including changes in products/services; (3) an explanation and quantification of investments and funding supporting the plan; and (4) a description of the role of administrative and management bodies.[88]

However, the CSDDD did not require Member States to monitor implementation of the plan or provide for remedies in case a company fails to follow through, and the transition plan was not subject to the Directive's special provisions on civil liability.[89] What is more, the provision became a victim of the Commission's drive to simplify EU regulation. Although the Commission only proposed to remove the requirement to "put into effect" transition plans, further amendments led to the scrapping of the entire provision.[90]

4.3 Consumer Law

As noted in Section 3 of this chapter, consumer protection law has been one of the areas where the development of EU private law has thrived. It is therefore not surprising that climate-specific legislation has developed in this area. However, the relevant laws go beyond merely *protecting* consumers (e.g., against unfair business practices) to also *empower* them to make the right choices (e.g., by withdrawing from a contract).[91]

At the Member State level, some laws regulate the claims made by companies about the climate contribution of their products. For instance, the French Climate and Resilience Law prohibits companies' use of the term "carbon neutral" unless they make underlying information available.[92] However, even if laws do not include such explicit prohibitions, courts can interpret general consumer protection laws to prohibit misleading green claims, as demonstrated by, for instance, the Germany's Act against Unfair Commercial Practices.[93] Moreover,

[86] Andreas Buser, 'Protecting the Climate through EU Supply Chain Legislation? Two Critiques and a Compromise' (2024) 3 European Law Open 617, 621–22. For instance, the Climate Change Convention and the Paris Agreement are not mentioned among the list of environmental instruments in Part II of the Annex to the CSDDD.

[87] CSDDD (n 10) art 22(1).

[88] ibid. As noted above, these transition plans need to be disclosed by companies covered by the CSRD, pursuant to the ESRS E1 reporting standard (n 67) para 14.

[89] ibid art 29. See Buser (n 86) 623.

[90] European Commission, 'Proposal for a Directive of the European Parliament and of the Council Amending Directives 2006/43/EC, 2013/34/EU, (EU) 2022/2464 and (EU) 2024/1760 as Regards Certain Corporate Sustainability Reporting and Due Diligence Requirements' COM(2025) 81 final, 26 February 2025, 41. Latham & Watkins (n 78). For a discussion, see Tim Bleeker, 'Corporate Climate Transition Planning after the Omnibus Overhaul: A Six-Question Guide' (1 January 2026) <https://papers.ssrn.com/sol3/papers.cfm?abstract_id=5552702> accessed 29 January 2026.

[91] Lucila de Almeida and Fabrizio Esposito, 'The Blinding Effect of EU Consumer Policy Overshadows the Role of Consumer Law in Delivering the Green Transition' in Marta Santos Silva and others (eds), *Routledge Handbook of Private Law and Sustainability* (Routledge 2024) 140, 142.

[92] *Loi no. 2021-1104 du 22 août 2021 portant lutte contre le dérèglement climatique et renforcement de la résilience face à ses effets*, art 12.

[93] BGH, I ZR 98/23 (27 June 2024), ECLI:DE:BGH:2024:270624UIZR98.23.0.

relevant rules are also laid down in self-regulation, such as the Dutch Sustainability Advertising Code.[94]

At the EU level, the 2024 Empowering Consumers for the Green Transition (ECGT) Directive[95] amends the Unfair Commercial Practices Directive to include certain new misleading actions. This includes the claim, "based on the offsetting of greenhouse gas emissions, that a product has a neutral, reduced or positive impact on the environment in terms of greenhouse gas emissions".[96] This inclusion means that companies need to be much more careful with claims about carbon neutrality if they intend to achieve this goal by means of carbon offsets.[97] Another type of prohibited claim is "making an environmental claim related to future environmental performance without clear, objective, publicly available and verifiable commitments set out in a detailed and realistic implementation plan that includes measurable and time-bound targets".[98] Such claims would include, for instance, broad claims to achieve carbon neutrality by 2050 without offering the necessary details or, for instance, having in place a climate transition plan.[99] The ECGT Directive also prohibits generic environmental claims (e.g., that a product is "climate-friendly") if the "trader is not able to demonstrate recognised excellent environmental performance relevant to the claim".[100] Also relevant to climate change, the ECGT Directive prohibits offsetting claims "that a product has a neutral, reduced or positive impact on the environment in terms of greenhouse gas emissions".[101] Such claims "mislead consumers by making them believe that such claims relate to the product itself or to the supply and production of that product, or give the false impression to consumers that the consumption of that product does not have an environmental impact".[102] Accordingly, they must "only be allowed when they are based on the actual lifecycle impact of the product in question, and not based on the offsetting of greenhouse gas emissions outside the product's value chain".[103]

The proposed EU Green Claims Directive would go beyond some of these provisions. The proposed Directive is particularly concerned with "climate-washing", as "[c]limate-related claims have been shown to be particularly prone to being unclear and ambiguous and to mislead consumers".[104] Unlike the Unfair Commercial Practices Directive (as amended by the ECGT Directive), the Green Claims Directive would require ex-ante substantiation, communication, and verification of environmental claims and labelling schemes in the form of a certificate of conformity issued by an independent verifier.[105] However, although the Directive would help to harmonise criteria for environmental claims across the EU, it is not intended to prejudge rulings by national courts, thereby clearly leaving the door open for

94 Stichting Reclame Code, 'Code voor Duurzaamheidsreclame (CDR)' <https://www.reclamecode.nl/nederlandse-reclame-code/bijzondere-reclamecodes/#code-voor-duurzaamheidsreclame--cdr-> accessed 28 June 2025.

95 Directive (EU) 2024/825 of 28 February 2024 amending Directives 2005/29/EC and 2011/83/EU as Regards Empowering Consumers for the Green Transition through Better Protection against Unfair Practices and Through Better Information [2024] OJ L2024/825 (ECGT Directive).

96 ibid Annex I, para 2, introducing a new para 4c to Annex I of Directive 2005/29/EC.

97 ibid.

98 ibid art 1(2)(b), introducing a new art 6(2)(d) to Directive 2005/29/EC.

99 Bert Keirsbilck, 'Empowering Consumers for the Green Transition: Overview of Directive (EU) 2024/825' (2024) 13(5) Journal of European Consumer and Market Law 205, 208.

100 ECGT Directive (n 95) Annex, amending Annex I to Directive 2005/29/EC, point 4a.

101 ibid Annex, amending Annex I to Directive 2005/29/EC, point 4c.

102 ibid recital 12.

103 ibid.

104 Green Claims Directive proposal (n 11) recital 12.

105 Keirsbilck (n 99) 206.

further litigation.[106] Moreover, given pushback among some political parties in Europe, the Commission announced its intention to withdraw the proposal in June 2025, and the future of the Green Claims Directive remains in the balance at the time of writing.[107]

5. EU Private Law and Climate Change: Judicial Approaches

European domestic courts have emerged as significant arenas for testing EU private law's capacity to address climate change, with judges interpreting traditional doctrines across tort law,[108] corporate due diligence,[109] and consumer protection.[110] These judicial developments reveal both the potential and limitations of private law approaches to climate governance as courts navigate the complex relationship between open-textured legal standards and the evolving regulatory landscape. Recent case law demonstrates courts grappling with fundamental questions: (1) How does regulatory compliance relate to private law duties? (2) How do human rights frameworks inform private obligations? and (3) How can due diligence legislation and climate litigation interact and possibly converge to strengthen corporate climate accountability?[111]

The emergence of climate litigation against private actors in the EU reflects a tension between regulatory compliance and broader societal expectations regarding corporate climate responsibility—whether mere compliance is sufficient or if broader obligations should be imposed on companies, particularly heavy emitters.[112] Courts in EU Member States have relied on established domestic causes of action, particularly the general duty of care in tort law, to examine whether private actors may be held liable for contributions to climate change or obliged to take measures to prevent future harm, beyond what is required through regulation. As these claims increase, courts must determine how legal standards in private law can internalise risk and develop mitigation pathways derived from climate science,[113] the Paris Agreement's long-term temperature goal,[114] and distributive principles such as intergenerational equity and fair shares of responsibility, while also addressing their interaction with existing EU and domestic climate legislation and policies. This has been particularly evident in tort cases where courts must interpret general standards of care in relation to specific climate obligations giving rise to new positive duties.[115]

[106] Jacquelyn MacLennan and William De Catelle, 'The Revision of EU Greenwashing Laws: A New Framework of Analysis' (2025) 10(2–3) Business and Human Rights Journal 456.

[107] Gerardo Fortuna, 'Five Political Takeaways from the EU Green Claims Directive Saga' (*Euronews*, 24 June 2025) <https://www.euronews.com/my-europe/2025/06/24/five-political-takeaways-from-the-eu-green-claims-directive-saga> accessed 29 June 2025.

[108] *Milieudefensie v Shell*, C/09/571932/HA ZA 19-379, 26 May 2021.

[109] *Notre affaire à tous et autres v TotalEnergies*, n° RG 23/14348, 18 June 2024.

[110] *Fossielvrij v KLM* C/13/719848/HA ZA 22-524, 20 March 2024.

[111] Rajavuori et al (n 81).

[112] Michael G Faure and André Nollkaemper, 'International Liability as an Instrument to Prevent and Compensate for Climate Change' (2007) 43(1) Stanford Journal of International Law 123, 151.

[113] See Intergovernmental Panel on Climate Change (IPCC), 'Summary for Policymakers' in Hoesung Lee and others (eds), *Climate Change 2023: Synthesis Report. Contribution of Working Groups I, II and III to the Sixth Assessment Report of the Intergovernmental Panel on Climate Change* (IPCC 2023) 1.

[114] Paris Agreement (adopted 12 December 2015, entered into force 4 November 2016) 55 ILM 740, art 2(1)(a).

[115] Roda Verheyen and Johannes Franke, 'Climate Change Litigation: A Reference Area for Liability' in Peter Gailhofer and others (eds), *Corporate Liability for Transboundary Environmental Harm* (Springer 2023) 353.

The *Milieudefensie v Shell* litigation in the Netherlands exemplifies these considerations, offering insight into how courts are interpreting, expanding, and constraining climate-related obligations within private law frameworks. In 2021, the Hague District Court interpreted Article 6:162 of the Dutch Civil Code, the unwritten standard of care in Dutch tort law, to impose a specific emissions reduction obligation on Royal Dutch Shell, a multinational fossil fuel corporation.[116] Drawing on evidence regarding national carbon budgets,[117] the Intergovernmental Panel on Climate Change (IPCC) reports, the Paris Agreement's long-term temperature goal, and business and human rights frameworks including the United Nations Guiding Principles on Business and Human Rights and the Organisation for Economic Co-operation and Development's (OECD) Guidelines for Multinational Enterprises, the court determined that Shell's duty of care required a 45% reduction in carbon dioxide emissions across all scopes by 2030 (relative to 2019 levels).[118]

This judgment expanded corporate climate obligations under Dutch tort law beyond regulatory compliance, finding that companies have individual responsibility to achieve reductions targets for the greenhouse gases they control and influence.[119] In addressing the separation of powers question, the court rejected Shell's argument that the claim was inadmissible because any decision would exceed judicial competence and encroach upon the legislative domain. Unlike jurisdictions with doctrines that limit judicial review of politically sensitive matters, Dutch law has no bars to admissibility that would prevent the court from addressing substantive climate obligations.[120] Instead, the court articulated a complementary relationship between judicial and regulatory approaches, holding that while climate regulation falls primarily to the legislature, the court retained the jurisdiction to interpret the unwritten standard of care in Dutch tort law.[121]

The District Court's approach to determining Shell's reduction obligation attracted extensive scholarly commentary.[122] Some questioned whether the court had adequately justified translating global emissions reduction targets into specific corporate obligations without sufficient consideration for sectoral practices, complex market realities, or differentiated responsibilities within the fossil fuel industry.[123] These methodological questions ultimately aligned with key aspects of the Court of Appeal's analysis. The Court of Appeal's 2024 reversal reflected these concerns about specificity. While recognising that "the social duty of care implies that companies also have an obligation to contribute to the mitigation of dangerous climate change",[124] the court determined that applying the general standard to Shell of a 45% reduction

116 *Milieudefensie v Shell* (n 108).

117 As ordered by the Dutch Supreme Court in *State of the Netherlands v Urgenda Foundation* (n 43).

118 *Milieudefensie v Shell* (n 108) para 5.3.

119 ibid para 4.4.47.

120 Marc-Philippe Weller and Mai-Lan Tran, 'Climate Litigation Against Companies' (2022) 1 npj Climate Action 14.

121 *Milieudefensie v Shell* (n 108) para 4.1.3.

122 See Benoit Mayer, 'The Duty of Care of Fossil-Fuel Producers for Climate Change Mitigation: Milieudefensie v. Royal Dutch Shell district court of The Hague (The Netherlands)' (2022) 11(2) Transnational Environmental Law 407; Phillip Paiement, 'Reimagining the Energy Corporation: *Milieudefensie and Others v Royal Dutch Shell Plc*' in Daniëlla Dam-de Jong and Fabian Amtenbrink (eds), *2021 Netherlands Yearbook of International Law* (Springer 2023) 281; Chiara Macchi and Josephine van Zeben, 'Business and Human Rights Implications of Climate Change Litigation: *Milieudefensie et al. v Royal Dutch Shell*' (2021) 30(3) Review of European, Comparative & International Environmental Law 409.

123 See, e.g., Mayer (n 122).

124 *Milieudefensie v Shell*, C/09/571932/HA ZA 19-379, 12 November 2024 at 7.55.

by the end of 2030 was not sufficiently case-specific.[125] The court emphasised that different reduction pathways are appropriate per sector, and they may also differ per country, suggesting that "Shell cannot be bound by a 45 per cent reduction standard (or any other percentage) agreed by climate science because this percentage does not apply to every country and every business sector individually".[126]

The Court of Appeal confirmed several important principles despite its reversal of the specific reduction target. The court explicitly acknowledged that the social duty of care in Dutch tort law encompasses corporate obligations to contribute to climate change mitigation and that fossil fuel companies bear heightened responsibilities in this domain.[127] Importantly, it affirmed that compliance with existing regulations alone does not fulfil the standard of care—a significant recognition of private law's complementary role alongside public law frameworks.[128] The court's reluctance to impose a specific percentage reduction stemmed primarily from evidentiary considerations: No sectoral standard for oil and gas could be established based on the evidence presented.[129] This reasoning suggests that while private law may recognise broader climate obligations, courts require robust and case-specific scientific evidence, where possible bolstered by intergovernmental consensus, to translate general climate targets into binding legal standards.

Finally, the Court of Appeal also emphasised that companies must consider the consequences of expanding fossil fuel supply when making investment decisions. This aspect of the judgment potentially provides a new legal framework for challenging fossil fuel proliferation through exploration and production projects—a significant development for legal efforts to constrain further fossil fuel development and lock in. The court's express recognition that Shell's planned investments in new oil and gas fields may be at odds with its duty of care suggests that private law offers avenues to contest expansion of fossil fuel infrastructure even where specific emissions reduction obligations cannot be imposed by the courts.[130] This judicial framework has already been operationalised, with Milieudefensie launching a separate case specifically aimed at stopping Shell's fossil fuel expansion, representing a strategic pivot towards supply-side mitigation.[131]

The *Milieudefensie* appeal reveals not only the evolving scope of corporate climate duties in tort law but also points to a broader phenomenon in EU climate jurisprudence: The transposition of public law principles into private law contexts. This legal transplantation is particularly evident in the way human rights and constitutional norms inform private law duties in the context of climate change. The case brought by KlimaSeniorinnen Schweiz (Senior Women

125 ibid para 7.111.

126 ibid paras 7.75 and 7.111.

127 ibid para 7.55.

128 ibid para 7.57.

129 ibid para 7.96.

130 ibid para 7.61. In February 2025, Milieudefensie formally appealed to the Dutch Supreme Court, specifically challenging the Appeal Court's finding that a mitigation pathway could not be formulated on the evidence presented. A ruling is expected in 2026 and may provide further clarification on the expanding scope of the duty of care for corporate climate impacts.

131 The new case represents the first-ever attempt at legally banning a company from all new oil and gas extraction, moving beyond emissions reduction targets to directly challenge fossil fuel expansion and exemplifies how private law can address upstream carbon lock-in effects that regulatory frameworks have yet to tackle. Milieudefensie, Letter to Shell Plc 'Notice of Liability and Announcement of New Legal Proceedings' (13 May 2025) <https://en.milieudefensie.nl/news/this-is-our-letter-to-shell> accessed 28 June 2025.

for Climate Protection Switzerland) before the European Court of Human Rights (ECtHR)[132] contributes substantively through the judicial recognition of climate protection as integral to the human rights guaranteed under the European Convention on Human Rights (ECHR). Though addressing state obligations, the *KlimaSeniorinnen* judgment clarifies that Articles 2 and 8 of the ECHR impose positive obligations to implement appropriate legislative and administrative frameworks to address foreseeable climate risks.[133] By affirming that the ECHR protects individuals from the serious adverse effects of climate change on life, health, and well-being, the ECtHR has articulated a rights-based approach to climate protection that domestic courts within the ECHR treaty space may reference when considering the horizontal application of these norms to non-state actors. This may occur through indirect horizontal effect or domestic doctrines that enable ECHR-consistent interpretation of private law.[134]

A clear example of this development can be traced through the relationship between *Urgenda v Netherlands* and *Milieudefensie v Shell.*[135] In *Urgenda*, the District Court of the Hague applied Articles 2 and 8 of the ECHR as a substantive basis to interpret the standard of care as imposing a requirement on the Dutch state to mitigate climate change under Article 6:162 of the Dutch Civil Code.[136] Although the Court of Appeal and Supreme Court upheld the outcome, they shifted the legal basis, grounding the duty directly in the ECHR and thereby avoiding further elaboration of domestic tort doctrine.[137] In *Milieudefensie*, the plaintiffs relied on the original *Urgenda* District Court judgment, arguing that the same Civil Code provision could support duties for corporate actors. The Hague District Court accepted this transposition, interpreting Shell's duty of care in light of, inter alia, human rights principles under the ECHR.[138] While the Court of Appeal subsequently overturned the specific reduction obligation, it affirmed that the social duty of care under Dutch tort law can be interpreted in light of Articles 2 and 8 of the ECHR, along with soft law instruments, recognising the relevance of human rights norms in assessing corporate climate responsibility.[139] This demonstrates how human rights principles originally established in state-focused litigation can influence the interpretation of private actors' obligations through open-textured private law concepts such as the duty of care.

These developments raise important questions about the appropriate relationship between judicially developed private law duties and the evolving EU regulatory landscape. As courts articulate climate-related obligations in tort, they do so in a legal environment increasingly shaped by supranational regulatory initiatives. Recent climate litigation before the EU courts increasingly reflects the interplay between emerging private law duties and the broader EU regulatory framework. Courts are not only interpreting the scope of private obligations but also assessing how these interact with regulatory schemes—most notably the EU ETS, the CSRD, and the CSDDD, which has already been addressed in case law.[140] Other instruments, including the ECGT Directive, are also likely to shape future claims and defences.

[132] ECtHR, Verein *KlimaSeniorinnen Schweiz and Others v Switzerland*, App No. 53600/20, Judgment (Grand Chamber), 9 April 2024.

[133] ibid para 550.

[134] See Olha O Cherednychenko and Boudewijn de Bruin, Chapter 45 of this handbook.

[135] *State of the Netherlands v Urgenda Foundation* (n 43).

[136] *Urgenda Foundation v the State of the Netherlands*, The Hague District Court (2015) C/09/456689/HA ZA 13-1396.

[137] Verheyen and Franke (n 115) 374.

[138] *Milieudefensie v Shell* (n 108).

[139] ibid para 7.6.1.

[140] *Milieudefensie v Shell*, Court of Appeal (n 124).

In *Milieudefensie v Shell*, the courts were required to assess whether compliance with the EU ETS could affect the existence or scope of a private law duty of care. Shell argued that its emissions were already regulated under the ETS, and that this should have an indemnifying effect. The Hague District Court rejected this argument, holding that the ETS applied to only a portion of Shell's emissions and provided an indemnifying effect only where the relevant interests were fully and correctly assessed by the issuing authority.[141] Outside of that scope, the EU ETS did not preclude the imposition of additional obligations under private law and the Court found that Shell may be required to go beyond regulatory compliance where the applicable reduction targets fall short of its duty of care.[142] The Court of Appeal affirmed the position, but expressed concern about imposing fixed, company-specific reduction targets where an EU-wide cap already governs emissions.[143] It found that the ETS achieves its objectives through a market-based ceiling on total emissions, not by requiring individual reductions from specific companies.[144] Therefore, while compliance with the ETS may inform the standard of care, the Court found, it does not exhaust it. This reasoning underscores the role of tort law in filling normative and regulatory gaps, even within the context of harmonised EU market-based instruments.

The German Higher Regional Court of Hamm's decision in *Lliuya v RWE* reinforced the principle that regulatory frameworks do not shield companies from private law liability for climate harms.[145] When the German utility RWE invoked its official permits and certificates under German emissions trading legislation as a defence, the Court rejected the defence, holding that permits do not create obligations for third parties to tolerate interference with their property rights, particularly where the affected parties are geographically distant from the emission source. The Court also directly addressed separation of powers concerns, summarily dismissing RWE's argument about judicial overreach by stating that the court's task is to apply German tort law, further demonstrating how European courts are defining private law's complementary role alongside regulatory frameworks.

Although the Court ultimately dismissed Lliuya's claim on evidentiary grounds, the judgment established that major greenhouse gas emitters can, in principle, be held liable under German civil law for climate-related harms abroad. The decision is final with no further appeal possible. Building on this precedent, in December 2025, 39 Pakistani farmers filed a lawsuit against RWE and Heidelberg Materials at the Heidelberg Regional Court, seeking compensation for losses suffered in the 2022 floods that devastated Pakistan's Sindh province.[146]

The litigation in *Notre Affaire à Tous v Total* offers another concrete example of how the contours of corporate due diligence obligations are beginning to take shape through judicial proceedings.[147] Brought under the French Duty of Vigilance Law, the case alleges that the fossil fuel company Total (now TotalEnergies) failed to identify and address the climate-related risks inherent in its business model. The plaintiffs argued specifically that the company's due

141 *Milieudefensie v Shell* (n 108) para 4.4.47.

142 ibid.

143 *Milieudefensie v Shell*, Court of Appeal (n 124) para 7.33.

144 ibid para 7.30.

145 *Lliuya v RWE*, Oberlandesgericht Hamm (28 May 2025), 5 U 15/17 (unofficial translation).

146 The farmers, supported by the European Center for Constitutional and Human Rights (ECCHR) and represented by the same lawyer who brought the *Lliuya* case, rely on §§ 906 and 823 of the German Civil Code. See 'Climate Lawsuit from Pakistan: Farmers Sue RWE and Heidelberg Materials' (ECCHR, 22 December 2025) <https://www.ecchr.eu/en/press-release/klimaklage-aus-pakistan-baeuerinnen-verklagen-rwe-und-heidelberg-materials/> accessed 27 January 2026.

147 *Notre affaire à tous et autres v TotalEnergies*, n° RG 23/14348, 18 June 2024.

diligence plan does not align with the emission reduction goals of the Paris Agreement, and therefore falls short of the statutory requirement under Article L.225-102-4 of the French Commercial Code to identify environmental hazards and adopt appropriate measures across the value chain.[148] The French Commercial Code establishes a general duty of care arising from the Charter for the Environment which is part of the French Constitution.[149] The plaintiffs seek judicial enforcement of a revised plan capable of aligning Total's operations with the Paris Agreement's mitigation goals. On 18 June 2024, the Paris Court of Appeal held that the claim was admissible, confirming that plaintiffs have standing to bring legal proceedings to require Total's compliance with both the statutory duty of vigilance and the general duty of environmental care.[150] In the meantime, the precise content of corporate climate due diligence under French law remains unsettled.

This evolving jurisprudence intersects with the legislative developments outlined in Section 4 of this chapter, particularly the entry into force of the CSDDD in July 2024. While the Directive sets harmonised minimum standards, it permits Member States to maintain or introduce more stringent requirements.[151] As a result, domestic regimes such as France's Duty of Vigilance Law may continue to apply where they impose higher obligations. In addition, obligations under the CSRD on climate-related financial disclosures are likely to inform the interpretation of corporate due diligence, including whether the obligations may include mitigation and alignment with the Paris Agreement, as courts begin to engage with climate-related diligence claims. Although the obligation in Article 22 of the CSDDD has been removed following the Omnibus process (see Section 4 of this chapter), this does not mean that litigation risks will subside. Indeed, as some legal experts suggest, companies may be at risk of more litigation in the absence of a harmonised EU framework.[152]

Finally, consumer protection law has become another site of interaction between climate litigation and regulation. In *FossielVrij NL and Reclame Fossielvrij v KLM*, the Amsterdam District Court found that fifteen of nineteen environmental claims made by Dutch airline KLM in its "Fly Responsibly" and CO_2ZERO marketing campaigns were misleading under the Dutch Unfair Commercial Practices Act and the EU Unfair Commercial Practices Directive (before the transposition of the ECGT Directive).[153] The Court determined that KLM's assertions about sustainable flying and the efficacy of carbon offsetting products conveyed an inaccurate impression to consumers regarding the environmental impact of air travel. The *KLM* judgment demonstrates that existing consumer protection frameworks can be interpreted to address greenwashing. This judicial approach operates in parallel with the emerging EU regulatory initiatives discussed in Section 4 of this chapter, which seek to establish more specific standards for environmental claims and increase transparency in climate-related marketing.

[148] *Notre affaire à tous et autres v TotalEnergies* (Complaint, English Version, unofficial translation) 28 January 2020.

[149] ibid 17.

[150] *Notre affaire à tous et autres v TotalEnergies* (n 147).

[151] European Coalition for Corporate Justice (ECCJ), 'Transposition of the Corporate Sustainability Due Diligence Directive: A Guide for National Advocates' (2024) <https://corporatejustice.org/wp-content/uploads/2024/11/ECCJ-Transposition-Guide_2024_online_version.pdf> accessed 28 June 2025.

[152] 'Legal Scholars: Abandoning Article 22 CSDDD Risks Policy Incoherence and Litigation Risk' (23 November 2025) <https://notreaffaireatous.org/wp-content/uploads/2025/11/Letter-from-legal-scholars-on-Art.-22-CSDDD.pdf> accessed 29 January 2026.

[153] *FossielVrij NL and Reclame Fossielvrij v Koninklijke Luchtvaart Maatschappij N.V. (KLM)*, Amsterdam District Court, Case No. C/13/710651/HA ZA 22-836.

German courts have similarly leveraged consumer protection law to address climate-related advertising claims. In the 2024 *BGH Katjes* decision, Germany's Federal Court of Justice established strict transparency requirements for environmental claims, holding that ambiguous terms like "climate neutral" must be clearly explained within advertisements themselves.[154] The Court rejected the defendant's offsetting-based climate neutrality claims, finding that reduction and compensation measures are not equivalent measures for achieving climate neutrality.[155] The BGH's approach has since been reinforced by the ECGT Directive, which, as discussed in Section 4 of this chapter, now explicitly prohibits claims of climate neutrality based solely on offsetting measures, illustrating the convergence between judicial interpretation and emerging regulatory frameworks in addressing greenwashing.

In France, the Paris Judicial Tribunal reached a comparable conclusion in October 2025, ruling that TotalEnergies had engaged in misleading commercial practices by promoting its "ambition to achieve carbon neutrality by 2050" and positioning itself as "a major player in the energy transition" without disclosing that its underlying strategy involved continued investment in oil and gas.[156] The court found that TotalEnergies claims constituted misleading commercial practices under Articles L.121-2 and L.121-3 of the French Consumer Code and ordered removal of the statements, awarding damages to the plaintiff NGOs. This was the first application of French consumer protection law to a major oil company's climate claims.

6. Conclusion

EU climate law is at a crossroads. In the past three decades, a complex mix of public law-based procedural and substantive regulation has emerged at the EU level to govern the transition to climate neutrality. The bloc remains a pioneer in the adoption and development of climate change law and policy, with the EU ETS and the related Carbon Border Adjustment Mechanism standing out as prime examples. But judicial challenges at both the EU and Member State levels show that the obligations flowing from this public law framework are not considered to be sufficient for either states or corporations. In this chapter, we have sketched how the emerging EU private law response to climate change is beginning to intersect with the EU's longer-standing public law framework. In particular, private law—and especially tort law—is acting as a gap-filler. Importantly, companies can no longer assume that compliance with the obligations imposed on them through public law frameworks (e.g., the EU ETS) will suffice, as shown by the *Milieudefensie* and *Lliuya* rulings. Further interactions can also be expected between litigation aimed at establishing corporate climate obligations and the CSDDD and CSRD. In the area of greenwashing, the ECGT Directive may similarly inform courts in greenwashing litigation, although the Directive is unlikely to pre-empt such litigation. To better understand the functioning of EU climate law in the future it will therefore be imperative to consider the myriad ways in which private law and public law approaches interact.

[154] BGH, 27.6.2024–IZR 98/23, ECLI:DE:BGH:2024:270624 UIZR98.23.0.

[155] Beate Gsell and Sebastian Meyer, 'How to Combat "Greenwashing": Comment on the Decision of the German Federal Court of Justice of June 27, 2024–BGH IZR 98/23 on Misleading Advertisement of Climate Neutrality' (2024) 32 Environmental Law Review 123.

[156] *Greenpeace France and Others v TotalEnergies SE*, Tribunal Judiciaire de Paris (23 October 2025) n° RG 22/02955.

CHAPTER 34

The United Kingdom

KIM BOUWER

1. Introduction

PRIVATE law will be implicated in the response to climate change in at least three ways. First, scholars and activists thinking about litigation are turning their attention to corporations and the role they play in causing climate change; the result is an increasing use of private law arguments in climate litigation against corporations.[1] In any event, activist climate cases have been brought in private law for some time, including actions against governments brought in tort.[2] Second, private law is implicated because its mechanisms and remedies will *inevitably* be relied upon as parties seek solutions to the problems climate change creates. This would include litigation "in the context of climate change" that is brought without activist intent, simply to protect the parties' interests;[3] as we seek to understand the relationship between private law and climate change, this could be where legal innovation takes place (as I explain below).

There is a third way in which private law—particularly the law of obligations—may be implicated in climate change. This arises in relation to law's response to transactions conducted either "in the shadow" of climate change regulatory regimes,[4] or the ways in which parties design or choose their own climate change actions.[5] This could refer to contracting parties undertaking certain climate change commitments as part of a broader agreement for some other endeavour, including where this might be imposed or recommended by a trade or industry body within a party's sector.[6] The above raises questions about whether and how existing legal rules will be able to accommodate both the need strategically to respond to climate change, but also the new risks and social pressures that climate change presents. It also raises the question of what legal effect of parties' own climate change actions might have.

[1] *Milieudefensive v Shell* ECLI:NL:RBDHA:2021:5339 (which was brought in Dutch tort law).

[2] Most famously *Urgenda Foundation v the Kingdom of the Netherlands (I)* ECLI:NL:RBDHA:2015:7196; or *Michael John Smith v Fonterra Co-operative group Ltd* [2024] NZSC 5.

[3] Kim Bouwer, 'The Unsexy Future of Climate Change Litigation' (2018) 30 Journal of Environmental Law 483.

[4] Elizabeth Fisher, Eloise Scotford, and Emily Barritt, 'The Legally Disruptive Nature of Climate Change' (2017) 80 Modern Law Review 173, 195–96.

[5] See Irina Sakharova, Chapter 6 of this handbook.

[6] In the UK context, regulators do play a significant role and action at the regulator level has proven to be more effective than court actions in governing the work of corporations. I do not discuss this in this chapter as, although governing private bodies, this refers to a public law function of regulation. For more detail, see Kim Bouwer, 'Global Perspectives on Corporate Climate Legal Tactics: UK National Report' (*British Institute of International and Comparative Law*, 2024) <https://www.biicl.org/documents/12174_global_perspectives_on_corporate_climate_legal_tactics_-_uk_national_report_v1.pdf> accessed 6 July 2025.

In this chapter, I consider the above intersections, examining whether, and how well, English private law has responded to the pressures caused by climate change. My thesis is that prospects of the courts changing or adapting doctrine in any significant way to decide a climate change case are slim. This is because the relevant legal structures—including fairly hard-baked protection of very specific interests—are not an easy fit with climate change problems, but the legal innovation that has been possible in other common law countries demonstrates that this rigidity is not simply a question of legal rules. I argue that English legal culture determines this rigidity, as much as the structure of the law. Legal culture can provide a useful lens to understand the contingency of courts' engagement with climate change laws and climate change problems.[7] I suggest here that the courts are conservative, rather than sceptical or informed by climate denial. They have not shied away from dealing with climate change issues where these can be managed within a (narrow) understanding of their institutional role, or compensating claimants when there is a need to do justice.

The chapter proceeds as follows. In Section 2, I briefly explain why climate change has been expected or observed to cause legal innovation and develop the idea of legal culture and specifically English legal culture, explaining how this can help us to understand the disruptive capacity of climate change in the English law context. In Section 3, I explore high-profile litigation, illustrating why an absence of tort litigation, and also a recent failure in relation to a statutory derivative action, make sense in context. I also highlight some cases where the courts have sought to deliver justice in the climate change context, both where claimants' rights have been affected due to climate change or environmental regulation, or where claimants have chosen their own enhanced mitigation actions. The final section serves as a conclusion.

2. Disruptive Climate Change, the Relevance of Legal Culture, and English Legal Culture

It has been argued that climate change can prove legally disruptive. Fisher and others demonstrate how in different contexts, climate change can shake the stability within legal systems.[8] Kysar, demonstrating the poor fit between climate change and tort law, argues that the social pressures that climate change presents could force changes in tort doctrine.[9] There have been some fairly high-profile legal changes and innovations in other common law countries. Most radically, in *Smith v Fonterra* the New Zealand Supreme Court has recognised the possibility of a new climate system damage tort, noting: "The common law, where it is not clearly excluded, responds to challenge and change in a considered way."[10] In the US, twenty years of sustained (albeit intermittent) attempts for claimants to proceed to a merits hearing in "holy grail" climate tort cases,[11] have finally borne fruit and with the first case permitted to proceed to a hearing.[12] While the action might not succeed, this suggests it is at least arguable. But there

[7] Sanja Bogojević, 'EU Climate Change Litigation, the Role of the European Courts, and the Importance of Legal Culture' (2013) 35 Law & Policy 184, 186.

[8] Fisher et al (n 4).

[9] Douglas Kysar, 'What Climate Change Can Do About Tort Law' (2012) 42 Environmental Law Reporter 10739.

[10] *Michael John Smith v Fronterra Co-operative group Ltd* [2024] NZSC 5.

[11] Bouwer, 'The Unsexy Future' (n 3) 489–91.

[12] *City & County of Honolulu v Sunoco* Case No. 20-cv-00163-DKW-RT (D. Haw. 5 March 2021).

are further instances in other common law jurisdictions where judges have employed climate conscious[13] interpretations of existing legal rules.[14]

Elsewhere, I have argued that it is almost unimaginable that either an English "holy grail" private law action,[15] or an action brought in relation to more mundane private law obligations,[16] would succeed. The former can be explained both by the structure of the law, and our cultural expectations of what law does; this must be fairly context-specific, or similar restraint would prevail across the common law world. The latter, I attribute to the fundamental underlying structure of tort law; that private law is designed around the creation and protection of private interests.[17] This does entail that private law is a poor fit for compensation for environmental harms; for instance compensation is only available for specific categories of damage, and may not always result in harms being fully rectified.[18] Climate change's more diffuse nature only amplifies these mismatches.[19]

This raises two questions: First, would the lower courts find themselves able to adjudicate in the context of climate change, and second, what difference would this make to the way cases were adjudicated? For instance, would the judges interpret existing legal duties in a "climate conscious" way if the facts of the case seemed to require it, or would they adapt legal rules to affect practical justice? Although there may be little space within *formal* legal structures to accommodate climate change arguments or harms, in other contexts it has been argued that rules can be distorted and compromised through mundane legal processes, where adjudicators seek to effect simple justice between the parties.[20] Over time, (particularly repeated) litigation could then be constitutive of changes to legal doctrine.[21] What is missing in the English context is a comprehensive analysis of this body of case law,[22] which could tell us something

[13] Kim Bouwer, 'Climate Consciousness in Daily Legal Practice' (*Journal of Environmental Law Blog*, 22 May 2015) <https://blog.oup.com/authors/kim-bouwer/> accessed 6 July 2025.

[14] See *Maharashtra State Electricity Distribution Company Limited v Adani Power Maharashtra Limited* 2023 SCC OnLine SC 233 (recognising the economic and operational implications that environmental policy changes can have on corporate activities). See Gonzalo Vial Fourcade, 'The Relevance of Climate Change to Contract Law' (2023) 16 Mexican Law Review 3.

[15] Kim Bouwer, 'Climate Change and the Individual in the United Kingdom' in Makane Mbengue and Francesco Sindico (eds), *Climate Change Litigation - A Comparative Approach* (Springer 2021).

[16] Kim Bouwer, 'When Gist Is Mist: Mismatches in Small Scale Climate Change Litigation' (2015) 27 Environmental Law and Management 11.

[17] Peter Cane, 'The Anatomy of Private Law Theory: A 25th Anniversary Essay' (2005) 25 Oxford Journal of Legal Studies 203. Interest based theories are one way—and a helpful way—of understanding the structure of private law and are used by textbook writers to describe their subject. See, e.g., Jenny Steele, *Tort Law: Text, Cases, and Materials* (5th edn, OUP 2022), ch 1.

[18] See, e.g., Sean Coyle and Karen Morrow, *The Philosophical Foundations of Environmental Law: Property, Rights and Nature* (Hart Publishing 2004); John Lowry and Rod Edmunds (eds), *Environmental Protection and the Common Law* (Hart 2000).

[19] Kysar (n 9).

[20] Simon Halliday, Jonathan Ilan, and Colin Scott, 'Street-Level Tort Law: The Bureaucratic Justice of Liability Decision-Making' (2012) 75 Modern Law Review 347.

[21] Susan M Sterett, *Litigating the Pandemic: Disaster Cascades in Court* (University of Pennsylvania Press 2023).

[22] Although see Chris Hilson, 'Climate Change Litigation in the UK: An Explanatory Approach (or, Bringing the Grievance Back In)' in Fabrizio Fracchia and Massimo Occhiena (eds), *Climate Change: La Riposta del Diritto* (Naples, Editorale Scientifica 2010); in the US context Susan M Sterett and Laura K Mateczun, 'Displacement, Legal Mobilization, and Disasters: Trial Courts and Legal Process' (2020) 11 Risk, Hazards & Crisis in Public Policy 348; Sterett (n 21); and in the Global South, see Birsha Ohdedar, 'Climate Adaptation, Vulnerability and Rights-Based Litigation: Broadening the Scope of Climate Litigation Using Political Ecology' (2022) 13 Journal of Human Rights and Environment 137; Jolene Lin

about the way legal rules adapt (or not) to social problems. If English legal culture prohibits high-profile, disruptive climate change cases—it may be that change happens more subtly from the bottom up. Here, I offer some discussion about some of the decided private law cases and offer a working hypothesis.

So, how might we understand legal culture? Karl Klare describes it as follows:

> By legal culture, I mean professional sensibilities, habits of mind, and intellectual reflexes: What are the characteristic rhetorical strategies deployed by participants in a given legal setting? What is their repertoire of recurring argumentative moves? What counts as a persuasive legal argument? What types of arguments, possibly valid in other discursive contexts (e.g., in political philosophy), are deemed outside the professional discourse of lawyers? What enduring political and ethical commitments influence professional discourse? What understandings of and assumptions about politics, social life and justice? What "inarticulate premises, [are] culturally and historically ingrained' in the professional discourse and outlook?"[23]

Legal culture can be understood as reflecting the "institutional, historical and power-related forces that find particular expressions in the legal language and traditions of a jurisdiction".[24] A "thick" conception of legal culture[25] includes a wide range of external elements, including the institutional factors, behavioural patterns and practices (including litigation rates and which litigation is brought), and values and attitudes towards the law within a specific jurisdiction.[26] The internally active elements of a legal culture include written law, scholarly commentary, judicial decisions, and the architecture of legal institutions.[27] This is heavily context specific: Legal culture is not monolithic and varies across societies and different fields,[28] embedded in larger frameworks of social structure and culture. But a defining feature is that the participants in a culture tend to accept its properties as normal, not perceiving the cultural specificity of their own argument—for instance, in relation to questions of legal convincingness,[29] or in relation to what counts as proper legal reasoning.[30] This does explain, for instance, the difficulties entailed in legal transfers, because legal culture would affect the outcome of a transfer of legal principles between different systems[31]—even where legal principles, policies, and doctrines were the same or similar.[32]

and Jacqueline Peel, *Litigating Climate Change in the Global South* (OUP 2024). It should be noted that although the cited studies look in depth at more mundane or incidental litigation, few of them examine the role of *private* law. My own work in progress monograph examines these cases.

[23] Karl Klare, 'Legal Culture and Transformative Constitutionalism' (1998) 14 South African Journal on Human Rights 146, 166–67.

[24] Eloise Scotford, *Environmental Principles and the Evolution of Environmental Law* (Hart Publishing 2017) 19.

[25] Jeremy Webber, 'Culture, Legal Culture, and Legal Reasoning: A Comment on Nelken' (2004) 29 Australian Journal of Legal Philosophy 27, 28–29.

[26] David Nelken, 'Using the Concept of Legal Culture' (2004) 29 Australian Journal of Legal Philosophy 1.

[27] ibid.

[28] ibid.

[29] Klare (n 23) 167.

[30] Hunt (n 17).

[31] Nelken (n 26). See also Roger Cotterrell, *Jurisprudence and Socio-Legal Studies* (Routledge 2024) 56–66, citing LeGrande.

[32] Although see Cotterrell (n 31) 59–60.

In general, common law legal culture is distinctive in that it is deeply rooted in precedent and most legal rules are laid down in judicial decisions.[33] Some legal rules and principles are introduced by Acts of Parliament or other forms of regulation.[34] Common law methods emphasise practical reasoning over abstract theory and, in general, common law systems tend to recognise tradition and develop the law incrementally where necessary. As such, "it was in resolving disputes rather than in laying down principles, that the English judge could see justice done".[35] This creates a legal culture that is both conservative in its respect for precedent but also adaptive, allowing incremental development and gradual evolution through judicial interpretation by analogy.

The ways in which specifically *English* legal culture differs from other parts of the common law world perhaps relate to a greater emphasis on tradition, and the class deference and social trust that operate within the broader profession.[36] More controversially, the English system has been associated with a greater degree of "prestige and elitism" than, say, the US.[37] Whatever the relative merits and other consequences of this, it potentially contributes to a high level of stability in a system in which the common law and techniques of common law reasoning are sanctified to some extent.[38] The number of vested interests in what is fundamentally a closed system has been associated with a high level of technical competence, predictable processes, and a low rate of error.[39]

Thick descriptions of legal culture encompass external factors such as the nature of funding arrangements and the architecture of institutions.[40] Both the costs and the cost risk of bringing litigation in the English courts are very high.[41] The Aarhus requirement that the costs of environmental litigation not be "prohibitively expensive" has been interpreted narrowly both in terms of the extent of the protection available[42] and in terms of the *kinds* of actions to which such protection applies. There is no protection for private law cases, and there are also some surprising limits on what counts as environmental judicial review.[43] To some extent, the strong elitism associated with English legal culture, as well as the split profession, could be contributing factors to the very high costs of litigation. But also, to some extent, costs could influence the culture of the legal system in terms of what might be perceived as the "net benefit" of litigation.[44] While the latter might be of less direct relevance in strategic public interest environmental litigation,[45] it would nevertheless influence legal culture more generally.

[33] Grant Lamond, 'Precedent and Analogy in Legal Reasoning' in Edward N Zalta (ed), *The Stanford Encyclopedia of Philosophy* (Stanford University 2016).

[34] AG Chloros, 'Common Law, Civil Law and Socialist Law: Three Leading Systems of the World, Three Kinds of Legal Thought' (1978) 9 Cambrian Law Review 11, 12.

[35] ibid 13.

[36] Richard Posner, *Law and Legal Theory in England and America* (OUP 1995), Lecture 3.

[37] ibid Lecture 1; see for instance Brian Abel-Smith and Robert B Stevens, *Lawyers and the Courts: A Sociological Study of the English Legal System 1750–1965* (Heinemann 1967) 7.

[38] Abel-Smith and Stevens (n 37) 325; also see the discussion in Webber (n 25) 30–31 as to how this contextual commonality is shaped by the practice of culture itself.

[39] Posner (n 36), Lecture 3; Chloros (n 34) 13.

[40] Webber (n 25) 28–29.

[41] See, for a more detailed discussion, Bouwer, 'Global Perspectives' (n 6) 50–59, and sources therein.

[42] Giselle Vega, 'Planning Challenges and Environmental Claims by Interested Parties Under Aarhus: Still Prohibitively Expensive?' (2021) 4 De Lege Ferenda 21.

[43] Bouwer, 'Global Perspectives' (n 6) 56–57; most recently *HM Treasury and another v Global Feedback Limited and another* [2025] EWCA Civ 624.

[44] Posner (n 36), Lecture 3.

[45] Lisa Vanhala, 'Legal Opportunity Structures and the Paradox of Legal Mobilization by the Environmental Movement in the UK' (2012) 46 Law & Society Review 523.

In terms of how this affects legal reasoning, while the common law is (perhaps) venerated, common law systems generally and the English system in particular are associated with a respect for the limits on judicial innovation and the need for restraint.[46] In very simple terms, it is recognised as foundational that although unelected judges do have capacity to make legal rules, they should exercise restraint in so doing, in order not to overstep their institutional role.[47] This is core to the understanding of the separation of powers, and the necessary deference this creates to Parliament.[48] In general, judicial tradition holds the judge to do what he is told to do, which involves trying to strike a balance between the interests of the litigants before him and what he is permitted to do within his institutional role. A long-term view of how this balance is struck reveals a fairly well-established culture of grumbling that judges defer too much to the lawmakers.[49] While the bench is not monolithic, there are shifts in judicial mood in terms of where this balance should be struck. At present, the bench in general is fairly conservative when it comes to the interpretation of existing legal duties and the scope to expand them.[50]

In relation to climate change judicial reviews, "judges have emphasised the supremacy of political accountability in negotiating the path to net zero", deprecating requests for strengthened forms of legal accountability.[51] There are a range of ways to understand the reasons for this, and relevant factors may include deference to lawmakers in climate change cases,[52] or the incompatibility of legal frameworks used in litigation with broader climate targets.[53] Neither would be incorrect, but it is my argument that this is not born of climate scepticism necessarily, but it part of a legal culture of deference to the lawmaking branches of government.[54] Climate change disputes may prompt particular conservatism because of the intensely political nature of the problem—although as has been pointed out, many of the public law cases do raise serious questions about statutory construction, which are firmly legal questions,[55] and therefore should be within a court's power to decide even if the broader context is political.[56] It should not be forgotten that the High Court has twice found a defendant department not to have complied with its procedural obligations under the Climate Change Act 2008, and required

46 On restraint, see Lewis Graham, 'Has the UK Supreme Court Become More Restrained in Public Law Cases?' (2024) 87 Modern Law Review 1073, 1057–77.

47 HLA Hart, 'Positivism and the Separation of Law and Morals' (1958) 71 Harvard Law Review 593.

48 Albert Venn Dicey, *An Introduction to the Study of the Law of the Constitution* (Palgrave Macmillan 1961).

49 Abel-Smith and Stevens (n 37) 306.

50 Graham (n 46). While there is no peer-reviewed scholarship taking a similar approach in private law, there are various areas where orthodoxy has been restored, for instance, in relation to the approach to the duty of care in negligence, see Donal Nolan, 'The Duty of Care After Robinson v Chief Constable of West Yorkshire Police' in Daniel Clarry (ed), *The UK Supreme Court Yearbook, Volume 9: 2017–2018 Legal Year* (Appellate Press 2019). Also see Graham (n 46), ftn 165 1094, although also see ftn 173 1095.

51 Joshua Kimblin, 'Climate Change, the Courts and the Constitution' (The Constitution Society 2022) 4.

52 ibid. This could also include not calling 'into question the decision-maker's exercise of evaluative judgment, except where . . . principles of . . . law allow', see *R (on the application of Sarah Finch on behalf of the Weald Action Group) v Surrey County Council and others* [2022] EWCA Civ 187 [3].

53 Sanja Bogojević, 'Squaring the Circle? Regional Airport Expansion, Climate Change and the Planning Regime' (2024) 87 Modern Law Review 967.

54 Graham (n 46) 1082–86.

55 Elizabeth Fisher, 'Climate Change and Statutory Construction: Administrative Law Expertise and "New" Emergencies' (2023) 27 Edinburgh Law Review 322.

56 *R (on the application of Miller and another) v Secretary of State for Exiting the European Union* [2017] UKSC 5 [2], [4], [5].

improved planning.[57] I do not think that the recent decision of *Finch*[58]—in which the Supreme Court established that all emissions resulting from burning oil and gas must be considered in a project's environmental impact assessment—reflects a significant change in judicial approach. This might have some impact on how projects are assessed,[59] but it was clear by the time *Finch* was handed down that the government's approach to oil and gas licensing would change fairly soon in any event, due to the then-imminent election.

3. English Private Law and Climate Change

In the proceeding section, I explained why the pressures caused by the changing climate could prompt legal innovation and introduced legal culture which could be understood as constraining the potential for significant legal disruption. To demonstrate this, I will consider some private climate litigation, before moving on to examine how law accommodates climate change problems in more subtle situations.

3.1 Classic Climate Litigation

The quintessential climate case is a private law action seeking compensation for loss and damage caused by climate change, the climate change "holy grail";[60] these cases present difficulties both doctrinally and constitutionally,[61] but they continue to be brought and progressed because they promise something no other kind of legal action can offer—the prospect of a damages award or injunction against a major emitter.[62] In the civil law world, (Dutch) tort law has been used as the basis for both actions against government as well corporate actions seeking increased ambition from major emitters in their emissions reductions.[63]

The prospects of a successful climate tort "holy grail" case in the English courts have never been particularly good, whether brought in torts[64] or under public trust doctrine,[65] and

[57] *R (on the application of Friends of the Earth Ltd and others) v Secretary of State for the Business, Energy and Industrial Strategy (Net Zero I)* [2022] EWHC 1841 (Admin); *R (oao Friends of the Earth, ClientEarth and Good Law Project) v Secretary of State for Energy and Net Zero (Net Zero II)* [2024] EWHC 995 (Admin); in Bouwer, 'Global Perspectives' (n 6) 10, I argue that these procedural victories could have substantive effects in time.

[58] *R (on the application of Finch on behalf of the Weald Action Group) v Surrey County Council and others* [2024] UKSC 20.

[59] Daria Shapovalova, 'The Legal Signifcance and Practical Implications of the Finch Decision of the UK Supreme Court: A New Hope for Climate or Business as Usual?' [2026] Journal of Environmental Law.

[60] Kim Bouwer, 'Lessons from a Distorted Metaphor: The Holy Grail of Climate Litigation' (2020) 9 Transnational Environmental Law 347.

[61] Kysar (n 9); Eduardo M Penalver, 'Acts of God or Toxic Torts - Applying Tort Principles to the Problem of Climate Change' (1998) 38 Natural Resources Journal 563; Maxine Burkett, 'Climate Justice and the Elusive Climate Tort' (2011) 121 Yale Law Journal Online 115 <https://www.yalelawjournal.org/pdf/1002_d3vqzbuq.pdf> accessed 7 July 2025.

[62] Shi-Ling Hsu, 'A Realistic Evaluation of Climate Change Litigation through the Lens of a Hypothetical Lawsuit' (2008) 79 University of Colorado Law Review 701; among other things, see Geetanjali Ganguly, Joana Setzer, and Veerle Heyvaert, 'If at First You Don't Succeed: Suing Corporations for Climate Change' (2018) 38 Oxford Journal of Legal Studies 841.

[63] *Urgenda Foundation v the Kingdom of the Netherlands (I)* (n 2); *Milieudefensive v Shell* (n 1).

[64] Giedre Kaminskaite-Salters, 'Climate Change Litigation in the UK: It's Feasibility and Prospects' in Michael Faure and Marjan Peeters (eds), *Climate Change Liability* (Edward Elgar Publishing 2011).

[65] Silke Goldberg and Richard Lord QC, 'England' in Richard Lord QC and others (eds), *Climate Change Liability: Transnational Law and Practice* (CUP 2011); Vedantha Kumar and Will Frank, 'Holding

whether brought as an action against national governments (as in New Zealand), by local or regional governments (as is now the case in the US), or against corporations.[66] A while ago, I wrote that it was "difficult to conceive" of a case like *Urgenda* even being *brought* in English law, let alone surviving a strike-out.[67] And indeed, the "systemic"[68] litigation focusing on government action as a whole was brought in public law.[69] Similarly, despite the fact that very many carbon majors are registered in the UK,[70] no action has been brought against a private party for their role in causing climate change (except obliquely in the two derivative actions discussed below). Yet the structure of the law is largely similar to that in New Zealand, Australia, and the US, where tort actions against corporations and/or government have been brought and (in the two former) achieved some success, at least for a time. The success of any "holy grail" tort case would require more doctrinal innovation than is likely at the moment; accordingly, any action would probably not be effective and would carry a significant risk of adverse costs.

Perhaps for the same reasons, actions for adaptation failures where climate risks materialise and the impacts are inadequately managed—which potentially lends itself well to tort law actions seeking compensation for damage[71]—were brought in public law. An action in which one claimant had lost his home due to storm damage and/or risk of coastal erosion,[72] which might then have constituted actionable damage as required in negligence, was brought as a challenge to the national adaptation programme. The claimants lost, which does raise questions as to why this largely unsuccessful strategy was used rather than a tort action.[73] Although in general no duty arises either in respect of omissions or failures to act,[74] or to protect others from physical harm arising "naturally",[75] a duty can arise in circumstances either where the defendant made a bad situation worse,[76] or failed to take adequate steps to protect the claimant's interests in a context there was a duty to do so. There also seems to be an on-point precedent. In the Court of Appeal case of *Holbeck Hall*, a "measured duty of care" could arise in relation to a naturally occurring nuisance when the hazard is known and the danger to the claimant's land is reasonably foreseeable; it is knowledge or presumed knowledge of a nuisance which could reasonably be abated, that gives rise to liability for allowing it to continue.[77] The issue then would be less whether the approach taken to adaptation policy generally was legal, and more a question of whether the defendant's behaviour towards the claimant had fallen below a certain standard. It would be a long shot, but so are most of the judicial review cases brought against

Private Emitters to Account for the Effects of Climate Change: Could a Case Like Lliuya Succeed under English Nuisance Laws' (2018) 2 Carbon & Climate Law Review 110.

[66] Bouwer, 'Climate Change and the Individual' (n 15); Bouwer, 'Global Perspectives' (n 6) 19–25.

[67] Bouwer, 'Climate Change and the Individual' (n 15).

[68] Lucy Maxwell, Sarah Mead, and Dennis Van Berkel, 'Standards for Adjudicating the next Generation of Urgenda-Style Climate Cases' (2022) 13 Journal of Human Rights and Environment 35.

[69] These (at the time rare) successful cases were judicial reviews, decided on the most narrow basis: *Net Zero I* (n 57); *Net Zero II* (n 57).

[70] Richard Heede, 'Tracing Anthropogenic Carbon Dioxide and Methane Emissions to Fossil Fuel and Cement Producers, 1854–2010' (2014) 122 Climatic Change 229.

[71] Bouwer, 'Climate Change and the Individual' (n 15).

[72] *R (oao Friends of the Earth, Kevin Jordan and Douglas Paulley) v the Secretary of State for Environment, Food and Rural Affairs* [2024] EWHC 2707 (Admin) [4].

[73] Very few of the climate change judicial reviews focusing on discrete projects or policy have succeeded, see Kimblin (n 51).

[74] Bouwer, 'Climate Change and the Individual' (n 15); Bouwer, 'Global Perspectives' (n 6) 19–21.

[75] *East Suffolk Rivers Catchment Board v Kent* [1941] AC 74.

[76] *Tindall v Chief Constable of Thames Valley Police* [2024] UKSC 33.

[77] *Holbeck Hall v Scarborough* [2000] 2 ALL ER 705.

the government over the last decade, and yet the latter continue. In contrast, for some reason no attempt has even been made to bring a private law action in any of the above—this cannot be a question of expertise,[78] and must be a question of strategic—or cultural—choice.

Now turning to corporate actions, the English courts had their *Milieudefensie* moment when the NGO ClientEarth brought a derivative claim under Section 260(1) of the Companies Act 2006 against the directors of Shell, in which it held a small number of shares.[79] ClientEarth claimed that Shell had, among other things, failed to promote the success of the company for the benefit of shareholders,[80] to have regard for the effect of the company's actions on the environment,[81] and to manage the material and foreseeable risks posed to the company by climate change. Another derivative action—*McGaughey and Davies v Universities Superannuation Scheme Limited*[82]—was brought around the same time as a multiple derivative claim on behalf of the Universities Superannuation Scheme pension fund's corporate trustee against its current and former directors, relying on common law principles analogous to the statutory provisions relied upon in the *Shell* case.[83] Because of the resemblances between the two, I shall discuss them together, dealing with the substantive obligations under the UK Companies Act 2006 upon which the claimants relied, and then the preliminary requirements that in the end, prevented both derivative actions from progressing.

The basis of ClientEarth's claim was that the Board's failure to adopt and implement an energy transition strategy—one that both gave appropriate weight and strategic consideration to climate risk and included mitigation commitments aligned with the Paris Agreement[84]—was a breach of directors' duties under the Companies Act 2006. The claimant also argued that the existing strategy excluded short- to medium-term targets to reduce Scope 3 emissions.[85] It also alleged that the Board's failure fully to comply with the *Milieudefensie* decision,[86] in terms of which (at the time) it was required to reduce its emissions, was a breach of its legal duties under English law.[87] In *McGaughey*, the fourth ground of action concerned the directors' failure to establish any kind of credible plan for dealing with climate change risks.[88] The claimants argued that the failure of the scheme's directors to create a credible plan for disinvestment from fossil fuel investments had, and would continue to, compromise the scheme, being in breach of various duties in the Companies Act 2006 and analogous concepts in equity.[89] In both, the

[78] English claimant public interest lawyers strategically use tort to remedy human rights breaches where damage has been caused by a defendant's breach of duty. See Richard Meeran, 'Tort Litigation against Multinational Corporations for Violation of Human Rights: An Overview of the Position Outside the United States' (2011) 3 City University of Hong Kong Law Review 1.

[79] This is an action brought by shareholders against the directors of a company for a breach of their duties. The rules applicable to derivative claims may be found in Part 11 of the Companies Act 2006.

[80] Companies Act 2006, s 172(1).

[81] Companies Act 2006, s 172(1)(d).

[82] *McGaughey v Universities Superannuation Scheme Ltd* [2022] EWHC 565 (Ch); *McGaughey v Universities Superannuation Scheme Ltd (CA)* [2023] EWCA Civ 873.

[83] *McGaughey v Universities Superannuation Scheme Ltd* (n 82) [30]; Lord Sales, 'Directors' Duties and Climate Change: Navigating the Shifting Landscape of Corporate Environmental Responsibility' (Durham Law School Institute for Commercial and Corporate Law Annual Lecture, Durham University, 27 February 2025) 10.

[84] These are outlined in *ClientEarth v Shell and others (July)* [2023] EWHC 1897 (Ch) [22].

[85] The specific breaches are set out in ibid [39].

[86] *Milieudefensive v Shell* (n 1).

[87] ibid [36].

[88] See Sawyer (n 33), 3.

[89] *McGaughey v Universities Superannuation Scheme Ltd (CA)* (n 82), [29] - [30], [42].

claimants were constrained to a consideration of *financial* risk, because legally the directors were required to prioritise shareholder value, which could not be compromised for "ethical" considerations.[90]

In both, the claimants relied upon two sections of the Companies Act that could be seen as relevant to management and climate change. These are Section 172, which provides that a director must act in the way he considers, in good faith, would most likely promote the success of the company for the benefit of its members as a whole, interpreted subjectively;[91] and Section 174, providing that a director must exercise reasonable care, skill, and diligence, which is interpreted mostly objectively, the relevant standard being what reasonably can be expected of a director.[92] It was never really anticipated that Section 172 would give rise to duties that could be legally enforced;[93] and the handful of examples where these have been arose from really bad behaviour.[94] Rather, Section 172 was intended to enhance and create opportunities for engagement through the usual channels of corporate governance,[95] creating scope for minority shareholders to raise challenges to decisions in meetings, and exert their influence there.[96] This is because courts will, in general, show restraint, embracing a business-judgment rule approach where they do not second-guess directors' decisions.[97]

In *ClientEarth*, Mr Justice Trower emphasised that "the law respects the autonomy of the decision making of the directors on commercial issues and their judgments as to how best to achieve results which are in the best interests of their members as a whole".[98] He noted that company actors were permitted a good deal of discretion in discharging their duties,[99] and the proper place for this kind of engagement is through the company structures, not in a legal challenge, and certainly not one against the directors personally.[100] Similarly, in *McGaughey* the court did not really engage with the discussion as to what the defendants *should* be doing in relation to climate change, but did remark that the relevant regulations required powers to be exercised so as to ensure the security, quality, liquidity, and profitability of pension investments, and that no breach of the regulations had been identified.[101] As such, the fossil fuels

90 Sales (n 83) 7, 10, discussing *Cowan v Scargill* [1985] Ch 270 (Ch). In relation to pension funds, see Philip Bennett, 'Would It Be a Breach of a Pension Fund Trustee's Investment Duties to Invest in "Green Gilts"?' (2021) 35 Trust Law International 133.

91 Ekaterina Aristova and Lionel Nichols, 'Climate Change on the Board: Navigating Directors' Duties' (2024) 24 Journal of Corporate Law Studies 479, 483. This chapter was completed before the Court of Appeal's decision in *Saxon Woods v Costa* [2025] EWCA Civ 708 was handed down.

92 Sales (n 83) 6.

93 Paul Davies, *Introduction to Company Law* (3rd edn, OUP 2020), 49: '[T]hose proposing what became section 172 did not suppose that litigation would be the main mechanism by which consideration of non-shareholder interests was enforced'.

94 Pablo Iglesias-Rodríguez, 'ClientEarth v Shell Plc and the (Un)Suitability of UK Company Law and Litigation to Pursue Climate-Related Goals' (2023) 35 Journal of Environmental Law 445, 450; Aristova and Nichols (n 91) 484–88.

95 Bouwer, 'Global Perspectives' (n 6) 35–7.

96 Aristova and Nichols (n 91) 491, 495.

97 Andrew Keay and Joan Loughrey, 'The Concept of Business Judgment' (2019) 39(1) Legal Studies 36, 37.

98 *ClientEarth v Shell and others (May)* [2023] EWHC 1137 (Ch), [47].

99 See *ClientEarth v Shell and others (July)* (n 84), [31]–[33], in relation to Section 174; see also the discussion in Richard Honey KC, 'ClientEarth v Shell Plc: Review and Lessons for Future Climate Litigation' (*Francis Taylor Building*, 1 September 2023) <https://www.ftbchambers.co.uk/elblog/view/clientearth-v-shell-plc-review-and-lessons-for-future-climate-litigation> accessed 5 July 2025.

100 *ClientEarth v Shell and others (May)* (n 98), 58; *ClientEarth v Shell and others (July)* (n 84), [53].

101 *McGaughey v Universities Superannuation Scheme Ltd (CA)* (n 82), [173].

claim was considered to be "an attempt to challenge the management and investment decisions of [the defendant] without any ground upon which to do so", which meant the action was bound to fail.[102]

As Lord Carnwath explains, it is "difficult to think of a company whose interests are more 'implicated by climate change effects' than a major fossil fuel operator such as Shell".[103] As such, this challenge to their climate change policies "could have been a valuable chance to examine the operation of the relevant Companies Act provisions, both in general and in the particular context of the fiduciary and due care obligations",[104] in relation to how these govern environmental decision-making. But, as Lord Sales has observed, the way the relevant duties have been interpreted would make this unfeasible. For instance, the (mostly) subjective nature of the Section 172 duty makes it difficult for a shareholder to attack the directors' approach to climate change management, unless the issue has been ignored entirely; similarly it might only be possible successfully to challenge a director's exercise of care and skill under Section 174 if the decision falls outside a reasonable range, which could be very difficult to prove.[105] Simply put, due to the general approach that refrains from interfering with directors' judgments, the situation in terms of their conduct would need to be fairly egregious before a court intervened.

As it turned out, in neither *ClientEarth* nor *McGaughey* did the courts take the opportunity to consider the operation of the above provisions. Due to the exceptional nature of derivative actions, the claimants faced a preliminary procedure to establish standing, which is complex but in essence seeks to establish whether it is in the interests of the company that the litigation be brought.[106] This is because the derivative action procedure is meant to be used sparingly to avoid development of a culture of litigation about directors' decision-making.[107] In both, the claimants were required to have established a prima facie case with respect to the claims made, the test for which was a higher than seriously arguable case, based on substantial evidence.[108] ClientEarth failed to satisfy the judge that it had done that, both on the papers and at an oral hearing,[109] and the claimants in *McGaughey* failed to satisfy either the High Court or the Court of Appeal that they had done so.[110] In *ClientEarth*, the court did take some exception to the framing of the claimant's case and, and in particular, the questions it raised about the defendant's board members' professional judgment.

As such, while the missed opportunity to examine further how far we can go with directors duties and climate change might be regrettable,[111] these two lost cases are not wildly out of step

[102] ibid [174]–[175]. It has also been suggested that making investment decisions aligned with any such policy might mean a trustee or investment manager was in breach of duty, Bennett (n 90).

[103] Robert Carnwath, 'ClientEarth v Shell: What Future for Derivative Claims?' (Grantham Research Institute on Climate Change and the Environment, London School of Economics 2024) 6 <https://www.lse.ac.uk/granthaminstitute/publication/clientearth-v-shell-what-future-for-derivative-claims/> accessed 6 September 2024.

[104] ibid.

[105] Sales (n 83) 10.

[106] Davies (n 93) 276. Companies Act 2006, s 263(2)(a).

[107] Jonathan Hardman, 'An Institutional Analysis of UK Ostensible Minority Shareholder Protection Mechanisms' (2023) 23 Journal of Corporate Law Studies 397, 407–08.

[108] Section 261(2) Companies Act 2006 for ClientEarth; under the 'proper plaintiff' rule in *Foss v Harbottle* (1843) 2 Hare 461 (Ch).

[109] *ClientEarth v Shell and others (May)* [2023] EWHC 1137 (Ch); *ClientEarth v Shell and others (July)* [2023] EWHC 1897 (Ch).

[110] *McGaughey v Universities Superannuation Scheme Ltd* (n 82); *McGaughey v Universities Superannuation Scheme Ltd (CA)* (n 82).

[111] Carnwath (n 103).

with the general law when it comes to directors' fiduciary duties and the means through which shareholders' minority interests are protected.[112] As much as the tranche of public law cases made very clear the courts' deference to Parliament and other decision-makers on challenging aspects of climate change law and policy, so too do the early cases against corporations reflect a level of deference to business. Having said that, it has been suggested that to some extent, in particular in *ClientEarth*, the decisions set a precedent for a more restrictive approach to derivative claims than was the norm.[113] Significantly, there was a punitive (and expensive) order as to costs.[114] The approach to costs is unprecedented,[115] deviating from the norm in derivative proceedings, where the defendant company would not normally be allowed to recover its costs if it participates voluntarily, as Shell did.[116] The risk of a hefty adverse costs order is bound to give pause to any future prospective claimants.

3.2 Climate Law in the Shadow of Regulation

Fisher and others identify a "category of legal disruption caused by regulatory schemes and legislative frameworks that have been created to address both the causes and the impacts of climate change . . . [and which will] give rise to new legal arrangements and novel legal questions, [leading] to legal uncertainty and thus legal disputes".[117] As the authors explain, the characteristics of climate change that make it difficult to govern do not go away with regulation; indeed, these "need to be accommodated within a legal culture, including through the implementation and interpretation of these regimes".[118] When litigation arises within the shadow of these regimes, the resultant cases are "legally disruptive when they concern regimes that are in . . . a state of flux, adjusting with the changing policy environment, but this gives rise to contested legal issues concerning their operation".[119] And indeed, flux has been a determining feature of climate change and energy policy under the previous three Parliaments.[120] They discuss a range of (mostly) judicial review cases, but there is one group of cases that concerns the protection of private rights, which is relevant for a discussion of private law and climate change.[121]

The *Breyer Group* litigation was brought in response to the Government's retrospective and retroactive modifications to a Feed-in-Tariff scheme.[122] In 2010, the (then) Department for Energy and Climate Change introduced the scheme, a financial incentive for domestic solar systems, to provide a financial cushion for householders to cover the high cost of installation.[123] The scheme created generation (subsidies paid for the generation of one's own

[112] Hardman (n 107), 411–17.

[113] Aristova and Nichols (n 91).

[114] *ClientEarth v Shell plc and others* [2023] EWHC 2182 (Ch).

[115] Carnwath (n 103) 6.

[116] Civil Procedure Rules Practice Directions 19 A para 2. Also see Aristova and Nichols (n 91) 499–501.

[117] Fisher et al (n 4) 192–93.

[118] ibid 192.

[119] ibid 193.

[120] Neil Carter and Mitya Pearson, 'From Green Crap to Net Zero: Conservative Climate Policy 2015–2022' (2024) 19 British Politics 1.

[121] Fisher et al (n 4) 193 ftn 144.

[122] *Breyer Group plc and others v Department of Energy and Climate Change* [2015] EWCA Civ 408. As to whether the modifications were retrospective or retroactive, see [45]–[48].

[123] Details of the FiT scheme and the relevant regulations may be found in the decision of the High Court *Breyer Group plc and others v Department of Energy and Climate Change* [2014] EWHC 2257 (QB) [6]–[17].

electricity) and export (for making electricity available to the grid) tariffs. And then, claiming budgetary reasons, the Secretary of State seriously modified the scheme at short notice.[124] This decision had a "catastrophic" impact on the solar industry,[125] and as such on the claimants, who were solar installation businesses. Following successful judicial review proceedings challenging the administrative action,[126] the claimants brought an action for damages for their lost profits relying on Article 1 of the First Protocol of the European Convention of Human Rights (A1P1).

It was already clear that a contract was capable of being a possession for the purposes of an A1P1 action,[127] and on appeal it was found that in *Breyer* the impact the policy change had on the claimants' contracts was an interference with their possessions. This applied in relation to concluded contracts which were tangible, assignable, and had a present economic value on their face.[128] The Court of Appeal confirmed that the interference with the claimants' rights was not justified by the savings achieved by the department as a result of the interference; very little consideration appeared to have been given by the department to the impact the changes would have on existing businesses.[129] This resulted in substantial damage payments to the claimants,[130] although this did not stop the collapse of the rooftop solar industry in England.

The decision of the Court of Appeal has been criticised for taking a very narrow approach to what constitutes the public interest, considering primarily budgetary constraints and questions about relative affordability during the period of government austerity.[131] But very little turned on this. The significant factor in *Breyer* was the weight placed on the claimants' tangible, assignable contracts—their installation contracts—for the purposes of determining whether their possessions had been affected. Subsequent actions by energy companies seeking to make similar claims in relation to the termination of other kinds of clean energy incentives have been less successful for this reason.[132] This is consistent with a common law system in

124 The facts may be found in ibid [18]–[25].

125 ibid [25].

126 *R (on the application of Homesun Holdings) v Secretary of State for Energy and Climate Change* [2011] EWHC 3575 (Admin); *R (Homesun Holdings Ltd) v Secretary of State* [2012] EWCA Civ 28.

127 *Murungaru v Secretary of State for the Home Department* [2008] EWCA Civ 1015 [48]–[49], [58].

128 In the High Court decision in *Breyer Group plc and others v Department of Energy and Climate Change* (n 123) [51], it is stated that they were part of the marketable goodwill of the company, [84]; this was approved in the Court of Appeal in *Breyer Group plc and others v Department of Energy and Climate Change* (n 122) [38], [42], [49]. But this approval did not extend to 'future contracts' or goodwill or any kind of expectation, as a tangible property right was required: see *Breyer Group plc and others v Department of Energy and Climate Change* (n 123) [98]–[107]; *Breyer Group plc and others v Department of Energy and Climate Change* (n 122) [43].

129 *Breyer Group plc and others v Department of Energy and Climate Change* (n 123) [144]–[150], specifically noting the impact on the environment; *Breyer Group plc and others v Department of Energy and Climate Change* (n 122) [88], [99]–[100].

130 Justine Thornton, 'Significant UK Environmental Law Cases 2015/16' (2016) 28 Journal of Environmental Law 359, 398.

131 Birsha Ohdedar and Steven McNab, 'Climate Change Litigation in the United Kingdom' in Wolfgang Kahl and Marc-Philippe Weller (eds), *Climate Change Litigation: A Handbook* (CH Beck 2020), Section 3(a)(bb).

132 *Drax Power Ltd and Infinis Energy Holdings v HM Treasury and Secretary of State for Climate Change* [2016] EWHC 228; *Infinis Energy Holdings Ltd v Her Majesty's Treasury and HM Revenue & Customs* [2016] EWCA Civ 1030 (legitimate expectations not possessions for the purposes of A1P1); see also discussion in Justine Thornton, 'Significant UK Environmental Law Cases 2016/17' (2017) 29 Journal of Environmental Law 367, 389; *Solaria Energy UK Ltd v Department for Business, Energy and Industrial Strategy* [2020] EWCA Civ 1625 (installation subcontracts not possessions for the purposes of A1P1 and in any event limitation had expired).

which significant weight is placed on the protection of private interests—which causes challenges for common law environmental protections.[133]

Another dispute that arose in the shadow of regulation arose due to the "defeat devices" fitted by car manufacturers. These devices were designed to ensure that new vehicles would emit a level of pollutants that was permitted in terms of the relevant EU regulations under testing conditions, but in the default or driving mode a higher level of emissions was the norm.[134] The English case of *Crossley* was brought in breach of statutory duty (the relevant EU regulations), fraudulent misrepresentation (deceit), breach of contract, and under various consumer legislation.[135] Although at the heart of the litigation, the issue was about the cars' nitrous oxide emissions, the actions were all about the loss to the claimants, with respect to the value and roadworthiness of their vehicles. Where reference is made to emissions, this is due to the implications for road tax and the financial implications of driving a cleaner car.[136]

The second reported case in the litigation was a strike out application which was brought due to uncertainty in the law of deceit as to the relationship between the defendants' representation and the claimant's conduct, specifically what level of awareness the claimant(s) had and how material this was to their decision-making. At the time, a recent decision—also in the High Court—of *Leeds City Council v Barclays Bank* had determined that "conscious awareness" of the exact nature of the representations made must have been that which induced the claimant to act,[137] in order to establish an action in deceit. Mr Justice Waksman was not bound, and also not prepared, to follow that approach in *Crossley*, finding that in some cases an assumption by the claimants could be sufficient.[138] The question of how much the lay claimants were expected to unravel in relation to their purchases was treated quite differently to *Leeds*—their sometimes unconscious assumptions that the vehicles would comply with relevant laws, were sufficient for the deceit claims to survive a strike out.[139] As above, this was in many respects a positive result for the environment,[140] subject to the inherent constraint that it is unclear how much of the claimants' compensation would be spent on remediation. But legally this could be seen as a judge taking a view on a specific point of law to ensure justice for lay claimants: The level of commercial and regulatory insight that could be expected of the claimants in *Leeds* simply would not have been fair to expect of the *Crossley* claimants, many of whom had not applied their minds in detail to what they expected and why, but nevertheless had been cheated.

3.3 Self-Directed Cases

Finally, there are of course numerous respects in which business arrangements are developed through which parties aim to meet or exceed environmental goals or standards. These

[133] Coyle and Morrow (n 18), Chapter 5.

[134] These cases are 'about' nitrogen oxide, but they can clearly be considered to be climate cases. See Bouwer, 'The Unsexy Future' (n 3).

[135] *Crossley and others v Volkswagen and others* [2021] EWHC 3444 [5].

[136] ibid [111], [119]–[125].

[137] [2021] EWHC 363 (Comm)

[138] *Crossley and others v Volkswagen and others* (n 135).

[139] ibid.

[140] A settlement of about £193m (excluding costs, for which a separate payment was made) were paid to 91,000 claimants. See 'Settlement of the English and Welsh VW NO_x Emissions Group Litigation' (Leigh Day, 25 May 2022) https://www.leighday.co.uk/news/news/2022-news/settlement-of-the-english-and-welsh-vw-nox-emissions-group-litigation/ accessed 6 July 2025.

might be completely chosen by the parties, for instance, a party to a contract might use their market power to compel better environmental performance from a lessor as a matter of choice,[141] or may be enacted to ensure compliance with any existing—or anticipated future—regulation. An example of this might be trying to incorporate pressure to reduce embodied carbon in construction or other long-term projects, where there would be a risk of asset stranding, as the proposed development may not be compliant with future standards and requirements.[142]

But parties are also free to choose how to behave in the conduct of their own businesses and may enter into agreements to support the design of a business relationship in such a way as to give effect to these ideals. A suite of contractual clauses developed by the Chancery Lane Project (TCLP) go beyond management of risk and include mitigation goals.[143] Model clauses might include requirements in relation to carbon disclosure (going beyond regulation or compelling parties to agree to comply with regulation by organisations that otherwise would not have to);[144] clauses committing to net-zero requirements; "green modifications" clauses in construction contracts to increase resilience against climate change; and agreements to improve energy efficiency.[145] A "green termination" clause allows the termination of a contract due to unsustainable activities.[146] To my knowledge there has not been any attempt to enforce such agreements, although the courts tend to hold parties to the bargains they have made.[147]

There is also now a precedent supporting charity trustees' freedom to choose an investment policy developed to give effect to climate change concerns and other social values. The claimants in *Butler-Schloss v Charity Commissioner* were charity trustees who approached the court in a "blessing or approval application"[148]; they asked the court to endorse a course of conduct, thus immunising them from future claims.[149] In this case, they wanted clarification as to whether it was permissible for them to pursue an investment policy that excluded investments that could be considered inconsistent with the Paris Agreement, even if it meant a lower rate of return. In both cases, environmental protection and the alleviation of poverty were part of their charitable purpose.[150] The court found that the trustees *were* entitled to adopt their respective policies, even if it meant a more modest return.[151] The case clarified that such actions

[141] Kathryn Janda and others, 'The Evolution of Green Leases: Towards Interorganizational Environmental Governance' (2016) 44 Building Research & Information 660.

[142] Bouwer, 'Global Perspectives' (n 6) 46.

[143] See Jennifer Ramos, 'Shifting the Mindset of Commercial Lawyers to Rewire Contracts, to Mitigate Climate Change More Effectively in Practice: The Chancery Lane Project' (2021) 23 Environmental Law Review 3. For the clauses, see The Chancery Lane Project <https://chancerylaneproject.org/> accessed 5 July 2025.

[144] ibid.

[145] Jennifer Ramos and The Chancery Lane Project, 'The Role of Contracts to Address Environmental Impacts in Supply Chains' in Susan A Maslow and David V Snyder (eds), *Contracts for Responsible and Sustainable Supply Chains: Model Contract Clauses, Legal Analysis, and Practical Perspectives* (ABA Publishing 2023), 183–84, 186.

[146] ibid.

[147] See Irina Sakharova, Chapter 6 of this handbook.

[148] *Sarah Butler-Schloss and others v The Charity Commissioner for England and Wales v The Attorney General* [2022] EWHC 974 (Ch).

[149] Richard Hoyle, 'The Fiduciary's Divestment Dilemma: ESG and the Era of Climate Change' (2023) Butterworths Journal of International Banking and Financial Law 612, 612.

[150] *Sarah Butler-Schloss and others v The Charity Commissioner for England and Wales v The Attorney General* (n 148) [13], [14].

[151] For more details, see Bouwer, 'Global Perspectives' (n 6) 47 - 8.

are within the range of discretion of a charity trustee acting to further the purposes of the trust.[152]

In previous litigation,[153] *pension* fund trustees had been permitted to exclude investments on moral grounds, where other options existed to support the financial purposes of the fund—a more restrictive policy would have conflicted with the duty of the fund trustees to safeguard the financial returns provided by the pension fund.[154] The picture was a little different with respect to charities, where trustees could choose to exclude investment categories on certain grounds provided that there was no risk of "significant financial detriment".[155] As such, in *Butler-Schloss*, the court afforded charitable trustees a "considerably wider latitude in determining a suitable investment policy" than they were previously thought to have.[156] This includes that trustees *are permitted to* exercise their discretion to exclude certain investments including on the basis that they conflict with a charitable purpose but where returns may be lower than otherwise. This might suggest that should it come to it, a court would support a party's choice when it came to their own policies and practices, although the significance of the charitable purpose here should not be understated. Questions remain about what might constitute a breach of duty in a context where a charitable or other trustee declines to exercise its discretion in a certain way.[157]

4. Conclusion

In this chapter I have considered a handful of English private law cases where judges have sought to solve problems arising in the context of climate change. There are not very many cases, and as such this chapter does to some extent provide provisional reflections; as a result my hypothesis may unravel in later years. In writing this, I have in mind a version of the question posed by Doug Kysar, asking how (private) law might respond to the challenges posed by climate change, but also, how and whether legal rules might change due to these pressures.[158]

The (provisional) answers to the above would appear to be that the way the English judges (and to some extent, the broader profession) have met this challenge is with restraint, but that this is not particularly out of step with English legal culture in general. So, while we may not see the creativity or climate conscious decision-making of other parts of the common law world, this is not inconsistent with legal decision-making in England in general, at present,

[152] *Sarah Butler-Schloss and others v The Charity Commissioner for England and Wales v The Attorney General* (n 148) [74].

[153] *Harries v Church Commissioners for England* [1992] 1 WLR 1241 (Ch).

[154] Sales (n 83) 7.

[155] *Harries v Church Commissioners for England* [1992] 1 WLR 1241 (Ch) [16]–[17]. See discussion in Bennett (n 90) 137.

[156] Cassandra Somers-Joce and Tim Koch, 'Butler-Sloss v The Charity Commission: The Pursuit of Charitable Purposes through ESG Investing' (*Property Law Blog*, 9 July 2022) <https://blogs.law.ox.ac.uk/property-law-blog/blog-post/2022/07/butler-sloss-v-charity-commission-pursuit-charitable-purposes> accessed 5 July 2025.

[157] Simon Bishop and others, 'Climate Conscious Investing and the Butler-Sloss Decision' (*Essex Court Chambers*, 8 November 2023) <https://essexcourt.com/publication/climate-conscious-investing-and-the-butler-sloss-decision-week-2-series-3/> accessed 17 February 2024.

[158] Kysar (n 9).

and so arguably this restraint is part of English legal culture. The literature about English legal culture highlights the possibilities for judges to enact practical justice in the way that issues between parties are resolved. And we do see this in the case law I have discussed. However, while on occasion these decisions do seem to fall on the side of the environment in some respects, legal innovation is geared towards delivering practical justice for claimants.

CHAPTER 35

The United States

JOHN C. DERNBACH

1. Introduction

THIS chapter focuses on the wide variety of state environmental, social, and governance (ESG) laws in the US and how they affect the private climate governance landscape. The term was coined in a 2004 United Nations report[1] to encourage and support corporate efforts that maintain and even improve financial performance by also considering and addressing environmental, social, and corporate governance issues. Since then, ESG activity and investing have grown rapidly. Globally, banks, mutual funds, and other financial institutions managed more than US$30 trillion in ESG assets in 2022. That figure is projected to grow to US$40 trillion in 2030, which would exceed one-fourth of all assets under management.[2] In the US, $6.5 trillion is managed as ESG or sustainability investments, which constitute about 12% of all assets under management.[3] "Climate change remains the dominant theme" of US ESG investing, "with a strong emphasis on clean energy transitions, carbon reduction, and nature restoration".[4] According to Professor Elizabeth Pollman "ESG is one of the most notable trends in corporate governance, management, and investment of the past two decades".[5] The greatest part of ESG is focused on actions that go beyond compliance with existing law. Thus, ESG plays a major role in private governance, including private climate governance. And the state laws opposing or supporting ESG are intended to discourage or encourage this form of private governance.

ESG in the US is also the subject of a backlash by politicians and others who view it as furthering an ideological agenda rather than, as it was intended, a way of managing risk and seizing opportunities.[6] Interpreted more charitably, these politicians view ESG as displacing what they see as their more-or-less exclusive role to make public decisions about climate change and other social and environmental issues. Interpreted less charitably, those opposing

[1] The Global Compact, *Who Cares Wins: Connecting Financial Markets to a Changing World* (United Nations 2004) <https://documents1.worldbank.org/curated/pt/280911488968799581/pdf/113237-WP-WhoCaresWins-2004.pdf> accessed 5 April 2005.

[2] 'Global ESG Assets Predicted to Hit $40 trillion by 2030, Despite Challenging Environment, Forecasts Bloomberg Intelligence' (*Bloomberg*, 8 February 2024) https://www.bloomberg.com/company/press/global-esg-assets-predicted-to-hit-40-trillion-by-2030-despite-challenging-environment-forecasts-bloomberg-intelligence/> accessed 5 April 2025 (hereinafter, Global ESG Assets).

[3] 'US Sustainable Investing Trends 2024/2025 - Executive Summary' (*US Sustainable Investment Forum*, 17 December 2024) https://www.ussif.org/research/trends-reports/us-sustainable-investing-trends-2024-2025-executive-summary> accessed 5 April 2025.

[4] ibid.

[5] Elizabeth Pollman (2024) 'The Making and Meaning of ESG' 14 Harvard Business Law Review 403, 403.

[6] ibid 431.

ESG seek to support incumbent fossil fuel and other interests by preventing corporations from taking actions that are in their own financial interest.

This chapter first describes the background and history of ESG. It then describes several relevant federal laws, which provide a framework for US financial markets, and efforts to address ESG at the federal level. All of this provides a foundation for this chapter's description and analysis of state ESG laws. States are the primary arena for ESG laws, with laws opposing ESG outnumbering those that support it. Most of these laws relate to state pension funds, which are governed first and foremost by the state pension fund trustees' fiduciary obligations to beneficiaries. Fiduciary duties limit the impact of both anti- and pro-ESG laws.[7]

This chapter then discusses three implications of these laws. First, it explains their significance for the role of private actors, particularly lawyers, in keeping up with a dynamic and ever-changing landscape. It suggests, among other things, that these laws illustrate the need for climate competence and sustainability competence in the practice of law. Second, ESG is a global phenomenon driven by private decisions about how best to address climate change, and private commitments are becoming more ambitious and better planned. State ESG laws in the US do not significantly alter that trend. Third, other national and regional (e.g., the EU) actors are adopting laws relating to climate change, sustainable development, and ESG, many of which are more ambitious than US laws. Corporations affected by these other laws will need to comply with them, whatever US state laws may say.

2. Sustainable Development, Climate Change, and ESG

ESG was coined to be distinct from sustainable development. Yet in practice, the two are often indistinguishable. Reducing greenhouse gas emissions and adapting to a changing climate, moreover, are essential features of sustainable development.

Sustainable development is the internationally recognised framework for maintaining and improving human well-being, freedom, and opportunity.[8] Its central decision-making principle requires the integration of economic development, social development, environmental protection, and, when applicable, peace and security.[9] Sustainable development, and the integrated decision-making framework, were a direct response to the tendency of countries and corporations to make decisions primarily on economic grounds, and deal with the social and environmental consequences of those decisions separately, if at all.[10] Countries around the world, including the US, committed to sustainable development at the 1992 UN Conference on Environment and Development in Rio de Janeiro, and have recommitted to it many times since then.

Corporations, however, are traditionally governed, at least in the Anglo-American jurisidictions, by the view that their primary purpose is to achieve a financial return for their shareholders. This nonetheless does not prevent corporations from engaging in some social

[7] See Seth Davis and Gregory Shaffer, Chapter 13 of this handbook.

[8] John C Dernbach and Federico Cheever, 'Sustainable Development and Its Discontents' (2015) 4 Transnational Environmental Law 247.

[9] John C Dernbach, 'Achieving Sustainable Development: The Centrality and Multiple Facets of Integrated Decisionmaking' (2003) 10 Indiana Journal of Global Legal Studies 247.

[10] Int'l Union for the Conservation of Nature and Natural Res., *World Conservation Strategy: Living Resource Conservation for Sustainable Development* (1980), <data.iucn.org/dbtw-wpd/edocs/WCS-004.pdf> accessed 5 April 2025.

and charitable actions, according to a line of cases on corporate governance that go back more than a century.[11] After the 1992 conference, many corporations began to "measure, document, and report a positive [return on investment] on all [of sustainability's] three bottom lines—economic, environmental, and social—as well as the benefits that stakeholders receive along the same three dimensions".[12]

Also after the 1992 conference, UN Secretary General Kofi Annan created the UN Global Compact, a voluntary association of corporations committed to advancing sustainable development as part of their business practices. In 2004, under the auspices of the UN, the Global Compact published a report, *Who Cares Wins*, which urged a wide variety of actors—including companies, investors and asset managers, pension fund trustees, regulators, consultants, analysts, and nongovernmental organisations—to further sustainable development by incorporating ESG factors into their decision-making.[13]

This report coined the term "ESG".[14] The report explained: "[W]e have refrained from using terms such as sustainability, corporate citizenship, etc., in order to avoid misunderstandings deriving from different interpretations of these terms".[15] To begin with, it limited governance to corporate governance, implicitly excluding public governance. It also limited the term to ESG issues "impacting company and investment value".[16] "Companies that perform better with regard to these issues", the report stated, "can increase shareholder value by, for example, properly managing risks, anticipating regulatory action or accessing new markets, while at the same time contributing to the sustainable development of the societies in which they operate. Moreover, these issues can have a strong impact on reputation and brands, an increasingly important part of company value".[17]

In spite of this effort to differentiate ESG from sustainable development, the two concepts are closely related. Besides the obvious overlap of E and S with sustainable development, both have integrated decision-making at their core. ESG was framed with the expectation that E, S, and G would be integrated into financial decision-making, although the report did not explain precisely how that is to occur.[18]

A particular legal issue—the fiduciary duty of pension funds and asset managers that held stock in these companies in trust—posed "a potentially thorny obstacle to spreading ESG".[19] These fiduciary duties include prudence and loyalty. The prudent investor rule spells out the duty of prudence for fund trustees. Essentially, the rule requires a trustee to manage a trust portfolio with "an overall investment strategy having risk and return objectives reasonably suited to the trust" and to "diversify the investments of the trust".[20] The duty of loyalty requires the trustee to manage the trust corpus "so as to accomplish the trust's purposes for the benefit

[11] Brian D Israel, Ellen Kay Fleishhacker, and Teresa L Johnson, 'Leaving the Lights Off: A Short History of the Legal Issues Related to ESG,' in Brian D Israel, Ellen Kaye Fleishhacker, and Teresa L Johnson (eds.), *Environmental, Social, Governance: The Professional's Guide to the Law and Practice of ESG* 3-16 (ABA 2023) (hereinafter, *Professional's Guide*).

[12] Andrew W Savitz with Karl Weber, *The Triple Bottom Line: How Today's Best-Run Companies Are Achieving Economic, Social, and Environmental Success—and How You Can Too* 5 (Jossey-Bass 2014).

[13] The Global Compact (n 1) i.

[14] Pollman (n 5) 413–17.

[15] The Global Compact (n 1) 1–2.

[16] ibid 6.

[17] ibid i.

[18] Pollman (n 5) 425.

[19] ibid 418.

[20] Max M Schanzenbach and Robert H Sitkoff, 'The Prudent Investor Rule and Market Risk: An Empirical Analysis' (2017) 14 Journal of Empirical Legal Studies 129, 130.

of the trust's beneficiaries".[21] Fiduciary duties—in the US and many other countries—led many portfolio managers and other trustees to conclude that consideration of ESG in investment decisions was legally impermissible.[22]

The law firm, Freshfields Bruckhaus Deringer, was thus commissioned to complete a report on whether consideration of ESG by trustees is consistent with their fiduciary duties. The firm conducted a detailed evaluation of trust law in nine countries, including the US. Because "the links between ESG factors and financial performance are increasingly being recognised", its report concluded, "integrating ESG considerations into an investment analysis so as to more reliably predict financial performance is clearly permissible and is arguably required in all jurisdictions".[23] The law firm's report has been enormously influential in furthering the use of ESG by institutional trustees.[24]

To implement the recommendations in *Who Cares Wins*, the UN Principles for Responsible Investment (PRI) were launched soon thereafter.[25] "The Principles were developed by investors, for investors."[26] There are six principles for investor action to which investors can voluntarily commit by publicly signing onto them. The first principle is: "We will incorporate ESG issues into investment analysis and decision-making processes."[27]

An increasingly important and visible part of ESG is represented by public corporate commitments to reduce greenhouse gas emissions. In 2017, PRI issued *A Blueprint for Responsible Investment* for the next ten years that among other things, encourages investors to "champion climate action".[28] Other entities, such as the Carbon Disclosure Project,[29] the Science Based Targets initiative,[30] the Task Force on Climate-Related Financial Disclosures,[31] and the International Standards Organization,[32] have established standards for accurate and uniform disclosure of voluntary corporate reporting of greenhouse gas reduction commitments and achievements. These and other similar initiatives could reduce corporate greenhouse gas emissions by half a billion tons of carbon dioxide equivalent per year.[33]

21 American Law Institute, *Restatement of the Law of Trusts (Third)* (2007) § 78.

22 Pollman (n 5) 418.

23 'A Legal Framework for the Integration of Environment, Social, and Governance Issues into Institutional Investment' (*UN Env't Programme Finance Initiative*) 13 (2005) < https://www.unepfi.org/wordpress/wp-content/uploads/2022/07/Freshfields-A-legal-framework-for-the-integration-of-ESG-issues-into-institutional-investment.pdf> accessed 3 April 2025.

24 Pollman (n 5) 418.

25 PRI, 'A Blueprint for Responsible Investment' (UN 2017) <https://www.unpri.org/download?ac=5330> accessed 29 March 2025 (hereinafter, PRI Blueprint).

26 PRI, 'What are the Principles for Responsible Investment?' <https://www.unpri.org/about-us/what-are-the-principles-for-responsible-investment> accessed 3 April 2025.

27 ibid.

28 PRI Blueprint (n 25) 5, 28.

29 'CDP Can Support Your Environmental Journey' (*Carbon Disclosure Project*) <https://www.cdp.net/en> accessed 29 March 2025.

30 'About Us' (*Science Based Targets Initiative*) <https://sciencebasedtargets.org/about-us> accessed 29 March 2025.

31 'Task Force on Climate-related Financial Disclosures' (*TCFD*) <https://www.fsb-tcfd.org/> accessed 29 March 2025.

32 International Standards Organization, 'Greenhouse Gases—Part 1: Specification with Guidance at the Organization Level for Quantification and Reporting of Greenhouse Gas Emissions and Removals' (2018) 14064–1:2018 <//www.iso.org/standard/66453.html> accessed 29 March 2025.

33 Michael P Vandenbergh and Jonathan M Gilligan, *Beyond Politics: The Private Governance Response to Climate Change* (CUP 2017) 180–81.

More than two decades have now passed since the term "ESG" was coined, and the analytic use of ESG has exploded. In March 2025, for example, the PRI had more than 5,000 signatories with total assets of some $128 trillion.[34] There are now "more than six hundred ESG ratings organizations and rankings worldwide", with "substantial variation among ratings".[35] ESG is driven by a wide variety of actors and stakeholders, with different but overlapping agendas. They include governments and regulatory agencies, to be sure. But most of the actors are nongovernmental, including but not limited to shareholders, boards of directors, management, employees, financial investors and lenders, customers, nongovernmental organisations, consultants, and the public.[36] Climate change and unsustainable development tend to be basic concerns of these actors. Historic corporate profitability, the unprecedented ability of corporations to outsource to suppliers in places with cheap labour and weak environmental and safety standards, and the growing salience of non-financial concerns to investors, customers, and other stakeholders are key factors driving ESG.[37] These factors "represent the most dynamic change in corporate ethos in lifetimes".[38]

Over these two decades, the historical origin and meaning of ESG have evolved into a variety of usages and understandings, including factors for investment analysis, risk management, corporate social responsibility, sustainability, and the expression of an ideological preference.[39] The latter, in particular, has sparked a political backlash against ESG.[40] The backlash, of course, is based on a failure to understand that "ESG was pitched from its beginning as aligning with financial materiality and the pursuit of long-term value maximization in capital markets".[41] But that has not stopped many states and the federal government from using the law to restrict the use of ESG. At the same time, a smaller number of state and federal legal efforts have attempted to support or clarify the use of ESG.

3. Federal Laws Relating to ESG

Federal law provides basic rules governing the US financial system that have a major effect on what state and local governments as well as private actors can do. This is exemplified by federal regulations applying federal securities law and the Employee Retirement Income Security Act (ERISA) to climate change and ESG. Although these regulations are not likely to survive in the near term, the statutes on which they are based will likely continue to have an effect on climate change disclosure and the use of ESG.

Federal securities law requires publicly traded corporations to publicly report information that is "material" to investors. According to the US Supreme Court, "[a]n omitted fact is material if there is a substantial likelihood that a reasonable shareholder would consider it important in deciding how to vote".[42] Publicly traded companies, for example, must publicly

[34] Principles for Responsible Investment, '2024 Annual Report' (2024) 17 <https://dwtyzx6upklss.cloudfront.net/Uploads/v/y/x/annualreport2024_final_98918.pdf> accessed 13 June 2025.

[35] Pollman (n 5) 437.

[36] Michael G Rowland, 'Stakeholders in the ESG Ecosystem' in *Professional's Guide* (n 11) 17–33.

[37] Andrew Waitman and Travis Miller, 'ESG and the Twenty-Second Century Corporation,' in Travis Miller and Todd Cort (eds.), *The Sustainable Corporation: A Legal and Business Centric Approach to ESG* (ABA 2023) 1, 3–4.

[38] ibid 4.

[39] Pollman (n 5) 424–33.

[40] ibid 431.

[41] ibid.

[42] TSC Industry, Inc v Northway, Inc, 426 U.S. 438, 449 (1976).

disclose "material pending legal proceedings" as well as expenditures that materially affect their financial condition.[43]

In 2021, the Securities and Exchange Commission (SEC) considered adopting regulations mandating disclosure of material ESG issues, but did not proceed with this effort.[44] The fact that the questions involved in such a rulemaking are "some of the most contested in the field of corporate and securities law", including "how to conceptualize the purpose of the corporation",[45] likely contributed to that outcome.

Instead, in March 2024, the SEC adopted a regulation to enhance and standardise climate-related disclosures for investors.[46] It applies to all companies that file reports with the SEC, including foreign private issuers. These companies must disclose all material climate-related matters, including Scope 1 greenhouse gas emissions (direct emissions from operations the company owns or controls) and Scope 2 emissions (indirect emissions "from the generation of purchased or acquired electricity, steam, heat, or cooling that is consumed by operations" the company owns or controls),[47] and their climate-related targets and goals. This information must be disclosed in the Regulation S-K[48] portion of the company's registration statement or annual report.

Challenges to the regulation were promptly filed by several organisations. In April 2024 the SEC voluntarily stayed implementation of the regulation pending resolution of these appeals.[49] In March 2025, the SEC voted to end its defence of the rule,[50] which means that decisions about the materiality of climate impacts and their disclosure will be made by private parties on a case-by-case basis.

ERISA establishes minimum standards for the operation of private sector employee benefit plans, including fiduciary responsibility rules.[51] Among other things, the act requires that ERISA plan trustees make paramount the plan's financial returns and risks to beneficiaries.[52] ERISA essentially codifies basic trust law, under which these trustees have fiduciary responsibilities for managing these funds on behalf of their beneficiaries.[53]

For years prior to 2020, the Department of Labor, which administers ERISA, recognised that investment in ESG funds could be consistent with these requirements.[54] In 2020, the

[43] George S Georgiev, 'Too Big to Disclose: Firm Size and Materiality Blindspots in Securities Regulation' (2017) 64 UCLA Law Review 602, 606–07.

[44] Gabrielle B Guliana, Note and Comment: 'The States Are the Answer to Requests for a Specific ESG Disclosure Mandate, not the SEC. . .Yet' (2023) 54 University of Toledo Law Review 263, 291–93.

[45] Amanda M Rose, 'A Response to Calls for SEC-Mandated ESG Disclosure' (2021) 98 Washington University Law Review 1821, 1821.

[46] *The Enhancement and Standardization of Climate-Related Disclosures for Investors*, 89 Fed. Reg. 21,668 (28 Mar. 2024).

[47] 'We Set the Standards to Measure and Manage Emissions' (*The Greenhouse Gas Protocol*) <https://ghgprotocol.org/> accessed 29 March 2025.

[48] 17 C.F.R. § 229. Regulation S-K can be found at 17 CFR Part 229. The March 2024 final rule added new subparts 1500–08 to Regulation S-K and new Article 14 to Regulation S-K regarding climate disclosures.

[49] *The Enhancement and Standardization of Climate-Related Disclosures for Investors; Delay of Effective Date*, 89 Fed. Reg. 25,804 (12 Apr. 2024).

[50] 'SEC Votes to End Defence of Climate Disclosure Rules' (*Securities and Exchange Commission*) <https://www.sec.gov/newsroom/press-releases/2025-58> accessed 4 April 2025.

[51] 29 U.S.C. §§ 1001–1461.

[52] ibid § 1104(a)(1).

[53] Chamber of Commerce of the US v US Dep't of Labor, 885 F.3d 360, 369 (5th Cir. 2018).

[54] *Prudence and Loyalty in Selecting Plan Investments and Exercising Shareholder Rights*, 87 Fed. Reg. 73,822, 73,822 (1 Dec. 2022) (amending 29 C.F.R.§ 2550 (2022)).

Department adopted a regulation requiring fiduciaries to make investment decisions "based solely on consideration of 'pecuniary factors,'" which was unmistakably aimed at investment in ESG funds.[55] In 2022, the Department, under a new administration, amended the rule by, among other things, eliminating the "pecuniary factors" requirement, permitting trustees to consider ESG factors as long as their decisions are consistent with their fiduciary duties. It determined that the 2020 rule was "inappropriate in light of research and investment practices suggesting that climate change and other ESG factors are material economic considerations".[56] In 2025, a federal district court upheld the 2022 regulation, reasoning that while the rule allows *consideration* of ESG factors, it nonetheless requires trustees to *act* for the sole benefit of beneficiaries.[57] In early 2025, with the second Trump administration, this regulation is widely recognised to be at risk of repeal or modification. Still, federal laws such as ERISA impose limits on what states can do with regard to ESG.[58]

4. State Laws Relating to ESG

Public pension and retirement funds operated by state and local governments are at the centre of state ESG legislation. While they are not subject to ERISA, their managers are nonetheless subject to the fiduciary duties of trustees, including prudence and loyalty. The existence and general meaning of these duties are not in dispute. Nor is their significance. In these funds, nearly two-third (63%) of the revenues are based on investment returns, with employer and employee contributions accounting for the rest.[59] But there is controversy over what they mean for the use of ESG in making investment decisions.

Most if not all state anti-ESG laws have been adopted since 2021.[60] About two-thirds of the ESG-related statutes enacted in 2024 were opposed to ESG, and about one-third were supportive. Over 90% of these laws were adopted in states where the same party controlled both houses of the legislature as well as the governor's office. For these laws, Republican states adopted the anti-ESG laws, and Democratic states adopted the pro-ESG laws.[61] This section summarises measures enacted as of 13 December 2024. It also includes selected decisions that

55 ibid 73,823.

56 ibid 73,826–27.

57 Utah v Micone, 766 F.Supp.3d 669 (N.D. Tex. 2025).

58 Securities Industry and Financial Markets Association v Ashcroft, 745 F.Supp.3d 783, 793–98 (W.D. Mo. 2024) (hereinafter, Ashcroft) (holding certain Missouri anti-ESG regulations pre-empted by federal law).

59 Office of the State Treasurer, *Material Factors in Public Finance and Investments: A Review of Laws in Other Jurisdictions and Their Impacts* (State of Washington 2024) 26 <https://app.leg.wa.gov/ReportsToTheLegislature/Home/GetPDF?fileName=2024_OST%20Report%20to%20the%20Legislature_Material%20Factors%20in%20Public%20Finance%20and%20Investments_afa807f7-338b-411c-825e-991395378f23.pdf> accessed 13 June 2025.

60 At least two online tracking platforms exist for ESG legislation. One is 'Reform Proposals Related to Environmental, Social, and Corporate Governance (ESG)' (*Ballotpedia*) <https://ballotpedia.org/Reform_proposals_related_to_environmental,_social,_and_corporate_governance_(ESG)#> accessed 9 March 2025. The other is 'Live Anti-ESG State Action Tracker' (*Pleiades Strategy*) <https://www.pleiadesstrategy.com/pleiades-anti-esg-bill-tracker-state-legislation-attacks-on-responsible-investing> accessed 9 March 2025. Unlike Ballotpedia, the latter does not cover pro-ESG proposals and laws.

61 James McAllister, 'Republican States Pass 17 Anti-ESG Laws, Democratic States Pass 8 Pro-ESG in 2024' (*Ballotpedia* 21 October 2024) <https://news.ballotpedia.org/2024/10/21/republican-states-pass-17-anti-esg-laws-democratic-states-pass-8-pro-esg-in-2024/> accessed 14 March 2025.

individual pension funds and other trustees have made regarding particular investments related to ESG.

4.1 Statutes Opposing ESG

Statutes opposing ESG can be grouped in four broad categories: statutes directed against consideration of ESG in managing state funds, statutes imposing fiduciary responsibilities on proxy advisors to public retirement systems and those voting on behalf of these systems, statutes directed against ESG-related boycotts, and statutes prohibiting the state use of ESG screens. To a large degree, these laws simply restate or emphasise traditional fiduciary duties, and do not significantly change the legal landscape. They do, however, create ambiguities in that landscape and differences in that landscape from state to state that require additional time and resources for corporations, investors, and lawyers to navigate. They also have reduced the willingness of investment funds to engage in certain public ESG activities.

4.1.1 Statutes Directed Against Consideration of ESG in Managing State Funds

At least thirteen states have adopted statutory provisions that prohibit public investment funds from considering ESG and other "nonpecuniary" factors in making their investment decisions.[62] South Carolina's law provides that the state's Retirement System Investment Commission "only shall consider pecuniary factors in making an investment decision or when allocating capital to an investment strategy".[63] Many of these laws define nonpecuniary factors to include "the furtherance of any social, political, or ideological interests".[64] Others are more nuanced, expressly recognising that ESG investments may have pecuniary value.[65]

Public reporting of adherence to fiduciary duties is a common feature in many of these statutes. New Hampshire requires a quarterly report to the legislature "regarding compliance with the duty to make all investment decisions solely in the interest of the participants and beneficiaries of the state retirement system".[66]

The cartoon version of ESG—that it is merely ideological—infuses many of these statutes. According to a survey by PRI, many political people supporting these measures "tended to repeat anti-ESG talking points but did not demonstrate an understanding of the investment

[62] See nn 63–65.

[63] S.C. Code Ann. § 9-16-50(A)(5) (2024). See also Tenn. Code Ann. § 9-4-1402 (2023) (requiring state department of treasury to 'invest, reinvest, manage, and select investment options for program assets for financial reasons for the exclusive benefit of the beneficiaries of the programs while maximizing longterm shareholder value'); Utah Code Ann. § 51-7-14(2)(b) (2023) (similar language).

[64] Fla. Stat. § 17.57 (2023). Other statutes are similar. Ark. Code Ann. § 24-2-803 (2023); Ga. Code Ann. § 47-20-88(b)(4) (2024); Idaho Code § 67-2345(1) (2022); Ind. Code § 5-10.2-14-1 to -13 (2023); Ky. Rev. Stat. Ann. § 94.030 (2023); N.C. Gen. Stat. § 147-69.7(5); N.D. Cent. Code §§ 21-10-08.1 and 26.1-04-03(7) (2023); S.C. Code Ann. § 9-16-10 (10) (2023); Tenn. Code Ann. §§ 9-4-1401 and 9-4-1402 (2023); Utah Code Ann. § 49-11-203(1)(q) (2023). But see *Ashcroft* (n 58) 800–02 (holding an anti-ESG Missouri regulation defining 'nonfinancial objective' to mean seeking an 'effect other than the maximization of financial return to the customer' to be void for vagueness because, among other reasons, the term could require high-return, high-risk investments that would be imprudent).

[65] Mont. Code Ann. § 17-6-232 (2023). See also Ky. Rev. Stat. Ann. § 21.450(2)(a) (2023); N.D. Cent. Code § 26.1-04-03(7) (2023); Tenn. Code Ann. § 9-4-1401(2)(C) (2023); W.V. Code § 12-6-11a(5) (2024).

[66] N.H. Rev. Stat. Ann. § 100-A:15, VIII(b) (2023). See also Fla. Stat. § 112.662(4) (2023).

process nor the practical implications of the demands they were making on managers".[67] Still, the guiding rule reflected in all of these statutes is adherence to fiduciary duties of prudence and loyalty to the beneficiaries. In that sense, these statutes do nothing more than restate in different words that trust fund managers must adhere to their pre-existing fiduciary duties. But these statutes also create ambiguities that require investment managers to spend more time explaining and documenting decisions.

The South Carolina statute, for example, defines "pecuniary factor" as "any factor or consideration that is collateral to or not reasonably likely to effect or impact the financial risk and return of the investment".[68] Because ESG factors are reasonably likely to affect financial risk and return on investment, they are pecuniary factors rather than nonpecuniary factors. So far, so good. But the statute goes on to say that nonpecuniary factors include "promotion, furtherance, or achievement of environmental, social, or political goals, objectives, or outcomes".[69] Many ESG investments also have such goals, but they provide financial returns as well. Financial returns of ESG investments are often comparable to those of non-ESG investments, but the data also indicates that returns depend on the particular mix of ESG investments and the rating system being employed.[70] The statute's apparent blanket characterisation of all ESG as nonpecuniary creates an interpretative challenge that requires time and effort to address.

4.1.2 Statutes Imposing Fiduciary Responsibilities on Proxy Advisors to Public Retirement Systems and Those Voting on Behalf of These Systems

Many states expressly impose fiduciary responsibilities on those voting on behalf of retirement funds, including proxies representing the fund. Thus, for example, under Arkansas law, shareholders and proxies must vote "solely in the pecuniary interest of the pension benefit plan participants". The statute adds: "Voting to further a nonpecuniary, environmental, social, political, ideological, or other benefit or goal is prohibited".[71]

In addition, some states have laws that require proxy advisors, investment managers, and contractors to the retirement fund to act as fiduciaries on behalf of the retirement fund.[72] That means, using Kansas as an example, that they must "discharge [their] duties solely in the financial interest of the participants and beneficiaries".[73] "Financial" is defined to mean "having been prudently determined by a fiduciary to have a material effect on the financial risk or the financial return of an investment", and excludes "any action taken or factor considered by a fiduciary with any purpose whatsoever to further social, political or ideological interests".[74]

States with such laws may also expressly prohibit the fund board from following the recommendations of a proxy advisor or other service provider if the service provider does not

[67] PRI, *Policy Briefing: Signatory Responses to State Anti-ESG Laws* (2024) <https://public.unpri.org/policy-reports/policy-briefing-signatory-responses-to-state-anti-esg-laws/12491.article> accessed 13 April 2026 (hereinafter, PRI Policy Briefing).

[68] S.C. Code Ann. § 9-16-10 (10).

[69] ibid.

[70] Pollman (n 5) 436–37.

[71] Ark. Code Ann. § 24-2-805(a) (2023). Other similar laws are Fla. Stat. § 112.662(3)((2023); Idaho Code § 67-2345(3) (2022); Ky. Rev. Stat. Ann. § 21.450(2)(b) (2023); Mont. Code Ann. § 17-6-233 (2023); W. Va. Code § 12-6-11a(d) (2023).

[72] Kan. Stat. Ann. § 75-42a03 (2024); Other similar laws are: Ark. Code Ann. § 24-2-805(b)(2) (2023); Fla. Stat. § 215.4755 (2023); Ind. Code § 5-10.2-14-10 (2023); Ky. Rev. Stat. Ann. § 21.450(2)(b) (2023); N.D. Cent. Code §21-10-08.1 (2023); S.C. Code Ann. § 9-16-30(G)(1)-(2) (2024); Tenn. Code Ann. §§ 9-4-1401(2) and 9-4-1403(a) and (b) (2023); W. Va. Code Ann. § 12-6-11a(c)-(e) (2023).

[73] Kan. Stat. Ann. § 75-42a03 (2023).

[74] ibid § 75-42a01(a)(7)(A) and (B).

commit to following proxy guidelines "that are consistent with the board's obligation to act based solely on pecuniary factors unless no economically practicable alternative is available".[75]

These laws contain several kinds of provisions to help ensure compliance. The periodic public reporting duties required for adherence to fiduciary duties by pension funds may also be applicable for these statutory provisions.[76] Several states require publication of all proxy votes on a publicly available webpage, including "a vote caption, the plan's vote, the recommendation of company management and, if applicable, the proxy advisor's recommendation".[77]

These statutes, too, are centred on adherence to the fiduciary duties of the trust fund managers. To that extent, they require nothing more than what is already required. For example, one can argue that the Arkansas statute prohibiting "[v]oting to further a nonpecuniary, environmental, social, political, ideological, or other benefit or goal"[78] simply recognises the pre-existing duties of prudence and loyalty to the beneficiaries. Still, like the statutes described above, characterising ESG in ideological terms creates some ambiguity about how to address ESG when it does provide comparable financial returns.[79]

Anti-ESG laws, and particularly the proxy aspects of these laws, may nonetheless have some chilling effect on voting for pro-ESG shareholder resolutions, particularly by large asset managers. BlackRock, Vanguard, Fidelity, and State Street are the largest such managers, holding a total of $29 trillion in public and private assets.[80] Their support for pro-ESG proxy resolutions significantly declined between 2021 and 2023, the same period when many anti-ESG laws were introduced and passed.[81] Significantly, many of these resolutions would have passed had they been supported by these actors.[82]

4.1.3 Statutes Directed Against ESG-Related Boycotts

Many investment firms further ESG by employing screens in selecting investments, boycotting or refusing to purchase securities from fossil fuel, tobacco, or firearms companies.[83] Several states have responded by adopting laws that generally prohibit public financial institutions from using the services of companies engaging in such boycotts. The fossil fuel boycott laws, of course, are of greatest relevance to this chapter. At least three states prohibit financial institutions from using the services of companies that boycott the fossil fuel industry. A Kentucky statute, for example, requires the state treasurer to divest from publicly traded financial services, banking, or investment companies that engage in an "energy company boycott".[84]

[75] Mont. Code Ann. § 17-6-233(3) (2023). For similar provisions, see Ark. Code Ann. §§ 24-2-802(1) (2023); Kan. Stat. ann. § 75-42a03(h) (2023); Ky. Rev. Stat. Ann. § 21.540(9)(b) (2023); N.D. Cent. Code § 54-06-39(2) (2023); W Va. Code § 12-6-11a(d)(1) (2023).

[76] Fla. Stat. § 112.662(4) (2023).

[77] Ark. Code Ann. § 24-2-805(e) (2023). For similar laws, see Kan. Stat. Ann. § 74-4921 (2023); Ind. Code § 5-10.2-14(11) (2023); S.C. Code Ann. § 9-16-320 (2024); W. Va. Code Ann. § 12-6-11a(f) (2023). Utah simply requires that proxy voting records be made available to the state treasurer upon request. Utah Code Ann. § 51-7-14(4)(a) (2023).

[78] Ark. Code Ann. § 24-2-805(a) (2023). Other similar laws are Fla. Stat. § 112.662(3)(2023); Idaho Code § 67-2345(3) (2022); Ky. Rev. Stat. Ann. Ann. § 21.450(2)(b) (2023); Mont. Code Ann. § 17-6-233(1) and (2) (2023); W.Va. Code § 12-6-11a(d) (2023).

[79] Similarly, the requirement that proxy advisors, investment managers, and contractors to retirement funds act as fiduciaries for the fund generally restates existing law.

[80] Office of the State Treasurer (n 59) 35.

[81] ibid 35–36.

[82] ibid 36.

[83] US Sustainable Investing Trends 2024/2025: Executive Summary (n 3).

[84] Ky. Rev. Stat. Ann. § 41.474(4) (2022).

Oklahoma and Texas have similar laws.[85] According to the Kentucky act, an "energy company boycott" includes a refusal to do business with a fossil fuel-based energy company that does not commit to environmental standards beyond state and federal law.[86]

The legislature's rationale is set out in findings that banks, institutional investors, large investment firms, and corporations are denying financing to fossil fuel companies in order to reduce their greenhouse gas emissions.[87] The legislature also stated: "Energy-producing states, when financially prudent, should avoid doing business with companies that are attacking the industries that substantially contribute to their state budgets."[88] The act requires the state treasurer to publish on its official web site a list of all companies the treasurer believes "have engaged in energy company boycotts", provide these companies an opportunity to show that they are not engaging in such boycotts and warning them of divestment if they do not cease doing so, and divesting from these companies if they do not comply.[89]

At least two states prohibit general public contracting with companies that engage in economic boycotts of fossil fuel companies "without an ordinary business purpose".[90] Utah's anti-boycott statute prohibits companies from coordinating or conspiring to boycott other companies on ESG grounds "with the specific intent of destroying a boycotted company and without an ordinary business purpose".[91]

Like the state anti-ESG laws described in previous sections, these statutes tend to be bounded by the law of fiduciary duties. The Kentucky act, for example, does not apply if the state "determines that the requirements would be inconsistent with its fiduciary responsibility with respect to the investment of entity assets or other duties imposed by law relating to the investment of entity assets".[92] The Utah statute is limited to actions that are taken "with the specific intent of destroying a boycotted company and without an ordinary business purpose", which provides plenty of leeway for actions that are taken to reduce risks, lower costs, or have other financial motives.

Still, these laws may compromise the fiduciary responsibility of retirement fund trustees. In 2024, an Oklahoma state district court held the state's Energy Discrimination Elimination Act to violate the state constitution's requirement that retirement funds held in trust be administered "for the exclusive purpose" of benefiting the retirement system, "and "not be encumbered for or diverted to any other purposes".[93] Under the statute, the state treasurer put six companies on its restricted financial companies list, and divested them, at a total cost to the system of $9.7 million.[94] The state treasurer stated that it was acting to counter "the political agenda"

[85] Okla. Stat. tit. 74, §§ 12001–12006 (2022); Tex. Gov't Code Ann. Ann. §§ 809.001(1), 2276.001-2276.002 (2021). On 3 February 2026, a federal district court held the Texas statute unconstitutional. The court held the act violates the Free Speech Clause of the First Amendment because it is facially overbroad, and violates the Due Process Claue of the Fourteenth Amendment 'it does provide persons of ordinary intelligence a reasonable opportunity to know what conduct is prohibited and does not provide explicit standards for determining compliance with the law'. American Sustainable Business Council v. Hegar, 2026 WL 300001, at *5, *6 (W.D. Tex. 4 February 2026).

[86] Ky. Rev. Stat. Ann. § 41.472(1)(c) (2022).

[87] ibid § 41.470(3)-(7).

[88] ibid § 41.470(8).

[89] ibid § 41.474(1)-(4).

[90] Ala. Code Ann. § 41-16-160 (2023). See also Idaho Code §§ 26-2155 and 67-2739 (2023) (similar statute applicable to banks and credit unions holding state funds).

[91] Utah Code Ann. § 13-63-201(1) (2023).

[92] Ky. Rev. Stat. Stat. § 41.472(3) (2022).

[93] Keenan v Russ, No. 2023-3021, Okla. Dist. Ct. (May 7, 2024) (temporary injunction); (Sept. 19, 2024) (permanent injunction) (both applying Okla. Const. art. 23, § 12).

[94] Keenan v Russ, No. 2023-3021, Okla. Dist. Ct. (May 7, 2024), paras 11 and 12.

of certain financial companies and "to assist the economic status of the oil and gas sector". All of this, the court held, violated the state constitution's directive that the fund be administered for the exclusive benefit of the beneficiaries.[95] The case is on appeal to the Oklahoma supreme court. Significantly, there is evidence that such laws in other states "can cost retirees and public institutional investors millions or billions of dollars".[96]

4.1.4 Statutes Prohibiting the State Use of ESG Screens

Other states prohibit the use of ESG screens in public contracting. Idaho law prohibits public entities from awarding a variety of construction and procurement contracts based on "environmental, social, and governance standards". The act defines these as "procurement standards that screen or score bids, in whole or in part, on subjective ethical or sustainability criteria unrelated to the specifications in a solicitation or the qualifications of a bidder".[97]

Florida prohibits any public body authorised by state law from issuing any ESG bonds, including general obligation bonds. ESG bonds are "any bonds that have been designated or labeled as bonds that will be used to finance a project with an ESG purpose", whether designated as such by the issuer or designated as such by a third-party verifier.[98] Florida also prohibits financial institutions that hold public funds from denying or cancelling their services to any person based on a list of activities that includes the person's engagement in the fossil fuel industry or the person's failure to comply with environmental or social governance standards not contained in applicable law.[99]

Texas prohibits insurers from using "an environmental, social, or governance model, score, factor, or standard to charge a rate different than the rate charged to another business or risk in the same class for essentially the same hazard".[100] But the act exempts an insurer "if the insurer's actions are based on an ordinary insurance business purpose, including the use of sound actuarial principles, or financial solvency considerations reasonably related to loss experience for the different types of risks and coverages made available by a particular insurer".[101]

The Texas statute may be the most obvious example of a statute where the "ordinary business purpose" exception swallows the rule, at least for climate change. The growing losses to insurers caused by climate change are well known, as are the increasing number of insurance policy cancellations for financial reasons in areas that are at serious risk of wildfires, hurricane damage, and other climate-related losses.[102]

State laws that restrict contracting also limit options for state and local government agencies in ways that may be adverse to them financially. State prohibitions against general contracting with companies that engage in boycotts have also reduced competition in the municipal bond

95 ibid paras 23 and 24.

96 Office of the State Treasurer (n 59) 26–28.

97 2023 Idaho Sess. Laws ch. 129 (compiled in various sections of Idaho Code). Similar laws are Fla. Stat. §§ 287.05701 and 1010.04 (2023); Kan. Stat. Ann. § 40-2c01 (2023); N.C. Gen. Stat. § 143–162.6 (c) (2023).

98 Fla. Stat. § 215.681(2023).

99 ibid § 280.025 (2023). Tennessee has a similar law, except that it applies only to financial institutions with more than $100 billion in assets. Tenn. Code Ann. § 45-1-128 (2024).

100 Tex. Ins. Code Ann. § 565.005 (2023). For similar laws, see N.D. Cent. Code § 26.1-04-03(7) (2023); Tenn. Code Ann. § 56-8-114 (2024).

101 Tex. Ins. Code Ann. § 565.006 (2023).

102 Christopher Flavelle, 'Insurers Are Deserting Homeowners as Climate Shocks Worsen' (*The New York Times* 18 December 2024) <https://www.nytimes.com/interactive/2024/12/18/climate/insurance-non-renewal-climate-crisis.html> accessed 29 June 2025.

market, increasing the costs of borrowing for municipalities in those states.[103] In addition, a federal district court has held that a Missouri law restricting contracts violated, among other things, the constitutional right to freedom of speech.[104]

The PRI survey on the effect of all state anti-ESG laws captures three key points that are relevant here. First, the investors who were surveyed said these laws were "vague and open to interpretation". They also described some as "counterfactual or contradictory, as generally accepted investment practice necessarily includes integration of E, S and G factors where investors believe they can improve risk-adjusted returns".[105] Second, they said that these laws had led many to limit the public presentation of their responsible investment practices in "website materials, proxy voting policies, and ESG integration procedures".[106] Finally, and most significantly, none "reported changing their fundamental investment practices, since their practices already are grounded in fiduciary duty, and their use of ESG information or engagement on ESG issues reflects efforts to fulfill that duty".[107]

BlackRock's experience with anti-ESG laws illustrates the latter two points. Between 2022 and 2024, nine states with these laws withdrew a total of almost $13.3 billion from BlackRock, the world's largest investment company.[108] Florida banned investment in BlackRock's sustainable investment funds but not other BlackRock funds, and BlackRock has nonetheless significantly increased its total ESG assets under management during the same period. Still, BlackRock has become less publicly visible as an advocate for ESG.[109]

4.2 Statutes Supporting ESG

A smaller number of states have adopted statutes supporting ESG. These statutes fall into two categories: statutes requiring consideration of ESG in managing state funds, and statutes directing divestment of fossil fuel assets.[110] Both are direct counterparts to many anti-ESG laws in that they govern state pension funds. These laws likely increase the attention of fund trustees to climate change and sustainability and reduce risks to fund assets from climate change. But they, too, are bounded by the fiduciary duties of trustees.

4.2.1 Statutes Requiring Consideration of ESG in Managing State Funds

At least three states have adopted legislation requiring consideration of ESG in management of state funds. Illinois requires the use of sustainability factors. Colorado and Maryland require consideration of climate change in investment decisions.

[103] Office of the State Treasurer (n 59) 28–29. See also Daniel G Garrett and Ivan T Ivanov, 'Gas, Guns, and Governments: Financial Costs of Anti-ESG Policies' [2023] Federal Reserve Bank of Chicago Working Papers < https://www.chicagofed.org/publications/working-papers/2023/2023-07> accessed 14 June 2025.

[104] *Ashcroft* (n 58) 798–800. See also Kali Venable, 'From Anti-BDS to Anti-ESG: The Next Generation of Boycotting the "Boycott" Is Only Slightly Less Problematic' (2024) 81 Washington & Lee Law Review 1687 (explaining that anti-ESG laws prohibiting or penalising clearly expressive speech may violate First Amendment).

[105] PRI Policy Briefing (n 67) 3.

[106] ibid.

[107] ibid 4.

[108] Office of the State Treasurer (n 59) 38.

[109] ibid 38–39.

[110] Other candidates for pro-ESG laws include California's greenhouse gas disclosure laws. For discussion of California and other jurisdictions' climate-related disclosure regimes, see Virginia Harper Ho, Chapter 23 of this handbook.

The Illinois Sustainable Investing Act requires each public agency to

> prudently integrate sustainability factors into its investment decision-making, investment analysis, portfolio construction, due diligence, and investment ownership in order to maximize anticipated financial returns, minimize projected risk, and more effectively execute its fiduciary duty.[111]

Sustainability factors include corporate governance and leadership, environmental, social capital, human capital, and business model and innovation.[112] The act also requires those seeking "selection as a fiduciary" for a public agency to disclose, prior to the award of a contract, their own process of integrating sustainability factors into investment and related decision-making.[113]

Colorado requires its Public Employees Retirement Association to submit to the legislature every five years a report describing, among other things, "the current or anticipated future risks that climate change poses" to its investment portfolio, "the impact climate has on the association's investment strategies, and any strategy changes that the association has implemented in response to such impact".[114] Similarly, Maryland requires the State Retirement and Pension System to "consider the potential system risks of the impact of climate change on" system assets, and to establish a process for regular assessment of climate risks to system assets.[115]

The Maryland statute also requires the system's chief investment officer to "identify environmentally sustainable investment opportunities to support a low-carbon economy", to "develop transition assessments relating to investments" in "high impact sectors responsible for greenhouse gas emissions", and to "evaluate whether internal and external investment managers are taking steps to transition to a more sustainable business model aligned with a low-carbon economy".[116]

These statutes certainly heighten attention to sustainability and climate change for fund managers and their contractors. They are nonetheless bounded by the trustees' traditional fiduciary duties. The Maryland act, for example, makes clear that it does not require any action "unless the board of trustees or other fiduciary determines, in good faith, that the action is consistent with" the board's fiduciary responsibilities.[117]

4.2.2 Statutes Directing Divestment of Fossil Fuel Assets

At least three states—California, Maine, and Oregon—have directed their state public employees retirement system to divest of certain large fossil fuel assets.[118] The California and Oregon statutes are directed at thermal coal—which California defines as "coal used to generate electricity".[119] The California law, adopted in 2015, prohibits the boards of the Public Employees' Retirement System (CalPERS) and the State Teacher's Retirement System from making or renewing investments in "thermal coal companies", which are publicly traded companies that generate 50% or more of their revenue from the mining of thermal coal.[120] It also

[111] 30 Ill. Comp. Stat. ch. 238, § 20(a) (2019).
[112] ibid § 20(b) (2019).
[113] ibid § 20(e) (2019).
[114] Colo. Rev. Stat. § 24-51-220(2)(b) (2023).
[115] Md. Code Ann. §§ 21-116.1(a) and (b)(3) (2022).
[116] ibid §§ 21-116.1(b)(1) and (d) (2022).
[117] ibid § 21-116.1(h) (2022).
[118] Cal. Gov't Code § 7513.75 (2015); Me. Rev. Stat. tit. 5, § 1957 (2024); Or. Rev. Stat. ch. 79 (2024).
[119] Cal. Gov't Code § 7513.75(b)(5) (2015).
[120] ibid §§ 7513.75(b)(6) and (c) (2015).

required liquidation of existing investments in thermal coal companies by July 1, 2017 unless the boards determined, after constructive engagement with each company, that it was "transitioning their business model to adopt to clean energy generation".[121] The Oregon statute, adopted in 2024, requires that the state public employees retirement fund, "try to ensure that moneys in subject investment funds are not invested in any thermal coal company, or any fund containing a thermal coal company".[122]

The Maine statute, signed into law in 2021, is directed more broadly at fossil fuel companies, which it defines to include "the 200 publicly traded companies with the largest fossil fuel reserves in the world", "the 30 largest public company owners in the world of coal-fired power plants", and companies whose "core business" is "the exploration, extraction, refining, processing or distribution of fossil fuels".[123] It prohibits new investment in fossil fuel companies, and requires the liquidation of fossil fuel company assets in state pension or annuity systems by January 1, 2026.[124]

The ability of these laws to achieve divestment, however, is explicitly constrained in all three statutes by the fiduciary duties of trustees.[125] This constraint has limited, but not prevented, movement towards divestment.

After the 2017 divestment deadline, CalPERS reported that it had divested from fourteen thermal coal companies but had not divested from three others, explaining that these three "had indicated plans to transition their business models to adapt to clean energy generation".[126] In 2022, a CalPERS consultant estimated the cumulative positive impact to the fund from thermal coal divestments to be $598 million.[127] The boards of the two systems disagree with anti-fossil-fuel advocacy groups about costs and benefits to the systems of divesting the remaining thermal coal assets, what fiduciary duty requires, and the value of continuing engagement with these companies on clean energy.[128] Still, in 2023, CalPERS announced a "sustainable investing strategy to accelerate moving the fund's portfolio toward net zero, where carbon emissions from investments are evenly balanced with carbon reductions".[129]

In 2024, Oregon's Treasury Department issued a plan containing an aspirational goal of a 60% reduction (from 2022 levels) in greenhouse gas emissions intensity from the retirement fund by 2035.[130] The plan explains the fund's fiduciary duty to seek opportunities and minimise

[121] ibid §§ 7513.75(d) and 7513.75(e)(2) (2015).

[122] Or. Rev. Stat. ch. 79 § 2(1) (2024).

[123] Me. Rev. Stat. tit. 5, § 1957.1(C) (2021).

[124] ibid §§ 1957.2 and 1957.3 (2021).

[125] Cal. Gov't Code § 7513.75(f) (2015); Me. Rev. Stat. tit. 5, § 1957.1(C) (2021); Or. Rev. Stat. ch. 79, § (2) (2024).

[126] California Public Employees' Retirement System, 'Public Divestiture of Thermal Coal Companies Act: Report to the California Legislature and Governor' 3 [July 14, 2017] <https://www.calpers.ca.gov/sites/default/files/spf/docs/forms-publications/public-divestiture-coal-companies-act-2017.pdf#> accessed 7 June 2025.

[127] Letter from Steven J Foresti, Wilshire Advisors, to David Miller, CalPERS (13 Oct. 2022) <https://www.calpers.ca.gov/documents/202211-invest-item06b-01-a/download> accessed 9 June 2025.

[128] 'CalSTRS Exaggerates Costs of Divestment' (*Owen Doyle, Lanie Goldberg, & Clair Brown, Fossil Free California* 3 May 2022) <https://fossilfreeca.org/calstrs-exaggerates-costs-of-divestment/> accessed 9 June 2025.

[129] 'CalPERS Announces $100 Billion Net Zero Pledge and New Climate Accountability Measures' (*CalPERS* 13 Nov. 2023) <https://www.calpers.ca.gov/newsroom/calpers-news/2023/calpers-announces-100-billion-net-zero-pledge-and-new-climate-accountability-measures#:~:text=CalPERS%20Announces%20$100%20Billion%20Net,New%20Climate%20Accountability%20Measures%20%7C%20CalPERS> accessed 9 June 2025.

[130] Oregon State Treasury, 'A Pathway To Net Zero: Positioning The Oregon Public Employees Retirement Fund For A Net Zero Carbon Future,' 3, 21 [2024] <https://www.oregon.gov/treasury/

risks from climate change, and requires "credible transition plans" from thermal coal companies.[131] In 2025, the Maine Public Employees Retirement System projected that its exposure to (investment in) fossil fuel will decline from 8.1% in 2020 to 3.9% by 2028. But it added that "further active divestment from fossil fuels" would "conflict with both the Trustees' duty of loyalty and its duty of prudence to our members".[132]

5. Implications

These laws have important implications for the role of private actors, particularly lawyers, but not necessarily for overall greenhouse gas emissions or companies affected by more ambitious laws in other countries.

5.1 Implications for Role of Private Actors, Including Lawyers

ESG is a growing global phenomenon driven by a variety of private actors. Lawyers, in particular, have played an important role in enabling and encouraging ESG. These laws heighten their role in navigating the ESG landscape. They also make clearer the need for lawyers to be climate competent and sustainability competent.[133]

While the private drivers for ESG are well known, the role of lawyers in facilitating and enabling ESG deserves greater attention. After all, it was the work of a private law firm, Freshfields Bruckhaus Deringer, that paved the way for ESG by concluding that traditional fiduciary duties allow and arguably require consideration and use of nonfinancial factors in financial decision-making. And in the less visible but important day-to-day decision-making related to ESG, lawyers also play a key role. If ESG represents a rethinking of the purpose or ethos of corporations, then the underlying challenges of climate change and sustainability that drive much of ESG are also forcing a rethinking of the role of lawyers.

ESG is a growing part of law practice.[134] An increasing number of books and other publications provide advice and guidance for lawyers on how to handle a wide variety of ESG issues, including goal setting, due diligence, public disclosure, and marketing.[135] Because the ESG landscape is dynamic and constantly evolving, it is also necessary for lawyers to be able to monitor new developments and advise clients on them. Among these developments, the various state ESG laws, both opposing and supportive, increase the number and complexity of issues that require legal assistance. This is particularly true for US and multinational corporations that must address the particularities of each state's laws.

Documents/Site-Documentation/Landing-Page-Documents/Sustainable-Investing/OST-Net-Zero-Plan.pdf> accessed 9 June 2025.

131 ibid 24–25.

132 Maine Public Employees Retirement System, 'Divestment Report: Public Law 2021, c. 231' 4 [2025] <https://www.mainepers.org/wp-content/uploads/pdfs/Reports/2025/2025-Divestment-Report-FINAL.pdf> accessed 9 June 2025.

133 See Camila Bustos, Chapter 43 of this handbook.

134 'Fast Rising Demand for ESG Expertise' (*Wolters Kluwer*, 24 October 2024) < https://www.wolterskluwer.com/en/expert-insights/rising-demand-for-esg-expertise-in-legal-industry#> accessed 7 April 2025. See also Camila Bustos, Chapter 43 of this handbook.

135 See, e.g., Katayun I Jafari and Stephen A Pike (eds), *ESG in the Boardroom: A Guidebook for Directors* (ABA 2022).

These laws also illustrate the growing need for lawyers to be climate competent and sustainability competent. A lawyer's duty to provide competent representation to clients is enshrined in the first rule of the American Bar Association (ABA) Model Rules of Professional Conduct.[136] Under the rule, "[c]ompetent representation requires the knowledge, skill, thoroughness and preparation reasonably necessary for the services".[137] As the effects of climate change mount and spread to nearly every sector of the economy, climate-competent lawyering is increasingly necessary in the practice of law.[138] As this chapter makes clear, climate change is now deeply embedded in business and corporate law, as well as insurance law and many other fields of law. Thus, in 2019, the ABA's House of Delegates—its chief policymaking body—adopted a resolution urging lawyers "to advise their clients of the risks and opportunities that climate change provides".[139] This, of course, applies to advising clients on ESG, including state laws related to ESG.

Climate competence entails more than knowledge of relevant laws and their effect on clients; it requires lawyers to understand the basic science of how climate change is transforming the physical world. In ESG and other climate-related work, for example, lawyers need to be able to explain not only liability risks but also physical risks and transition risks (business and other risks arising from the transition to a low-carbon economy).[140]

Because measures to reduce greenhouse gas emissions and adapt to climate change invariably have economic, social, and even peace and security dimensions, lawyers must also be sustainability-competent.[141] Sustainable development, like climate change, affects nearly every area of law practice, including healthcare and environmental law.[142] In addition, ESG issues are almost always sustainable development issues. Thus, in 2024, the ABA House of Delegates adopted a resolution that is similar in some ways to the climate change resolution; it urges lawyers "to learn about sustainable development, and to counsel their clients on related risks and opportunities".[143]

To be sure, there is now in the US significant political pushback against ESG at the federal and state levels. But this pushback increases the need for lawyers to be climate competent and sustainability competent. The real-world trends that fuel ESG—deteriorating environmental and social conditions—are not going to disappear because some people look the other way. In addition, while the US is an important country, it is only one of many, and it must compete in an international market where, for example, prices for renewable electricity and battery storage are plummeting. The need for lawyers to be climate competent and sustainability competent is also important in countries with less developed public laws, where creative use of private law may be needed to fill gaps.

136 ABA, Model Rules of Professional Conduct, r 1.1 ('A lawyer shall provide competent representation to a client').

137 ibid.

138 Irma S Russell, John C Dernbach, and Matthew Bogoshian 'The Lawyer's Duty of Competence in a Climate-Imperiled World' (2023) 92 UMKC Law Review 859, 859.

139 ABA House of Delegates, 'Resolution 111' (2019) <https://www.americanbar.org/content/dam/aba/directories/policy/annual-2019/111-annual-2019.pdf> accessed 14 June 2025.

140 Jonathan S Martel and Sandra Rizzo, 'Key Principles Related to Climate Risk,' in *Professional's Guide* (n 11) 87, 87–91.

141 Amy L Edwards and John C Dernbach, 'Sustainability-Competent Lawyering in the International Context' (2025) 93 UMKC Law Review 857, 857.

142 John C Dernbach, 'Sustainable Development in Law Practice: A Lens for Addressing All Legal Problems' (2017) 95 Denver Law Review 123, 123.

143 ABA House of Delegates, 'Resolution 513' (2024) <https://www.americanbar.org/content/dam/aba/directories/policy/annual-2024/513-annual-2024.pdf> accessed 14 June 2025.

5.2 Implications for Climate Change

Increasingly ambitious corporate commitments to reduce greenhouse gas emissions are an integral part of ESG. State anti-ESG laws may have some dampening effect on these commitments and how publicly they are made but are highly unlikely to change the overall trajectory of these commitments. Similarly, pro-ESG laws may encourage ESG investments, but are not likely to significantly affect the overall trajectory of ESG investment.

According to the 2025 PricewaterhouseCoopers decarbonisation report, more than 4,000 of nearly 7,000 companies "indicated climate commitments", nine times the number that indicated such commitments five years earlier.[144] More than a third of these companies have increased their greenhouse gas reduction goals, while only 16% have decreased them.[145] The report explained:

> These findings may be surprising, given the headlines that amplify news of companies retreating on their climate commitments. But we are entering an era of quiet progress, where companies avoid publicizing climate pledges that can open them up to unwanted scrutiny and instead focus on making progress far from the spotlight.[146]

The report explains how many companies are working to reduce not only their Scope 1 and Scope 2 emissions, but also their Scope 3 emissions (all other indirect emissions, including purchased goods and services that do not fall under Scope 2), particularly by working through suppliers.[147] Companies with strong governance, the report also found, are more likely to be able to meet their commitments.[148] Corporate sustainability initiatives, it added, are also becoming more rigorous.[149]

Against this background, what difference do US state anti- and pro-ESG laws make? The short answer is that they probably change private corporate commitments to further sustainable development and reduce greenhouse gas emissions a little, but not a lot. The traditional fiduciary duty of pension fund trustees is a guardrail against deviation, and it limits what laws in both directions can achieve. As explained above, these laws nonetheless create some ambiguities about what represents departure from fiduciary duty, which requires considered judgments about what is lawful and prudent under a variety of circumstances. Almost certainly, these laws lead to individual judgments about particular investments that would not be made under identical circumstances in a state without such laws. In other words, these laws have some effect on the margins, but not on the overall direction, of state investments. But by drawing attention to ESG investments, laws both opposing and supporting ESG likely increase the rigor of ESG analysis.

5.3 Implications for Other Countries

The EU has the world's largest share of corporate ESG and climate change commitments, followed by the US, and the EU's share is projected to grow much more rapidly than that of the

144 PwC's Second Annual State of Decarbonization Report (*PricewaterhouseCoopers*) (2025) 5 <https://www.pwc.com/us/en/services/esg/library/assets/pwc-sustainability-decarbonization-2025.pdf> accessed 7 April 2025.

145 ibid.

146 ibid.

147 ibid 6.

148 ibid 16.

149 ibid 24.

US in the years ahead.[150] Australia, Canada, and Japan have smaller but fast growing ESG markets.[151] In the rest of the world, ESG commitments are less significant. The world's ESG leader in other words, is not the US; it is the EU, and that is likely to remain true for the foreseeable future.[152]

In the EU, sustainable development and climate change are having a profound effect on business and corporate law. The EU has been taking the lead in sustainability and climate-disclosure requirements by moving past voluntary disclosure standards to mandatory disclosure standards. Of particular importance are the 2022 Corporate Sustainability Reporting Directive (CSRD)[153] and the 2024 Corporate Sustainability Due Diligence Directive (CS3D).[154] As this chapter goes to press, the EU has postponed the effective date of these measures and is considering an omnibus package that would streamline reporting under them.[155]

Still, a brief description is helpful in understanding their potential scope and meaning. The CSRD as originally adopted incorporates a double materiality standard. Companies must report on the sustainability impacts of their operations on people and the environment (including from their value chain) over the short, medium, and long term (impact materiality). They must also report on the impact of sustainability issues on the company's financial matters, such as its financial position, cash flow, ability to access financing, cost of capital, or financial performance (financial materiality). Sustainability matters include environmental, social, and human rights and governance factors. This materiality standard is different from the single materiality standard contained in US securities law, which focuses on financial materiality. As originally adopted, the other key directive, the CS3D, would require specified companies to identify, prevent, mitigate, and end environmental and human rights harms, both in the company's operations and in its supply chain. CS3D also requires these companies to adopt climate transition plans. Both of these directives would apply to large EU companies as well as companies that do significant business in the EU. Significantly, these impacts will be felt not just by US companies that meet the EU thresholds, but also by their suppliers.

It is quite likely that many US corporations will be subject to both the final form of these EU laws as well as some state anti-ESG laws. Even within the US, in other words, law from other jurisdictions will likely affect what states can dictate regarding ESG. A significant number of other jurisdictions are also considering climate and sustainability disclosure laws. What all of this means in countries other than the US is more or less the same as what this means in the US: Corporations operating in a particular country will nonetheless find themselves needing to comply with these other laws, regardless of US state ESG laws.

150 Global ESG Assets (n 2).

151 ibid.

152 See Harro van Asselt and Jessica Crow, Chapter 33 of this handbook.

153 Parliament and Council Directive 2022/2464, 2022 O.J. (L 322) <https://eur-lex.europa.eu/legal-content/EN/TXT/PDF/?uri=CELEX:32022L2464> accessed 14 June 2025.

154 Parliament and Council Directive 2024/1760, 2024 O.J. (L 5.7.24) <https://eur-lex.europa.eu/legal-content/EN/TXT/PDF/?uri=OJ:L_202401760> accessed 14 June 2025). See also Barbara Pozzo, Chapter 29 of this handbook.

155 'EU Delays Corporate Sustainability Rules as Businesses Push Back' *Environmental Health News* (7 April 2025) <https://www.ehn.org/eu-delays-corporate-sustainability-rules-as-businesses-push-back#> accessed 7 April 2025. See also Harro van Asselt and Jessica Crow, Chapter 33 of this handbook.

6. Conclusion

Corporations cannot ignore, and are increasingly cognisant of, the basic physics of climate change and how climate change affects their risks and opportunities. The same is true of societal expectations about how they should respond to ESG and sustainable development. US state ESG laws likely have little effect over the trajectory of ESG in the US and the rest of the world. They illustrate the limited ability of US states to encourage or discourage a global private governance phenomenon that is based on investment returns from achievement of nonfinancial goals.

CHAPTER 36

India

UMAKANTH VAROTTIL

1. Introduction

AT a global level, litigation has emerged to the forefront in combating the adverse effects of climate change.[1] In one type of litigation, claimants assert "horizontal" rights against private actors (such as companies emitting greenhouse gases) that are based on private law.[2] These actions are generally brought before the civil courts invoking principles of tort, property, contract, or corporate law.[3] In another litigation type, claimants champion "vertical" rights premised in public law against the state whose actions are found to be inadequate in curbing the ill-effects of climate change.[4] From a normative perspective, the private–public law paradigm in the context of climate litigation offers elegant conceptual clarity, but a positive account reveals constant boundary-blurring.[5] The goal of this chapter is to demonstrate the point using India as a case study.

The chapter finds significant challenges in parties' ability to bring private law claims of the conventional type grounded in common law in the context of India. Not only are there substantive barriers in the form of requirements relating to causation and measure of damages, but significant procedural hurdles such as high litigation costs and inordinate delays in India's ordinary civil courts tend to stymie claimants' efforts. Therefore, no private law claims have arisen in India yet in the realm of climate change.[6]

At the same time, private law concepts and principles have guided India's higher judiciary while dealing with public law claims relating to the environment (and, by extension, to matters pertaining to climate change). These include the polluter pays principle, the precautionary principle, the rule of absolute liability in matters of tort law, and the notions of stakeholder rights and corporate social responsibility in matters of corporate law.[7] In that sense, while private law has been inactive on a standalone basis, it has formed the bedrock of public law

[1] Anita Foerster, 'Climate Justice and Corporations' (2019) 30 King's Law Journal 305, 306.

[2] Robert F Blomquist, 'Comparative Climate Change Torts' (2012) 46 Valparaiso University Law Review 1053, 1053.

[3] Monika Hinteregger, 'Civil Liability and the Challenges of Climate Change: A Functional Analysis' (2017) 8(2) Journal of European Tort Law 238, 245; Jim Rossi and J B Ruhl, 'Adapting Private Law for Climate Change Adaptation' (2023) 76 Vanderbilt Law Review 827, 831.

[4] Marc-Phillipe Weller and Mai-Lan Tran, 'Climate Litigation Against Companies' (2022) 1:14 Climate Action 1, 2–3.

[5] Lee Godden and others, 'Law, Governance and Risk: Deconstructing the Public–Private Divide in Climate Change Adaptation' (2013) 36 University of New South Wales Law Journal 224, 224.

[6] Shibani Ghosh, 'Climate Litigation in India' in F Sindico and M M Mbengue (eds), *Comparative Climate Litigation: Beyond the Usual Suspects* (Springer 2021) 347, 347.

[7] These are discussed in detail in Section 3 and Section 4 of this chapter.

adjudication in dealing with issues pertaining to the environment, thereby performing a supporting role rather than playing the lead act.

The dominance of public law in climate litigation is attributable not only to claimants' choice of invoking the writ jurisdiction of High Courts and the Supreme Court (applicable to constitutional cases), which do not suffer as much from the inadequacies faced by civil courts, but also to the judicial elasticity displayed by judges of higher courts in framing innovative solutions in constitutional law to intractable social and economic problems. Approaches adopted by the higher judiciary have also permeated the specialist National Green Tribunal (NGT) that has been legislatively tasked with adopting tort law ideas such as the polluter pays principle.

Overall, the chapter finds that the cross-over of private law into the public law domain, while conceptually unsatisfying, holds promise in overcoming barriers to corporate climate litigation in India. At a conceptual level, as the chapter demonstrates, courts have veered away from well-established principles in tort law and corporate law, such as causation, measure of damages, and the content of directors' duties, in devising somewhat unsystematic approaches on matters of environmental litigation, thereby further stultifying the growth of private law in the climate arena. At the pragmatic level, however, the reshaping of private law principles in the hands of India's constitutional courts while adjudicating public law rights and duties could lead to further advancements in addressing climate change issues where private law could play but a secondary role.[8] Equally, novel developments in public law in the climate space could infuse fresh life into private law concepts relevant to corporate climate litigation.

Section 2 of this chapter offers a background to the private–public law divide in India in the context of climate change, highlighting the nature of the interrelationship between the two legal bodies. Moving to specific areas of private law, Section 3 focuses on the evolution of tort law principles in public law litigation, but by drawing upon and extending doctrinal principles from common law. Section 4 addresses the debates in corporate law involving the stakeholder orientation of corporate boards in India under company law, as well as the concept of social responsibility in tackling climate issues. Section 5 touches upon how contracts can not only be interpreted to address climate issues but also how regulatory nudges in the contractual arena can motivate parties to achieve net-zero goals through the adoption of renewable energy. Section 6 brings all these areas of private law together and finds a cross-pollination of ideas with public law, the combination of which would provide a unique legal environment for corporate climate litigation in India. Section 7 briefly concludes.

2. Climate Change and the Private–Public Law Divide in India

In 2024, the Supreme Court in *MK Ranjitsinh v Union of India*[9] (*Ranjitsinh 2024*) recognised a "right against the adverse effects of climate change" as a fundamental right under the Indian Constitution (hereinafter, "climate right"). It noted with reference to the Constitution:

> Article 21 recognises the right to life and personal liberty while Article 14 indicates that all persons shall have equality before law and the equal protection of laws. These articles are important sources of the right to a clean environment and the right against the adverse effects of climate change.[10]

[8] Pia Rebelo and Xavier Rebelo, 'Rights-Based Climate Change Litigation Against Private Actors' in Kim Bouwer and others (eds), *Climate Litigation and Justice in Africa* (Bristol University Press 2024) 191.

[9] 2024 INSC 280.

[10] *Ranjitsinh 2024* (n 9) [20].

This landmark ruling follows nearly four decades of Indian jurisprudence that recognised the right to a pollution-free environment.[11] In *Ranjitsinh 2024*, the Supreme Court took a monumental step by extending the right to a clean environment to the broader remit of climate change. While recognising a distinct climate right, the Court observed that "this right and the right to a clean environment are two sides of the same coin".[12] This approach reemphasises that the jurisprudence surrounding environmental law continues to hold considerable sway in an analysis of the law regarding climate change.[13]

A key follow-on question, one that is central to this chapter, is whether the so-called climate right is exercisable by affected parties only against the state (i.e., vertically) or even against private parties such as corporations that operate in a manner that amounts to a breach of the constitutional right (i.e., horizontally). The exercise of horizontal constitutional rights by affected parties would offer claimants an additional opportunity to assert their claim over and above horizontal rights they may have under private (common) law.

In an earlier ruling in *Kaushal Kishor v State of Uttar Pradesh* (*Kaushal Kishor*),[14] the Supreme Court had occasion to examine whether constitutional rights have an impact over relationships between private actors (whether individuals or corporations). A five-judge (constitution) bench of the Court ruled that a fundamental right under Article 21 of the Constitution "can be enforced even against persons other than the State or its instrumentalities".[15] Such an approach grants the Indian judiciary's imprimatur to the horizontal application of the fundamental rights enshrined under the Indian Constitution.

A conjoint reading of the rulings of the Supreme Court in *Ranjitsinh 2024* and *Kaushal Kishor* leaves open the possibility that the constitutional climate right as articulated by the Supreme Court would be justiciable not just against the state but also against errant corporations,[16] in the latter case through the "horizontal effect".[17] Hence, victims of actions or inactions by corporations in the climate context can either bring a constitutional claim for breach of fundamental rights or can assert claims under private law (to the extent available).

An enthusiast of private law might be keen to determine the possibility of asserting climate rights through common law (or statute as applicable to private parties), but that question is less interesting in the Indian context for reasons this chapter elaborates later on. The more important question is how Indian private law will help shape the exercise of the constitutional climate right. The reason is that through a longstanding tradition of public interest litigation, the Indian courts have used tort law principles in cases involving acts or omissions by the state,

11 See *Rural Litigation and Entitlement Kendra, Dehradun v State of U.P.* 1985 INSC 49.

12 *Ranjitsinh 2024* (n 9) [24].

13 Parul Kumar, 'Striving Towards the "The Good Life": What Environmental Litigation in India Can Tell Us About Climate Litigation in the Global South' (2024) 13 Transnational Environmental Law 636, 647.

14 2023 INSC 4.

15 ibid [78] (V. Ramasubramanian J). However, a separate opinion cautioned that fundamental rights may not be justiciable horizontally in a constitutional case except where those rights have been statutorily recognised. ibid [43] (B V Nagarathna J).

16 Maya Nirula, 'Pioneering Decision from the Indian Supreme Court Recognizing Freedom from the Adverse Effects of Climate Change as a Fundamental Right' (*Climate Law: A Sabin Center Blog*, 28 August 2024) <https://blogs.law.columbia.edu/climatechange/2024/08/28/guest-blog-pioneering-decision-from-the-indian-supreme-court-recognizing-freedom-from-the-adverse-effects-of-climate-change-as-a-fundamental-right/> accessed 4 June 2025.

17 Stephen Gardbaum, 'Horizontal Effect' in Sujit Choudhary, Madhav Khosla, and Pratap Bhanu Mehta (eds), *The Oxford Handbook of the Indian Constitution* (OUP 2016) 609–10. See also Boudewijn de Bruin and Olha Cherednychenko, Chapter 45 of this handbook.

as they enable courts to award compensations to victims of violations of fundamental rights.[18] Effectively through a "merger of constitutional law and tort law",[19] the Indian Supreme Court's "approach in public interest litigation cases [has] started bearing a stark resemblance to traditional private-law based tort claims".[20] At the same time, the Court's innovative focus on constitutional jurisprudence has led to the dereliction of substantive private law, especially tort law.[21] This conundrum has been exacerbated by the fact that when faced with the prospect of choosing between public law remedies and private law ones, claimants are prone to resort to constitutional actions because they are not only brought directly before the Supreme Court and the High Courts by way of writ actions, but the higher judiciary has also demonstrated a track record of devising innovative mechanisms for remedying breaches of constitutional rights.

Given this scenario, private law concepts under Indian law are likely to play a greater role enunciating horizontal constitutional claims brought against the state to which non-state actors such as corporations could be added as defendants against whom appropriate remedies are sought. In that sense, private law principles under Indian law are likely to support constitutional climate actions. While the possibility of standalone private law actions on climate matters continue to remain, they are likely to be more the exception than the norm.[22]

Against this backdrop, the chapter delves into three areas of Indian private law, viz., tort law, corporate law, and contract law, to demonstrate how they have formed the bases for constitutional litigation under environmental law and, by extension, are relevant to the assertion of the climate right.[23]

3. Tort Law in India: Compensatory and Preventive Mechanisms

Some scholars and advocates have suggested that tort law could play a crucial role in combating the adverse effects of climate change. Its potential benefits include a compensatory effect that allows victims to redress losses suffered as a result of actions or omissions of tortfeasors, and a preventive effect that will disincentivise potential greenhouse gas emitters from jeopardising their long-term commercial interests.[24] In at least one jurisdiction, tort law has been utilised to impose a duty on private actors with regard to the risks emanating from climate change, albeit with the precise, enforceable content of that duty still to be developed.[25] In the Indian context,

[18] Shyamkrishna Balganesh, 'The Constitutionalisation of Indian Private Law' in Sujit Choudhary, Madhav Khosla, and Pratap Bhanu Mehta (eds), *The Oxford Handbook of the Indian Constitution* (OUP 2016) 686.

[19] ibid.

[20] ibid 687.

[21] ibid 691–92.

[22] There have been but rare instances of cases involving negligence and nuisance, both public and private. See, e.g., *Municipal Council, Ratlam v Vardhichand* 1980 INSC 138.

[23] A fourth area of private law, viz., property law, is omitted from the analysis not only because of its limited utility in the Indian climate context, but also due to constraints of space. At the same time, it is noteworthy that courts have evolved concepts such as the public trust doctrine which are relevant in climate arena. See, e.g., *M.C. Mehta v Kamal Nath* 1996 INSC 1482 [17].

[24] Monika Hinteregger, 'Climate Change and Tort Law' in Eva Shulev-Steindl and others (eds), *Climate Change, Responsibility and Liability* (Nomos 2022) 385.

[25] *Shell Plc v Milieudefensie and others*, ECLI:NL:GHDHA:2024:2100 (Court of Appeals, The Hague, 12 November 2024) (unofficial English translation)(the Appeal Judgment) <https://climatecasechart.com/wp-content/uploads/non-us-case-documents/2024/20241112_8918_judgment.pdf>. See also Jolene

though, tort law is replete with impediments (both substantive and procedural) that have prevented its extensive use as a private law remedy.[26] Most notably, the inadequacies of the Indian tort system came to the fore in the aftermath of the Bhopal gas tragedy.[27]

Through some deft manoeuvring, the Indian Supreme Court converted the shortcomings of the Indian private law of torts into an opportunity by shifting the ground to public law. In a series of rulings, the Court adopted principles of Indian tort law in constitutional cases and moulded them to overcome the traditional shackles. In doing so, it revolutionised the use of tort law principles in cases involving environmental matters, but through the lens of public law.

3.1 Innovative Tort Law Concepts in the Environmental Context

The first indication of the Supreme Court's novel approach emerged in *M.C. Mehta v Union of India* (*Oleum Leak Case*),[28] where a public interest litigant[29] filed a constitutional claim before the highest court[30] for environmental damage seeking the award of compensation for the victims of escape of oleum gas from the facility belonging to a company. After finding that the court has the power to award compensation to victims of breach of fundamental rights in exceptional circumstances, the Supreme Court developed the standard of "absolute liability" by departing from the narrower "strict liability" rule propounded in the common law decision in *Rylands v Fletcher*.[31] The absolute liability rule applies "where an enterprise is engaged in a hazardous or inherently dangerous activity and harm results to anyone on account of an accident in the operation of such hazardous or inherently dangerous activity".[32] To ensure a deterrent effect on polluting enterprises, the Court noted that the "measure of compensation" in such circumstances "must be co-related to the magnitude and capacity of the enterprise".[33] It sought

Lin, 'Milieudefensie et al. v. Shell: Analysis and Commentary of the Hague Court of Appeal's Decision' Climate Change Law Blog (18 November 2024) < https://cil.nus.edu.sg/blogs/milieudefensie-et-al-v-shell-analysis-and-commentary-of-the-hague-court-of-appeals-decision/> accessed 7 July 2025.

[26] Marc Galanter, 'India's Tort Deficit: Sketch for a Historical Portrait' in David M Engel and Michael McCann (eds), *Fault Lines: Tort Law as Cultural Practice* (Stanford University Press 2009) 47; Deepa Badrinarayana, 'The Jewel in the Crown: Can India's Strict Liability Doctrine Deepen Our Understanding of Tort Law Theory?' (2017) 55 Louisville Law Review 25, 26.

[27] S Muralidhar, 'Unsettling Truths, Untold Tales: The Bhopal Gas Disaster Victims "Twenty Years" of Courtroom Struggles for Justice' (2004) International Environmental Law Research Centre Working Paper 2004/5 <https://www.ielrc.org/content/w0405.pdf> accessed 29 May 2025. Note that tort law in India is uncodified and relies on common law principles, except in specific areas that have witnessed partial codification, for example through the Public Liability Insurance Act, 1991 and the National Green Tribunal Act, 2010.

[28] 1986 INSC 281.

[29] The concept of public interest litigation in India allows an individual or group to represent victims of breaches of fundamental rights under India's Constitution who are unable to represent themselves before a court. See, e.g., Sarbani Sen, 'The "Public Interest" in India: Contestation and Confrontation before the Supreme Court' (2015) 60 Diogenes 27.

[30] Such constitutional claims are filed before the Supreme Court in exercise of its writ jurisdiction under Article 32 of the Constitution. The High Courts too similarly enjoy writ jurisdiction under Article 226 of the Constitution.

[31] (1868) LR 3 HL 330.

[32] *Oleum Leak Case* (n 28) [31].

[33] ibid [32].

to impose a higher measure of compensation on enterprises that are "larger and more prosperous".[34] Thus emerged a succession of public law cases that adapted tort law principles to address environmental harms in public law actions.

Nearly a decade later, the Supreme Court extended the concept of absolute liability from the *Oleum Leak Case* to formulate the "polluter pays" principle. In *Indian Council for Enviro-Legal Action v Union of India* (*Indian Council for Enviro-Legal Action*),[35] the Court was concerned with damage to soil and underground water caused by chemical plants in the State of Rajasthan. It observed that the "polluter pays" principle has "gained almost universal recognition", apart from the fact that it has been stated in absolute terms in the *Oleum Leak Case*.[36] Hence, the "polluter pays" principle was set out as the law of the land.

Subsequently, in *Vellore Citizens Welfare Forum v Union of India* (*Vellore Citizens Welfare Forum*),[37] the Supreme Court articulated the nexus between the absolute liability and polluter pays principles. It noted:

> The "Polluter Pays" principle as interpreted by this Court means that the absolute liability for harm to the environment extends not only to compensate the victims of pollution but also the cost of restoring the environmental degradation. Remediation of the damaged environment is part of the process of "Sustainable Development" and as such polluter is liable to pay the cost to individual sufferers as well as cost of reversing the damaged ecology.[38]

Vellore Citizens Welfare Forum is also known for its enunciation of the "precautionary principle" which requires the state to "anticipate, prevent and attack the causes of environmental degradation".[39] Here, the Court categorically stated that "the precautionary principle and the polluter pays principle are part of the environmental law of the country".[40]

In a subsequent line of cases, the Supreme Court adopted a flexible approach towards determination of compensation in public law cases involving environmental damage, thereby refraining from adhering to age-old concepts in tort law on measure of damages. For instance, in *T.N. Godavarman Thirumulpad v Union of India*,[41] the Court observed:

> The damage to the environment is a damage to the country's assets as a whole. Ecology knows no boundaries. It can have impact on the climate. The principles and parameters for valuation of the damage have to be evolved also keeping in view the likely impact of activities on future generation[s].[42]

A few years later, the Supreme Court wholeheartedly embraced the flexibility it availed in determining compensation in environmental claims under public law in a number of different ways. For instance, in *Goa Foundation v Union of India* (*Goa Foundation*),[43] where ecological

[34] ibid. This is also referred to as the 'deep pocket' theory. See Usha Tandon, 'Green Justice and the Application of the Polluter-Pays Principle: A Study of India's National Green Tribunal' (2020) 13 OIDA International Journal of Sustainable Development 35, 42.

[35] 1996 INSC 237.

[36] ibid [69].

[37] 1996 INSC 952

[38] ibid [12].

[39] ibid [11].

[40] ibid [14].

[41] 2005 INSC 439.

[42] ibid [80]. This ruling also alluded to the 'public trust' doctrine and the principle of 'intergenerational equity', which are recognised under Indian law. A discussion of these is beyond the scope of this chapter.

[43] (2014) 6 SCC 590.

damage was alleged due to mining activity, the Court ordered that "10% of the sale proceeds of the iron ore excavated in the State of Goa" ought to be appropriated towards a fund earmarked "for the purpose of sustainable development and inter-generational equity" in the State of Goa.[44] In another high profile case of *Sterlite Industries (India) Ltd v Union of India*,[45] the Court assessed the "magnitude, capacity and prosperity" of the defendant company and imposed a liability of INR 1 billion (equivalent in present terms of USD 11.8 million) for polluting the environment in the vicinity of the plant which was operated without the requisite permits.[46]

The environmental tort law principles devised by India's apex court also received statutory recognition. In 2010, the Indian Parliament enacted the National Green Tribunal Act (NGT Act) to establish a separate tribunal for dealing with cases pertaining to "environmental protection and conservation of forests and other natural resources".[47] This followed calls for a separate judicial apparatus for dealing with environmental matters that possesses the requisite expertise and is also free from the delays and other challenges faced by the ordinary civil and criminal courts.[48] The NGT has jurisdiction to deal with civil cases arising out of a direct violation of a statutory environmental obligation, including the enforcement of rights pertaining to the environment.[49] More interestingly, the NGT Act stipulates that the NGT "shall, while passing any order or decision or award, apply the principles of sustainable development, the precautionary principle and the polluter pays principle",[50] thereby statutorily espousing the environmental (and by extension climate-related) doctrines framed by the Supreme Court using the foundations of tort law.[51] In terms of remedial actions, the NGT is authorised by statute to exercise its jurisdiction to "provide compensation or relief to the claimants and for restitution of the damaged property or environment",[52] as well as to order relief or compensation for any death, injury, or damage under several specified heads.[53]

Over the last decade and a half, the NGT has moved the Supreme Court's expansion of compensatory jurisprudence forward in cases involving environmental law. For instance, in *Goel Ganga Developers India Pvt Ltd v Union of India* (*Goel Ganga Developers*),[54] the tribunal imposed damages of the higher of INR 1 billion or 10% of the project cost for construction carried out in violation of the environmental clearance granted.[55] Similarly, damages were imposed on bottling units of a corporation for illegal groundwater extraction.[56] In a high-profile case, though, the NGT's award of compensation has attracted criticism on the ground that the compensation was reduced to INR 50 million (equivalent to approximately USD 0.6 million) from

44 ibid [63].
45 2013 INSC 204.
46 ibid [39].
47 See NGT Act, Preamble.
48 See *Indian Council for Enviro-Legal Action* (n 35) [70].
49 NGT Act, ss 2(m), 14.
50 NGT Act, s 20.
51 Charu Sharma and Vishavjeet Chaudhary, 'Liability' in Phillipe Cullet, Lovleen Bhullar, and Sujith Koonan (eds), *The Oxford Handbook of Environmental and Natural Resources Law in India* (OUP 2024) 186.
52 NGT Act, s 15(4).
53 NGT Act, s 17(1) read with Schedule II.
54 2018 INSC 696.
55 ibid [59].
56 *Sushil Bhatt v Moon Beverages Ltd* 2022 SCC OnLine NGT 76 [381].

an initial estimate of INR 1.2 billion (equivalent to approximately USD 14.1 million) to address the impact of a mass cultural event on a riverbank and floodplain.[57]

While the judicial innovation in the use and extension of tort law principles to public law to address serious environmental concerns is evident, questions arise about the credibility of such an approach utilised by India's higher judiciary as well as the NGT. In its zeal to overcome the constraints imposed by conventional tort law, the expanded jurisprudence in the public law domain may have had the effect of muddying the doctrinal waters in tort law. This arguably does a disservice to the core of private law jurisprudence, but it might also represent a unique window of opportunity in the legal fight against climate change, albeit principally in the public law domain.

3.2 Doctrinal Distortions in Tort Law: Challenges and an Opportunity

Globally, considerable challenges confront the use of tort law to address climate change. These include (1) identifying appropriate causes of action, (2) proving causation, and (3) determining the amount of compensation payable in a specific case.[58] Climate litigants have encountered challenges in tort-based climate actions in other jurisdictions.[59] Commentators have therefore cautioned that if corporate climate litigation is to be effective under private law, "the elements of tort law need to be interpreted in a loose way".[60] While the Indian outlook to tort law in the environmental context has attracted a great deal of criticism on the ground that it is unprincipled and somewhat arbitrary,[61] the judiciary's approach to unshackle itself from some of the vestiges of narrow tort law doctrines could very well present an exceptional chance to push the boundaries of tort law in the climate context, whether grounded in private law or extended to the public law domain (as normally occurs in Indian jurisprudence). Each of the specific facets of a tort law action mentioned earlier is discussed in sequence.

First, the now well-established precautionary principle, the polluter pays principle, and the absolute liability rule constitute judicially conceived causes of action in tort law that are capable of being asserted in private law tort claims as well as in public law constitutional actions, in each case horizontally against greenhouse gas emitters. While the jurisprudence in this arena thus far is limited to environmental law, the Supreme Court has already opened the door for extension of such principles to climate change by establishing a close nexus between the two concepts.[62] Hence, Indian tort law (albeit derived via public law) already provides a strong jurisprudential platform for initiation of climate-related tort actions. Unlike what may be seen

[57] *Manoj Mishra v Delhi Developmental Authority* 2016 SCC OnLine NGT 114. For a critique of this ruling, see Raghuveer Nath and Armin Rosencranz, 'Determination of Environmental Compensation: The Art of Living Case' (2019) 12 National University of Juridical Sciences Law Review 1.

[58] See Hinteregger, Climate Change and Tort Law (n 24) 386; Centre for Climate Engagement, Hughes Hall, University of Cambridge, 'Tort Law and Climate Change' (*Law and Climate Atlas*, July 2024) <https://lawclimateatlas.org/resources/tort-law-and-climate-change/> accessed 29 May 2025.

[59] See, e.g., *Shell plc* (n 25).

[60] See, e.g., Riccardo Fornasari, 'The Legal Form of Climate Change Litigation: An Inquiry into the Transformative Potential and Limits of Private Law' (2024) 4 Journal of Law and Political Economy 820, 823.

[61] Madhuri Parikh, 'Global Perspectives on Corporate Climate Legal Tactics: India National Report', *British Institute of International and Comparative Law* (February 2024), 41; Nath and Rosencranz (n 57) 14.

[62] See, *Ranjitsinh 2024* (n 9).

in the context of other jurisdictions, the Indian courts do not need to go so far as to carve out a new tort that imposes a climate duty.[63]

Second, upon finding a specific duty, one needs to assess the element of causation, which "requires a sufficient causal link between the defendant's activity and the harm sustained by the victim".[64] This is often difficult to establish in a climate change scenario as the loss may be attributable to several different factors apart from the actions or omissions of a single business enterprise.[65] Hence, there has been a global momentum to ease the knotty issues involving causation that are steeped in the complexity of the scientific evidence.[66] Thus far, while Indian courts have adhered to the general principles of causation in customary tort actions,[67] they have not had the occasion to expound on the matter in environmental or climate-related actions.[68] Although how the Indian judiciary will react on the issue of causation in climate litigation is essentially a matter of speculation, its track record so far on environmental matters leaves considerable room for possible innovation and modernisation of approach to keep pace with scientific developments in the climate arena.[69]

Third, concerns abound regarding the methodology for quantification of damages for climate-related harms. While the matter of quantification has yet to receive the required attention worldwide, the Indian courts and tribunals have followed a diversity of approaches in determining the amount of compensation to be awarded once an environmental harm has been established. The Supreme Court has adopted several methods.[70] The first involves the "deep pockets" theory, which correlates with the magnitude of the business of the violator of an environmental (or climate) right and the financial capacity of the relevant enterprise. The second involves pegging the quantum of the compensation either as a percentage of the sale proceeds[71] or the project cost.[72] Third, the Court has adopted a delegation approach whereby rather than determining the quantum of the compensation itself, it appoints a committee of experts to investigate matters and determine the compensation payable. In some cases, it has even delegated the quantification responsibility to the appropriate government or regulatory officials.[73]

These methods have percolated to the quantification of damages by the NGT as well. As critics have noted, not only does the estimation often lack scientific analysis,[74] but the judicial bodies admittedly cannot measure compensation "with exactitude and precision", thereby

[63] *Shell plc* (n 25); *Smith v Fonterra* [2024] NZSC 5.

[64] Hinteregger, Civil Liability (n 3) 254.

[65] Blomquist (n 2) 1057.

[66] Jim Rossi and Michael Panfil, 'Climate Resilience and Private Law's Duty to Adapt' (2022) 100 North Carolina Law Review 1135, 1206; Fornasari (n 60) 2.

[67] *Rajkot Municipal Corporation v Manjulben Jayantilal Nakum* 1997 INSC 34 [63].

[68] Lovleen Bhullar, 'The Polluter Pays Principle: Scope and Limits of Judicial Decisions' in Shibani Ghosh (ed), *Indian Environmental Law: Key Concepts and Principles* (Orient Black Swan 2019).

[69] For a discussion on the application of the precautionary principle despite the absence of scientific certainty, see Kanika Jamwal, 'Precautionary Principle and Its Tryst with the Indian Judiciary' (*Mongabay*, 19 August 2020) <https://india.mongabay.com/2020/08/commentary-precautionary-principle-and-its-tryst-with-the-indian-judiciary/> accessed 29 May 2025.

[70] Dhvani Mehta and Debadityo Sinha, 'Penalties and Compensation' in Phillipe Cullet (ed), *The Oxford Handbook of Environmental and Natural Resources Law in India* (OUP 2024) 793.

[71] See, e.g., *Goa Foundation* (n 43).

[72] See, e.g., *Goel Ganga Developers* (n 54).

[73] Sroyon Mukherjee, 'How Much Should the Polluter Pay? Indian Courts and the Valuation of Environmental Damage' (2023) 35 Journal of Environmental Law 331, 343.

[74] Nath and Rosencranz (n 57) 11.

resulting in "hypothesizing or guess work".[75] In the absence of any prescribed formula for computing compensation for environmental and climate torts, there would be a greater onus on the judicial bodies to offer reasons for arriving at a quantification.[76] But on occasion, no reasoning is offered at all,[77] leading to considerable uncertainty. Such an ad hoc approach to the quantification of damages would likely have a deleterious effect in bringing as well as defending tort actions relating to climate change, whether under public law or private law. On the one hand, the uncertainty might disincentivise claimants from bringing otherwise worthy actions, thereby adversely affecting their ability to redress climate-related grievances. On the other, it could alter the deterrent effect on climate-agnostic business enterprises by either overreaching or underreaching through incorrect quantification of the compensation.

3.3 Procedural Considerations in Tort-Based Actions

Before concluding this section, it would be useful to address certain procedural considerations in bringing tort actions before the Indian courts. Tort actions under private law (especially those arising in common law) are asserted before the regular civil courts. These cases undergo a full-fledged trial with appeals available in justifiable cases to the High Courts and thereafter to the Supreme Court. Given that India's regular court system is overburdened with an astonishingly large number of pending cases,[78] there is bound to be significant delays in achieving judicial resolution in ordinary tort cases in private law. Moreover, claimants bringing regular civil suits are required to incur the cost of court fees and stamp duties, which vary from state to state.[79] Judges in ordinary civil courts tend to adhere closely to the procedural law with limited flexibility.[80] Most civil suits are decided at the level of the lower courts. Only some of them make it to the High Court, while even fewer are appealed all the way to the Supreme Court. Hence, the opportunity to the higher judiciary in "laying down the law" in the private law arena is rather limited. These procedural factors could play a significant role in inhibiting claimants from seeking private law remedies for climate-related claims.[81]

Turning to the public law arena, procedural ramifications vary drastically. Litigants can directly petition the relevant High Court[82] or the Supreme Court[83] for breach of fundamental rights under the Constitution. In that sense, the higher judiciary is seized of the matter at the outset in the exercise of its writ jurisdiction. The delays and costs the litigants suffer in such

[75] Harshita Singhal and Sujit Koonan, 'Polluter Pays Principle in India: Assessing Conceptual Boundaries and Implementation Issues' (2021) 7 Rajiv Gandhi National University of Law Student Law Review 33, 42.

[76] Tandon (n 34) 42.

[77] Mukherjee (n 73) 350.

[78] According to Government statistics, there are nearly 5.8 million civil suits pending before various Indian courts. National Judicial Data Grid, <https://njdg.ecourts.gov.in/njdgv3/> accessed 25 March 2025.

[79] Saiesh Kamath, 'Court Fees and Access to Justice: A Re-Examination' (*Journal of Indian Law and Society Blog*, 10 February 2021) <https://jilsblognujs.wordpress.com/2021/02/10/court-fees-and-access-to-justice-a-re-examination/> accessed 4 June 2025.

[80] Code of Civil Procedure, 1908.

[81] Wherever there is a demonstrable violation of specific environmental statutes, parties do have the option of seeking redress before the NGT, which does not suffer from the level of delays and costs as the regular court system.

[82] Constitution of India, art 226.

[83] Constitution of India, art 32.

public law claims are of a much lower of magnitude compared to private law claims before the regular courts. Other procedural advantages for litigants before the constitutional courts include a considerable relaxation of the prerequisites regarding standing for claimants, which has enabled an upsurge in public interest litigation in India. Evidentiary requirements are less stringent in public law actions, as cases are decided based on affidavit evidence without requiring testimony from witnesses.[84] High Courts and the Supreme Court are able to exercise the flexibility to mould the relief suited to the circumstances that the lower civil courts lack.[85]

Combined with the substantive differences, the wide gulf in the procedural requirements lends more reason for litigants to access the public law remedies for climate-related torts rather than to rely on private law. Hence, while theoretically climate change can be addressed through corporate litigation involving the private law of torts, there is a greater likelihood that litigants will rely on invoking the writ jurisdiction of the higher judiciary, which has more than keenly displayed its propensity to adopt tort law mechanisms to address constitutional issues on matters concerning environmental law, and it is not unreasonable to expect the courts to adopt a similar approach on matters of climate change.

4. Corporate Law in India: Stakeholder Responsibility

Another tool available in climate litigation against corporations lies under corporate law, particularly the duties of directors on corporate boards "to act on climate change, to transition away from carbon-intensive business models, to invest capital and resources in clean energy practices".[86] Unlike tort law duties that are more remedial in nature, corporate law duties seek to regulate ex ante the conduct of business to ensure it meets with the requisite climate goals.[87] While corporate law duties are useful on a standalone basis, anecdotal evidence indicates that the directors' duties under corporate law may be embellished through "the use of human rights as a reflexive interpretative tool".[88]

Although there has been no climate-related corporate law claim that has been brought before the Indian courts, the role of corporate law in addressing climate risks has been the subject matter of considerable attention both from academics as well as practitioners.[89] Among others, two specific aspects of Indian corporate law are relevant in the climate change context. The first relates to the duties of directors on corporate boards. Section 166(2) of the Companies Act, 2013 states as follows:

84 Balganesh (n 18) 687.

85 See, e.g., Constitution of India, art 142 (which stipulates that the Supreme Court 'in the exercise of its jurisdiction may pass such decree or make such order as is necessary for doing complete justice in any cause or matter pending before it').

86 Foerster (n 1) 307.

87 ibid.

88 See, e.g., Rebelo and Rebelo (n 8) 212 (discussing the example of South Africa).

89 See, e.g., Umakanth Varottil, 'Directors' Liability and Climate Risk: White Paper on India' (Commonwealth Climate and Law Initiative 2021) <https://commonwealthclimatelaw.org/wp-content/uploads/2022/05/CCLI-Directors-Liability-and-Climate-Risk-White-Paper-on-India.pdf> accessed 4 June 2025; Shyam Divan, Sugandha Yadav, and Ria Singh Sawhney, 'Legal Opinion: Directors' Obligations to Consider Climate Change-Related Risk in India' (7 September 2021) <https://commonwealthclimatelaw.org/wp-content/uploads/2022/05/CCLI_Legal_Opinion_India_Directors_Duties.pdf> accessed 4 June 2025.

> A director of a company shall act in good faith in order to promote the objects of the company for the benefit of its members as a whole, and in the best interests of the company, its employees, the shareholders, the community and for the protection of environment.

This provision not only requires the directors to act in the long-term interest of the company, but the fact that "the protection of the environment" commands its own space in the statutory provision is indicative of the fact that directors are obligated to garner their attention towards the topic of climate regardless of the associated financial implications. In other words, Section 166(2) now treats climate change, which has already gained a status of eminence within the environmental discourse under Indian law, as an end in itself rather than merely as a financial risk. In this sense, Indian corporate law is arguably different from that of other Commonwealth jurisdictions, wherein the treatment of directors' duties in the context of climate change is etched in the detection and treatment of financial risk.

The second aspect of Indian company law relates to corporate social responsibility (CSR) in terms of Section 135 of the Companies Act, 2013. By virtue of this statutory provision, India is one of only a handful of jurisdictions to require large companies to spend a stipulated amount—at least 2% of average net profits made during the three immediately preceding financial years—in pursuance of their CSR policy towards specified activities, which include "ensuring environmental sustainability, ecological balance, protection of flora and fauna".[90] At a broad level, these mechanisms make Indian corporate law stakeholder-oriented rather than purely shareholder-centric.[91]

Similar to the phenomenon witnessed in tort law, the Indian Supreme Court has enunciated these corporate law duties, albeit in a public law action. In *M.K. Ranjitsinh v Union of India*[92] (*M.K. Ranjitsinh 2021*), the Supreme Court was faced with a writ petition to protect a rare species of bird called the Great Indian Bustard (GIB). In particular, the existence of overhead power lines in the State of Rajasthan posed a hazard to the GIB as the birds regularly collided with the power lines due to their limited frontal vision and lack of manoeuvrability, thereby resulting in their deaths. The petitioners sought that wherever possible "diverters" be installed on existing power lines in the near term and that the lines be undergrounded in the long term to protect this rare species. A principal concern arose that these measures would involve a significant outlay by the power companies involved. In dealing with this constitutional case, the Supreme Court invoked the CSR obligations and the directors' duties under the Companies Act, 2013. In particular, the Court noted that the "word 'environment', though not defined in the Companies Act, has to be given the meaning assigned to it under the Environment (Protection) Act, 1986".[93]

The width of this definition is adequately capable of accommodating the risks corporations face due to climate change. In their legal opinion, legal counsel Divan, Yadav, and Sawhney underscore the significance of the Court's ruling:

[90] Companies Act, 2013, sch VII. See also, *MK Ranjitsinh v Union of India* 2025 INSC 1472 [38] (alluding to the fact that the concept of 'social responsibility' ought to encompass 'environmental responsibility').

[91] Mihir Naniwadekar and Umakanth Varottil, 'The Stakeholder Approach towards Directors' Duties under Indian Company Law: A Comparative Analysis' in Mahendra Pal Singh (ed.), *The Indian Yearbook of Comparative Law* (OUP 2016).

[92] 2021 INSC 257.

[93] ibid [14]. Section 2(a) of the Environment (Protection) Act, 1986 defines the word 'environment' to include the 'inter-relationship which exists among and between water, air and land, and human beings, other living creatures, plants, micro-organisms and property'.

> The Supreme Court's order in the Bustard case is the first to explain the broad scope of directors' duty to the environment under section 166. The Bustard case demonstrates that there is no fixed hierarchy in the duties owed to the company and other stakeholders identified under section 166. A decision taken seemingly in the financial interest of the company and its shareholders, but which is detrimental to the environment, may transgress section 166. Such a decision may additionally expose the company to litigation risk, transition risk from tightening regulations, and render the company's assets stranded.[94]

Hence, consideration of matters such as climate risk and other environmental protection is not merely an option for directors of Indian companies that they may account for on a voluntary basis, but it is an obligation, which they can afford to ignore only at risk of liabilities for breach. *M.K. Ranjitsinh 2021* is therefore salient because the Supreme Court seized the opportunity available to it under a public law dispute to expound on the duties of directors of Indian companies in protecting the environment (and, by implication, in climate mitigation and adaptation). In that sense, the broader interpretation of Section 166 adopted by the Court in *M.K. Ranjitsinh 2021* would guide how directors of Indian companies ought to incorporate an analysis of climate risk in the board decision-making.

Although the stakeholder-oriented duties of corporate directors in India have been devoid of extensive judicial analysis as yet, their public (rather than mere private) nature has attracted attention even in corporate disputes. In the high-profile corporate (private law) litigation in *Tata Consultancy Services Limited v Cyrus Investments Pvt. Ltd.(Tata Consultancy Services Limited)*,[95] the Supreme Court accepted the opportunity to expound on the "public" elements of Indian company law, especially directors' duties. The Court noted that "the history of evolution of the corporate world shows that it has moved from the (i) familial to (ii) contractual and managerial to (iii) a regime of social accountability and responsibility".[96] In doing so, it continued the tradition of the Supreme Court recognising the nature of an Indian corporation to be very different from the shareholder-orientation displayed in Anglo-American corporate law. For example, over three decades ago, the Court articulated this somewhat unique approach in India, observing that "the old nineteenth century view which regarded a company merely as a legal device adopted by shareholders for carrying on trade or business as proprietors has been discarded and a company is now looked upon as a socio-economic institution wielding economic power and influencing the life of the people".[97] Section 166(2) of the Companies Act, 2013 as interpreted by the Supreme Court very much adopts this tenor. In fact, in *Tata Consultancy Services Limited*, the Court went on to state that "[w]hat is ordained under section 166(2) is a combination of private interest and public interest".

The limited jurisprudence available in India regarding the duties of corporate directors to consider matters pertaining to the environment or climate reveals a bi-directional relationship between private law and public law. Signals emanating from *M.K. Ranjitsinh 2021* clearly indicate that in dealing with public law issues, the Supreme Court is willing to not only draw upon private law principles such as the statutorily codified directors' duties but that it is also keen to use the opportunity to expound on the interpretation of Section 166(2) in the environmental context. Concomitantly, in dealing with a private dispute in *Tata Consultancy Services Limited*, the Court has unhesitatingly clarified the "public" nature of company law, including directors' duties.

[94] Divan et al Opinion (n 89) 13.
[95] 2021 INSC 217.
[96] ibid [19.25].
[97] *National Textile Workers' Union v PR Ramakrishnan* 1983 INSC 57 [4].

The procedural constraints in corporate law are less stark compared to tort law. Most corporate disputes are litigated before the National Company Law Tribunal (NCLT) (which is the equivalent of the NGT, but in the corporate law realm). At the same time, the jurisdiction of the NCLT is quite narrow and confined to pure corporate law disputes in the private arena. Climate litigants may encounter constraints in seeking to resort to the NCLT when they can instead assuage concerns by bringing public law disputes through the assertion of constitutional rights to be protected against the adverse effects of climate change. Hence, it is reasonable to assume there will be greater application of corporate law concepts from the private domain being used to support public law dispute resolution, much in a similar way one expects with tort law.

5. Contractual Arrangements: Regulatory Nudges

Existing literature suggests that contract law can address issues pertaining to climate change in two distinct ways. First, climate change might affect existing contracts, for instance, where performance may be made impossible due to climate events.[98] Second, contractual mechanisms may have the effect of facilitating contracts that propel companies towards a net-zero transition.[99] In the latter case, the facilitation may occur through government regulation that mandates companies enter climate-friendly contracts. While the first category of cases falls largely within the exclusive domain of private law, the second category attracts an admixture of private and public laws, as evident in the context of India.

With existing contracts, companies could face climate transition risks that make the performance of such contracts financially unprofitable or even unviable if the risks threaten the continued operation of the company's business. These cases would be governed by customary *force majeure* and "change in law" clauses, apart from the deployment of the frustration principle, which under Indian law is governed by Section 56 of the Contract Act, 1872. Although key issues pertaining to these clauses have made their way up to the Supreme Court,[100] none involve issues related to the environment or climate change.

On the other hand, the Indian Supreme Court has confronted disputes where government regulation has mandated that companies contract for renewable energy in specific circumstances with a view to facilitate energy transition. Understandably, companies subject to governmental regulation have mounted a challenge on constitutional grounds, leading this otherwise contractual private law matter to spill over into the domain of public law. In *Hindustan Zinc Ltd v Rajasthan Electricity Regulatory Commission*,[101] the Court had to decide the constitutional validity of certain regulations issued by the Rajasthan Electricity Regulatory Commission (RERC) that required captive power generation companies and certain open access consumers to purchase a minimum quantity of energy from renewable sources or,

[98] Centre for Climate Engagement, Hughes Hall, University of Cambridge, 'Contract Law and Climate Change' (*Law and Climate Atlas*, July 2024) <https://climatehughes.org/law-and-climate-atlas/contract-law-and-climate-change/> accessed 26 March 2025

[99] ibid; David Howarth, 'Environmental Law and Private Law' in Emma Lees and Jorge E Viñuales (eds), *The Oxford Handbook of Comparative Environmental Law* (OUP 2019) 1096.

[100] See, e.g., *Energy Watchdog v Central Electricity Regulatory Commission* 2017 INSC 338; *Maharashtra State Electricity Distribution Co. Limited v Adani Power Maharashtra Limited* 2023 INSC 400.

[101] (2015) 12 SCC 611.

alternatively, to pay a surcharge to the extent of shortfall in the renewable energy commitment.[102] Having established its own captive generation plant, Hindustan Zinc refused to take up the renewable energy commitment and challenged the validity of the RERC regulations. The Supreme Court observed that the said regulations were framed to "encourage generation and consumption of green energy", bearing in mind that the government must discharge its fundamental duties to protect and improve the environment.[103] It noted:

> The impugned Regulations have been enacted in order to effectuate the object of promotion of generation of electricity from renewable sources of energy as against the polluting sources of energy . . . The provisions requiring purchase of minimum percentage of energy from renewable sources of energy have been framed with an object of fulfilling the constitutional mandate with a view to protect the environment and prevent pollution in the area by utilizing renewable energy sources as much as possible in the larger public interest.[104]

More interestingly, the Court was cognisant of the financial implications of such a ruling. It noted that with the promotion of renewable energy, "larger public interest must prevail over the interest of the industry herein which will in any case pass on the extra burden, if any, . . . as part of the cost of its products".[105]

Another ruling of the Supreme Court involving contractual interpretation in a regulatory context was premised on the push towards renewable energy. *Gujarat Urja Vikas Nigam Limited v Renew Wind Energy (Rajkot) Private Limited*[106] involved a scenario where a party to a power purchase agreement (PPA) concerning renewable energy sought modifications to the PPA upon an amendment to the relevant electricity regulations that had an impact on the computation of an applicable tariff. In denying such modifications, the Court relied on the push towards "solar and other renewables [to] potentially transform the energy landscape".[107] Implicit in the Court's outlook is an eye on addressing the issues arising from climate change and impelling a net-zero transition.

Contract law has received limited attention as a form of private law measure in addressing climate change matters in India. However, regulatory nudges pushing companies to facilitate transition measures through contracting for renewable energy have generally been affirmed, signifying the indirect contractual green impetus galvanised by the Indian Supreme Court, albeit through the use of public law measures.

6. The Future of Climate Change and Private Law in India

Across the world, a discourse has emerged as to the extent to which private law will motivate climate mitigation and adaptation. In the United States, scholars have argued

> that doctrines and practices central to the private law of torts, property, and contracts will and should play an important role in developing policy and resolving disputes regarding how individuals, businesses, and other private actors respond to and manage the harms of climate change.[108]

102 ibid [3].
103 ibid [15], [16], [29].
104 ibid [44].
105 ibid [49].
106 2023 INSC 366.
107 ibid [38].
108 Rossi and Ruhl (n 3) 832.

A wave of litigation, admittedly much of it yet unsuccessful, has been initiated in various jurisdictions under various forms of private law, predominantly tort law and corporate law, and the efforts may likely continue in this direction. However, scholars have cautioned that climate litigation in the Global North and the Global South "differs because of its context and content".[109] The narrow focus on private law that is prevalent in the Global North in addressing issues of climate change may not work in jurisdictions in the Global South despite the fact that "the legacies (and persistence) of colonialism and imperialism have partially crafted those legal systems on the model of the western ones".[110] For instance, in the South African context, it has been argued that the interpretation of the Constitution, particularly its horizontal application to private parties, would open the door for a more flexible rights-based private climate litigation by offering a legal framework for "greening private law".[111] The argument asserts that the interpretation of the bill of rights under the South African constitution would operate as a catalyst for more private rights-based litigation in the climate context.[112]

At the outset, it is difficult to be entirely sanguine about the role of corporate climate litigation on its own in fostering the transition towards a net-zero economy in India. While claims under tort, corporate, contract, or property law are eminently possible in the Indian context, they suffer from hurdles as discussed in this chapter. It is not the case that pure private law remedies are unavailable in India, but just that the likelihood of private law's effective use in the climate context ought to be viewed with some level of scepticism. This is attributable to two reasons. First, private law remedies are subject to constraints, both substantive and procedural, as outlined in this chapter. Second, and more importantly, there is a strong culture spanning decades of the use of public law remedies to stimulate social change, especially when it comes to matters of the environment. Hence, it is realistic to expect litigation, even of the variety that is brought against corporations in the climate change space, to occur in the public law arena through the exercise of horizontal rights against private defendants invoking the writ jurisdiction of the constitutional courts.

At the same time, it is reasonable to deduce that private law principles will have an important role to play in the climate context, albeit in conjunction with public law rather than on a standalone basis. This story suggests a cross-pollination of ideas, philosophies, and doctrines between Indian public law and private law through a bi-directional symbiotic relationship between the two bodies of law. On the one hand, private law has already provided (and will likely continue to provide) the intellectual legal foundations for the evolution of novel public law remedies. In that sense, private law has strongly supported the evolution of Indian environmental (and, in turn, climate) jurisprudence from the outside by way of a reinforcement mechanism to help evolve suitable public law remedies. On the other hand, the idea flow is likely to occur in the reverse direction as well, whereby the well-established public law mechanisms are likely to propel a wider and more flexible interpretation of private law concepts (whether in statute or common law) to place them in a greater state of readiness to address climate change. This requires a reorientation of several private law concepts, whether by an expansive reading of statutory provisions or novel ways of shaping common law doctrines, if private law were to be the focus of achieving climate transition. Here, already demonstrated innovations in public law will likely provide the impetus in private law actions, were they to be brought into India in the climate space.

[109] Fornasari (n 60) 5.
[110] ibid.
[111] Rebelo and Rebelo (n 8) 191.
[112] ibid 217.

As examined in detail in this chapter, the Supreme Court painstakingly developed a rich jurisprudence surrounding environmental law by not only adopting but also expanding private law principles in adjudicating public law cases. In doing so, its innovative approaches resulted in the evolution of principles such as absolute liability, which were stretched from the well-known tort law rule of strict liability. In other instances, the Court incorporated then-established international concepts such as the precautionary principle and the polluter pays principle and entrenched them as an integral part of Indian law. This judicially designed law was then statutorily codified in the NGT Act, 2010, following which the NGT has also been implementing these principles germinated from private law.

Given the Indian higher judiciary's track record, there is sufficient reason to believe that advancements in the jurisprudence surrounding climate litigation are likely to emanate more effectively in public law cases than private law ones. As one commentator astutely observes:

> The constitutional and statutory powers of Indian courts are broadly worded and allow them to exercise jurisdiction in innovative ways in situations that are not necessarily governed by black letter law. Indian courts have not shied away from using this discretionary space in adjudicating environmental disputes, and they are likely to extend this proactive approach to climate claims as well. The framework of environmental rights and legal principles that the Indian judiciary has developed over the past three decades is well placed to support climate litigation.[113]

This is more so given that the Indian Supreme Court has recognised horizontal litigation in constitutional law matters against private actors. This will offer more opportunity for claimants to initiate constitutional claims using the writ jurisdiction of the High Courts and the Supreme Court in the climate context against companies that are emitters of greenhouse gases. Not only is the enforcement of public law measures likely to be swifter, but they may very well be comparatively more effective. If the incremental measures devised by the Indian higher judiciary over the last few decades in environmental law are anything to go by, one can expect a similar approach in the area of climate change as well. The exercise of writ jurisdiction by the higher courts offers ample opportunity for the judiciary to make modest but crucial improvements. For instance, one set of authors argues "that the Indian judiciary through a step-change or a small win process underpinned by the environmental rule of law contributes towards an evolving climate change transformation".[114]

While its utility is likely to be marginalised by the expansion of constitutional rights, private law actions would continue to hold some limited sway in corporate climate litigation. Actions in tort law using the absolute liability or polluter pays principles or those in corporate law involving breaches of directors' duties to consider stakeholder interests are not altogether out of the question. If at all these actions become prevalent, they are likely to draw heavily from the public law jurisprudence already developed by the courts. For instance, one can imagine that any tort law action would rely heavily on public law jurisprudence that has taken the narrow common law of breaches of duty, causation, and quantification of damages and stretched them considerably in the environmental context. Hence, defendants in private law actions might be inhibited from relying extensively on the doctrinal constriction of tort law concepts in private

[113] Shibani Ghosh, 'Litigating Climate Claims in India' in Symposium on Jacqueline Peel and Jolene Lin, 'Transnational Climate Litigation: The Contribution of the Global South' (2020) 114 American Journal of International Law Unbound 45, 49.

[114] Gitanjali N Gill and Gopichandran Ramachandran, 'Sustainability Transformations, Environmental Rule of Law and the Indian Judiciary: Connecting the Dots Through Climate Change Litigation' (2021) 23 Environmental Law Review 228, 239.

law in evading potential climate claims. In that sense, the constitutionalisation of tort law in India has expanded the boundaries of common law doctrine. Another example is that the recognition of the fundamental right to be protected against the adverse effects of climate change in *Ranjitsinh 2024* could be used imaginatively to form the bulwark in the assertion of a private climate right in an action under tort law or corporate law. This way, the removal of at least some of the substantive constraints of private law doctrine in the climate space by infusion of doctrinal nourishments from public law could potentially lead to a greater utility of private law in corporate climate litigation. This, of course, assumes that some of the procedural hurdles of private law are also removed, if not by the regular courts, then at least by the specialist NGT.

7. Conclusion

Private law is receiving greater recognition as a tool in the action against climate change. In the Global North, companies are facing the prospect of increased private law litigation. In countries such as India, however, private law is likely to play a rather unconventional role in corporate climate litigation. Given that most advancements in environmental law have occurred in public law in the Indian context (albeit by borrowing heavily from private law concepts), one can reasonably anticipate the same trend to continue in the climate space as well. At the same time, it would be imprudent to forsake the utility of private law on its own. Private law would likely play a greater role in moderating the behaviour of private actors, like corporations, to address ex ante the challenges arising from climate change. This suggests that in addition to playing a secondary role in supporting the development of public law, the concepts in tort, contract, property, and corporate law in India have to be re-engineered to the extent they can be deployed in the mitigation and adaptation of climate risks.

CHAPTER 37

Australasia

JACQUELINE PEEL

1. Introduction

THE Australasian region has emerged as a key area for understanding the developing interface between climate change and private law. "Australasia" in this chapter is understood as comprising principally the common law jurisdictions of Australia and New Zealand.[1] Within the region, Australia has seen rapid evolution of the intersection between climate change and private legal avenues, mediated through the lens of a growing body of corporate climate litigation. This litigation—numbering nearly sixty cases that utilise a wide array of private law causes of action (including corporate and financial law, consumer law, and tort law)[2]—has inspired similar cases in neighbouring New Zealand, such as the landmark *Smith v Fonterra* lawsuit,[3] and emerging consumer protection claims.[4]

This chapter considers developments in corporate climate litigation in Australasia as a means of exploring intersections between climate change and private law. It argues that this jurisprudence is demonstrating both the potential for existing private law avenues utilised in the region's corporate climate litigation to play a role in addressing climate change, and also

[1] C Gibson, 'Australasia' in Rob Kitchin and Nigel Thrift (eds), *International Encyclopaedia of Human Geography* (Elsevier 2009) 225–33, explaining that 'Australasia' is 'less a concretely defined physical region, than an imagined geography of a diverse part of the world'. The term generally encompasses Australia and New Zealand, sometimes in combination with other neighbouring countries that are 'south of Asia, and west of the Pacific'. Pacific Island states are yet to see the emergence of corporate climate litigation meaning the jurisdictional focus of this Chapter is limited to Australia and New Zealand.

[2] The Australian and Pacific Climate Change Litigation Database maintained by Melbourne Climate Futures records over 100 cases in the 'corporate accountability' category across Australia and New Zealand. These cases utilise a range of public and private legal claims and litigation strategies covering topics like disputes over carbon credits and offsets, corporate form, environmental harm, greenwashing, nuisance and negligence, renewable energy certification, and transparency and disclosure; see Australian and Pacific Climate Change Litigation Database, Melbourne Climate Futures, <https://law.app.unimelb.edu.au/climate-change/index.php#litigation> accessed 19 May 2025. The subset of these claims using private law avenues in corporate and financial law, consumer law and tort law consists of sixty cases (not all of which have yet reached the stage of court determination), fifty-seven of which are from Australia. There are also a further two complaints lodged on behalf of Australian Torres Strait Islanders with banks and superannuation funds alleging human rights violations because of their fossil fuel investments.

[3] *Smith v Fonterra Co-Operative Group Limited* [2024] NZSC 5 (Supreme Court of New Zealand, 7 February 2024). For an overview, see Sam Bookman, '*Smith v Fonterra* and the Climatisation of Tort Law' (2025) 88(1) Modern Law Review 192–204. See also David Bullock, Chapter 7 of this handbook.

[4] *Lawyers for Climate Action & Ors v Firstgas*, Advertising Standards Complaint Board, Complaint 21/194, Decision 6 July 2021 and *Consumer NZ Inc v Z Energy Ltd*, filed with the High Court of New Zealand in November 2023.

how private law doctrines are themselves undergoing adaptation in ways that could make them more suitable for managing climate impacts. As the New Zealand Supreme Court put it in *Smith v Fonterra*:

> The common law has not previously grappled with a crisis as all-embracing as climate change. But in the 19th and 20th centuries it had to deal with another existential crisis, albeit one of lesser scale, when the industrial revolution dramatically enlarged the risk of accidents through the mechanisation of factories, transportation and mining. The law's response was a mixture of the flawed . . . and the inspired.[5]

In its decision to reinstate a claim in tort relating to damage caused by climate change, the New Zealand Supreme Court in *Smith v Fonterra* applied established principles governing strike out to create the space necessary for robust judicial reconsideration of the doctrinal underpinnings of tortious legal concepts (such as causation and proximity) in the context of climate change. Although tort claims have not featured prominently in Australian corporate climate litigation, the more prevalent cases concerning corporate disclosure obligations and the prevention of misleading and deceptive statements by companies about their climate performance equally illustrate the inherent flexibility of private law avenues to be moulded to fit new circumstances, including those presented by climate disruption. In this way, the corporate climate litigation experience of these two common law jurisdictions in Australasia presents a microcosm of broader efforts to understand the developing private law–climate interface.

The remainder of the chapter proceeds as follows. Section 2 elaborates the understanding of "corporate climate litigation" employed in the chapter, noting that while attracting growing attention in the literature, the category does not yet have a settled scope or meaning.[6] Section 3 examines corporate climate litigation developments in Australia and their utilisation of different private law avenues, analysing the way that courts are adapting private law doctrines to accommodate climate change. Section 4 then compares and contrasts this experience with parallel developments in New Zealand. This section highlights the tort law case of *Smith v Fonterra*, as well as emerging cases focused on consumer protection. It also expands the comparative analysis to consider the degree of transference of litigation strategies between Australia and New Zealand. The concluding section, Section 5, summarises the chapter's reflections on how private law is evolving in response to climate change across the different doctrinal areas (directors' duties, disclosure, consumer protection, and tort) explored in Australasian corporate climate litigation. It posits that rather than fundamentally transforming these private law doctrines, climate change—as mediated through corporate climate cases—is facilitating their incremental adaptation in ways that make private law more suitable for application in a climate changed world.

2. Corporate Climate Litigation

Corporate climate litigation has been identified as an emerging area of growth in the broader field of climate change litigation.[7] The Grantham Research Institute's "Global Trends" annual "snapshot" reports show that while governments remain the primary focus of climate

[5] *Smith v Fonterra* (n 3) (Williams and Kós JJ) [156].

[6] See Jacqueline Peel, Rebekkah Markey-Towler, and Thea Shields, 'Global Perspectives on Corporate Climate Legal Tactics: Australia National Report' (*BIICL*, February 2024) <https://www.unimelb.edu.au/__data/assets/pdf_file/0006/4886484/12176_global_perspectives_on_corporate_climate_legal_tactics_-_australia_national_report_v1.pdf> accessed 2 March 2025.

[7] UNEP, *Global Climate Litigation Report: 2023 Status Review* (Nairobi, 2023), 90.

litigation, a significant proportion of cases now target private actors like companies (20% of cases filed in 2024).[8] This trend is even more pronounced outside of the US;[9] for "global" cases (i.e., those filed in countries other than the US) the Grantham Research Institute found 40% of such cases in 2023 "involved corporate actors among the defendants".[10]

Although corporate climate litigation is attracting more interest from scholars, activists, and practitioners,[11] there remains no settled definition of the concept. In part this is because the field is just emerging, and litigants are experimenting with many different legal avenues. Highlighting the "rise of corporate climate change litigation", scholars such as Rajavuori, Severesi, and van Asselt, thus note that "[t]his emergent practice of climate change litigation targeting corporate actors builds on a variety of legal arguments and strategies", from private law areas of contract, tort law, and financial regulation, to public law doctrines drawn from constitutional or human rights law.[12] More broadly, corporate climate litigation claims are emerging across all the component climate policy areas of mitigation (focused on emissions reduction), adaptation (focused on managing or reducing climate impacts), and loss and damage (focused on responses to address climate-related economic and non-economic losses and harms).[13]

The growth in corporate climate litigation globally is often attributed to the goal of "targett[ing] corporations in an attempt to identify their corporate responsibility to mitigate [greenhouse gas] emissions".[14] The British Institute of International and Comparative Law's (BIICL) Global Toolbox on Corporate Climate Litigation, which draws from national reports produced for seventeen jurisdictions, hence describes "efforts to hold companies accountable for their impacts on climate change" as "the essence of corporate climate litigation".[15]

A more specific definition of corporate climate litigation is found in the Australia National Report produced for the BIICL project, which provides that:

> corporate climate change litigation is distinguished by: (a) having/involving a corporation as the defendant of the claim; and/or (b) having a cause of action drawn from corporate, commercial, or financial law.[16]

[8] Joana Setzer and Catherine Higham, *Global Trends in Climate Change Litigation: 2025 Snapshot* (LSE Grantham Research Institute on Climate Change and the Environment, June 2025), 26.

[9] Joana Setzer and Catherine Higham, *Global Trends in Climate Change Litigation: 2024 Snapshot* (LSE Grantham Research Institute on Climate Change and the Environment, June 2024), 19. The Global Trends 2025 Snapshot notes that the trend of 'a higher proportion of corporate cases filed outside the US rather than within it' was also evident in the 2024 case dataset: ibid. On US corporate climate litigation more generally, see Lisa Benjamin, 'The Road to Paris Runs Through Delaware: Climate Litigation and Directors' Duties' (2020) Utah Law Review 313.

[10] Global Trends 2024 (n 9).

[11] See the developments noted in Global Trends 2024 (n 9), including the BIICL Global Toolbox on Corporate Climate Litigation Project (for the Australian contribution to this Project, see (n 6)).

[12] Mikko Rajavuori, Annalisa Savaresi, and Harro van Asselt, 'Mandatory Due Diligence Laws and Climate Change Litigation: Bridging the Corporate Climate Accountability Gap?' (2023) 17 Regulation & Governance 944–53, 945.

[13] Karen S Sokol, 'Bringing Courts into Global Governance in a Climate-Disrupted World Order' (2023) 108 Minnesota Law Review 163–239.

[14] UNEP 2023 Status Review (n 7) 90.

[15] BIICL, Global Toolbox on Corporate Climate Litigation Toolbox, Introduction, Section 1, <https://www.biicl.org/global-toolbox-corporate-climate-litigation> accessed 2 March 2025.

[16] Peel, Markey-Towler, and Shields (n 6) 7.

It is acknowledged by the authors of the Australia National Report that this is "a very broad definition" that captures administrative, environmental, and planning law cases utilising public law avenues to address climate change, where such cases are brought by or otherwise involve corporate defendants.[17] Such cases have been characterised as part of a "first generation" of climate litigation in Australia, concerned with challenges to individual projects with climate impacts.[18] These cases can be contrasted with "next generation" corporate climate cases, which are "focused on ensuring the direct accountability of [company] defendants for their contribution to climate change".[19] It is the latter category of cases that tend to rely on private law causes of action as part of "strategic" lawsuits "filed with the aim of influencing the broader debate around climate action".[20]

In discussing relevant lawsuits, the remainder of the chapter focuses on such "next generation" corporate climate cases.[21] These claims are often brought by litigants with the express purpose of testing the utility of private law doctrines to apply beyond their usual bounds to circumstances of climate change.[22] Hence, they provide the greatest insights in understanding how this litigation is influencing the interface of climate change and private law across Australasia.

3. Australia's Corporate Climate Litigation Experience

Within the Australasian region (and arguably, globally), Australia has emerged as an innovative "testbed" for corporate climate change litigation.[23] In a set of "next generation" cases that have emerged since 2017, private law causes of action in company and financial law, and consumer law, are particularly coming to the fore.[24] Causes of action in tort law have also featured in this next generation litigation, although, to date, these cases have targeted government actors, such as the federal environment minister in the challenge by Anjali Sharma and other children to decision-making approving a new coal mine extension.[25]

The following sections discuss the different private law pathways utilised in Australian corporate climate change litigation, with examples of how particular cases have treated the interface between private law and climate change concerns. The aim of this analysis is to highlight the ways in which Australian litigants and courts, through their arguments and decisions in these legal disputes, are adapting a broad array of private law doctrines to accommodate climate change.

17 ibid.

18 Jacqueline Peel, Hari Osofsky, and Anita Foerster, 'Shaping the "Next Generation" of Climate Change Litigation in Australia' (2017) 41(2) Melbourne University Law Review 793.

19 Peel, Markey-Towler, and Shields (n 6) 8.

20 Global Trends 2024 (n 9) 7.

21 For a similar understanding of corporate climate litigation as involving strategic private climate litigation see Geetanjali Ganguly, Joana Setzer, and Veerle Heyvaert, 'If at First You Don't Succeed: Suing Corporations for Climate Change' (2018) 38(4) Oxford Journal of Legal Studies 841–68.

22 Geetanjali Ganguly, 'Breaking New Ground in Private Climate Litigation' in Francesco Sindico and others (eds), *Research Handbook on Climate Change Litigation* (Edward Elgar Publishing 2024) 123–44.

23 Peel, Markey-Towler, and Shields 2024 (n 6) 5.

24 ibid.

25 *Sharma by her litigation representative Sister Marie Brigid Arthur v Minister for Environment* [2021] FCA 560; *Minister for Environment v Sharma* [2022] FCAFC 35.

3.1 Pathways in Corporate and Financial Law

3.1.1 Evolving Directors' Duties to Include Action on Climate

Reliance on corporate and financial law pathways in Australian corporate climate litigation is founded on the increasing acceptance of climate change as posing not just environmental risks but also creating financial and reputational risks for firms.[26] This trend, which had its origins in the Paris Agreement negotiations and the work of the G20 Taskforce on Climate-Related Financial Disclosures (TCFD),[27] was first given legal significance in Australia via a series of legal opinions issued from 2016 onwards by leading commercial barristers, Noel Hutley QC and Sebastian Hartford-Davis. The "Hutley opinions",[28] as they have become known, put forward the position that company directors who fail to consider and disclose material financial risks relating to climate change could be liable for breaching their duty of care and diligence under Section 180(1) of the Corporations Act 2001 (Cth) (Corporations Act). This duty—much like fiduciary duties owed by company directors in other jurisdictions[29]—provides:

> A director or other officer of a corporation must exercise their powers and discharge their duties with the degree of care and diligence that a reasonable person would exercise if they:
> (a) were a director or officer of a corporation in the corporation's circumstances; and
> (b) occupied the office held by, and had the same responsibilities within the corporation as, the director or officer.[30]

Supplementary Hutley opinions have recognised that the standard for directors to establish the requisite degree of care and diligence has continued to rise as global action on climate increases in line with Paris Agreement targets, and that "greenwashing" (i.e., misleading statements or disclosures regarding a company's green or climate credentials) is likely to be a key litigation risk for entities.[31] In a statement that set off ripples of concern across Australian boardrooms, the original Hutley opinion concluded:

[26] Sarah Barker, 'Directors' Liability and Climate Risk: Australia: Country Paper' (*Commonwealth Climate and Law Initiative*, April 2018) <https://commonwealthclimatelaw.org/wp-content/uploads/2021/12/CCLI-Australia-Paper-Final.pdf> accessed 2 March 2025.

[27] TCFD, 'Recommendations of the Task Force on Climate-Related Financial Disclosures' (June 2017) <https://assets.bbhub.io/company/sites/60/2021/10/FINAL-2017-TCFD-Report.pdf> accessed 2 March 2025.

[28] Centre for Policy Development, '2021 Hutley opinion on directors duties and climate change' (25 April 2021) <https://cpd.org.au/work/2021-hutley-opinion-greenwashing-repor/> accessed 2 March 2025 (2021 Hutley Opinion); Centre for Policy Development, '2016 Hutley opinion on directors duties and climate change' (30 October 2016) <https://cpd.org.au/work/2016-hutley-opinion-directors-duties-climate/> accessed 2 March 2025 (2016 Hutley Opinion).

[29] See the work of the Commonwealth Climate and Law Initiative (CCLI), which produces the 'Directors' Duties Navigator' in collaboration with the Climate Governance Initiative (CGI). The fourth edition of the online Navigator covers 33 countries and the EU. Commonwealth Climate and Law Initiative and Climate Governance Initiative, 'Directors' Duties Navigator: Climate Risk and Sustainability Disclosures' (26 September 2024) < https://commonwealthclimatelaw.org/directors-duties-navigator-climate-risk-and-sustainability-disclosures-fourth-edition-2024> accessed 13 June 2025.

[30] The federal Corporations Act, s 181(1) provides further duties on directors and other corporate officers to 'exercise their powers and discharge their duties: (a) in good faith in the best interests of the corporation; and (b) for a proper purpose'.

[31] 2021 Hutley Opinion (n 28) [50].

> It is likely to be only a matter of time before we see litigation against a director who has failed to perceive, disclose or take steps in relation to a foreseeable climate-related risk that can be demonstrated to have caused harm to a company (including, perhaps, reputational harm).[32]

Despite that prediction, Australia is yet to see a climate case founded on a breach of corporate directors' duties. Nonetheless, this avenue continues to be explored as a potential basis for future corporate climate claims against Australian companies,[33] drawing inspiration from jurisprudence in other common law countries, such as the *ClientEarth v Shell* case in the United Kingdom.[34]

In another indication of the potential for this pathway to shape private law doctrines in a climate context, a similarly framed case was taken forward in 2018 in respect of the duties owed by superannuation (i.e., pension) fund trustees in the lawsuit of *McVeigh v Retail Employees Superannuation Pty Ltd* (REST case).[35] In the REST case, Mr McVeigh—a then twenty-three-year-old member of the REST superfund—commenced proceedings against the fund's corporate trustee for allegedly failing to provide him with information regarding the financial risks posed to his accounts by climate change, in breach of the trustee's legal duties under the Superannuation Industry (Supervision) Act 1993 (Cth) (SIS Act) and the Corporations Act.[36] In addition, McVeigh sought to compel REST to act on climate risks in managing the investments in its portfolio in order to ensure that the best interests of the fund's members were protected from future losses due to climate change (for instance, as a result of "stranding" of fossil fuel assets with tightening climate regulatory requirements).[37]

The REST case settled before trial on terms very favourable to McVeigh.[38] This included REST issuing a statement acknowledging that the Australian superannuation industry—as a cornerstone of the country's economy—was exposed to economic risks (i.e., financial, physical, and transition impacts) associated with climate change.[39] REST's statement also recognised climate change as a "material, direct and current financial risk" to the superfund and acknowledged the importance of the fund trustee "actively" identifying and managing these risks and continuing to develop "systems, policies and processes" for mitigating and managing those risks "having regard to the goals of the Paris Agreement and other international efforts to limit climate change".[40] Further, the fund committed to implementing "a long-term objective to achieve a net zero carbon footprint for the fund by 2050".[41]

[32] 2016 Hutley Opinion (n 28), [51].

[33] See CCLI and CGI, Directors' Duties Navigator (n 29).

[34] *ClientEarth v Shell's Board of Directors* [2023] EWHC 1137 (Ch); [2023] EWHC 1897 (Ch); [2023] EWHC 2182 (Ch). While the case was dismissed by successive UK courts, the legal theory put forward by the plaintiffs has generated legal commentary and attracted substantial interest from Australian litigators: see, e.g., Ekaterina Aristova and Lionel Nichols, 'Climate Change on the Board: Navigating Directors' Duties' (2024) 24(2) Journal of Corporate Law Studies 479–514.

[35] It is common for Australian superannuation schemes to have a single trustee that is a company.

[36] Relevant duties under the SIS Act in ss 52(2)(b) and (c) include those for trustees 'to exercise, in relation to all matters affecting the entity, the same degree of care, skill and diligence as a prudent superannuation trustee would exercise in relation to an entity of which it is trustee and on behalf of the beneficiaries of which it makes investments' and 'to perform the trustee's duties and exercise the trustee's powers in the best financial interests of the beneficiaries'.

[37] See further George Semieniuk and others, 'Stranded Fossil-Fuel Assets Translate to Major Losses for Investors in Advanced Economies' (2022) 12 Nature Climate Change 532–38.

[38] REST, Statement from REST, Media Release (2 November 2020) <https://equitygenerationlawyers.com/wp/wp-content/uploads/2020/11/Statement-from-Rest-2-November-2020.pdf> accessed 2 March 2025.

[39] ibid.

[40] ibid.

[41] ibid.

The REST case received wide attention both nationally and internationally.[42] Although the settlement limited the precedential value of the case, it nevertheless provides an affirmation of the relevance of climate-related financial risks to the interpretation of directors' duties under Australian corporate and financial law,[43] justifying commentators' warnings that the REST litigation will lead to "increasing pressure on companies and businesses and investment and infrastructure asset owners to address climate risks".[44]

3.1.2 Extending Disclosure Requirements to Climate Risk

While the REST case combined arguments around (trustee) directors' duties and disclosure, other Australian climate cases utilising corporate and financial law pathways have focused solely on disclosure requirements. The theory of change underlying these cases is that greater disclosure by companies of information concerning the climate risks faced by their businesses to shareholders, investors, and the general public will motivate action by companies to address and mitigate these risks. An early example of litigation in this vein was the case of *Abrahams v Commonwealth Bank of Australia* (Abrahams case).[45] Shareholders of the Commonwealth Bank of Australia (CBA) commenced proceedings against the bank alleging that CBA had violated several provisions of the Corporations Act by failing to disclose climate-related financial risks in its annual reporting. Like the REST case, the Abrahams case settled before trial.[46] However, as a practical matter, the lawsuit appeared to achieve its desired impact with a substantial improvement in CBA's disclosure of climate-related risks in subsequent annual reports, likely driven by the bank's desire to avoid further litigation.[47]

A similar, more recent, case is that of *Catherine Rossiter v ANZ Group Holdings Limited*.[48] It was brought by an ANZ Bank shareholder, Ms Rossiter, who filed an application for preliminary discovery in the Federal Court of Australia on 9 November 2023 seeking access to ANZ's internal risk management framework to assess whether the bank was adequately addressing

[42] See, e.g., Esmeralda Colombo, 'From Bushfires to Misfires: Climate-Related Financial Risk after *McVeigh v. Retail Employees Superannuation Trust*' (2022) 11(1) Transnational Environmental Law 173–99.

[43] Brian J Preston, 'The Influence of the Paris Agreement on Climate Litigation: Causation, Corporate Governance and Catalyst (Part II)' (2021) 33(2) Journal of Environmental Law 227–56.

[44] Tony Zhang, 'Rest Super Climate Lawsuit Has Far-Reaching Implications' (*Lawyers Weekly*, 6 November 2020) <https://www.lawyersweekly.com.au/biglaw/29907-rest-super-climate-lawsuit-has-far-reaching-implications> accessed 2 March 2025.

[45] The court record for the litigation is available from the Federal Court, Victorian Registry, <https://www.comcourts.gov.au/file/Federal/P/VID879/2017/actions> accessed 2 March 2025.

[46] Another case was brought by Guy and Kim Abrahams against CBA in 2021 seeking access under s 247A of the Corporations Act to CBA's internal documents relating to funding of seven oil and gas projects and alleging instances of greenwashing in the company's documents: *Abrahams v CBA (No 2)* NSD864/2021 <https://comcourts.gov.au/file/Federal/P/NSD864/2021/actions> accessed 2 March 2025. This proceeding was finalised in 2023, with the Federal Court ordering in favour of the Abrahams: Federal Court of Australia, *Abrahams v CBA*, Consent Order, 13 April 2023 <https://comcourts.gov.au/file/Federal/P/NSD864/2021/3921677/event/31377494/document/2089025> accessed 2 March 2025.

[47] See, e.g., Commonwealth Bank of Australia, Annual Report 2024, 26-28 <https://www.commbank.com.au/content/dam/commbank-assets/investors/docs/results/fy24/2024-Annual-Report_spreads.pdf> accessed 2 March 2025.

[48] NSD1315/2023. The court file can be accessed at <https://comcourts.gov.au/file/Federal/P/NSD1315/2023/actions>. The case parallels *Beere v National Australia Bank*, NSD715/2024, brought by a long-term shareholder in National Australia Bank (NAB) against the company requesting to 'inspect books' and review internal company documentation on financing of companies with new thermal coal projects.

the risks posed by climate change and biodiversity loss.[49] Four days later, on 13 November 2023, ANZ released its 2023 annual report, disclosing that on the same day Rossiter's action was filed, its Board Risk Committee had designated "climate risk" as a key material risk. The report also outlined ANZ's commitment to strengthening its enterprise-wide approach to managing climate risk, with further updates expected in its 2024 reporting.[50] Additionally, ANZ acknowledged its ongoing efforts to refine its strategy, policies, and services to better manage risks and opportunities related to climate change and biodiversity loss. The case was later discontinued by mutual agreement in April 2024. Shortly thereafter, ANZ announced it would no longer provide project finance for new or expanded oil and gas projects.[51]

While this series of corporate law, disclosure-related cases against banks has not received judicial consideration due to the litigants' (and lawyers') preference to settle ahead of a court hearing, their effectiveness in forcing the targeted companies to disclose relevant climate risks to their businesses, and how those risks are being internally managed, illustrates the capacity to adapt this private legal pathway to climate ends. This in turn has encouraged further efforts by climate litigants to expand this pathway to target superannuation (pension) funds and their management of climate risks posed to members' investment portfolios.[52]

In addition to cases brought by shareholders or pension fund members, an increasing number of climate-related actions relying on corporate and financial law disclosure requirements have been brought by regulators such as the Australian Securities and Investments Commission (ASIC). Following release of an information sheet on misleading climate disclosures in June 2022,[53] ASIC announced a new enforcement posture for the agency focused on "greenwashing" in respect of investment products and corporate net-zero commitments. ASIC has since issued several infringement notices to companies about alleged greenwashing.[54]

ASIC has also undertaken successful enforcement actions against Vanguard Investments Australia, Active Super, and Mercer Superannuation for making false or misleading representations in breach of the ASIC Act.[55] In a judgment issued in August 2024 by the Federal Court

[49] Equity Generation Lawyers, 'Catherine Rossiter v ANZ Group Holdings Limited', Media Release <https://equitygenerationlawyers.com/case/catherine-rossiter-v-anz-group-holdings-limited/> accessed 2 March 2025.

[50] ANZ, Annual Report (2024) <https://www.anz.com.au/content/dam/anzcom/shareholder/ANZGHL-2024-Annual%20Report.pdf> accessed 2 March 2025. This report articulates the bank's approach to climate change on page 17.

[51] Ben Potter, 'ANZ Hardens Policy Against Bankrolling Oil and Gas Projects' (*Australian Financial Review*, 9 May 2024) <https://www.afr.com/policy/energy-and-climate/anz-hardens-policy-against-bankrolling-oil-and-gas-projects-20240508-p5hbu4> accessed 2 March 2025 (noting this decision effectively precluded the bank's direct financing of Santos 'troubled' $15bn Papua LNG project, a joint venture with TotalEnergies, ExxonMobil and JX Nippon).

[52] These claims are at an earlier 'pre-litigation' stage, taking the form of legal letters sent by environmental public interest law firm—the Environmental Defenders Office (EDO)—to pension funds such as UniSuper and HESTA, claiming that their investments in fossil fuel companies, Santos and Woodside, amount to a breach of the companies' obligations to manage climate risk and that they may therefore be liable. For details, see Australian and Pacific Climate Change Litigation Database (n 2).

[53] Information Sheet 271, 'How to Avoid Greenwashing When Offering or Promoting Sustainability-related Products' (*Australian Securities and Investments Commission*, June 2022) <https://asic.gov.au/regulatory-resources/financial-services/how-to-avoid-greenwashing-when-offering-or-promoting-sustainability-related-products/> accessed 2 March 2025.

[54] ASIC has issued over $AUD300,000 in infringement notices in response to concerns about alleged greenwashing, which include those against Tlou Energy Limited, Vanguard Investments Australia, Diversa Trustees Limited, Black Mountain Energy, Future Super, Morningstar, and Fertoz Limited.

[55] *Australian Securities and Investments Commission v Vanguard Investments Australia Ltd* [2024] FCA 308; *Australian Securities and Investments Commission v LGSS Pty Ltd (Active Super)* [2024] FCA

of Australia, Mercer was ordered to pay a $AUD11.3 million penalty after it admitted to making misleading statements about the sustainable nature and characteristics of some of its superannuation investment options.[56] In his judgment, Justice Horan pointed out that enforcement action to address the new category of misleading green or climate disclosures is underpinned by standard commercial rationales foundational to private law doctrines focused on protecting consumers and safeguarding fair competition.[57] As His Honour opined:

> Greenwashing practices have the potential to reduce consumer confidence in environmental, social and corporate governance (ESG) claims, which undermines the efforts of businesses that are pursuing ESG goals accurately and fairly. In addition to harming consumers by depriving them of information relevant to making choices in accordance with environmental, social and ethical values or objectives, false or misleading ESG claims may confer unfair competitive advantages on companies in marketing their financial products and services.[58]

3.2 Consumer Law Pathways

3.2.1 Anti-Greenwashing Action by Consumer Protection Regulators

ASIC's anti-greenwashing enforcement actions are illustrative of a broader trend in Australian corporate climate litigation focused on using private law avenues to safeguard against misleading corporate disclosures or statements regarding corporate climate credentials or practices that may harm consumers.[59] This trend has also seen Australia's consumer protection scheme under the Corporations Act and the Australian Consumer Law (ACL)[60] increasingly used to mount climate litigation and legal interventions against corporations. As Parker and Johnson note, applying consumer law in a climate context is intended to drive positive action on this environmental problem through "climate conscious consumption" whereby "the more consumers purchase climate-friendly products, the more businesses are incentivised to take climate action to attract more consumers".[61] While themselves sceptical of the

587; *Australian Securities and Investments Commission v Mercer Superannuation (Australia) Limited* [2024] FCA 850.

56 Media Release 24-173MR, 'ASIC's First Greenwashing Case Results in Landmark $11.3 Million Penalty for Mercer' (*Australian Securities and Investments Commission*, 2 August 2024) <https://asic.gov.au/about-asic/news-centre/find-a-media-release/2024-releases/24-173mr-asic-s-first-greenwashing-case-results-in-landmark-11-3-million-penalty-for-mercer/> accessed 2 March 2025. In the Vanguard case, Vanguard was ordered to pay $12.9M in penalties. Media Release 24-213MR, 'ASIC's Vanguard Greenwashing Action Results in Record $12.9 Million Penalty' (*Australian Securities and Investments Commission*, 25 September 2024) <https://asic.gov.au/about-asic/news-centre/find-a-media-release/2024-releases/24-213mr-asic-s-vanguard-greenwashing-action-results-in-record-12-9-million-penalty/> accessed 2 March 2025.

57 See Stephanie Law and others, 'Private Law, Private International Law and Public Interest Litigation' (2024) 13(1) *Global Constitutionalism* 1–12, 3: 'It has generally been accepted that private law must also be understood to encompass regulatory fields that touch upon concerns of a broader public interest, including consumer and labour law.'

58 *Australian Securities and Investments Commission v Mercer Superannuation (Australia) Limited* [2024] FCA 850, [4].

59 Christine Parker and Hope Johnson, 'Climate-Related Greenwashing and Australian Consumer Law' in Julia Dehm, Nicole Graham, and Zoe Nay (eds), *Becoming a Climate Conscious Lawyer: Climate Change and the Australian Legal System* (La Trobe University 2024), 294–316.

60 The ACL is found in a Schedule to the Competition and Consumer Act 2010 (Cth).

61 Parker and Johnson (n 59) 299. See also Eric Ortz, Chapter 5 of this handbook.

validity of climate conscious consumption as a strategy for addressing climate change, Parker and Johnson explain that this approach

> relies on consumers having meaningful and accurate information about the climate credentials of different products and services to inform their choices. In this ideal of environmentally responsible consumption, consumer law therefore has an important role to play in ensuring that the marketing information consumers receive is accurate and meaningful.[62]

Like ASIC, Australia's competition and consumer regulator—the Australian Competition and Consumer Commission (ACCC)—has issued announcements and guidance that indicate that misleading climate or environmental marketing of products is a priority for its oversight, and warning companies against making environmental claims without proper backing. In March 2023, ACCC issued a media statement following an internet sweep it had conducted where it found 57% of the businesses surveyed had made potential greenwashing claims about their environmental credentials.[63] In December 2023, ACCC issued a guide for business on making environmental claims.[64]

As yet, the ACCC has not initiated any enforcement actions to address corporate claims that may mislead consumers about the climate credentials of Australian businesses. The closest analogue is the ACCC's proceedings against Volkswagen for breaches of Section 29 of the ACL by making false representations about the vehicle manufacturer's compliance with Australian diesel emissions standards.[65] The Volkswagen litigation built on earlier greenwashing cases taken by ACCC in 2008 against Saab[66] and V8 Supercars. Before the latter case proceeded to court, V8 Supercars Australia Pty Ltd acknowledged the ACCC's concerns that its claim that carbon emissions would be entirely offset by the planting of trees may have been misleading or deceptive.[67]

3.2.2 Civil Society Litigation Targeting Corporate Climate Claims

Rather than action by regulators, the principal examples of Australian climate litigation using consumer law avenues involve claims brought by civil society actors. There are now several such cases and complaints afoot,[68] with a far-reaching settlement concluded in the EnergyAustralia case, discussed further below, in May 2025.

62 ibid.

63 Media Release, 'ACCC 'Greenwashing' Internet Sweep Unearths Widespread Concerning Claims' (*Australian Competition and Consumer Commission*, 3 March 2023) <https://www.accc.gov.au/media-release/accc-%E2%80%98greenwashing%E2%80%99-internet-sweep-unearths-widespread-concerning-claims> accessed 2 March 2025.

64 Making environmental claims: A guide for business (*Australian Competition and Consumer Commission*, December 2023) <https://www.accc.gov.au/about-us/publications/making-environmental-claims-a-guide-for-business> accessed 2 March 2025.

65 *Australian Competition and Consumer Commission v Volkswagen Aktiengesellschaft* [2019] FCA 2166; [2021] FCAFC 49.

66 Media Release, 'Saab 'Grrrrrreen' Claims Declared Misleading by Federal Court' (*Australian Competition and Consumer Commission*, 18 September 2008) <https://www.accc.gov.au/media-release/saab-grrrrrreen-claims-declared-misleading-by-federal-court> accessed 2 March 2025.

67 Media Release, 'V8 Supercars Australia Pty Ltd - s.87B Undertaking' (*Australian Competition and Consumer Commission*, 16 September 2008) <https://www.accc.gov.au/public-registers/undertakings-registers/section-87b-undertakings-register/v8-supercars-australia-pty-ltd-s87b-undertaking> accessed 2 March 2025.

68 In addition to the EnergyAustralia and Santos claims discussed below see: (1) *Greenpeace Australia Pacific Limited v Woodside Energy Group Ltd* NSD1520/2023; Greenpeace, Media Release, 'Greenpeace Australia Pacific Takes Woodside To Court Alleging Misleading Climate Claims (Offsets

A common thread in this litigation is challenges to an entity's net-zero or carbon neutrality claims as misleading or deceptive for consumers based on alleged deficiencies in the actions being taken by the companies concerned to reduce their greenhouse gas emissions and climate impacts. This approach invites courts to consider what actions and processes companies must put in place to avoid greenwashing in a climate context, including issues which have evaded consensus in other areas of climate law, such as the extent to which indirect or "Scope 3" emissions must be included in net-zero pledges,[69] and the allowability of "carbon offsets" as a means to meet emissions reduction targets.[70] In this way, these cases stand to contribute not just to evolving the application of consumer law to climate issues but also to developing notions of corporate accountability under climate law.

Two examples—the settled litigation against EnergyAustralia—and the ongoing lawsuit against gas giant, Santos, illustrate the broader point. In the EnergyAustralia case, the grassroots advocacy group, Parents for Climate sued the energy retailer, EnergyAustralia, for allegedly misleading consumers with its "Go Neutral" electricity and gas products. The Go Neutral product relied on purchased carbon offsets to achieve carbon neutrality rather than reductions in sourcing electricity produced through the combustion of fossil fuels. These offsets were alleged by the plaintiff to be primarily "avoidance" credits that did not neutralise emissions, lacked "additionality", did not address existing emissions and might worsen climate impacts (e.g., through methane flaring).[71] A two-week hearing in early May 2025 before the Federal Court considered expert evidence on carbon offsetting and the consumer understanding of "carbon neutral" to determine if EnergyAustralia's marketing was misleading and deceptive in breach of the ACL.[72]

In a statement released by EnergyAustralia on 19 May 2025, following the parties agreeing to a settlement, the energy company acknowledged that "carbon offsetting is not the most effective way to assist customers to reduce their emissions" and apologised to customers misled by marketing of its Go Neutral products.[73] The company specifically conceded that "offsets do not prevent or undo the harms caused by burning fossil fuels for a customer's energy use",

Greenwashing)' (*Greenpeace Australia Pacific*, 14 December 2023) <https://www.greenpeace.org.au/news/greenpeace-australia-pacific-takes-woodside-to-court-alleging-misleading-climate-claims/> accessed 2 March 2025; and (2) Media Release, 'Formal ACCC complaint lodged against Qantas for allegedly misleading sustainability claims' (*Environmental Defenders Office*, 16 October 2024) https://www.edo.org.au/2024/10/16/formal-accc-complaint-lodged-against-qantas-for-misleading-sustainability-claims/ accessed 2 March 2025. In addition, a suite of complaints has been lodged with Australia's advertising regulator, Ad Standards, by various individuals over alleged greenwashing advertisements from companies including Ampol and Glencore. For details see the Australian and Pacific Climate Change Litigation Database (n 2).

[69] See, e.g., Alexis McGivern and others, 'Defining Net Zero: How Do Climate Criteria Align Across Standards and Voluntary Initiatives?' (*Smith School of Enterprise and the Environment, University of Oxford*, 2022) <https://netzeroclimate.org/wp-content/uploads/2022/10/SUMMARY-REVIEW-21-OCT-FINAL.pdf> accessed 2 March 2025.

[70] See, e.g., Clemens Kaupa, 'Scrutinizing Net Zero: The Legal Problems of Counting Greenhouse Gas Emissions, Removals and Offsets Together' (2022) 31(3) Review of European, Comparative and International Environmental Law 447–57.

[71] Equity Generation Lawyers, 'Parents for Climate v EnergyAustralia (Offsets Greenwashing)' <https://equitygenerationlawyers.com/case/ap4ca-v-energyaustralia/> accessed 8 June 2025.

[72] ibid.

[73] Energy Australia, 'Go Neutral Litigation: EnergyAustralia Acknowledges Issues with "Offsetting" and Moves Away from Carbon Offsets for its Residential Customer Products' (*News*, 19 May 2025) <https://www.energyaustralia.com.au/about-us/media/news/go-neutral-litigation-energyaustralia-acknowledges-issues-offsetting-and-moves> accessed 20 May 2025.

noting that "[e]ven with carbon offsetting, the emissions released from burning fossil fuels for a customer's energy use still contribute to climate change".[74] It acknowledged "the importance of consumers understanding the climate impact of products and services offered to them and that offsets are not the most effective means of reducing greenhouse gas emissions", and also recognised the importance of organisations "provid[ing] clear and transparent information to consumers on where and how offsets have been used and what those offsets can achieve".[75] Accordingly, the company stated that it was withdrawing its Go Neutral product and has now "shifted its focus to direct emissions reductions".[76]

The other major example of civil society initiated anti-greenwashing litigation in Australia is the lawsuit filed in 2021 by the Australasian Centre for Corporate Responsibility (ACCR) against the large gas company, Santos, over its claims in annual reports and investor briefings that natural gas is a "clean fuel" and that the company has a credible pathway to reach net-zero emissions by 2040.[77] ACCR has alleged that Santos's claims in this regard amount to misleading or deceptive conduct in breach of the Corporations Act and the ACL. The litigation is still ongoing, with a merits hearing before the Federal Court held in October 2024.[78] The court's decision is expected to address the issue of what is necessary for a company to make a credible net-zero emissions claim.[79]

3.3 Emerging Anti-regulatory Uses of Private Law to Resist Climate Action

It should be noted that efforts to use private law avenues in climate litigation are not solely undertaken by progressive climate actors. In what might be described as a SLAPP suit (strategic lawsuits against public participation),[80] the energy company AGL commenced proceedings against Greenpeace in 2021 arguing that the environmental group breached its intellectual property (trademark and copyright) when using AGL's brand in Greenpeace's "AGL is Australia's biggest corporate climate polluter" and "Australia's greatest liability" campaigns. AGL Energy failed in both its trademark infringement and its copyright infringement claim for all uses of the logo but succeeded in relation to its claims on three social media posts, as well as some photographs and placards, although Judge Burley of the Federal Court denied AGL's request for the award of damages.[81]

The AGL case is representative of a broader trend emerging in corporate climate litigation—most especially in the US—in which corporate actors bring cases designed to challenge efforts seeking to enhance climate action through private law (e.g., ESG disclosure standards).[82] Such

[74] ibid.

[75] ibid.

[76] ibid.

[77] *Australasian Centre for Corporate Responsibility v Santos Ltd* NSD858/2021.

[78] Media Release, 'Greenwashing Proceedings in Federal Court' (*Australasian Centre for Corporate Responsibility*, 24 October 2024) <https://www.accr.org.au/news/greenwashing-proceedings-in-federal-court/> accessed 8 June 2025.

[79] Media Release, 'World-First Federal Court Case Over Santos' "Clean Energy" & Net Zero Claims' (*Environmental Defenders Office*, 26 August 2021) <https://www.edo.org.au/2021/08/26/world-first-federal-court-case-over-santos-clean-energy-net-zero-claims/> accessed 8 June 2025.

[80] Robert Abrahams, 'Strategic Lawsuits against Public Participation (SLAPP)' (1989–1990) 7 Pace Environmental Law Review 33–44.

[81] *AGL Energy Limited v Greenpeace Australia Pacific Limited* [2021] FCA 625.

[82] Taylor Nchako and Lisa Benjamin, 'ESG Backlash in the United States: Investor Concerns or 'Red Scare'? (2025) 5(2) Journal of Law and Political Economy 268. See also John Dernbach, Chapter 35 of this handbook.

legal actions often rest on claims that ESG strategies violate private law requirements, such as corporate law fiduciary duties, anti-trust (competition) laws, or consumer protection standards.[83] While these cases are yet to emerge in Australia, they illustrate the potential for the private law–climate change interface in corporate climate litigation to cut both ways, promoting, but also potentially constraining, progressive action on climate change.

3.4 Pathways in Tort Law: Duty of Care in Negligence

The previous discussion of pathways in corporate and financial, and consumer, law points to the private law avenues that have been successfully explored under Australian law to hold corporate actors accountable for climate-related harms. However, these avenues are limited to circumstances of harms to the companies, shareholders, or pension fund members (corporate and financial law pathways) or consumers affected by misleading corporate disclosures (consumer protection law pathways). For a corporation to be held to account for climate-related harms by a wider group of actors, including members of the public, "liability must be pursued via a different route".[84] This leads to a discussion of private law pathways in tort law, particularly using the tort of negligence.[85]

The starting (and perhaps end) point for negligence-based climate claims in Australia is the case of *Sharma v Minister for Environment*, although this litigation is principally concerned with the legal duties of governmental authorities. The case brought by Sister Marie Brigid Arthur on behalf of eight Australian children argued that the federal Minister for Environment owed a novel duty of care in tort when exercising her statutory approval powers for a new coal mine extension applied for by Whitehaven Coal. At first instance, Justice Bromberg of the Federal Court ruled that the Environment Minister indeed owed the children a duty of care in negligence on the basis that the risk of harm to Australian children from the mine emissions was reasonably foreseeable, that the Minister had control over the risk, that Australian children are vulnerable to the risk of harm from climate change, and that they are reliant on the Minister for assistance.[86] Justice Bromberg made a declaration that this duty required the Minister to take reasonable care to avoid causing personal injury or death to Australian children arising from carbon emissions into the Earth's atmosphere, including from the coal mine extension at issue in the case.[87]

However, despite success at first instance, this ruling was unanimously overturned on appeal.[88] All three judges on appeal provided different reasons for overturning the finding of a novel duty of care, including that there was an insufficient "closeness" between the Minister and the children, that harm to the children from the extension of the coal mine was not reasonably foreseeable, and that a novel duty of this kind would be inconsistent and incoherent

[83] Global Trends 2025 (n 8).

[84] Tina Popa and others, 'Do Emerging Trends in Climate Litigation Signal a Potential Cause of Action in Negligence against Corporations by the Australian Public? (2022) 12 Climate Law 185–215, 197.

[85] There have only been limited uses of tort law in Australian corporate climate litigation. In the Australian and Pacific Climate Change Litigation Database (n 2), the only recorded corporate cases are *Sanda v PTTEP Australasia (Ashmore Cartier) Pty Ltd* (where a $192.5 million settlement was reached in a class action negligence suit involving damage from an oil well spill affecting coastal areas and agriculture) and the nuisance case of *Uren v Bald Hills Wind Farm Pty Ltd* [2022] VSC 145 (concerning amenity complaints of neighbouring residents relating to noise from operation of the wind farm).

[86] *Sharma by her litigation representative Sister Marie Brigid Arthur v Minister for the Environment* [2021] FCA 560 [91ff].

[87] ibid [491].

[88] *Minister for the Environment v Sharma* [2022] FCAFC 35.

with the purpose and duties in the relevant environmental statute under which the Minister was required to make a decision.[89] Concerns were also raised by the court that the relationship between the Minister and the children in the case was one between government and governed rather than between "neighbours in the legal sense amenable to responsibility in the private law of torts".[90]

The *Sharma* appeal judgment most likely constrains avenues for using negligence as a basis for future Australian climate litigation, including against companies,[91] although the reasoning Justice Bromberg applied in determining the existence of a duty of care could plausibly be extrapolated to corporate actors.[92] The greater significance of the *Sharma* case may lie outside the Australian jurisdiction where it has inspired efforts to use tort law in other litigation, such as the pioneering New Zealand case of *Smith v Fonterra*, discussed in the following part of the chapter.

4. Developments in New Zealand

Unlike Australia, New Zealand has not experienced an exponential growth in corporate climate litigation. Nevertheless, the cases that have developed in New Zealand illustrate both the influence of the jurisprudence of its westward neighbour in the Australasian region, as well as the emergence of different ways of framing the private law–climate change intersection. The following sections illustrate these contrasting relationships between New Zealand and Australian corporate climate litigation focusing, first, on the similar framing of anti-greenwashing complaints and, second, on the different approach to the applicability of tort law claims to climate harms, as illustrated by the New Zealand Supreme Court's decision in the case of *Smith v Fonterra*.

4.1 Emerging Anti-Greenwashing Complaints

The Australian and Pacific Climate Change Litigation Database maintained by the University of Melbourne records two New Zealand cases involving anti-greenwashing complaints. The first is a 2021 complaint brought by Lawyers for Climate Action New Zealand against the LPG distributor, Firstgas, regarding its television advertising. The complaint, made to the Advertising Standards Authority (the New Zealand equivalent of Australia's Ad Standards which has also received several similar complaints),[93] claimed that Firstgas' advertisement asserting, "we're ensuring our gas is going zero carbon", amounted to greenwashing. The Complaints Board of the Advertising Standards Authority found that the advertisement

[89] ibid, in the separate judgments of Allsop CJ (e.g., [7], [267]), Beach J (e.g., [363], [473]), Wheelahan J (e.g., [869ff]).

[90] ibid; see particularly the separate judgment of Allsop CJ, [346].

[91] The Court of Appeal's decision in *Sharma* 'abruptly checked the momentum generated by the trial judgment in the case'. See Popa et al (n 84) 192. That said, there is another negligence-based claim on foot in *Pabai v Commonwealth of Australia* (Federal Court of Australia, VID622/2021), which involves First Nations' leaders from the Torres Strait Islands challenging the Australia's failure to cut emissions and asserting that the government's inaction will force their communities to migrate to new areas. At first instance, the plaintiff's tort claim was dismissed by the Federal Court (see *Pabai Pabai v Commonwealth of Australia* [2025] FCA 796) but is being appealed to the Full Court of the Federal Court.

[92] See the analysis by Popa et al (n 84) 206 (discussing the potential to found a corporate duty of care under Australian negligence law in respect of climate harms, focusing on the 'salient features' of 'reasonable foreseeability, control, vulnerability and indeterminacy').

[93] See n 68.

breached rules of the Advertising Standards Code requiring "truthful presentation" and was misleading. Specifically, the Complaints Board

> said the impression that consumers will not need to do anything differently to avoid adding any carbon to the atmosphere, combined with the implication that the proposed change to zero carbon gas was imminent, was not supported by the evidence provided.[94]

Firstgas was accordingly required to remove the advertisement.[95]

The second case of *Consumer NZ v Z Energy* was filed with the High Court of New Zealand in 2023 and raises claims of misleading and deceptive conduct in breach of New Zealand's consumer protection law, paralleling the strategy of anti-greenwashing complaints brought by civil society actors in Australia.[96] Like the *EnergyAustralia* and *ACCR v Santos* cases in Australia, the corporate target of the *Consumer NZ v Z Energy* filing is a major energy company described in the plaintiff's statement of claim as the largest retailer of petroleum products in New Zealand and the country's second largest emitter of carbon dioxide and equivalent GHG emissions.[97] The plaintiffs claim that statements made by Z Energy, inter alia, about its emissions reduction pathway, and that it is "getting out" of the petroleum business are misleading and deceptive, in breach of Section 9 of New Zealand's Fair Trade Act, because the company is not making changes to its business that would materially reduce its total emissions or decrease its sales of petroleum products.

4.2 *Smith v Fonterra*: Pathways in Tort Law

In contrast to the anti-greenwashing claims described above, which converge with the Australian experience, the tort law case of *Smith v Fonterra* illustrates the potential for a divergent pathway.[98] The plaintiff in the case, Mr Smith, is an elder of Ngāpuhi and Ngāti Kahu, and a climate spokesperson for the Iwi Chairs Forum, a national forum of tribal leaders.[99] In August 2019, he filed a lawsuit against seven New Zealand companies including Fonterra, which owns and operates eight dairy factories in New Zealand that burn coal to generate energy, and Genesis, which operates the Huntly Power Station, the largest power station in the country which relies on coal and natural gas combustion to generate electricity.[100] Smith's central claim is that these defendant companies have contributed materially to the climate emergency and have damaged, and will continue to damage, his whenua (ancestral land) and

94 *Lawyers for Climate Action and others v Firstgas Group*, Complaint No. 21/194, ASA Complaints Board Decision, 6 July 2021, 4.

95 Lawyers for Climate Action, New Zealand, 'Advertising Standards Board rules "Zero Carbon Gas" Advertising Campaign Is Misleading' (22 July 2021) <https://www.lawyersforclimateaction.nz/news-events/firstgas-decision> accessed 28 May 2025.

96 Lawyers for Climate Action, New Zealand, 'LCANZI, Consumer NZ and ELI File NZ's First Greenwashing Case Against Z Energy' (30 November 2023) <https://www.lawyersforclimateaction.nz/news-events/lcanzi-consumer-nz-and-environmental-law-initiative-file-nzs-first-greenwashing-case-against-z-energy> accessed 5 June 2025.

97 Statement of Claim, *Consumer NZ & Ors v Z Energy*, 24 November 2023, High Court of New Zealand <https://static1.squarespace.com/static/5cf3039126905000011c02b0/t/6566b70e7a2e7e1948020607/1701230391387/Statement+of+claim+%28endorsed%29+%28CIV-2023-485-771%29.pdf> accessed 5 June 2025. In *Consumer NZ & Ors v Z Energy*, [2024] NZHC 2018, the plaintiff was ordered to file an amended statement of claim.

98 Bookman (n 3).

99 *Smith v Fonterra* (n 3) [3].

100 ibid [51].

moana (ocean), including places of customary, cultural, historical, nutritional, and spiritual significance to him and his whānau (extended family).[101]

Smith raised three causes of action in tort: public nuisance, negligence, and a proposed new climate system damage tort. In the High Court, Justice Wylie determined that the claims in public nuisance and negligence were not reasonably arguable and struck them out, while declining to strike out the claim based on the proposed climate system damage tort.[102] On appeal, the Court of Appeal struck out all three causes of action, taking the view that

> the magnitude of the crisis which is climate change simply cannot be appropriately or adequately addressed by common law tort claims pursued through the courts. It is quintessentially a matter that calls for a sophisticated regulatory response at a national level supported by international coordination.[103]

In this regard, the Court of Appeal's judgment echoed that of the Australian Full Federal Court in *Sharma*, which also cast doubt on the suitability of a court-designed novel duty of care as an appropriate judicial response to issues of climate policy. The *Smith v Fonterra* case then reached the Supreme Court which, succinctly put, applied established principles governing strike out to conclude that the plaintiff's claims should be allowed to proceed to trial rather than being pre-emptively struck out.

The High Court Rules 2016 provide that the court may strike out all or part of a pleading if it "discloses no reasonably arguable cause of action".[104] The Supreme Court focused on a particular passage in the Court of Appeal's statement of the applicable principles governing strike out where the court stated:

> We must be certain that the claim is so untenable it cannot succeed and slow to strike out claims in any developing area of law.[105]

The Supreme Court reaffirmed this finding and added that its approach would be a measured one where a claim is novel but at least founded on seriously arguable, non-trivial harm. Responding to the defendants' argument that the claim must fail because it is almost impossible to attribute the harm caused by climate change to individual defendants, the Supreme Court held that in such cases, "the common law should lean towards receipt of the claim, and full evaluation based on evidence and argument at trial, over pre-emptive elimination".[106] The case was thus referred back to the High Court to proceed to trial.[107]

It is noteworthy that the Supreme Court in *Smith v Fonterra* case did not accept the defendant companies' argument that climate change legislation and regulation, such as an emissions trading scheme, displaces private law and precludes common law actions on damage caused by GHG emissions. In this respect, the Court followed a line of reasoning similar to the Netherlands' Hague Court of Appeal's decision in *Milieudefensie v Shell*.[108] It found that the New Zealand Parliament

101 ibid [3].

102 ibid [7].

103 *Smith v Fonterra Co-Operative Group Limited* [2021] NZCA 552 (Court of Appeal of New Zealand, 21 October 2021) [16].

104 Rule 15.1(1)(a) of the High Court Rules.

105 *Smith v Fonterra 2021* (n 103) [38].

106 *Smith v Fonterra* (n 3) [83].

107 A decision on the merits had not been reached at the time of writing.

108 See the Hague Court of Appeal's decision in *Milieudefensie v Shell*, 12 November 2024, ECLI:NL:GHDHA:2024:2100.

> has left a pathway open for the common law to operate, develop and evolve ... amid a statutory landscape that does not displace the common law by the interposition of permits, immunities, policies, rules and resource consents.[109]

It is important to scrutinise this argument to appreciate the tensions that underlie corporate climate litigation pursuing a torts pathway. From the defendant company's perspective, its business activities are lawful as they comply with applicable statutory laws and regulations. Attempts to use private law (specifically tort law) to declare such business activities unlawful are strongly resisted using the language of separation of powers, ineffective and incoherent regulation when private and public law are both in play, and undue exposure to open-ended liability which would have economically disruptive consequences.[110] Similar arguments—although raised in the context of a government rather than a corporate defendant—were persuasive for the Full Federal Court in *Sharma*. The different conclusions reached by the Supreme Court in *Smith v Fonterra* highlight an important policy question: Is it distorting the role of tort law if it is used to discourage businesses from selling products that release GHG emissions when consumed, thereby effectively forcing such companies to change their business model? This is how some critics have phrased the question, condemning corporate climate litigation as a frivolous abuse of the law to advance an "ulterior motive".[111]

However, it can be argued that such ways of framing the legal issues are unhelpful and unnecessarily so. Noting that private rights are being infringed by the activities of companies that contribute to causing climate change, and that the current state of climate legislation in most countries is incomplete or inadequate, it is not far-fetched for individuals to seek a remedy in the courts, just as individuals have approached the courts for remedies in cases ranging from medicines that have caused fatal or life-threatening consequences to the harmful effects of social media on youths.[112]

4.3 Comparing the Australian and New Zealand Experience

Little direct evidence from the pleadings or judgments in the New Zealand corporate climate cases to date suggests that there have been active efforts to transfer private law strategies across the region. That said, there are undoubtedly similarities between the approach taken in emerging New Zealand anti-greenwashing claims and those that have been filed in Australia. In each jurisdiction, there are efforts to hold large corporate emitters to account for the public statements they are making about their decarbonisation pathway, both to ensure consumers and shareholders are not misled, and ultimately to ensure that these companies "walk the talk" on their climate commitments.

The seemingly different pathway that might be pursued in New Zealand with respect to climate actions taken in torts as opposed to the (likely) closing of that door in Australia, reflects different approaches by common law courts in balancing their competing roles as guardians of the separation of powers doctrine and forums for the judicial development of common law doctrines to embrace new situations. The New Zealand Supreme Court decision in *Smith*

[109] *Smith v Fonterra* (n 3) [101].

[110] See, for example, ibid [11], summarising submissions of the respondents.

[111] Quoting the language of Trower J in the decision refusing to permit ClientEarth to proceed with its shareholder derivative action against Shell's board of directors: see *ClientEarth v Shell*, [2023] EWHC 1897 (Ch) [92].

[112] In a similar vein, see Douglas Kysar, 'What Climate Change Can Do About Tort Law' (2011) 41 Environmental Law 1–71.

v Fonterra signals a judicial openness to novel tort arguments to address climate harms.[113] Specific features of the different legal systems also appear to be influential. A notable element of the *Smith v Fonterra* Supreme Court judgment, for instance, was the court's discussion of the relevance of *tikanga* (cultural connection to land under Māori customary law) in informing the formulation of tort claims, particularly in considering the concept of "special damage".[114] By comparison, Australian law has no comparative deference to Indigenous customary law and Australian courts are yet to see the creation of novel torts dealing directly with climate harms.

5. Conclusion

This chapter has discussed corporate climate litigation developments in the Australasian jurisdictions of Australia and New Zealand as a means of understanding the evolution of the climate change-private law interface occurring in this region. The jurisprudence demonstrates the potential for existing private law requirements, such as directors' duties, disclosure requirements, consumer protection laws, and torts, to be deployed in aid of enhanced climate outcomes through holding companies to account for their commercial decisions that may be contributing to climate harms, as well as the commitments they are making to address the problem. The Australian corporate climate litigation has been particularly innovative in this regard, exploring the way a range of private law tools can be repurposed to climate ends. This case law is already seeing echoes in New Zealand, with a similar approach to Australia's anti-greenwashing cases, but a potentially different pathway being forged regarding the applicability of tort law and the possibilities for development of a novel tort addressing climate harms.

The overwhelming success of corporate climate litigation claims in Australasia suggests it is an effective approach for enhancing the accountability of corporate action to address climate change. Overall, across the different doctrinal areas being explored in Australasian corporate climate litigation (directors' duties, disclosure, consumer protection, and tort) there is evidence that these private law areas are proving adaptable to climate ends. What is occurring—with the possible exception of the still-to-be determined New Zealand torts case of *Smith v Fonterra*—is an adaptation of private law doctrines to deal with the new issues posed by climate change, rather than a fundamental transformation. In other words, across Australasia, courts are finding ways to comfortably extend key requirements of private law to deal with new situations posed by businesses operating in a climate context. This helps to make private law doctrines more suitable for application in a climate-changed world but does not fundamentally disrupt private law,[115] or question its role in facilitating the conditions of climate

[113] Beyond the *Smith v Fonterra* case example, however, it is acknowledged with regard to New Zealand's private law framework and climate change that the courts have adopted a highly deferential 'supremacy of parliament' doctrine while operating on the embedded presumption of effectiveness when legal challenges involve regulatory elements: Feroze Brailsford, 'Foreseeable sea-level rise and climate change causation: A discussion of tort law's role in providing relief and attributing liability for climate change-induced harms' (2022) 26 New Zealand Journal of Environmental Law 91–113. See also Georgina Lyes, 'Climate Change and the Role of the Courts: Litigation and Mitigation in Aotearoa: New Zealand' (2023) 30 Canterbury Law Review 231–78.

[114] *Smith v Fonterra* (n 3) [188].

[115] Cf Elizabeth Fisher, Eloise Scotford, and Emily Barritt, 'The Legally Disruptive Nature of Climate Change' (2017) 80(2) Modern Law Review 173–201.

change through safeguarding private entitlements that promote the externalisation of environmental harms.[116]

Even so, it would be imprudent to conclude that private law avenues deployed in corporate climate litigation offer a panacea to the problem of ensuring the accountability of companies for the contributions they make to greenhouse gas emissions and climate change. Already there are some signs of an anti-regulatory litigation trend, such as the AGL case against Greenpeace in Australia; of court hesitancy to extend private law doctrines beyond their conventional understandings, as in the *Sharma* appeal decision; and of the potential for corporate adverse reaction to increased greenwashing regulatory scrutiny and litigation to take the form of greenhushing or greenrinsing,[117] rather than more ambitious action to realise net zero and other climate commitments. With worsening climate change, we should be prepared for "bitter conflict over the planetary imperative that individual freedoms must be sacrificed to collective exigencies".[118] This points to the importance of embedding legal reform and litigation in a broader socio-political recognition of the need for departure from corporate business-as-usual pathways to address the existential risks for humanity, societies, and our environment posed by climate change.[119]

116 Nicole Graham, 'Teaching Private Law in a Climate Crisis' (2021) 40(3) University of Queensland Law Journal 403–19.

117 ESG Voices, Greenwashing Terms: Greenhushing, Greenshifting, and More, 15 February 2024 <https://www.esgvoices.com/post/green-claims-terms-greenwashing-greenshifting-and-more-explained> accessed 2 March 2025.

118 Graham (n 116), 419.

119 See also Ryan Gunderson and Claiton Fyock, 'The Political Economy of Climate Change Litigation: Is There a Point to Suing Fossil Fuel Companies?' (2022) 27(3) New Political Economy 441–54.

CHAPTER 38

East and Southeast Asia

JOLENE LIN

1. Introduction

Asia is a large geographic region comprising jurisdictions including Bhutan, Nepal, Japan, the United Arab Emirates, Vietnam, and Malaysia, which are at different levels of social and economic development and span across the common law and civil law traditions.[1] As it is impossible to cover the entire region in a single chapter, this chapter focuses on climate change law developments in East and Southeast Asia, excluding India and China which are discussed in Chapters 36 and 40 (hereinafter "Asia").

It is not easy to avoid falling into the trap of broad-brush generalisations when proper and nuanced legal analysis would require in-depth knowledge of a specific jurisdiction's laws. A caveat that this author would therefore make is that this chapter does not seek to be a comprehensive and in-depth overview of climate change law developments in Asia. Selected legal and regulatory developments are discussed even though these developments are at early stages compared to those occurring elsewhere (e.g., within Australia and the European Union), because they signal the direction of travel and raise interesting legal questions that merit scholarly attention. In some cases, such as the Philippine Corporate Accountability Bill, these developments are novel and unique. One of the aims of this chapter is to draw attention to the unique contributions that Asian jurisdictions are making towards climate law and

[1] The United Nations traditionally organises countries into five regional groups: the African States, Asia-Pacific States, Eastern European States, Latin American and the Caribbean States, and the Western European and Other States; https://www.un.org/dgacm/en/content/regional-groups. The Intergovernmental Panel on Climate Change (IPCC) adopts a more helpful and practical schematic of the regions of the world. The IPCC's Sixth Assessment report contains regional chapters and Asia is defined as 'land and territories of 52 countries/regions. It can be broadly divided into six subregions based on geographic position and coastal peripheries': Central Asia, East Asia, North Asia, South Asia, Southeast Asia, and West Asia; Intergovernmental Panel on Climate Change (IPCC), *Climate Change 2022: Impacts, Adaptation and Vulnerability—Contribution of Working Group II to the Sixth Assessment Report* (CUP 2022) ch 10 (Asia): https://www.ipcc.ch/report/ar6/wg2/. The population of Asia was reported to be 4.8 billion people in 2024, which is about 60% of the world's population; https://repository.unescap.org/server/api/core/bitstreams/29538ee8-a43d-4b95-84a3-fe37595659c0/content. The gross domestic product (GDP) per capita ranged from US$2,690 (Bangladesh) to US$33,960 (Japan) in 2025; https://www.imf.org/en/Countries. The common law jurisdictions in Asia include Hong Kong, Singapore, Malaysia (which also incorporates aspects of Islamic law), and India. The civil law jurisdictions include South Korea, China, Vietnam, and Bahrain (which also incorporates aspects of Islamic law). There are also jurisdictions like Bhutan, The Philippines, and Sri Lanka, which have mixed legal systems that draw from both common law and civil law traditions. Asia is highly vulnerable to climate change impacts largely due to a lack of adaptive capacities. For analysis, see IPCC's Sixth Assessment Report. All websites in this footnote accessed 3 June 2025.

governance in the private law context, thereby enriching comparative climate legal scholarship and practice.

Across Asia, and the Global South more broadly, climate change litigation is at early stages of development, often emerging because the courts are the only available institution thorough which civil society (and citizens, more broadly) can engage in and influence climate governance.[2] Apart from India and Pakistan, and to a lesser extent, the Philippines—which are jurisdictions that have an established history of environmental public interest litigation that has created a pathway for climate litigation to emerge—there are a small handful of climate cases across the rest of Asia.[3] This relative paucity of climate litigation can be explained by, inter alia, hefty legal costs, judicial backlog that means that plaintiffs may wait many years before they have their day in court, low levels of public trust in some judicial systems plagued by corruption, and difficulties enforcing judgments. These factors greatly reduce the incentives for citizens to go to court.[4] In some jurisdictions such as Japan, there is a strong preference for alternative, non-litigation dispute resolution.[5] In Thailand, the Philippines, Malaysia, and Indonesia, the proliferation of SLAPPs (Strategic Lawsuits Against Public Participation) and related defamation lawsuits against journalists, human rights activists, and environmental defenders has had a chilling effect on civic engagement and legal advocacy.[6]

[2] Jolene Lin and Jacqueline Peel, *Litigating Climate Change in the Global South* (OUP 2024) 94.

[3] In a systematic examination of cases in Global South jurisdictions up to May 2023, 128 cases were identified of which 46 were filed or decided in Asia; ibid 56. It can be argued that in India and Pakistan which have an established tradition of public interest environmental litigation, court action is a matter of course. It has been said that 'almost every major environmental issue that has made the news ends up before the High Court or the Supreme Court through a petition or is taken up by the Supreme Court of its own volition under its suo motu jurisdiction'; Waqqas Ahmad Mir, 'From Shehla Zir to Asghar Leghari: Pronouncing Unwritten Rights is More Complex than a Celebratory Tale" in Jolene Lin and Douglas A Kysar (eds), *Climate Change Litigation in the Asia Pacific* (CUP 2020) 286.

[4] For discussion of these factors, see for example, Sameer Yasir, "'A Lifelong Nightmare': Seeking Justice in India's Overwhelmed Courts" *The New York Times* (13 January 2024) <https://www.nytimes.com/2024/01/13/world/asia/india-judicial-backlog.html> accessed 5 June 2025; Manaswini Rao, *Frontline Courts as State Capacity: Micro-Evidence from India* (12 February 2022) <https://thedocs.worldbank.org/en/doc/40736ea1c916001d483b833b356c952d-0050022022/original/Frontline-Courts-as-Stata-Capacity.pdf> accessed 3 June 2025; Simon Butt, *Judicial Dysfunction in Indonesia* (Melbourne University Publishing 2023); S M Solaiman, 'Prevention of Judicial Corruption in Bangladesh: Cutting the Gordian Knot by Ensuring Accountability' (2023) 19 University of Pennsylvania Asian Law Review 27.

[5] Tomoko Otake, 'Climate Litigation Remains a Tough Sell in Japan Despite Wins Overseas' *The Japan Times* (17 September 2023) <https://www.japantimes.co.jp/environment/2023/09/17/climate-change/japan-climate-litigation/> accessed 3 June 2025; Also see contra Tom Ginsburg and Glenn Hoetker G, 'The Unreluctant Litigant? An Empirical Analysis of Japan's Turn to Litigation' (2006) 35(1) Journal of Legal Studies 31.

[6] For discussion, see International Commission of Jurists, 'Indonesia, Malaysia, Thailand, the Philippines: Experts Call for Legal Reforms to Address Abusive Lawsuits Targeting Human Rights and Public Interest Advocates (SLAPPs)' (9 December 2021) <https://www.icj.org/indonesia-malaysia-thailand-the-philippines-experts-call-for-legal-reforms-to-address-abusive-lawsuits-targeting-human-rights-and-public-interest-advocates-slapps/> accessed 3 June 2025. A landmark SLAPP case in the Philippines is *FCF Minerals Corporation v Lunag and Others* (896 Phil 806; 119 OG No 36, 6997, 4 September 2023) <https://elibrary.judiciary.gov.ph/thebookshelf/showdocs/1/67292> accessed 3 June 2025. In this case, a mining company sought to portray itself as the victim of a SLAPP. The court rejected this, reaffirming that 'SLAPP is a defence that may only be invoked by individuals who become target of litigation due to their environmental advocacy. It is not a remedy of powerful corporations to stifle the actions of ordinary citizens who seek to make them accountable'. Indonesia's anti-SLAPP provisions also only provide protection against SLAPPS for environmental issues and there are significant weaknesses

As these issues are likely to remain in play over the short to medium term, it can be argued that litigation is unlikely to become a significant driver of climate governance in Asia, which also means that there will be few opportunities for private law's encounter with climate change. However, climate litigation is likely to increase in Asia as more youths, civil society groups, and other members of society become increasingly frustrated with the pace of legislative and executive climate action. This is most likely to occur in Asian jurisdictions where the above-mentioned obstacles to access to justice are less prominent. Many of these cases are likely to engage public law, but there will be cases that attempt to use private law pathways to compel private actors to be accountable for their contribution towards causing climate harm. Secondly, as more jurisdictions across Asia introduce climate change legislation and regulatory regimes such as corporate climate disclosure obligations, greenhouse gases (GHG) emissions trading schemes (or carbon markets), and greenwashing regulations, there will simply be more bases to hold public and private actors "climate accountable". There will, in short, be more "hooks" for climate cases—both public and private—in the coming years.

Against this background, this chapter focuses on a few areas of law that are potentially promising avenues for achieving corporate climate accountability in Asia and draws out the implications for the broader discussion about climate change and private law. Section 2 of this chapter focuses on climate litigation against private actors. Section 3 turns to greenwashing and the limited role of private law in addressing it across Asia. Section 4 focuses on a unique piece of (proposed) corporate accountability legislation, which is the Philippine Corporate Accountability Bill. The legislation is unique because it goes beyond the typical suite of disclosure obligations and seeks to promote accountability for loss and damage through both public and private litigation.

2. Taking Companies to Court Over Climate Change

The use of law as an instrument to achieve wider social objectives is not a recent phenomenon. In their seminal work "Pressure through Law", Carol Harlow and Richard Rawlings argue that lawsuits filed by groups advocating for social change can be identified in Britain as early as 1749, when abolitionists used the courts to test conflicting views of slavery in the common law.[7] In the early 2000s, climate litigation that sought to assign responsibility for causing climate change to the "carbon majors"—the world's largest corporate producers of industrial carbon emissions—had already started in the United States, but there were, at least during that early US wave, no successful cases.[8] In the past ten years, there has been a significant rise in climate litigation worldwide and climate lawsuits have been filed in, for example, Brazil, South Africa, Kenya, Indonesia, Nepal, and Guyana.[9] Most of these cases are strategic litigation and

which hinder their effectiveness. Linda Yanti Sulistiawati, 'Strategic Lawsuit Against Public Participation (SLAPP) in Indonesia: When Defenders Became Defendants' *Tempo* (10 May 2025) <https://en.tempo.co/read/2005751/strategic-lawsuit-against-public-participation-slapp-in-indonesia-when-defenders-became-defendants> accessed 3 June 2025.

[7] Carol Harlow and Richard Rawlings, *Pressure through Law* (Routledge 2016).

[8] For discussion, see Geetanjali Ganguly, Joana Setzer, and Veerle Heyvaert, 'If at First You Don't Succeed: Suing Corporations for Climate Change' (2018) 38(4) Oxford Journal of Legal Studies 841.

[9] In 'Global Trends in Climate Change Litigation: 2024 Snapshot', the authors report that their dataset currently contains 2,666 cases. Around 70% of these cases have been filed since 2015, the year the Paris Agreement was adopted. Climate cases from 55 countries have been identified, including cases filed in

tend to rely on public law (including constitutional law, administrative law, environmental laws, planning laws) for their causes of action.[10]

While climate litigation is at an emergent stage across Asia, the climate accountability landscape is far from being dormant. There are several efforts to use a broader set of legal interventions that may precede formal court proceedings, including complaints to regulators, shareholder/investor engagement, letters issued to corporate actors to warn of potential litigation, and legal opinions to inform companies and their officers of their climate change-related legal duties.[11] Such activities can be understood to be forms of legal mobilisation, which extend to "any process by which individuals or collective actors invoke legal norms, discourse or symbols to influence policy or behaviour", including, for example, the use of law in advocacy campaigns or lobbying.[12] While some of these efforts are led by global non-governmental organisations (which are well-resourced and have highly qualified staff, including lawyers and communication strategists), local grassroots citizen groups and youths also lead legal mobilisation efforts across Asia.[13]

It can be argued that legal mobilisation is likely to be more effective than litigation against a carbon major in Asia, such as Petronas and Pertamina, which are Malaysian and Indonesian

2023 for the first time in Panama and Portugal; Joana Setzer and Catherine Higham, *Global Trends in Climate Change Litigation: 2024 Snapshot* (Grantham Research Institute on Climate Change and the Environment, London School of Economics and Political Science, 2024) <https://www.lse.ac.uk/granthaminstitute/wp-content/uploads/2024/06/Global-trends-in-climate-change-litigation-2024-snapshot.pdf> accessed 5 June 2025.

[10] For example, in *Save Lamu et al. v National Environmental Management Authority and Amu Power Co. Ltd.* (2017), the plaintiff environmental group pursued a judicial review of the national environmental agency's decision to grant Amu Power Company a license to construct a coal-fired power plant, arguing that the company had not conducted an adequate environmental impact assessment (EIA); Save Lamu and Others v National Environmental Management Authority and Amu Power Co Ltd [2019] KLR (High Court of Kenya). A copy of the decision can be found here: < https://climatecasechart.com/wp-content/uploads/non-us-case-documents/2019/20190626_Tribunal-Appeal-No.-Net-196-of-2016_decision-1.pdf> accessed 23 June 2025.

[11] See, for example, the guide 'Net Zero Engagement in Asia: A Guide to Shareholder Climate Resolutions', which is a resource for Asia-focused investors considering shareholder resolutions as part of corporate engagement. The guide was produced by ClientEarth (an environmental law NGO) with the support of the Asia Investor Group on Climate Change: <https://www.clientearth.asia/media/i32jbwe1/net-zero-engagement-in-asia-a-guide-to-shareholder-climate-resolutions-2022.pdf>. The Commonwealth Climate and Law Initiative (CCLI), a global NGO that 'examines the legal basis for directors and trustees to consider, manage and report on climate change and broader environmental risks' has commissioned legal opinions from experts around the world. In Asia, opinions have been commissioned for Japan, Singapore, Hong Kong, the Philippines, Indonesia, Malaysia and India. These opinions have played a significant role in galvanising academic and public discourse on directors' duties in relation to climate change; CCLI: <https://commonwealthclimatelaw.org>. 'Towards Net Zero: Legal Aspects of Corporate Climate Action in Asia', held in Singapore on 17 October 2024, was the first conference in Asia to bring together lawyers, judges, directors, regulators, investors and academics to examine the legal issues around corporate climate action: <https://law.nus.edu.sg/apcel/media/towards-net-zero-conference-legal-aspects-of-corporate-climate-action-in-asia/>. All websites in this footnote accessed 3 June 2025.

[12] Lisa Vanhala and Jacqui Kinghan, *Literature Review on the Use and Impact of Litigation* (Public Law Project Research Paper, 2023) 5 <https://publiclawproject.org.uk/content/uploads/2023/11/Litigation-Lit-Review-PLP.pdf>.

[13] See Lin and Peel (n 2), Chapter 5 for an analytical overview of the constellation of key actors in Global South (which includes several jurisdictions in Asia) and their climate change legal mobilisation efforts.

state-owned enterprises (SOEs), respectively.[14] First, these SOEs have deep pockets to support lengthy court battles that plaintiff organisations will struggle to match. Secondly, these SOEs serve public functions such as the maintenance of energy security and generating public funds for development. In this context, litigating against these SOEs in Asia runs the risk of public backlash, as the narrative behind the quest for climate justice and corporate accountability can be distorted to be one of the pursuits of elite and partisan interests against national security and development. While any analysis of potential backlash is necessarily fact-sensitive, and it is not the case that all SOEs should not be sued on this basis, the point here is that litigation could be a risky proposition.[15] In any case, legal mobilisation can help create favourable conditions to leverage the impact of future litigation if pursued. An important feature of legal mobilisation is that its main objective need not be winning a case, but it is part of a broader advocacy strategy to draw attention to an issue, to start a debate, or even to enable the media to write about something that they could not otherwise address.

This section discusses two recent cases that have been filed in Japan and Korea with a view to elucidating the interaction between private law and climate change.

2.1 Youth Climate Case Japan for Tomorrow

In August 2024, sixteen Japanese youths filed a case in the Nagoya District Court against ten thermal power companies. The plaintiffs sought injunctive relief to compel the companies to reduce their greenhouse gas (GHG) emissions.[16] The youth plaintiffs relied on Articles 709 and 719 of the Japanese Civil Code, which provide the legal basis for compensation for tortious loss or damage.[17] In their complaint, the plaintiffs alleged that the power companies had a legal obligation to reduce their GHG emissions so as to be in line with the carbon budgets established by the Intergovernmental Panel on Climate Change (IPCC). They argued that compliance with the IPCC carbon budgets constituted a legal obligation not to "infringe the rights or legally protected interests of another person" referred to in Article 709 of the Civil Code.

[14] Carbon Majors Database, 'Petronas' <https://carbonmajors.org/Entity/Petronas-84>; 'Pertamina' <https://carbonmajors.org/Entity/Pertamina-78> accessed 3 June 2025.

[15] On the other hand, as argued by Lim in Chapter 18 of this handbook, the broader societal obligations of directors and managers of SOEs might also afford them important leeway in pursuing climate mitigation and adaption goals that are harder to justify under the narrow, firm-specific shareholder wealth maximisation ideals of private companies.

[16] 'Guest Blog: First Youth Climate Lawsuit Brought in Japan' (Columbia Law School, Sabin Center for Climate Change Law Blog, 15 August 2024). <https://blogs.law.columbia.edu/climatechange/2024/08/15/guest-blog-first-youth-climate-lawsuit-brought-in-japan/> accessed 3 June 2025; 'Youth Climate Case (Japan): For Tomorrow' (Climate Case Chart) <https://climatecasechart.com/non-us-case/youth-climate-case-japan-for-tomorrow/> accessed 3 June 2025. For discussion of climate litigation in Japan more generally, see Kenichiro Konishi, 'Climate Change Litigation in Japan: In Search of an Effective Remedy' (2023) 7(2) Chinese Journal of Environmental Law 214.

[17] Civil Code (Japan), arts 709 and 719 (English translation available online at <https://www.japaneselawtranslation.go.jp/en/laws/view/2154> accessed 3 June 2025. Article 709 (Compensation for Loss or Damage in Torts) states '[a] person that has intentionally or negligently infringed the rights or legally protected interests of another person is liable to compensate for damage resulting in consequence'. Article 719 (Liability of Joint Tortfeasors) states '(1) If more than one person has inflicted damage on another person by a joint tort, each of them is jointly and severally liable to compensate for the damage. The same applies if it cannot be ascertained which of the joint tortfeasors inflicted the damage. (2) A person who has abetted or aided a perpetrator is deemed to be a joint tortfeasor, and the provisions of the preceding paragraph apply.'

This line of argument is similar to that pursued by the plaintiffs in *Milieudefensie et al. v Royal Dutch Shell plc*.[18]

It has been argued that the "infringement of a right" in Article 709 should not be interpreted to limit protection only to cases of actual infringement, but to also confer protection to victims of "unlawful" conduct even if the conduct does not infringe any right. Accordingly, "unlawfulness" should be determined by considering the type and nature of the infringed interest, and the manner of the infringement.[19] Furthermore, it has been pointed out that judges often refer to the notions of "unlawfulness", "infringement of a right", "legally protected interest", and "fault" interchangeably and it is not often clear from their decisions how the various elements relate to each other (if at all).[20] To the extent that such ambiguity exists, it creates space for legal argumentation about the scope of the legally protected rights/interests or, in the alternative, what constitutes unlawfulness.

In *Milieudefensie et al. v Royal Dutch Shell plc*, the Hague District Court had to determine the applicable standard of care. Book 6 Section 162 of the Dutch Civil Code stipulates that "acting in conflict with what is generally accepted according to unwritten law is unlawful". In conducting this open-ended enquiry of determining the standard of care with reference to a range of factors, including public international law, business and human rights codes of conduct, and human rights law, the Hague District Court concluded that Shell had a duty to reduce its GHG emissions (otherwise its conduct would fall below the standard of care and would therefore be unlawful). On appeal, the Hague Court of Appeal ruled that Shell has a duty of care to reduce its GHG emissions but declined to specify a target or timeline for the company's obligation to reduce Scope 3 emisions, which constitute about 95% of its emissions. The Court of Appeal also declined to make specific orders for Shell's reduction of its Scope 1 and 2 emissions on the basis that the company appeared to be on track to keeping its reduction commitments.[21] While the Court of Appeal's decision is a step back from the District Court's because of its unwillingness to set Shell a clear target for reducing its Scope 3 emissions, it nonetheless upheld (and further elaborated upon) the lower court's finding that a duty of care existed on the basis of, inter alia, constitutional law, human rights law, and international law.[22] The plaintiffs in *Youth Climate Case Japan for Tomorrow* have invited the Japanese courts to follow the pioneering lead of the Dutch courts with respect to corporate climate accountability.

Tort law scholars have already identified several challenges to the use of tort law in climate litigation. They can be broadly grouped into four categories: the plaintiff, the defendant, causation, and the harm.[23] This chapter will not seek to revisit that body of intellectual work. What

[18] *Milieudefensie et al. v Royal Dutch Shell plc* (2021) District Court of The Hague, Case No C/09/571932/HA ZA 19-379, Judgment of 26 May 2021, unofficial English translation available at <https://uitspraken.rechtspraak.nl/#!/details?id=ECLI:NL:RBDHA:2021:5339> accessed 5 June 2025.

[19] Emi Matsumoto, 'Tort Law in Japan' in Mauro Bussani and Anthony J Sebok (eds), *Comparative Tort Law: Global Perspectives* (Edward Elgar Publishing 2021) 365.

[20] ibid 369.

[21] *Milieudefensie* et al (n 18) para 7.65.

[22] For analysis of the Hague Court of Appeal's decision, see Jolene Lin, *Milieudefensie et al. v Shell:* Analysis and Commentary of the Hague Court of Appeal's Decision (*CIL Dialogues* 18 November 2024) <https://cil.nus.edu.sg/blogs/milieudefensie-et-al-v-shell-analysis-and-commentary-of-the-hague-court-of-appeals-decision/> accessed 3 June 2025.

[23] Douglas A Kysar, 'What Climate Change Can Do About Tort Law' (2011) 41 Environmental Law Reporter 1; Martin Spitzer and Bernhard Burtscher, 'Liability for Climate Change: Cases, Challenges and Concepts' (2017) 8 Journal for European Environmental & Planning Law 137; Christopher W Callahan and Justin S Mankin, 'Carbon Majors and the Scientific Case for Climate Liability' (2025) *Nature* <https://www.nature.com/articles/s41586-025-08751-3> accessed 3 June 2025.

the following discussion seeks to highlight is that tort-based climate litigation is creating the space for the interplay between private law and public law concepts. The "standard of care" is an open-ended norm that must be judicially interpreted considering contemporary social values. In doing so, judges may refer to various normative sources, including constitutional and human rights law. This means that even though the constitution does not impose obligations on companies directly, fundamental rights can be given indirect horizontal effect and shape the contours of a private duty/right, as elucidated by de Bruin and Cherednychenko in Chapter 45 of this handbook. In interpreting whether the defendant company's conduct has been "unlawful", it should also be noted that these companies are regulated by administrative laws and permitting systems. Prevailing environmental laws and regulations (public law) should be considered in determining the lawfulness of the defendant company's conduct; but it is not a foregone conclusion that compliance with public law means that the defendant company has not infringed upon the plaintiff's legal interests that can be protected by private law.[24]

Such interplay between public law and private law is novel, if not controversial, in most instances. In the UK, for example, it has been said that the use of tort law to address corporate accountability for human rights abuses "has initiated a silent revolution within tort law".[25] At the same time, academics have critiqued how such instrumental use of tort law—"tools used in private bilateral quarrels between victims and perpetrators"—is fundamentally changing the notion of human rights.[26] Both the use of human rights law in a tort case and the use of tort law to achieve human rights goals appear to invite criticism. Within the context of climate litigation, this author takes the view that the borrowing of legal doctrines across the public–private boundary to address society's greatest challenges should be encouraged rather than frowned upon in the name of doctrinal purity. Further, one can ask: What ultimately does tort law protect? It has been argued that tort law is a primary legal mechanism "for the recognition and protection of some of the most fundamental human rights" and by "fundamental", what is meant is that these rights are the bedrock of a social order and its legal system.[27] This would all sound familiar to a constitutional law scholar. As such, the boundary between private and public is perhaps not as clear as often depicted and therefore should not act as a barrier for urgently needed creative climate lawyering.

2.2 Korean Youths Seek Civil Injunction Against POSCO

POSCO is a South Korean steel manufacturer headquartered in Pohang, South Korea. With a production of 38 million tonnes in 2023, it was ranked the seventh largest steel-producing company in the world.[28] The steel sector is the largest emitter of GHG emissions of all South Korea's industries, representing approximately 39% of industrial emissions and 13% of total GHG emissions.[29] Steel production is an energy-intensive process. In South Korea, about

[24] To the extent that the permits (public law) do not contain any GHG reduction obligations, the absence of public regulation can be recognised as a case of the state shirking its legal obligations to address climate change.

[25] Dalia Palombo, 'Business, Human Rights and Climate Change: The Gradual Expansion of the Duty of Care' (2024) 44 Oxford Journal of Legal Studies 889.

[26] ibid.

[27] Allan Beever, 'What Does Tort Law Protect?' (2015) 27 Singapore Academy of Law Journal 626, 638.

[28] World Steel Association, 'Top Steel-Producing Companies 2023/2022' <https://worldsteel.org/data/top-producers/> accessed 3 June 2025.

[29] Climate Transparency, *South Korea: Climate Transparency Report 2022* (October 2022), 14: <https://www.climate-transparency.org/wp-content/uploads/2022/10/CT2022-South-Korea-Web.pdf> accessed 3 June 2025.

70% of steel is produced by using coal-powered Blast Furnace-Basic Oxygen Furnace (BF-BOF) systems. Regulatory efforts to reduce industrial GHG emissions, including a national emissions trading scheme, have been ineffective, as GHG emissions continue to rise.[30] Steel production also has significant adverse impacts on air quality and public health (respiratory illnesses and premature deaths linked to prolonged exposure to toxic air pollutants).[31] A study has shown that air pollution from South Korea's three BF-BOF plants was related to approximately 506 premature deaths in 2021.[32]

Ten youths in South Korea, aged eleven to eighteen, filed a civil lawsuit in February 2025 against POSCO seeking an injunction to stop the company from replacing the lining of its blast furnace (which is a necessary process to extend the furnace's operational lifespan).[33] Relying in part on *Do-Hyun Kim et al v South Korea*, a decision handed down by the Korean Constitutional Court on 29 August 2024 declaring part of Korea's Framework Act on Carbon Neutrality and Green Growth for Coping with the Climate Crisis unconstitutional, the youth plaintiffs in this case argue that POSCO is violating their constitutional right to healthy environment by failing to reduce its GHG emissions and by continuing to expand its coal-fired steel furnace capacity for another fifteen years.[34]

While *Do-Hyun Kim et al v South Korea* was a constitutional challenge against the state for not fulfilling its duty to guarantee the right to live in a healthy environment, inter alia, and therefore not directly applicable in the context of litigation against private actors like a steel company, courts in other jurisdictions (e.g., the Netherlands, South Africa, and India) have used human rights, constitutional rights, and obligations to Indigenous communities to interpret the scope of private law obligations such as the duty of care in negligence claims or directors' duties.[35] Much of the earlier discussion about the interplay between public law and private law (Section 2.1) is relevant here. It can be argued that this interpretative approach could be taken in this case, which is the first in the world to specifically target the steel industry's carbon-intensive production methods. It is worth noting that this is an ambitious test case and the prospects of success (i.e., that the Korean court will impose GHG reduction obligations on the company) are unclear. In *Do-Hyun Kim et al v South Korea*, the constitutional court

[30] 'South Korea's Biggest Polluters Made Millions from Carbon Sales' *The Japan Times* (26 February 2024) <https://www.japantimes.co.jp/business/2024/02/26/companies/south-korea-polluters-carbon-sales/> accessed 3 June 2025.

[31] Centre for Research on Energy and Clean Air (CREA), *Unveiling the Truth Behind Blast Furnace Pollution in South Korea* (2024) <https://energyandcleanair.org/publication/unveiling-the-truth-behind-blast-furnace-pollution/> accessed 3 June 2025.

[32] ibid.

[33] For Our Climate, 'POSCO's Blast Furnace Expansion Accelerating Climate Crisis: Future Generations Take It to Court' (25 April 2024) <https://forourclimate.org/newsroom/1038> accessed 3 June 2025.

[34] ibid. *Constitutional Court of South Korea, Do-Hyun Kim and 18 others v South Korea*, judgment of 29 August 2024; For discussion of this landmark decision, the first time a court in Asia has declared a climate law unconstitutional and ordered the legislative body to amend the law, see: Aleydis Nissen, 'Green Court: South Korean Constitutional Court Rules Landmark Climate Judgement', EJIL:Talk! 29 April 2025 <https://www.ejiltalk.org/green-court-south-korean-constitutional-court-rules-landmark-climate-judgement/> accessed 5 June 2025.

[35] In the case of India, while this interpretive technique has been adopted, it is likely that private law will stay at the sidelines of the development of Indian climate jurisprudence because the legal opportunity structure strongly favours public interest litigation and/or litigation premised on public law causes of action; see Lin and Peel (n 2), 97–109, and Umakanth Varottil, Chapter 36 of this handbook. Also see David Bullock, Chapter 7 of this handbook; Elbert de Jong, Chapter 9 of this handbook; and Olha Cherednychenko and Boudewijn de Bruin, Chapter 45 of this handbook.

was not willing to declare that the 2030 GHG reduction target in the Korean legislation was insufficient and it ruled that it could not identify a single standard that can be used as a legal standard.[36] It declared the legislation unconstitutional on only one ground, that is, the failure to adopt GHG reduction targets after 2030 up to 2050 would place an excessive mitigation burden on future generations and therefore amounted to the State violating its duty to protect the plaintiffs' right to a healthy environment.[37] The court's reasoning was that its constitutional role was to identify (and prescribe remedies) for omissions in the legislation that would infringe upon the constitutional rights of Korean citizens but it would go beyond its constitutional ambit to rule on the specific GHG reduction pathways that the Korean state should adopt because such decisions should be made by the executive branch of government and its expert agencies, and subject to debate and adoption by the legislature.[38]

This line of reasoning, which speaks to democratic legitimacy and the view of the Korean constitutional court of its rightful role in climate governance, is relevant to thinking about how the civil court might rule on the plaintiffs' request for an injunction to stop POSCO from relining its blast furnance. In one scenario, the civil court might take a view similar to that of the constitutional court, that it would be interfering in the proper governance of the company's affairs by stepping in to stop the company from doing what seems to be in the normal course of its business operations, which is to replace the lining of its blast furnace and proper maintenance of its equipment. In an alternative scenario, the civil court might take cognizance of the significance of POSCO's operations in terms of its share of global GHG emissions as well as the local harm caused by air pollution. The court could be willing to take the unprecedented step of considering the horizontal effects of constitutional duties on companies, specifically in this case, the right to a healthy environment. As the case was filed only sixteen weeks ago at the time of writing, much remains to be seen of this test case.

3. Greenwashing

Business firms and other private actors are confronted with public regulation as well as private environmental governance in the face of the reality that urgent action to address climate change is required. Half of the world's largest publicly listed companies have set themselves a net-zero target, including Trafigura (a Singapore-based commodities company that is the world's second-largest oil trader), Samsung Electronics (a Korean company that is the fourth-largest technology company globally), and the Mitsubishi Group (a large Japanese conglomerate that generated about US$135 billion in revenue in 2024).[39] Many financial sector firms have formed or joined initiatives such as the Glasgow Financial Alliance for Net Zero (GFANZ) which provides "financial institutions with tools, frameworks, and voluntary guidance to support the net-zero transition to bolster economic growth and manages the financial risks of climate change". In the span of three years, GFANZ has grown its membership from about 160 (in 2021) to 700 members (in 2024).[40] Investment funds that are marketed as "green"

[36] Plan 1.5, 'Unofficial Translation of *Constitutional Court of South Korea, Do-Hyun Kim and 18 others v South Korea*, judgment of 29 August 2024' <https://climatecasechart.com/wp-content/uploads/non-us-case-documents/2024/20240829_NA_decision-1.pdf> accessed 18 July 2025, 22.

[37] ibid 30–31.

[38] ibid.

[39] Zero Tracker, 'Tracking Net Zero Commitments' <https://zerotracker.net> accessed 3 June 2025.

[40] Glasgow Financial Alliance for Net Zero (GFANZ), 2024 Progress Report (November 2024) 4 <https://assets.bbhub.io/company/sites/63/2024/11/GFANZ-Progress-Report-2024.pdf> accessed 3 June 2025. In 2025, following the Trump election, there was an exodus of American lenders which also led to

or "socially responsible" have grown exponentially, though this growth has been dampened by an "ESG backlash" primarily in the United States, but with knock-on effects in the rest of the world including Asia.[41] The corporate pledges and public statements are typically focused on climate action ("Paris aligned" being a popular buzzword) but can include commitments to address a range of environmental issues including biodiversity loss, plastics pollution, and air pollution.

This proliferation of environmental marketing claims has raised concerns about their truthfulness. Greenwashing generally refers to the practice of companies making false or misleading environmental claims.[42] These claims about the environmental impact of a product, service, or a company's business model are usually made to gain a commercial advantage as many consumers are willing to pay more for a product that is ecologically less harmful or, to put it simply, "better for our planet".[43] As consumer demand for environmentally less harmful products and services has grown globally, many businesses have responded in part by marketing their products and services as being environmentally less harmful (or even beneficial).

Studies have shown that contrary to oft-held assumptions, a significant majority of people living in Asia are concerned about climate change and express willingness to pay more for

lenders elsewhere to reconsider their membership of GFANZ. As a result of this upheaval, GFANZ is in a weaker position today. For analysis, see Simon Mundy, 'The Unravelling of a $130tn Climate Alliance' *Financial Times* (15 January 2025) < https://www.ft.com/content/82c193c9-a52d-41fa-a945-e91273754 1b0> accessed 18 July 2025; Cynthia Williams, Chapter 30 of this handbook.

[41] Mark Segal, 'BlackRock Exits Net Zero Coalition, Says Move Won't Change How It Manages Investments' *ESG Today* (10 January 2025) <https://www.esgtoday.com/blackrock-exits-net-zero-coalit ion-says-move-wont-change-how-it-manages-investments/> accessed 3 June 2025; 'From Boom to Backlash: The Evolving ESG Narrative' *Nanyang Business School* (20 February 2025) <https://www.ntu.edu.sg/business/news-events/news/story-detail/from-boom-to-backlash--the-evolving-esg-narrative> accessed 3 June 2025.

"ESG Fund Outflows Hit Record as Sustainable Investing Backlash Grows" *Financial Times* (25 April 2025) <https://www.ft.com/content/9f425c25-4fc3-45de-bcc5-e9c75d6d14d3> accessed 3 June 2025).

[42] See, for example, paragraph 1 of the preamble in 'Empowering consumers for the green transition: European Parliament legislative resolution of 17 January 2024 on the proposal for a directive of the European Parliament and of the Council on amending Directives 2005/29/EC and 2011/83/EU' as regards empowering consumers for the green transition through better protection against unfair practices and better information (COM(2022)0143-C9-0128/2022-2022/0092 (COD)). For analysis of greenwashing claims in the Global South, see Tiffanie Chan, Juliana Vélez Echeverri, Joana Setzer, and Catherine Higham, Chapter 11 of this handbook.

[43] Centre for Climate Engagement, *Summary Report: Greenwashing: Legal Risks and Opportunities* (1 July 2024) <https://climatehughes.org/greenwashing/#:~:text=In%20a%20private%20sector%20 context,to%20gain%20a%20commercial%20advantage> accessed 3 June 2025; United Nations' High-Level Expert Group on the Net Zero Emissions Commitments of Non-State Entities, *Integrity Matters: Net Zero Commitments by Businesses, Financial Institutions, Cities and Regions* (United Nations 2022) <https://www.un.org/sites/un2.un.org/files/high-level_expert_group_n7b.pdf> accessed 3 June 2025. It should be noted that while there is significant attention paid to greenwashing by businesses, less attention is paid to greenwashing by universities and public agencies which can also be highly detrimental. For discussion, see Temitope Tunbi Onifade, '"State Greenwashing": An Overlooked Phenomenon?" 2025 Journal of Environmental Law (Advance Access 10 May 2025) <https://academic.oup.com/jel/advance-article/doi/10.1093/jel/eqaf008/8129420?searchresult=1> accessed 3 June 2025; Alice Venn, 'Climate Litigation, Equality and Unfulfilled Promises: Illuminating Greenwashing in the Public Sector' (2025) Journal of Environmental Law 1 <https://doi.org/10.1093/jel/eqaf011> accessed 3 June 2025.

goods and services that have less negative environmental impacts.[44] However, these studies also show that there is a significant intention-action gap across most Asian jurisdictions. The intention-action gap, which refers to the situation in which a person expresses clear intention or plans to do something but fails to translate that intention into actual behaviour, can be explained by the generally low levels of awareness of environmental and ecological sustainability across Asia, the overwhelming choices available to the environmentally conscious consumer that leads to decision paralysis, and the high costs of environmentally friendly products.[45] In these surveys, many consumers also express mistrust about many environmental claims, which hinders their willingness to make those purchases, confirming the negative effects of greenwashing.

Across Asia, regulatory efforts to tackle rampant greenwashing are uneven and sporadic. Regulation has also largely not come from environmental and climate change policymakers, but from financial market regulators and government agencies responsible for consumer welfare and the promotion of competition and fair trading. In Indonesia, for example, the legal basis for regulating greenwashing is the Consumer Protection Act No. 8 of 1999. Article 4(3) of this Act stipulates that consumers have the right to accurate, clear, and honest information about the conditions of goods and services. Article 8 prohibits businesses from misleading considers by claiming that their products or services meet certain standards when they do not. However, lack of enforcement and low penalties for non-compliance have been identified as barriers to effective regulation of greenwashing in Indonesia.[46]

Another example is Singapore, where greenwashing is rampant and there is "light touch" regulation, if at all. A study on greenwashing in online marketing that was commissioned by the Competition and Consumer Commission of Singapore (CCCS) and that showed that 51% of online product claims to be "environmentally friendly", "sustainable", "natural", and "good for Earth" were vague and unsubstantiated. In response, the CCCS informed Parliament that it would issue guidelines "to help companies make fair and accurate claims about the 'green' credentials of their products".[47] It is interesting to note that the regulatory agency's position is that these guidelines are intended to "help companies to avoid unintentional greenwashing that could amount to unfair practices under the Consumer Protection (Fair Trading) Act".[48] As of May 2025, the guidelines have not been published and there have only been two reported cases of the Advertising Standards Authority finding companies in breach of the Singapore

[44] Karine Trinquetel, 'How to Avoid Your Brand Being Inadvertently Tarred with the "Greenwashing Brush"' *Kantar* (31 March 2024) <https://www.kantar.com/inspiration/the-negative-impact-of-greenwashing-and-how-to-keep-your-marketing-aligned-with-the-un-sdgs> 3 June 2025.

[45] ibid; see also Ridho Bramulya Ikhsan, 'Greenwashing Raises Red Flags among Indonesian Consumers' *Eco-Business* (2 October 2024) <https://www.eco-business.com/opinion/greenwashing-raises-red-flags-among-indonesian-consumers/> accessed 3 June 2025.

[46] Caecilia Patrice Yonandi and Gunardi Lie, 'Greenwashing in Indonesia: Deceptive Claims and Corporate Social Responsibility (CSR)' (2025) 11(2.A) Jurnal Ilmiah Wahana Pendidikan 112–13 <https://jurnal.peneliti.net/index.php/JIWP/article/view/9786> accessed 3 June 2025.

[47] Lawrence Loh and others, *Promoting Best Practices in Online Marketing* (Centre for Governance and Sustainability, November 2023) <https://bschool.nus.edu.sg/cgs/wp-content/uploads/sites/7/2023/11/CGS-Report-on-Promoting-Best-Practices-in-Online-Marketing-November-2023.pdf> accessed 3 June 2025; Singapore Ministry of Trade and Industry, *Written Reply to Parliamentary Question on CCCS' Guidelines on Product Marketing to Avoid Greenwashing* (5 February 2024) <https://www.mti.gov.sg/Newsroom/Parliamentary-Replies/2024/02/Written-reply-to-PQ-on-CCCS-guidelines-on-product-marketing-to-avoid-greenwashing> accessed 3 June 2025.

[48] Singapore Ministry of Trade and Industry (n 47).

Code of Advertising Practice, which is a set of guidelines for the advertising industry to self-regulate in the interests of promoting ethical advertising.[49] The Zero Greenwashing Alliance is an early-stage civil society initiative to identify and stop cases of greenwashing.[50] Of the four cases of greenwashing that the Alliance has acted on, two companies (City Energy and Shell Singapore) did not respond to the Alliance's emails. In the remaining two cases (involving carbon offset claims by Scoot Airlines and Singapore Airlines), the Singapore Airlines Group responded with a commitment "to improve the carbon offset information on SIA and Scoot's communication channels and VCOP microsites".[51]

The brief discussion above shows that public regulation of greenwashing is currently weak, even in Singapore, which has high state enforcement capacity. Limited public awareness of the harms of misleading environmental claims, business actors not being clear about the boundary between creative marketing and misleading advertising, and regulators only starting to tackle greenwashing—these three factors combine such that there are insufficient reputational and enforcement risks to deter greenwashing. Steps are being taken across Asia to address these factors through, for example, consumer education and issuance of guidelines to businesses. Ratcheting up of enforcement action is happening in South Korea, but there is limited evidence of that happening elsewhere. Against this context, is there a role for private law to play?

So far, we have discussed greenwashing in its traditional paradigm, which is that of businesses trumpeting their environmental credentials to individual consumers. In the traditional paradigm, private litigation by individual consumers based on fraudulent or negligent misrepresentation can be a pathway to tackle greenwashing. In the US, for example, private actions against greenwashing commenced in the 1970s and continue today.[52] However, regulation through litigation is an expensive and challenging proposition in many Asian jurisdictions. In Singapore and Hong Kong, for example, there is an absence of formal class action litigation procedures, and there are restrictions on contingency or conditional fees and third-party litigation funding.[53] This chapter would therefore advocate for greenwashing legislation and stronger enforcement of these laws by regulators across Asia.[54]

[49] James Darley, 'Inside VietJet's Controversial "Greenwashing" Campaign' *Sustainability Magazine* (10 January 2025) <https://sustainabilitymag.com/articles/the-story-of-vietjets-controversial-greenwashing-campaign> accessed 3 June 2025; Carmen Sin, 'Prism+ Air-Con Ad Deemed "Greenwashing" by S'pore Watchdog; Company Defends It as "Tongue-in-Cheek"' *The Straits Times* (18 December 2023) <https://www.straitstimes.com/singapore/prism-air-con-ad-accused-of-greenwashing-is-removed-after-s-pore-watchdog-deems-it-misleading> accessed 3 June 2025.

[50] Zero Greenwashing Alliance <https://www.zerogreenwashingalliance.com> accessed 3 June 2025.

[51] Zero Greenwashing Alliance, *Case File: S/T/02—Scoot* (2023) <https://9b2d2d75-7adf-4ea5-8c47-1b96d3a7eaf6.filesusr.com/ugd/a4715a_70413f2a7aeb4ae5a63c7eabaa4b9f0a.pdf>; Zero Greenwashing Alliance, *Case File: S/T/03—Singapore Airlines* (2023) <https://9b2d2d75-7adf-4ea5-8c47-1b96d3a7eaf6.filesusr.com/ugd/a4715a_13a04187f5cb4deba13fc3dc9a93cc86.pdf> both accessed 3 June 2025.

[52] For discussion, see Eric L Lane, 'Greenwashing 2.0' (2013) 38 Columbia Journal of Environmental Law 279, 280–95.

[53] In Singapore, the key procedural rules for representative proceedings is found in Order 4, Rule 6 of the Rules of Court 2021. A class action is defined as 'where numerous persons have a common interest in any proceedings, such persons may sue or be sued as a group with one or more of them representing the group'. Third-party funding is not permitted for representative or class actions except those commenced in the Singapore International Commercial Court. Contingency fee arrangements are prohibited in Singapore. Conditional fee arrangements are permitted only for cases commenced in the Singapore International Commercial Court or generally in arbitration matters; <https://www.mlaw.gov.sg/files/Council_GN_Third_Party_Funding.pdf>.

[54] For discussion of regulatory enforcement against greenwashing in Australia, see Jacqueline Peel, Chapter 37 of this handbook.

The clean technology revolution—a significant period of development and commercialisation of low-carbon technologies and equipment—has meant that green marketing has expanded beyond the advertising of products to individual consumers into business-to-business communications regarding clean technology products and services.[55] As such, it has been argued that greenwashing analysis should also contemplate legal actions by and on behalf of corporate consumers and three new categories of commercial consumer greenwashing cases have been identified: breach of contract or breach of warranty clauses involving energy generation equipment and projects, trademark infringement actions involving branded clean technology equipment, and fraud cases in connection with renewable energy credits.[56] All three categories arise as some clean technology businesses are tempted to make false, misleading, or deceptive claims about the environmental benefits of their products and projects.[57] There are currently no reported cases in these categories in Asia. It is likely that many of these disputes have been resolved through arbitration, which is frequently the dispute resolution mechanism of choice for cross-border transactions, particularly when a party is a state or state-owned entity. It is also the mechanism of choice where confidentiality and privacy are important to the parties in dispute, which is often the case with contracts involving technology and innovation. While commercial arbitration offers confidentiality to the parties, it makes it difficult to track the extent to which climate-related issues are already being raised.[58]

In line with global trends, sustainability reporting and climate disclosure rules have been introduced across several jurisdictions in Asia. In Singapore, for example, sustainability reporting on key environmental, social, and governance (ESG) metrics and climate-related disclosures, consistent with the Task Force on Climate-related Financial Disclosures (TCFD) recommendations, which have been incorporated into the International Sustainability Standards Board (ISSB) standards, has been introduced in phases, with mandatory reporting by all Singapore-listed companies starting from the 2025 financial year.[59] A similar approach has been adopted in Hong Kong, Malaysia, and Japan, for example.[60] Mandatory reporting on ESG and climate change risks is often seen as a step forward in fostering corporate accountability and, in putting a price on carbon and other forms of environmental pollution, will help to internalise environmental costs and force businesses to pay the true costs of their operations. However, there is also significant room for misleading climate-related claims in disclosure reports, which can lead to both regulatory enforcement and shareholder litigation.[61]

[55] Lane (n 52).

[56] ibid 303.

[57] ibid.

[58] For discussion, see Ying Zhu, Chapter 25 of this handbook.

[59] Rules 711A and 711B, Mainboard Rules, Singapore Stock Exchange: <https://rulebook.sgx.com/rulebook/sustainability-report> accessed 6 June 2025.

[60] The Stock Exchange of Hong Kong, 'Climate Change': <https://www.hkex.com.hk/Listing/Sustainability/ESG-Academy/ESG-in-Practice/Climate-Change?sc_lang=en>; Sustainability Standards Board of Japan, 'SSBJ Issues Inaugural Sustainability Disclosure Standards to Be Applied in Japan' (press release, Tokyo, 5 March 2025): <https://www.ssb-j.jp/jp/wp-content/uploads/sites/7/news_release_20250305_e.pdf>; Bursa Malaysia, 'Bursa Malaysia Requires Sustainability Reporting Using the IFRS Sustainability Disclosure Standards' (Press Release, 23 December 2024) <https://www.bursamalaysia.com/sites/5bb54be15f36ca0af339077a/content_entry5c11a9db758f8d31544574c6/6768e229e6414a4ba0eb9f4d/files/23122024__MEDIA_RELEASE_BURSA_MALAYSIA_REQUIRES_SUSTAINABILITY_REPORTING_USING_THE_IFRS_SUSTAINABILITY_DISCLOSURE_STANDARDS.pdf?1734927108> all accessed 8 June 2025.

[61] Perhaps the most well-known example is the first case brought by the US Securities and Exchange Commission (SEC)'s Climate and ESG Task Force, which was against Vale S.A., a Brazilian mining

4. Corporate Accountability Legislation

In a legal innovation that is globally a first of its kind, the Climate Accountability (CLIMA) Act is a bill that was put forward by some members of the Philippines House of Representatives in November 2023.[62] House Bill 9609 is an ambitious attempt to create a holistic corporate accountability framework in the Philippines—one that is backed by legal sanctions and will provide climate change victims effective compensation and other remedies. As stated in its preamble, this legislation seeks "[t]o institute policies and systems to address climate change, establishing the necessary institutional mechanisms for the protection of most vulnerable communities from loss and damage in the country, providing for corporate and state accountabilities and reparations for violation thereof, and other purposes".[63] The proposed CLIMA Act can also be seen as an initiative by a climate-vulnerable state to complement the work that is being done on loss and damage in the sphere of international law (i.e., the United Nations Framework Convention on Climate Change (UNFCCC) regime).[64]

The bill consists of four chapters. The following discussion highlights the key features of each chapter.

Chapter 1 is one of general provisions. There are three noteworthy definitions. First, Section 2 declares that the United Nations Guiding Principles on Business and Human Rights is the basis for the establishment of minimum standards of behaviour for corporate actors operating in the Philippines. Secondly, Section 2 defines what a business is and specifically what "carbon majors" refer to, that is, "businesses that are multinational or state-owned producers, traders, and refineries of crude oil, natural gas, coal, and cement, that significantly contribute to global greenhouse gas emissions, without taking climate accountability, and therefore primarily drive climate change". Thirdly, the section defines reparations as "the amends for a tort or injury inflicted, especially, in the context of this bill, compensation, relocation, and rehabilitation and recovery for victims/survivors of climate loss and damage".

Chapter 2 sets out the framework for corporate accountability. The reporting obligations and measures that businesses must undertake in order to fulfil their due diligence standard of care are far-reaching. Section 4 clearly states that a business that exceeds established thresholds for GHG emissions can be held liable in negligence. Notably, Section 5 imposes obligations on companies to make climate-related financial disclosures, measure their GHG emissions throughout their value chains, respect and protect human rights, and comply with the Indigenous Peoples' Rights Act of 1997. Section 8 provides for who can sue. Standing is conferred on climate change victims or survivors who seek redress for the harm caused by

company whose American depository shares and notes are registered with the SEC and publicly traded on the New York Stock Exchange; US SEC, 'Brazilian Mining Company to Pay $55.9 Million to Settle Charges Related to Misleading Disclosures Prior to Deadly Dam Collapse' (Press Release, Washington, DC, 28 March 2023) <https://www.sec.gov/newsroom/press-releases/2023-63> accessed 8 June 2025.

[62] A copy of House Bill No. 9609 can be found at <https://www.greenpeace.org/static/planet4-philippines-stateless/2023/11/720d51c3-hb09609.pdf>. For discussion about the context of climate loss and damage in the Philippines, see Legal Rights and Natural Resources Center, 'Submission to the UN Special Rapporteur on the Right to Development regarding Climate Justice in Loss and Damage', 29 March 2024 <https://www.ohchr.org/sites/default/files/documents/issues/development/sr/cfi-2024-reports/subm-2024-sr-development-cso-legal-ri-lrc-lrc.pdf> both accessed 10 June 2025.

[63] House Bill No. 9609 (n 63).

[64] Jameela Joy Reyes, 'Loss and Damage: Perspectives from Inside and Outside the UNFCCC' (Heinrich Boll Stiftung, Southeast Asia, 9 July 2024) <https://th.boell.org/en/2024/07/09/loss-and-damage-perspectives-inside-and-outside-unfccc> accessed 9 June 2025.

non-compliance with the CLIMA Act, minors, generations yet unborn, and biodiversity. The bill clearly states that the filing of a petition pursuant to the CLIMA Act is without prejudice to international dispute resolution and administrative redress. Citizen suits are also encouraged to enforce the act. Section 11 states that the doctrine of last clear chance applies to this act, "whereby carbon majors' knowledge of their significant contribution to climate change compels them to substantially reduce greenhouse gas emissions to be faithful to their duty of care. Failure to do so implicates them in exacerbating and thus makes them accountable for significantly contributing to the climate crisis".

Chapter 3 establishes the climate change reparations fund that is to be administered by an independent board. The operating costs of the fund will be borne by the government as well as donations, grants, and other funds generated by international loss and damage mechanisms. Chapter 4 sets out fines of up to 15% of a business's gross income reported in their latest regulatory disclosure for the offences of greenwashing, climate denialism, and exceeding GHG emissions thresholds that are determined in accordance with the Philippines' Paris Agreement Nationally Determined Contribution. All collected fines will be channelled to the climate change reparations fund.

At the time of writing, House Bill No. 9609 is still pending with the Committee on Climate Change (19th Congress).[65] Many provisions in the bill will require refinement before they can be translated into laws and policies.[66] It is, after all, an ambitious piece of legislation that sets the high water mark in the quest for corporate climate accountability globally. The hope is that the CLIMA Act will soon become law, thereby creating a robust legal framework that combines private litigation, public enforcement, international law, and climate science to achieve corporate accountability for climate change and human rights.

5. Conclusion

This chapter has sought to provide a snapshot of some legal and regulatory developments in Asia that are truly innovative as well as promising in their attempt to advance corporate accountability for climate change. The challenges are immense. Many of the countries in Asia struggle with issues of poverty, ethnic and religious tensions, corruption, and lack of access to basic human needs, including water and energy. Against this background, corporate accountability mechanisms have tended to emerge in the more developed jurisdictions in Asia. Yet, at the same time, corporate climate accountability takes on a more existentialist and moral dimension when one considers that there are millions of vulnerable victims and survivors of climate-related extreme weather events in Asia.

For a long time, policymakers and scholars have recognised that there is a role for private actors in reducing GHG emissions, but governments are conceived of as the primary actors leading efforts to limit climate change. The Paris Agreement is an instrument of public international law and its architecture of "Nationally Determined Contributions", supported by transparency and capacity-building mechanisms, seeks to galvanise state action. This focus on governments and public law as instrumental to addressing climate change is replicated across all jurisdictions globally. However, since 2015 (the year in which the Paris Agreement entered into force), there has been a surge of interest in making private actors assume responsibilities

[65] Senate of the Philippines, Legislative Digital Resources: <https://issuances-library.senate.gov.ph/bills/house-bill-no-9609-19th-congress> accessed10 June 2025.

[66] See, for example, recommendations made by the Republic of the Philippines, Commission on Human Rights in its 'Position Paper on the Draft Climate Accountability Bill' <https://chr.gov.ph/chr-resource/position-paper-2023-6/> accessed 10 June 2025.

to limit climate change as well as creating incentives (usually financial) to encourage their participation in limiting climate change. It is in this space where scholars interested in private law's intersections with the societal project of decarbonisation, climate adaptation, and loss and damage have found examples of the relevance of private law. This chapter shows that these examples are rare in Asia as the "public" still looms large in climate law and governance. However, this chapter has also shown that as more climate-related laws and regulations are put in place, private litigation and private contracting will increase to complement the public in the quest for climate justice in Asia.

CHAPTER 39

Africa

UZUAZO ETEMIRE

1. Introduction

As the world races to stem the tide of climate change, scholarly conversations about appropriate responses to its drivers and impact at the national and supranational levels continue to emerge with much vigour. The relevance of this conversation for Africa cannot be overemphasised, especially as the continent was assessed in the latest report of the Intergovernmental Panel on Climate Change (IPCC) as the most vulnerable region to climate change in the world.[1]

To be sure, Africa is currently experiencing significant and worsening ecological, economic, and social impacts from climate change.[2] In the last sixty years, Africa has recorded a warming trend generally beyond the global average,[3] and over 110 million people in the continent are said to have been directly impacted by climate change-related disasters in 2022 alone. These natural hazards caused over US$8.5 billion in economic damages.[4] Already, "tens of millions of Africans" are suffering climate change-related health problems, in the form of health stress and the increased transmission of infectious diseases.[5] African countries are also losing annually an average of 2%–5% of their GDP suffering from and responding to climate extremes, with the annual cost of adaptation to climate change in sub-Saharan Africa estimated at US$30–US$50 billion over the next decade.[6] And if adequate response measures are not established and promoted, WMO estimates that by 2030, "up to 118 million extremely poor people (living on less than US$1.90 per day) will be exposed to drought, floods and extreme heat in Africa", among other negative impacts.[7]

[1] IPCC, 'Poverty, Livelihoods and Sustainable Development', *Climate Change 2022: Impacts, Adaptation and Vulnerability: Working Group II Contribution to the Sixth Assessment Report of the Intergovernmental Panel on Climate Change* (CUP 2023) 1171, 1199. See also Ayansina Ayanlade and others, 'Complex Climate Change Risk and Emerging Directions for Vulnerability Research in Africa' (2023) 40 Climate Risk Management 1, 3.

[2] See World Meteorological Organization (WMO), *State of the Climate in Africa 2019* (WMO, 2020); United Nations Environment Programme, *Climate Change Challenges for Africa: Evidence from selected EU-Funded Research Projects* (Briefing, April 2012); and Janani Vivekananda, 'Climate Change: Conflict and Crisis in Lake Chad' (2018) 2 European Security and Defence Union Journal 23.

[3] WMO, *State of the Climate in Africa 2023* (WMO, 2024) ii.

[4] WMO, *State of the Climate in Africa 2022* (WMO, 2023) 16.

[5] Giuliana Viglione, 'In-Depth: How Climate Change affects Health in Africa' (*Carbon Brief*, 22 June 2023) <https://www.carbonbrief.org/in-depth-how-climate-change-affects-health-in-africa/> accessed 5 June 2025.

[6] WMO (n 3) 17.

[7] ibid.

The regulatory efforts of African governments aimed at tackling the drivers and impacts of climate change within the continent have generally not produced the desired result.[8] The major reasons for this include the complicity of most governments in actions and omissions that contribute to climate change in their push for economic development,[9] and their penchant to see required far-reaching mitigation and adaptation measures as "expensive, unnecessary, futile, and remote from policies that yield immediate and politically popular economic benefits".[10] This failure by governments in Africa and beyond has significantly contributed to the emergence of the now-popular complementary measure of "climate change litigation"[11] whereby non-state actors seek to fill the gap created by deficient regulatory state action by approaching the court for climate-related remedies. Globally, the majority of climate litigation cases have been against governments.[12] This is also the case in Africa, where more than 90% of climate litigation cases on the continent, as archived in the database of the Sabin Center for Climate Change Law, target governments.[13]

In those cases, private entities deploy public law mechanisms under constitutional law and other legislative schemes in their efforts to hold the respective governments accountable for the drivers and impacts of climate change.[14] This global predominance of public (or vertical) climate litigation is understandable, considering, among other reasons, that the traditional and primary responsibility of protecting the environment and the public from avoidable harm—including in relation to contributions to climate change by private businesses—rests on the government.[15] On the other hand, private (or horizontal) climate litigation,[16] whereby private litigants seek to hold other private actors legally accountable for their climate-harmful activities using private law tools, has lagged. Past efforts aimed at suing private entities for climate wrongs were largely unsuccessful due to difficulties in scaling the hurdles created by restrictive rules on the likes of standing, proof of harm, and causation.[17] However, the mix of the rapid evolution of climate science in a manner that eases the evidentiary burden and widespread legal reforms have given rise to "a new wave"[18] of private climate litigation, which has

[8] Lotsmart Fonjonga, Frank Matoseb, and David A Sonnenfeld, 'Climate Change in Africa: Impacts, Adaptation, and Policy Responses' (2024) 89 Global Environmental Change 1, 3.

[9] Uzuazo Etemire, 'The Future of Climate Change Litigation in Nigeria: COPW v NNPC in the Spotlight' (2021) 15(2) Carbon & Climate Law Review, 158.

[10] Michael Burger and Justin Gundlach, *The Status of Climate Change Litigation: A Global Review* (Sabin Centre for Climate Change Law, Columbia Law School, and UN Environment 2017) 6, 8.

[11] Climate change litigation includes 'cases that raise *material issues* of law or fact *relating to* climate change mitigation, adaptation, or the science of climate change'. UNEP, *Global Climate Litigation Report: 2020 Status Review* (UNEP 2020) 6 (emphasis added).

[12] Burger and Gundlach (n 10) 14.

[13] See entries for the African countries on The Sabin Center for Climate Change Law, *Climate Change Litigation Databases* <https://climatecasechart.com/non-us-jurisdiction/> accessed 5 June 2025.

[14] ibid.

[15] Working Group on the issue of human rights and transnational corporations and other business enterprises, 'Information Note on Climate Change and the Guiding Principles on Business and Human Rights' (UN, June 2023) [7–8] <https://www.ohchr.org/sites/default/files/documents/issues/business/workinggroupbusiness/Information-Note-Climate-Change-andUNGPs.pdf> accessed 5 June 2025.

[16] For emphasis, 'private or horizontal climate litigation' as used in this chapter generally refers to a climate change case where the principal parties in the case are both private entities.

[17] Geetanjali Ganguly, Joana Setzer, and Veerle Heyvaert, 'If at First You Don't Succeed: Suing Corporations for Climate Change' (2018) 38(4) Oxford Journal of Legal Studies 841.

[18] ibid.

seen a private law-facilitated growth in private actors, especially corporations, being cited as defendants in suits.[19]

In light of this development, this chapter seeks to respond to the question: Why *should*, and to what extent *have* and *can*, private law mechanisms be engaged to hold private actors in Africa climate-accountable through the courts at the national level? To unravel this query, the next section will address the question of the importance of horizontal climate litigation for Africa. Section 3 will broadly assess the extent to which private law has fostered or has been used in climate litigation in Africa. Then, Section 4 will inquire into the extent to which emerging national climate-specific legislation in Africa includes private law mechanisms and makes room for horizontal litigation on the continent. Section 5 provides a conclusion.

2. Why Horizontal Climate Litigation in Africa?

Compared to other regions, Africa has one of the lowest numbers of climate change litigation cases indicated in databases such as those of the Sabin Center for Climate Change Law. While these databases are arguably not exhaustive concerning African climate litigation,[20] they clearly indicate that such cases in the continent are on the rise. Most of these cases, as noted earlier, relate to litigants seeking to hold governments climate-accountable using public law mechanisms under national constitutions, as well as environmental and climate change statutes. South Africa, for instance, hosts several of such cases where its government's decisions approving potential climate-harmful projects—such as a coal-fired power plant[21] and urban development in a horticultural area[22]—have been successfully challenged for failing to reflect adequate consideration of climate change. Also, there are two interesting vertical climate (adaptation and mitigation) lawsuits pending in Uganda—a victims-led action against the government for non-fulfilment of its positive obligations under climate change and disaster management laws to manage the risk of landslides in the Bududa district;[23] and another action where, on behalf of four minors, the state is being sued for the breach of its obligation to mitigate climate change pursuant to its constitutional public trust duty and obligation to protect the interest of the present and future generations.[24]

It is important for this dominant trend of vertical climate litigation in Africa to continue, and even be encouraged, as it is effective in pressuring governments that arguably bear the

[19] Joana Setzer and Catherine Higham, *Global Trends in Climate Change Litigation: 2021 Snapshot* (Grantham Research Institute on Climate Change and the Environment and Centre for Climate Change Economics and Policy, London School of Economics and Political Science 2021) 23, 27–30.

[20] Some reasons for this may include the fact that (1) some of such cases may have '"taken place largely below the radar' of scholarly attention", or may not have made it into the public domain due to the relatively weak internet presence of many African judicial institutions, and (2) some cases that may be considered to be climate litigation in the African context may fall outside the ambits of how these mostly Global North databases define a climate case. Jacqueline Peel and Hari M Osofsky, 'Climate Change Litigation' (2020) 16 (1) Annual Review of Law and Social Science, 21, 28.

[21] *Earthlife Africa Johannesburg v Minister of Environmental Affairs* (65662/16) [2017] ZAGPPHC 58.

[22] *Philippi Horticultural Area Food & Farming Campaign v MEC for Local Government, Environmental Affairs and Development Planning: Western Cape* (16779/17) [2020] ZAWCHC 8.

[23] *Tsama William and Others v Uganda's Attorney General and Others*, Miscellaneous Cause No. 24 of 2020 (High Court of Uganda, Mbale).

[24] *Mbabazi v The Attorney General and National Environmental Management* Civil Suit No. 283 of 2012 (High Court of Kampala).

primary responsibility for addressing climate change and its impacts to take the necessary actions. Nevertheless, there is now a heightened need to also subject private actors with climate-significant activities in Africa under the same burden and a similar level of judicial scrutiny through the instrumentality of private law in its broadest form. This is primarily because the private actors in Africa are not only a major force for socio-economic development, accounting generally for "90% of jobs, 70% of gross domestic product, and 70% of all investment" on the continent;[25] they are also key players in the sectors that contribute the most to climate change, such as Africa's hydrocarbon exploration that has attracted the direct participation of more than 500 private oil companies.[26] Importantly, these companies are neither responding responsibly to the visible negative impacts of climate change in Africa nor to the growing international laws and commitments aimed at addressing the phenomenon. In fact, their role as frontline economic actors, especially in the development of fossil fuel infrastructure in Africa, has continued to expand rapidly in recent years.

Buttressing that point, a research report by a group of NGOs found in sub-Saharan Africa *alone* 964 fossil fuel projects between 2016 (the year in which the Paris Agreement entered into force[27]) and 2021 that were "owned or supported by 406 companies, the majority headquartered in Europe, the US and China".[28] In a separate report, they identified 200 oil, gas, and coal companies that were at the forefront of fossil fuel expansion in Africa in 2022, "exploring or developing new fossil reserves, building new fossil transport infrastructure or developing new gas- and coal-fired power plants" in forty-nine of Africa's fifty-five countries.[29] Apart from private energy companies, other private investors, especially private financial institutions, are complicit in this fossil fuel expansion in the continent: Between 2019 and July 2022, 352 commercial banks channelled over US$98 billion (mostly from banks headquartered in US, Europe, and Asia) to companies developing new fossil projects in Africa—71% of which sum ironically came from banks that are members of the Net Zero Banking Alliance.[30] It was on the strength of these studies that the African Union (AU) in its recent communication with the International Court of Justice (ICJ) stressed that the duty to tackle climate change "requires vigilance vis-à-vis the activities of private operators".[31] Thus, if climate litigation in Africa will be effective as a tool for addressing climate change on the continent, it cannot mostly focus on government and largely ignore the role of private actors; it must be applied comprehensively so that private actors in Africa are made to share in the climate responsibility that follows their rapidly evolving and dominant role in Africa's development story.

An additional point is that beyond their direct contribution to climate change, private actors in Africa are also indirectly responsible for much of the climate-harmful decisions of

[25] African Development Bank Group (AFDB), *Private Sector Development Strategy 2021–2025* (AFDB, 2021) 5, 5.

[26] KPMG, *Oil and Gas in Africa: Reserves, Potential and Prospects of Africa* (KPMG, 2014) 1.

[27] Paris Agreement to the United Nations Framework Convention on Climate Change (adopted 12 December 2015, entered into force 4 November 2016) T.I.A.S. No. 16-1104.

[28] Isabelle Geuskens and Henrieke Butijn, *Locked Out of a Just Transition: Fossil Fuel Financing in Africa* (BankTrack, Milieudefensie, and Oil Change International, March 2022) 4.

[29] Heffa Schücking, *Who Is Financing Fossil Fuel Expansion in Africa?* (BankTrack, urgewald, 350.org Africa, Africa Coal Network and others, November 2022) 39. See also ROAPE, 'Climate Cynicism: Fossil Fuel Growth in Africa' (*Review of African Political Economy*, 23 October, 2023) <https://roape.net/2023/10/23/climate-cynicism-fossil-fuel-growth-in-africa/> accessed 5 June 2025.

[30] ibid 41, 44.

[31] *African Union's Answers to the Questions from the Court* (under the Advisory Proceedings of the ICJ on the Obligations of States in Respect of Climate Change, 20 December 2024) 3, 7 <https://www.icj-cij.org/sites/default/files/case-related/187/187-20241220-oth-01-00-en.pdf> accessed 5 June 2025.

government. Indeed, over the years, private actors with large financial bases have become a lot more influential than governments and their regulators in economic sectors that contribute significantly to climate change.[32] This is especially prevalent in Africa, where many countries are relatively poor and characterised by weak public institutions that lack adequate autonomy, as well as the legal and bureaucratic ethos of "impersonality, impartiality and rationality", making them uninsulated from and prone to "private capture" or regulatory agency capture.[33] This phenomenon of capture is even more prevalent in sectors with large carbon footprints that require huge investments and technical expertise that governments in the continent mostly lack; and because, more often than not, these sectors constitute the economic backbone of most African countries, the governments tend to be more beholden to major private actors, especially multination companies, that possess the necessary financial power and technical know-how. For instance, regarding the Nigerian oil and gas sector, Amnesty International has noted how "powerful business actors whose word appears to be law in some cases" have escaped effective regulation by the regulators.[34] Hence, climate litigation targeting these private interests as they make efforts to reap from the climate-harmful decisions that they have engendered through government bodies and regulators is just as, if not more, important than going after government decision-makers that are many times simply the "agents" of private actors.

Moreover, there is currently a growing trend across Africa—the privatisation of state-owned enterprises, many of which are carbon majors.[35] In Angola, for instance, its Privatisation Programme was launched in 2019, under which the government has commenced the process of, and is on track to, privatise its national oil company, Sonangol, alongside dozens of other government companies and assets by 2026.[36] Similarly, in 2022, Nigeria transformed its national oil company from a government agency established by legislation to a limited liability company in the private sphere called the Nigerian National Petroleum Company Limited (NNPC Ltd), pursuant to the historic Petroleum Industry Act 2021 (PIA).[37] The core objective

[32] Danwood Mzikenge Chirwa, 'The Horizontal Application of Constitutional Rights in a Comparative Perspective' (2006) 10(2) Law, Democracy & Development 21.

[33] Eghosa E Osaghae, *Crippled Giant: Nigeria since Independence* (Hurst & Co Publishers Ltd 1998) 23. 'Private capture' or 'agency capture' refers to a situation where a regulatory government agency becomes dominated or significantly influenced by the industry (actors) it is supposed to regulate; here a 'public regulatory agency aligns itself with the industry it is charged with regulating usually to the detriment of its ability to perform its regulatory or public duties'. Uzuazo Etemire, *Law and Practice on Public Participation in Environmental Matters: The Nigerian Example in Transnational Comparative Perspective* (Routledge 2015) 111.

[34] Amnesty International, *Nigeria: Petroleum, Pollution and Poverty in the Niger Delta* (Amnesty International Publications, 2009) 39, 48.

[35] Chipo Muwowo, 'Africa Looks to a New Wave of Privatisation' (*FDI Intelligence*, 13 October 2023) <https://www.fdiintelligence.com/content/2b7bcdc9-a24f-5462-97b4-e9aeecbb6261> accessed 5 June 2025.

[36] See Energy Capital Power, 'Angola to Complete Privatization of Sonangol by 2026' (*Energy Capital & Power*, 27 June 2023) <https://energycapitalpower.com/angola-to-complete-privatization-of-sonangol-by-2026/> accessed 5 June 2025; and Oladehinde Oladipo, 'Angola Speeds Up State Oil IPO as Nigeria's NNPC Drags' (*Business Day*, 3 February 2025) <https://businessday.ng/energy/article/angola-speeds-up-state-oil-ipo-as-nigerias-nnpc-drags/> accessed 5 June 2025.

[37] PIA, No. 6, Federal Republic of Nigeria Official Gazette, Vol 108, No 142, 27 August 2021. See Oghogho Makinde and Olagoke Kuye, 'The Nigerian National Petroleum Company Limited: 'Privatising' the NNPC' (*Aluko & Oyebode*, June 2022) <https://www.aluko-oyebode.com/insights/the-nigerian-national-petroleum-company-limited-privatising-the-nnpc/> accessed 5 June 2025.

of NNPC Ltd is to—without government funding as before—"carry out petroleum operations on a commercial basis, comparable to private companies in Nigeria".[38] Even though ownership of all shares in NNPC Ltd was vested in the government at incorporation,[39] there are clear provisions in the PIA,[40] and imminent plans to ultimately allow private ownership of the new enterprise.[41] In the context of this trend, the issue of climate liability and accountability for past and future actions of these former government entities is another reason why an enabling legal environment for private climate litigation is important in Africa.

The above discussion on the necessity of horizontal climate litigation in Africa requires a shift in the mindset of African climate litigants, who have been mostly fixated on state actors, as well as an assessment of the robustness and adequacy of private law mechanisms that can effectively form the basis for climate action against relevant private actors. This accords with the position of the AU expressed in its substantive intervention in the advisory proceedings of the ICJ on "the obligations of states with respect to climate change".[42] While highlighting the primary responsibility of states to address climate change, the AU, in its written statement, drew strong attention to data showing how fossil fuel and cement companies are the primary cause of "63% of cumulative worldwide emissions of industrial CO2 and methane between 1751 and 2010"; and on this basis, it noted that states, as part of their primary responsibility, were required "to adopt legislative and other appropriate measures to protect against violations linked to business activities, as well as to provide victims of corporate abuses with access to effective remedies".[43] It is in this context that the next section will assess the extent to which available private law mechanisms have been used by victims of climate-harmful activities to hold private actors in Africa accountable.

3. Horizontal Climate Litigation in Africa: Progress and Problems

As stated above, vertical climate litigation has been the dominant approach of litigants in Africa seeking to ensure climate justice through the courts. Nevertheless, there have been a few known cases of horizontal climate litigation on the continent where the activities of the private actors have been challenged in court. These private climate claims have primarily been founded on three causes of action: tort law, environmental law (EIA), and human rights law. While these cases—which, incidentally, all emanated from Nigeria—will be reviewed below, the potency of the respective causes of action to effectively ground future horizontal climate litigation in Africa will also be assessed.

[38] PIA, s 64(a).

[39] PIA, s 53(3).

[40] See, e.g., PIA, s 53(5)–(6).

[41] See Camillus Eboh, 'Nigeria's NNPC in 'Final' Stages of Preparations for IPO, Says Official' (*Reuters*, 27 March 2025) <https://www.reuters.com/world/africa/nigerias-nnpc-final-stages-preparations-ipo-says-official-2025-03-27/> accessed 5 June 2025; Damilola Aina, 'Breaking: NNPCL Set to Sell Shares' (*Punch*, 27 March 2025) <https://punchng.com/breaking-nnpcl-set-to-sell-shares/> accessed 5 June 2025.

[42] *Written Statement of the African Union* (regarding the Advisory Proceedings of the ICJ on the Obligations of States in Respect of Climate Change, 22 March 2024) 4, 81 <https://www.icj-cij.org/sites/default/files/case-related/187/187-20240322-wri-10-00-en.pdf> accessed 5 June 2025.

[43] Richard Heede, 'Tracing Anthropogenic Carbon Dioxide and Methane Emissions to Fossil Fuel and Cement Producers: 1854–2010' (2014) 122 Climatic Change 229, 229.

3.1 Tort Law

About a third of African countries, especially those with a history of British colonial rule, have, as the cornerstone of their tort law, the common law mechanisms of trespass, negligence, and nuisance, among others. These private law causes of action have historically provided a platform for private victims and communities in Africa to participate in ensuring environmental justice and protection, usually against other private actors.[44] One case, however, is noteworthy for shedding some light on the usefulness of these common law mechanisms in facilitating, specifically, horizontal climate litigation in Africa: the Nigerian case of *Chinda & Ors v Shell Petroleum Development Co. Ltd*.[45] In this case, suing under negligence, the plaintiffs aimed to stop the defendant's gas flaring activities negatively affecting their communities. They claimed that as a result of the defendant's negligent management and control of their gas flaring infrastructure, they suffered excessive heat, noise, vibration, and damage to their properties. But for reasons that include their inability to prove to the court's satisfaction that the defendant breached its duty of care—for example, by non-compliance with good industry practice, standards, and guidelines—regarding the management of their gas flare equipment, the court held that the plaintiffs' action in negligence must fail.

This case reflects the limited potency of common law torts to facilitate horizontal climate litigation in Africa. Referencing the *Chinda* case, Frynas noted that unlike other environmental cases, it was particularly "difficult to prove negligence" in cases of "gas flaring", not least because of the "technical nature of oil operations" over which the "oil industry normally has a superior technical knowledge compared to individual litigants. Consequently, it may often be difficult for the plaintiff to argue [successfully with proof] that the oil company was unreasonably negligent or did not adopt accepted standards during its operations",[46] the proof of which may be within the exclusive knowledge of the oil company. This significant disparity in access to information is a core reason why modern approaches, including within the African human rights jurisprudence,[47] favour, in deserving cases, the reversal of the burden of proof to achieve justice.[48] However, this trend is yet to be embraced by courts in Africa in the administration of common law torts. Beyond this, common law torts are generally reactive and not proactive in nature, as they can only provide remedies for injured parties post-pollution,[49] and are thus ill-suited for preventing activities that are potentially harmful to the climate. There are also broader issues, including causation and attribution of responsibility for harm, regarding

[44] See George Agyemang Sarpong, *Ghanaian Environmental Law: International and National Perspectives* (Wildy, Simmonds & Hill Publishing 2018) 66; and Kenneth Kakuru and Irene Ssekyana, *Handbook on Environmental Law in Uganda* (2nd edn, Greenwatch and Environmental Law Institute 2009) 6.

[45] (1974) 2 RSLR 1.

[46] Jedrzej George Frynas, 'Legal Change in Africa: Evidence from Oil-Related Litigation in Nigeria' (1999) 43(2) Journal of African Law 121, 124.

[47] See, for example, the following decisions of the African Court of Human and Peoples' Rights (AfCHPR): *Kennedy Gihana and others v Republic of Rwanda*, App no 017/2015, AfCHPR (28 November 2019), paras 84–85; and *Robert John Penessis v United Republic of Tanzania*, App no 013/2015, AfCHPR (28 November 2019), para 92.

[48] See Christopher Roberts, 'Reversing the Burden of Proof Before Human Rights Bodies' (2022) 25 (10) International Journal of Human Rights Law 1682–1703; and Article 8(3)(e) of the 2018 Regional Agreement on Access to Information, Public Participation and Justice in Environmental Matters in Latin America and the Caribbean, C.N.195.2018, TREATIES-XXVII.18 of 9 April 2018.

[49] Damilola S Olawuyi, *The Principles of Environmental Law in Nigeria* (Afe Babalola University Press 2015) 81.

which common law torts rules are grossly insufficient in the context of climate change, as aptly adumbrated by Kysar:

> Nuisance and other traditional tort theories are overwhelmed by the magnitude and the complexity of the climate change conundrum. Built as it is on a paradigm of harm in which A wrongfully, directly, and exclusively injures B, tort law seems fundamentally ill-equipped to address the causes and impacts of climate change: diffuse and disparate in origin, lagged and latticed in effect, anthropogenic greenhouse gas emissions represent the paradigmatic anti-tort, a collective action problem so pervasive and so complicated as to render at once both all of us and none of us responsible.[50]

Nonetheless, there is some value in the argument that common law torts, as is, may be useful for establishing standards of foresight and responsibility relevant to cases of climate change adaptation.[51] One can also hardly disagree with the desirability, expressed by scholars, of courts evolving the rules of common law torts to effectively capture and accommodate the intricacies and uniqueness of climate change litigation.[52] However, among African jurists and scholars, there appears to be little or no motivation to take steps or advocate the need for common law to be more responsive to (horizontal) climate change issues. This posture is not unconnected with: (1) the subsisting colonial heritage of African courts that were established in the learnings of "the British common law system, with its *minimalist* constitutional conception of the role of judges", whereby the latter, being ultraconservative, are generally averse to radical departures from well-established norms even in light of new circumstances;[53] and (2) the growing African alternatives for grounding private climate claims in (a) hundreds of (human rights and environmental) laws whose provisions can more easily be (re-)interpreted and applied to climate concerns,[54] and (b) specialised, stand-alone climate change legislation.[55]

3.2 Environmental Legislation

Historically, there has been a penchant to treat private law as a subject matter that lies exclusively in the domain of common law, including as it relates to torts, but with the global "emergency of the modern administrative state . . . several domains of horizontal interaction between private actors [and private causes] are today governed entirely [or substantially] by statutory law[s]" underpinned by private law principles.[56] Thus, several environmental statutes across various countries in Africa potentially provide fertile ground for horizontal climate

[50] Douglas A Kysar, 'What Climate Change Can Do About Tort Law' (2011) 41 Environmental Law 12, 3–4. See also David Bullock, 'Public Nuisance and Climate Change: The Common Law's Solutions to the Plaintiff, Defendant and Causation Problems' (2022) 85(5) Modern Law Review 1136, 1137.

[51] JB Ruhl, 'Climate Change Adaptation and the Structural Transformation of Environmental Law' (2010) 40 Environmental Law 363, 401.

[52] Kysar (n 50).

[53] Hakeem O Yusuf, 'The Judiciary and Political Change in Africa: Developing Transnational Jurisprudence in Nigeria' (2009) 7 (654) International Journal of Constitutional Law 654, 664 (emphasis added).

[54] See the Climate Change Laws of the World, a database hosted by the Grantham Research Institute on Climate Change and the Environment at the London School of Economics, UK <https://climate-laws.org/?q=Climate+framework+laws> accessed 5 June 2025.

[55] As discussed in Section 4 of this chapter.

[56] Shyamkrishna Balganesh, 'Private Law Statutory Interpretations' (2019) 92 Southern California Law Journal 949, 950.

litigation. This point is exemplified by legislation on environmental impact assessment, which usually aims to mainstream environmental-related concerns into development decisions on a wide range of potential GHG-emitting projects proposed by public and private entities.[57] If properly applied, the EIA procedure could lead to the rejection or alteration of a proposed project or activity that would otherwise significantly contribute to climate change.

The above point is clearly exemplified by the horizontal climate case of *Oronto Douglas v Shell Petroleum Development Company Nigeria Limited and Ors.*[58] The plaintiff in that case sued the defendants, which included a consortium of oil companies, for non-compliance with the procedural requirements of the Nigerian EIA Decree No. 86 of 1992 (now an Act[59]) in the process of establishing the Nigeria Liquified Natural Gas (NLNG) project. To be sure, the NLNG project is largely a "greening" mechanism that converts gas that would have been flared (in the process of crude oil production) to cleaner fuel for domestic and industrial use.[60] However, it could also be a source of GHG emissions (in the course of gas production and transportation).[61] Yet, the Federal High Court struck out the matter on the basis that the plaintiff, who had a private interest in the suit as a native of a village affected by the project and a public interest as a well-known environmentalist, had no standing to sue. The court, applying the age-long, unduly restrictive Nigerian standing rule to discard the plaintiff's claim, held that "the plaintiff shows no *prima facie* evidence that his [private] right was affected nor any direct injury caused to him" by the non-compliance with the EIA Act.[62]

The number of potential horizontal climate claims which that archaic standing rule has discouraged over the years is unclear. However, the Nigerian Supreme Court, in the recent case of *Centre for Oil Pollution Watch (COPW) v Nigerian National Petroleum Corporation (NNPC)*[63] has now liberalised this restrictive standing rule by allowing for public interest litigation in environmental and climate matters. The Supreme Court reached this decision in consideration of global trends regarding standing, the writings of academic scholars,[64] and—as the court expressly stated—the need for the court to play a role in addressing the challenges of "climate change" and "global warming".[65] Such a liberal approach to standing will likely encourage

57 See Uzuazo Etemire, *Law and Practice on Public Participation in Environmental Matters: The Nigerian Example in Transnational Comparative Perspective* (Routledge 2016) 196.

58 Unreported Suit No: FHC/L/CS/573/96 (17 February 1997).

59 Cap E12, Laws of the Federation of Nigeria, 2004.

60 See NLNG, 'Who We Are' <https://www.nigerialng.com/the-company/Pages/Who-We-Are.aspx> accessed 9 June 2025; and Chineme Okafor, 'Between NLNG and Nigeria's Global Warming Challenges' (*ThisDay*, 12 November 2020) <https://www.thisdaylive.com/index.php/2019/11/12/between-nlng-and-nigerias-global-warming-challenges/> accessed 5 June 2025.

61 See Collins NC Ugochukwu and Jürgen Ertel, 'Negative Impacts of Oil Exploration on Biodiversity Management in the Niger Delta Area of Nigeria' (2008) 26(2) Impact Assessment and Project Appraisal 139, 144.

62 *Oronto Douglas v Shell & Ors* (n 58) 2. Although, on appeal, the Nigerian Court of Appeal set aside this decision and remitted the case back to the Federal High Court for retrial on the grounds that the trial court had breached a number of procedural rules, the retrial did not proceed because the project had been completed by the time the Court of Appeal delivered its decision in December 1998. Rhuks Temitope Ako 'The Judicial Recognition and Enforcement of the Right to Environment: Differing Perspectives from Nigeria and India' (2010) 3 NUJS Law Review 423, 439.

63 (2019) 15 NWLR 1666.

64 ibid 548–71.

65 ibid 580–81.

more horizontal climate litigation.[66] In other words, a future "Oronto Douglas" in Nigeria will no longer have their climate change-related actions struck out for want of proof of any effect of private and other entities on their "private legal rights".

The Supreme Court, in that case, also acknowledged that recognising public interest litigation will help to address some other barriers to access to justice, including better ensuring climate justice for poor people without "the financial muscle to sue"[67] the likes of much richer carbon major companies—a problem that plagues much of Africa,[68] especially considering its status as the continent with the highest percentage of poor people in the world.[69] While several African countries, like Kenya, have adopted similar broad-standing rules,[70] sadly, some others, like Tanzania[71] and Botswana[72] have not—this being a possible contributory factor to the relatively low rate of horizontal and even vertical climate change litigation in the continent.

3.3 Human Rights Law

Traditionally, human rights have been considered as applying only in the public, and not the private sphere, whereby only states, and not private entities, are bound by it.[73] This age-old position continues to persist for the most part in the international sphere, such that private actors, like transnational corporations, can generally not be found liable under international law for gross violation of human rights even though they have been complicit in such acts in various countries of the world.[74] However, with the gradual evolution of human rights jurisprudence and/or the adoption of new constitutions in several modern African states, it is now possible to legally hold private entities in those countries accountable for human rights violations.[75] This is the case in the likes of South Africa and Kenya, where their post-2010 constitutions provide for the horizontality of human rights, as well as Nigeria, where the judges have simply read horizontality into its constitutional bill of rights, mostly on the grounds of reasonability and

[66] See Emeka Polycarp Amechi, Uzuazo Etemire, and Agent Ihua-Maduenyi, 'Access to Justice through Environmental Public Interest Litigation: Exploring Contemporary Trends in Nigeria' (2021) 54(3) World Comparative Law 398.

[67] *COPW v NNPC* (n 63) 581.

[68] Carolyn Logan, 'Ambitious SDG Goal Confronts Challenging Realities: Access to Justice is still Elusive for Many Africans' (March 2017) <https://www.afrobarometer.org/wp-content/uploads/migrated/files/publications/Policy%20papers/ab_r6_policypaperno39_access_to_justice_in_africa_eng.pdf> accessed 5 June 2025.

[69] Luca Ventura, 'Poorest Countries in the World 2024' (*Global Finance*, 6 May 2024) <https://gfmag.com/data/economic-data/poorest-country-in-the-world/> accessed 5 June 2025.

[70] See Lydia A Omuko-Jung 'The Evolving Locus Standi and Causation Requirements in Kenya: A Precautionary Turn for Climate Change Litigation?' (2021) 15(2) Carbon and Climate Law Review 171.

[71] See Massawe Martin Patrice, 'Legal Dissection of the Doctrine of Locus Standi and Marine Environmental Pollution: Tanzania as a Case Study' (2024) 9(1) African Journal of International Energy & Environmental Law 67.

[72] Tinashe Madebwe, Emma Chitsove, and Jimcall Pfumorodoz, 'Giving Effect to the Human Right to a Clean Environment in Botswana' (2021) 23(1) Environmental Law Review 23, 36.

[73] Danwood Mzikenge Chirwa, 'The Horizontal Application of Constitutional Rights in a Comparative Perspective' (2006) 10(2) Law, Democracy & Development 21.

[74] Danwood Mzikenge Chirwa, 'The Long March to Binding Obligations of Transnational Corporations in International Human Rights Law' (2006) 22 South African Journal on Human Rights 76.

[75] Brian Sang YK, 'Horizontal Application of Constitutional Rights in Kenya: A Comparative Critique of the Emerging Jurisprudence' (2018) 26 African Journal of International and Comparative Law 1.

absence of any constitutional provision inhibiting this broad approach.[76] And, indeed, this liberal approach accords with the traditional African philosophy of human rights, which lends strong credence to the idea that human rights obligations are not only borne by state actors, but non-state actors as well.[77]

To be sure, the drivers and impacts of climate change often culminate in widespread breaches of human rights, especially in Africa, where the capacity to avoid and mitigate climate-related harm is weak due to high rates of indices like poverty and illiteracy.[78] Thus, the aforementioned liberal approach to the application of human rights opens the door for private entities, especially corporations, to be held legally accountable for their actual or proposed and impending climate-harmful activities. This much was reflected in the AU's intervention in the ICJ's advisory proceedings on climate change, where it emphasised, in the context of climate harm, that "the private sector, including multinational companies, share the responsibility to respect human rights, independently of the capacity or the determination of states to protect human rights".[79] But despite the widespread complicity of private corporations in climate-harmful activities that undermine or threaten human rights across Africa, horizontal human rights litigation in such situations remains rare in the continent. In fact, the 2005 Nigerian case of *Gbemre v Shell Petroleum Development Company Nigeria Ltd and Ors*[80] is the only known private climate litigation in Africa where the court horizontally applied relevant human rights provisions against the climate-harmful activities of oil companies.

In that case, the plaintiff, suing for himself and on behalf of members of his community, alleged that the flaring of gas by the defendant company in the course of its oil production activities violated their human rights to life and dignity. Importantly, the plaintiff cited, among others, the contribution of gas flaring to climate change and its negative impact on their healthy and immediate environment as a basis for their constitutional and human rights claims. Agreeing with the plaintiff, the Federal High Court held, inter alia, that: (1) the rights to life and dignity of the human person guaranteed under Sections 33(1) and 34(1) of the Nigerian Constitution,[81] and reinforced by Articles 4 (on right to life), 16 (on right to health) and 24 (on to a healthy environment) of the African Charter Act,[82] "inevitably included the right to clean poison-free, pollution-free and healthy environment"; (2) the failure of the defendants to carry out an EIA on the impact of their gas flaring activity on the plaintiff's community was a violation of the EIA Act and contributed to the violation of the plaintiff's fundamental rights to life and dignity; and (3) the actions of the defendants in continuing to flare gas in the course of

[76] See Pia Rabelo and Xavier Rabelo, 'Rights- Based Climate Change Litigation Against Private Actors' in Kim Bouwer and others (eds), *Climate Litigation and Justice in Africa* (Bristol University Press 2024) 189, 200–11; and Oluwatimilehin Ayobola Opabola, 'Horizontal Application of the Freedom from Discrimination in Kenya, Nigeria, and South Africa' (LLM Thesis, Central European University 2023).

[77] Danwood Mzikenge Chirwa, 'In Search of Philosophical Justifications and Suitable Models for the Horizontal Application of Human Rights' (2008) 8(2) African Human Rights Law Journal 294, 303; Kwame Gyekye, *An Essay on African Philosophical Thought: The Akan Conceptual Scheme* (Temple University Press 1987) 154; Bonny Ibhawoh, 'Cultural Relativism and Human Rights: Reconsidering the Africanist Discourse' (2001) 19 Netherlands Quarterly of Human Rights 43, 53–54. See also Boudewijn de Bruin and Olha Cherednychenko, Chapter 45 of this handbook.

[78] Michael Addaney, Elsabe Boshoff, and Bamisaye Olutola, 'The Climate Change and Human Rights Nexus in Africa' (2017) 9(3) Amsterdam Law Forum 5.

[79] *Written Statement of the African Union* (n 42) 75.

[80] Unreported, Suit No: FHC/B/CS/53/05 (14 November 2005).

[81] Cap 23, Laws of the Federation of Nigeria, 2004.

[82] Cap A9, Laws of the Federation of Nigeria, 2004.

their oil production activities in the plaintiff's community "is a violation of their rights to life (including healthy environment) contained in the aforementioned statutory provisions".[83]

Thus, the court ordered the defendant oil company to stop gas flaring in the plaintiff's community.[84] It also ordered the federal government of Nigeria to take steps to legally prohibit gas flaring in Nigeria while declaring that Section 3 of the (now repealed) Associated Gas Re-Injection Act[85] (and any other Regulations thereunder) under which gas flaring may be and was being permitted in Nigeria, was inconsistent with the aforementioned provisions of the Nigerian Constitution and the African Charter Act, and is thus null and void by virtue of Section 1(3) of the Nigerian Constitution.[86] The appeal that the dissatisfied defendants were said to have filed at the time was shrouded in uncertainties and never heard.[87] Also, efforts by the plaintiff's counsel to enforce the judgment are reported to have failed,[88] in a manner that suggests the complicity of law enforcement agencies and the judiciary, considering perhaps the wider impact that the decision would have had on the operations of other corporate actors in the industry.[89] Surprisingly, according to recent newspaper reports, the defendants in 2021 instituted an appeal against the trial court's decision in the Court of Appeal, and the case was scheduled for hearing in January 2023.[90] Many now look forward to the exhaustion of the appellate process as it "will arguably create an opportunity for the Nigerian judiciary to provide more clarity on the implications of the *Gbemre* case for environmental justice (including climate justice) in the country".[91] But considering that the Nigerian Supreme Court in the 2019 case of *COPW v NNPC* has already given extensive validation to the constitutional human rights approach to environmental and climate protection as set in *Gbemre's* case, hopes are high that the position of the trial court in the latter case will likely receive support on appeal.[92]

However, Nwauche has drawn attention to the "uncertainty about the possibility of the horizontal application of human rights in . . . [several] African national courts".[93] To be sure, in many African countries—including Burkina Faso, Chad, and Botswana—the horizontal applicability of human rights is neither recognised in the national constitution nor espoused and established by judicial pronouncements;[94] and even in some countries, like Malawi, where

83 *Gbemre v Shell* (n 80) 30.

84 ibid 31.

85 Cap A25 Laws of the Federation of Nigeria, 2004.

86 *Gbemre v Shell* (n 80) 30

87 Kaniye SA Ebeku 'Constitutional Right to a Healthy Environment and Human Rights Approaches to Environmental Protection in Nigeria: Gbemre v Shell Revisited' (2007) 16(3) Review of European Community and International Environmental Law 312, 319.

88 ibid.

89 Friends of the Earth (FOE), 'Shell Fails to Obey Gas Flaring Court Order' (FOE 2 May 2007) <http://www.foe.co.uk/resource/press_releases/shell_fails_to_obey_gas_fl_02052007.html> accessed 1 June 2021. See also Uzuazo Etemire, 'Climate Change Litigation in Nigeria: Challenges and Opportunities' in Francesco Sindico and Makabe Moïse Mbegue (eds), *Comparative Climate Change Litigation: Beyond the Usual Suspects* (Springer 2021) 409.

90 E Addeh, 'Shell Challenges Judgement Ordering Halt to Gas Flaring in N'Delta Community' (*ThisDay*, 26 December 2021) <https://www.thisdaylive.com/2021/12/29/shell-challenges-judgement-ordering-halt-to-gas-flaring-in-ndelta-community/> accessed 5 June 2025

91 Eghosa O Ekhator and Edward O Okumagba, 'Climate Change, Multinationals and Human Rights in Nigeria: A Case for Climate Justice' in Kim Bouwer and others (eds), *Climate Litigation and Justice in Africa* (Bristol University Press 2024) 247, 268.

92 Etemire (n 9) 168–70.

93 Enyinna S Nwauche, 'The ECOWAS Community Court of Justice and the Horizontal Application of Human Rights' (2013) 13 African Journal of Human Rights 30, 37–38.

94 Oyeniyi Abe, *The State of Business and Human Rights in Africa* (Friedrich-Ebert-Stiftung 2022).

the constitution provides for the horizontal application of the bill of rights, doubts and uncertainties remain as to the extent of its application considering how the relevant provision was couched.[95] Thus, in such nations, the possibility of horizontal climate litigation based on applicable human rights provisions for now remains questionable or narrow at best and non-existent at worst. This will remain until there is a constitutional or judicial change in position on the scope of application of human rights law that aligns with the modern progressive trend on the subject.

4. Potentials for Horizontal Litigation under Africa's Evolving National Climate Legislation

As demonstrated above, common law, environmental legislation, and human rights law are the only known causes of action that have provided legal bases for a limited number of horizontal climate lawsuits in Africa, considering their nature and shortcomings. However, "[w]ith more available knowledge on the scope and urgency of legislative action required to address climate change, it has become important for countries across the world to move beyond general environmental [human and common] laws and provide clear and comprehensive . . . [legal] frameworks on climate change".[96] With African countries gradually buying into this idea, the recent emergence of specific national climate legislation in Africa has been argued as holding the potential to boost and more easily support climate litigation on the continent, including in its horizontal form.[97] This potential is premised on the characteristic propensity of such laws to—unlike other legal regimes with only indirect and tangential relations to climate change—expressly and clearly confer enforceable climate obligations on diverse entities, including private ones, and provide for the enforcement of those obligations by a spectrum of stakeholders.[98] Also, according to Averchenkova and others, such laws are valuable for their ability to make "action on climate change more predictable, more structured and more evidence-based".[99] In practice, nonetheless, how does the evolving national climate legislation in Africa stand with regard to its potential to meaningfully and effectively support horizontal climate litigation?

95 Sibo Banda, 'Constitutional Mimicry and Common Law Reform in a Rights-Based Post-Colonial Setting: The Case of South Africa and Malawi' (2009) 53(1) Journal of African Law 142.

96 Damilola S Olawuyi, 'Nature and Sources of Climate Change Law and Policy in MENA Region' *Climate Change Law and Policy in the Middle East and North Africa Region* (Routledge 2022) 1, 4.

97 Muhammed Tawfiq Ladan, 'A Review of Nigeria's 2021 Climate Change Act: Potential for Increased Climate Litigation' (IUCN, 28 March 2022) <https://iucn.org/news/commission-environmental-economic-and-social-policy/202203/a-review-nigerias-2021-climate-change-act-potential-increased-climate-litigation> accessed 5 June 2025.

98 See Alina Averchenkova and others, *Impacts of Climate Framework Laws: Lessons from Germany, Ireland and New Zealand* (Grantham Research Institute on Climate Change and the Environment, London School of Economics and Political Science 2024) 14; Catherine Higham, Joana Setzer, and Emily Bradeen, *Challenging Government Responses to Climate Change through Framework Litigation* (Grantham Research Institute on Climate Change and the Environment and Centre for Climate Change Economics and Policy, London School of Economics and Political Science 2022).

99 Alina Averchenkova, Sam Fankhauser, and Jared Finnegan, 'The Impact of Strategic Climate Legislation: Evidence from Expert Interviews on the UK Climate Change Act' (2020) 21(2) Climate Policy 251.

The first national climate-specific legislation in Africa occurred in Kenya in 2016 (with amendments in 2023)—just under a decade ago; since then, Benin (2018), Mauritius (2020), Nigeria, Uganda, Gabon (2021), South Africa, and Zambia (2024) have gone on to develop climate-specific legislation as well.[100] In other words, only eight (or 13%) of fifty-four African countries have specific climate change legislation at present, with no country from North Africa on the list despite being one of the regions in the world most severely impacted by climate change.[101] Nonetheless, more of this specialised climate legislation are being prepared and expected to emerge in Africa, with that of Eswatini, for instance, having reached an advanced level.[102] Thus, it is important to broadly analyse the potential of the extant climate legislation to engender effective horizontal climate litigation, especially as they may serve—beyond their domestic impacts—as models for other African countries looking to enact such laws.[103] The focus of this analysis will be on the climate legislation of all those listed above except Benin and Gabon.[104] But then, some of the countries in focus that possess climate-specific legislation are also among the biggest GHG emitters in Africa.[105] Importantly, the ensuing discussion will aim to unravel the following three key issues that are necessary for broadly determining the possibility, as well as the quality of horizontal litigation that this climate legislation can engender: (a) Do private actors bear climate obligations? (b) Can private actors enforce those obligations? and (c) What remedies are available upon the breach of those obligations?

The first issue is whether African national climate legislation imposed enforceable climate responsibilities on private actors. The accurate response to this query is neither a straightforward yes nor a no. Rather, the climate legislation of the countries under review (1) empowers designated public authorities to impose enforceable procedural and substantive climate obligations—including GHG reporting and emissions reduction duties—on private actors through the subsequent promulgation of certain measures and (2) refers to non-state actors with different terminologies that create a wide range of variations in the scope of private actors upon which such obligations can be imposed.[106] Regarding the first point, it is noteworthy that while some of the climate legislation, as in Nigeria and South Africa, commendably mandates

[100] African Group of Negotiators Experts Support (AGNES), 'African Lawmakers Validate Landmark Model Climate Change Model Law in Abuja' (*AGNES*, 2 February 2025 <https://www.agnesafrica.org/african-lawmakers-validate-landmark-model-climate-change-law-in-abuja/> accessed 5 June 2025. For copies of these legislation, see Climate Change Laws of the World (n 57).

[101] Olawuyi (n 96).

[102] Business Eswatini, 'Invitation to Review and Comment on the Draft Climate Change Bill' (*Business Eswatini*, 18 February 2025) <https://business-eswatini.co.sz/invitation-to-review-and-comment-on-the-draft-climate-change-bill/> accessed 5 June 2025.

[103] The AR Initiative, 'Advancing Climate Change Policies in Africa: A Review of Regulatory Frameworks and Key Considerations' (*The AR Initiative*, 31 May 2023) <https://www.arinitiative.org/insights/advancing-climate-change-policies-in-africa-a-review-of-regulatory-frameworks-and-key-considerations> accessed 5 June 2025.

[104] The exclusion of both countries is due to language challenges; the official English language translation of their climate legislation was not found.

[105] Intelpoint, 'Top Ten African Countries' Contribution to CO2 Emission from Fossil Fuel (2023)' (*Intelpoint*, 2023) <https://intelpoint.co/insights/top-ten-african-countries-contribution-to-co2-emission-from-fossil-fuel-2023/> accessed 5 June 2025.

[106] See generally, Catherine Higham, Anirudh Sridhar, and Emily Bradeen, 'Innovations in Climate Change Acts: Kenya, Uganda and Nigeria in Focus' (*Commonwealth Parliamentary Association*, 2023) <https://www.cpahq.org/knowledge-centre/blogs/climate-change-acts-in-kenya-uganda-and-nigeria/> accessed 5 June 2025.

the public authority to take the necessary action required to impose such obligations,[107] others, such as Mauritius and Zambia, leave it largely to their discretion.[108] Furthermore, even though some of these statutes have been in existence for a few years now, one finds that the relevant public authorities have yet to implement the prescribed measure that imposes the said climate responsibilities on any private actor. For instance, in Kenya, the draft Climate Change (Duties and Incentives) Regulations 2021 designed to impose climate duties on private entities is still pending enactment into law.[109] And in Nigeria, key provisions in its climate legislation remain unimplemented, including those requiring and/or empowering the relevant authority to produce a National Climate Change Action Plan (Sections 20 and 24(1)),[110] publish a notice in the government's gazette (Section 24(3)), and make regulations (Sections 32) to activate and/or prescribe different types of climate duties for private entities.

On the second point, some of the climate legislation employs terminology that potentially includes all natural and artificial private actors—a ready example being the Zambian climate legislation, which seeks to impose climate obligations on "a private body and individual",[111] and goes on to define "private body" to mean "a private entity or a non-state actor that emits greenhouse gases".[112] Nigeria, Uganda, and Kenya also take a similarly expansive approach.[113] It is, however, unfortunate that others have used words and phrases that exclude a section of private actors with potentially significant carbon footprints. In South Africa, for instance, climate obligations will rest only on "any person that conducts an activity listed" in a government notice of activities which emit or potentially emits, beyond a specified threshold, any GHG published in a government list of GHGs "which the Minister reasonably believes" might cause or exacerbate climate change.[114] There is no gainsaying the risk that in the complexity and abundant discretion of this provision, several major private carbon emitters will find themselves outside the ambits of any climate obligation imposed under the legislation. Even under the Nigerian climate legislation where, as alluded to above, the authorities are generally empowered to impose climate obligation on "public entities" broadly, the law, however, imposed only on "[a]ny private entity *with employees numbering 50 and above*" the particular obligation to "put in place measures to achieve the annual carbon emission reduction target in line with the Action Plan", and designate an officer to report to[115] regularly on its efforts in this regard. The rationale for this limiting provision is seriously undermined by the fact that a private entity with half that number of staff could possibly be a bigger carbon emitter.

The second issue is the all-important question of whether private actors can enforce the climate obligations imposed on other non-state actors under Africa's national climate legislation. In Kenya and Uganda, the answer is a straightforward "yes", as their climate legislation clearly permits any person to approach the court for the enforcement of anyone's climate duties and

[107] Nigeria Climate Change Act 2021, ss 20 and 24.

[108] Mauritius Climate Change Act 2020, s 16; Zambia Green Economy and Climate Change Act 2024, s 46.

[109] Omondi Owino, *Global Perspectives on Corporate Climate Legal Tactics: Kenya National Report* (British Institute of International and Comparative Law 2024) 6–7.

[110] Anthony Aileman, 'Buhari Approves Work Plan for Climate Change Council' (*Business Day*, 11 February 2023) <https://businessday.ng/news/article/buhari-approves-work-plan-for-climate-change-council/#google_vignette> accessed 5 June 2025.

[111] Zambia Green Economy and Climate Change Act 2024, s 46(2)(o).

[112] ibid s 1.

[113] Nigeria Climate Change Act 2021, ss 24(3), 32 and 35; Uganda National Climate Change Act 2021, ss 1 and 23; Kenya Climate Change Act 2016, ss 2 and 16.

[114] South Africa Climate Change Act 2024, ss 26 and 27(1).

[115] Nigeria Climate Change Act 2021, s 24(1)-(2) (emphasis added).

obligations whether or not the plaintiff has suffered any harm or injury from the action or omission of the defendant.[116] Although the Nigerian climate legislation is silent on the subject, the Nigerian Supreme Court, in the case of *COPW v NNPC*, has already confirmed that any person, including NGOs, can bring an action against public *and private entities*, to ensure "the due performance of statutory functions or enforcement of statutory provisions or public laws, especially laws designed to protect human lives, public health and [the] environment".[117] The South African climate legislation is also silent on the subject, without more, as with those of Zambia and Mauritius, which only provide for the enforcement of their climate legislation by public officers on behalf of the state.[118] In other words, the climate legislation of Kenya, Uganda, and Nigeria bears clear potential to support horizontal climate litigation, but those of South Africa, Zambia, and Mauritius do not.

The latter point is reinforced by the response to the third and last query with respect to the stipulated remedies. The climate statutes of South Africa, Zambia, and Mauritius provide for only public law criminal remedies, such as fines and terms of imprisonment,[119] which are traditionally within the exclusive purview of the state to pursue, leaving no room for horizontal enforcement. But, *in addition* to these criminal remedies,[120] Nigeria and Uganda obviously followed the Kenyan approach, where its climate legislation in Section 23 provides for robust private law remedies that will support and contribute to the effectiveness of horizontal litigation under the law in the following manner:

1) A person may . . . apply to . . . Court alleging that a person has acted in a manner that has or is likely to adversely affect efforts towards mitigation and adaptation to the effects of climate change.
2) Where an application is made under sub-section (1), the Court may make an order or give directions that it considers appropriate to—
   a) prevent, stop or discontinue an act or omission that is harmful to the environment;
   b) compel a public officer to take measures to prevent or discontinue an act or omission that is harmful to the environment; or
   c) provide compensation to a victim of a violation relating to climate change duties.[121]

5. Conclusion

The discussion above reveals that existing government efforts to tackle the drivers and impacts of climate change in Africa are largely inadequate. It demonstrated that Africa is in dire

[116] Kenya Climate Change Act 2016, s 23; Uganda National Climate Change Act 2021, s 26.

[117] *COPW v NNPC* (n 63) 595 (emphasis added).

[118] Zambia Green Economy and Climate Change Act 2024, s 32; Mauritius Climate Change Act 2020, s 25.

[119] Section 44, Zambia Green Economy and Climate Change Act 2024; Mauritius Climate Change Act 2020, s 28.

[120] Nigeria Climate Change Act 2021, s 34(1); e.g., Uganda National Climate Change Act 2021, ss 13(4) and 18(7); Kenya Climate Change Act 2016, ss 17(3)–(4) and 33.

[121] A similar provision is contained in Nigeria Climate Change Act 2021, s 34(2); Uganda National Climate Change Act 2021, s 26. See Pedi Obani, 'Climate Litigation in South Africa and Nigeria: Legal Opportunities and Gender Perspectives' in Bouwer and others (eds), *Climate Litigation and Justice in Africa* (Bristol University Press 2024) 291, 306.

need of increased horizontal climate litigation that allows private actors to judicially hold other private entities climate-accountable, considering, among other reasons, the sharp rise of private entities as major players in, or contributors to, carbon-intensive industries on the continent, against whom African governments are usually unwilling to act. While Africa has witnessed some horizontal climate litigation based on torts law, environmental legislation, and human rights law, only very few are known—all of which are from Nigeria—and their impact is limited due to a mixture of factors like the nature and shortcomings of the aforementioned causes of action. These legal platforms retain, to an extent, some potential to facilitate effective horizontal climate litigation in Africa. But their inadequacies, especially in the context of a contemporary challenge like climate change, give room for the gradual emergence of national climate-specific legislation in Africa, considering, unlike other regimes, the latter's direct, more comprehensive, and coherent engagement with the subject matter.

Regarding their potential to ground horizontal climate litigation, the analysis above shows that national climate legislation in Africa is a mixed bag—while an allowance is made for horizontal action in the Kenyan, Nigerian, and Ugandan laws, those of South Africa, Zambia, and Mauritius only enable vertical action. However, with reference to climate legislation that allows for horizontal action, the designated public authorities are yet to implement the relevant provision in the law that will activate and/or prescribe climate responsibilities for private entities on which bases legal action can be brought against them, where necessary. While this inaction may have so far hindered the materialisation of horizontal litigation under the respective statutes, the calls by civil society for its implementation are getting louder, and some governments are beginning to take the prescribed steps to realise climate obligations for private entities under their legislation. Yet, on a broader view, the diverging development of national climate legislation in Africa, with particular regard to the potential for horizontal application, is worrisome. Considering the espoused value of horizontal climate litigation for Africa, the time is ripe for the African Union—as it has done successfully in other areas—to execute a model law on climate change, both to motivate African countries without climate legislation to develop one, and to ensure the coherent development of such legislation across Africa, containing basic provisions that will guarantee their effectiveness, including making reasonable allowance for the possibility of horizontal climate litigation under such laws.

CHAPTER 40

China

YUE ZHAO AND YI FENG

1. Introduction

CLIMATE change litigation has emerged as an essential tool in the global response to the climate crisis. As governments, industries, and citizens increasingly confront the impacts of climate change, courts are playing a crucial role in holding parties accountable for climate consequences. Central to many climate change lawsuits is the use of "open norms"—legal principles that are not strictly defined, offering flexibility for judicial interpretation in response to evolving climate challenges. Judges worldwide are increasingly turning to open norms in adjudicating climate cases, as climate change litigation often involves complex and evolving issues where specific climate legislation is insufficient to address them.

In rights-based climate litigation, to support human rights claims,[1] numerous open-ended norms, such as the concept of a "duty of care", are increasingly being invoked as legal grounds to hold both governments and private entities accountable for their role in climate change. In the landmark case *Urgenda Foundation v State of the Netherland*,[2] the court applied the concept of "due care", which requires the government to take reasonable steps to protect the environment and public welfare. The court found that the Dutch Government had a duty of care under Dutch Constitutional Law and Articles 2 and 8 of the European Convention on Human Rights law[3] to protect citizens against the foreseeable harms of climate change, which it had failed to meet by setting emissions reduction targets that were too low to comply with international agreements such as the Paris Agreement. Moreover, in reaching the conclusion, the court also cited other open-ended norms (without directly applying them), such as principles under the European Convention on Human Rights, the "no harm" principle of international law, the principle of fairness, the precautionary principle, and the sustainability principle embodied in the UN Framework Convention on Climate Change. Similarly, in *Milieudefensie v Royal Dutch Shell plc*,[4] the Hague District Court found that the private sector—not just governments—has a duty of care towards citizens regarding carbon emissions. The legal ground for this decision was Dutch tort law, specifically the standard of care, which stipulates that "acting in conflict with what is generally accepted according to unwritten law is unlawful".[5] Though the appeal court refused to impose a specific emission reduction target for Shell in 2024, the appeal still

[1] Jacqueline Peel and Hari M Osofsky, 'A Rights Turn in Climate Change Litigation?' (2018) 7 Transnational Environmental Law 37.

[2] *Urgenda Foundation v State of the Netherlands* [2019] C/09/00456689 (HAZA).

[3] European Convention on Human Rights [1950] ETS5, art 2 and 8.

[4] *Milieudefensie and others v Royal Dutch Shell plc* [2024] 200.302.332/01 (Court of Appeal The Hague).

[5] Dutch Civil Code, Book 6 s 162.

endorsed the finding of the Court of first instance that Shell has a legal duty of care to curb dangerous climate change.[6]

In the US, many states have been attempting to bring public nuisance claims against carbon majors, alleging that their contributions to climate change have caused significant harm to public resources, property, and human health.[7] Alongside conspiracy and failure to warn claims, the nuisance theory has become a cornerstone of the second wave of climate tort litigation. In *Lliuya v RWE*,[8] the German nuisance law was also invoked as the legal foundation for the litigation.[9] Nuisance law often relies on open-ended legal principles like "unreasonableness" or "substantial harm" that are not always clearly defined, allowing for judicial flexibility. This flexibility enables courts to adapt these legal principles in response to evolving climate challenges, particularly when dealing with global environmental harms that are not explicitly addressed in existing legislation. In Australia, the concept and principle of "ecologically sustainable development"[10] and the "precautionary principle"[11] have been the legal grounds for many climate litigation cases. The use of open-ended norms is especially relevant in Global South countries where specific climate legislation is usually lacking.[12] In Nepal's landmark climate litigation,[13] the principle of *parens patriae* was invoked to clarify that climate mitigation and adaptation are the responsibility of the state. In Pakistan, based on the precautionary principle and the principle of *in dubio pro natura* (when in doubt, favour nature), the judge made a ruling protecting the environment.[14]

In these climate cases, plaintiffs around the world have argued that States and corporations have general obligations to mitigate climate change that arise from open-ended legal norms under tort law, human rights law, or customary international law.[15] By providing flexibility and judicial discretion, open-ended norms allow courts to respond to the urgent and evolving challenges posed by climate change. Despite the absence of specific, well-defined legal obligations, these open norms enable courts to apply legal principles to complex environmental issues, expand access to justice, and promote greater accountability for climate action.

Unlike the rights-based approaches to global climate change litigation, China's climate justice follows a contract-based mode[16] centred on policy implementation.[17] Compared to directly holding the government and major carbon emitters accountable for climate

[6] *Milieudefensie* (n 3).

[7] Maximillian Scott Matiauda, 'Rising Tide: The Second Wave of Climate Torts' (2022) 30 University of Miami International and Comparative Law Review 194.

[8] *Lliuya v RWE AG* [2025] (Higher Regional Court Hamm).

[9] Vedantha Kumar and Will Frank, 'Holding Private Emitters to Account for the Effects of Climate Change: Could a Case Like *Lliuya* Succeed under English Nuisance Laws' (2018) 12 Carbon and Climate Law Review 110.

[10] Jacqueline Peel 'Ecologically Sustainable Development: More than Mere Lip Service?' (2018) 12 Australasian Journal of Natural Resources Law and Policy 1.

[11] *Gippsland Coastal Board v South Gippsland Shire Council* [2008] 1545 (VCAT).

[12] Jolene Lin and Jacqueline Peel, *Litigating Climate Change in the Global South* (OUP 2024).

[13] *Shrestha v Office of the Prime Minister and others* (2018) 074-WO-0283 (Supreme Court of Nepal).

[14] See Jolene and Jacqueline (n 12) 58; see also *D. G. Khan Cement Company v Government of Punjab* [2019] C.P.1290-L/2019 (Supreme Court of Pakistan).

[15] Benoit Mayer, 'Prompting Climate Change Mitigation through Litigation' (2023) 72 International & Comparative Law Quarterly 233.

[16] Yue Zhao, Shuang Lyu, and Zhu Wang, 'Prospects for Climate Change Litigation in China' (2019) 8 Transnational Environmental Law 349.

[17] Mingzhe Zhu, 'The Rule of Climate Policy: How do Chinese Judges Contribute to Climate Governance without Climate Law?' (2022) 11 Transnational Environmental Law 119.

consequences, Chinese judges place greater emphasis on guiding market entities, including citizens, businesses, and investors, through judicial rulings. This approach encourages market entities to change their lifestyles, business practices, and consumption patterns, promoting the implementation of national climate policies and achieving an overall low-carbon transformation of society.[18] This approach has significantly reshaped the legal landscape of China's civil law, particularly in carbon-related disputes. Among the various legal principles, an open-ended norm, the Green Principle, is the most frequently applied as the legal foundation of judgments in these carbon-related civil disputes. Introduced in 2017, the *General Principles of Civil Code* included the so-called Green Principle (Article 9), which facilitates environmental protection through civil law. The establishment of the Green Principle in China's *Civil Code* marks a critical step in the "publicisation of private law"[19] and serves as a prime example of the integration of public and private law. It reflects the growing societal demand for a low-carbon transition and acknowledges the urgent need for environmental protection within the legal framework. This chapter explores the role of the Green Principle as an open-ended norm in climate-related civil disputes, discussing its utility, challenges, and broader implications for climate justice and China's private law.

Three issues will be examined: First, what the normative requirements of the Green Principle are and how this principle is different from other principles of China's civil law. Second, how the Green Principle has been applied in adjudicating carbon/climate-related cases to help implement China's Dual Carbon Policy. Third, whether the open-textured nature of the Green Principle is consistent with the requirements laid down in the judicial decisions.

2. Green Principle: Introduction of a Positive Obligation in China's Civil Code

According to Article 9 of the *General Principles of the Civil Code*, "Civil entities engaging in civil activities shall be conducive to the conservation of resources and the protection of the ecological environment". The phrase "shall be conducive to" is particularly innovative within the framework of fundamental principles, as it requires entities to "act in a manner that facilitates environmental protection", which goes beyond the minimum obligations typically associated with compliance to law, public order, and morals.

Many interpret the phrase "shall be conducive to" as imposing a positive obligation to take proactive action, thereby introducing a new "encouraging" normative model within civil law principles (Table 40.1).

Notably, in the basic principles outlined in Articles 4 to 9 of the Civil Code, all principles—except for the "principle of equality" in Article 4—are framed in obligatory terms. These provisions impose binding requirements using expressions such as "shall adhere to", "shall not violate", or "shall be conducive to". However, the behavioural requirements associated with "shall be conducive to" are more stringent than those associated with "shall adhere to", which, in turn, are higher than those tied to "shall not violate", as "shall be conducive to" could be seen as encompassing both negative obligations, which set the baseline for acceptable behaviour,

[18] Fred Steward, 'Transformative Innovation Policy to Meet the Challenge of Climate Change: Sociotechnical Networks Aligned with Consumption and End-use as New Transition Arenas for a Low-carbon Society or Green Economy' (2012) 24 Technology Analysis & Strategic Management 331.

[19] Igor Szpotakowski, 'The New Chinese Civil Code and its Contribution to Sustainable Development' (March 2020) Transformacje Prawa Prywatnego 233 <https://ssrn.com/abstract=3824602> accessed 16 July 2025.

TABLE 40.1 Comparison of the Fundamental Principles of the Civil Code

Principle	Disposition	Model
Equality	Article 4 "All civil entities are equal in their legal status in civil activities."	Descriptive Norm
Voluntariness	Article 5: "Civil entities engaging in civil activities shall adhere to the principle of voluntariness and establish, modify, or terminate civil legal relationships in accordance with their own intentions."	Imperative obligatory norm
Fairness	Article 6: "Civil entities engaging in civil activities shall adhere to the principle of fairness and reasonably determine the rights and obligations of all parties."	Discretionary
Good faith	Article 7: "Civil entities engaging in civil activities shall adhere to the principle of good faith, upholding honesty and honoring commitments."	Imperative obligatory norm
Public order and morals	Article 8: "Civil entities engaging in civil activities shall not violate the law and shall not contravene public order and morals."	Negative mandatory obligation
Green Principle	Article 9: "Civil entities engaging in civil activities shall be conducive to the conservation of resources and the protection of the ecological environment."	Positive mandatory obligation

and positive obligations that urge proactive actions. To put it another way, "shall be conducive to" implies that civil activities must neither be "harmful" nor "detrimental" to the protection of the environment and conservation of resources; they should not even be "neutral" in their impact. By directing attention towards the duty of taking positive actions, the phrase "conducive to" sets a higher standard for behaviour. Therefore, if civil conduct fails to meet the standard of being conducive to resource conservation and environmental protection, it may lead to legal consequences.

In other words, unlike most fundamental principles, which, when applied to specific civil law rules, are often discretionary or negative mandatory norms, Article 9 of the General Principles of the Civil Code potentially introduces a positive mandatory obligation, which is quite uncommon in China's civil law. Due to concerns about excessive state interference in private autonomy, China's civil law rarely incorporates such mandatory obligations. Articles 5 to 7 typically operate through discretionary norms. These are supported by prohibitive mandatory norms designed to safeguard rights and freedoms; moreover, since civil rights can usually be waived, these norms allow for a degree of discretion, providing rights holders with some flexibility in their decisions. For example, the "principle of voluntariness" (Article 5) stipulates that civil entities shall establish rights and obligations according to their own will within the bounds of the law. However, it also ensures that no organisation or individual can unlawfully interfere with this freedom. If a civil entity decides to waive its right, private law does not impose any interference.[20] This flexibility is similarly applied to the principles of equality, fairness, voluntariness, and good faith, where the law allows for a degree of autonomy in how these principles are exercised, provided that no unlawful interference occurs.

[20] Contract Law, art 54.

However, the principle of public order and morals differs slightly. Its phrases "shall not violate" and "shall not violate/contravene" refer to purely negative mandatory obligations,[21] and do not involve rights that can be waived at the discretion of the parties. This is primarily because other principles often pertain to the rights and interests of specific parties, whereas the principle of public order and morals addresses the conflict between individual interests and the public good, which cannot be waived or transferred. Similarly, the public interest purpose of Article 9 aligns with the principle of public order and good morals, and therefore also points to mandatory obligations. However, unlike conventional public order norms, which are limited to annulling agreements that contravene legal prohibitions (expressed as a negative obligation), the Green Principle transcends passive prohibition by creating affirmative duties *ex lege*. These include mandating the recycling of used goods (Article 558), and mandating assistance in pile installation (electric vehicle or EV charging station) (Article 509), among others—even absent explicit contractual stipulations.

In civil adjudication, this principle may function analogously to the principle of *in dubio pro natura* (when in doubt, favour nature),[22] especially where ecological preservation prevails in cases of legal ambiguity or conflicting interests, guiding courts to resolve interpretive uncertainties through an ecocentric lens. Such an evolutionary approach reconceptualises the Green Principle from a static prohibition against environmental harm into a dynamic imperative for proactive ecological stewardship, requiring actors not merely to avoid damage but to actively "prevent, mitigate, or regenerate" compromised ecosystems.

3. The Use of Open Norms in China's Policy-Driven Climate Justice

In China, the "when in doubt, favour nature" tendency is increasingly being expressed as "when in doubt, favour climate" under the country's Dual Carbon Policy.

3.1 Dual Carbon Goals and Significant Legislative Gap

In 2020, China announced that it will strive to peak carbon dioxide emissions before 2030 while achieving carbon neutrality by 2060. Later that year, the Central Committee of the Communist Party of China and the State Council jointly issued the *Opinions on Fully, Accurately, and Comprehensively Implementing the New Development Concept to Achieve Carbon Peaking and Carbon Neutrality* (hereinafter referred to as the *Dual Carbon Opinions*),[23] which outlined key tasks and initiated a nationwide effort towards realising these goals. The *Dual Carbon Opinions* established specific targets for 2030/2060. By 2060, China aims to establish a green, low-carbon, and circular economic system alongside a clean, low-carbon, safe, and efficient energy system. Energy efficiency will achieve internationally advanced standards, non-fossil energy will constitute over 80% of total energy consumption, and the nation will achieve carbon neutrality. The adoption of the dual carbon goals signals that China has

[21] Civil Code, art 153.

[22] Ridwan Arifin and Siti Hafsyah Idris, 'In Dubio Pro Natura: in Doubt, should the Environment Be a Priority? A Discourse of Environmental Justice in Indonesia' (2023) 6 Jambe Law Journal 143; see also Marko Ahteensuu, *In Dubio Pro Natura* (Oldenbourg 2008).

[23] Communist Party of China and the State Council, 'Opinions on Fully, Accurately, and Comprehensively Implementing the New Development Concept to Achieve Carbon Peaking and Carbon Neutrality' (22 September 2021).

entered into a new phase of high-quality economic and social development, centred on accelerating a green and low-carbon transformation. However, this ambitious dual carbon transition faces significant challenges, particularly due to a lack of robust legal support.

At the legislative level, the absence of a comprehensive legal framework significantly hinders efforts to achieve the dual carbon goals. Currently, China lacks specialised, integrated legislation on climate change. The proposed Climate Change Response Law remains at the academic proposal stage. In September 2023, the National People's Congress included the "codification of an Environmental (Ecological) Code and other mature areas" in its legislative agenda as a first-class project (indicating laws considered mature and expected to be submitted during the current legislative term). This step marked a transition from academic discussion to legislative preparation for the Environmental (Ecological) Code. A dedicated chapter on addressing climate change has been included in the ongoing compilation of the Environmental Code. However, without a concrete legislative timeline and with the comprehensive environmental legislation still centred on pollution control, integrating carbon-related provisions with existing laws, such as energy and natural resource regulations, remains a challenge. Consequently, the proposed Environmental (Ecological) Code could probably only provide a broad framework for carbon-related norms, lacking the specificity needed to address all aspects in detail. Therefore, when statutory frameworks suffer from structural deficiencies or lag behind policy imperatives, courts—through creative interpretation and on a case-by-case basis—become indispensable legal engines for achieving China's dual carbon goals.

3.2 Concept and Methodology

First, what constitutes carbon-related civil cases? How they are different from periphery climate litigation?

In a narrow sense, in the judicial context of China, carbon-related civil cases refer to civil cases falling under the category of climate change response cases. Around 2015, the Supreme Court of China (SCC) began promoting the specialisation of environmental judicial adjudication. To define the scope of environmental courts' jurisdiction, the SCC classified environmental and resource-related cases into five types, one of which is climate change response cases.[24] However, in 2023, in response to the national Dual Carbon Policy, the Supreme Court issued the *Supreme People's Court Guidelines on Judicial Services for Carbon Neutrality (2023)*,[25] marking the shift from the climate change response justice to dual carbon justice. As a result, the scope of carbon-related civil cases has expanded beyond the climate change response cases within environmental resource cases. More broadly, carbon-related civil cases now encompass fundamental and overarching themes such as comprehensive green transformation of economic and social development, industrial restructuring, low-carbon energy transition, and carbon trading market mechanisms. Therefore, in a broader sense, carbon-related civil cases refer to contract, tort, and property disputes involving industrial restructuring, low-carbon

[24] According to the SCC's Specifications on the Types and Statistics of Environmental Resource Cases (Trial), 'climate change response cases' include civil cases under 'climate change mitigation cases' such as 'industrial restructuring in key carbon-emitting sectors and the development and utilisation of new energy, energy-saving services, and other energy-saving and emission-reduction cases', 'carbon sink trading cases', and 'cases promoting sustainable transportation, land use change management, and forestry'.

[25] Supreme People's Court, 'Opinions of the Supreme People's Court on Implementing the New Development Philosophy Fully, Accurately, and Comprehensively to Provide Judicial Services for the Steady and Active Advancement of Carbon Peak and Carbon Neutrality' (Fa Fa No.5, 2023).

energy transition, and social green transformation in the context of dual carbon construction. This chapter adopts this broader definition of carbon-related civil cases.

Having delineated the concept of carbon-related civil cases, the authors tried to identify them in databases. The authors used terms such as "green principle", "Article 9 of the Civil Code", and "civil", combined with case types like tort disputes, "contract disputes", and "property disputes", to search databases such as the Judgment Document Database and the Peking University Law Database. The time frame for the search ranged from October 1, 2017, when the original General Principles of Civil Law came into effect, to 20 November 2024. After reviewing and filtering carbon-related cases, and excluding invalid or duplicate ones, a total of eighty-one valid cases were identified. These included fifty-seven carbon-related contract disputes, sixteen carbon-related property disputes, and eight carbon-related tort disputes.

Carbon-related contract disputes adjudicated under the Green Principle mainly involve disputes over virtual currency-mining contracts and property service contracts related to the installation of charging piles in residential underground parking lots. In such cases, due to the lack of clear legal provisions, the Green Principle is often invoked alongside other civil law principles and policy documents as the basis for court judgments. Carbon-related property disputes, mainly involving the installation of charging piles, raise legal issues related to accession and building ownership. In these cases, the application of the Green Principle has altered traditional adjudication logic, introducing the principle of "when in doubt, favour climate" into the application of property law, so that judicial decisions not only focus on the ownership and use of property but also emphasise green and low-carbon goals. Carbon-related tort disputes are primarily civil public interest lawsuits related to air pollution, based on the Green Principle, and atmospheric polluters are required to bear punitive damages. Considering that these cases often involve specific private interests with minimal climate impact when examined in isolation, they can be viewed as even more marginal than "periphery cases".[26] However, given the strong judicial inclination of Chinese courts in implementing the dual carbon policy, the judgment in certain types of cases may have a broader societal impact on climate change response compared to periphery cases.

Due to the large number of Bitcoin mining contract disputes and charging pile installation disputes and their close relation to the dual-carbon policy, this chapter first focuses on these two types of cases for in-depth analysis of the regulatory role played by the Green Principle and the legal application issues that arise.

4. Green Principle and Bitcoin Mining Contract Disputes

Chinese courts invoke the Green Principle to evaluate the validity of contracts, especially in civil disputes involving Bitcoin mining contracts. Some regions in China, such as Sichuan, Yunnan, and Inner Mongolia, are rich in hydropower, wind power, and coal power resources, resulting in low electricity costs that attracted a large number of mining farms. At one point, China accounted for half of the global Bitcoin mining hashrate.[27] However, in 2021, the National Development and Reform Commission and other departments issued the *Notice on*

[26] Popielarski, Mark, 'Climate Change Litigation: Regulatory Pathways to Cleaner Energy' (2016) 108 Law Library Journal 301.

[27] MacKenzie Sigolos, 'China is Kicking Out More Than Half the World's Bitcoin Miners—and a Whole Lot of Them Could be Headed to Texas' *CNBC* (July 20 2021) <https://www.cnbc.com/2021/06/15/chinas-bitcoin-miner-exodus-.html>.

Rectifying Virtual Currency Mining Activities,[28] which listed mining activities as an eliminated industry under the *Interim Provisions on Promoting Industrial Restructuring*,[29] leading to a nationwide ban on Bitcoin mining activities. Local governments also issued policy documents to shut down virtual currency mining projects. Despite this, China still lacks clear legal provisions defining the nature of mining activities. In this context, judges have relied on the open-ended norms of the Civil Code to fill legal gaps, applying principles as the basis for judgment. In terms of adjudicatory methods, judges commonly refer to both the Green Principle and the Public Order and Good Morals Principle to determine the validity of contracts.

4.1 The Validity of Bitcoin Mining Contract

Before 2021, courts typically upheld the validity of Bitcoin mining contracts and typically made rulings based on the agreements between the parties and the rules of contract law.[30] However, after 2021, a significant number of Bitcoin mining contracts were ruled invalid. This chapter analysed twenty-one Bitcoin mining contract cases, of which twenty were deemed invalid. In the 2022 case of *Xinjiang Xintao Silicon Industry Co., Ltd. v Yang Peng et al.*, the court ruled that the Bitcoin mining contract was invalid, as "[b]itcoin mining activities consume a huge amount of electricity, with the defendant using over 700 million kWh in just one year and four months. This is clearly detrimental to energy conservation, emission reduction, and the achievement of carbon peak and carbon neutrality goals; furthermore, the production and trading of virtual currencies, including Bitcoin, pose significant risks, have become speculative tools, and may threaten national financial security and social stability".[31] In its ruling, the court invoked both Article 9 of the Civil Code (the Green Principle) and Article 153, Paragraph 2 (the Public Order and Good Morals Principle), concluding that the contract was inconsistent with the legislative spirit of the Civil Code, violated mandatory administrative regulations and regulatory requirements, and infringed the public order and good morals principle, thereby declaring the contract invalid.

From the court's reasoning, it is clear that the primary basis for evaluating the validity of Bitcoin mining contracts remains the traditional Public Order and Good Morals Principle. The Green Principle serves as a supplementary foundation, broadening the scope of public order to include ecological and environmental protection as well as resource conservation. This enables the Public Order and Good Morals Principle to play a role in evaluating the validity of civil activities in carbon-related contract disputes. By applying the Green Principle, judges create relevant legal norms to fill gaps in the law, allowing regulatory measures tied to dual carbon goals in policy documents to be integrated into civil judicial decisions. This approach provides a special interface for extending public law norms into the realm of private law,[32] ultimately supporting the achievement of regulatory objectives under the dual carbon policy.

[28] National Development and Reform Commission and other Relevant Government Departments, 'Notice on Rectifying Virtual Currency Mining Activities' (Fa Gai Yun Xing No.1283, 2021).

[29] State Council of the People's Republic of China, 'Interim Provisions on Promoting Industrial Restructuring' (Guo Fa No. 40, 2005).

[30] *Zhangxin v Yifeng* [2019] No. 37355 Jing 0102 Min Chu (Xicheng District People's Court of Beijing Municipality).

[31] *Xinjiang Xintao Silicon Industry Co., Ltd. v Yang Peng* [2022] NO.2201 Xin 2105 Min Chu (Yizhou District People's Court, Hami, Xinjiang Uygur Autonomous Region, China).

[32] C X Liu, 'Minfa lvse yuanze jieshi de fangxiang yu lujin [The Direction and Path of the Interpretation of the Green Principle of Civil Law]' (2023) 5 Faxue pinglun 141.

4.2 The Legality of Lawmaking Application of the Green Principle

However, is the Green Principle appropriate as a basis for determining the validity of civil acts? This chapter argues that the Green Principle should not be used as a basis for evaluating the validity of civil acts for the following reasons.

First, as mentioned in Section 4.1, among the various principles of civil law, only the Public Order and Good Morals Principle can explicitly serve as a basis for determining the validity of civil acts (Article 153).[33] The Public Order and Good Morals Principle aims to protect social public interests and uphold basic moral standards, ensuring that civil acts not only comply with legal requirements, but also align with mainstream social values. In contrast, the Green Principle, in terms of its normative expression and functional orientation, is more promotional and is generally considered to have weaker mandatory force.

Second, the Green Principle is primarily a hortatory norm, urging civil subjects to "act positively" rather than setting boundaries for prohibited civil acts. Unlike the Public Order and Good Morals Principle, which uses prohibitive language, the Green Principle employs the affirmative phrase "shall be conducive to resource conservation and environmental protection". If "shall not violate" represents the minimum requirement, then "shall be conducive to" establishes a higher standard, requiring not only the avoidance of harm but also the active contribution to positive outcomes. Such a higher standard of ambition typically is associated with a lesser degree of binding judicial enforcement than narrower prohibitive principles.

Third, when legal prohibitions are in place, even within the context of ecological and environmental protection and dual-carbon administrative regulations, Article 153, Paragraph 2 of the Civil Code can be directly invoked to declare civil acts invalid for violating public order and good morals, without needing to reference the Green Principle. However, in the absence of specific legal prohibitions related to dual carbon goals, and given the broad scope of these goals, hastily invoking the Green Principle to invalidate civil acts could introduce legal uncertainty, undermining the predictability and stability of the law.

5. Green Principle and Charging Pile Installation Disputes

In addition to applying the Green Principle to assess the validity of civil acts, Chinese courts also invoke it in carbon-related contract disputes to determine the owners' rights of underground parking lots and ancillary obligations associated with contract performance. Around 2010, China promoted new energy vehicles as a strategic industry,[34] leading to a surge in the number of new energy vehicles and a corresponding explosion in charging demand. However, the installation of charging piles in older residential areas could not keep up with the demand, leading to disputes.

33 Civil Code, art 153.

34 State Council of the People's Republic of China, 'Decision of the State Council on Accelerating the Cultivation and Development of Strategic Emerging Industries' (Guo Fa No.32, 2010).

5.1 The Green Principle and the Ownership of Underground Parking Lots

In civil disputes over the installation of charging piles in residential areas, in addition to property service contract disputes involving ancillary obligations, when the party refusing to assist in the installation procedures is the homeowners' association or some homeowners, building ownership disputes may arise.

In such cases, courts would sometimes invoke the Green Principle as a basis for judgment, requiring the homeowners' association to assist in the installation. For example, in the case of *Yu Tianrong v Kaiping Changsha Yunding Huating Residential Area Homeowners' Association*,[35] the court invoked Article 240 of the *Civil Code*, which states that "the owner of a property has the right to possess, use, and dispose of their immovable or movable property in accordance with the law", as the primary basis for judgment, ruling that the plaintiff's installation of a charging pile in their dedicated parking space was a necessary means of using a new energy vehicle and did not violate property use regulations. In the meanwhile, the court also invoked the Green Principle, stating that "civil activities should be conducive to resource conservation and environmental protection", and that "the promotion of new energy vehicles and charging piles has a positive impact on environmental protection, aligning with the Green Principle". The court ultimately ruled that the defendant homeowners' association should assist the plaintiff in the installation procedures within five days.

Notably, these cases inherently possessed more direct legal basis, such as the explicit provisions of Article 240. In this context, the Green Principle is applied neither as a gap-filling rule, nor as a substitute for existing rules, but as a normative amplifier to reinforce the low-carbon transition. In fourteen cases, the defendant argued that the installation of charging piles required a vote by the homeowners' assembly. In eight of these cases, the court ruled that the installation of charging piles was not a matter requiring a decision by the homeowners' assembly, as this argument "confused the distinction between exclusive and common areas in building ownership". The installation of charging piles in individual parking spaces is an exercise of the owner's rights over their exclusive area and does not change the use of common areas. Therefore, the property company's argument that the installation of charging piles in individual parking lots required a decision by the homeowners' assembly had no legal basis.

In these cases, while the Green Principle's invocation here did not alter the substantive outcome, it served a critical interpretive bridging function: Embedding decarbonisation imperatives into the hermeneutics of property rights. This signals a deliberate judicial pivot towards low-carbon infrastructure prioritisation, even within conventional civil disputes.

5.2 The Ancillary Obligations in Property Service Contracts

In judicial practice, issues related to ancillary obligations in the performance of carbon-related contracts mainly arise in property service disputes over the installation of new energy vehicle charging piles. When these disputes reached the courts, judges faced a lack of legal basis. On the one hand, while the state issued policies requiring property companies to cooperate with the installation of charging piles (such as the Notice on Accelerating the Construction of Electric Vehicle Charging Infrastructure in Residential Areas), local implementation rules

[35] *Yu Tianrong v The Owners Committee of Yunding Huating Community* [2022] No. 4810 Yue 0783 Min Chu (Kaiping City People's Court of Guangdong Province).

were unclear, and property companies' understanding and execution of the policies varied. Some property companies refused to cooperate, citing "no clear regulations" and the absence of explicit provisions in the initial property service contracts. On the other hand, Article 272 of the Civil Code addresses the ownership, use, and disposal of building areas, but it cannot be directly applied as a basis for judgment because, even if the owner's right to use the parking space is confirmed, it must be exercised "without endangering building safety or harming the legitimate rights and interests of other owners".[36] In some residential areas, the installation of charging piles indeed poses safety risks and technical obstacles. Therefore, property rights alone cannot directly imply the ancillary obligations of property service contracts related to charging pile installation, as the Civil Code lacks clear legal provisions supporting the obligation of property companies to assist in the installation of charging piles.

Among the thirty-six charging pile contract disputes identified in this study, sixteen judgments invoked both the Green Principle and the principle of good faith as the basis for judgment, while twenty invoked only the Green Principle as the primary basis. Additionally, thirty judgments invoked the Green Principle as the primary basis, with policy documents serving as supplementary basis.[37] This shows that in disputes over charging pile installation, the Green Principle is invoked as a basis for judgment primarily due to the lack of clear legal provisions, allowing the Green Principle to fill legal gaps and implement the government's dual carbon policies.

This analysis reveals that judges applying the Green Principle in their rulings have broadened the scope of ancillary obligations in property service contracts. Ancillary obligations refer to additional duties that parties must fulfil during the execution of a contract, beyond the main contractual obligations, in order to ensure its smooth performance, maintain its fundamental purpose, and avoid causing unnecessary harm to the other party. These obligations include notification, assistance, and confidentiality (Article 509 of the Civil Code). Traditionally, ancillary obligations are derived from the principle of good faith, aimed at filling gaps in contract terms and ensuring a balance of interests between the parties. A breach of ancillary obligations may constitute a breach of contract (Article 577 of the Civil Code), leading to compensation for damages, with the traditional standard for determining a breach being whether good faith has been violated.

Is the Green Principle compatible with the ancillary obligations derived from the principle of good faith? The answer is yes. Article 509 of the Civil Code states that "parties shall perform their obligations in accordance with the contract and in good faith, and shall fulfil obligations such as notification, assistance, and confidentiality based on the nature, purpose, and transaction practices of the contract. During the performance of the contract, parties shall avoid wasting resources, polluting the environment, and damaging the ecosystem". The last clause reflects the requirements of the Green Principle. However, as previously noted, the Green Principle encourages parties to "act positively", thus creating a new model of "encouraging" obligations within civil law principles. Therefore, the "shall be conducive to" requirement of

36 *Shang Siming v Luoyang Yingfu Property Management Co., Ltd.* [2022] No. 2821 Yu 0303 Min Chu (Xigong District People's Court of Luoyang City, Henan Province).

37 The majority of the cited policy documents are the 'Notice on Accelerating the Construction of Electric Vehicle Charging Facilities in Residential Areas' (NDRC Energy [2016] No. 1611), jointly issued by the National Development and Reform Commission, the National Energy Administration, the Ministry of Industry and Information Technology, and the Ministry of Housing and Urban-Rural Development on 25 July 2016. In very few cases, locally issued relevant policy documents are cited, such as the 'Implementation Rules for the Construction of New Energy Vehicle Charging and Swapping Facilities in Huizhou City (Interim)' (Huizhou Development and Reform (2015) No. 251).

the Green Principle not only encompasses the need to "avoid wasting resources, polluting the environment, and damaging the ecosystem" but also imposes higher standards regarding the manner and effect of actions. Among the few civil law norms that require parties to take positive actions beyond the contract terms, the "assistance obligation" specified in the Civil Code stands out.

Before 2020, when the Green Principle was not yet codified and China's dual carbon policy had not been officially introduced, courts often did not support property owners' requests for property companies to assist in the installation of charging piles. In a 2017 property service contract dispute,[38] the plaintiff requested the court to order the defendant to fulfil the property service contract, sign a written parking lot maintenance service agreement, and clarify the defendant's obligations and liabilities for breach in the installation of electric vehicle charging infrastructure. However, the court ruled that "the plaintiff's request to clarify the installation of electric vehicle charging infrastructure requires the submission of an application to the relevant departments if the residential area meets the conditions for installation, and the court will not address this claim".

After the Green Principle was introduced into the Civil Code, courts began to interpret and apply contract terms based on the Green Principle in contract disputes, also invoking relevant policy documents as supplementary bases for judgment, leading to different outcomes. For example, in the 2023 case of *Zhao v Siping Fengyi Property Management Co., Ltd.*,[39] the plaintiff, after purchasing a new energy vehicle, applied to install a charging pile in their dedicated parking space. The defendant requested the plaintiff to provide a feasibility assessment from the power company and refused to assist in the installation procedures. Due to the lack of clear legal provisions, the court invoked the Green Principle in its reasoning, stating that "the purchase and use of new energy vehicles are strongly encouraged and advocated by the state and society, and are of significant positive importance for promoting resource conservation and environmental protection. Charging piles are essential infrastructure for promoting the development of new energy vehicles and are a necessary equipment for individual users of new energy vehicles". Therefore, the property company should follow the Principle of Good Faith and the Green Principle stipulated in the Civil Code and provide active cooperation. The court ruled that the property company should assist the owner in providing materials and procedures for the installation of the charging pile. In fact, by invoking the Green Principle, most judgments after 2021 supported the owners' claims regarding the ancillary obligations of property service contracts. In all thirty-six charging pile installation contract disputes identified in this chapter, the courts supported the owners' claims.

In fact, even in the absence of policy documents as supplementary bases for judgment, the Green Principle can be invoked alone as the basis for determining ancillary obligations in contract performance. In one charging pile installation contract dispute, the main issue was whether the defendant should provide the necessary documents for the installation of the charging pile. The court first invoked Article 272 of the Civil Code, clarifying that the owner has the right to possess, use, and dispose of their exclusive building area without endangering building safety or harming the legitimate rights and interests of other owners. However, the court further invoked the Green Principle in its reasoning, stating that "according to the Green

[38] *Hua Jianwei v Guangdong Zhong'ao Property Management Co., Ltd.* [2017] No. 12202 Zhe 0109 Min Chu (Xiaoshan District People's Court of Hangzhou City).

[39] *Zhao v Siping Fengyi Property Management Co., Ltd.*[2023] No. 3588 Ji 0303 Min Chu (Tiedong District People's Court of Siping City, Jilin Province); *Shang Siming v Luoyang Yingfu Property Management Co., Ltd.* [2022] No. 2821 Yu 0303 Min Chu (Xigong District People's Court of Luoyang City, Henan Province).

Principle, the vigorous development of electric vehicles is of great significance for ensuring energy security, promoting energy conservation and emission reduction, and preventing air pollution", and that "the installation of charging piles is indispensable for the use of electric vehicles, and the plaintiff has the right to install a charging pile in their parking space for their vehicle". The court ruled that "the defendant, as the property service provider, should assist the plaintiff in the procedures for installing the charging pile in the underground parking space". This shows that the court's requirement was not based on property rights but on the public interest of low-carbon transformation, reflecting the Green Principle's function as a conduit for public law values into the private law system.

5.3 Boundaries and Exceptions of the Green Principle in Defining Ancillary Obligations

The application of the Green Principle in resolving disputes during contract performance should consider the following issues.

First, the application of the Green Principle should have its boundaries and exceptions. In charging pile installation contract disputes, the application of the Green Principle is not absolutely prioritised over other civil law principles. When there are legitimate reasons (such as objective technical limitations or public safety risks—for example, a power department's certification of overload), the rights and obligations of civil subjects must be balanced. Objectively, many older residential areas were not designed to accommodate the electrical load of new energy vehicle charging, and the cost and time required for electrical capacity expansion are high. In such cases, the installation of charging piles indeed poses a risk of electrical overload, and courts should not rule that property companies are obligated to assist in the installation. In twenty-nine cases, the defendant property companies argued that the residential areas did not meet the conditions for installation, that the installation of charging piles would occupy residential electrical capacity, exceed the electrical load, affect normal electricity use, and create safety and fire hazards. In twenty-six of these cases, the courts ruled that the issues of fire safety, electrical conditions, and insufficient electrical capacity related to the installation of charging piles were "specific and substantive matters to be determined by relevant functional departments (such as the power supply department) based on work rules and technical regulations after on-site feasibility assessments". In two cases, the courts ruled that the defendant should bear the burden of proof and did not accept the defence due to the defendant's failure to provide evidence of safety hazards. In one case, the court, based on the response from the State Grid Sichuan Electric Power Company Chongzhou Branch and the power load curve chart of the residential area, found that the electrical capacity of the residential area had significant surplus and did not accept the defence. In all twenty-nine cases, the plaintiffs' claims were fully supported by the courts, resulting in favourable rulings.

Second, the specific contents of property companies' ancillary obligations in property service contracts related to charging pile installation under the Green Principle should be clarified. Specifically, according to the requirements of the Notice, property companies have a preliminary review obligation for charging pile installation, meaning they must conduct a formal review of the owner's installation application (such as proof of parking space ownership and electrical qualifications) but are not responsible for substantive technical feasibility assessments. They must also assist owners in liaising with the power supply and fire departments and provide necessary documents such as the residential area's electrical layout. Additionally, property companies have a risk notification obligation, meaning they must clearly inform owners that they are responsible for the safety and maintenance costs of the charging pile after installation. If property companies claim that there are objective obstacles such as insufficient electrical capacity or fire hazards, they must provide written certification from third-party professional institutions (such as the power supply company or fire department). In judicial practice, in twenty-six judgments, the courts ruled that the issues of fire safety, electrical conditions, and insufficient electrical capacity related to the installation of charging piles were specific and substantive matters to be determined by the owner, with the assistance of the property company, through on-site feasibility assessments by relevant functional departments (such as the power supply department) based on work rules and technical regulations. Therefore, the burden of proof still lies with the owner. However, in two cases, the courts ruled that the property company should bear the burden of proof regarding the existence of safety hazards.[40] This shows that when defining the specific content of ancillary obligations based on the Green Principle, due to the ambiguity of adjudication rules and the unclear content of property companies' assistance obligations, different judgments may be reached in similar cases.

6. Categorisation of the Application Modes of the Green Principle

Based on the different ways the Green Principle was invoked, the cases can be categorised into the following three application scenarios.

6.1 First Mode: Declaratory Function of the Green Principle

In carbon-related civil disputes where there are clear, specific, and directly applicable civil legal norms, courts typically apply these norms directly as the basis for judgment, while invoking the Green Principle in the reasoning to serve a declaratory function. Since there are directly applicable provisions, the judgment outcomes are generally clear and predictable. This declaratory invocation does not substantially affect the case outcome, but it often enhances the judicial function of environmental education. In six carbon-related civil judgments, the Green Principle does not appear in the listed legal bases but serves only a declaratory and guiding role in the reasoning. In such cases, the Green Principle is regarded as an advocacy tool, primarily promoting environmental awareness, enhancing environmental education, and extending the environmental impact of the judgment. This type of invocation is rare, accounting for only 7.4% of the cases in this study, as shown in Figure 40.1.

In carbon-related tort disputes, primarily civil public interest lawsuits related to air pollution, given the clarity of relevant tort law rules, courts often invoke the Green Principle in their judgments as a basis for reasoning, mainly serving a declaratory function.[41] The application of the Green Principle typically does not affect the outcome of the case. However, in some cases, courts may apply the Green Principle to impose heavier burdens of proof and liability on

40 *Ma Hong. Chengdu Zhonghewei Property Group Co., Ltd.* [2022] No. 3673 Xin 0109 Min Chu (Midong District People's Court of Urumqi City, Xinjiang Uygur Autonomous Region); *Fan Min v Jinke Smart Service Group Co., Ltd.* [2022] No. 2470 Chuan 0105 Min chu (Qingyang District People's Court of Chengdu City).

41 *Fujian Green Home Environmental Friendliness Center v Zhao'an Hanxin Stone Co., Ltd.* [2021] No. 3932 Min 06 Min Zhong (Zhangzhou Intermediate People's Court of Fujian Province); *Fujian Green Home Environmental Friendliness Center v Dingyu Building Materials (Zhangzhou) Co., Ltd.* [2021] No. 3933 Min 06 Min Zhong (Zhangzhou Intermediate People's Court of Fujian Province).

polluters in the absence of clear legal provisions. In such cases, the Green Principle can also be invoked as a basis for reasoning, assisting in the interpretation of laws and enhancing the persuasiveness of the judgment.

In Guangdong's first environmental civil public interest lawsuit applying the Green Principle, *Beijing Fengtai District Source Enthusiasts Environmental Research Institute and others v Shenzhen Shenchao Optoelectronics Co., Ltd.*,[42] the defendant repeatedly exceeded emission standards for air and water pollutants, causing severe environmental pollution. The court invoked the Green Principle, stating that:

> Article 9 of the Civil Code establishes the Green Principle, providing guidance for legal application, interpretation, and the filling of legal gaps in judicial practice, as well as for value judgments and choices in cases of conflicting interests. Courts should sanction environmental polluters in accordance with the law, impose heavier burdens of proof on polluters, and properly adjudicate environmental public interest lawsuits to demonstrate the state's determination to protect the environment through judicial rulings.

Accordingly, the court ruled that the defendant's excessive emissions had caused environmental damage and that the defendant's failure to publicly disclose its emission levels and pollution control measures made it difficult to accurately determine the actual extent of the pollution. Therefore, the court shifted the burden of proving the facts related to the pollution from the plaintiff to the defendant and, after considering the specific circumstances of the pollution, the defendant's degree of violation, and subjective fault, ordered the defendant to pay a total of ten million yuan in ecological restoration costs.

6.2 Second Mode: The Green Principle as a Basis for Normative Interpretation and Selection

This scenario typically arises when the legal norms applicable to the case are vague, overly broad, or even contradictory, requiring the judge to exercise interpretative judgment based on case-specific circumstances. The term "normative interpretation and application" refers to situations where a civil norm is applicable, but its application may conflict with the Green Principle of the Civil Code. In such cases, the Green Principle can serve as a reason or reinforcing factor for legal interpretation. Normative selection applies when multiple conflicting civil norms are potentially applicable. Judges may invoke the Green Principle to justify rulings favouring environmental protection.

For instance, in property disputes, the ownership of accessions affects how they are handled, and in such disputes, courts can either apply Article 97 of the Contract Law, requiring restoration to the original state, or apply Article 322 of the Property Law, determining the ownership of the accessions and awarding compensation. In such cases, the Green Principle guides civil subjects to handle accessions in a more environmentally friendly and resource-efficient manner. Before the Green Principle was codified in the Civil Code, courts often applied Article 97 of the original Contract Law[43] to decide whether to remove accessions based on the specific circumstances of the case. In the 2016 case of *Fuzhou Railway Building Co., Ltd.*

[42] *Beijing Fengtai District Source Lovers Environmental Research Institute and others v Shenzhen China Optoelectronics (Shenzhen) Co., Ltd.* [2019] No. 3509 Yue 03 Min Chu (Shenzhen Intermediate People's Court of Guangdong Province).

[43] Contract Law, art 97.

v Fuzhou Federal Commercial Co., Ltd.,[44] the court confirmed that the lease contract between the parties had been terminated in 2004. The defendant had installed automatic escalators, sightseeing elevators, and central air conditioning units that had not become attached to the building, and the plaintiff requested their removal and restoration of the original state. The court applied Article 97 of the original Contract Law, ruling that the defendant should remove and relocate the central air conditioning units and related facilities, supporting the plaintiff's claim. This ruling, while respecting the parties' contractual freedom and property rights protection, was clearly detrimental to resource conservation and environmental protection, as the removal and relocation of these facilities would result in significant waste of building materials and potentially generate additional environmental pollution and carbon emissions during the disposal process, contradicting the sustainable development goals advocated by the Green Principle.

After the Green Principle was codified in the Civil Code, courts have tended to confirm the ownership of accessions, making rulings that favour low-carbon and environmentally friendly outcomes. For example, in the 2022 case of *Qingdao Moore Property Management Co., Ltd. v Qingdao Gome Electrical Appliances Co., Ltd.*,[45] the plaintiff, Moore Property, had installed central air conditioning for business purposes under a lease contract with the defendant, Gome Electrical Appliances. After a dispute arose and the lease contract was terminated, the court ordered Moore Property to vacate the premises. Moore Property claimed that movable items had been removed and sought to offset rent with fixed decorations and facilities, but the parties could not reach an agreement. Moore Property requested that Gome Electrical Appliances pay for the use of the air conditioning, while Gome Electrical Appliances argued that the central air conditioning belonged to them under the contract's provision that "unremoved items are deemed abandoned". The court invoked Article 322 of the Civil Code, applying the accession rule to determine the ownership of the central air conditioning, and cited the Green Principle, stating that "civil activities should be conducive to resource conservation and environmental protection. If restoration to the original state is not feasible or reasonable, the ownership of the new property should be confirmed". Accordingly, the court ruled that the central air conditioning, as a movable property attached to immovable property, belonged to Gome Electrical Appliances but required compensation to Moore Property. This case, guided by the Green Principle, refined the adjudication logic and reflected the principles of resource conservation and environmental protection.

6.3 Third Mode: The Green Principle as a Tool for Filling Legal Gaps

The Green Principle also plays lawmaking role in civil adjudication to fill existing legal gaps in carbon-related civil adjudication. According to our research, Chinese courts sometimes would even invoke the Green Principle as a basis for judgment when there is a lack of clear legal provisions or when existing laws are insufficiently specific. In such cases, judges use legal principles to create law and fill in the legal gaps.

44 *Fuzhou Railway Building Co., Ltd. v Fuzhou Federal Commercial Co., Ltd.* [2016] No. 7871 Min 0102 Min Chu (Gulou District People's Court of Fuzhou City, Fujian Province).

45 *Qingdao Moore Property Management Co., Ltd. and Qingdao Gome Electrical Appliances Co., Ltd.* [2022] No. 1868 Lu 0203 Min Ch (Shibei District People's Court of Qingdao City, Shandong Province).

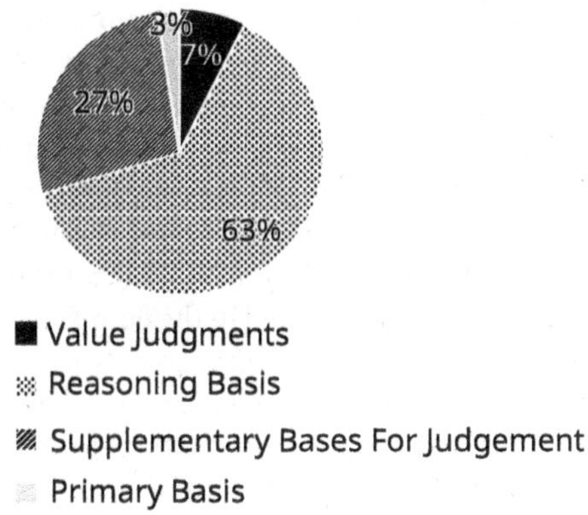

FIGURE 40.1 Percentage of the modes of application of the green principle

In the case of *Huang v Xiamen [Property Management Company]*[46] regarding a property service contract dispute, the plaintiff, Huang, requested the court to order the defendant property management company to assist in installing a new energy charging pile. The court held that Huang's request to install a new energy vehicle charging pile aligns with the Green Principle established by this provision. The request essentially concerns the property owner's rights to possess and use the exclusive parts of the building. In addition, the court referred to a policy document,[47] which states: "Property service enterprises should play an active role. During the installation of charging infrastructure in residential areas, property service enterprises should cooperate with the owner or the construction unit commissioned by the owner, promptly provide relevant drawings and information, and actively assist with site surveys and construction." The court ruled that the company should fulfill its duty by assisting Huang in handling the installation procedures for the new energy charging pile.

6.4 Challenges and Risks in Applying the Green Principle in Judicial Rulings

The three modes of applying the Green Principle reflect the reluctance of judges in a civil law system like China when it comes to judicial lawmaking, as under the premise of clear legal provisions, judges usually do not directly apply the Green Principle in their rulings; yet they also reflect Chinese judges' proactive attitude when implementing the State's dual-carbon policy by using open norms to fill legal gaps. In a civil law system, there is a strong emphasis on the clarity and stability of written laws. Judges are generally expected to strictly interpret and apply existing laws, rather than engaging in judicial creativity. Therefore, when faced with legal gaps, the use of the Green Principle as a tool for judicial lawmaking highlights the judges' struggle to adapt in the face of insufficient legislative guidance; it reflects Chinese judiciary's effort to follow the pathway "when in doubt, favour climate", addressing pressing climate concern in the absence of comprehensive legislation. Consequently, what might appear as routine property

[46] *Huang Moukai v Xiamen XX Property Management Co., Ltd.* [2022] No. 11758 Min 0203 Min Chu (Siming District People's Court of Xiamen City, Fujian Province).

[47] Notice on Accelerating the Construction of Electric Vehicle Charging Infrastructure in Residential Areas, 2016.

law adjudication becomes a strategic vector for institutionalising ecological governance, transforming case-by-case disputes into catalysts for systemic environmental transformation.

However, this attempt to invoke open-ended norms and fill legal gaps also carries risks. Given the open-endedness of the Green Principle, the application of the Green Principle can hardly be uniform across all courts. Different courts may interpret the principle differently, leading to inconsistent rulings. This inconsistency could create confusion and undermine public trust in the legal system, as parties involved in similar cases might receive different outcomes based on the same legal issue. As mentioned in the empirical research of Bitcoin mining contract disputes, among twenty-one cases ruled after 2021, twenty judicial decisions declared the invalidity of the targeted mining contract, however, in the 2021 case of *Deng Peng*[48] the court ruled that the Bitcoin mining machine sales contract formed between the parties was valid, as the law had not explicitly prohibited the trading of mining machines. In contrast, in most other judicial decisions, the court ruled that the mining machine sales contract was invalid because the mining activities were energy-intensive and carbon-emitting, detrimental to national industrial restructuring, energy conservation, emissions reduction, and the achievement of carbon peak and carbon neutrality, thus violating the Green Principle and harming social public interests.

There have also been other instances where similar cases resulted in opposite rulings especially when the Green Principle was applied as a basis for normative selection, as explained in Section 6.2. In the case of *Wu v a Real Estate Company in Henan*,[49] the defendant real estate company failed to deliver the house on time as per the contract. The plaintiff sought damages for the delay, while the defendant argued that during the construction period, a severe pollution weather alert was issued, and they received a work suspension notice from the local government and environmental protection authorities, which led to construction delays and ultimately prevented timely delivery. The defendant argued that this situation constituted force majeure and should be exempt from liability. The court, however, rejected the defendant's defence and supported the plaintiff's claim, citing Article 9 of the General Principles of Civil Law. A similar case was filed in a court in Tianjin,[50] with nearly identical facts. The defendant also used the argument of severe pollution weather during the construction period and the work suspension notice from local government authorities. Yet, the two cases resulted in completely opposite rulings, with the court citing Article 9 of the General Principles of Civil Law to reject the plaintiff's claim in this case. These two cases both invoked the Green Principle, resulted in opposite rulings, highlighting the potential for legal uncertainty and inconsistent adjudication standards when using open-ended norms like the Green Principle as a basis for evaluating the validity of civil acts. This also reflects the arbitrariness and discretionary nature of judicial decisions when judges apply open-ended norms in case rulings.

7. Conclusion

There is a widespread insufficiency of climate legislation globally, particularly in the Global South. In this context, the challenge of how courts can bridge this gap and proactively address the urgent demands for climate change mitigation and social low-carbon transformation has

48 *Deng Peng v Cheng Tianjie* [2021] No. 3356 Chuan 0682 Min Chu (Shifang City People's Court of Sichuan Province).

49 *Wu Lingjie v Henan Hongjiang Real Estate Development Co., Ltd.* [2018] No. 696 Yu 0102 Min Chu (Zhongyuan District People's Court of Zhengzhou City, Henan Province).

50 *Li Ruirui v Tianjin Binhai Real Estate Management Co., Ltd.* [2018] No. 3451 Jin 0116 Min Chu (Binhai New Area People's Court of Tianjin Municipality).

become a universally complex issue. In global rights-based climate litigation, courts in various countries have started to seek breakthroughs in climate change regulation by relying on open-ended norms, urging governments to implement effective mitigation and adaptation measures. However, climate response and carbon reduction transformation do not solely pertain to governmental duties; they encompass all aspects of social and economic life, necessitating the participation of society at large. Market entities, in particular, must alter their conventional business models, consumption patterns, and even lifestyles. In this context, the question arises whether open-ended norms can be similarly applied in the adjudication of ordinary civil cases involving resource recycling, energy transformation, and low-carbon economic restructuring to guide the green and low-carbon behaviour of civil entities.

In response, Chinese courts have utilised the Green Principle in the Civil Code to effect low-carbon value proclamations, normative interpretation or selection, and legal gap-filling in ordinary civil cases, such as contract, property, and tort disputes. Article 9 of the Chinese Civil Code, the Green Principle, mandates that civil activities should be conducive to resource conservation and ecological protection, reflecting the characteristics of public law, such as public interest purpose, affirmative nature, and compulsory nature. This represents the integration of public law values into the private law system. The application of open-ended norms reflecting public law values in civil disputes demonstrates the proactive judicial attitude of Chinese judges in implementing national climate and dual-carbon policies through judicial rulings. It is important to note that Chinese judicial organs do not possess lawmaking functions, judicial rulings are not precedents, and there is no principle of stare decisis. However, this does not hinder Chinese judges from proactively applying the law in the absence of explicit legislative provisions to address the practical needs of social development.

Nevertheless, the application of open-ended norms must remain consistent with the legislative intent of lawmakers. First, if explicit legal provisions already exist, and the application of these provisions does not contravene legal principles, courts should not disregard them in favour of applying legal principles. In other words, a fundamental condition for applying the Green Principle is the absence of corresponding regulatory provisions within existing laws. Second, the Green Principle in Article 9 of the Civil Code is a hortatory norm; its purpose is to urge civil entities to actively act rather than establish boundaries for prohibiting civil legal actions. Thus, it is inappropriate to invalidate civil acts solely based on the Green Principle. Finally, given the open-ended nature of the Green Principle, it is essential to issue judicial interpretative documents clarifying its scope and application methods at an appropriate time. This would help mitigate the risks of inconsistent rulings in similar cases, judicial arbitrariness, and non-standardised judgments arising from divergent interpretations of the Green Principle, which could undermine judicial fairness and the credibility of the courts.

CHAPTER 41

Brazil

DANIELLE DE ANDRADE MOREIRA

1. Introduction

THE global and hyper-complex nature of climate risks highlights the importance attributed to climate-environmental law,[1] and therefore, the urgency of adjusting existing legal structures to address the need for effective liability for the damages associated with climate change.[2]

Although the repercussions and risks of industrial society have already led to changes in normative structures, the peculiarities of post-industrial (or risk) society demand a significant updating of the "dominant relations of definition".[3] Legal rules and instruments must be updated to be capable of guaranteeing the prevention and reparation of harm resulting from causes dispersed or dissolved among a multiplicity of actors, conditions, reactions, and counter-reactions.[4] Without this restructuring, given the increasing number of climate-related calamities, "the law-as-usual" would mean "authorising" "business-as-usual", and thus the worsening of climate risks, legitimising their "anonymous" character and therefore the impossibility of holding accountable those who cause or contribute to such a scenario, and profit from it, at the expense of society as a whole and of the planet. In sum, such a scenario would expose the so-called organised irresponsibility.[5]

[1] I refer to climate-environmental law as the scientific specialisation that has been attributed to climate law, as a subdiscipline of environmental law. It is based on the premise that 'climate matters are already included in Brazilian environmental legislation and, therefore, that the right to a stable climate is embedded in the fundamental human right to an ecologically balanced environment, expressly provided for in article 225 of the Brazilian Federal Constitution (CRFB/88)'. Danielle de Andrade Moreira, *Sumário de fundamentos para a litigância climática no Brasil: Argumentos jurídicos para a inserção da variável climática no licenciamento ambiental* (Editora PUC-Rio 2022) 11.

[2] 'As with earlier periods of societal evolution in response to suffering that is uncompensated, undeterred, and unrationalised, tort law will not be exempt from this necessity of reevaluation. Put bluntly, tort law will be forced to adapt or perish, much like life itself in a warming world.' Douglas A Kysar, 'What Climate Change Can Do About Tort Law' (2011) 41 Environmental Law 71, 7.

[3] For Ulrich Beck, dominant relations of definition encompass the rules, institutions, and instruments that determine the identification and recognition of risks, whether within a nation-state or in the relationship between two states, constituting the legal, epistemological, and cultural matrix of power in which risks are organised. See Ulrich Beck, *Ecological Politics in the Age of Risk* (Polity Press 1995).

[4] See Richard Lazarus, 'Super Wicked Problems and Climate Change: Restraining the Present to Liberate the Future' (2009) 94 Cornell Law Review 1153 (2009).

[5] According to Ulrich Beck, a scenario of 'general irresponsibility' manifests itself in a context in which the multiplication in the production and distribution of risks is seen as 'normal', bringing the idea that 'you can do something and continue doing it without having to take personal responsibility for it'. Ulrich Beck, *La sociedad del riesgo: hacia una nueva modernidad* (Jorge Navarro Pérez, Daniel Jiménez, and Maria Rosa Borrás trs, Paidós 1998) 39 (author's translation).

In this chapter, I propose a re-reading of the civil liability regime in Brazil in light of the challenges posed by climate change. The starting point is the changes already made to its classic structure to adapt it to the peculiarities of environmental damage. Even greater complexities are identified in climate-environmental damage—the dimension of environmental harm that either stems from greenhouse gases (GHG) emissions or is created (or intensified) by climate change.[6]

This chapter is divided into three sections. Section 1 presents the specificities of environmental civil liability in the Brazilian legal system, focusing on the transformations already implemented to adjust the traditional doctrine to the unique characteristics of the environmental harm. Section 2 explores how the Brazilian environmental civil liability regime can be applied to climate-related damages. Section 3 analyses how civil liability is being used and can be applied in Brazilian climate litigation, based on available data from the Brazilian Climate Litigation Platform, to map potential opportunities and hurdles to the development of the topic in Brazil.

2. Main Features of Environmental Civil Liability in Brazil

Originally, civil liability served as a mechanism for addressing tangible, easily pinpointable harm affecting a specific victim, arising from the culpable (e.g., negligent or reckless) conduct of one or a few wrongdoers. These harms were typically pecuniary in nature and recognised through a clear, linear causal link between the wrongdoing and the resulting injury.

Significant changes have been made to the structure of civil liability to adapt it to the inherent complexity of environmental damage. An analysis of the peculiarities of environmental damage reveals the limitations of traditional civil liability, leading to the development of the specific contours and characteristics of what is now referred to as environmental civil liability. This evolution seeks to transform it into an effective instrument for addressing environmental harm, whether by ensuring its full reparation or by preventing its occurrence or aggravation.

Understanding the complexity inherent to environmental damage begins with recognising the nature of the legal interest protected by law—and, more specifically, by civil liability: the environment. The environment, under Article 225 of the Brazilian Constitution,[7] is conceived as a collective and systemic *macrobem*—understood as the environment as a whole, from a holistic or systemic perspective, surpassing the isolated consideration of ecological elements (such as air, fauna, flora, water, and soil) and explicitly recognising their essential interconnections.[8] It thus constitutes an autonomous and intangible legal interest, intrinsically linked

[6] Within the broad legal category of 'environmental damage', this climate dimension is assessed on a case-by-case basis, in accordance with article 14 of Resolution 433/2021 of the National Council of Justice (BR), which requires consideration of the impacts of environmental damage on global climate change. On the peculiarities and complexities that tort law poses in the context of climate change, see Douglas A Kysar, 'The Public Life of Private Law: Tort Law as a Risk Regulation Mechanism' (2018) 9 European Journal of Risk Regulation 48, 53–54.

[7] 'Art. 225. Everyone has the right to an ecologically balanced environment, an asset for the common use of the people and essential to a healthy quality of life, imposing on the public authorities and the community the duty to defend and preserve it for present and future generations.' Constitution of the Federative Republic of Brazil (1988) (author's translation).

[8] Danielle de Andrade Moreira, 'A Panorama of Climate Litigation in Brazil' in Maria Antonia Tigre, Armando Luis Silva Rocha and Délton Winter de Carvalho (eds), *Brazil and Climate Justice* (Brill 2025) 55–56. Antonio Herman Benjamin states that: 'It is upon this basic concept of 'environmental quality' that the recognition of a unitary and macro notion of the environment is founded, an identity detached

to the full exercise of the right to life and respect for human dignity.[9] It is a human and fundamental right, recognised on behalf of present and future generations—intergenerational solidarity.[10] As will be explained in this section, the judiciary in Brazil has made protection of the *macrobem* based on fundamental principles, such as the principles of prevention, precaution, polluter-pays, and full reparation.

In addition to the nature of the legal interest at stake, the complexity inherent in the environmental damage becomes immediately apparent. Among its defining features are: (1) the potential involvement of multiple parties on both the active (polluters) and passive (victims) sides of a dispute; (2) the presence of varied causal factors (i.e., different causes contributing to a single harm or set of related harms); (3) the spatial and temporal dispersion of the damage; (4) the cumulative and/or synergistic effects of harmful events; and (5) significant evidentiary challenges, which undermine the applicability of traditional standards of certainty in establishing both the existence and causation of harm. These and other traits underscore the need for substantial adjustments to the classical doctrinal framework of civil liability when applied to environmental harm.

Indeed, environmental damage is often the result of multiple, gradual, and "invisible" actions that accumulate over years, sometimes decades, and produce synergistic effects. Frequently, the harmful consequences of a given activity or condition only become apparent in the future and/or manifest across a wide spatial scope, surpassing the territorial boundaries of municipalities, states, countries, or even continents. The absence of complete scientific knowledge regarding the full extent or nature of the harm often compounds these challenges. In such contexts, the characterisation of the causal link becomes especially complex, as it is frequently weakened or contested by the temporal and/or spatial distance between the harmful conduct and the manifestation of damage, as well as by the multiplicity of polluting sources and the diffuse nature of the affected victims.[11]

The elusive and dynamic nature of environmental damage renders the task of proving and delimiting its existence, scope, causal link, and the identification of the perpetrator(s) and victim(s) particularly complex. Compounding these challenges is the fact that regardless of its material or immaterial consequences, whether individual or collective, the victim of environmental harm is always the community as a whole, including future generations, as the holder of the violated right: the *direito difuso* ("diffuse right" or collective right) to an environment

from its material manifestations, and the acceptance, from a legal perspective, of an equally unitary form of environmental protection. . . . It is, as a *macrobem* (a macro-level legally protected interest or value), with a public nature. As a *bem* (legally protected interest), perceived as a true *universitas corporalis*, it is not to be confused with any singular material entity, asset or resource (forest, river, sea, historic site, protected species, etc.) that composes it; rather, it manifests itself as the complex of aggregated *bens* (interests) that make up environmental reality.' Antonio Herman Benjamin, 'Função Ambiental' in Antonio Herman Benjamin (ed), *Dano ambiental: Prevenção, Reparação e Repressão* (Revista dos Tribunais 1993) 75 (author's translation). See also Tiago Fensterseifer, *Direitos Fundamentais e Proteção do Ambiente: A Dimensão Ecológica da Dignidade Humana no Marco Jurídico-Constitucional do Estado Socioambiental de Direito* (Livraria do Advogado 2008) 165.

[9] José Rubens Morato Leite and Danielle de Andrade Moreira, 'Sociedade de Risco, Danos Ambientais Extrapatrimoniais e Jurisprudência Brasileira' in José Rubens Morato Leite and Paulo Roney Ávila Fagúndez (eds), *Biossegurança e Novas Tecnologias na Sociedade de Risco: Aspectos Jurídicos, Técnicos e Sociais* (Conceito Editorial 2007).

[10] See Danielle de Andrade Moreira and others, 'Rights-Based Climate Litigation in Brazil: An Assessment of Constitutional Cases Before the Brazilian Supreme Court' (2024) 16 Journal of Human Rights Practice 47, 48–49.

[11] See Mark Geitsfeld and Sandy Steel, Chapter 8 of this handbook.

ecologically balanced. Just as such right cannot be divided or individualised, neither can the damage resulting from its violation, which must therefore be characterised as a *dano difuso* ("diffuse harm" or collective harm).

In response to these peculiarities, several structural changes have been introduced to the Brazilian liability regime over the past decades. The first and most significant was the adoption, in 1981, of the *responsabilidade objetiva* (strict liability), which dismisses fault as a requirement for establishing the duty to repair environmental damages. The National Environmental Policy Act establishes that "the polluter is obliged, regardless of fault, to indemnify or repair the damage caused to the environment and to third parties affected by its activity".[12] Thus, in the field of environmental law one is not concerned with identifying guilty parties, a notion that has become anachronistic, but rather with identifying those who, having caused or contributed to the damage, can and should be held liable for the harm.

Another fundamental aspect of the environmental civil liability is identifying the parties responsible for the damage. In this regard, the definition of "polluter" under Brazilian law is notably broad, which significantly expands the range of actors who may be held liable for environmental harm. Polluter is defined as "any natural or legal person, public or private, directly or indirectly responsible for an activity that causes environmental degradation".[13] Thus, both direct and indirect polluters are strictly liable for environmental damages, with no distinction being made between them, and, as a general rule, without consideration for gradations of liability. This is because the liability of direct and indirect polluters is grounded in the principle of joint and several liability (solidarity, *responsabilidade solidária*), applicable whenever the damage results from multiple contributing causes or parties. The benefit (or, from the perspective of those held accountable, the burden) of solidarity, as established in Article 942 of the Brazilian Civil Code (2002), allows any of the polluters to be required to repair the damage fully. This liability framework is based on the premise that in environmental damage involving multiple polluters, the causal link is collective, given that the damage is diffuse and thus indivisible, reflecting the notion of the environment as an "unfragmentable unit".[14] Accordingly, the same causal link gives rise to, and defines, the legal bond that connects both direct and indirect polluters.

The Brazilian Superior Court of Justice (STJ)[15] has consistently recognised the liability of indirect polluters and the joint and several nature of liability in actions seeking reparation for environmental damage. This understanding is consolidated in Issues 30 and 257 of the publication *Jurisprudência em Teses* (Legal Theses from Case Law), which state that liability for environmental damage is joint and several among all polluters, whether direct or indirect.[16] One

[12] Lei 6.938/1981, art 14, para 1. This provision was retained by the Brazilian Constitution (1988), which, in art 225, para 3, declares: 'Conducts and activities deemed harmful to the environment shall subject their offenders, whether natural or legal persons, to criminal and administrative sanctions, independently of the obligation to repair the damage caused' (author's translation).

[13] Lei 6.938/1981, art 3, IV (author's translation).

[14] Antonio Herman de Vasconcellos e Benjamin, 'Responsabilidade civil pelo dano ambiental' (1998) 3 Revista de Direito Ambiental: RDA 5, 38 (author's translation).

[15] The Brazilian Superior Court of Justice (*Superior Tribunal de Justiça, STJ*) functions as the country's highest court for the uniform interpretation of federal infra-constitutional law. Positioned hierarchically below the Federal Supreme Court (*Supremo Tribunal Federal, STF*), which is reserved for constitutional matters, the STJ hears special appeals (*recursos especiais*) when a lower federal or state court has misapplied federal statutes or when divergent interpretations among different courts lead to legal non-uniformity.

[16] STJ, 'Jurisprudência em Teses' (Direito Ambiental n. 30), 2015 7; STJ, 'Jurisprudência em Teses' (Responsabilidade por Dano Ambiental II n. 257), 2025 4 7.

important consequence of these consolidated theses is the recognition that due to the joint and several nature of environmental civil liability, the causal link does not depend on determining percentages of contribution or assessing the degree of participation of each party in causing the damage. Were it otherwise, the very effectiveness of the doctrine—particularly its role in facilitating access to justice for victims—would be undermined.[17]

Brazil's highest courts have also recognised the polluter-pays principle as a fundamental guideline for conduct and as a normative framework for shaping reparatory measures. This principle is grounded in both economic and ethical reasoning, encapsulated in the maxim that "those who reap the rewards must bear the burden". In this regard, for instance, the Brazilian Supreme Court has affirmed that

> environmental law is guided by various principles, among them the polluter-pays principle, which underpins the reparation (and prevention) of environmental damage. According to this principle, the entrepreneur must internalise the external social costs of production. In other words, it is not equitable for entrepreneurs to retain the profits generated by their activity while society absorbs the resulting environmental harm (i.e., negative externalities).[18]

In the same vein, the STJ has held that:

> The polluter is therefore obliged, by virtue of the polluter-pays principle, to bear the costs of preventing, suppressing, and repairing pollution. This model ensures greater protection of the environment as a whole—a *macrobem*—by requiring economic agents to internalise external costs within the investment dynamics of their private activities, thus avoiding the "privatisation of profits and the socialisation of losses".[19]

Also deserving attention is the debate concerning the theory of risk applicable to environmental civil liability. In Brazilian environmental law, the prevailing interpretation is that the traditional grounds for excluding liability, such as unforeseeable circumstances, force majeure, acts of third parties, or the exclusive fault of the victim,[20] are not admissible in cases involving environmental damage. As a result, the strict liability is applied under the modality known as the *teoria do risco integral* ("integral-risk theory" or absolute liability). According to the STJ, "[l]iability for environmental damage is strict, informed by the integral-risk theory, with the causal link serving as the unifying factor that integrates the risk into the unity of the act. It is therefore unreasonable for the company responsible for the environmental harm to invoke traditional exclusions from civil liability to avoid its duty to indemnify".[21]

Rejecting the integral-risk theory in the context of environmental damage would mean accepting the disproportionate and unjust generation of negative environmental externalities. Environmental harm is, by its very nature, a negative externality[22] that should not be borne

[17] STJ 2ª Turma REsp 1.236.863/ES Rel. Min. Herman Benjamin (DJe 27/02/2012).

[18] STF Tribunal Pleno RE 654.833/AC Rel. Min. Alexandre de Moraes (DJe 24/06/2020). Decided unanimously (author's translation).

[19] STJ 3ª Turma REsp 1.612.887/PR Rel. Min. Nancy Andrighi (DJe 07/05/2020) (author's translation).

[20] The sole paragraph of Article 393 of the Brazilian Civil Code (2002) states that 'unforeseeable circumstances or force majeure occur in the case of a necessary event, the effects of which could not be avoided or prevented' (author's translation).

[21] Jurisprudência em Teses (n 16) 10; STJ, 'Jurisprudência em Teses' (Responsabilidade por Dano Ambiental n. 119), 2019 1.

[22] '[Environmental] damage directly affects third parties, regardless of their participation in the production and consumption chain from which the harmful conduct originated. The victim of environmental damage is always the community, *outsiders* to the market relations that gave rise to the damage. In this sense, . . . "environmental damage is a typical case of externality, because in its impact

by the community at large but rather internalised by those who engage in polluting activities, under the polluter-pays principle.[23] Indeed, there appears to be no legitimate justification for allowing an individual or entity to enjoy the positive outcomes of their activities while shifting the resulting environmental harm, that is, the negative externality, onto society.

The same peculiarities of environmental damage that justify the developments discussed thus far must also be considered when identifying the causal link in environmental civil liability. Establishing a cause-and-effect relationship between the conduct of the polluter(s) (whether direct or indirect) and the environmental harm to be remedied can be an extremely complex task. This complexity arises from factors already pointed out above, such as the temporal and/or spatial distance between the harmful act and its effects, the multiplicity of polluting sources and affected parties, and the existence of scientific uncertainties or limitations.

This scenario underpins a growing trend towards a more flexible—indeed elastic—approach to causation in environmental liability, prompting courts to loosen traditional causal requirements. An example of this broader understanding of causation is found in a 2009 decision by the STJ, which has since been reiterated in several subsequent rulings. In that decision, the Court stated that: "For the purpose of determining the causal link in environmental damage, those who act, those who fail to act when they should, those who allow others to act, those who are indifferent to the actions of others, those who finance the harmful conduct, and those who benefit from it—all stand on equal footing."[24]

It is also important to highlight the role of the precautionary principle and its interpretive guideline: *in dubio pro natura*. Although "it is complex—as well as costly and time-consuming—to produce expert evidence capable of proving that a specific environmental harm is in fact the result of a particular potentially polluting activity, such difficulties should not benefit the likely polluter, thereby shifting to society the burden—often impossible to meet—of establishing the alleged facts with absolute certainty and precision".[25] Indeed, the ongoing " '(r)evolution' in theories of causation aims to adapt them to the realities of environmental harm, emphasising the shift from certainty to probability, and from truth to verisimilitude. . . . truth is replaced by plausibility; certainty gives way to probability".[26]

on third parties, there is no mediation; it is direct, without any market or legal mechanism" ' (author's translation). Danielle de Andrade Moreira, *Responsabilidade Ambiental Pós-Consumo: Prevenção e Reparação de Danos à Luz do Princípio do Poluidor-Pagador* (Letras Jurídicas Editora PUC-Rio 2015) 105.

[23] 'The polluter-pays principle dictates the need for activities that potentially cause environmental degradation to internalise all the social costs arising from their operation.' The aim is to 'charge the polluter with the social cost of the pollution it generates or that it is capable of generating'. ibid 85 and 114. In Brazilian case law, this is a principle that has stood out as 'an important driving force for change and subsequent pacification of understandings that are more protective of the environment when it comes to repairing environmental damage, promoting the improvement of the interpretation of the main characteristics of environmental civil liability' (author's translation). Danielle de Andrade Moreira, Letícia Maria Rêgo Teixeira Lima and Izabel Freire Moreira, 'O Princípio do Poluidor-Pagador na Jurisprudência do STF e do STJ: Uma Análise Crítica' (2019) 16 Revista Veredas do Direito: Direito Ambiental e Desenvolvimento Sustentável 367, 399.

[24] See, among many others, STJ 2ª Turma REsp 650.728/SC Rel. Min. Herman Benjamin (DJe 02/12/2009) (author's translation).

[25] Danielle de Andrade Moreira, 'A Produção de Prova na Ação Civil Pública Ambiental: Alguns Aspectos Polêmicos e a Garantia da Efetividade da Tutela Jurisdicional à Luz da Jurisprudência do Superior Tribunal de Justiça' in Flavia Moreira Guimarães Pessoa, Natercia Sampaio Siqueira and Paulo Roberto Coimbra Silva (eds), *Processo, Jurisdição e Efetividade da Justiça* (CONPEDI 2015) 5.

[26] Branca Martins da Cruz, 'Responsabilidade Civil pelo Dano Ecológico: Alguns Problemas' (1997) 2 Revista de Direito Ambiental: RDA 5, 33 (author's translation, internal quotation marks omitted).

Thus, when there is serious and well-founded evidence of environmental degradation and its connection to a specific activity, the burden of proof must be reversed. It is the potential polluter who must demonstrate the absence of a causal link or environmental harm in the specific case.[27]

Moreover, the Brazilian Code of Civil Procedure now expressly adopts the technique of dynamic distribution of the burden of proof. Paragraph 1 of Article 373 provides for the possibility of shifting the burden of proof in cases provided for by law, or when specific circumstances of the case make it either impossible or excessively difficult for the plaintiff to discharge the burden of proving the facts constituting their claim—particularly when the opposing party is in a better position to produce the relevant evidence.

The STJ endorses this interpretation, having established in its *Súmula* 618 (Precedent) that "[t]he reversal of the burden of proof applies to actions concerning environmental degradation".[28]

Another key feature of environmental civil liability is its functional reorientation: It now operates not only to compensate victims ex post (after), but also to deter and prevent environmental harm ex ante (before).[29] To better fulfil its role in environmental matters, the civil liability regime has set aside what was once a core premise: that harm must be certain and already realised. Because environmental harm is often diffuse, cumulative, and latent, the "certain-and-present" requirement is no longer viable.

The complexity surrounding the "timing of damage" in environmental matters has led to the recognition of future environmental harm. As a result, the concept of reparable damage has evolved to encompass not only existing harm, but also the likely future consequences of current environmental risks or the future impacts of already-occurring damage.[30]

Equally significant are the difficulties related to valuing environmental damage, particularly in light of the legal imperative for its full reparation. The complex task of adequately assessing environmental harm necessarily involves recognising its extra-patrimonial or moral dimension. The intangible relationship between the environment and the community is inherent to its status as a *macrobem* and reflects the systemic and integrated approach underpinning the Brazilian legal-environmental framework. Accordingly, environmental damage is understood to encompass both pecuniary losses—arising from ecological harm, economic loss, and the financial costs associated with restoration—and non-pecuniary (non-material) losses, commonly referred to as moral damages, which may extend to cultural, ethnic, and even spiritual dimensions.

The extra-patrimonial (moral) environmental damage arises from the intrinsic value attributed to the environment as a *macrobem*—upon whose integrity the enjoyment of a dignified life depends. Such damage also derives from the environment's status as part of the collective ideal heritage of society, or from the existential dimension evident in situations where environmental degradation prevents the community from enjoying the level of environmental quality to which it is fundamentally entitled.[31]

[27] Danielle de Andrade Moreira, 'Responsabilidade Civil por Danos Ambientais no Direito Brasileiro' in Flavio Ahmed and Ronaldo Coutinho, *Curso de Direito Ambiental* (Lumen Juris 2012) 243.

[28] Author's translation.

[29] See Kysar (n 6).

[30] Future environmental harm must not be misunderstood as hypothetical or merely possible harm. Indeed, 'the harm must be sufficiently concrete and foreseeable to avoid slipping into the realm of the speculative or purely eventual'. Alvaro Luiz Valery Mirra, *Ação Civil Pública e a Reparação do Dano ao Meio Ambiente* (Juarez De Oliveira 2002) 101 (author's translation).

[31] 'Once environmental harm has been established, collective moral damages are presumed; in other words, no evidence of pain, suffering, revulsion, or indignation on the part of the affected community is

Therefore, given the peculiarities inherent in environmental damage, adjustments and adaptations to the traditional structure of civil liability are essential for this legal regime to be truly effective in addressing harm caused to the environment. Considering this, it is relevant to examine whether environmental civil liability, as currently understood in both doctrinal and case law, can, and indeed should, be applied as a legal framework for addressing climate-related damage. This issue is explored in the following section.

3. How Can Tort Law be Applied to Tackle Climate Change in Brazil?

Identifying how environmental civil liability can be applied to climate damage begins with recognising the broad scope of the concept of environmental damage itself. It is through the normative and jurisprudential foundations on which environmental civil liability has been built, along with the intrinsic specificities of the subject, that the full extent of what constitutes environmental harm can be properly understood. This expansive interpretation is precisely what allows, on a case-by-case basis, the identification of a climate dimension within environmental damage. From this perspective arises the concept of climate-environmental damage.

As previously discussed, environmental damage affects the community as a whole, which holds the fundamental constitutional right to an ecologically balanced environment. Such damage gives rise not only to ecological harm per se but also to patrimonial and existential losses. The STJ case law recognises that in addition to the obligation to restore the environment to its *status quo ante* (original condition), multiple dimensions of environmental harm are subject to compensation.[32] These include: (1) *danos interinos* (intermediary or temporary losses), referring to the losses incurred during the time interval between the occurrence of the environmental harm and its full restoration; (2) residual damage, denoting irreversible degradation that persists despite recovery efforts; and (3) collective moral damage, understood as the impairment of the community's well-being and quality of life. Furthermore, the party responsible for the environmental harm may also be ordered to return the economic gains obtained through the degrading activity in an unduly manner. This measure reflects the principle of disgorgement of profits, which seeks to prevent unjust enrichment and reinforce the polluter pays principle.

This understanding arises from the recognition that environmental damage inevitably possesses multiple dimensions. In other words, environmental harm is inherently multifaceted—"ethically, temporally, ecologically, and patrimonially speaking, and also in light of the diversity of the vast universe of victims, ranging from isolated individuals to society as a whole, future generations, and even ecological processes themselves".[33] Given this multidimensional nature, the reparation of environmental damage must be carried out as comprehensively as

required.' Jurisprudência em Teses (n 16) (author's translation). On the recognition and characteristics of extra-patrimonial environmental damage, see also Annelise Monteiro Steigleder, *Responsabilidade Civil Ambiental: as Dimensões do Dano Ambiental no Direito Brasileiro* (Livraria do Advogado 2017); José Rubens Morato Leite, *Dano Ambiental: Do Individual Ao Coletivo Extrapatrimonial* (Editora Revista dos Tribunais 2003); Leite and Moreira (n 9); Mirra (n 30); Danielle de Andrade Moreira, 'Dano Ambiental Extrapatrimonial: Dissertação de Mestrado Em Direito Da Cidade' (Faculdade de Direito da Universidade do Estado do Rio de Janeiro 2003).

32 As an illustration of this approach, see STJ 2ª Turma REsp 1.145.083/MG Rel. Min. Herman Benjamin (DJe 04/09/2012).

33 STJ 2ª Turma REsp 1.198.727/MG Rel. Min. Herman Benjamin (DJe 09/05/2013) (author's translation).

possible. This may include, for instance, the imposition of obligations to act or to refrain from acting, cumulatively with pecuniary compensation,[34] in line with the principles of full reparation of environmental harm and the polluter-pays.[35]

To identify the climate-related dimension of environmental damage within this multidimensional framework, it is important to revisit some of the foundational concepts established in Brazil's National Environmental Policy Act (*Política Nacional do Meio Ambiente*, Lei 6.938/1981) and the National Policy on Climate Change (*Política Nacional sobre Mudança do Clima*, Lei 12.187/2009), as well as the text of the United Nations Framework Convention on Climate Change (UNFCCC).[36]

Since the enactment of the National Environmental Policy Act in 1981, the concept of the environment has been understood to include the set of biotic and abiotic elements, as well as the dynamic and complex interactions among them that make life possible.[37] This broad and systemic definition inherently encompasses elements that would later be scientifically identified as components of the climate system.[38]

In addition to the concept of the environment, the law also provides a broad definition of pollution, which includes the degradation of environmental quality[39] and embraces not only ecological factors but also social, economic, and cultural aspects. This definition covers any direct or indirect adverse alteration of the environmental characteristics, thereby reinforcing the integrative and holistic approach adopted by Brazilian environmental law.[40]

GHG emissions can thus be classified as a form of pollution, insofar as the environmental degradation resulting from these emissions adversely affects biotic elements, endangers human health and quality of life, and creates harmful conditions for social and economic activities. Examples include the increased frequency and intensity of extreme weather events, the proliferation of diseases, biodiversity loss, and declines in agricultural productivity. These impacts directly jeopardise the integrity of the environment and its constituent elements, particularly when the atmosphere's natural absorption capacity is exceeded.[41]

It is for this reason that Lei 12.187/2009 affirms that everyone has a duty to act, for the benefit of present and future generations, to reduce the impacts of anthropogenic interference on the climate system.[42] These impacts have already produced and continue to produce significant adverse effects over the course of decades. Such effects now exceed the natural adaptive

[34] *Súmula* (precedent) 629 of the STJ: 'With regard to environmental damage, it is permissible to sentence the defendant to an obligation to do or not to do combined with an obligation to compensate' STJ 'Súmula 629' (Dje 17/12/2018). See also Jurisprudência em Teses 30 (n 16) 1: 'The simultaneous and cumulative condemnation of the obligations to do, not to do and to indemnify in the integral reparation of the environment is admitted' (author's translation).

[35] Moreira, 'A Panorama of Climate Litigation in Brazil' (n 8) 63–64.

[36] The UNFCCC, signed in New York on May 9, 1992, was enacted in Brazil by Decreto 2.652/1998.

[37] Lei 6.938/1981, art 3, I.

[38] The climate system is defined by the UNFCCC as the 'totality of the atmosphere, hydrosphere, biosphere and geosphere and their interactions' (art 1, 3 of the Anexo ao Decreto 2.652/1998, which promulgates the UNFCCC in Brazil (author's translation).

[39] Degradation of environmental quality consists of any type of adverse alteration in the characteristics of the ecologically balanced environment (Lei 6.938/1981, art 3, II).

[40] According to Lei 6.938/1981, art 3, III, pollution is the degradation of environmental quality resulting from activities that directly or indirectly harm the health, safety and well-being of the population; create adverse conditions for social and economic activities; adversely affect biota; affect the aesthetic or sanitary conditions of the environment; and release materials or energy in disagreement with established environmental standards.

[41] Danielle de Andrade Moreira, *Litigância climática no Brasil: Argumentos jurídicos para inserção da variável climática no licenciamento ambiental* (Editora PUC-Rio 2021) 23, 37.

[42] Lei 12.187/2009, art 3.

capacity of the climate system to absorb the cumulative load of GHG emissions giving rise to what can be legally and scientifically characterised as climate damage.[43]

In fact, the best available science attests categorically that anthropogenic GHG emissions have caused a rise in the planet's average temperature, with devastating consequences that are already being witnessed and are, alarmingly, expected to worsen. Current scientific research leaves no room for doubt: Humanity, primarily through GHG emissions over the past two centuries, is responsible for disrupting the Earth's regular functioning climate system.[44] Although the climate system is naturally resilient, the rapid and unprecedented increase in atmospheric GHG concentrations and the corresponding spike in global average temperatures within a relatively short period has undermined its stability. This disruption poses a serious risk to the survival of innumerable species of fauna and flora, and at the very least, to the continuity of society as we know it.

Climate damage should therefore be understood as a dimension of environmental damage, characterised by both: (1) the intolerable negative impact on the functioning of the climate system caused by anthropogenic GHG emissions (direct climate damage); and (2) the adverse repercussions resulting from disruptions to the climate system (indirect climate damage, or so-called loss and damage associated with climate change).[45]

According to Annelise Steigleder, climate damage can be divided into "damage to the climate itself", resulting from the emission of GHGs, and "damage resulting from climate change". These categories are, in her view, "intertwined, since damage to the climate produces global warming, which in turn alters climatic conditions, triggering a succession of new negative impacts that are clearly perceptible and harmful to legally protected interests".[46]

In other words, direct climate damage refers to harm inflicted upon the climate system as a *macrobem*. This type of damage manifests continuously and possesses a cumulative and synergistic nature, as it is exacerbated by ongoing GHG emissions. Given the recognition of the climate system as a *macrobem*—that is, an autonomous and indivisible legal interest—its violation or threat of violation does not depend on injury suffered by a specific individual or identifiable social group.[47] In legal terms, it constitutes *dano difuso* (diffuse harm).[48]

[43] 'For the purposes of this law, the following definitions shall apply: . . . II - adverse effects of climate change: changes in the physical environment or biota resulting from climate change that have significant deleterious effects on the composition, resilience or productivity of natural and managed ecosystems, on the functioning of socio-economic systems or on human health and well-being'. ibid art 2.

[44] 'Intergovernmental Panel on Climate Change (IPCC), Climate Change 2023: Synthesis Report. Contribution of Working Groups I, II and III to the Sixth Assessment Report of the Intergovernmental Panel on Climate Change [Core Writing Team, H Lee and J Romero (Eds.)]. IPCC, Geneva, Switzerland.' (Intergovernmental Panel on Climate Change 2023) 42 <https://doi.org/10.59327/IPCC/AR6-9789291691647>.

[45] Danielle de Andrade Moreira, Victória Lourenço de Carvalho e Gonçalves and Maria Eduarda Segovia Barbosa Neves, 'Aspectos Conceituais e Práticos da Responsabilização Civil por Dano Ambiental-climático no Brasil' (2024) 29 Revista de Direito Ambiental: RDA 341, 351–52.

[46] Annelise Monteiro Steigleder, 'A Imputação da Responsabilidade Civil por Danos Ambientais Associados às Mudanças Climáticas' in Paula Lavratti and Vanêsca Buzelato Prestes (eds), *Responsabilidade Civil e Mudanças Climáticas* (Instituto O Direito por um Planeta Verde 2010) 23.

[47] In the words of Rafaela da Rosa: 'Climate damage, therefore, as damage directly suffered by the macro-good [*macrobem*] climate system, is not a divisible damage because the legal good [legal public interest] is not a fraction or part of the environment. The climate system cannot be fragmented into species of fauna and flora, for example. The climate system is not just the atmosphere, the oceans, or the cryosphere. The climate system is a factual totality, already regulated as a totality, and its violation or threat of violation should be legally respected and translated in this totality condition'. Rafaela Santos Martins da Rosa, *Climate Damage: Concept and Accountability. Insights from a Brazilian Federal Judge.* (2nd edn, Tirant Lo Blanch Brasil 2024) 272.

[48] As Rafaela da Rosa explains: 'Climate damage is inherently diffuse and extends beyond the verifiable damage to the natural elements and components of the system. It is not just damage to the

It is sufficient to observe that the adverse effects of human interference with climate stability wear away the resilience of the system as a whole, and—indirectly and reflexively—may also impair the ability of humanity and other living beings to adapt to the new conditions resulting from such instability. Thus, even if it is possible, to a reasonable extent, to individualise the contributions of a particular polluting source, direct climate damage arises from the global sum of individual emissions that when aggregated alter the functioning of the climate system.[49]

Indirect climate damage, in turn, refers to the harmful impacts resulting from ongoing direct climate damage. Anthropogenic climate change gives rise to a wide range of environmental, social, and economic consequences, including rising sea levels; the melting of glaciers; ocean acidification; losses in food production due to heatwaves or disproportionately intense rainfall; expanded geographical reach, seasonality, and intensity of disease transmission; an increase in the frequency, intensity, and magnitude of extreme weather events; and biodiversity loss. These consequences, although indirectly linked to anthropogenic climate change in terms of causation, result in both individual and collective harm, including pecuniary and non-pecuniary losses. They exemplify how direct disruptions to the climate system can generate tangible, cascading effects on ecosystems, human health, livelihoods, and the enjoyment of fundamental rights.[50]

In cases of indirect climate damage, there is a violation of the rights of individuals and social groups to life, health, physical integrity, private property, and others rights, as they are harmed by the adverse effects of global warming and climate system destabilisation.[51] Beyond the duty to compensate for such harms, these negative effects can—and indeed should—be prevented or minimised through mitigation measures (aimed at reducing GHG emissions) and adaptation strategies (focused on protecting communities, ecosystems, and biomes from the consequences of climate change).

Notably, the Brazilian legal system already acknowledges the extent and severity of the consequences of anthropogenic GHG emissions by defining the adverse effects of climate change as "changes in the physical environment or biota resulting from climate change that have significant deleterious effects on the composition, resilience, or productivity of natural and managed ecosystems, on the functioning of socio-economic systems, or on human health and well-being".[52] It also stipulates that any measures adopted under the climate policy must be calibrated to the socio-economic context in which they are applied, ensuring that the burdens and costs of implementation are shared equitably among economic sectors, populations and communities.

A forward-looking approach is also essential to ensure preventive measures are adopted to avoid or mitigate future climate damage resulting from the cumulative effect of GHG emissions. This entails the adoption of present-day actions with future-oriented

atmosphere, the oceans, to one or other particular natural resource (fauna, flora). It is damage to the functionality of the system that is compatible with human habitability, both current and future'. ibid 364.

49 ibid 268, 273.

50 ibid 300–01.

51 ibid 391.

52 Lei 12.187/2009 (n 42), art 2, II.

objectives—specifically, actions capable of reducing GHG emissions to prevent the continuation and intensification of climate damage, which may otherwise reach a point of irreversible harm.[53]

The traits of climate-related damage demand the application of the special liability regime already developed for environmental damage. Unlike conventional doctrines, this regime is better suited to address the diffuse, gradual, and often future-oriented manifestations of climate-related harm, whose consequences can occur far from the location and time of the original polluting conduct.

Given the global and indivisible nature of the climate system, the damage to it results from the aggregated contributions of countless sources, which makes individualised attribution and accountability inherently difficult. While recent advances in attribution science offer tools to trace the specific contribution of emitters, the causal link remains complex, especially when emissions occurred in compliance with existing regulations. In this context of causal dispersion, where multiple sources act simultaneously or successively, establishing individualised liability becomes a particularly challenging task.[54]

Because climate damage constitutes one facet of the broader category of environmental harm[55]—a concept already well-established in Brazilian case law—it is appropriate to refer to this phenomenon as climate-environmental damage.[56] Although subsumed under environmental harm, climate damage presents particular issues that call for tailored legal responses. The following section analyses how civil liability actions involving climate-environmental damage have, so far, reached Brazilian courts, charting the profile of these cases and the main emerging trends.

4. Climate-Environmental Damage in Brazilian Climate Litigation

Brazil currently holds the highest number of reported climate cases in the Global South and ranks second globally, behind only the US.[57] As of January 2026, the Brazilian Climate Litigation Platform had registered 352 cases.[58] The number of climate lawsuits filed before the

[53] Rafaela da Rosa (n 47), 262, 391.

[54] Cláudia Lima Marques and Annelise Monteiro Steigleder, 'A Aplicação da Pollution Share Liability no Direito Brasileiro: Reflexões a Partir das Contribuições de Antonio Herman de Vasconcellos e Benjamin Para a Responsabilidade Civil Ambiental' (2010) 25 Revista de Direito Ambiental: RDA 27.

[55] Álvaro Luiz Valery Mirra, 'A Dimensão Climática do Dano Ambiental: Condições de Reparabilidade do Dano e Aspectos do Nexo Causal' in Alexandre Burmann, Annelise Steigleder, and Gabriel Wedy (eds), *Litigância Climática na Visão da Academia, Advocacia, Judiciário e do Ministério Público* (Thoth 2026) 518–520; Ana Maria de Oliveira Nusdeo, 'Nota técnica sobre o art. 14 da Resolução CNJ 433/2021' (2024) 29 Revista de Direito Ambiental: RDA 419, 419–22.

[56] Moreira et al (n 45) 351–52.

[57] Data as of 30 January 2026 were drawn from 'Plataforma de Litigância Climática no Brasil' <https://www.juma.jur.puc-rio.br/base-dados-litigancia-climatica-no-brasil> accessed 30 January 2026, and 'Climate Change Litigation Databases' <https://climatecasechart.com/> accessed 30 January 2026.

[58] Although the concept of climate litigation may embrace a wider spectrum of disputes, for the purposes of building the Brazilian Climate Litigation Platform and related studies in the country, we define climate litigation as lawsuits directly related to climate change. This includes two categories: (1) cases where climate change constitutes a main issue, or (2) cases where climate change is mentioned but serves only as contextual background rather than a central discussion point. For a better understanding of the methodology regarding selection criteria and classification of cases, see Danielle de Andrade Moreira and others, *Plataforma de litigância climática no Brasil: Metodologia para Seleção e Categorização de Casos Climáticos Brasileiros* (Lucas Melara & Companhia 2022) 4.

Brazilian judiciary has increased significantly, particularly since 2019.[59] Although Brazilian climate litigation presents a plural and diverse profile—involving a variety of objectives, biomes, and GHG emission sectors—a significant and growing number of these cases, especially among routine ones,[60] include at least one measure addressing the reparation of climate-environmental damage. This trend indicates not only the expansion of climate litigation in quantitative terms, but also the increasing centrality of damage-based claims within the broader climate legal landscape in Brazil.[61]

Of the 352 cases registered on the Platform, 254 involve claims related to civil liability for climate damage. In these cases, the link between environmental harm and climate change is articulated to varying degrees. While the majority—236 cases—explicitly develop the argument of climate damage,[62] which needs to be specifically measured and addressed, there are others in which the climate dimension of environmental harm is not explored in detail, even though the alleged damage is demonstrably linked to GHG emissions and climate change.[63]

Deforestation in the Amazon region is by far the most frequently challenged activity within the 236 Brazilian climate lawsuits that explicitly develop the argument of climate damage, and specifically seek its valuation and reparation, in addition to compensation for other aspects of the environmental harm at issue. The prevalence of damage-based litigation in land-use change and forestry closely mirrors Brazil's overall emissions profile.[64] Only one of these cases

[59] See Danielle de Andrade Moreira and others, *Panorama da Litigância Climática no Brasil: Relatório de 2025* ((Law, Environment and Justice in the Anthropocene Research Group (JUMA/PUC-Rio) 2025) 17–18 <https://juma.jur.puc-rio.br/publicacao/panorama-da-litigancia-climatica-no-brasil-relatorio-de-2025-11-2025> accessed 30 July 2025; and Danielle de Andrade Moreira and others, *Brazilian Climate Litigation Bulletin 2024* (Law, Environment and Justice in the Anthropocene Research Group (JUMA/PUC-Rio) 2024) 5 <https://juma.jur.puc-rio.br/pesquisas-litigancia-climatica> accessed 1 July 2025.

[60] 'Systemic cases are classified as those that involve more complex and broader discussions, such that an occasional judicial decision has the potential to have an impact on the functioning of a system or microsystem . . . such as public policies or the production and consumption chains of a large company with GHG emissions.' On the other hand, 'routine cases challenge specific acts or enterprises in court and usually have direct impacts restricted to the particular case in question. These legal actions are more routine litigation models and provide strategies and arguments that can be replicated in other cases . . . While systemic cases are characterised by efforts to contain environmental and climate setbacks, diverse themes appear in routine actions'. Danielle de Andrade Moreira and others, *Climate Litigation in Brazil: 2024 Report* (Law, Environment and Justice in the Anthropocene Research Group (JUMA/PUC-Rio) 2024) 41–44 <https://juma.jur.puc-rio.br/pesquisas-litigancia-climatica> accessed 1 July 2025.

[61] According to the classifications adopted by the Brazilian Climate Litigation Platform, different measures can be demanded in lawsuits, including civil liability for climate damage. The other measures that can be identified are mitigation, adaptation and climate risk assessment. On this topic, see Moreira et al, *Brazilian Climate Litigation Bulletin 2024* and *Panorama da Litigância Climática no Brasil: Relatório de 2025* (n 59).

[62] Among these is a batch of 195 Public Civil Actions, filed between November and December 2024 by the Federal Public Prosecutor's Office (MPF) as part of the fourth phase of 'Amazônia Protege', an MPF initiative aimed at securing reparation for environmental damage caused by deforestation in the Amazon.

[63] In other words, there are a group of these lawsuits that although 'based on questioning GHG emissions, when they pursue reparations for associated harm, they often reference environmental damage in general terms without constructing a detailed argument to distinguish its specific climate dimension (climate damage)'. Moreira, 'A Panorama of Climate Litigation in Brazil' (n 8) 64.

[64] According to the System for Estimating Greenhouse Gas Emissions and Removals (*Sistema de Estimativas de Emissões e Remoções de Gases de Efeito Estufa*, SEEG), in 2023: 'Land-use change once again produced the largest share of Brazil's gross greenhouse-gas emissions, accounting for 46 per cent, or 1.062 billion tonnes of CO_2-equivalent. It was followed by agriculture, at 631 $MtCO_2e$ (28 per cent); energy, at 420 $MtCO_2e$ (18 per cent); waste, at 92 $MtCO_2e$ (4 per cent); and industrial processes,

contests the environmental licensing of a thermoelectric coal plant and seeks compensation for the GHG emissions left unaddressed in that licensing process.[65]

Geographically, proceedings are heavily concentrated in the Amazon region and are primarily brought by the Federal Public Prosecution Office (MPF)[66] and the federal environmental agency (*Instituto Brasileiro do Meio Ambiente e dos Recursos Naturais Renováveis*—IBAMA).[67] The lawsuits target both the deforesters themselves—direct polluters—and the actors further along the deforestation chain who play an indirect role in the harmful activity (e.g., depositing timber without an environmental licence) indirect polluters.[68] In each instance, the claim encompasses the full range of environmental impacts generated by a single polluting operation, including harm to the climate system, and demands comprehensive reparation.

Although the degree to which each claim draws on traditional principles of environmental civil liability depends on its particular facts, all 236 cases are nonetheless anchored in strict liability. Every case also draws on at least one further pillar of Brazil's liability framework—for example, the expansive definition of "polluter" (encompassing both direct and indirect polluters), joint and several liability, and recognition of the multilayered nature of environmental harm. Each lawsuit affirms the duty of *in integrum* reparation (full reparation), demanding remedies that reach beyond the in-kind restoration typically ordered in deforestation cases. Accordingly, plaintiffs may seek intermediary or *danos interinos* (intermediary or temporary losses), compensation for residual harm, collective moral damages, and, in some instances, disgorgement of unlawful gains. Valuing climate-environmental damage, however, remains one of the most difficult tasks in current Brazilian damage-based climate litigation as plaintiffs adopt varied methodologies to quantify the climate dimension of environmental harm.[69]

The set of Brazilian cases seeking compensation for climate-environmental damage, which advance distinct valuation methodologies, has yet to receive a final judicial determination. Indeed, so far, the few decisions that address this issue are first-instance judgments, the vast majority of them remaining subject to further appeals, and diverge on whether distinct climate-damage awards are appropriate. In each, the evidentiary record proves pivotal in confirming the scale of injury and the proportionality of any monetary remedy. Some judgments

at 91 $MtCO_2e$ (also 4 per cent)' (author's translation). David Tsai and others, 'Análise Das Emissões de Gases de Efeito Estufa e Suas Implicações Para as Metas Climáticas Do Brasil 1970–2023' (SEEG 2024) 4 (author's translation).

65 See *Instituto Arayara v Copel, Instituto Água e Terra e outros* (UTE Figueira), ACP 5015788-26.2024.4.04.7001/PR, TJDFT. Information about the above-mentioned case law is available at '*Plataforma de Litigância Climática no Brasil*' <https://litigancia.biobd.inf.puc-rio.br/visualizacao_caso/601/0/> accessed 15 July 2025.

66 Under art. 127–130 of the Brazilian Constitution, the Public Prosecutor's Office (Ministério Público) is established as a permanent institution, indispensable to the State's judicial function and entrusted with the defence of the legal order, the democratic regime and social and individual interests that are inalienable, as well as vested with the authority to initiate public civil actions, including those for the protection of the environment.

67 In lawsuits brought by IBAMA, the federal agency is represented by the Attorney General's Office, which uses the agency's administrative violation records as the basis for pursuing civil damages for environmental harm.

68 Data as of 30 January 2026 were drawn from *Plataforma de Litigância Climática no Brasil* < https://litigancia.biobd.inf.puc-rio.br/visualizacao_caso/601/0/> accessed 1 July 2025.

69 See Danielle de Andrade Moreira, Fernanda Leite Barbosa and Victória Lourenço de Carvalho e Gonçalves, 'Valoração da Dimensão Climática do Dano Ambiental no Brasil' (2024) 29 Revista de Direito Ambiental: RDA 407.

(in nineteen cases) have recognised the existence of climate damage (direct climate damage)[70] and awarded compensation in line with the valuation methodology put forward in each case. In others (4 cases), however, the courts have held that the quantification of climate damage lacks consensus and objective benchmarks, since scientific uncertainties, the absence of case law, statutory or doctrinal guidance, and the dearth of technical studies preclude the setting of a definitive monetary figure.[71]

To address the difficulties and methodological complexities involved in valuing environmental damage, among other purposes, the National Council of Justice (*Conselho Nacional de Justiça*—CNJ) adopted Resolution 433/2021, whose Article 14 instructs courts to consider three further factors when quantifying such harm: the contribution to global climate change, the diffuse losses suffered by affected communities, and the deterrent required to internalise externalities. To operationalise these directives, the CNJ adopted, in October 2024, a Protocol for Judging Environmental Lawsuits, offering concrete parameters for appraising climate impacts in cases involving harm to flora, especially deforestation and forest fires.[72] The recent adoption of parameters for quantifying climate-environmental damage is expected to guide judicial practice and help litigants frame claims more effectively.

Finally, it is noteworthy that nearly all the 254 cases asserting civil liability for climate damage—whether or not they articulate the argument of climate damage in depth—centre on direct climate harm, seeking to hold defendants responsible for harm resulting from increased concentrations of GHGs in the atmosphere and the consequent destabilisation of the climate system. Only one case examines adverse effects that go beyond harm to the environment and the climate system as *macrobens* (autonomous collective legal interests), thereby engaging the category of indirect climate damage—that is, loss and damage associated with climate change. This case involves a *litígio estrutural* (structural litigation)[73] brought by the Federal Public Prosecutor's Office against the Federal Government, the State of Rio Grande do Sul, and nine municipalities in response to climate-related events that occurred between September and

[70] Several of these favourable judgments rely on the following findings: 'In the present case, the damage arose from deforestation and forest degradation, which constitute the direct and identifiable cause of the unlawful removal of carbon stocks and sinks, as well as of illegitimate greenhouse-gas emissions that add to other emissions, thereby contributing effectively and directly to an abnormal and deleterious interference with the climate system' (author's translation). *Ministério Público Federal e INCRA v Joel de Souza (Desmatamento e dano climático no PAE Antimary) Justiça Federal da 1a Região 7ª Vara Federal Ambiental e Agrária da* SJAMP ACP 1022425-07.2021.4.01.3200. Sentença (judgment) 6–7. Information about the above-mentioned case law is available at '*Plataforma de Litigância Climática no Brasil*' <https://litigancia.biobd.inf.puc-rio.br/visualizacao_caso/530/0/> accessed 15 July 2025.

[71] In four cases the judgments partially granted the claim but rejected the climate-damage request. In one case the judgment left it unaddressed, and in other six cases the judgments dismissed the action without adjudication on the merits.

[72] Conselho Nacional de Justiça (Brasil). 'Protocolo para Julgamento das Ações Ambientais: Parâmetros para Mensuração do Impacto do Dano na Mudança Global do Clima (Art. 14 da Res. CNJ 433/2021) Diretrizes para ações judiciais sobre danos à flora: desmatamento e incêndio florestal. Segundo Escopo' <https://atos.cnj.jus.br/files/compilado1920182024100967o6d7724dee1.pdf> accessed 12 June 2025.

[73] The case is considered a *processo estrutural* (structural litigation) because it seeks formal recognition of governmental omission and inefficiency in the disasters that have occurred, together with structural measures to improve coordination among federal, state, and municipal authorities in implementing public policies on climate adaptation, disaster preparedness, risk management, and emergency response.

November 2023 and again between April and May 2024.[74] Although the complaint does not explicitly develop the concept of climate damage, it emphasises the foreseeability of the events and the role of human action in exacerbating the disaster. Based on these elements, the plaintiffs argued for the civil liability of the *Poder Público* (State) and rejected the applicability of exclusions based on causality. Nevertheless, it remains an isolated case and does not substantiate indirect climate damage or expressly seek compensation for it.[75]

Therefore, Brazilian climate litigation has not yet incorporated broader discussions concerning compensation for losses related to or resulting from the intensification of climate change. This includes, for example, damages associated with the increased frequency and severity of extreme weather events, as well as reduced agricultural productivity due to elevated temperatures.

It is nonetheless expected that actions of this nature—seeking redress for indirect climate-related harm (commonly referred to as climate damage, loss and damage claims, or climate liability litigation)[76]—is likely to be brought before Brazilian courts, in line with developments already taking place internationally. To date, more than fifty of such cases have been filed, predominantly in the United States, but with notable claims also initiated by Global South litigants before European courts.[77]

Among these cases, *Lliuya v RWE*[78] stands out. Recently adjudicated by the Higher Regional Court of Hamm, in Germany, the case brought to an end a legal dispute that had spanned ten years. Although the claimant's request was ultimately dismissed, the final decision nonetheless represents a significant milestone.

In summary, the German court concluded that there was insufficient concrete evidence to demonstrate that the risk of harm alleged by the claimant was sufficiently serious and imminent to warrant imposing upon the defendant a legal duty to prevent or mitigate it. Nevertheless, the court recognised that the defendant had made a contribution—specifically 0.38%—to the total stock of GHGs currently present in the atmosphere; and this contribution is, in principle, capable of giving rise to liability for the mitigation or remediation of concrete harm, proportionate to the defendant's share. Crucially, the court rejected a number of key defences advanced by the defendant, including that: (1) its emissions were lawful, duly

[74] *Ministério Público Federal e ANAB v União e outros* (Litígio estrutural sobre desastre climático no RS). Tribunal Regional Federal ACP 5001898-69.2024.4.04.7114. Information about the above-mentioned case law is available at '*Plataforma de Litigância Climática no Brasil*'<https://litigancia.biobd.inf.puc-rio.br/visualizacao_caso/580/0/> accessed 12 June 2025.

[75] Because this is a form of structural litigation, its primary aim is to compel the effective management of extreme climate events through coordinated action across sectoral policies and all tiers of government, federal, state, and municipal, so as to prevent further disasters and restore the affected areas. Accordingly, the claim calls for a restructuring plan together with a standing monitoring committee, comprising representatives of civil-society groups and the relevant government bodies.

[76] See the analysis on the polluter-pays cases in Joana Setzer and Catherine Higham, 'Global Trends in Climate Change Litigation: 2025 Snapshot' (Grantham Research Institute on Climate Change and the Environment, London School of Economics and Political Science 2025) <https://www.lse.ac.uk/granthaminstitute/wp-content/uploads/2025/06/Global-Trends-in-Climate-Change-Litigation_2025-Snapshot.pdf> accessed 1 July 2025. On the so-called loss and damage litigation, see Olivia Otilia Nemeth and Jacob Metz-Lerman, 'Report: Loss and Damage Litigation Against Carbon Majors - CLX - Climate Law Accelerator Toolkit' (TERRA Program at NYU Law, Climate Law Accelerator NYU School of Law 2025) <https://clxtoolkit.com/publications/report-loss-and-damage-litigation-against-carbon-majors/> accessed 13 June 2025.

[77] Otilia Nemeth and Metz-Lerman (n 77) 4–5.

[78] *Lliuya v RWE AG* (2018) Case No 5 U 15/17 (OLG Hamm).

licensed, and resulted from the generation of electricity, an activity undertaken in the public interest; (2) it would be neither lawful nor reasonable to hold a single emitter—responsible for less than 0.5% of total global emissions—liable for harm resulting from the cumulative impact of innumerable emitters and multiple contributing factors, both anthropogenic and natural; and (3) it would be legally unsustainable to impose liability for emissions lawfully produced in Germany over several decades in relation to consequences allegedly materialising in a distant country, such as Peru, given both the geographical and temporal remoteness between the emissions and their claimed effects. The court dismissed these arguments and held that: (1) the defendant's contribution amounted to adequate causation, since—as the largest energy company in Germany and described by the court as an "optimal observer"—the defendant could, and indeed should, have recognised as early as the mid-1960s that anthropogenic greenhouse gas emissions would drive global warming and its associated consequences;[79] and (2) insofar as the defendant's emissions contributed to climate change—even if amounting to less than 0.5% of the total—the defendant might be held liable for the proven consequences arising from that contribution, proportionate to its share.[80]

Climate litigation, both in its theoretical underpinnings and practical applications, has made significant strides globally and in Brazil. At least in principle, the ruling of the German court would not be incompatible with the Brazilian legal system, which is grounded in the polluter-pays principle, strict liability, the duty to prevent, mitigate or compensate for environmental harm, and the requirement of full reparation for environmental damage.

5. Conclusion

The challenge is both singular in its peculiarities and global in scale. The existence and aggravation of climate-environmental damage, with dramatic ecological and socio-economic repercussions, are expanding in scope and severity, marked by daunting levels of complexity.

Examining civil liability through the lens of these contemporary challenges, most notably the climate-related damages, exposes the need for a renewed normative and conceptual reading of the regime within Brazilian law. The classical tort framework, conceived to address individual, patrimonial losses based on direct causation and measurable by relatively simple methods, falls short when confronted with damage that is diffuse, cumulative and synergistic, and whose relationship with time and space is inherently non-linear.

However, decades of Brazilian environmental law, shaped by both doctrine and case law, have generated a robust body of principles capable of invigorating climate litigation. The country's tort-liability regime for environmental harm, refined through sustained scholarly debate and judicial practice, now offers a mature legal architecture and well-tested pathways for redressing climate-environmental damage attributable to private actors and the State alike.

This evolution is borne out empirically. Brazilian climate litigation proceeds on the premise that climate harm constitutes a facet of environmental harm—hence the use of the expression climate-environmental damage—and most claims rest on doctrinal tenets already tested and accepted by the courts. The remaining hurdles, particularly the quantification of climate impacts and establishing causation in indirect-damage cases, are only beginning to be addressed and must still be confronted decisively by Brazil's courts.

[79] *Lliuya v RWE AG* (n 75) Verdict 49. The unofficial translation of the verdict is available at <https://rwe.climatecase.org/en/legal#legaldocs> accessed 15 June 2025.

[80] ibid 6, 27, 47, 49–53, 61.

Looking ahead, the convergence of Brazil's mature environmental liability framework with its evolving procedural protocol for measuring the climate dimension of environmental damage offers a genuine pathway to meaningfully addressing at least direct climate damage. Overcoming the remaining obstacles will require doctrinal clarity on indirect harms, methodological consensus on damage valuation and strengthened technical capacity in the courts. If litigants marshal robust scientific evidence, Brazil's existing legal toolkit can not only hold polluters to account, but also catalyse the preventive, adaptive, and restorative measures essential to fulfilling both the country's Paris Agreement obligations and domestic climate commitments.

Finally, one might reasonably ask why, despite its extensive legal arsenal for tackling environmental harms, including their climate dimension, Brazil still shows such discouraging results in effectively holding polluters to account and, consequently, in securing tangible advances in prevention and remediation. What explains the gap between law on the books and law in action? The principal cause appears to lie in the endemic slowness of Brazil's judicial system, a challenge faced by many other jurisdictions, whose effects are magnified in cases of high complexity, such as those involving climate-environmental issues. Protracted proceedings are compounded by significant hurdles to enforcing judgments—a topic that lies beyond the scope of this chapter. Even so, the doctrinal and case law trends surveyed here suggest a more promising outlook: Brazil's superior courts, guided by the polluter-pays principle and informed by robust attribution science, are increasingly willing to impose liability on polluters for climate-environmental damage.

PART VI

Emerging Issues

CHAPTER 42

Legal Education

CANDIDA LEONE

1. Introduction

OVER the past decade or so, the relationship between climate change and legal education has received (at least for a while) growing attention in educational practice as well as in the literature.[1] Reflection in both corners has focussed on both legal (doctrinal and theoretical) contents and pedagogical/educational tools. Furthermore, scholars have drawn attention to the relationship between law schools and the legal professions, whose role as enablers of large polluters—and more recently of strategic litigation—is of course a subject of independent (but not unrelated) discussion.[2] In this chapter, I do not wish to retrace all these discussions, but to advance one more specific argument: Namely, that to meet its responsibility in facing the climate crisis, legal education should, in any event, *decouple* from perpetuating the idea of necessary (especially economic) growth.

The analysis, and related argument, take place in three broad steps: First, outlining the plausible responsibility of law schools to avoid naturalising growth (Section 2); second, indicating how to look for entanglements to be undone in the curriculum (Sections 3–5); lastly, reflecting on what the premises laid in the analysis mean for the institutional outlook of (at least some) law schools (Section 6). A final section concludes the chapter.

[1] See for the first, e.g., Irish Rule of Law International, 'Climate Change & Sustainability: Why Legal Education in IRL Needs an Overhaul' (*Irish Rule of Law International*, 1 November 2021) <https://www.irishruleoflaw.ie/climate-change-sustainability-why-legal-education-in-irl-needs-an-overhaul> accessed 27 June 2025; see The Society of Legal Scholars, 'The Law School adn the Climate Crisis' (*The Society of Legal Scholars*) <https://www.legalscholars.ac.uk/the-law-school-and-the-climate-crisis/ > accessed 15 July 2025. As for literature, to quote only some particularly prominent English-language contributions, see John C Dernbach, 'The Essential and Growing Role of Legal Education in Achieving Sustainability' (2010) 60 Journal of Legal Education 489; Margaret A Young, 'Climate Change and Law: A Global Challenge for Legal Education' (2021) 40 University of Queensland Law Journal 351. For reflections on concrete interventions, see Kim Bouwer and others, '"Climate Change Isn't Optional": Climate Change in the Core Law Curriculum' [2022] Legal Studies 1; David Mohan Ong, 'Prospects for Integrating an Environmental Sustainability Perspective within the University Law Curriculum in England' (2016) 50 The Law Teacher 276. The author of this chapter has also previously written on the subject of sustainable legal education, see Candida Leone, 'Who's Afraid of Sustainability? A Primer for Mainstreaming Sustainability in Private Law Education' in Marta Santos Silva and others (eds.), *Routledge Handbook of Private Law and Sustainability* (Routledge 2024); Candida Leone, 'A Private Law Theory for Sustainable Legal Education?' (2022) 23 German Law Journal 881.

[2] See Camila Bustos, Chapter 43 in this handbook.

2. From "Sustainability" or "Climate Conscious" Legal Education to "Growth Agnostic" Education

In the context of the current environmental and climate crisis, it has been argued that legal education has an important responsibility in raising a new generation of much more "climate conscious" lawyers.[3] It has been claimed in this respect that "we are all climate lawyers",[4] meaning environmental concerns should not be limited to niches but integrated into *all* areas of legal education.[5] There are by now, of course, a variety of dedicated master's programmes, specialisations, and, in countries that offer law degrees at both the graduate and undergraduate level, dedicated modules within specific masters all aiming to equip students with sustainability-related knowledge and competences beyond the occasional environmental and climate law course. As with general discussions on sustainability policy, interventions incorporating sustainability into law curricula tend to be agnostic on the controversies around the term, particularly on the debate that is commonly summarised as "strong" versus "weak" sustainability. In the sections that follow, this lack of engagement is problematised.

2.1 Strong and Weak Sustainability, Green Growth, and Post-Growth

On the tail of the 2015 United Nations Sustainable Development Goals (SDGs), climate and planet consciousness often fall under the notion of sustainability. I understand this move—from climate change to sustainability—as an attempt, in practical more than theoretical terms, to move from a rough fact to a normative standard, or more commonly, policy goal (or set of policy goals). It reflects a concern with the unsustainability of current human socio-techno-economic arrangements without committing to any specific solution. Sustainability, however, is a contested notion, including in the context of the SDGs. Broadly speaking, "weak" notions of sustainability claim that it is possible to decouple questions of economic growth and sustained prosperity from direct engagement with planetary boundaries,[6] whereas strong sustainability pleads for the non-substitutable nature of (finite) natural capital. Strong sustainability, as a consequence, implies abandoning growth as the overarching imperative, on the argument that it is impossible to envisage pathways to continued growth for affluent countries

[3] See for an extensive overview of calls from different corners Young (n 1). Also, Bouwer et al (n 1). In this volume, see Bustos (n 2).

[4] See American Society of International law, 'International Law and Climate Change: We Are All Climate Lawyers Now | ASIL' <https://www.asil.org/topics/signaturetopics/climate-change> accessed 21 July 2025.

[5] This is acknowledged also by those who focus on climate law as a distinct discipline, see, e.g., Michael Mehling and others, 'Teaching Climate Law: Trends, Methods and Outlook' (2020) 32 Journal of Environmental Law 417, 418–19.

[6] As synthesised by Pelenc, Ballet, and Dedeurwaerdare, weak sustainability 'assumes that natural capital and manufactured capital are essentially substitutable and considers that there are no essential differences between the kinds of well-being they generate'. See Jérôme Pelenc and Ballet, 'Weak Sustainability versus Strong Sustainability (pp. 1–4). Brief for GSDR 2015. United Nations (UN), 2005' <https://sustainabledevelopment.un.org/content/documents/6569122-Pelenc-Weak%20Sustainability%20versus%20Strong%20Sustainability.pdf>.

that are not both unsustainable and unjust towards, in any case, humans in less affluent parts of the world,[7] and in some versions towards non-human beings and future generations.

In this direction, a growing body of literature explores ideas of "prosperity without growth",[8] seeks to lay out the contours of "steady-state economies",[9] and discuss how affluent countries could walk a path of "sustainable degrowth".[10] This would allow less affluent countries to "develop", or, in any event, still grow their economies and provide safety to their citizens, while refraining from worsening the already grave pressures on Earth's ecosystems. "Degrowth" points to a "radical political and economic reorganization leading to drastically reduced resource and energy throughput".[11] Affluent economies should "abandon growth of gross domestic product (GDP) as a goal, scale down destructive and unnecessary forms of production to reduce energy and material use, and focus economic activity around securing human needs and well-being".[12] Even though jokes have been made that the Spring 2025 US administration tariff policy could, under some definition, be understood in line with degrowth, proponents of degrowth would highlight that degrowth requires planning and deliberate choices in a way that is incompatible with the chaotic deployment that has characterised the second Trump administration's early forays into renovating trade policy.

When I talk about growth here, I mean something both broader and more specific than profit, even though there is obvious proximity between the two concepts in a private law context. Political economist Gareth Dale speaks of the "growth paradigm" as the "idea that 'the economy' exists as an identifiable sphere of society, that it possesses an inherent tendency to grow, that its growth is imperative, continuous (even, essentially, limitless), and that growth is an acknowledged social goal and a fundamental social good—even indeed the principal remedy for a catalogue of social ills".[13] While the idea of private profit has obviously existed for a much longer time, he explains, only at the turn of the seventeenth century has this individual ambition been decoupled from negative connotations of greed and, in fact, endowed with positive characteristics first at individual and then at societal levels. Dale identifies the Puritan idea of improvement as the key nexus for this transition, which first glorified labour as a means of "gardening Eden"[14] on Earth (or, more specifically, in the Americas) and later allowed the abstraction of this virtue from the collective to the social level under the guise of "private vice, public virtue" reasoning.[15]

From these intellectual origins, which are important because they immediately show a connection to the way we think about core private law institutions, growth was gradually

[7] Joyeeta Gupta and others, 'A Just World on a Safe Planet: A Lancet Planetary Health–Earth Commission Report on Earth-System Boundaries, Translations, and Transformations' (2024) 8 The Lancet Planetary Health e813.

[8] Tim Jackson, 'Prosperity Without Growth' in Philip Lawn (ed), *Globalisation, Economic Transition and the Environment: Forging a Path to Sustainable Development* (Edward Elgar Publishing 2013) 105–28.

[9] Herman E Daly, *From Uneconomic Growth to a Steady-State Economy* (Edward Elgar Publishing 2014).

[10] Joan Martínez-Alier and others, 'Sustainable De-Growth: Mapping the Context, Criticisms and Future Prospects of an Emergent Paradigm' (2010) 69 Ecological Economics, 1741–47.

[11] Giorgos Kallis and others, 'Research on Degrowth' (2018) 43 Annual Review of Environment and Resources 291.

[12] Jason Hickel and others, 'Degrowth Can Work—Here's How Science Can Help' (2022) 612 Nature 400, 400.

[13] Gareth Dale, 'Seventeenth-Century Origins of the Growth Paradigm' in Iris Borowy and Matthias Schmelzer (eds), *History of the Future of Economic Growth* (Routledge 2017).

[14] ibid 35.

[15] ibid 45.

institutionalised to the point where we are today, where the model is both contested and absolutely dominant. A notable milestone in this respect is the establishment of the GNP (gross national product), later replaced by the GDP (gross domestic product),[16] which was formalised after the Second World War as a means of measuring economic activity for States. Among all the critiques of GDP that are known or less known to readers, one is worth mentioning here because of its tight connection to private law—namely, what we can label the "feminist" or care critique. This line of criticism observes how GDP devalues unpaid work, and in particular unpaid care (and in rather crude terms!), by considering the same work—such as caring for children or elderly persons—as productive or non-productive depending on whether it is done for wages or inside the household.[17]

2.2 The Responsibility to Decouple

Failure to address the tension between strong and weak sustainability conceptions is partially explained by the observation that most policy mixes will likely be positioned between the two ideal poles of this dichotomy. At the same time, not acknowledging the fundamentally different assumptions underlying the two paradigms means, ultimately, to avail a fallacy: Because we assume that societies are not willing to take the collective action that strong sustainability would require, we omit to engage with its theoretical and scientific premises regardless of whether they are more or less plausible than those underlying "weak" conceptions of sustainability. In doing so, however, we implicitly take sides with the theory that least challenges the status quo. This is problematic from a variety of perspectives. As shown by a recent large-scale expert survey, there is no clear consensus that green growth is possible on Earth.[18] Even more, the same study showed that a majority of experts in relevant fields such as Earth, planetary, biological, and agricultural sciences—and notably excluding economists, engineers, and materials scientists—believe that decoupling economic growth from excessive material degradation is not possible.[19] One of the factors that most strictly correlates with belief in green growth is the parallel belief that growth is necessary to achieve human well-being. In other words, the study suggests that experts are more likely to believe that green growth is possible when they believe that prosperity without growth is *not* possible, and thus that growth itself is an unquestioned good.[20]

Against the plausibility of the strong sustainability hypothesis, engaging with "sustainable education" while essentially avoiding discussion of the plausible unsustainability of the growth

[16] Jean-Baptiste Fressoz and Christophe Bonneuil, 'Growth Unlimited: The Idea of Infinite Growth from Fossil Capitalism to Green Capitalism' in Iris Borowy and Matthias Schmelzer (eds), *History of the Future of Economic Growth* (Routledge 2017) 58–59.

[17] Nancy Fraser, *Cannibal Capitalism: How Our System Is Devouring Democracy, Care, and the Planet and What We Can Do About It* (Verso Books 2023). Nancy Folbre, 'Measuring Care: Gender, Empowerment, and the Care Economy' (2006) 7 Journal of Human Development 183. See also Frances Flanagan, Chapter 26 of this handbook.

[18] Manuel Suter and others, 'Green Growth Beliefs: Investigating Factors Associated with Expert Opinions on Green Growth' (2025) 4 PLOS Climate e0000597.

[19] Interesting in this respect that geology is also the discipline credited with having once 'rescued' growth from the limits of the 'organic' (that is, mostly wood-based) economy, see Fressoz and Bonneuil (n 16) 54.

[20] Lawyers were not among the professional groups considered in the survey. However, Günter Frankenberg has long cautioned us against our lawyerly versions of motivated reasoning and 'belief in a just world'. Günter Frankenberg, 'Human Rights and the Belief in a Just World' (2014) 12 International Journal of Constitutional Law 35.

paradigm is problematic. First, it produces a disconnection that we would not accept in respect of other areas of science: We would not, in less systematically consequential domains, accept the naturalisation of other controversial hypotheses coming from non-legal disciplines. Second, by implicitly providing students with overly optimistic view of our climate future, it sets them up for likely disappointment, confusion, and feelings of betrayal to ensue rather soon. Third, it reinforces the very problem we as educators often complain about—that voters do not sufficiently appreciate climate urgency to make it central to their political choices.

For this chapter, I do not substantively engage with this controversy but rather take a different type of middle ground. Given the urgency of slowing down anthropogenic degradation of the climate and broader environment, and the role that "there is no alternative" ideas about economic growth play in slowing down climate action, I contend that law schools have a responsibility to achieve a degree of agnosticism not towards sustainability paradigms, but towards *growth*. This responsibility rests on law schools as higher education institutions but also, more specifically, in their function as trainers of the last generalists whose task is to translate scientific findings into actionable, somewhat coherent, and socially acceptable policies. That is both the academically integer route to take and one of the main things we, as educators, can do to achieve the "democratic shift" that is required to overcome the disconnect between what the global majority expects of governments and the electoral politics incentives that push governments not to act.[21]

Based on the assumption that a strong sustainability paradigm is at least as plausible as a weak one, and taking a shortcut that associates weak sustainability with so-called green growth paradigms, on the one hand, and strong sustainability with "degrowth", on the other, I put forward the following core question: How can legal education be made *truly* agnostic with respect to growth? Answering this question first requires understanding to what extent private law education is currently aligned with the growth paradigm to subsequently investigate, tentatively, what it could mean to break this relationship. I am, in this chapter, most interested in what happens within the *core* law curriculum, which is both a result of integration concerns[22] and a result of the chapter's starting hypothesis that law schools *structurally* entrench growth, with the contention that they should stop doing so. In this sense, climate-conscious specialisations offered against a growth-dominated core curriculum, while important, are liable to create cognitive dissonance among students other than those falling squarely within such programmes' target groups.[23] Such programmes may ultimately benefit institutional profiling more than their declared goals.

One could think that this is a non-starter as we teach law, not growth. At a very broad level, however, there is little doubt that the way we have come to think about law (legislation, interpretation, practice, etc.) is enmeshed with ideas of growth. Below, I give two examples—the European Commission's president's latest attempt to woo tech companies with a 28th system of private law and (of course!), and the discussions that started with the World Bank "Doing Business" report and legal origins theory. But what about law schools? Since there is no such

[21] United Nations Development Programme, 'Peoples' Climate Vote' (*Peoples' Climate Vote*, 2024) <https://peoplesclimate.vote> accessed 27 June 2025.

[22] Phillipa C McCormack and Michelle Lim, 'Future Lawyers, Future Laws: Reimagining Legal Education for Sustainability in a World "Governing Through Goals"' in Kim Beasy, Caroline Smith, and Jane Watson (eds), *Education and the UN Sustainable Development Goals*, vol 7 (Springer Nature Singapore 2023) <https://link.springer.com/10.1007/978-981-99-3802-5_7> accessed 15 June 2025.

[23] See for a similar argument in the context of sustainable consumption, Clemens Kaupa, 'Smoke Gets in Your Eyes: Misleading Fossil Fuel Advertisement in the Climate Crisis' (2021) 1 Journal of European Consumer and Market Law 21.

thing as one model of "private law education",[24] I cannot give a reliable account of the sheer diversity of institutional arrangements, varieties of positivism, and educational priorities among thousands of law schools worldwide, so the chapter tries to give examples to point to where to look for entanglements. First, I divide the curriculum into content, skills, and attitudes.[25] The distinction provides a breakdown of the so-called competence framework, which seems suitable here as it is often used to make educational programmes comparable and intelligible across systems. It is worth mentioning here that to use this framework means already, to an extent, accepting a premise that some may disagree with in the context of higher education but is never entirely out of the picture in *legal* education, namely that university education contains at least an element of vocational training.[26] Second, I locate further entanglements in the institutional politics and survival strategies of contemporary law schools. However, before undertaking these examinations, we first need to define what growth (and degrowth) means for the purposes of the analysis.

3. Private Law Education Without Growth?

3.1 Where We Stand: Private Law for Growth

> Today, the European Single Market still has too many national barriers. Sometimes companies are dealing with 27 national legislations. We will offer instead to innovative companies to operate all across our Union under one single set of rules. We call it the 28th regime. Corporate law, insolvency, labour law, taxation—one single and simple framework across our Union. This will help bring down the most common barriers to scaling up all across Europe. Because continental scale is our greatest asset in a world of giants.[27]

This is not the first time that the European Union has pitched harmonised private law, and even the specific idea of a 28th private law regime as key to unlocking growth: A similar narrative surrounded the later abandoned Common European Sales Law project.[28] What is remarkable about the EU's instrumentalisation of private law is how explicitly the connection is laid at

[24] I am directly familiar with two such models, both based in Europe but significantly different from each other—the Italian and Dutch models—and have some understanding of other European models based on short attendance as a student in France and insights from colleagues and students, but most of my understanding of non-European law schools comes from literature.

[25] I follow, in my understanding of this tripartition, the same understanding as, e.g., Mak, who speaks of 'knowledge, competences, and ethical mind-set of legal professionals'. Chestermann, in contrast, talks of doctrines, perspectives, and skills, including legal ethics under the latter. I believe setting out 'attitudes' as a separate category does more justice to the emotional and more generally 'human' components of the related educational endeavours and objectives. See Simon Chesterman, 'Doctrine, Perspectives and Skills for Global Practice' in William van Caenegem and Mary Hiscock (eds), *The Internationalisation of Legal Education* (Edward Elgar Publishing 2014); Elaine Mak, *The T-Shaped Lawyer and Beyond* (Eleven International Publishing 2017).

[26] Universities working in the competence framework will work on defining high-level 'learning attainments' that all together form a programme's exit profile: the competences that all graduates are supposed to have achieved. Such competences, in turn, will be categorised along the lines I follow here.

[27] European Commission, 'Special Address by President von der Leyen at the World Economic Forum' (21 January 2025) <https://ec.europa.eu/commission/presscorner/detail/en/speech_25_285> accessed 28 June 2025.

[28] Martijn W Hesselink, 'Progress in EU Contract Law' (2022) 18 European Review of Contract Law 281.

policymaking and even at the highest political levels, but of course we know that this is not an isolated example.

The law and economics (L&E) movement's emphasis on efficiency is a particularly clear example, and maybe even more so the specific strand of this movement that has been at the core of the "legal origins" saga. By equating to a large extent "better" outcomes to supposedly more efficient ones and, in turn, equating greater efficiency with wealth maximisation (due to the difficulty of quantifying utility on different bases), L&E is a classic example of ways in which a growth paradigm—since efficiency is mostly comparative, in the sense that it *improves* wealth vis-à-vis the previous situation[29]—gets embedded into our way of thinking about private law. This applies, crucially, to both so-called normative L&E and positive L&E, which, while allowing for the idea that legislators may want to pursue other goals, effectively sidesteps all these considerations in foregrounding one type of—reductionist—analysis.[30] Quite crucially, this reductionism is also very attractive for law and policymakers: As Collins observed over two decades ago,[31] it is much easier to conceptualise the specific form of regulatory rationality that seeks to enhance welfare qua efficiency than to put trust in the effectiveness of different interventions—the "constructivist" ethos much despised by the likes of Friederich Hayek.[32]

Whereas the "efficiency" of institutions like criminal punishment may not be immediately connected to economic growth, the link seems obvious when private law, and particularly its patrimonial core, is considered. Nevertheless, the connection between private law and growth has not always been a given. Both more recent scholarship, such as Katharina Pistor's account of land-as-capital from the enclosure movement to twentieth-century reforms,[33] and classic accounts of contract law through the middle ages—showing how Aristotelian "equality in exchange" doctrines for a long time stood in the way of thinking of contracts as a way of producing value—serve to remind us that growth has long not been a concern of private law (and hence, by plausible historical extension, of much law).[34] That the notion of "exchange value", in other words, has come to be entwined with the supposed individual utility through offer and demand, and hence, we have come to think that mutually beneficial exchanges *increase welfare* rather than just maintain it, is a relatively recent insight. This digression is all meant to say that it seems possible to teach private law in a way that is not immediately committed to economic

[29] This is true for both Pareto and Kaldor-Hicks's efficiency criteria.

[30] Julia Black, 'Critical Reflections on Regulation' (2002) 27 Australian Journal of Legal Philosophy 1.

[31] Hugh Collins, 'Justifications and Techniques of Legal Regulation of the Employment Relation' in Hugh Collins, Paul L Davies, and Roger W Rideout (eds), *Legal Regulation of the Employment Relation* (Kluwer Law International 2000).

[32] As observed in Marija Bartl, Towards the imaginary of collective prosperity in the European Union (EU): reorienting the corporation (2022) 1 European Law Open 957 at 963–964. See for a very clear articulation of 'spontaneous' and (legally) 'constructed' orders in Hayek's thought Antoine Vandenbulke, 'La Legal Origins Theory: Droit, Économie, Idéologie' (2017) 30 Revue internationale de droit économique 79.

[33] See Chapter 2, 'Coding Land' in Katharina Pistor, *The Code of Capital* (Princeton University Press 2019).

[34] See Atiyah's insightful reflections: 'Smith's views about prices are a great advance on the scholastic ideas about "just prices" in that he allows for fluctuations in market prices, and does not assume that everything always has one fixed just price. At the same time Smith by no means adopted Hobbe's sweeping argument that a price agreed to by the parties is always a just price merely by virtua of the agreement. Nevertheless, he did give substantial support to those who wished to argue like Hobbes: for Smith provided a rational and scientific explanation of why it was in general desirable that prices should rise and fall in the market.' Patrick Selim Atiyah, *The Rise and Fall of Freedom of Contract*, vol 1 (OUP 1979) 298.

growth. This comes down to both selecting topics that are taught and considering how they are taught.

3.2 Teaching Private Law for Growth

Legal complexity keeps increasing at a breakneck pace in affluent and less affluent jurisdictions. Together with the challenges coming from digitalisation, including most recently generative AI applications, this complexity has the advantage of bringing attention to the choices that we collectively and individually make in setting up law curricula.[35] Subjects and topics falling under the broad umbrella of private law that are explored in this handbook typically constitute a very significant part of any legal curriculum. This is so often the case that we sometimes fail to interrogate the significance of this choice and how reasons for inclusion affect, or should affect, subsequent choices. Interrogating curricular and scholarly omissions in the context of climate change and towards growth-agnosticism may be the first step towards deeper understanding of what more globally sustainable legal education entails.

This handbook, for instance, includes no chapters on family law. This is remarkable since the impact of climate change on family planning, the stability of family arrangements, and issues of custody in cases of forced displacement, among others, seems already significant and is only likely to increase its impact on the lives of law's addressees.[36] Irrespective of the process and dynamics that may have led to this specific omission, this observation is aligned with tendencies to dismiss family law as insufficiently doctrinally sophisticated or not relevant enough to deserve the same attention paid to, say, company law. Bar qualification standards sometimes include general or more specific references to private law subjects that need to be included in the curriculum. For instance, in England and Wales, students need to have acquired basic knowledge of the law of obligations (contracts, restitution, and torts), property law, as well as the law of trusts as a specific element of foundations of equity.[37] Family law is not covered as such, nor is employment law.

Thus, the first debate to examine is to what extent more obviously GDP-relevant private law is given outsized space or prominence in the law curricula. The imbalance may be obvious at first glance, but even more if one looks more closely *within* subjects: In this sense, a typical suggestion would be to reconsider the respective space allocated to for profit and social enterprises, investment or conservation land arrangements, and so on. This reconsideration is not rendered less relevant even if one accepts the contention that first understanding the workings of law in contemporary global economies is a necessary premise to challenging the ways in which (transnational and private) legal arrangements entrench unsustainability or injustices.[38]

[35] As Germelmann aptly observed, 'In fact, legal teaching is constantly facing the problem of an information overload', which should trigger very careful and explicit selection (supported by academic freedom and integrity). See Claas Friedrich Germelmann, 'Challenges and Approaches to Modern Legal Education in a European Perspective' in Claas Friedrich Germelmann (ed), *Innovative Teaching in European Legal Education* (Nomos Verlag 2021) 21.

[36] See, e.g., Jessica Rizzo, 'The Children's Hour: Climate Change, Law, and the Family' (2021) 27 Hastings Environmental Law Journal 79 <https://repository.uchastings.edu/hastings_environmental_law_journal/vol27/iss2/3> accessed 27 June 2025.

[37] Solicitors Regulation Authority, 'Academic Stage Handbook' (*Solicitors Regulation Authority*, 2014) <https://www.sra.org.uk/globalassets/documents/students/academic-stage/academic-stage-handbook.pdf?version=4a1ac3> accessed 27 June 2025.

[38] See Oscar Vilhena Vieira and José Garcez Ghirardi, 'The Unstoppable Force, the Immovable Object: Challenges for Structuring a Cosmopolitan Legal Education in Brazil' in Bryant Garth and Gregory Shaffer (eds), *The Globalization of Legal Education* (OUP 2022) 267–68. This tension is most

The second question to be explores is how we discuss the topics that we do teach. I will elaborate here on only one example taken from the area I am most comfortable with—contract law—and only briefly mention examples offered by colleagues more versed in other areas of private law.[39] The point here is not to be comprehensive but to offer an idea of how one can *go about* the process of questioning how their own educational practices entrench growth ideologies.

Section 3.1 discussed how the marginalist revolution in economic theory, which shifted focus from labour and material costs to the subjective utility market actors might attach to (exchange of) goods and services, has been key to conceptualising economic growth. How does this shift connect to contract law? Until quite late, mainstream economic doctrine looked at production as the combination of productive factors—chiefly land, labour, and capital. *Circulation* of such factors, as such, was not considered a productive activity. This changed with the advent of marginalism, which conceptualised exchange surplus as the added utility deriving from things being transferred from someone who valued them less to someone who valued them more.[40] Modern freedom of contract is typically justified on the European continent on the grounds of individual autonomy and hence not only self-responsibility but also the inscrutability of individual conceptions of the good. This paradigm only makes limited sense outside of the marginalist framework—and indeed, the idea that the *price* of a good as set in a contract would never be subject to judicial or otherwise public control found a coherent theoretical articulation around the same time when marginalism developed. This is, incidentally, some time after private money creation, which decoupled money from specific (and limited) material resources, had made growth much more conceivable in the first place, as Christine Desan's work has convincingly argued.[41] These developments have consequences not only for our foundational understanding of freedom of contract, but also for specific doctrines.[42]

The common law doctrine of "expectation damages" for breach of contract, in this sense, is illustrative on two different grounds: On the one hand, because damages in lieu of specific performance seem to underscore that what needs to be preserved is the *utility* of the bargain, expressed as the expectation interest of the non-breaching party; on the other hand, because the choice for *expectation* rather than reliance interest ultimately seems to rely on the same assumption. It is then no surprise that neo-Aristotelians like James Gordley reject the idea of expectation interest as the touchstone for contract remedies.[43]

A very similar observation can be made regarding contract law's extraordinary deference to price arrangements, even where non-price terms are subject to some degree of scrutiny.

openly discussed in the context of Third World Approaches to International Law ("TWAIL"). See Tony Anghie, 'Critical Pedagogy Symposium: Critical Thinking and Teaching as Common Sense—Random Reflections' (*Opinio Juris*, 31 August 2020) <https://opiniojuris.org/2020/08/31/critical-pedagogy-symposium-critical-thinking-and-teaching-as-common-sense-random-reflections/> accessed 20 August 2021. See also Srinivan Burra, 'Teaching Critical International Law: Reflections from the Periphery' (*TWAILR*, 12 March 2021) <https://twailr.com/teaching-critical-international-law-reflections-from-the-periphery/> accessed 21 July 2025.

[39] This section has benefitted from insights of participants in the October 2024 ACT symposium *Social Justice, Private Law and Europe (?) 2004–2044: Keeping the Hope Alive* as well as email exchanges (and dinner interrogations!) with several colleagues in the Netherlands and abroad.

[40] Fressoz and Bonneuil (n 16) 57.

[41] Christine Desan, *Making Money: Coin, Currency, and the Coming of Capitalism* (OUP 2014).

[42] On which, see for all Atiyah (n 34).

[43] James Gordley, 'The Myth of "Expectation Interest"' (2020) 52 University of the Pacific Law Review 77.

Besides the area of standard terms,[44] this can be seen in the doctrines concerning mistake, which exclude mistakes on *value* from the circumstances that may entitle the mistaken party to relief. Besides language of self-responsibility and legal certainty, this deference relies on the idea, cemented through the marginalist revolution, that the price is set according to individual preferences, making the idea of a "just price" vain. Besides the fact that this assumption doesn't necessarily reflect thinking about prices in other areas of the law,[45] the inscrutability of (contractual) price is also challenged by contemporary institutionalist literature.[46] Historicising, contextualising, and ultimately questioning the self-evident nature of these basic rules is an important step.

Similar questions could be asked for "basic" rules and doctrines in other subfields. In corporate law, for instance: Given the significant externalities generated by corporate negligence, are the very high thresholds usually applicable to directors' liability—normally justified by the wish not to over-deter risk-taking—still a good idea if we do not put a very high prize on (potential) economic growth? In property and tort law, we see comparable issues. Nuisance or "voisinage" rules have been relaxed over time to accommodate growing industries. Is it responsible to simply accept Calabresi and Melamed's view of the "cathedral", equating tort and property rules in matters of pollution, without pointing with equal articulation to the qualitative differences between prevention and damage compensation? The distinction is critical in a world where "dilution" is no longer an answer to pollution?[47] We may even extend the questioning to personal injury law: How does considering future earnings and statutory interest in the awarding of damages for personal injury project individual and societal economic progress? All the colleagues I have challenged to come up with examples of how economic growth was entrenched in doctrines they *taught* over the past year were startled at first. However, they were later surprised by how often the connection became visible once one started looking.

Naturalisation of certain doctrines, and particularly their connection to growth, sometimes happens in the *narratives*—in the way we talk about private law institutions. Most explicit in this sense may be the justification of the free choice of law in private international law articulated in the US Supreme Court case, *The Bremen v Zapata*, namely that:

> The expansion of American business and industry will hardly be encouraged if, notwithstanding solemn contracts, we insist on a parochial concept that all disputes must be resolved under our laws and in our courts.[48]

Sometimes, these narratives are less explicit but equally telling—take the Dutch example of the most adopted first-year introduction to patrimonial private law.[49] While all other chapters in

[44] Hans Erich Brandner and Peter Ulmer, 'The Community Directive on Unfair Terms in Consumer Contracts: Some Critical Remarks on the Proposal Submitted by the EC Commission' (1991) 28 Common Market Law Review 495.

[45] An obvious example is that of competition law disputes, that routinely seek to calculate what the 'actual' competitive price of certain goods or services would be. See also for a broad reconstruction William Boyd, 'Just Price, Public Utility, and the Long History of Economic Regulation in America' (2018) 35 Yale Journal on Regulation 721.

[46] See, e.g., for an avowedly *non-Aristotelian*, institutional, view: Robert C Hockett and Roy Kreitner, 'Just Prices' (2017) 27 Cornell Journal of Law & Public Policy 771.

[47] Environmental law has more principles for private lawyers to engage with beyond polluter-pays: see Nicolas De Sadeleer, *Environmental Principles: From Political Slogans to Legal Rules* (OUP 2020). A similar point has been made long ago in Douglas A Kysar, 'Sustainability, Distribution, and the Macroeconomic Analysis of Law' (2001) 43 Boston College Law Review. 1.

[48] *The Bremen v Zapata Off-Shore Co.*, 407 U.S. 1 (1972).

[49] J H Nieuwenhuis, *Hoofdstukken vermogensrecht* (13th edn, Wolters Kluwer 2022).

the book have consistently dry titles like "Transfer of Title" or "Performance", the chapter on representation is called "Carl and August's Dream" ("De droom van Carl en August"). In this chapter of the Dutch standard text, August and Carl need a representative because otherwise their company cannot *grow*. Apparently, growing a business is the only thing that deserves to get romanticised, and hence made relatable, when introducing basic legal concepts to students just out of high school.

Similar examples could likely be identified in countless syllabi, first-year introduction handbooks, and more. None of this is necessary for students to understand basic concepts of private law, even though, on occasion, it may help explain (and predict) developments in specific contexts. Critically highlighting those contexts—for instance, historicising *The Bremen v Zapata* instead of just repeating its arguments—is a crucial exercise.

4. Skills for Growth/Beyond Growth

The degree to which skills are paid attention to in law curricula varies greatly across and within legal systems and academic traditions, along with the range of skills that are contemplated.[50] Examination practices, accordingly, vary wildly across faculties and systems in ways that are sometimes under-acknowledged. Besides the distinction between oral and written exams, the emphasis could be on multiple-choice questions, open-ended knowledge reproduction questions, essays, or case-based questions. The latter often entails some more explicit skills training with the assumption often being that the skills required for other types of questions are ultimately an extension of those that should have been acquired in previous education.[51] In contrast, case-based questions require system-specific and typical *legal* reasoning skills. This rather casual attitude to critical thinking skills stands in remarkable contrast to pedagogical practices in the humanities and social sciences and has been subject to criticism.[52] Over the past decades, partially under external pressure to improve graduates' practical competences,[53] more explicit skills training has made its way in many programmes. One traditional approach to skills takes the form of *moot courts*. Moot courts are a specific way of training both drafting and advocacy skills together (depending on the case) with an understanding of specific rules and dynamics of proceeding before a specific court. More recently, law *clinics* have become an alternative way of introducing skills.

All these endeavours share some common features and assumptions. Attention to skills, first of all, aims to make explicit what for a long time has been implicit in legal education, transmitted more as a matter of habitus than as an explicit pedagogical endeavour.[54] In this

[50] For instance, Finch and Fafinski's 'best selling' legal skills manual ranges from finding sources to dissertation writing, from brief and memo drafting conventions such as IRAC to negotiation. See Emily Finch and Stefan Fafinski, *Legal Skills* (7th edn, OUP 2023).

[51] The connected criticality being that many observe that such skills have often *not* been acquired to a sufficient extent: see for the US context Cara R Shaffer, 'Context at the Periphery: The Rise of the Critical-Contextual Legal Education Reform Movement' (2023) 30 Cardozo Journal of Equal Rights & Social Justice 55, 92. Colleagues from many other jurisdictions will likely recognise the challenge.

[52] See again, for an extensive reconstruction in the US context, Shaffer (n 51).

[53] ibid.

[54] Famously Pierre Bourdieu, *Outline of a Theory of Practice* (Richard Nice tr, CUP 2013). For an explicit reflection on the tensions this awareness entails in the context of (legal) education, see, e.g., Lucille A Jewel, 'Bourdieu and American Legal Education: How Law Schools Reproduce Social Stratification and Class Hierarchy' (2008) 56 Buffalo. Law Review 1155, 1158. In similar fashion, Duncan Kennedy, *Legal Education and the Reproduction of Hierarch: A Polemic Against the System* (New York University Press 2004) (originally self-published 1983). For a recent reflection on pedagogical practices as aiming for a different socialisation, Willem-Jan Kortleven, Nina Holvast, and Alma Bešić, 'From

sense, such a focus aims to democratise access to the social and economic capital that comes with legal education. Attention to first-generation students confirms the role of education, and in particular legal education, as an instrument of social mobility. Experiences with legal education reform across the globe show how "better", or more skills-oriented, training has been used (with diverging degrees of success) to undermine existing legal hierarchies based on class and familial connections.[55] This also means that focus on skills is tightly connected with a meritocratic ethos that has largely displaced more result-egalitarian understandings of social justice in many contemporary societies.[56]

There are, to be sure, many good things about this push to abandon traditional hierarchies and strive for more inclusive educational practices.[57] There is also a very real risk, however, in making marketable skills—rather than education as such—the emancipatory focus of institutionally sanctioned pedagogies. This applies to some skills practices more than to others. Take the example of mooting: In addition to existing critiques of its competitiveness and hierarchy-performative nature, mooting runs the risk of—without some thick embedding in an understanding of deliberative practices—turning into the worst possible version of the "marketplace of ideas" fallacy or the "both-sideism" that we have seen applied to so many controversial issues in journalistic and other spheres. Clinics, especially when *actually* connected to the needs of local justice demands, are obviously more open to bringing students in contact with the very real impacts of climate change and other ongoing crises affecting people and communities.[58]

To an extent, however, *all standardised skills training* reflects an individualistic and limited understanding of practical experience.[59] They are also, one has to admit, very expensive to install and maintain without fully relying on external sponsors.[60] This contributes to driving tuition fees up at fee-based schools and puts great strain on less well-funded institutions, reinforcing the division between "good" and less good schools.[61] For law schools offering mass education, the sheer numbers that characterise many of these exercises stand in the way of responsibly engaging in the forms of insurgent pedagogies that are often advocated in the Anglo-American (fee-based) graduate school context.[62] In this setting, it is difficult to create the safe class environment that critical pedagogies are based on, and it is even more difficult to introduce workable assessment mechanisms. In resource-constrained contexts, skills

Adaptive to Reflective Law School Socialisation: A Theoretical and Empirical Contribution from the Netherlands' (2024) 27 Legal Ethics 63.

[55] Bryant G Garth, *Law as Reproduction and Revolution: An Interconnected History* (University of California Press 2021).

[56] Stuart Tannock, 'On Education and Degrowth' (2025) 46 British Journal of Sociology of Education 454, 460.

[57] Stuart Tannock, 'The Question of International Tuition Fees: Cash Cows and Silent Elephants' in Stuart Tannock, *Educational Equality and International Students* (Springer International Publishing 2018) <https://link.springer.com/10.1007/978-3-319-76381-1_6> accessed 15 June 2025.

[58] McCormack and Lim (n 22).

[59] See the navel-gazing, borderline narcissistic traits of many of the imaginary 'cause' lawyers described in Gerald P López, *Rebellious Lawyering: One Chicano's Vision of Progressive Legal Practice* (Westview Press 1992).

[60] My own institution, which by continental European standards counts as exceptionally well-ranked and reasonably well-funded, has recently suffered very significant financial set-back from an ambitious attempt to introduce 'skills' training, including some forms of mooting and clinical education, throughout the LLB.

[61] Hans-Wolfgang Micklitz, 'The Bifurcation of Legal Education: National vs Transnational' in Christopher Gane and Robin Hui (eds), *Legal Education in the Global Context* (Routledge 2017).

[62] McCormack and Lim (n 22).

modules often come at the cost of investing in contextual education, diverse contents, and ultimately, without proper embedding, critical thinking.[63] Practical skills that are not embedded in rigorous academic inquiry are quite different from the more nuanced, embedded normative and systems thinking skills required by sustainability education (which are, in contrast, quite more compatible with critical-contextual education).[64] They are also unlikely to be very *durable*, in the sense of proving their value beyond a very short period. Take a very urgent example, AI literacy skills are unlikely to be sustainable if they are reduced to prompting rather than grounded in an overall understanding of the social, technological, and legal stakes involved in past, current and future technologies.[65]

Crucially, too much emphasis on institution-imparted skills will come at the cost of depreciating the skills that students learn by virtue of community. The latter include cause-based and political organisation, which is, if not at all times, often explicitly opposed and disciplined by university bureaucracies and certainly made over-expensive for most non-privileged students as a result of tuition fees, social and institutional expectations of quick graduation, and quick return on investment thanks to early acquisition of market-relevant skills. Less *standardisation* of skills beyond the academic core, that is, less ambition to *scale up* skills, may hence allow more diversity of skills—in line with post-growth precepts of fostering diverse, non-marketised forms of human flourishing.

5. Growth Embedded in Developing Professional Roles and Attitudes

Due to its connection to a distinct set of professional activities, legal education always relies on and implicitly reinforces certain understandings about "the ideal jurist". These understandings vary across legal cultures and have shifted over time.[66]

The past decades have seen the rise of the corporate lawyer as the apex of the legal-professional hierarchy. This is increasingly a global development,[67] although it is taking place with varying impacts and speeds in different jurisdictions. Garth and Shaffer describe how the US context provided the backbone for moulding the image of the "corporate lawyer-statesman", where particularly successful lawyers at large firms would "move from time to time to government positions where they help the law to regulate but not disrupt their powerful clients".[68] This happened through a combination of prestige, economic incentives, and direct

[63] This 'competition' for the space left or created next to doctrine is also extensively observed by Shaffer (n 51).

[64] See Leone (n 1); Margherita Paola Poto and Emily Margaret Murray, 'Achieving a Common Future for All Through Sustainability-Conscious Legal Education and Research Methods' (2024) 24 Global Jurist 157.

[65] For a first attempt at grounding the discussion: Michael Veale and others, 'Artificial Intelligence, Education and Assessment at UCL Laws: Current Thinking and Next Steps for the UK Legal Education Sector' (2025) UCL Legal Studies Research Paper Series 04/2025.

[66] See the various chapters in Bryant G Garth and Gregory C Shaffer, *The Globalization of Legal Education: A Critical Perspective* (OUP 2022). These images are often implicit but clearly codified. They also do not necessarily overlap with one specific legal *profession*: as Elaine Mak observes, the early continental European 'lawyer-statesman' typified a set of qualities (with Mak: 'intellectual skills but also emotional and perceptual power, that is: "capacity for judgment"' that could apply to judges, advocates, academic lawyers alike; see Mak (n 25) 14. In contemporary terms, this approach would come closest to aligning with images of ideal (civil law) judges, and in some contexts with a majority of academics.

[67] See the extensive introductory chapter by the editors in Garth and Shaffer (n 66).

[68] ibid 20.

action in developing countries by US public and private actors.[69] Across systems, tradition operates its resistance through social structures as well as legal arrangements. In Italy, for instance, the replicability of the big law model is still, to an extent, actively wedged by legal arrangements: Lawyers cannot be *employees* because they are expected to maintain their professional independence at any time (due to their obligations towards both clients and the legal system), which is against the notion of subordination.[70] This, however, is a rearguard defence.[71]

The corporate lawyer (without the particular pretence of statespersonship referred to above), has certainly been very much on the rise in the Netherlands, where US-style law firms have blossomed and competition for high-profile corporate law jobs is relatively mild. This has happened in parallel with a steep decline in the ideal—and socio-economic position—of small-shop generalists and social lawyers. This development has been both a matter of academic reflection and of concern among both scholars and practitioners.[72] Worries about how many of the ambitious students pursuing private law master's degrees in the Netherlands end up acting, as highlighted in press reports, as "butlers of the Zuidas",[73] working within large corporate law firms, are a frequent theme in my conversations with colleagues interested in sustainability. While many young lawyers may enter these big commercial law firms with high ideals of changing the system from within, gaining experience, stability, and connections to move on to something different and better after a few years and so on, there is generally no space within firms for conscientious objection vis-à-vis individual clients. Furthermore, professional socialisation makes it difficult not to gradually normalise choices that may have seemed reprehensible from the vantage point of a young student.

Much like other capitalist enterprises, the global law firm depends on ever-larger *scale*. It needs to grow. This underlying factor is reinforced by digitalisation. Investment in technologies, which characterises the strategy as well as the marketing language of many large firms, requires capital. Accumulation of such capital depends crucially on transactional practice, meaning it also relies on a certain model of financialised global capitalism.[74] Foregrounding this professional archetype, in short, means de facto endorsing its extractive business model.[75]

[69] Garth and Shaffer (n 66). In the same volume, see in particular Ron Levi, Ronit Dinovitzer, and Wendy H Wong, 'Strategic Philanthropy and International Strategies: The Ford Foundation and Investments in Law Schools and Legal Education' in Bryant Garth and Gregory Shaffer (eds), *The Globalization of Legal Education: A Critical Perspective* (OUP 2022).

[70] Lastly reaffirmed by the Italian Supreme Court in its decision of 4 November 2024, n. 28274/2024.

[71] The same applies to other countries in the European French-inspired tradition, such as France and Romania.

[72] Iris van Domselaar, 'Where Were the Law Schools? On Legal Education as Training for Justice and the Rule of Law (against the "Dark Sides of Legality")' (2021) 50 Netherlands Journal of Legal Philosophy 3.

[73] See '"Corporate lawyers": de butlers van de Zuidas' (*De Groene Amsterdammer*, 24 February 2021) <https://www.groene.nl/podcasts/de-groene-amsterdammer-podcast/afleveringen/corporate-lawyers-de-butlers-van-de-zuidas> accessed 15 June 2025. 'Zuidas' designates the sprawling business district to the South of Amsterdam, where much of the financial/trading services and many of the major law firms have their offices.

[74] Thomson Reuters, 'Law Firms Saw Double-Digit Profit Growth to Close an Incredible 2024: Thomson Reuters Law Firm Financial Index' (*Thomson Reuters Institute*, 10 February 2025) <https://www.thomsonreuters.com/en-us/posts/innovation/law-firms-saw-double-digit-profit-growth-to-close-an-incredible-2024-thomson-reuters-law-firm-financial-index/> accessed 15 June 2025.

[75] See Garth and Shaffer's conclusion that '"global educational reforms are closely related to the remarkable spread of the US-style corporate law forms around the globe that service global business'. Garth and Shaffer (n 66) 7.

As I am writing this chapter, the corporate lawyer-statesman image *may* be undergoing an existential crisis. Scott Cummings has pointed to lawyers' role in undermining the rule of law in the context leading up to the 2025 US constitutional crisis.[76] This anti-democratic ethos, however, has long been detectable at the (internal) periphery of the US empire and of other empires. Free trade liberal legalism has worked well to globalise elite legal practice but less so to undermine or prevent authoritarian legalism.[77] The climate crisis is a test for democratic resilience. A recent example is the startling $660 million claim against Greenpeace awarded by a jury in North Dakota.[78] As pointed out by Eckes and Paiement, "these judicial actions go after the civil society actors that organize non-institutional interest representation in the democratic process".[79] This is not a side effect but the *goal* of lawsuits of this kind. To the extent that law schools contribute to equating traditional partisanship notions with "anything goes"—that is, describing ethically minimalist attitudes in corporate counselling and advocacy as the neutral default and "cause lawyering" as exceptional—we are implicitly colouring professional responsibility with personal and corporate greed.

6. Can We Wean Law Schools of Their Addiction to Growth?

Generally speaking, letting go of the growth paradigm does not require *less* education, and arguably also not less formalised higher education—even the contrary may be possible.[80] In light of what we have discussed above, however, this may not be true of law schools. Law school demographics display different trends in different countries. In general, though, there seems to be a sustained interest in pursuing legal education at institutions targeting international students. Not only has the popularity of LLMs not shown any sign of decline, but growing numbers of students are pursuing a degree in a country or jurisdiction other than the one where they have been studying until then. In Europe, international or European LLBs have proliferated over the past years, with some countries hitting the limits to growth (in particularly worrisome ways in the country where I live and work, where universities are currently under pressure to severely restrict English-language instructions in the Bachelor's phase) and others still hoping to tap into the global trends and explore their growth potential.[81]

In the US, law school applications also do not seem to have been discouraged by ever-growing fees, a supposed shift in valuing of work-life balance by younger generations, or

[76] Scott L Cummings, 'Why Do Lawyers Attack the Rule of Law? Trajectories of "Trump Lawyers"' (2025) 32 International Journal of the Legal Profession 19.

[77] Garth and Shaffer (n 66) 31.

[78] Mary Steurer, 'Jury Finds Greenpeace at Fault for Protest Damages, Awards Pipeline Developer More than $660 Million' (*North Dakota Monitor*, 19 March 2025) <https://northdakotamonitor.com/2025/03/19/jury-finds-greenpeace-at-fault-for-protest-damages-awards-pipeline-developer-hundreds-of-millions/> accessed 21 July 2025.

[79] Christina Eckes and Phillip Paiement, 'Silencing Greenpeace: Can the EU Prevent the Chilling Effect on Democracy from Crossing the Atlantic?' (*VerfBlog*, 31 March 2025) <https://verfassungsblog.de/greenpeace-slapp-energy-transfer/> accessed 27 June 2025.

[80] See Tannock (n 47) 457 ('When thinking about the implications of degrowth for education as a social institution and field of practice, the emphasis should clearly be on growth, not degrowth').

[81] See the volume, *Globalisation of Legal Education*, with instructive chapters on 'global law schools' across the world. Garth and Shaffer (n 64). For recent developments in Europe, see the English-language LLB 'global law' recently established at Bocconi, Italy's leading private university, as well as the very new LLM in comparative and global law at the University of Münster, Germany.

any other of the multiple factors that could be contributing to a cooling down in interest for studying law.[82] Globally, the rise of the US-inspired JD—as opposed to undergraduate or bachelor's legal education—has contributed to enabling the kind of skills focus and pedagogical ambitions discussed in Section 4 by increasing both student maturity and preparation levels and the fees that (especially private) law schools could charge.[83] Faced with shrinking budgets, public (or publicly funded) universities have meanwhile also tried to grow revenues by attracting more (international) students, chasing "better" students, and hoping that they perform better.[84] Roughly speaking, what publicly funded or less selective institutions do chiefly by means of numbers, elite institutions seem to do by means of fees—but ultimately, the goal remains growth. In both cases, to sustain institutions' attractiveness to students, ambitions have grown in both education and research, despite (or in response to) the often-heard complaint that student preparation or dedication has not. One important factor driving this development is, of course, the role of rankings, which are crucial to both fee-paying students and their families, as well as to scholarship-funding institutions.[85] As Tamanaha pointed out already some time ago in the US context,[86] the interdependence between high-paying jobs at fancy law firms and especially elite legal education is a point of very painful fragility. Elite law schools charge ever-higher fees on account of the salaries that future graduates will be able to draw from law firms. This makes them vulnerable to the same perverse incentives that affect those law firms. A letter by law school deans repeating the until recently rather mainstream take that "the government should not punish lawyers and law firms for the clients they represent, absent specific findings that such representation was illegal or unethical"[87] stood out, among other things, because the list of signatories was largely populated by deans of public universities. On the other hand, largely publicly subsidised Australian and UK universities have been targeted with demands to shrink their international population, as have the Dutch ones. This also means that hitherto less English-language-oriented countries still have space to—well—grow in their international ambitions.

The legal professional attitude that is currently fostered—the typical image of the "amoral lawyer"—has been developed for a different profession than the one that currently dominates.[88] Furthermore, it does little to inform and support the very different roles that law

[82] 'Law School Applications Surge: Trends and Opportunities' (*Educations.com*, 17 June 2025) <https://www.educations.com/higher-education-news/law-school-applications-surge-trends-and-opportunities-for-2024> accessed 15 June 2025.

[83] Garth and Shaffer (n 66) 3.

[84] The growth of executive education would deserve separate consideration, but readers of this chapter will not find it too challenging to extrapolate the analysis.

[85] Many scholarships, especially but not exclusively from funders in the majority world, are only awarded on condition of a student's admission/enrolment at institutions placed within a certain range of recognised rankings.

[86] Brian Z Tamanaha, *Failing Law Schools* (University of Chicago Press 2012). Particularly instructive in this respect is the chapter about lateral admissions, and similarly, the *Globalisation of Legal Education* chapter about New York University's law school, highlighting how the school discourages students from spending a semester abroad if they have not secured an offer of permanent employment by their third year.

[87] Madeline Yingling, 'US Law School Deans Sign Letter Condemning Trump Sanctions on Law Firms' (*Jurist*, 27 March 2025) <https://www.jurist.org/news/2025/03/us-law-school-deans-sign-letter-condemning-trump-sanctions-on-law-firms/> accessed 15 June 2025.

[88] See for reflections on a recent attempt to reflect this in professional rules, James E Moliterno, 'Place-Based versus Practice-Based Norms for American Lawyers: "It's the End of the World as We Know It (and I Feel Fine)"' (2022) 74 South Carolina Law Review 739.

graduates go on to take, for instance, providing little guidance to government lawyers, in-house counsels of (problematic) organisations, and so forth.[89] This is even more problematic if we take into account that this rather un-civic view of law's practice will also be transmitted to and propagated by graduates that end up doing non-legal professions. Law schools should both actively reflect on the broader palette of professional roles that graduates may go on to take and, crucially, decouple their fortunes from those of big law. So far, even the dramatic acceleration of a rule of law crisis in the US context has not led to significant shifts in the law school-law firm alignment, with most of the pushback still coming from engaged students.[90] But law schools (and universities) have also not done great on their own merits in the current US constitutional crisis. While some have suggested that the vulnerability of higher education came from excessive reliance on *public* funding, I would like to suggest that it is the overall capital-intensity of higher education and law school (and with that, our ever-expanding ambitions) that needs to be tamed.[91]

7. Conclusion

This chapter has argued that a growth paradigm is entwined with private law education at crucial levels—in particular in determining core contents of private law curricula, in embracing skills education as a route to social mobility and meritocracy, and in terms of the domination of amoral corporate lawyering among the paradigm-setting professional attitudes that are cultivated or reinforced. More diversification in both areas—emphasis on the legal arrangements underlying non-economic exchanges and diverse economies, a reflection of a wider variety of legal professional images, and, ultimately, opening up of role morality to a variety of responsibilities beyond the client are required in order to decouple private law education from the growth paradigm. Less emphasis on social mobility as the ultimate justification for the system-preserving traits of higher education and attention to diverse and collective practices is something that can be seen as a task for law schools as well as for other areas of higher education.

More controversially, however, I have argued that for law schools, decoupling from entrenching growth requires a conscious choice of degrowth or abandoning the growth paradigm *for law faculties as institutions themselves*: On the one hand, because they cannot plausibly keep growing against demographics, the development of diverse areas of high-quality education in emerging countries, and the digitalisation and diversification of labour markets; on the other hand, because taking the responsibility of legal education in the climate crisis seriously means making certain choices that are just not profitable and do not fit the current business model. In other words, to *decouple* their curriculum and fates from unsustainable growth paradigms, many law faculties themselves need to prepare for degrowth or at

[89] See, among others, Domselaar (n 72).

[90] See the very public cancellation of a networking event with—and paid for by—Skadden by the Georgetown Energy Law Group; Maria Gracia Santillana Linares, 'Law Students Push Back on Firms That Have Capitulated To Trump' (*Forbes*, 4 April 2025) <https://www.forbes.com/sites/mariagraciasantillanalinares/2025/04/04/law-students-push-back-on-firms-that-have-capitulated-to-trump/> accessed 15 June 2025.

[91] See Jeannie Suk Gersen, 'Why Harvard Decided to Challenge Donald Trump' (*The New Yorker*, 2025) <https://www.newyorker.com/news/the-lede/why-harvard-decided-to-challenge-donald-trump> accessed 15 June 2025.

least post-growth—in numbers, fee levels, and ambitions. This process does not need to be all misery: To give a concrete example inspired by Jennifer Nedelsky's proposition of *Part-Time for All*,[92] less insatiable institutional ambition may leave space for different forms of fulfilment by faculty, including creating more support for academia by fostering less technocratic forms of impact than those imposed by rankings and ranking-oriented financing.

92 Jennifer Nedelsky and Tom Malleson, *Part-Time for All: A Care Manifesto* (OUP 2023).

CHAPTER 43

Lawyers and Law Firms

CAMILA BUSTOS

1. Introduction

CLIMATE change has been called the "crisis of our times". Put simply, our house is on fire. Against the projections of devastating climate impacts, several professions have begun to rethink how to respond and transform under this new reality.[1] In parallel, the so-called enablers of climate disruption have faced scrutiny for their role in upholding the status quo and failing to effectively respond to a warming world. Climate advocates have targeted financial institutions for their role in funding fossil fuel projects despite the scientific consensus to shift away from carbon-intensive energy sources.[2] Campaigners have similarly targeted public relations firms, demanding that these firms decline to work on behalf of the fossil fuel industry as part of a broader refusal to erode their social license to operate.[3]

A similar trend is now shaping the legal industry. Because "[l]awyers are everywhere in the context of climate change",[4] the legal profession has begun to reckon with climate change and its impact on legal practice.[5] Some scholars and advocates have called for a "climate-conscious" approach to lawyering,[6] which seeks to integrate climate change as a cross-cutting

[1] See, e.g., 'Doctors from Around the World Unite to Call for Urgent Climate Action' (*The Guardian*, 28 October 2023) <https://www.theguardian.com/environment/2023/oct/28/doctors-from-around-the-world-unite-to-call-for-urgent-climate-action> accessed 13 June 2025.

[2] Rainforest Action Network and others, 'Banking on Climate Chaos: Fossil Fuel Finance Report 2024' (2024) <https://www.bankingonclimatechaos.org/wp-content/uploads/2024/07/BOCC_2024_vF3.pdf> accessed 15 March 2025 (finding that the world's 60 largest banks continue to fund fossil fuel infrastructure, reaching USD $6.9 trillion).

[3] Clean Creatives, 'The Future of Creativity Is Clean' <https://cleancreatives.org/> accessed 15 March 2025 (describing 'a movement of advertisers, PR professionals, and their clients cutting ties with fossil fuels').

[4] Steven Vaughan, 'Climate Change and the Rule of Law(yers): What Thinner and Thicker Accounts Might Require of Those in Practice' (2022) University College London Research Paper Series No 11/2022; Achinthi C Vithanage and Nadia Ahmad, 'ABA at COP28: Calling on the Legal Community for a Common Cause' (*American Bar Association*, 1 March 2024). <https://www.americanbar.org/groups/environment_energy_resources/resources/trends/2024-march-april/aba-at-cop28/> accessed 15 March 2025 (observing that lawyers are 'adjudicators, drafters, negotiators, advisers, mediators, and translators of complex scientific data and goals into actionable policies and legal frameworks . . . Most of all, they are professionally mandated to deliver on the quality of justice').

[5] See, e.g., John C Dernbach, Matthew Bogoshian, and Irma S Russell, 'Sustainability Essentials: A Leadership Guide for Lawyers' (*Environmental Law Institute*, 2022).

[6] Brian J Preston, 'Climate Conscious Lawyering' (2021) 95(51) Australian Law Journal; John C Dernbach, Tracy D Hester, and Amy L Edwards, 'ABA Encourages Climate-Conscious Lawyering at COP27' (*American Bar Association*, 3 March 2023). <https://www.americanbar.org/groups/environment_energy_resources/publications/trends/2022-2023/march-april-2023/aba-encourages-climate-conscious> accessed 15 March 2025; Kim Bouwer has similarly called for a 'climate-conscious' approach in the

issue impacting *all* areas of legal practice. At the same time, recent efforts by bar associations, law firms, and civil society organisations have focused on the role of lawyers in tackling climate change, exploring the ways in which lawyers as service providers can either exacerbate the crisis by upholding current structures or combat climate change by aligning the profession with a climate-survivable future.[7]

Several bar associations around the world have released statements on the importance of tackling climate change and developed initiatives to reflect their commitment to sustainable development more broadly. In parallel, law firms have launched initiatives to reduce the carbon footprint of their business model, primarily by tackling direct emissions from their operations and reducing the environmental impact of their services. For example, the Legal Sustainability Alliance (LSA) in the UK—a group of 300 law firms—has pledged to work collaboratively to improve the environmental sustainability of their operations and activities.[8] Similar initiatives promoting sustainable practices across the legal sector exist in the US and Australia.[9]

This chapter provides an overview of how the legal profession has responded to increased calls to align legal practice with climate change and sustainable development goals writ-large, exploring how lawyers and law firms can increase climate ambition. I examine existing and potential private environmental governance[10] initiatives and ultimately argue that lawyers have a duty to address climate change by meaningfully supporting a transition away from a carbon-intensive model. I specifically look at seven potential actions law firms can take to move the climate agenda forward, namely (1) reducing operational emissions, (2) supporting advised emissions schemes, (3) assisting clients with climate regulations, (4) avoiding greenwashing, (5) seeking clients promoting decarbonisation, (6) reconsidering representation of climate-harmful entities, and (7) reforming professional responsibility rules.

2. Environmental, Social, and Governance (ESG) Principles and Law Firms

In the last decade or so, major law firms have developed Environmental, Social, and Governance (ESG) practice areas to support corporate clients seeking to minimise the human rights and environmental impacts of their operations. This move reflects a broader shift in corporate practice as clients nudge law firms to provide ESG-aligned advice and to demonstrate

context of climate litigation, which 'demands awareness of the interfaces between the subject matter of the litigation and climate change issues'. Kim Bouwer, 'Climate Consciousness in Daily Legal Practice' (*OUPblog*, 22 May 2015) <https://blog.oup.com/2015/05/climate-consciousness-daily-legal-practice/> accessed 15 March 2025.

[7] Brian J Preston, 'Climate Conscious Lawyering' (2021) 95 Australian Law Journal 51.

[8] See, e.g., Legal Sustainability Alliance, 'LSA Membership Principles' (2019) <https://legalsustainabilityalliance.com/about-us-2/principles/>.

[9] Some examples include Australian Legal Sector Alliance, 'About AusLSA' <https://www.legalsectoralliance.com.au/about> accessed 15 March 2025; Legal Sustainability Network, 'About Us' <https://legalsustainabilitynetwork.org/> accessed 15 March 2025.

[10] Michael P Vandenbergh, 'The Emergence of Private Environmental Governance' (2014) 44 Environmental Law Reporter 10125; Joshua Galperin, 'Foreword: Private, Environmental, Governance' (2018) 9 George Washington Journal of Energy & Environmental Law 1 (recognising the incredible growth of private environmental governance as an area of study in the legal academy). See also Michael P Vandenbergh and Paul Stern, Chapter 31 of this handbook.

ESG credentials.[11] Although private environmental governance efforts such as ESG metrics have primarily focused on business and industry actors, "lawyers are equally important actors because of the role that their clients play (positively and negatively) in climate change, and the impact their advice and legal assistance can have".[12] Indeed, an industry survey indicated that 87% of legal industry members regularly receive requests for proposals asking for information about the firm's environmental practices, initiatives, and results.[13] Further, 53% of those surveyed stated that their current or new clients feel environmental sustainability is "very important".[14] It is not then surprising that ESG-related risks are often cited as having high risk potential by in-house lawyers.[15]

Yet these trends may be seeing a reversal as ESG faces increasing pushback.[16] After significant growth in popularity, ESG seems to, at the very least, be facing a retreat. According to survey results, ESG-related statements have declined, with some actors using different terms altogether like "transition investing".[17] In 2022, the Vanguard Group—the world's biggest mutual fund manager—withdrew from a net-zero industry initiative.[18] J. P. Morgan announced it would also quit a similar initiative in 2024, while BlackRock scaled down its commitment.[19] The general critique has been that climate pledges may cause asset managers to act inconsistently with their fiduciary duties to maximise their clients' financial interests.[20] In the United States, more than twenty states sued the Department of Labor under the Biden administration, seeking to set aside rules integrating climate change and ESG considerations in retirement

[11] Olivia Adam, 'Opinion: Client Demand Pushes Law Firms to Demonstrate ESG Credentials' (*IFLR*, 20 November 2023) <https://www.iflr.com/article/2ch86mm061y5yz0u7v30g/opinion-client-demand-pushes-law-firms-to-demonstrate-esg-credentials> accessed 15 June 2025; Todd D Amaral, 'Conflicting Goals: The Ethics and Accountability of Law Firm Environmental, Social, and Governance (ESG) Policies' (2024) 29 Roger Williams University Law Review 323 (noting that 'the realization of the importance of ESG has led many law firms to establish multi- disciplinary advisory practices to help clients address the policy and corporate governance aspects of ESG').

[12] John C Dernbach and others, 'The Role of Lawyers, Bar Associations, and Law Societies in Combatting Climate Change' (2023) 38(1) ABA, Natural Resources & Environment.

[13] Erin Brereton, 'Law Firms' Evolving Take on Sustainability' (Legal Management, April 2022) <https://www.alanet.org/legal-management/2022/april/features/law-firm-evolving-take-on-sustainability> accessed 15 June 2025. One global law firm recently noted that it had received 50 requests from RFPs to share the firm's ESG information, including carbon emissions, between October 2022 and March 2023. Gayatri Joshi, 'How Law Firms are Calculating their Greenhouse Gas Emissions' (*Reuters*, 23 May 2023) <https://www.reuters.com/legal/legalindustry/how-law-firms-calculate-greenhouse-gas-emissions-2023-05-23/> accessed 9 January 2025.

[14] ibid.

[15] ibid.

[16] John Norberg, 'The Slow Death of ESG and DEI' (*FirstThings*, 4 February 2025) <https://firstthings.com/the-slow-death-of-esg-and-dei/> accessed 15 June 2025; John Dernbach, Chapter 35 of this handbook.

[17] Mary Foley, 'Reports of the Death of ESG Are Greatly Exaggerated' (*Forbes*, 6 March 2024) <https://www.forbes.com/sites/maryfoley/2024/03/06/reports-of-the-death-of-esg-are-greatly-exaggerated/> accessed 15 June 2025.

[18] Ross Kerber and Noor Zainab Hussain, 'Vanguard Quits Net Zero Climate Effort, Citing Need for Independence' (*Reuters*, 7 December 2022) <https://www.reuters.com/business/sustainable-business/vanguard-quits-net-zero-climate-alliance-2022-12-07/> accessed 15 June 2025.

[19] Patrick Temple-West and Brooke Masters, 'JP Morgan and State Street Quit Climate Group as BlackRock Scales Back' (*Financial Times*, 15 February 2024) <https://www.ft.com/content/3ce06a6f-f0e3-4f70-a078-82a6c265ddc2> accessed 15 June 2025.

[20] It is also likely that many of these firms are responding to Republican-led efforts that perceive climate pledges as a 'boycott' of the fossil fuel industry. ibid.

plan management.[21] Texas and West Virginia—two US states with significant fossil fuel interests—have blocked certain financial companies from operating in their states.[22] Across the country, Republican majorities at the state level introduced over 150 anti-ESG bills in 2024 in state legislatures.[23]

That said, outside the United States, the momentum towards ESG might endure. Responsible investing may continue to garner support, with an increase in sustainable global fund assets and sustainable finance regulations worldwide.[24] For example, Norway's sovereign wealth fund has retained its focus on ESG and divested from dozens of companies due to ESG-related risks.[25] Firms will have to navigate changing regulatory landscapes across jurisdictions, particularly those operating in jurisdictions with seemingly contradictory directions such as the US and the European Union.

At the same time as law firms wrestle with an uncertain ESG landscape, the Trump administration has launched an unprecedented attack on law firms and lawyers perceived as threats because of past clients or causes.[26] The American Bar Association (ABA) has rejected these attacks, calling upon the legal profession to speak against intimidation and defend the rule of law, judicial independence, and due process.[27] Several firms have struck deals with President Trump,[28] agreeing to provide pro-bono legal services to causes favoured by the administration in exchange for keeping access to federal buildings and suspending federal investigations into the firms' human resources practices.[29] The response among law firms has varied, with an apparent split between firms oriented towards transactional versus litigation work. Law firms entering deals with the government have significant transactional work, while firms with more prominent litigation dockets have resorted instead to filing legal challenges. This fragmented response demonstrates that law firms are not monolithic and respond to external pressures

21 Timbre Shriver, 'State AGs Challenge Department of Labor Rule on ESG Investing' (*National Law Review*, 18 March 2024) <https://natlawreview.com/article/state-ags-challenge-department-labor-rule-esg-investing> accessed 15 June 2025.

22 Interestingly, Texas has also been sued over its ESG law for violating free speech. Jonathan Stempel, 'Texas Is Sued over Anti-ESG law' (*Reuters*, 29 August 2024) <https://www.reuters.com/legal/texas-is-sued-over-anti-esg-law-2024-08-29/> accessed 15 June 2025. For a more detailed account of the ethical implications of this ESG backlash, see Victor B Flatt, 'Getting "Woke" Out of Business? Is Attorney Anti-ESG Anti-Ethical?' (2025) Case Legal Studies Research Paper No. 2025-9 <https://ssrn.com/abstract=5211562 or http://dx.doi.org/10.2139/ssrn.5211562> accessed 15 June 2025.

23 Richa Naidu, 'Companies Walk ESG Tightrope, Under Fire from All Sides Over Disclosures' (*Reuters*, 28 February 2024) <https://www.reuters.com/sustainability/boards-policy-regulation/companies-walk-esg-tightrope-under-fire-all-sides-over-disclosures-2024-02-29/> accessed 15 June 2025.

24 Foley (n 17).

25 Kari Lundgren, 'Norway $1.8 Trillion Fund Hones ESG Focus, Cut 49 Companies' (*Bloomberg*, 6 February 2025) <https://www.bloomberg.com/news/articles/2025-02-06/norway-1-8-trillion-fund-quit-49-companies-for-esg-risk-in-2024?embedded-checkout=true> accessed 15 June 2025.

26 Carrie Johnson, 'Trump's Deals with Law Firms Are Like Deals "Made with a Gun to the Head," Lawyers Say' (*NPR*, 31 May 2025) <https://www.npr.org/2025/05/31/nx-s1-5406173/trump-deals-law-firms> accessed 15 June 2025 (some of the targets include firms who have represented the Democratic National Committee).

27 William R Bay, 'The ABA Rejects Efforts to Undermine the Courts and the Legal Profession' (*ABA*, 3 March, 2025) <https://www.americanbar.org/news/abanews/aba-news-archives/2025/03/aba-rejects-efforts-to-undermine-courts-and-legal-profession/> accessed 15 June 2025.

28 ibid.

29 Sam Levine, 'US Lawyers Set Up Own Firms to Lead Legal Fightback in Face of Trump Onslaught' (*The Guardian*, 18 May 2025) <https://www.theguardian.com/us-news/2025/may/18/trump-administration-law-firms> accessed 15 June 2025.

according to their different position in the legal market, internal cultures, and firm priorities. As law firms face pressure not only to move away from ESG or climate-aligned programmes, but also to terminate diversity, equity, and inclusion (DEI) initiatives and cease providing pro-bono work for "unpopular" causes (such as legal services to immigrants), lawyers will have to reevaluate how to uphold the values of the legal profession with competing demands.

3. The Legal Profession's Response to Climate Change

Emerging efforts by bar associations have focused on how climate change shapes lawyers' professional obligations. In 2019, the American Bar Association (ABA) adopted a climate change resolution urging the legal profession to take greater action to reduce greenhouse gas emissions "to net zero or below".[30] In 2024, the ABA built on prior resolutions to "urge[] lawyers to learn about sustainable development, and to counsel their clients on related risks and opportunities".[31] The ABA has also created a task force exploring the role of practitioners in integrating climate considerations into legal practice, illustrating how climate advocates are leveraging bar associations to drive crucial conversations on the profession's responsibility in the context of climate change.

Similar efforts recognising climate change's magnitude and the role of lawyers in addressing climate-related challenges are taking place in England and Wales, Scotland, Canada, and Australia.[32] The Law and Society of England and Wales—a professional association representing solicitors—has produced by far the most comprehensive and cutting-edge climate change guidance for solicitors' practices, legal firms, and in-house employers.[33] The guidance helps firms understand and reduce clients' and their own climate impact, explore the types of risks that climate change poses, and assess the impact of climate change's legal risks on professional duties.[34] Significantly, the guidance recognises that firms might consider whether "to advise on matters that are incompatible with the 1.5°C goal".[35] Similar guidance is being developed by the Bar Council's Climate Crisis Working Group to advise the Bar Council on the role of barristers in the context of the climate crisis.[36]

[30] The 2019 resolution highlighted the need for a just transition towards renewable energies for communities reliant on carbon-intensive industries and urged lawyers to play an active role in supporting said efforts to mitigate and adapt, both through pro bono activities and through their for-profit client matters. ABA House of Delegates, Resolution 111 (2019) <https://www.americanbar.org/content/dam/aba/directories/policy/annual-2019/111-annual-2019.pdf>.

[31] American Bar Association, Resolution 513 (2024) <https://www.americanbar.org/content/dam/aba/directories/policy/annual-2024/513-annual-2024.pdf>.

[32] The Law Council of Australia (LCA) also released a climate change policy statement in November of 2021, addressing the profound impacts of climate change on legal frameworks and the profession, urging lawyers to understand and respond to wide-ranging legal implications. Inside Australia, the Law Society of New South Wales has established a working group on climate change and has suggested that there is 'an evolving duty of care owed by solicitors to their clients to provide advice regarding a legal problem which meaningfully addresses any climate change issues and related consequences'. The Law Society of NSW, 'The Legal Implications of Climate Change' <https://www.lawsociety.com.au/legal-implications-climate-change> accessed 15 March 2025.

[33] The Law Society of England and Wales, 'The Impact of Climate Change on Solicitors' (19 April 2023) <https://www.lawsociety.org.uk/topics/climate-change/impact-of-climate-change-on-solicitors> accessed 15 March 2025.

[34] ibid.

[35] ibid.

[36] Communication with the author.

Civil society and industry efforts to align the profession with a climate-stable future primarily fall into three advocacy models: (1) collaboration, (2) accountability, and (3) technocracy. Under the collaboration model, advocates (often other lawyers) work alongside law firms to decarbonise their operations, expand work on behalf of renewable energy firms, and overall support climate ambition. Supporters of this model see themselves able to assist and even nudge law firms towards a more environmentally sustainable practice. Under the collaboration model, advocates are working *with* law firms. This approach does not question the neutral conception of lawyers, whereby attorneys' professional duties can only be met by allowing lawyers to remain morally non-accountable for their clients' actions. Ultimately, the collaboration model seeks to facilitate climate ambition while still adhering to the standard conception of lawyers as service providers, whose actions are independent from their client.

The Net Zero Lawyers Alliance (NZLA) is an illustrative example of the collaboration model. The NZLA is a voluntary initiative composed of thirty-five member firms encompassing more than 100,000 lawyers across over forty jurisdictions.[37] NZLA supports legal professionals with the knowledge and expertise necessary to assist their clients in decarbonising, consisting of "setting emissions reduction targets, providing pro-bono services, setting targets for capacity building, and aligning legal services with net zero".[38] This initiative reflects the belief that lawyers providing competent counsel to corporate actors—including and perhaps most importantly to big emitters—is an essential part of a transition towards a stable climate.[39] Under this logic, competent counsel should result in increased compliance and ultimately, steer clients away from environmentally or socially damaging behaviour.

In contrast, a second set of initiatives under the accountability model has taken a more antagonistic role, at least with respect to large law firms, by leveraging arguments grounded in ordinary morality and moral stigma. The accountability model critiques the traditional conception of lawyers and legal ethics broadly, positing attorneys can, in fact, be morally accountable for the clients they choose and the outcomes of said legal representation. This advocacy model seeks to reorient legal practice by arguing lawyers are morally obligated to wield their professional roles in service of climate action.

Law Students for Climate Accountability (LSCA) and Lawyers Are Responsible (LAR) are examples of the accountability model in practice. LSCA utilises a naming-and-shaming strategy[40] by producing an annual climate scorecard that assigns letter grades to the Vault 100 law firms based on the amount of litigation, transactional, and lobbying work these law firms perform on behalf of fossil fuel companies versus renewable energy companies.[41] The

[37] Net Zero Lawyers Alliance, 'About Us' <https://www.netzerolawyers.com/about-us> accessed 15 October 2024. NZLA members 'commit to reducing operational emissions, contributing pro bono time to projects to achieve climate objectives, building capacity among all their lawyers, and providing net zero aligned advice'. Net Zero Lawyers Alliance, 'Our Commitment' <https://www.netzerolawyers.com/commitments/our-commitment> accessed 15 October 2024.

[38] ibid.

[39] Katie Kouchakji, 'How the Climate Crisis is Changing the Legal Profession' (*IBA*, 28 September 2021) <https://www.ibanet.org/How-the-climate-crisis-is-changing-the-legal-profession> accessed 15 March 2025.

[40] Sharon Yadin, *Fighting Climate Change Through Shaming* (CUP 2023) 41.

[41] Law Students for Climate Accountability, 'Who We Are' <www.ls4ca.org> accessed 25 October 2024; 'Vault 100' <https://vault.com/best-companies-to-work-for/law/top-100-law-firms-rankings> accessed 15 March 2025; LSCA has also produced research on the UK and Canadian legal sectors: Law Students for Climate Accountability, 'The Carbon Circle: The UK Legal Industry's Ties to Fossil Fuel Companies' (*LSCA*, 10 May 2023) <https://www.ls4ca.org/blog-show-all/the-carbon-circle> accessed 15 March 2025; Law Students for Climate Accountability, 'The Canadian Law Firm Climate Impact Report'

organisation has expanded outside the United States and is moving towards a global approach to greater accountability in the legal industry. LSCA ultimately questions the notion that attorneys are neutral service-lenders and cannot be held accountable for their clients' actions. Through its naming-and-shaming technique, LSCA seeks to "pressure firms by undermining their social license, thereby improving compliance and strengthening climate social norms relating to corporate behaviour".[42] Under the accountability model, the "threat of public pressure is also meant to function as a deterrent of undesired climate actions".[43]

Another initiative leveraging moral stigma is LAR, which has led efforts in the UK to shame law firms such as Slaughter & May for their role in representing fossil fuel companies, including Premier Oil.[44] LAR has also called for lawyers to pledge to withhold their services supporting new fossil fuel projects and to defy the bar by declaring they would not prosecute climate protesters.[45] The signatories of the Declaration of Conscience even self-referred themselves to the Bar Standards Board (BSB) for breaching their duty under the cab-rank rule.[46] The self-referral is significant given that the cab-rank rule, which ostensibly imposes the obligation to accept all clients seeking their service, is seen as central to protecting access to justice and stability in the profession.[47]

In the UK, other examples of the accountability model involve demonstrations against law firms seen as upholding the fossil fuel industry by lending legal services to fossil fuel companies. For instance, in 2023, a group of lawyers and advocates orchestrated a climate action at the Royal Courts of Justice in London. The group projected a message directly onto the building that houses the Royal Courts: "An urgent and radical transformation is needed to seriously tackle the climate crisis."[48]

(*LSCA*, 6 November 2023) <https://www.ls4ca.org/blog-show-all/canadianimpactreport> accessed 15 March 2025.

42 Sharon Yadin, *Fighting Climate Change Through Shaming* (CUP 2023) 34.

43 ibid 41.

44 'Slaughter and May Advised Premier Oil on Its Merger with Chrysaor' (*Slaughter and May*, 1 April 2021) <https://www.slaughterandmay.com/recent-work/premier-oil-on-its-proposed-merger-with-chrysaor/> accessed 15 March 2025.

45 Jack Womack, 'Slaughter and May Agrees to Meet Lawyers Climate Group' (*Law.com*, 11 September 2023) <https://www.law.com/international-edition/2023/09/11/slaughter-and-may-agrees-to-meet-lawyer-climate-pressure-group/> accessed 15 March 2025; Lawyers Are Responsible, 'Declaration of Conscience, Lawyers Are Responsible' <https://www.lar.earth/sign/> accessed 6 January 2025; Daniel Gayle, 'Top Lawyers Defy Bar to Declare They Will Not Prosecute Peaceful Climate Protesters' (*The Guardian*, 24 March 2023) <https://www.theguardian.com/environment/2023/mar/24/top-lawyers-defy-bar-declare-will-not-prosecute-peaceful-climate-protesters> accessed 15 March 2025; Jerome Entwisle, 'Climate Change and the Cab Rank Rule' (*Bar News*, 2023) <https://bn.nswbar.asn.au/article/climate-change-and-the-cab-rank-rule> accessed 15 March 2025.

46 Lawyers Are Responsible, 'Declaration of Conscience, Lawyers Are Responsible' <https://www.lar.earth/sign/> accessed 6 January 2025.

47 Neil Rose, 'Lawyers' Eco-Declaration Sparks Cab-Rank Rule Row' (*Legal Futures*, 24 March 2023) <https://www.legalfutures.co.uk/latest-news/lawyers-eco-declaration-sparks-cab-rank-rule-row> accessed 15 March 2025. Meanwhile, attorneys in the US generally maintain freedom to decline representation as a matter of principle, except in criminal law. Though the cab-rank rule has not been formally adopted in the US, attorneys broadly subscribe to the notion that 'everyone deserves representation'.

48 Law Students for Climate Accountability, 'The Carbon Circle: The UK Legal Industry's Ties to Fossil Fuel Companies' (*LSCA*, 10 May 2023) <https://www.ls4ca.org/blog-show-all/canadianimpactreport> accessed 15 March 2025.

Finally, under the technocracy model, advocacy efforts focus on measuring the climate impact of law firms through their direct and indirect emissions. The technocratic model focuses on technical approaches to decarbonising the legal industry, taking no position on how lawyers may be complicit or not in contributing to climate change. As opposed to the first two models, the underlying presumption of this approach is that information is in itself valuable and that developing sophisticated models to calculate a firm's impact is a necessary step in moving the legal profession towards a more sustainable practice.

Dozens of law firms have implemented sustainability strategies and sought to reduce their Scope 1 and Scope 2 emissions.[49] More recently, several scholars and practitioners have called for law firms to account for their "advised" or "serviced" emissions,[50] which refers to indirect emissions stemming from the representation or provision of legal services as opposed to direct emissions from a firm's operations.[51] The model has partly resulted from clients "challenging [legal] advisers to demonstrate they can help them in their transition to low or no emissions and that they are committed to this, not just in the advice they provide, but in not providing advice which contributes to harmful practices by others."[52] In parallel to these efforts, the Net Zero for Professional Service Providers Working Group—which is part of the UN Race to Zero—issued Draft Guiding Principles for Serviced Emissions in 2024.[53]

Another example of a technocratic approach is the Legal Charter 1.5, a joint initiative between several firms "to reduc[e] greenhouse gas emissions at the speed and scale necessary to restrict global temperature increases to no more than 1.5°C by 2030".[54] The initiative is led by a coalition of corporate law firms[55] and supports the development of a framework for measuring advised emissions (Principle 2) as well as a commitment to annual reporting on progress (Principle 5).[56]

Finally, The Chancery Lane Project has created a "net zero toolkit", a large collection of contract clauses that can be incorporated into standard law firm contracts and other commercial agreements, as well as a "collection of tools that align contractual drafting with net zero".[57]

[49] Scope 1 emissions refer to direct emissions resulting from sources that are under the direct control or ownership of the emitter, while Scope 2 emissions are indirect emissions resulting from the purchase of electricity, heating, or cooling. Advised emissions are *indirect* emissions stemming from the provision of legal services as opposed to direct emissions from a firm's operations. US EPA, *Scope 1 and Scope 2 Inventory Guidance* (EPA Center for Corporate Climate Leadership) <https://www.epa.gov/climateleadership/scope-1-and-scope-2-inventory-guidance> accessed 6 January 2025.

[50] Tracy Hester, 'Can Counselors Be Complicit?' (2024) 41 Environmental Law Institute 38 <https://www.eli.org/the-environmental-forum/can-counselors-be-complicit> accessed 15 June 2025; UNFCCC, 'Professional Service Providers in a Net Zero Future' <https://climatechampions.unfccc.int/system/net-zero-for-professional-service-providers/> accessed 12 November 2024. Scope 3 emissions 'are not explicitly included in the GHG Scope 3 protocol as downstream emissions relate to products not services'. Matthew Gingell, 'Measuring "Advised Emissions": A Framework for Assessing the Carbon Footprint of a Law Firm's Advice' (*Oxygen House*, 2023) <https://legalsustainabilityalliance.com/wp-content/uploads/2023/09/Measuring-Advised-Emissions-final-200923.pdf> accessed 12 November 2024.

[51] David Hunter, 'Advised Emissions: Assessing the Impact' (*Law Society Gazette*, 28 April 2023) <https://www.lawgazette.co.uk/practice-points/advised-emissions-assessing-the-impact/5115871.article> accessed 12 November 2024.

[52] ibid.

[53] Hester (n 51).

[54] Legal Charter 1.5, 'Inspiring Ambitious Transformative Action to Combat the Climate Crisis' <https://legalcharter1point5.com/> accessed 3 January 2025.

[55] ibid.

[56] ibid.

[57] Legal Charter 1.5, 'Legal Charter 1.5' <https://legalcharter1point5.com/wp-content/uploads/2024/01/The-Legal-Charter-1.5-.pdf> accessed 3 January 2025.

While most of these clauses are based on United Kingdom law, they are also being drafted for other jurisdictions, including the US.[58]

4. Climate Best Practices for the Modern Law Firm

4.1 Law Firm's Direct and Indirect Emissions

4.1.1 Reduce the Direct Impact of Law Firm Operations

Unsurprisingly, the most straightforward contribution to a stable climate is a commitment followed by concrete actions to reduce Scope 1 and Scope 2 emissions. Firms looking to increase sustainability can engage in several best practices like document digitisation, robust in-office recycling, reduced travel, and energy conservation practices.[59] Many law firms have already begun to take steps to reduce their environmental impact, as demonstrated by the Legal 500 annual Green Guide, which ranks different firms based on their sustainability initiatives.[60]

4.1.2 Meaningfully Support an Advised or Serviced Emissions Scheme

Perhaps one of the most comprehensive and long-term actions that law firms can take to support a just transition is to develop a robust advised emissions scheme establishing a uniform methodology to measure a firm's climate impact. It is possible that the advised emissions stemming from a firm's advice to a fossil fuel company may exceed any reductions achieved through the reduction of emissions directly traceable to the firm's operations. Calculating serviced emissions—with a rigorous methodology and publicly available data—can contribute to climate ambition. Indeed, the Law Society of England and Wales' guidance recognises that "advised emissions associated with matters on which a solicitor provides legal advice are attracting increased attention in relation to professional services, including legal services",[61] and recommends that lawyers prepare for accounting of advised emissions of their work.

The Draft Guiding Principles for Serviced Emissions provide a starting point for service providers considering how to tackle their advised emissions. However, the Draft Principles contain some significant limitations. They fail to discuss or explain how service providers may reduce their serviced emissions in the near term by declining or phasing out work that is incompatible with limiting warming to 1.5°C. Moreover, the Draft Principles' vagueness limits their ability to effectively curb greenwashing. Service providers can claim to be supporting corporate clients in transitioning away from fossil fuels or carbon-intensive activities, or to be working to reduce their serviced emissions, but not actually take any action to reduce their work on high-emitting projects. As recent announcements by major fossil fuel companies demonstrate, many energy companies are not actually committed to transitioning away from

[58] ibid.

[59] Beth Cooper, 'How Can Law Firms Become More Sustainable?' (*Interlink Recruitment*, 9 January 2025) <https://www.interlinkrecruitment.com/blog/how-can-law-firms-become-more-sustainable> accessed 3 January 2025.

[60] Legal 500, 'The Legal 500 Green Guide: United States 2025' <https://www.legal500.com/editions/global-green-guide-united-states-2025/> accessed 3 January 2025.

[61] The Law Society of England and Wales, 16 'The Impact of Climate Change on Solicitors' (19 April 2023) <https://www.lawsociety.org.uk/topics/climate-change/impact-of-climate-change-on-solicitors> accessed 15 March 2025.

fossil fuels or seriously considering renewables.[62] New oil, gas, or coal resource development risks locking in emissions for decades, as fossil fuel companies have the economic incentive to continue to extract or operate for the lifetime of the investment. Another related concern stems from the likelihood that service providers will wait for a finalised serviced emissions methodology before taking action to reduce serviced emissions. As written, the Draft Principles do not clearly state that choosing not to engage high-emitting clients and projects is a viable way to reduce serviced emissions.

The Law Society of England and Wales supported the Draft Principles but critiqued their reliance upon "quantitative methodology that currently does not exist" and argued they could go further by clarifying how they apply and interact with other frameworks. Significantly, the Law Society acknowledged the Draft Principles will only be feasible for large service providers given how expensive their development and implementation will be and given a lack of current client demand.[63] This raises tricky questions for mid-size and smaller firms with fewer resources to develop an advised emissions scheme.

The Draft Principles—like many other climate-related targets or goals—incorporate a net-zero approach, aiming to align service providers' advised emissions with the goal of "net zero emissions no later than 2050".[64] While outside the scope of this chapter, it is important to note there are significant problems with relying on net-zero emissions pledges, which have generally been kept vague and can perpetuate climate inequities.[65] Net-zero approaches create the risk that law firms will attempt to use their work on renewable energy or carbon sinks to offset or justify continued work on carbon intensive projects.[66] Furthermore, offsets come with all sorts of implementation problems, some of which include achieving pledged emission reductions at a certain point in time that is dependent upon factors outside of the organisation's control (e.g., carbon sequestration timelines vary depending both on the project and external factors such as wildfires). Emissions accounting, verification, and reporting are also notoriously complex. Furthermore, net zero often allows emitters in the Global North to offset their carbon emissions by funding projects in the Global South and in low-income communities. Carbon offsetting projects may contribute to the displacement of communities and ignore harmful localised impacts.

The Legal Charter 1.5, an initiative led by major law firms that also supports promoting an advised emissions framework, suffers from similar critiques. The language of the Charter does not contemplate any specific timeline or pledge, raising questions regarding the firms'

[62] Simon Jack and Faarea Masud, 'BP Shuns Renewables in Return to Oil and Gas' (*BBC*, 26 February 2025) <https://www.bbc.com/news/articles/c3374ekd11po> accessed 15 March 2025.

[63] The Law Society of England and Wales, 'UN Race to Zero's Draft Guiding Principles for Serviced Emissions: Law Society Response' <https://www.lawsociety.org.uk/campaigns/consultation-responses/un-race-to-zero-draft-guiding-principles-for-serviced-emissions> accessed 15 March 2025.

[64] Oxford Net Zero & Race to Zero, 'Professional Service Providers: Consultation on Draft Guiding Principles for Serviced Emissions' (Draft Working Paper 7, 2023) 3 <https://climatechampions.unfccc.int/wp-content/uploads/2023/12/Professional-Service-Providers-draft-working-pap er-for-upload.pdf> accessed 15 March 2025.

[65] Shelley Welton, 'Neutralizing the Atmosphere' (2022) 132 Yale Law Journal 171 <https://www.yalelawjournal.org/feature/neutralizing-the-atmosphere> accessed 15 July 2025; Courtney Lindwall, 'The Promise and Pitfalls of Net Zero Pledges' (*NRDC*, 3 February 2022) <https://www.nrdc.org/stories/promise-and-pitfalls-net-zero-pledges> accessed 15 March 2025.

[66] Corporate Accountability, 'The Big Con: How Big Polluters are Advancing a "Net Zero" Climate Agenda to Delay, Deceive, and Deny' (Corporate Accountability, 2021) <https://www.corporateaccountability.org/wp-content/uploads/2021/06/The-Big-Con_EN.pdf> accessed 15 March 2025.

commitment to disclose their advised emissions and to decarbonise their portfolio by reducing representation involving fossil fuel clients, steering their clients away from carbon-intensive activities, or developing a clear climate standard to guide their future business.

Overall, while developing a robust advised emissions framework holds great potential for moving the legal profession towards a more sustainable future, the current initiatives appear to lack concrete commitments to transform the status quo.

4.2 Law Firm's Work Vis-à-vis Clients

4.2.1 Assist Clients with Climate-Related Regulatory Developments

While law firms generally are not publicly traded companies, they often represent clients who are and who therefore will need to be aware of and comply with a landscape of changing regulations on corporate disclosures and climate change law. For example, under the Biden administration, the Securities and Exchange Commission (SEC) finalised a rule that required public companies to disclose climate-related information on their annual reports.[67] The rule, which was stayed by a federal court, would have required companies to disclose information like (1) material climate-related risks, both current and future, and their impact on the company's strategy and financial performance; and (2) how their board and management oversee and govern climate-related risks.[68] While the SEC climate disclosure rule was not operationalised,[69] and as ESG trends evolve across jurisdictions, lawyers will be expected to advise their clients on corporate performance and risk management. Some scholars have even observed attorneys have a duty of competence to provide climate-sound advice when relevant across areas of practice.[70] For example, law firms may explain how a client's current or proposed activities will exacerbate climate change or expose the client to future climate liability and other legal risks.

4.2.2 Avoid Greenwashing

Law firms that engage in greenwashing whether by boasting how "green" they are or by helping their clients obfuscate the real impact of their business model should desist from these efforts. Ethics rules across jurisdictions already discourage misleading statements, such as ABA Model Rule 4.1 (encouraging truthfulness in statements to others). The Law Society of England and Wales' guidance includes specific language on greenwashing, observing that firm marketing materials "should not mischaracterize or overstate" the firm's "targets, or progress".[71]

[67] US Securities and Exchange Commission, 'SEC Adopts Amendments to Modernize Reporting of Fund Fees and Expenses', Press Release No. 2024-31 (SEC, 8 February 2024) <https://www.sec.gov/newsroom/press-releases/2024-31> accessed 1 January 2025.

[68] ibid.

[69] John C Dernbach and others, 'The Role of Lawyers, Bar Associations, and Law Societies in Combatting Climate Change' (2023) 38(1) Natural Resources & Environment 3.

[70] John Dernbach, Irma Russell, and Matthew Bogoshian, 'The Lawyer's Duty of Competence in a Climate-Imperiled World' (2024) 92 University of Missouri-Kansas City Law Review 859 (arguing that 'the increasing pace of the climate crisis, and the increasingly sophisticated tools and practices that lawyers now have to address the crisis, expand what lawyers should reasonably do for clients').

[71] Although many would like to see the ABA lead a similar effort, there is scepticism that such a broad and politically diverse organisation may be able to issue a similar document. 'The Roles of Lawyers and Bar Associations in Combating Climate Change' (*Climate Week*, 18 September 2023) <https://www.climateweeknyc.org/events/roles-lawyers-and-bar-associations-combating-climate-change> accessed 15 March 2025.

The guidance also advises lawyers to "ensure any such communications cannot give rise to claims of misrepresentation or greenwashing".[72] The guidance encourages firms that describe their services as sustainable or aligned with specific climate goals like net zero or the Paris Agreement's 1.5°C target to consider "whether those claims can stand up to external, objective scrutiny".[73] Katrina Kuh and Lissa Griffin have argued that attorneys involved in public disinformation campaigns should exercise caution to avoid violating ethical rules, observing that

> the deep public harms from disinformation efforts as well as the unpalatability of the notion that attorneys may ethically deploy their stature and skills to advance corporate deception when not otherwise specifically prohibited by law suggests, at a minimum, that the profession should seriously evaluate the scope of its obligations in this regard.[74]

In sum, lawyers should consider how greenwashing may create regulatory, litigation, and reputational risks for their clients and themselves. Even in instances where clients or firms may have good intentions, counsel should consider how specific claims or engagement with net-zero pledges, carbon offsets, and other green initiatives will withstand external scrutiny. Lawyers should be able to provide advice on how to evaluate and reduce these risks.[75]

4.2.3 Seek and Support Clients Promoting Decarbonisation and Climate-Positive Activities

Law firms can directly support decarbonisation efforts by securing and advising clients whose actions ultimately move society away from carbon-intensive industries, such as renewable energy companies, businesses working towards improving energy efficiency and conservation, or sustainable investment firms. Whether through traditional representation or pro bono work, law firms can use their resources to directly help climate mitigation or adaptation efforts by assisting with contracts, transactions, financing, and regulatory approvals.

Firms may also consider increasing the amount of pro bono work they do on behalf of climate organisations, offering criminal defence to climate protesters, supporting projects that reduce greenhouse gas emissions, or supporting frontline communities interested in bringing legal challenges or leveraging other legal tools against environmental harm. In jurisdictions where climate work is being targeted, law firms may consider providing support to organisations facing challenges to their tax-exempt status or whose governmental grants are being terminated, as has been the case for environmental and climate justice organisations under the first months of the Trump administration.[76]

[72] ibid.

[73] The Law Society of England and Wales, 'The Impact of Climate Change on Solicitors' (19 April 2023) <https://www.lawsociety.org.uk/topics/climate-change/impact-of-climate-change-on-solicitors> accessed 15 March 2025.

[74] Lissa Griffin and Katrina F Kuh, 'Chapter 5: Professional Responsibility and the Corporate Hoodwink: Using the Climate Disinformation Campaign to Examine the Ethical Responsibilities of Attorneys When Corporate Clients Mislead the Public to Avoid Government Regulation' in Keith Hirokawa and Jessica Owley (eds), *Environmental Law, Disrupted* (Edward Elgar Publishing 2021) 107.

[75] Allen & Gledhill LLP, 'What Greenwashing Risks Mean for the Legal Profession' (*Legal 500*, 5 February 2025) <https://www.legal500.com/developments/thought-leadership/what-greenwashing-risks-mean-for-the-legal-profession/> accessed 15 March 2025.

[76] Oliver Milman, 'Trump Has Launched More Attacks on the Environment in 100 Days Than His Entire First Term' (*The Guardian*, 1 May 2025) <https://www.theguardian.com/environment/2025/may/01/trump-air-climate-pollution-regulation-100-days> accessed 15 June 2025.

One consideration is potential conflicts of interest that may arise when a law firm is already lending representation to a party directly opposed. For example, a firm will be unable to provide representation to a community hoping to sue an oil refinery if the firm is already representing said refinery. In the context of law firms entering agreements with the Trump administration to conduct pro bono work on behalf of military veterans, trade deals, immigration enforcement, and police officers,[77] it is possible that firms would undertake representation on behalf of clients that would render them unable to take on climate-friendly work. For smaller firms where pro-bono might not be an option, low-bono representation could still prove to be meaningful.

4.2.4 Reconsider and Potentially Decline Representation of "Climate Wreckers"

Lawyers play a crucial role in upholding a carbon-intensive economic model. Legal counsel is essential to secure and facilitate high-emitting activities like fossil fuel production, extraction, and combustion, as well as methane-emitting operations, such as meat production and processing. Lawyers assist clients across projects by employing transactional, regulatory, or contractual skills. The 2025 Climate Change Scorecard found that "[f]rom 2020–2024, Vault 100 firms engaged in 623 climate-exacerbating representations, earned $35,839,000 [USD] for lobbying on behalf of fossil fuel interests, and facilitated over $2 trillion [USD] in transactions supporting fossil fuel work".[78] The report also found that in 88% of climate cases reported, the Vault 100 firms worked on behalf of the fossil fuel industry.[79]

I have argued elsewhere that the legal profession must reconsider its role amidst the climate crisis, including by examining professional responsibility rules and principles considering the scale of the challenge.[80] Specifically, I have questioned the notion that lawyers are neutral actors and thus bear no ethical responsibility (beyond complying with professional ethics rules) in who they represent. Several scholars, practitioners, and advocates have similarly weighed in on the proper role of lawyers and the ethical questions arising when lawyers represent so-called climate wreckers or climate villains.[81] The Law Society of England and Wales has observed that solicitors have "wide discretion in choosing whether to accept instructions" because they are "not obliged to provide advice to every prospective client that seeks it."[82] Regarding the decision of solicitors to choose clients, the guidance further clarifies that "[s]ome solicitors may also choose to decline to advise on matters that are incompatible with the 1.5°C goal, or for clients actively working against that goal if it conflicts with your values or your firm's stated objectives".[83]

[77] Johnson (n 26).

[78] Law Students for Climate Accountability, '2025 Climate Change Scorecard' (2025) 17–18 <https://www.ls4ca.org/s/LSCA_2025_CLIMATE_SCORECARD-3.pdf> accessed 15 June 2025.

[79] ibid 18.

[80] For a US application, see Camila Bustos, 'Representing Climate Wreckers' (2025) 33 NYU Environmental Law Journal 157.

[81] ibid. For a UK application, see Steven Vaughan, 'Existential Ethics: Thinking Hard About Lawyer Responsibility for Client's Environmental Harms' (2023) 76 Current Legal Problems 1. For a general discussion grounded in moral philosophy, see Eric Boot, 'Climate Change and Complicit Lawyers' (2025) (work in progress) <https://link.springer.com/article/10.1007/s10892-025-09539-3>.

[82] The Law Society of England and Wales, 'The Impact of Climate Change on Solicitors' (19 April 2023) <https://www.lawsociety.org.uk/topics/climate-change/impact-of-climate-change-on-solicitors> accessed 15 March 2025.

[83] ibid.

While my prior analysis has primarily focused on fossil fuel corporations and trade associations that have engaged in public disinformation campaigns to stall climate action and sow doubt regarding climate science,[84] law firms should consider broadly how their representation ultimately enables or hinders the goal of decarbonisation. The conventional conception of lawyers as neutral actors misses the mark by failing to account for the scale of the existential crisis in which we find ourselves.[85] In this context, I have argued how the different conceptions of the lawyer's role as "zealous advocate", "officer of the court", or "legitimising agent" have frustrated private governance efforts to persuade attorneys to fulfil their duty to the rule of law by securing a transition away from fossil fuels. Too many lawyers are comfortable invoking the principle that climate wreckers, however defined, have a right to counsel to justify their choice of clients, which in turn distorts foundational legal principles, and allows lawyers to remain unaccountable to the broader public for the ultimate outcomes of said representation.

This particular approach stands in stark contrast with the *collaborative model* arguments discussed earlier, whereby attorneys see themselves fulfilling their professional responsibility duties when they offer competent and zealous counsel to high emitters. Bradley Wendel explains that whatever moral views one may have of a client's conduct, if the transaction or activity is lawful, "that counts for something in the evaluation of the lawyer's decision to assist the client".[86] However, the climate record of major law firms regarding their clients leaves much to be desired.

For example, Baker McKenzie's website notes that it is "at the cutting edge of climate change law and climate finance developments".[87] However, Baker Makenzie lawyers engage in lobbying on behalf of the fossil fuel industry.[88] Another global firm, Ashurst, identifies itself as a leader in the energy transition, despite being the leading firm litigating on behalf of the coal industry in Australia.[89] Similarly, Latham Watkins's website boasts that the firm "established the first dedicated climate change law practice in 2008, years before most other firms" and "advise[s] on the largest, most significant, and most innovative climate change transactions in the world".[90] At the same time, the firm is ranked among the worst five firms on litigation for

[84] There has been extensive research documenting the role of the fossil fuel industry in promoting climate denialism or scepticism. Naomi Oreskes, *Merchants of Doubt* (Bloomsbury Publishing 2015); Benjamin Franta, 'Early Oil Industry Disinformation on Global Warming' (2021) 30 Environmental Politics 663. More recently, members of the US Congress have urged the Department of Justice to investigate whether these companies' deception campaigns violated federal law. 'Rep. Lieu and Sen. Blumenthal Lead Bicameral Letter Urging DOJ to Investigate Big Oil's Climate Lies', Press Release (25 July 2023) <https://lieu.house.gov/media-center/press-releases/rep-lieu-and-sen-blumenthal-lead-bicameral-letter-urging-doj> accessed 15 March 2025.

[85] Bustos (n 80); Vaughan (n 81).

[86] Bradley Wendel, 'The Rule of Law and Legal-Process Reasons in Attorney Advising' (2019) 99 Boston University Law Review 148.

[87] Baker McKenzie, 'Environment and Climate Change' <https://www.bakermckenzie.com/en/expertise/practices/environment-and-climate-change> accessed 15 July 2025.

[88] Law Students for Climate Accountability, 'Climate Change Scorecard 2024' (2024) 14 <https://static1.squarespace.com/static/646e3b899493ae261720e957/t/66798b882489016ae073aac5/1719241628165/FINAL_2024_Climate_Scorecard_LSCA.pdf>. The report notes that 'lawyers from Akin Gump, Baker McKenzie, Linklaters, and Norton Rose Fulbright lobbied specifically on behalf of the International Emissions Trading Association. The IETA helped shape the concept of the carbon market and has a long history with BP and other fossil fuel companies'. ibid 167.

[89] ibid 24.

[90] Latham & Watkins LLP, 'Climate Change' <https://www.lw.com/en/practices/climate-change> accessed 9 January 2025.

its fossil fuel work.[91] Latham & Watkins was also among the top eight firms lobbying on behalf of carbon capture technology, which has been heavily criticised for its cost and for potentially stalling decarbonisation of the energy system.[92] During a recent United Nations Conference of the Parties (COP), Latham & Watkins lawyers lobbied on behalf of carbon capture technology. They were not alone, as firms like Slaughter and May—which has committed to reduce its emissions by 50% by 2030 and 90% by 2040[93]—represented fossil fuel interests at COP28 in Dubai.[94]

It is with this context in mind that law firms should at the very least consider whether their representation will result in the development of new "carbon bombs", meaning facilities or projects that will get us closer to climate disaster by exceeding scientifically accepted temperature limits.[95] If the direct impact of a particular representation will exacerbate climate change by contributing additional emissions, those lawyers should not be able to use "access to justice" arguments to insulate themselves from criticism. Law firms should not enable further planetary disruption by enabling or facilitating new fossil fuel projects against scientific consensus to keep fossil fuels in the ground. I share Dean Vaughan's observation that lawyers have distorted the principles of "public interest" and "rule of law", utilising them as rhetorical devices to justify their choice of clients.[96] Law firms with serious climate commitments should review and reconsider representing clients whose activities may be legal but are in direct opposition to our future. This argument is particularly salient in the context of transactional work.[97]

The first objection to this approach is that increased scrutiny will block some actors from securing legal counsel, hindering access to the legal system. However, the practical realities of capitalism make it so that corporate clients who can afford a lawyer have access to representation. Indeed, companies often have several firms at their disposal, in addition to in-house counsel. Lawyers who decide to represent clients who conduct environmental harm are often responding to the logic of the market and "financial, psychological, and organisational pressures of law practice . . . [rather than] the rules of legal ethics".[98] Furthermore, at least in the US and the UK, there is no such thing as a constitutional right to counsel in civil matters or a right to the representation of a specific lawyer or law firm. The importance of the right to counsel in criminal matters is vastly different than in the civil context, where disputes often arise

91 Law Students for Climate Accountability (n 87) 36.

92 ibid 15, 17.

93 Slaughter and May, 'Climate Action' <https://www.slaughterandmay.com/our-firm/responsible-business/climate-action/> accessed 9 January 2025.

94 Law Students for Climate Accountability (n 87) 17–18.

95 Damian Carrington and Matthew Taylor, 'Revealed: the "Carbon Bombs" Set to Trigger Catastrophic Climate Breakdown' (*The Guardian*, 11 May 2022) <https://www.theguardian.com/environment/ng-interactive/2022/may/11/fossil-fuel-carbon-bombs-climate-breakdown-oil-gas> accessed 15 January 2025.

96 Vaughan (2022); Vaughan (2023); Steven Vaughan, 'The Unethical Environmental Lawyer', Inauguration Speech at University College London (13 October 2022), in University College London Research Paper Series, No 18/2022 (30 October 2022) 5 <https://ssrn.com/abstract=4253980> accessed 15 January 2025 (noting that 'lawyers often wave the rule of law around like a flag, assuming that it—the rule of law—is this neat, easy, agreed-upon thing and that it also supports whichever particular argument they are trying to make').

97 There are distinct concerns arising in the transactional and the litigation context since the checks of the adversarial system are not present in the former as they are in the latter. For an in-depth discussion of the importance of the adversarial system, see Bustos (n 81) 192.

98 Vaughan (n 81) 30 (citing T Schneyer, 'Moral Philosophy's Standard Misconception of Legal Ethics' (1984) Wisconsin Law Review 1529, 1543).

over profits as opposed to human life or liberty. In the case of "climate wreckers", legal representation involves corporations as opposed to individuals, meaning due process concerns are distinct. While the principle of neutrality and non-accountability can serve a function by guaranteeing that unsavoury *criminal* defendants have counsel, the corporate civil context is quite different.[99]

The second concern stems from fears about how public scrutiny in the form of boycotts or naming and shaming efforts may undermine the rights of corporate actors. However, these efforts are leveraging public opinion and concepts of ordinary morality to raise the reputational costs of representing climate wreckers. Unlike some of the efforts by the Trump administration to leverage the state's monopoly on violence to threaten political opponents, sanction attorneys, and block access to federal buildings, these efforts remain private tools by civil society actors to erode the social license of climate wreckers to operate.

The third concern relates to fears over the independence of the legal profession and adherence to professional responsibility norms. But in the US and many other jurisdictions, there is no obligation to accept a particular client unless there is a court order to do so. Law firms often *choose* to represent clients whose business is inherently at odds with a survivable climate. Furthermore, attorneys should not equate environmental compliance with climate-sound advice. While it is possible that in some instances, attorneys may help shape their client's actions to align with climate goals, this may be simply impossible when the client's goal is to perpetuate fossil fuel infrastructure or methane-releasing operations in meat production. BP's announcement to abandon renewable energy production and its commitment to transition away from fossil fuels, along with similar behaviour by other corporate actors, should give pause to lawyers who believe their work is in fact facilitating decarbonisation.[100] Indeed, the International Energy Agency, an independent intergovernmental organisation providing policy recommendations on energy policy, has observed that oil companies' investments in clean energy are "marginal".[101]

Concerns related to lawyers' professional obligation to remain neutral, non-partisan, and non-accountable for their clients' choices lose force in a context of lobbying and transactional work as opposed to litigation. First, in the context of lobbying and transactions, the adversarial system's checks do not operate in the same way. Because there is no dispute to resolve and no opposing sides, the standard conception of the attorney as a "zealous advocate" is much different than in the context of adversarial matters.[102] Second, arguments related to the right to counsel to conduct multi–million-dollar transactions or lobby against climate change

[99] Vaughan (n 81) 25; see also Abbie Smith, 'Defending Defending: The Case for Unmitigated Zeal on Behalf of People Who Do Terrible Things' (1999) 28 Hofstra Law Review 925.

[100] Kate Aronoff, 'Whatever Happened to "Net-Zero"?' (*The New Republic*, 8 October 2024) <https://newrepublic.com/article/186883/bp-oil-production-emissions-net-zero> accessed 15 March 2025.

[101] International Energy Agency, 'The Oil and Gas Industry in Net Zero Transitions' (*IEA*, 2023) 13, 224 <https://iea.blob.core.windows.net/assets/41800202-d427-44fa-8544-12e3d6e023b4/TheOilandGasIndustryinNetZeroTransitions.pdf> accessed 15 March 2025 ('[T]hese producers face pivotal choices about their role in the global energy system.' Many of these companies have launched campaigns promoting 'minimal investments in clean or renewable energy'); Jeff Brady, 'Exxon Lobbyist Caught on Video Talking About Undermining Biden's Climate Push' (*NPR*, 1 July 2021) <https://www.npr.org/2021/07/01/1012138741/exxon-lobbyist-caught-on-video-talks-about-undermining-bidens-climate-push> accessed 27 June 2025.

[102] David Luban and Bradley W Wendel, 'Philosophical Legal Ethics: An Affectionate History' (2017) 30 Georgetown Journal of Legal Ethics 337, 329 (noting that the standard conception of a lawyer 'has its origins in the adversarial structure of adjudication').

legislation seem less compelling than in the paradigmatic case of the accused individual facing the all-powerful state in a criminal proceeding.

Within the confines of their jurisdictions, lawyers should examine the notion that they have a duty to represent a particular client absent a court-appointment.[103] Law firms already representing some of these actors may consider withdrawing from existing representation when there is good cause, and withdrawal will not impose an adverse material effect on the client. A noteworthy exception remains barristers bound by the cab-rank rule.[104]

Beyond representing climate wreckers, law firms should be careful not to lend their services in support of strategic lawsuits against public participation (SLAPP) efforts and other questionable tactics trying to discourage climate advocacy. A recent investigation by the Guardian revealed the extent to which fossil fuel lobbyists orchestrated a campaign to adopt SLAPP legislation against climate protesters.[105] Greenpeace is one of the organisations that has become a recurring target of this tactic.[106] In an interesting turn, now firms like Gibson Dunn are weaponising anti-SLAPP statutes, which are intended to protect advocates, to seek dismissal of climate litigation against the fossil fuel industry.[107] In the United States, even some academics working on climate accountability have faced legal challenges due to their scholarly research. US law professor Rachel Rothschild's work, which inspired laws to hold the fossil fuel industry accountable, is now facing pressure from conservative groups weaponising public records laws to access her private files.[108]

While these attacks are not entirely new as other academics and attorneys have been previously targeted—as have hundreds of human rights and environmental defenders in the Global South[109]—these efforts demonstrate a continuing repressive atmosphere. Lawyers who enable this type of intimidation should be wary of using their professional identity to further repress freedom of speech, assembly, and peaceful protest. In a consultation paper on "Upholding Professional Ethical Duties", the UK Legal Services Board recognised that attorneys facilitating

[103] Bradley Wendel, 'Lawyer Shaming' (2022) University of Illinois Law Review 175 ('In contrast with the English "cab-rank" rule, under which barristers are obligated to accept all clients who seek their services, there is no requirement in the rules of professional conduct for lawyers which require them to accept the representation of any particular client').

[104] This exception is relevant in legal systems where there is a distinction between solicitors and barristers, whereby the former may be free to take on or decline clients whereby in the latter, barristers are often limited by the cab-rank rule. Common law jurisdictions such as England and Wales as well as Australia prohibit a barrister from refusing to represent any client under the cab-rank rule, which is understood as essential to secure access to justice.

[105] Hilary Beaumont and Nina Lakhani, 'Revealed: How the Fossil Fuel Industry Helps Spread Anti-protest Laws Across the US' (*The Guardian*, 26 September 2024) <https://www.theguardian.com/us-news/2024/sep/26/anti-protest-laws-fossil-fuel-lobby?CMP=share_btn_url> accessed 15 March 2025.

[106] Emily Sanders, 'The Law Firm Helping Big Oil Weaponize the First Amendment' (*DeSmog*, 5 January 2024) <https://www.desmog.com/2024/01/05/gibson-dunn-chevron-dapl-oil-free-speech/> accessed 15 March 2025.

[107] ibid.

[108] Coral Davenport, 'She Inspired Laws to Hold the Fossil Fuel Industry Accountable. Now She's a Target' (*NYT*, 27 March 2025) < https://www.nytimes.com/2025/03/27/climate/she-inspired-laws-to-hold-the-fossil-fuel-industry-accountable-now-shes-a-target.html> accessed 15 June 2025.

[109] Global Witness, 'Almost 2,000 Land and Environmental Defenders were Killed Between 2012 and 2022 for Protecting the Planet' (13 September 2023) <https://www.globalwitness.org/en/press-releases/almost-2000-land-and-environmental-defenders-killed-between-2012-and-2022-protecting-planet/> accessed 15 June 2025.

"the misuse of non-disclosure agreements (NDAs), and Strategic Lawsuits against Public Participation (SLAPPs)" can "undermine professional ethics and the rule of law".[110]

4.3 Legal Ethics and Lawyer's Role

4.3.1 Promote Greening of Professional Responsibility Rules

Law firms and individual lawyers can support a transition to a low-carbon future by fostering efforts to modify professional responsibility standards to include a commitment to sustainable development. While proposals to integrate such a substantive commitment may receive criticism, professional norms often involve implicit or explicit commitments to broader social values like transparency, inclusion, and the rule of law, among others. In this context, some scholars have suggested amendments that would import "green ethics" to the ABA Model Rules.[111] Some even argue that the professional and ethical duty of competence means that lawyers have a duty to respond to climate change.[112] John Dernbach, Irma Russell, and Matt Bogoshian argue that the lawyer's duty of competence requires lawyers to keep up with evolving legal obligations and the new reality of climate change.[113] They argue that the duty of competence supports "lawyers to do what reasonably should be done for the client, the rule of law, and our system of justice".[114] Relatedly, Katrina F. Kuh has raised the concept of "malignant normality"[115] to illustrate the ways "legal professional norms may frustrate an efficacious response by the profession to climate change".[116] Indeed, current ethics rules offer little guidance to attorneys on how to respond to the climate crisis. In this context, law firms can engage in conversations about the ethics of legal advice that enables climate change, whether it be in the form of litigation, arbitration, or transactional work. Victor Flatt observes that states' ethics law could be interpreted "to require, or at least permit, attorneys to disclose client activity relating to greenhouse gas emissions".[117] Flatt explains that "[b]ecause of the lack of any

[110] Legal Services Board, 'Upholding Professional Ethical Duties' (6 March 2025), para 22; 86 <https://legalservicesboard.org.uk/wp-content/uploads/2025/03/PERL-Consultation-Document-February-2025.pdf> accessed 15 June 2025 ('Our evidence shows that this type of conduct is being used to silence or intimidate individuals from bringing valid public interest claims, characterised by abuse of legal processes to harass or intimidate, and often involves power imbalances between well-resourced claimants and less well-resourced defendants'); ibid at para 29.

[111] Tom Lininger, 'Green Ethics for Lawyers' (2016) 57 Boston College Law Review 61 <https://lira.bc.edu/files/pdf?fileid=7a8fbea6-3a12-4d7e-ad27-c3c2f25e7967> accessed 9 January 2025.

[112] John Dernbach, Irma Russell, and Matthew Bogoshian, 'The Lawyer's Duty of Competence in a Climate-Imperiled World' (2024) 92 University of Missouri-Kansas City Law Review 859.

[113] ibid.

[114] ibid 891.

[115] Katrina Fischer Kuh, 'Malignant Normality' (*Environmental Law Prof Blog*, 11 November 2018) <https://lawprofessors.typepad.com/environmental_law/2018/11/malignant-normality.html> accessed 15 March 2025.

[116] ibid; David Luban, *Legal Ethics and Human Dignity* (CUP 2007) 44–47 (describing how zealous advocacy as traditionally understood may often conflict with 'ordinary morality'); Norman S Spaulding, 'The Rule of Law in Action: A Defense of Adversary System Values' (2008) 93 Cornell Law Review 137, 138 (observing that according to Luban, the adversary system 'permits, and even sometimes invites obfuscation . . . encourages lawyers to press for advantages that exceed the entitlements of their clients and infringe upon the rights of their adversaries . . . [ultimately] allow[ing] lawyers to manipulate the scales').

[117] Victor Byers Flatt, 'Disclosing the Danger: State Attorney Ethics Rules Meet Climate Change' (2020) Utah Law Review 569.

comprehensive federal regulatory scheme to address major greenhouse gas emissions and the scale of the problem, climate change is fundamentally different from an ethics standpoint than more traditional, heavily regulated pollution like hazardous waste releases".[118]

In the US, Oregon has considered adopting a rule imposing an obligation for attorneys to protect the environment.[119] Other jurisdictions may consider and adopt similar rules, from a general rule encouraging attorneys to consider a climate-conscious lawyering approach to more specific rules prohibiting specific actions, such as supporting greenwashing, misinformation, or any type of consumer deception. Jurisdictions ascribing to the cab-rank rule may also consider proposing reforms to make it easier for barristers to refuse to engage in work that undermines the climate. However, the limitations of self-governance may seem increasingly evident if professional standards continue to allow planetary disruption at such a significant scale.

5. Conclusion

The legal profession stands at a critical crossroads in addressing climate change. As this analysis demonstrates, lawyers possess both significant influence and responsibility in shaping climate outcomes through their professional choices. The proposed actions for law firms—from reducing operational emissions to reforming professional ethics—provide a practical framework for meaningful climate engagement that goes beyond superficial commitments.

While ESG initiatives represent important progress, their vulnerability to political headwinds highlights the need for more deeply embedded climate consciousness throughout legal practice. The varying approaches of bar associations worldwide, particularly the comprehensive guidance from the Law Society of England and Wales, illustrate both the growing recognition of climate imperatives, the uneven development of professional standards in this area, and the metes and bounds of private law addressing climate change in the legal profession.

Looking forward, the legal profession must move beyond viewing climate change as merely another practice area and instead recognise it as a fundamental consideration that intersects with all aspects of legal service. By leveraging their unique position as advisors, facilitators, and gatekeepers in economic and regulatory systems, lawyers can either perpetuate carbon-intensive models or accelerate the transition to sustainable alternatives. The profession's willingness to embrace this responsibility and implement substantive changes in practice will significantly influence the global capacity to achieve climate goals within increasingly urgent timeframes.

[118] ibid 575.

[119] Oregon has also been the first state in the country to create a Sustainable Future Section. 'About' (Oregon State Bar: Sustainable Future Section) <https://sustainablefuture.osbar.org/about/> accessed 7 January 2025.

CHAPTER 44

Artificial Intelligence

JAN-ERIK SCHIRMER

1. Introduction

ARTIFICIAL intelligence (AI) and climate change are arguably the two greatest challenges of our time. While long considered in isolation, a more integrated perspective of a "twin transformation" is gaining traction in public debate and the social sciences.[1] However, little of this has found its way into legal discourse.[2] This is particularly true of corporate governance scholarship. While contributions on the respective impacts of AI or climate change are ubiquitous, there is limited engagement with how the two are interrelated. This chapter aims to address this gap through three contributions: First, it links the siloed debates on AI and climate change to spark a common conversation in corporate governance. Second, it shows how uncritical calls for more AI in the boardroom pose significant climate risks and run counter to the aims of corporate climate governance. Third, it provides concrete examples of how AI, if used selectively, could enhance corporate climate governance.

By "corporate climate governance", I mean a particular approach to corporate governance. Unlike conventional corporate governance, which typically focuses on reducing agency problems and costs,[3] corporate climate governance reflects on how corporate laws, concepts, and policies could be (re)designed to help curb climate change—either through climate-oriented legislation or doctrinal reinterpretation.[4] Note that I do not argue that corporate governance should necessarily be climate-oriented. While it is true that corporate laws, concepts, and

[1] See, e.g., European Commission, Shaping Europe's Digital Future (Publications Office of the European Union, 2020); Matthijs Mouthaan and others, 'Systemic Sustainability Effects of Contemporary Digitalization: A Scoping Review and Research Agenda' (2023) 149 Futures 103142; Tilman Santarius and Josephin Wagner, 'Digitalization and Sustainability: A Systematic Literature Analysis of ICT for Sustainability Research' (2023) 32 GAIA 21; Anne-Sophie Christmann and others, 'The Twin Transformation Butterfly' (2024) Business & Information Systems Engineering 489.

[2] But see Amy L Stein, 'Artificial Intelligence and Climate Change' (2020) 37 Yale Journal on Regulation 890; Herbert Zech, 'Nachhaltigkeit und Digitalisierung im Recht' (2022) 2 ZfDR 123; Philipp Hacker, 'Sustainable AI Regulation' (2024) 61 Common Market Law Review 345; Michael von Landenberg-Roberg and Arne Pilniok (eds), *Recht der digitalen und ökologischen Transformation* (Mohr Siebeck 2025).

[3] This is, of course, a very vague description that I use here for illustrative purposes only, for details see, e.g., John Armour, Henry Hansmann, and Reinier Kraakman, 'Agency Problems and Legal Strategies' in John Armour and others (eds), *The Anatomy of Corporate Law: A Comparative and Functional Approach* (3rd edn, OUP 2017).

[4] In a similar vein, Virginia E Harper Ho, 'Corporate Climate Governance' (2024) European Corporate Governance Institute Law Working Paper No 804/2024 <https://www.ecgi.global/publications/working-papers/corporate-climate-governance> accessed 22 January 2026, 14, 54.

policies can be responsive to broader societal goals such as climate neutrality or sustainability,[5] corporate climate governance is only one of many possible approaches to corporate governance. Whether corporate climate governance (or the conventional approach) is the "right" way to go is not the subject of this chapter.[6] Rather, I sidestep that fundamental (and very controversial) question and move directly to more practical issues: Assuming that corporate climate governance is the right approach and that corporate governance should be climate-oriented, what risks and potentials does the advent of AI bring?

The remainder of this chapter is structured as follows: Section 2 introduces the fundamentals of AI that are critical to understanding its climate risks. Section 3 examines these risks in more detail and considers the role of corporate governance in shaping these risks. In this context, I also develop the concept of *AI pragmatism*, which calls on legal scholars to more carefully consider the climate risks of AI when interpreting (corporate) law. Section 4 explores the climate potentials of AI for corporate climate governance, using corporate climate reporting and corporate climate planning as examples. Section 5 concludes.

2. Fundamentals of AI

To understand the climate risks associated with AI, it is essential to first grasp how AI is developed, what it can (and cannot) do, and what its future trajectory might look like.

2.1 Development of AI

While AI research is broad and rapidly evolving, most state-of-the-art models today are based on deep learning, a specific technique of machine learning.[7] Instead of programming precise rules for each task, deep learning uses large amounts of data and computing power to train artificial neural networks that gradually learn to recognise patterns and make sense of new information—ultimately enabling powerful decision-making capabilities. Getting to this point requires months of training and immense computing power, often utilising tens of thousands of graphics processing units and specialised AI chips. Once training is complete, the AI model is combined with interfaces, safety mechanisms, and other components to develop it into an AI system. At this stage, the model becomes operational, ensuring that the AI can be used effectively in real-world applications. For example, while GPT-4o is a general-purpose AI model, only ChatGPT—the fully developed AI system—turns it into a functional product.[8]

[5] With regard to private law in general, see Jan-Erik Schirmer, *Nachhaltiges Privatrecht* (Mohr Siebeck 2023).

[6] But see, e.g., Alessio M Pacces, 'Sustainable Corporate Governance: The Role of the Law' in Danny Busch, Guido Ferrarini, and Seraina Grünewald (eds), *Sustainable Finance in Europe: Corporate Governance, Financial Stability and Financial Markets* (Springer 2021) (arguing in favour); Lucian A Bebchuk and Roberto Tallarita, 'The Illusory Promise of Stakeholder Governance' (2020) 106 Cornell Law Review 91 (arguing against).

[7] Instructive Stuart J Russel and Peter Norvig, *Artificial Intelligence: A Modern Approach* (4th edn, Pearson 2021) 801–35.

[8] AI Safety Institute, *International AI Safety Report* (UK Department for Science, Innovation and Technology, 2025) 35–36. The Regulation (EU) 2024/1689 of the European Parliament and of the Council of 13 June 2024 laying down harmonised rules on artificial intelligence and amending Regulations (EC) No 300/2008, (EU) No 167/2013, (EU) No 168/2013, (EU) 2018/858, (EU) 2018/1139 and (EU) 2019/2144 and Directives 2014/90/EU, (EU) 2016/797 and (EU) 2020/1828 (EU AI Act) follows a similar approach regarding AI systems in Article 3 (1).

2.2 Capabilities of AI

AI systems have reached remarkable levels of performance in several domains.[9] This is particularly true for general-purpose systems based on large language models, such as ChatGPT or Gemini.[10] Less than ten years ago, leading models struggled to produce coherent text and often failed basic reasoning tasks—including counting to ten.[11] Today, AI systems can, among other things, assist programmers in writing and debugging code, generate high-quality images and videos, and engage in fluent conversations in multiple languages. Unsurprisingly, demand has surged. Again, ChatGPT is a case in point: Within five days of its launch, it had one million users; after two months, the number had grown to 100 million.[12]

In multiple fields, AI systems nowadays perform tasks (almost) as good as human experts. For example, AI systems score on average in the 90th percentile of humans taking the Unified Bar Exam,[13] almost similar results are being reported for coding tasks (89th percentile) and undergraduate-level chemistry tests (92nd percentile).[14] State-of-the-art AI systems perform so strongly in the American Invitational Mathematics Examination that they qualify for the Math Olympiad;[15] another study attests them as comparable to expert PhD-level performance on science questions.[16] However, two important caveats remain: When experiments are rerun or applied on different data, evaluations of AI performance often do not replicate.[17] And in many other areas AI systems still perform remarkably poorly. They often struggle with unusual scenarios, subtle factual distinctions, or common-sense tasks.[18] AI systems also continue to hallucinate, generating false or fabricated citations and facts.[19]

[9] Russel and Norvig (n 7) 46–48.

[10] Unlike narrow (or weak) AI, general-purpose AI can adapt to new challenges and interact with various types of input. Because general-purpose AI has advanced particularly rapidly in recent years and has been widely deployed, most of today's discussion concerns this type of AI. For example, the legislation of the EU AI Act was strongly influenced by the rapid development of general-purpose AI, and the AI Act contains numerous provisions in this regard (Article 53–55). See also Serena Quattrocolo and Ernestina Sacchetto, 'EU and AI: Lessons to Be Learned' in Ernest Lim and Phillip Morgan (eds), *The Cambridge Handbook of Private Law and Artificial Intelligence* (CUP 2024).

[11] For (rather disappointing) examples of state-of-the-art models in the late 2010s see Russel and Norvig (n 7) 926–29.

[12] AI Safety Institute (n 8) 25.

[13] Daniel Martin Katz and others, 'GPT-4 Passes the Bar Exam' (2024) 382 Philosophical Transactions of the Royal Society A: Mathematical, Physical and Engineering Sciences 20230254.

[14] Open AI, 'Learning to Reason with LLMs' (2024) <https://openai.com/index/learning-to-reason-with-llms/> accessed 22 January 2026.

[15] Trieu H Trinh and others, 'Solving Olympiad Geometry without Human Demonstrations' (2024) 625 Nature 476.

[16] Epoch AI, 'AI Benchmarking Dashboard' (2025) <https://epoch.ai/data/ai-benchmarking-dashboard> accessed 22 January 2026. The latest version of a leading AI model even outperformed many human experts in these tasks, see AI Safety Institute (n 8) 11–12.

[17] Moritz Herrmann and others, 'Position: Why We Must Rethink Empirical Research in Machine Learning' (2024) 235 Proceedings of the International Conference on Machine Learning 18228.

[18] See, e.g., Zhaofeng Wu and others, 'Reasoning or Reciting? Exploring the Capabilities and Limitations of Language Models Through Counterfactual Tasks' (Proceedings of the 2024 Conference of the North American Chapter of the Association for Computational Linguistics: Human Language Technologies, vol 1, Mexico City, Association for Computational Linguistics 2024) 1819.

[19] Ziwei Ji and others, 'Survey of Hallucination in Natural Language Generation' (2023) 55 ACM Computing Surveys 1.

2.3 Future of AI

The recent performance breakthroughs are associated with a novel chain-of-thought technique, in which AI systems break down complex tasks into small steps.[20] However, these and other improvements are largely dependent on what is known in the industry as *scaling up*: AI models perform better because they can draw on ever-greater datasets and computing power. Recent estimates suggest that since 2010, training datasets have grown on average by a factor of 2.5 per year, and computing power by a factor of 4 per year. In contrast, training efficiency and hardware efficiency have increased at lower rates, by a factor of 3 and 1.3, respectively. As a result, energy consumption has roughly tripled annually. If current trends continue uninterrupted, by 2030 AI models could require up to 10,000 times more computing power than the most advanced models of 2023.[21] While new architectures and efficiency gains could slow this trend,[22] most AI experts believe that continued scaling will remain the primary driver of progress. In fact, some even argue that AI development is dominated by what they call the "Law of Scaling".[23]

3. Climate Risks of AI

As AI systems become more advanced, they pose several risks to society, such as cybercrime, disinformation, or job loss. While most of these issues are well known and are increasingly being addressed by researchers and policymakers worldwide,[24] one of the most pressing risks has received comparatively little attention:[25] AI also poses significant risks to the global climate. This section examines these climate risks in more detail before turning to the role of corporate governance in shaping them.

3.1 Specific Risk

AI's growing capabilities can be used for damaging the climate. Studies show that AI systems can significantly accelerate the extraction of fossil fuels such as oil and gas and enhance sales, leading to increased GHG emissions.[26] Even seemingly benign AI applications can turn out to be harmful to the climate. For instance, AI-driven livestock management systems often aim to optimise productivity, which can lead to larger herd sizes. This contributes to increased

[20] AI Safety Institute (n 8) 42–43.

[21] See ibid 46–57 (with further references).

[22] With DeepSeek being the today's most prominent example. However, whether DeepSeek actually uses fewer resources (or was able to reduce training effort by 'distilling' large portions of ChatGPT) is still debated, see Mark Sweney and Dan Milmo, 'OpenAI 'Reviewing' Allegations That Its AI Models Were Used to Make DeepSeek' *The Guardian* (London, 29 January 2025) <https://www.theguardian.com/technology/2025/jan/29/openai-chatgpt-deepseek-china-us-ai-models> accessed 22 January 2026.

[23] Tom Henighan and others, 'Scaling Laws for Autoregressive Generative Modeling' (2020) arXiv <https://ui.adsabs.harvard.edu/abs/2020arXiv201014701H> accessed 22 January 2026.

[24] See especially, AI Safety Institute (n 8).

[25] Likewise, Hacker (n 2) 345. For example, the leading textbook on AI does not mention climate (or environmental) risks, cf Russel and Norvig (n 7) 49–50. While this neglect can be explained to some extent by the fact that the book was published in 2021 and AI has only become widespread in recent years, the growing problem of AI's energy intensity was already well-known at the time.

[26] Lynn H Kaack and others, 'Aligning Artificial Intelligence with Climate Change Mitigation' (2022) 12 Nature Climate Change 518, 522; David Rolnick and others, 'Tackling Climate Change with Machine Learning' (2022) 55 ACM Computing Surveys 1, 4; AI Safety Institute (n 8) 135.

methane emissions, a highly potent GHG. Given that cattle farming already accounts for approximately 9% of global GHG emissions and is also associated with biodiversity loss through monocultures and land degradation, such optimisation strategies pose a serious climate risk.[27]

3.2 Systemic Risk

Beyond specific use cases, however, the mere existence of AI is already a significant threat to the climate. As discussed above, developing AI requires huge amounts of energy. Although many AI developers are increasingly turning to climate-friendly sources such as solar or nuclear power, large portions of this energy still come from fossil fuel-based sources.[28] Reports from Meta's recently developed AI models provide some perspective: Meta estimates that the training phase alone resulted in GHG emissions equivalent to the annual energy consumption of nearly 1,500 US households.[29] However, this figure likely underestimates the true carbon footprint. The reported emissions only account for the direct energy use of computing hardware, omitting the significant energy required for powering and cooling data centres and processing training data—the latter of which can make up as much as 30% of the energy used during AI development.[30] Importantly, AI's thirst for energy does not end once development is complete. The operation of AI systems requires constant data transmission and computation, which also consumes vast amounts of electricity.[31] In fact, there is growing evidence that the everyday operation of AI systems now consumes more energy than its development.[32]

However, because not all AI companies disclose how much power they consume and where it is generated, it is not (yet) possible to measure the carbon footprint of AI precisely. Still, conservative estimates based on data centre extrapolations suggest that AI is currently responsible for between 0.06 and 0.17% of global annual GHG emissions.[33] This puts AI's climate impact somewhere between that of countries like Jordan and Belgium.[34]

And this impact is expected to rise sharply. As noted earlier, AI experts believe that scaling—using more and more data and computing power—will continue to be the key driver for further progress. This creates a dangerous feedback loop: To advance, AI needs more

[27] Kaack et al (n 26) 522.

[28] Alexandra Sasha Luccioni and Alex Hernandez-Garcia, 'Counting Carbon: A Survey of Factors Influencing the Emissions of Machine Learning' (2023) arXiv <https://ui.adsabs.harvard.edu/abs/2023arXiv230208476S> accessed 22 January 2026.

[29] Meta reported 11,380 tons of CO2 equivalent, which were converted using the EPA's Greenhouse Gas Equivalencies Calculator, see AI Safety Institute (n 8) 130.

[30] ibid 130; David Patterson and others, 'The Carbon Footprint of Machine Learning Training Will Plateau, Then Shrink' (2022) 55 Computer 18.

[31] Which leads, in addition to climate-damaging GHG emissions, also to high water consumption. According to a recent study, a single ChatGPT conversation involving 10–50 exchanges consumes approximately half a litre of water, see Pengfei Li and others, 'Making AI Less "Thirsty": Uncovering and Addressing the Secret Water Footprint of AI Models' (2023) arXiv <https://ui.adsabs.harvard.edu/abs/2023arXiv230403271L> accessed 22 January 2026.

[32] Alexandra Sasha Luccioni, Yacine Jernite, and Emma Strubell, 'Power Hungry Processing: Watts Driving the Cost of AI Deployment?' (2024) Proceedings of the 2024 ACM Conference on Fairness, Accountability, and Transparency 85. For companies like Google and Meta, day-to-day AI usage now accounts for 60%–70% of their total AI-related energy consumption.

[33] AI Safety Institute (n 8) 130; for details on the available data and the estimation method see Kaack et al (n 26) 520.

[34] See European Commission, 'Emissions Database for Global Atmospheric Research (EDGAR): CO_2 Emissions 2023' <https://edgar.jrc.ec.europa.eu/report_2024#emissions_table> accessed 22 January 2026.

energy—which in turn leads to even more GHG emissions. Recent improvements to Google's AI model, for example, were a key factor behind a 37% increase in the company's GHG emissions between 2022 and 2023.[35] While gains in technological efficiency and fossil-free energy deployment may have some offsetting effect, they are unlikely to outpace the rapidly growing energy demand of AI.[36] Additional rebound effects are projected from the further deployment of AI systems; recent findings suggest that AI systems are following the same pattern as video streaming, where a surge in demand has outpaced per-unit energy efficiency gains.[37] In sum, unless development strategies change, AI will continue to heat up the planet—simply by getting bigger and better.

3.3 Risk by Legal Design

If the climate risks of AI stem from specific, climate-damaging applications and systemic effects, then "law's guiding hand" comes into play.[38] As an essential part of the social fabric, law embeds and shapes technological revolutions.[39] This includes the climate risks posed by AI: Since it is the law that regulates the use of AI—either by permitting certain applications or by neglecting to restrict them—it is also the law that explicitly or implicitly determines whether and how AI systems can be used for climate-damaging purposes.[40] The same is true for the systemic risks that arise from GHG-intensive development and operation. Again, by either permitting scaling or neglecting to restrict it, the law determines whether and how GHG-intensive AI development and operation will proceed.[41] This applies even to areas of law that do not explicitly deal with AI. Take copyright law: Only if copyright law allows AI developers to easily collect and use ever-increasing amounts of protected data will they be able to assemble datasets large enough to improve their AI models.[42] Or take contract law: AI systems can only engage in autonomous transactions involving the sale and purchase of coal and gas if

[35] Google, *Environmental Report 2024* (Google 2024) <https://sustainability.google/reports/google-2024-environmental-report/> accessed 22 January 2026.

[36] AI Safety Institute (n 8) 133–35. Even in optimistic best-case scenarios, GHG emissions are not expected to decline until the 2030s, see Patterson et al (n 30).

[37] Kaack et al (n 26) 522; Alexandra Sasha Luccioni, Emma Strubell, and Kate Crawford, 'From Efficiency Gains to Rebound Effects: The Problem of Jevons' Paradox in AI's Polarized Environmental Debate' (2025) arXiv <https://ui.adsabs.harvard.edu/abs/2025arXiv250116548S> accessed 22 January 2026; AI Safety Institute (n 8) 133. For rebound effects regarding video streaming (and other digital technologies), see Santarius and Wagner (n 1) 26.

[38] See generally, Katharina Pistor, *The Code of Capital* (Princeton University Press 2019) 6; regarding AI see, e.g., Kai Ebert and others, 'AI, Climate, and Regulation: From Data Centers to the AI Act' (2025) arXiv <https://ui.adsabs.harvard.edu/abs/2024arXiv241006681E> accessed 22 January 2026.

[39] Horst Eidenmüller, 'Machine Performance and Human Failure: How Shall We Regulate Autonomous Machines' (2019) 15 Journal of Business and Technology Law 109, 114–24 (using the example of a purely welfare-economic approach); see also Iris H-Y Chiu and Ernest WK Lim, 'Technology vs Ideology: How Far Will Artificial Intelligence and Distributed Ledger Technology Transform Corporate Governance and Business?' (2021) 18 Berkeley Business Law Journal 1, 35–38; with respect to the Industrial Revolution see famously John Fabian Witt, *The Accidental Republic* (Harvard University Press 2009).

[40] This is similar to the legal rules that created the modern internet by protecting platforms from lawsuits based on user-generated content, see Jeff Kosseff, *The Twenty-Six Words That Created the Internet* (Cornell University Press 2019).

[41] With respect to EU law see Hacker (n 2) 379–81.

[42] Mark A Lemley and Bryan Casey, 'Fair Learning' (2020) 99 Texas Law Review 743; Pamela Samuelson, 'Generative AI Meets Copyright' (2023) 381 Science 158.

non-humans can form valid contracts.[43] But as we will see below, the extent to which legal designs shape the climate risks of AI is also evident in corporate law, especially in the context of corporate governance.

3.3.1 Conventional Corporate Governance: AI Enthusiasm

Although AI systems are also being used to write private thank-you notes or wedding invitations, much of their widespread adoption has occurred in the business sector. According to a 2023 IBM study, 38% of large companies worldwide already integrate AI systems into their business operations, and another 42% are exploring doing so.[44] In practice, AI systems assess the risks of financial transactions in mergers and acquisitions, develop new products, or select employees. Many other business applications exist, and given the tremendous recent improvements in AI, more are expected to emerge in the near future.[45]

Conventional corporate governance has embraced this trend with little resistance. On the contrary, AI's growing capabilities and optimisation potential have sparked a veritable *AI enthusiasm*.[46] A prime example is the scholarly debate about AI in the boardroom.[47] According to the prevailing opinion in German law, for example, directors[48] have a broad discretion as to whether and how to use AI systems.[49] As long as they do not take over core management tasks and no other laws prohibit their use,[50] directors can delegate day-to-day business decisions to AI systems—just as they can rely on human employees to assess financial risks or to develop new products. Directors can then limit their efforts to monitoring the AI system. Both delegation and monitoring are subject to the business judgment rule. This means that as long as

[43] Jan-Erik Schirmer, 'Artificial Intelligence and Legal Personality: Introducing "Teilrechtsfähigkeit": A Partial Legal Status Made in Germany' in Thomas Wischmeyer and Timo Rademacher (eds), *Regulating Artificial Intelligence* (Springer 2020) 129–30, 136–38; T T Arvind, 'Contract Law and AI: AI-Infused Contracting and the Problem of Relationality: Is Trustworthy AI Possible?' in Ernest Lim and Phillip Morgan (eds), *The Cambridge Handbook of Private Law and Artificial Intelligence* (CUP 2024).

[44] IBM, *IBM Global AI Adoption Index 2023* (Morning Consult 2023) 8.

[45] See Massimo Bertolini and others, 'Machine Learning for Industrial Applications: A Comprehensive Literature Review' (2021) 175 Expert Systems with Applications 114820; from the legal literature, see John Armour and Horst Eidenmüller, 'Self-Driving Corporations?' (2020) 10 Harvard Business Law Review 87, 96–99; Stein (n 2) 900–16.

[46] See, e.g., Jan Lieder, 'From Corporate Governance to Algorithm Governance: Artificial Intelligence as a Challenge for Corporations and Their Executives' in Silja Voeneky and others (eds), *The Cambridge Handbook of Responsible Artificial Intelligence: Interdisciplinary Perspectives* (CUP 2022) 312 (calling for a 'time for digital initiative'). For more examples see Anne-Christin Mittwoch, 'Digitalisierung und Nachhaltigkeit: Praktische Konvergenzen zweier Leitdiskurse im Unternehmensrecht' (2023) 78 JuristenZeitung 376, 380.

[47] It remains largely an scholarly debate because there is (yet) no relevant case law or codified corporate law, see for Europe European Commission, *European Enterprise Survey on the Use of Technologies Based on Artificial Intelligence: Final Report* (Publications Office of the European Union 2022) 41–42, 45–51; for the US, see Christopher Bruner, 'Artificially Intelligent Boards and the Future of Delaware Corporate Law' (2022) 22 Journal of Corporate Law Studies 783, 790.

[48] Strictly speaking, the German Stock Corporation Act (AktG) refers to members of the Management Board and not directors. For the sake of clarity, however, I will use the internationally more common term 'directors'.

[49] For a comprehensive overview, see Lieder (n 46) 335–39.

[50] Prohibitions result in particular from the EU AI Act (e.g., Article 5 (1) a), which prohibits the use of manipulative or deceptive AI systems. Beyond that, German (or EU) law rarely regulates the use of AI systems (but see Securities Trading Act 1998 (WpHG), s 80 (2–5) (regarding algorithmic trading)). Where such regulations on the use of AI do exist, directors must of course comply with them.

directors are using a state-of-the-art AI system, are adequately informed about its capabilities and limitations, and check the plausibility of its output, directors will not breach their duties to the corporation if the AI system's decision turns out to be financially damaging.[51] Moreover, many German scholars go even further, arguing that directors' discretion is increasingly becoming a duty: Since directors must act in the best interests of the corporation, and since AI systems are getting better and better at optimising business operations, directors should use them regularly—and must provide plausible reasons if they do not.[52]

This is by no means a German *Sonderweg*. Apart from differences in detail, the debates in other jurisdictions are moving in a similar direction.[53] In France and the United Kingdom, for example, it is widely accepted that directors may delegate day-to-day business decisions to AI systems, provided they carefully select and monitor them and retain ultimate decision-making authority.[54] In Italy, directors are generally not permitted to delegate decisions to others, but they may rely on AI systems to support the decision-making process—which essentially amounts to the same broad discretion.[55] And much like in Germany, a growing number of scholars in these countries do not stop there, claiming that the duty to act in the best interest of the company may actually oblige directors to rely on the optimisation capabilities of AI systems.[56] This parallels the debate in the US, where it is argued that the fiduciary duty may require directors to use AI systems if they can improve informed decision-making (as they increasingly do).[57] Given this consistent global trend in conventional corporate governance, all signs point to Florian Möslein's prediction being correct: Relying on AI systems is becoming

[51] See, e.g., Katja Langenbucher, 'Künstliche Intelligenz in der Leitungsentscheidung des Vorstands' (2023) 187 Zeitschrift für das gesamte Handelsrecht und Wirtschaftsrecht 723, 728–37; but see for a more restrictive approach Elena Dubovitskaya and Annika Buchholz, 'The Management and the Advice of (Un)Explainable AI' (2023) European Company and Financial Law Review 794, 805–15.

[52] See, e.g., Georg Langheld and Christian Haagen, 'Einsatz Künstlicher Intelligenz bei unternehmerischen Entscheidungen' (2023) Neue Zeitschrift für Gesellschaftsrecht 1535, 1537–38; in a similar vein Lieder (n 46) 340: '[In] a complex and calculation-intensive decision [. . . the directors] will hardly be able to justify not using AI'.

[53] Instructive Florian Möslein, 'AI and Corporate Law' in Larry A DiMatteo, Cristina Poncibò and Michel Cannarsa (eds), *The Cambridge Handbook of Artificial Intelligence* (CUP 2022) 76–79.

[54] Karine Lemercier, 'L'impact de l'intelligence artificielle sur l'organisation et le fonctionnement des sociétés' in Alexandra Mendoza-Caminade (ed), *L'entreprise et l'intelligence artificielle: Les réponses du droit* (Presses de l'Université Toulouse Capitole 2023) para 5–6 (for France); Deirdre Ahern, 'Corporate Law, Corporate Governance and AI: Are We Ready for Robots in the Boardroom?' in Ernest Lim and Phillip Morgan (eds), *The Cambridge Handbook of Private Law and Artificial Intelligence* (CUP 2024) 422–23 (for the UK).

[55] Gian Domenico Mosco, 'AI and the Board Within Italian Corporate Law: Preliminary Notes' (2020) 17 European Company Law Journal 92–95.

[56] Lemercier (n 54) [11] (arguing for the establishment of a statutory or regulatory procedure for prior consultation with AI, the non-observance of which would constitute a breach of management duty); Assaf Hamdani and others, 'Technological Progress and the Future of the Corporation' (2018) 6 Journal of the British Academy 230 (proposing the director's duty to report to the shareholders if it decides not to follow AI regarding the selection of a CEO); ibid 96 (arguing that the capabilities of AI lead to an obligation to use that directors cannot neglect).

[57] Floris Mertens, 'The Use of Artificial Intelligence in Corporate Decision-Making at Board Level: A Preliminary Legal Analysis' Financial Law Institute Working Paper Series 2023-01 <https://financiallawinstitute.ugent.be/wp-content/uploads/2023/11/2023-01.pdf> accessed 22 January 2026 (regarding Delaware General Corporation Law).

less and less optional for directors, and the "development of a corporate law duty to make appropriate use of [them] is therefore foreseeable".[58]

But the AI enthusiasm is not limited to calls for more AI in the boardroom. Despite the fact that most national corporate laws require directors to be natural persons,[59] some scholars suggest replacing human directors with AI systems altogether. Here, too, optimisation considerations are cited: Since AI systems—unlike human directors—are assumed to be free from cognitive biases and opportunistic behaviour, they are considered less prone to agency problems.[60] As Tobias Ponßen aptly puts it: "The debate is no longer about *whether* corporations should be run by machines, but *when*."[61]

3.3.2 Corporate Climate Governance: AI Pragmatism

Given AI's impressive capabilities, the widespread AI enthusiasm in conventional corporate governance is understandable.[62] AI's optimisation potential also fits well with the dominant efficiency paradigm.[63] But there is a major blind spot in the debate. Similar to the long-standing neglect of environmental concerns in AI research,[64] the climatic consequences of AI in the boardroom are mostly left out. If corporate law encourages—or even requires—directors to delegate decision-making to AI systems, this will further stimulate demand. Not only will companies that do not already use AI systems be incentivised to do so, but by requiring directors to use state-of-the-art systems, corporate law will also spur demand for the continued development of AI.[65] This will be all the more true if corporate law allows AI systems to replace human directors altogether.[66] Thus, simply by interpreting existing corporate law in an AI-enthusiastic way, conventional corporate governance creates a legal design that implicitly helps AI get bigger and better—and ultimately adds to its large carbon footprint.

In contrast, corporate climate governance suggests a different perspective. If corporate laws, concepts, and policies are understood as an integral part of curbing climate change, this calls for *AI pragmatism*. Of course, given AI's immense potential to optimise business operations, this does not mean that AI should be banned from the boardroom altogether. Nor would that be good for the climate. As we will see below in more detail,[67] AI can help curb climate change in many ways. Rather, AI pragmatism requires keeping climate impacts in mind. When debating whether and how directors should use AI systems (or whether they should replace

[58] Möslein (n 53) 79; likewise Ahern (n 54) 424: 'Future doctrinal developments of the duty of care could see courts consider that being suitably informed prior to board decision-making should be shaped by the availability of recourse to AI systems to provide high sophisticated analysis.'

[59] See, e.g., German Stock Corporation Act 1965, s 76(3); French Code de Commerce 1807, art L225-51-51; UK Companies Act 2006, s 156A (1); or Delaware General Corporation Law 1899, s 141(b).

[60] See in particular Armour and Eidenmüller (n 45) 105–14; Ahern (n 54) 418–22. However, this view is likely overly optimistic, as it overlooks that AI is prone to all kinds of other (unique) analytical issues, including discriminatory biases, hallucinations, miscalculations, etc.

[61] Tobias Ponßen, *Der Menschenvorbehalt* (Mohr Siebeck 2024) 323 [translated from German, JES].

[62] However, there is likely to be an optimism bias at play, leading (as in other epistemic communities) to a systematic overestimation of digital tools and AI systems, see Mouthaan et al (n 1) 9.

[63] Chiu and Lim (n 39) 11–16, 49–56.

[64] See para 9.

[65] Eidenmüller (n 39) 119: 'This is "fertile ground" for the advent of smart AI-powered systems' (with respect to the functionally similar Bolam test in English tort law). See also Ahern (n 54) 429.

[66] In a similar vein (regarding systemic risks in general) Chiu and Lim (n 39) 31.

[67] See para 24–38.

humans), corporate governance scholarship must account for AI's systemic contributions to climate change.[68]

Note that this does not imply that AI pragmatism calls for a welfarist calculus that weighs the social benefits of AI systems against their (climate) costs.[69] While such a calculus may be theoretically appealing, it does not work well in practice—neither as a guide for directors nor as a regulatory approach.[70] First, like all cost-benefit exercises, it is typically far too complex at the micro level of the firm. In reality, directors have neither the expertise nor the time to gather all the relevant information needed to weigh the expected benefits of using the AI system against the climate costs.[71] Second, even if directors were willing to invest the time and effort, in most cases they would not end up with sufficiently robust numbers. As explained above, it is not (yet) possible to accurately measure the carbon footprint of AI due to a lack of data. While educated estimates of global annual GHG emissions exist, attributing GHG emissions to a *specific* AI system would require detailed company-level information that is not widely disclosed.[72] Third, this limited data also makes it largely impossible to perform the calculus at the macro level of society as a whole. Given that the contribution of AI to global annual GHG emissions is estimated to be between 0.06 and 0.17%, the associated climate costs of AI are also in a wide range. Thus, even if one could quantify the climate costs of AI—let alone its benefits—the initial variables are so volatile that the calculus would remain largely speculative.[73]

Instead, AI pragmatism calls for less enthusiastic and more cautious interpretative strategies. When designing corporate law by doctrinal interpretation (or any other area of the law, for that matter), scholars should reflect on the climate risks of AI.[74] Although one cannot be sure of the exact magnitude of these risks, given how AI is being developed and operated, *one can be certain that they are real.* This leads directly to a rule of thumb: Less AI is often more. Legal designs that incentivise the extensive and uncritical use of AI are the wrong way to go.

This rule of thumb can provide guidance in current debates. Consider the question, common across jurisdictions, of whether directors are free to use AI systems or whether they should be required to do so. The latter interpretation makes the use of AI the default option. To avoid detailed explanations or even liability, directors have a strong incentive to rely on AI systems even if this offers little to no advantage—likely resulting in increased demand and

[68] In a similar vein Mittwoch (n 46) 380; Harper Ho (n 4) 54; see also Gry Hasselbalch and Aimee Van Wynsberghe, 'Artificial Intelligence, Power and Sustainability' in Nathalie A Smuha (ed), *The Cambridge Handbook of the Law, Ethics and Policy of Artificial Intelligence* (CUP 2025) 117 (highlighting the need to 'avoid getting caught up in the hype, power dynamics, and competition surrounding this technology').

[69] But see Kaack et al (n 26) 520; Hacker (n 2) 381–83 (both suggesting a cost-benefit analysis for the use of AI systems); Ahern (n 54) 422 (arguing directors should balance cost and benefits before using AI).

[70] Eidenmüller (n 39) 124–25.

[71] The situation of directors is therefore similar to that of judges, who also lack the capacity to carry out a cost-benefit analysis in every case to be decided, see Horst Eidenmüller, *Effizienz als Rechtsprinzip* (2nd edn, Mohr Siebeck 1998) 426–31.

[72] See para 12.

[73] See generally, Duncan Kennedy, 'Cost-Benefit Analysis of Entitlement Problems: A Critique' (1981) 33 Stanford Law Review 387; Douglas A Kysar, *Regulating From Nowhere: Environmental Law and the Search for Objectivity* (Yale University Press 2010) 71–98 (focusing on environmental risks and harm).

[74] I focus here (only) on scholars because the debate about AI in the boardroom is yet a mostly scholarly debate (see para 16–18); whether (and to what extent) courts and legislators should apply AI pragmatism is a question that is beyond the scope of this chapter. However, given that more and more constitutions aim at sustainability (e.g., German Grundgesetz, art 20a; TFEU, art 3, 11), there is much to suggest that courts and legislators should all the more reflect on the climate risks of AI.

higher GHG emissions. The former interpretation, by contrast, leaves directors with full discretion. While it still allows the use of AI systems, it creates less pressure to do so. This makes it more likely that AI systems will only be used for specific tasks where directors expect tangible advantages—leading to lower overall GHG emissions. Or take the debate on whether AI systems should be allowed to become directors. In addition to serious moral objections (should far-reaching business decisions really be made without any human oversight?),[75] AI pragmatism highlights the climate risks of this proposal. Unlike AI systems, human brains operate naturally and, aside from their basic sustenance needs, do not generate additional GHG emissions. Assuming that some decisions in human-led companies will continue to be made without AI, this alone should result in fewer emissions. This suggests that scholarly proposals to replace human directors with AI should be met with scepticism.

4. Climate Potentials of AI

But AI is not only a risk to the climate. As mentioned above, the increasing capabilities of AI can help combat climate change in many ways. For example, with regard to society's overall transition to climate neutrality, AI systems can be used to coordinate renewable energy sources and stabilise power grids, reduce manufacturing waste, or optimise shipping routes in global supply chains.[76]

While these broader societal potentials are increasingly being recognised,[77] the important role that AI systems can play in enhancing corporate climate governance has received far less attention. At the same time, companies around the world are increasingly subject to climate-related obligations and market expectations, many of which could benefit significantly from AI support. Two examples illustrate this: corporate climate reporting and corporate climate planning.

4.1 Corporate Climate Reporting

Despite recent political backlash, a growing number of market participants still want to do business with climate-friendly companies. Customers like to buy from them, employees like to work for them, and investors like to invest in them.[78] But because it is often difficult and time-consuming to distinguish "green" from "brown" companies, market participants need transparency to make informed decisions. This is where corporate disclosure and reporting requirements come into play.

The European Union has been a pioneer in this area.[79] Since 2017, companies of a certain size have been required to report information on sustainability matters, particularly environmental matters. In 2024, the EU significantly expanded reporting obligations by implementing the Corporate Sustainability Reporting Directive (CSRD). As part of their

[75] See, e.g., Stephen M Bainbridge, 'Corporate Directors in the United Kingdom' (2017) 59 William & Mary Law Review Online 75–83; Ahern (n 54) 427–29; for a fundamental critique see Ponßen (n 61).

[76] Rolnick et al (n 26).

[77] See, e.g., Stein (n 2) 900–16.

[78] See, e.g., Matthias Pfister, 'Corporate Social Responsibility and Organizational Attraction: A Systematic Literature Review' (2020) 20 American Journal of Management 96; Michal Carrington and others, 'Consumption Ethics: A Review and Analysis of Future Directions for Interdisciplinary Research' (2021) 168 Journal of Business Ethics 215.

[79] See Magnus Habighorst, 'Corporations, Climate, Governance: German Status Quo Perspectives' (2024) 2 Transatlantic Law Journal 261, 261–63.

overall sustainability reporting, companies that are subject to the CSRD[80] must now provide information on how their business activities materially impact the climate (so-called inside-out effects) and, conversely, how the climate materially impacts their business activities (so-called outside-in effects).[81] What impacts are considered material is specified in the European Sustainability Reporting Standards (ESRS), a delegated act that sets EU-wide guidelines on what exactly needs to be reported and how.[82] For example, companies must disclose their gross Scope 1, 2, and 3 GHG emissions[83] and report on climate-related hazards in their sustainability report, which must be published in a machine-readable format.[84] As the revised CSRD now follows the principle of "alternative materiality", the reporting requirement is triggered as soon as either material inside-out effects *or* material outside-in effects occur.[85] Thus, a GHG-emitting company would have to report on the climate-related hazards of its business activities, even if those hazards are unlikely to affect its assets or financial performance.[86] This ultimately shifts the CSRD from sustainability-related financial reporting to financially (un) related sustainability reporting.

These European developments are mirrored by similar trends in the US. In 2024, one year after California moved forward with a state-level climate disclosure framework, the Securities and Exchange Commission (SEC) adopted the Rules for the Enhancement and Standardization of Climate-Related Disclosures for Investors.[87] Similar to the reporting requirements under the CSRD, companies subject to these rules are required to disclose material GHG emissions and climate-related risks.[88] However, there are two key differences: First, the SEC's disclosure rules cover only Scope 1 and 2 GHG emissions; Scope 3 emissions were excluded due to doubts about the reliability and robustness of the relevant data. Second, in contrast to the CSRD's alternative approach, the SEC's rules follow the principle of "single materiality": Only material climate impacts to the company (outside-in effects) trigger reporting. Apart from disclosing GHG emissions, companies that are subject to the SEC's rules are not required to provide information on the climate-related hazards of their business activities.[89]

While it is true that the SEC suspended the effectiveness of its rules in April 2024 due to the uncertainty created by multiple lawsuits (and there is little to suggest that this will change for

[80] In principle, the CSRD applies (for financial years starting on or after 1 January 2027) to EU companies employing on average over 1,000 employees and with a net annual turnover of over €450 million; non-EU companies may also be subject if they generated more than €450 million in net turnover in the EU in each of the last two financial years and have a subsidiary or a branch in the EU that recorded net turnover of more than €200 million in the preceding financial year.

[81] CSRD, art 19a (1). As with all European directives, the CSRD does not have direct effect but is still subject to transposition into national law by the Member States.

[82] See ESRS 1, s 3.4.–3.5.

[83] That is, both direct emissions from own sources (e.g., factories) and indirect emissions from the distribution and value chain (e.g., product use).

[84] See ESRS E1, s 20 (b) and ESRS 1, s 8.1.

[85] This is often referred to as the principle of 'double materiality' but given that one effect is sufficient to trigger the reporting obligation, this term seems rather confusing, similar Michael Nietsch, 'Von der nichtfinanziellen Berichterstattung zur Nachhaltigkeitsberichterstattung' (2022) Zeitschrift für Wirtschaftsrecht 449, 454.

[86] See ESRS 1, s 3.4. and ESRS E1, s 1.

[87] SEC, Enhancement and Standardization of Climate-Related Disclosures for Investors (28 March 2024) 17 CFR 210, 229, 230, 232, 239, and 249 (US).

[88] Contrary to the CSRD, only the largest companies are subject to GHG emissions disclosure; so-called Emerging Growth Companies and Small Reporting Companies were exempted (but are nevertheless required to report on climate risks). See, ibid Item 1505, 21736 and Rule 14–01(a), 21823.

[89] For more details, see Harper Ho (n 4) 18–19, 26–28.

the remainder of the Trump presidency),[90] it would be premature to assume that corporate climate disclosure is politically doomed. The more legally robust California framework remains in place, and with it the far-reaching California effect.[91] As for Europe, although the scope of reporting companies has been significantly narrowed,[92] the climate-related reporting requirements under the CSRD have largely remained unchanged.[93] Companies subject to climate reporting and disclosure rules are therefore well advised to (continue to) comply by disclosing all required information,[94] not least to avoid disappointing their climate-sensitive customers, employees, and investors.[95]

4.2 Corporate Climate Planning

Also in 2024, the EU adopted the Corporate Sustainability Due Diligence Directive (CSDDD), which, while primarily focused on supply chain monitoring, was initially designed to have far-reaching implications for corporate climate governance. In its original form, the CSDDD would have required companies within its scope[96] to adopt and put into effect a climate transition plan aimed at ensuring, through best efforts, that the business model and strategy of the company are compatible with the 1.5°C target of the Paris Agreement and the EU-wide goal of climate neutrality by 2050.[97] Among other things, the plan was to include five-year, time-bound climate targets based on conclusive scientific evidence and an explanation of how the company's governing bodies would contribute to its implementation.[98] Again, the ESRS were intended to provide more details, such as requiring GHG emission reduction targets to be

[90] SEC, The Enhancement and Standardization of Climate-Related Disclosures for Investors; Delay of Effective Date (12 April 2024) 17 CFR 210, 229, 230, 232, 239, and 249 (US); SEC, 'SEC Votes to End Defense of Climate Disclosure Rules' (SEC 27 March 2025) <https://www.sec.gov/newsroom/press-releases/2025-58> accessed 22 January 2026.

[91] Harper Ho (n 4) 16. Once again, state-level rules could insofar act as a barrier to climate backsliding, see generally William W Buzbee, 'Federalism Hedging, Entrenchment, and the Climate Challenge' (2017) 2017 Wisconsin Law Review 1037, 1101. It should be noted, however, that the California framework is currently under judicial review, and the enforcement of climate-related financial risk disclosures has been suspended.

[92] The initial version of the CSRD applied to companies either listed on an EU regulated market or employing more than 250 people, as well as to non-EU companies generating more than €150 million in turnover within the EU.

[93] However, the EU Commission is planning to revise the ESRS and substantially reduce the number of data points, see European Commission,' Proposal for a Directive of the European Parliament and of the Council amending Directives 2006/43/EC, 2013/34/EU, (EU) 2022/2464, and (EU) 2024/1760 as regards certain corporate sustainability reporting and due diligence requirements' COM (2025) 81 final.

[94] There is also increasing pressure to comply from climate litigation, see Thomas Marts, 'SEC Proposed Climate Disclosures: Preparing for a New Era of Climate Litigation in Idaho and beyond' (2024) 60 Idaho Law Review 91, 101–02.

[95] This should also explain why the total number of disclosing companies across all categories has increased from 221 companies in 2003 to 23,000 in 2023, see Carbon Disclosure Project, *CDP States and Regions: Summary Report 2023* (2023).

[96] In principle, the CSDDD applies to EU companies with more than 5,000 employees and a worldwide net turnover of more than €1.5 billion; non-EU companies may also be subject if they generate this turnover in the EU.

[97] CSDDD, art 22 (initial version).

[98] The climate plan must be reviewed and updated annually. See CSDDD, art 22 (1) and (3).

disclosed separately for Scope 1, 2, and 3 GHG emissions.[99] However, following intense criticism from the business community, the EU has recently scaled back the CSDDD significantly. As a result, the directive no longer imposes a substantive obligation on companies to adopt and put into effect a climate transition plan.[100]

In this respect, the EU framework has effectively converged with the situation in the US, where there has never been a general obligation to adopt such a plan.[101] Yet, given the market dynamics at play, this lack of legal obligation may ultimately not be that crucial. Both in the EU and the US, a clear trend toward *voluntary* corporate climate planning can be observed. A growing number of EU and US companies are committing to climate transition plans in response to investor expectations and stakeholder pressure.[102] Companies that choose to do so often rely on guidelines such as those issued by the US Environmental Protection Agency (EPA), which largely mirror the original approach of the CSDDD and the ESRS. For example, the EPA guidelines require companies to include GHG emission reduction targets in their climate transition plans, along with strategies for achieving these targets within a specified timeframe.[103]

4.3 Support From AI

Disclosing GHG emissions, reporting on climate-related hazards, or developing climate transition plans is no easy task. Not only does it require the collection of vast amounts of data, but companies must also rely on sophisticated climate models to turn that data into meaningful information. Here, AI can provide valuable assistance.

4.3.1 Determining Emissions

Whether companies need to set emission reduction targets for their transition plan or just have to disclose their current emissions, the first step is always to determine total emissions. This is harder than it may seem. Emissions—whether they are Scope 1, 2, or 3—cannot simply be measured at a smokestack or tailpipe but must be extrapolated based on known parameters (such as the amount of fuel purchased, average fuel economy of a vehicle, etc.). Traditionally, companies have mainly used third-party calculation models, such as the MSCI ESG Carbon Metrics, or developed their own models, such as the Volkswagen Group's DKI

99 See ESRS E1, s 34. When the GHG emissions targets are disclosed combined for all scopes, the company must disclose which GHG emission Scopes (1, 2, and/or 3) are covered by the target, the share related to each respective GHG emission scope and which GHGs are covered.

100 Contrary to the European Commission's initial plans, which envisaged only a limited modification of the obligation, the European Parliament removed CSDDD, art 22 in its entirety.

101 However, companies that voluntarily adopt a climate transition plan are required under the SEC's rules to describe the plan and disclose any material impacts on financial performance, see SEC (n 87), Item 1502(e)(1 and 2), 854; Harper Ho (n 4) 19. The SEC rules (Item 1500, 851) define a transition plan under Item 1500 as 'a strategy and implementation plan to reduce climate-related risks, which may include a plan to reduce its greenhouse gas emissions in accordance with its own obligations or the obligations of jurisdictions in which it conducts significant business'. However, as with the rest of the SEC's climate disclosure rules, these reporting requirements are currently suspended.

102 In 2023, nearly 6,000 companies had a climate transition plan at place, an increase of 44% since the year before, see Carbon Disclosure Project, *The State of Play: 2023 Climate Transition Plan Disclosure* (2024). For a review of legal efforts within the United States to discourage voluntary corporate climate actions, see John Dernbach, Chapter 35 of this handbook.

103 EPA, 'Climate Transition Planning' (December 2025) <https://www.epa.gov/climateleadership/climate-transition-planning#key> accessed 22 January 2026.

Decarbonization Index.[104] However, not only are these models based on multiple input parameters and limited to statistical calculations (making them rather complex and expensive to operate), but they are also frequently inaccurate. As a result, NGOs often arrive at different emissions figures than companies themselves.[105]

Several studies show that AI-driven emission models promise improvements on both fronts.[106] For example, a recently developed AI-powered model can determine emissions much more cheaply and accurately than traditional models. This is particularly true for predicting future emissions, which is essential for setting scientifically robust reduction targets in climate transition plans. The model developers report that their AI-driven predictions are about 30% more accurate than conventional models.[107] Ironically, AI can even help measure its own carbon footprint.[108] AI companies subject to climate disclosure rules could use their own AI systems to better determine how many GHG emissions result from AI development and operation—thereby adding missing pieces to the puzzle of AI's overall climate impact.

4.3.2 Identifying Climate-Related Risks

In Europe and the US, companies are required to report on material climate-related risks that affect their assets or financial performance (outside-in effects); companies covered by the CSRD must also provide information on the climate-related hazards of the company's business activities (inside-out effects).[109] While advances in climate science have made it possible to identify both effects with increasing certainty and accuracy, they require sophisticated climate modelling.[110] Consider outside-in effects: Only when a model tells a company where, how, and when climate change will affect its business can it provide meaningful information. The same goes for inside-out effects: To report on climate-related hazards, climate models are not only needed to determine the company's specific contribution to climate change (i.e., the extent to which it contributes to annual global GHG emissions, land use, and other climate factors), but also to assess the extent to which that contribution leads to rising sea levels or heat waves. However, conventional climate models rely heavily on physical laws, global climate data, and

[104] Quyen Nguyen, Ivan Diaz-Rainey, and Duminda Kuruppuarachchi, 'Predicting Corporate Carbon Footprints for Climate Finance Risk Analyses: A Machine Learning Approach' (2021) 95 Energy Economics 105129. The company's own models are often based on existing metrics such as the models used by VW and BASF, see <https://www.volkswagen-group.com/de/publikationen/weitere/dekarbonisierung-2348>; <https://www.basf.com/global/en/who-we-are/sustainability/our-contributions-to-enabling-the-green-transformation/carbon-footprint/corporate-carbon-footprint> accessed 22 January 2026.

[105] A case in point is Greenpeace's allegations that TotalEnergy's emissions are nearly four times higher than reported. See Greenpeace, Press Release, <https://www.greenpeace.org/international/press-release/56491/greenpeace-finds-totalenergies-emissions-almost-4-times-higher-than-reported/> accessed 22 January 2026. However, the accusations failed in court on procedural grounds, see TotalEnergies v Greenpeace France <https://climatecasechart.com/non-us-case/totalenergies-v-greenpeace-france-slapp-case/> accessed 22 January 2026.

[106] Rolnick et al (n 26) 35–40, 43–53; Kaack et al (n 26) 522.

[107] Nguyen, Diaz-Rainey and Kuruppuarachchi (n 104).

[108] Kaack et al (n 26) 522–23.

[109] See para 27.

[110] Richard A Betts, 'Heed Blame for Extreme Weather' (2021) 589 Nature 493; for a detailed analysis, see Michael Burger, Jessica Wentz, and Radley Horton, 'The Law and Science of Climate Change Attribution' (2020) 45 Columbia Journal of Environmental Law 57, 66–139.

statistical calculations, making each run a complex and computing-intensive endeavour. As a result, identifying climate-related risks is time-consuming and costly.[111]

As with determining GHG emissions, AI-driven climate models promise some relief. Many studies have shown that AI's deep learning approach allows the models to run significantly faster and cheaper than traditional climate models. For example, one research group trained an AI model to simulate cloud behaviour and found that it produced similar results in less time and at a fraction of the cost.[112] Another study presented an AI-powered climate model that can simulate the expansion of glaciers 1,000 times faster.[113] In addition to improving efficiency, AI can also improve the accuracy of climate models. Recent studies have reported that their AI-driven models showed better prediction results for climate-related hazards such as tropical cyclones, atmospheric rivers, and extreme temperatures.[114] According to a comprehensive meta-study, all of this makes AI particularly helpful for companies that need to identify climate-related inside-out and outside-in effects.[115]

4.3.3 Reducing Information Overload

But AI can do more than just support companies in disclosing emissions or identifying climate-related risks. It can also help stakeholders to better process the information provided. The importance of this should not be underestimated. Climate and sustainability reporting is often rightly criticised for failing to achieve its goal of greater transparency for stakeholders, because customers, employees, or investors are overwhelmed by the unstructured "flood of reports".[116]

AI systems can greatly reduce this information overload. There are numerous tools that automatically analyse and summarise emissions and sustainability reports. Instead of having to manually review a large number of reports and compare the risks presented in them, stakeholders can delegate most of the work to AI-powered tools such as ClimateBERT.[117] So far, the scope of these tools has been quite limited, for example in their focus on specific financial climate-related risks.[118] According to the tool developers, this is mainly due to the fact that emissions and sustainability reports are not yet standardised, which makes it difficult for the tools to detect and process the relevant information.[119] However, this problem is expected

111 Likewise, Jens Ekkenga, 'Externe Nachhaltigkeitsberichterstattung nach der neuen CSRD' (2023) 187 Zeitschrift für das gesamte Handels- und Wirtschaftsrecht 228, 254–55.

112 Pierre Gentine and others, 'Could Machine Learning Break the Convection Parameterization Deadlock?' (2018) 45 Geophysical Research Letters 5742.

113 Ching-Yao Lai and others, 'Machine Learning for Climate Physics and Simulations' (2024) arXiv <https://ui.adsabs.harvard.edu/abs/2024arXiv240413227L> accessed 22 January 2026.

114 Remi Lam and others, 'Learning Skillful Medium-Range Global Weather Forecasting' (2023) 382 Science 1416; Kaifeng Bi and others, 'Accurate Medium-Range Global Weather Forecasting with 3D Neural Networks' (2023) 619 Nature 533; D Kochkov and others, 'Neural General Circulation Models for Weather and Climate' (2024) 632 Nature 1060.

115 Rolnick et al (n 26) 35–40; Kaack et al (n 26) 522.

116 See Wolfgang Schön, 'Nachhaltigkeit in der Unternehmensberichterstattung' (2022) Zeitschrift für die gesamte Privatrechtswissenschaft 207; Ekkenga (n 111) 253–54.

117 David Friederich and others, 'Automated Identification of Climate Risk Disclosures in Annual Corporate Reports' (2021) arXiv <https://arxiv.org/abs/2108.01415> accessed 22 January 2026; Nicolas Webersinke and others, 'ClimateBert: A Pretrained Language Model for Climate-Related Text' (2022) arXiv <https://arxiv.org/abs/2110.12010> accessed 22 January 2026.

118 See, e.g., Julia Anna Bingler and others, 'Cheap Talk and Cherry-Picking: What ClimateBert Has to Say On Corporate Climate Risk Disclosures' (2022) 47 Finance Research Letters 102776.

119 Friederich et al (n 117).

to diminish significantly. First, tools are constantly improving through machine learning. Second, reporting frameworks such as the CSRD and ESRS are increasingly providing the missing standardisation by requiring reports to be published in a machine-readable format—enabling AI tools to unlock their full potential.

5. Conclusion

AI has both beneficial and adverse effects on climate change. As this chapter has shown, this dual role is also evident in corporate governance. So far, it has been largely overlooked that calls for more AI in the boardroom implicitly contribute to the growth and intensification of AI use—thereby increasing its already large carbon footprint. From the perspective of corporate climate governance—that is, a perspective that regards corporate laws, concepts, and policies as an integral part of curbing climate change—this suggests a shift from rather uncritical AI enthusiasm to more cautious AI pragmatism: When interpreting corporate law, scholars should take the climate risks of AI into account. Legal designs that incentivise the extensive and unreflective use of AI are the wrong way to go.

Of course, given AI's immense optimisation potential, this does not mean that companies should avoid it altogether. On the contrary, if used selectively, AI can meaningfully enhance corporate climate governance. As demonstrated by the examples of corporate climate reporting and corporate climate planning, AI can not only help companies disclose emissions and identify climate-related risks more efficiently and accurately; it can also reduce information overload and support stakeholders in better processing the information provided in emissions and sustainability reports.

CHAPTER 45

The Horizontal Effect of Fundamental Rights

OLHA O. CHEREDNYCHENKO AND BOUDEWIJN DE BRUIN

1. Introduction

Fundamental rights (or human rights) enshrined in national constitutions and international instruments, such as the International Covenant on Civil and Political Rights (ICCPR) and the European Convention on Human Rights (ECHR), have been increasingly invoked in climate change litigation.[1] In most cases brought before national or supranational courts across the globe, so far, these rights have been relied upon by citizens against states to compel them to take appropriate action to avert climate change, and with some success. For example, the Dutch supreme court (*Hoge Raad*) ordered the Dutch State in the *Urgenda* case to cut its greenhouse emissions by 25% in 2020 compared with 1990 levels based on its positive obligations to protect the right to life (Article 2, ECHR) and the right to respect for private and family life (Article 8, ECHR).[2] The European Court of Human Rights (ECtHR) ruled in *Verein KlimaSeniorinnen Schweiz v Switzerland* that Switzerland had failed to comply with its positive obligations to protect the right to private and family life (Article 8, ECHR) by not taking sufficient action against climate change.[3] And the South Korean constitutional court found that the existing national legislation was contrary to the state's duty to protect the right to a healthy and pleasant environment (Article 35, Constitution of the Republic of Korea).[4]

However, apart from vertical climate lawsuits instigated by private individuals against state actors, horizontal climate lawsuits have also been on the rise.[5] The latter are typically brought by private individuals against companies under private law, particularly tort law, to require these non-state actors to contribute to the fight against climate change. Like vertical climate

[1] See, e.g., Annalisa Savaresi, 'Plugging the Enforcement Gap: The Rise and Rise of Human Rights in Climate Change Litigation' (2021) 77 Questions of International Law 1; Joana Setzer and Lisa Benjamin, 'Climate Litigation in the Global South: Constraints and Innovations' (2020) 9 Transnational Environmental Law 77; Laura E Burgers, 'Representing Future Generations through European Private Law Climate Change Litigation' in Chantal Mak and Betül Kas (eds), *Civil Courts and the European Polity: The Constitutional Role of Private Law Adjudication in Europe* (Hart Publishing 2023).

[2] *The State of the Netherlands (Ministry of Economic Affairs and Climate Policy) v Stichting Urgenda* [2019] Supreme Court of the Netherlands 19/00135, ECLI:NL:HR:2019:2006.

[3] *Verein KlimaSeniorinnen Schweiz and others v Switzerland* App no 53600/20 (ECtHR, 9 April 2024).

[4] Press Release, Case on the National Greenhouse Gas Reduction Targets Addressing the Climate Crisis (2024) Application No. 2020Hun-Ma389 2021Hun-Ma1264, 2022Hun-Ma854, 2023Hun-Ma846 (consolidated) (*The Constitutional Court of Korea*, 29 August 2024) <https://climatecasechart.com/wp-content/uploads/non-us-case-documents/2024/20240829_NA_press-release.pdf> accessed 9 June 2025.

[5] See, e.g., Marc-Philippe Weller and Mai-Lan Tran, 'Climate Litigation against Companies' (2022) 1 Climate Action 1.

lawsuits, horizontal climate lawsuits may also rely on fundamental rights. A notable example is the *Shell* case before the lower Dutch civil courts in which several non-governmental organisations (NGOs) invoked, in particular, the right to life (Article 2, ECHR) and the right to private and family life (Article 8, ECHR) in support of their claim that the oil and gas company Shell should reduce its greenhouse gas emissions.[6] While fundamental rights were originally conceived as individual defences against the state, reliance on such rights in horizontal climate lawsuits fits the general trend towards the constitutionalisation of private law, whereby fundamental rights influence this part of law.[7] This development also corresponds with the growing influence of soft law instruments, such as the United Nations Guiding Principles on Business and Human Rights (UNGPs)[8] and the OECD Guidelines for Multinational Enterprises on Responsible Business Conduct.[9]

Against this backdrop, this chapter examines the role of fundamental rights in private law disputes on climate-related issues, focusing on the horizontal effect of such rights in general private law. Our central question is: How and to what extent can and should fundamental rights influence private law in climate change cases? We begin by exploring the link between fundamental rights and climate change, given the normative foundations of such rights. Subsequently, we revisit the well-established concepts of direct and indirect horizontal effect to assess the legal implications of each for the relationship between fundamental rights law and private law in the context of climate change litigation. We then turn to an inquiry into the challenges and opportunities that arise when claimants seek to ground climate-related claims in fundamental rights. Finally, we draw together our findings, reflecting on their significance and outlining avenues for further research.

2. Fundamental Rights and Climate Change

Can climate change adversely affect fundamental rights? If so, can an individual company be held responsible for a fundamental rights violation by contributing to climate change? To answer these questions, in the following, we will identify fundamental rights which can be potentially relevant in climate change litigation and highlight the complexity of establishing their breach in the context of debates on corporate responsibility.

[6] *Vereniging Milieudefensie and others v Royal Dutch Shell Plc* [2021] Hague District Court, C/09/571932/HA ZA 19-379, ECLI:NL:RBDHA:2021:5337; *Shell and others v Vereniging Milieudefensie and others* [2024] Hague Court of Appeal, 200.302.332/01, ECLI:NL:GHDHA:2024:2099. See, e.g., Benoit Mayer, 'The Duty of Care of Fossil-Fuel Producers for Climate Change Mitigation: *Milieudefensie* v. *Royal Dutch Shell*' (2022) 11 Transnational Environmental Law 407; Elbert de Jong, Chapter 9 of this handbook.

[7] In more detail see, e.g., Daniel Friedmann and Daphne Barak-Erez, 'Introduction' in Daniel Friedmann and Daphne Barak-Erez (eds), *Human Rights in Private Law* (Hart Publishing 2001); Olha O Cherednychenko, *Fundamental Rights, Contract Law and the Protection of the Weaker Party: A Comparative Analysis of the Constitutionalisation of Contract Law, with Emphasis on Risky Financial Transactions* (Sellier European Law Publishers 2007); Hugh Collins, 'On the (In)compatibility of Human Rights Discourse and Private Law' in Hans-W Micklitz (ed), *Constitutionalization of European Private Law* (OUP 2014).

[8] John Ruggie, Report of the Special Representative of the Secretary-General on the Issue of Human Rights and Transnational Corporations and Other Business Enterprises, 'Guiding Principles on Business and Human Rights: Implementing the United Nations "Protect, Respect and Remedy" Framework' (*UN Digital Library*, 21 March 2011) <https://digitallibrary.un.org/record/705860?v=pdf> accessed 9 June 2025.

[9] OECD, *Guidelines on Multinational Enterprises* (OECD Publishing 2017).

2.1 Potentially Relevant Fundamental Rights

Since the turn of the millennium, concerns about the impact of global warming on the exercise of fundamental rights have been increasingly raised by scholars,[10] intergovernmental bodies,[11] and NGOs.[12] Two distinct lines of argument have taken shape, each steering the discourse in a different direction. One presses for the recognition of new fundamental rights—a line of thought that can be traced at least as far back as Karel Vasak's 1977 notion of "third-generation" rights.[13] The other, in contrast, seeks to address climate-related harms within the framework of already established fundamental rights. Yet for all their differences, both approaches rest on the view that as climate change brings about forms of harm previously unrecognised, fundamental rights law must adapt to new circumstances.[14] This perspective aligns with the idea that fundamental rights instruments function as "living instruments" to be interpreted in the light of "present-day conditions".[15]

Simon Caney's 2005 seminal paper represents the first approach.[16] Following Joseph Raz's theory of rights,[17] Caney starts from the premise that we have a right to something whenever it constitutes a fundamental interest that is sufficiently weighty to induce obligations on others. Observing that we have a fundamental interest not to suffer from such things as droughts and crop failures, deaths as a result of heatstroke, infectious diseases such as malaria, floods,

[10] See, e.g., Simon Caney, 'Cosmopolitan Justice, Responsibility, and Global Climate Change' (2005) 18 Leiden Journal of International Law 747; Tim Hayward, *Constitutional Environmental Rights* (OUP 2005); John Knox, 'Linking Human Rights and Climate Change at the United Nations' (2009) 33 Harvard Environmental Law Review 477; Svitlana Kravchenko, 'Right to Carbon or Right to Life: Human Rights Approaches to Climate Change' (2008) 9 Vermont Journal of Environmental Law 513; Eric A Posner, 'Climate Change and International Human Rights Litigation: A Critical Appraisal' (2007) 155 University of Pennsylvania Law Review 1925; Amy Sinden, 'Climate Change and Human Rights' (2007) 27 Journal of Land, Resources & Environmental Law 255; Steve Vanderheiden, *Atmospheric Justice: A Political Theory of Climate Change* (OUP 2008). An early critical appraisal is a special issue of Georgia Journal of International and Comparative Law, introduced by Daniel Bodansky, 'Climate Change and Human Rights: Unpacking the Issues' (2010) 38 Georgia Journal of International and Comparative Law 511. See also Margaretha Wewerinke-Singh, 'Remedies for Human Rights Violations Caused by Climate Change' (2019) 9 Climate Law 224.

[11] E.g., the Human Rights Council (HRC) recognised the relevance of the issue in its resolutions 7/23 ("the link between the enjoyment of human rights and the protection of the environment"), 10/4 and 18/22 ("climate change-related impacts have a range of implications, both direct and indirect, for the effective enjoyment of human rights").

[12] See, e.g., Petition to the Inter American Commission on Human Rights Seeking Relief from Violations Resulting from Global Warming Caused by Acts and Omissions of the United States (7 December 2005) (Inuit Petition). See also Hari M Osofsky, 'The Inuit Petition as a Bridge? Beyond Dialectics of Climate Change and Indigenous Peoples' Rights' (2007) 31 American Indian Law Review 675.

[13] Karel Vasak, 'A 30-Year Struggle: The Sustained Efforts to Give Force of Law to the Universal Declaration of Human Rights' (1977) November UNESCO Courier 29.

[14] See, e.g., Milka Sormunen, 'Rethinking Effective Remedies to the Climate Crisis: A Vulnerability Theory Approach' (2023) 24 Human Rights Review 171 and Vincent Bellinkx and others, 'Addressing Climate Change through International Human Rights Law: From (Extra)Territoriality to Common Concern of Humankind' (2022) 11 Transnational Environmental Law 69.

[15] E.g., *Tyrer v the United Kingdom* App no 5856/72 (ECtHR, 25 April 1978) [31]. See Przemysław Siwior, 'The Potential of Application of the ECHR in Climate Change Related Cases' (2021) 23 International Community Law Review 197.

[16] Caney (n 10) 767–68.

[17] Joseph Raz, *The Morality of Freedom* (OUP 1986) 192.

relocation, and further dramatic changes to our world, Caney goes on to argue, based on information provided by the Intergovernmental Panel on Climate Change (IPCC), that climate change will cause these effects, which leads him to the conclusion that we have a "human right not to suffer from the disadvantages generated by global climate change".[18] While Caney later argued that climate change affects existing rights, such as the rights to life, health, and subsistence,[19] his early proposal seems to put forward a new right specifically tailored to climate change. This approach aligns with other scholars defending a fundamental right to climatic stability[20] or to an adequate environment,[21] and is also reflected in the 2007 Malé Declaration on the Human Dimension of Global Climate Change by representatives of Small Island Developing States.[22] A recent advisory opinion of the International Court of Justice on state obligations with respect to climate change, which recognises the fundamental right to a clean, healthy, and sustainable environment, further cements this development.[23]

The second approach arises from the climate-related claims of an Indigenous people who stand among the first to bear the full weight of a warming planet—the Inuit of the Arctic. In 2005, they brought a petition before the Inter-American Commission on Human Rights (IACHR) seeking relief from fundamental rights violations by the United States. While making a passing reference to the right to a healthy environment, the core argument is far broader.[24] The Inuit petition sets out in painstaking detail how various consequences of climate change have encroached upon a wide array of rights enshrined in the American Declaration of the Rights and Duties of Man, including the rights to life, physical security and integrity, health, personal and intellectual property, means of subsistence, the use and enjoyment of traditionally occupied lands, the benefits of culture, residence and freedom of movement, and the inviolability of the home.[25] Consider, for instance, how the Inuit petition describes the effects of climate change on their right to life:

> Individual Inuit lives are at risk due to the effects of climate change . . . [T]he sea ice, an important resource for travel and hunting . . . is thinner because of climate change . . . The thinner ice . . . cause[s] hunters and other travelers to fall through the ice and be injured or drowned.[26]

Although the IACHR ultimately decided not to process the Inuit petition,[27] there could perhaps be no clearer illustration of how the right to life can be affected by climate change. Moreover, in many climate change cases that have been filed worldwide, the right to life and other existing fundamental rights have in fact been successfully relied upon against states. For example, the Federal High Court of Nigeria ruled that by failing to stop Shell from engaging in massive and intense gas flaring for decades, the Nigerian government had violated the fundamental rights to life and human dignity (Sections 33 and 34, Nigerian Constitution), which

[18] Caney (n 10) 768.

[19] Simon Caney, 'Climate Change, Human Rights and Moral Thresholds' in Simon Caney (ed), *Climate Ethics: Essential Readings* (OUP 2010).

[20] Vanderheiden (n 10) 241.

[21] Hayward (n 10).

[22] Malé Declaration on the Human Dimension of Global Climate Change (14 November 2007).

[23] International Court of Justice, Obligations of States in Respect of Climate Change, Advisory Opinion No. 187, 23 July 2025 [387–93].

[24] See, e.g., Inuit Petition (n 12) 72–74.

[25] Inuit Petition (n 12).

[26] Inuit Petition (n 12) 91.

[27] Decision of the Inter-American Commission on Human Rights on the Inuit petition, 16 November 2006.

include the right to a clean and healthy environment.[28] The Supreme Court of India acknowledged India's commitment to achieve about 50% cumulative electric power installed capacity from non-fossil fuel-based energy resources by 2030, deriving a "right against the adverse effects of climate change" from the right to life and personal liberty (Article 21, Constitution of India) and the right to equality before law (Article 14, Constitution of India).[29] And, as noted above, in *Urgenda* and *Verein KlimaSeniorinnen Schweiz v Switzerland*, the right to life (Article 2, ECHR) and the right to respect for private and family life (Article 8, ECHR) were successfully invoked against the Dutch and Swiss governments, respectively. According to the ECtHR, the right to respect for private and family life encompasses "a right for individuals to effective protection by the State authorities from serious adverse effects of climate change on their life, health, well-being and quality of life".[30] The impact of climate change thus reaches beyond the basic conditions of subsistence, creeping into the private sphere.[31]

Other existing fundamental rights may potentially also play a role in climate change litigation. A notable example is the *Duarte Agostinho and others v Portugal and others* case currently pending before the ECtHR in which applicants argue that the effects of global warming, such as heatwaves and wildfires, harm their well-being and mental health, violating, among other rights, the prohibition of torture and inhuman or degrading treatment (Article 3, ECHR).[32] Some scholars have suggested that climate-related mental health impacts could fall within the scope of this prohibition, given that young people not only witness the tangible effects of climate change, but also face the prospect of bearing its long-term burdens.[33] Others have framed the issue in terms of autonomy, arguing that the suffering imposed by climate change constrains the ability of young people to shape their own futures.[34] But whether such arguments will gain traction remains to be seen.

2.2 **Corporate Responsibility**

Before moving forward, it is worth pausing to consider the difficulty of framing climate change as a fundamental rights *violation*.[35] While it is clear that global warming threatens the fundamental rights of present and future generations, it is far from obvious who, if anyone, can be identified as a violator. The challenge of causation looms large.[36] Even the world's largest emitters contribute only a fraction of global emissions, and climate change is the cumulative result of innumerable individual actions. If causation can be established, additional questions

[28] Federal Court of Nigeria, 14 November 2005, Suit No. FHC/B/CS/53/05. This case is discussed by Uzuazo Etemire, Chapter 39 of this handbook.

[29] Constitutional Court of India, *MK Ranjitsinh v Union of India* 2024 INSC 280 [20]. See Umakanth Varottil, Chapter 36 of this handbook.

[30] *Verein KlimaSeniorinnen Schweiz* (n 3) 7.

[31] See, e.g., Hari M Osofsky, 'Learning from Environmental Justice: A New Model for International Environmental Rights' (2005) 24 Stanford Environmental Law Journal 71, discussing, e.g., *Lopez Ostra v Spain* App no 16798/90 (ECtHR, 9 December 1994).

[32] *Duarte Agostinho and Ors v Portugal and others* App no 39371/20 (ECtHR, 9 April 2024).

[33] Corina Heri, 'Climate Change before the European Court of Human Rights: Capturing Risk, Ill-Treatment and Vulnerability' (2022) 33 European Journal of International Law 925, 947. See also Milka Sormunen, 'Rethinking Effective Remedies to the Climate Crisis: A Vulnerability Theory Approach' (2023) 24 Human Rights Review 171.

[34] Jelena Belic, 'Climate Change as Inhuman Treatment' (2022) 14(2) Global Justice 1.

[35] See, e.g., Knox (n 10) 484–90, Alexander Zahar, 'Human Rights Law and the Obligation to Reduce Greenhouse Gas Emissions' (2022) 23 Human Rights Review 385.

[36] See Mark Geitsfeld and Sandy Steel, Chapter 8 of this handbook.

arise, such as whether interference with fundamental rights can be justified.[37] Such obstacles to climate litigation might seem insurmountable for now,[38] particularly in horizontal climate lawsuits against individual companies.

One approach to addressing these questions is offered by Kristian Høyer Toft,[39] who builds on the work of Henry Shue[40] and Iris Marion Young,[41] whose contributions have shaped debates on corporate responsibility.[42] Toft proposes a typology of corporate responsibility that distinguishes between backward-looking duties, such as the polluter pays principle, and forward-looking ones, such as the no harm principle and the principle of beneficence. The polluter pays principle and the no harm principle may align with existing soft law instruments, such as the UNGPs, which emphasise corporate responsibility for minimising harm. The principle of beneficence, however, goes further, extending beyond a company's obligation to prevent or mitigate fundamental rights violations directly linked to its operations. Drawing on Young's theory of structural injustice,[43] the corporate responsibility to "do good" that follows from this principle might entail an obligation for companies to actively engage in climate change mitigation, adaptation, and redress, regardless of their past contributions and even in the absence of direct linkage between their actions and climate change.[44] Young's insights, developed in her work on global supply chains in the apparel industry, are particularly relevant here. She argues that when the complexity of supply chains makes it difficult to trace specific harms to individual companies, businesses may still have a forward-looking duty to act as part of a shared responsibility to address structural injustice. In her view, this responsibility does not depend on whether a company has violated the no harm principle but arises from the broader influence and power—or "leverage", as the UNGPs call it[45]—that the company holds. In climate governance, this reasoning suggests that businesses with significant leverage should play an active role in reducing harm—with power comes responsibility.[46]

Young's approach also addresses a closely related challenge of determining where along the causal chain responsibility should be assigned.[47] This issue becomes particularly pressing in discussions about corporate accountability for scope 3 emissions (i.e., emissions generated

[37] John H Knox, 'Human Rights Principles and Climate Change' in Kevin R Gray, Richard Tarasofsky, and Cinnamon P Carlarne (eds), *The Oxford Handbook of International Climate Change Law* (OUP 2016); Linnéa Nordlander, *Human Rights and Climate Change* (Routledge 2024) 70.

[38] cf Mattias Gunnemyr, 'Causing Global Warming' (2019) 22 Ethical Theory and Moral Practice 399.

[39] Kristian Høyer Toft, 'Climate Change as a Business and Human Rights Issue: A Proposal for a Moral Typology' (2020) 5 Business and Human Rights Journal 1.

[40] Henry Shue, 'Responsible for What? Carbon Producer CO2 Contributions and the Energy Transition' (2017) 144 Climatic Change 591. See also Henry Shue, *Basic Rights and Climate Change* (PUP 2020).

[41] Iris Marion Young, 'Responsibility and Global Labor Justice' 12 Journal of Political Philosophy 365.

[42] John G Ruggie, 'Business and Human Rights: The Evolving International Agenda' (2007) 101 American Journal of International Law 839.

[43] Young (n 41). See also Robyn Eckersley, 'Responsibility for Climate Change as a Structural Injustice' in Teena Gabrielson and others (eds), *The Oxford Handbook of Environmental Political Theory* (OUP 2016).

[44] See Florian Wettstein, 'Normativity, Ethics, and the UN Guiding Principles on Business and Human Rights: A Critical Assessment' (2015) 14 Journal of Human Rights 162 for a critical discussion of the principle of beneficence and the UNGPs.

[45] UNGPs, Principle 19.

[46] See also Simon Caney, 'Two Kinds of Climate Justice: Avoiding Harm and Sharing Burdens' (2014) 22 Journal of Political Philosophy 125, 141–42.

[47] See Bodanski (n 10); Douglas Kysar, 'What Climate Change Can Do About Tort Law' (2011) 41 Environmental Law 1, 11–12.

indirectly, for example, by consumers using the company's products).[48] Caney draws a distinction between "producer-based" and "consumer-based" approaches to assigning responsibility, ultimately favouring a model that distributes responsibility in proportion to power and leverage, with producers bearing the greatest share.[49] This view gains further weight when considering, as Toft observes, that consumers have been far less informed about climate change than the corporations responsible for large-scale emissions, not only in the past, but even now.[50]

3. The Degree of Fundamental Rights Horizontality

As the foregoing analysis has shown, climate change can adversely affect fundamental rights, and individual companies may have a responsibility to mitigate climate change in this context. However, relations between companies and other private persons are governed by private law, which brings us to the question of how fundamental rights relate to private law. The relationship between fundamental rights law and private law in a particular legal order largely depends on the extent to which fundamental rights affect horizontal relationships between individuals. In public law, fundamental rights are conceived as having direct vertical effect. An individual can exercise his or her rights by bringing a claim for breach of those rights directly against a public authority. But can an individual exercise his or her fundamental rights in a similar way against another individual in private law? In particular, can individuals, groups of individuals, and NGOs seeking to combat climate change directly invoke fundamental rights against, for instance, oil and gas companies, or against banks financing projects with a negative environmental impact? Or should they ground their claims in existing private law rules, such as duties of care in tort? And what is at stake here for the relationship between fundamental rights law and general private law? The debate on these issues has so far been dominated by the conceptual distinction between the direct and indirect horizontal effect of fundamental rights that originated in German legal scholarship and case law.[51] Although this distinction is not clear cut,[52] it is still useful for analysing the degree of fundamental rights horizontality in the context of climate change litigation under general private law.

3.1 Direct Horizontal Effect

In the case of the direct horizontal effect, a private party has, in his or her action against another private party, a claim or a defence which is based on a fundamental right which overrides an otherwise applicable rule of private law. The theory of direct horizontal effect was developed by Hans Nipperdey, who justified its adoption in Germany by the fact that the fundamental rights

[48] See, e.g., *Vereniging Milieudefensie and others v Royal Dutch Shell Plc* (n 6) [4.4.19].

[49] Simon Caney, 'Justice and the Distribution of Greenhouse Gas Emissions' (2009) 5 Journal of Global Ethics 135.

[50] Toft (n 39) 14.

[51] For more details, see Cherednychenko (n 7) s. 3.2.

[52] See further ibid s. 9.2.2, who, for the sake of conceptual clarity, distinguishes between three forms of the horizontal effect of fundamental rights in private law—*direct* horizontal effect, *strong indirect* horizontal effect, and *weak indirect* horizontal effect.

enshrined in the German Constitution embody a value system for the whole legal order and that there is thus no strict divide between public and private law.[53] As Olha Cherednychenko has argued, the direct horizontal effect of fundamental rights in fact leads to the subordination of private law to fundamental rights law.[54] After all, this form of horizontal effect implies that just as judges apply fundamental rights to the acts of public authorities under public law, so too they apply such rights to private conduct under private law. The substantive outcome of a dispute between private parties is determined by fundamental rights rather than private law. In the case of a violation of fundamental rights, the role of private law is limited to providing remedies. Fundamental rights law thus *governs* private law, thereby enjoying priority over the latter's internal principles of interpersonal justice.

While the German federal constitutional court ultimately did not adopt Nipperdey's approach, it resorted to the "state duties to protect constitutional rights" ("*grundrechtliche Schutzpflichten*") in private law—a concept which had previously only been applied in the context of public law. These *positive* obligations of the state differ from its *negative* obligations to respect constitutional rights. While the latter imply that the state should refrain from action so as not to interfere with the individual's constitutional rights, the former oblige the state to act when the constitutional rights of one individual are violated by another individual. In particular, following Claus-Wilhelm Canaris's theory of state duties to protect constitutional rights in private law,[55] the constitutional court ruled that in cases involving the inequality of bargaining power between the parties to a contract, the legislator is obliged to introduce mandatory rules in order to protect the constitutional rights of the weaker party against infringement by the stronger party, and where the legislator fails to do so, civil courts are obliged to control the terms of the contract based on the general clauses in the German Civil Code (*Bürgerliches Gesetzbuch* (*BGB*)), such as good faith (§ 242 BGB) and good morals (§ 138(1) BGB).[56] The courts' duty to protect fundamental rights of the weaker party implies that what is contrary to good faith or good morals is practically determined at the level of fundamental rights law rather than that of private law. The effect of imposing the duties to protect fundamental rights through contract or tort law on the civil courts may therefore not differ much from the outcome of the direct horizontal effect of such rights: In both cases, private law becomes subordinate to fundamental rights law.

Similarly, the subordination of private law to fundamental rights law is manifest in the case law of the ECtHR. Like the German constitutional court, the ECtHR has formulated positive obligations of the state not only under public law,[57] but also under private law, notably family law.[58] In particular, national civil courts may be required to interpret private law instruments,

[53] Hans C Nipperdey, *Grundrechte und Privatrecht* (Scherpe 1961) 13. cf Mattias Kumm, 'Who is Afraid of the Total Constitution? Constitutional Rights as Principles and the Constitutionalization of Private Law' (2006) 7 German Law Journal 341.

[54] For more details, see Cherednychenko (n 7) ch 3; Olha O Cherednychenko, 'Fundamental Rights and Private Law: A Relationship of Subordination or Complementarity?' (2007) 3 Utrecht Law Review 1.

[55] Claus-Wilhelm Canaris, 'Grundrechte und Privatrecht' (1984) 84 Archiv für civilistische Praxis 201; Claus-Wilhelm Canaris, *Grundrechte und Privatrecht* (Walter de Gruyter 1999).

[56] See, e.g., BVerfG 7 February 1990, *BVerfGE* 81, 242 (*Handelsvertreter*); BVerfG 19 October 1993, *BVerfGE* 89, 214 (*Bürgschaft*); 18 BVerfG 9 February 1994, BVerfGE 90, 27 (*Parabolantenne*). For more details, see Cherednychenko (n 7) s. 3.2.3.

[57] See, e.g., *X and Y v The Netherlands*, ECHR (1985) Series A, No. 91.

[58] See, e.g., *Marckx v Belgium*, ECHR (1979) *Series A*, No. 31; *Airey v Ireland*, ECHR (1979) *Series A*, No. 32.

such as wills, contracts, or constituent documents, in conformity with the ECHR.[59] Thus, although the ECtHR has not granted the direct horizontal effect to Convention rights, it may achieve a similar result in terms of those rights' actual effect on national private law by imposing positive obligations to protect them between individuals in the civil courts.

These developments in the case law of national and supranational courts are also echoed in international soft law instruments, notably the UNGPs. The latter include "the state duty to protect human rights", which requires taking appropriate steps to prevent, investigate, punish, and redress human rights abuses within a country's territory or jurisdiction by third parties, including companies, through legislation and adjudication.[60] Moreover, the UNGPs also impose the responsibility to respect fundamental rights on companies.[61] According to the UNGPs, companies should not only "[a]void causing or contributing to adverse human rights impact through their own activities, and address such impacts when they occur".[62] In addition, they should also "[s]eek to prevent and mitigate adverse human rights impacts that are directly linked to their operations, products or services by their business relationships, even if they have not contributed to those impacts".[63] The imposition of these responsibilities on corporations, which in effect amounts to granting the direct horizontal effect to fundamental rights, is justified as follows:

> The actions of business enterprises, just like the actions of other non-State actors, can affect the enjoyment of human rights by others, either positively or negatively. Enterprises can affect the human rights of their employees, their customers, workers in their supply chains or communities around their operations. Indeed, experience shows that enterprises can and do infringe human rights where they are not paying sufficient attention to this risk and how to reduce it.[64]

To the best of our knowledge, there have so far been no climate lawsuits against private parties in which fundamental rights were explicitly or implicitly granted the direct horizontal effect. Given the developments outlined above, however, this scenario is not unthinkable. Where private law is subordinated to fundamental rights law through the direct horizontal effect of fundamental rights or the state duties to protect such rights between individuals, an environmental NGO, for instance, could exercise the fundamental rights, such as the right to life, the right to respect for private and family life, or the right to a clean, healthy, and sustainable environment, against a company in a similar way as against the state. However, unlike in vertical climate change litigation, where only one party—in our example, the NGO—can rely on a fundamental right, in horizontal climate change litigation, *both* parties can typically claim that their fundamental rights are at stake. In order to have a chance of success in litigation in the scenario of the subordination of private law to fundamental rights law, the alleged tortfeasor, such as an oil and gas company or a bank, could rely, for example, on the freedom to conduct a business. This economic right is explicitly mentioned in Article 16 of

[59] See, e.g., *Pla and Puncernau v Andorra*, ECHR (2004) *Reports* 2004-VIII (2006) 42 EHRR 25, para 59; *Dimici v Turkey*, No. 70133/16, 5 July 2022. See Richard S Kay, 'The European Convention on Human Rights and the Control of Private Law' (2006) EHRLR 466; Olha O Cherednychenko, 'Towards the Control of Private Acts by the European Court of Human Rights?' (2006) 13 Maastricht Journal of European and Comparative Law 195; Collins (n 7) 53.

[60] UNGPs, Principle 1.

[61] UNGPs, Principle 11.

[62] UNGPs, Principle 13 under (a).

[63] UNGPs, Principle 13 under (b).

[64] United Nations Human Rights Office of the High Commissioner 2012, *The Corporate Responsibility to Respect Human Rights: Interpretive Guide*, United Nations 2012, 10.

the Charter of Fundamental Rights of the EU (EUCFR) or may be derived from other fundamental rights. As discussed in Section 4.1, the possibility of clashing rights raises difficult jurisprudential issues.

3.2 Indirect Horizontal Effect

In the case of the indirect horizontal effect of fundamental rights, in contrast, the private party's claim or defence is based on a private law rule which is influenced by the relevant fundamental right. The theory of indirect horizontal effect was first put forward by Günter Dürig as an alternative to Nipperdey's theory of direct horizontal effect.[65] Dürig defended his standpoint, emphasising the need to preserve the autonomy of private law from constitutional law, and thus protect private autonomy, which, in his view, would be reduced to zero if constitutional rights were to have direct horizontal effect.[66] In essence, the indirect horizontal effect of fundamental rights in this sense presupposes what Olha Cherednychenko has called a complementary relationship between fundamental rights law and private law, whereby relations between private parties are substantially governed by private law as a conceptually distinct and autonomous category, which is only *influenced* by fundamental rights.[67] A judge should take fundamental rights into account when interpreting and applying well-established private law rules, such as duties of care in tort, in a dispute between private parties. At the same time, private law remains decisive for the substantive outcome of such a dispute, which is resolved in accordance with its own requirements of interpersonal justice.

In fact, Dürig's theory of indirect horizontal effect was adopted by the German federal constitutional court in the famous *Lüth* case decided by it more than half a century ago.[68] In this case, the court ruled that constitutional rights, as objective values for the whole legal order, were to influence private law by affecting the interpretation of the existing rules, particularly general clauses, and that a dispute between private parties was to remain "*substantively* and procedurally a *private law* dispute".[69] While the *Lüth* formula of the indirect horizontal effect was never formally overruled, it is doubtful whether the German federal constitutional court actually adheres to it, given the adoption of the duties to protect constitutional rights in its later case law, noted above. However, the theory of indirect horizontal effect has shaped the relationship between fundamental rights law and private law in many other legal systems in Europe and beyond. For instance, it has been consistently, albeit implicitly, followed by the civil courts in the Netherlands,[70] where, in contrast to Germany, domestic constitutional rights do not have a monopoly position as a source of fundamental values for the entire legal order. In the UK, judges tend to favour a similar approach, accommodating the values

[65] Günter Dürig, 'Grundrechte und Zivilrechtsprechung' in Theodor Maunz (ed.), *Vom Bonner Grundgesetz zur gesamtdeutschen Verfassung: Festschrift zum 75. Geburtstag von Hans Nawiasky* (Isar 1956).

[66] ibid 164, 183.

[67] In more detail see Cherednychenko (n 7), ch. 3; Cherednychenko, Fundamental Rights and Private Law (n 54).

[68] BVerfG 15 January 1958, BVerfGE 7, 198 (*Lüth*).

[69] *Lüth*, 205 (our translation and emphasis).

[70] See, e.g., *Mensendieck I* HR 31 October 1969, NJ 1970, 57; *Maimonides* HR 22 January 1988, NJ 1988, 891; *Aidstest II* HR 12 December 2003, NJ 2004, 117. For more details, see Cherednychenko (n 7) s. 3.3.

behind the ECHR within the existing common law rules, in line with the general culture of incrementalism.[71]

A notable example of the indirect horizontal effect of fundamental rights in the context of climate change litigation is the recent ruling of the Dutch second instance civil court, the Hague Court of Appeal, in the *Shell* case.[72] This case arose from the claim by Milieudefensie, an association established under Dutch law to pursue the public interest in a healthy environment for current and future generations, and several other NGOs. The claimants sought a court order requiring Shell to prevent climate change by reducing its CO_2 emissions into the atmosphere by 45% by the end of 2030 compared with 2019 levels based on Shell's duty of care in tort (Article 6:162, Dutch Civil Code). In support of their claim, Milieudefensie and other NGOs relied in particular on the right to life (Article 2, ECHR) and the right to private and family life (Article 8, ECHR) of Dutch residents, the inhabitants of the Wadden region, and the world population. The first instance court, the Hague District Court, upheld the collective claim on behalf of the current and future generations of Dutch residents and inhabitants of the Wadden region.[73] It ordered Shell to meet the reduction target of 45% by cutting the emissions generated by the activities of the Shell group (Scope 1), its energy suppliers (Scope 2), and the consumers of its products (Scope 3). However, this decision was overturned by the Hague Court of Appeal.

Recalling the aforementioned ruling of the Dutch supreme court in the *Urgenda* case and the decision of the ECtHR in *Verein KlimaSeniorinnen Schweiz v Switzerland*, as well as the case law outside Europe and resolutions of the United Nations, the Hague Court of Appeal reaffirmed the fundamental right to "protection against dangerous climate change" under Articles 2 and 8 of the ECHR.[74] It also reiterated that this right has an indirect horizontal effect, influencing the interpretation of the unwritten standard of care in tort (Article 6:162, Dutch Civil Code).[75] When determining what this private law standard requires of large multinational companies like Shell, the fundamental right to protection against dangerous climate change should therefore be taken into account among other factors, such as the severity of a particular threat, the contribution to the emergence of the threat, and the ability to contribute to combating the threat, as well as relevant soft and hard law.[76] The second instance court noted that particularly those companies that have contributed significantly to climate change and that have the ability to contribute to combating it, bear responsibility towards other inhabitants of Earth in achieving the goals of the Paris Agreement on climate change. This interpretation of the duty of care in tort marks a significant expansion of corporate responsibility under soft law instruments, such as the UNGPs, aligning it more closely with the principle of beneficence, noted above.[77] According to the court, companies like Shell thus have an obligation under private law to reduce CO_2 emissions in order to combat dangerous climate change,

[71] See, e.g., *Douglas v Hello! Ltd* [2001] QB 967 C.A.; *Campbell v MGN Newspaper Ltd* [2004] UKHL 22. For more details, see Cherednychenko (n 7), s. 3.4. cf Collins (n 7), 41.

[72] *Shell and others v Vereniging Milieudefensie and others* [2024] (n 6).

[73] *Vereniging Milieudefensie and others v Royal Dutch Shell Plc* [2021] (n 6). The claim on behalf of the world population was considered inadmissible. In the district court's view, the interests of the current and future generations of the world population are not 'similar' and thus not suitable for bundling in accordance with Article 3:305a of the Dutch Civil Code on collective action because there are big differences in the time and manner in which those generations in various places will be affected by global warming.

[74] *Shell and others v Vereniging Milieudefensie and others* [2024] (n 6), [7.6–7.17].

[75] ibid [7.18, 7.24–7.25].

[76] ibid [7.24–7.26, 7.54].

[77] ibid [7.26–7.27].

even where public regulation does not require them to do so.[78] This obligation could entail that they consider the negative consequences of a further expansion of fossil fuel supply for the energy transition when investing in new oil and gas fields.[79] In the court's view, therefore, by going ahead with planned investments in these fields, Shell might act in breach of its duty of care in tort.[80]

At the same time, the Hague Court of Appeal rejected the claim by Milieudefensie and other NGOs that Shell's duty of care implies that the company should cut its greenhouse gas emissions by 45% or any other percentage, which was at issue in these proceedings. The court observed that the EU climate-related legislation did not impose specific reduction obligations on individual companies like Shell.[81] With respect to Scope 1 and Scope 2 emissions, it noted that Shell had already taken concrete measures to reduce them by at least 45% by the end of 2030 compared with 2019 levels and that the claimants did not demonstrate that this target would not be met.[82] With respect to Scope 3 emissions, which form the largest part of Shell's greenhouse gas emissions, the court argued that "objective starting points",[83] in particular the precautionary principle and climate science, provided "insufficient support" to oblige the company to reduce them by a specific percentage.[84] In addition, it could not be established that imposing such an obligation on a particular company would be effective because while that company would disappear from the value chain, fossil fuels would still reach consumers via another intermediary.[85]

The decision of the Hague Court of Appeal in the *Shell* case has been appealed, and it remains to be seen whether it will be upheld by the Dutch supreme court. And yet, it stands as a landmark judgment delivered by an ordinary civil court. While reflecting the rise of public interest litigation in Europe to tackle climate change, the ruling shows how the indirect horizontal effect of fundamental rights enables judges to accommodate fundamental rights within traditional private law discourse, thus fostering the complementarity between the two. In contrast to *Urgenda* and *Verein KlimaSeniorinnen Schweiz v Switzerland*, which imposed positive obligations to protect the right to life and the right to private and family life on states, *Shell* made it clear that these fundamental rights can also be relied upon against a private company to require it to fulfil its private law duty of care by contributing to the fight against climate change. When interpreting the unwritten standard of care in tort, the Dutch court took into account the compelling public interest in climate change mitigation supported by fundamental rights, among other factors, including those related to the role of oil and gas companies in climate change and energy transition, in line with the original concept of indirect horizontal effect.

4. Challenges and Opportunities

The horizontal effect of fundamental rights in private law presents both challenges and opportunities for efforts to prevent climate change. In this section, we discuss these challenges

[78] ibid [7.27].
[79] ibid [7.61 and 7.62].
[80] ibid [7.61]. However, whether this is indeed the case was not at issue in these proceedings.
[81] ibid [7.51 and 7.56].
[82] ibid [7.63–7.66].
[83] ibid [7.2] (our translation). According to the court, these include, in particular, legislation, general principles of law, fundamental rights, case law, and expert reports.
[84] ibid [7.91 and 7.96] (our translation).
[85] ibid [7.106 and 7.110].

and opportunities in the context of two major controversies surrounding the growing role of fundamental rights in climate change litigation in general and in horizontal climate lawsuits in particular: the judicial balancing exercise between competing interests and the role of courts as semi-regulators.

4.1 Balancing Conflicting Interests

The horizontal effect of fundamental rights—either direct or indirect—ultimately involves a complex balancing exercise to be performed by a court. Where a case is decided at the level of fundamental rights law, along the lines of the subordination of private law thereto, a court needs to determine the relevant fundamental rights of both parties and balance the competing interests against each other in the light of these rights. In contrast, where a case is decided at the level of private law, which is complemented by fundamental rights law, a court needs to identify relevant fundamental rights and rights under private law on both sides and weigh the countervailing interests protected by those rights within the framework of open-textured norms of private law. In the former case, both parties need to demonstrate that their interests have a fundamental rights dimension in order to have a chance of success in litigation. In the latter case, however, this will not be necessary, because the interests supported by fundamental rights will not automatically override the interests protected by private law, and both will be weighed against each other.

This may seem obvious in theory, but this balancing exercise is far from straightforward in practice. In the first place, courts rarely explain why some fundamental rights are explicitly referred to in particular contexts, whereas others are not mentioned at all. Judges often proceed from the existence of fundamental rights of one party to a private law dispute, failing to acknowledge that the interests of the other party are also protected by fundamental rights. In doing so, they might be merely responding to the lawyers' arguments. However, if judges do not consistently raise relevant fundamental rights on their own motion, some interests and policies could be jeopardised. Second, even where competing rights on both sides are identified, it remains unclear how, in general, courts carry out the weighing process based on the broadly formulated fundamental rights which were not conceived with horizontal relationships in mind.

The direct horizontal effect of fundamental rights is particularly problematic in this respect. After all, the difficult question that courts will face in this scenario is how to resolve a conflict between the competing fundamental rights on both sides, such as the right to life, the right to private and family life, or the right to a clean, healthy, and sustainable environment, on the one hand, and the freedom to conduct a business, on the other hand. To tackle this challenge, courts cannot simply apply the usual proportionality test in public law. Instead, they should measure competing rights against each other at the level of fundamental rights law, but the latter is not well-equipped to resolve a conflict between them. A possible solution might be provided by the "ultimate balancing test", also known as "the double proportionality test", developed by the English courts,[86] in which the rights of each party are qualified according to their weight in a particular context.[87] However, this test has not been widely applied so far. Therefore, while the direct horizontal effect of fundamental rights results in the subordination of private law to fundamental rights law, effectively sidelining tort law in the climate space,

[86] *Re S (Identity: Restrictions on Publication)* [2004] UKHL 47 [17]; *A Local Authority v W* [2005] EWHC 1564 (Fam).

[87] See Collins (n 7) 49.

fundamental rights law on its own may not be an appropriate framework for an intricate balancing act in horizontal climate lawsuits.

In allowing judges to accommodate fundamental rights within private law, the indirect horizontal effect circumvents the need to balance such rights within fundamental rights law and thus avoids the dominance of fundamental rights over tort law. As the Dutch *Shell* case shows, by following this approach in climate change cases, courts can explicitly take into account a wide range of factors, which not only include fundamental rights, but also more tort law-specific factors, such as the alleged tortfeasor's contribution to global warming, its awareness of climate change, and the point at which it acquired such knowledge, as well as the ability or leverage to contribute to limiting it. In the *Shell* case, such a balancing exercise has led the court to reject, for the time being, the existence of any specific reduction obligation on the part of Shell based on its duty of care in tort. At the same time, the court's reasoning in this case opened the door for broadening the scope of the company's private law duty of care to include an obligation to contribute to the fight against global warming.

The indirect horizontal effect of fundamental rights in climate change cases may thus lead to the departure from the conventional understanding of the tort law system as an individual dispute resolution mechanism, which is exclusively concerned with justice in a bipolar relationship between the tortfeasor and the victim, prompting civil courts to reconsider the boundaries of the private sphere and reinterpret open-textured private law norms in response to the climate crisis. At the same time, the extent to which tort law ultimately contributes to the pursuit of the public interest in climate change mitigation underpinned by fundamental rights is ultimately determined by the tort law itself in accordance with the principles of interpersonal justice. Accordingly, fundamental rights do not supersede tort law but rather infuse new life into traditional tort law concepts relevant to climate change litigation.

4.2 Courts as Semi-Regulators

It is widely acknowledged today that the horizontal effect of fundamental rights enables judges to step beyond positive legal rules in private law adjudication and make value judgments, addressing broader, often politically sensitive, issues.[88] As the Dutch *Shell* case shows, reliance on fundamental rights may lead courts to go beyond the existing public regulation and engage in what some authors call "judge-made risk regulation"[89] to tackle complex distributive issues raised by climate change in the pursuit of the public interest in a healthy environment and intergenerational justice.[90] The concept of judge-made risk regulation acknowledges that tort adjudication may have implications beyond the private interests of the litigating parties and have the effect of risk regulation by incentivising one of the parties to change its behaviour. However, the court's role as a semi-regulator with respect to climate-related risks in a democratic society has proven particularly controversial.

[88] cf, e.g., Ronald Dworkin, *Taking Rights Seriously* (HUP 1977); Duncan Kennedy, *A Critique of Adjudication: Fin de Siècle* (HUP 1997).

[89] Elbert de Jong and others, 'Judge-Made Risk Regulation and Tort Law: An Introduction' (2018) 9 European Journal of Risk Regulation 6.

[90] For a comprehensive analysis of the interplay between fundamental rights, public regulation and private law in the context of climate change and beyond, see Olha O Cherednychenko, *Market Regulation and Private Law* (CUP 2026) ch. 7.

For some, this role is justified to resolve the tragedy of the commons, where the enjoyment of fundamental rights is threatened by the democratic majority.[91] For others, it amounts to impermissible judicial activism, which cannot resolve the tragedy of the commons.[92] In particular, some scholars have warned that framing climate change within a fundamental rights framework risks depoliticising the issue, potentially narrowing public debate, sidelining broader political discourse on climate policy, and undermining the coherence of such policy.[93] As Surabhi Ranganathan argues, climate is a "global common" and the "common heritage of mankind", and while outsourcing the protection of fundamental rights may play a role within a broader policy framework for safeguarding these commons by using litigation risk to incentivise businesses to take responsibility, relying solely on public interest litigation may create the illusion that the issue is adequately addressed, which in turn, may undermine the need for further political or public action.[94] Ultimately, the most pressing challenge posed by depoliticisation is not so much that the complex normative dimensions of climate change are insufficiently addressed within the political process, but rather that the problem remains unsolved altogether.

To better grasp what is at stake in the debate over the role of courts as semi-regulators in climate change litigation against companies, it is helpful to turn to a broader theoretical framework, one that distinguishes between ideal and non-ideal approaches to justice. This distinction, which was first suggested by John Rawls[95] and later refined by Amartya Sen,[96] provides a lens through which to assess the reliance on fundamental rights in private law adjudication as a strategy for addressing climate change. The idea behind the distinction is that while political ideologies may set forth a vision of a just society under ideal conditions, there is a need for a complementary framework (non-ideal theory) to account for the practical steps required to move towards that vision. In the face of deep and widespread injustice, the chief concern should not be to define an abstract ideal of justice and chart a direct path to its realisation. Rather, the task of a theory of justice is to function as a practical tool: a means of shaping and assessing policies not by their alignment with some distant ideal, but by their capacity to bring about meaningful and incremental improvements in existing conditions. The key question in non-ideal theory, then, is how to engage with weak or unjust legal systems and societies. While much of the discourse focuses on more radical responses, such as civil disobedience, we suggest that judge-made risk regulation may be seen as a more moderate and institutionally grounded alternative.

Although Rawls and Sen did not formulate this distinction between ideal and non-ideal approaches to justice with horizontal climate lawsuits in mind, it provides a useful framework

[91] See, e.g., Laura Burgers, 'Should Judges Make Climate Change Law?' (2020) 9 Transnational Environmental Law 55.

[92] Gerhard Wagner, 'The Climate Judges' in Andreas Engert and others (eds), *Business Law and the Transition to a Net Zero Economy* (Beck, Hart and Nomos 2022) 69.

[93] See, e.g., Rebecca Ploof, 'Can Rights be Enough? Depoliticization, Human Rights, and Climate Change' (2024) 14 Global Justice 121. See also Sarah Seck, 'Revisiting Transnational Corporations and Extractive Industries: Climate Justice, Feminism, and State Sovereignty' (2017) 26 Transnational Law and Contemporary Problems 383; Sarah Downs, 'Civil Liability for Climate Change? The Proposed Tort in *Smith v Fonterra* with Reference to France and the Netherlands' (2024) 33 Review of European Community and International Environmental Law 31; Guillaume Laganiere, 'Choice of Law Issues in Tort-Based Climate Change Litigation' (2023) 74 University of New Brunswick Law Journal 33, 58.

[94] Surabhi Ranganathan, 'Global Commons' (2016) 27 European Journal of International Law 693.

[95] John Rawls, *A Theory of Justice* (HUP 1971) 351.

[96] Amartya Sen, 'What Do We Want from a Theory of Justice?' (2006) 103 Journal of Philosophy 215. See also Christopher Thompson, 'Ideal and Nonideal Theory in Political Philosophy' in (2020) *Oxford Research Encyclopedia of Politics*.

for assessing the role of fundamental rights in efforts to avert climate change through private law. In an ideal world, a global problem of this magnitude would be addressed through democratic decision-making that considers all relevant present and future interests. Policies would be implemented effectively, legal rules would be properly enforced, and both the powerful and the vulnerable would be held to the same standards. Where sacrifices in living standards were necessary, they would be accepted without dispute. Yet we do not live in that ideal world. Under non-ideal circumstances, there may be a strong justification for resorting to non-ideal means. The judicial reinterpretation of open-textured private law norms, such as a duty of care in tort, in the light of fundamental rights to tackle climate change certainly raises concerns about the separation of powers, particularly when it concerns private companies rather than states. However, this critique overlooks the reality that we live in today: The executive has largely failed to take decisive action, and public frustration over government inaction, which threatens the enjoyment of fundamental rights, is growing. The indirect horizontal effect of fundamental rights in general private law allows civil courts to legitimise their semi-regulatory role in the climate space under non-ideal circumstances.[97]

5. Conclusion

This chapter has explored the role of fundamental rights in climate change litigation, focusing on the horizontal effect of such rights in general private law. It has shown that a link between fundamental rights and climate change has been firmly established not only in the current policy discourse and scholarly work, but also in the case law of many national and supranational courts. There is growing consensus that climate change poses a threat to our fundamental rights, such as the right to life, the right to private and family life, or the right to a clean, healthy, and sustainable environment, and that both state and non-state actors have a responsibility to take action. But while climate change litigation against companies is on the rise, many questions still exist as to how and to what extent fundamental rights can and should influence private law, particularly tort law, in this context.

To address this key issue, it is helpful to distinguish between the direct and indirect horizontal effect of fundamental rights and the two corresponding models of the relationship between fundamental rights and private law—subordination and complementarity. In the case of the direct horizontal effect, a private party has, in his or her action against another private party, a claim or a defence which is based on a fundamental right which overrides an otherwise applicable rule of private law, resulting in the subordination of private law to fundamental rights law. In the case of the indirect horizontal effect, in contrast, the private party's claim or defence is based on a private law rule which is influenced by the relevant fundamental right, which enables the complementarity between fundamental rights law and private law.

The horizontal effect of fundamental rights—either direct or indirect—poses major challenges in the context of climate change litigation. In particular, one may point to the complexity of the judicial balancing exercise between competing interests supported by such rights or private law. One may also express concern about the role of courts as semi-regulators and the resulting depoliticisation of climate policy. The subordination of private law to fundamental rights through the direct horizontal effect of the latter is especially controversial, given

[97] cf Jürgen Habermas, *Between Facts and Norms: Contributions to a Discourse Theory of Law and Democracy* (John Wiley & Sons 2015) 263–64, who argues that when fundamental rights are threatened, judicial activism is justified to protect democracy itself.

that fundamental rights law is less equipped to resolve conflicts between the competing interests of the parties in horizontal climate lawsuits than private law.

And yet, the indirect horizontal effect of fundamental rights presents opportunities for civil society and private law to contribute to the fight against climate change in the face of persisting government inaction, while preserving the autonomy of private law from fundamental rights law. The assertion of private law claims based on fundamental rights may prompt civil courts to reinvigorate a duty of care in tort and other well-established private law concepts in order to address climate change. The complementarity between fundamental rights law and private law could thus allow tort law to combine its traditional concern about interpersonal justice with the concerns about distributive justice in a particular society or between generations, providing legitimacy for the courts' role as semi-regulators with respect to climate-related risks. Further research is needed into how the interests supported by fundamental rights and private law could be weighed against each other in order to enable tort law to reconcile these competing concerns.

CHAPTER 46

Indigenous Peoples

SAM BOOKMAN

1. Introduction

MANY Indigenous groups occupy a precarious double space: as *vulnerable* to the effects of climate change, and as *agents* both in leading global responses to mitigate and adapt to the crisis and in holding its largest contributors accountable. In many respects, Indigenous peoples play an outsize role in global climate governance.[1]

The displacement and marginalisation of Indigenous peoples has left many particularly vulnerable to the impacts of climate change. Many Indigenous peoples live in exposed territories and with access to few material resources.[2] Yet as Indigenous scholars and activists have pointed out,[3] the causes of climate change are deeply intertwined with the same processes of colonisation, imperial expansion, and economic extraction which led to the conquest and subjugation of Indigenous peoples. At the heart of colonisation is the alienation of Indigenous peoples from their lands and land-based lifeways. The laws, knowledge, and practices of Indigenous peoples are therefore perhaps unsurprisingly looked to by many non-Indigenous scholars and activists as a source of leadership and inspiration in the fight against climate change and the broader economic and political systems that produce it.[4] This

[1] For the purposes of this chapter, Indigenous peoples are those 'living descendants of pre-invasion inhabitants of lands now dominated by others. They are culturally distinct groups that find themselves engulfed by other settler societies born of forces of empire and conquest'. *See* James Anaya, *Indigenous Peoples in International Law* (2nd edn, OUP 2004) 3. Indigeneity may continue to exist even after independence from colonial rule. For an example of one such jurisdiction, see Bridget Fa'amatuainu, 'Indigenising Private Law: Lessons from Samoa' (2023) 4 Journal of Commonwealth Law 101. See also Nicole Graham, Chapter 15 of this handbook.

[2] For discussion of the disproportionate impacts of climate change on Indigenous peoples, *see* IPCC, *Climate Change 2023: Synthesis Report. Contribution of Working Groups I, II and III to the Sixth Assessment Report of the Intergovernmental Panel on Climate Change* (2023) 50–51; 62; 99; 101.

[3] See, e.g., Kyle Whyte, 'Indigenous Climate Change Studies: Indigenizing Futures, Decolonizing the Anthropocene' (2017) 55 English Language Notes 1, describing climate change as a form of 'intensified colonialism'; Leonie Hayden, 'Te taio Under Threat: Indigenous Voices Speak Up on Climate Change' *The Spinoff* (New Zealand, 3 November 2021) <https://thespinoff.co.nz/atea/03-11-2021/te-taiao-under-threat-indigenous-voices-speak-up-on-climate-change> accessed 27 May 2025, quoting Māori activist India Logan-Riley.

[4] For prominent examples, see, e.g., Anita Hofschneider, 'The Key to Better Climate Outcomes? Respecting Indigenous Land Rights and Autonomy' *Grist* (23 May 2024) <https://grist.org/indigenous/the-key-to-better-climate-outcomes-respecting-indigenous-land-rights-and-autonomy/> accessed 27 May 2025; Maria Antonia Tigre, 'Climate Change and Indigenous Groups: the Rise of Indigenous Voices in Climate Litigation' (2022) 9(3) E-Publica 214; Randall S Abate and Elizabeth Ann Kronk Warner, 'Introduction' in Randall S Abate and Elizabeth Ann Kronk Warner (eds), *Climate Change and Indigenous Peoples: The Search for Legal Remedies* (Edward Elgar Publishing 2013).

move is supported by empirical evidence which points to positive environmental outcomes in Indigenous-managed lands.[5] Decolonisation—including the decolonisation of *legal* systems—is justifiably seen as a central component of any meaningful attempt to address both the effects and root causes of the climate crisis.

At the same time, Indigenous peoples are no monolith. They instead comprise almost 500 million people from 5000 distinct groups, with a wide variety of interests, values, and legal systems.[6] While many Indigenous peoples have led global action on climate change, some Indigenous groups have countervailing economic interests in the development of their lands and resources—resources often reclaimed only after prolonged struggles against post-colonial states.[7] Attempts to equate Indigenous and environmental interests can end in harmful romanticisation. And despite the significant role of Indigenous peoples in global climate action, pinpointing the specific role of Indigenous *private law* is a challenging one. Defining and identifying a globally coherent category of "Indigenous law" is itself challenging, let alone isolating a portion of that corpus as exclusively "private". Indeed, any attempt to do so risks reifying colonial legal taxonomies and categories.

Rather than establishing a uniform conception of Indigenous private law, Section 2 of this chapter canvasses a range of possibilities. This chapter discusses the use of state private law by Indigenous peoples.[8] But it also engages with Indigenous private law as a set of laws and legal practices whose origins predate or differ from state law, and which might interact with state law in a range of different ways. Indigenous private law may be integrated into state law through statute or judicial reasoning (as in Aotearoa/New Zealand), occupy a separate domain of authority (as in the US), or lack state recognition altogether. These different possibilities foreground the application of Indigenous private law to climate change.

Section 3 maps the field of Indigenous private law and climate change, as well as the use of state private law by Indigenous peoples in the pursuit of climate-related goals. It begins with the question of liability for climate harm, discussing cases in which Indigenous peoples have held large emitters to account for their outsize contributions to greenhouse gas emissions. It then discusses the uses of Indigenous laws and lands in two contexts: the *mitigation* of climate change (in reducing greenhouse gas emissions and preserving carbon sinks); and the use of Indigenous lands for *adaptation* efforts. While the precise contours of such efforts will depend on the relationship between Indigenous and state law, the survey reveals that Indigenous private laws and legal concepts have a life and vitality beyond the state system.

This chapter continues in Section 4 by identifying future frontiers for the engagement between Indigenous private law and climate change. I discuss three possibilities. First, this chapter canvasses the model of fiduciary relationships between state governments and Indigenous peoples, referred to in some contexts as "trust obligations" or "the honour of the

5 See, e.g., Neil Dawson and others, 'Is it Just Conservation? A Typology of Indigenous Peoples' and Local Communities' Roles in Conserving Biodiversity' (2024) 7 One Earth 1007.

6 'Indigenous Peoples', United Nations <https://www.un.org/en/fight-racism/vulnerable-groups/indigenous-peoples> accessed 8 April 2025.

7 For example, see Matthew Brown and Felicia Fonseca, 'Boom in Native American Oil Complicates Biden Climate Push' *Associated Press* (24 June 2021) <https://apnews.com/article/joe-biden-lifestyle-travel-science-native-americans-c8ff51f166d815acfd6057ca86f6808a> accessed 27 May 2025, describing three Native American tribes which have earned $1.5 billion USD in revenue from oil extraction, and observing that some Native American groups have opposed efforts to reduce oil extraction.

8 'State law' or 'state private law' is used in this chapter to denote the state-sanctioned private law of a national legal system, in most cases established through a process of colonial conquest or settlement.

Crown".[9] Such relationships at once invoke state *public* law, but are also grounded in concepts and applications of *private* law. Secondly, this chapter considers private law models of reparations owed to Indigenous peoples. Third, this chapter considers the relevance of private regimes related to traditional ecological knowledge, and the possibility of Indigenous legal systems themselves as resources vulnerable to extraction. This chapter concludes by considering the challenges and risks for ongoing Indigenous engagement with private law in the context of climate change. Many Indigenous peoples face the hard choice of whether to pursue claims for self-determination and the development of autonomous Indigenous private law or repurpose and adapt state law for Indigenous environmental interests.

My training in Indigenous law (as a non-Indigenous scholar) is primarily grounded in tikanga Māori—the first law of Aotearoa/New Zealand. This contribution accordingly leans heavily on tikanga Māori concepts and principles, some of which may have resonance in other Indigenous legal systems, and many which may be more specific and limited. Regrettably, owing to limitations of space and expertise, this chapter contains little reference to Indigenous traditions beyond those of today's Anglophone settler-states. Generalisations to "Indigenous peoples" should be treated with care. For a fuller picture, readers are encouraged to engage with the work of Indigenous legal scholars from other legal systems, including those of Latin America, Scandinavia, Africa, and Asia.

2. What Is Indigenous Private Law?

Much has been written about the role of Indigenous peoples in climate law and litigation. Indeed, one of the first instances of climate litigation was brought by an Indigenous group: the Alaskan Native village of Kivalina, which brought suit against several fossil fuel companies,[10] and later the US government.[11] Most scholarly attention on Indigenous peoples and climate law, however, deals with *public* law, and in particular, claims by Indigenous peoples asserting their treaty, constitutional, or human rights claims against national governments.[12] The literature on Indigenous peoples, climate change, and *private* law is much sparser, and beset by conceptual challenges.

2.1 Definitional Challenges

Private law is itself a contested concept. No field of law is entirely free of state regulation. Even the traditional private law fields of tort, contract, and property each have a public law dimension.[13] And the absence or presence of private or state parties is not dispositive of whether the

[9] See, e.g., *Guerin v R* [1984] 2 SCR 335; *Proprietors of Wakatū v Attorney-General* [2017] NZSC 17, [2017] 1 NZLR 423.

[10] *Native Village of Kivalina v ExxonMobil Corp.*, 696 F.3d 849 (9th Cir. 2012).

[11] *Petition to the Inter American Commission on Human Rights Seeking Relief from Violations Resulting from Global Warming Caused by Acts and Omissions of the United States* (7 December 2005) <https://climatecasechart.com/wp-content/uploads/non-us-case-documents/2005/20051208_na_petition.pdf> accessed 27 May 2025.

[12] For example, see Sam Bookman, 'Climate Litigation in Anglophone Settler-Colonial States' *Verfassungsblog* (25 March 2022) <https://verfassungsblog.de/indigenous-climate-litigation-in-anglophone-settler-colonial-states/> accessed 4 July 2025; Tigre (n 4); Louise du Toit, Caiphas Soyapi, and Louis J Kotze, 'David versus Goliath? Indigenous People, Carbon Majors and Climate Litigation in South Africa' (2024) 33 Review of European, Comparative and International Environmental Law 326.

[13] For example, see Gregory C Keating, 'Is Tort Law "Private"?' in Paul B Miller and John Oberdiek (eds), *Civil Wrongs and Justice in Private Law* (OUP 2020).

relevant legal field is public or private—states themselves are subject to private law obligations in tort, contract, and property law.

If there is doubt as to the coherence of private law writ large, so much more so for the concept of Indigenous private law. Two challenges are particularly difficult. First, the binary between public and private law is often premised on a particular division of labour between government regulation and private ordering. This division pervades the courts, codes, precedents, and bureaucracies of colonial and European legal systems: institutions that do not exist in many Indigenous societies. Instead, Indigenous legal systems tend to be grounded in customary practices and institutions such as spiritual beliefs, relational obligations, and place-based interactions. A recent attempt by New Zealand's Law Commission to map tikanga Māori—defined as the "set of values, principles, understanding, practices, norms and mechanisms from which a person or community can determine the correct action"—identifies concepts of connection, equilibrium, entity-status, and responsibility, arising from sources and institutions as diverse as creation stories, customary norms, expert knowledge, spiritual worldviews, kinship ties, and ritual protocols.[14] Such institutions do not easily map on to either public or private descriptors. They are, however, "jural": "involv[ing] rights, duties, liabilities, and other interests or restrictions that govern relationships".[15] Rather than a set of obligations pertaining to interactions with either (1) the state or (2) atomised individuals, Indigenous legal systems (such as tikanga Māori) are more likely to involve communally embedded relational obligations derived from—and applying to—a diverse and decentralised set of actors.

Secondly, the legal institutions of many Indigenous peoples have been deliberately suppressed by ongoing processes of colonisation. Institutions such as chiefly authorities, spiritual leaders, and formal decision-making and adjudicative protocols have, in many cases, been actively outlawed.[16] To the extent that any demarcation between public and private law *institutions* may exist, they have been diminished or recently reconstructed.

These two challenges are not universal to all Indigenous legal systems. Some, such as those of federally recognised US Indian tribes, more closely mirror the legal institutions of Western states, with constitutionally established lawmaking processes, written codes, and tribal courts. But for the majority of the world's Indigenous peoples whose self-determination is not formally recognised by states, the concept of Indigenous private law is a complex one.

2.2 Indigenous Private Law

"Indigenous private law" is used in this chapter to denote the norms of conduct and action-guiding values which derive from within Indigenous legal systems—and specifically, those norms which relate to interactions between communally embedded groups or individuals, rather than interaction with state institutions or formal Indigenous governments. Functionally, then, this chapter often uses "Indigenous private law" to refer to norms that bear some resemblance to subject matter governed by state tort, contract, or property law, though the content of such norms will often be very different.

States interact with Indigenous private law in different ways. One useful three-part taxonomy identified by some scholars such as Jacob Levy[17] is between those systems where (1)

[14] New Zealand Law Commission, *He Poutama* (Study Paper 24, 2023) [3.16]. See also David Bullock, Chapter 7 of this handbook.

[15] ibid [3.13].

[16] See for example the Tohunga Suppression Act 1907 (NZ).

[17] Jacob T Levy, 'Three Modes of Incorporating Indigenous Law' in Will Kymlicka and Wayne Norman (eds), *Citizenship in Diverse Societies* (OUP 2000).

Indigenous peoples have some form of self-government, (2) Indigenous law is integrated into state law, or (3) Indigenous law lacks formal recognition.

Even where Indigenous law lacks formal recognition, it may still be relevant in specific adjudication. As Levy observes, in such systems "the Indigenous identities and practices of individuals may be relevant to legal adjudication under state law" (for instance, where Indigenous land practices meet the criteria for adverse possession).[18] Where Indigenous law is integrated into state law (what Aotearoa/New Zealand Supreme Court Justice Joseph Williams describes as an "integrate to perpetuate" model),[19] there will be a closer connection between the two systems. This may include statutory tests for native title property rights requiring evidence of customary usage (as in Australia's Native Title Act 1993), or recognition of customary practices as a source of common law norms (as in Aotearoa/New Zealand,[20] Samoa,[21] and Hawai'i[22]). Although a stronger form of pluralism and integration, this model falls short of Indigenous sovereignty or self-determination. Recognition of customary land rights generally—though not always[23]—falls short of freehold title (for instance, involving restraints on alienation or being limited to usufructuary rights), and Indigenous peoples lack the ability to directly legislate and apply private law norms through their own institutions. Where states recognise Indigenous self-government, however, Indigenous peoples have formal territorial sovereignty and can enact enforce their own private law norms. This approach is most developed in the US, where federally recognised Indian tribes are sovereign over their tribal territories, a model Williams describes as "separate to survive".[24] How Indigenous peoples and laws interact with climate change will depend in large part on the model of a particular state.

2.3 Private Law and Indigenous Peoples

Some examples discussed in this chapter, however, do not involve Indigenous law in this strict sense. Instead, they relate to what might more accurately be described as private law and Indigenous peoples, that is, the use of state private law by Indigenous peoples, generally acting as collectives of citizens rather than expressing their own legal norms and values. Because state recognition of Indigenous law in many regimes is so weak, it may be that Indigenous peoples have no choice but to adopt the tools and categories of state private law. In other cases, Indigenous peoples might conclude that state private law tools offer a greater prospect of success. In many of the examples discussed in Sections 3 and 4, Indigenous peoples are faced with trade-offs: using state law to their advantage while reinforcing its primacy, or working outside the system of state law while sacrificing the potential efficacy of their campaigns. This trade-off is discussed further at the end of this chapter.

[18] ibid.

[19] Joseph Williams, 'Lex Aotearoa: An Heroic Attempt to Map the Māori Dimension in Modern New Zealand Law' [2013] Waikato Law Review 2.

[20] See *Takamore v Clarke* [2012] NZSC 116; *Ellis v R* [2022] NZSC 114; *Trans-Tasman Resources Ltd v Taranaki Whanganui Conservation Board* [2021] NZSC 127; *Smith v Fonterra* [2024] NZSC 7.

[21] Fa'amatuainu, (n 1) 116, citing Section 111 of the Constitution of Samoa.

[22] See HRS § 1-1: '[t]he common law of England' is 'the common law of the State of Hawai . . . except as otherwise . . . established by Hawaiian usage'.

[23] For example, in the Canadian case of *Tsihqot'in Nation v British Columbia* [2014] 2 SCR 257 (SCC) the Supreme Court of Canada issued a declaration awarding 'ownership rights similar to those associated with fee simple'. See generally John Borrows, 'Aboriginal Title and Private Property' (2015) 71 Supreme Court Law Review 91.

[24] Williams (n 19).

3. Indigenous Peoples, Private Law, and Climate Change: The State of the Field

Current private law developments relating to Indigenous peoples can be roughly grouped into three issues. The first is liability for climate harm. In this category, Indigenous peoples have sought to hold private parties liable under tort law for their contributions to global greenhouse gas emissions. While such claims generally rely on state private law, they may also incorporate elements of Indigenous law, as in the ongoing case of *Smith v Fonterra* in Aotearoa/New Zealand. The other two categories relate to land use and either climate *mitigation* or *adaptation*. Each category is discussed in turn below.

3.1 Liability for Climate Harm

As extensively documented elsewhere in this handbook, private law—and in particular, tort law—is an important site of litigation where plaintiffs seek to hold major emitters responsible for their historic and ongoing contributions to climate change.[25] While it would be incorrect to speak of Indigenous private law as possessing a directly analogous notion of torts, Indigenous legal systems nevertheless include a range of action-guiding values, norms, and practices relevant to interpersonal relationships. Indigenous peoples have long participated in tort suits in state law systems and, more recently, have advanced Indigenous legal norms and practices.

Indigenous peoples were among the first to attempt to use tort law as a tool to hold large greenhouse gas emitters accountable. In *Kivalina v ExxonMobil Corporation*, the Alaskan Native village of Kivalina sued several large oil corporations.[26] The village, located on a barrier island extremely vulnerable to rising sea levels and extreme weather, sought damages to fund its relocation. The case was grounded primarily in public nuisance law.

The plaintiffs were ultimately unsuccessful. A district court dismissed the claim, finding that it lacked subject matter jurisdiction over an essentially political question, and that the village would not be able to establish a sufficient chain of causation between the defendants' actions and climate-related harms. But the case was significant: It was the first of dozens of tort suits against large greenhouse gas emitters brought across the US, many of which remain ongoing.[27] Two of those ongoing cases have been brought by Native American tribes: *Makah Indian Tribe v ExxonMobil* and *Shoalwater Bay Indian Tribe v ExxonMobil*.[28] Both cases are grounded in state private law arguments, including public nuisance and failure to warn. Although based on state law, the two cases highlight the impact of climate change on Native American populations, particularly those living in coastal areas facing rising sea levels, depleted fish stocks, and, ultimately, the threat of relocation.

Claims such as those in *Kivalina*, *Makah Indian Tribe*, and *Shoalwater Bay Indian Tribe* have been brought by Indigenous peoples, but do not necessarily involve *Indigenous* private law. Instead, they necessarily rely on state private law. US courts have been reluctant to recognise

[25] David Bullock, Chapter 7 of this handbook; Elbert de Jong, Chapter 9 of this handbook.

[26] *Kivalina* (n 10).

[27] 'Big Oil Accountability Lawsuits', *Center for Climate Integrity* <https://climateintegrity.org/lawsuits> accessed 5 May 2025.

[28] Both cases were remanded to state court after an unsuccessful attempt by defendants to remove them to federal court. *Makah Indian Tribe v ExxonMobil Corp.*, Case No. 2:24-cv-157 (Dist. Ct Wash, 26 March 2025) <https://climatecasechart.com/wp-content/uploads/case-documents/2025/20250326_docket-224-cv-00157_order.pdf> accessed 27 May 2025.

the legal relevance of Indigeneity in state law tort claims. In tort litigation concerning the Exxon Valdez oil spill, for instance, federal courts awarded damages to tribal plaintiffs, but did not make any special award or allowance for additional damages related to the destruction of cultural lifeways.[29] As Rebecca Tsosie argues, such an approach reflects an individualised vision of private law "in which citizens are perceived as having a primary identity based on their shared civic values and in which their religious and cultural differences are confined to the 'private' sphere".[30] Such an approach leaves little room for the relevance of Indigenous private law beyond tribal courts and reservations.

The situation may be different, however, where Indigenous law is incorporated into state private law. In recent years, courts in Aotearoa/New Zealand have increasingly recognised tikanga Māori as a source of private common law norms.[31] In *Smith v Fonterra*, New Zealand's Supreme Court expressly applied these norms in the context of liability for greenhouse gas emissions.[32] Smith, a Māori iwi (tribal) leader, brought a case against the country's seven largest greenhouse gas emitters. As in *Kivalina*, the case included a public nuisance claim. Smith did not argue that tikanga Māori gave rise to a new cause of action in state courts. But he did argue that it should inform the court's application of private law. He pointed to whakapapa (genealogical) and whanaungatanga (kinship) connections to land and water that were harmed by climate change, as well as injuries related to "customary, historical, spiritual and nutritional values" held by him and his descendants.[33] In other words, as the court observed, "the specific loss pleaded by Mr Smith in this case is in part tikanga-based".[34] After refusing to strike out the case, the Supreme Court directed a future trial court to "engage with tikanga", including the "need to consider the potential effect of tikanga on any special damage requirement in public nuisance . . . and . . . whether tikanga-related harm is a cognizable form of loss".[35] The court pointed out that such an approach had a long pedigree dating back to mid-ninteenth-century cases contesting ownership of natural resources.[36] Ultimately, a trial court will[37]

> need to grapple with the fact that Mr Smith purports to bring proceedings not merely as an alleged proprietor who has suffered loss, but as a kaitiaki [guardian] on behalf of the whenua [land], wai [water] and moana [ocean]—distinct entities in their own right. And it must consider some tikanga concepts of loss that are neither physical nor economic. In other words, addressing and assessing matters of tikanga simply cannot be avoided.

Indigenous private law concepts may also be relevant in litigation against public entities. In *Pabai v Commonwealth of Australia*, for example, members of a Torres Strait Islander community argue that the Australian government has negligently breached a duty of care owed towards them.[38] They argue that such a duty arises in part because of their status as holders of native title in the Islands, and that the government's breach of that duty threatens the very

[29] *In re Exxon Valdez*, 1994 W.L. 182856 (D. Alaska); affirmed 104 F.2d 1196 (9th Cir., 1997).

[30] Rebecca Tsosie, 'Climate Change and Indigenous Peoples: Comparative Models of Sovereignty' (2013) 26 Tulane Environmental Law Journal 239, 249.

[31] See cases cited at n 20.

[32] *Smith v Fonterra* [2024] NZSC 7.

[33] ibid [177].

[34] ibid [182].

[35] ibid [182].

[36] ibid [184].

[37] ibid [188].

[38] *Pabai v Commonwealth of Australia* VID6222/2021 (Statement of Claim, 26 October 2021) available at https://www.fedcourt.gov.au/__data/assets/pdf_file/0003/96609/2021.10.26-Statement-of-Claim.pdf.

existence of Ailan Kastom: the ability to live lives in accordance with Indigenous legal, spiritual, and action-guiding norms.[39] The plaintiffs argue that the destruction of these norms and way of life, rooted in "a unique spiritual and physical connection with the Torres Strait Islands and surrounding waters",[40] amounts to a negligent breach of duty. At the time of writing (June 2025), a decision by the Federal Court of Australia is reserved.

Cases such as *Smith* and *Pabai* potentially open new legal frontiers in Indigenous private law and climate change. Though no such claim has been advanced to date, another possibility arises in environmental and climate tort claims adjudicated in Indigenous tribal courts, such as those operated by federally recognised tribes in the US. The jurisdiction of such courts is largely restricted to activities that occur on tribal reservations or concerning the conduct of tribal members.[41] Nevertheless, some opportunities could potentially arise where (as in the US) tribal courts have jurisdiction over private parties who enter into commercial relationships with tribes, or where non-member activities pose an existential threat to the tribe's welfare and security.[42] These possibilities, however, remain untested.

3.2 Indigenous Private Law, Land Use, and Climate Mitigation

The discussion above concerned the law of torts, or its analogues in Indigenous private law: action-guiding values and norms governing conduct in interpersonal relationships. The following two sections concern norms governing relationships with *land*. While in state private legal systems these norms would generally be called "property law", such a descriptor would be a misnomer in many Indigenous legal systems, which instead are more likely to stress duties of stewardship, specific place-based connections, and long-term kinship obligations—thus complicating the sharp dividing line between natural objects and human subjects. Indeed, state-based property law has proven to be one of the most violent tools of colonisation, enabling the rapid transfer of communally used land into private individual title, and removing the ability of Indigenous peoples to maintain sovereignty or governorship over their traditional lands. As Joseph Williams observes, "where tikanga Māori was recognised during the colonial period, it was recognised only to the extent necessary to succeed in extinguishing it".[43]

In many Indigenous legal systems, the relationship between land and legal norms is reciprocal: Legal norms *apply to* but are also *derived from* the land.[44] Norms are typically derived through spiritual and kinship ties, as well as customary practices and traditional ecological knowledge. In many Indigenous legal systems, land is assigned spiritual significance,

[39] The *Pabai* plaintiffs describe Ailan Kastom as including 'connection to the marine and terrestrial environment, including as part of cultural ceremony; participant in cultural ceremony; use of plants and animals for food, medicine and cultural ceremony; burying Torres Strait Islanders in local cemeteries and performing mourning rituals; visiting sacred sites, including on uninhabited islands; and dugong and marine turtle hunting, and other marine hunting and fishing'. ibid [55].

[40] ibid 19.

[41] *Montana v United States*, 450 U.S. 544 (1981).

[42] ibid; see also *Dollar General Corp. v Mississippi Band of Choctaw Indians*, 578 U.S. 545 (2016).

[43] *Williams* (n 19) 12.

[44] Kathleen Birrell, Lee Godden, and Maureen Tehan, 'Climate Change and REDD+: Property as a Prism for Conceiving Indigenous Peoples' Engagement' (2012) 3 JHRE 196, 206: 'In Aboriginal Australian societies, for instance, knowledge, including law, is literally manifest in the landscape, which is broadly described as "country", such that "Aboriginal law is 'grown' not 'made'". The landscape is spiritually animated'.

producing a set of reciprocal relationships and duties. As Rebecca Tsosie describes, "in the world view of many indigenous peoples, the relationship of human beings to the natural world must be premised on an ethics of respect and reciprocity, sometimes linked up to a model of 'stewardship' rather than the Western property-based notion of 'dominion' ".[45] Importantly, such relationships usually arise between particular groups and particular lands, grounded in specific place-based ties.[46] Indigenous laws and action-guiding norms are often based on spiritual beliefs and practices, viewing non-human objects as entities deserving of respect, protection, or stewardship. The principle of Ubuntu, recognised as a protected legal norm under South African law, offers one such example.[47] Land-based norms are derived relationally, with relationships extending beyond individual persons and instead encompassing broader kinship ties, future and past generations, non-human beings, and the land itself.[48] Such norms differ from concepts of ownership inherent in most state law systems.[49] Indeed, some scholars have suggested that fiduciary *duties* might be a stronger analogue for Indigenous property law systems than the concept of *ownership*.[50]

A case study of tikanga Māori illustrates the point. Interactions with land are grounded in the norm of kaitiakitanga. As succinctly defined by Justice Williams, kaitiakitanga implies that:[51]

> No right in resources can be sustained without the right holder maintaining an ongoing relationship with the resource. No relationship, no right. The term that describes the legal obligation is kaitiakitanga. This is the idea that any right over a human or resource carries with it a reciprocal obligation to care for his, her or its physical and spiritual welfare. Kaitiakitanga is then a natural (perhaps even inevitable) off-shot of whanaungatanga [obligations derived from family ties]. The point is that whanaungatanga was, in traditional Māori society, not just about emotional and social ties between people and with the environment. It was just as importantly about economic rights and obligations.

In many countries, Indigenous peoples have significant interests in land. Such interests generally fall short of full-fledged self-determination: that is, the ability to govern those lands in accordance with Indigenous laws and norms, free from the overriding power or veto of the colonial state. Instead, such interests usually take some form of property interest, still subject to overriding state law. Even where their rights over land fall short of territorial self-determination, Indigenous peoples may possess large tracts of land in freehold title, or in country-specific native title arrangements (which generally involve restraints on alienation

[45] Tsosie (n 30) 84.

[46] ibid 85: 'In sum, the traditional laws of Native peoples acknowledge a unique relationship between the indigenous peoples and the specific places and landscapes that have facilitated their existence for thousands of years. The very identity of many Native peoples is circumscribed by particular landforms and waterways. For example, in the Southwest, the Navajo people perceive their world to be bounded by four sacred mountains, as do the Tewa people. In the Pacific Northwest, the Native people are tied to a landscape that reflects the importance of the oceans (for example, the Salish Coastal Sea) and inland waterways, such as the Columbia River and Snake River.'

[47] Du Toit et al (n 12) 329, citing *Maledu v Itereleng Bakgatla Mineral Resources* [2018] ZACC 41; *Gonggose v Minister of Agriculture* [2018] ZASCA 87.

[48] Birrell et al (n 44) 247.

[49] ibid 208: '[T]he concept of "ownership" as understood in Western law may not exist in many Indigenous societies.'

[50] Kristen A Carpenter, Sonia K Katyal, and Angela R Riley, 'In Defense of Property' (2008) 118 Yale Law Journal 1022, 1074.

[51] Williams (n 19) 4.

and title to underlying land and minerals). In Australia, for example, Indigenous peoples have rights or interests in over 50% of the country's land, though in many cases such rights are non-exclusive.[52] Such lands are often those on the periphery, unwanted by colonial settlers. In other cases, Indigenous peoples have been pushed into reservations, in many cases hundreds of miles from the lands to which they have spiritual, familial, and ultimately legal ties. In still other cases, Indigenous interests in land may arise from treaty settlements which return public lands to some form of Indigenous ownership, though such arrangements rarely include return of land in private hands.

In many instances, Indigenous lands possess large reserves of natural resources, including fossil fuels, carbon sinks, and minerals used for renewable energy. The Indigenous legal norms governing the use of such lands, and the conflicts produced between stewardship norms and economic development imperatives, has a potentially dramatic effect on global climate mitigation. Many Indigenous peoples have pursued economic development through resource extraction, including the extraction of fossil fuels. In the US, for example, 5% of domestic oil production and 8% of domestic gas production as of 2014 occurs on Native American lands—an outsize contribution, given that such lands cover only 2% of the US.[53] Such lands also contain significant untapped reserves.[54]

Indigenous lands have also been caught up in the private governance of another kind of resource: carbon credits. Such credits are often purchased by companies as part of compulsory or voluntary schemes to offset their greenhouse gas-emitting activities. A particularly common form of credit is derived from the maintenance or restoration of forests. Many Indigenous peoples hold interests in old-growth or recently planted forests, and some have sought to participate in these carbon markets. The Yurok Tribe in the northwestern US, for example, has negotiated an agreement with the state government of California to receive credits for forest preservation on tribal land, and used those funds to purchase back its former lands.[55] While such projects are rarely conducted in accordance with Indigenous private law, they are an example of Indigenous peoples engaging in private law and governance in relation to climate change.

These projects, however, have attracted significant criticism. Some argue that carbon credits do little to address climate change, because they are beset by accounting challenges, are liable to gaming, and can be used as excuses to delay more tangible cuts in emissions.[56] The

[52] 'Environment and Land', *National Indigenous Australian Agency* <https://www.niaa.gov.au/our-work/environment-and-land> accessed 6 May 2025. See also Indigenous ownership of forest lands in India. Shomona Khanna, 'Forest Rights and the Forest Rights Act' in Philippe Cullet, Lovleen Bhullar, and Sujith Koonan(eds), *The Oxford Handbook of Environmental and Natural Resource Law in India* (OUP 2024).

[53] Elizabeth Ann Kronk Warner, 'Examining Tribal Law' (2014) 39 Columbia Journal of Environmental Law 42, 49–50.

[54] ibid 50.

[55] The agreement is controversial and has in some cases converted claims for greater tribal sovereignty into a strategy to raise money to purchase former lands under fee simple title. Carolyn Kormann, 'How Carbon Trading Became a Way of Life for California's Yurok Tribe' (*The New Yorker* 10 October 2018) <https://www.newyorker.com/news/dispatch/how-carbon-trading-became-a-way-of-life-for-californias-yurok-tribe> accessed 27 May 2025.

[56] For various criticisms of forestry offset schemes, see Julia Dehm, *Reconsidering REDD+: Authority, Power and Law in the Green Economy* (CUP 2021); G Cornelis van Kooten and Craig MT Johnston, 'The Economics of Forest Carbon Offsets' (2016) 8 Annual Review of Resource Economics 227 (2016); Keith Hyams and Tin Fawcett, 'The Ethics of Carbon Offsetting' (2013) 4 Wiley Interdiscplinary Reviews: Climate Change 91. See also Tiffanie Chan et al, Chapter 11 of this handbook.

Indigenous Environmental Network, a global environmental network of Indigenous peoples, has criticised such schemes (and carbon pricing more generally) as a license to pollute, arguing they "not only . . . legitimize and expand a clearly unsustainable economic system based on extraction but also as a source of further profit and land grab".[57] For Indigenous peoples in particular, such market-driven schemes might conflict with models of land use less centred on individual ownership and commodification. Forestry-related offset schemes in particular have often led to conflicts with Indigenous peoples, as governments and corporations seek to use traditional Indigenous lands for carbon credit programmes.[58] Similar conflicts also arise with other efforts to use Indigenous lands to support climate mitigation aims, including the siting of renewable projects[59] and the mining of minerals necessary for batteries, renewables, and electrification.[60]

Where Indigenous land-based private law lacks normative power—either because it is not incorporated into state law, or because Indigenous peoples lack self-determination—Indigenous peoples are left with a difficult choice. They can push for law reform which recognises Indigenous legal norms in state law; make use of state private law tools to approximate Indigenous norms or sovereignty; or pursue direct demands for self-determination, as with the growing "land back" movement in many postcolonial societies. While the latter would ultimately grant Indigenous peoples a greater measure of justice in reclaiming sovereignty after colonial dispossession, the former two strategies will often be more immediately realisable, and potentially more effective.

Some legal systems have integrated Indigenous land-based legal norms into state property regimes. Typically, such integration comes via public law environmental statutes which condition the operation of private property rights. Aotearoa/New Zealand's Resource Management Act 1991, which governs development consents, requires all decisions to have regard to "the relationship of Māori and their culture and traditions with their ancestral lands", "the protection of protected customary rights", and "kaitiakitanga". While not private law norms per se, these public law environmental restrictions incorporate Indigenous legal principles as limits on the otherwise unfettered disposition of property, including the exploitation of natural resources and fossil fuels.

Indigenous peoples might also use state law tools to protect lands from resource extraction, including practices harmful to the climate (such as deforestation, mining, and oil extraction). This includes engagement by Indigenous peoples with private law conservation tools.[61] In the US, for example, there exist at least twenty-five Native American private conservation

[57] 'Carbon Pricing is a False Solution to Climate Chaos' *Indigenous Environmental Network* https://www.ienearth.org/carbon-pricing/ accessed 8 May 2025.

[58] Julia Dehm, 'Indigenous Peoples and REDD Safeguards: Rights as Resistance or as Disciplinary Inclusion in the Green Economy?' (2016) 7 Journal of Human Rights and the Environment 170.

[59] Annalisa Savaresi et al, 'Conceptualising Just Transition Litigation' (2024) 7 Nature Sustainability 1379.

[60] Thea Riofrancos, 'The Rush to 'Go Electric' Comes with a Hidden Cost: Destructive Lithium Mining" *The Guardian* (14 June 2021) <https://www.theguardian.com/commentisfree/2021/jun/14/electric-cost-lithium-mining-decarbonasation-salt-flats-chile> accessed 27 May 2025.

[61] Alisa White, 'Private Law for Land Back' (2025) 51 Ecological Law Quarterly <https://papers.ssrn.com/sol3/papers.cfm?abstract_id=4748991> accessed 5 July 2025; Mary Christina Wood and Zachary Welcker, 'Tribes as Trustees Again (Part I): The Emerging Tribal Role in the Conservation Movement' (2008) 32 Harvard Environmental Law Review 373; Mary Christina Wood and Zachary Welcker, 'Evaluating Four Models of Tribal Participation in the Conservation Trust Movement' (2008) 27 Stanford Environmental Law Journal 477.

trusts, relying on instruments such as cultural access and conservation easements.[62] While falling short of self-determination or fee simple title, such measures enable Indigenous peoples to "access land and reinscribe non-Western forms of care, relationship and law with that land".[63] As Alisa White argues, such tools can provide a measure of reparation and return to Indigenous peoples, and cultivate a set of land-use norms grounded in stewardship and Indigenous worldviews.[64]

Ultimately, however, Indigenous law concerning land cannot take effect without Indigenous self-determination over those lands. Empirical studies show that Indigenous systems of tenure and land-related legal norms consistently lead to positive environmental outcomes.[65] Maintaining Indigenous self-determination (or at least co-governance) over land allows for Indigenous private law norms to take effect through social practices, as well as through formally sanctioned law. The property law framework set out in the Navajo Tribal Code, for instance, establishes that Navajo Nation members have "the sacred obligation and duty to respect, preserve and protect all that was provided for we were designated as the steward for these relatives".[66] The Code's environmental regulation chapter likewise codifies tribal land-based legal norms, including obligations owed to future generations and the interconnectedness of all Navajo-related entities to the natural environment.[67] Such codification can also be found in the laws of other Native American tribes.[68] Even where full sovereignty cannot be established, co-management or co-stewardship programmes may allow for a measure of Indigenous law to be applied to land management.[69]

Such codification is consequential. Courts can apply and enforce formally enacted Indigenous law, including where it conflicts with harmful environmental development. Tribal courts in the US have sometimes invoked specific Indigenous legal standards and values, such as the obligation to ensure that land transactions do not jeopardise the "spiritual health" of a tribe.[70] And the protection of Indigenous lands through recognised self-determination is not just instrumentally valuable in securing environmental or climate outcomes. It is also valuable in and of itself as a form of redress for the past wrongdoings of colonial dispossession and subjugation—processes intimately bound up with the same forces which have ultimately produced the climate crisis.

3.3 Indigenous Private Law, Land Use, and Climate Adaptation

Indigenous private law norms are relevant not only to climate mitigation (reducing the impacts of climate change by lowering greenhouse gas emissions and protecting carbon sinks).

[62] White (n 61) 17.
[63] ibid 47.
[64] ibid 49.
[65] Neil Dawson and others, 'The Role of Indigenous Peoples and Local Communities in Effective and Equitable Conservation' (2021) 26 Ecology and Society 19.
[66] Navajo Nation Code tit. I, § 205(D) (2005).
[67] Navajo Nation Code Ann. Tit. 4 § 901 (2010).
[68] Dean B Suagee, 'Tribal Environmental Policy Acts and the Landscape of Environmental Law' [2009] Natural Resources & Environment 13.
[69] Nazune Menka, 'The LandBack Movement: Native Nations and the Restoration of Ancestral Lands' 39 Natural Resources & Environment 23 (2025); Te Awa Tupua (Whanganui River Claims Settlement) Act 2017 s 13 (NZ) (establishing a management body over New Zealand' Whanganui River co-nominated by the government and local Māori, which is to be managed in accordance with a set of intrinsic values (Tupua te Kawa) derived from tikanga Māori).
[70] *Hoover v Colville Confederated Tribes*, 3 CTCR 43, 6 CCAR 16 (2002) [90]–[92].

They are also relevant to *adapting* to the inevitable impacts of climate change. As noted in Section 1, Indigenous peoples are particularly vulnerable to such impacts, especially where they are located in small islands, coastal areas, and polar regions, or maintain traditional practices of fisheries or pastoralism.[71]

Adapting to these impacts is a key challenge. Indigenous legal norms and customary land practices comprise part of what is often referred to as "traditional ecological knowledge" (TEK): "a cumulative body of knowledge and beliefs, handed down through generations by cultural transmission, about the relationship of living beings (including humans) with one another and with their environment".[72] Forest management practices, such as protocols and norms concerning controlled burns and fires, offer one such example of how Indigenous communities have drawn on traditional customs and jural norms in adapting to the impacts of climate change, as forest protection becomes a greater imperative, and wildfires become a greater threat.[73]

Ultimately, however, the efficacy of interpersonal Indigenous *private* law norms may be limited. This is particularly true given the devastating impacts of colonisation. For many Indigenous peoples, a significant portion of the challenge they face is to recover and regain action-guiding norms and practices. And coordinated planning has become essential in the face of escalating climate related impacts. It is here that Indigenous self-determination—rather than incorporation of Indigenous law within state legal systems—may be a preferred model. Where such self-determination exists, some tribal agencies have drawn on or codified Indigenous legal norms in tribal adaptation plans.[74] Climate adaptation plans have proliferated significantly among Native American tribes in the US.[75] And in many of those plans, tribal leaders have tried to translate traditional, decentralised environmental practices and customary law into more formal policy and planning agendas. In many cases, such plans aim as a starting point to rebuild understandings of Indigenous customs, knowledge, and law to facilitate better climate adaptation.[76] Importantly, many Indigenous peoples acknowledge the

[71] Victoria Reyes-Garcia and others, 'Indigenous Peoples and Local Communities Report Ongoing and Widespread Climate Change Impacts on Local Social-ecological Systems' (2024) 5 Nature Communications Earth & Environment 29.

[72] Fikret Berkes, quoted in 'Traditional Ecological Knowledge', *US Department of the Interior: Indian Affairs* <https://www.bia.gov/service/fuels-management/traditional-knowledge> accessed 7 May 2025.

[73] ibid.

[74] For example, the Swinomish Tribe in the Northwest US developed a comprehensive tribal adaptation plan including a a strategy for integrating tribal knowledge, tradition and custom. 'Swinomish Climate Change Initiative: Climate Adaptation Plan' (October 2010), 24 *Swinomish Indian Tribal Council* <https://www.swinomish-climate.com/swinomish-climate-change-initiative> accessed July 4, 2025.

[75] For a full database collecting tribal adaptation plans from across the US (maintained by the University of Oregon), see 'Adaptation Plans', *Tribal Climate Change Guide* <https://tribalclimateguide.uoregon.edu/index.php/adaptation-plans> accessed 6 May 2025.

[76] 'A Climate Adaptation Plan for the Sicangu Lakota Oyate' *Rosebud Sioux Tribal Council* (June 2022), <https://www.rosebudsiouxtribe-nsn.gov/_files/ugd/ed1fef_53c3d954c1ef4c9d8d8ce441f58cb55c.pdf>, accessed 4 July 2025, describing interviews conducted with tribal elders to understand traditional adaptation practices, and listing 10 Lakota laws relevant to climate adaptation: Unsikicilapi (humility), Wowacintanka (perseverance), Wawoohola (respect), Wayuonihan (honour), Cantognake (love), Iciciupi (sacrifice), Wowicake (truth), Waunsilapi (compassion), Woohoitike (bravery), Cantewasakae (fortitude), Canteyuke (generosity), and Woksape (wisdom).

need to combine these traditional knowledge bases and legal systems with new forms of knowledge and regulation in light of the accelerating impacts of climate change.[77]

In the absence of full self-determination, agreements between state governments and Indigenous peoples may provide opportunities for the application of Indigenous law in climate adaptation. Such agreements, often referred to as "co-management", "co-governance", or "co-stewardship" agreements,[78] are becoming increasingly common in jurisdictions such as Australia, Aotearoa/New Zealand, and the US, and often blur the boundaries of public agreements and private contracts.[79] While in some cases such agreements permit only limited application of Indigenous law and knowledge, in other cases they may allow for greater application—though rarely to the same degree as self-determination.[80]

4. Future Frontiers

The three-way collision between Indigenous law, private law, and climate change produces a wide (and sometimes surprising) constellation of possibilities and outcomes. As Section 3 revealed, these already find expression in a broad gamut of climate-related issues. In this section, I consider three further issues produced by this collision which are yet to receive a full airing in practice. These include the possibilities of fiduciary law, the question of climate reparations owed to Indigenous peoples (and their link to private law concepts), and the potential property rights of Indigenous peoples in their own ecological knowledge. Each is considered only briefly as suggestions for further inquiry and action.

4.1 Taking Fiduciary Law Seriously

Governmental duties towards Indigenous peoples are typically thought of as arising from treaty or human rights obligations. But many courts have also recognised *fiduciary* obligations owed towards Indigenous peoples. This is particularly true in common law courts in former British settler-colonies.

The first recognition of such obligations came from the Supreme Court of Canada in 1984. In *Guerin v R*, the Court found that the Canadian government owed a judicially enforceable

[77] 'National Inuit Climate Change Strategy', *Inuit Tairiit Kanatami* (2019) 14 <https://www.itk.ca/wp-content/uploads/2019/06/ITK_Climate-Change-Strategy_English.pdf> accessed 4 July 2025, acknowledging that '[t]raditional knowledge no longer always adequate' and calling for '[i]ncreased capacity, coordination and information sharing . . . to benefit climate decision-making . . . by improving climate research and educational goals, and enabling more effective use of Inuit knowledge'.

[78] The three descriptors have somewhat different meanings within and between different jurisdictions.

[79] Helen Ross and others, 'Co-Management and Indigenous Protected Areas in Australia: Achievements and Ways Forward" (2009) 16 Australasian J of Env Management 242; 'Principles for effectively co-governing natural resources', Auditor General of New Zealand (2016), available online at <https://oag.parliament.nz/2016/co-governance/docs/co-governance-amended.pdf> accessed 4 July 2025; Clarita Lefthand-Begay and others, 'From Paternalism to Self-determination: Examining Evolving Tribal-federal Relationships and Co-management Arrangements through Three Case Studies' (2025) 12 Humanities and Social Science Communications 30.

[80] See for example the developing practice in Aotearoa/New Zealand of recognising natural phenomena as legal entities with governance boards with majority or exclusive Indigenous representation. Examples include Te Urewera Act 2014, Te Awa Tupua (Whanganui River Claims Settlement) Act 2017, and Te Ture Whakatupua mō Te Kāhui Tupua 2025.

equitable obligation to deal with Indigenous land "for the benefit of" Indigenous people.[81] While the Canadian government has discretion to the determine those interests, such discretion is subject to a fiduciary duty owed towards Indigenous peoples—a duty importing a private law "strict standard of conduct".[82] Such a duty continues where Indigenous land is surrendered to the Crown, and means, among other things, that governments must act in accordance with the wishes and understanding of groups surrendering that land, and cannot act unconscionably.[83] Subsequent Canadian cases have confirmed this fiduciary duty, related to a broader requiring (among other things) that Canadian governments consult with First Nations,[84] including in matters with environmental impacts on Indigenous lands (such as seismic testing).[85] Even where the narrower and stricter fiduciary duty is not imposed, the Crown is still subject to a broader freestanding duty—the "honour of the Crown"[86]—present in all dealings with Indigenous peoples and incorporating the obligation to consult.[87]

Versions of the Canadian honour of the Crown and fiduciary duty jurisprudence can also be found elsewhere in the world. In some cases, the concept alludes to trust-like frameworks and high-level principles flowing from treaties and public law duties, while in other jurisdictions it refers to more concrete private law fiduciary obligations. In Aotearoa/New Zealand, for example, the Supreme Court has expressly recognised that in particular circumstances, the Crown owed ongoing fiduciary obligations after acquiring Māori land, and agreed with the Supreme Court of Canada that such obligations were enforceable private law duties.[88] In the US, the "federal trust responsibility" incorporates common obligations of good faith, loyalty, and protection owed by the federal government towards native American tribes.[89]

Two cases adjudicating these trust obligations have implicated climate-related concerns. In *Smith v Attorney-General*, the same plaintiff in *Smith v Fonterra* argued that New Zealand's government had breached fiduciary duties owed towards him in failing to take sufficient action on climate change. He argued that a fiduciary duty arose both from New Zealand's Treaty of Waitangi, as well as the Crown's "significant power (kāwanatanga) that was capable of being exercised in a way that would adversely affect the property rights of Māori".[90] This was a novel claim, as it went beyond particular historical fact-specific fiduciary relationships previously recognised by New Zealand courts, and instead suggested a broad climate-related obligation owed to all Māori. Ultimately, it proved too novel for New Zealand courts to accept.[91] In narrower circumstances, in *Tsleil-Waututh Nation v Canada*, Canada's Federal Court of Appeals overturned a government agency's approval of an oil pipeline system on the basis that the government "failed . . . to engage, dialogue meaningfully and grapple with the real concerns" of Indigenous peoples.[92] While these were largely limited to localised environmental harms, such

81 [1984] 2 SCR 335, 336–37.

82 ibid.

83 ibid.

84 *Mikisew Cree First Nation v Canada* [2018] 2 SCR 765.

85 *Clyde River (Hamlet) v Petroleum Geo-Services Inc.* [2017] 1 SCR 1069.

86 *R v Sparrow* [1990] 1 SCR 1075.

87 *Haida Nation v British Columbia* [2004] 3 SCR 511.

88 *See Proprietors of Wakatū v Attorney General* [2017] NZSC 17, [2017] 1 NZLR 423.

89 Daniel ISJ Rey-Bear and Matthew LM Fletcher, '"We Need Protection from Our Protectors": The Nature, Issues, and Future of the Federal Trust Responsibility to Indians' (2017) 6 Michigan Journal of Environmental & Administrative Law 397.

90 *Smith v Attorney-General* [2024] NZCA 692 at [159].

91 ibid [162]–[167].

92 2018 FCA 153 at [6].

projects also have potentially catastrophic climate impacts for both local Indigenous peoples, as well as Indigenous and non-Indigenous peoples worldwide. The project at issue in *Tsleil-Waututh Nation*, for instance, would generate approximately 400,000 tonnes of greenhouse gas emissions annually.[93]

The impact of the decision in *Tsleil-Waututh Nation*, however, proved to be limited. After the Canadian government carried out further consultation, Canadian courts were ultimately satisfied that it had discharged its fiduciary duty.[94] There is a risk that the stricter fiduciary duties owed by governments to Indigenous groups might be swallowed up by the broader procedural honour of the Crown duties: duties which can be discharged largely through consultation, rather than rather than substantive duties to protect Indigenous groups from the harmful effects of climate change. But depending on the context, Indigenous peoples could argue that Crown actions concerning climate change breach not only public law, but also private law fiduciary duties owed towards them. This could involve both climate *mitigation* arguments (such as the development of carbon infrastructure threatening Indigenous lands and interests), as well as climate *adaptation* issues (for instance, where governments fail to act in the best interests of climate-threatened Indigenous groups).[95] The precise contours of such arguments, as well as their chances of success, would depend on the legal, factual, and historical context of any particular dispute.

4.2 Private Law as a Model of Reparations

In addition to climate mitigation and adaptation obligations, a third set of claims advanced by climate justice advocates are those related to *loss and damage*. Such claims articulate the view that excessive releases of greenhouse gases have *already* harmed particular groups in ways that cannot be addressed only by reducing future emissions and assisting with adaptation efforts. Instead, groups who are disproportionately affected by climate change—but who have contributed a disproportionately small share of global emissions—argue that they should receive compensation. Indigenous peoples, who are typically responsible for a small share of global emissions but are vulnerable to the effects of climate change, are often among those groups demanding reparations.[96] Such claims often intersect with other demands of Indigenous justice, including the return of Indigeous lands.

As Cass Sunstein argues, these claims often replicate the core logic of private tort law.[97] Demands for climate reparations are essentially claims of corrective justice, widely recognised as a basis for compensation in both common law tort and civil law wrongs. Though politically challenging, demands by climate advocates at the international level are essentially extensions of this same principle. As Sunstein puts it, "[i]f you're injuring someone, you should stop—and pay for the damage you've caused. Why . . . does this simple proposition, generally accepted,

[93] 'Greenhouse Gas Emissions from the Trans Mountain Project', *Environment and Climate Change Canada* (18 June 2019) <https://www.canada.ca/en/environment-climate-change/news/2019/06/greenhouse-gas-emissions-from-the-trans-mountain-project.html> accessed 4 July 2025.

[94] *Coldwater First Nation v Canada* 2020 FCA 34.

[95] Erika Chamberlain, 'The Crown's Fiduciary Duties to Aboriginal Peoples as an Aspect of Climate Justice' (2012) 30 Windsor Yearbook of Access to Justice 289.

[96] Dorothy Guerrero, 'Colonialism, Climate Change, and Climate Reparations', *Global Justice Now* (4 August 2023) <https://www.globaljustice.org.uk/blog/2023/08/colonialism-climate-change-and-climate-reparations/>.

[97] Cass R Sunstein, *Climate Justice: What Rich Nations Owe the World—and the Future* (MIT Press, 2025).

not apply to climate change?"[98] The central insight of climate justice claims is that a *wrong* must be *righted*, and that reparations might offer one such way of righting those wrongs.

Indigenous private law systems also possess conceptual frameworks for righting relational wrongs. D Kapua'ala Sproat argues that restorative justice principles in Native Hawai'ian legal ordering could provide a basis for addressing claims of climate-related harms to Indigenous peoples.[99] Importantly, Sproat points out that addressing such claims must go beyond basic compensatory private law principles: They must be contextualised in historic and ongoing processes of colonisation and restoration must address "cultural destruction, land dispossession, [and] the loss of self-governance", harms which can only be restoratively addressed through recognition of self-determination in the spheres of cultural integrity, lands and natural resources, social welfare and development, and self-government.[100] Scholars in Aotearoa/New Zealand have suggested that the tikanga Māori principle of utu (reciprocity/obligation) as a basis for environmental redress[101] or a framework for international obligations.[102] And scholars in sub-Saharan Africa have long argued that the principle of Ubuntu could inform global schemes of reparations and restoration, both in environmental and other contexts.[103] As *reparations* continue to be advanced as an essential component of the global response to climate change, Indigenous conceptions of interpersonal justice could provide a powerful source of legal norms.

4.3 Property Interests in Ecological Knowledge

As this chapter has suggested, Indigenous private law norms have much to offer in the context of the climate crisis. Yet there is a risk that well-meaning attempts to engage Indigenous knowledge systems might themselves amount to extraction and misappropriation by legal scholars, policymakers, and scientists.[104] Indigenous knowledge systems—including Indigenous legal systems themselves—are the products of careful intellectual labour, empirical observation, and ethical stewardship across centuries. In many cases, such systems have been maintained and preserved against attempts by colonial powers to dismantle them. It would indeed prove ironic if the inheritors of the systems and institutions that colonised the world now turned to Indigenous law and knowledge in a desperate attempt to avoid their own destruction.

[98] ibid.

[99] D Kapua'ala Sproat, 'An Indigenous People's Right to Environmental Self-Determination: Native Hawaiians and the Struggle Against Climate Change Devastation' (2016) 35 Stanford Environmental Law Journal 157, 183–84.

[100] ibid 160.

[101] *He Poutama* (n 14) [3.60]–[3.70]; [3.126]–[3.127]; [4.81]–[4.90].

[102] Nichoals Ross Smith and Bonnie Holster, 'Conceptualizing Utu as a Foreign Policy Doctrine for Aotearoa New Zealand' (2025) 16 Global Policy 568.

[103] Mofihli Teleki and Serges Djoyou Kamga, 'Recognizing the Value of the African Indigenous Knowledge System: The Case of Ubuntu and Restorative Justice' in Samuel Ojo Oloruntoba, Adeshina Afolayan, and Olajumoke Yacob-Haliso (eds), *Indigenous Knowledge Systems and Development in Africa* (Springer Nature 2020); Mechtild Nagel and others, 'Ubuntu and Ethical Implications for Global Transformative Justice Movements' in Ezra Chitando and others (eds), *The Palgrave Handbook of Ubuntu, Inequality and Sustainable Development* (Springer Nature 2025).

[104] Fiona Batt, 'The Vulnerability of African Indigenous Peoples' Traditional Meteorological Knowledge in the Climate Change Debate' in Kim Bouwer and others (eds), *Climate Litigation and Justice in Africa* (Bristol University Press 2024)

In this context, another field of private law may be relevant: intellectual property. Debates have long raged as to how essentially Western systems of intellectual property law can recognise the contributions of Indigenous knowledge systems to art, design, and medicine.[105] The same is true of Indigenous and traditional knowledge concerning ecosystems. Indigenous knowledge—including customary practices and laws—might provide valuable guidance in more climate-friendly forest protection or agricultural methods. But the unauthorised or uncontrolled use of such knowledge can fail to economically and morally recognise the property rights of Indigenous peoples, produce cultural harm, or even destabilise the systems that produce such knowledge.[106] Just as Indigenous *lands* can be destabilised even by well-meaning attempts to address climate change (for instance, through carbon markets or reforestation schemes), so too can Indigenous *knowledge* and *law itself*.

These concerns have been squarely expressed by Indigenous peoples worldwide. The 2009 Anchorage Declaration issued by Indigenous representatives from across the globe declared that "[w]e offer to share with humanity our Traditional Knowledge, innovations, and practices relevant to climate change, provided our fundamental rights as intergenerational guardians of this knowledge are fully recognized and respected".[107]

In this context, Indigenous peoples may draw on private law tools to protect such knowledge, including Indigenous legal norms themselves. As Ruth Okediji argues, these can range from privacy laws to contracts, trade secrets, and native title claims.[108] Such claims are likely to sit alongside international and public law claims, such as those under the Convention on Biodiversity and TRIPS Agreement.

5. Conclusion

This chapter has surveyed many points of intersection between Indigenous peoples, private law, and climate change. It is perhaps unsurprising that three fields of rich practice and scholarly inquiry would raise such a wide range of issues. But rather than conclude with a confident normative payoff, this chapter ends by reemphasising two central dilemmas facing the primary actors situated at this intersection: Indigenous peoples themselves, in many circumstances faced with serious challenges not of their own making, and a legal framework historically hostile to their rights and interests.

The first dilemma arises from the natural resources located on Indigenous lands. Such lands often contain rich deposits of fossil fuels, offering Indigenous groups a revenue stream and prospects of prosperity following decades or centuries of dispossession and disadvantage arising from colonialism. In other cases, Indigenous peoples stand to benefit from forestry or the extraction of minerals such as lithium. Indigenous peoples would be well within their rights to argue that climate change is not a problem of their making, and that exploiting such resources could even produce funds that would assist in adapting to the serious impacts of climate change, even as they come with both local and global environmental costs. Yet such an approach may conflict with

105 For a summary of such debates, see Ruth L Okediji, 'Traditional Knowledge and Private Law' in Andrew S Gold and others (eds), *The Oxford Handbook of the New Private Law* (OUP 2020).

106 Okediji (n 105) 438–39; Rebecca Tsosie, 'Cultural Challenges to Biotechnology: Native American Genetic Resources and the Concept of Cultural Harm' (2007) 35 Journal of Law, Medicine & Ethics 396.

107 Anchorage Declaration 20–24 April 2009, Alaska <https://unfccc.int/resource/docs/2009/smsn/ngo/168.pdf> accessed 4 July 2025.

108 Okediji (n 105) 440–43.

Indigenous legal norms and contribute to a problem that disproportionately affects Indigenous peoples across the world.

The second dilemma is the question of how to interact with Western private law systems. Such systems were imposed on Indigenous peoples, and only recently (and sporadically) have come to recognise Indigenous legal systems or self-governance. Yet as this chapter has shown, such systems may offer Indigenous peoples opportunities to advance their rights and interests. At the same time, acceptance and recognition of colonial law may undercut Indigenous claims for self-governance or self-determination. In some cases, Indigenous peoples may choose to partially sidestep this dilemma, advancing the integration of Indigenous law within private law systems: what Williams describes as the "integrate to perpetuate" model.[109]

This chapter does not purport to solve these dilemmas. In all cases, their resolution will depend on local circumstances, the existing position of both Indigenous and colonial law, and most importantly, the choices of Indigenous peoples. Sproat perhaps frames it best when she argues that:[110]

> Responses to climate change must be driven by native peoples' choices. But those choices will inevitably entail interaction with state, local, or tribal agencies, tribal businesses, and non-indigenous residents. In large part, the local legal regime's handling of natural resources and indigenous peoples' claims will frame these interactions particularly when such claims clash with western-imposed values and practices. That clash, even today, is nearly always about more than competing land or water uses. It is steeped in a history of conquest, confiscation, cultural suppression, betrayal, and halting reparative initiatives.

Questions of colonialism and climate change are deeply interconnected, and private law frequently sits at the heart of both issues. Neither can be addressed without addressing the other.

[109] Williams (n 19) 32.

[110] Sproat (n 99) 158–59.

INDEX

For the benefit of digital users, indexed terms that span two pages (e.g., 52–53) may, on occasion, appear on only one of those pages.

Tables and figures are indicated by an italic *t* and *f* following the page number.

A
Active Super, 652–53
ad coelum doctrine, 236
Adler, Jonathan H., 104n.7
Africa. *See also specific country*
generally, 11, 682, 695–96
climate change litigation in
generally, 681–82
environmental legislation and, 687–89
evolving legislation and, 692–95
horizontal litigation, 682–85, 696
human rights law and, 689–92
tort law, 686–87
vertical litigation, 682–83, 696
environmental damage in, 680
African Union (AU), 683, 685
agency capture, 684n.33
"age of empire," 454n.75
AGL Energy, 656–57
Agreement of Trade-Related Aspects of Intellectual Property Rights (TRIPS Agreement), 269–70, 275–76
Ahern, Deirdre, 782n.58
AI. *See* artificial intelligence
Alvarez-Armas, Eduardo, 562–63
American Declaration of the Rights and Duties of Man, 794
Amu Power Company, 667n.10
Anchorage Declaration (2009), 825
Angola
climate change litigation in, 684–85
Privatisation Programme, 684–85
Anker, Kristen, 253–54, 255
Annan, Kofi, 344, 609
ANZ Bank, 651–52
arbitration. *See* international commercial arbitration
Aristova, Ekaterina, 6
Arnold-Dwyer, Franziska, 10
Arrojo Agudo, Pedro, 266
artificial intelligence
generally, 11–12, 774–75, 790
adaptability of, 776n.10
capabilities of, 776
climate potentials of
generally, 784
climate-related risks, identification of, 788–89
corporate climate planning, 786–87
corporate climate reporting, 784–86
emissions, determination of, 787–88
information overload, reduction of, 789–90
climate risks of
generally, 777
legal design, risk by, 779–84
specific risk, 777–78
systemic risk, 778–79
water consumption, 778n.31
corporate law and governance and
generally, 779–80
AI enthusiasm, 780–82
AI pragmatism, 775, 782–84
development of, 775
France, in, 781–82
future of, 777
Germany, in, 780–81
UK, in, 781–82
US, in, 785–86, 787
Ashurst (law firm), 768–69
Asia Investor Group on Climate Change (AIGCC), 523–24, 667n.11
Association of Southeast Asian Nations (ASEAN), 401–2
Association of Southeast Asian Nations (ASEAN) – Australia–New Zealand Free Trade Agreement (AANZFTA), 485
Atiyah, Patrick Selim, 743n.34
attorneys. *See* legal profession
Australia
anti-regulatory use of private law to resist climate action, 656–57
ASIC Act, 652–53
Australasian Centre for Corporate Responsibility (ACCR), 656
Australian Competition and Consumer Commission (ACCC), 654
Australian Consumer Law (ACL), 653–54, 655, 656
Australian Council of Trade Unions (ACTU), 448–50, 454
Australian Institute of International Affairs, 267

Australia (*cont.*)
Australian Securities and Investments Commission (ASIC), 652–54
Builders Labourers Federation, 448–49
climate change litigation in
generally, 646, 648, 662–63
anti-greenwashing action, 653–54
civil society litigation, 654–56
climate disclosure, 651–53
consumer protection and, 653–56
defined, 647–48
director duties, 649–51
Hutley opinions, 649
negligence, duty of care in, 657–58
New Zealand compared, 661–62
climate disclosure in, 651–53
climate-washing litigation in, 175–77
common law torts in, 110–11
Competition and Consumer Act 2010, 363
Competition Commission, 363
competition law in, 363
consumer protection in
anti-greenwashing action, 653–54
civil society litigation, 654–56
corporate law and governance in, 649–51
Corporations Act 2001 (Cth), 649, 650, 651, 651n.46, 653–54, 656
environmental clauses, 449n.40
Environmental Defenders Office (EDO), 652n.52
environmental offsetting in, 485n.94
Fair Work Act, 455
forum non conveniens in, 560
Hazards Insurance Partnership, 357n.103
Indigenous Peoples in, 812, 814–15, 815n.39, 816–17, 821
insurance law in, 384
ISDS, phase-out of coal and, 484, 488
kinship systems in, 253
labour law in, 448–50, 455
land use and ownership in, 259
Law Council of Australia (LCA), 759n.32
legal education in, 751–52
legal profession in, 759, 768–69
National Emergency Management Agency, 357n.103
Native Title Act, 812
negligence, duty of care in, 657–58
precautionary principle in, 698
public nuisance in, 110–11
Queensland Mining and Energy Union, 455n.77
Resource Management Act 1991, 818
REST superfund, 650–51
securities regulation in, 414
Superannuation Industry (Supervision) Act 1993 (Cth) (SIS Act), 650, 650n.36
tort law in, 657–58
Australian and Pacific Climate Change Litigation Database, 645n.2
Austria
competition law in, 371n.76
corporate law and governance in, 580
public internationa law in, 555
Azienda Elettrica Ticinese (AET), 483, 486, 487

B
Babcock, Helen, 281
Baker McKenzie (law firm), 768–69
Bali Action Plan, 342n.12
Bank of America, 529
Bank of England Biennial Exploratory Scenario, 179
Bank of Montreal (BMO), 529
bankruptcy law
generally, 10, 416–18, 425
absolute priority rule, 418
automatic stay, 418
Center of Main Interest (COMI), 422
channeling instructions, 418
classes of creditors, 418–19
collective action problems and, 416
cross-purposes with environmental law, 416–17
enforcement actions against distressed firms, reluctance to bring, 416–17
global challenges, 421–24
asset collection, 421
forum shopping, 421, 423–24
jurisdictional issues, 421
strategic asset restructuring, 423
modified universalism, 422
non-adjusting creditors
generally, 419
piercing corporate veil and, 419
super priority claims, 417
vulnerability to strategic behaviour by debtors and other creditors, 419
past versus future environmental claimants, 417, 420
preference rules, 418
purpose of, 418–19
recommendations, 424–25
insurance, 424–25
investment funds, 425
non-recognition of foreign proceedings, 424
surety bonds, 424–25
reorganisation versus liquidation, 420–21
generally, 418
continuation bias, 420
political considerations, 420–21
UNCITRAL Model Law on Cross- Border Insolvency, 422–23
US, in, 418–19, 421, 422
Baron, David, 539
Barry, Wendell, 83
Beck, Ulrich, 716n.5
Belgium
choice of law in, 563–64
climate-washing litigation in, 175–76
corporate law and governance in, 580

private international law in, 553
Bendell, Jem, 251
Benin, environmental legislation in, 693
Benjamin, Antonio Herman, 717n.8
Benoit, Philippe, 315
Bernstein, Anita, 168
Bhopal chemical leak (1985), 515
Biber, Eric, 251
Biden, Joe, 71–72, 218–19, 545, 757–58
bilateral investment treaties (BITs), 472, 473, 490
Binder, Jens-Hinrich, 224
Bitcoin mining contract disputes
generally, 703–4, 714
legality of application of Green Principle, 705
Public Order and Good Morals Principle and, 704, 705
validity of contracts, 704
BlackRock, 6, 219–20, 359, 523–24, 529, 616, 619, 757–58
Blessing, Marc, 436n.63
Bloomberg, Michael, 518
"blue lining," 357
BMW, 143
BNP Paribas, 553–54
Bogoshian, Matt, 772–73
Bolton, Patrick, 525–26
Bonatti Group, 431
Bookman, Sam, 11, 287–88
Boskovic, Olivera, 563
Botswana
environmental legislation in, 689–90
human rights law in, 691–92
Bourdieu, Pierre, 36
Bouwer, Kim, 7, 755–56n.6
Brazil
generally, 10–11
Amazon, deforestation of, 728–29
arbitration in, 440
Brazilian Development Bank, 326
climate change litigation in, 666–67
generally, 717, 732–33
affirmative duty to act, 724–25
burden of proof, 722
causation, 721
climate-environmental damage, 727–32
compensation, 723
forward-looking approach, 726–27
indirect polluters, 719–20
joint and several liability (*responsabilidade solidaria*), 719–20
legal status of environment, 717–18, 724
limitations of traditional civil liability, 717
"polluter pays" principle, 720–21, 721n.23
pollution defined, 724
precautionary principle, 721
strict liability, 719, 729
structural litigation (*processo estrutural*), 730n.73
climate disclosure in, 325–27
generally, 322, 337
Global North compared, 333–35, 334*t*, 336, 339*t*
regulatory standards, 337
climate-environmental damage, 727–32
Climate Litigation Platform, 727–28, 727n.58, 728n.61
climate-washing litigation in, 175–76, 177, 179–80, 182–85, 187–88, 189, 190, 191
Ecomapua Project, 183–84
environmental damage
climate damage as, 725–27
climate-environmental damage, 727–32
complexity of, 718–19, 723–24
direct climate damage, 725–26
extra-patrimonial (moral) damages, 722
indirect climate damage, 726
timing of, 722
valuation of, 722
Extractive Reserves, 183
Extractive Reserves of Mapua (AMOREMA), 183
Federal Public Prosecution Office (MPF), 729, 730–31
fiduciary law in, 7
Financial Innovation Laboratory (Laboratorio de Inovacao Financeira), 326
Instituto Brasileiro do Meio Ambiente e dos Recursos Naturais Renovaveis (IBAMA), 729
Instituto de Defesa do Consumidor, 185
National Council of Justice (CNJ), 730
National Environmental Policy Act, 719, 724
National Policy on Climate Change, 724
National Register of Conservation Units (CNUC), 183
National System of Conservation Units (SNUC), 183
Operation Greenwashing, 190
private international law in, 555
Protocol for Judging Environmental Lawsuits, 730
Securities Commission (Comissao de Valores Mobiliarios) (CVM), 325–26
Specialised Office of the Federal Attorney General, 325–26
Superior Tribunal de Justica (Superior Court of Justice) (STJ), 719n.15
Terra Grande-Pracuuba (AMORETGRAP), 183
trust law in, 290
British Airways, 180
British Petroleum (BP), 201–2, 770
Broad, Robin, 515–16, 523
Bronin, Sarah, 234
Brundtland Report, 492
Brussels I Regulation
applicable law, 562n.96, 567
jurisdiction, 556, 557, 558, 559
"Brussels effect," 75–76
Bullock, David, 8, 9, 129, 170
Burkina Faso, human rights law in, 691–92
Bustos, Camila, 6
but-for causation
attenuated-causation problem and, 121–24
beyond but-for test, 126–27
causal-proof problem and, 124–25

C

Calabresi, Guido, 746
Canada
  Alberta Climate Leadership Plan, 483
  causation in tort in, 134–35
  choice of law in, 564–65
  climate-washing litigation in, 175–76
  Indigenous Peoples in, 812n.23, 821–23
  IP in, 270
  ISDS, phase-out of coal and, 483–84, 488
  legal profession in, 759
  Library of Parliament, 267
  private international law in, 555
  securities regulation in, 414
  Sustainable Finance Action Council, 347n.46
Canaris, Claus-Wilhelm, 797–98
Caney, Simon, 793–94, 796–97
carbon capture and storage (CCS), 235–37, 240
Carbon Disclosure Project (CDP)
  ESG and, 610
  PEG and, 533–34, 537–38, 539, 542, 545–46
  private standard-setting and, 516–17, 518, 520–21
  securities regulation and, 400–1
  Sustainability Disclosure Framework, 519
Carbon Majors Database, 301, 317–18
Carbon Social Standard, 184
Carbon Streaming, 429
Carney, Mark, 518, 528
Cashore, Benjamin, 524–25, 531
Casino (French supermarket), 553–54
Catholic Church, 539
causation in tort
  generally, 7, 119–21, 136–37
  asbestos cases, 134–35
  attenuated-causation problem
    generally, 119–20
    adddressing, 120–21
    beyond but-for test, 126–27
    but-for causation and, 121–24
    causal grouping and, 131–32
    dynamic nature of climate change and, 123
    individual carbon emitters and, 120, 121–24
    joint and several liability and, 130
    making contribution, 127–28
    multiple conditions and, 127
    Necessary Element of a Sufficient Set (NESS) and, 127–30
    "no worse off" limitation and, 131–32
    probability-raising and, 129–30
    substantial or material contribution, 128–30
    threshold of toxicity and, 123
    tipping point and, 127
    "two fires" problem, 126
    type of harm and, 123–24
  but-for causation
    attenuated-causation problem and, 121–24
    beyond but-for test, 126–27
    causal-proof problem and, 124–25
  causal-proof problem
    generally, 120
    adddressing, 120–21, 132–36
    background risks and, 120, 124
    but-for causation and, 124–25
    individual carbon emitters and, 120, 124–25
    material increase in risk and, 133–34
    multiple breach rule, 134
    risk exposure as compensable harm, 125
  DES cases, 134, 135–36
  factual causation, 121
  Germany, in, 122
  individual carbon emitters
    attenuated-causation problem and, 120, 121–24
    causal-proof problem and, 120, 124–25
  joint and several liability, 130
  legal causation, 121
  liability, relation to, 119
  proximate causation, 121
  UK, in, 126, 134–35
  unjust enrichment and, 194–95, 203–4
  US, in, 133–34, 135–36
Cavanagh, John, 515–16, 523
Centre for International Legal Cooperation, 434
CERES, 520, 521, 523–24
Chad, human rights law in, 691–92
Chan, Tiffanyie, 2
charity trusts, 604–5
ChatGPT, 775–76, 778n.31
Cheng, Thomas, 6
Cherednychenko, Olha O., 4, 576n.54, 797–98, 800
Chevron, 188, 201–2
Chia, Yaru, 355
China
  generally, 8
  Banking and Insurance Regulatory Commission i, 348
  Bitcoin mining contract disputes
    generally, 703–4, 714
    legality of application of Green Principle, 705
    Public Order and Good Morals Principle and, 704, 705
    validity of contracts, 704
  charging pile installation disputes
    generally, 705
    boundaries of and exceptions to Green Principle, 709–10
    Notice on Accelerating the Construction of Electric Vehicle Charging Infrastructure in Residential Areas, 706–7
    property service contracts, ancillary obligations in, 706–9
    underground parking lot ownership, 706
  China Securities Regulatory Commission (CSRC), 329–30
  Chinese Revolution, 68n.10
  Climate Change Response Law (proposed), 702
  climate disclosure in, 329–31

generally, 321, 322, 328
Global North compared, 333–35, 334*t*, 336, 339*t*
regulatory standards, 337
Contract Law, 711–12
corporate law and governance in, 298–99, 306–7, 313–16, 317–18
Corporate Sustainability Disclosure Standards—Basic Standards (Trial) (CSDS), 331
emitters in, 207
Environmental (Ecological) Code (proposed), 702
fiduciary law in, 7
Green Principle
generally, 8, 698–99, 714–15
bitcoin mining contract disputes, 703–5
charging pile installation disputes, 705–10
declaratory function, 710–11
gap-filling and, 712–13
judicial rulings, application in, 713–14
modes of application, 710–14, 713*f*
normative interpretation and selection and, 711–12
other principles of Civil Code compared, 700*t*
positive obligation under, 699–701
Hong Kong
Arbitration Ordinance, 438
choice of law in, 564–65
greenwashing in, 675
International Arbitration Centre (HKIAC), 438
Securities and Futures Ordinance (SFO), 440
Ministry of Ecology and Environment (MEE), 329–30
open norms in policy-driven climate justice
generally, 701
carbon-related civil claims, 702–3, 705n.34
concept of, 702–3
dual carbon goals, 701–2
legislative gap, 701–2
methodology, 702–3
private international law in, 555
Property Law, 711–12
Public Order and Good Morals Principle, 704, 705
securities regulation in, 401–2
Shanghai Stock Exchange (SSE), 330–31
Shenzhen Stock Exchange (SZSE), 330–31
SOEs in, 298–99, 306–7, 313–16, 317–18
State-Owned Assets Supervision and Administration Commission of the State Council (SASAC), 313–14, 329, 330
CIBC, 529
Citigroup, 529
City Energy, 674–75
civil law torts
generally, 7, 138–39, 143, 155
autonomy of liability law
generally, 140, 148
high level of autonomy, 149
low level of autonomy, 148–49
RWE case, 150
Shell case, 150
common features of climate change litigation, 139–42
corporate mitigation duties and, 138
damages and, 138–39
effectiveness of liability law
generally, 151
duty-centred effectiveness, 154–55
problem-solving effectiveness, 152–54
EU, in, 146
factual regulatory effects, 142
Germany, in (*see* Germany, *subheading* "climate change litigation in")
institutional competence of civil courts
generally, 139–40, 143
legal protectors, courts as, 146–48
risk regulators, court as, 144–46
legal regulatory effects, 141–42
Netherlands, in (*see* Netherlands, *subheading* "climate change litigation in")
New Zealand, in (*see* New Zealand, *subheading* "climate change litigation in")
Claflin Doctrine, 291–92
Clark, Alex, 315
Clean Development Mechanism, 429
ClientEarth, 598–99, 600, 667n.11
Climate Action 100+.
climate disclosure and, 212–13, 219–20
PEG and, 538–39
private standard-setting and, 523–24, 527
Climate Bond Initiative (CBI), 514, 520, 520n.49, 523–24, 529–30
Climate Change Litigation Databases, 175–76, 180, 186
Climate Change Scorecard (2025), 767
climate disclosure. *See also specific country*
generally, 3, 319–23, 337–38
artificial intelligence and, 784–86
finance law and, 346
Global South, in
Global North compared, 320–22, 333–36, 334*t*
regulatory tendencies, 336–37
international standards, 323–25
securities regulation and
corporate climate governance, 403–5
disclosure-driven climate governance, 405–6
evolution of, 400–1
Climate Disclosure Standards Board (CDSB), 400–1
Climate Policy Initiative (CPI), 340–41
climate-washing litigation
generally, 2, 173–74, 190–91
carbon credit claims, 177–78
case selection, 179–81
climate neutrality claims
generally, 181–82
AMOREMA, 182–85
Gran Cumbal, 185–86
Pira Paraná, 185–86
defined, 175
distinct legal phenomenon, as, 174–75

climate-washing litigation (*cont.*)
Global North trend, as, 175–77
impacts of, 178–79
implications of
generally, 187
mediation approach, 190
public–private divide, challenging, 188–90
strategic framing, 187–88
coal-fired power plants (CFPPs), 354–55
Coalition for Environmentally Responsible Economies (CERES), 517–18
Coase, Ronald, 17
Coastal GasLink, 431
Cole, Luke, 45–46
Colino, Sandra Marco, 373
collective action problems
bankruptcy law and, 416
consumer climate contracts and, 78
law and economics and, 23
securities regulation and, 407–8
collective bargaining, 449–50
Colombia
climate-washing litigation in, 185–86, 187–88, 189, 190, 191
labour law in, 450
Ministry of Environment, 186
National Registry of Greenhouse Emissions Reduction, 186
SOEs in, 356n.98
Columbia University, 548
commercial arbitration. *See* international commercial arbitration
Commission on International Trade Law (UNCITRAL)
Arbitration Rules, 435, 436, 439
bankruptcy law and, 422
international commercial arbitration and, 434–35, 436, 439
ISDS and, 476
Rules of Transparency in Treaty-Based Investor–State Arbitration, 439
common law torts
generally, 8
Australia, in, 110–11
causation problem, 108–9 (*see also* causation in tort)
defendant problem, 106–8
de minimis non curat lex, 107
"first wave" of climate change litigation, 109–13
flexibility of, 103
future directions, 117–18
historical background, 104–6
judges, role of, 103–4
negligence, 51, 51n.9, 105
non-binary nature of, 103–4
"paradigmatic anti-tort," climate change as, 104
plaintiff problem, 106
pollution and, 105–6
public nuisance (*see* public nuisance)
public rights and, 106–7
tikanga Māori (system of laws) compared, 114–17
UK, in, 108–9, 110–11
US, in, 109–10, 591–92
Commonwealth Bank of Australia (CBA), 651
Commonwealth Climate and Law Initiative (CCLI), 667n.11
compensation funds, 24n.37
competition law
generally, 6, 359–60, 375–76
Australia, in, 363
Austria, in, 371n.76
cartel enforcement, fostering climate change goals through, 363–65
consumer welfare standard and
generally, 360, 365
by-object restrictions, 365–67
closely related or connected markets approach, 374–75
closer look, 365–68
collective benefits, 371–72, 374
discount rate, 375
fostering climate change goals through, 364–65
individual non-use value benefits, 371–72, 373–74
individual use value benefits, 371–72, 373
innovation and, 374–75
other climate collaborations, 370–75
procompetitive sustainability standards, 369–70
damages in, 746n.45
EU, in (*see* European Union)
France, in, 364
overview of law, 360–63
sustainability and, 360
Switzerland, in, 363
TFEU and, 360–62, 365–66, 370, 371, 375
UK, in, 371n.76
US, in (*see* United States)
Comprehensive and Progressive Agreement for a Trans-Pacific Partnership, 489–90
Comte, Auguste, 36
ConocoPhillips, 201, 349–50, 441
conservation easements, 239
Conservation Law Foundation, 166
conservation trusts, 280, 285–87, 818–19
consumer climate contracts
generally, 5, 69, 83–84
activism and, 77
alienation and, 77
challenges to public climate law and, 69–72
citizens as consumers, 73, 77–79
collective action problems, 78
consumer climate cooperatives, 81–83
consumers as citizens, 73, 76, 77–79
empowering pro-climate consumers
consumer lawsuits, 80
consumer produced climate information, 80
procurement policies, 80
engagement and, 77
externalities and, 74
firms and, 2

good faith of government and, 76
hybrid cooperatives, 82
informational regulation and, 75–76
need for private law alternatives and, 69–72
"nudging," 75–76
producers versus consumers, 73–75, 74n.50
reconcilement and, 76
renewable energy cooperatives, 82–83
social contract theory and, 67–69
consumer climate cooperatives, 81–83
consumer protection
Australia, in
anti-greenwashing action, 653–54
civil society litigation, 654–56
climate-washing litigation (*see* climate-washing litigation)
consumer climate contracts (*see* consumer climate contracts)
EU, in, 581–83, 588–89
France, in, 581–82
Germany, in, 581–82, 589
Netherlands, in, 581–82, 588
Consumer Reports, 78
contract law
generally, 6, 85–88, 102
climate commitments
joint project contracts, 99–101
quid pro quo contracts, 98–99, 100–2
relational theory of contract and, 97–98, 98n.74
consumer climate contracts (*see* consumer climate contracts)
contract governance, 91
effectiveness of climate clauses, 90–91
enforceability of climate clauses
generally, 88–92
agreed remedies, 94–96
charitable donations, 94, 95–96
commercial contracts, 88
damages, 92–93
judicial remedies, 92–94
specific performance, 93–94, 95
termination, 94
expectation damages, 745
force majeure clauses, 85–86, 640
foreseeability, 85–86, 85n.6
frustration, 85–86
growth paradigm and, 743–44
India, climate change litigation in, 640–41
force majeure clauses and, 640
regulatory context, in, 640–41
legislation and, 91n.35
mandatory rules, 86–87
prevalence of climate clauses, 89–90
price arrangements and, 745–46
public interest and, 96n.68
sustainability clauses, 86n.8, 90–92, 98n.77
teaching private law for growth and, 745–46
tort law compared, 97
voluntary undertaking of obligations
generally, 87–88
external pressure versus internal motivation, 89
reasons for, 88–89
Convention on the Recognition and Enforcement of Foreign Arbitral Awards (New York Convention), 426, 432–34, 435, 436–37, 477
corporate law and governance. *See also specific country*
generally, 3, 297–99, 316–18
artificial intelligence and
generally, 779–80
AI enthusiasm, 780–82
AI pragmatism, 775, 782–84
climate change, arguments in favour of directors addressing
generally, 307
corporate constitution, incorporating nature into, 298, 307–9
ESG and, 309, 310, 311
fiduciary duties, aligning, 312–16
shareholder preferences, catering to, 298, 309–11
SOEs and, 312–16
enforcement of director duties, 300
external dimension of director duties generally, 300–1
importance of addressing external dimension of director duties
generally, 301–2
CSDDD and, 304, 305–6
CSRD and, 304–6
SOEs and, 306–7
universal ownership, 302–3
internal dimension of director duties, 299–300
securities regulation and (*see* securities regulation)
shareholder governance
generally, 406
collective action problems, 407–8
engagement, 406–7
voting rights, 407
state-owned Enterprises and
generally, 298, 317
China, in, 298–99, 313–16, 317–18
climate change, arguments in favour of directors addressing, 312–16
importance of addressing external dimension of director duties, 306–7
teaching private law for growth and, 746
universal ownership
generally, 297–98, 302–3
addressing negative externalities, 304
internalising negative externalities, 303
corporate social responsibility (CSR), 499–500, 638–39
corporate sustainability
CSDDD (*see* Corporate Sustainability Due Diligence Directive (CSDDD))
CSRD (*see* Corporate Sustainability Reporting Directive (CSRD))
EU, in (*see* European Union)
externalities and, 493
Germany. in, 496
Netherlands. in, 496

Corporate Sustainability Due Diligence Directive (CSDDD)
generally, 3, 140
artificial intelligence and, 786–87, 786n.96, 788
autonomy of liability law, 148, 150, 151
climate change litigation and, 586, 588, 589
corporate law and governance and, 298, 304, 305–6, 580–81
corporate sustainability generally, 508–9
ESG and, 625
fiduciary law and, 214, 222, 224
future directions, 510
"green finance" and, 508–9
private international law and, 554, 566
private standard-setting and, 527–28
securities regulation and, 415
Corporate Sustainability Reporting Directive (CSRD)
generally, 3, 140
artificial intelligence and, 784–86, 785n.80, 788–90
autonomy of liability law, 148, 150
climate change litigation and, 586, 589
climate disclosure and, 324–25, 332, 336
corporate law and governance and, 298, 304–6
corporate sustainability and, 505–7
ESG and, 625
fiduciary law and, 221, 222
finance law and, 578
future directions, 510
"green finance" and, 505–7
private standard-setting and, 527–28
securities regulation and, 415
Corpus Juris Civilis, 576
corrective justice, 55–56
Cotterrell, Roger, 249–50
courts, role in private law, 7–8
critical and social theory
generally, 12, 36–38, 47–48
defining, 36–37, 36–37n.2, 37n.3
environmental justice movement and, 45
interventions, 37
property law as obstacle to addressing climate change, 41–47
collective action versus property rights, 46–47
community-led resettlement, 44
community needs versus private property, 41–42
displacement and, 45–47, 48
floodplains, home construction in, 45–48
inequities, 41
land use, limits on control of, 41–42
sea level rise and, 42–44
race, intersectionality with private law and environment, 38–41
Crow, Jessica, 3
CSDDD. *See* Corporate Sustainability Due Diligence Directive (CSDDD)
CSRD. *See* Corporate Sustainability Reporting Directive (CSRD)
Cummings, Scott, 751
Czechia, private international law in, 555

D
Dade County wetlands mitigation project, 286–87
Dale, Gareth, 739
damages
civil law torts and, 138–39
competition law, in, 746n.45
contract law, in, 92–93, 745
expectation damages, 745
extra-patrimonial (moral) damages, 722
insurance law, mitigation damages in, 391–94
liquidated damages, 54
punitive damages, 60–61n.43
da Rosa, Rafaela, 725–26nn.47–48
Davies, Martin, 10
Davis, Adrienne, 38–39, 39n.7
Davis, Seth, 3, 292–93
de Andrade Moreira, Danielle, 10–11
de Bruin, Boudewijn, 4
de Jong, E.R., 7
Deloitte, 184
Delta Air Lines, 177
de minimis non curat lex, 107
Denmark
climate disclosure in, 328
climate-washing litigation in, 175–76
Depoorter, Ben, 29
Dernbach, John C., 5, 772–73
design defects, 159–60, 161–62, 163
Dibley, Arjuna, 6
disclosure. *See* climate disclosure
discounted cash flow (DCF) method of valuation, 477–78
"Disney's Law," 537
DKI Decarbonization Index, 787–88
Doha Declaration on the TRIPS Agreement and Public Health, 269–70
Dorfman, Avihay, 8, 9
double-edged sword, private law as, 5–7
Draghi Report, 574–75
Dürig, Günter, 800–1
Durkheim, Emile, 36
DuVivier, K.K., 235n.32

E
East and Southeast Asia. *See also specific country*
generally, 7–8, 664–66, 678–79
climate change litigation in, 665n.3, 666–68
demographics of, 664n.1
greenwashing in, 672–76
ECHR. *See* European Convention on Human Rights (ECHR)
Eckes, Christina, 751
Eco-Patent Commons, 262–63, 272–73
Ecuador, labour law in, 450
Edison (Italian utility), 431
Eichel, Florian, 562–63

Emission Allowances Single Trade Agreement (STA), 430
Emission Reduction Purchase Agreements (ERPAs), 429
EnergyAustralia, 655–56
Energy Charter Treaty (ECT)
  international commercial arbitration and, 434
  ISDS and, 472–73, 475–76, 481–82, 483, 490
Energy Research Institute, 516
Environmental, Social, and Governance (ESG)
  corporate law and governance and, 309, 310, 311
  EU, in, 214, 221, 224
  fiduciary law and, 609–10
  finance law and, 341, 344–45
  legal profession and, 756–59, 765, 773
  origins of term, 609
  PEG and, 541, 546
  securities regulation and, 401–2, 406–7, 408–9, 410, 413–14
  sustainable development and, 608–11
  trust law and, 291
  US, in (*see* United States)
Environmental Defense Fund, 538, 545–46
environmental justice movement, 45
equality
  generally, 53
  corrective justice versus, 55–56
  "entire fairness" standard, 53–54
  fairness, 50–51, 53–55, 59
  formal conception of, 55–56
  substantive conception of, 56–59
  tort law and, 49, 50–52
Equator Principles, 533–34, 537–38
equitable deviation, 292
ESG. *See* Environmental, Social, and Governance (ESG)
estate tax, 293–94
Etemire, Uzuazo, 11
European Central Bank, 348
European Commission. *See* European Union
European Convention on Human Rights (ECHR)
  civil law torts and, 150–51
  climate change litigation and, 585–86, 601–2
  direct horizontal effect and, 798–99, 801–2
  duty of care and, 697–98
  fiduciary law and, 223
  human rights law and
    mental health, 795
    right to life, 791–92, 794–95
    right to respect for private and family life, 791–92, 794–95
  ISDS and, 481n.71
European Court of Human Rights (ECtHR), 585–86, 791, 795, 798–99, 801–2
European Economic Community, 491
European Environment Agency, 492–93
European Free Trade Area (EFTA), 556, 567–68
European Union. *See also specific country*
  generally, 571–72, 589
  Accounts Modernisation Directive, 577–78
  Action Plan, 412–13
  Action Plan on Financing Sustainable Growth, 502, 504
  automobile emissions reduction in, 497
  Better Regulation Agenda, 492
  Capital Markets Union (CMU) Action Plan, 502
  Carbon Border Adjustment Mechanism, 574–75, 589
  Charter of Fundamental Rights of the EU (EUCFR), 491, 799–800
  choice of law in, 561–62, 563
  Circular Economy Action Plan, 499
  civil law torts in, 146
  Clean Industrial Directive, 574–75
  climate change litigation in, 583–89 (*see also specific country*)
    consumer protection and, 588–89
    duty of care and, 584, 587–88
    ECHR and, 585–86
    Emissions Trading System (ETS) and, 587
    regulation and, 586–87
    separation of powers and, 584
    strategic litigation, 575
  Climate Delegated Act, 503
  climate disclosure in, 322, 328, 336–37
  climate law in
    industry competitiveness and, 574–75
    market-based instruments and, 573–74
    market orientation of, 572–75
    strategic litigation, 575
  Climate Transition Benchmarks, 578–79
  Commercial Practices Directive, 582–83
  Common European Sales Law, 742–43
  competition law in
    generally, 375
    by-object restrictions, 365–67
    cartel enforcement, 364
    consumer welfare standard, 362–67
    other climate collaborators, 370–72, 374–75
    procompetitive sustainability standards, 370
    public interest exception, 363
    TFEU and, 360–62, 365–66, 370, 375
    two-step analysis, 360–61
  Competitiveness Compass, 574–75
  consumer protection in, 581–83, 588–89
  corporate law and governance in, 580–81
  corporate social responsibility (CSR) in, 499–500
  corporate sustainability in
    generally, 11, 510–12
    command-and-control instruments, 493
    CSDDD and, 508–9
    CSRD and, 505–7
    Delegated Regulation and, 503–4
    Green Deal and, 500–1
    green economy versus linear economy, 498–99
    historical background, 491–92
    liability for environmental damage, 495

European Union (*cont.*)
market-based instruments, 492–95
Sustainable Finance Disclosure Regulation (SFDR) and, 504–5
Taxonomy Regulation and, 502–4
tradable pollution rights, 495–96
voluntary agreements, 496–98
crisis management in, 377
Critical Raw Materials Act, 574–75
CSDDD (*see* Corporate Sustainability Due Diligence Directive (CSDDD))
CSRD (*see* Corporate Sustainability Reporting Directive (CSRD))
Ecodesign Directive, 499
Eighth Environmental Action Programme, 494
Emissions Trading System (ETS)
generally, 573, 574–75, 589
civil law torts and, 140, 148, 150
climate change litigation and, 586–87
ISDS and, 487
maritime law and, 459–60, 467–68, 470–71
Empowering Consumers for the Green Transition (ECGT) Directive, 582–83, 589
Environmental Liability Directive, 22
European Climate Law, 412–13, 501, 573–74, 581
European Green Bond, 578–79
European Sustainability Reporting Standards (ESRS)
artificial intelligence and, 784–85, 786–87, 789–90
climate disclosure and, 324–25, 332, 334–35
finance law and, 578
"green finance" and, 506
fiduciary law in, 221–25
generally, 7
Action Programme, 222
ESG and, 214, 221, 224
Fifth Environmental Action Programme, 493, 497
finance law in, 577–80
Green Bond Regulation, 578–79
Green Claims Directive (proposed), 187–88, 582–83, 589
Green Deal
generally, 574–75
corporate sustainability and, 500–1
"green finance" and, 502
private standard-setting and, 521–22
securities regulation and, 412–13, 472–73
green economy and, 498–99
"green finance" and
generally, 501–2
CSDDD and, 508–9
CSRD and, 505–7
Sustainable Finance Disclosure Regulation (SFDR) and, 504–5
Taxonomy Regulation and, 502–4
Green Papers
Corporate Social Responsibility, 500
Greenhouse Gas Emissions Trading within the European Union, 496
Market-based Instruments for Environment and Related Policy Purposes, 494
Remedying Environmental Damage, 495n.26
High-Level Experts Group (HLEG), 501–2
Horizontal Cooperation Guidelines, 367
informational regulation in, 75–76
Intra-EU BIT Termination Agreement, 490
Maastricht Treaty (1992), 491
Member States Experts Group (MSEG), 502
natural hazards, insuring against, 381
Net Zero Industry Act, 574–75
Non-Financial Reporting Directive (NFRD), 336–37, 501, 505–6, 507, 577–78
Paris-aligned Benchmarks, 578–79
private law in
acquis communautaire, 576
development of, 576–77
historical background, 576
ius commune, 576
public law distinguished, 576n.54
private standard-setting in, 521–22
securities regulation in, 400–2, 408, 410–11, 412–13, 414–15
Seventh Environmental Action Programme, 494
Sixth Environmental Action Programme, 493–94
Strategy for Sustainable Development, 492
Strategy for Sustainable Finance, 501–2
Strategy 2011–14 for Corporate Social Responsibility, 500
Sustainable Finance Disclosure Regulation (SFDR), 214, 408, 504–5, 578–80
Sustainable Finance Platform, 503
Taxonomy Regulation, 502–4, 578–80
Technical Experts Group (TEG), 502
2020 Strategy, 492
Unfair Commercial Practices Directive, 588
Verified Emissions Report (VER), 471
Waste Directive, 499
expectation damages, 745
externalities
consumer climate contracts and, 74
corporate sustainability and, 493
securities regulation and, 403–5
universal ownership and
addressing negative externalities, 304
internalising negative externalities, 303
extra-patrimonial (moral) damages, 722
ExxonMobil, 201–2
Exxon Valdez oil spill (1989), 813–14
Exxon Valdez Oil Spill Trustee Council, 286–87

F
factual causation, 121
Fairfax, Lisa, 513–14, 518
fairness
non-human life, tort duties to, 50–51, 53–55, 59

relational justice and, 50–51, 53–55, 59
family law, 744
Faure, Michael, 4
Feng, Yi, 8
Fermeglia, Matteo, 478
Ferris, Nick, 201nn.55–56
Fiduciary Duty in the 21st Century (UNEP), 2, 3, 7
fiduciary law. *See also specific country*
generally, 3, 207–9, 225
barriers to normative settlement
generally, 215, 216
interface problem, 217–18
legitimacy trap, 217
sword-and-shield problem, 216–17
ESG and, 609–10
EU, in (*see* European Union)
features of
generally, 209
capital flows, 212–13
common code across common and civil law jurisdictions, 209
fiduciary mandates, 209–11
investment fiduciaries, 212–13
public trust doctrine, 211–12
regulation of corporations and states, 211–12
Indigenous Peoples and, 809–10, 821–23
recursive change within law
actor mismatch and, 216
charity and, 215
compromise and, 215
consensus and, 215
transnational legal ordering (TLO) around climate change, 213–14
trust law compared, 6
US, in (*see* United States)
finance law
generally, 6, 342, 358
carbon liability-shifting
housing mortgage market compared, 350n.64
information-based market failures. moving beyond, 353–56
leakage, undermining of climate alignment through, 349–50
state-owned enterprises and, 355–56
climate alignment, effect of sustainable finance agenda on private law response to
generally, 342–43
information-based market failures and, 344–48
Paris Agreement and, 343–44, 347
climate disclosure and, 346
climate risk-shifting
generally, 341–42
"blue lining," 357
information-based market failures. moving beyond, 356–58
"insurance retreat" and, 350–51
leakage, undermining of climate alignment through, 350–51
ESG and, 341, 344–45
EU, in, 577–80
green labels and certifications, 347
information-based market failures
generally, 341
carbon liability-shifting and, 353–56
climate alignment, effect of sustainable finance agenda on private law response to, 344–48
climate risk-shifting and, 356–58
leakage, undermining of climate alignment through
generally, 341–42, 348–49
addressing problems versus abandoning climate information, 352
carbon liability-shifting and, 349–50
climate risk-shifting and, 350–51
sustainable finance taxonomies, 346
Financial Stability Board (FSB), 323–24, 398–99, 518
Fink, Larry, 523–24
Firstgas, 658–59
First Peoples. *See* Indigenous Peoples
Fisher, Elizabeth, 591–92, 601
Flanagan, Frances, 10
Flatt, Victor, 772–73
force majeure clauses, 85–86, 640
foreign judgments, 566–68
foreseeability, 85–86, 85n.6
forum non conveniens, 560–61
forum shopping
bankruptcy law, in, 421, 423–24
international commercial arbitration, in, 435–37
Foster, Sheila, 45–46
Fraley, Jill, 41–42, 46–47, 48, 48n.48
Framework Convention on Climate Change (UNFCCC) (1992)
duty of care and, 697–98
environmental damage and, 724
finance law and, 342–43, 342n.11, 344
international commercial arbitration and, 428
ISDS and, 472–73
maritime law and, 459–60
private standard-setting and, 521–22
products liability law and, 168
Race to Zero Starting Line and Leadership Practices 3.0, 521–22
Standing Committee on Finance, 472–73
France
artificial intelligence in, 781–82
Charter for the Environment, 587–88
Climate and Resilience Law, 581–82
climate change litigation in, 587–88
climate disclosure in
generally, 322, 339*t*
Global South compared, 333–35, 334*t*
regulatory standards, 336–37
climate-washing litigation in, 175–76
Commercial Code, 337n.159, 587–88
consumer protection in, 581–82
corporate law and governance in, 580

France (*cont.*)
Duty of Vigilance Law of 2017, 222, 222n.85, 225, 508, 553–54, 565–66, 580, 587–88
Energy Transition Law, 336–37
extraterritoriality in, 565–66
fiduciary law in, 7, 222, 222n.85, 225
French Revolution, 68
joint project contracts in, 100
private international law in, 555
Frankenberg, Günter, 740n.20
Frankfurt School, 36
Franzen, Jonathan, 251
Freshfields Bruckhaus Deringer (law firm), 610
Frumhoff, Peter C., 201n.58
Fuller, Lon, 281
fundamental rights. *See* human rights law

G
Gabon, environmental legislation in, 693
Galperin, Joshua, 104n.9
Garth, Bryant G., 749–50
Gary, Susan, 291, 292
Geistfeld, Mark A., 7
general jurisdiction, 557
generation-skipping tax (GST), 293–94
Germany
Act against Unfair Commercial Practices, 581–82
Act against Unfair Competition, 176
artificial intelligence in, 780–81
causation in tort in, 122
choice of law in, 563–64
climate change litigation in
generally, 138–39, 731–32
autonomy liability law, 147–48, 150
consumer protection and, 589
institutional competence of civil courts, 139–41, 143
regulation and, 587
climate disclosure in
generally, 322
Global South compared, 333–35, 334*t*, 339*t*
climate-washing litigation in, 175–76
consumer protection in, 581–82, 589
cooperatives in, 82–83
corporate law and governance in, 580
corporate sustainability in, 496
fiduciary law in, 7, 221, 222
human rights law in, 797–98, 800–1
Insurance Contact Law Act (Versicherungsvertrags gesetz), 392–93
insurance law in, 392–93
ISDS, phase-out of coal and, 482–83, 486–87, 488, 490
joint project contracts in, 100
labour law in, 450
private international law in, 552, 555
private standard-setting in, 521–22
public nuisance in, 698
Supply Chain Due Diligence Act of 2021, 222, 508, 580
tort law in, 59
Germelmann, Claas Friedrich, 744n.35
Gerrard, Michael, 535
GFANZ. *See* Glasgow Financial Alliance for Net Zero (GFANZ)
Gibbons, John, 537
Gilboa, Maytal, 3, 203n.65
Givens, Rachel, 234–35n.30
Glasgow Financial Alliance for Net Zero (GFANZ)
greenwashing and, 672–73, 672–73n.40
private standard-setting and, 514, 516–17, 523–24, 525, 528–29, 530–31
Global GHG Accounting and Reporting Standard for the Financial Industry, 516–17
Global Reporting Initiative (GRI)
climate disclosure and, 323, 324–25, 326–27, 332, 334–35
finance law and, 578
private standard-setting and, 517–18
Global Toolbox on Corporate Climate Litigation, 647
Global Trends 2025 Snapshot, 646–47, 647n.9
Gold, Andrew, 210
Gold, E. Richard, 276
Goldman Sachs, 529
Gollier, Christian, 28
Gol Linhas Aereas, 185
Gome Electrical Appliances, 712
Goulder, Larry, 537
Gözlügöl, Alperen A., 355
Graham, Mary, 252–53
Graham, Nicole, 8–9, 287–88
Grantham Research Institute on Climate Change and the Environment, 521, 646–47
green economy, 498–99
Greenhouse Gas (GHG) Protocol, 323, 336, 516
Greenpeace, 656, 751, 788n.105
greenwashing
climate-washing litigation and, 174–75, 179
defined, 673
East and Southeast Asia, in, 672–76
legal profession avoiding, 765–66
PEG and, 535, 540–41, 546
Griffin, Lissa, 766
growth paradigm
contract law and, 743–44
law and economics and, 743
legal education and, 739, 742–44
Grušić, Uglješa, 6
Guiding Principles on Business and Human Rights (UNGPs)
generally, 3
climate change litigation and, 584
corporate sustainability and, 503, 508
human rights law and, 791–92, 796, 799, 801–2
Guyana, climate change litigation in, 666–67

H
Hague Judgments Convention (2019), 549, 558–59, 567

Hague Rules on Business and Human Rights Arbitration, 434
Halliday, Terence C., 213, 215, 216
Harlow, Carol, 666–67
Harper, Virginia, 10
Hart, Oliver, 298, 309
Hayek, Friedrich, 743
Head, Lesley, 258
Heede, Richard, 555
Hester, Tracy D., 353–54
Higgins, Henry Bournes, 452–53, 454
Higham, Catherine, 2
Hindustan Zinc, 640–41
Ho, Virginia Harper, 329
Hobbes, Thomas, 67
Hohfeld, Wesley, 256
hold harmless and indemnity principle, 390–91
homeowner associations (HOAs), 238–39
Hong Kong
- Arbitration Ordinance, 438
- choice of law in, 564–65
- greenwashing in, 675
- International Arbitration Centre (HKIAC), 438
- Securities and Futures Ordinance (SFO), 440

Honneth, Axel, 447–48
humanism, 62–63
human rights law. *See also specific country*
- generally, 4, 791–92, 806–7
- Africa, and climate change litigation in, 689–92
- balancing of conflicting interests, 803–4
- climate change and
  - generally, 792
  - corporate responsibility, 795–97
  - Indigenous Peoples and, 794
  - mental health, 795
  - potentially relevant rights, 793–95
  - right to life, 791–92
  - right to respect for private and family life, 791–92
  - "third-generation" rights, 793
- double proportionality test, 803–4
- ECHR (*see* European Convention on Human Rights (ECHR))
- horizontal effect of fundamental rights
  - generally, 797
  - direct horizontal effect, 797–800, 806–7
  - indirect horizontal effect, 800–2, 806–7
- mental health and, 795
- relationship to IP and climate change (*see* intellectual property (IP))
- semi-regulators, courts as, 804–6
- theories of justice and, 805–6
- ultimate balancing test, 803–4

Hurricane Katrina, 26, 30
Hurricane Maria, 156
hybrid cooperatives, 82

I

IMO. *See* International Maritime Organization (IMO)
India
- generally, 4
- Business Responsibility and Sustainability Report (BRSR), 328
- Business Responsibility Report (BRR), 327–28, 336–37
- choice of law in, 564–65
- Clean Development Mechanism, 327–28
- climate change litigation in
  - generally, 627–28, 644, 671–72, 671n.35
  - contract law, 640–41
  - corporate law and governance, 637–40
  - future directions, 641–44
  - "horizontal effect," 629
  - human rights law and, 794–95
  - private law versus public law, 628–30
  - stakeholder responsibility, 637–40
  - tort law, 630–37
- climate disclosure in, 327–28
  - generally, 322
  - Global North compared, 333–34, 334*t*, 335, 339*t*
  - regulatory standards, 336–37
- Companies Act, 2039, 637–39
- Contract Act, 1872, 640
- contract law, climate change litigation and, 640–41
  - *force majeure* clauses and, 640
  - regulatory context, in, 640–41
- corporate law and governance, climate change litigation and, 637–40
  - corporate social responsibility (CSR), 638–39
  - duties of directors, 637–38
- Corporate Social Responsibility Voluntary Guidelines (CSR Guidelines), 327
- emitters in, 207
- Environmental Protection Act, 1986, 638n.93
- fiduciary law in, 211–12
- human rights law in, 794–95
- Ministry of Corporate Affairs (MCA), 327–28
- mix of instruments in, 21–22
- National Company Law Tribunal (NCLT), 640
- National Green Tribunal Act (NGTA), 633, 643
- National Green Tribunal (NGT), 628, 633–34, 635–36, 640, 643
- National Guidelines on Responsible Business Conduct, 328
- National Voluntary Guidelines (NVGs), 327–28
- private international law in, 555
- Rajasthan Electricity Regulatory Commission (RERC) t, 640–41
- Securities and Exchange Board of India (SEBI), 327–28
- tort law, climate change litigation and
  - generally, 630–31
  - absolute liability, 631–32, 634–35
  - causation and, 635
  - constitutional claims, 631–32, 631n.30
  - damages and, 635–36
  - "deep pocket" theory, 632n.34

India (*cont.*)
doctrinal distortions, 634–36
innovative concepts, 631–34
"polluter pays" principle, 632, 634–35
precautionary principle, 632, 634–35
procedural considerations, 636–37
public interest litigation, 631–32, 631n.29
public trust doctrine, 632n.42
Indigenous Environmental Network, 817–18
Indigenous Peoples
Australia, in, 812, 814–15, 815n.39, 816–17, 821
Canada, in, 812n.23, 821–23
carbon credits and, 817
climate-washing litigation and (*see* climate-washing litigation)
community-led resettlement, 44
defined, 808n.1
defining private law and, 810–11
fiduciary law and, 809–10, 821–23
Free, Prior, and Informed Consent (FPIC), 182, 185
human rights law and, 794–95
Indigenous private law, 811–12
Isle de Jean Charles Choctaw Nation of Louisiana, 42–44, 46
land use and ownership and (*see* land use and ownership)
liability for climate harm, 813–15
Māori people (*see* Māori people)
mineral rights and, 816–17, 825
Navajo Tribal Code, 287–88, 819
New Zealand, in (*see* Māori people)
private law generally, 11, 808–10, 812, 825–26
property law as obstacle to addressing climate change
community-led resettlement, 44
sea level rise and, 42–44
Quinault Indian Reservation, 288–89
reparations and, 809–10, 820–24
self-governance, 824, 826
traditional ecological knowledge (TEK)
climate adaptation and, 820
property interests in, 809–10, 824–25
Tribal Holder model, 288–89
trust law and, 287–89, 818–19
US, in (*see* United States)
Yainix Ranch, 288–89
Yurok Tribe, 817
individualism, interconnectedness and, 8–9
Indonesia
climate change litigation in, 666–67
climate disclosure in, 333–34, 334*t*, 339*t*
climate-washing litigation in, 180–81
Consumer Protection Act No. 8 of 1999, 674
greenwashing in, 674
ministry of Environment, 180–81
private international law in, 555
state-owned enterprises in, 667–68
Strategic Lawsuits Against Public Participation (SLAPPs) in, 665, 665–66n.6
Industrial Democracy (Webb & Webb), 453
Industrial Revolution, 103, 105, 117
Infinite-Earth, 429
ING (Dutch bank), 141
Ingram, John Kell, 451–53, 454
Institutes (Justinian), 281
Institutional Investor Group on Climate Change (IIGCC), 520, 521, 523–24
insurance law
generally, 10, 379, 395–96
Australia, in, 384
ex ante role of, 378
financing loss prevention
generally, 390
hold harmless and indemnity principle, 390–91
mitigation damages, 391–94
subrogation, 394–95
sue and labour costs, 391–94
Germany, in, 392–93
justifications for loss prevention, 384–86
knowledge sharing
generally, 387–88
contractual information dutie3s, 389–90
pre-contractual information dutie3s, 388
limitations of traditional insurance
generally, 382
betterment principle, 383–84
coverage exclusions, 382
deductibles, 382
limits, 382
notice of loss requirement, 383
post-event claims payments, 383–84
price-signalling, 382
risk mitigation terms, 382–83
loss prevention
generally, 386–87
financing, 390–95
knowledge sharing, 387–88
natural hazards, insuring against
generally, 379–80
cost of, 377, 380
insurability, 380–81
protection gaps, 381–82
terminology, 379
New Zealand, in, 383–84
Switzerland, in, 392–93
UK, in (*see* United Kingdom)
"insurance retreat," 350–51
intellectual property (IP)
generally, 2
Canada, in, 270
COVID-19 vaccines and, 276
environmentally sound technologies (EST), 261–63, 271–73, 276–77
human rights approach to IP and climate change
generally, 263–65, 276–77

application of, 271–73
digital technologies and, 269
gender, impact of climate change on, 268
impact of, 273–76
lack of success, 270–71
limitations of, 275–76
relationship between IP and human rights, 268–71
right to food, 266, 273–74
right to health, 266, 274
right to housing, 266
right to safe, clean, health, and sustainable environment, 267
right to self-determination, 267, 274–75
right to water, 266
trade and, 269
US, in, 270
Inter-American Commission on Human Rights (IACHR), 794–95
Inter-American Development Bank, 326
Interfaith Center on Corporate Responsibility (ICCR), 523
Inter-Governmental Maritime Consultative Organization (IMCO), 460–61
Intergovernmental Panel on Climate Change (IPCC)
generally, 22
Africa and, 680
carbon budgets, 668–69
climate change litigation and, 584
East and Southeast Asia and, 664n.1
human rights law and, 794
ISDS and, 472–73
maladaptation and, 244
Sixth Assessment Report (AR6), 265
International Accounting Standards Board (IASB), 514–15, 519
International Arbitration Survey (2025), 426–27, 435–36n.62
International Association of Classification Societies (IACS), 464
International Association of Insurance Supervisors (IAIS), 384–85
International Bar Association (IBA), 430
International Centre for the Settlement of Investment Disputes (ICSID), 476, 477
International Chamber of Commerce (ICC)
arbitrability, 433–34
Arbitration Rules, 426, 435, 439
Commission on Arbitration and ADR, 428
dispute resolution, 432
international commercial arbitration
generally, 4, 426–27, 441
ad hoc arbitration, 426n.2
climate-related disputes
generally, 427–28
carbon market disputes, 428–30, 428–29n.10
contractual clauses, 430–31
mergers and acquisitions (M&A) and, 430–31
projects, 428–30
third-party interests, 431
dispute-based perspective, 427–28
dispute resolution
generally, 431–33
arbitrability, 433–34
efficient mechanism, 432
forum shopping, 435–37
multiple jurisdictions, 432–33
party autonomy, 435–37
procedural flexibility, 432
public policy exception, 435–37
regulatory arbitrage, 435–37, 435n.61
third-party participation, 437–41
transparency, 437–41
institutional arbitration, 426n.2
sector-based perspective, 428
International Convention for Prevention of Pollution by Oil 1954 (OILPOL 54), 460
International Convention for the Prevention of Pollution from Ships (MARPOL)
generally, 461
Annex VI generally, 462–63
enforcement of Annex VI
carbon intensity indicator (CII), 463–64
classification societies, 464–65
decarbonisation strategy, 462–63
flag state control, 463–64
memoranda of understanding (MoUs), 466–67
Paris Memorandum of Understanding on Port State Control (the Paris MoU), 466–67
port state control, 465–67
Protection and Indemnity Associations (P&I Clubs), 465n.36
International Convention for the Safety of Life at Sea 1974 (SOLAS), 465, 466
International Cooperative Alliance, 81
International Court of Justice (ICJ), 448–49, 683, 685, 690, 794
International Covenant on Civil and Political Rights (ICCPR), 791
International Emission Trading Association (IETA), 429–30
International Energy Agency, 770
International Finance Corporation, 329–30n.91
International Financial Reporting Standards (IFRS), 514–15, 518, 519, 525
International Financial Reporting Standards (IFRS) Foundation, 324, 514–15, 518
International Framework (Integrated Reporting), 518
International Group of P&I Clubs, 465n.36
International Integrated Reporting Council (IIRC), 326, 518
International Labour Organization, 503
International Maritime Organization (IMO)
generally, 460
carbon intensity indicator (CII), 468–69, 470
direct compliance target (DCT), 470
Energy Efficiency Existing Ship Index (EEXI), 468

International Maritime Organization (IMO) (*cont.*)
GHG fuel intensity (GFI), 470
Legal Committee, 461
Marine Environment Protection Committee (MEPC), 461, 462–63, 467–68, 469–70
Regulations with Effect from 1 March 2027, 469–70
Ship Energy Efficiency Management Plan (SEEMP), 468
Sustainable Fuel Certification Scheme, 470
2023 Regulations, 459, 467–69
International Monetary Fund (IMF), 323–24, 460, 477–78
International Organization for Standardization (ISO), 369, 515, 521–22
International Organization of Securities Commissioners (IOSCO)
climate disclosure and, 324, 325–26
securities regulation and, 400, 409–10
International Organization of Securities Commissions, African Finance Ministers, and Finance Ministers and Central Bank Governors, 518
International Sustainability Standards Board (ISSB)
climate disclosure and, 322, 324, 325–26, 329, 332, 334–35, 336, 337
corporate law and governance and, 299
PEG and, 542, 543, 544
private standard-setting and, 514, 518, 519–20, 523–24
securities regulation and, 400–1, 405, 405n.55
Sustainability Disclosure and Climate Disclosure Standards, 517
TCFD and, 676
International Trade Union Confederation (ITUC), 448–49
International Transport Federation, 448–49
investment law. *See* finance law
Investor Group on Climate Change (IGCC), 523–24
Investors' Network on Climate Risk, 523
investor–state dispute settlement (ISDS)
generally, 4, 472–73, 489–90
basis for climate-related claims
generally, 473
fair and equitable treatment (FET), 474–75, 481–82
indirect expropriation, 475
non-discrimination, 473–74
sunset clauses, 475–76
bilateral investment treaties (BITs), 472, 473, 490
carbon capture and storage (CCS) and, 480–81, 487
coal, phase-out of
generally, 480–81
analysis, 485–88
Australia, in, 484, 488
Canada, in, 483–84, 488
Germany, in, 482–83, 486–87, 488, 490
neoliberalism and, 487
Netherlands, in, 481–82, 486, 488, 490
right to compensation versus right to regulate, 486–88
speculative futures, 487–88
discounted cash flow (DCF) method of valuation, 477–78
"double-hatting," 476, 476n.27
foreign direct investment (FDI) and, 479–80
New Zealand and, 480, 489–90
outcomes, 477–78
Pakistan and, 477–78
process, 476
Spain and, 479–80
types of climate-related claims, 478–80
IP. *See* intellectual property (IP)
IPCC. *See* Intergovernmental Panel on Climate Change (IPCC)
Ireland, private international law in, 555
ISDS. *See* investor–state dispute settlement (ISDS)
Isle de Jean Charles Choctaw Nation of Louisiana, 42–44, 46
ISSB. *See* International Sustainability Standards Board (ISSB)
Italy
climate-washing litigation in, 175–76
private international law in, 552, 555

J
Japan
climate change litigation in, 668–70
climate disclosure in
generally, 322, 337
Global South compared, 333–34, 334*t*, 336, 339*t*
fiduciary law in, 7
private international law in, 552, 555
tort law in, 668–70, 668n.17
Jerolleman, Alessandra, 42–43, 45–48
Jessee, Nathan, 42–43, 45–48
Johnson, Hope, 653–54
joint and several liability
Brazil, in, 719–20
causation and, 130
products liability and, 159, 168, 169
Joint Implementation Mechanism, 429
joint project contracts, 99–101
J.P. Morgan, 757–58
JPMorganChase, 529
Judgment Document Database, 702
jurisdiction in private international law (PIL)
generally, 556
forum non conveniens, 560–61
general jurisdiction, 557
judicial discretion, 560–61
special/specific jurisdiction, 558–59
Just Energy Transition Partnerships (JETPs), 480–81

K
Kacperczyk, Marcin, 525–26
Kaplan, Yotam, 3
Kazakhstan, private international law in, 555
Kenya
Climate Change (Duties and Incentives) Regulations 2021, 693–95

climate change litigation in, 666–67, 696
climate-washing litigation in, 182
environmental legislation in, 689–90, 693–95
human rights law in, 689–90
Kieninger, Eva-Maria, 562–63
Klare, Karl, 593
KlimaSeniorinnen Schweiz (Senior Women for Climate Protection Switzerland), 585–86
KLM (Dutch airline), 588
Korsgaard, Christine, 68
Kuh, Katrina F., 766, 772–73
Kunreuther, Howard, 31
Kurtz, Thilo, 224
Kyoto Protocol (1997)
emissions targets, 136
goals of, 573–74
international commercial arbitration and, 429
tradable pollution rights and, 496
Kysar, Douglas A., 3, 104, 104n.9, 117–18, 142, 591–92, 605, 686–87

L

labour law
generally, 10, 444, 457–58
Australia, in, 448–50, 455
climate responsibility, traditional labour law and
generally, 454
alignment between industrial and societal interests, presumption of, 454–55
redistribution of industrial citizenship between sectors, limits on, 456
Colombia, in, 450
Ecuador, in, 450
Germany, in, 450
Nigeria, in, 450
Norway, in, 450, 455
private law dimensions of
generally, 444–45
employees versus independent contractors, 445–46
employment contracts and, 445–46
failures of, 457
internal versus external to, 445
limitations to climate change mitigation, 445–46
public law versus, 444–45
public law dimensions of
collective bargaining, 449–50
health and safety protections, 447
leave entitlements, 447–48
private law versus, 444–45
procedural entitlements, 448–51
substantive entitlements, 447–48
successes of, 457–58
trade unions, 448–49
tension with climate change mitigation, 443–44, 450
theoretical justifications
generally, 442–43
democracy and, 453
inequal bargaining power, 451–53
non-commoditisation of labour, 442n.3, 451–53
UK, in, 450
US, in, 446
Lancet Planetary Health Commission, 522, 526–28
land use and ownership
generally, 8–9
Australia, in, 259
Indigenous Peoples and
generally, 246–48
climate adaptation and, 819–21
climate mitigation and, 815–19
emergence of, 246–47
forced removal and, 255–56
legal norms, 815–16, 818
mineral rights, 816–17, 825
place-based legal culture, as, 246–48, 252–55
legal cultures
legal attitudes, 250
legal consciousness, 250
legal mobilisation, 250
legal practices, 250
radical intervention, need for, 250
reframing of changes in, 251–52
significance of, 249–52
place-based legal cultures
generally, 246–48, 259
determinism, avoiding, 255
First Peoples law as, 246–48, 252–55
kinship systems and, 252–53
place as being, 252
placeless legal cultures, tension with, 257
primitivism fallacy, avoiding, 254–55
reductive narratives, avoiding, 254–55, 260
reflective engagement and, 253–54
relational ontologies and, 252–53
role of humans in, 252
variety in, 254, 255
placeless legal cultures
generally, 247–48, 259–60
climate change and, 257–58
commoditization of property, 257
dephysicalised model, 256–57
destructive nature of, 247–49
place-based legal cultures, tension with, 257
reassessment of, 258
settler colonial law as, 247–48, 255–58
planetary health, relation to, 248–49
settler colonial law
emergence of, 247
placeless legal culture, as, 247–48, 255–58
UK, in, 255–56
Langille, Brian, 444–45
Latham Watkins (law firm), 768–69
Latin American Center for Investigative Journalism a, 188
law and economics
generally, 4, 34–35
adaptation and compensation for harm generally, 17–18, 24

law and economics (*cont.*)
causal uncertainty, 23–24
collective action problems, 23
compensation funds, 24n.37
efficiency and, 743
ex post governmental compensation
effect on prevention, 28–29
fitness for climate change, 29
instrument, 27
problems with, 27–28, 34
first party insurance
compensation, 29–30
effect on prevention, 30
fitness for climate change, 30–31
instrument, 29
preference for, 34
free-riding, 23
gap-filling, 17
government intervention as reinsurer
compensation, 32
effect on prevention, 32–33
fitness for climate change, 33
instrument, 31–32
growth paradigm and, 743
liability rules
compensation, 25–26
complementary role of, 20–21
effect on prevention, 26
fitness for climate change, 26–27
instrument, 24–25
problems with, 34
lobbying, 19–20
market failures and, 17
mitigation of climate change emissions
effectiveness of private law, increasing, 22–24
liability rules, complementary role of, 20–21
mix of instruments, choice of, 21–22
private interest perspective, 19–20
regulation, preference for, 18–19
transaction costs, 17
law firms. *See* legal profession
law schools. *See* legal education
Law Students for Climate Accountability (LSCA), 760–61
lawyers. *See* legal profession
Lawyers Are Responsible (LAR), 760–61
Lawyers for Climate Action New Zealand, 658–59
LeafScore, 78–79
legal causation, 121
Legal Charter 1.5, 762, 764–65
legal education
generally, 12, 737, 753–54
Australia, in, 751–52
decoupling from economic growth, 740–42, 753–54
green growth, 738–40
growth paradigm and, 739, 742–44
Netherlands, in, 746–47, 751–52
post-growth, 738–40
professional roles and attitudes, economic growth embedded in development of, 749–51
skills for moving beyond economic growth, 747–49
strong versus weak sustainability, 738–40
"sustainable degrowth" and, 739
teaching private law for economic growth, 744–47
contract law and, 745–46
corporate law and governance and, 746
disproportionate attention to, 744
property law and, 746
tort law and, 746
UK, in, 751–52
US, in, 751–53
legal profession
generally, 6, 755–56, 773
accountability model, 760–61
Australia, in, 759, 768–69
cab-rank rule, 91, 93n.47, 771nn.103–104
Canada, in, 759
climate-related regulatory developments, assisting clients with, 765
"climate wreckers," declining representation of, 767–72
collaboration model, 760, 768
decarbonisation and climate-positive activities, seeking clients supporting, 766–67
direct impact of law firm operations, reducing, 763
emissions scheme, meaningful support for, 763–65
ESG and, 756–59, 765, 773
greenwashing, avoiding, 765–66
legal education (*see* legal education)
Netherlands, in, 750
professional responsibility rules, promoting greening of, 772–73
response to climate change, 759–63
technocracy model, 762–63
UK, in, 759, 761–62
US, in
accountability model, 760–61
climate disclosure and, 765
ESG, implications of, 622–23
professional responsibility rules, promoting greening of, 773
zealous advocacy and, 768
Lehmann, Matthias, 562–63
Leone, Candida, 12
Lessa, Maria Eduarda, 3
Levmore, Saul, 32
Levy, Jacob, 811–12
Lim, Ernest, 3, 668n.15
Lin, Jolene, 7–8
linear economy, 498
liquidated damages, 54
Lisbon European Council, 499
Lliuya, Saul Luciano, 23–24, 122, 138–39, 147–48
Localiza, 185
Locke, John, 67, 446
Logue, Kyle D., 32
London Court of International Arbitration (LCIA), 438

London School of Economics and Political Science (LSE), 521
Looney, Adam, 287–88
Luban, David, 772n.116
Luxembourg, private international law in, 555

M
Maastricht Treaty (1992), 491
Macey, Joshua C., 10
Magna Carta, 281
Mak, Elaine, 742n.25, 749n.66
maladaptation, 244
Malawi, human rights law in, 691–92
Malaysia
  climate disclosure in, 328
  state-owned enterprises in, 667–68
  Strategic Lawsuits Against Public Participation (SLAPPs) in, 665, 665–66n.6
Male Declaration on the Human Dimension of Global Climate Change by representatives of Small Island Developing States, 794
manufacturing defects, 159–60, 161
Māori people
  generally, 809
  fiduciary law and, 822–23
  historical background, 114
  reparations and, 824
  tikanga Māori (system of laws)
    generally, 8, 814
    common law torts compared, 114–17
    future directions, 118
    judicial recognition of, 116
    kaitiakitanga, 114, 118, 816
    mana, 114
    tapu, 114
    whakapapa, 114, 115
    whanaungatanga, 114, 115
Marie Brigid Arrthur, Sister, 657
Marine Stewardship Council's (MSC), 533–34, 543
Marino, Elizabeth, 42–43, 45–48
maritime law
  generally, 10, 459–60, 471
  carbon intensity indicator (CII), 463–64, 468–69, 470
  classification societies, 464–65
  decarbonisation strategy, 462–63
  direct compliance target (DCT), 470
  EU Emissions Trading System (ETS) and, 459–60, 467–68, 470–71
  flag state control, 463–64
  GHG fuel intensity (GFI), 470
  IMO (*see* International Maritime Organization (IMO))
  MARPOL (*see* International Convention for the Prevention of Pollution from Ships (MARPOL))
  memoranda of understanding (MoUs), 466–67
  port state control, 465–67
market failures
  finance law, information-based market failures and
    generally, 341
    carbon liability-shifting and, 353–56
    climate alignment, effect of sustainable finance agenda on private law response to, 344–48
    climate risk-shifting and, 356–58
  law and economics and, 17
MARPOL. *See* International Convention for the Prevention of Pollution from Ships (MARPOL)
Marrakesh Treaty to Facilitate Access to Published Works for Persons Who Are Blind, Visually Impaired, or Otherwise Print Disabled, 269–70
Marx, Karl, 36
Mauritius
  climate change litigation in, 696
  environmental legislation in, 693–95
Mehranvar, Ladan, 479–80
Mehta, M.C., 21–22
Melamed, A. Douglas, 746
Melbourne Climate Futures r, 645n.2
Mendes Filho, Francisco Alves (Mendes, Chico), 183
Mercedes-Benz, 143
Mercer Superannuation, 652–53
Merry, Sally, 250, 260
Meta (US technology firm), 302
Mexico
  climate disclosure in
    Global North compared, 333–35, 334*t*, 336, 339*t*
    regulatory standards, 337
  climate-washing litigation in, 175–76, 179–80
  private international law in, 555
Miazad, Amelia, 374
Michaels, Ralf, 563
Milieudefensie. *See* Netherlands, *subheading* "climate change litigation in"
Miller, Paul, 210
Minerology Canada Acquisition Corp., 484–85
mitigation footprint, 239
Mitsubishi Group, 672–73
Model Mine Development Agreement (MMDA), 430
Mongabay Latam, 188
Montreal Protocol on Substances that Deplete the Ozone Layer (1987), 214
Moore Property, 712
Moreira, Danielle de Andrade, 720–21nn.22–23
Morgan Stanley, 529
Möslein, Florian, 781–82
MSCI ESG Carbon Metrics, 787–88
Musk, Elon, 82

N
Nader, Ralph, 78
Napoleon, Val, 260
National Bank (Canada), 529
natural hazards, insuring against
  generally, 379–80
  cost of, 377, 380
  insurability, 380–81
  protection gaps, 381–82
  terminology, 379

Natural Resources Defense Council (NRDC), 520
Navajo Tribal Code, 287–88, 819
Necessary Element of a Sufficient Set (NESS), 127–30
negligence, 51, 51n.9, 105, 657–58
Nepal, climate change litigation in, 666–67, 698
Netherlands
choice of law in, 563–64
climate change litigation in
generally, 138, 139–40, 660–61, 669, 671–72
autonomy of liability law, 147, 148, 150
collective action, 801, 801n.73
consumer protection and, 588
duty of care and, 584, 697–98
ECHR and, 585–86
effectiveness of liability law, 152–55, 153n.79
Emissions Trading System (ETS) and, 587
human rights law and, 791–92, 794–95, 801–2, 804
institutional competence of civil courts, 140–41
judicial approaches to, 573n.19, 584–85
separation of powers and, 584
climate-washing litigation in, 175–76
Coal Ban Act, 481–82
consumer protection in, 581–82, 588
corporate law and governance in, 580
corporate sustainability in, 496
fiduciary law in, 221, 223–24, 225
"greenwashing" in, 588
human rights law in, 800–2, 804
ISDS, phase-out of coal and, 481–82, 486, 488, 490
legal education in, 746–47, 751–52
legal profession in, 750
mix of instruments in, 22, 22n.24
private international law in, 551–52
Sustainability Advertising Code, 581–82
Unfair Commercial Practices Act, 588
unjust enrichment in, 200–1n.52
Net Zero Asset Managers, 529
Net Zero Banking Alliance, 538–39, 683
Net Zero Banking Assessment Framework (NZBAF), 521
Net Zero Lawyers Alliance (NZLA), 760
Nevitt, Mark, 41–42, 46–47, 48, 350–51
New Climate Institute, 521–22
New York Convention. *See* Convention on the Recognition and Enforcement of Foreign Arbitral Awards (New York Convention)
New Zealand
Advertising Authority, 658–59
climate change litigation in
generally, 104, 106–7, 591–92, 645–46, 658, 662–63, 814
anti-greenwashing action, 658–59
Australia compared, 661–62
case law, 109–10n.44, 111–13, 117–18
defined, 647–48
effectiveness of, 152
negligence, 660
new tort, development of, 113–17, 660
public nuisance, 109–10n.44, 111–13, 660
risk regulators, courts as, 145–46
tort law, pathways in, 659–61
climate-washing litigation in, 175–76
Fair Trade Act, 659
Indigenous Peoples in (*see* Māori people)
insurance law in, 383–84
ISDS and, 480, 489–90
Iwi Chairs Forum, 659–60
Law Commission, 811
Māori people in (*see* Māori people)
private standard-setting in, 518
products liability law in, 170
Resource Management Act 1991, 818
supremacy of parliament doctrine, 662n.113
tort reform in, 50
Treaty of Waitangi, 822–23
Ngāpuhi, Ngāti Kahu (Smith, Mike), 111–13, 116, 145, 659–60, 814
Nigeria
African Charter Act, 690–91
Climate Change Act 2021, 695n.121
Climate Change (Duties and Incentives) Regulations 2021, 695
climate change litigation in, 684–85, 686–87, 688–89, 688n.62, 690–91, 694–95, 696, 794–95
EIA Act, 688, 691
environmental legislation in, 688–89, 693–94
human rights law in, 689–90, 794–95
labour law in, 450
National Climate Change Action Plan, 693–94
Nigeria Liquified Natural Gas (NLNG), 688
Nigerian National Petroleum Company Limited (NNPC Ltd), 684–85
Petroleum Industry Act 2021 (PIA), 684–85
tort law in, 686–87
Nipperdey, Hans, 797–98, 800
Nishitani, Yuko, 562–63
non-human life, tort duties to
generally, 49, 62–63
condition and, 57–58
equality and, 49, 50–52
fairness and, 50–51, 53–55, 59
formal conception of equality and, 55–56
instrumental approach, 58–59
judicial versus legislative authority, 58–59
rights of action in proper context, 50–51
standing and, 49–51, 52–53
substantive conception of equality and, 56–59
value and, 57
Norsk Hydro, 516
North American Free Trade Agreement (NAFTA), 489–90
Norway
ESG in, 758
Industri Energi, 455
labour law in, 450, 455
LO-Norway, 455

Norwegian Union of Municipal and General Employees, 455
Nowag, Julian, 6
"nudging," 75–76
nuisance. *See* public nuisance
Nwauche, Enyinna S., 691–92

O
Obama, Barack, 71–72
Oberlin College, 81–82
OECD. *See* Organisation for Economic Co-operation and Development (OECD)
Okediji, Ruth I., 270–71, 273, 277
Olson, Mancur, 19
OMV Group, 434
Optional Rules for Arbitration of Disputes Relating to Natural Resources and/or the Environment in 2001 (Environmental Rules), 432, 435
Organisation for Economic Co-operation and Development (OECD)
  automobile emissions reduction and, 497
  Contact Points, 551
  Guidelines for Multinational Enterprises on Responsible Business Conduct, 3, 503, 584, 791–92
  insurance law and, 387–88
  ISDS and, 472–73, 489
  state-owned enterprises and, 306–7
Orts, Eric W., 5, 171, 188
Ostrom, Elinor, 532–33, 537–38, 539, 542, 546, 547
Our Children's Trust, 211

P
Paiement, Phillip, 751
Pakistan
  fiduciary law in, 211–12
  ISDS and, 477–78
  precautionary principle in, 698
Palmer, Clive, 484
Pappas, Michael, 350–51
parens patriae, 698
Parents for Climate, 655
Parfit, Derek, 67n.3
Pargendler, Mariana, 3
Paris Agreement (2015)
  generally, 69–70, 84
  climate change litigation and, 584
  climate-washing litigation in and, 190
  corporate law and governance and, 581
  fiduciary law and, 3, 222
  finance law and, 340–41, 343–44, 347, 358
  GHG emissions and, 516
  goals of, 241, 340–41, 378, 536, 786–87, 801–2
  "green finance" and, 501
  intellectual property (IP) and, 264, 267–68
  international commercial arbitration and, 428
  ISDS and, 472–73, 486
  legal profession and, 766
  Nationally Determined Contributions, 678–79
  New Collective Quantified Goal, 343
  private standard-setting and, 521–22
  securities regulation and, 399
  SOEs and, 306
  trust law and, 290
  unjust enrichment and, 201–2
  US and, 70–72
Park, K-Sue, 12
Parker, Christine, 653–54
Parr, Adam, 176n.19
Partnership for Carbon Accounting Financials (PCAF), 516–17
Pasqua, Marco, 563
Paz, Joseph, 793–94
Peel, Jacqueline, 7
PEG. *See* private environmental governance (PEG)
Peking University Law Database, 702
Pelenc, Jérôme, 738n.6
Permanent Court of Arbitration (PCA), 429, 432, 434, 440–41
Pertamina, 667–68
Petersen Wenner, Madeliene, 562
Petronas, 667–68
Pew Center on Global Climate Change, 516
Phang, Rachel, 355
Philippines
  Climate Accountability (CLIMA) Act, 664–65, 666, 677–78
  climate disclosure in, 328
  Indigenous Peoples' Rights Act of 1997, 677–78
  Paris Agreement Nationally Determined Contribution, 678
  Strategic Lawsuits Against Public Participation (SLAPPs) in, 665, 665–66n.6
Pigou, Arthur C., 19–20
PIL. *See* private international law (PIL)
Pistor, Katharina, 207–8, 743–44
Platt River Whooping Crane Preservation Trusts, 286
Poland
  climate-washing litigation in, 175–76
  PIL in, 555
Pollman, Elizabeth, 607
"polluter pays" principle, 632, 634–35, 720–21, 721n.23
pore space, 235–37
Porter, George Richardson, 453
POSCO, 670–72
Potsdam Institute for Climate Impact Research, 522
Pozzo, Barbara, 11
precautionary principle, 632, 634–35, 698, 721–22
Premier Oil, 761
PRI. *See* Principles for Responsible Investment (PRI)
PriceWaterhouseCoopers, 519–20, 624
Princen, Thomas, 201n.57

Principles for Responsible Investment (PRI)
generally, 7
corporate law and governance and, 310
ESG and, 610, 611, 619
fiduciary law and, 213
finance law and, 344–47
private standard-setting and, 522–24, 525
securities regulation and, 407–8
Principles of European Tort Law, 23–24, 23n.33
private environmental governance (PEG)
generally, 5, 532–33, 547
actors in, 533–34
climate change private ordering
generally, 535–36
beyond small groups, 537–39
challenge of, 536–37
defined, 533–35
examples of, 533–34
future directions, 546–47
government market mechanisms distinguished, 534
model of, 539–42
beyond small groups, 542–44
climate mitigation, effect on, 544
efficiency and, 541
employee recruitment and retention and, 541
ESG and, 541, 546
limitations of, 545–46
market and non-market reactions, 540*f*
principles of, 542–44
private environmental governance pressure, 539–40, 540*f*
public governance, effect on, 544–45
other concepts compared, 534–35
privatisation distinguished, 534
US, in, 537–38
private international law (PIL). *See also specific country*
generally, 6, 548–50, 568
analysis of transnational climate change litigation, 554–55
applicable law
generally, 561
choice of law, 561–65
extraterritoriality, 565–66
foreign judgments, 566–68
international law distinguished, 549
jurisdiction
generally, 556
forum non conveniens, 560–61
general jurisdiction, 557
judicial discretion, 560–61
special/specific jurisdiction, 558–59
non-US case studies
generally, 551
climate change damage reduction, 552–53
duty of vigilance/due diligence, breach of, 553–54
GHG emission reduction, 551–52
US case studies, 550–51
private standard-setting
generally, 5, 513–14, 531
climate change and
climate disclosure, 517–20
climate disclosure standard (S2), 519
"financed emissions," 516–17
GHG emissions, measurement, 516–17
investor coalitions, 522–23
sustainability disclosure standard (S1), 519
technical climate standards, 520–22
corporate accountability and, 514–16
EU, in, 521–22
Germany, in, 521–22
investor leadership in, 514, 523–28
"least common denominator" phenomenon, 527
New Zealand, in, 518
reasonable expectations of, 514, 528–31
roles of government in, 513n.2
securities regulation and, 413–15
socially responsible investors (SRI) and, 515–16
UK, in, 518
US, in, 518, 529–30
producer cooperatives, 81n.100
products liability law
generally, 3, 158, 171–72
actors and networks, 168–69
alternative design analysis, 162–63
causal connection between breach and harm, 165–66
consumer expectation test, 163–64, 171–72
consumption and, 171
design defects, 159–60, 161–62, 163
effect of climate change on, 166–71
electricity and, 162
end users, 169
evolving purpose of, 167
"failure to adapt" theory, 166–67
historical background, 159–61
joint and several liability, 159, 168, 169
manufacturing defects, 159–60, 161
misrepresentation and, 160–61, 164
motor vehicles and, 166–67, 168, 169
New Zealand, in, 170
pharmaceuticals and, 166–67
privity of contract not required, 159, 165–66
product versus conduct, 160, 170–71
Puerto Rico, in, 157, 161–62, 164–65
relevance to climate change, 161–66
sewers and, 164–65
supply chain responsibility and, 157–58, 167–68
US, in, 159, 160, 166, 169–70
warning defects, 159–60, 161–62, 164–65
The Progress of the Nation (Porter), 453
Project Gigaton, 541
property law
generally, 1, 9
adaptation footprint
generally, 232, 240–42, 245
adaptation, adapting to, 242, 244–45
evolving risks, adapting to, 242–43
excessive and novel risks, adapting to, 242, 243–44
maladaptation, 244
public law versus private law, 242
sea-level rise and, 243–44

stress tests, 244
ad coelum doctrine, 236
Earth system non-stationary law
generally, 230–31
advent of, 232
evolution of property law doctrine and, 232–33
intellectual property (IP) (*see* intellectual property (IP))
land use and ownership (*see* land use and ownership)
mineral extraction and, 229
mitigation footprint
generally, 232, 245
carbon capture and storage (CCS), 235–37, 240
conservation easements, 239
homeowner associations (HOAs), 238–39
novel property disputes, 233, 240
ownership design, 233–37
pore space, 235–37
solar rights, 234
subsurface rights, 235–37
use restrictions, 233, 238–39
wind rights, 234–35
nature and, 229–30
obstacle to addressing climate change, as (*see* critical and social theory)
public nuisance and, 40n.12, 244
reasonable actor standard, 242
rule of capture, 229
teaching private law for growth and, 746
trust law (*see* trust law)
waste doctrine and, 242–43, 244
proximate causation, 121
prudent investor rule, 292, 609–10
public law, relationship to private law, 2–4
public nuisance
generally, 104, 117
climate change litigation, 109–13
future directions, 117–18
pollution and, 106
property law and, 40n.12, 244
public trust doctrine, 211–12, 280–84, 632n.42
Puerto Rico, products liability law in, 157, 161–62, 164–65
punitive damages, 60–61n.43

Q
quid pro quo contracts, 98–99, 100–2
Quinault Indian Reservation, 288–89

R
Rabin, Yale, 45
race
intersectionality with private law and environment, 38–41
property law as obstacle to addressing climate change
collective action versus property rights, 46–47
displacement and, 45–47, 48
floodplains, home construction in, 45–48
Rajagopal, Balakrishnan, 266
Rajavuori, Mikko, 647
Ranganathan, Surabhi, 805
Rawlings, Richard, 666–67
Rawls, John, 54n.17, 68, 278, 805–6
Rees, William, 251
relational justice
generally, 8, 49–51, 62–63
equality and
generally, 53
corrective justice versus, 55–56
"entire fairness" standard, 53–54
fairness, 50–51, 53–55, 59
formal conception of, 55–56
substantive conception of, 56–59
tort law and, 49, 50–52
non-human life, tort duties to (*see* non-human life, tort duties to)
standing and, 49–51, 52–53
relational theory of contract, 97–98, 98n.74
renewable energy cooperatives, 82–83
Responsible Care Initiative, 515
Restatement of Conflicts of Law, 564–65
Restatement (Third) of Restitution and Unjust Enrichment, 192–93n.5
Restatement (Third) of Torts
causation and, 128–29, 129n.42, 130
physical and emotional harm, 193n.8
products liability and, 160n.20, 160–61, 162n.29, 163
Reynolds. Graham, 2
Ringe, Wolf-Georg, 355
Rio Declaration (1992), 210
Rivers, Camereon K., 234–35nn.30–31
Rockhopper, 475–76
Rome II Regulation
applicable law, 561–63, 562n.96, 564–65, 567
jurisdiction, 556, 558, 559
private international law generally, 551–52, 553, 568
Rossi, Jim, 9
Rothschild, Rachel, 771
Roughton, Abby, 235n.33
Rousseau, Jean-Jacques, 67
Royal Dutch Shell. *See* Netherlands, *subheading* "climate change litigation in"
Ruhl, J.B., 9
Rule Against Perpetuities, 293–94
Rules and Regulation of the Amalgamated Society of Engineers, 453
Russell, Irma, 772–73
Russia
environmental backsliding by, 84
illiberalism in, 71
private international law in, 555
Russian Revolution, 68n.10
RWE, 23–24. *See* Germany, *subheading* "climate change litigation in"

S
Sabin Center for Climate Change Law, 175–76, 175–76n.15, 180, 186, 548, 550, 681
Sachs, Lisa E., 479–80
"sacrifice zones," 442–43, 443n.5
Sakharova, Irina, 6
Santos (Australian gas company), 655, 656
Sarel, Roee, 3
SBTi. *See* Science Based Targets initiative (SBTi)
Schafer, Hans-Bernd, 23
Schapiro, Mary, 518
Schirmer, Jan-Erik, 11–12, 162
Science Based Targets initiative (SBTi)
  ESG and, 610
  PEG and, 538, 539, 543, 544
  private standard-setting and, 520–22, 523–24, 531
Scott, Austin Wkaeman, 279
sea level rise
  adaptation footprint and, 243–44
  property law as obstacle to addressing climate change, 42–44
securities regulation
  generally, 10, 397–98, 415
  anti-fraud regulation, 401–2
  Australia, in, 413–14
  Canada, in, 414
  China, in, 401–2
  climate disclosure and
    corporate climate governance, 403–5
    disclosure-driven climate governance, 405–6
    evolution of, 400–1
  corporate climate governance and
    generally, 405
    climate disclosure, 403–5
    climate externalities, 403–5
    coordination, 409–10
    disclosure-driven climate governance, 405–6
    gatekeeper regulation, 408–9
    harmonisation, 409–10
    public versus private enforcement, 410–11
    standardisation, 409–10
  defined, 398
  ESG and, 401–2, 406–7, 408–9, 410, 413–14
  EU, in, 400–2, 408, 410–11, 412–13, 414–15
  evolution of, 398–403
  fund labelling, 401–2
  gatekeeper regulation, 402, 408–9
  intermediary regulation, 402
  market stability, 403
  policy support for climate action, 412–13
  potential impact on climate change, 403–11
  private standard-setting and, 413–15
  public law versus private law, 398, 398n.5
  regulatory versus market driven approaches, 412
  relevance of, 411–15
  shareholder governance and
    generally, 406
    collective action problems, 407–8
    engagement, 406–7
    voting rights, 407
  systemic risk, 403
  taxonomies, 401–2
  UK, in, 408, 412, 414
  US, in (*see* United States)
Sen, Amartya, 805–6
Serres, Michel, 68
Setzer, Joana, 2
Severesi, Annalisa, 647
Shaffer, Gregory C., 3, 213, 215, 216, 292–93, 749–50
shareholder governance
  generally, 406
  collective action problems, 407–8
  engagement, 406–7
  voting rights, 407
Shavell, Steven, 18–19, 21, 23–24
Sherwin, Emily, 196n.24
Shoemaker, Jessica, 257
Shue, Henry, 796
Simard, Justin, 40
Sinclair, Upton, 70
Singapore
  Advertising Standards Authority, 674–75
  choice of law in, 564–65
  class actions in, 675n.53
  Code of Advertising Practice, 674–75
  Competition and Consumer Commission of Singapore (CCCS), 674–75
  Consumer Protection (Fair Trading) Act, 674–75
  ESG in, 676
  greenwashing in, 674–75
  Zero Greenwashing Alliance, 674–75
Singapore Airlines Group, 674–75
Singapore–Australia Free Trade Agreement, 484–85
Single European Act, 491
Sinzheimer, Hugo, 453, 453–54n.74
Slaughter and May (law firm), 768–69
Smith, Adam, 452
Smith, Lionel, 210
Smith, Mike (Ngāpuhi, Ngāti Kahu), 111–13, 116, 145, 659–60, 814
social contract theory, 67–69, 67n.3
SOEs. *See* state-owned enterprises (SOEs)
Solvay, 431
South Africa
  bill of rights, 642
  climate change litigation in, 666–67, 671–72, 696
  climate disclosure in, 331–33
    generally, 322, 328, 337
    regulatory standards, 336–37
  environmental legislation in, 693–94, 695
  human rights law in, 689–90
  Johannesburg Stock Exchange (JSB), 326–27, 331, 332
  King Code, 331–33, 336–37
  King IV Guidance Paper on the Responsibilities of Governing Bodies in Responding to Climate Change, 331–32
  private international law in, 555

Sustainability Disclosure Guidance and Climate Disclosure Guidance, 332
South Korea
climate change litigation in, 670–72, 791
Framework Act on Carbon Neutrality and Green Growth for Coping with the Climate Crisis, 671
greenwashing in, 675
tort law in, 670–72
Spain
climate-washing litigation in, 175–76
ISDS and, 479–80
private international law in, 555
special/specific jurisdiction, 558–59
specific performance, 93–94, 95
Spivack, Carla, 6
Sproat, D Kapua'ala, 824, 826
standard-setting. *See* private standard-setting
standing
non-human life, tort duties to, 49–51, 52–53
relational justice and, 49–50, 52–53
Stapleton, Jane, 122–23
state-owned enterprises (SOEs)
carbon liability-shifting and, 355–56
corporate law and governance and
generally, 298, 317
China, in, 298–99, 313–16, 317–18
climate change, arguments in favour of directors addressing, 312–16
importance of addressing external dimension of director duties, 306–7
State Street, 6, 219, 616
Steel, Sandy, 7
Steigleder, Annelise, 725
Stern, Paul C., 5
Stiglitz, Joseph, 472
Stockholm Chamber of Commerce (SCC), 429, 438
Strategic Lawsuits Against Public Participation (SLAPPs), 665, 665–66n.6, 771–72
Strine, Leo, 212
subrogation, 394–95
sue and labour costs, 391–94
Sunstein, Cass, 823–24
Sustainability Accounting Standards Board (SASB), 326, 335, 400–1, 518, 519, 523–24
sustainability clauses, 86n.8, 90–92, 98n.77
Sustainability Tracker, 78–79
Sustainable Carbon, 184
Sweden, SOEs in, 306–7
Switzerland
Cartel Act, 363
climate change litigation in, 794–95
climate-washing litigation in, 175–76
Code of Obligations, 552–53
competition law in, 363
Insurance Contract Act (Versicherungsvertragsges etz), 392–93
insurance law in, 392–93
private international law in, 552–53, 555

T
Tanzania, environmental legislation in, 689–90
Task Force on Climate-Related Financial Disclosures (TCFD)
climate disclosure and, 323–24, 326, 334–35, 336
corporate law and governance and, 649
ESG and, 610
ISSB and, 676
private standard-setting and, 514, 518, 519, 523–24, 525, 528, 529–30, 531
securities regulation and, 398–99, 400–1, 406
Taskforce on Nature-related Financial Disclosures (TNFD), 519–20
TC Energy, 431
TCFD. *See* Task Force on Climate-Related Financial Disclosures (TCFD)
TD Bank Group, 529
Tellus Institute, 517–18
Tesla, 82
Thailand
private international law in, 555
Strategic Lawsuits Against Public Participation (SLAPPs) in, 665, 665–66n.6
Tienhaara, Kyla, 4
Toft, Kristian Høyer, 796
Toronto School, 52, 55n.20, 61
Torrey Canyon oil spill (1967), 461
tort law
Africa, and climate change litigation in, 686–87
causation in tort (*see* causation in tort)
civil law torts (*see* civil law torts)
common law torts (*see* common law torts)
contract law compared, 97
harmful battery, 59
joint and several liability
Brazil, in, 719–20
causation and, 130
products liability and, 159, 168, 169
negligence, 51, 51n.9, 105, 657–58
non-human life, duties to (*see* non-human life, tort duties to)
products liability law (*see* products liability law)
public nuisance
generally, 104, 117
climate change litigation, 109–13
future directions, 117–18
pollution and, 106
punitive damages, 60–61n.43
rights of action in proper context
generally, 50–51
autonomy and, 60–62
deliberate wrongdoing, 60–61
impaired relationship, 61
instrumental value, 60–62
types of rights, 60
strict liability, 719
teaching private law for growth and, 746
unjust enrichment (*see* unjust enrichment)

TotalEnergies, 201–2, 553, 587–88
tradable pollution rights, 495–96
traditional ecological knowledge (TEK)
  climate adaptation and, 820
  property interests in, 809–10
transaction costs, 17
Transition Pathway Initiative (TPI), 521, 524, 531
Treaty of Rome (1957), 573
Treaty on the Functioning of the European Union (TFEU), 360–62, 365–66, 370, 371
TRIPS Agreement (Agreement of Trade-Related Aspects of Intellectual Property Rights), 269
Trump, Donald
  anti-climate policies of, 82, 537–38
  ESG and, 218–19, 220
  legal profession and, 758–59, 766
  Paris Agreement and, 70–72
  procurement policies and, 80
  Russia and, 71
  securities regulation and, 405n.53, 413
  trade policy and, 739
trust law
  generally, 6, 278–80, 294
  ameliorating climate change
    generally, 279–80
    civil law systems, in, 290–91
    conservation trusts, 280, 285–87, 818–19
    Indigenous Peoples and, 287–89
    public trust doctrine, 280–84
    waste and, 280, 289–90
  Brazil, in, 290
  charity trusts, 604–5
  Claflin Doctrine, 291–92
  conservation trusts, 280, 285–87, 818–19
  definition of trust, 279
  double-edged nature of trusts, 279
  Earth as held in trust for future generations, 278
  ESG and, 291
  fiduciary law compared, 6
  historical background, 281–82
  Indigenous Peoples and, 287–89, 818–19
  inimical to climate preservation
    generally, 280
    equitable deviation and, 292
    fiduciary duty rule and, 291
    modification of trust terms, 291–92
    prudent investor rule and, 292, 609–10
    Rule Against Perpetuities and, 293–94
    tax avoidance and, 293–94
  legal ambiguity of trusts, 279
  legal fiction, trusts as, 281
  split title, concept of, 278
  Uganda, in, 290–91
  UK, in
    modification of trust terms, 292
    public trust doctrine, 281–82
    tax avoidance and, 293
  US, in (*see* United States)
  waste doctrine and, 280, 289–90
Tsosie, Rebecca, 813–14, 815–16, 816n.46
Two Treatises of Government (Locke), 446

U
Ubuntu, 815–16
Uganda
  climate change litigation in, 682, 696
  environmental legislation in, 694–95
  trust law in, 290–91
Ukraine, private international law in, 555
Ulfbeck, Vibe, 142
UNCITRAL. *See* Commission on International Trade Law (UNCITRAL)
UNFCCC. *See* Framework Convention on Climate Change (UNFCCC) (1992)
UNGPs. *See* Guiding Principles on Business and Human Rights (UNGPs)
Uniform Prudent Investor Act, 291, 481n.71, 487
Union Carbide, 515
United Kingdom
  generally, 7
  artificial intelligence in, 781–82
  Bar Council, 759
  Bar Standards Board (BSB), 761
  British Institute of International and Comparative Law (BIICL), 647
  causation in tort in, 126, 134–35
  The Chancery Lane Project (TCLP), 89–90, 91–92, 604, 762–63
  Charter of the Forest of 1217, 281–82
  choice of law in, 561–62, 563
  Climate Change Act 2008, 595–96
  climate change litigation in
    generally, 591, 605–6
    adaptation failures, 597–98
    charity trusts and, 604–5
    classic litigation, 596–601
    common law and, 594, 595
    corporate actions, 598–601
    English legal culture and, 591–96
    lack of success, 596–97
    other countries compared, 596–97
    pension funds and, 605
    regulation and, 601–3
    relevance of legal culture, 591–96
    self-directed cases, 603–5
    "thick" legal culture and, 593, 594
  Climate Crisis Working Group, 759
  climate disclosure in
    generally, 322
    Global South compared, 333–34, 334*t*, 335, 336, 339*t*
    regulatory standards, 336–37
  climate-washing litigation in, 175–76, 177–78
  Code of Non-broadcast Advertising and Direct & Promotional Marketing, 176
  common law torts in, 108–9, 110–11

Commonwealth Conciliation and Arbitration Act 1904, 452
Companies Act 2006, 307–8, 598–99, 600
Competition and Markets Authority, 359
competition law in, 371n.76
Consumer Rights Act 2015, 383n.39
contractual climate clauses in, 89–90, 95
Coronavirus Job Retention Scheme (CJRS), 395
corporate law and governance in
corporate constitution, incorporating nature into, 298, 307–9
enforcement of director duties, 300
Department for Energy and Climate Change, 601–2
emitters in, 207
English Revolution, 68
fiduciary law in, 225
Financial Conduct Authority, 383n.39
foreign judgments in, 567
forum non conveniens in, 560
general jurisdiction in, 557
GMB Union, 450
Green Agreements Guidance, 359, 371n.76
human rights law in, 800–1
insurance law in
"basis of settlement" clauses, 384
betterment principle, 383–84
hold harmless and indemnity principle, 390–91
mitigation damages, 391–92
subrogation, 395
labour law in, 450
land use and ownership in, 255–56
Law Society of England and Wales, 363, 764, 766, 767
legal education in, 751–52
legal profession in, 759, 761–62
Legal Services Board, 771–72
Magna Carta, 281
Marine Insurance Act (MIA) 1906, 386, 391
Miners' Federation of Great Britain, 453
private international law in, 555
private standard-setting in, 518
public nuisance in, 110–11
right to counsel in, 769–70
securities regulation in, 408, 412, 414
specific jurisdiction in, 558, 559
Strategic Lawsuits Against Public Participation (SLAPPs) in, 771–72
Sustainability Disclosure Requirements (SDR), 408
tort law in, 670
trust law in
modification of trust terms, 292
public trust doctrine, 281–82
tax avoidance and, 293
unjust enrichment in, 195n.19
United Nations
Committee on Economic, Social and Cultural Rights, 273–74
Conference on Environment and Development (Rio Conference) (1992), 498–99, 608
Conference on Trade and Development (UNCTAD), 322n.22, 369
Convention on the Law of the Sea (UNCLOS), 463, 466
Convention on Transparency in Treaty-Based Investor–State Arbitration (Mauritius Convention), 439, 439n.87
Declaration on the Rights of Indigenous Peoples, 182
Draft Guiding Principles for Serviced Emissions, 762, 763–64
Environment Programme (UNEP), 7, 213, 344, 523
Forum on Sustainability Standards, 369
General Recommendation No. 37 (2018) on the Elimination of Discrimination against Women, 268
Global Compact, 344, 520–21, 523–24, 609
High-Level Expert Group, 521–22
Human Rights Council (HRC), 265–66, 267–68
Model Law on Cross- Border Insolvency, 422–23
Net Zero for Professional Service Providers Working Group, 762
Office of the High Commissioner of Human Rights (OHCHR), 264, 266, 273–74
PRI (*see* Principles for Responsible Investment (PRI))
Principles for Sustainable Insurance, 385
Race to Zero, 528–29, 762
Rio Declaration (1992), 210
Special Envoy for Climate Change and Finance, 323–24
Special Rapporteur on Adequate Housing as a Component of the Right to an Adequate Standard of Living, and on the Right to Non-Discrimination in this Context, 266
Special Rapporteur on the Human Rights to Safe Drinking Water and Sanitation, 266
Sustainable Development Goals (SDGs), 3, 326–27, 344, 501, 522, 738–39
2030 Agenda for Sustainable Development, 264, 522
UNCITRAL (*see* Commission on International Trade Law (UNCITRAL))
UNFCCC (*see* Framework Convention on Climate Change (UNFCCC) (1992))
UNGPs (*see* Guiding Principles on Business and Human Rights (UNGPs))
United States
generally, 5
ad coelum doctrine in, 236
Agency for International Development (USAID), 303
Alien Tort Statute (ATS), 566
American Bar Association (ABA), 369, 623, 758–59, 759n.30, 765n.71, 766, 772–73
American Law Institute, 160
American Revolution, 68
America Petroleum Institute, 161–62
antitrust law in
generally, 361, 375

United States (*cont.*)
cartel enforcement, 364
consumer welfare standard, 362–63, 365, 367–68
other climate collaborators, 372–75
per se rule, 361–62
procompetitive sustainability standards, 369
public interest exception, 363
quick look analysis, 362
Rule of Reason, 361–62, 365, 367, 368, 369, 372–73
sliding scale of legal standards, 361–62
Arkansas, fiduciary duties of proxy advisors and voters in public retirement systems in, 616
artificial intelligence in, 785–86, 787
Bankruptcy Abuse Prevention and Consumer Protection Act of 2005, 422
bankruptcy law in, 418–19, 421, 422
California
climate disclosure in, 619n.110
Consumers Legal Remedies Act, 176
divestment of fossil fuel assets in, 620–21
Public Employees' Retirement System (CalPERS), 620–21
State Teacher's Retirement System, 620–21
causation in tort in, 133–34, 135–36
Chamber of Commerce, 386
Chevron deference, 414n.108
choice of law in, 564–65, 746
civil rights movement, 38–39
Clean Air Act, 39, 110, 495–96
Clean Water Act, 166
climate disclosure in
generally, 322, 337–38
Global South compared, 333–34, 334*t*, 335, 336, 339*t*
legal profession and, 765
securities regulation and, 400–1, 404–5
climate-washing litigation in, 175–76, 177
Colorado
consideration of ESG in management of state funds in, 619, 620
Public Employees Retirement Association, 620
common law torts in, 109–10, 591–92
corporate law and governance in
ESG and, 309, 310, 311
securities regulation and, 405
universal ownership, 302–3
Delaware Corporate Law, 311
Department of Hawaiian Homelands, 286–87
Department of Housing and Urban Development, 42–43
Dodd–Frank Act, 398n.6, 405
emitters in, 207
Employee Retirement Income Security Act (ERISA), 219–20, 611, 612–13
Endangered Species Act, 39, 79
environmental backsliding by, 84
Environmental Protection Agency (EPA), 38, 110, 201–2, 535, 538, 787, 788
ESG in (*see also specific state*)
generally, 6, 607–8, 626
anti-ESG backlash, 607–8, 672–73, 757–58
climate change, implications for, 624
corporate law and governance, 309, 310, 311
divestment of fossil fuel assets, 620–22
ESG-related boycotts, 616–18
ESG screens, 618–19
federal laws relating to, 611–13
fiduciary law, 212–13, 218–21
lawyers, implications for, 622–23
other countries, implications for, 624–25
private actors, implications for, 622–23
public retirement systems, fiduciary duties of proxy advisors and voters, 615–16
state funds, consideration in management of, 614–15, 619–20
state laws relating to, 613–22
statutes opposing, 614–19
statutes supporting, 619
ESG Task Force, 410
estate tax, 293–94
extraterritoriality in, 566
Federal Trade Commission, 79, 174–75
Federal Trade Commission Act, 174–75
FEMA, 42–43
fiduciary law in, 218–21
ESG and, 6, 212–13, 218–21
legitimacy trap, 217
public trust doctrine, 211–12
Fifth Amendment, 283, 556
First Amendment, 264
Florida, ESG screens in, 618
forum non conveniens in, 560
fossil fuel industry in, 70–72
Fourteenth Amendment, 556
general jurisdiction in, 557
generation-skipping tax (GST), 293–94
homeowner associations (HOAs) in, 238
Illinois
consideration of ESG in management of state funds in, 619–20
Sustainable Investing Act, 619–20
Indigenous Peoples in
generally, 811
carbon credits and, 817
climate adaptation and, 820–21
climate change litigation and, 810, 813–14
codification of laws, 819
conservation trusts, 818–19
fiduciary law and, 822
property law and, 42–44, 46, 287–88
reparations and, 824
separate legal domain of authority, 809
Inflation Reduction Act (IRA), 537, 539–40, 574–75
Infrastructure Investment and Jobs Act (IIJA), 537, 539–40
IP in, 270

Isle de Jean Charles Choctaw Nation of Louisiana, 42–44, 46
Kansas, fiduciary duties of proxy advisors and voters in public retirement systems in, 615
Kentucky, ESG-related boycotts, 616–17
labour law in, 446
legal education in, 751–53
legal profession in
accountability model, 760–61
climate disclosure and, 765
ESG, implications of, 622–23
professional responsibility rules, promoting greening of, 773
Louisiana Office of Community Development (OCD), 44
Maine, divestment of fossil fuel assets in, 620–21
Maryland
consideration of ESG in management of state funds in, 619, 620
State Retirement and Pension System, 620
Missouri
consideration of ESG in management of state funds in, 614n.64
ESG screens in, 618–19
Montana Environmental Protection Act, 219n.68
National Academy of Sciences, 162
National Cooperative Research and Production Act, 369
National Disaster Resilience Competition, 42–43
National Environmental Policy Act, 533–34, 537–38
New Hampshire, consideration of ESG in management of state funds in, 614
New Jersey
Consumer Fraud Act, 176
Industrial Site Recovery Act, 353
Oklahoma
Energy Discrimination Elimination Act, 617
ESG-related boycotts, 616–17
Oregon, divestment of fossil fuel assets in, 620–22
Paris Agreement and, 70–72
PEG in, 537–38
private international law in, 550–51, 555
private standard-setting in, 413–15, 518
products liability law in, 159, 160, 166, 169–70
Public Company Accounting Oversight Board (PCAOB), 402–3n.33
public nuisance in, 109–10, 698
Puerto Rico, products liability law in, 157, 161–62, 164–65
right to counsel in, 769–70
Sarbanes-Oxley Act, 398n.6, 402–3n.33, 405
Securities and Exchange Commission (SEC)
artificial intelligence and, 785–86, 787
Climate and ESG Task Force, 676–77n.61
climate disclosure and, 333–34, 335, 338, 765
ESG and, 612
fiduciary law and, 219–20
PEG and, 537–38
private standard-setting and, 518
Rules for the Enhancement and Standardization of Climate-Related Disclosures for Investors, 785–86, 787
securities regulation and, 400, 401–2, 404–5, 407–8, 410, 413–15, 415n.110
securities regulation in
climate disclosure and, 400–1, 404–5
corporate law and governance and, 405
evolution of, 400
fund labelling, 401–2
oversight, 402
policy support for climate action, 413
private standard-setting and, 413–15
public versus private enforcement, 410–11
regulatory versus market-driven approaches, 412–13
shareholder governance and, 406–8
Sherman Act, 361, 364, 375
South Carolina, consideration of ESG in management of state funds in, 614, 614n.63, 615
specific jurisdiction in, 558, 559
Standards Development Organization Act of 2004, 369
surety bonds in, 419n.8
Tennessee, ESG screens in, 618n.99
Texas
ESG-related boycotts, 616–17
ESG screens in, 618
tradable pollution rights in, 495–96
trust law in
Claflin Doctrine, 291–92
conservation trusts, 285–87
Indigenous Peoples and, 287–89
modification of trust terms, 291–92
public trust doctrine, 282–84
tax avoidance and, 293–94
Tribal Holder model, 288–89
universal ownership in
generally, 302–3
addressing negative externalities, 304
internalising negative externalities, 303
Utah, ESG-related boycotts, 617
workers compensation in, 50
unjust enrichment
causation element, 194–95, 203–4
climate change litigation and
generally, 3, 192–93, 205–6
advantages of, 202–5
carbon budgets and, 199–201
challenges of, 193–95, 202–5
extractors versus emitters, 192–93, 199, 200–2, 203–5, 206
gain-based litigation, 196, 197, 203–5
loss versus gain, 200
profitability, relevance of, 197–98, 201–2, 205
public dominion, resources in, 198–99
traditional tort law compared, 203, 205

unjust enrichment (*cont.*)
  doctrine, 195–97
  enrichment element, 195
  harm element, 194
  Netherlands, in, 200–1n.52
  principles, 195–97
  UK, in, 195n.19
  unjust element, 195–96
  wrongful conduct element, 194
  wrongful enrichment versus, 196–97, 197n.34

V

Value Reporting Framework, 519–20
van Asselt, Harro, 3, 173, 647
Vandenbergh, Michael P., 5
VanDuzer, J. Anthony, 474
Vanguard Group, 757–58
Vanguard Investments, 6, 176–77, 219, 529, 616
Vanguard Investments Australia, 652–53
van Loon, Hans, 562–63
Varottil, Umakanth, 4
Vasak, Karel, 793
Vaughan, Dean, 769
V8 Supercars Australia Pty Ltd, 654
Vélez Echeverri, Juliana, 2
Verra, 181–82
Volkswagen, 143, 654

W

Walmart, 73–74, 538
Walters, Jonathan, 315
Waratah Coal, 484–85
warning defects, 159–60, 161–62, 164–65
waste doctrine
  property law, in, 242–43, 244
  trust law, in, 280, 289–90
Webb, Beatrice, 453–54
Webb, Sidney, 453–54
Weber, Max, 36
Weinrib, Ernest J., 55
Weller, Marc-Philippe, 562, 564
Westmoreland Coal Company, 484, 487
Williams, Cynthia A., 5
Williams, Joseph, 115, 812, 815, 816
Williams, Patricia, 38–39
WIPO GREEN, 262–63, 272–73
Wood, Stepan, 513–14, 513n.2
World Bank, 322n.22, 335, 460
World Business Council for Sustainable Development (WBCSD), 323, 516, 542
World Economic Forum (WEF), 519–20
World Federation of Exchanges, 409–10
World Intellectual Property Organization (WIPO), 262–63, 269–70, 272–73
World Meteorological Organization (WMO), 680
World Resources Institute/World Business Council on Sustainable Development Greenhouse Gas Standard, 537–38
World Resources Institute (WRI), 323, 515, 516, 520–21, 542, 545–46
World Trade Organization (WTO), 269
World Wide Fund for Nature, 186
World Wildlife Fund (WWF), 515, 516, 520–21, 545–46
Wright, Richard, 127–28
wrongful enrichment, 196–97, 197n.34

Y

Yainix Ranch, 288–89
Year of Cooperatives (2025), 81
Yin, Ivy, 180n.45
Young, Iris Marion, 796–97
Yurok Tribe, 817

Z

Zambia
  climate change litigation in, 696
  environmental legislation in, 693–95
Zeh, Samuel, 563
Zeph Investments, 484–85, 485n.95
Zhao, Yue, 8
Zhu, Ying, 4
Zingales, Luigi, 298, 309
Zurich Insurance Company, 529
Zurich Risk Advisor, 389